# MARITIME ECONOMICS

Winner of the Chojeong Book Prize 2005 for 'making a significant contribution to the development of maritime transport academically and practically'

'In its breadth, this book is a tour de force and anyone who reads it cannot but be better informed about the shipping world'

*Lloyds List*, 17th December 1997

For 5,000 years shipping has served the world economy and today it provides a sophisticated transport service to every part of the globe. Yet despite its economic complexity, shipping retains much of the competitive cut and thrust of the 'perfect' market of classical economics. This blend of sophisticated logistics and larger than life entrepreneurs makes it a unique case study of classical economics in a modern setting.

The enlarged and substantially rewritten *Maritime Economics* uses historical and theoretical analysis as the framework for a practical explanation of how shipping works today. Whilst retaining the structure of the second edition, its scope is widened to include:

- lessons from 5,000 years of commercial shipping history;
- shipping cycles back to 1741, with a year by year commentary;
- updated chapters on markets, shipping costs, accounts, ship finance and a new chapter on the return on capital;
- new chapters on the geography of sea trade, trade theory and specialized cargoes;
- updated chapters on the merchant fleet shipbuilding, recycling and the regulatory regime;
- a much revised chapter on the challenges and pitfalls of forecasting.

With over 800 pages, 200 illustrations, maps, technical drawings and tables, *Maritime Economics* is the shipping industry's most comprehensive text and reference source, whilst remaining, as one reviewer put it, 'a very readable book'.

**Martin Stopford** has enjoyed a distinguished career in the shipping industry as Director of Business Development with British Shipbuilders, Global Shipping Economist with the Chase Manhattan Bank N.A., Chief Executive of Lloyds Maritime Information Services, Managing Director of Clarkson Research Services and an executive Director of Clarksons PLC. He lectures regularly at Cambridge Academy of Transport and is a Visiting Professor at Cass Business School, Dalian Maritime University and Copenhagen Business School.

# MARITIME ECONOMICS

## Third edition

## Martin Stopford

Routledge
Taylor & Francis Group

LONDON AND NEW YORK

First published by Allen and Unwin 1988
Second edition published 1997
Third edition published 2009 by Routledge
2 Park Square, Milton Park, Abingdon, Oxon OX14 4RN

Simultaneously published in the USA and Canada
by Routledge
270 Madison Avenue, New York, NY 10016

*Routledge is an imprint of the Taylor & Francis Group,
an informa business*

© 2009 Martin Stopford

Typeset in Times New Roman by Keyword Group Ltd.
Printed and bound in Great Britain by MPG Books Ltd, Bodmin,
Cornwall

*British Library Cataloguing in Publication Data*
A catalogue record for this book is available from the British Library

*Library of Congress Cataloging in Publication Data*
A catalog record for this book has been requested,

ISBN10: 0-415-27557-1 (hbk)
ISBN10: 0-415-27558-X (pbk)
ISBN10: 0-203-89174-0 (ebk)

ISBN13: 978-0-415-27557-6 (hbk)
ISBN13: 978-0-415-27558-3 (pbk)
ISBN13: 978-0-203-89174-2 (ebk)

# Contents

*Preface to the Third Edition*      xi
*Synopsis*      xiii
*Abbreviations*      xix
*Fifty Essential Shipping Terms*      xxi

**PART 1: INTRODUCTION TO SHIPPING**      **1**

Chapter 1 Sea Transport and the Global Economy      3
    1.1 Introduction      3
    1.2 The origins of sea trade, 3000 BC to AD 1450      7
    1.3 The global economy in the fifteenth century      12
    1.4 Opening up global trade and commerce, 1450–1833      13
    1.5 Liner and tramp shipping, 1833–1950      23
    1.6 Container, bulk and air transport, 1950–2006      35
    1.7 Lessons from 5,000 years of commercial shipping      44
    1.8 Summary      45

Chapter 2 The Organization of the Shipping Market      47
    2.1 Introduction      47
    2.2 Overview of the maritime industry      48
    2.3 The International transport industry      50
    2.4 Characteristics of sea transport demand      53
    2.5 The sea transport system      61
    2.6 The world merchant fleet      68
    2.7 The cost of sea transport      73

# CONTENTS

2.8  The role of ports in the transport system          81
2.9  The shipping companies that run the business        83
2.10 The role of governments in shipping                 89
2.11 Summary                                             89

## PART 2:  SHIPPING MARKET ECONOMICS                    91

Chapter 3  Shipping Market Cycles                        93
3.1  Introducing the shipping cycle                      93
3.2  Characteristics of shipping market cycles           94
3.3  Shipping cycles and shipping risk                  101
3.4  Overview of shipping cycles, 1741–2007             104
3.5  Sailing ship cycles, 1741–1869                     108
3.6  Tramp market cycles, 1869–1936                     110
3.7  Bulk shipping market cycles, 1945–2008             118
3.8  Lessons from two centuries of cycles               130
3.9  Prediction of shipping cycles                      131
3.10 Summary                                            133

Chapter 4  Supply, Demand and Freight Rates             135
4.1  The shipping market model                          135
4.2  Key influences on supply and demand                136
4.3  The demand for sea transport                       139
4.4  The supply of sea transport                        150
4.5  The freight rate mechanism                         160
4.6  Summary                                            172

Chapter 5  The Four Shipping Markets                    175
5.1  The decisions facing shipowners                    175
5.2  The four shipping markets                          177
5.3  The freight market                                 180
5.4  The freight derivatives market                     193
5.5  The sale and purchase market                       198
5.6  The newbuilding market                             207
5.7  The demolition (recycling) market                  212
5.8  Summary                                            213

## PART 3:  SHIPPING COMPANY ECONOMICS                   215

Chapter 6  Costs, Revenue and Cashflow                  217
6.1  Cashflow and the art of survival                   217
6.2  Financial performance and investment strategy      219
6.3  The cost of running ships                           225

6.4 The capital cost of the ship     236
6.5 The revenue the ship earns     242
6.6 Shipping accounts – the framework for decisions     246
6.7 Four methods of computing the cashflow     252
6.8 Valuing merchant ships     262
6.9 Summary     266

Chapter 7 Financing Ships and Shipping Companies     269
7.1 Ship finance and shipping economics     269
7.2 How ships have been financed in the past     270
7.3 The world financial system and types of finance     276
7.4 Financing ships with private funds     285
7.5 Financing ships with bank loans     285
7.6 Financing ships and shipping companies in the capital markets     296
7.7 Financing ships with special purpose companies     303
7.8 Analysing risk in ship finance     310
7.9 Dealing with default     314
7.10 Summary     316

Chapter 8 Risk, Return and Shipping Company Economics     319
8.1 The performance of shipping investments     319
8.2 The shipping company investment model     324
8.3 Competition theory and the 'normal' profit     329
8.4 Pricing shipping risk     338
8.5 Summary     342

PART 4: SEABORNE TRADE AND TRANSPORT SYSTEMS     345

Chapter 9 The Geography of Maritime Trade     347
9.1 The value added by seaborne transport     347
9.2 Oceans, distances and transit times     348
9.3 The maritime trading network     356
9.4 Europe's seaborne trade     365
9.5 North America's seaborne trade     368
9.6 South America's seaborne trade     371
9.7 Asia's seaborne trade     373
9.8 Africa's seaborne trade     378
9.9 The seaborne trade of the Middle East, Central Asia and Russia     379
9.10 The trade of Australia and Oceania     383
9.11 Summary     383

Chapter 10 The Principles of Maritime Trade     385
10.1 The building-blocks of sea trade     385

## CONTENTS

10.2 The countries that trade by sea 389

10.3 Why countries trade 393

10.4 Differences in production costs 395

10.5 Trade due to differences in natural resources 399

10.6 Commodity trade cycles 404

10.7 The role of sea transport in trade 411

10.8 Summary 415

Chapter 11 The Transport of Bulk Cargoes 417

11.1 The commercial origins of bulk shipping 417

11.2 The bulk fleet 418

11.3 The bulk trades 419

11.4 The principles of bulk transport 422

11.5 Practical aspects of bulk transport 427

11.6 Liquid bulk transport 432

11.7 The crude oil trade 434

11.8 The oil products trade 442

11.9 The major dry bulk trades 445

11.10 The minor bulk trades 457

11.11 Summary 466

Chapter 12 The Transport of Specialized Cargoes 469

12.1 Introduction to specialized shipping 469

12.2 The sea transport of chemicals 473

12.3 The liquefied petroleum gas trade 478

12.4 The liquefied natural gas trade 483

12.5 The transport of refrigerated cargo 488

12.6 Unit load cargo transport 492

12.7 Passenger shipping 499

12.8 Summary 503

Chapter 13 The Transport of General Cargo 505

13.1 Introduction 505

13.2 The origins of the liner service 506

13.3 Economic principles of liner operation 512

13.4 General cargo and liner transport demand 514

13.5 The liner shipping routes 524

13.6 The liner companies 532

13.7 The liner fleet 537

13.8 The principles of liner service economics 539

13.9 Pricing liner services 550

13.10 Liner conferences and cooperative agreements 555

13.11 Container ports and terminals 559

13.12 Summary 562

**PART 5:  THE MERCHANT FLEET AND TRANSPORT SUPPLY**          **565**

Chapter 14  The Ships that Provide the Transport                      567
  14.1  What type of ship?                                            567
  14.2  Seven questions that define a design                          571
  14.3  Ships for the general cargo trades                            581
  14.4  Ships for the dry bulk trades                                 590
  14.5  Ships for liquid bulk cargoes                                 596
  14.6  Gas tankers                                                   604
  14.7  Non-cargo ships                                               608
  14.8  Economic criteria for evaluating ship designs                609
  14.9  Summary                                                       610

Chapter 15  The Economics of Shipbuilding and Scrapping              613
  15.1  The role of the merchant shipbuilding and scrapping industries  613
  15.2  The regional structure of world shipbuilding                 614
  15.3  Shipbuilding market cycles                                    625
  15.4  The economic principles                                      628
  15.5  The shipbuilding production process                          638
  15.6  Shipbuilding costs and competitiveness                      644
  15.7  The ship recycling industry                                  648
  15.8  Summary                                                      652

Chapter 16  The Regulation of the Maritime Industry                 655
  16.1  How regulations affect maritime economics                   655
  16.2  Overview of the regulatory system                           656
  16.3  The classification societies                                658
  16.4  The law of the sea                                          663
  16.5  The regulatory role of the flag state                       666
  16.6  How maritime laws are made                                  675
  16.7  The International Maritime Organization                     678
  16.8  The International Labour Organization                       684
  16.9  The regulatory role of the coastal and port states         685
  16.10  The regulation of competition in shipping                  688
  16.11  Summary                                                    692

**PART 6:  FORECASTING AND PLANNING**                               **695**

Chapter 17  Maritime Forecasting and Market Research               697
  17.1  The approach to maritime forecasting                        697
  17.2  Key elements of the forecast                                702
  17.3  Preparing for the forecast                                  705
  17.4  Market forecasting methodologies                            709

# CONTENTS

17.5  Market research methodology                                   712
17.6  Freight rate forecasting                                      715
17.7  Developing a scenario analysis                                723
17.8  Analytical techniques                                         724
17.9  Forecasting problems                                          738
17.10  Summary                                                      742

Appendix A:  An Introduction to Shipping Market Modelling          745
Appendix B:  Tonnage Measurement and Conversion Factors            751
Appendix C:  Maritime Economics Freight Index, 1741–2007           755

*Notes*                                                            759
*References and suggested reading*                                 783
*Index*                                                            793

# Preface to the Third Edition

The third edition of *Maritime Economics*, like the previous editions, aims to explain how the shipping market is organized and answer some practical questions about how it works. Why do countries trade by sea? How is sea transport organized? How are prices and freight rates determined? How are ships financed? Are there market cycles? What returns do shipping companies make? How can a shipping company survive depressions? What influences ship design? And, of course, is it possible to make reliable forecasts?

Much has changed in the twenty years since the first edition was published in 1988. Then the industry was struggling out of a deep recession and the second edition, which appeared in 1997, was written in a more prosperous but still disappointing market. However the third edition, on which work started in 2002, coincided with one of the great booms in the industry's history. These contrasting decades provided a unique opportunity to study shipping in feast and famine and I hope the substantially revised third edition has benefited from the insights it provided.

This edition retains the structure of its predecessors, but there are many changes and additions. A major innovation is the chapter on the economic history of the maritime business. Introducing an economics book with history is risky, but shipping has five thousand years of documented commercial history. If you've got it, why not flaunt it? There is a certain comfort in knowing that others have navigated the same seas many times before and there a lesson to learn. Maritime history surges forward with all the momentum of a VLCC, flattening anything in its path, so shipping investors in their commercial sailboats must keep a sharp lookout for the 'secular trend', as well as more immediate, but less threatening, shipping market cycles.

The analysis of shipping cycles now extends back to 1741 and the markets chapter includes an expanded section on derivatives which are more widely used than a decade ago. The theoretical supply demand analysis has been updated to introduce vertical mobility of the supply curve. A new chapter tackles the tricky issue of the return on capital in shipping, focussing on the microeconomics of the industry and introducing the 'risky asset pricing' (RAP) model. There is also a new chapter on the geography of maritime trade which deals with the physical world in which shipping operates and another on specialised shipping. The other chapters have all been updated, extended and revised where appropriate.

*Maritime Economics: third edition* now has seventeen chapters, the contents of which are summarized in the next section.

In producing the three editions I am grateful for the help from many people. For the first and second editions I would like to repeat my thanks to Efthimios Mitropoulos, now Secretary-General of the International Maritime Organization, Professor Costas Grammenos, Pro-Vice Chancellor of City University, London, the late Peter Douglas of Chase Manhattan Bank, Professor Harry Benford of Michigan University, Professor Rigas Doganis, Professor Michael Tamvakis of CASS Business School, the Rt Hon. Gerald Cooper, Dr John Doviak of Cambridge Academy of Transport, Professor Henk Molenaar, Mona Kristiansen of Leif Hoegh & Company, Captain Philip J. Wood, Sir Graham Day, Alan Adams of Shell International Marine, Richard Hext, CEO of Pacific Basin Shipping Ltd, Rogan McLellan, Mark Page Director of Drewry Shipping Consultants, Professor Mary Brooks of Dalhousie University, Bob Crawley, Betsy Nelson, Merrick Raynor, Jonathan Tully, Robert Bennett, John Ferguson and Paul Stott. All provided comments, suggestions and insights from which the present volume benefits.

For help with the third edition my thanks are due to Professor Peter B. Marlow, Rawi Nair, and Kiki Mitroussi of Cardiff University, Bill Ebersold, now retired from MARAD, Alan Jamieson, Peter Stokes of Lazards, Jeremy Penn, Chief Executive of the Baltic Exchange, Tony Mason, Secretary General of the International Chamber of Shipping, Richard Greiner, Partner of Moore Stephens, Rogan McLellan, Captain Robert W. Sinclair, Sabine Knapp of IMO, Niels G. Stolt-Nielsen, Sean Day, Chairman of Teekay Shipping Corporation, Susan Cooke, Finance Director of Global Ship Lease, Jean Richards, Director of Quantum Shipping Services, Trevor Crowe and Cliff Tyler, Directors of Clarkson Research Services Ltd, Nick Wood and Tom White of Clarksons newbuilding desk, Bob Knight and Alex Williams of Clarksons Tanker Division, Nick Collins of Clarksons Dry Cargo Division, Alan Ginsberg, CFO of Eagle Bulk Shipping, John Westwood of Douglas-Westwood Ltd, Dorthe Bork and her colleagues at Odense Steel Shipyard, Jarle Hammer of Fearnleys, Professor Roar Adland of Clarksons Fund Management, Dr Peter Swift, MD of Intertanko, Professor Knick Harley of Oxford University, Professor Alan Winter of the University of Sussex,, Hamid Seddighi of the University of Sunderland and Erik Bastiensen. Also I would like to thank Randy Young of the US Office of Naval Intelligence (ONI) for his help and enthusiasm in extending the freight cycle statistics back to 1741, my brother John Stopford for many thoughtful discussions and my editor at Routledge, Rob Langham.

Finally, finishing this much enlarged book was a daunting task and I owe special thanks to Tony Gray of Lloyds List, Professor Ian Buxton of Newcastle University and Charlie Norse of Massachusetts Maritime Academy for their encouragement, time, knowledge and advice.

Martin Stopford,
London, 2008

# Synopsis

## PART 1 INTRODUCTION TO SHIPPING

*Part 1 addresses the questions of where shipping has come from and where it is now.*

*Chapter 1: Sea Transport and the Global Economy*

Shipping plays a central part in the global economy, and its well-documented history, stretching back for 5,000 years, gives maritime economists a unique perspective on the way the industry's economic mechanisms and institutions have evolved. We find that today's trading world has evolved over many centuries and history demonstrates the regional center of sea trade is constantly on the move – we call its path the 'Westline'. By examining the trade of the Atlantic and Pacific Oceans we can see where the 'Westline' is today.

*Chapter 2: The Economic Organization of the Shipping Market*

We give an overview of the market covering the transport system, the demand for sea transport, the merchant fleet, how transport is provided, the role of ports, shipping company organization and political influences.

## PART 2 SHIPPING MARKET ECONOMICS

*Part 2 sets out the macroeconomic structure of the shipping market to show the role of market cycles, the forces that drive them, and the commercial environment in which the industry operates.*

*Chapter 3: Shipping Market Cycles*

Shipping market cycles dominate the industry's economic thinking. A discussion of the characteristics of shipping cycles leads on to a review of how experts have explained the shipping cycle. The 22 cycles since 1741 are identified from statistical series and contemporary market reports. A brief account is provided of each cycle, drawing attention to the economic mechanism which drove the market up or down and the underlying secular trend. The chapter ends with some thoughts on the return on capital in shipping and the prediction of shipping cycles.

*Chapter 4: Supply, Demand and Freight Rates*

We now take a more detailed look at the economic model of the shipping market which underlies the cyclical nature of the business. The model consists of three components: supply, demand and the freight rate mechanism. The first half of the chapter discusses the ten key variables which influence the supply and demand functions for the shipping industry. The second half examines how freight rates link supply and demand. Emphasis is placed on market dynamics.

*Chapter 5: The Four Shipping Markets*

In this chapter we review how the markets actually work. Shipping business is conducted through four related markets dealing in different commodities, freight, second-hand ships, new ships and ships for demolition. We discuss the practicalities of each market and the dynamics of how they are connected by cashflow. As cash flows in and out of shipowners' balance sheets it influences their behaviour in these markets.

## PART 3 SHIPPING COMPANY ECONOMICS

*Turning to microeconomics, we discuss the practical issues facing a firm. How are shipping costs and revenues structured? How are ships financed? How does the industry make a commercial return on investment?*

*Chapter 6: Costs, Revenue and Financial Performance*

This chapter discusses the costs and revenues of operating merchant ships. Costs are divided into voyage costs and operating costs. Capital costs are also discussed, though the main review of financing is contained in the next chapter. The final section focuses on company accounts, including the income statement, balance sheet and cashflow statement. We finish with a discussion of cashflow analysis.

*Chapter 7: Financing Ships and Shipping Companies*

Finance is the most important item in the shipowner's cashflow budget. The chapter starts with a review of the many ways ships have been financed in the past, followed by a brief explanation of the world capital markets, showing where the money comes from. Finally the chapter discusses the four main ways of financing ships: equity, debt, newbuilding finance, and leasing.

*Chapter 8: Risk, Return and Shipping Company Economics*

Shipping has a history of offering very mediocre returns over long periods, interspersed by bursts of profitability. This chapter examines the shipping company investment model and applies the theory of the firm to shipping companies, to establish what determines return on investment in shipping and how the shipping industry prices risk.

## PART 4 SEABORNE TRADE AND TRANSPORT SYSTEMS

*We turn our attention to cargo and the transport systems which carry it. We begin with the geographical framework of trade, moving on to trade theory and the economic forces that govern trade. Then we examine how the shipping industry transports cargo today, focusing on the three main segments: bulk shipping, specialized shipping and liner shipping.*

*Chapter 9: The Geography of Maritime Trade*

The shipping industry adds value by exploiting arbitrages between global markets, and there is a physical dimension to shipping economics, so we must be aware of the geography of maritime trade. This chapter examines the physical world within which this trade takes place, covering the oceans, distances, transit times and the maritime trading network. It concludes with a review of the trade of each of the major economic regions.

*Chapter 10: The Theory of Maritime Trade*

Shipping depends on trade, so we must understand why countries trade and why trading patterns change. We start with a short summary of trade theory, identifying the various explanations for trade. This is followed by a discussion of the supply–demand model used to analyse natural resource based commodity trades. Turning to the actual sea trade of 105 countries, we review the evidence for a relationship between trade and land area, population natural resources and economic activity. Finally, we review the 'trade development cycle' and the relationship between sea trade and economic development.

*Chapter 11: Bulk Cargo and the Economics of Bulk Shipping*

The widespread use of bulk transport systems to reduce the cost of shipping raw materials reshaped the global economy in the twentieth century. The first part of the chapter analyses the principles of bulk transport and bulk handling. It covers the transport system, the transport characteristics of commodities and the development of transport systems for bulk handling. This is followed by a brief account of the various commodities shipped in bulk, their economic characteristics and the transport systems employed.

*Chapter 12: The Transport of Specialized Cargoes*

In this chapter we study the shipping segments which have been developed to transport those cargoes which can benefit from specialized transport systems. The chapter covers chemicals, liquefied gas, refrigerated cargo, unit labour cargoes, and passenger shipping.

*Chapter 13: The Economics of Liner Shipping*

Containerization of liner services was one of the great commercial innovations of the twentieth century. Faster transport and lower costs have made it possible for businesses to source materials and market their products almost anywhere in the world. This chapter discusses the organization of the liner system, the characteristics of demand and the way the liner business deals with the complex economic framework within which it operates.

## PART 5  THE MERCHANT FLEET AND TRANSPORT SUPPLY

*Part 5 is concerned with three key aspects of the supply of merchant ships: the fleet of vessels; shipbuilding and demolition; and the regulatory framework which influences the cost of operating ships and the conditions under which ships can be traded.*

*Chapter 14: The Ships that Supply the Transport*

In this chapter we discuss the design of merchant ships. The aim is to focus on the way designs have evolved to meet technical and economic objectives. The chapter starts from the three objectives of ship design: efficient cargo containment, operational efficiency and cost. There follows a discussion of each of the main categories of ship design: liner vessels, liquid bulk, dry bulk, specialist bulk, and service vessels.

*Chapter 15: The Economics of Merchant Shipbuilding and Scrapping*

The shipbuilding and ship scrapping industries play a central part in the shipping market model. This chapter starts with a regional review of the location of shipbuilding capacity. This is followed by a discussion of shipping market cycles in production and prices. A section on the economic principles is followed by a discussion of the technology of the business. Finally there is a section on ship scrapping.

*Chapter 16: The Regulation of the Maritime Industry*

This chapter examines the impact of regulation on shipping economics. We identify three key regulatory institutions: the classification societies, the flag states and the coastal states. Each plays a part in making the rules which govern the economic activities of shipowners. The classification societies, through the authority of the 'class certificate', supervise the technical safety of the merchant ships. The flag states make the laws which govern the technical and commercial activities of shipowners registered with them. Finally, the coastal states police the 'good conduct' of ships in their waters, notably on environmental issues.

## PART 6: FORECASTING AND PLANNING

*Decision makers need to decide what is the best thing to do, and that means analysis and forecasting (though the two are different). Part 6 consists of a single chapter which examines the use of maritime economics to answer these questions.*

*Chapter 17: Maritime Forecasting and Market Research*

The 'forecasting paradox' is that businessmen do not really expect forecasts to be correct, yet they continue to use them. There are two different types of 'forecasts' used in the shipping industry: market forecasts and market research. Market forecasts cover the market in general, whilst market research applies to a specific decision. Different techniques are discussed covering each type of study. We conclude with a review of common forecasting errors.

**Appendix A:** An Introduction to Shipping Market Modelling

**Appendix B:** Tonnage Measurement and Conversion Factors

**Appendix C:** Maritime Economics Freight Index, 1741–2007

# Abbreviations

| | |
|---|---|
| ACF | annual cashflow analysis |
| AG | Arabian Gulf |
| bt | billion tons |
| btm | billion ton miles |
| BTX | benzene, toluene, xylene |
| cgrt | compensated gross registered tonnage |
| COA | contract of affreightment |
| cgt | compensated gross tonnage |
| dwt | deadweight tonnage |
| EEC | European Economic Community |
| FEFC | Far East Freight Conference |
| FFA | forward freight agreement |
| FPC | forest products carrier |
| GATT | General Agreement on Tariffs and Trade |
| GDP | gross domestic product |
| GNP | gross national product |
| GRI | general rate increase |
| grt | gross registered tonnage |
| gt | gross tonnage |
| IACS | International Association of Classification Societies |
| ILO | International Labour Organization |
| IMCO | Inter-governmental Maritime Consultative Organization |
| IMO | International Maritime Organization |
| IPO | initial public offering |
| IRR | internal rate of return |
| ISO | International Organization for Standardization |

## ABBREVIATIONS

| | |
|---|---|
| ITF | International Transport Workers' Organization |
| LCM | lateral cargo mobility |
| LNG | liquefied natural gas |
| LOA | length overall |
| lo-lo | lift on, lift off |
| LPG | liquefied petroleum gas |
| MCR | maximum continuous rating |
| m.dwt | million tons deadweight |
| MPP | multi-purpose |
| mt | million tons |
| MTBE | methyl tert-butyl ether |
| NPV | net present value |
| OBO | oil/bulk/ore carrier |
| OECD | Organization for Economic Co-operation and Development |
| OPEC | Organization of Petroleum Exporting Countries |
| P&I | protection and indemnity- |
| PCC | pure car carrier |
| PCTC | pure car and truck carrier |
| PSD | parcel size distribution function |
| RFR | required freight rate |
| ROI | return on investment |
| ro-ro | roll on, roll off |
| SDR | Special Drawing Right |
| TEU | twenty-foot equivalent unit |
| tm | ton mile |
| ULCC | ultra large crude carrier |
| UN | United Nations |
| UNCTAD | United Nations Conference on Trade and Development |
| VCF | voyage cashflow analysis |
| VLCC | very large crude carrier |
| WS | Worldscale |

# Fifty Essential Shipping Terms

(See also Box 5.1 in Chapter 5 for a glossary of essential chartering terms.)

1. **Aframax**. Tanker carrying around 0.5 million barrels of oil, but usually applied to any tanker of 80,000–120,000 dwt (name derived from old AFRA chartering range).

2. **Auxiliary engines**. Small diesel engines on the ship used to drive alternators providing electrical power. They generally burn diesel oil. Ships generally have between three and five, depending on electricity requirements.

3. **Ballast**. Sea water pumped into carefully located ballast tanks, or cargo spaces, when the ship is not carrying cargo, to lower the ship in the water so that the propeller is sufficiently submerged to perform efficiently.

4. **Berth**. Designated area of quayside where a ship comes alongside to load or discharge cargo.

5. **Bulk carrier**. Single-deck ship which carries dry cargoes such as ore, coal, sugar or cereals. Smaller vessels may have their own cranes, whilst larger sizes rely on shore based equipment.

6. **Bare boat charter**. Similar to a lease. The vessel is chartered to a third party who to all intents and purposes owns it for the period of the charter, provides the crew, pays operating costs (including maintenance) and voyage costs (bunkers, port dues, canal transit dues, etc.), and directs its operations.

7. **Bunkers**. Fuel oil burned in ship's main engine (auxiliaries use diesel)

8. **Capesize**. Bulk carrier too wide to transit the Panama Canal. Usually over 100,000 tonnes deadweight, but size increases over time, currently 170,000–180,000 dwt.

9. **Charterer**. Person or company who hires a ship from a shipowner for a period of time (time charter) or who reserves the entire cargo space for a single voyage (voyage charter).

10. **Classification society**. Organization, such as Lloyd's Register, which sets standards for ship construction; supervises standards during construction; and inspects the hull and machinery of a ship classed with the society at regular intervals, awarding the 'class certificate' required to obtain hull insurance. A ship with a current certificate is 'in class'.

11. **Container**. Standard box of length 20 or 40 ft, width 8 ft and height 8 ft 6 in. High cube containers are 9 ft 6 in. high, and container-ships are usually designed to carry some of these.

12. **Container-ship**. Ship designed to carry containers, with cell guides in the holds into which the containers are lowered. Containers carried on deck are lashed and secured.

13. **Compensated gross ton (cgt)**. Measure of shipbuilding output based on the gross tonnage of the ship multiplied by a cgt coefficient reflecting its work content (see Appendix B).

14. **Deadweight (dwt)**. The weight a ship can carry when loaded to its marks, including cargo, fuel, fresh water, stores and crew.

15. **Freeboard**. Vertical distance between waterline and top of hull.

16. **Freight rate**. Amount of money paid to a shipowner or shipping line for the carriage of each unit of cargo (lonne, cubic metre or container load) between named ports.

17. **Freight alt kinds (FAK)**. The standard rate charged per container, regardless of what commodity it is carrying, e.g. FAK rate of $1500 per TEU.

18. **FEU**. Forty-foot container (see TEU).

19. **Gas tanker**. Ship capable of carrying liquid gas at sub-zero temperatures. Cargo is kept cold by pressure, insulation, and/or refrigeration of 'boil-off gas' which is returned to the cargo tanks (see Chapter 14).

20. **Gross ton (gt)**. Internal measurement of the ship's open spaces. Now calculated from a formula set out in the IMO Tonnage Convention.

21. **Handy bulker**. Bulk carrier at the smaller end of the range of sizes associated with this type of ship, typically up to 30,000–35,000 tonnes deadweight. Most have their own cargo-handling gear.

22. **ice class 1A**. Ship certified to transit ice of 0.8 m thickness.

23. **IMO**. International Maritime Organization, the UN agency which is responsible for maritime regulations.

24. **Lay-up**. This describes a ship that has been taken out of service because freight rates are too low to cover its operating and maintenance costs Not a well-defined condition, it often just means that the ship has not moved for, say, 3 months.

25. **Lashing**. Used with twist-locks to stop containers moving in heavy seas. Lashing wires may be secured, for example, from the top corners of the first tier and bottom corners of the second tier.

26. **LIBOR**. London Inter-bank Offered Rate, the interest rate at which banks raise funds on the eurodollar market.

27. **Lightweight (light displacement tonnage, lwt)**. Weight of a ship's hull, machinery, equipment and spares. This is the basis on which ships are usually sold for scrap, e.g. $200 per lwt.

28. **MARPOL**. International Convention for the Prevention of Pollution from Ships (see Chapter 16).

29. **Off-hire**. Time, usually measured in days, during which charter hire payments are suspended because the vessel is not available to trade, for example because of a breakdown or routine repair time.

30. **Operating costs (OPEX)**. Expenses involved in the day-to-day running of the ship and incurred whatever trade the ship is engaged in. These include crew wages and expenses, victuailing, stores, spares, repairs and maintenance, lubricants, and insurance.

31. **P&I club**. Mutual society which provides third party insurance to shipowner members.

32. **Panamax**. Bulk carrier which can transit Panama Canal where the lock width of 32.5 m is the limiting factor. Vessels of 60,000–75,000 tonnes deadweight fall into this category. 'Panamax' is also used to refer to tankers of 60,000–70,000 deadweight.

33. **Reefer**. Insulated cargo ship for carrying refrigerated food, either frozen or chilled.

34. **Reefer container**. Insulated container for carrying refrigerated cargo. Some have integral electric refrigeration plant run from a plug on the ship or shore facility. Others receive cold air from central refrigeration unit on ship.

35. **Seller's commission**. Fee or commission payable by a seller of a vessel to the broker(s) who has secured her sale.

36. **Service agreement**. Agreement between container line and shipper to provide freight transport on specified terms.

37. **Shipbroker**. Individual with current market knowledge who acts as intermediary between buyers and sellers in return for a percentage commission on the transaction. There are several types of these – for example, chartering brokers deal with cargo; sale and purchase brokers buy and sell ships; newbuilding brokers place contracts for new ships.

38. **SOLAS**. Safety of Life at Sea Convention. Important convention setting out the safety regulations with which all merchant ships must comply (see Chapter 16).

39. **Special survey**. Mandatory examination of the ship's hull and machinery carried out every five years, or on a rolling basis, by the classification society with which the vessel is classed.

40. **Spot rate**. Negotiated rate per unit (tonne, cubic metre, etc.) of cargo paid to the shipowner to carry specific cargo between two ports, say US Gulf to Japan. Voyage costs are paid by the shipowner.

41. **String (of container-ships)**. The number of container-ships needed to maintain a regular service on a specific route ('loop'). For example, a string of four ships is needed to run a transatlantic loop.

42. **Suezmax**. Tanker able to transit Suez Canal fully loaded; carries about 1 million barrels of oil. Tankers of 120,000–200,000 dwt are grouped into this category.

43. **Tanker**. Ship designed for the carriage of liquid in bulk with cargo space consisting of several tanks. Tankers carry a wide variety of products, including crude oil, refined products, liquid gas and wine. Parcel tankers have a separate pump and cargo lining for each tank so that many cargo parcels can be carried separately in the ship.

44. **TEU**. Twenty-foot equivalent unit (a 40 ft container is 2 TEU).

45. **Time charter**. A transportation contract under which the charterer has the use of the vessel for a specific period. A fixed daily or monthly payment is made for the hire of the vessel, for example $20,000 per day. Under this arrangement, the owner manages the day-to-day running of the ships, and pays the operating and capital costs. The charterer pays fuel, port charges, loading/discharging fees and other cargo-related costs, and directs the ship operations.

46. **Time charter equivalent**. The spot freight rate (e.g. $20 per tonne for a 40,000 tonne cargo) converted into a daily hire rate for the voyage (e.g. $20,000 per day) by deducting voyage costs from the gross freight and dividing by the days on the voyage, including necessary ballast time.

47. **Tonne**. Metric ton, equivalent to 1,000 kilograms or 2,240 lbs.

48. **Twist-lock**. Devices used to join and lock containers to those above and below them by clamping the adjacent corner castings together. 'Cones' fit into apertures in the corner castings and turn to lock them in place. Used with lashing wires and bars.

49. **VLCC**. Very large crude carrier, generally carries about 2 million barrels of oil, but all tankers over 200,000 dwt are grouped into this category.

50. **Voyage costs**. The cost of fuel, port expenses and canal costs which are specific to the voyage. On a voyage charter where the ports are specified they are generally included in the negotiated spot rate and paid by the shipowner. On a time charter where the ports are not known in advance they are paid by the charterer.

# Part 1

# INTRODUCTION TO SHIPPING

# 1

# Sea Transport and the Global Economy

*Wonders are many on earth, and the greatest of these*
*Is man, who rides the ocean and takes his way*
*Through the deeps, through wind-swept valleys of perilous seas*
*That surge and sway.*

(The chorus in *Sophocles' Antigone, 422 BC*, trans. R.C. Jebb)

## 1.1 INTRODUCTION

### Characteristics of the business

Shipping is a fascinating business. Since the first cargoes were moved by sea more than 5,000 years ago it has been at the forefront of global development. The epic voyages of Columbus, Diaz and Magellan opened the maritime highways of the world, and the same pioneering spirit brought supertankers,[1] container-ships, and the complex fleet of specialized ships which each year transport a ton of cargo for every person in the world. No business is more exciting. The great shipping boom of 2004 swept the industry from rags to riches in little more than a year, making its fortunate investors some of the wealthiest people in the world. This sort of volatility created superstars like Niarchos and Onassis, and a few villains like Tidal Marine, which built up a 700,000 dwt (dead-weight tonnage) shipping fleet in the early 1970s and were indicted with a number of their bankers for fraudulently obtaining more than $60 million in loans.[2]

Our task in this book is to understand the economics of the industry. What makes it so interesting to economists is that the shipping investors who grapple with shipping risk are so visible, and their activities so well documented, that we can blend theory and practice. For all their flamboyance, they operate within a strict economic regime, which would be immediately recognizable by nineteenth-century classical economists. It is, more or less, the 'perfect' market place at work, an economic Jurassic Park where the dinosaurs of classical economics roam free and consumers get a very good deal – there are not many monopolies in shipping! Occasionally the investors miscalculate, as in the remarkable episode in 1973 when investors in the tanker market ordered over 100 million tons deadweight (m.dwt) of supertankers, for which there turned out to be no demand.

Some went from the builder's yard straight into lay-up, and few ever operated to their full economic potential. Or occasionally they run short of ships and rates go sky high, as they did during the booms of 1973 and 2004–8. But generally they 'deliver the goods' economically as well as physically at a cost which, on average, has increased surprisingly little over the years.[3]

Because shipping is such an old industry, with a history of continuous change, sometimes gradual and occasionally calamitous, we have a unique opportunity to learn from the past. Time and again we find that shipping and trade greased the slipway[4] from which the world economy was launched on new voyages in whatever political and economic vessel history had devised for it. No other industry had played such a central part in these economic voyages over thousands of years – the airline industry, shipping's closest counterpart, has barely 50 years of economic history to study! So before we plunge into the details of the shipping business as it is today, we will spend a little time studying the history of this ancient global industry to see how the economics worked in practice and where the industry is today in its latest epic voyage of globalization.[5]

## The role of sea trade in economic development

The importance of sea transport in the early stages of economic development is well known to economists. In Chapter 3 of *The Wealth of Nations*, published in 1776, Adam Smith argued that the key to success in a capitalist society is the division of labour. As productivity increases and businesses produce more goods than they can sell locally, they need access to wider markets. He illustrated the point with the famous example of making pins. Working alone, ten craftsmen can produce less than 100 pins a day, but if each specializes in a single task, together they can produce 48,000 pins a day. This is far too many to sell locally, so unlocking the power of 'division of labour' depends on transport, and this is where shipping had a crucial part to play:

> As by means of water carriage a more extensive market is opened to every sort of industry than what land carriage alone can afford it, so it is upon the sea-coast, and along the banks of navigable rivers, that industry of every kind naturally begins to subdivide and improve itself, and it is frequently not until a long time after that those improvements extend themselves to the inland parts of the country.[6]

In primitive economies shipping is generally more efficient than land transport, allowing trade to get started earlier. Adam Smith paints a graphic picture of the economic benefits offered by sea transport in the eighteenth century:

> A broad wheeled wagon attended by two men and drawn by eight horses in about six weeks time carries and brings back between London and Edinburgh nearly 4 tons weight of goods. In about the same time a ship navigated by six or eight men, and sailing between the ports of London and Leith, frequently carries and brings back 200 ton weight of goods.[7]

That is a labour productivity benefit of 15 times. By exploiting economies of scale and integrated transport systems, shipping continues to demonstrate Adam Smith's insight. Today a lorry carrying one 40-foot container from Felixstowe to Edinburgh might be competing with a small container-ship carrying 200 containers. Or a truck hauling 40 tons of oil along our congested highways competes with a coastal oil tanker carrying 4,000 tons of oil by sea. Ships now travel at speeds that trucks can hardly match on congested urban roads and at a fraction of the cost. No wonder the oceans are the highways of economic development, an aspect of the business which hardly changes with the centuries. Many practical aspects of the business have not changed either. For example the bill of lading from AD 236 in Box 1.1 shows that Roman shipowners worried just as much about demurrage as shipowners do today. But new generations of shipowners also face new challenges, and shipping companies that do not adapt, however big or prestigious they may be, soon discover how ruthless the shipping market is in forcing the pace of change.

## History of maritime development – the Westline

So in this chapter we are not just concerned with history. Winston Churchill said 'the further backward I look the further forward I can see',[8] and if he was right, the shipping industry is in a unique position to learn from its past about the economics of the maritime business. The evolution of sea transport is a well-travelled road which we can even plot on a map. Over 5,000 years, whether by chance or some deeply hidden economic force, the commercial centre of maritime trade has moved west along the line shown by the arrows in Figure 1.1. This 'Westline' started in Mesopotamia in 3000 BC, and progressed to Tyre in the eastern Mediterranean then to Rhodes, the Greek mainland and Rome. A thousand years ago Venice (and soon after Genoa) became the crossroads for

> ### BOX 1.1  A BILL OF LADING, AD 236
>
> This bill of lading is given by Aurelius Heracles, son of Dioscorus of Antaeopolis, master of his own ship of 250 artabae burden, without any figurehead, to Aurelius Arius, son of Heraclides, senator of Arsinoe, capital of Fayum, for the carriage of 250 artabae of vegetable seed, to be conveyed from the haven of the Grove to the capital of Arisonoe in the haven of Oxyrhynchus, the freightage agreed on being 100 clean silver drachmae, whereof he has received 40 drachmae, the remaining 60 drachmae he is to receive when he lands the cargo; which cargo he shall land safe and undamaged by any nautical mishap; and he shall take for the journey two days, from the 25th, and likewise he shall remain at Oxyrhynchus four days; and if he be delayed after that time he, the master, shall receive 16 drachmae per day for himself; and he the master shall provide a sufficient number of sailors and all the tackle of the ship; and he shall receive likewise for a libation at Oxyrhynchus one ceramion of wine. This bill of lading is valid, in the third year of Emperor Caesar Gaius Julius Verus Maximus the Pious, the fortunate, the 22nd of Phaophi (Oct. 19th).
> Source: The British Museum, London

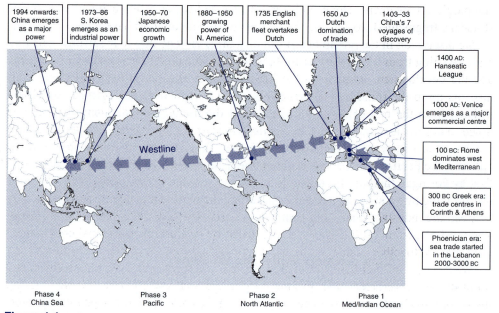

**Figure 1.1**

The Westline: 5,000 years of maritime trading centres

Source: Stopford (1988)

trade between the Mediterranean and the emerging north-western European centres of Cologne, Bruges, Antwerp and Amsterdam. Meanwhile the Hanseatic towns were opening up trading links with the Baltic and Russia. The two streams merged in Amsterdam in the seventeenth century and London in the eighteenth. By the nineteenth century steamships carried the Westline across the Atlantic, and North America became a leading centre of sea trade. Finally, in the twentieth century commerce took another giant step west across the Pacific as Japan, South Korea, China and India picked up the baton of growth.

This evolution of maritime trade was led successively by Babylon, Tyre, Corinth, Rhodes, Athens, Rome, Venice, Antwerp, Amsterdam, London, New York, Tokyo, Hong Kong, Singapore and Shanghai. At each step along the Westline there was an economic struggle between adjacent shipping super-centres as the old centre gave way to the new challenger, leaving a trail like the wake of a ship that has circumnavigated the world. The maritime tradition, political alignments, ports, and even the economic wealth of the different regions are the product of centuries of this economic evolution in which merchant shipping has played a major part.

In this chapter we will try to understand why Europe triggered the expansion rather than China, India or Japan, which were also major civilizations during this period. Fernand Braudel, the French trade historian, distinguished *the* world economy from *a* world economy which 'only concerns a fragment of the world, an economically autonomous section of the planet able to provide for most of its own needs, a section to which its internal links and exchanges give a certain organic unity'.[9] From this perspective shipping's achievement, along with the airlines and telecommunications, was to link Braudel's fragmented worlds into the single global economy we have today.

The discussion in the remainder of this chapter is divided into four sections. The first era, stretching from 3000 BC to AD 1450, is concerned with the early history of shipping, and the development of trade in the Mediterranean and north-western Europe. This takes us up to the middle of the fifteenth century when Europe remained completely isolated from the rest of the world, except for the trickle of trade along the Silk and Spice routes to the east. In the second period we start with the voyages of discovery and see how the shipping industry developed after the new trading routes between the Atlantic, the Pacific and the Indian Ocean were discovered. Global trade was pioneered first by Portugal, then the Netherlands and finally England. Meanwhile North America was growing into a substantial economy, turning the North Atlantic into a superhighway between the industrial centres of East Coast North America and north-western Europe. The third era, from 1800 to 1950, is dominated by steamships and global communications which together transformed the transport system serving the North Atlantic economies and their colonies. A highly flexible transport system based on liners and tramps was introduced and productivity increased enormously. Finally, during the second half of the twentieth century liners and tramps were replaced by new transport systems making use of mechanization technology – containerization, bulk and specialized shipping.

## 1.2 THE ORIGINS OF SEA TRADE, 3000 BC TO AD 1450

### The beginning – the Arabian Gulf

The first sea trade network we know of was developed 5,000 years ago between Mesopotamia (the land between the Tigris and Euphrates rivers), Bahrain and the Indus River in western India (Figure 1.2). The Mesopotamians exchanged their oil and dates

for copper and possibly ivory from the Indus.[10] Each river system probably had a population of about three quarters of a million, more than ten times as great as the population density in northern Europe at that time.[11] These communities were linked by land, but sheltered coastal sea routes provided an easy environment for maritime trade to develop. Bahrain, a barren

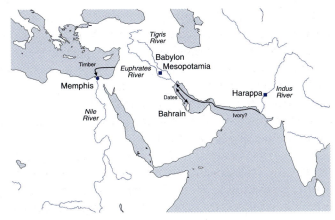

**Figure 1.2**
Early sea trade, 2000 BC

island in the Arabian Gulf, played a part in this trade, but it was Babylon which grew into the first 'super-city', reaching a peak in the eighteenth century BC under Hammurabi, the sixth Amorite king. By this time the Mesopotamians had a well-developed maritime code which formed part of the 3600-line cuneiform inscription, the legal Code of Hammurabi, discovered on a diorite column at Susa, the modern Dizful in Iran.[12] The Code required ships to be hired at a fixed tariff, depending on the cargo capacity of the vessel. Shipbuilding prices were related *pro rata* to size and the builder provided a one-year guarantee of seaworthiness. Freight was to be paid in advance and the travelling agent had to account for all sums spent. All of this sounds very familiar to modern shipowners, though there was obviously not much room for market 'booms' under this command regime of maritime law! About this time seagoing ships were starting to appear in the eastern Mediterranean where the Egyptians were active traders with the Lebanon.

## Opening Mediterranean trade

Tyre in the Lebanon, located at the crossroads between the East and the West, was the next maritime 'super-city'. Although founded in 2700 BC, Tyre did not become a significant sea power until after the decline of Egypt 1700 years later.[13] Like the Greeks and Norwegians who followed in their steps, the poor, arid hinterland of this island encouraged its inhabitants to become seafarers.[14] Their trading world stretched from Memphis in Egypt through to Babylon on the Euphrates, about 55 miles south of Baghdad. Tyre, which lay at the crossroads of this axis, grew rich and powerful from maritime trade. The Phoenicians were shipbuilders and cross-traders (carriers of other people's merchandise) with a trade portfolio that included agricultural produce, metals and manufactures. By the tenth century BC they controlled the Mediterranean trade routes (Figure 1.3), using ships built from cedar planks, usually with a crew of four. Agricultural trades included honey from Crete, wool from Anatolia, plus timber, wine and oil. These were traded for manufactures such as Egyptian linen, gold and ivory, Anatolian wool, Cypriot copper and Arabian resins.[15]

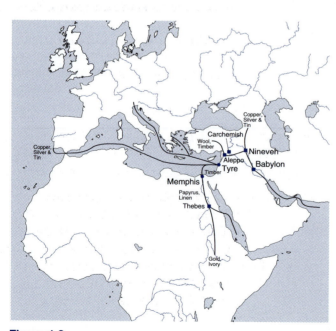

**Figure 1.3**
Phoenician trade, 1000 BC

This traffic grew steadily in the first millennium BC, and as local resources were depleted they travelled further for trading goods. After the discovery of Spain and the settlement of Sades (Cadiz) around 1000 BC, the Iberian peninsula became a major source of metal for the economies of the eastern Mediterranean, consolidating Tyre's commercial domination in the Orient. On land, the domestication of camels made it possible to establish trade routes between the Mediterranean and the Arabian Gulf and Red Sea, linking with the sea trade between the Ganges and the Persian Gulf. In about 500 BC King Darius of Persia, keen to encourage trade, ordered the first Suez Canal to be dug so that his ships could sail direct from the Nile to Persia. Finally, the city of Tyre was captured by Alexander the Great after a long siege and the Phoenician mastery of the Mediterranean came to an end.

## The rise of Greek shipping

By 375 BC the Mediterranean was much busier and was ringed by major towns: Carthage in North Africa, Syracuse in Sicily, Corinth and Athens in Greece, and Memphis in Egypt (Figure 1.4). As the Phoenician merchants declined, the more centrally placed Greeks with their market economy took their place as the leading maritime traders. As Athens expanded, the city imported grain to feed its population, one of the earliest bulk trades.[16] Two hundred years later the eastern Mediterranean had become an active trading area dominated by the four principal towns of Athens, Rhodes, Antioch and Alexandria. The latter two grew particularly strong, thanks to their trading links to the East through the Red Sea and the Arabian Gulf.

The Greeks traded their wine, oil and manufactures (mostly pottery) for

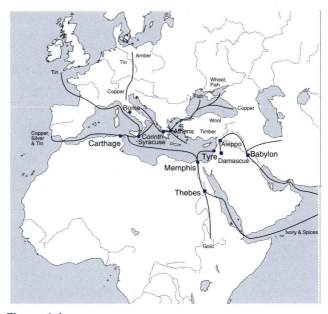

**Figure 1.4**
Mediterranean trade, 300 BC

Carthaginian and Etruscan metals and the traditional products of Egypt and the East. Initially Corinth was the leading town, benefiting from its position on the Isthmus, but subsequently Athens became more prominent thanks to the discovery of silver in nearby Laurion (c.550 BC). This paid for the navy which triumphed at Salamis, liberating the Ionians and guaranteeing safe passage to grain ships from the Black Sea on which the enlarged city came to depend.[17] Grain and fish were shipped in from the Black Sea where, by 500 BC, Greece had founded more than 100 colonies. Carthage held most of the western Mediterranean, including the coast of North Africa, southern Spain, Corsica and western Sicily. However, this was not a developed area with less trade than the eastern Mediterranean.

### Mediterranean trade during the Roman Empire

As Greece declined and Rome grew in economic and political importance, the centre of trade moved to Italy, and the Roman Empire built up a widespread trade network. Rome imported minerals from Spain, and more than 30 million bushels of grain a year from the grain lands of northern Africa, Sicily and Egypt.[18] To carry this trade a fleet of special grain ships was built. Manufactures were traded from the eastern Mediterranean and over the next 200 years the Roman Empire controlled the coasts of the Mediterranean and Black Sea, as well as southern Britain. Under the *Pax Romana,* Mediterranean trade expanded, though there were more towns and trade routes in the East than the West. The towns of the East imported minerals from the 'developing' countries of Spain and Britain, corn from North Africa, Egypt and the Black Sea, and manufactures from the still thriving commercial centres of the Lebanon and Egypt, where the eastern trade routes entered the Mediterranean. An insight into the mature commercial system employed is provided by the bill of lading from AD 236 for a cargo of seed carried up the Nile by a Roman boat (Box 1.1).

### The Byzantine Empire

Towards the end of the fourth century AD the 'Westline' took a step backwards. In about AD 390 the failing Roman Empire, under attack from all sides, was split for administrative purposes into the Western Roman Empire and the Eastern Roman Empire. In modern-day jargon the Eastern Roman Empire contained the economically 'developed' world, while the Western Roman Empire, consisted mainly of 'underdeveloped' territories. The Eastern Roman Empire, with its new capital of Constantinople, grew into the Byzantine Empire, but by AD 490 the Western Roman Empire had fragmented into kingdoms controlled by the Vandals, Visigoths, Slavs, Franks, Saxons and others. Ships could no longer trade safely in the western Mediterranean, and sea trade in the West declined as Europe entered the Dark Ages. For three centuries its economy stagnated.[19]

Over the next 200 years the more stable Eastern Roman Empire, with its capital in Constantinople on the Black Sea, controlled an empire stretching from Sicily in the West to Greece and Turkey in the East. In about AD 650 its administration was overhauled, and because of growing Greek influence on its language and character it is subsequently referred to as the Byzantine Empire.[20] Gradually, by AD 700 the Arab Caliphate controlled the southern and eastern shores of the Mediterranean, and since their trade was principally by land, passage through the Mediterranean became safer. Mediterranean trade was re-established. Sea trade centred on Constantinople, which imported corn from the Black Sea and Sicily as well as commodities such as copper and timber, with shipping routes to Rome and Venice and the Black Sea, whilst the Eastern trade by land followed the Silk and Spice routes, both through Baghdad – a clear demonstration of how much shipping and trade depend on political stability.

## Venice and the Hanseatic League, AD 1000–1400

By AD 1000 the economy of North Europe had begun to grow again, based particularly on the expansion of the wool industry in England and the textile industry in Flanders. As towns grew and prospered in NW Europe, trade with the Baltic and the Mediterranean grew rapidly, leading to the emergence of two important maritime centres, Venice and Genoa in the Mediterranean and the Hanseatic League in the Baltic.

Cargoes from the East arrived in the Mediterranean by the three routes marked on Figure 1.5. The southern route (S) was via the Red Sea and Cairo; the middle route (M) through the Arabian Gulf, Baghdad and Aleppo; whilst the northern route (N) was through the Black Sea and Constantinople. The cargoes were then shipped to Venice or Genoa, carried over the Alps and barged down the Rhine to northern Europe. The commodities shipped west included silk, spices and high-quality textiles from northern Italy which had become a prosperous processing centre. The trade in the other direction included wool, metals and timber products.

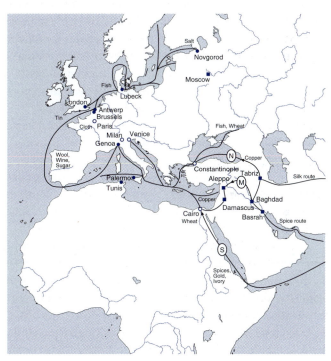

In the Mediterranean, Venice emerged as the major maritime entrepôt and super-city, with Genoa as its main rival. Venice

**Figure 1.5**
North-west Europe opens up, 1480

was helped initially by its political independence, its island sites and the commercial links with the Byzantine Empire which was by then in economic decline, with little interest in sea trade. State legislation, which enforced low interest rates for agricultural reasons, discouraged the Byzantine merchants from entering the business and the Byzantine seafarers could not compete with the low-cost Venetians, even on internal routes. So gradually the Venetian network replaced the native Byzantine one.[21] By accepting Byzantine suzerainty

Venice was able to control the East–West trade. In return for their shipping services they procured preferential tax rates, and in 1081 they won the right to trade anywhere within the Byzantine Empire, without restriction or taxation of any kind. This was an early example of outsourcing sea transport to an independent flag. We will come across many other examples, especially in the twentieth century.

But by the beginning of the thirteenth century the epicentre of maritime trade started to move west. The weakened Byzantine Empire had lost control of Anatolia to the Seljuk Turks, and by 1200 Venice's privileged position with the Byzantine Empire was fading. But this was its peak as a maritime power[22] and as the economy of NW Europe grew, Venice and Genoa's commercial position gradually declined. The sacking of Constantinople by the Ottoman's in 1453 blocked the busy northern trade routes through the Black Sea, increasing the risks and diminishing the returns of the East–West trade. Meanwhile Bruges in Belgium was emerging as Venice's successor. It had an excellent position on the River Zwin estuary, and its monopoly in the English wool trade was strengthened when the direct sea route with the Mediterranean was opened. After the first Genoese ships put in at Bruges in 1227, trade gradually bypassed Venice and the arrival of sailors, ships and merchants from the Mediterranean brought an influx of goods and capital along with commercial and financial expertise. Bruges became the new maritime entrepôt, with a huge trading network covering the Mediterranean, Portugal, France, England, Rhineland and the Hansa ports. Its population grew rapidly from 35,000 inhabitants in 1340 to 100,000 in 1500.[23]

The other strand was NW Europe's need for raw materials to support its economic growth. Russia and the Baltic states were the primary source, exporting fish, wool, timber, corn and tallow, which was replacing vegetable oil in lamps. As this trade grew, Hamburg and Lübeck, which were at the crossroads between the NW Atlantic and the Baltic, grew prosperous and organized themselves into the Hanseatic League.

## 1.3 THE GLOBAL ECONOMY IN THE FIFTEENTH CENTURY

By the fifteenth century there were four developed areas of the world: China, with a population of 120 million; Japan, with 15 million; India, with a population of 110 million; and Europe, with a population of about 75 million. But the only links between them were the tenuous silk and spice routes through Constantinople and Tabriz to China, and the spice route through Cairo and the Red Sea from India.

In terms of wealth and economic development, the Chinese Empire had no rival, with a bureaucracy of indestructible traditions and a history going back 3,000 years.[24] China's seagoing expertise was also in some areas significantly ahead of Europe's. In 1403 the Ming Emperor Zhu Di ordered the construction of an imperial fleet, under the command of Admiral Zheng He. This fleet undertook seven voyages between 1405 and 1433, with over 300 ships and 27,000 men (the need to supply the ships so quickly which must have triggered quite a shipbuilding boom). Contemporary Ming texts suggest that the treasure ships were over 400 feet long with a beam of 150 feet, four times the size of European ocean-going ships, which were typically

100 feet long with 300 tons capacity, but there are doubts about whether such large wooden hulls could have been built.[25] However, the Chinese vessels were certainly technically advanced, with multiple masts, a technique only just developed by the Portuguese, and up to 13 watertight compartments. In sail technology, the Europeans still relied on square sail rigs on their ocean vessels, whilst the Chinese had been using fore-and-aft lugsails in ocean-going ships since the ninth century, giving them a great advantage when sailing upwind. During the seven voyages the great fleet visited Malaysia, the Indian subcontinent, the Arabian Gulf, and Mogadishu in East Africa, travelling about 35,000 miles. There is also some evidence that on one of the voyages the fleet sailed into the South Atlantic and mapped the Cape of Good Hope.[26]

Although by the fifteenth century Chinese mariners were ahead of Europe in some areas of ocean-going ship technology and had the ships and navigational skills to explore and trade with the world, they chose not to do so. In 1433 the expeditions were halted, the ships destroyed and laws passed banning further construction of ocean-going ships, leaving the way open for European seafarers to develop the global sea transport system we have today. What followed was a major shift in global trade as the nations of NW Europe, whose route to the East was now blocked by the Ottoman Empire, discovered the sea route round the Cape and used their naval superiority to create and control global trade routes.

## 1.4 OPENING UP GLOBAL TRADE AND COMMERCE, 1450–1833

### Europe discovers the sea route to Asia

In just a few years in the late fifteenth century, Europe laid the foundation for a global sea trade network which would dominate shipping for the next 500 years. It is hard to imagine the impact which the voyages of discovery (Figure 1.6) must have had, penetrating the Atlantic Ocean and turning sea trade into a global business.[27] The goal was economic: to find a sea route to Asia, the source of the precious spices and silk traded along the spice and silk routes from the east. Marco Polo's 'Description of the World' published in 1298 had publicized the East as an economically attractive destination. He reported that the 'spice islands' consisted of

> 7,488 islands, most of them inhabited. And I assure you that in all these islands there is no tree that does not give off a powerful and agreeable fragrance and serves some useful purpose. There are, in addition, many precious spices of various sorts. The islands produce pepper as white as snow and in great abundance, besides black pepper. Marvellous indeed is the value of the gold and other rarities found in these islands.[28]

No wonder the fabulous 'Spice Islands' gripped the imagination of the European kings and adventurers.

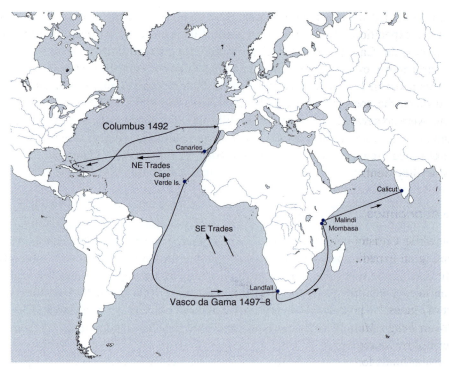

**Figure 1.6**
The European voyages of discovery 1492–98

The problem was getting there. The overland trade was increasingly difficult, and a map drawn by Ptolemy in the second century AD showed the Indian Ocean as being landlocked. However, information gleaned from Moorish traders who had crossed the Sahara hinted that this might not be the case. It was difficult to find out because the South Atlantic was a challenging barrier for sailing ships. Currents and winds opposed ships sailing south,[29] and there were few landfalls on the African coast between Guinea and the Cape. But by the fifteenth century the European explorers had some technical advantages, including the compass, and the astrolabe had been developed in 1480.[30] This navigational instrument allowed sailors to calculate their latitude by measuring the angle between the horizon and the Sun or the pole star, and looking up the latitude for that angle in sea tables. With it explorers could accumulate knowledge about the position of land masses they visited and gradually they built up the knowledge about the Atlantic they needed to make the journey to the east.

## The Portuguese expeditions

At first progress was slow. In the early 1400s Henry 'the Navigator', King of Portugal, a small barren land with a lengthy coastline on the southern tip of Atlantic Europe, became obsessed with finding a way around Africa.[31] His first success came in 1419 when an expedition was blown off course and discovered Madeira. Discovery of the Azores, the Canaries and the Cape Verde Islands soon followed,[32] providing the fifteenth-century explorers with a base for their voyages into the Atlantic. Another big step was taken in 1487 when the Portuguese explorer Bartholomew Diaz successfully sailed down the coast of Africa and rounded the Cape of Good Hope. However, the storms were so severe (he christened it the 'Cape of Storms', but the King of Portugal renamed it the 'Cape of Good Hope') that after making landfall just beyond the Cape his exhausted crew persuaded him to turn back, which they did, mapping the African coast as they went.

## The economics of discovery

Meanwhile Christopher Columbus, a Geonese trader, seafarer and mapmaker, was planning an expedition to reach the Spice Islands by a different route. From ancient writings,[33] his own travels in the North Atlantic and intelligence from the seafaring community – including reports that trees and canes were washed up in Madeira by westerly gales[34] – he concluded that Asia could be reached by sailing west. Using the tables in *Imago Mundi*[35] he calculated that Cipangu, one of the wealthy Spice Islands described by Marco Polo, lay 2400 miles across the Atlantic.[36]

Raising funds for such a speculative scheme proved difficult. In 1480 he appealed to the Portuguese crown but the *junto* appointed to look into his scheme rejected it. However, they secretly instructed a vessel to test the theory by sailing west from Cape Verde. It was not a success and after a few days the mariners, terrified by the rough weather and the vastness of the ocean, turned back. When he heard of this duplicity Columbus left Portugal[37] and, after trying Venice, in 1485 he arrived in Spain penniless and got an audience with Ferdinand and Isabella.

After six years of procrastination Columbus's project was again rejected by the Spanish crown's advisory committee in January 1492. Then an influential courtier named Luis de Santangel took up his case. Spain had just occupied Granada, and the young nobles who had fought were expecting to be rewarded with land. Since there was not enough land in Spain, Santangel's idea was to look west as Columbus suggested. The agreement signed on 17 April 1492 appointed Columbus admiral, viceroy, governor and judge of all islands and mainlands he discovered and awarded him 10% of any treasure and spices he obtained. A royal decree was issued requiring Andalusian shipowners to provide three vessels ready for sea, and two shipping families, the Pinzons and the Ninos, finally invested in the modest expedition. Two caravels and a larger vessel set sail for the Canaries where they spent six weeks fitting out, finally setting sail for the great island of Cipangu on 6 September 1492. The NE Trades carried them across the Atlantic and at 2 a.m. on 12 October they sighted land (Figure 1.6). In reality the landfall was Watling Island (now San Salvador) in the Bahamas, but it was 20 years before anyone knew for sure that it was not the Indies.[38] Anyway there were no spices or fabulous cities, so from a trade perspective it was a false start.

## The Portuguese trade network

Columbus's discovery shocked the Portuguese who had been trying to reach Asia for nearly a century, as the Spanish appeared to have found it at their first attempt. They redoubled their efforts and on 3 August 1497 Vasco da Gama set off from Lisbon with a fleet of four ships, 170 men, three months' supplies, the maps of Africa prepared by Diaz and a new navigational strategy. After calling at Cape Verde, instead of coast-hopping as Diaz had done and beating against the SE Trades, he swung south-west into the Atlantic for 10 weeks, sailing until he reached the latitude of the Cape of Good Hope, and then turned east (see Figure 1.6). It worked brilliantly, and three months after setting sail he made landfall 1° north of the Cape! A great victory for the astrolabe. Rounding the Cape, he landed at Mombasa where he was not well received, so he sailed up the coast to Malindi where he got a better reception and found a pilot. Twenty-seven days later, in May 1497, he arrived at Calicut in India, 9 months after leaving Lisbon.

Although the voyage was a success, the trade was not. After a lavish welcome by the Zamorin of Calicut, things went downhill fast. Diaz's modest gifts were ridiculed by the wealthy Calicut merchants, who had no intention of sharing their business with impoverished adventurers. Da Gama scraped together a cargo by selling his trade goods at a fraction of their cost in Portugal and bought cloves, cinnamon and a few handfuls of precious stones.[39] Discouraged, they careened their ships in Goa and headed back. The return voyage took a year and they limped back to Portugal in August 1499 with only 54 of the 170 who had set out with the expedition. But the welcome was tumultuous. The trade route was established and although the cargo was sparse, da Gama brought an invaluable piece of commercial information. The hundred-weight of pepper sold in Venice for 80 ducats could be purchased in Calicut for 3 ducats! All that was needed was to eliminate the Muslim grip on the trade and build a new commercial empire.

The Portuguese set about doing this. Six months later an expedition of 13 ships and 1300 men was despatched under Pedro Alvares Cabral to set up a depot, so that spices could be purchased and stored, ready to load when ships arrived. This time they reached Calicut in just 6 months and their lavish gifts impressed the Zamorin, who signed a trade treaty. However, after only two ships had been loaded the resentful Moslem traders rioted and stormed the depot, killing most of the staff. Cabral retaliated by bombarding Calicut, setting fire to part of the city, then moved on to Cochin where he set up a new trading post and depot, with a garrison, before returning to Portugal. Although he had lost half his ships and men, the voyage was tremendously profitable and the basis of the Portuguese trading empire had been laid. Over the next decade the Portuguese established strongholds on the East African coast and in 1510 seized the town of Goa which grew into a thriving community of 450 settlers. A year later they took Malacca, now in Malaysia, a vital spice emporium, and Hormuz on the doorstep of the Persian Gulf. The trickle of trade between East and West turned into a torrent, as cargo ships, each carrying a few hundred tons of cargo, plied the new trade route around the Cape of Good Hope.

## New directions in European trade

In less than a decade Europe had established sea routes to every part of the globe and set about turning these discoveries to its advantage. Most trade in medieval Europe was in local goods, and trading opportunities were limited by the rather similar climate and technology of these countries. The voyages of discovery opened new markets for European manufactured goods and new sources of raw materials such as wool, dyestuffs, sugar, cotton, tea, coffee and of course the much sought-after spices. Over the next century the European explorers, with their improving navigational techniques and superior weapons, set about developing these trades.[40] The Cape route to the Spice Islands had an immediate commercial impact, but the Americas, which were more easily reached from Europe by exploiting the Trade winds, added a completely new dimension to the trade revolution that was taking place. These were sparsely populated territories, rich in raw materials, and provided an endless source of trade goods, a market for European manufactures, and near-perfect conditions for economic development. Over the next 200 years the trading triangle shown in Figure 1.7 developed in the North Atlantic. Manufactures were shipped from Europe to West Africa and slaves to the West Indies, the ships returning with sugar, rum, tobacco and cotton.

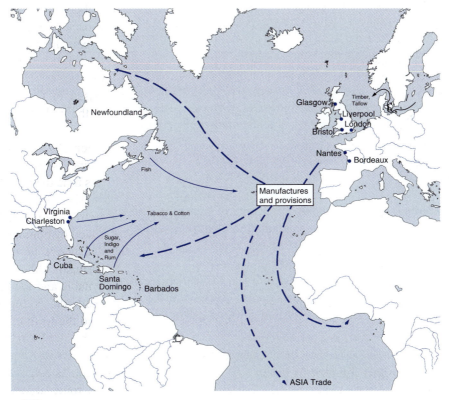

**Figure 1.7**
Sea trade in the eighteenth century

Trading in this enlarged world economy made NW Europe rich, and the new wealth soon produced a flourishing financial system with joint stock companies, bourses (stock exchanges), central banks and insurance markets. It also transformed the shipping business. Transport was still expensive (coal in London cost five times as much as it did at the pit head in Newcastle), and shipping was mainly an archaic business 'where the men who built the boats themselves loaded goods on board and put to sea with them, thus handling all the tasks and functions occasioned by maritime trade'.[41] Much more was needed to develop the new world economy. Deep-sea trade needed bigger ships, capital to finance the long voyages, and specialization.

## The rise of Antwerp

Although Portugal developed the important eastern trade, and Spain the Americas, the next maritime capital was not Lisbon or Seville, but Antwerp on the River Scheldt. Situated at the heart of the new overseas trading network and benefiting from an inland trade network built up during the Hapsburg occupation of the Low Countries, it became the most important market place for the rapidly developing global trade. In the late fifteenth century Antwerp had started to take over the distribution of Venetian cargoes from Bruges, whose harbour was silting up, and in 1501 the first Portuguese ship laden with Indian pepper, nutmeg, cinnamon and cloves berthed in Antwerp. It was a logical step for the Portuguese who were carrying the huge cost of sending ships to the Indies, and preferred to leave the wholesale distribution to the established Antwerp merchants who already handled the Venetian trade. Other trades followed. English merchants traded English cloth and wool; the southern German bankers (Fuggers, Welsers) traded cloth, spices and metals with Germany and Italy, while Spanish merchants from Cadiz brought cargoes of wool, wine and silver, with backhaul cargoes of cloth, iron, coal and glass. By 1520 Antwerp had become the market place for trade with the Mediterranean and the East.[42]

Antwerp also grew into a financial centre. The money market which it created between 1521 and 1535 played a major part in financing the Spanish development of the Americas. Merchants became expert at such capitalist techniques as double-entry bookkeeping, joint-stock companies, bills of exchange, and stock markets.[43] The efficiency of this new society was apparent in its most essential aspect – shipping. In 1567 Luigi Guicciardini counted 500 vessels moored before the roadstead in Antwerp and was impressed by the mighty crane on the wharf.[44]

However, Antwerp's dominant position as the leading maritime centre was short-lived. In 1585 the city was sacked by Spanish troops and the Scheldt was blocked by the Dutch. Many of the merchants fled to Amsterdam, which rapidly took over as the maritime capital.

## Amsterdam and the Dutch trade

Amsterdam's advantage was both geographical and economic. Its location as a maritime centre was excellent, with the Zuider Zee providing superb protected access for big ships, though it was difficult to navigate. It also had the support of the whole Dutch seaboard open to maritime trade, and between 1585 and 1620 took over from Genoa in the South and Antwerp in the North as the centre of a network of sea trade stretching from the Baltic to India. By 1701 a French guide reported 8,000 ships in Amsterdam harbour 'whose masts and rigging were so dense that it seems the sun could hardly penetrate it',[45] and the Amsterdam Gazette reported dozens of boats leaving and arriving every day. The Dutch fleet was estimated in 1669 to consist of 6,000 ships, of roughly 600,000 tons, the equivalent of all the other European fleets put together.[46]

However, the commercial advantages of the Dutch entrepreneurs should not be overlooked. As the Dutch became the entrepreneurs, merchants, bankers and 'cross-traders' of the newly emerging global trade there was much talk of the 'Dutch miracle'. This small, bare country had a population of about 1 million in 1500, half living in towns, far more than elsewhere in Europe, and they were 'so given to seafaring that one might think water rather than land their element'.[47] Dutch shipping's success owed much to their low costs, at least a third less than anyone else. To carry the growing bulk trade the Dutch developed an ocean-going merchantman, the *fluyt* or 'flyboat'. These vessels had 20% more cargo capacity and needed only seven or eight crew on a 200-ton vessel, compared with 10 or 12 on an equivalent French boat. The Dutch also had a very competitive shipbuilding industry[48] and a thriving sale and purchase market for second-hand ships.[49] With the cheap freight rates provided by the flyboat, the Dutch expanded in the bulk trades in corn, timber, salt and sugar. One great success was the Baltic grain trade, which increased rapidly as the growing population of NW Europe created a demand for imports.

By 1560 the Dutch had three-quarters of the Baltic bulk trade,[50] trading grain, forest products, pitch, and tar. Amsterdam became 'the corn bin of Europe'. Next they opened trade with the Iberian peninsula, trading wheat, rye and naval stores for salt, oil, wine and silver. Amsterdam's position as a financial centre developed with the opening of the Bourse (stock exchange), and with their lower costs they were able to squeeze out the northern Italian merchants, whose strategic position was already weakened.[51] Venetian ships had stopped sailing to the Netherlands, and 50 years later the Mediterranean to North Europe trade was being serviced by English and Dutch vessels, with half the Venetian fleet being built in Dutch shipyards.

However their greatest success was in the East where, after a slow start, they established a dominant position. Initially the Dutch merchants made little headway against Portuguese, English and Asian merchants. They needed large ships for the long voyages, fortified trading posts and military strength to deal with local opposition from natives and other traders. Individuals could not capitalize ventures on this scale, and their solution was to set up a company to provide capital and manage the trade. The Dutch East India Company was founded in 1602 with capital of 6,500,000 florins raised from the public. Its charter permitted it to trade 'westward into the Pacific from the Straits of Magellan to the Cape of Good Hope' with total administrative and judicial authority.[52] This strategy was very successful and the company rapidly grew in influence, obtaining a monopoly in the trade with Malaysia, Japan and China.

C
H
A
P
T
E
R
1

By 1750 Amsterdam's position as an entrepôt was waning as more trade went direct and the industrial revolution moved the hub of maritime trade to Britain. The steam engine made it possible to use coal to power machinery and as machines replaced people in manufacturing, the output of goods increased. The most immediate application was in that staple of international trade, textiles. Over the next 50 years, British manufacturers automated all the most skilled and time-consuming aspects of textile manufacture, radically reducing the cost of cotton cloth. After Hargreaves invented the 'spinning jenny', a machine for manufacturing cotton thread, the price of cotton yarn fell from 38 shillings per pound in 1786 to under 10 shillings per pound in 1800. Arkwright's water frame (1769), Crompton's 'mule' (1779) and Cartwright's power loom extended the automation to cloth manufacture. By 1815 exports of cotton textiles from Britain accounted for 40% of the value of British domestic exports.[53] New raw materials were introduced. The two most important were coal, which freed iron makers from the dependence on forests for charcoal, and cotton, which opened up a new market for clothing.

## Sea trade in the eighteenth century

Sea trade, dominated by textiles, woollen cloth, timber, wine and groceries, grew rapidly and British foreign trade (net imports and domestic exports) grew from £10 million in 1700 to £60 million in 1800.[54] As the century progressed the character of imports changed. Semi-tropical foodstuffs and raw materials from the Americas appeared and after 1660 London, with its growing exports of manufactures and range of financial and shipping services, gradually moved into a leading position.[55] The long-haul Asian trade was still controlled by the English and Dutch East India Company monopolies, but the Atlantic trade was served by small traders operating in the Baltic, the Mediterranean, the West Indies, East Coast North America, and sometimes West Africa and Brazil. An idea of the size of these trades and the number of ships in them is given by the statistics of ships entering and cleared for foreign trade in Great Britain in 1792 (Table 1.1).

The trade with the Baltic, Germany, Poland, Russia and Scandinavia was one of the biggest. In 1792, 2700 ships entered Britain carrying shipbuilding materials, hemp, tallow, iron, potash and grain. Much of this trade was carried in Danish and Swedish vessels. If the ships performed three voyages a year, which seems likely given that little winter trade was possible in these northerly waters, a thousand ships would have been needed to service this trade. An equally important trade for merchants was the West Indies. Colonial produce, including sugar, rum, molasses, coffee, cocoa, cotton and dyes, was shipped home, whilst some vessels performed a triangular voyage, sailing to the Guinea Coast to pick up slaves for transport to the West Indies. In 1792 between 700 and 900 ships were employed in the trade.[56] London, Liverpool and Bristol were the chief ports in the West Indies trade. Trade with the United States employed about 250 British vessels, with an average size of around 200 tons, carrying outward cargoes of British manufacturers and re-exports of Indian and foreign products and returning with tobacco, rice, cotton, corn, timber and naval stores. There was also an active trade with British North America and Newfoundland to supply the needs of the fishermen in Hudson's Bay.

**Table 1.1** British ships entered and cleared in foreign trade, 1792

| | Number of ships | | | % | Average Tonnage |
|---|---|---|---|---|---|
| | Entered | Cleared | Total | | |
| Baltic trades[a] | 2,746 | 1,367 | 4,113 | 27% | 186 |
| Holland and Flanders | 1,603 | 1,734 | 3,337 | 22% | 117 |
| France | 1,413 | 1,317 | 2,730 | 18% | 126 |
| Spain, Portugal | 975 | 615 | 1,590 | 10% | 126 |
| Mediterranean | 176 | 263 | 439 | 3% | 184 |
| Africa | 77 | 250 | 327 | 2% | 202 |
| Asia | 28 | 36 | 64 | 0% | 707 |
| British North America | 219 | 383 | 602 | 4% | 147 |
| USA | 202 | 223 | 425 | 3% | 221 |
| West Indies | 705 | 603 | 1,308 | 9% | 233 |
| Whale Fisheries | 160 | 135 | 295 | 2% | 270 |
| Total | 8,304 | 6,926 | 15,230 | | 2,519 |

[a] Russia, Scandinavia, Baltic, Germany

Source: Fayle (1933, p. 223)

Shorter-haul trades with Spain, Portugal, Madeira and the Canaries provided employment for around 500 or 600 small vessels carrying wine, oil, fruit, cork, salts, and fine wool from Spain. There was also a long-distance trade to Greenland and the South Sea whale fisheries. Whaling was an extremely profitable industry with about 150 ships sailing annually for the whaling grounds from English and Scottish ports. Finally, there was the coasting trade. A fleet of small vessels of about 200 tons plied the east coast between the Scottish ports and Newcastle, Hull, Yarmouth and London carrying coal, stone, slate, clay, beer and grain. These were the ships that Adam Smith used to illustrate the efficiency of sea transport in *The Wealth of Nations*. Coal was by far the most important cargo, by the late eighteenth century employing around 500 vessels, of around 200 tons, making eight or nine round voyages a year.

Finally, there was the passenger trade. In addition to cargo, many of the merchant ships in the Atlantic carried a few passengers for a price agreed with the master. Most passengers, however, travelled by the Post Office packets, fast-sailing vessels of about 200 tons which carried the mail weekly to Spain, Portugal and the West Indies and at longer intervals to Halifax, New York, Brazil, Surinam and the Mediterranean. In 1808 there were 39 Falmouth packets, carrying 2,000–3,000 passengers a year. As the fare from Falmouth to Gibraltar was 35 guineas (£36.75), the command of a packet was a profitable job.

### The rise of the independent shipowner

In the late eighteenth century the Atlantic trade was still mainly controlled by merchants and private partnerships. A syndicate would build or charter a ship, provide it with a cargo, and take their profit from trade or by carrying freight for hire. A 'supercargo' generally travelled with the ship to handle the business affairs, though this was sometimes left to the master, if he was qualified. The supercargo bought and sold cargoes and could, for example, order the vessel to a second port of discharge, or to sail in ballast to a port where a cargo might be available. As trade increased, this speculative approach gradually gave way to a more structured system, with some companies specializing in the trade of specific areas like the Baltic or the West Indies and others in the ownership and operating of ships, so the roles of trader and shipowner gradually grew apart.

Some voyages undertaken by Captain Nathaniel Uring in the early eighteenth century illustrate how the trading system worked in practice.[57] In 1698 he loaded groceries in Ireland and sailed to Barbados where he sold them and purchased rum, sugar and molasses for the Newfoundland fishermen, from whom he intended to purchase a cargo of fish for Portugal. However, when he reached Newfoundland, the market was overstocked with colonial products and fish prices were so high that he sailed back to Virginia where he sold his cargo and bought tobacco. On another voyage in 1712, in the 300-ton *Hamilton*, he was instructed to load logwood at Campeachy, to be sold in the Mediterranean. He called first at Lisbon, where he sold 50 tons of logs and filled up with sugar for Leghorn (Livorno) in Italy. At Leghorn he consulted the English consul as to the respective advantages of Leghorn and Venice as markets for logwood, finally selling the cargo at Leghorn, where he entered into a charter party to carry 100 tuns of oil at Tunis for Genoa. When he arrived in Tunis the Bey compelled him to make a short coastal voyage to fetch timber from Tabarca, after which he loaded the oil and, seeing no bargains about, he filled the ship with 'other goods I could procure upon freight' for Genoa. In Genoa he contracted 'For the freight of a lading of wheat, which I was to carry first to Cadiz, and try the market there; and if that did not answer, to proceed to Lisbon'. But the winds were unfavourable for entering Cadiz, so he sailed direct to Lisbon. After delivering the wheat and 'finding the ship perfectly worn-out with age' he then sold it to Portuguese shipbreakers 'as I was empowered to do'. Quite a voyage!

Uring was both a trader and a carrier, but by the end of the century the distinction between the shipowning and trading interests was becoming clearer. The term 'shipowner' first appeared in the shipping registers in 1786,[58] and early nineteenth-century advertisements for the General Shipowner's Society laid special emphasis on the fact that their members' business was confined to running ships, with no outside interests.[59] This change was accompanied by a rise in the numbers of shipbrokers, marine underwriters and insurance brokers, whose business was involved with shipping. In 1734 *Lloyd's List* was published as a shipping newspaper, primarily for marine underwriters, and soon afterwards in 1766 Lloyd's Register of Shipping published shipping's first register of ships.[60]

Although the transport system was improving, the ships and the standards of navigation remained so inefficient that sea passage times were very long. For example, Samuel Kelly recorded that in the 1780s the voyage time from Liverpool to Philadelphia took between 43 and 63 days, whilst the return voyage from Philadelphia to Liverpool took between 29 and 47 days. Similarly, the trip from Liverpool to Marseilles was 37 days. His worst experience was a winter passage from Liverpool to New York, which took 119 days.[61] The ships were generally around 300–400 tons in size, though the East India

Company operated a fleet of 122 vessels averaging 870 tons. This unsatisfactory state of affairs was about to change.

## 1.5  LINER AND TRAMP SHIPPING, 1833–1950

### Four innovations transform merchant shipping

In the nineteenth century shipping changed more than in the previous two millennia. A Venetian master sailing into London in 1800 would soon have felt at home. The ships were bigger, with better sails, and the navigation techniques had improved, but they were still wooden sailing ships. A century later he would have been in for a shock. The river would have been crammed with enormous steel ships, belching steam and sailing against wind and tide in response to instructions cabled across the world. In a few decades shipping was transformed from a loose system run by traders like Captain Uring to a tightly run industry specializing in the transport of cargo by sea.

This transformation was part of the industrial revolution taking place in Great Britain and Europe at this time. As manufacturing productivity increased, especially in textiles, output could not possibly be consumed locally and trade became a necessary part of the new industrial society. The engineering technology which transformed textile manufacturing also produced a new transport system to carry the manufactures to new markets and to bring in the raw materials and foodstuffs that the growing industrial population required. Many factors contributed to this change, but four were of particular importance: first, steam engines which freed ships from dependence on the wind; second, iron hulls which protected cargo and allowed much larger vessels to be built; third, screw propellers which made merchant ships more seaworthy, and fourth, the deep sea cable network which allowed traders and shipowners to communicate across the world.

As canals, railways and steamships merged into a global transport network, in the second half of the nineteenth century the shipping industry developed a completely new transport system which raised transport speed and efficiency to new heights. This new system had three parts: 'passenger liners' which transported mail and passengers on regular services between the economic 'hubs' of North America, Europe and the Far East; 'cargo liners' which transported cargo and some passengers on a widespread network of regular services between the developed and imperial markets; and the tramp shipping business which carried 'spot' cargoes on routes not served by liner services, or when cargo became available and they could offer cheaper freight.

### Growth of sea trade in the nineteenth century

The scale of the change is illustrated by the speed of trade growth. Sea trade increased from 20 million tons in 1840 to 140 million tons in 1887, averaging 4.2% per year (Table 1.2). Ton miles also increased as the trades with the Baltic and the Mediterranean were

**Table 1.2** Merchandise carried by sea, annual totals 1840 to 2005 (thousands of tons)

|  | 1840 | 1887 | 1950 | 1960 | 1975 (1) | 2005 |
|---|---|---|---|---|---|---|
| Crude oil |  | 2,700 | 182,000 | 456,000 | 1,367,000 | 1,885,000 |
| Products |  | n.a. | n.a. | n.a. | 253,700 | 671,000 |
| Liquefied gas |  |  |  |  | 21 | 179,000 |
| Total oil |  | 2,700 | 216,000 | 456,000 | 1,620,700 | 2,556,000 |
| Iron ore |  |  |  | 101,139 | 291,918 | 661,000 |
| Coal | 1,400 | 49,300 |  | 46,188 | 127,368 | 680,000 |
| Grain | 1,900 | 19,200 |  | 46,126 | 137,202 | 206,000 |
| Bauxite and alumina |  |  |  | 15,961 | 41,187 | 68,000 |
| Phosphate |  |  |  | 18,134 | 37,576 | 31,000 |
| Total |  |  |  | 227,548 | 635,251 | 1,646,000 |
| Iron and steel | 1,100 | 11,800 |  |  | 55,000 | 226,000 |
| Timber | 4,100 | 12,100 |  |  | 77,500 | 170,000 |
| Sugar | 700 | 4,400 |  |  | 17,291 | 48,000 |
| Salt | 800 | 1,300 |  |  | 8,700 | 24,000 |
| Cotton | 400 | 1,800 |  |  | 2,315 | 7,800 |
| Wool | 20 | 350 |  |  | 1,200 |  |
| Jute |  | 600 |  |  | 450 | 382 |
| Meat |  | 700 |  |  | 3,200 | 26,640 |
| Coffee | 200 | 600 |  |  | 3,134 | 5,080 |
| Wine | 200 | 1,400 |  |  | 1,217 |  |
| Other | 9,180 | 33,750 | 334,000 | 426,452 | 646,042 | 2,412,098 |
| Total seaborne trade | 20,000 | 137,300 | 550,000 | 1,110,000 | 3,072,000 | 7,122,000 |
| % increase since previous period |  | 4.2% | 2.2% | 7.3% | 7.0% | 2.8% |

Source: Craig (1980, p. 18); UN *Statistical Yearbook* 1967 onwards; *Fearnleys Review* 1963 onwards; Maritime Transport Research (1977); CRSL, *Dry Bulk Trade Outlook*, Dec. 2007 and *Oil Trade & Transport*, Dec. 2007 edition. The statistics are not precisely comparable and only provide a rough idea of trade developments over this long period.

replaced by long-haul trades with North America, South America and Australia. For the first time industrial cargoes appeared on the market in very large quantities, the most important being the coal trade. For many years coal had been shipped from the north-east of England as a domestic fuel, but in the nineteenth century large quantities started to be used by industry and as bunkers for steamships. The tonnage of trade increased from 1.4 million tons in 1840 to 49.3 million tons in 1887. During the same period the trade in textile fibres, notably cotton, wool and jute also grew rapidly to supply the new textile industries of industrial Britain. After the repeal of the Corn Laws in 1847, the grain trade increased from 1.9 million tons in 1842 to 19.2 million tons in 1887. Initially the trade came from the Black Sea, but as railways opened up North and South America, the trades with the US East Coast, the Gulf and South America, especially River Plate, became equally important. Timber and the trades with the Baltic also grew and in 1887 we see the first petroleum cargoes, just 2.7 million tons, the beginning of a trade which in due course would reach over 2 billion tonnes.

In addition to cargo, as global trade developed so did passenger traffic and mail and there was tremendous commercial pressure to speed up these services. With a 60-day round-voyage time on the North Atlantic, doing business was difficult and there was a market for fast transit. The passenger trade was also swelled by emigrants from Europe to the USA and Australia. Numbers increased from 32,000 a year between 1825 and 1835 to 71,000 a year between 1836 and 1845, and 250,000 a year between 1845 and 1854, following the 1847 California gold rush. Although this pace was not continued, the trade remained brisk until the 1950s.

## Steam replaces sail in the merchant fleet

As the nineteenth century progressed, steamship technology improved dramatically. In the first half of the century sail set the pace and competition between shipyards in Britain and the United States produced some of the most efficient merchant sailing ships ever built. Until the 1850s the fledgling steamships could not compete, mainly because the engines were so inefficient. For example, in 1855 the 900 dwt steamship shown in Table 1.3 burnt 199 lb of fuel per thousand ton miles at 7.5 knots. On an Atlantic crossing it would use 360 tons of coal, occupying 40% of its cargo space. As a result, steamers were still too inefficient to be economic on deep-sea routes (see Table 1.3) and in 1852 only 153 were listed in *Lloyd's Register*.[62] But by 1875 the steam engines were using only 80 lb per thousand cargo ton miles and for the first time the shipbuilders were offering steamships well able to compete with sail in the deep sea trades.[63] The opening of the Suez Canal in 1869 was well timed to generate a surge of investment innovation, trebling the world merchant fleet from 9 m.grt in 1860 to 32 m.grt in 1902 (Figure 1.8).

The 650-ton *John Bowes*, built in Jarrow in 1852 for the coastal coal trade, and one of the first modern bulk carriers, demonstrates the way the new technology, when used in the right trade, increased transport efficiency (see Section 6.2 and, in particular, Table 6.1). On her first trip she loaded 650 tons of coal in four hours; in 48 hours she

**Table 1.3** Fuel consumption of typical cargo ships

| Year built | Gross registered tonnage | Dead weight tonnage | Cargo tons | Speed knots | Engine type | Horse-power | Fuel type | Tons per day | Cargo | lb fuel/ 1,000 ton miles |
|---|---|---|---|---|---|---|---|---|---|---|
| 1855 | 700 | 900 | 750 | 7.5 | Steam 1 | 400 ihp | coal | 12 | 63 | 199.1 |
| 1875 | 1,400 | 1,900 | 1,650 | 8.5 | Steam 2 | 800 ihp | coal | 12 | 138 | 79.9 |
| 1895 | 3,600 | 5,500 | 4,900 | 9.5 | Steam 3 | 1,800 ihp | coal | 25 | 196 | 50.1 |
| 1915 | 5,300 | 8,500 | 7,500 | 11 | Steam 3 | 2,800 ihp | coal | 35 | 214 | 39.6 |
| 1935 | 6,000 | 10,000 | 9,000 | 12.5 | Steam 3 | 4,000 ihp | oil | 33 | 273 | 27.4 |
| 1955 | 7,500 | 11,000 | 10,000 | 14 | Diesel | 6,000 bhp | oil | 25 | 400 | 16.7 |
| 1975 | 13,436 | 17,999 | 17,099 | 16 | Diesel | 9,900 bhp | oil | 37 | 462 | 12.6 |
| 2006 | 12,936 | 17,300 | 16,435 | 15 | Diesel | 9,480 bhp | oil | 25 | 657 | 9.5 |

Key: Steam 1 = steam reciprocating simple, Steam 2 = Steam reciprocating compound, Steam 3 = steam reciprocating triple expansion

Source: British Shipbuilding Database (Prof. Ian Buxton, Newcastle University)

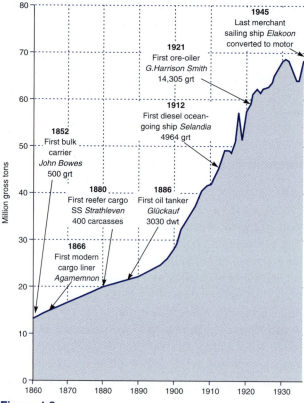

**Figure 1.8**

World fleet and design innovation, 1860–1930

Sources: Craig (1980, pp. 7, 12); Kummerman and Jacquinet (1979, p. 127); Hosking (1973, p. 14); Dunn L. (1973, p. 95); Britannic Steamship Insurance Association (2005, p. 24); Kahre (1977, p. 145); *Lloyd's Register* 1900–30.

arrived in London; she took 24 hours to discharge her cargo; and in 48 hours she was back in the River Tyne.[64] Compared with the five weeks taken by a sailing ship, this five-day round trip increased productivity by 600%. In addition to speed and reliability, the iron hulls were more consistently water-tight, reducing cargo damage, and the cargo payload was 25% bigger than a wooden ship. By 1875 a 'Handy' vessel had increased to 1400 grt (1900 dwt), and by the end of the nineteenth century ships of 4600 grt were common-place. This phase of technical progress peaked in the early decades of the twentieth century with high-speed ocean liners like the 45,000 grt *Aquitania*, built in 1914 to carry passengers and cargo between North Europe and North America. Passenger traffic had become a central feature of the maritime trade, not just for the big passenger liner operators, but also for the cargo liners and even some tramps.

But despite their productivity advantage, steamships were so expensive to build and operate that the transition from sail to steam took over 50 years. In 1850, 2,000 grt fast clippers could easily compete with the early steamships which burned so much coal that there was little cargo space on long voyages. Triple expansion steam engines solved this problem, and between 1855 and 1875 fuel consumption fell 60% from 199 pounds per thousand cargo ton miles to 80 pounds, and by 1915 it had halved again (see Table 1.3). In 1915, a 5300 grt cargo tramp used only 35 tons of coal per day and consumed only 40 pounds per cargo ton mile. Steel hulls allowed bigger ships to be built, and the opening of the Suez Canal in 1869 shortened the vital sea route between the East and Europe by 4,000 miles, with plenty of bunkering stations, giving the steamships a major advantage. With each step forward in steam technology the economic pressure on sailing ships increased, but they proved surprisingly resilient in long-haul bulk trades such as wool, rice, grain, nitrates and coal. For example, in 1891 there were still 77 sailing vessels in

Sydney loading wool for London and the last merchant sailing ship, the *Elakoon*, was not converted to motor power until 1945. There were other technical changes along the way, though none so fundamental. The first deep sea diesel-powered ship, the *Selandia*, went into service in 1912, and over the next 50 years the diesel engine replaced the steam engine, except in the most powerful ships. In the 1930s welding started to replace rivets in hull construction, and in the 1970s automation halved the number of crew required to staff a deep sea vessel.

During the next 50 years a steady stream of specialized ships were developed to carry particular types of cargo (see Figure 1.8): the *Agamemnon*, the first cargo liner in 1866; the first reefer in 1880; the first tanker, the *Glückauf* in 1886; the first diesel ship in 1912; and the first ore-oiler in 1921. However, the passenger liners were the outstanding development of this era. These vessels, designed to carry passengers and mail at great speed across the Atlantic and the Imperial routes, first appeared in the second half of the nineteenth century and reached their peak immediately before the First World War, reducing the Atlantic crossing from 17 days to five and a half days in the process (see Table 1.4).

## Deep-sea cables revolutionize shipping communications

Of equal importance in transforming the shipping industry in the nineteenth century was the undersea cable network linking the continents. Until the 1860s international communication was by letter and little was heard of a ship until she returned, the 'Supercargo' or the master being relied upon to attend to business.[65] Ships could sit for weeks waiting for a return cargo. Businesses needed better information about the availability of ships and cargoes and invested heavily in trying to achieve this. In 1841, P&O introduced a fast mail service to India, sailing to Suez by sea, crossing the isthmus by camel staging posts, and then on to India by sea.[66] This allowed a bill of lading to arrive in India ahead of the cargo. Then in 1855 the first Atlantic cable was laid. The signal was feeble and after 40 days it stopped working, but it showed what could be done. A land cable across Siberia to Bombay was opened in 1865 but messages took 10 days to pass along the staging posts.[67]

Then in the 1865 the first successful transatlantic cable[68] was laid by the *Great Eastern*, Brunel's 18,915 grt iron steamship. It could manoeuvre more effectively than the sailing ships used in 1855 and was big enough to carry a cable long enough to stretch from Ireland to Newfoundland, with a mechanism to control the cable as it was paid out. On the first expedition in 1865 the cable parted in mid-ocean, and was lost along with $3 million of its investor's money, about $180 million in today's terms.[69] However, in 1866 it laid a new cable and retrieved and repaired the 1865 cable. Within a decade a network of cables linked the major cities of the world[70] and, by 1897, 162,000 nautical miles of cable had been laid, with London at the heart of the network.[71] This communications network transformed the shipping business, for the first time allowed transport to be planned. So in the end Brunel's commercial 'white elephant', the *Great Eastern*, made a far greater contribution to shipping as a humble cable layer than it could possibly have done carrying passengers.

**C H A P T E R 1**

**Table 1.4** Evolution of Atlantic liners, 1830–1914

| Name | Length (feet) | Gross tonnage | Indicated horse power | Knots per hour | Consumption tons/day | Hull material | Propulsion system | Engine design | Built | Transit days |
|---|---|---|---|---|---|---|---|---|---|---|
| Royal William | 176 | 137 | 180n | 7 | | Wood | Aux Paddle | Steam | 1833 | 17.0 |
| Sirius | 208 | 700 | 320n | 7.5 | | Wood | Paddle | Steam | 1838 | 16.0 |
| Great Western | 236 | 1,320 | 440n | 9 | 28 | Wood | Paddle | Steam | 1838 | 14.0 |
| Britannia[a] | 207 | 1,156 | 740 | 8.5 | 31.4 | Wood | Paddle | Steam | 1840 | 14.3 |
| Great Britain | 302.5 | 2,935 | 1,800 | 10 | 35-50 | Iron | Screw prop | Steam | 1843 | |
| America | 251 | 1,825 | 1,600 | 10.25 | 60 | Wood | Paddle | Steam | 1848 | |
| Baltic | 282 | 3,000 | 800 | | | Wood | Paddle | Steam | 1850 | 9.5 |
| Persia | 376 | 3,300 | 3,600 | 13.8 | 150 | Iron | Paddle | Steam | 1856 | 9.5 |
| Great Eastern | 680 | 18,914 | 8,000 | 13.5 | 280 | Iron | Screw and Paddle | Steam | 1858 | 9.5 |
| Russia | 358 | 2,959 | 3,100 | 14.4 | 90 | Iron | Single screw | Compound | 1867 | 8.8 |
| Britannic | 455 | 5,004 | 5,000 | 15 | 100 | Iron | Single screw | Compound | 1874 | 8.2 |
| City of Berlin | 488.6 | 5,490 | 4,779 | 15 | 120 | Iron | Single screw | Compound | 1875 | 7.6 |
| Servia | 515 | 7,391 | 10,000 | 16.7 | 200 | Steel | Single screw | Compound | 1881 | 7.4 |
| Umbria | 500 | 7,718 | 14,500 | 18 | | Steel | Single screw | Compound | 1884 | 6.8 |
| City of Paris | 527.5 | 10,699 | 18,000 | 19 | 328 | Steel | Twin screw | Triple expansion | 1888 | 6.5 |
| Teutonic | 565.7 | 9,984 | 16,000 | 19 | | Steel | Twin screw | Triple expansion | 1888 | 6.5 |
| Campania | 600 | 12,950 | 30,000 | 21 | 458 | Steel | Twin screw | Triple expansion | 1893 | 5.9 |
| Kaiser Wilhelm II | 678 | 19,361 | 45,000 | 23.5 | 700 | Steel | Twin screw | Quad. expansion | 1901 | 5.4 |
| Mauretania | 787 | 31,938 | 70,000 | 25 | 1000 | Steel | Quad screw | Turbines | 1907 | 5.0 |
| Aquitania | 901 | 45,647 | 60,000 | 23 | 850 | Steel | Quad screw | Turbines | 1914 | 5.5 |

[a]Consumption reported as 450 tons for the crossing of 14.3 days; n = nominal horse power, about half ihp pre-1850

Sources: Kirkaldy (1914), Appendix XVIII; British Shipbuilding Database (Prof. Ian Buxton, Newcastle University).

## The liner and tramp shipping system emerges

The steamships and the communications revolution set the scene for a new and more sophisticated shipping system. As trade grew, and the complexity of the transport operation increased, the market gradually divided into three segments: passenger liners, cargo liners and tramp shipping. The basic model is illustrated in Figure 1.9. The range of cargoes being shipped by sea in the mid- to late nineteenth century is shown at the top of the diagram and included bulks, liquids, general cargo, passengers and, later in the century, refrigerated cargo. Passengers were the cream cargo which was most sought after, and one segment of the business, the passenger liners, was designed to provide fast transport on the busy routes across the Atlantic and to the Far East. The passenger liners built for these trades were fitted with passenger accommodation and were usually relatively fast, operating to a published schedule. Cargo liners also operated on regular schedules and were often designed for specific routes. Typically they had several decks to allow them to load and discharge cargo in many ports, and they would often have provision for specialist cargoes such as refrigerated cargo and heavy lift. Finally, the tramps carried bulk cargoes such as coal and grain on a voyage by

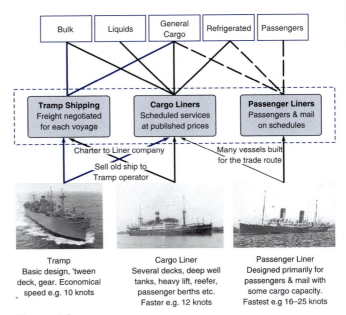

**Figure 1.9**

The liner and tramp shipping system, 1869–1950

voyage basis. They were usually of a very basic design, often with just a single 'tween deck and an economical speed and cargo-handling gear. However, some were sufficiently versatile to carry general cargo and be chartered by liner companies when they were short of capacity, and the more sophisticated tramps were designed with this in mind.

## The passenger liner services

Once reliable steamships were available, travel between regions became far more manageable and a network of passenger liner services rapidly developed. Initially the focus was on speed to carry mail and passengers between the continents, and the North Atlantic was the showpiece for the development of nineteenth-century shipping technology. Early liner services used sailing ships and the competition stimulated efficiency. In 1816 the Old Black Ball Line, the first liner service, was set up by Isaac Wright, a US owner. Using much-admired American sailing clippers, it offered fortnightly departures between New York and London, in competition with the Swallowtail Line, a New Bedford company. Although a great improvement, over the first 10 years the transit still averaged 23 days from New York to Liverpool and 43 days from Liverpool to New York.[72] Eventually they carried a thousand passengers a week, but by the 1850s they were eclipsed by the screw steamers of Great Britain which reduced the transit time to less than 10 days in each direction (see Table 1.4).[73]

As the century progressed the 'passenger liners' evolved into big, fast, luxurious ships with limited cargo capacity, built for the fast transport of passengers and mail and the important emigrant trade from Europe to the USA.[74] The improving technology of ships used on the North Atlantic is demonstrated in Table 1.4, which shows that between 1833 and 1914 every aspect of ship design changed. The hull grew from 176 ft to 901 ft, and gross tonnage from 137 tons to 45,647 tons. Hull construction switched from wood to iron in the 1850s, and from iron to steel in the 1880s, whilst paddle propulsion was replaced in the 1850s by screws driven by steam engines. Triple expansion steam engines arrived in the 1880s and turbines from 1900. Speed increased from 7 knots per hour in 1833 to 25 knots per hour in 1907, and fuel consumption from around 20 tons a day to 1,000 tons a day, with a significant improvement in thermal efficiency.

Cunard developed steamships for the North Atlantic capable of offering speed and reliability in all weathers. These services were obviously highly valued by businesses. For example, when Cunard's 1156 grt paddle steamer *Britannia* was frozen in Boston harbour in 1843–4, local merchants paid for a seven-mile channel to be cut to get her out.[75] The *Britannia* had a speed of 8.5 knots on 31.4 tons of coal a day, but 30 years later in 1874 the 4566 grt *Bothnia* had a speed of 13 knots on 63 tons a day and capacity for 340 passengers, in addition to 3,000 tons of cargo (Table 1.5). By the early twentieth century these passenger liners had evolved into sophisticated vessels. The 25 knot, 31,938 grt *Mauretania,* with its 350 stokers and 1,000 tons per day bunker consumption probably used more fuel than any ship ever built. However, not all passenger liners were so exotic. The *Balmoral Castle,* built in 1910 for the South Africa trade, was a four-deck ship of 13,361 gross tons, with two quadruple expansion engines of 12,500 ihp and a more modest speed of 17.5 knots. It could carry 317 first-class, 220 second-class and 268 third-class passengers.

The companies in this business, such as Cunard, White Star, North German Lloyd, and Holland America Line, were household names and their ships were symbols of national engineering prowess. From the 1880s onwards there was much latent competition for the transatlantic speed record, the Blue Riband, and it was probably this as much as commercial considerations which led to the construction of the most extreme ships such as Hamburg America's *Deutschland* (which suffered extreme vibration), North German Lloyd's record-breaking *Kaiser Wilhelm II,* and Cunard's turbine driven sister ships *Mauritania* and *Lusitania.*

**Table 1.5** Performance of Cunard cargo ships, 1840–1874

| | Gross tons | Built | Speed knots | Coal tons/day | Cargo | Passengers | Bunkers |
|---|---|---|---|---|---|---|---|
| *Britannia* | 1,139 | 1840 | 8 | 38 | 225 | 90 | 640 |
| *Persia* | 3,300 | 1855 | 13 | 150 | 1,100 | 180 | 1,640 |
| *Java* | 2,697 | 1865 | 13 | 85 | 1,100 | 160 | 1,100 |
| *Bothnia* | 4,556 | 1874 | 13 | 63 | 3,000 | 340 | 940 |

Source: Fayle (1933, p. 241)

## The cargo liner services

The rapidly growing trade in manufactures and raw materials across the Atlantic and between the European states and their empires in the Far East, Oceania, Africa and South America created a demand for fast, cheap and regular cargo transport services. To deal with this the shipping industry developed a sophisticated system of cargo liner services using ships designed to transport the complex mix of passengers, mail and cargoes appearing as the international economy grew in the nineteenth century, supported by a fleet of tramp ships which carried the bulkier cargoes and supplemented the liners when the need arose (see Figure 1.9). They were the backbone of world trade, providing a reliable and flexible outward transport for general cargo, and often returning with a bottom cargo of logs, copra, grain and other minor bulks, topped up with passengers and whatever specialist cargoes they could pick up. As an economic solution to a complex problem the system worked well for a century and was every bit as revolutionary as containerization in the twentieth century.

From the 1870s onwards a network of liner services spread across the world, especially between Europe and its colonies, served by a new generation of steam cargo liners. These vessels were less elaborate and slower than the passenger liners. They were built for moderate speed, with several decks for stacking general cargo, bottom holds where bulk cargoes could be stowed on the return voyage, and special features such as refrigerated holds and deep well tanks for oils. There was often accommodation for some passengers. For example, the 6690 dwt *Ruahine* (1891) had accommodation for 74 first-class, 36 second-class and 250 emigrants. However, by the end of the century many cargo liners did not carry a Board of Trade Passenger Certificate. Vessel size gradually increased, as illustrated by the Ocean Steam Ship Company fleet. The 2200 grt *Agamemnon,* built in 1865, was 309 ft long with a 945 horsepower engine and with coal consumption of only 20 tons per day, allowing it to steam to the Far East. By 1890 the *Orestes* was 4653 grt, with a 2600 horsepower engine, and by 1902 the *Keemun* was 9074 grt with a 5,500 hp twin triple expansion engine. Finally, the *Nestor* built in 1914 was 14,000 grt. This more or less defined the liner vessel, and sizes did not increase significantly for the next 40 years.

The liner trades were complicated by the need for multi-port loading and discharge as well as the need for the service operator to offer trans-shipment to other ports not served directly by the liner. These operations were expensive and made the job of stowing and discharging cargo more complicated than a simple tramping operation. The cargo manifest for the 2849 grt cargo liner SS *Scotia*, carrying 5061 tons of cargo, shown in Table 1.6, illustrates this point. On the voyage in question the ship loaded 28 different commodities in bags, bales, cases and casks.

By the 1950s there were 360 liner conferences in the deep-sea trades, each with between 2 and 40 members which regulated sailings and freight rates.[76] The new liner companies were highly visible organizations with offices or agencies in the ports they served. Companies such as P&O, Blue Funnel, and Hamburg Süd became household names. Their prestigious office buildings housed teams of administrators, naval architects and operations staff who planned and directed fleets of a hundred ships or more as

**Table 1.6** Cargo of SS *Scotia*, 1918

| Item | Unit | Number |
|------|------|--------|
| Skins | Bales | 128 |
| Turmeric | Bags | 150 |
| Tea | Cases | 90 |
| Shellac | Cases | 208 |
| Goat Skins | Bales | 15 |
| Shellac | Cases | 175 |
| Tea | Cases | 1,386 |
| Linseed | Bags | 1,159 |
| Hides | | |
| Coffee | Casks | 11 |
| Gunnies | Bales | 68 |
| Fibre | Bales | 605 |
| Wheat | Bags | 3,867 |
| Tea | Cases | 2,851 |
| Goat Skins | Barrels | 330 |
| Gunnies | Bales | 194 |
| Wheat | Bags | 4,321 |
| Poppy seeds | Bags | 1,047 |
| Rapeseed | Bags | 682 |
| Potash | Bags | 152 |
| Wheat | Bags | 1,086 |
| Shellac | Cases | 275 |
| Copra | Cases | 530 |
| Coconuts | Bags | 1,705 |
| Hides | Bales | 60 |
| Gunnies | Bales | 90 |
| Gunnies | Bales | 100 |
| Linseed | Bags | 2,022 |

Source: Captain H. Hillcoat, *Notes on Stowage of Ships*, (London, 1918), reproduced in Robin Craig (1980)

they plied back and forth on their trades. Naturally the ships were registered locally, and the companies were generally publicly quoted, even though the stock was usually held by family members. In short, liner shipping became a prominent and highly respectable business, and young men joined the industry confident in the knowledge that they were serving national institutions.

## Tramp shipping and the global market place

The other component in the nineteenth-century sea transport system was tramp shipping, a very different business. Tramps filled the gaps in the transport system, carrying the bulk and general cargoes not catered for by the liner services. They were the direct descendants of Captain Uring, working from port to port carrying grain, coal, iron ore, and whatever was available. However, they had two important advantages which made them much more efficient than their eighteenth-century counterparts. First, they were steamships, usually with a 'tween deck for stacking cargo, offering speed and flexibility. Second, through the cable system they had access to the Baltic Exchange, so they could fix cargoes ahead without waiting or making speculative ballast voyages as Captain Uring had to do.

The growth of the Baltic Exchange was a response to the high cost and inflexibility of the early cable network. In 1866 a transatlantic cable cost 4*s*. 3*d*. (about $1.25) per word.[77] To put that in perspective, in 1870 a seaman earned about $12.50 (£2 2*s*.) a month.[78] Although rates soon fell, in 1894 communicating with outlying areas such as South and East Africa still cost over $1.25 per word. This favoured a central market place where cargoes could be 'fixed' by local brokers and agents and the terms communicated to their clients by cable. London was at the heart of the cable network and the Baltic exchange became the market place where trade was done. The Virginia and Baltic Coffee House had been a popular shipping venue for a century, in 1744 advertising itself as the place 'where all foreign and domestic news are taken in; and all letters or parcels, directed to merchants or captains in the Virginia or Baltic trade will be carefully delivered according as directed and the best attendance given'.[79] By 1823 it had a committee, rules and an auction room where tallow was traded,[80] and when cables arrived in the 1860s it rapidly became the trading floor for the world tramp fleet.

Brokers circulated details of ships and cargoes at the Baltic, struck deals and cabled the terms to their principals in the briefest possible form.

London shipbroking companies were the intermediaries in the system.[81] The history of H. Clarkson & Co. Ltd records that in the 1870s Leon Benham, the company's leading broker, 'was in constant attendance at the Baltic Exchange. Several times a day he would return to the office to despatch telegrams, invariably drafted from jottings on the stiff cuff of his shirt'.[82] In 1869 Clarksons spent more on telegrams than on wages.[83] The Baltic reached a peak in 1903 when it opened the new exchange building in St Mary Axe. As long as international messaging remained cumbersome and expensive the Baltic was guaranteed a position as the global clearing house for shipping business.[84]

The shipping companies which operated in the tramp market were very different from the liner companies, though there was some overlap. Large tramp companies would sometimes establish liner services if they spotted a gap in the market and the liner companies sometimes engaged in 'tramping'. However, most of the tramp business was carried on by small companies. In 1912 over a third of the British tramp companies had only one or two ships, and by 1950 this had increased to more than half (Table 1.7). These businesses were often very small, relying heavily on outsourcing various skilled tasks. For example, marine and engineering superintendents were now available

**Table 1.7** Size of British ocean tramp companies

| | Number of companies | | |
| Number of ships | 1912 | 1950 | % of total 1950 |
| --- | --- | --- | --- |
| 1 | 25 | 37 | 29% |
| 2 | 12 | 28 | 22% |
| 3 | 9 | 20 | 16% |
| 4 | 12 | 15 | 12% |
| 5 | 7 | 7 | 5% |
| 6+ | 34 | 22 | 17% |
| Total | 99 | 129 | 100% |

Source: Gripaios (1959, Table 5)

in most ports to deal with technical matters such as breakdowns and dry dockings; shipbrokers and agents chartered the ships for a commission; and chandlers provided deck and engine stores and victuals. Bunkers were readily available at advertised prices; crewing agencies supplied officers and crews; and insurance brokers and protection and indemnity (P&I) clubs were available to cover the various risks. In these circumstances a tramp owner really could 'carry his office under his hat'.[85] Some ships were owned by the captain or a syndicate using the system whereby the holding company was split into 64 shares (see Section 7.2).

Although the British were initially the biggest tramp owners, towards the end of the nineteenth century the Greek shipowners, who had built up thriving cargo shipping businesses on the commerce of the Black Sea and the Mediterranean, started to set up offices in London.[86] Soon they became an important part of the international tramp shipping scene. The Norwegians took a while to move from sail to steam and were less in evidence. Operating fleets of multi-deck vessels, these owners worked from port to port, carrying whatever cargoes became available, though by the early twentieth century they were mainly carrying bulk commodities. The breakdown of cargoes in

**Table 1.8** British deep-sea tramp shipping cargoes, 1935

| Cargo | Voyages | Cargo tons |
|---|---|---|
| Coal and coke | 1,873 | 12,590,000 |
| Grain | 1,200 | 8,980,000 |
| Grain and timber | 105 | 890,000 |
| Timber | 196 | 1,345,000 |
| Timber and other cargo | 19 | 110,000 |
| Ore | 398 | 2,830,000 |
| Fertilizers | 207 | 1,535,000 |
| Sugar | 204 | 1,425,000 |
| Other cargoes | 610 | 3,785,000 |
| Totals | 4,812 | 33,490,000 |

Source: Isserlis (1938).

Table 1.8 shows that by 1935 coal and grain accounted for two-thirds of the tonnage of cargo shipped, with timber, ores, fertilizers and sugar making up another quarter.

A typical tramp itinerary in the 1930s illustrates how the tramp business worked. The ship was chartered to carry rails from Middlesbrough to Calcutta. From there it loaded jute gunny-bags for Sydney, then ballasted to Newcastle, NSW, to load coal for Iquiqui in Chile, expecting to load nitrate. However, there were many ships waiting in the nitrate ports, so instead, after an exchange of cables, the ship ballasted to the River Plate where the maize harvest would soon be coming forward and demand was expected to be brisk. However, by the time the ship reached Buenos Aires many ships had recently arrived with coal from Britain and were looking for a backhaul, so supply exceeded demand. After waiting a couple of weeks it was eventually fixed at a slightly higher rate by a maize trader with an option to discharge in London, Rotterdam or Genoa, for each of which a freight was specified. The ship was to call for orders at St Vincent in the Cape Verde Isles, where the master learned he was to proceed to Rotterdam, then load coal for Genoa. From Genoa he was instructed to proceed to Algeria and load iron ore for the Tees. The permutations were endless, but at each stage owners and shipbrokers worked furiously to find the best cargo for the next leg and cable instructions to the ship's master and it is easy to see why the Baltic Exchange played such an important part in coordinating the activities of the tramp fleet.[87]

When not tramping, tramp ships would often be chartered to cargo liner companies in need of extra capacity, thus providing a link between the bulk and liner businesses. This was possible because both segments of the market used similar ships. Generally the tramp operators invested in basic multi-deck vessels of between 5,000 and 10,000 dwt, with a 'tween deck to stack general cargo and bottom holds designed to carry bulk. Some more expensive tramps were designed with liner charters in mind, with a slightly faster speed and special features such as refrigerated holds, deep well tanks to carry vegetable oils, cabins for 20 or more passengers and heavy lift cranes for awkward cargoes. However, the basic tramp design was instantly recognizable.

## Regulation of shipping

As the volume of business increased so did the framework of regulations imposed by the insurance industry. In the eighteenth century the London insurance industry developed a system to check that the ships they insured were soundly built and in good condition. By the early nineteenth century Lloyd's Register, which had started life in the 1760s as a register of ships, had assumed the role of setting standards and issuing classification certificates. After a major reorganization in 1834, 63 surveyors were appointed and they made a complete resurvey of the 15,000 ships in the Register. Any new vessel for which an A1 classification was sought must undergo 'a survey under construction', which meant in practice that its progress was closely inspected at least three times while its hull was on the stocks. In 1855 Rules for Iron Ships were issued by the Society, and subsequently committees were established to set construction standards for new ships and the network of surveyors monitored their implementation. Several other countries set up classification societies, among them the American Bureau of Shipping and Det Norske Veritas, and by the end of the nineteenth century the industry's technical regulatory system was in place.

Governments also became involved in regulating shipping, particularly the British government. After a series of scandals involving ships used in the emigrant trade, the Merchant Shipping Act 1854 was passed. This set out a legal framework for the registry of ships; tonnage measurement; survey of ships and equipment; carriage of dangerous goods; safety and seaworthiness of ships; protection of seamen; and inspection of provisions. From time to time it was extended, often in the face of opposition from the shipping industry; for example, the recommendation of the 1874 Royal Commission on unseaworthy ships that a load line (for many years known as the 'Plimsoll mark') should be introduced to prevent ships being overloaded was opposed by British owners who complained it would give them an unfair disadvantage. The body of maritime laws developed at this time, when Britain controlled half the world merchant fleet, was used by many other countries as the template for enacting their own maritime law providing the basis for a maritime legal system which was reasonably consistent between countries. The first formal step in this direction was the Law of the Sea conference held in Washington in 1896, listing an agenda of items to regularize shipping activities.

## 1.6 CONTAINER, BULK AND AIR TRANSPORT, 1950–2006

### The rationale for sea transport integration

By 1950 the liner and tramp system had worked successfully for a century and it was hard to believe that it could suddenly disappear, but that is exactly what happened. Although it was immensely flexible, it was far too labour-intensive to survive in the post-1945 global economy where rising labour costs made mechanization inevitable. This meant replacing expensive labour with cheaper capital equipment and increasing the size of transport operations to take advantage of economies of scale.[88] As a result, 30 years later there was nothing left of the proud, conservative shipping industry which sailed confidently into the 1950s. The passenger liners disappeared in a decade, or were converted into cruise ships, and the cargo liners and tramps were gradually replaced by

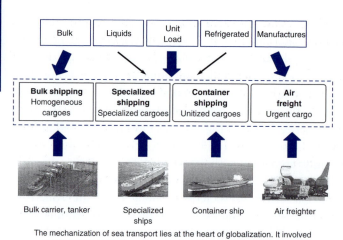

The mechanization of sea transport lies at the heart of globalization. It involved splitting transport into four segments where investment could be applied.

**Figure 1.10**

The bulk and container shipping system after 1950

the new transport systems illustrated in Figure 1.10, using technology already well established in land-based industries such as car manufacture. The new system reduced costs by replacing expensive labour with cheaper and more efficient capital equipment and by treating sea transport as part of an integrated through-transport system. Standardization, automation of cargo handling, economies of scale, and developing ship designs adapted for efficient cargo stowage and handling all played a part in this process.

Homogeneous bulk cargoes were now carried by a fleet of large bulk carriers operating between terminals designed to mechanize cargo handling; general cargo was containerized and transported by a fleet of cellular container-ships; and five new specialized shipping segments evolved to transport chemicals, liquefied gases, forest products, wheeled vehicles, and refrigerated cargoes, each with its own fleet of specially designed ships. One side effect of automation was that shipping, which had previously been one of the world's most visible industries, became virtually invisible. The busy ports with miles of wharves were replaced by deserted deep water terminals handling cargo in hours, not weeks, and the shipping companies which had become household names were replaced by independent shipowners operating under 'flags of convenience'.

Many factors contributed to these changes. The airlines took over the passenger and mail trades from the passenger liners and the European empires were dismantled, removing two of the liner companies' most important revenue streams. American, European and Japanese multinationals relying on imported raw materials actively encouraged the new bulk shipping industry by offering time charters, and with this security it was easy to access investment funds from the emerging eurodollar market. Improved communications, including telex, fax, direct-dial phone calls and later e-mail and cheap inter-regional air travel, all helped to create an even more efficient global market place for shipping services. Thus the foundations were laid for a more efficient shipping business, combining economies of scale with an unprecedented ability to apply technology and logistics to the ever-changing pattern of seaborne trade.

## The new trade environment created at Bretton Woods

The change started with the new trade strategy adopted by the Western nations after the Second World War. Since the early 1940s the United States had been determined that after the war the restrictions of the colonial system should be removed, providing free access to global markets and raw materials. In July 1941 a memorandum from the US Council on Foreign Relations argued that to achieve this, the world needed financial institutions capable of 'stabilising currencies and facilitating programmes of capital investment in backward and underdeveloped regions'.[89] At the Bretton Woods Conference in 1944 the US Secretary of the Treasury, Henry Morgenthau, outlined the objective of creating 'a dynamic world economy in which the peoples of every nation will be able to realise their potentialities in peace and enjoy increasingly the fruits of material progress of an earth infinitely blessed with natural riches'.[90] By the end of the meeting the World Bank and the International Monetary Fund had been founded and the groundwork had also been laid for the General Agreement on Tariffs and Trade (GATT).

This policy had a profound effect on the maritime industry. By the end of the 1960s almost all of the European colonies had been given independence and they were encouraged to open their borders and transform their economies from self-sufficiency to export production. Trade agreements negotiated through GATT opened economies in both North and South to the free movement of goods and money. Capital flows were liberalized and multinational corporations systematically developed raw materials, manufacturing capacity and local consumer markets. Since the whole system depended on trade, efficient shipping played a central part in creating this new global economy and the imperially based liner system was not well positioned to meet the needs of the new order.

## Growth of air transport between regions

During the same period the airlines became serious competitors for the passenger and mail markets, one of the mainstays of the liner system. In 1950 ships still carried three times as many passengers across the Atlantic as aircraft, and in 1952 Cunard-White Star had nine vessels in the New York trade, with another four working out of Southampton to Canadian ports.[91] However, with the arrival of passenger jets the economics moved decisively in favour of the airlines. A passenger liner needed 1,000 crew and 2,500 tons of fuel to deliver 1,500 passengers to New York once a week. Even a first-generation jet carrying 120 passengers could make eight or nine crossings in a week, delivering almost 1,000 passenger crossings, but with only 12 crew and burning only 500 tons of fuel.[92] The flight time of 6 hours was an added bonus for busy travellers. On these economic considerations there was no contest. In 1955 almost 1 million passengers crossed the Atlantic by sea and about 750,000 by air, but by 1968 over 5 million travelled by air but only 400,000 by sea.[93] When jumbo jets arrived in 1967 the longer routes followed, and between 1965 and 1980 air traffic increased from 198 billion passenger kilometres to 946 billion.[94]

The last great passenger liner, the *Queen Elizabeth 2*, was ordered at John Brown's shipyard on Clydeside in 1963 as a dual-purpose passenger and cruise vessel for the Atlantic service, but two years after it was delivered in 1968 the jumbo jets came into service and it mainly served as a cruise liner. The passenger liners of the 1950s, built for speed, either went to the scrapyard or were converted into cruise liners offering a mobile leisure environment in which speed is irrelevant, bringing to an end the era of the great passenger liner.

## Growth of seaborne trade, 1950–2005

Meanwhile sea trade was growing faster than at any time since the early nineteenth century, with imports increasing from 500 million tonnes in 1950 to 7 billion tonnes in 2005 (Figure 1.11). This growth was led by Europe and Japan. Both had been badly damaged during the war, and set about the reconstruction of their economies. Released from their colonial empires, the European multinationals set about post-war reconstruction. Expansion of heavy industries such as steel and aluminium, combined with the substitution of imported oil for domestic coal in power stations, railway locomotives and rising car ownership, produced rapidly growing imports, particularly of bulk commodities. This growth persisted through the 1960s and the upward trend in imports was reinforced by the switch from domestic to imported sources for key raw materials such as iron ore, coal and oil. By the early 1970s the

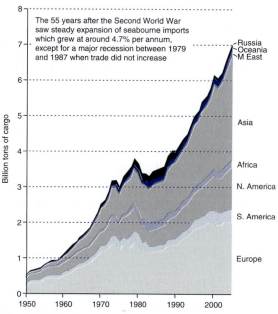

**Figure 1.11**
Sea trade by region, 1950–2005
Source: United Nations Statistical Yearbooks

European economy was maturing and demand for raw material intensive goods such as steel, aluminium and electricity stabilized.

The growth of Japan followed a similar pattern, but changed the focus of world shipping, because it was the first major industrial economy in the Pacific region. Development had started in the late nineteenth century, but after 1946 the Japanese economy was reorganized and the 'trading houses' took over the traditional coordinating role of the *zaibatsu*. Leading industries such as shipbuilding, motor vehicles, steel and shipping were selected by the Ministry of International Trade and Industry which coordinated growth for development, and during the 1960s the Japanese economy embarked upon a programme of growth which made it the world's leading maritime nation. Between 1965 and 1972 Japan generated 80% of the growth of the deep-sea dry cargo trade, and by the early 1970s it built half the world's ships and, taking account of open registry vessels, controlled the world's largest merchant shipping fleet.

In the 1970s the two oil crises coincided with the end of the European and Japanese growth cycle and the lead in trade growth switched to the Asian economies – notably

South Korea, which embarked on a programme of industrial growth. Emulating Japan, it rapidly expanded its heavy industries such as steel shipbuilding and motor vehicles. Then, in the 1980s, after two decades of total isolation and many centuries of restricted contact with the West, the Chinese economy opened its doors to capitalism and trade. There followed a period of remarkable economic growth, coupled with a move towards a more Westernized capitalist economic system.

The world economy was entering a new consumer-driven era, and during the 1960s the flow of motor cars, electronic products and a host of others increased very rapidly and the framework of trade widened, bringing in Asian economies and a more extensive trade with Africa and South America. This turned sea trade into a complex network connecting the three industrial centres in the temperate latitudes of the Northern Hemisphere – North America, western Europe and Japan – which generated about 60% of the trade, and drawing in raw materials and exporting manufactures.

## Shipping's 'industrial revolution'

Trade expansion on this scale would not have been possible without a major reform of the transport system. The new transport model that emerged gradually over 20 years had the three segments shown in Figure 1.10: bulk shipping, specialized shipping and containerisation. During the next 35 years many new ship types were developed, including bulk carriers, supertankers, liquefied gas tankers, chemical tankers, vehicle carriers, lumber carriers and, of course, container-ships.

## The development of bulk transport systems

The new bulk shipping industry was mainly masterminded by the multinationals, especially the oil companies and steel mills. Until the early 1950s the oil trade was still quite small and oil was mainly shipped as products in small tankers. However, as markets grew the strategy changed to shipping crude in large volumes to refineries located near the market, and this allowed bigger ships to be used (see Section 12.2). At the same time the steel mills were moving to coastal sites and developing overseas iron ore and coalmines to supply them. For the new generation of bulk carriers constructed for this trade, the only restrictions on size were the size of cargo parcels and the depth of water at the terminals, both of which increased rapidly. Commodities like oil, iron ore and coal were used in sufficiently large quantities to make cargo parcels of 100,000 tons or more practical and cargo shippers built deep-water terminals with automated cargo-handling systems. By investing in big ships and high-speed cargo-handling systems, it was decisively cheaper to import raw materials by sea from suppliers thousands of miles away than by land from suppliers only a few hundred miles away – for example, the rail freight for a ton of coal from Virginia to Jacksonville, Florida, was almost three times the sea freight from Hampton Roads to Japan, a distance of 10,000 miles.

Tankers illustrate the evolution in ship size (Figure 1.12). The 12,500 dwt *Narraganset* was built in 1903, and this remained a very acceptable size of vessel until 1944 when the largest tanker was the *Phoenix* of 23,900 dwt. During the Second World War the T2

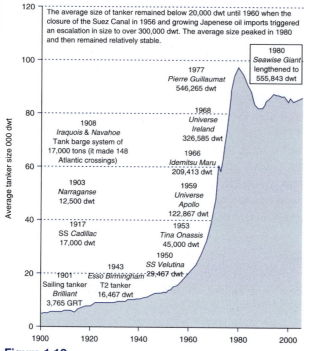

The average size of tanker remained below 20,000 dwt until 1960 when the closure of the Suez Canal in 1956 and growing Japanese oil imports triggered an escalation in size to over 300,000 dwt. The average size peaked in 1980 and then remained relatively stable.

1980
Seawise Giant lengthened to 555,843 dwt

1977
Pierre Guillaumat
546,265 dwt

1968
Universe Ireland
326,585 dwt

1908
Iraquois & Navahoe
Tank barge system of 17,000 tons (it made 148 Atlantic crossings)

1966
Idemitsu Maru
209,413 dwt

1903
Narraganse
12,500 dwt

1959
Universe Apollo
122,867 dwt

1917
SS Cadillac
17,000 dwt

1953
Tina Onassis
45,000 dwt

1950
SS Velutina

1943
SS Birmingham
29,467 dwt

1901
Sailing tanker Brilliant
3,765 GRT

Esso Birmingham
T2 tanker
16,467 dwt

Average tanker size 000 dwt

**Figure 1.12**

Average size of tanker, 1900–2005

Source: Complied by Martin Stopford from various sources

tanker, a 16,500 dwt vessel, had been mass-produced, and that remained the workhorse size, mainly shipping products from refineries based near the oil-fields. Then in the 1950s tanker sizes started to increase. By 1959 the largest tanker afloat was the *Universe Apollo* (122,867 dwt), and in 1966 the first very large crude carrier (VLCC), the *Idemitsu Maru* 209,413 dwt followed, just two years ahead of the *Universe Ireland* (326,585 dwt) the first ultra large crude carrier (ULCC) in 1968. This upward trend peaked in 1980 when the *Seawise Giant* was extended to 555,843 dwt. Overall the increase in ship size probably reduced unit shipping costs by at least 75%.

In dry bulk shipping, the move into large bulk vessels was equally pronounced. Although 24,000 dwt ore carriers were used in the 1920s, in 1950 most bulk cargo was still carried in tramps of between 10,000 and 12,000 dwt. The move to bigger ships followed the same pattern as tankers, and by the 1970s vessels of 200,000 dwt were widely in use on the high-volume routes, while the first generation of 300,000 dwt vessels started to come into service in the mid-1980s. There was also a steady upward movement in the size of ships used for the transport of commodities such as grain, sugar, non-ferrous metal ores and forest products. Taking the grain trade as an example, in the late 1960s most of the grain shipped by sea was in vessels under 25,000 dwt.[95] It seemed inconceivable to shippers in the business that vessels of 60,000 dwt could ever be used extensively in the grain trade, although by the early 1980s this is precisely what had happened.

Technical improvements, though less dramatic than previously, were significant. Hatch designs, cargo-handling gear and navigation equipment all improved in efficiency. During the 1980s the fuel efficiency of diesel engines increased by 25%. Shipbuilders became more adept at fine-tuning hull designs, with the result that for some ship types the steel weight was reduced by 30%; hull coatings improved to give the submerged hull better smoothness and improved longevity for tank structures.

Bulk shipping also benefited from improving communications. During this period the position of the Baltic Exchange as a central market for shipping was undermined by improved communications including direct-dial telephony, broadcast telex, fax and e-mail. It was no longer necessary to meet face-to-face to fix ships. Instead owners, brokers and cargo agents used telex messages to distribute cargo/position lists and negotiations were handled by phone. In the 1970s computerized work stations allowed telex or fax messages to be sent by the user and also provided access to databases of ship positions, vessel details and voyage estimating programs. PC networks, which appeared in the 1980s, made these facilities available cheaply to even the smallest companies, and modems gave access to the office workstation from home. The final link in the virtual market place was the cellular telephone, which allowed a broker to go out for lunch even while he was 'working' a ship – now that really *was* progress!

As the fleet of tankers and bulk carriers grew and the independent owners became more established, the multinationals gradually reduced their owned and chartered fleets, relying more on independent shipowners and the rapidly growing charter market. As information technology improved in the 1970s, the market started to segment by ship type – VLCCs, products tankers, Handy bulkers, Panamax, Capesize, chemicals, etc. Teams of specialist brokers developed an in-depth knowledge of their sector – its ships, charterers, ports and cargoes – and combined this with the 'soft' information gained from daily networking to gain negotiating leverage. By allowing market specialization, cheap, fast communications took the business a step forward in terms of logistic efficiency. The result was the highly efficient transport system for bulk cargoes we have today.

### The containerization of general cargo

Developing a new system for shipping general cargo was left to the shipowners and it took much longer to get started. By the 1960s congested ports and labour difficulties were slowing transit times, and cargo shipped from Europe to the United States took months to arrive. Industry observers could see that 'the old methods had reached the end of the line',[96] but the way forward was not obvious. The problem facing the liner companies when they finally started to investigate unitization in 1960 was that liners had always been flexible in the cargo they carried and some cargoes were difficult to containerize. Containerization, which excluded all cargoes that would not fit in a standard 20-foot box, seemed an extreme solution, and even in 1963 the debate was not resolved. Companies experimented with flexible systems such as cargo palletization and ro-ro ships, which combined unitization with the flexibility to carry bulk cargoes like forest products. But in reality containerization was not just about ships. It was a completely new way of organizing transport, involving massive capital investment and an end to the control of trade by separate shipping companies working within a closed conference system.[97] The first transatlantic service was started on 23 April 1966 by Sea-Land, a new US company which had been developing the concept since 1956 (see Chapter 13). Transporting general cargo in standard boxes had a more fundamental impact than even its most ardent advocates anticipated. Just a few days after leaving the factory in the Midlands of England, a container wagon could be arriving at its destination in East Coast USA with its cargo safe from damage or pilferage and readily transferable to rail or barge with the minimum of delay and effort. By adopting containerization the industry opened the floodgates for global commerce (see Chapter 12 for more history).

Containerization was made possible by developments in communications and information technology. Until the 1960s, liner services were very fragmented, and managers in one service knew little of what was going on in others. When containerization arrived in the 1960s, the pendulum swung to the other extreme because it 'could not have been accomplished without computer control systems for controlling the movement of containers, taking bookings, printing out bills of lading and invoices and transmitting advice and information'.[98] Only large companies could afford the mainframe computer systems needed to run a container service, so 'the dominance of the mainframe computer, development of data bases and rationalisation of systems predicated central control for a major operator'.[99] By the mid-1990s the system for handling containers had become very sophisticated and was squeezing more value out of the transport business, pioneered by operators such as OCL in the 1970s. These developments were immensely productive, reducing cycle times by 40%, errors by 30% and saving $5 per document.[100] This was a great leap forward for those big enough to be able to afford it.

## Transport of specialized cargoes

Some cargoes did not fit comfortably in either the container or the bulk shipping systems, and gradually specialized shipping services developed to carry them. The five commodity groups which became the focus for specialized shipping operations were: forest products; chemicals; refrigerated cargo; cars and wheeled vehicles; and liquefied gases. Previously these had all been carried in liners or tramps, often with the help of some special investment such as refrigerated holds and deep tanks for liquid chemicals and vegetable oil. However, the standard of service was often poor. For example, vehicles were very expensive to transport and were often damaged in transit. As the volume of these cargoes grew, shippers and owners often worked together to improve the economics of the service, creating a period of tremendous innovation in ship design. From 1950 onwards the innovations came thick and fast. The first chemical parcel tanker, the *Marine Dow Chem* was built in the United States in 1954, and this was soon followed by the first container-ship, a conversion, in 1956. In the same year Wallenius lines built the first car carrier, the *Rigoletto*, designed for the carriage of 260 cars, and the first open hatch bulk carrier, designed with wide hatches to carry pre-packaged timber was built in 1962, for use in the paper trade. The first purpose-built liquefied natural gas (LNG) tanker came in 1964 and the first liquefied petroleum gas (LPG) tanker in 1955.

Each of these pioneer ships eventually grew into a fleet, and a new business sector for the shipping industry arose. In most cases the mode of operation was dramatically different from the 'quayside to quayside' business of the preceding century. The defining feature of these specialized segments is that they focus on the transport of a single cargo which permits, or requires, specialist investment to improve efficiency. As a result, the ships are closely integrated with the industries they served, often a small group of charterers. Chemical tankers carried small parcels of chemicals between industrial plants; car carriers became an integral part of the international motor business; and LNG tankers are shuttled between specially built terminals. The investment and organization behind these projects created the new concept of specialized shipping which became one of the building-blocks of the post-war global economy.

## Changing shipping company organization

As the shipping industry changed, so did the companies that ran it. Out of the top 10 UK liner companies in 1960, none remained 50 years later and there were no tramp companies left. The change in registration is very apparent from the fleet statistics in Table 1.9. In 1950, 71% of the world fleet was registered in Europe and the United States, and 29% under overseas flags. By 2005 the share of the European and US flags had fallen to 11%, whilst other countries, particularly flags of convenience such as Liberia and Panama, accounted for 89%. Part of this change is explained by the growth of new economies, particularly Japan, South Korea and China, whose national fleets grew rapidly. For example, the Japanese fleet grew from 1.9 million grt in 1952 and 18.5 million grt in 1997. However, a more important explanation is the growing importance of independent shipowners in

**Table 1.9** World merchant fleet by country (millions of tons)

| Start of year | 1902 | 1950 | 2005 |
|---|---|---|---|
| *W Europe & USA* | | | |
| Britain | 14.4 | 18.2 | 9.8 |
| USA | 2.3 | 16.5 | 12.5 |
| US Reserve | 0.3 | 11.0 | n/a |
| Holland | 0.6 | 3.1 | 5.7 |
| Italy | 1.2 | 2.6 | 11.1 |
| Germany | 3.1 | 0.5 | 9.1 |
| Belgium | 0.3 | 0.5 | 3.5 |
| France | 1.5 | 3.2 | 4.3 |
| Spain | 0.8 | 1.2 | 2.2 |
| Sweden | 0.7 | 2.0 | 3.6 |
| Denmark | 0.5 | 1.3 | 0.7 |
| Danish International | | | 6.9 |
| **Total** | **25.7** | **60.0** | **69.4** |
| **% world fleet** | **80%** | **71%** | **11%** |
| *Other flags* | | | |
| Liberia | 0.0 | 0.2 | 55.2 |
| Panama | 0.0 | 3.4 | 136.1 |
| Greece | 0.3 | 1.3 | 32.7 |
| Japan | 0.6 | 1.9 | 12.7 |
| Norway | 1.6 | 5.5 | 3.6 |
| Others | 4.0 | 12.3 | 342.8 |
| **Total** | **6.5** | **24.6** | **583.1** |
| **% world fleet** | **20%** | **29%** | **89%** |
| **WORLD** | **32.2** | **84.6** | **652.5** |

Source: *Lioyd's Register*, Clarkson Research

the post-Bretton Woods world and their preference for open registries such as Liberia and Panama as a way of reducing costs.

The independent shipowners of this new generation were descendants of the tramp operators who had served the liner companies for the last century, supplemented by a new generation of businessmen such as Onassis, Niarchos, Pao and Tung who saw the opportunities in shipping. As the established national shipping companies struggled to adapt, weighed down by wealth, tradition and the wrong ships, the 'tramp' operators of Norway, Greece and Hong Kong were quick to spot that their new clients were the multinational oil companies, steel mills, aluminium producers, etc. These large companies needed the raw materials available in Africa, South America and Australasia, and that meant cheap sea transport. Whilst the established and cash-rich shipping companies were not attracted by this risky, low-return business, the independents were only too willing. Using time charters from the multinationals as security to raise finance, they rapidly built up the fleets of tankers, bulk carriers and specialized ships that were needed. Since the charters were subject to intense competition, to keep costs low they used an invention of American tax lawyers, the 'flag of convenience'. By registering the ships in a country such as Panama or Liberia, they paid only a fixed registration fee, and no further taxes were payable (see Chapter 16).

So once again the character of the shipping industry changed. The shipping companies were transformed from high-profile pillars of imperial respectability into intensely private businesses run by entrepreneurs. The change was compounded during the long recession of the 1980s (see Chapter 4) when even the most efficient shipowners had to 'flag out' and cut corners to survive. To the reputation for privacy was added the image of running ships that were 'old and corroded, structurally weak'.[101] By the 1990s governments, which had raised no real objection to the growth of the independent shipping industry during the earlier period, became concerned about the quality standards and the safety of the ships which operated in their national waters.

## 1.7 LESSONS FROM 5,000 YEARS OF COMMERCIAL SHIPPING

So that brings us to the end of the Westline. From the early sea trade in the Lebanon 5,000 years ago, the line has now arrived at China, and is heading through SE Asia to India, the Middle East, Central Asia, Russia and eastern Europe. The shipping industry has a unique opportunity to study its commercial history, and there are many lessons which we could draw, but three stand out.

The first is the central part which shipping has played in the global economy. At every stage in its development, sea transport has figured prominently, and the shipping industry, with its distinctive international flavour, has played a central role.

Second, the basic economics of the business have not changed all that much over the years. The messages gleaned from the Mesopotamian Maritime Code, the Roman bill of lading or even Captain Uring's exploits in the eighteenth century all tell the same story of a business driven by the laws of supply and demand. The ships, technology and customers change, but the basic principals of maritime commerce seem immutable. Although there is continuity in the economic model, the circumstances can change with remarkable speed. The break-up of the Roman Empire; the voyages of discovery in the sixteenth century, steam and the colonial system in the nineteenth century, and the mechanization of shipping in the second half of the twentieth century all dramatically changed the world in which shipowners operated. In the process, shipping today has become more than ever before an integral part of the process of globalization.

Third, shipping prospers during periods of political stability when the world is prosperous and stable. For example, we saw how the Mediterranean trade prospered when the Roman Empire provided safe passage, and declined when the *Pax Romana* broke down in the third century. Similarly the stability provided by the European empires from 1850 to 1950 created a framework in which the liner and tramp system could operate. Then a new period of globalization in the post-Bretton Woods era following the Second World War did the same sort of thing and once again the shipping business had to adapt. So the lesson is that the starting-point for any future analysis is not economics but the geopolitical environment and where that is going.

But change was not always gradual. The step changes in knowledge and technology were often followed by longer transitional periods as the commercial infrastructure was developed to put the changes into practice. As a result, revolution was softened into a more gradual evolution. Thus the voyages of discovery at the end of the fifteenth century took just a couple of decades, but it took centuries for the new global commercial trading system to grow out of them. Similarly, the transition from sail to steam started in the 1820s but it was almost a century before steamships had completely taken over merchant shipping from sail. More recently, containerization started in the 1950s but it was 25 years before its full potential as a global transport system was felt in world trade. So although change is sudden, the implementation of change is often a long and tedious business.

Pulling all this together, our task as maritime economists is to understand where we are at any point of time, so that we can see where things might go next. We must also understand the evolutionary nature of change. The die may be cast, but it is often many years before the real consequences of change become apparent. Today we are in a phase of transition created by globalization which is, in its own way, as revolutionary as the voyages of discovery five hundred years ago.

## 1.8 SUMMARY

In this chapter we examined how shipping developed over the last 5,000 years. It turns out that today's trade network is just a snapshot taken as the world economy creeps jerkily along its evolutionary path. The pace is usually too slow for contemporaries to see the trend, but from a historical perspective the progress is evident. The central role of shipping in this process was obvious to early economists such as Adam Smith, who recognized that shipping offers the transport needed to promote economic development. Indeed, shipping, trade and economic development all go hand in hand.

We divided the history of trade into three phases. The first started in the Mediterranean, spreading west through Greece, Rome and Venice, to Antwerp, Amsterdam and London. During this phase a global trading network gradually developed between the three great population centres in China, India and Europe. At first this trade was by land and was slow and expensive, but when the voyages of discovery opened up global sea routes in the late fifteenth century, transport costs fell dramatically and trade volumes escalated.

The second phase was triggered by the industrial revolution in the late eighteenth century. Innovations in ship design, shipbuilding and global communications made it possible for shipping to be conducted as a global industry, initially through the Baltic Exchange, whilst reliable steamships and technical innovations such as the Suez Canal made it possible for liner companies to operate regular services. For the next century trade grew rapidly, focused around the colonial empires of the European states and the framework of sea trade was radically changed.

Finally in the second half of the twentieth century another wave of economic and technical change was triggered by the dismantling of the colonial empires which were replaced by the free trade economy initiated at Bretton Woods. Manufacturers set out to track down better sources of raw materials and invested heavily in integrated transport systems which would reduce the cost of transporting these goods. During this period we saw the growth of the bulk carrier markets, the containerization of general cargo and specialist shipping operations transporting chemicals, forest products, motor vehicles, gas, etc. An important part of this revolution was the move of shipping away from the nation states which had dominated previous centuries towards flags of convenience. This brought greater economies and changed the financial framework of the industry, but it also raised regulatory problems.

The lesson is that shipping is constantly changing. It is a business that grew up with the world economy, exploring and exploiting the ebb and flow of trade. Today it has become a tightly knit global business community, built on communications and free trade. Perhaps that will change. But it is hard to disagree with Adam Smith that, whatever the circumstances 'such therefore are the advantages of water transport that ... this conveniency opens the whole world to the produce of every sort of labour'.[102]

# 2 The Organization of the Shipping Market

*Shipping is an exciting business, surrounded by many false beliefs, misconceptions and even taboos … The facts of the matter are straightforward enough and, when stripped of their emotional and sentimental overtones in clinical analysis, are much less titillating than the popular literature and maritime folklore lead one to expect.*

(Helmut Sohmen, 'What bankers always wanted to know about shipping but were afraid to ask', address to the Foreign Banks' Representatives Association, Hong Kong, 27 June 1985. Reprinted in *Fairplay*, London, 1 August 1986)

## 2.1 INTRODUCTION

Our aim in this chapter is to sketch the economic framework of the shipping industry. Like the street map of a city, it will show how the different parts of the maritime business fit together and where shipping fits into the world economy. We will also try to understand exactly what the industry does and identify the economic mechanisms that make the shipping market place operate.

We start by defining the maritime market and reviewing the businesses that are involved in it. This leads on to a discussion of the demand for international transport and its defining characteristics. Who are its customers, what do they really want and what does transport cost? The overview of the demand is completed with a brief survey of the commodities traded by sea. In the second half of the chapter we introduce the supply of shipping, looking at the transport system and the merchant fleet used to carry trade. We also make some introductory comments about ports and the economics of supply. Finally, we discuss the shipping companies that run the business and the governments that regulate them. The conclusion is that shipping is ultimately a group of people – shippers, shipowners, brokers, shipbuilders, bankers and regulators – who work together on the constantly changing task of transporting cargo by sea. To many of them shipping is not just a business. It is a fascinating way of life.

## 2.2 OVERVIEW OF THE MARITIME INDUSTRY

In 2005 the shipping industry transported 7.0 billion tons of cargo between 160 countries. It is a truly global industry. Businesses based in Amsterdam, Oslo, Copenhagen, London, Hamburg, Genoa, Piraeus, Dubai, Hong Kong, Singapore, Shanghai, Tokyo, New York, Geneva and many other maritime centres compete on equal terms. English is the common language, which nearly everyone speaks. Ships, the industry's main assets, are physically mobile, and international flags allow shipping companies to choose their legal jurisdiction, and with it their tax and financial environment. It is also ruthlessly competitive, and some parts of the industry still conform to the 'perfect competition' model developed by classical economists in the nineteenth century.

Merchant shipping accounts for roughly a third of the total maritime activity as can be seen from Table 2.1, which divides the maritime business into five groups: vessel operations (i.e. those directly involved with ships); shipbuilding and marine engineering; marine resources, which include offshore oil, gas, renewable energy and minerals; marine fisheries, including aquaculture and seafood processing; and other marine activities, mainly tourism and services. When all these businesses are taken into account the marine industry's annual turnover in 2004 was over $1 trillion. Although these figures contain many estimates, they make a useful starting point because they put the business into context and provide a reminder of the other businesses with which shipping shares the oceans. Many of them use ships too – fishing, offshore, submarine cables, research and ports are examples – providing diversification opportunities for shipping investors.

In 2004 merchant shipping was much the biggest, with a turnover of about $426 billion. The business had grown very rapidly during the previous five years, due to the freight market boom which was just starting in 2004. In 2007 it operated a fleet of 74,398 ships, of which 47,433 were cargo vessels. Another 26,880 non-cargo merchant vessels were engaged in fishing, research, port services, cruise and the offshore industry (see Table 2.5 for details). This makes shipping comparable in size with the airline industry, which has about 15,000 much faster aircraft.

It employs about 1.23 million seafarers, of whom 404,000 are officers and 823,000 are ratings,[1] with smaller numbers employed onshore in the various shipping offices and services. These are relatively small numbers for a global industry.

Naval shipping is worth about $170 billion a year, which includes personnel, equipment and armaments. Although not strictly involved in commerce, navies are responsible for its protection and preserving open lines of commercial navigation on the major waterways of the world.[2] About 9,000 naval vessels, including patrol craft, operate worldwide with annual orders for about 160 new vessels. Cruise and ports complete the vessel operations section. There are over 3,000 major ports and terminals around the world, with many thousands of smaller ones engaged in local trades. So this is a major industry.

Supporting these core activities are the shipbuilding and marine equipment industries. There are over 300 large merchant shipyards building vessels over 5,000 dwt worldwide, and many more small ship- and boatbuilding yards with a turnover of

**Table 2.1** Marine activities, 1999–2004

| US$ millions | Turnover US$ m.[a] | | Growth 99–04 (% p.a.) | Share in 2004% |
|---|---|---|---|---|
| | **1999** | **2004** | | |
| **1. Vessel operations** | | | | |
| Merchant shipping | 160,598 | 426,297 | 22% | 31% |
| Naval shipping | 150,000 | 173,891 | 3% | 13% |
| Cruise industry | 8,255 | 14,925 | 12% | 1% |
| Ports | 26,985 | 31,115 | 3% | 2% |
| Total | 345,838 | 646,229 | 13% | 47% |
| **2. Shipbuilding** | | | | |
| Shipbuilding (merchant) | 33,968 | 46,948 | 7% | 3% |
| Shipbuilding (naval) | 30,919 | 35,898 | 3% | 3% |
| Marine equipment | 68,283 | 90,636 | 6% | 7% |
| Total | 133,170 | 173,482 | 5% | 13% |
| **3. Marine resources** | | | | |
| Offshore oil and gas | 92,831 | 113,366 | 4% | 8% |
| Renewable energy | — | 159 | | 0% |
| Minerals and aggregates | 2,447 | 3,409 | 7% | 0% |
| Total marine resources | 95,278 | 116,933 | 4% | 8% |
| **4. Marine fisheries** | | | – | |
| Marine fishing | 71,903 | 69,631 | –1% | 5% |
| Marine aquaculture | 17,575 | 29,696 | 11% | 2% |
| Seaweed | 6,863 | 7,448 | 2% | 1% |
| Seafood processing | 89,477 | 99,327 | 2% | 7% |
| Total marine fisheries | 185,817 | 206,103 | 2% | 15% |
| **5. Other marine related activities** | | | | |
| Maritime tourism | 151,771 | 209,190 | 7% | 15% |
| Research and Development | 10,868 | 13,221 | 4% | 1% |
| Marine services | 4,426 | 8,507 | 14% | 1% |
| Marine IT | 1,390 | 4,441 | 26% | 0% |
| Marine biotechnology | 1,883 | 2,724 | 8% | 0% |
| Ocean survey | 2,152 | 2,504 | 3% | 0% |
| Education and training | 1,846 | 1,911 | 1% | 0% |
| Submarine telecoms | 5,131 | 1,401 | –23% | 0% |
| **Total other activities** | 179,466 | 243,898 | 6% | 18% |
| **Total marine activities** | 939,570 | 1,386,645 | 8% | 100% |

[a] The information in this table is based on many estimates and should be regarded as no more than a rough indication of the relative size of the various segments of the maritime business. The totals include some duplication, for example marine equipment is double-counted.

Source: Douglas-Westwood Ltd

around $67 billion in 2004. In the 1990s the annual investment in new cargo ships was $20 billion, but in 2007 $187 billion's worth of new ships were ordered and shipbuilding capacity was growing rapidly.[3] Another $53 billion was spent on second-hand ships, a very large figure in comparison with previous years.[4] In addition, a network of ship repair yards maintain merchant, naval and offshore ships. The shipyards are supported by the marine equipment manufacturers, paint manufacturers and suppliers of the host of equipment needed to construct and maintain the complex mechanical structures which we refer to as merchant ships. Their turnover in 2004 was about $90 billion.

A third group of businesses are concerned with marine resources, mainly oil and gas which turns over about $113 billion per annum. Marine fisheries, the fourth group, are also very significant, including fishing, aquaculture, seaweed and seafood processing. Marine tourism is larger still, but this group includes a wide range of activities, including research, surveys, IT, and submarine telecoms. Finally, there are the marine services such as insurance, shipbroking, banking, legal services, classification and publishing. Whilst it is doubtful whether any of these global figures are very accurate, they provide a starting point by putting the businesses we will study in this volume into the context of the marine industry as a whole.

## 2.3 THE INTERNATIONAL TRANSPORT INDUSTRY

The modern international transport system consists of roads, railways, inland waterways, shipping lines and air freight services, each using different vehicles (see Table 2.2). In practice the system falls into three zones: inter-regional transport, which covers deep-sea shipping and air freight; short-sea shipping, which transports cargoes short distances and often distributes cargoes brought in by deep-sea services; and inland transport, which includes road, rail, river and canal transport.

### Deep-sea shipping and air freight

For high-volume inter-regional cargoes deep-sea shipping is the only economic transport between the continental landmasses. Traffic is particularly heavy on the routes between the major industrial regions of Asia, Europe and North America, but the global transport network is now very extensive, covering many thousands of ports and offering services ranging from low-cost bulk transport to fast regular liner services. Air freight started to become viable for transporting high-value commodities between regions in the 1960s. It competes with the liner services for premium cargo such as

**Table 2.2** International transport zones and available transport modes

| Zone | Area | Transport sector | Vehicle |
|------|------|------------------|---------|
| 1 | Inter-regional | Deep-sea shipping | Ship |
|   |   | Air freight | Plane |
| 2 | Short-sea | Coastal seas | Ship/ferry |
| 3 | Land | River and canal | Barge |
|   |   | Road | Lorry |
|   |   | Rail | Train |

Source: Martin Stopford 2007

electronic goods, processed textiles, fresh fruit, vegetables and automotive spare parts. Since the 1960s air freight has grown at over 6% per annum, reaching 111 billion ton miles (btm) by 2005. Maritime trade has been growing more slowly, averaging 4.2% growth per annum over the same period, but the volume of cargo is much larger. Compared with the 28.9 trillion ton miles of maritime cargo in 2005, air freight still accounted for only 0.4% of the volume of goods transported between regions.[5] Its contribution has been to widen the range of freight transport by offering the option of very fast but high-cost transport.

## Short-sea shipping

Short-sea shipping provides transport within regions. It distributes the cargo delivered to regional centres such as Hong Kong or Rotterdam by deep-sea vessels, and provides a port-to-port service, often in direct competition with land-based transport such as rail. This is a very different business from deep-sea shipping. The ships are generally smaller than their counterparts in the deep-sea trades, ranging in size from 400 dwt to 6,000 dwt, though there are no firm rules. Designs place much emphasis on cargo flexibility.

Short-sea cargoes include grain, fertilizer, coal, lumber, steel, clay, aggregates, containers, wheeled vehicles and passengers. Because trips are so short, and ships visit many more ports in a year than deep-sea vessels, trading in this market requires great organizational skills:

> It requires a knowledge of the precise capabilities of the ships involved, and a flexibility to arrange the disposition of vessels so that customers' requirements are met in an efficient and economic way. Good positioning, minimisation of ballast legs, avoiding being caught over weekends or holidays and accurate reading of the market are crucial for survival.[6]

The ships used in the short-sea trades are generally smaller versions of the ships trading deep-sea. Small tankers, bulk carriers, ferries, container-ships, gas tankers and vehicle carriers can be found trading in most of the regions on short-haul routes. Short-sea shipping is also subject to many political restrictions. The most important is cabotage, the practice by which countries enact laws reserving coastal trade to ships of their national fleet. This system has mainly been operated in countries with very long coastlines, such as the United States and Brazil, but is no longer as prevalent as it used to be.

## Land transport and the integration of transport modes

The inland transport system consists of an extensive network of roads, railways, and waterways using trucks, railways and barges. It interfaces with the shipping system through ports and specialist terminals, as shown in Table 2.2, and one of the aims of modern transport logistics is to integrate these transport systems so that cargo flows smoothly and with minimum manual handling from one part of the system to another.[7] This is achieved in three ways: first, by adopting international standards for the units in which cargoes are transported, and these standards are applied to containers, pallets, packaged lumber, bales (e.g. of wool) and bulk bags; second, by investing in integrated handling systems designed to move the cargo efficiently from one transport mode to another; and third, by designing the vehicles to integrate with these facilities – for example, by building rail hopper cars which speed up the discharge of iron ore and building open-hatch bulk carriers with holds that exactly comply with the standards for packaged lumber.

As a result, transport companies operate in a market governed by a mix of competition and cooperation. In many trades the competitive element is obvious: rail competes with road; short-sea shipping with road and rail; and deep-sea shipping with air freight for higher-value cargo. However, a few examples show that the scope of competition is much wider than appears possible at first sight. For example, over the last 50 years bulk carriers trading in the deep-sea markets have been in cut-throat competition with the railways. How is this possible? The answer is that users of raw materials, such as power stations and steel mills, often face a choice between use of domestic and imported raw materials. Thus, a power station at Jacksonville in Florida can import coal from Virginia by rail or from Colombia by sea. Or container services shipping from Asia to the US West Coast and then transporting the containers by rail to the East Coast are in competition with direct services by sea via the Panama Canal. Where transport accounts for a large proportion of the delivered cost, there is intense competition. But cost is not the only factor, as shown by the seasonal trade in perishable goods such as raspberries and asparagus. These products travel as air freight because the journey by refrigerated ship is too slow to allow delivery in prime condition. However, the shipping industry has tried to recapture that cargo by developing refrigerated containers with a controlled atmosphere to prevent deterioration.

Although the different sectors of the transport business are fiercely competitive, technical development depends upon close cooperation because each component in the transport system must fit in with the others by developing ports and terminals designed for efficient cargo storage and transfer from one mode to another. There are many examples of this cooperation. Much of the world's grain trade is handled by a system of barges, rail trucks and deep-sea ships. The modal points in the system are highly automated grain elevators which receive grain from one transport mode, store it temporarily and ship it out in another. Similarly, coal may be loaded in Colombia or Australia, shipped by sea in a large bulk carrier to Rotterdam, and distributed by a small short-sea vessel to the final consumer. The containerization of general cargo is built around standard containers which can be carried by road, rail or sea with equal facility. Often road transport companies are owned by railways and vice versa. One way or another, the driving force which guides the development of these transport systems is the quest to win more business by providing cheaper transport and a better service.

## 2.4 CHARACTERISTICS OF SEA TRANSPORT DEMAND

### The sea transport product

The merchant shipping industry's product is transport. But that is like saying that restaurants serve food. It misses out the qualitative part of the service. People want different food for different occasions, so there are sandwich bars, fast-food chains and cordon bleu restaurants. The Rochdale Report, one of the most thorough investigations of the shipping industry ever carried out, commented on these sectoral divisions within the industry as follows:

> Shipping is a complex industry and the conditions which govern its operations in one sector do not necessarily apply to another; it might even, for some purposes, be better regarded as a group of related industries. Its main assets, the ships themselves, vary widely in size and type; they provide the whole range of services for a variety of goods, whether over shorter or longer distances. Although one can, for analytical purposes, usefully isolate sectors of the industry providing particular types of service, there is usually some interchange at the margin which cannot be ignored.[8]

Like restaurateurs, shipping companies provide different transport services to meet the specific needs of different customers, and this gives rise to three major segments in the shipping market, which we will refer to as liner, bulk and specialized shipping. The liner business carries different cargoes, provides different services and has a different economic structure than bulk shipping, whilst the 'specialist' market segments which focus on the transport of cars, forest products, chemicals, LNG and refrigerated produce each have their own, slightly different, characteristics. But as Rochdale points out, they do not operate in isolation. They often compete for the same cargo – for example, during the 1990s the container business won a major share of the refrigerated trade from the reefer fleet. In addition, some shipping companies are active in all the shipping sectors and investors from one sector will enter another if they see an opportunity.

So although there is some market segmentation, these markets are not isolated compartments. Investors can, and do, move their investment from one market sector to another,[9] and supply–demand imbalances in one part of the market soon ripple across to other sectors. In what follows we will first explore the characteristics of the world trade system which creates the demand for different types of transport service; then we discuss how this translates into price and qualitative aspects of the transport product; and finally, we discuss how this has led to segmentation in the shipping business (ground we have already covered historically in Chapter 1, but which we will now examine in a more structured way). Is shipping one industry or several?

### The global sea transport demand model

Shipping companies work closely with the companies that generate and use cargo. As we saw in Chapter 1, today's multinational companies source raw materials where they are cheapest and locate manufacturing facilities in any low-cost corner of the world, however remote, drawing many towns and cities into the global economy. These oil companies, chemical producers, steel mills, car manufacturers, sugar refiners, consumer goods manufacturers, retail chains and many others are the shipping industry's biggest customers.

These businesses need many different types of transport, and Figure 2.1 gives a bird's-eye view of how shipping serves their global businesses.[10] On the left are the four primary producing sectors of the world economy: energy, including coal, oil and gas; mining, including metal ores and other crude minerals; agriculture, including grain and oilseeds, refrigerated foods, vegetable oils, and live animals; and forestry. These commodities are the building-blocks of economic activity, and transporting them from areas of surplus to areas of shortage, usually in the largest parcels possible to reduce transport costs, is a major market for the shipping industry.

Most of these raw materials need primary processing, and whether this takes place before or after transport makes a major difference to the trade. The principal industries involved are listed in the centre of Figure 2.1. At the top are oil refining, chemicals, and steel; the corporations that control these heavy industrial plants are major users of bulk transport and their policies change. For example, oil may be shipped as crude or products, with very different consequences for the transport operation. The more important manufacturing industries shown in the lower part of the middle column include vehicle manufacturing, light engineering, food processing, textiles, and wood and paper processing. They import semi-manufactures such as steel products, pulp, petroleum, chemicals, vegetable oils, textile fibres, circuit boards and a host of other products. Although these products still travel in large quantities, the cargo parcels are usually smaller and the commodities are more valuable. For example, iron ore is worth about $40 per tonne, but steel products are worth about $600–1,000 per tonne. They may also use special ships and cargo-handling facilities, as in the case of forest products and chemicals tankers.

Manufactured goods are often shipped several times, first to assembly plants and then on to other plants for finishing and packaging. This is a very different business from the raw materials and semi-manufactures discussed in previous paragraphs. Physical quantities are generally much smaller, and the components shipped around the world from one fabricator to another are increasingly valuable. For many products tight inventory control calls for fast, reliable and secure shipment, often in relatively small parcels, and transport now plays a central part in the world business model. A recent development in trade theory argues that comparative advantage is driven by clusters of expertise scattered around the globe.[11] Clusters of companies specializing in a particular business, say manufacturing ski boot clamps (or maritime equipment for that matter) develop a 'comparative advantage' in that product.[12] With the right communications and transport, these clusters can market their products globally, leading to a broader trade matrix, improved global efficiency and in the process giving shipowners more cargo. This is a theme we will develop in Chapter 10 where we examine the principles underlying maritime trade. For the present we can simply note that these remote clusters of expertise are reliant on cheap and efficient transport to deliver their products to market, and

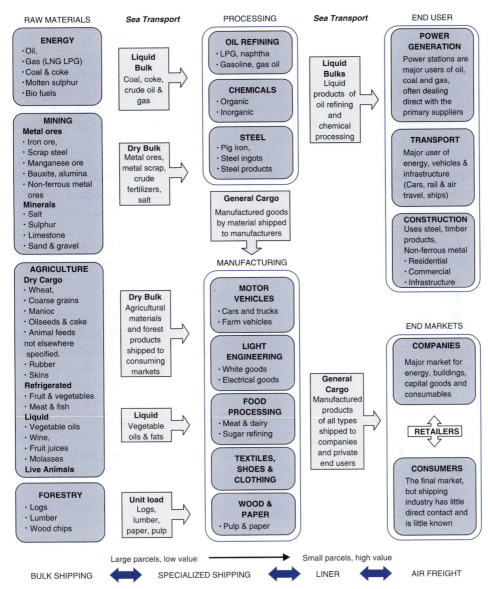

**Figure 2.1**
International transport system showing transport requirements
Source: Martin Stopford, 2007

the transport network developed by the container companies in the second half of the twentieth century must have contributed significantly to the growth of manufacturing in these areas.

In the right-hand column of Figure 2.1 are listed the final customer groups for the processed and manufactured products. At the top are three very important industries: power generation, transport and construction. These use large quantities of basic materials such as fuel, steel, cement and forest products. They are usually very sensitive to the business cycle. Below them are listed the end markets for the goods and services produced by the world economy, loosely classified as companies and consumers.

This diversity of cargo makes analysing trade flows between these industries complex. Whilst primary materials, such as oil, iron ore and coal, move from areas of surplus to areas of shortage, and are quite simple to analyse, specialist cargoes are often traded for competitive reasons rather than supply and demand deficit – for example, the United States produces motor vehicles locally, but is also a major export market for manufacturers in Asia and Europe. In fact, when we view trade from the viewpoint of the underlying economic forces which drive it, there are three quite different categories. First, there is deficit trade, which occurs when there is a physical shortage of a product in one area and a surplus in another, leading to a trade flow which fills the gap in the importing country. This is very common in the raw material trades but also for semi-manufactures, for example when there are difficulties in expanding processing plant. Second, there is competitive trade. A country may be capable of producing a product, but cheaper supplies are available overseas. Or consumers or manufacturers may wish for diversity. For example, many cars are shipped by sea because consumers like a greater choice than domestic car manufacturers can offer. Third, there is cyclical trade which occurs in times of temporary shortages, for example due to poor harvests, or business cycles, leading to temporary trade flows. Steel products, cement and grain are commodities which often exhibit this characteristic. These are all issues which come up in discussing the trades in Part 4. This chapter simply introduces the transport systems that have developed to carry the cargoes.

The job of the shipping industry is to transport all these goods from place to place. There are about 3,000 significant ports handling cargo, with a theoretical 9 million routes between them. Add the complex mix of commodities and customers outlined above (a ton of iron ore is very different from a ton of steel manufactured into a Ferrari!) and the complexity of the shipping industry's job becomes all too apparent. How does it organize the job?

## The commodities shipped by sea

We can now look more closely at the commodities the industry transports. In 2006 the trade consisted of many different commodities. Raw materials such as oil, iron ore, bauxite and coal; agricultural products such as grain, sugar and refrigerated food; industrial materials such as rubber, forest products, cement, textile fibres and chemicals; and manufactures such as heavy plant, motor cars, machinery and consumer goods. It covers everything from a 4 million barrel parcel of oil to a cardboard box of Christmas gifts.

One of the prime tasks of shipping analysts is to explain and forecast the development of these commodity trades, and to do this each commodity must be analysed in the context of its economic role in the world economy. Where commodities are related to the same industry, it makes sense to study them as a group so that interrelationships can be seen. For example, crude oil and oil products are interchangeable – if oil is refined before shipment then it is transported as products instead of crude oil. Similarly, if a country exporting iron ore sets up a steel mill, the trade in iron ore may be transformed into a

**Table 2.3** World seaborne trade by commodity and average growth rate

| | Million tonnes of cargo | | | | % growth p.a. |
| --- | --- | --- | --- | --- | --- |
| | 1995 | 2000 | 2005 | 2006 | 1995–2006 |
| **1. Energy trades** | | | | | |
| Crude oil | 1,400 | 1,656 | 1,885 | 1,896 | 2.8% |
| Oil products | 460 | 518 | 671 | 706 | 4.0% |
| Steam coal | 238 | 346 | 507 | 544 | 7.8% |
| LPG | 34 | 39 | 37 | 39 | 1.3% |
| LNG | 69 | 104 | 142 | 168 | 8.5% |
| Total | 2,201 | 2,663 | 3,242 | 3,354 | 3.9% |
| | | Share of total in 2006 | | | 44% |
| **2. Metal industry trades** | | | | | |
| Iron ore | 402 | 448 | 661 | 721 | 5.5% |
| Coking coal | 160 | 174 | 182 | 185 | 1.3% |
| Pig iron | 14 | 13 | 17 | 17 | 1.8% |
| Steel product | 198 | 184 | 226 | 255 | 2.3% |
| Scrap | 46 | 62 | 90 | 94 | 6.7% |
| Coke | 15 | 24 | 25 | 24 | 4.4% |
| Bauxite/alumina | 52 | 54 | 68 | 69 | 2.6% |
| Total | 887 | 960 | 1,269 | 1,366 | 4.0% |
| | | Share of total in 2006 | | | 18% |
| **3. Agricultural trades** | | | | | |
| Wheat/coarse grain | 184 | 214 | 206 | 213 | 1.3% |
| Soya beans | 32 | 50 | 65 | 67 | 7.0% |
| Sugar | 34 | 37 | 48 | 48 | 3.2% |
| Agribulks | 80 | 88 | 97 | 93 | 1.4% |
| Fertilizer | 63 | 70 | 78 | 80 | 2.2% |
| Phosphate rock | 30 | 28 | 31 | 31 | 0.2% |
| Forest products | 167 | 161 | 170 | 174 | 0.3% |
| Total | 590 | 648 | 695 | 706 | 1.6% |
| | | Share of total in 2006 | | | 9.4% |
| **4. Other cargoes** | | | | | |
| Cement | 53 | 46 | 60 | 65 | 1.9% |
| Other minor bulk | 31 | 36 | 42 | 44 | 3.2% |
| Other dry cargo | 1,116 | 1,559 | 1,937 | 2,016 | 5.5% |
| Total | 1,200 | 1,641 | 2,039 | 2,125 | 5.3% |
| | | Share of total in 2006 | | | 28% |
| memo: Containerized | 389 | 628 | 1,020 | 1,134 | |
| | 4,878 | 5,912 | 7,246 | 7,550 | 4.1% |

Source: CRSL, *Dry Bulk Trades Outlook*, April 2007, *Oil & Tanker Trades Outlook*, April 2007, *Shipping Review & Outlook*, April 2007

smaller trade in steel products. To show how the various seaborne trades interrelate, the main seaborne commodity trades are shown in Table 2.3, arranged into four groups reflecting the area of economic activity to which they are most closely related. The growth rate of each commodity between 1995 and 2006 is also shown in the final column, illustrating the difference in character of the different trades. These groups can be summarized as follows.

- *Energy trades*. Energy dominates bulk shipping. This group of commodities, which by weight accounts for 44% of seaborne trade, comprises crude oil, oil products, liquefied gas and thermal coal for use in generating electricity. These fuel sources compete with each other and non-traded energy commodities such as nuclear power. For example, the substitution of coal for oil in power stations in the 1980s transformed the pattern of these two trades. The analysis of the energy trades is concerned with the world energy economy.

- *Metal industry trades*. This major commodity group, which accounts for 18% of sea trade, represents the second building-block of modern industrial society. Under this heading we group the raw materials and products of the steel and non-ferrous metal industries, including iron ore, metallurgical grade coal, non-ferrous metal ores, steel products and scrap.

- *Agricultural and forestry trades*. A total of seven commodities, accounting for just over 9% of sea trade, are the products or raw materials of the agricultural industry. They include cereals such as wheat and barley, soya beans, sugar, agribulks, fertilizers and forest products. The analysis of these trades is concerned with the demand for foodstuffs, which depends on income and population. It is also concerned with the important derived demand for animal feeds. On the supply side, we are led into the discussion of land use and agricultural productivity. Forest products are primarily industrial materials used for the manufacture of paper, paper board and in the construction industry. This section includes timber (logs and lumber) wood pulp, plywood, paper and various wood products, totalling about 174 mt. The trade is strongly influenced by the availability of forestry resources.

- *Other cargoes*. There are a wide range of commodities which together account for 28% of sea trade. Some are industrial materials such as cement, salt, gypsum, mineral sands, chemicals and many others. But there are also large quantities of semi-manufactures and manufactures such as textiles, machinery, capital goods and vehicles. Many of these commodities have a high value so their share in value is probably closer to 50%. They are the mainstay of the liner trades and the memo item at the bottom of the table estimates the volume of containerized cargo at 1.1 billion tons in 2006.

Viewing the trade as a whole, over 60% of the tonnage of seaborne trade is associated with the energy and metal industries, so the shipping industry is highly dependent upon developments in these two industries. But although these trade statistics convey the scale of the merchant shipping business, they disguise its physical complexity. Some shipments are regular, others irregular; some are large, others are small; some shippers are in a hurry, others are not; some cargoes can be handled with suction or grabs, while others are fragile; some cargo is boxed, containerized or packed on pallets, while other cargo is loose.

## Parcel size distribution

To explain how the shipping industry transports this complex mix of cargoes, we use the parcel size distribution (PSD) function. A 'parcel' is an individual consignment of cargo for shipment, for example 60,000 tonnes of grain that a trader has bought; 15,000 tonnes of raw sugar for a sugar refinery; 100 cases of wine for a wholesaler in the UK; or a consignment of auto parts. The list is endless. For a particular commodity trade, the PSD function describes the range of parcel sizes in which that commodity is transported. If, for example, we take the case of coal shown in Figure 2.2(a), individual shipments ranged in size from under 20,000 tons to over 160,000 tons, with clusters around 60,000 tons and 150,000 tons. However, the PSD for grain, shown in Figure 2.2(b), is very different, with only a few parcels over 100,000 tons, many clustered around 60,000 tons and a second cluster around 25,000 tons. Figure 2.2(c) shows two even more extreme trades – iron ore is almost all shipped in vessels over 100,000 dwt, with the largest cluster of cargoes around 150,000 dwt, whilst bulk sugar, a much smaller trade, clusters around 25,000 tons.

There are hundreds of commodities shipped by sea (see Table 11.1 in Chapter 11 for more examples of the bulk commodities) and each has its own PSD function, the shape of which is determined by its economic characteristic. Three factors which have a particular impact on the shape of the PSD function are the stock levels held by users (e.g. a sugar refinery with an annual throughput of 50,000 tons is hardly likely to import raw sugar in 70,000 ton parcels); the depth of water at the loading and discharging terminals; and the cost savings by using a bigger ship (economies of scale become smaller as ship size increases and eventually using a bigger ship may not be worth the trouble). From these factors shipping investors have to sort out the mix of cargo parcels they think will be shipped in future and from this decide what size of ship to order. Will the average size of iron ore cargoes move up from 150,000 tons

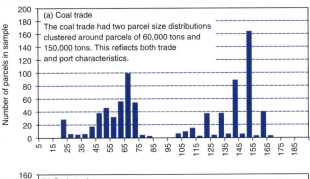

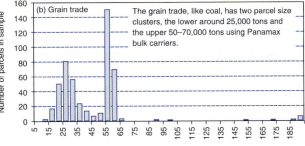

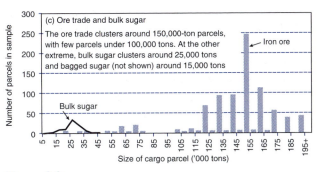

**Figure 2.2**

Parcel size distribution for coal, grain, ore and bulk sugar
Source: Sample of 7,000 dry cargo fixtures 2001–2

to 200,000 tons? If so, they should be ordering bigger Capesize bulk carriers. These are all subjects that we discuss more extensively in Part 4; for the present, we simply establish the principle that it is quite normal for the same commodity to be shipped in many different parcel sizes.

The importance of the PSD function is that it answers the question of which cargoes go in which ships. Cargoes of similar size and characteristics tend to be transported in the same type of shipping operation. One important division is between 'bulk cargo', which consists of large homogeneous cargo parcels big enough to fill a whole ship, and 'general cargo', which consists of many small consignments, each too small to fill a ship, that have to be packed with other cargo for transport. Another concerns ship size. Some bulk cargoes travel in small bulk carriers, while others use the biggest ships available. Each commodity trade has its own distinctive PSD, with individual consignments ranging from the very small to the very large.[13]

For many commodities the PSD contains parcels that are too small to fill a ship – for example, 500 tons of steel products – and that will travel as general cargo, and others – say, 5,000 tons of steel products – that are large enough to travel in bulk. As the trade grows, the proportion of cargo parcels large enough to travel in bulk may increase and the trade will gradually switch from being a liner trade to being predominantly a minor bulk trade. This happened in many trades during the 1960s and 1970s, and as a result the bulk trade grew faster than general cargo trade. Because many commodities travel partly in bulk and partly as general cargo, commodity trades cannot be neatly divided into 'bulk' and 'general' cargo. To do this it is necessary to know the PSD function for each commodity.

## Product differentiation in shipping

In addition to the parcel size, there are other factors which determine how a cargo is shipped. Although sea transport is often treated as a 'commodity' (i.e. all cargoes are assumed to be the same), this is an obvious oversimplification. In the real world different customer groups have different requirements about the type and level of service they want from their sea transport suppliers, and this introduces an element of product differentiation. Some just want a very basic service, but others want more. In practice there are four main aspects to the transport service which contribute to the product 'delivered' by shipping companies:

- *Price.* The freight cost is always important, but the greater the proportion of freight in the overall cost equation, the more emphasis shippers are likely to place on it. For example, in the 1950s the average cost of transporting a barrel of oil from the Middle East to Europe was 35% of its c.i.f. cost. As a result, oil companies devoted great effort to finding ways to reduce the cost of transport. By the 1990s the price of oil had increased and the cost of transport had fallen to just 2.5% of the c.i.f. price, so transport cost became less important. In general, demand is relatively price inelastic. Dropping the transport cost of a barrel of oil or a container load of sports shoes has little or no impact on the volume of cargo transported, at least in the short term.

- *Speed*. Time in transit incurs an inventory cost, so shippers of high-value commodities prefer fast delivery. The cost of holding high-value commodities in stock may make it cheaper to ship small quantities frequently, even if the freight cost is greater. On a three-month journey a cargo worth $1 million incurs an inventory cost of $25,000 if interest rates are 10% per annum. If the journey time can be halved, it is worth paying up to $12,500 extra in freight. Speed may also be important for commercial reasons. A European manufacturer ordering spare parts from the Far East may be happy to pay ten times the freight for delivery in three days by air if the alternative is to have machinery out of service for five or six weeks while the spares are delivered by sea.
- *Reliability*. With the growing importance of 'just in time' stock control systems, transport reliability has taken on a new significance. Some shippers may be prepared to pay more for a service which is guaranteed to operate to time and provides the services which it has promised.
- *Security*. Loss or damage in transit is an insurable risk, but raises many difficulties for the shipper, especially when the parcels are high in value and fragile. In this case they may be prepared to pay more for secure transportation with lower risk of damage.

Together these introduce an element of differentiation into the business.

## 2.5  THE SEA TRANSPORT SYSTEM

### The economic model for sea transport

In Chapter 1 we saw that over the last 50 years the shipping industry has developed a new transport system based on mechanization and systems technology. Within this system the economic pressures arising from the parcel size distribution and demand differentiation create the demand for different types of shipping service. Today's shipping market has evolved into three separate but closely connected segments: bulk shipping, specialized shipping and liner shipping. Although these segments belong to the same industry, each carries out different tasks and has a very different character.

The transport model is summarized in Figure 2.3. Starting at the top of this diagram (row A), world trade splits into three streams – bulk parcels, specialized parcels and general cargo parcels – depending on the PSD function for the commodity and service requirements of each cargo parcel. Large homogeneous parcels such as iron ore, coal and grain are carried by the bulk shipping industry; small parcels of general cargo are carried by the liner shipping industry; and specialized cargoes shipped in large volumes are transported by the specialized shipping industry. These three cargo streams create demand for bulk transport, specialized transport and liner transport (row B). The lower half of the diagram shows how the supply of ships is organized. A major distinction is drawn between the fleets of ships owned by the companies moving their own cargo in their own ships (row C) and the ships owned by independent shipowners (row D) and chartered

# THE ORGANIZATION OF THE SHIPPING MARKET

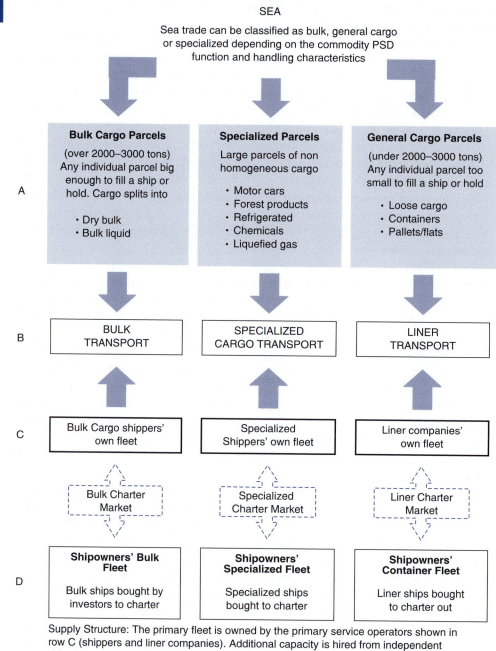

WORLD    TRADE

SEA

Sea trade can be classified as bulk, general cargo
or specialized depending on the commodity PSD
function and handling characteristics

A

**Bulk Cargo Parcels**

(over 2000–3000 tons)
Any individual parcel big
enough to fill a ship or
hold. Cargo splits into

• Dry bulk
• Bulk liquid

**Specialized Parcels**

Large parcels of non
homogeneous cargo

• Motor cars
• Forest products
• Refrigerated
• Chemicals
• Liquefied gas

**General Cargo Parcels**

(under 2000–3000 tons)
Any individual parcel too
small to fill a ship or hold

• Loose cargo
• Containers
• Pallets/flats

B

BULK
TRANSPORT

SPECIALIZED
CARGO TRANSPORT

LINER
TRANSPORT

C

Bulk Cargo shippers'
own fleet

Specialized
Shippers' own fleet

Liner companies'
own fleet

Bulk Charter
Market

Specialized
Charter Market

Liner Charter
Market

D

**Shipowners' Bulk
Fleet**

Bulk ships bought by
investors to charter

**Shipowners'
Specialized Fleet**

Specialized ships
bought to charter

**Shipowners'
Container Fleet**

Liner ships bought
to charter out

Supply Structure: The primary fleet is owned by the primary service operators shown in
row C (shippers and liner companies). Additional capacity is hired from independent
shipowners who buy ships to charter out. The 'charter market' arrows go both ways
because shippers may charter their ships out as well as in.

## Figure 2.3
The sea transport system, showing cargo demand and three shipping market segments
Source: Martin Stopford, 2008

to the cargo owners in Row C. Between rows C and D are the charter markets where rates for transport are negotiated. This is a highly flexible structure. For example, an oil company might decide to buy its own fleet of tankers to cover half of its oil transport needs and meet the other half by chartering tankers from shipowners. The same applies to the specialized and liner markets.

The bulk shipping industry on the left of Figure 2.3 carries large parcels of raw materials and bulky semi-manufactures. This is a very distinctive business. Bulk vessels handle few transactions, typically completing about six voyages with a single cargo each year, so the annual revenue depends on half a dozen negotiations per ship each year. In addition, service levels are usually low (see the discussion of pools in Section 2.9) so little overhead is required to run the ships and organize the cargo. Typically bulk shipping companies have 0.5–1.5 employees in the office for every ship at sea, so a fleet of 50 ships worth $1 billion could be run by a staff of 25–75 employees, depending on how much of the routine management is subcontracted. In short, bulk shipping businesses focus on minimizing the cost of providing safe transport and managing investment in the expensive ships needed to supply bulk transport.

The liner service shown on the right of Figure 2.3 transports small parcels of general cargo, which includes manufactured and semi-manufactured goods and many small quantities of bulk commodities – malting barley, steel products, non-ferrous metal ores and even waste paper may be transported by liner. For example, a container-ship handles 10,000–50,000 revenue transactions each year, so a fleet of six ships completes 60,000–300,000 transactions per annum. Because there are so many parcels to handle on each voyage, this is a very organization-intensive business. In addition, the transport leg often forms part of an integrated production operation, so speed, reliability and high service levels are important. However, cost is also crucial because the whole business philosophy of international manufacturing depends on cheap transport. With so many transactions, the business relies on published prices, though nowadays prices are generally negotiated with major customers as part of a service agreement. In addition, cargo liners are involved in the through-transport of containers. This is a business where transaction costs are very high and the customers are just as interested in service levels as price.

Specialized shipping services, shown in the centre of Figure 2.3 transport difficult cargoes of which the five most important are motor cars, forest products, refrigerated cargo, chemicals and liquefied gas. These trades fall somewhere between bulk and liner – for example, a sophisticated chemical tanker carries 400–600 parcels a year, often under contracts of affreightment (COAs), but they may take 'spot' (i.e. individually negotiated) cargoes as well. Service providers in these trades invest in specialized ships and offer higher service levels than bulk shipping companies. Some of the operators become involved in terminals to improve the integration of the cargo-handling operations. They also work with shippers to rationalize and streamline the distribution chain. For example, motor manufacturers and chemical companies place high priority on this and in this sector the pressure for change often comes from its sophisticated clients.

So although the three segments of the shipping industry shown in Figure 2.3 all carry cargo in ships, they face different tasks in terms of the value and volume of cargo, the number of transactions handled, and the commercial systems employed. Bulk shipping carries the high-volume, price-sensitive cargoes; specialized shipping carries those higher-value 'bulk' cargoes such as cars, refrigerated cargo, forest products and chemicals; the container business transports small parcels; and air freight does the rush jobs. But these segments also overlap, leading to intense competition for the minor bulk cargoes such as forest products, scrap, refrigerated cargo and even grain.

### Definition of 'bulk shipping'

Bulk shipping developed as the major sector in the decades following the Second World War. A fleet of specialist crude oil tankers was built to service the rapidly expanding economies of Western Europe and Japan, with smaller vessels for the carriage of oil products and liquid chemicals. In the dry bulk trades, several important industries, notably steel, aluminium and fertilizer manufacture, turned to foreign suppliers for their high-quality raw materials and a fleet of large bulk carriers was built to service the trade, replacing the obsolete 'tweendeckers previously used to transport bulk commodities. As a result, bulk shipping became a rapidly expanding sector of the shipping industry, and bulk tonnage now accounts for about three-quarters of the world merchant fleet.

Most of the bulk cargoes are drawn from the raw material trades such as oil, iron ore, coal and grain, and are often described as 'bulk commodities' on the assumption that, for example, all iron ore is shipped in bulk. In the case of iron ore this is a reasonable assumption, but many smaller commodity trades are shipped partly in bulk and partly as general cargo; for example, a shipload of forest products would be rightly classified as bulk cargo but consignments of logs still travel as general cargo in a few trades. There are three main categories of bulk cargo:

- *Liquid bulk* requires tanker transportation. The main ones are crude oil, oil products, liquid chemicals such as caustic soda, vegetable oils, and wine. The size of individual consignments varies from a few thousand tons to half a million tons in the case of crude oil.
- The five *major bulks* – iron ore, grain, coal, phosphates and bauxite – are homogeneous bulk cargoes which can be transported satisfactorily in a conventional dry bulk carrier or multi-purpose (MPP) stowing at 45–55 cubic feet per ton.
- *Minor bulks* covers the many other commodities that travel in shiploads. The most important are steel products, steel scrap, cement, gypsum, non-ferrous metal ores, sugar, salt, sulphur, forest products, wood chips and chemicals.

### Definition of 'liner shipping'

The operation of liner services is a very different business. General cargo consignments are too small to justify setting up a bulk shipping operation. In addition, they are often high-value or delicate, requiring a special shipping service for which the shippers prefer a fixed tariff rather than a fluctuating market rate. There are no hard-and-fast rules about what constitutes general cargo – boxes, bales, machinery, 1,000 tons of steel products, 50 tons of bagged malting barley are typical examples. The main classes of general cargo from a shipping viewpoint are as follows:

- Loose cargo, individual items, boxes, pieces of machinery, etc., each of which must be handled and stowed separately. All general cargo used to be shipped this way, but now almost all has been unitized in one way or another.
- Containerized cargo, standard boxes, usually 8 feet wide, often 8 feet 6 inches high and mostly 20 or 40 feet long, filled with cargo. This is now the principal form of general cargo transport.
- Palletized cargo, for example cartons of apples, are packed onto standard pallets, secured by straps or pallet stretch film for easy stacking and fast handling.
- Pre-slung cargo, small items such as planks of wood lashed together into standard-sized packages.
- Liquid cargo travels in deep tanks, liquid containers or drums.
- Refrigerated cargo, perishable goods that must be shipped, chilled or frozen, in insulated holds or refrigerated containers.
- Heavy and awkward cargo, large and difficult to stow.

Until the mid-1960s most general cargo (called 'break-bulk' cargo) travelled loose and each item had to be packed in the hold of a cargo liner using 'dunnage' (pieces of wood or burlap) to keep it in place. This labour-intensive operation was slow, expensive, difficult to plan and the cargo was exposed to the risk of damage or pilferage. As a result cargo liners spent two-thirds of their time in port and cargo-handling costs escalated to more than one-quarter of the total shipping cost,[14] making it difficult for liner operators to provide the service at an economic cost, and their profit margins were squeezed.[15]

The shipping industry's response was to 'unitize' the transport system, applying the same technology which had been applied successfully on the production lines in manufacturing industry. Work was standardized, allowing investment to increase productivity. Since cargo handling was the main bottleneck, the key was to pack the cargo into internationally accepted standard units which could be handled quickly and cheaply with specially designed equipment. At the outset many systems of unitization were examined, but the two main contenders were pallets and containers. Pallets are flat trays, suitable for handling by fork-lift truck, on which single or multiple units can be packed for easy handling. Containers are standard boxes into which individual items are packed. The first deep-sea container service was introduced in 1966 and in the next 20 years containers came to dominate the transport of general cargo, with shipments of over 50 million units per year.

## Definition of 'specialized shipping'

'Specialized' shipping sits somewhere between the liner and the bulk shipping sectors and has characteristics of both. Although it is treated as a separate sector of the business, the dividing line is not particularly well defined, as we will see in Part 4. The principal distinguishing feature of these specialized trades is that they use ships designed to carry a specific cargo type and provide a service which is targeted at a particular customer group. Buying specialized ships is risky and is only worthwhile if the cargoes have handling or storage characteristics which make it worth investing in ships designed to improve transport performance of that specific cargo.

Over the years new ship types have been developed to meet specific needs, but many specialist cargoes continue to be carried in non-specialist ships. A brief review of the development of ship types designed for a specific commodity is provided in Table 2.4. Starting with the *John Bowes*, the first modern collier built in 1852, we have in rapid succession the cargo liner, the oil tanker, refrigerated cargo ships, the chemical parcel tanker, the container-ship, the LPG tanker, the forest products carrier, and the LNG tanker. Some of these trades have now grown so big that they are no longer regarded as being specialized, for example crude oil tankers. Today the five main specialized sectors are as follows.

- *Motor vehicles.* Perhaps the best examples of a specialized transport sector. The cars are large, high-value and fragile units which need careful stowage. In the early days of the trade they were shipped on the deck of liners or in specially converted bulk carriers with fold-down decks. Apart from being inefficient, the cars were often damaged and in the 1950s purpose-built vessels were developed with multiple decks. The first car carrier was the 260 vehicle *Rigoletto* (see Table 2.4).

**Table 2.4** Development of ship types designed for a specific commodity, 1852–2008

| Date | First specialized ship of class | Name | Commodity | Size |
|------|----------------|------|-----------|------|
| 1852 | Bulk Carrier | SS *John Bowes* | Coal | 650 dwt |
| 1865 | Cargo liner | SS *Agamemnon* | General cargo | 3,500 dwt |
| 1880 | Reefer | SS *Strathleven* | Frozen meat | 400 carcasses |
| 1886 | Oil Tanker | SS *Glückauf* | Oil | 3,030 dwt |
| 1921 | Ore-Oil Carrier | *G.Harrison Smith* | Iron ore/oil | 14,305 grt |
| 1926 | Heavy Lift Ship | *Belray* | Heavy cargo | 4,280 dwt |
| 1954 | Chemical Parcel Tanker | *Marine Dow-Chem* | Chemical parcels | 16,600 dwt |
| 1950 | LPG Tanker (Ammonia) | *Heroya* | Ammonia | 1,500 dwt |
| 1956 | Car Carrier | *Rigoletto* | Wheeled vehicles | 260 cars |
| 1956 | Containership (conversion) | *Ideal-X* | Containers/oil | 58 TEU |
| 1962 | Forest Products Carrier | *MV Besseggen* | Lumber | 9,200 dwt |
| 1964 | LNG Tanker (purpose built) | *Methane Princess* | LNG | 27,400 m$^3$ |

Source: Martin Stopford 2007

Modern pure car and truck carriers (PCTCs) carry over 6,000 vehicles (see Chapter 14 for technical details).

- *Forest products*. The problem with logs and lumber is that although they can be carried easily in a conventional bulk carrier, cargo handling is slow and stowage is very inefficient. To deal with this the shippers started to 'package' lumber in standard sizes and built bulk carriers with holds designed around these sizes, hatches which opened the full width of the ship, and extensive cargo-handling gear. The first was the *Besseggen*, built in 1962. Companies such as Star Shipping and Gearbulk have built up extensive fleets of this sort of vessel.
- *Refrigerated foods*. The practice of insulating the hold of a ship and installing refrigeration equipment so that chilled or frozen food could be carried was developed in the nineteenth century. The first successful cargo was carried in the *Strathleven* in 1880. There has always been competition between the specialist 'reefer' operators and the liner service operators who used refrigerated holds or, more recently, refrigerated containers.
- *Liquid gas*. To transport gases such as butane, propane, methane, ammonia or ethylene by sea it is necessary to liquefy them by cooling, pressure or both. This requires specially built tankers and high levels of operation.
- *Chemical parcels*. Small parcels of chemicals, especially those which are dangerous or need special handling, can be carried more efficiently in large tankers designed with large numbers of segregated tanks. These are complex and expensive ships because each tank must have its own cargo-handling system.

The important point is that 'specialization' is not just about the ship design, it is about adapting the shipping operation to the needs of a specific customer group and cargo flow. Setting up a specialized shipping operation is a major commitment because the ships are often more expensive than conventional bulk vessels, with a restricted second-hand market, and provision of the service generally involves a close relationship with the cargo shippers. As a result, specialist shipping companies are easier to recognize than they are to define.

## Some limitations of the transport statistics

An obvious question is: 'What is the tonnage of bulk, specialized and general cargo shipped by sea?' Unfortunately there is a statistical problem in determining how the commodities are transported. Because we only have commodity data, and transport of some commodities is carried out by more than one segment, the volume of trade in general cargo cannot be reliably calculated from commodity trade statistics. For example, we may guess that a parcel of 300 tons of steel products transported from the UK to West Africa will travel in containers, whereas a parcel of 6,000 tons from Japan to the USA would be shipped in bulk, but there is no way of knowing this for certain from the commodity statistics alone. As we have already noted, some commodities (such as iron ore) are almost always shipped in bulk and others (such as machinery) invariably travel as general cargo, but many commodities (such as steel products, forest products and non-ferrous metal ores) straddle the two. In fact, as a trade flow grows it may start off being shipped as general cargo but eventually become sufficiently large to be shipped in bulk.[16] The difficulty of identifying bulk and general cargo trade from commodity trade statistics is very inconvenient for shipping economists, since seaborne trade data are collected mainly in this form and very little comprehensive information is available about cargo type.

## 2.6 THE WORLD MERCHANT FLEET

### Ship types in the world fleet

In 2007 the world fleet of self-propelled sea-going merchant ships was about 74,398 vessels over 100 gt, though because there are many small vessels, the exact number depends on the precise lower size limit and whether vessels such as fishing boats are included. In Figure 2.4 the cargo fleet is divided into four main categories: bulk (oil tankers, bulk carriers and combined carriers), general cargo, specialized cargo and non-cargo. Although these groupings seem well defined, there are many grey areas. Merchant ships are not mass-produced like cars or trucks and classifying them into types relies on selecting distinguishing physical characteristics, an approach which has its limitations. For example, products tankers are difficult to distinguish from crude tankers on physical grounds, or ro-ro vessels which can be used in the deep-sea trades or as ferries, so which category does a particular ship belong in?

Detailed statistics of various ship types are shown in Table 2.5, which splits the fleet into 47,433 cargo ships and 26,880 non-cargo vessels. In the bulk cargo fleet there were 8040 oil tankers trading in July 2007, with the ships over 60,000 dwt mainly carrying crude oil and the smaller vessels carrying oil products such as gasoline and fuel oil. Note that there is also a fleet of chemical tankers which generally have more tanks and segregated cargo-handling systems, and these are included in the specialized

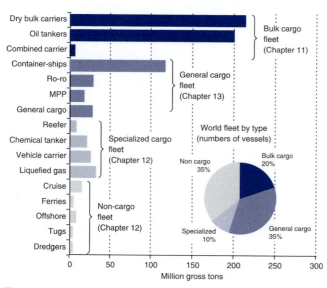

**Figure 2.4**
Merchant fleet classified by main cargo type. July 2007
Source: Clarkson Register, July 2007, CRS London

**Table 2.5** Commercial shipping fleet by ship type, July 2007

| No. | Name | Size | Numbers | Fleet size Mill. GT | Mill. Dwt | Dwt/ GT | Age | Comment |
|-----|------|------|---------|---------|-----------|---------|-----|---------|
| **1. Bulk Cargo Fleet** | | | | | | | | |
| | *Tankers over 10,000 dwt* | dwt | | | | | | |
| 1 | VLCC over 200,000 dwt | Over 200,000 | 501 | 77.5 | 147.0 | 1.9 | 9.1 | Long haul crude oil |
| 2 | Suezmax | 120–199,999 | 359 | 29.0 | 54.2 | 1.9 | 9.1 | Medium haul crude |
| 3 | Aframax | 80–120,000 | 726 | 41.1 | 74.2 | 1.8 | 9.3 | Some carry products |
| 4 | Panamax | 60–80,000 | 329 | 13.2 | 23.0 | 1.7 | 8.8 | Very short haul |
| 5 | Handy | 10–60,000 | 1,496 | 33.0 | 53.1 | 1.6 | 13.5 | Mainly products, some chemicals |
| 6 | Total over 10k | | 3,411 | 193.7 | 351.4 | 1.8 | | |
| 7 | Small tankers | <10,000 | 4,629 | 6.8 | 10.6 | 1.6 | 26.6 | |
| 8 | **Total tankers** | | **8,040** | **200** | **362** | **1.8** | **20.0** | |
| | *Bulk carriers over 10,000 dwt* | dwt | | | | | | |
| 9 | Capesize | Over 100,000 | 738 | 64.4 | 125.7 | 2.0 | 11.1 | Mainly carry ore and coal |
| 10 | Panamax | 60–100,000 | 1,453 | 57.0 | 106.0 | 1.9 | 11.7 | Coal, grain, few geared |
| 11 | Handymax | 40–60,000 | 1,547 | 44.8 | 74.1 | 1.7 | 11.6 | Workhorse, mainly geared |
| 12 | Handy | 10–40,000 | 2,893 | 47.8 | 77.1 | 1.6 | 20.7 | Smaller workhorse |
| 13 | Total dry bulk | | 6,631 | 214 | 382.9 | 1.8 | 15.6 | |
| | *of which:* | | | | | | | |
| 14 | Open hatch | | 481 | | 16.6 | | | Designed for unit loads |
| 15 | Ore carrier | | 51 | | 8.8 | | | Low cubic (0.6 m³/tonne) |
| 16 | Chip carrier | | 129 | | 5.9 | | | High cubic (2 m³/tonne) |
| 17 | Cement carrier | | 77 | | | | | |
| | *Combined carriers* | | | | | | | |
| 18 | Bulk/oil/ore | | 85 | 4.7 | 8.2 | 1.8 | 19.3 | Dry and wet |
| | **Total bulk fleet** | | **14,756** | **419** | **753** | **5.4** | | |
| **2. General cargo fleet** | | | | | | | | |
| 19 | Container-ship fleet | size (TEU) | | | | | | |
| 20 | Large | Over 3,000 | 1,207 | 72.1 | 79.6 | 1.1 | 7.0 | Fast (25 knots), no gear |
| 21 | Medium | 1,000–2,999 | 1,747 | 37.2 | 45.9 | 1.2 | 11.2 | Faster, some geared |
| 22 | Small | 100–999 | 1,251 | 8.2 | 10.2 | 1.2 | 14.9 | Slow, geared |
| 23 | Total container-ship fleet | | 4,205 | 117 | 136 | 1.2 | 11.1 | |
| 24 | Ro-ro fleet | 100–50,000 | 3,848 | 28.0 | 12.7 | 0.5 | 23.7 | Ramp access to holds |
| 25 | MPP fleet | 100–2,000 | 2,618 | 17.7 | 23.9 | 1.3 | 16.1 | Open hatch, cargo gear |
| 26 | Other general cargo | | 15,113 | 27.8 | 39.1 | 1.4 | 27.2 | Liner types, tramps, coasters |
| 27 | **Total general cargo fleet** | | **25,784** | **191** | **211** | **1.1** | | |
| **4. Specialized cargo fleet** | | | | | | | | |
| 28 | Reefer | | 1,800 | 7.6 | 7.7 | 1.0 | 23.9 | Refrigerated, palletized |
| 29 | Chemical tankers | | 2,699 | 18 | 29 | 1.6 | 14.6 | Chemical parcels |
| 30 | Specialized tankers | | 511 | 2 | 3 | 1.5 | 24.5 | |
| 31 | Vehicle carrier | | 651 | 24.8 | 9.1 | 0.4 | 14.7 | Multiple decks |
| 32 | LPG | | 1,082 | 10.1 | 11.9 | 1.2 | 17.7 | Several freezing systems |
| 33 | LNG | | 235 | 21.2 | 16.1 | 0.8 | 12.0 | −161 degrees Celsius |
| 34 | **Total specialized cargo fleet** | | **6,978** | **84** | **77** | | | |
| | memo: Total cargo ships | | 47,433 | 689 | 1,033 | 1.5 | | |
| **5. Non-cargo fleet** | | | | | | | | |
| 35 | Tugs | | 11,097 | 2.9 | 1.0 | 0.4 | 23.8 | Port or deep sea transport |
| 36 | Dredgers | | 1,812 | 3.0 | 3.6 | 1.2 | 26.8 | Dredging ports and aggregates |
| 37 | Offshore tugs and supply | | 4,394 | 4.6 | 5.0 | 1.1 | 22.7 | Offshore support functions |
| 38 | Other offshore support | | 2,764 | 4.2 | 2.5 | 0.6 | 22.5 | |
| 39 | Floating, production, storage and offloading system Drill ships, etc. | | 500 | 20.3 | 33.8 | 1.7 | 25.4 | Development and production |
| 40 | Cruise | | 452 | 13.1 | 1.5 | 0.1 | 21.8 | Holidays and travel |
| 41 | Ferries | | 3,656 | 2.6 | 0.6 | 0.2 | 24.4 | Passengers and vehicle transport |
| 42 | Miscellaneous | | 2,205 | 9.2 | 5.7 | 0.6 | 23.0 | |
| 43 | **Total non cargo fleet** | | **26,880** | **60** | **54** | **0.9** | | |
| **5. Total commercial fleet** | | | **74,398** | **753.6** | **1,094.8** | **1.5** | **21.8** | |

Source: Clarkson Register July 2007, CRSL, London    Note: average ages are weighted by numbers, not capacity

cargo ships category; though there is some overlap with the products tankers (see Chapter 12). The tanker fleet is split into five segments known in the industry as VLCCs, Suezmax, Aframax, Panamax, Handy (sometimes called 'Products') and small tankers. These different sizes operate in different trades, with the bigger vessels working in the long-haul trades, but there is much overlap. There were 6631 dry bulk carriers in July 2007, divided into four groups: Capesize, Panamax, Handymax and Handy. Within these groups are some specialized hull designs including open hatch, ore carriers, chip carriers and cement carriers. These bulk carriers carry homogeneous dry cargoes, mainly in parcels over 10,000 dwt. Bulk carriers have steel hatch covers with hydraulic opening mechanisms and most vessels under 50,000 dwt have cranes or derricks.

The table shows 25,784 general cargo ships, of which the most important are the 4205 container-ships. These ships have box-shaped holds and cell guides so that containers can be lowered securely into place below deck without the need for locking devices, reducing loading times to a matter of minutes. In recent decades it has been by far the most dynamic segment of the shipping market. Ro-ro ships provide access to the cargo holds by ramp, allowing wheeled vehicles such as fork-lift trucks to load cargo at high speed, whilst MPP vessels have open holds and cargo-handling gear, but not cell guides, so they can carry bulk and project cargoes. There is still a large fleet of 15,113 general cargo ships including tramps and many small vessels operating in the short sea trades.

Specialized vessels include reefers, chemical and specialized (e.g. for molasses) tankers, vehicle carriers, and gas tankers, with a fleet of 6,978 ships (note that Chapter 12 on specialized cargoes includes some other vessel types – see Table 12.1). All of these ships are related to vessels found in other categories, but their design has been modified to improve efficiency in carrying a specific cargo. For example, chemical tankers have many parcel tanks and special coatings for carrying small parcels of specialized liquid cargoes, but they are really a subset of the tanker fleet.

Finally, the non-cargo fleet includes 26,880 vessels used in various related maritime business activities. Tugs are mainly used in ports, though more powerful ones are used for deep-sea towage of heavy lift barges. Dredgers are used for clearing shipping channels or dredging material such as aggregates from the sea floor for construction or land fill. There is a large fleet of offshore support vessels used by the oil industry, whilst cruise ships and ferries carry people.

The table also shows that the average age of the fleet is 21.8 years, though the average varies between the fleet segments. For example, the fleet of deep-sea tankers averages about 9 years old, and bulk carriers about 11 years, no doubt reflecting regulatory pressures in the last decade. But many of the fleets of small vessels and service craft average over 20 years of age. Making the best use of this diverse fleet, built over so many years, to transport the thousands of commodities is not straightforward. Unfortunately, we cannot just say that bulk cargo goes in bulk carriers and general cargo goes in containers because shipping companies use the ships that are available and sometimes the old ships are very different from their modern counterparts – for example, general cargo ships which pre-date containerization. The task of the shipping market is to find commercial opportunities for even the sub-optimal ships in the fleet, and it achieves this by adjusting the price and earnings of each market segment and relying on shipping investors to seek out profitable opportunities for the marginal ships which they can buy cheap. When no opportunities can be found they may come up with a project to modify or convert the ship, for example by converting an old tanker into an offshore storage vessel or even a bulk carrier. In this way the maximum economic value is extracted from even the oldest ships.

## Ownership of the world fleet

Ownership is a major commercial issue in the shipping business. A merchant ship must be registered under a national flag, and this determines the legal jurisdiction under which it operates. For example a ship registered in the United States is subject to the laws of the United States, whilst if it chooses the Marshall Islands or the Bahamas it is subject to their maritime laws. Of course the shipowner is also subject to the international conventions to which the flag of registration is a signatory, and when it sails into the territorial waters of another country it becomes subject to their laws. As we saw in Chapter 1, low-cost flags have been used for many years, one of the earliest examples being the Venetians shipping Byzantine trade. A more detailed account of these issues can be found in Chapter 16. For the present, it is sufficient to note that the business does not have close national affiliations. For this reason it is useful when analysing the national ownership of vessels to recognize that the fleets registered in a particular country are not necessarily a true indication of the fleet controlled by nationals of that country.

We can take as an example the fleets of the 35 leading maritime countries (Table 2.6). In January 2006 they controlled 95 per cent of the total world fleet, so the analysis only excludes 5% of the total. Out of a total fleet of 906 m.dwt in 2006, 303 m.dwt was registered under the national flag of the owner, and 603 m.dwt was registered under a foreign flag. In many cases the ships on foreign registers were under 'flags of convenience', though there may be other reasons for registering abroad. For example, a Belgian shipowner with a ship on time-charter to a French oil company might be required to register the ship in France. The table also shows that the world's biggest shipowning nation is Greece, which controls 163 m.dwt of ships, but with only 47.5 m.dwt registered under the Greek flag. For Japan the ratio is even greater, with 91% registered under foreign flags and only 12 m.dwt under the Japanese flag. This diversity of registration has become an increasingly important issue in shipping industry over the last 20 years.

## Ageing, obsolescence and fleet replacement

The continuous progress in ship technology, combined with the costs of ageing over the twenty- or thirty-year life of a ship, presents the shipping industry with an interesting economic problem. How do you decide when a ship should be scrapped? Ageing and obsolescence are not clearly defined conditions. They are subtle and progressive. A great deal of trade is carried by ships which are obsolete in some way or other. It took

**Table 2.6** The 35 most important maritime countries, January 2006

| | Million deadweight | | | % under foreign flag |
|---|---|---|---|---|
| | National | Foreign | Total | |
| **Asia** | | | | |
| Japan | 11.8 | 119.9 | 131.7 | 91% |
| China | 29.8 | 35.7 | 65.5 | 54% |
| Hong Kong, China | 18.0 | 25.9 | 43.8 | 59% |
| Republic of Korea | 12.7 | 17.0 | 29.7 | 57% |
| Taiwan | 4.8 | 19.6 | 24.4 | 80% |
| Singapore | 14.7 | 8.3 | 23.0 | 36% |
| India | 12.5 | 1.3 | 13.8 | 9% |
| Malaysia | 5.5 | 4.2 | 9.6 | 43% |
| Indonesia | 3.8 | 2.4 | 6.2 | 39% |
| Philippines | 4.1 | 1.0 | 5.0 | 19% |
| Thailand | 2.4 | 0.5 | 2.9 | 16% |
| Total | 120.0 | 235.6 | 355.6 | 66% |
| **Europe** | | | | |
| Greece | 47.5 | 115.9 | 163.4 | 71% |
| Germany | 13.1 | 58.4 | 71.5 | 82% |
| Norway | 13.7 | 31.7 | 45.4 | 70% |
| United Kingdom | 9.0 | 12.3 | 21.3 | 58% |
| Denmark | 9.2 | 10.3 | 19.6 | 53% |
| Italy | 10.2 | 4.3 | 14.5 | 30% |
| Switzerland | 0.8 | 11.0 | 11.8 | 93% |
| Belgium | 5.9 | 5.7 | 11.6 | 49% |
| Turkey | 6.8 | 3.5 | 10.3 | 34% |
| Netherlands | 4.5 | 4.3 | 8.8 | 49% |
| Sweden | 1.7 | 4.7 | 6.4 | 73% |
| France | 2.2 | 2.7 | 4.9 | 55% |
| Spain | 0.9 | 3.2 | 4.1 | 79% |
| Croatia | 1.7 | 1.0 | 2.7 | 37% |
| Total | 127.1 | 269.0 | 396.1 | 68% |
| **Middle East** | | | | |
| Saudi Arabia | 1.0 | 10.4 | 11.4 | 91% |
| Iran (Islamic) | 8.9 | 0.9 | 9.8 | 10% |
| Kuwait | 3.7 | 1.4 | 5.0 | 27% |
| UAE | 0.6 | 3.9 | 4.5 | 88% |
| Total | 14.1 | 16.6 | 30.7 | |
| **Other** | | | | |
| Israel | 0.9 | 1.8 | 2.7 | 68% |
| United States | 10.2 | 36.8 | 46.9 | 78% |
| Canada | 2.5 | 4.0 | 6.5 | 61% |
| Brazil | 2.6 | 2.2 | 4.8 | 46% |
| Russian Federation | 6.8 | 9.9 | 16.7 | 59% |
| Australia | 1.4 | 1.3 | 2.6 | 48% |
| Total | 24.3 | 54.1 | 77.5 | |
| Total (35 countries) | 285.5 | 575.3 | 860.0 | 95% |
| World total | 303.8 | 603.0 | 906.8 | 100% |

Source: *UNCTAD Yearbook*, 2006 Table 16, p. 33

fifty years for steamships to drive sailing ships from the sea. Yet somehow the industry has to decide when to scrap the old ships and order new ones.

This is where the sale and purchase market comes in. When an owner has finished with a ship, he sells it. Another shipping company buys it at a price at which it believes it can make a profit. If no owner thinks he can make a profit, only the scrap dealer will bid. As the ship grows old or obsolete it trickles down the market, falling in value, until at some stage, usually between 20 and 30 years, the only buyer is the demolition market. This whole process is eased forward by shipping market cycles. By driving freight rates and market sentiment sharply upwards (when new ships are ordered) and downwards (when old ships are scrapped) the cycles make poorly defined economic decisions much clearer. In case there is any doubt, it reinforces economics with sentiment. Owners are more likely to make the decision to sell for scrap if they feel gloomy about the future. Thus, cycle by cycle, fleet replacement lurches forward. We discuss cycles in Chapter 3 and the four markets which are involved in the fleet replacement process in Chapter 5.

## 2.7 THE COST OF SEA TRANSPORT

### World trade and the cost of freight

One of the contributions of shipping to the global trade revolution has been to make sea transport so cheap that the cost of freight was not a major issue in deciding where to source or market goods. In 2004 the value of world import trade was $9.2 trillion and the cost of freight was $270 billion, representing only 3.6% of the total value of world trade.[17] Since these statistics cover both bulk and liner cargoes, and would normally include inland distribution, they probably overstate the proportion of sea freight in the total cost.

In fact coal and oil cost little more to transport in the 1990s than 50 years earlier as can be seen from Figure 2.5, which shows freight costs in the money of the day. In 1950 it cost about $8 to transport coal from East Coast North America to Japan. In 2006 it costs $32. Along the way there were nine market cycles, peaking in 1952, 1956, 1970, 1974, 1980, 1989, 1995, 2000 and 2004, but the average transport cost was $12.30 per ton. The cheapest year for shipping coal was 1972 when it cost $4.50 per ton, while the most expensive was 2004 when it cost $44.80 per ton. The oil trade shows the same long-term trend, with transport costs fluctuating between $0.50 and $1 per barrel. The highest cost was during the 2004 boom when the cost went up to $3.37 per barrel. In four years, 1949, 1961, 1977 and 1994, it fell to $0.50 per barrel and in 2002 it fell to $0.80 per barrel before increasing to $2.20 per barrel in 2006.

Compared with other sectors of the economy, the transport industry's achievement is exceptional. Average dollar prices in 2004 were six times higher than in 1960 (Table 2.7). A basic Ford motor car had increased in price from $1385 to $13,430; the UK rail fare from London to Glasgow from $23.50 to $100; the price of a ton of domestic coal in the UK from $12 to $194; and the price of a barrel of crude oil increased from $1.50 to $50. The three products with the smallest increase in prices are air fares, rail fares and

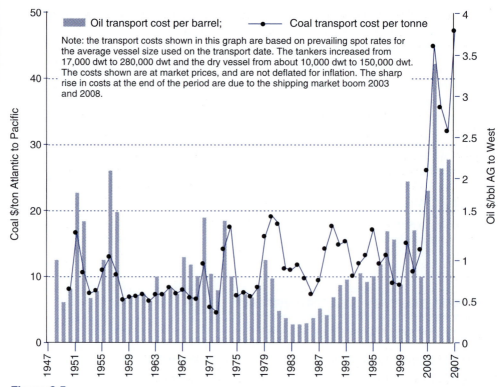

**Figure 2.5**
Transport cost of coal and oil, 1947–2007
Source: Compiled by Martin Stopford from various sources

a man's suit, illustrating the impact of Chinese exports on the clothing business. Seaborne oil freight and dry bulk freight came second and third in the table, but it is not really a fair comparison because 2004 was a high point in the shipping cycle, with the highest freight rates for a century (see Chapter 3 for discussion of cycles). The fact that air fares head the list provides an insight into why shipping lost the passenger transport business during this period.

This demonstrates that the shipping business was very successful in maintaining costs during a period when the cost of the commodities it carried increased by 10 or 20 times. As a result, for many commodities freight is now a much smaller proportion of costs than it was 30 years ago. For example, in 1960 the oil freight was 30% of the cost of a barrel of Arabian light crude oil delivered to Europe.[18] By 1990 it had fallen to less than 5% and in 2004 it was about the same, making the tanker business less important to the oil companies. This cost performance was achieved by a combination of economies of scale, new technology, better ports, more efficient cargo handling and the use of international flags to reduce overheads. These are the topics which we will address in the remainder of this chapter.

**Table 2.7** Prices of goods, services and commodities 1960–2004 at current market prices

| | Unit | 1960 | 1990 | 2004 | Average increase 1960–2004 (% p.a.) |
|---|---|---|---|---|---|
| Atlantic air fare[a] | $ | 432.6 | 580.9 | 230.0 | –1% |
| Rail fare[b] | $ | 23.5 | 106.1 | 99.8 | 3% |
| Men's suit (Daks) | $ | 84 | 484 | 478 | 4% |
| Oil freight Gulf/West | $/barrel | 0.55 | 0.98 | 3.30 | 4% |
| Coal freight Hampton Roads/Japan | $/ton | 6.9 | 14.8 | 44.8 | 4% |
| Ford car[c] | $ | 1,385 | 11,115 | 13,430 | 5% |
| Dinner at the Savoy[d] | $ | 7 | 52 | 96 | 6% |
| Household coal | $/ton | 12 | 217 | 194 | 6% |
| Bread (unsliced loaf) | cents | 6.7 | 75.5 | 115.2 | 6% |
| Postage stamp[e] | cents | 4 | 67 | 83 | 8% |
| Crude oil (Arabian Light) | $/barrel | 1.5 | 20.5 | 50.0 | 8% |
| memo: US consumer prices | Index | 100.0 | 442.0 | 640.0 | 4% |
| exchange rate $ per £ | | 2.8 | 1.8 | 1.9 | –1% |

Source: 'Prices down the years', *The Economist*, 22 December 1990, updated.

Notes
[a]London to New York return
[b]London to Glasgow, 2nd class, return
[c]Cheapest model
[d]Soup, main course, pudding, coffee
[e]London to America
[f]Average % increase 1960–2004

Although less easily documented, the achievements of the container business are equally impressive. The cost of shipping 7,500 pairs of trainers on the main leg from the Far East to UK in 2004 was 24 cents a pair. On the return leg the cost of shipping 15,500 bottles of scotch whisky in a 20-foot container from the UK to Japan fell from $1660 in 1991 to $735 in 2004. That works out at 4.7 cents a bottle.[19]

## Ship size and economies of scale

Economies of scale played a major part in keeping sea transport costs low. We have already noted that many sizes of ships are required to deal with differing parcel sizes, water depths and distance over which cargo is shipped (see Table 2.5). For example, tankers range in size from 1,000 dwt to over 400,000 dwt and separate market segments have developed, differentiated by ship size. Tankers evolved into VLCCs (over 200,000 dwt) which work on the long-haul routes; Suezmaxes (199,999 dwt) for medium-haul crude oil trades; Aframaxes (80,000–120,000 dwt) for the short-haul crude trade; Panamax tankers (60,000–80,000 dwt) for very short-haul crude and dirty products; and products tankers (10,000–60,000 dwt). In the dry bulk market, Capesize bulk carriers of

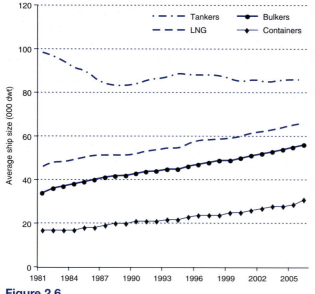

**Figure 2.6**
Ship size trends, 1980–2006
Source: Compiled from fleet data

around 170,000 dwt special-ize in the coal and iron ore trade, whilst Panamax bulk carriers carry grain, coal and small iron ore parcels and Handy bulkers (20,000–60,000 dwt) do smaller parcels of minor bulks. Over time the average size of ship in each of these size bands tends to edge upwards. For example, the cutting edge Handy-sized bulk carrier being delivered was 25,000 dwt in 1970, 35,000 dwt in 1985, and 50,000 dwt in 2007. Ship size increased because businesses were able to handle larger parcels of cargo, and port facilities were developed to accommodate bigger ships. Much the same sort of size escalation is taking place in tankers and, of course, container-ships. As can be seen in Figure 2.6, over the 25 years from 1981 to 2006 the size trend was generally up. For example, the average bulk carrier increased in size from 34,000 dwt to 56,000 dwt. But sizes do not always increase. The average size of tanker fell from 96,000 dwt in 1981 to 86,000 dwt in 2005 as a result of structural changes in the fleet, caused by a switch from long-haul to short-haul oil.[18]

## The sea transport unit cost function

We can see why investors go for bigger ships when we examine the unit cost function. The unit cost of transporting a ton of cargo on a voyage is defined as the sum of the capital cost of the ship (*LC*), the cost of operating the ship (*OPEX*) and the cost of han-dling the cargo (*CH*), divided by the parcel size (*PS*), which for bulk vessels is the tonnage of cargo it can carry:

$$\text{Unit Cost} = \frac{LC + OPEX + CH}{PS}$$

In calculating capital and operating costs, time spent repositioning the ship between cargoes must be taken into account. The unit cost generally falls as the size of the ship increases because capital, operating and cargo-handling costs do not increase proportionally with the cargo capacity. For example a 330,000 dwt tanker only costs twice as much as an 110,000 dwt vessel, but it carries three times as much cargo (we examine this in more detail in Chapter 6), so the cost per tonne of shipping a 110,000 tonne parcel of oil is much higher than shipping a 330,000 tonne parcel. If the cargo parcel is too small to occupy a whole ship the cost escalates further because of the high cost of handling and stowing small parcels. For example, crude oil can be transported 12,000 miles from the Arabian Gulf to the USA for less than $1 per barrel using a 280,000 dwt tanker, whereas the cost of shipping a small parcel of lubricating oil from Europe to Singapore in a small parcel can be over $100 a tonne.

The shape of the unit cost function is illustrated in Figure 2.7 which relates the cost per tonne of cargo transported (vertical axis) to the parcel size (horizontal axis). Unit costs escalate significantly as the parcel size falls below the size of a ship and the cargo slips into the liner transport system. There is clearly a tremendous incentive to ship in large quantities, and it is the slope of the unit cost curve which creates the economic pressure which has driven parcel sizes upwards over the last century. It also explains why containerization has been so successful. By packing 10 or 15 tonnes of cargo into a 20-foot container which can be loaded onto a containership of 8,000 twenty-foot equivalent units (TEU) in a couple of minutes it is possible to reduce the freight to around $150 per tonne, which is not much more than some

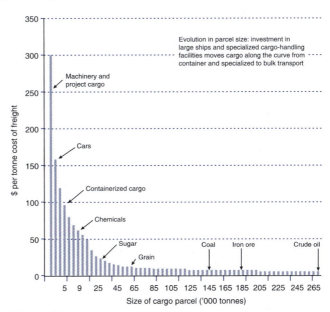

small bulk parcels. Imagine having to load the 1300 cases of scotch whisky that the container carries and then pack them into the hold (not to mention the damage and pilferage).

**Figure 2.7**
Shipping unit cost function: parcel size and transport cost
Source: Compiled by Martin Stopford from various sources

Liner and bulk shipping companies, which operate at opposite ends of the unit cost function, carry out fundamentally different tasks. Liner companies have to organize the transport of many small parcels and need a large shore-based staff capable of dealing with shippers, handling documentation and planning the ship loading and through-transport operations. The bulk shipping industry, in contrast, handles fewer, but much larger cargoes. A large shore-based administrative staff is not required, but the few decisions that have to be made are of crucial importance, so the owner or chief executive is generally intimately involved with the key decisions about buying, selling and chartering ships. In short, the type of organizations involved, the shipping policies, and even the type of people employed in the two parts of the business are quite different. The nature of the liner and bulk shipping industries is discussed in detail in Chapters 11

C
H
A
P
T
E
R
2

and 13, so the comments in this chapter are limited to providing an overview of these two principal sectors of the shipping market.

These differences in the nature of demand provide the basis for explaining the division of the shipping industry into two quite different sectors, the bulk shipping industry and the liner shipping industry. The bulk shipping industry is built around minimizing unit cost, while the liner shipping industry is more concerned with speed, reliability and quality of service.

## Bulk shipping economics

The bulk shipping industry provides transport for cargoes that appear on the market in shiploads. The principle is 'one ship, one cargo', though we cannot be too rigid about this. Many different ship types are used for bulk transport, but the main ones fall into four groups: tankers, general-purpose dry bulk carriers, combined carriers, and specialist bulk vessels. The tankers and bulk carriers are generally of fairly standard design, while combined carriers offer the opportunity to carry dry bulk or liquid cargo. Specialist vessels are constructed to meet the specific characteristics of difficult cargoes. All of these ship types are reviewed in detail in Chapter 14.

Several different bulk cargoes may be carried in a single ship, each occupying a separate hold or possibly even part of a hold in a traditional 'tramping operation', though this is less common than it used to be. The foundation of bulk shipping is, however, economies of scale (Figure 2.8). Moving from a Handy bulk carrier to a Handymax saves about 22% per tonne, whilst upsizing to a Panamax bulk carrier saves 20% and the much bigger jump to a Capesize an additional 36%. So the biggest dry bulk ships can more than halve the cost of transport, though this analysis depends on many assumptions which we will discuss in depth in Chapter 6 (see, in particular, Table 6.1). A shipper with bulk cargo to transport can approach the task in several different ways, depending on the cargo itself and on the nature of the commercial operation – his choices range from total involvement by owning his own ships to handing the whole job over to a specialist bulk shipper.

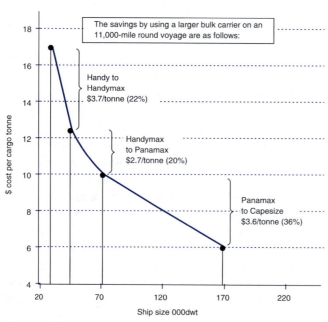

**Figure 2.8**
Economies of scale related to ship size for bulk carriers
Source: based on 11,000-mile round voyage from Table 10.5, Chapter 10

Large companies shipping substantial quantities of bulk materials sometimes run their own shipping fleets to handle a proportion of their transport requirements. For example, in 2005 the major oil companies collectively owned approximately 22.7 m.dwt of oil tankers, representing 7% of the tanker fleet. Steel companies in Japan and Europe also run fleets of large bulk carriers for the transport of iron ore and coal. This type of bulk shipping operation suits shippers running a stable and predictable through-transport operation.

One of the first examples of modern dry bulk transportation was the construction for Bethlehem Steel of two ore carriers to carry iron ore from Chile to the newly con-structed coastal steel plant in Baltimore, USA (see Chapter 11). The whole transport operation was designed to minimize transport costs for that particular plant, and this pattern is still followed by heavy industrial operations importing bulk cargo. Some industrial shippers in the oil and steel business still follow this practice to optimize the shipping operation and ensure that basic transport requirements are met at a predictable cost without the need to resort to the vagaries of the charter market.

The main problem raised by this strategy is the capital investment required and the question of whether owning ships reduces transport costs.[21] If the shipper has a long-term requirement for bulk transport but does not wish to become actively involved as a shipowner, he may charter tonnage on a long-term basis from a shipowner. Some companies place charters for 10 or 15 years to provide a base load of shipping capacity to cover long-term material supply contracts – particularly in the iron ore trade. For example, the Japanese shipping company Mitsui OSK ships iron ore for Sumitomo, Nippon Kokan and Nippon Steel on the basis of long-term cargo guarantees and operates a fleet of ore carriers and combined carriers to provide this service. In the early 1980s the company was carrying about 20% of Japanese iron ore imports.[22] In such cases, the contract is generally placed before the vessel is actually built. Shorter-term time charters for 12 months or 3–5 years are obtained on the charter market and this practice has not changed significantly over the last thirty years.

However, some shippers have only an occasional cargo to transport. This is often the case in agricultural trades such as grain and sugar where seasonal factors and the volatility of the market make it difficult to plan shipping requirements in advance, or where the cargo is a consignment of prefabricated buildings or heavy plant. In such cases, bulk or multi-deck tonnage is chartered for a single voyage at a negotiated freight rate per ton of cargo carried.

Finally, the shipper may enter into a long-term arrangement with a shipowner who specializes in a particular area of bulk shipping supported by suitable tonnage. For example, Scandinavian shipowners such as Star Shipping and the Gearbulk Group are heavily involved in the carriage of forest products and run fleets of specialist ships designed to optimize the bulk transportation of forest products. Similarly, the trans-portation of motor cars is serviced by companies such as Wallenius Lines, which runs a fleet of pure vehicle carriers and transports 2 million vehicles around the world each year.

The service offered in specialist bulk trades involves adherence to precise timetables, using ships with a high cargo capacity and fast cargo handling. Such an operation requires close cooperation between the shipper and the shipowner, the latter offering a better service because he is servicing the whole trade rather than just one customer. Naturally, this type of operation occurs only in trades where investment in specialist tonnage can provide a significant cost reduction or quality improvement as compared with the use of general-purpose bulk tonnage.

## Liner shipping economics

Liner services provide transport for cargoes that are too small to fill a single ship and need to be grouped with others for transportation. The ships operate a regular scheduled service between ports, carrying cargo at fixed prices for each commodity, though discounts may be offered to regular customers. The transport of a mass of small items on a regular service faces the liner operator with a more complex administrative task than the one facing the bulk shipowner. The liner operator must be able to:

- offer a regular service for many small cargo consignments and process the associated mass of paperwork;
- charge individual consignments on a fixed tariff basis that yields an overall profit – not an easy task when many thousands of consignments must be processed each week;
- load the cargo/container into the ship in a way that ensures that it is accessible for discharge (bearing in mind that the ship will call at many ports) and that the ship is 'stable' and 'in trim';
- run the service to a fixed schedule while allowing for all the normal delays – arising from adverse weather, breakdowns, strikes, etc.; and
- plan tonnage availability to service the trades, including the repair and maintenance of existing vessels, the construction of new vessels and the chartering of additional vessels to meet cyclical requirements, and to supplement the company's fleet of owned vessels.

All of this is management-intensive and explains why, in commercial terms, the liner business is a different world than bulk shipping. The skills, expertise and organizational requirements are very different.

Because of their high overheads and the need to maintain a regular service even when a full payload of cargo is not available, the liner business is particularly vulnerable to marginal cost pricing by other shipowners operating on the same trade routes. To overcome this, liner companies developed the 'conference system', which was first tried out in the Britain to Calcutta trade in 1875. In the 1980s there were about 350 shipping conferences operating on both deep-sea and short-sea routes. However, the prolonged market recession in the 1980s, the changes brought about by containerization, and regulatory intervention weakened the system to such an extent that liner operators started to look for other ways of stabilizing their competitive position. Liner operations are discussed extensively in Chapter 13.

## 2.8 THE ROLE OF PORTS IN THE TRANSPORT SYSTEM

Ports are the third component in the transport system and provide a crucial interface between land and sea. It is here that much of the real activity takes place. In the days of cargo liners and tramps the activity was obvious. Ports were crowded with ships and bustling with dockers loading and unloading cargo. Artists loved to paint these busy scenes, and the waterfronts were famous for the entertainment they provided to sailors during their long portcalls. Anyone could see what was going on. Modern ports are more subtle. Ships make fleeting calls at highly automated and apparently deserted terminals, often stopping only a few hours to load or discharge cargo. The activity is less obvious, but much more intense. Cargo-handling speeds today are many times higher than they were fifty years ago.

Before discussing ports, we must define three terms: 'port', 'port authority' and 'terminal'. A port is a geographical area where ships are brought alongside land to load and discharge cargo – usually a sheltered deep-water area such as a bay or river mouth. The port authority is the organization responsible for providing the various maritime services required to bring ships alongside land. Ports may be public bodies, government organizations or private companies. One port authority may control several ports (e.g. Saudi Ports Authority). Finally, a terminal is a section of the port consisting of one or more berths devoted to a particular type of cargo handling. Thus we have coal terminals, container terminals, etc. Terminals may be owned and operated by the port authority, or by a shipping company which operates the terminal for its exclusive use.

Ports have several important functions which are crucial to the efficiency of the ships which trade between them. Their main purpose is to provide a secure location where ships can berth. However, this is just the beginning. Improved cargo handling requires investment in shore-based facilities. If bigger ships are to be used, ports must be built with deep water in the approach channels and at the berths. Of equal importance is cargo handling, one of the key elements in system design. A versatile port must be able to handle different cargoes – bulk, containers, wheeled vehicles, general cargo and passengers all require different facilities. There is also the matter of providing storage facilities for inbound and outbound cargoes. Finally, land transport systems must be efficiently integrated into the port operations. Railways, roads and inland waterways converge on ports, and these transport links must be managed efficiently.

Port improvement plays a major part in reducing sea transport costs. Some of this technical development is carried out by the shipping companies which construct special terminals for their trade, or shippers such as oil companies and steel mills. For example, the switch of grain transport from small vessels of about 20,000 dwt to vessels of 60,000 dwt and above depended upon the construction of deep-water grain terminals with bulk handling and storage facilities. Similarly, the introduction of container services required container terminals. However, the port industry provides much of the investment itself. It has its own market place which is every bit as competitive as the shipping markets. The ports within a region are locked in cut-throat competition to attract the cargo moving to inland destinations or for distribution within the region.

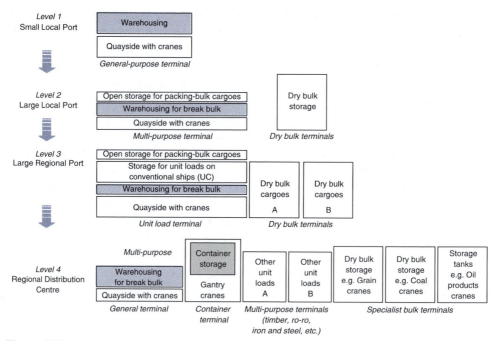

**Figure 2.9**
Four levels of port development
Source: Compiled by Matin Stopford from various sources

Hong Kong competes with Singapore and Shanghai for the Far East container distribution trade. Rotterdam has established itself as the premier European port in competition with Hamburg, Bremen, Antwerp and, in earlier times, Liverpool. Investment in facilities plays a key part in the competitive process.

The facilities provided in a port depend on the type and volume of cargo which is in transit. As trade changes, so do the ports. There is no such thing as a typical port. Each has a mix of facilities designed to meet the trade of the region it serves. However, it is possible to generalize about the type of port facilities which can be found in different areas. As an example, four types of port complex are shown in Figure 2.9, representing four different levels of activity. In very rough terms, the blocks in these diagrams represent, in width, the number of facilities or length of quay wall, and in height, the annual throughput of each.

- Level 1: *Small local port*. Around the world there are thousands of small ports serving local trade. They handle varied cargo flows, often serviced by short-sea vessels. Since the trade volume is small the facilities are basic, consisting of general-purpose berths backing on to warehouses. Only small ships can be accommodated and the port probably handles a mixture of containers, break-bulk cargo plus shipments of commodities in packaged form (e.g. part loads of packaged timber or oil in drums) or shipped loose and packaged in the hold prior to discharge. Cargo is unloaded from the ship on to the quayside and stored in the warehouses, or on the quayside until collected. Ports like this are found in developing countries and in the rural areas of developed countries.

- Level 2: *Large local port*. When the volume of cargo is higher, special investment becomes economic. For example, if the volume of grain and fertilizers increases, a dry bulk terminal may be constructed with the deeper draft required to handle bigger bulk carriers (e.g. up to 35,000 dwt), a quayside with grab cranes, apron space to stack cargo, railway lines and truck access. At the same time the break-bulk facilities may be expanded to handle regular container traffic, for example, by purchasing container handling equipment and strengthening the quayside.

- Level 3: *Large regional port*. Ports handling high volumes of deep-sea cargo require heavy investment in specialized terminal facilities. Unit loads such as pallets, containers or packaged timber are handled in sufficient volume to justify a unit-load terminal with cargo-handling gear such as gantry cranes, fork-lift trucks and storage space for unit-load cargo. For high-volume commodity trades, moving in volumes of several million tons a year, special terminals may be built (e.g. coal, grain, oil products terminals) capable of taking the bigger ships of 60,000 dwt and above used in the deep-sea bulk trades.

- Level 4: *Regional distribution centre*. Regional ports have a wider role as distribution hubs for cargo shipped deep sea in very large ships, and requiring distribution to smaller local ports. This type of port, of which Rotterdam, Hong Kong and Singapore are prime examples, consists of a federation of specialist terminals, each dedicated to a particular cargo. Containers are handled in container terminals; unit-load terminals cater for timber, iron and steel and ro-ro cargo. Homogeneous bulk cargoes such as grain, iron, coal, cement and oil products are handled in purpose-built terminals, often run by the cargo owner. There are excellent facilities for trans-shipment by sea, rail, barge or road.

Ports and terminals earn income by charging ships for the use of their facilities. Leaving aside competitive factors, port charges must cover unit costs, and these have a fixed and variable element. The shipowner may be charged in two ways, an 'all-in' rate where, apart from some minor ancillary services, everything is included; or an 'add-on' rate where the shipowner pays a basic charge to which extras are added for the various services used by the ship during its visit to the port. The method of charging will depend upon the type of cargo operation, but both will vary according to volume, with trigger points activating tariff changes.

## 2.9 THE SHIPPING COMPANIES THAT RUN THE BUSINESS

### Types of shipping company

A striking feature of the shipping business to outsiders is the different character of the companies in different parts of the industry. For example, liner companies and bulk shipping companies belong to the same industry, but they seem to have little else in common, a fact we shall discuss more extensively in later parts of the book. In fact there are several different groups of companies involved in the transport chain, some directly and others indirectly. The direct players are the cargo owners, often the primary producers such as oil companies or iron ore mines and the shipowners (shipping companies). However, in the last 20 years they have been joined by two other increasingly important groups: the traders who buy and sell physical commodities such as oil, for which they need transport, making them major charterers; and the 'operators' who charter ships against cargo contracts for an arbitrage. Ship managers and brokers are also involved in the day-to-day commercial operation of the business. Each has a slightly different perspective on the business.

In 2004, 5518 shipping companies owned the 36,903 ships carrying the world's deep-sea trade, an average of seven ships per company (Table 2.8). There are some very big companies, at least when measured by the number of ships owned, and one-third of the fleet was owned by 112 companies with over 50 ships. Amongst the biggest companies are the national shipping companies such as China Ocean Shipping Company (COSCO), China Shipping Group, the Indian government, and MISC. Then there are the large corporates, such as the Japanese trading houses (Mitsui OSK, NYK, K-Line), the Korean shipping groups and some very large independent companies such as Maersk, Teekay and the Ofer Group. Another third was owned by 716 companies operating 10–49 ships, many of which are privately owned companies, and the remainder was owned by 4690 companies with an average of 2.3 ships each. To really understand what is going on in those supply–demand curves that we will study in Chapter 4, or to track and forecast the cycles in shipping, we must understand what really drives these companies.

**Table 2.8** Size of shipping companies, 2004[a]

| No. of ships in fleet | No. of | | % fleet (No. of ships) | Ships per company |
|---|---|---|---|---|
| | Companies | # Ships | | |
| Over 200 | 10 | 4074 | 11% | 407 |
| 100–200 | 22 | 2754 | 7% | 125 |
| 50–99 | 80 | 5538 | 15% | 69 |
| 20–49 | 256 | 7520 | 20% | 29 |
| 10–19 | 460 | 6211 | 17% | 14 |
| 5–9 | 669 | 4389 | 12% | 7 |
| Under 5 | 4021 | 6417 | 17% | 2 |
| Grand total | 5518 | 36,903 | 100% | 7 |

[a]Includes deep-sea vessels, including bulk, specialized and liner.
Source: CRSL

In the background are the suppliers, including managers, ship repairers, shipbuilders, equipment manufacturers and shipbreakers. Each of these is a distinctive business with its own special culture and objectives. Ship finance forms another category, again with distinctive subdivisions, as do lawyers and other associated services such as ship surveying, insurance and information providers.

## Who makes the decisions?

Because the business is internationally mobile, shipowners can choose to register their companies in the Bahamas, Liberia, the Marshall Islands or Cyprus. These countries have maritime laws that, as we discuss in Chapter 16, offer a favourable commercial environment. Several different types of company structure are used, including sole proprietorship, partnerships and corporate structures.

Within the bulk and liner shipping industries there are many different types of business, each with its own distinctive organizational structure, commercial aims and strategic objectives. Consider the examples in Box 2.1. This is by no means an exhaustive account of the different types of shipowning companies, but it illustrates the diversity of organizational types to be found and, more importantly, the different pressures and constraints on management decision-making.

The Greek shipowner with the private company runs a small tight organization which he controls, making all the decisions and having a direct personal interest in their outcome. In fact, the number of important decisions he makes is quite small, being concerned with the sale and purchase of ships and decisions about whether to tie vessels up on long-time charters. He is a free agent, dependent on his own resources to raise finance and beat the odds in the market place.

The other examples show larger structures where the top management are more remote from the day-to-day operation of the business and are subject to many institutional pressures and constraints in operating and developing the business. The container company has a large and complex office staff and agency network to manage, so there is an unavoidable emphasis on administration. The oil company division reports to a main board, whose members know little about the shipping business and do not always share the objectives of the management of the shipping division. The shipping corporate is under pressure from its high profile with shareholders and its vulnerability to take-over during periods when the market does not allow a proper return on capital employed. Each company is different, and this influences the way it approaches the market.

## Joint ventures and pools

One of the methods used by smaller shipping companies to improve their profitability is to form pools which allow them to reduce overheads, use market information more efficiently and compete more effectively for contracts with shippers who require high service levels. A shipping pool is a fleet of similar vessel types with different owners, in the care of a central administration.[23] Pools often use an organization of the type shown in Figure 2.10. The pool manager markets the vessels as a single fleet and collects the earnings which, after deducting overheads, are distributed to pool members under a pre-arranged 'weighting' system ('distribution key') which reflects each ship's revenue-generating characteristics. The revenue-sharing arrangements are of central importance, and for this reason pools are almost always restricted to ships of a specific type so that the revenue contribution of each vessel can be assessed accurately.

CHAPTER 2

## BOX 2.1 EXAMPLES OF TYPICAL SHIPPING COMPANY STRUCTURES

**Private bulk company** A tramp company owned by two Greek brothers. They run a fleet of five ships, three products tankers and two small bulk carriers. The company has a two-room office in London, run by a chartering manager with e-mail, a mobile phone and a part-time secretary. Its main office is in Athens, where two or three staff do the accounts and administration and sort out any problems. Three of the ships are on time charters and two are on the spot market. One of the brothers is now more or less retired and all the important decisions are taken by the other brother, who knows from experience that the real profits are made from buying and selling ships rather than from trading them on the charter market.

**Shipping corporate** A liner company in the container business. The company operates a fleet of around 20 container-ships from a large modern office block housing about 1,000 staff. All major decisions are taken by the main board, which consists of 12 executive board members along with representatives of major stockholders. In addition to the head office, the company runs an extensive network of local offices and agencies which look after their affairs in the various ports. The head office has large departments dealing with ship operations, marketing, documentation, secretariat, personnel and legal. In total the company has 3,500 people on its payroll, 2,000 shore staff and 1,500 sea staff.

**Shipping division** The shipping division of an international oil company. The company has a policy of transporting 30% of its oil shipments in company-owned vessels, and the division is responsible for all activities associated with the acquisition and operation of these vessels. There is a divisional board, which is responsible for day-to-day decisions, but major decisions about the sale and purchase of ships or any change in the activities undertaken by the division must be approved by the main board. The vice president is responsible for submitting an annual corporate plan to the board, summarizing the division's business objectives and setting out its operating plans and financial forecasts. In particular, company regulations lay down that any items of capital expenditure in excess of $2 million must have main board approval. Currently the division is running a fleet of ten VLCCs and 36 small tankers from an organization that occupies several floors in one of the company's office blocks.

**Diversified shipping group** A company which started in shipping but has now acquired other interests. It runs a fleet of more than 60 ships from its head office in New York, though operations and chartering are carried out from offices in other more cost-effective locations. The company is quoted on the New York Stock Exchange and the majority of shares are owned by institutional investors, so its financial and managerial performance is closely followed by investment analysts who specialize in shipping. In recent years the problems of operating in the highly cyclical shipping market have resulted in strenuous efforts to diversify into other activities. Recently the company was the subject of a major takeover bid, which was successfully resisted, but management is under constant pressure to increase the return on capital employed in the business.

**Semi-public shipping group** A Scandinavian shipping company started by a Norwegian who purchased small tankers in the early 1920s. Although it is quoted on the Stock Exchange, the family still owns a controlling interest in the company. Since the Second World War the company has followed a strategy of progressively moving into more sophisticated markets, and it is involved in liner shipping, oil tankers, and the carriage of specialist bulk cargoes such as motor vehicles and forest products, in both of which markets it has succeeded in winning a sizeable market share and a reputation for quality and reliability of service. To improve managerial control the tanker business was floated as a separate company. The company runs a large fleet of modern merchant ships designed to give high cargo-handling performance, and is based in an Oslo office with a sizeable staff.

From the owner's viewpoint participating in a pool is rather like having the ship on time charter, but with variable freight earnings. When a ship enters the pool its distribution key is agreed and this determines its share of the net earnings. It is generally based on the vessel's earning capacity compared with other ships in the pool and will typically take account of cargo capacity, equipment (cranes, types of hatches, etc.), speed and consumption. The ship is chartered into the pool which pays all voyage-related costs such as port costs, cargo handling and bunkers, whilst the owner continues to pay capital costs, manning and maintenance. After deducting overheads and commission, the net earnings of the pool are distributed between the participants. The pool agreement generally includes a non-competition clause which prevents the participant using other ships he owns or controls outside the pool to compete with pool vessels. Finally, for a pool to work there must be cultural understanding. For example, a small private shipping company may not fully

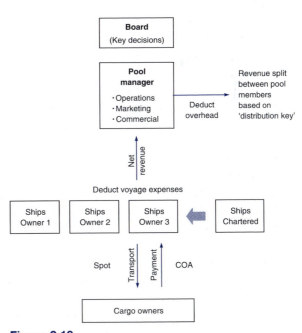

**Figure 2.10**
Structure of typical shipping pool
Source: Martin Stopford 2007

understand the constraints faced by a shipping company which is part of a large corporation, leading to frustration and misunderstanding. There must be benefits for both sides.

Shipping pools of this type are found in almost all segments of the tramp/non-liner shipping market, including product tankers, parcel tankers, chemical tankers, gas tankers and VLCCs, segments of the bulk carrier market (Handy, Handymax, Panamax and Capesize), reefers, LPG tankers, and forest product trades (lumber and wood chip carriers, etc.).

The pool may be managed by one of the participants, often the one who started the pool, or an independent manager. A pool agreement gives the manager control of day-to-day affairs, whilst a board nominated by participants takes decisions on chartering strategy, admission of new members and revision of the 'pool points' distribution key. The owners generally continue to be responsible for the crewing, maintenance and technical management of their ships, with defined terms of exit. Leaving the pool generally involves giving notice – typically 3–6 months – and settling obligations. However, there is a great deal of variation. Some pools are loose, whilst others are highly integrated, operating more like a joint venture. Participants prefer a short notice period, allowing them to withdraw their vessels if they feel the pool is not operating effectively or if they decide to sell the ship.

The pool manager has four main tasks. Firstly, he arranges employment for the fleet, including spot freight negotiations, time charters and in the longer term arranging COAs. Increasingly large shippers tender out large transportation contracts which pools, with their large fleet and specialist staff, are better positioned to win. In some cases the pools become an integrated logistics arm of the shippers. Secondly, he collects freight and pays voyage costs out of the earnings. Thirdly, he manages the fleet's commercial operations, including issuing instructions to the ships, nominating agents, keeping customers updated on vessel movements, issuing freight and demurrage invoices, collecting claims and ordering bunkers. Fourthly, he distributes the net earnings of the pool to participants in accordance with the distribution key.

To succeed the pools usually specialize in a specific trade or ship type where it is possible to offer members better than average earnings, more effective marketing of COAs, and time charters with lower marketing costs per ship, long-term planning, cost savings and economies of scale. For example, a large fleet may be able to significantly reduce its ballast time by arranging COAs to cover backhauls by providing return cargo, chartering additional vessels when members' ships are not available, and provide performance guarantees which an individual owner would not be able to undertake. By offering ships in the relevant areas, letters of credit can be arranged more quickly.

Organizations of this sort must comply with the competition laws of the states in which they trade. These laws generally make it illegal for pool members to collude to prevent or restrict competition. For example, in many countries agreements to fix prices, tenders, allocate customers between pool members or carve up geographical markets are illegal. In the last decade various governments, including the USA and the European Union (EU), have taken steps to tighten the application of these regulations to the shipping industry, initially liner conferences, but subsequently to the large companies and pools operating in the bulk shipping industry. The regulation of competition in shipping, including pools, is discussed in Section 16.10.

## 2.10  THE ROLE OF GOVERNMENTS IN SHIPPING

Finally, we cannot ignore national and international political aspects of the business. Because shipping is concerned with international trade, it inevitably operates within a complicated pattern of agreements between shipping companies, understandings with shippers and the policies of governments. From the Plimsoll Act (1870), which stopped ships being overloaded, to the US Oil Pollution Act (1990), which set out stringent regulations and liabilities for tankers trading in US national waters, politicians have sought to limit the actions of shipowners. The regulations they have developed have ranged from the efforts of the Third World countries to gain entry to the international shipping business through the medium of UNCTAD in the 1960s, to the subsidizing of domestic shipbuilding, the regulation of liner shipping and the increasing interest in safety at sea, pollution and crew regulations.

Just as these subjects cannot easily be understood without some knowledge of the maritime economy, an economic analysis cannot ignore regulatory influences on costs, prices and free market competition. These subjects will be discussed in later chapters.

## 2.11 SUMMARY

In this chapter we have concentrated on the maritime industry as a whole and shipping's part in it. During the last 50 years the cost of transporting commodities by sea has fallen steadily, and in 2004 accounted for 3.6% of the value of imports. Our aim is to show how this has been achieved and how the different parts of the shipping market – the liner business, bulk shipping, the charter market, etc. – fit together. We have discussed the transport system and the economic mechanisms which match a diverse fleet of merchant ships to an equally diverse but constantly changing pattern of seaborne trade.

Because shipping is a service business, ship demand depends on several factors, including price, speed, reliability and security. It starts from the volume of trade, and we discussed how the commodity trades can be analysed by dividing them into groups which share economic characteristics, such as energy, agricultural trades, metal industry trades, forest products trades and other industrial manufactures. However, to explain how transport is organized we introduced the subject of parcel size distribution. The shape of the PSD function varies from one commodity to another. The key distinction is between 'bulk cargo', which enters the market in ship-size consignments, and 'general cargo', which consists of many small quantities of cargo grouped for shipment.

Bulk cargo is transported on a 'one ship, one cargo' basis, generally using bulk vessels. Where trade flows are predictable, for example, servicing a steel mill, fleets of ships may be built for the trade or vessels chartered on a long-term basis. Some shipping

C
H
A
P
T
E
R
2

companies also run bulk shipping services geared to the transport of special cargoes such as forest products and cars. To meet marginal fluctuations in demand, or for trades such as grain where the quantities and routes over which cargo will be transported are unpredictable, tonnage is drawn from the charter market.

General cargo, either loose or unitized, is transported by liner services which offer regular transport, accepting any cargo at a fixed tariff. Containerization transformed loose general cargo into a homogeneous commodity which could be handled in bulk. This changed the ships used in the liner trades, with cellular container-ships replacing the diverse fleet of cargo liners. However, the complexity of handling many small consignments remained and the liner business is still distinct from the bulk shipping business. They do, however, go to the charter market to obtain ships to meet marginal trading requirements.

Specialized shipping falls midway between general cargo and bulk, focusing on high-volume but difficult cargoes such as motor vehicles, forest products, chemicals and gas. Their business strategy is generally to use their specialist investment and expertise to give the company a competitive advantage in these trades. However, few specialist markets are totally segregated and competition from conventional operators is often severe.

Sea transport is carried out by a fleet of 74,000 ships. Since technology is constantly changing and ships gradually wear out, the fleet is never optimum. It is a resource which the shipping market uses in the most profitable way it can. Once they are built, ships 'trickle down' the economic ladder until no shipowner is prepared to buy them for trading, when they are scrapped.

Ports play a vital part in the transport process. Mechanization of cargo handling and investment in specialist terminals have transformed the business.

Finally, we discussed the companies that run the business. They have very varied organization and decision-making structures, a fact which market analysts are well advised to remember.

# Part 2

# SHIPPING MARKET ECONOMICS

# 3 Shipping Market Cycles

## 3.1 INTRODUCING THE SHIPPING CYCLE

Market cycles pervade the shipping industry. As one shipowner put it: 'When I wake up in the morning and freight rates are high I feel good. When they are low I feel bad'.[1] Just as the weather dominates the lives of seafarers, so the waves of shipping cycles ripple through the financial lives of shipowners. Considering the sums of money involved, it is not surprising that they are so prominent. Take the transport of grain from the US Gulf to Rotterdam. After operating expenses a Panamax bulk carrier trading spot would have earned $1 million in 1986, $3.5 million in 1989, $1.5 million in 1992, $2.5 million in 1995 and $16.5 million in 2007! A new Panamax would have cost $13.5 million in 1986, $30 million in 1990, $19 million in 1999 and $48 million in 2007.

These shipping cycles roll out like waves hitting a beach. From a distance they look harmless, but once you are in the surf it's a different story. No sooner has one finished than another starts and, like surfers waiting for a wave, shipowners cluster in the trough, paddling to keep afloat and anxiously scanning the horizon for the next big roller. Sometimes it is a long wait. In 1894, in the trough of a recession, a shipbroker wrote: 'The philanthropy of this great body of traders, the shipowners, is evidently inexhaustible, for after five years of unprofitable work, their energy is as unflagging as ever, and the amount of tonnage under construction and on order guarantees a long continuance of present low freight rates, and an effectual check against increased cost of overseas carriage'.[2] He was right. It was 1900 before he could write: 'The closing year of the century has been a memorable one for the shipping industry. It would be hard to find any year during the century which could compare in respect of the vast trade done and the large profits safely housed'.[3]

Comments of this sort appear time and again in shipping market commentaries and they make shipping investors sound short-sighted and incompetent as they scramble to over-order ships, triggering yet another recession. But appearances can be deceptive. Despite the industry's apparent inability to learn from history, its performance in providing transport has been excellent (see Chapter 2). If we set aside the volatility, over the last century there has been an impressive reduction in shipping costs. In 1871 it cost $11.40 to ship a ton of coal from Wales in the United Kingdom to Singapore.[4] In the 1990s the average freight cost to ship a ton of coal from Brazil to Japan, a roughly similar distance, was still $9.30, both figures reported in market prices.

As far as shipowners are concerned the cycles are like the dealer in a poker game, dangling the prospect of riches on the turn of each card. This keeps them struggling through the dismal recessions which have occupied so much of the last century and upping the stakes as the cash rolls in during booms. Investors with a taste for risk and with access to finance need only an office, a telex, and a small number of buy, sell or charter decisions to make or lose a fortune.[5] They become players in the world's biggest poker game, in which the chips are valued in tens of millions of dollars, betting on ships which may or may not be needed. If trade is to be carried, somebody has to take this risk, and the analogy with poker is appropriate because both activities involve a blend of skill, luck and psychology. Players must know the rules, but success also depends on their skill in playing the shipping cycle, a game shipowners have been playing for hundreds of years. This is the model we will explore in this chapter.

## 3.2 CHARACTERISTICS OF SHIPPING MARKET CYCLES

### The components of economic cycles

Cycles are not unique to shipping, they occur in many industries. Sir William Petty, writing in the 1660s, noticed a 7-year cycle in corn prices and commented that 'the medium of seven years, or rather of so many years as make up the Cycle, within which Derths and Plenties make their revolution, doth give the ordinary Rent of the Land in Corn'.[6] Later economists analysed these cycles more deeply, and found that they often had several components which could be separated statistically using a technique known as 'decomposition'.[7] For example Cournot, the French economist, thought that 'it is necessary to recognise the *secular* variations which are independent of the *periodic* variations'.[8] In other words, we should distinguish the long-term trend from the short-term cycle. This approach is illustrated in Figure 3.1, which identifies three components of a typical cyclical time series. The first is the *long-term cycle* (referred to by Cournot as the 'secular trend'), shown by the dashed line. The long-term trend is of importance if it is changing, and the big issue here is whether, for example, the underlying cycle is moving upwards, which is good for business, or moving downwards, which is bad. The example in Figure 3.1 shows a long-term trend with upswings and downswings lasting 60 years. The second component is the *short-term cycle*, sometimes referred to as the 'business cycle'. It is the one that corresponds more closely to most people's notion of a shipping cycle. In Figure 3.1 these short cycles are shown superimposed on the long-term trend. They fluctuate up and down, and a complete cycle can last anything from 3 to 12 years from peak to peak. This is the form economic business cycles take and they are important drivers of the shipping market cycle. Finally, there are *seasonal cycles*. These are regular fluctuations within the year. For example, in shipping the dry bulk market is often weak during July and August when relatively little grain is being shipped. Similarly, there is a seasonal cycle in the oil trade relating to stock building for the

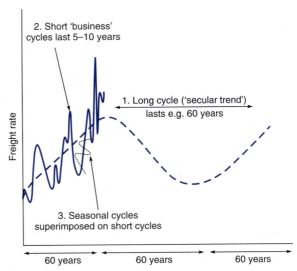

**Figure 3.1**

Seasonal, short and long cyclical components
Compiled by Martin Stopford from various sources

Northern Hemisphere winter. In the following subsections we will briefly review each of these three cyclical components. The techniques for identifying cycles statistically are discussed in Chapter 17.

## Long shipping cycles (the 'secular trend')

At the heart of the cyclical mechanism is the long-term cycle which 'ferries along with it other cycles which have neither its longevity, serenity nor unobtrusiveness'.[9] These long-term cycles are driven by technical, economic or regional change. This makes them of great importance, even if they are more difficult to detect.

The long-cycle theory of the world economy was developed by the Russian economist, Nikolai Kondratieff. He argued that in the major Western countries, between 1790 and 1916, there were three periods of slow expansion and contraction of economic activity, averaging about fifty years in length. After studying 25 statistical series, of which ten concerned the French economy, eight the British, four the US, one (coal) the German and two (pig iron and coal production) the world economy as a whole, he identified the three cycles with the initial upswings starting in 1790, 1844 and 1895. The peak-to-trough length of the cycles was 20–30 years, with an overall trough-to-trough length of approximately 50 years. Writing shortly after Kondratieff, the economist J.A. Schumpeter argued that the explanation of the long-wave cycles could be found in technological innovation.[10] He suggested that the upturn of the first Kondratieff cycle (1790–1813) was largely due to the dissemination of steam power, the second (1844–74) to the railway boom and the third (1895–1914/16) to the joint effects of the motor car and electricity. The upswing which started in the 1950s may be attributed to a combination of major innovations in the chemical industries, aircraft and the electrical/electronic industries. Unfortunately these Kondratieff cycles do not fit well with the long-term freight cycles we will review in Figure 3.5. For example, 1790 was a peak in the long shipping cycle, not the beginning of an upswing, and in general the shipping cycle looks much longer, with a downswing that lasted for the whole of the nineteenth century.

The French historian, Fernand Braudel, identified much longer cycles lasting a century or more, with peaks in the European economy occurring in 1315, 1650, 1817 and 1973. This analysis matches the cycles in Figure 3.5 more closely. Whatever the exact timing, the history of the shipping industry in Chapter 1 made it clear that the long-term technical, social and political changes we observed are precisely the sort of developments that might well drive long-term shipping cycles.[11] For example, the period from 1869 to 1914 saw a downward spiral in freight rates which was driven by the increasing efficiency of steamships and the phasing out of the much less efficient sailing ships. Similarly, from 1945 to 1995 the mechanization of the bulk and liner shipping businesses using bigger ships and more efficient cargo-handling technology produced a fall in real freight rates. So these long cycles deserve a place in our analysis, even if we cannot define them precisely.

## Short cycles

The study of short economic cycles started in the early nineteenth century after a series of severe 'crises' in the UK economy in 1815, 1825, 1836–9, 1847–8, 1857 and 1866. Observers came to the conclusion that these 'crises' formed part of a wavelike mechanism in the economy and they started to refer to them as cycles.[12] These short cycles 'shoot up and down, and are easy, indeed conspicuous to see. Everyday life, today as in the past, is punctuated by the short-lived movements which must be added to the trend in order to estimate them as a whole'.[13] However, they also spoke of the 'periodicity' of cycles, by which they meant that they consisted of a sequence of phases, irrespective of duration. For example, the nineteenth-century banker, Lord Overstone, observed that 'the state of trade revolves apparently in an established cycle of quiescence, improvement, prosperity, excitement, overtrading, convulsion, pressure, stagnation and distress'.[14] This periodicity theory does not require cycles to be of equal length.

It is easy to identify Overstone's phases with the different stages in modern shipping cycles, an example of which is shown in Figure 3.2. The short cycle has four main stages (see Box 3.1): a market trough (stage 1) is followed by a recovery (stage 2), leading to a market peak (stage 3), followed by a collapse (stage 4). In this example the trough lasts 4 years, reaching a peak 7 years after the first market peak, then falling sharply. However, during the trough in year 8 the market starts to recover, but fails and slowly subsides back to recession levels in year 10. Abortive recoveries of this sort are quite common, and in shipping are often the result of counter-cyclical ordering. Investors anticipate the recovery and order large volumes of cheap ships, so that supply dampens off the recovery. A dashed line superimposed on the chart illustrates what might have happened if investors had been less aggressive. In that case the

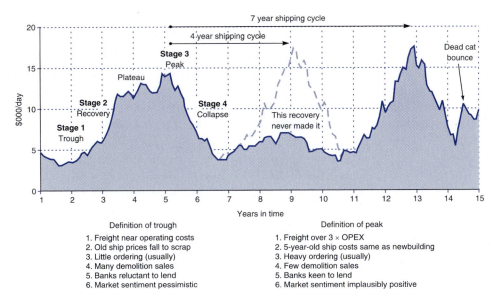

**Figure 3.2**
Stages in a typical dry cargo shipping market cycle
Source: Martin Stopford

shipping cycle lasts 4 years, not 7. In fact there is a strong case for supposing that the longer cycles of the sort shown in Figure 3.2 are often produced by a build-up of supply capacity during a succession of very profitable market spikes as a result of which the market 'jumps' a cyclical upswing, due to the pure weight of supply. Obviously the opposite effect can occur during these long recessions. These are important points we will come back to when we discuss past shipping cycles in Section 3.4. For example, does that abortive recovery in year 8 of Figure 3.2 count as a peak? And what about the 'dead cat bounce' in year 15? Frankly it is not easy to decide, but the cycles in Table 3.1 were compiled on the basis that neither counts.

## Seasonal cycles

Seasonal cycles occur quite widely in shipping, and are the fluctuations in freight rates which occur within the year, usually at specific seasons, in response to seasonal patterns of demand for sea transport. There are numerous examples, some of which are far more prominent than others. In the agricultural trades, there is a noticeable cycle in freight rates for ships carrying grain, caused by the timing of harvests. Typically there is a surge in grain movements during late September and October as the North American harvest reaches the sea for shipment. Then there is a quieter period during the early summer as shipment of the previous season's stock runs down. Similarly, there is a strong seasonal cycle in the reefer trade, associated with the movement of fresh fruit during the harvest in the Northern Hemisphere. Another example is the stocking up of oil for periods of peak demand in the winter.

## BOX 3.1 STAGES IN A 'TYPICAL' SHIPPING CYCLE

**Stage 1:** *Trough*. A trough has three characteristics. Firstly, there are clear signs of surplus shipping capacity with ships queuing at loading points and sea slow-steaming to save fuel. Secondly, freight rates fall to the operating cost of the least efficient ships, which move into lay-up. Thirdly, as low freight rates and tight credit produce negative cashflow, financial *pressures* build up, leading to stagnation as tough decisions are put off, and finally distress as market pressures overwhelm inertia. In extreme cycles banks foreclose and shipping companies are forced to sell modern ships at *distress* prices well below their book value, to raise cash. The price of old ships falls to the scrap price, leading to an active demolition market and the seeds of recovery are sown. As the wave of difficult decisions passes and the market starts to correct, a state of *quiescence* sets in.

**Stage 2:** *Recovery*. As supply and demand move towards balance, freight rates edge above operating costs, and laid up tonnage falls. Market sentiment remains uncertain, but gradually *confidence grows*. Spells of optimism alternate with doubts about whether a recovery is really happening (sometimes the pessimists are right, as shown by the false recovery in periods 7 to 9 in Figure 3.2). As liquidity improves, second-hand prices increase and sentiment firms as markets become *prosperous*.

**Stage 3:** *Peak/Plateau*. As the surplus is absorbed supply and demand tighten. Only untradable ships are laid up and the fleet operates at full speed. Freight rates rise, often two or three times operating costs, or on rare occasions as much as ten times. The peak may last a few weeks (see periods 5–6 in Figure 3.2) or several years (see periods 12–15 in Figure 3.2), depending on the balance of supply–demand pressures, and the longer it lasts the more the excitement increases. High earnings generate excitement, increasing liquidity; banks are keen to lend against strong asset values; the international press reports the prosperous shipping business with talk of a 'new era'; and shipping companies are floated on the stock market. Eventually this leads to *over-trading* as second-hand prices move way above their replacement cost, modern ships sell for more than the newbuilding price and older ships are bought without inspection. Newbuilding orders increase, slowly at first, and then rapidly until the only berths left are three or four years ahead, or in unattractive shipyards.

**Stage 4:** *Collapse*. As supply overtakes demand the market moves into the collapse (convulsion) phase and freight rates fall precipitately. This is often reinforced by the business cycle downturn, but other factors contribute, for example the clearing of port congestion, the delivery of vessels ordered at the top of the market, and in depressions we generally find these factors reinforced by an economic shock. The oil crises of 1973 and 1979 are prominent examples. Spot ships build up in key ports. Freight rates fall, ships reduce operating speed and the least attractive vessels have to wait for cargo. Liquidity remains high and there are few ship sales since owners are unwilling to sell their ships at a discount to recent peak prices. Market sentiment is initially confused, changing with each rally in rates and reluctant to accept that the peak is over.

## Analysts' views of short cycles in shipping

By the end of the nineteenth century the concept of cycles had spread to shipping and in January 1901 a broker noted in his annual report that 'the comparison of the last four cycles (10 year periods) brings out a marked similarity in the salient features of each component year, and the course of prices'. He went on to observe that the cycles seemed to be getting longer: 'a further retrospect shows that in the successive decades the periods of inflation gradually shrink, whilst the periods of depression correspondingly stretch out'.[15]

But as the understanding of the shipping market model increased, it became evident that in concentrating on length as the primary defining characteristic, analysts were 'putting the cart before the horse'. At first the perception was murky, though Kirkaldy cast some light on economic process when he defined the cycles as a succession of prosperous and lean periods which sorted out the wealthy shipowners from their less fortunate colleagues.

> With the great development of ocean transport, which commenced about half a century ago, competition became very much accentuated. As the markets became increasingly normal, and trade progressively regular, there was from time to time more tonnage available at a given port than there was cargo ready for shipment. With unlimited competition this led to the cutting of rates, and at times shipping had to be run at a loss. The result was that shipping became an industry enjoying very fluctuating prosperity. Several lean years would be followed by a series of prosperous years. The wealthy ship-owner could afford to put the good years against the bad, and strike an average; a less fortunate colleague after perhaps enjoying a prosperous time, would be unable to face the lean years, and have to give up the struggle.[16]

Viewed in this way, shipping market cycles have a Darwinian purpose. They create an environment in which weak shipping companies are forced out, leaving the strong to survive and prosper, fostering a lean and efficient shipping business.

Whilst Kirkaldy dwelt on the competition between owners and the part played by cashflow pressures, E.E. Fayle had more to say about the mechanics of the cycle. He suggested that the build-up of a cycle is triggered by the world business cycle or random events such as wars which create a shortage of ships. The resulting high freight rates attract new investors into the industry, and encourage a flood of speculative investment, thus expanding shipping capacity.

> The extreme elasticity of tramp shipping, the ease with which new-comers can establish themselves, and the very wide fluctuations of demand, make the owner-ship of tramp steamers one of the most speculative forms of all legitimate business. A boom in trade or a demand for shipping for military transport (as during the South African War) would quickly produce a disproportion between supply and demand; sending freight soaring upwards. In the hope of sharing the profits

of the boom, owners hastened to increase their fleet and new owners come into the business. The world's tonnage was rapidly increased to a figure beyond the normal requirements, and the short boom was usually followed by a prolonged slump.[17]

This analysis suggests cycles consist of three events: a trade boom, a short shipping boom during which there is overbuilding, followed by a 'prolonged' slump. However, Fayle was not confident about the sequence, since he says the boom is 'usually' followed by a prolonged slump. He thought the tendency of the cycles to overshoot the mark could be attributed to the lack of barriers to entry. Once again the cycle is more about people than statistics. Forty years later, Cufley also drew attention to the sequence of three key events common to shipping cycles: first, a shortage of ships develops, then high freight rates stimulate over-ordering of the ships in short supply, which finally leads to market collapse and recession.

> The main function of the freight market is to provide a supply of ships for that part of world trade which, for one reason or another, does not lend itself to long term freighting practices … In the short term this is achieved by the interplay of market forces through the familiar cycle of booms and slumps. When a shortage of ships develops rising freights lead to a massive construction of new ships. There comes a point either when demand subsides or when deliveries of new vessels overtake a still increasing demand. At this stage freights collapse, vessels are condemned to idleness in laying up berths.[18]

This is a neat synopsis of the way cycles pump ships in and out of the market in response to changes in freight rates. However, Cufley is convinced that the pumping action is too irregular to forecast, though he thought the underlying trends were more predictable.

> Any attempt to make long-term forecasts of voyage freights (as distinct from interpreting the general trend in growth of demand) is doomed to failure. It is totally impossible to predict when the open market will move upwards (or fall), to estimate the extent of the swing or the duration of the phase.[19]

One reason the cycles are so unpredictable is that the investors themselves can influence what happens. Hampton, in his analysis of long and short shipping cycles, emphasizes this point:

> In today's modern shipping market it is easy to forget that a drama of human emotions is played out in market movements … In the shipping market, price movements provide the cues. Changes in freight rates or ship prices signal the next round of investment decisions. Freight rates work themselves higher and trigger orders. Eventually excess orders undermine freight rates. Lower freight rates stall orders and encourage demolition. At the low point in the cycle, reduced ordering and increased demolition shrink the supply and set the stage for a rise in freight rates. The circle revolves.[20]

Hampton goes on to argue that groups of investors do not necessarily act rationally, which explains why the market repeatedly seems to over-react to the price signals.

> In any market, including the shipping market, the participants are caught up in a struggle between fear and greed. Because we are human beings, influenced to varying degrees by those around us, the psychology of the crowd feeds upon itself until it reaches an extreme that cannot be sustained. Once the extreme has been reached, too many decisions have been made out of emotion and a blind comfort which comes from following the crowd rather than objective fact.[21]

All these descriptions of the shipping cycle have a common theme. They describe it as a mechanism devoted to removing imbalances in the supply and demand for ships. If there is too little supply, the market rewards investors with high freight rates until more ships are ordered. When there are too many ships it squeezes the cashflow until the owners of the oldest ships give up the struggle and ships are scrapped. Looked at in this way, the cycles last as long as is necessary to do the job. It is possible to classify them by length, but this is not very helpful as a forecasting aid. If investors decide that an upturn is due and decide not to scrap their ships, the cycle just lasts longer. Since shipowners are constantly trying to second-guess the cycle, and the crowd psychology to which Hampton refers often intervenes to drive the decision process, each cycle has a distinctive character.

## Conclusions

Pulling all this together, shipping cycles are not there to irritate shipowners (though they do a good job in that respect), they are a crucial part of the market mechanism and we highlighted five points. First, shipping cycles have different components – long, short and seasonal. Second, the function of the short shipping cycle is to coordinate supply and demand in the shipping market. They are the shipping market's engine room telegraph (think about it) and as long as there are fluctuations in supply or demand there will be cycles. Third, a short cycle typically has four stages. A market trough (stage 1) is followed by a recovery (stage 2), leading to a market peak (stage 3), followed by a collapse (stage 4). Fourth, these stages are 'episodic', with no firm rules about the timing of each stage. Regularity is not part of the process. Fifth, there is no simple formula for predicting the 'shape' of the next stage, far less the next cycle. Recoveries can stall half way and slump back into recession in a few months or last for five years. Market collapses may be reversed before they reach the trough. Troughs may last six months or six years. Peaks may last a month or a year. Sometimes the market gets stuck in the middle ground between trough and recession.

## 3.3 SHIPPING CYCLES AND SHIPPING RISK

Since shipping cycles lie at the heart of *shipping risk*, we should now say something about what that risk involves. Technically, shipping risk can be defined as the 'measurable liability for any financial loss arising from unforeseen imbalances between the supply and demand for sea transport'.[22] In other words, we are concerned with who shoulders the financial burden if the supply of ships does not exactly match the demand and a loss results. For example, if too few ships are built and oil companies cannot supply their refineries, steel mills run out of iron ore, and manufactured exports are stranded in the ports, who pays? Or if too many ships are built and many earn nothing on their multi-million-dollar capital investment, who pays?

The answer is that the primary risk takers are the shipowners (the investors who own the equity in the ships offered for hire) and the cargo owners (also called the *shippers*) who between them perform the balancing act of adjusting supply to demand. They are on opposite sides of the shipping risk distribution, and when supply and demand get out of balance, one or the other loses money. Figure 3.3 shows how movements in freight rates (the vertical axis) over time (the horizontal axis) determine who pays. The break-even cost of transport is shown by the line $T_1$ – in a perfect market this should reflect the long-term cost curve for operating ships, and if supply and demand were always precisely in balance freight rates would follow this line (we discuss this in Chapter 8). But in practice supply and demand are rarely exactly in balance, so freight rates fluctuate around $T_1$, as shown by the short-term cycle $F_1$. When cargo owners get it wrong and have too many cargoes, rates shoot above the trend

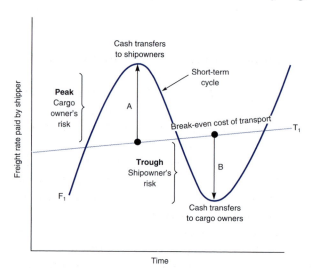

**Figure 3.3**
Key risk features of the shipping cycle
Compiled by Martin Stopford from various sources

cost, transferring cash to shipowners who respond by ordering more ships (point A in Figure 3.3). Conversely, when the owners get it wrong and there are too many ships, rates swing below trend. Shipowners find themselves subsidizing the cargo owners and they cut back on investment (point B in Figure 3.3). In this way the cycles exert financial pressure to correct the situation and bring rates back to the trend. Eventually if business is to continue, the freight cashflow should average out at the break-even cost of transport, so across the whole market shipping risk is primarily about the *timing* of receipts.

## Shipping risk and market structure

But that does not apply to the shipping risk of individual companies. As a group, cargo owners and shipowners face mirror-image risk distributions, so the volatility of the cycles allows individual companies to 'play the cycle' and in so doing vary their individual risk profile. As cargo owners and shipowners adjust their exposure to shipping risk they can determine who actually controls the way the supply side of the market cycle develops. We will discuss the economics of this process in Chapter 4; the point here is simply to emphasize how the supply side decision process is determined. Since the shippers have the cargo, they take the lead in this process, and the diagram in Figure 3.4 illustrates the three main 'options' open to them.

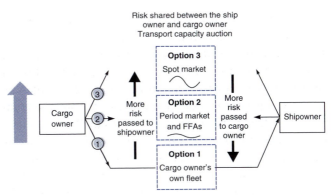

**Figure 3.4**
Risk management options in bulk shipping
Compiled by Martin Stopford from various sources

If cargo owners feel very confident about their future cargo flows and want to control the shipping, they may decide on option 1, which involves buying and operating their own ships. In doing this they cut the shipowner out of the equation (though they may use a shipping company to manage the vessels) and take all the shipping risk themselves. If all cargo owners do this, the spot market phenomenon disappears and the role of independent shipowners shrinks. There are many examples of this. For example, most LNG schemes were set up using vessels owned or leased by the project and until 1990 almost all the container-ship fleet was owned by the liner companies.

However, if they are reasonably certain about future cargo volumes, but feel independent shipowners can do the job cheaper, they may prefer option 2, which involves taking long-term charters from independent owners. They pay an agreed daily rate, regardless of whether the ship is needed, whilst leaving the cost management and the residual risk with the shipowner. For example, Japanese corporations often arrange for foreign owners to build ships in Japanese yards and charter them back on long-term contracts. These are known as 'tie-in' ships or *shikumisen*.[23] Raw materials such as iron ore, coal, bauxite, non ferrous metal ores and coal are often shipped in this way. The longer the charter, the more risk is taken by the cargo owner and the less by the shipowner, and long charters became so common that in the early 1970s that Zannetos commented: 'I know of few industries that are less risky than the oil tankship transportation business. Relatively predictable total requirements, time-charter agreements, and, because of the latter, availability of capital mitigate the risks involved in the industry'.[24] In this business the challenge is to win the contract and deliver the service at a cost which leaves the shipowner with a profit. Although the shipowner is freed from market risk, that does not remove all risk. Charterers strike a hard bargain, often leaving the owner vulnerable to inflation, exchange rates, the mechanical performance of the ship and, of course, the ability of the shipper to pay his hire. As an alternative to a physical contract, charterers could take financial cover using the derivatives market and, for example, a forward freight agreement (FFA). This form of hedging (or speculating) is discussed in Chapter 6.

Finally, cargo owners can pass all the shipping risk to the shipowner by using the spot market (option 3 in Figure 3.4). They hire the ships they need on a cargo by cargo basis, so if for some reason there is no cargo, the shipowner carries all the cost of the ships which are unemployed. However, everything has a price and when ships are in short supply, cargo owners with no cover must pay a premium. Both the period and the spot markets have cycles, but the spot cycles are the most volatile. We discuss the workings of the spot and period markets and the economics of freight rates in detail in Chapter 6.

## Risk distribution and shipping strategy

These three options do not change the amount of shipping risk; they just redistribute it between the cargo owners, who take all the downside risk under option 1 and none under option 3, and the shipowners, who take no risk (except possibly as ship manager) under option 1, take time-charter risk under option 2, and become primary shipping risk takers under option 3. So shipowners have very different strategic options. They can trade on the spot market and become risk managers or become subcontractors and ship managers, focusing on cost and management. Cargo owners have strategic choices, too. The distribution of risk between the spot and period markets is a matter of policy, and the balance will change with circumstances. Oil transport provides a good example. In the 1950s and 1960s the oil companies owned or time-chartered most of the ships they needed, taking only 5–10% from the voyage charter market, so in 1973 there was 129 m.dwt of independent tanker tonnage on time charter and only 20 m.dwt on the spot market (see Figure 5.2 in Chapter 5).[25] However, after the oil crisis in 1973 the oil trade became more volatile and oil shippers, which now included many traders, started to switch to the spot market, so by 1983 the tonnage trading spot had increased to 140 m.dwt and only 28 m.dwt was on time-charter. So in 10 years tanker shipping risk was completely redistributed. One benefit of this was that with such a large spot market there was increased liquidity, making it a more viable transport source for shippers than the tiny spot market in the early 1970s.

## 3.4 OVERVIEW OF SHIPPING CYCLES, 1741–2007

The freight index in Figure 3.5 allows us to see how freight cycles have behaved over a 266-year period. This freight index was derived from a number of sources. Coal rates for the English trade covering the period from 1741 to 1869 were spliced together with a long dry cargo freight index compiled by Isserlis.[26] The post-1950 data came from several published sources of dry cargo data. But overall we get a reasonable indication of what was going on each year in the shipping market. Identifying the shipping cycles from these data is not entirely straightforward, since it was necessary to distinguish the many small fluctuations from the significant peaks and troughs. Over the 266-year period 22 shipping cycles were identified. The initial market peak of each of the

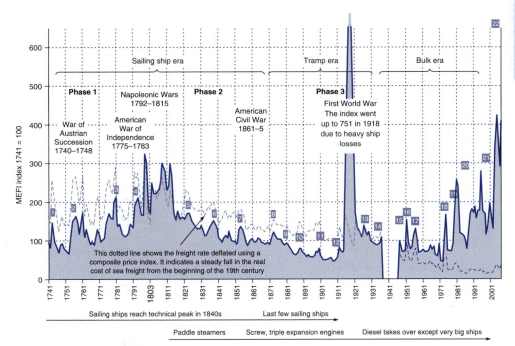

**Figure 3.5**
Dry cargo shipping cycles (mainly coal), 1741–2007
Source: Based on Appendix C.

22 cycles is numbered in Figure 3.5, ignoring the minor year-to-year fluctuations and focusing on major peaks. From 1869 it was possible to confirm the status of the identified peaks and troughs by referring to contemporary brokers' reports, and this resulted in 1881 and 1970 being treated as peaks although they are not prominent in statistical terms.

Table 3.1 provides a statistical analysis of the length of the 22 cycles since 1741 and shows that they vary enormously in length and severity. Between 1741 and 2007 there were 22 cycles lasting 10.4 years on average, though only one actually lasted 10 years. Three cycles were over 15 years, three lasted 15 years; one lasted 14 years; one 13 years; three 11 years; one 10 years; three 7 years; two 6 years; two 5 years; one 4 years; and one 3 years. In statistical terms, the standard deviation was 4.9 years, so with a mean of 10.4 years we can be 95% certain that cycles will last between 0 and 20 years. Table 3.1 also shows the length of the peaks and the troughs of each cycle. The start, end and total length of each cyclical peak is shown in columns 2–4, and the same information for each market trough in columns 5–7. Finally, column 8 shows the total length of each cycle, including both the peak and the trough. Finally, note that between 1741 and 2007 there were three major wars – the Napoleonic Wars, the First World War and the Second World War – and numerous lesser wars and revolutions, so it was a pretty bumpy ride. Since the major wars disrupted the market, the freight statistics for these periods are excluded from the analysis. The longest cyclical peak, defined as a period when

C
H
A
P
T
E
R
3

**Table 3.1** Dry cargo freight cycles, 1741–2007

| (1) | | (2) | (3) | (4) | (5) | (6) | (7) | (8) |
|---|---|---|---|---|---|---|---|---|
| | | | Peak | | | Trough | | Total |
| Cycle Number | | Start | End | Length | Start | End | Length | Cycle |
| 1 | | 1743 | 1745 | 3 | 1746 | 1753 | 7 | 10 |
| 2 | | 1754 | 1764 | 11 | 1765 | 1774 | 9 | 20 |
| 3 | Sail era 1741–1871 | 1775 | 1783 | 9 | 1784 | 1791 | 7 | 16 |
| 4 | | 1791 | 1796 | 6 | 1820 | 1825 | 5 | 11 |
| | | 1792 | 1813 | | Napoleonic Wars | | | |
| 5 | | 1821 | 1825 | 5 | 1826 | 1836 | 10 | 15 |
| 6 | | 1837 | 1840 | 4 | 1841 | 1852 | 11 | 15 |
| 7 | | 1853 | 1857 | 5 | 1858 | 1870 | 12 | 17 |
| 8 | | 1873 | 1874 | 2 | 1875 | 1879 | 5 | 7 |
| 9 | | 1880 | 1882 | 3 | 1883 | 1886 | 4 | 7 |
| 10 | Tramp era 1872–1947 | 1887 | 1889 | 3 | 1890 | 1897 | 8 | 11 |
| 11 | | 1898 | 1900 | 3 | 1901 | 1910 | 10 | 13 |
| 12 | | 1911 | 1913 | 3 | First World War | | | |
| 13 | | 1919 | 1920 | 2 | 1921 | 1925 | 4 | 6 |
| 14 | | 1926 | 1927 | 2 | 1928 | 1937 | 9 | 11 |
| | | 1939 | 1946 | | Second World War | | | |
| 15 | | 1947 | 1947 | 1 | 1948 | 1951 | 4 | 5 |
| 16 | | 1952 | 1953 | 2 | 1954 | 1955 | 2 | 4 |
| 17 | | 1956 | 1957 | 2 | 1958 | 1969 | 12 | 14 |
| 18 | Bulk era 1947–2007 | 1970 | 1970 | 1 | 1971 | 1972 | 2 | 3 |
| 19 | | 1973 | 1974 | 2 | 1975 | 1978 | 4 | 6 |
| 20 | | 1979 | 1981 | 1 | 1982 | 1987 | 6 | 7 |
| 21 | | 1988 | 1997 | 10 | 1998 | 2002 | 5 | 15 |
| 22 | | 2003 | 2007 | 5 | | | | 5 |
| Average | | | | 3.9 | | | 6.8 | 10.4 |

| Summary | | Av. Peak | | Av. Trough | Total |
|---|---|---|---|---|---|
| Sail era | 1741–1871 | 6.1 | | 8.7 | 14.9 |
| Tramp era | 1871–1937 | 2.6 | | 6.7 | 9.2 |
| Bulk era | 1947–2007 | 3.0 | | 5.0 | 8.0 |
| 1741–2007 | | 3.9 | | 6.8 | 10.4 |

Source: Complied by Martin Stopford from the data in Appendix C and other sources

the freight index was consistently above the long-term trend, was 10 years, whilst the longest trough was also 10 years. However, there were many cycles which lasted only 1 year, and 2-year troughs were particularly frequent.

Figure 3.6, which plots the cycles in chronological order by length, reveals two interesting points. Firstly, cycles were longer in the sailing ship era than during the

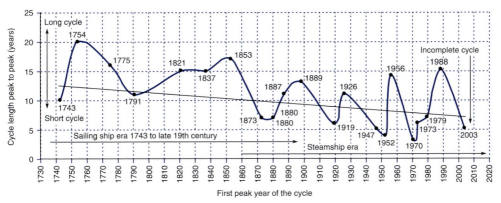

**Figure 3.6**
Length of shipping cycles, 1740–2007
Source: Compiled by Martin Stopford from various sources

steamship era which followed, and the average length of cycle fell from 12.5 years in 1743 to 7.5 years in 2003. This could be associated with the technology. Or possibly global communications which first appeared in 1865 could have affected the dynamic adjustment process. So for the present there may be some merit in the industry rule of thumb that shipping cycles last about 7 years. Secondly, the graph suggests that the length of cycles was itself cyclical. The long cycles of 12–15 years were generally separated by a sequence of short cycles, sometimes lasting less than 5 years. For example, the long cycle in 1956 was preceded two short cycles and the 1988 long cycle was preceded by three short cycles. Although the pattern is not regular, there could, for example, be a dynamic mechanism which produces alternating long and short cycles. But there are clearly no firm rules and the main conclusion is that shipping investors who rely on rules of thumb about the length of cycles are asking for trouble. We need to dig deeper for an explanation of what drives these cycles.

## Shipping cycles in practice

Having looked at cycles from a number of different perspectives, we can take advantage of the shipping industry's long and well-documented history to see how cycles have behaved in the past. In the following sections we will review the cycles illustrated in Figure 3.5 in the context of developments in the world economy and the contemporary comments made by brokers and other commentators. The three periods taken as the basis for this review are the sailing ship era (1741–1869); the liner and tramp era which started when efficient steamships became available in the 1860s – and lasted until the Second World War; and the bulk shipping era which started after the second world war as the shipping industry transport system was mechanized and purpose-built bulk carriers started to be used. The commentary focuses on dry cargo until the third period, when the tanker market is introduced into the discussion.

## 3.5 SAILING SHIP CYCLES, 1741–1869

The period 1741–1869 covers the final years when sailing ships dominated sea transport. The freight index in Figure 3.7, which tracks the cycles during this period, is based on coal freight rates from Newcastle upon Tyne to London in shillings per ton. The freight increased from 6s. 8d. per ton in 1741 to 18s. 16d. in 1799, during the Napoleonic Wars, then declined to 7s. per ton in 1872. Most of the early increase between 1792 and 1815 was due to wartime inflation; this period has been excluded from the cycle analysis and market prices have been retained for comparability. Although this was the sailing era, there was a clear pattern of cycles over the period which was not so different from later times, though the cycles were longer. There were seven peaks, not counting the Napoleonic war period, averaging 6.1 years each, and seven troughs, which averaged 8.7 years each, so the average cycle lasted 14.9 years. Although the graph in Figure 3.7 shows a clear cyclical pattern, the cycles varied enormously in length and the number of cycles depends on how you classify them. One very obvious issue is that there were seven 'mini-peaks' which occurred mid-way through the troughs, in 1749, 1770, 1789, 1816, 1831, 1847, and 1861. These mini-peaks barely reached the dotted trend line in Figure 3.7 and for this reason were not included as market peaks. Possibly they are examples of the 'recovery that never made it' illustrated in Figure 3.6.

This was a period of continuous trade growth as the industrial revolution took hold in Britain, but it was also a politically unsettled period, with a series of wars which

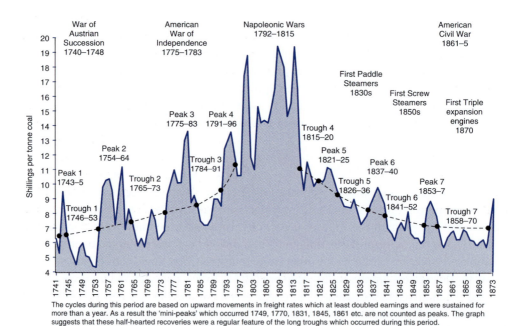

The cycles during this period are based on upward movements in freight rates which at least doubled earnings and were sustained for more than a year. As a result the 'mini-peaks' which occurred 1749, 1770, 1831, 1845, 1861 etc. are not counted as peaks. The graph suggests that these half-hearted recoveries were a regular feature of the long troughs which occurred during this period.

**Figure 3.7**

Sailing ship market cycles, 1741–1873: coal freight rates from Newcastle upon Tyne to London
Source: Compiled by Martin Stopford from various sources

certainly affected freight rates. At the start of the period there was a seven-year trough from 1746 to 1753. This coincided with the War of Austrian Succession and the 1739–48 War of Jenkins' Ear with Spain. Davis comments that 'In 1739–48 … the armed conflict was holding back trade … The peace of 1748, therefore, found England ripe for an extraordinary increase in the volume of export trade'.[27] This increase is reflected in contemporary trade statistics which show that the volume of English commodity exports increased by 40% between 1745 and 1750.[28] Possibly this prepared the way for the boom which started in 1754 and lasted until 1764.

Generally this was a period of relatively strong alternating peaks and troughs. The strong boom of 1754–64 was followed by a mirror image recession from 1765 to 1773. The strength of the boom almost precisely matched the depth of the recession. After a 'mini-peak' in 1770 there was another strong boom from 1775 to 1783. In fact this coincided with the American War of Independence and between 1775 and 1881 English commodity exports fell by 30% from £15.2 million to £10.5 million.[29] The result was a nine-year recession from 1782 to 1791. This is one of the most severe recessions on record and was caused by the disruption to trade arising from the American War. Before the war there was a well-balanced three-leg trade consisting of general cargo from the UK to the Caribbean, followed by a trading leg with plantation produce, from the Caribbean to East Coast North America from where a backhaul to the UK could be obtained. It worked well, but after the American War of Independence, the backhaul cargoes completely disappeared, and the focus of trade switched from the North Atlantic to the Baltic, leaving surplus shipping capacity. The recovery came with the fourth peak, which lasted from 1791 to 1796.

From the end of the Napoleonic wars in 1815 the trend in freight rates was strongly downwards. The dry cargo freight rate started at £11 8s. per ton in 1815 and by 1871 it had fallen by 40% to £7 per ton. This falling trend makes it difficult to identify the cycles precisely during this period and creates a particular problem when assessing the severity of cycles. In fact the cycles were probably not particularly extreme. Although these freight rates are not adjusted for inflation, this is probably evidence that sea transport was becoming more efficient and cheaper. Some of this efficiency was certainly due to the intense competition between sailing ships, which, as we noted in Chapter 1, reached new peaks of efficiency during the first half of the nineteenth century. However, the paddle steamers became more economic with each decade and by the end of the period had evolved into screw-driven ships with more efficient steam engines. In addition, improvements in shipbuilding and greater industrial activity resulted in ship sizes increasing steadily during the period. For example, in the eighteenth century a 300 grt vessel was a good size, but by 1865, a 2,000 grt vessel built of iron was a more common size.

During the period following 1815 there were four cycles, with peaks averaging 4–5 years each and troughs averaging 10–12 years. On that basis the average length of cycle was 15 years, which is similar to the earlier period. The fifth peak from 1821 to 1825 was followed by a 10-year trough, but with a 'mini-peak' in 1831. Then there was another strong peak between 1837 and 1840 followed by an 11-year trough from 1841 to 1852, with a 'mini-peak' in 1847 when rates reached £8 14s. per ton. The seventh peak lasted from 1853 to 1857 with the final long trough from 1858 to 1870, again with a couple of 'mini-peaks' in 1861 and 1864. This was a period of rapidly changing technology in the coal trade as new steam colliers forced their way into the trade and the owners of old and obsolete sailing ships may have suffered badly during the troughs, whilst the owners of more modern vessels faced less pressure, due to their greater productivity. In general this was a period of well-defined cycles pushing the industry forward during an era of changing technology.

## 3.6 TRAMP MARKET CYCLES, 1869–1936

The next seventy years provide a fascinating example of the interplay between short-term cycles and long-term trends, with just about every shape of cycle appearing. During this period the tramp steamer dominated the freight market. At the start efficient steam-driven tramps were just beginning to appear, and they reached their peak during the Second World War with the mass production of Liberty ships. The pattern of freight rates in Figure 3.8 shows a long-term downward trend, during which the freight index fell from 94 in 1869 to 53 in 1914.[30] Onto this long-term trend was superimposed a series of five shorter cycles which averaged 9.8 years in length.

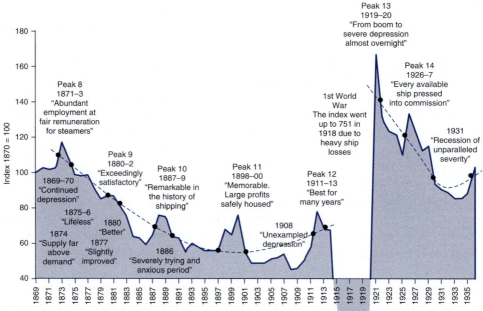

It is difficult to identify the cycles clearly in the period 1921–40. Cycle 5 started with a strong peak in 1921 and, arguably, ended with the short peak in 1926. On this interpretation cycle 6, which included the shipping depression of the 1930s, lasted 11 years. An alternative interpretation would be to count the period 1926–9 as a separate cycle.

**Figure 3.8**
Tramp shipping market cycles, 1871–1937
Source: Compiled by Martin Stopford from various sources

Like the cycles in the first half of the nineteenth century, it is difficult to disentangle the short cycles from the long-term trend. Once again we see rapidly falling freight rates resulting in cyclical peaks at rates which, in terms of their deviation from the trend, are in absolute terms lower than rates experienced in troughs just a few years earlier. Fortunately the availability of brokers' reports from 1869 onwards means that it is possible to validate the estimated cycles against market reports.

The cycles continued relentlessly, despite the rapid advances in technology. The best peak came in the early 1870s and there were two relatively severe troughs. The first was between 1866 and 1871, but the most severe was the trough between 1902 and 1910. Contemporary records confirm that this was indeed a very difficult time for the shipping industry, probably triggered by over-building as a result of the preceding boom in 1900. In 1902 'the result of the past year's trading, as far as 80 percent of British shipping is concerned, is an absolute loss, or at best the bare covering of out of pocket expenses' and 1904 was 'the fourth year of unprofitable work'. By 1907 the brokers noted 'the enormous difficulties which beset the shipowner in his efforts to find employment for his tonnage as will not involve him in a heavy loss', and it was not until 1909 that the reports state that, 'having passed through times of utmost stress, one can with some confidence state that the worst is over'.[31]

## The technological trend in freight rates, 1869–1913

The fall in freight rates between 1869 and 1913 was driven by technical change which steadily reduced costs. This trend is well documented in both academic and shipping literature. Lecturing at Oxford in 1888, Professor James Rogers commented:

> There is perhaps no branch of human industry in which the economy of cost has been so obviously exhibited as in the supply of transit. The voyage across the Atlantic is completed in less than half the time it took forty years ago, a great saving in motive power and labour. The same is true on voyages to and from India, China and other distant places. The process of loading and unloading ships does not take a third of the time, a third of the labour and a third of the cost which it did a few years ago.[32]

Shipyards were gaining confidence in steel shipbuilding and production grew rapidly. Between 1868 and 1912 the shipbuilding output of the shipyards on the Wear trebled from 100,000 grt to 320,000 grt. The ships became bigger and more efficient. In 1871 the largest transatlantic liner was the *Oceanic*, a 3800 grt vessel with a 3000 hp engine capable of 14.75 knots. It completed the transatlantic voyage in nine and a half days. By 1913 the largest vessel was the 47,000 grt *Aquitania*. Its 60,000 hp engines drove it at 23 knots. The transatlantic voyage time had fallen to under five days. These vessels were comparable in length with a 280,000 dwt tanker and vastly more complex in terms of mechanical and outfitting structure.

Perhaps the most important technical improvement was in the efficiency of steam engines. With the introduction of the triple expansion system and higher-pressure boilers, the cargo payload of the steamships increased rapidly.[33] The economic advantage of steamships was compounded by economies of scale. The average size of merchant ships launched on the River Wear grew from 509 gross tons in 1869 to 4324 gross tons in 1913.[34] Finally, the opening of the Suez Canal in 1869 gave steamships the economic advantage they needed to oust sail as the preferred type of newbuilding.

Between 1870 and 1910 the world fleet doubled from 16.7 million grt to 34.6 million grt and the continuous running battle between the new and old technologies dominated market economics as each generation of more efficient steamers pushed out the previous generation of obsolete vessels. The first to come under pressure were the sailing ships, which were replaced by steamers. In 1870 steamers accounted for only 16% of the tonnage (Table 3.2) but by 1910 they accounted for 76% of the world merchant fleet.[35] The competition was long and hard fought. Sailing ships with their low overheads managed to survive recessions and even occasionally win back a little ground.

**Table 3.2** World merchant fleet by propulsion

|  | Steam | Sail | Total |
|---|---|---|---|
| 1870 | 2.6 | 14.1 | 16.7 |
| 1910 | 26.1 | 8.4 | 34.5 |
| Growth pa | 6% | −1% |  |

Source: Kirkaldy (1914 Appendix XVII).

Change is never easy, and the market used a series of short cycles to alternately draw in new ships and drive out old ones. At a time when the shipping industry was growing rapidly and making great technical strides forward, shipbrokers saw little of the current of technical progress on which the market was being swept along. Their reports focus on the charter market where each generation of marginal tonnage struggled for survival against the new-cost effective vessels. They paint a picture of almost continuous gloom as year after year the better and bigger high-technology ships drove out the obsolete tonnage.[36] Yet by the end costs had fallen, the fleet had grown and enormous volumes of cargo had been shipped. The following brief review of the cycles is drawn from several sources, but principally Gould, Angier & Co., supplemented by the details of the cycles in shipbuilding output on the River Wear, at that time one of the world's most active merchant shipbuilding areas.

### Cycle 8: 1871–9

There were three good years in 1871–3. The first was described as a year with 'abundant employment at very fair remuneration for steamers, but restricted employment at very low remuneration for sailing ships'.[37] This theme of steamers driving sailing ships from the market was to persist for the next decade. The following two years were patchy, though brokers described them as better than expected.

The recession started in 1874 and lasted 5 years until 1879. By 1876 the market was 'still stagnant', but started improving in 1877, a trend that is clear from the pick-up in shipbuilding output on the River Wear. Steamers were gradually winning the battle with sail. According to McGregor '1878 can be regarded as the last year in which sail figured at the same equality as steam in the China trade'.[38] Although the market was weak, it was not a particularly severe recession. Rates were seasonal, and the words 'dull', 'lifeless' and 'stagnant' were repeatedly used in contemporary reports to describe business. Shipbuilding deliveries were running well below the peak of 1872. On the Wear launches fell from a peak of 134,825 grt in 1872 to 54,041 grt in 1876, after which they recovered to 112,000 grt in 1878.

## Cycle 9: 1881–9

The next cycle also lasted 8 years, spanning most of the 1880s. The boom picked up in the autumn of 1879 when rates showed 'considerable firmness' and 'in almost every trade a fair amount of business is doing which leaves more or less profit, and there is a better state of things than could be noted during several winters past'.[39] Firm rates continued until 1882, driven by an expanding trade cycle. The strength of this boom is apparent from the sharp rise in shipbuilding launches. This was a real shipbuilding boom. Output on the Wear was 108,626 grt in 1880 and, following heavy ordering in 1880–1, doubled to a peak of 212,313 grt in 1883.

After a slow start in 1883 the recession gathered force in 1884. 'The rates at which steamers have been chartered are lower than have ever before been accepted. This state of things was brought about by the large over-production of tonnage during the previous three years, fostered by the reckless credit given by banks and builders, and over-speculation by irresponsible and inexperienced owners. The universal contraction of trade also aggravated the effect of the above causes'. It continued this way until 1887, making it a four-year trough. In fact, the recession was coming to an end, but, as so often happens, the transition from recession to boom was somewhat drawn out. Three years into the recession the volume of shipbuilding output in the UK had fallen sharply from a peak of 1.25 million grt in 1883 to a trough of 0.47 million grt in 1886.

## Cycle 10: 1889–97

The third cycle was of similar length, spanning 1889–1897. The 1880s ended with a real freight boom, described as 'remarkable in the history of shipping'. In fact 1888 opened quietly, but in the autumn the freight index, which had fallen to 59 in 1886, peaked at 76, a 29% increase. In 1889 freights remained at this level and prices for completed cargo steamers rose by 50% from £6.7 to £9.9 per deadweight ton. Shipbuilding output continued to grow, with launches on the Wear in 1889 reaching 217,000 grt, higher than the previous peak of 212,000 grt in 1883. In total the peak lasted a little over 18 months.

In 1890 the market moved sharply into recession. By the end of the year observers commented on 'The sudden relapse of all freights and all values of steam property from the high points reached in 1889 to about the lowest figures touched during the long recession from 1883 to 1887 ... The rates now ruling leave a heavy loss in working for all but cheaply-bought new steamers ... The only sure means of improving the position was a wholesale laying-up of steamers in order to reduce the amount of trading tonnage by 25%'.[40]

The recession which followed lasted most of the decade. There was a modest recovery in 1895 and the market progressively improved during the next three years. Once again attention is focused on the shipbuilding scene, where the level of production had not fallen as sharply as in the previous recession. Launches on the Wear reached 215,887 grt in 1896, almost back to the 1889 peak.

### Cycle 11: 1898–1910

The fourth and last cycle before the First World War was also the longest, lasting 12 years. After the protracted recession of the early 1890s, there was a three-year freight market boom, starting in 1898. That year opened with a distinctly firm market as 'the effect of the long stoppage of work in the engine shops and shipyards caused by the engineers' strike of 1897, and a general awakening of trade, but the actual advance in prices was so gradual that purchasers were able to get in contracts for an immense amount of tonnage at cheap rates'.[41]

The year 1899 proved less profitable than expected, but far from unsatisfactory. Bad crops in India and Russia reduced the exports from these areas, undermining the anticipated boom. Then 1900 was a memorable year for the shipping industry: 'It would be hard to find any year during the century which could compare in respect of the vast trade done and the large profits safely housed'.[42] The freight index reached the highest level since 1880 and, as a result of orders placed during this period, in 1901 shipbuilding launches on the Wear were close to 300,000 grt.

A major factor during 1900 was the large amount of government transport taken for the South African war, but also for India and China. By the last quarter the market was starting to run out of steam. 'The last quarter witnessed a general sobering down, showing distinctly that the flood tide was spent, and a gradual ebb commenced. The general conditions of the world's trade point to no sudden contraction or slump, but to a continuance of steady and widespread business for some time to come, though at gradually reducing margins of profit'.[43]

Things did not work out quite so well. By 1901 the market was back in recession. Starting from a decline of 20–30% from the best rates fixed in 1900, there was a further fall of 20–30%. By the autumn of 1901 rates were 50% below the peak levels in 1900. The year 1901 was poor and in 1902 'the result of the year's trade, as far as the 80% of British Shipping is concerned, was an absolute loss to the vast majority of ships, or at best the bare covering of out of pocket expenses. Of the remaining 20% of tonnage, consisting of "liners" proper, only the few most favoured companies have done well, viz. those with good mail contracts'.[44] The market remained more or less in depression until 1909.

Despite the recession, by 1906 shipbuilding launches on the Wear reached 360,000 grt, an all-time record. Considering the level of freight rates, the newbuilding boom is difficult to explain. It may have been triggered by the large cash reserves built up during the previous market boom and anticipation of a market upturn. Shipbuilders trying to maintain their business volume may also have contributed. Angier thought so, commenting that in 1906 'The knowledge that many fleets of steamers were owned far more by the builders than by the registered owners [has] become a commonplace, but this year we have seen a shipbuilder's syndicate entering directly into competition with shipowners and securing a mail contract from Australia. This action was received with natural annoyance on the part of the established lines'.[45]

## Cycle 12: 1911–14

Finally, in 1911 the industry moved into a period of better trading conditions during which most owners made modest profits. This improvement was 'contributed to by the general improvement in the trade of the world, the cessation of building brought about by the lockout of the boiler makers by the shipbuilders, and the removal from freight markets of a number of obsolete steamers which their owners have been driven, by the prohibitive premiums demanded by underwriters, to sell for breaking up'.[46] In 1911 freights were higher than in any year since 1900, though returns on capital were not much more than 'would have been made by the investing of a like amount in first class securities, involving no labour or retention'.[47] The year 1912 witnessed a 'boom' in freights which enabled shipowners to make a real profit. The freight market collapse started again in 1913 but was interrupted by war.

## Shipping cycles between the wars (1920–40)

The period between the First and Second World Wars had a very different character. It was not a particularly prosperous period for shipowners, and Jones comments: 'For most of the period between the wars it appears from the statistics of laid up tonnage that the world was over-stocked with shipping'.[48] In fact the period falls into two separate decades, the first poor and the second disastrous. The first, from 1922 to 1926, was volatile and from time to time shipping was modestly profitable. The second, from 1927 to 1938, was dominated by the great shipping depression of the 1930s.

In terms of cycles, it was a very strange period. In 1920 there was one of the most extreme market booms in the history of shipping. Freight rates went to record levels, and the General Council of British Shipping index jumped 140, four times the normal level. But the extent of the boom is best illustrated by the escalation of ship prices. A modern cargo ship, which had cost £55,000 in September 1914 at the start of the war, jumped in price from £169,000 in 1918 to 232,500 at the end of 1919. But two years later the price was back down to £60,000, where it stayed for the rest of the decade.[49] So that got the period off to a quirky start. According to Jones, the explanation of this boom was wartime reparations.

During the war, losses of merchant shipping to submarine warfare on the North Atlantic had become so severe that shipbuilding production had become a major strategic issue. In the United Kingdom, at that time the world's leading shipbuilder, capacity was expanded and between 1917 and 1921 the United States set up the first mass-production facility for merchant ships at Hog Island. The facility, which had 50 slipways, was designed to build 7800 dwt freighters for the war effort. However, it did not come into production until a few months before the end of the war, and it helped to swell surplus capacity. The result was that shipping in the 1920s was under a cloud of shipyard overcapacity, making it difficult to disentangle the cycles. The index shows little change over the 20 years, with just three short peaks and two lengthy troughs. The average length of cycle was 7.8 years. Contemporary records show that the first cyclical trough started in 1921 and continued until 1925. During this period the market was weak, though this is not fully reflected in the annual statistics. In 1926 there was a brief boom, triggered by the coalminers' strike in the UK, plus a revival in business activity. By the end of 1927 rates were slipping again and the market moved into a seven-year trough, one of the longest on record.

### Cycle 13: 1921–5

The 1920s started with a boom and in 1921 the Economist freight index reached 200. After this spectacular start to the decade, the market was never really strong. By 1922 the freight index had fallen to 110. From then onwards freights fluctuated throughout the 1920s, creating conditions which, though not wildly profitable for shipowners, provided a modest living from year to year.[50] There was a brief recession in 1924–5 followed by a brief 'boom' when freight rates touched 170 in 1926, when demand was driven up by heavy coal imports from the USA to the UK during the miners' strike of that year. This is taken as the end of the fifth cycle, though the precise timing is debatable. After a spectacular start to the decade, second-hand prices were relatively stable, offering no opportunity for asset play profits. The Fairplay price index for a standard 7,500 dwt vessel opened at £258,000 in the first quarter of 1920. By spring 1921 it had fallen to £63,750, where it stayed, with the exception of a brief fall to £53,000 in 1925, until December 1929.

There were three developments which gave this period its distinctive character. By far the most important were the boom and bust cycle in sea trade. Between 1922 and 1931 the volume of seaborne trade increased by more than 50% from 290 million tons to 473 million tons, before falling precipitously to 353 million tons in 1934 (Figure 3.9). The second was shipyard overcapacity. During the First

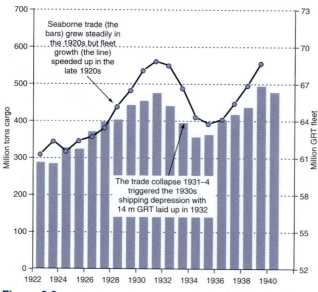

**Figure 3.9**
Sea Trade, 1922–38
Source: Sturmey (1962) Lloyd's Register

World War the shipyards had built up capacity to replace heavy wartime losses of merchant ships, especially in the North Atlantic. The annual merchant tonnage launched during the war was 3.9 million gt, compared with only 2.4 million grt annual launches in 1901–14. After record production of 4.45 million grt in 1921, output fluctuated between 2 and 3 million grt. The lowest year was 1926, when production fell to 1.9 million grt. This was the best year of the decade for freight rates. Third, this was a period of moderate technical change. Internal combustion engines were starting to replace steam engines; oil was replacing coal as a primary fuel; and specialist ships such as tankers were being built in greater numbers.

### Cycle 14: 1926–37 (The Great Depression)

A patchy market in the 1920s turned into the 1930s depression. Ironically, in 1929 some shipowners were predicting a return to more favourable market conditions, but the Wall Street Crash of October 1929 and the subsequent recession in world trade plunged the shipping industry into a major depression which lasted until the late 1930s. There is no doubt about the cause of the depression. Between 1931 and 1934 the volume of sea trade fell by 26%, and this coincided with a phase of rapid expansion of the merchant fleet, as can be seen in Figure 3.9. As a result laid-up tonnage increased from the 'normal' level of 3 million gt in June 1930, to a peak of 14 million gt by June 1932, representing 21% of the world fleet, after which heavy scrapping started to remove the surplus.

The financial consequences for the shipping industry were severe. The Economist freight index, which had averaged 110 in the 1920s and had never fallen below 85, fell to 80 points and stayed there. The fall in second-hand ship prices was even more severe, reaching a trough in the first half of 1933. Jones comments:

> Ship values fell by 50% in 1930. Similar depreciation is disclosed in the sale records of post-war vessels of every type and size. Single- and two-deck steamers built in the early post war period, which at the time were valued at between £200,000 and £280,000, were being sold for £14,000 in 1930. A number of these vessels were sold during 1933 and during the early part of the year these were changing hands for between £5,000 and £6,000. There was a slight recovery in the autumn, and in December the S.S. *Taransay*, a single-deck steamer, was sold for £11,500.[51]

By 1933 financial pressures had become so great, and market sentiment so adverse, that financially weak owners were forced to sell their ships at the distress prices which distinguish a depression from a recession. The banks played a leading role in forcing down prices and 'the market was hammered into insensibility by the ruthless and incredible course pursued by British banks in 1931 and thereafter'.[52] This trough in prices created an active speculative market and, 'values having reached such an unprecedented low level, extraordinary activity was recorded in the ship sale market. Foreign buyers recognized the opportunity to acquire tonnage at bargain prices. Greek buyers were especially prominent'.[53] Between 1935 and 1937, 5 million gt of ships were scrapped.

This was coupled with the renewed growth of sea trade, which finally passed its 1929 peak in 1937 and by January 1938 ships in lay-up had fallen to 1.3 million gt. As a result the freight index had shot up from 80, where it had been for the previous five years, to 145.

This 'boom' did not last long. The position deteriorated rapidly due to a decline in trade in 1938 and a recovery of shipbuilding deliveries to 2.9 million tons in 1937 and 2.7 million tons in 1938. Within 6 months, laid-up tonnage increased by over a million tons (on 30 June 1938, out of 66.9 million tons in existence, 2.5 million tons was laid up). Further details of the cycles during the inter-war period can be found in the discussion of shipbuilding market cycles in Chapter 15.

## 3.7 BULK SHIPPING MARKET CYCLES, 1945–2008

In the fifty-year period following the Second World War, the seven dry cargo freight market cycles were shorter, averaging 6.7 years each. During this period the bulk shipping markets developed, and we need to track developments in the tankers market as well as the dry cargo cycles. Dry cargo freight rates are shown in Figure 3.10 which continues the sequence of dry freight cycles, starting with cycle 15 in 1947 and ending with cycle 23 in 2003–8, whilst the tanker spot rates are shown in Figure 3.11. Although there are similarities in the timing of cycles, the shape is different. The dry cargo cycles are more clearly defined and the peaks tend to be longer, while the tanker cycles are

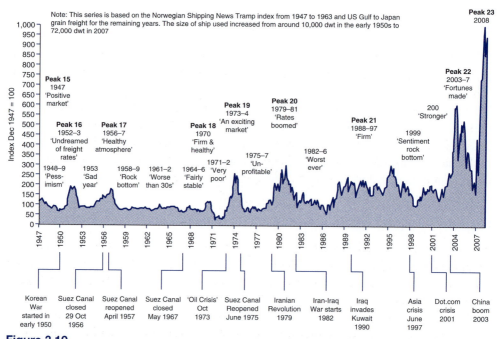

**Figure 3.10**

Bulk carrier shipping market cycles, 1947–2008

Source: Compiled by Martin Stopford from various sources

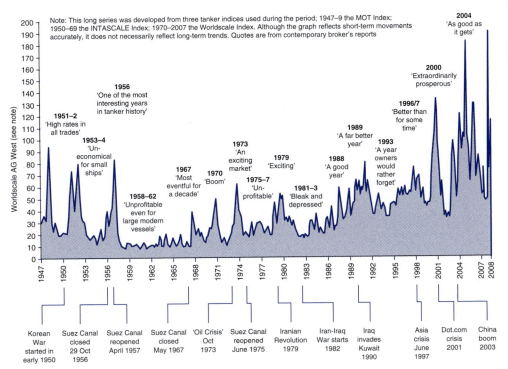

**Figure 3.11**
Oil tanker shipping market cycles, 1947–2008
Source: Compiled by Martin Stopford from various sources

more 'spiky'. Since freight rates do not tell the whole story, the graphs are annotated to show the terms in which shipbrokers were describing the market at each point. Changing technology made new markets possible and the liner and tramp markets which dominated the previous period gave way to a range of specialized bulk shipping markets. The main markets which developed during this period were tanker, bulk carrier, LPG, LNG, container, offshore, cruise and sophisticated ferries. In the bulk market the multi-deck tramp ships which had dominated the business for a century were progressively replaced by more efficient specialized ships.

## The technological trend, 1945–2007

During the post-war period the freight trend line, adjusted to constant prices using a US inflation index, fell from 15 to less than 5. This is clear evidence that the period was one of extreme technical change, and these changes have been documented elsewhere. Bigger ships, specialized vessels, improved on-board technology and more efficient engines combined to reduce the cost of freight by about two-thirds. Quite an achievement.

The first twenty-five years after the Second World War saw extraordinary growth in sea trade (Figure 3.12), which increased from 500 million tons in 1950 to 3.2 billion tons in 1973. Once again this was a period of great technical change in the shipping

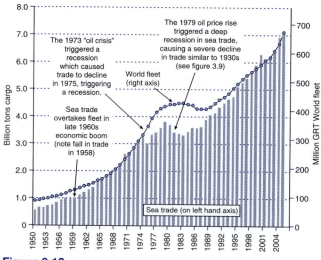

**Figure 3.12**

Sea Trade, 1949–2005

Source: *United Nations Yearbook* (various years)

industry, though the emphasis was on organization as much as hardware. Major shippers in the energy and metal industries took the initiative in developing integrated transport operations designed to reduce their transport costs. The trend towards specialization was continuous and pervasive. In 1945 the world merchant fleet consisted of passenger ships, liners, tramps and a small number of tankers. Few vessels used for cargo transport were larger than 20,000 dwt. By 1975 the fleet had changed out of all recognition and all the major trades had been taken over by specialized ships. Dry bulks were carried by a fleet of bulk carriers, oil by crude tanker, and general cargo for the most part by container-ships, vehicles in car carriers, forest products in open hatch lumber carriers and chemicals in chemical parcel tankers. Specialization allowed the size of ship to increase. The largest cargo ships in 1945 were not much more than 20,000 dwt. By the mid-1990s the specialist bulk fleets contained many ships over 100,000 dwt and in the liner trades the largest container-ships were four or five times the capacity of their multi-deck ancestors. Thus the familiar theme of large modern ships forcing out small obsolete vessels continued just as it had in the nineteenth century.

In addition, the market was disrupted by a series of political developments: the Korean War which started in 1950; the nationalization and subsequent closure of the Suez Canal in 1956; the second Suez closure in 1967; the Yom Kippur War in 1973; the second oil crisis in 1979; the Gulf War in August 1990; and the Iraq invasion in 2003. Although the pattern of freight peaks and troughs coincided with fluctuations in the OECD industrial trade cycle, the effects of these political influences were also apparent.

In the mid-1970s the shipping environment changed. There was a fall in sea trade, followed by a major dip in the early 1980s. The scale of this downturn in trade rivalled that of the 1930s in its severity. In the tanker market the sprint for size lost momentum and the fleet, which had previously been young and dynamic, grew old and sluggish. Shippers became less confident about their future transport requirements, and the role of tanker owners as subcontractors gave way to an enlarged role as risk takers. In other parts of the shipping market the technical evolution continued. Bulk carriers continued to increase in size, with volume cargoes such as iron ore and coal moving up into Capesize vessels of over 100,000 dwt. A fleet of car carriers was built, with the largest able to carry 6,000 vehicles. Chemical parcel tankers grew in size to 55,000 dwt.

Container-ships increased from 2,000 TEU in the early 1970s to 6,500 TEU in the mid-1990s, and by 2007 vessels of over 10,000 TEU were being delivered. Ship technology improved with the unmanned engine room, satellite navigation, anti-fouling paint finishes, more efficient diesel engines, vastly improved hatch covers and a host of other technical improvements in the design and construction of merchant ships.

## Short-term cycles, 1945–2007

However, it is the short-term cycles that are of real interest. During the period 1947–2007 there were eight dry cargo cycles, and compared to previous periods their average duration was quite short: the peaks averaged 2.4 years and the troughs 3.2 years, so the average cycle was 5.6 years. However, the cycles varied in shape and intensity. Most peaks lasted 2 years but there was a long drawn-out peak from 1988 to 1997, and finally a very long one which started in 2003 and was still going on at the beginning of 2008, making it the best boom in 264 years. On the negative side, there were two very severe recessions, from 1958 to 1964 and from 1982 to 1987, the latter ranking alongside the 1930s recession as the worst of the century. On some measures it was the most extreme since 1775, which helps to put things into perspective.[54]

## Cycle 15: 1945–51

The post-war market got off to a good start in 1945: 'As a result of scarcity of tonnage and the tremendous need for transportation, the freight quotations were soon at a sky high level and seemed fantastic compared with pre-war rates'.[55] The market remained firm in 1946. In 1947 it started a downward trend, reaching a trough in 1949 when 'pessimism prevailed. Generally speaking there was ample tonnage and consequently falling rates'.[56] The year 1950 was quiet until the autumn when 'there was a considerable lack of tonnage in a great many trades resulting in a sudden rise in the market'.[57]

## Cycle 16: 1952–5

In 1951 anxieties raised by the Korean War sparked a wave of panic stock building. Seaborne trade grew by 16% in the year, creating a market 'undreamed of only one year ago'. The peak only lasted a year and by spring 1952 freights had fallen by up to 70% as the reaction to the panic of 1951 set in. By 1953 laid-up tonnage was increasing as import restrictions and the overstocking of 1951 continued to make themselves felt. Second-hand prices give a clear idea of the extreme nature of this cycle. The price of a reasonably prompt Liberty ship built in 1944 increased from £110,000 in June 1950 to £500,000 in December 1951. By December 1952 it was back down to £230,000.[58] The year 1954 demonstrated once again how unpredictable the shipping industry can be: 'The freight market went from bad (1953) to worse (in the first half of 1954) and then to a considerable improvement in the last half of 1954'.[59] In the autumn of 1954 the market started to tighten and by year's end rates were up 30%. The improving trend continued through 1955 and when the Suez Canal closed in November 1956, diverting

Suez traffic to the longer journey round the Cape, there was a tremendous boom in rates and time-charter activity.

## Cycle 17: 1957–69

The events which followed the Suez crisis provide a case study of the 'shipping game' at its most exciting, as the 1956 boom was suddenly followed by a severe recession (see Chapter 8). Platou comments:

> The year 1957 shows how almost impossible it is to predict the future of the shipping industry. The forecasts made at the end of 1956 by leading shipping personalities were fairly optimistic. Nobody seemed to expect the recession which subsequently occurred, a depression which must be considered the worst since middle thirties. From sky high rates at the end of 1956 they fell throughout 1957 to what can only be termed an almost rock bottom level…There were few people, if any, who imagined that, with small changes, it would turn out to be a ten year depression only relieved by a second and more lasting closure of the Suez Canal in 1967.[60]

A complex range of economic and political variables conspired to produce the lengthy recession. Tugenhadt describes the part which the oil companies played in creating a tanker investment boom which drove the market down.

> It was during the 1956 Suez crisis that owners made their biggest killings. When the canal was closed and tankers had to be rerouted round the Cape of Good Hope there were not enough available to carry the oil that was needed, and charter rates rose astronomically. The companies, believing like everybody else that the Egyptians would be incapable of running the canal after it had been cleared, thought the shortage would last well into the 1960s until new ships had been built. They therefore signed contracts in which they not only hired tankers for immediate work at the high prevailing rate but also agreed to terms for chartering ships which had not yet been built for work in the 1960s. … When the Egyptians showed they could operate the canal efficiently the bottom fell out of the tanker market, but the companies were stuck with the contracts.[61]

Several other factors contributed to the over capacity which developed in dry cargo in 1958. Platou singles out stockbuilding, overbuilding, more efficient ships and the world economy:

> The reasons for this decline were many. Stockpiles in Europe at the end of 1956 made it possible to slightly reduce the demand for tramp tonnage in the early months of 1957. The rate of completion of new tramps had increased enormously and these were rapidly replacing the Liberty vessels. These new tramps, averaging 3,000 tons higher capacity than the war-built ships, and faster by four knots, were carrying considerably

more cargo than the Liberty ships they were designed to replace. Also contributing to the decline were the restrictions on trade imposed in a number of countries caused by shortage of foreign exchange. Other contributory causes were the accelerating tendency towards self-sufficiency in shipowning, chartering, and shipbuilding in hitherto non-maritime countries, and the fact that Japan suddenly became an important supplier of tramp tonnage to the world's merchant fleet. Last, but not least, the recession in world trade helped to force rates down to well below operating levels.[62]

The severe recession in the world economy certainly played a major part. OECD industrial production fell by 4% in 1958, producing the first decline in seaborne trade since 1932 (Figure 3.12). The reopening of Suez reduced tanker demand and coincided with record deliveries of newbuildings ordered during the strong market of 1955–6. However, the cause of this long recession was not primarily a lack of demand. After the setback in 1958, seaborne trade grew from 990 million tons in 1959 to 1790 million tons in 1966, an increase of 80% in seven years. The real problem was on the supply side. After the shortages of the 1950s, shipbuilding output more than doubled, and an expanding flow of large modern vessels was largely responsible for keeping charter rates down. It was not until the closure of the Suez Canal in 1967 that tanker freight rates returned to really profitable levels. However, this second Suez crisis was not really a rerun of its predecessor because supply had become more flexible:

> So many ships were ordered in the aftermath of the 1956 crisis that for several years before the canal closed again in 1967 there was a considerable surplus of tankers, and many of them had to be converted into grain carriers to find employment. As a result, the shipowners were unable to repeat their coup. Within a few weeks of the closure some 200 tankers totalling 5 million tons had been brought back into oil carrying, and Europe's supplies were assured. The companies therefore refused to charter vessels for more than two or three voyages at a time, instead of for several years ahead. Nevertheless, the crisis was highly profitable for owners…The Norwegian Sigval Bergesen showed what this meant in overall terms when he chartered the 80,000 ton *Rimfonn* to Shell for two voyages that brought in £1m.[63]

In short, the decade following the 1956 Suez boom was less prosperous for the shipping industry. Sizeable losses were made by owners trading on the spot market during the first half and, although in the second half the market improved, demand never got sufficiently far ahead of supply to push rates to acceptable profitable levels.

## Cycle 18: 1970–2

The Six Day War between Israel and Egypt in 1967 and the subsequent closure of the Suez Canal marked the start of seven prosperous years for shipowners in the charter market. There were three freight market booms, and at various times owners were able to fix time charters at highly profitable rates. Since oil was the largest cargo moving through the Suez Canal at this time, the main impact of its closure was felt in the tanker market.

The dry cargo market benefited indirectly from improved rates for ore carriers owing to combined carriers switching into oil trading but, in general, the increase in rates was less noticeable than in the tanker market. The booms of 1970 and 1973 both coincided with exceptional peaks in the industrial trade cycle, reinforced by political events such as the closure in May 1970 of Tap Line, the oil pipeline running from the Arabian Gulf to the Mediterranean, which cut back the availability of oil from Sidon by 15 million tons. Later in the year the restrictions on Libyan oil production by the new regime gave a further boost to the market. A similar pattern occurred when the nationalization of Libyan oil supplies in August 1973 made oil companies cut back their take-up of Libyan oil in favour of the more distant Middle East sources.

However, the real cause of the buoyant market was an unprecedented growth of trade. Seaborne trade increased by 78% from 1807 million tons in 1966 to 3233 million tons in 1973. The increased requirement for ships during this seven-year period was greater than in the previous 16 years. Despite rapidly expanding shipbuilding capacity, the shipyards had difficulty keeping pace with demand. There was a recession in 1971, but it proved short-lived, and many owners were covered by profitable time charters contracted in 1970. It was, therefore, a period of great prosperity and expansion in the shipping industry.

### Cycle 19: (bulk carriers) 1973–8

The year 1973 was one of the great years in shipping, comparable with the 1900 boom triggered by the South African war. During the summer the time-charter rate for a VLCC doubled from $2.5 per deadweight per month ($22,000 per day) to $5 per deadweight per month ($44,000 per day). The extremity of conditions sowed the seeds for a spectacular bubble in ship prices. Hill and Vielvoye describe the price spiral in the following terms:

> The upward movement in ship prices began at the end of 1972, and during 1973 the price of all types of ships rose by between 40 and 60 per cent compared with the previous year, with the most significant increase being paid for tanker tonnage. Owners were prepared to pay vastly inflated prices as a result of premiums on ships with an early delivery ... In this situation a very large crude carrier which had been ordered in 1970 or 1971 at a cost of about $26.4 million could realize a price of between $61m and $73.5m.[64]

The tanker market collapsed following the Yom Kippur War in 1973, but the dry cargo market held up through 1974 and for small bulk carriers into 1975, spurred on by buoyant economic growth, a phase of stockbuilding in the world economy as a result of commodity price inflation, and the heavy congestion in the Middle East and Nigeria resulting from the boom in these areas triggered by the increased oil revenue. This is an interesting example of a dry cargo peak outlasting a downturn in the world economy.

Between 1975 and 1995 the dry cargo market followed a different pattern from tankers. For bulk carriers the cycle 19 trough only lasted 3 years from 1975 to 1978.

The very firm market in 1973–4 allowed owners to fix time charters that yielded profits for several years after. However, the spot market moved into recession in 1975 and the 3 years from 1975 to 1978 were very depressed for all sizes of vessels. Although there was some seasonal fluctuation, on average, freight rates were not sufficient to cover running costs. By 1977 many owners were experiencing severe liquidity problems.[65]

In the autumn of 1978 the dry cargo recovery started, leading to a very firm market in 1979–80. By the end of 1978 freight rates had risen 30%, and they continued their climb through 1979 to a higher level than the 1974 peak. There were several reasons for strength of this recovery. The stage was set by a sharp improvement in the fundamentals. Trade in the major bulk commodities grew by 7.5% in 1979, but supply increased by only 2.5% due to the low ordering during the previous recession. On top of this came the knock-on effect of the 1979 oil price increase. Power utilities around the world switched from oil to coal, giving a major boost to the thermal coal trade. This effect was reinforced by congestion. According to *Fearnleys Review*, 'the backbone of the freight market in 1980 was the heavy congestion in important port areas. In the last quarter of the year the waiting time for coal carriers in US ports soared up to 100 days which in fact trebled the need for tonnage in these trades'.[66] The congestion was widespread, particularly in the Middle East and West Africa where traditional port facilities could not cope with the flood of trade. Rates climbed further in 1980 and at the end of December were 50% over the good average reached in 1979.

In the tanker market, the Yom Kippur War ushered in a structural depression which lasted until 1988, relieved by only a brief market improvement in 1979. There were essentially three problems which contributed to the depth of this recession. The first was the oversupply of tankers resulting from the speculative investment in the early 1970s. During the peak year of 1973, the operational tanker fleet was 225 million dwt, but so many new tanker orders were placed that, despite the decline in tanker demand during the next two years, the fleet actually increased to 320 million dwt, creating surplus tanker capacity of 100 million dwt. Secondly, the world shipbuilding industry was now able to build 60 million dwt of merchant ships each year. This was far more than was required to meet the demand for new ships even if the trend of the 1960s had continued. Shipyard capacity was not easily reduced and it took a decade of over-production to cut capacity to a level more in line with demand. Thirdly, the oil price rises in 1973 and 1979 dramatically reduced the demand for oil imports. The market crashed to a trough.

The transformation from boom to bust in 1973 was one of the most spectacular ever recorded in a shipping market. Over the summer rates for VLCCs soared to more than Worldscale (WS) 300, and stayed there until October. Then in October OPEC introduced a 10% embargo on all exports to the West, and the market crashed precipitately, with VLCC rates falling to WS 80 in December. The decline continued through 1974 and by April 1975 the rate for a VLCC from the Gulf to Europe had sunk to WS 15. However, it took nearly a year for the seriousness of the position to sink in. In March 1974, five months after the crisis broke, a 270,000 dwt tanker was fixed for 3 years at a firm $28,000 per day, but eight months later in November a similar fixture was reported at only $11,000 per day.[67] There was little sale and purchase activity, but by year's end prices had already fallen by more than 50%. For example, the second-hand price of a 1970-built 200,000 dwt VLCC fell from $52 million in 1973 to $23 million in 1974. This proved to be only the beginning. In 1975 the price fell to $10 million, in 1976 to $9 million in 1976 and in mid-1977 to $5 million.

After two years there was a modest recovery in the tanker market. A recovery in the world economy in 1979 started to push rates up, though only to a peak of Worldscale 62 in July 1979. Laid-up tonnage fell from 13.4 million dwt to 8.6 million dwt in 1979. However, this was a poor sort of recovery and VLCC rates did little more than cover voyage expenses. Second hand prices also edged up, and the price of a 200,000 dwt VLCC rose to $11 million. An intermission in a long recession, rather than a market peak.

## Cycle 20: (bulk carriers) 1979–87 (the 1980s depression)

The dry cargo freight boom lasted until March 1981 when a sharp fall set in. The daily earnings of a Panamax fell from $14,000 per day in January to $8,500 per day in December. The initial trigger for the fall was a US coalminers' strike which caused a decline in the Atlantic market.[68] The more fundamental problem was the start of a severe recession in the world economy. Falling oil prices, a stagnant coal trade and elimination of congestion pushed rates down to levels that by 1983–4 some brokers were describing as the worst ever experienced.

The following year, 1982, brought a further halving of freight rates. By December 1982 the earnings of a Panamax bulk carrier were down to $4200 per day. In the time-charter market a great number of time charters negotiated in the previous year had to be renegotiated to allow the charterers to survive, and many charterers failed to meet their commitments altogether, which resulted in premature redeliveries and further difficulties for shipowners.[69] Freight rates improved slightly in the spring of 1983, but fell to the bottom level in the summer and stayed there. Although freight rates were very depressed, in 1983–4 large numbers of orders were placed for bulk carriers. The whole process was started by Sanko Steamship, a Japanese shipping company, which secretly placed orders for 120 ships. Their example was soon followed by a flood of orders from international shipowners, particularly Greeks and Norwegians. The explanation of this counter-cyclical ordering, which resembles a similar event in 1905–6, is complex. Shipowners had accumulated large cash reserves during the 1980 boom; banks, which had large deposits of petrodollars, were keen to lend to shipping; and ships were cheap because the shipyards still had overcapacity and no tankers were being ordered. In addition, the shipyards were offering a new generation of fuel-efficient bulk carriers which looked very attractive at the prevailing high oil price. The yen was favourable, making ships ordered in Japan look cheap. Finally, owners ordering in 1983 expected the cycle to last 6 years as its predecessor had done, so they would take delivery in the next cyclical upswing which on that calculation was due in 1985.

If so many owners had not had the same idea, this would have been a successful strategy. Expectations that trade would improve were fulfilled. In 1984 the business cycle turned up and there was a considerable increase in world trade. However, the combination of heavy deliveries of bulk carrier newbuildings, many ordered speculatively in the previous two years, and the fact that the combined carrier fleet could find little employment in the tanker market ensured that the increase in rates was very limited. Panamax bulk carrier freight rates struggled up to $6,500 per day in 1985, then collapsed under a flood of deliveries with the result that, as *Fearnleys* commented, 'shipowners lived through another year without being able to cover their costs'.[70] Just to make matters worse, by this time the yen had strengthened and bulk carriers ordered in yen but paid for in dollars cost more than expected.[71] Many shipowners who had borrowed heavily to invest in newbuildings now faced acute financial problems. Bank foreclosures and distress sales were common and second-hand prices fell to distress levels.

In financial terms the market trough was reached in mid-1986 when a five-year-old Panamax bulk carrier could be purchased for $6 million, compared with a newbuilding price of $28 million in 1980, identifying this as a depression rather than a recession.[72] As trade started to grow and scrapping increased, the dry market moved into balance, with freight rates in both markets reaching a peak in 1989–90. Freight rates for a Panamax bulk carrier increased from $4400 per day in 1986 to $13,200 per day in 1989. This stimulated one of the most profitable asset play markets in the history of the bulk carrier market.[73]

## Cycle 20: (tankers) 1979–87

For the tanker market this period was a disaster. The Iranian revolution in 1979 pushed the price of oil from $11 a barrel to almost $40 a barrel, triggering a massive response from oil consumers and an appalling tanker cycle. During the previous five years much research had been devoted to finding alternative energy sources, and many power stations had taken steps to permit the use of coal as an alternative energy source. When the oil price increased, there was an immediate reaction and the seaborne trade in oil fell steadily from 1.4 billion tonnes in 1979 to 900 million tonnes in 1983. This laid the foundation for an extreme recession in the tanker market, with a surplus approaching 50% developing as this fall in demand combined with the over-building of the 1970s.

By 1981 brokers commented:

> the tanker freight market in 1981 could very well be described by two words, bleak and depressed. The previous 5 years gave an acceptable return to owners of tonnage up to 80,000 dwt, and even occasionally some encouragement to larger tankers through periodic increases in demand. However 1981 cannot have given any tanker owner with ships on the spot market anything but net losses. The rates for VLCC and ULCC tonnage showed an overall slide. At rates hovering around WS 20 the transport of crude oil is virtually subsidised by the tanker owners by hundreds of thousands of dollars per voyage.[74]

The result was a severe depression as the market squeezed cashflow until sufficient tankers had been scrapped to restore market balance. By April 1983 the rate for a VLCC trading from the Arabian Gulf to Europe had fallen to WS 17 and prices had fallen dramatically. Because there were few old tankers for scrap, especially in the bigger sizes where the surplus was concentrated, this took years to achieve and eventually many younger vessels were scrapped. For example in November 1983 the 8-year-old *Maasbracht*, a 318,707 dwt tanker, was sold for scrap at $4.65 million.

Laid-up tanker tonnage increased to 40 million dwt in 1982 and 52 million dwt in 1983. By this time tanker prices were back to scrap levels and, even at these prices, ships that were 5 or 6 years old could not always attract a bidder. In the autumn VLCCs were sold for little over $3 million. The statistics do not do justice to the difficulties faced by tanker owners trading on the charter market during this period. In 1985 sentiment hit 'rock bottom':

> The last ten years of capital drain in the tanker industry have no historical precedent and we have witnessed a decimation of shipping companies which has probably no parallel in modern economic history, even taking into account the depression of the 1930s. The surviving members of the independent tanker fleets must be akin to those of the world's endangered species whose survival appeared questionable in a changing and hostile environment, but have instead shown a remarkable ability to adapt.[75]

If nothing else, this demonstrates that in a free shipping market the adjustment of supply is a long-drawn-out, uncomfortable and expensive business, however simple it may look in theory. In 1986 the market showed the first signs of starting to pick up. Over the year freight rates increased by 70% and the price of an 8-year-old 250,000 dwt VLCC doubled from $5 million to $10 million. This was the start of a spiral of asset price appreciation, and by 1989 the vessel was worth $38 million, despite being three years older. Inevitably this triggered heavy investment in new tankers and the great tanker depression of 1974–88 ended as it had begun with a phase of speculative building.

## Cycle 21: 1988–2002

After the market bottomed out for tankers in 1985 and bulk carriers in 1986, rates rose steadily to a new market peak which was reached in 1989, coinciding with a peak in the world business cycle. During the next five years the tanker and bulk carrier markets developed very differently, due mainly to the different attitudes of investors in the two markets.

In the tanker market the freight peak was accompanied by three years of heavy ordering, from 1988 to 1991, during which there were orders for 55 m.dwt of new tankers. This rush of investment was based on three expected developments in the tanker market. Firstly, the fleet of ageing tankers built during the 1970s construction boom was expected to be scrapped at 20 years of age, creating heavy replacement demand in the mid-1990s. Secondly, shipbuilding capacity had shrunk so much in the 1980s that many observers thought there would be a shortage when the replacement of the 1970s-built tanker fleet built up in the 1990s. Rapidly increasing newbuilding prices seemed to support this view. For example, in 1986 a new VLCC had cost less than

$40 million, but by 1990 the price was over $90 million. Thirdly, growing oil demand was expected to be met from long-haul Middle East exports, creating rapidly increasing demand for tankers, especially VLCCs. As it turned out none of these expectations were realized. Most of the 1970s-built tankers continued to trade beyond 20 years; by the mid-1990s shipbuilding output had more than doubled from 15 m.dwt to 33 m.dwt; and Middle East exports stagnated as technical innovation allowed oil production from short-haul sources to increase faster than expected. Delivery of the tanker orderbook pushed the market into a recession which lasted from early 1992 to the middle of 1995 when a recovery finally started and freight rates moved onto a steady improving path.

Conditions in the dry bulk market took the opposite path. This was one of the rare periods when there was no clear cycle. Dry bulk freight rates peaked along with tankers in 1989, but over the three years from 1988 to 1991 when tanker investors ordered 55 m.dwt, only 24 m.dwt of bulk carriers were ordered. When the world economy moved into recession in 1992 bulk carrier deliveries had fallen to only 4 m.dwt per annum, compared with 16 m.dwt of tanker deliveries. This tonnage was easily absorbed and, after a brief dip in 1992, dry bulk freight rates recovered, reaching a new peak in 1995. By this time five years of relatively strong earnings had triggered heavy investment in bulk carriers and, in the three years from 1993 to 1995, 55 m.dwt of bulk carriers were ordered. As deliveries built up in 1996 the dry bulk market moved into recession. Things started to go wrong for the bulk shipping market in June 1997 when the 'Asia crisis' triggered a recession in the Asian economies. During the first half of 1997 industrial production boomed, growing by 9% in the Pacific region. By the spring of 1998 it had slumped to −5% growth, halting inward investment into the emerging Chinese economy. It was widely expected that recovery would take several years and freight rates in both the tanker and dry bulk markets slumped. Crude tanker earnings slumped from $37,000 a day in June 1997 to less than $10,000 a day in September 1999, and bulk carriers and containerships followed suit. Brokers commented in September 1999 that the 'last six months were memorable in shipping markets for their consistency. Just about every market segment was in recession'.[76]

As so often happens in shipping cycles, things did not develop as anticipated, and during the next two years the market experienced a classic boom and bust cycle. The Asian economies only remained in recession for a few months, and by the spring of 2000 industrial production was growing faster than ever, at up to 11% per year. Meanwhile the negative sentiment in the tanker market had triggered heavy scrapping of the 1970s tankers which were coming to the end of their life and as a result the tanker and bulk carrier fleets grew very slowly. In response tanker freight rates surged to a new peak, with VLCCs achieving earnings of $80,000 a day in December 2000. The dry bulk market also edged upwards, but less forcefully than the tanker market. But overall the shipping market saw its first real boom for 25 years. Unfortunately it did not last too long. In early 2001 the collapse of internet stocks triggered a deep recession in the Atlantic and Asian economies, and by the end of 2002 industrial production in both the Atlantic and the Pacific was declining. In response freight rates slumped, with VLCC earnings down to $10,000 a day and Capesize bulk carriers to $6000 a day.

Owners and analysts felt that this was perfectly normal, and were grateful to have had one fantastic year.

## Cycle 22: 2003-7

Which brings us to the final cycle, which started with a peak which turned out to be one of the most extreme in the period under review. During the previous six years China had been developing its economy, employing an open-market model which attracted inward investment. In early 2003 it moved into a period of serious infrastructure development, and this required enormous quantities of raw materials. Between 2002 and 2007 China's steel production grew from 144 million tons a year to 468 million tons a year, adding capacity equivalent to that of Europe, Japan and South Korea. Combined with growth of oil imports and exports of minor bulks, in the autumn of 2003 this created an acute shortage of ships. Tanker and bulk carrier rates were propelled to new highs and, despite some volatility, stayed at these high levels for the following four years.

## 3.8 LESSONS FROM TWO CENTURIES OF CYCLES

Well, that's the history of shipping cycles since steamships and cables opened up the global market. What are the lessons? There seem to be two main conclusions to be drawn from this analysis. The first is that shipping cycles definitely exist and the shipping industry's 'rule of thumb' that cycles last 7 years is certainly supported by the statistics. Shipping cycles last 8 years if you take the last fifty years as the base. The second is that each cycle is different. None of the cycles actually lasted 7 years. Four cycles lasted only 5–6 years from peak to peak, two lasted 8 years, and six lasted over 9 years, all with 5-year troughs. So it would be hard to devise a more dangerous business decision tool. Try telling your bank manager cycles only last 7 years when you run out of cash in a nine-year cycle!

### Fundamentals set the tone for good and bad decades

There is no mystery about why these cycles are so irregular. Our analysis demonstrates that they are driven by an undercurrent of economic fundamentals of supply and demand which determines the 'market tone' at any point in time, and in retrospect it is clear that each period has a very different character. To illustrate this point, Table 3.3 shows an assessment of these factors during the period under review, ranked by the relative prosperity of the shipping industry:

1.  *Prosperity*. Two periods were prosperous, the 1950s and 1998–2007. In both cases rapidly growing demand coincided with a shortage of shipbuilding capacity.
2.  *Competitiveness*. There were three periods of intensely competitive activity characterized by growing trade and shipbuilding capacity that expanded fast enough to keep up with demand.

3. *Weakness*. There was a weak market in the 1920s when growing demand was damped by overcapacity in the shipbuilding market.

4. *Depression*. There were two depressions, in the 1930s and the 1980s when falling trade coincided with shipbuilding overcapacity.

**Table 3.3** Shipping market fundamentals analysis

|  | Demand growth | Supply tendency | Market tone |
|---|---|---|---|
| 1998–2007 | Very fast | Shortage | Prosperous |
| 1945–1956 | Very fast | Shortage | Prosperous |
| 1869–1914 | Fast | Expanding | Competitive |
| 1956–1973 | Very Fast | Expanding | Competitive |
| 1988–1997 | Slow | Expanding | Competitive |
| 1920–1930 | Fast | Overcapacity | Weak |
| 1930–1939 | Falling | Overcapacity | Depressed |
| 1973–1988 | Falling | Overcapacity | Depressed |

Clearly, supply and shipbuilding capacity have a part to play in setting the tone for a decade, but are not the whole story. This 'supply-side management' is an area where maritime economists do have something to contribute. The challenge is to help the shipping industry remember the past and anticipate the future. To do this we must improve the clarity of our message, with better information, improved analysis, clearer presentation and greater relevance to the decisions made in the commercial shipping market and, most of all, an open mind. Three centuries of shipping cycles prove that just about anything is possible.

## 3.9 PREDICTION OF SHIPPING CYCLES

The problem is that although everyone knows about cycles, it is very difficult to believe in them. As each cycle progresses, doubts set in. This time it will be different. The fact that the cycles are never exactly the same just complicates matters. But the harsh reality is that investors who want to make an annual return of more than 4–5% per annum must be prepared to take some 'shipping risk'. They must find a strategy for dealing with the cycles we have discussed at such length. One obvious strategy is to exploit the volatility of freight rates by taking positions based on the expected development of the cycle. The strategy described, for example, by Alderton[77] is to spot-charter on a rising market and, when the peak is reached, to sell or take a time charter long enough to carry the vessel through the trough. Ship acquisitions are made at the bottom of the market when ships are 'cheap'.[78] Few would argue with the principle of buying low and selling high. The skill lies in the execution. Most analysts have been caught out too often to believe they can forecast accurately. However, there is some middle ground.

First we must restate the truth so evident from shipping history, that cycles are not 'cyclical' if by this we mean 'regular'.[79] In the real world shipping cycles are a loose sequence of peaks and troughs. Because the timing of each stage in the cycle is irregular, simple rules like the 'seven-year cycle', although statistically correct over a very long period, are far too unreliable to be worthwhile as a decision criterion. Cufley's warning that 'it is totally impossible to predict when the market will move upwards (or fall)'[80] deserves to be taken seriously. As he goes on to point out, 'Even reasoned and intelligent assessments, made by experts and covering only a few months, can be made to appear foolish by the turn of events'. So we must carefully weigh up what we can say about the future. There are a few positive factors. Our review in this chapter of the last 12 cycles demonstrates that the same explanations of cyclical peaks and troughs appear again and again. Economic conditions, the 'business cycle', trade growth and the ordering and scrapping of ships are the fundamental variables which can be analysed, modelled and extrapolated. Careful analysis of these variables removes some, but not all, of the uncertainty and reduces the risk. But to these must be added the 'wild cards' which often trigger the spectacular booms and slumps. The South African War in 1900, closure of the Suez Canal, stockbuilding, congestion and strikes in the shipyards have all played a part.

The difficulty of analysing these factors is daunting. The world economy is complex and we often have to wait years for the detailed statistics which tell us precisely what happened. Many of the variables and relationships in the model are highly unpredictable, so the prediction process should be seen as clarifying risk rather than creating certainty. In this respect shipowners are in much the same position as other specialist commodity market traders. Those playing the market must try to understand the cycles and take a risk. That is what they are paid for. An essential part of weighing up this risk is to form a realistic view of what is driving each stage in the cycle – reading the signs as the market progresses through the stages in the cycle, extrapolating the consequences and, when the facts support it, being prepared to act against market sentiment. It is not necessary to be completely right. What matters is being more right than other traders. There is a long history of ill-advised shipping investments which, over the years, have provided a welcome source of income for more experienced investors who buy ships cheap during recessions and sell expensively during booms.

## The importance of market intelligence

The whole thrust of this argument is to direct our attention towards the process of obtaining information about what is going on in the shipping market and understanding the implications of any actions we take. Research suggests that successful business decisions are based upon careful consideration of all the relevant facts, while bad decisions often flow from inadequate consideration of the facts. For example, Kepner and Tregoe, in their study of business decisions, made the following comments:

> In the course of our work, we witnessed a number of decisions in government agencies and private industry that ranged in quality from questionable to catastrophic. Wondering how such poor decisions ever came to be made, we decided to look into their history. We found that most of these decisions were bad because certain important pieces of available information had been ignored, discounted or given insufficient attention. We concluded that the process of gathering and organising information for decision making needed improvement.[81]

These observations, which can hardly be at variance with most people's practical experience, emphasize the importance of collecting and interpreting information.

## The challenge of successful risk management

So where does this leave us in terms of predicting freight cycles? There are three conclusions to be drawn. First, in shipping cycles, as in poker, for every winner there must be a loser. This aspect of the business is about risk management, not carrying cargo. Shipping is not quite a zero-sum game, but we will see in Chapter 8 that the financial returns average out at a fairly modest level. Second, shipping cycles are not random. The economic and political forces which drive them, although highly complex, can be analysed, and the information used to improve the odds in the players' favour. But remember that if everyone has the same idea, it will not work. Third, like poker, each player must assess his opponents, take a view on how they will play the game, and work out who will be the loser this time. In the end, no loser means no winner.

We should not be surprised that this makes shipping sound more like a gambling game than a sober transport business. It *is* a gambling game. Shippers turn to the shipping market because they do not know how much shipping capacity they will need in future. Nobody does. The job of the shipowner is to make the best estimate he can and take a gamble. If he is wrong, he loses. These decisions are complex and often require decisive action which flies in the face of market sentiment. That is why individuals are often more successful than large companies. Imagine playing poker under the direction of a board of directors. For shipowners with many years in the business, the instinct that drives their decisions probably derives from the experience of past cycles, reinforced by an understanding of the international economy and up-to-date information obtained from the international grapevine. For those without a lifetime of experience, either newcomers to the industry or outsiders, the problems of decision-making are daunting. Many bad decisions have been made because of a misunderstanding of the market mechanism. Our aim in the following three chapters is to examine the economic structure of the markets in which sea transport is traded and the fundamentals which drive them.

## 3.10 SUMMARY

In this chapter we have discussed the economic role of cycles in the shipping industry.

We started with the characteristics of cycles, identifying the secular trend, short cycles and seasonal cycles. Then we moved on to define shipping risk. This is the risk that the investment in the hull of a merchant ship, including the return on the capital employed, is not recovered during a period of ownership. Shipping risk can be taken by the shipper (industrial shipping) or the shipowner (shipping market risk). The market cycle dominates shipping risk. Although the existence of cycles is undisputed, their character is 'episodic' rather than regular. We identified four stages (i.e. episodes) in a cycle: a trough, a recovery, a peak, and a collapse. Although we found that cycles averaged 8 years, there are no firm rules about the length or timing of these stages. The cyclical mechanism must be flexible to do its job of managing shipping investment.

The short-term cyclical model is an important part of the market mechanism. When ships are in short supply freight rates shoot up and stimulate ordering. When there is a surplus, rates fall and remain low until enough ships have been scrapped to bring the market into balance. Each stage is periodic, continuing until its work is completed. As a result shipping cycles, like shipowners, are unique individuals. In each 'cycle', supply lurches after demand like a drunk walking a line that he cannot see very clearly.

There is also a longer-term cycle or secular trend driven by technology. Technical developments such as the triple expansion engine or containerization stimulate investment in new ships. As the new ships are delivered they set a new standard for efficiency. The more there are, the bigger the commercial impact. The transition from one technology to another can take 20 years to complete, during which time it affects the economics of the business. Over the last century there has been a succession of these cycles – steam replacing sail, diesel replacing steam, better boilers, containerization, and the bulk shipping revolution.

Analysis of short cycles over the period 1741–2007 illustrates the 'work pattern' of the shipping cycle. There were 22 cycles, averaging 10.4 years each, though when we analysed them into three periods – sail, tramp and bulk – we found the length of cycles reduced, from 14.9 years in the sail era to 9.2 years in the tramp era and 8 years in the bulk era. Each cycle developed within a framework of supply and demand, so common features such as cycles in the economy and over-ordering of ships crop up again and again. As a rule supply has no difficulty keeping up with demand, so the big freight 'booms' are often the result of unexpected events, such as the closing of the Suez Canal, stockpiling or congestion. Recessions tend to be driven by economic shocks which cause an unexpected decline in trade (as in 1930, 1958, 1973, 1982, 1991, 1997 and 2001). Overinvestment also plays a part.

Against this background, predicting cycles and the timing of changes is difficult, especially in the heightened sentiment that accompanies the peaks and troughs of each cycle. The framework of each cycle is set by economic fundamentals. Within this framework it is left to shipowners and market sentiment to 'play the game'. In a low-return industry, one investor's fortune is another investor's loss, so the stakes are high. When outsiders look at the low average returns, they often ask: 'Why would anyone want to invest in shipping?' But the shrewdest and most adaptable owners know that they will survive to make massive profits the next time some unforeseen event turns the market on its head – a case of 'devil take the hindmost'.

# 4 Supply, Demand and Freight Rates

*The price of freight*
*Today is great*
*Because the ships, you'll understand,*
*Are high priced too,*
*Costing when new*
*Far more than they used to*

*If you'd know why*
*Their price is high,*
*Consider this, berth costs are great*
*Because the trade,*
*On which freight's paid*
*Grows faster than ships can be made*

*Only one thing left to know,*
*What it is that makes trade grow.*
*The world needs its grain and ore;*
*Sometimes less, but mostly more.*
*When judging if the price is high*
*What matters most is ... when you buy*

(Martin Stopford 2007)

## 4.1 THE SHIPPING MARKET MODEL

### The search for signposts

Now it is time to examine the economic mechanisms which control the shipping cycles discussed in the previous chapter. Shipowners have two jobs. One is to operate ships, a worthy task but not one that brings riches. The other is to be in the right place at the right time, to rake in the money at the peak of a cycle. Each twist of the cycle confronts shipping investors with a new opportunity or threat. In the space of a few months a shipowner's cashflow can swell from a trickle to a flood, and the market value of his fleet can change by millions of dollars. This is how the market manages investment in a difficult and uncertain world, and it presents shipping company management with quite a challenge.

The aim is to take advantage of the cycles to buy low and sell high. This is fair enough, as far as it goes, but this aspect of shipping is a game of skill and playing the cycles depends on being able to recognize – or, better still, predict – the peaks and troughs on the freight chart. Just being right is not enough. An investor may correctly predict a market peak, but if the charterers take the same view there will be no long-term contracts. Similarly, in market troughs owners may be ready to buy cheap ships, but who is willing to sell for a loss? As Michael Hampton pointed out, consensus is generally not a good signpost.[1] The best opportunities go to those who can judge when the other players in the market are wrong, and that means digging below the surface to understand the consequences of current developments (see Chapter 17 for a full discussion of forecasting).

From an economic viewpoint, each shipping cycle is unique. If we are to improve our understanding of what is going on in the market, we must now develop a theoretical explanation of how the freight market cycles are generated. To do this we will use the supply and demand model, a technique often used by economists to analyse commodity markets. The term 'model' is used here in just the same way as when we talk about a model ship – it is a smaller version of the real thing, leaving out those details that are not relevant to the present subject. The aim of the exercise, which is often referred to as 'fundamentals analysis', is to explain the mechanisms which determine freight rates in a consistent way.

## 4.2 KEY INFLUENCES ON SUPPLY AND DEMAND

The maritime economy is enormously complex, so the first task is to simplify the model by singling out those factors that are most important. This is not to suggest that detail should be ignored, but rather to accept that too much detail can hinder a clear analysis. In the initial stages at least we must generalize. From the many influences on the shipping market we can select ten as being particularly important, five affecting the demand for sea transport and five affecting the supply. These are summarized in Table 4.1.

**Table 4.1** Ten variables in the shipping market model

| Demand | Supply |
| --- | --- |
| 1. The world economy | 1. World fleet |
| 2. Seaborne commodity trades | 2. Fleet productivity |
| 3. Average haul | 3. Shipbuilding production |
| 4. Random shocks | 4. Scrapping and losses |
| 5. Transport costs | 5. Freight revenue |

As far as the demand for sea transport is concerned (the 'demand function'), the five variables are the world economy, seaborne commodity trades, average haul, random shocks and transport costs. To explain the supply of shipping services (the 'supply function'), we focus on the world fleet, fleet productivity, shipbuilding deliveries, scrapping and freight revenues. The way in which these variables fit together into a simple model of the shipping market is shown in Figure 4.1. This model has three components, demand (module A), supply (module B), and the freight market (module C) which links the demand and supply by regulating the cashflow flowing from one sector to another.

How does the model work? The mechanics are very simple. In the demand module (A) the world economy, through business cycles and regional growth trends, determines

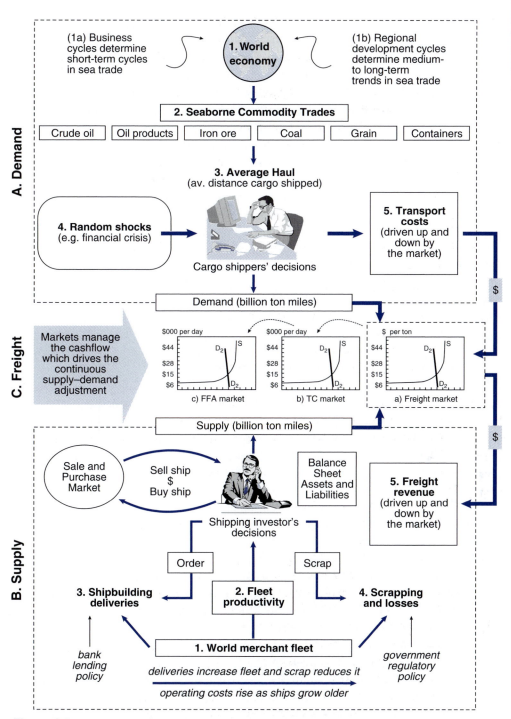

**Figure 4.1**
The shipping market supply and demand model
Source: Martin Stopford, 2008

the broad volume of goods traded by sea. Developments in particular commodity trades may modify the growth trends (e.g. development in the steel industry may influence the iron ore trade), as may changes in the average haul over which the cargo is transported. The final demand for shipping services measured in ton miles. (i.e. the tonnage of cargo multiplied by the average haul). The use of ton miles as a measure of demand is technically more correct than simply using the deadweight of cargo ships required, since it avoids making a judgement about the efficiency with which ships are used. That belongs more properly to the supply side of the model.

Turning to the supply module (B), in the short term, the world merchant fleet provides a fixed stock of transport capacity. When demand is low only part of this fleet may be trading and some ships will be laid up, or used for storage. The fleet can be increased by new-building and reduced by scrapping. The amount of transport this fleet provides also depends on the logistical efficiency with which ships are operated – in particular, speed and waiting time (see below). For example, a fleet of tankers steaming at 11 knots and returning from each cargo voyage in ballast carries less cargo in a year than the same size fleet of bulk carriers steaming at 14 knots and carrying a backhaul for all or part of its journey. This efficiency variable is generally referred to as 'fleet productivity' and is expressed in cargo ton miles per dwt per annum. Finally, the policies of banks and regulators have an impact on how the supply side of the market develops.

## Dynamic links in the model

People play a central part in this shipping market model. At the heart of the demand module (A) are the *cargo shippers*. Their decisions over the sourcing of raw materials and the location of processing plant such as oil refineries determine how trade develops and, of course, they negotiate freight rates, time charters and FFAs. Many shippers are large corporations trading raw materials and manufactures, but in recent years they have been joined by commodity traders and operators who have cargo contracts for which ships are needed. The people who play a central part in supply module (B) are the *shipping investors*. The term 'shipping investor' is used because although many decision-makers will be private shipowners or shipping companies there are other important players – for example, German Kommanditgeseichllschaft (KG) companies which own containerships; oil traders which own tankers; and major oil companies with their own fleets. These shipping investors sit on the other side of the table from the cargo shippers in the freight negotiation and they also have the crucial task of ordering the new ships and scrapping old ones.

Imbalances between the supply and demand modules feed through into the third part of the model, the freight market (C), where freight rates are constantly adjusting in response to changes in the balance of supply and demand. This freight module is a 'switchbox' controlling the amount of money paid by shippers to shipowners for the transport of cargo, and it is this flow of money which drives the shipping market. For example when ships are in short supply, freight rates are bid up and the cash which flows into the bank accounts of shipowners affects the behaviour of both the cargo shippers and shipping investors (we discuss this 'behavioural' part of the model in more detail in Chapter 17). As the earnings of their ships rise, shipping investors rush to buy more second-hand ships, bidding up prices and then when second-hand ships become too expensive they turn to ordering new ships. As the new ships are delivered supply expands, but only after the time lag required to deliver the new ships – usually 18 months to 3 years. Meanwhile cargo shippers are responding to the high freight rates by looking for ways to cut transport costs by delaying cargoes, switching to closer supply sources or using bigger ships. But by this stage in the market cycle there is not a great deal they can do, and they have to grit their teeth and pay up.

When there are too many ships the process is reversed. Rates are bid down and shipowners have to draw on reserves to pay fixed costs such as repairs and interest on loans. As their reserves diminish, some owners are forced to sell ships to raise cash. If the downturn persists, eventually the price of older ships falls to a level where shipbreakers offer the best price and supply gradually reduces. Changes in freight rates may also trigger a change in the performance of the fleet, through adjustments to speed, or ships may be put into lay-up.

This model gives shipping market cycles their characteristic pattern of irregular peaks and troughs. Demand is volatile, quick to change and unpredictable; supply is ponderous and slow to change; and when the market is tightly balanced the freight mechanism amplifies even small imbalances at the margin. Thus the 'tortoise' of supply chases the 'hare' of demand across the freight chart, but hardly ever catches him. In a market with these dynamics we must expect 'balance', in the sense of steady earnings over several years, to be quite rare.

One final throught. At the heart of the model are people – shipping investors and cargo shippers. Their task is to negotiate the rate for each ship and inevitably the rates they agree vary depending on how the negotiating parties feel. A ship might be fixed for $20,000 per day on Monday, but the sister ship might be fixed for $30,000 per day on Tuesday because charterers got panicky overnight, perhaps due to some rumour they heard. Mathematical models cannot hope to simulate this sort of freight auction, so in the short term at least psychology is as important as fundamentals.

This, in summary, is the market model which controls shipping investment. In the remainder of this chapter we will examine the three sections of the model. Our main interest is not in the value of the variables themselves – we discuss this in later parts of the book. Rather it is to examine why each variable changes and the relationships between them. The model is dynamic in the sense that supply and demand are determined separately, with the two modules linked by the freight negotiation. But it is important to remember that the primary aim of the market mechanism is not to fix the freight rate, it is to coordinate the growth of supply and demand for sea transport in the hopelessly complex world in which shipping operates.

## 4.3 THE DEMAND FOR SEA TRANSPORT

We have suggested that ship demand, measured in ton miles of cargo, is mercurial and quick to change, sometimes by as much as 10–20% in a year. Ship demand is also subject to longer-term changes of trend. Looking back over the last two or three decades, there have been occasions when ship demand has grown rapidly over a sustained period, as happened in the 1960s, and others when ship demand stagnated and declined – notably, for example, the decade following the 1973 oil crisis.

## The world economy

Undoubtedly, the most important single influence on ship demand is the world economy. It came up repeatedly in our discussion of shipping cycles in Chapter 3. Seventy years ago, in his review of the tramp market, Isserlis commented on the similar timing of fluctuations in freight rates and cycles in the world economy.[2] That there should be a close relationship is only to be expected, since the world economy generates most of the demand for sea transport, through either the import of raw materials for manufacturing industry or the trade in manufactured products. It follows that judging trends in the shipping market requires up-to-date knowledge of developments in the world economy. The relationship between sea trade and world industry is not, however, simple or direct. There are two different aspects of the world economy that may bring about change in the demand for sea transport: the business cycle and the trade development cycle.

The *business cycle* lays the foundation for freight cycles. Fluctuations in the rate of economic growth work through into seaborne trade, creating a cyclical pattern of demand for ships. The recent history of these trade cycles is evident from Figure 4.2, which shows the close relationship between the growth rate of sea trade and GDP over the period 1966–2006. Invariably the cycles in the world economy were mirrored by

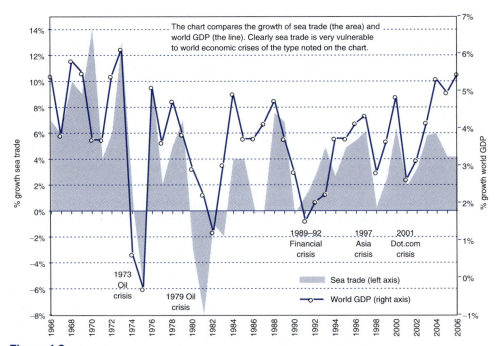

**Figure 4.2**
World GDP cycles and sea trade
Source: World Bank, *Fearnleys Review*

cycles in sea trade. Note, in particular, that the deep sea trade recessions in 1975, 1983 and 1988 coincided with recessions in the world economy. Since world industrial production creates most of the demand for commodities traded by sea, this is hardly surprising. Clearly the business cycle is of major importance to anyone analysing the demand side of the shipping market model.

Nowadays most economists accept that these economic cycles arise from a combination of external and internal factors. The external factors include events such as wars and sudden changes in commodity prices such as crude oil, which cause a sudden change in demand. Internal factors refer to the dynamic structure of the world economy itself, which, it is argued, leads naturally to a cyclical rather than a linear growth path. Among the more commonly quoted causes of business cycles are the following:

- *The multiplier and accelerator*. The main internal mechanism which creates cycles is the interplay between consumption and investment. Income (gross national product or GNP) may be spent on investment goods or consumption goods. An increase in investment (e.g. road building) creates new consumer demand from the workers hired. They spend their wages, creating even more demand (the investment multiplier). As the extra consumer expenditure trickles through the economy, growth picks up (the income accelerator), generating demand for even more investment goods. Eventually labour and capital become fully utilized and the economy over-heats. Expansion is sharply halted, throwing the whole process into reverse. Investment orders fall off, jobs are lost and the multiplier and accelerator go into reverse. This creates a basic instability in the economic 'machine'.[3]

- *Time-lags*. The delays between economic decisions and their implementation can make cyclical fluctuations more extreme. The shipping market provides an excellent example. During a market boom, shipowners order ships that are not delivered until the market has gone into recession. The arrival of the new ships at a time when there is already a surplus further discourages new ordering just at the time when shipbuilders are running out of work. The result of these time-lags is to make booms and recessions more extreme and cyclical.

- *Stockbuilding* has the opposite short-term effect. It produces sudden bursts of demand as industries adjust their stocks during the business cycle. The typical stock cycle, if such a thing exists, goes something like this. During recessions financially hard-pressed manufacturers run down stocks, intensifying the downturn in demand for sea transport. When the economy recovers, there is a sudden rush to rebuild stocks, leading to a sudden burst of demand which takes the shipping industry by surprise. Fear of supply shortages or rising commodity prices during the recovery may encourage high stock levels, reinforcing the process. On several occasions shipping booms have been driven by short-term stockbuilding by industry in anticipation of future shortages or price rises. Examples are the Korean War in 1952–3, the dry cargo boom of 1974–5, and the tanker mini-booms in 1979 and summer 1986, both of which were caused by temporary stockbuilding by the world oil industry.

- Some economists argue that cycles are intensified by *mass psychology*. Pigou put forward the theory of 'non-compensated errors.[4] If people act independently, their errors cancel out, but if they act in an imitative manner a particular trend will build up to a level where they can affect the whole economic system. Thus periods of optimism or pessimism become self-fulfilling through the medium of stock exchanges, financial booms and the behaviour of investors.

All of the above factors contribute to the cyclical nature of the world economy, but in terms of the shipping markets the peaks and troughs they produce are not generally severe enough to threaten the survival of well run businesses. The severe cycles shown in Figure 4.2 are almost all associated with 'random shocks' which fall outside the normal business cycle mechanism. From the analyst's viewpoint this distinction is important because the random shocks trigger extreme market conditions. We will discuss random shocks in more detail later in this section.

To help in predicting business cycles, statisticians have developed 'leading indicators' which provide advance warning of turning points in the economy. For example, the OECD publishes an index based on orders, stocks, the amount of overtime worked and the number of workers laid off, in addition to financial statistics such as money supply, company profits and stock market prices. It is suggested that the turning point in the lead index will anticipate a similar turning point in the industrial production index by about 6 months. To the analyst of short-term market trends such information is useful, though few believe that business cycles are reliably predictable. Two quotations serve to illustrate the point:

> No two business cycles are quite the same; yet they have much in common. They are not identical twins, but they are recognisable as belonging to the same family. No exact formula, such as might apply to the motions of the moon or of a simple pendulum, can be used to predict the timing of future (or past) business cycles.[5]
>
> A remark that can perhaps be made about industrial cycles in general is certainly applicable to the shipping industry: it is certain that these cycles exist; their periodicity – the interval from peak to peak – is variable; and their amplitude is variable; the position of the peak or of the trough of a cycle in progress is not predictable. An ad hoc explanation can usually be found for each period of prosperity and for each phase of the cycle if sufficient knowledge is available of the conditions at the time ... but it is impossible to predict the occurrence of the successive phases of a cycle which is in progress, and still more so in the case of a cycle which has not yet commenced.[6]

In conclusion, the 'business cycle' in world industry is the most important cause of short-term fluctuations in seaborne trade and ship demand. However business cycles, like the shipping cycles to which they contribute, do not follow in an orderly progression. We must take many other factors into account before drawing such a conclusion, in particular drawing a distinction between the business cycles and random shocks.

We now turn to the long-term relationship between seaborne trade and the world economy. Over a period of years does sea trade grow faster, slower, or at the same rate as industrial output? There are two reasons why, over long periods, the trade growth of individual regions will probably change.

One major reason is that the economic structure of the countries generating seaborne trade is likely to change over time – countries, like people, mature as they age! For example, changes in the industrial economies of Europe and Japan in the 1960s had a major impact on sea trade, producing a period of rapid growth from 1960 to 1970, followed by an equally sudden stagnation in the 1970s, as shown in Figure 4.3. A similar pattern occurred in the early 1990s, as South Korea and other Asian countries moved along the industrial

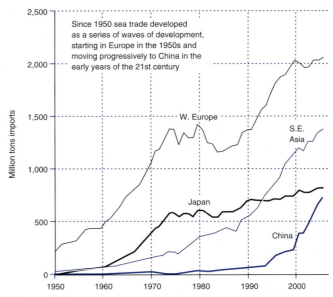

**Figure 4.3**
Regional trade development cycles, 1950–2005
Source: United Nations

path, producing the very high trade growth. By the early twenty-first century China was moving along the same path. These changes in trade are driven by changes in demand for bulk commodities such as iron ore. As industrial economies mature, economic activity becomes less resource-intensive, and demand switches from construction and stock-building of durables, such as motor cars, to services, such as medical care and recreation, with the result that there is a lower requirement for imported raw materials.[7] This contributed to the slower import growth of Europe and Japan during the 1970s and 1980s and will be important for China in the future. This sequential approach to development, known as the trade development cycle, is discussed in more detail in Chapter 10.

The second influence the world economy has on trade concerns the ability of local resources of food and raw materials to meet local demand. When domestic raw materials are depleted users turn to foreign suppliers, boosting trade – for example, iron ore for the European steel industry during the 1960s and crude oil for the USA market during the 1980s and 1990s. Or the cause may be the superior quality of foreign supplies, and the availability of cheap sea transport.

## Seaborne commodity trades

To find out more about the relationship between sea trade and the industrial economy we turn to the second demand variable, the seaborne commodity trades. The discussion falls into two parts: short-term and long-term.

An important cause of short-term volatility is the *seasonality* of some trades. Many agricultural commodities are subject to seasonal variations caused by harvests, notably grain, sugar and citrus fruits. Grain exports from the US Gulf reach a trough in the summer then build up in September as the crop is harvested. Trade may increase by as much as 50% between September and the end of the year. In the oil business there is also a cycle that reflects the seasonal fluctuation in energy consumption in the Northern Hemisphere, with the result that more oil is shipped during the autumn and early winter than during the spring and summer. Much the same seasonality is found in the liner trade, with seasonal peaks and troughs coinciding, for example, with major holidays such as the Chinese New Year and Christmas.

Seasonality has a disproportionate effect on the spot market. Transport of seasonal agricultural commodities is difficult to plan, so shippers of these commodities rely heavily on the spot charter market to meet their tonnage requirements. As a result, fluctuations in the grain market have more influence on the charter market than some much larger trades such as iron ore where tonnage requirements are largely met through long-term contracts. Some agricultural produce, such as fruit, meat and dairy produce, require refrigeration. For this trade, special 'reefer' ships and reefer containers are required.

Long-term trends in commodity trade are best identified by studying the economic characteristics of the industries which produce and consume the traded commodities. This is a topic we will examine in Chapters 11 and 12. Although every business is different, there are four types of change to look out for: changes in the demand for that particular commodity (or the product into which it is manufactured); changes in the source from which supplies of the commodity are obtained; changes due to a relocation of processing plant which changes the trade pattern; and finally changes in the shipper's transport policy.

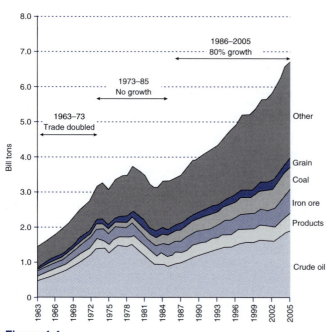

A classic example of *changes in demand* is the trade in crude oil, which Figure 4.4 shows is the largest individual commodity traded by sea. During the 1960s, crude oil demand grew two or three times as fast as the general rate of economic growth because oil was cheap and the economies of western Europe and Japan switched from coal to oil as their primary energy source. Imported oil replaced domestic coal, and the trade elasticity was very high. However, with the increase in oil prices during the 1970s, this trend was reversed and the

**Figure 4.4**
Major seaborne trades by commodity
Source: *Fearnleys Review*

demand for crude oil first stagnated and then declined. Coal regained some of its original market share and the oil trade elasticity fell.

The oil trade also provides a good illustration of the importance of *changes in supply sources*. In the 1960s the main source of crude oil was the Middle East. However, in the 1970s new oil reserves near to the market, such as the North Sea and Alaska, came on stream, reducing the need for deep sea imports. Depletion of local resources provides another example of how changing supply sources affect seaborne trade. An example is provided by Chinese iron ore imports. Until the 1990s China relied on iron ore produced locally to supply its steel industry. However, with the expansion of the steel industry in the 1990s, it became increasingly difficult to meet demand from this source and, as high-grade iron ore was shipped in from Brazil and Australia, domestic supplies were progressively replaced by imports. This run-down of local supplies, combined with rapidly growing demand, resulted in spectacular growth of iron ore imports.

*Relocation of the processing* of industrial raw materials can also affect the volume of cargo shipped by sea and the type of ship required. Take, for example, the aluminium industry. The raw material of aluminium production is bauxite. It takes about 3 tons of bauxite to produce 1 ton of alumina and 2 tons of alumina to produce 1 ton of aluminium. Consequently, a commercial decision to refine bauxite to alumina before shipment reduces the volume of cargo shipped by sea by two-thirds. Alumina has a higher value and is used in smaller quantities than bauxite, so the transport requirement switches from larger vessels suitable for the bauxite trade to smaller bulk carriers suitable for alumina. Another example is the refining of crude oil to products before shipment by exporters. This does not affect the volume transported, but it affects the parcel size and the tank coatings required.

Sometimes processing does not actually reduce the volume of cargo but changes the shipping requirement. In the early days of the oil trade, crude oil was refined at source and transported as oil products in products carriers. In the early 1950s, the oil companies moved towards the transport of crude oil, locating their refineries at the market. This led to the construction of very large crude carriers. Similarly, forest products were originally shipped as logs, but with developing sophistication in the industry there has been a trend towards processing logs into sawn lumber, woodchips, panels or wood pulp prior to shipment. While this did not have a major impact upon the volume of cargo, it resulted in the construction of special forest product carriers.

Finally, we come to the fourth long-term item, the shipper's *transport policy*. This is well illustrated by the oil industry. Until the 1970s the major oil companies planned and controlled the sea transport of oil. The oil companies planned their tonnage requirements, building ships or signing long-time charters with shipowners. The oil trade grew regularly and any minor errors in their planning would quickly be corrected. In this highly structured environment the role of the spot market was relegated to less than 10% of total transport requirements. It was there to cover seasonal fluctuations, minor misjudgements in the speed of trade growth and the occasional mishap such as the closure of the Suez Canal.

After the 1973 oil crisis the oil trade became more volatile and oil company policy changed. Faced with uncertainty over trade volume, the oil shippers relied more heavily on the spot market for their transport requirements. By the 1990s the spot market's share of oil shipments had increased from 10% to almost 50%. This trend was reinforced by a change in the commercial structure of the oil business. After 1973 the control of oil transport changed. Producers, oil companies in industrializing areas such as South Korea and oil traders, who had less incentive to become directly involved in oil transport, started to play a bigger part.

The commodity developments outlined above are not usually of major significance when considering short-term cycles in ship demand, since changes of this type do not take place overnight. They are, however, of considerable importance when judging the medium-term growth of demand and the employment prospects for particular ship types. As a result, any thorough medium-term analysis of the demand for sea transport needs to consider carefully the development of the commodity trades. Further discussion of the major commodity trades can be found in Chapters 10 and 11.

## Average haul and ton miles

Transport demand is determined by a precise matrix of distances which determine the time it takes the ship to complete the voyage. A ton of oil transported from the Middle East to western Europe via the Cape travels five times as far as a ton of oil shipped from Ceyhan in Turkey to Marseilles. This distance effect is generally referred to as the 'average haul' of the trade. To take account of average haul, it is usual to measure sea transport demand in terms of 'ton miles', which can be defined as the tonnage of cargo shipped, multiplied by the average distance over which it is transported.

The effect on ship demand of changing the average haul has been dramatically illustrated several times in recent years by the closure of the Suez Canal, which increased the average distance by sea from the Arabian Gulf to Europe from 6,000 miles to 11,000 miles. As a result of the sudden increase in ship demand there was a freight market boom on each occasion. Another example was the closure of the Dortyol pipeline from Iraq to Turkey when Iraq invaded Kuwait in 1990. As a result 1.5 million barrels per day of oil which had previously been shipped from the East Mediterranean had to be shipped from the Arabian Gulf.

In most trades we find that the average haul has changed over the last few decades. Figure 4.5 shows the average haul of crude oil, oil products, iron ore, coal and grain during the period 1963–2005. In the crude oil trade, the average haul jumped from 4,500 miles in 1963 to over 7,000 miles a decade later, fell precipitately back to 4,500 in 1985 and then increased to 5400 miles. The products trade was stable at about 3800 miles until the early 1980s when long-haul exports from Middle East refineries pushed the average up to 5,000 miles. There was also rapid growth in the average haul in the iron ore and coal trades, both of which increased steadily from about 3,000 miles in 1963 to over 5,000 by the early 1980s.

Analysing changes in the average haul of a commodity trade can be extremely complex, requiring information in the form of detailed trade matrices, but very often the key issue is simply the balance between long-haul and short-haul suppliers.

For example, in the oil trade some oil producers are located close to the major consuming markets: Libya, North Africa, the North Sea, Mexico, Venezuela and Indonesia are all located close to their principal markets in western Europe, Japan and the United States. Oil not obtained from these sources is, of necessity, shipped from the Middle East, which is about 11,000 miles from western Europe and the USA and

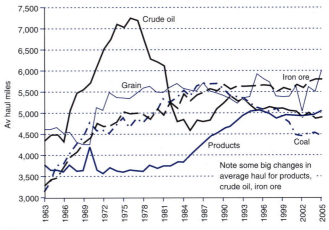

**Figure 4.5**
Average haul of commodity trades 1963–2005
Source: Fearnleys *World Bulk Trades*

about 6,500 miles from Japan. Consequently, the average haul in the oil trade depends upon the balance of output from these two groups of suppliers. The rapidly increasing haul during the 1960s can be explained by the growing share of the Middle East in total oil exports, while the declining haul during the mid-1970s reflected the cut-back in Middle East supplies as new short-haul sources such as Alaska, the North Sea and Mexico came on stream against the background of a declining oil trade.

A similar pattern can be found in the iron ore, and bauxite trades. In the early 1960s the major importers drew their supplies from local sources – Scandinavia in the case of iron ore and the Caribbean for bauxite. As the demand for imports increased, more distant supplies became available, the cost being offset to a large extent by the economies of scale obtainable from the use of large bulk carriers. Thus the European and Japanese iron ore markets came to be supplied principally from long-haul sources in Brazil and Australia and the bauxite market from Australia and West Africa.

## The impact of random shocks on ship demand

No discussion of sea transport demand would be complete without reference to the impact of politics. *Random shocks* which upset the stability of the economic system may contribute to the cyclical process. Weather changes, wars, new resources, commodity price changes, are all candidates. These differ from cycles because they are unique, often precipitated by some particular event, and their impact on the shipping market is often very severe.

The most important influence on the shipping market are economic shocks. These are specific economic disturbances which are superimposed on business cycles, often with dramatic effects. A prominent example was the 1930s depression which followed the Wall Street Crash of 1929 and caused trade to decline. More recent examples, the effects of which are clearly visible in Figure 4.2, are the two oil price shocks which

C
H
A
P
T
E
R
4

happened in 1973 and 1979. On both occasions, industrial output and seaborne trade suddenly declined, setting off a shipping depression. Some economists think the whole cyclical process can be explained by a stream of random shocks which make the economy oscillate at its 'resonant frequency'. The US financial crisis of the early 1990s, the Asia Crisis of 1997 and the stock market crash in 2000 are other examples. The singular feature of these economic shocks is that their timing is unpredictable and they bring about a sudden and unexpected change in ship demand.

In addition to economic shocks, from time to time political events such as a localized war, a revolution, the political nationalization of foreign assets or strikes can disrupt trade. Events of this type do not necessarily impact directly on ship demand; it is generally their indirect consequences that are significant. The various wars between Israel and Egypt had important repercussions, owing to the proximity of the Suez Canal and its strategic importance as a shipping route between the Mediterranean and the Indian Ocean. The more protracted and extensive war between Iran and Iraq had no such effect, and if anything probably reduced the demand for sea transport by encouraging oil importers to obtain their supplies from other sources, most of which were closer to the market. The impact of the Korean war in the early 1950s was felt through its effect on commodity stockpiling, while the invasion of Kuwait by Iraq in 1990 created a short tanker boom because speculators started to use tankers for oil storage.

Having made these reservations, the regularity with which political events have, by one means or another, turned the shipping market on its head is quite striking. Leaving aside the First and Second World Wars, since 1945 there have been at least nine political incidents that have had a significant influence on ship demand:

- The Korean War, which started in early 1950. Although cargo associated directly with the war was mainly transported by ships of the US reserve fleet, political uncertainty sparked off a stockbuilding boom in Western countries.
- The Suez crisis, the nationalization of the Suez Canal by the Egyptian government in July 1956 and the subsequent invasion of Egypt and closure of the canal in November. Oil tankers trading to Europe were diverted round the Cape, and this created a sudden increase in ship demand.
- The Six Day War between Israel and Egypt in May 1967 resulted in the closure of the Suez Canal. European oil imports were again diverted round the Cape.
- The closure of the Tap Line oil pipeline between Saudi Arabia and the Mediterranean in 1970 redirected crude oil previously shipped through the pipeline around the Cape.
- The nationalization of Libyan oil assets in August 1973 resulted in the oil companies turning to the more distant Middle East producers for oil supplies.
- The Yom Kippur War in October 1973 and the OPEC production cut-back triggered the collapse of the tanker market. The associated oil price rise had an effect on the world economy and the shipping market that was to last more than a decade.

- The 1979 Iran Revolution and the temporary cessation of Iranian oil exports precipitated a major increase in the price of crude oil, with significant repercussions for the world economy and the shipping market.
- The 1990–1 Gulf War which resulted in the closure of the Dortyol pipeline and a phase of short-term oil stockbuilding. Both increased tanker demand.
- The Venezuelan oil strike in 2002–3 which reduced Venezuela's exports to almost nothing for several months, requiring US imports to be sourced from more distant suppliers

Other political events have had a more localized effect on the shipping market. For example, the Falklands War in 1982 resulted in the British government chartering ships from UK owners. In the early 1960s, the Cuban crisis resulted in Cuban sugar exports being diverted to the USSR and China, while US importers obtained their supplies from other sources, again causing some disruption of the shipping market. The Iran–Iraq War of 1982 had localized effects on the tanker market.

On this evidence it is clear that any balanced view of the development of the shipping market must take account of potentially important facts of a political nature. Information of this type is often outside the experience of market analysts, with the result that few market forecasts take very much account of such factors. However, in this case, the facts speak for themselves in emphasizing the importance of this topic as a regular contributor to the mercurial behaviour of ship demand.

## Transport costs and the long-run demand function

Finally, we come to the cost of sea transport. Many of the developments in sea trade of the type discussed in the previous section depend on the economics of the shipping operation. Raw materials will only be transported from distant sources if the cost of the shipping operation can be reduced to an acceptable level or some major benefit is obtained in quality of product. This makes transport costs a significant factor for industry – according to an EEC study, in the early 1980s transport costs accounted for 20% of the cost of dry bulk cargo delivered to countries within the Community.[8]

Over the last century, improved efficiency, bigger ships and more effective organization of the shipping operation have brought about a steady reduction in transport costs and higher quality of service. In fact the cost of shipping a ton of coal from the Atlantic to the Pacific, which hardly changed between 1950 and 1994, was achieved by using bigger ships (Figure 4.6). In 1950 the coal would have travelled in a 20,000 dwt vessel at a cost of $10–15 per ton. Forty years later a 150,000 dwt bulker would be used, still at $10–15 per ton. There can be little doubt that this has contributed materially to the growth of international trade. Developing this point, Kindleberger comments: 'what the railway did for the development of national markets in England and France the development of cheap ocean shipping has done for world trade. New channels of trade have been opened up, new links forged.'[9] Although transport costs may not appear to have such a dramatic influence upon seaborne trade as the world economy, their long-term effect on trade development should not be underrated.

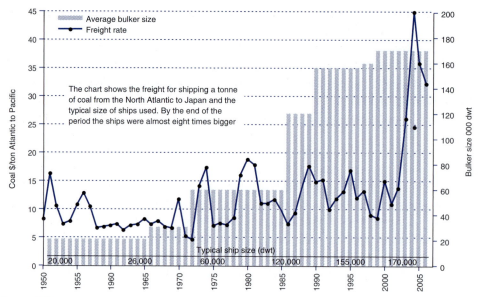

**Figure 4.6**
Coal transport costs from Hampton Roads to Japan, 1950–2006
Source: Compiled by Martin Stopford from various broker's reports

## 4.4 THE SUPPLY OF SEA TRANSPORT

In the introduction to this chapter we characterized the supply of shipping services as being slow and ponderous in its response to changes in demand. Merchant ships generally take about a year to build and delivery may take 2–3 years if the shipyards are busy. This prevents the market from responding promptly to any sudden upsurge in demand. Once built, the ships have a physical life of 15–30 years, so responding to a fall in demand is a lengthy business, particularly when there is a large surplus to be removed. Our aim in this section is to explain how this adjustment process is controlled.

### The decision-makers who control supply

We start with the decision-makers. The supply of ships is controlled, or influenced, by four groups of decision-makers: shipowners, shippers/charterers, the bankers who finance shipping, and the various regulatory authorities who make rules for safety. Shipowners are the primary decision-makers, ordering new ships, scrapping old ones and deciding when to lay up tonnage. Shippers may become shipowners themselves or influence shipowners by issuing time charters. Bank lending influences investment and it is often banks who exert the financial pressure that leads to scrapping in a weak market. Regulators affect supply through safety or environmental legislation which affects the transport capacity of the fleet. For example, the update to International Maritime Organization (IMO) Regulation 13G introduced in December 2003 requires single hull tankers to be phased out by 2010, leaving shipowners with no choice over the life extension of their ships.[10]

At this point, a warning is needed. Because the supply of shipping capacity is controlled by this small group of decision-makers, the supply-side relationships in the shipping model are behavioural. If we draw an analogy with a poker game, there are many ways of playing a particular hand. The player may be cautious, or he may decide to bluff. All his opponent can do is make the best judgement he can based on an assessment of character and how he played previous hands. Exactly the same problem faces shipping analysts trying to judge the relationship between, for example, freight rates and newbuilding orders. The fact that high freight rates have stimulated orders in the past is no guarantee that the relationship will hold in future. Market behaviour cannot be explained in purely economic terms. In 1973, when freight rates were very high, shipowners ordered more tankers than could possibly have been required to meet even the most optimistic forecast of oil trade growth. Similarly, in 1982–3 and 1999 when freight rates were low, there was an ordering boom for bulk carriers. It is in situations like this that clear-sighted analysts have something to say.

## The merchant fleet

The starting point for a discussion of the supply of sea transport is the merchant fleet. The development of the fleet between 1963 and 2005 is shown in Figure 4.7. Although it was a bumpy ride, this was a period of rapid growth and the merchant fleet increased from 82 m.dwt in 1963 to 740 m.dwt in 2004. It was a period of great change, and over the forty years the ship type composition of the fleet changed radically.

In the long run scrapping and deliveries determine the rate of fleet growth. Since the average economic life of a ship is about 25 years, only a small proportion of the fleet is scrapped each year, so the pace of adjustment to changes in the market is measured in years, not months. A key feature of the shipping market model is the mechanism by which supply adjusts when ship demand does not turn out as expected. Looking back over the last three decades we find examples of the merchant fleet in both expansion and contraction phases. It can be seen in Figure 4.7 that the adjustment process involved changes in the type of ship within the fleet.

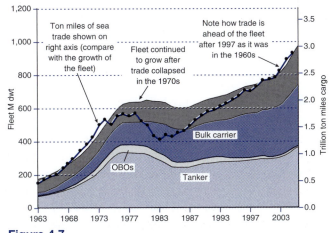

**Figure 4.7**
World fleet by ship type 1973–2006
Source: *Fearnleys Annual Review* (cargo)

Starting in the early 1960s, the *oil tanker fleet* went through a cycle of growth and contraction that took over 20 years to achieve. Between 1962 and 1974 the demand for seaborne oil transport, measured in ton miles, almost quadrupled and, despite the expansion of shipyard capacity, by the late 1960s supply could not keep up with demand (compare sea trade growth with fleet growth in Figure 4.7). As a result, there was an acute shortage of tanker capacity; in the early 1970s tankers were in such short supply that ships were sold 'off the stocks' for twice their original contract price – in the peak freight market of 1973 the profits on a few voyages were sufficient to pay off the investment in the ship. This led to record orders for new ships.

In the mid-1970s the whole process was thrown into reverse. Over the next decade tanker demand fell by 60% and the tanker market was confronted with the problem of bringing supply and demand into balance. It took about 10 years for supply to adjust to such a major change in demand. The fleet statistics in Figure 4.7 show what happened. After the collapse of the trade in 1975, the fleet continued to grow as the orders placed in 1973 were delivered, reaching a peak of 336 m.dwt in 1977. Scrapping did not start until the owners of the vessels became convinced that there was no future for them. This position was reached in the early 1980s when the second-hand price of VLCCs, some of which had cost $50–60 million to build in the mid-1970s, fell to $3 million. There was so little demand that sometimes ships put to auction did not attract a bid. The only buyers were shipbreakers. As scrap sales increased the fleet started to decline, reaching a trough in 1985. When the oil trade recovered in the late 1980s, supply and demand grew closer together, and freight rates increased. The whole cycle took about 14 years and by 2007 the tanker fleet was still only 354 m.dwt.

The *combined carrier fleet* links the wet and dry markets. Combination tonnage was pioneering in the early 1950s to obtain high cargo performance by carrying oil in one direction with a return load of dry cargo. However, real growth of the fleet was sparked off by the closure of the Suez Canal in 1967, when combined carrier owners, who had previously traded mainly in dry cargo, were able to take advantage of the very favourable oil freight market. Many orders were placed in the next few years and the fleet reached a peak of 48.7 m.dwt in 1978 and then declined to below 20 m.dwt in the 1990s. Most of the fleet is in the 80,000–200,000 dwt size group, which limits its activities in dry bulk to the larger bulk cargoes such as iron ore, or part cargoes of grain and coal.

Dry *bulk carriers* started to appear in the shipping market in the late 1950s, and between 1963 and 1996 the bulk fleet grew from 17 m.dwt to 237 m.dwt. The use of large bulk carriers played an integral part in the growth of major deep-sea bulk trades such as iron ore and coal, because economies of scale allowed these raw materials to be imported at very low cost. During the same period, there was a progressive switch of cargoes such as grain, sugar, minor ores, and steel products, which had previously been carried in'tweendeckers or as bottom cargo in liners, into dry bulk carriers. The market widening meant that the market share of bulk tonnage grew steadily during the 1960s and 1970s at the expense of the multi-deck fleet, with a progressive upward movement in ship size and none of the chronic overcapacity problems encountered in the oil market.

**Table 4.2** The world cargo fleet at 1st January (m.dwt)

| | Size of fleet (m.dwt) | | | | % growth rate per annum | | |
|---|---|---|---|---|---|---|---|
| | 1980 | 1990 | 2000 | 2007 | 1980–90 | 1990–2000 | 2000–2007 |
| Bulk carriers | 140.7 | 203.4 | 266.8 | 369.7 | 4% | 3% | 5% |
| Oil tankers | 339.3 | 262.9 | 307.0 | 363.9 | –3% | 2% | 2% |
| Combined carriers | 47.4 | 30.3 | 14.9 | 9.4 | –4% | –7% | –6% |
| Containerships | 9.9 | 26.3 | 64.7 | 128.0 | 10% | 9% | 10% |
| MPP | 8.5 | 16.8 | 19.0 | 23.6 | 7% | 1% | 3% |
| Reefer | 5.8 | 7.4 | 8.0 | 7.3 | 3% | 1% | –1% |
| Car carriers | 1.9 | 4.0 | 5.7 | 8.7 | 8% | 3% | 6% |
| Ro-Ro | 3.7 | 6.6 | 8.1 | 9.5 | 6% | 2% | 2% |
| LPG | 5.1 | 6.9 | 10.2 | 11.9 | 3% | 4% | 2% |
| LNG | 2.9 | 3.9 | 7.1 | 15.2 | 3% | 6% | 11% |
| Sub total | 565.1 | 568.6 | 711.6 | 947.2 | 0% | 2% | 4% |
| General cargo | — | — | 42.8 | 38.9 | — | — | –1% |
| Grand total | — | — | 754.4 | 986.1 | — | — | 4% |

Source: CRSL, *Shipping Review and Outlook*

In recent years the major change in the deep-sea liner trades was the replacement of traditional liners by cellular container ships. The first containership went into service in 1966. By 2007 the fleet had grown to 128 m.dwt, averaging 10% per annum growth during the previous 27 years (Table 4.2). The fleet of MPP vessels, which are specifically fitted for the carriage of containers, also grew at 3% per annum and the reefer fleet stayed about the same size. However, the general cargo fleet, which consists mainly of small multi-deck vessels being made obsolete by containerization, declined from 42.8 m.dwt in 2000 to 38.9 m dwt in 2007 (note that the definitions of ship type categories in Table 4.2 differ slightly from those in Table 2.5).

In practice, the different ship types discussed above do not operate in separate and self-contained markets. Although there is much specialization in the shipping market, there is also a high degree of substitution between ship types. In a volatile market, flexibility is desirable and some ships, such as 'tweendeckers and combined carriers, are built with the objective of being flexible. This leads us to the important principle of lateral mobility (which is discussed further in Section 14.2): shipowners redeploy surplus vessels into more profitable applications in other sectors of the market. An example of the way this works in practice is provided by the following extract from a broker's report:

> Larger vessels of 40,000 dwt and above were particularly economical on the long hauls, and charterers now quoted substantially reduced rates for such trades. This pressed medium-sized bulk carriers of about 30,000 dwt into finding employment in trades previously serviced by vessels of 10–20,000 dwt and in the scrap trade from US to Japan units of 25–35,000 dwt were successfully introduced … with tankers and large dry cargo vessels taking care of the main part of the grain

movements a new market was created for Liberty type vessels as barges in India and Pakistan where ports cannot accommodate large vessels.[11]

Thus ships move freely from one market sector to another. As we have noted, combined carriers are built for this purpose and were used very successfully in 1967 when the Suez Canal was closed, as the following quotation suggests:

> The improvement in freights was mainly brought about by the many combined carriers which switched to oil transportation as did the majority of tankers employed in the grain trades. Heavy demand for large conventional bulk carriers to replace the combined carriers caused a considerable number of this kind of newbuilding in the 50–100,000 dwt class to find a very favourable market when commissioned.[12]

Perhaps the most striking feature of the world merchant fleet during the last 30 years has been the rapid escalation of ship sizes, particularly in the bulk sector of the fleet. In the tanker market there was a steady increase in the average size of tankers until the early 1980s when the size structure stabilized. In bulk carriers there was a similar upward movement in ship size, but the pattern was more evenly spread between the different ship size groups with the fleets of Handy vessels (20,000–40,000 dwt), Panamax (40,000–80,000 dwt) and large bulk carriers over 80,000 dwt all expanding. Larger and more efficient ships have progressively pushed their way into the market and depressed rates for smaller sizes. At the same time investment for specialization, as in the case of car carriers and chemical tankers, played an important part in the development of the fleet. These apparently conflicting objectives emphasize the complexity of the investment decisions facing the modern shipowner.

## Fleet productivity

Although the fleet is fixed in size, the productivity with which the ships are used adds an element of flexibility.[13] Past productivity statistics in Figure 4.8 show how much the productivity of the various sections of the fleet has changed over the past decade. For example, productivity expressed in terms of ton miles per deadweight reached a peak of 35,000 in 1973, but by 1985 this had fallen to 22,000; in other words, productivity had fallen by over a third. A few years later it had increased by nearly half to 32,000. The productivity in tons per deadweight shows a similar pattern, peaking at 8 in the early 1960s, falling to a trough of 4.6 in 1983, and then reaching 7.5 in 2005. The major swings in productivity in Figure 4.8 are mainly due to the deep recessions in the 1970s and 1980s when ships were very cheap and as a result were used inefficiently. In normal times the average ship carries about 7 tons of cargo per deadweight and does around 35,000 tanker ton miles.

The nature of these productivity changes becomes more apparent when we look in detail at what merchant ships actually do. Carrying cargo is just one small part of the story. As an illustration Figure 4.9 shows what the 'average' VLCC was doing during a typical year, 1991. Surprisingly, it spent only 137 days carrying cargo – little more than one-third of its time. What happened to the rest? Ballast time accounted for 111 days and cargo handling for 40 days. The remaining 21% of the time was spent in non-trading activities. This included incidents (i.e. accidents), repair, lay-up, waiting, short-term storage and long-term storage. When we analyse these activities more systematically, it becomes apparent that some are determined by

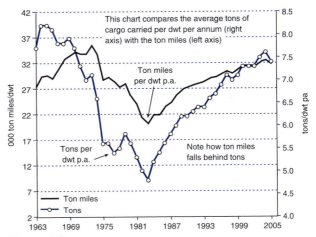

**Figure 4.8**
Performance of the world merchant fleet, 1963–2005
Source: *Fearnleys Review*

both the physical performance of the fleet, and market forces. In a tight market the time on other activities would reduce, increasing supply, but even in the very tight market of 2007 an average of 200 days at sea per ship across a mixed fleet of tankers and bulk carriers was reported.[14]

The productivity of a fleet of ships measured in ton miles per deadweight depends upon four main factors: speed, port time, deadweight utilization and loaded days at sea (see Section 6.5 for a more detailed discussion of productivity and its financial implications for the shipping company).

First, *speed* determines the time a vessel takes on a voyage. Tracking surveys show that, owing to a combination of operational factors, even in good markets ships generally operate at average speeds well below their design speed. For example, in 1991 the fleet of tankers over 200,000 dwt had an average design speed of 15.1 knots, but the average operating speed between ports was 11.5 knots.[15] The speed of the fleet will change with time. If new ships are delivered with a lower design speed, this will progressively reduce the transport capacity of the fleet. Similarly, as ships age,

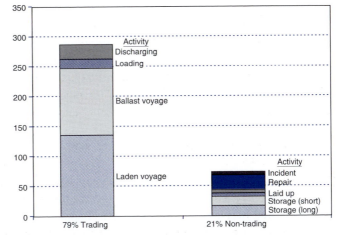

**Figure 4.9**
VLCC operating performance: time use of average VLCC
Source: Clarkson Research Studies, VLCC Quality Survey (1991)

unless exceptionally well maintained, hull fouling will gradually reduce the maximum operating speed.

Second, *port time* plays an important part in the productivity equation. The physical performance of the ships and terminals sets the upper limit. For example, the introduction of containerization dramatically reduced port time for liners. Organization of the transport operation also plays a part. After the oil crisis in 1973, changes in the oil industry reduced the opportunities for maximizing the efficiency of tanker operations by the transport planning departments of the major oil companies. Congestion produces temporary reductions in performance. Middle East port congestion absorbed large amounts of shipping in the mid-1970s, and in 1980 there was heavy congestion at Hampton Roads, USA, with queues of over 100 bulk carriers waiting to load coal. This congestion reduced the supply of ships available for trading.

Third, *deadweight utilization* refers to the cargo capacity lost owing to bunkers, stores, etc. which prevent a full load from being carried. A rule-of-thumb estimate of 95% for bulk carriers and 96% for tankers is derived from surveys. During the recessions of the 1970s and 1980s there was an increasing tendency for owners to carry part cargoes, reducing deadweight utilization to well below these levels. For example, *the World Tanker Fleet Review* estimated that at the end of 1986 about 16.6 m.dwt of tanker capacity was lost owing to part cargoes.

Finally, a vessel's time is divided between *loaded days at sea* and 'unproductive' days (in ballast, port, or off hire). A reduction in unproductive time allows an increase in loaded days at sea, and one can interpret changes in this variable in terms of changes in port time, etc. Vessels designed for cargo flexibility can improve their loaded time at sea because they are able to switch cargoes for backhauls. The fleet's operating performance changes in response to market conditions, as is clearly demonstrated by the changes in tanker productivity shown in Figure 4.8. Faced with a depressed freight market, the first response of the merchant fleet is generally to reduce its pace of operation. To save bunker costs, owners reduce the operating speed and, since cargoes are less readily available, waiting times increase. Eventually ships that are too expensive to operate are laid up. Tankers are frequently used for oil storage, either in port or in offshore installations. Bulk carriers may be used to store coal or grain. Some tankers in storage are on contracts lasting only a few months, after which they will become available for trading. Others used in offshore oil production may be employed on long contracts, so for practical purposes they are no longer part of the trading fleet.

## Shipbuilding production

The shipbuilding industry plays an active part in the fleet adjustment process described in the previous paragraphs. In principle, the level of output adjusts to changes in demand – and over long periods this does happen. Thus, in 1974, shipbuilding output accounted for about 12% of the merchant fleet, whereas in 1996 it had fallen to 4.7%, but by 2007 it was back up to 9%. Adjustments in the level of shipbuilding output on this scale do not take place quickly or easily. Shipbuilding is a long-cycle business, and the time-lag between ordering and delivering a ship is between 1 and 4 years, depending on the size of orderbook held by the shipbuilders. Orders must be placed on the basis of an estimate of future demand and in the past these estimates have often proved to be wrong, most dramatically in the mid-1970s when deliveries of VLCCs continued for several years after demand had gone into decline. In addition, downward adjustments in shipbuilding supply may be seriously hampered by political intervention to prevent job losses.

From the point of view of the shipping industry, the type of ship built is important because peaks and troughs in the deliveries of specific ship types have an impact on their market prospects. In recent years there have been major changes in the product range of ships built by the merchant shipbuilding industry. These are illustrated graphically in Figure 4.10.

Tanker production illustrates the extreme swings which can occur in shipping investment. Tanker newbuilding dominated the period 1963–75, increasing from 5 m.dwt in 1963 to 45 m.dwt in 1975, when it accounted for 75% of shipbuilding output. The collapse of the tanker market after the 1973 oil crisis reversed this trend and tanker output fell to a trough of 3.6 m.dwt in 1984, accounting for only 1% of the tanker fleet. In the absence of VLCC orders, the tanker deliveries during the period 1978–84 were principally products tankers or 80,000–120,000 dwt crude oil tankers. As the

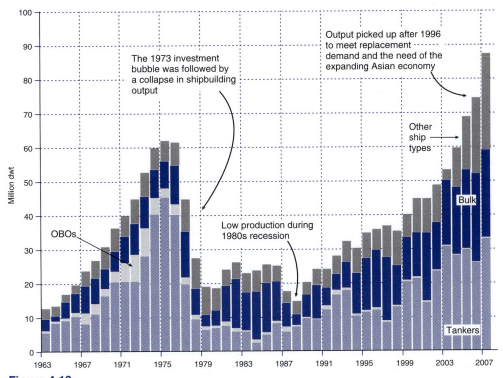

**Figure 4.10**
World shipbuilding deliveries by type, 1963–2007
Source: Fearnleys, Clarkson Research

tanker fleet built in the 1970s needed to be replaced the trend was again reversed, and by 2006 tanker production had increased to 25.8 m.dwt.

Compared with oil tankers, the dry bulk carrier newbuilding market has been comparatively stable since the mid-1960s. However, investment has been cyclical, with deliveries fluctuating between 5 and 15 m.dwt per annum. A very low output of 4 m.dwt in 1979 was followed by the 'mini-boom' in the dry cargo market during 1979–80. Heavy ordering resulted in peak deliveries of 14.7 m.dwt in 1985, accounting for 59% of total world shipbuilding output in deadweight tonnage terms. In a very real sense bulk carriers took over the dominant role in the shipbuilding market previously occupied by VLCCs, and by the mid-1980s were facing the same problems of overpro-duction and chronic surplus. One consequence of this heavy investment was a deep recession in the mid-1980s. Ordering stopped and deliveries of bulk carriers fell to 3.2 m.dwt in 1988. By 2006 deliveries were back up to 26 m.dwt, and so the cycles continued.

The remaining category of shipbuilding output comprises an enormous range of mer-chant cargo and service vessels – ro-ros, container ships, conventional general cargo vessels, fishing boats, ferries, cruise liners, tugs, etc. The total tonnage of deliveries in 2007 was 22.7 m.dwt, accounting for 32% of total output, and the newbuilding trend in this sector has been comparatively stable over the last two decades at about this level. Although these ship types account for only a third of the total merchant shipbuilding output in deadweight terms, in terms of work content they are much more important – for example, a deadweight ton of ferry tonnage may contain four or five times as much work as a deadweight ton of tanker tonnage. For this reason, the various ship types in this category are substantially more important to the shipbuilding industry than might appear at first sight.

## Scrapping and losses

The rate of growth of the merchant fleet depends on the balance between deliveries of new ships and deletions from the fleet in the form of ships scrapped or lost at sea. This balance changed radically during the late 1970s, as can be seen from Figure 4.11. In 1973, only about 5 m.dwt of vessels were scrapped, compared with deliveries of over 50 m.dwt, with the result that the fleet grew rapidly. By 1982, scrapping had overtaken deliveries for the first time since the Second World War, accounting for 30 m.dwt compared with 26 m.dwt of deliveries. Thus scrapping, which appeared to be of little significance in 1973, was of major importance by the early 1980s.

Whilst it is clear that scrapping has a significant part to play in removing ships from the market, explaining or predicting the age at which a ship will actually be scrapped is an extremely complex matter, and one that causes considerable difficulties in judging the development of shipping capacity. The reason is that scrapping depends on the balance of a number of factors that can interact in many different ways. The main ones are age, technical obsolescence, scrap prices, current earnings and market expectations.

Age is the primary factor determining the tonnage of vessels scrapped. Ships deteriorate as they grow older and the cost of routine repairs and maintenance increases; thus the

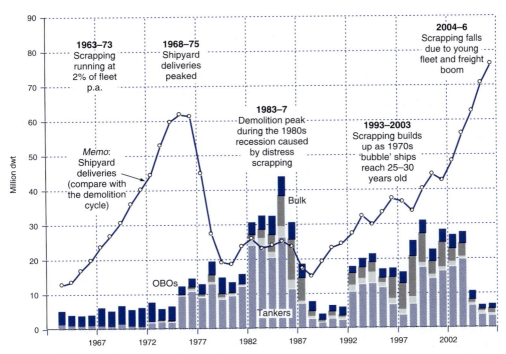

**Figure 4.11**
World ship demolition sales by type, 1963–2006
Source: *Fearnleys Review*, Clarkson Research

owners of elderly vessels face the combination of heavier costs and more time off hire for planned and unplanned maintenance. Because physical deterioration is a gradual process, there is no specific age at which a ship is scrapped; a look through *Lloyd's Demolition Register* generally reveals a few examples of vessels scrapped with an age of over 60 or 70 years, and at the other extreme tankers sold for demolition at as little as 10 years. In 2007, when 216 vessels were scrapped, the average scrapping age was 27 years for tankers and 32 years for dry cargo vessels. In each case there was a wide spread.

Technical obsolescence may reduce the age at which a particular type of vessel is scrapped because it is superseded by a more efficient ship type. For example, the high scrapping rate of multi-deckers in the late 1960s is attributable to these vessels being made obsolete by containerization. Obsolescence also extends to the ship's machinery and gear – tankers fitted with inefficient steam turbines were among the first to go to the scrapyard when prices rose in the 1970s.

The decision to scrap is also influenced by the scrap prices. Scrap ships are sold to shipbreakers, who demolish them and sell the scrap to the steel industry. Scrap prices fluctuate widely, depending upon the state of supply and demand in the steel industry and the availability of scrap metal from sources such as shipbreaking or the demolition of vehicles, which form the largest sources of supply. A period of extensive ship scrapping may even depress prices of scrap metal – a process that is accentuated by the fact that shipping surpluses often occur simultaneously with trade cycle downswings in the industrialized regions when demand for steel is also depressed.

Most importantly, the scrapping of a ship is a business decision and depends on the owner's expectations of the future operating profitability of the vessel and his financial position. If, during a recession, he believes that there is some chance of a freight market boom in the reasonably near future, he is unlikely to sell unprofitable ships for scrap because the possible earnings during a freight market boom are so great that they may justify incurring a small operating loss for a period of years up to that date. Naturally the oldest ships will be forced out by the cost of repairs but, where vessels are still serviceable, extensive scrapping to remove surplus capacity is only likely to occur when the shipping community as a whole believes that there is no prospect of profitable employment for the older vessels in the foreseeable future, or when companies need the cash so urgently that they are forced into 'distress' sales to shipbreakers. It follows that scrapping will occur only when the industry's reserves of cash and optimism have been run down.

## Freight revenue

Finally, the supply of sea transport is influenced by freight rates. This is the ultimate regulator which the market uses to motivate decision-makers to adjust capacity in the short term, and to find ways of reducing their costs and improving their services in the long term. In the shipping industry there are two main pricing regimes, the freight market and the liner market. Liner shipping provides transport for small quantities of cargo for many customers and is essentially a retail shipping business[16], accepting cargo from a wide range of customers and a very competitive one. In contrast bulk shipping is a wholesale operation, selling transport for shiploads of cargo to a small number of industrial customers at individually negotiated prices. By standardizing the cargo units containerization has brought the two segments closer together in economic terms, and in both cases the pricing system is central to the supply of transport. In the short run, supply responds to prices as ships adjust their operation speed and move to and from lay-up, while liner operators adjust their services. In the longer term, freight rates contribute to the investment decisions which result in scrapping and ordering of ships. How this works in the bulk market is the subject of the next section. Liner pricing, which has a different economic structure, is discussed in Chapter 13.

## 4.5. THE FREIGHT RATE MECHANISM

The third part of the shipping market model, labelled C in Figure 4.1, is the freight market. This is the adjustment mechanism linking supply and demand. The way it operates is simple enough. Shipowners and shippers negotiate to establish a freight rate which reflects the balance of ships and cargoes available in the market. If there are too many ships the freight rate is low, while if there are too few ships it will be high. Once this freight rate is established, shippers and shipowners adjust to it and eventually this brings supply and demand into balance. We will use the perfect competition model to analyse the shipping market, and the economic concepts we will use to analyse this process more formally are the supply function, the demand function and the equilibrium price.[17]

## The supply and demand functions

The *supply function* for an individual ship, shown in Figure 4.12a, is a J-shaped curve describing the amount of transport the owner provides at each level of freight rates. The ship in this example is a 280,000 dwt VLCC. When the freight rate falls below $155 per million ton miles the owner puts it into lay-up, offering no transport. As freight rates rise past $155 per million ton miles he breaks lay-up but, to save fuel, steams at the lowest viable speed of 11 knots per hour. If he trades loaded with cargo at this speed for 137 days per annum (the loaded operating days we discussed in Figure 4.9), he will supply 10.1 btm of transport in a year (i.e. $11 \times 24 \times 137 \times 280,000$). At higher freight

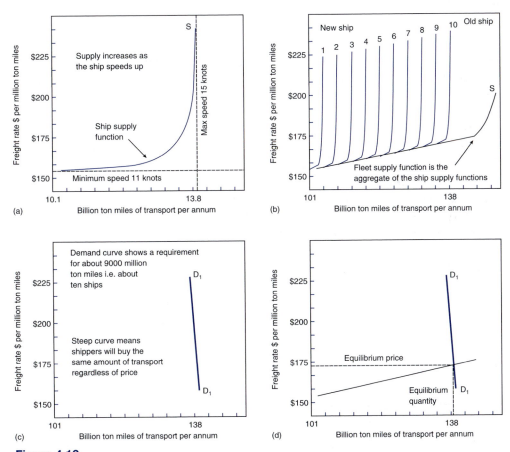

**Figure 4.12**
Shipping supply and demand functions: (a) supply function for single ship (VLCC); (b) supply function for fleet of ten VLCCs; (c) oil transport demand function; (d) supply–demand equilibrium
Source: Martin Stopford 2005

rates he speeds up until at about $220 per million ton miles the ship is at full speed of 15 knots and supplying 13.8 btm of sea transport per year (a lot of transport for just one ship!). Thus by increasing freight rates the market has obtained an extra 36% supply. Evidence of this process at work can be seen in Figure 4.8, which shows how the productivity of the world fleet peaked in 1973 when freight rates were very high, fell in the early 1980s when freight rates were very low, and then increased again in the 1990s as freight rates improved.

Economic theory can help to define the shape of the supply curve. Provided the market is perfectly competitive, the shipowner maximizes his profit by operating his ship at the speed at which marginal cost (i.e. the cost of providing an additional ton mile of transport) equals the freight rate. The relationship between speed and freight rates can be defined as follows:[18]

$$S = \sqrt{\frac{R}{3p.k.d}} \qquad (4.1)$$

where $S$ is the optimum speed in miles per day, $R$ the voyage freight rate, $p$ the price of fuel, $k$ the ship's fuel constant, and $d$ = distance. This equation defines the shape of the supply curve. In addition to freight rates the optimum speed depends on the price of fuel, the efficiency of the ship and the length of the voyage. We will discuss these costs in Chapter 6.

In reality the supply function is more complex than the simple speed–freight rates relationship described in the previous paragraphs. Speed is not the only way supply responds to freight rates. The owner may take advantage of a spell of low freight rates to put his ship into dry dock, or fix a short-term storage contract. At higher rates he may decide to ballast back to the Arabian Gulf through the shorter Suez Canal route rather than taking the longer 'free passage' round the Cape. All of these decisions affect supply. Similarly, freight rates are not the only way the market adjusts shipowners' revenue. During periods of surplus ships have to wait for cargo or accept small cargo parcels. This reduces the operating revenue in just the same way as a fall in freight rates, a factor often forgotten by owners and bankers doing cashflow forecasts on old ships. They may predict freight rates correctly but end up with an embarrassing cash deficit due to waiting time and part cargoes.

The next step is to show how the market adjusts the supply provided by a *fleet of ships*. To illustrate this process, the supply function for a fleet of 10 VLCCs is shown in Figure 4.12b. The fleet supply curve (S) is built up from the supply curves of individual ships of varying age and efficiency. In this example the age distribution of the fleet ranges from 2 to 20 years in intervals of 2 years. Ship 1 (the newest ship) has low daily operating costs and its lay-up point is $155 per million ton miles. Ship 10 (the oldest) has high operating costs and its lay-up point is $165 per million ton miles.

The *fleet supply function* works by moving ships in and out of service in response to freight rates. If freight rates fall below the operating costs of ship 10, it goes into lay-up and supply is reduced by one ship. Ship 9 breaks even and the other eight ships make a margin over their fixed expenses, depending on how efficient they are. If shippers only need five ships they can drop their offer to $160 per million ton miles, the lay-up point of ship 5. In this way supply responds to movements in freight rates. Over a longer period the supply can be increased by building new more efficient ships and reduced by scrapping old ones.

The slope of the short-term supply curve depends on three factors which determine the lay-up cost of the marginal ship. First, old ships generally have higher operating costs so the lay-up point will occur at a higher freight rate. We discuss this in Chapter 5. Second, bigger ships have lower transport costs per ton of cargo than small ships, so if big and small ships are competing for the same cargo, the bigger ship will have a lower lay-up point and will generally drive the smaller ships into lay-up during recessions. If the size of ships has been increasing over time, as has happened for most of the last century, the size and age will be correlated and there will be quite a steep slope to the supply curve which becomes very apparent during recessions. Third, the relationship between speed and freight rates is described in equation (4.1) above.

The *demand function* shows how charterers adjust to changes in price. The demand curve ($D_1$) in Figure 4.12c is almost vertical. This is mainly supposition, but there are several reasons why this shape is likely for most bulk commodities. The most convincing is the lack of any competing transport mode. Shippers need the cargo and, until they have time to make alternative arrangements, must ship it regardless of cost. Conversely cheap rates will not tempt shippers to take an extra ship. The fact that freight generally accounts for only a small proportion of material costs reinforces this argument.[19]

## Equilibrium and the importance of time

The supply and demand curves intersect at the equilibrium price. At this point buyers and sellers have found a mutually acceptable price. In Figure 4.12d the equilibrium price is $170 per million ton miles. At this price buyers are willing to hire 10 ships and owners are prepared to make 10 ships available. The equation balances.

But that is not the end of the story. If our aim is to understand why freight rates behave the way they do, it is just the beginning. We must be precise about *time-frame*. It is an additional dimension present in every decision because market, prices are a blend of the present and the future expectations, the short run and the long. In the real world the price at which buyers and sellers are prepared to trade depends on how much time they have to adjust their positions. There are three time periods to consider: the *momentary* equilibrium when the deal must be done immediately; the *short run*, when there is time to adjust supply by short-term measures such as lay-up, reactivation, combined carriers switching markets or operating ships at a faster speed; and there is the *long run*, when shipowners have time to take delivery of new ships and shippers have time to rearrange their supply sources. We will look at each of these in turn.

### MOMENTARY EQUILIBRIUM

Momentary equilibrium describes the freight rate negotiated for 'prompt' ships and cargoes. It is the spot market that owners and charterers deal with day by day. The ships are ready to load, the cargoes are awaiting transport and a deal must be done. The shipowner

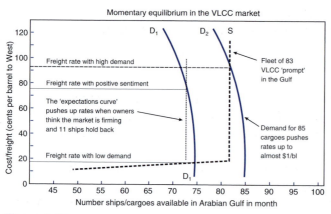

**Figure 4.13**
Momentary equilibrium in the VLCC market
Source: Martin Stopford 2007

is in the same position as a farmer when he arrives at market with his pig (see Section 5.8). Within this time frame the shipping market is highly fragmented, falling into the regions so familiar in brokers' reports – the Arabian Gulf, the Caribbean, the United Stated Atlantic Coast, the Pacific, and the Atlantic, etc. Local shortages and surpluses build up, creating temporary peaks and troughs which show up as spikes on the freight chart. This is the market that owners are constantly trying to anticipate when selecting their next cargo, or deciding whether to risk a ballast voyage to a better loading point.

Once these decisions are taken and the ship is in position, the options are very limited. The owner can 'fix' at the rate on offer, or sit and lose money. Charterers with cargoes face the same choice. The two parties negotiate to find a price at which supply equals demand. Figure 4.13 illustrates how this works out in practice. Suppose there are about 75 cargoes on offer in the loading zone during the month. The demand curve, marked $D_1$, intercepts the horizontal axis at 75 cargoes, but as the freight rate rises it curves to the left because at very high freight rates a few cargoes may be withdrawn or perhaps amalgamated to allow a different size of ship to be used.

There are 83 ships available to load and the supply curve S (the dotted line) slopes gently up from 15 cents a barrel to 21 cents a barrel until all 83 ships are contracted and then it goes vertical. In this case demand is only for 75 ships, so there are more ships than cargoes. Since the alternative to fixing is earning nothing, rates fall to operating costs, which for 75 cargoes equates to 20 cents a barrel, shown by the intersection of S and $D_1$. If the number of cargoes increases to 85 ($D_2$) there are more cargoes than ships. Charterers bid desperately to find a ship and the freight rate shoots up to almost $1 per barrel. A swing of 10 cargoes is quite common, but the effect on rates is dramatic.

But never forget that this is an auction and in this very short-term situation market sentiment is often the real driver. If there are a few more ships than cargoes, but owners believe that rates are rising, they may decide to wait. Suddenly there are more cargoes than ships and rates rise, at which point the reticent owners enter the market and fix at 'last done'. This is shown by the 'expectation curve' in Figure 4.13. Sometimes owners attempt to hide their ships from charterers by reporting the presence of only one ship in their fleet, or waiting outside the loading area. But the fundamentals have the last word. If the surplus of ships persists, the owners holding back may be unable to fix at all and as they start to haemorrhage cash, rates quickly collapse. So when supply and demand are roughly balanced the shape of the supply curve is determined by sentiment rather than fundamentals, a problem that sometimes misleads analysts and traders.

## THE SHORT-RUN EQUILIBRIUM

In the 'short run' there is more time for owners and charterers to respond to price changes by moving ships in and out of lay-up, so the analysis is a little different.

The short-run supply curve shown in Figure 4.14a plots, for a given size of fleet, the ton miles of transport available at each level of freight rates. The transport supply is measured in thousands of billion ton miles per annum and the freight rate in dollars per thousand ton miles of cargo transported.

At point A, the supply offered is only 50,000 btm per annum because the least efficient ships are laid up; at point B, all ships are back in operation and the supply has risen to about 85,000 btm per annum; at point C, the fleet is at maximum speed and the whole fleet is at sea; finally, at point D, no further supply is obtained by increasing freight rates and the supply curve becomes almost vertical. Very high freight rates may tempt out a few remaining unutilized ships. For example, during the 1956 boom, 'A number of vessels half a century old and barely seaworthy obtained freights of up to five times the rate obtained a year earlier.'

If we now bring the *short-run demand curve* into the picture we can explain how freight rates are determined. The market settles at the freight rate at which supply equals demand. Consider the three different equilibrium points marked A, B and C in Figure 4.14b. At point A demand is low and the freight rate settles at point $F_1$. A major increase in demand to point B only pushes the freight rate up slightly because ships immediately come out of lay-up to meet increasing demand.[20] However, a small increase in demand to point C is sufficient to treble the level of freight rates because the

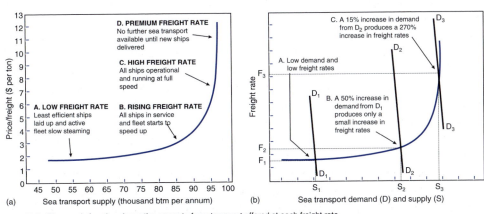

Note: The supply function shows the amount of sea transport offered at each freight rate

**Figure 4.14**
Short-run equilibrium: (a) short-run supply function; (b) short-run adjustment
Source: Martin Stopford 2007

market rate is now set by the oldest and least efficient ships which need very high freight rates to tempt them into service. Finally, with no more ships available charterers bid against each other for the available capacity. Depending on how badly they need transport, rates can go to any level. However, this is an unstable situation. Shippers look for cheaper supply sources and the high freight rates almost always trigger frenzied investment activity by owners and shippers.

### THE LONG RUN

Finally, we must consider the long run during which the size of the fleet can be adjusted by ordering new ships and scrapping old ones. The longer-term adjustment mechanism balances supply and demand through the three other markets we will discuss in Chapter 5: the sale and purchase market, the newbuilding market and the demolition market. As freight rates fall during a recession, the profitability of ships – and, consequently, their second-hand value – also falls. Eventually the price of the least efficient ships falls to the scrap price. Ships are scrapped, removing them permanently from the market and reducing the surplus. Falling second-hand prices also make new uses of the surplus tonnage financially viable; the use of supertankers for oil storage and the conversion of single hull tankers to ore carriers or offshore vessels are examples. In these ways the price mechanism gradually reduces the supply of ships to the market. Conversely, when a shortage of ships pushes up freight rates this works through to the sale and purchase market. Shipowners are keen to add to their fleets and, because there is a shortage of ships, shippers may decide to expand their own shipping operations. With more buyers than sellers, second-hand prices rise until used ships become more expensive than new-buildings. Frustrated shipowners turn to the newbuilding market and the orderbook expands rapidly. Two or three years later the fleet starts to grow.

To illustrate this process we can take the example of the adjustment of the tanker market over the period 1980–1992. Figure 4.15 shows the position of the supply–demand chart in 1980 (a), 1985 (b), 1991 (c) and 1992 (d). The freight rate is shown on the vertical axis measured in dollars per day and as an indicator of transport supply the tanker fleet is shown on the horizontal axis, measured in millions of tons dead weight. Neither of these units of measurement is strictly correct[21] but they illustrate the point. Figure 4.15e is a freight chart which shows the level of freight rates in each of the four years. Our aim is to explain how the supply and demand curves moved between the 4 years. In 1980 (Figure 4.15a) freight rates were moderately high at $15,000 per day, with the demand curve intersecting the 'kink' of the supply curve. By 1985 (Figure 4.15b) the supply curve has moved to the left as heavy scrapping reduced the tanker fleet from 320 m.dwt to 251 m.dwt, but demand had fallen even more to below 150 m.dwt due to the collapse in the crude oil trade after the oil price rises in 1979. This left 60 m.dwt of tankers laid up, extensive slow steaming, and the demand curve intersecting the supply curve way down its span at $D_{85}$. Freight rates averaged about $7,000 per day, close to operating costs.

Between 1985 and 1991 (Figure 4.15c), despite heavy scrapping, the tanker fleet fell by only 7 m.dwt, due to increased newbuilding in the late 1980s. As a result the supply

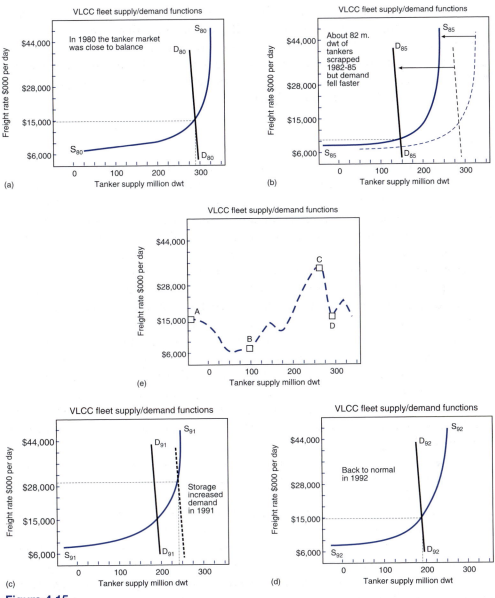

**Figure 4.15**
Long-term adjustment of supply and demand, 1980–92
Source: Martin Stopford 2004

curve moved very slightly to the left to $S_{91}$, but a growing oil trade increased demand by 30% to $D_{91}$, suggesting an equilibrium freight rate of about $15,000 per day. However, in 1991 another factor intervened. After the invasion of Kuwait in August 1990 oil traders used tankers as temporary storage, moving the demand curve temporarily to the right, shown by the dotted line in Figure 4.15c. Freight rates increased to $29,000 per day. Then in 1992 supply increased due to heavy deliveries and the demand curve

C
H
A
P
T
E
R
4

moved back to its 'normal' position as the temporary storage market disappeared. This was enough to drive freight rates down to $15,000 per day (Figure 4.15d).

It is the combination of volatile demand and a significant time-lag before supply adjusts to demand that creates the framework for shipping market cycles. Shipowners tend to base investment on the current state of the market – they order more ships when freight rates are high and fewer when freight rates are low. The delay in delivering these ships means, however, that demand may have changed by the time the ships are delivered so any cyclical tendency is amplified.[22] Our analysis of the length of shipping cycles in Chapter 3 showed that over half a century the average cycle was about 8 years long, which is about the length you would expect in a market with the adjustment mechanism we have discussed. It takes 2–3 years for new orders to be delivered, 2–3 years for scrapping to catch up, and 2–3 years for the market to build up a head of steam for the next round of ordering. In the 1930s Jan Tinbergen noticed this relationship and thought it might be modelled using a periodic model.[23]

### The effect of sentiment on the supply curve

There is a final issue to consider, the effect of sentiment on the supply function. The supply curves we have discussed so far (for example in Figure 4.15) move *horizontally* backwards and forwards, driven by the physical fundamentals as ships are scrapped and delivered. But changes in sentiment during the ongoing freight auction between charterers and shipowners can also move the curve *vertically*. For example if charterers are strong, confident and well informed they may be able to drive the curve down, whilst if owners are more confident, better informed and ready to hold back ships they may be able to drive the curve up so that for any given balance of supply and demand they get higher earnings.

To illustrate how this works in practice, Figure 4.16 plots Aframax tanker earnings against a rough estimate of the shipping capacity balance, measured as percentage surplus or deficit, between 1990 and 2007. The points are shown as diamonds, linked by a dotted line. The supply curve S1 is fitted to these points as a polynomial function. But the fit is not good. The years 1998, 1999, 2002 and 2003 (all weak years in the market) fall well below S1, whilst the good years 2000, 2005, 2006 and 2007 are way above. Linking the low points, which correspond to years of recession, produces a second supply curve S2. Similarly linking the high points, which occurred in strong markets, produces supply curve S3. It suggests that in the recession the supply curve moved down to S1, whilst in the boom it moved up to S2. Note also that in the very strong year 2004 the curves converged.

This complicates the freight model because the assumption in Figure 4.15 that earnings are uniquely defined by the percentage of surplus capacity is not necessarily correct. We now have two different supply curves S2 and S3, each giving different earnings levels for a given market balance. For example when the market is exactly in balance on the horizontal axis of Figure 4.16, S2 shows owners earning $19,000 per day whilst S3 says $37,000 per day, almost twice as much. This significant difference has a simple explanation. In years of recession the negotiation goes in the charterer's favour whilst in the boom the owners get the upper hand. During a sequence of good or

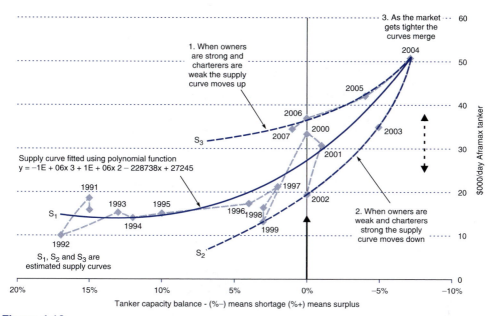

**Figure 4.16**
Analysis of vertical movement of the shipping supply curve
Source: Aframax earnings CRSL SRO Autumn 207; tanker capacity balance calculated by Martin Stopford for the tanker market as a whole

bad years the prevailing sentiment becomes part of the supply curve and continues to determine its shape until something changes sentiment, for example an economic shock. This happens in booms and recessions, so to predict earnings we need to know how sentiment has moved the supply curve. Unfortunately this makes forecasting freight rates a much more complex task because sentiment is harder to predict and changes much more quickly than the physical supply and demand fundamentals

## The shipping cycle model

Although periodic cyclical models of the type proposed by Tinbergen are theoretically attractive, the review of almost three centuries of cycles in Chapter 3 and the underlying economics make it unlikely that this sort of model will be very helpful in practical situations. In the course of this discussion we mentioned many of the factors which contemporaries thought were important. The same factors tend to appear time and again but rarely in the same form. Business cycles in the world economy, economic shocks, misjudgements by shipowners, shipyard overcapacity, and most importantly sentiment. Our task as economists is to reduce this apparently disorganized jumble of causes and effects to a more structured form which will help us to analyse the influences on cycles, and if we are lucky predict what might happen next.

One of the main reasons why shipping cycles are irregular is that they are not driven by a single economic model; they are produced by the interaction of five separate models, described in Figure 4.17. We will describe this as the shipping cycle

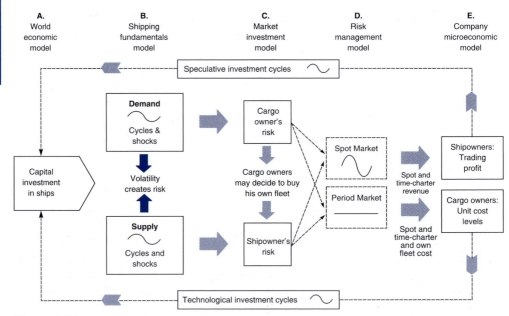

**Figure 4.17**
The shipping cycle composite mode
Source: Martin Stopford 2007

composite model. Segment A is the world economic model, segment B the shipping fundamentals model; segment C the market investment model; segment D the risk management model and Segment E the company microeconomic model. We will briefly discuss each of these in turn to show how it fits into the composite model.

The world economic model provides the main stimulus to the shipping cycles. Shipping is about sea transport, and the main purpose of the shipping cycle, as was discussed in Section 4.1, is to adjust the fleet to changes in the volume and composition of world seaborne trade. Thus segment A of the model simply recognizes that if we are to come to terms with shipping cycles, we must recognize the factors which may change demand for the product. This is a micro-economic model, and so we are less interested in the finer points of demand, which are dealt with in segment B, than with the overall changes. It is convenient to divide these changes into three types. Firstly there are business cycles. Unfortunately (or fortunately for shipping, depending on how you look at it) the world economy does not go in a straight line, as we saw in Figure 4.2. Over the last century it has experienced cycles rather similar to those in shipping, with periods of boom alternating with periods of bust. This gives rise to short-term changes in the demand for sea transport, and is a major contributor to shipping cycles. Secondly, there are economic shocks. These are important because they generally produce major changes of trend, and extreme changes in shipping demand. Wars, political crisis, and sudden changes in the economics of some major commodity such as oil have all contributed to major shifts in the demand for sea transport. Finally, there are the 'secular trends'. These are the major economic changes of direction which may accompany the development of a new technology (steam, electricity, information technology) or the emergence of a new major region (e.g. Japan, South Korea, China), so secular trends are the ones which underlie the long-term cycles and are perhaps the most neglected of the three. Partly it is because such trends are concealed due to their slow development. All three of these contributors to the changes in sea trade represent major topics in their own right, and they often seem too distant from the more specialist world of shipping to be of great importance. However, ultimately this is the focal point of the shipping cycle. Its purpose is to compensate for these changes in the world economy, so understanding this segment is a task that must be taken seriously.

Segment C of the model brings together the economic forces which press cargo owners and ship owners to adjust their behaviour in response to market circumstances with sentiment which, in the absence of reliable forecasts, is one of the main business drivers. This section of the shipping cycle composite model is well defined, and forms the main subject of Chapter 5 where we will discuss the factors which contribute to demand, supply and the all-important freight rates model. Parts of this model are so well documented in terms of shipping data that it is possible to develop a deterministic model which shows how the variables interact. But the role of sentiment is not well documented.

Finally stage D in the model introduces risk management. Of course shipping risk is intimately connected with the market investment model discussed under segment C, but it is such an important area that it deserves separate attention in the discussion of shipping cycles. Because the world economy generates uncertainty about how much trade will be carried in future years, somebody has to carry that risk. To take an extreme case, between 1979 and 1983, as we will see in Chapter 11 page 437, the demand for crude oil tankers fell by almost 50%. Such events do not occur frequently, but when they do they are very expensive. Who should take the risk, and how should they be rewarded for doing so? These are the issues which the shipping risk model addresses. If, for example, charterers decided that it is cheaper to take the risk themselves, they may decide to purchase large fleets and award secure time charters to shipowners. That reduces the size of the spot market, and creates a business which is more concerned with 'industrial shipping' than shipping market cycles. However, if charterers decide that they do not want a long-term commitment to shipping, then they may decide to use the charter market. During the 1990s the tonnage of container ships chartered by the 30 top liner companies increased from 15% to almost 50% of the fleet. This resulted in the rapid growth of the charter market for container ships, and a completely different market structure. Segment D is concerned with explaining these structural shifts which take place from time to time in the shipping market.

## The dynamic adjustment process

Although this is straightforward, there are four aspects of the adjustment process which result in a complex process. First, the shipbuilding time-lag complicates the adjustment process. Orders placed at the top of the cycle, when rates are very profitable, have no effect on current rates, so investors keep on ordering. But when the ships are delivered a couple of years later the surge of supply drives down rates, encouraging owners to under-order. Second during the delivery time-lag ship demand often changes direction in a way investors did not anticipate when they placed their orders, so by the time the new ships hit the market they upset the balance even more. Third, the peaks and troughs of the cycles are fraught with emotion, leading to a tendency for investors to react to the violent and often unexpected swings in freight rates. Fourth, every so often a major crisis creates the need for a much greater adjustment in the supply of ships than can be achieved by these minor adjustments in the tonnage of ships delivered or scrapped. This dynamic economic adjustment model is well known to economists.

### Long-run prices and costs

What determines the long-run freight rate in the shipping market? Where will earnings average out? Will the average be high enough to pay for a new ship? This is a matter of great interest to investors who, quite reasonably, want to know what return they can expect in the long term, taking one cycle with another.

The early economists argued that there is a built-in tendency for prices to cover costs. For example, Adam Smith distinguished between the *market price*, which could be very variable, and the *natural price* which just covered the cost of production. He argued that the natural price is 'the central price towards which the prices of all commodities are continually gravitating'.[24] This is a comforting idea for investors, since it suggests that if they wait long enough the market will ensure that they will earn a proper return. It is, however, a very dangerous concept.

Marshall warned against placing too much faith in the idea of a 'natural' price which, in the long run, covers costs. It is not that the theory is wrong, but that it only works 'if the general conditions of life were stationary for a run of time long enough to enable [economic forces] to work out to their full effect.[25] The natural price is unlikely to prevail because the world is constantly changing. Demand and supply schedules are constantly on the move as technology and events change and the unexpected intervenes long before the 'natural' price has been achieved. This is the common-sense view. The world is far too mercurial for the concept of a long-run equilibrium price to be significant in an industry where the product has a life of 20 years or more. Investors cannot expect any comfort from this quarter. They must back their judgement that on this occasion prices will cover their real costs. Economic theory offers no guarantees, and, as we saw in Chapter 2, the returns have, on average, tended to be rather low. This discussion of the Return on Shipping Investment (ROSI) model is developed in Chapter 8, pages 325–338.

### 4.6 SUMMARY

We started this chapter with the idea that shipping companies should approach the shipping market from a competitive viewpoint, 'i.e. playing other players'. The rules of the shipping market game are set by the economic relationships which create freight cycles. To explain them we discussed the economic 'model' of the shipping market. This model has two main components, supply and demand, linked by freight rates which, through their influence on the actions of shippers and shipowners, bring supply and demand into balance. Because the demand for ships changes rapidly but supply is slow and ponderous, freight cycles are generally irregular.

We identified five key demand variables: the world economy, commodity trades, average haul, political events and transport costs. The demand for ships starts with the world economy. We found that there is a close relationship between industrial production and sea trade, so close scrutiny of the latest trends and lead indicators for the world economy provide some warning of changes in the demand for ships. The second important demand variable is the structure of the commodity trades, which can lead to changes in ship demand. For example, a change in the oil price in the 1970s had a major impact on the oil trade. Distance (average haul) is the third demand variable and here again we found that there have been substantial changes in the past. Political events were the fourth variable, since wars and disturbances often have repercussions for trade. Finally transport costs play an important part in determining the long-term demand.

On the supply side we also singled out five variables: the world fleet, productivity, shipbuilding production, scrapping and freight rates. The size of the world fleet is controlled by shipowners who respond to the freight rates by scrapping, newbuilding and adjusting the performance of the fleet. Because the variables in this part of the model are behavioural, the relationships are not always predictable. Market turning points depend crucially on how owners manage supply. Although the orderbook provides a guide to the size of the world fleet 12–18 months ahead, future ordering and scrapping are influenced by market sentiment, and are very unpredictable. Because shipping investors sometimes do things which economists find difficult to understand, relying too much on economic logic can be dangerous.

Freight rates link supply and demand. When supply is tight freight rates rise, stimulating shipowners to provide more transport. When they fall, it has the opposite effect. We looked in detail at the dynamics of the mechanism by which freight rates are determined and found that time-scale is important in reaching an equilibrium price. Momentary equilibrium describes the day-to-day position as 'prompt' ships in a particular loading area compete for the available cargoes. Short-run equilibrium describes what happens when ships have time to move around the world, adjust their operating speed or spend time in lay-up. In shipping the long-term is set by the time taken to deliver new ships – say, 2–3 years. This characteristic certainly influences the 7–8 year duration of freight cycles.

Our analysis of supply–demand charts showed that the short-term supply function has a characteristic J shape, and in the short term demand is inelastic. Freight cycle peaks and troughs are produced by the inelastic demand curve moving along the supply curve. When it arrives at the 'kink' of the supply curve, freight rates move above operating costs and become very volatile. Beyond this point economics can tell us little about the level of freight rates; it is entirely based on the auction between buyers and sellers for the available capacity.

In the long term the volatile freight cycles ought to average out at a 'natural' freight rate which gives investors a fair return on capital. Although this is true in theory,

Alfred Marshall warned that we should not rely on it. In a constantly changing world long-term average earnings are not subject to rules. In the past the over-eagerness of shipping investors has tended to keep market returns low, as we saw in Chapter 2, yet enough shipping fortunes have been made to keep hopeful investors in the business. We will discuss the return on shipping assets more fully in Chapter 8, where we introduce the risky assets pricing (RAP) model.

No amount of statistical analysis can reduce this complex economic structure to a simple predictive 'rule of thumb'. The requirements of success in the shipping cycle game are a lifetime's experience in the shipping industry, a direct line to the world economic and political grapevine, and a sharp eye for a bargain. Decision-makers without the advantage of experience must rely on what they can glean from books.

# 5 The Four Shipping Markets

*Economists understand by the term Market, not any particular market place in which things are bought and sold, but the whole of any region in which buyers and sellers are in such free intercourse with one another that the prices of the same goods tend to equality easily and quickly.*

(Antoine-Augustin Cournot, *Researches Into the Mathematical Principles of the Theory of Wealth*, 1838 (Trans. N.T. Bacon 1897))

## 5.1 THE DECISIONS FACING SHIPOWNERS

A shipowner had a difficult decision to make. He was about to take delivery of two 300,000 dwt VLCCs which an oil company was prepared to charter for 5 years at $37,000 per day each. This would guarantee revenue to cover his finance costs for the 5 years of the ship's life, but the return on his equity worked out at only 6% per annum. Not much for the risk he had taken in ordering the ships. In addition, the time charter would shut him out from the tanker boom he felt sure would happen in the next few years.

He decided to wait and trade the ships on the spot market, but because of the high level of debt service for those two years he entered into some VLCC forward freight agreements (FFAs) to hedge his earnings at $40,000 per day for those two years. This turned out to be a good decision, since the ships were delivered into a falling market and the positive settlement of the FFAs topped up his falling spot market income. Unfortunately the next three years proved to be very poor and the vessels earned only $25,000 per day each. To meet bank payments the owner was forced to sell two old Suezmax tankers. Since there were no offers from trading buyers he eventually sold them to a breaker for $5 million each. Two years earlier they had been valued at $23 million each.

In this example the shipowner trades in four different markets:

- the *newbuilding market* where he ordered the ships;
- the *freight market* where he chartered them and concluded FFAs;
- the *sale and purchase market* where he tried to sell the Suezmax tankers;
- the *demolition market* where he finally sold them.

## BOX 5.1 GLOSSARY OF CHARTERING TERMS

**Shipper** Individual or company with cargo to transport.

**Charterer** Individual or company who hires a ship.

**Charter-party** Contract setting out the terms on which the shipper contracts for the transportation of his cargo or the charterer contracts for the hire of a ship.

**Voyage charter** Ship earns freight per ton of cargo transported on terms set out in the charter-party which specifies the precise nature and volume of cargo, the port(s) of loading and discharge and the laytime and demurrage. All costs paid by the shipowner.

**Consecutive voyage charter** Vessel hired to perform a series of consecutive voyages between A and B.

**Contract of Affreightment (COA)** Shipowner undertakes to carry quantities of a specific cargo on a particular route or routes over a given period of time using ships of his choice within specified restrictions.

**Period charter** The vessel is hired for a specified period of time for payment of a daily, monthly or annual fee. There are three types, time charter, trip charter and consecutive voyage charter.

**Time charter** Ship earns hire, monthly or semi-monthly. The shipowner retains possession and mans and operates ship under instructions from charterer who pays voyage costs (see Chapter 3 for definition).

**Trip charter** Fixed on a time charter basis for the period of a specific voyage and for the carriage of a specific cargo. Shipowner earns 'hire' per day for the period determined by the voyage.

**Bare boat charter** The owner of the ship contracts (for a fee, usually long-term) to another party for its operation. The ship is then operated by the second party as if he owned it.

**Laytime** The period of time agreed between the party to a voyage charter during which the owner will make ship available for loading/discharging of cargo.

**Demurrage** The money payable to the shipowner for delay for which he is not responsible in loading and/or discharging beyond the laytime.

**Despatch** Means the money which the owner agreed to repay if the ship is loaded or discharged in less than the laytime allowed in the charter-party (customarily demurrage).

*Common abbreviations*

**c.i.f.** The purchase price of the goods (by importer) includes payment of insurance and freight which is arranged by the exporter.

**f.o.b.** Goods are purchased at cost and the importer makes his own arrangement for insurance and freight.

The aim of this chapter is to explain how these four markets work from a practical view-point and to identify the differences between them. In Chapter 4 we discussed the bare bones of supply–demand analysis, showing how the supply and demand curves interact to determine freight rates and prices, so now we will put some flesh on the bones. How are ships actually chartered? How can FFAs be used to manage freight market risk? How does the sale and purchase market operate and what determines the value of a ship at a particular point in time? What is the difference between buying a new ship and buying a second-hand one? How does selling a ship for scrap differ from selling it for continued trading? And how do these markets interact? An understanding of these practical questions should provide a deeper insight into how the market economics really work. A list of the more important specialist terms often used in these markets is provided in Box 5.1.

## 5.2 THE FOUR SHIPPING MARKETS

### Definition of a market

Markets play such a big part in the operation of the international sea transport business that we must start by clarifying what a market actually is. Jevons, the nineteenth-century economist, provided a definition which, a century later, still serves very well for shipping:

> Originally a market was a public place in a town where provisions and other objects were exposed for sale; but the word has been generalized, so as to mean any body of persons who are in intimate business relations and carry on extensive transactions in any commodity. A great city may contain as many markets as there are important branches of trade, and these markets may or may not be localized. The central point of a market is the central exchange, mart or auction rooms where traders agree to meet and transact business … But this distinction of locality is not necessary. The traders may be spread over a whole town, or region or country and yet make a market if they are … in close communication with each other[1]

Although the scale of markets has changed and communications have freed traders from the need for physical contact, the basic principles described by Jevons are still valid, though we can refine the model.

### Shipping's four market places

Today sea transport services are provided by four closely related markets, each trading in a different commodity: The freight market trades in sea transport; the sale and purchase market trades second-hand ships; the newbuilding market trades new ships; and the demolition market deals in ships for scrapping. Beyond this there is no formal structure. This is an important point which calls for a warning. Although this chapter provides guidance on how the markets operate, we are not dealing with immutable laws. The fact that traders behaved in a particular way in the past is no guarantee that they will do so in future. Because markets consist of people going about their business, the best commercial opportunities often arise when the market behaves inconsistently. For example, ordering ships at the top of the market cycle is usually bad business, but if for some reason few ships are ordered, the rule will not apply. Commercial judgements must be based on an understanding of market dynamics, not economic principles taken out of context.

## How the four shipping markets integrate

Because the same shipowners are trading in all four markets their activities are closely correlated. When freight rates rise or fall the changing sentiment ripples through into the sale and purchase market and from there into the newbuilding market, with the balance sheets of the companies trading in the different markets acting as a link. The way this works is illustrated in Figure 5.1. The focal point is the industry balance sheet, shown at the centre of the chart, which is the consolidation of individual company balance sheets. Cash flows in and out of the balance sheets of the various shipping companies as they trade in the four shipping markets (represented by the squares) which respond to the cycles in trade.

The freight market (market 1) provides *freight revenue*, the main source of cash for shipping companies. In fact there are three sectors to this market: the *voyage market* which trades transport for a single voyage; the *time-charter market* which hires out the ship for a defined period; and the *freight derivatives market* which deals in forward contracts settled against an index. Freight rates earned in these markets are the primary motivating force driving the activities of shipping investors. The other cash inflow comes from the demolition market (market 4). Old or obsolete vessels sold to scrap dealers provide a useful source of cash, especially during recessions. The sale and purchase market (market 2) has a more subtle role. Investing in a second-hand ship involves a transaction between a shipowner and an investor. Because the investor is usually another shipowner, money changes hands but the transaction does not affect the amount of cash held by the industry. The sale of a tanker for $20 million just transfers $20 million cash from one shipping bank account to another, leaving the aggregate cash balance unchanged.[2] In this sense the sale and purchase market is a zero-sum game. For every winner there is a loser. The only real source of wealth is trading cargo in the freight market.[3] In the case of the newbuilding market (market 3) cash flows in the opposite direction. Cash spent on new ships flows out of the shipping industry because the shipyard uses it to pay for materials, labour and profit.

These waves of cash flowing between the four markets drive the shipping market cycle. At the beginning of the cycle freight rates rise and cash starts to pour in, allowing shipowners to pay higher prices for second-hand ships. As prices are bid up, investors turn to the newbuilding market which now looks better value. With the confidence created by bulging wallets they order many new ships. A couple of years later the ships arrive on the market and the whole process goes into reverse. Falling freight rates squeeze the cash inflow just as investors start paying for their newbuildings. Financially weak

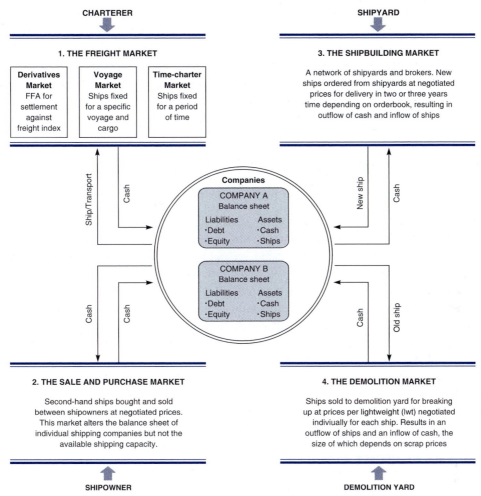

**Figure 5.1**
The four markets that control shipping
Source: Martin Stopford, *Maritime Economics* 3rd edition 2007
Note: This diagram shows how the four shipping markets are linked together by the cash flowing through the balance sheets of the companies in the middle. The freight market generates cash; the sale and purchase market moves it from one balance sheet to another; the newbuilding market drains it out of the market in return for new ships; and the demolition market produces a small inflow in return of old ships

owners who cannot meet their day-to-day obligations are forced to sell ships on the second-hand market. This is the point at which the asset play market starts for those shipowners with strong balance sheets. In extreme circumstances, – such as those of 1932 or 1986 – modern ships change hands at bargain prices, though shipowners pursuing the strategy of 'buying low and selling high' are often disappointed because in short recessions there are few bargains. For older ships there will be no offers from trading buyers, so hard-pressed owners are obliged to sell for demolition. As more ships are scrapped the supply falls, freight rates are bid up and the whole process starts again.

The whole commercial process is controlled and coordinated by cashflow between markets. Cash is the 'stick and carrot' which the market uses to drive activity in the required direction. Whether they like it or not, shipowners are part of a process which controls the price of the ships they trade and the revenue they earn. An important aspect of this competitive process is the continuous movement of companies in and out of the markets. One of the main purposes of the market cycle is to squeeze out the inefficient companies, and allow new and efficient companies to enter the market and gain market share. This is how the market mechanism steadily improves efficiency, and in most markets the top companies are continuously changing.

## The different characters of the four markets

The markets we discuss in this section share some very distinctive characteristics. Because of the international nature of the shipping business and the mobility of assets, they are globally competitive and very close to the perfect competition model described by classical economists (see Chapter 8, Section 8.2 for a discussion of this point). However the markets are not homogeneous. Over time various sub-market segments have developed trading specialist cargoes and the ships that carry them (we discuss these trades in Chapter 12). These markets have a different business character, but there is still competition between them for cargo. Finally there are many small entrepreneurial companies and it is easy for companies to enter and leave the market, making the whole structure very cost-effective and responsive to changes in shippers' needs. In all, a fascinating case study of market economics at work.

## 5.3 THE FREIGHT MARKET

### What is the freight market?

The freight market is one of the markets Jevons must have had in mind when he wrote the definition cited in the previous section. The original freight market, the Baltic Shipping Exchange, first started to trade as a commodity and shipping exchange in the mid-nineteenth century, though as we saw in Section 1.5 its functions had long been performed, in a less organized way, by the Baltic Coffee House. The Baltic operated in exactly the way Jevons described. At this institution merchants looking for transport met ships' captains looking for cargo. The freight market today remains a market place in which sea transport is bought and sold, though the business is mainly transacted by telephone, e-mail and messaging services rather than on the floor of the Baltic. Nowadays there is a single international freight market but, just as there are separate sections for cows and pigs in the country market, there are separate markets for different ships in the freight market. In the short term the freight rates for tankers, bulk carriers, container-ships, gas tankers, and chemical tankers behave quite differently, but because it is the same broad group of traders, what happens in one sector eventually ripples through into the others. For example, combined carriers switch between tanker and bulk markets. Also, because it takes time for ships to move around the world, there are separate regional markets which are only accessible to ships ready to load cargo in that area. We discussed how this influences the theory of short-term and long-term freight rate determination in Section 6.4.

The freight market has two different types of transaction: the *freight contract* in which the shipper buys transport from the shipowner at a fixed price per ton of cargo; and the *time charter* under which the ship is hired by the day. The freight contract suits shippers who prefer to pay an agreed sum and leave the management of the transport to the shipowner, while the time charter is for experienced ship operators who prefer to manage the transport themselves.

## Arranging employment for a ship

When a ship is chartered or a freight rate is agreed, the ship is said to be 'fixed'. Fixtures are arranged in much the same way as any major international hiring or subcontracting operation. Shipowners have vessels for hire, charterers have cargo to transport, and brokers put the deal together. Let us briefly consider the part played by each of these.

The shipowner comes to the market with a ship available, free of cargo. The ship has a particular speed, cargo capacity, dimensions and cargo-handling gear. Existing contractual commitments will determine the date and location at which it will become available. For example, it may be a Handymax bulk carrier currently on a voyage from the US Gulf to deliver grain to Japan, so it will be 'open' (available for hire) in Japan from the anticipated date at which the grain has been discharged, say 12 May. Depending upon his chartering strategy, the shipowner may be looking for a short charter for the vessel or a long charter.

The shipper or charterer may be someone with a volume of cargo to transport from one location to another or a company that needs an extra ship for a period of time. The quantity, timing and physical characteristics of the cargo will determine the type of shipping contract required. For example, the shipper may have a cargo of 50,000 tons of coal to ship from Newcastle, New South Wales, to Rotterdam. Such a cargo might be very attractive to a bulk carrier operator discharging coal in Japan and looking for a cargo to reposition into the North Atlantic, because he has only a short ballast leg from Japan to Australia and then a full cargo back to Europe. So how does the shipper contact the shipowner?

Often the principal (i.e. the owner or charterer) will appoint a shipbroker to act for him. The broker's task is to discover what cargoes or ships are available; what expectations the owners/charterers have about what they will be paid or pay; and what is reasonable given the state of the market. With this information they negotiate the deal for their client, often in tense competition with other brokers. Brokers provide other services, including post-fixture processing, dealing with disputes, and providing accounting services in respect of freight, demurrage, etc. Some owners or shippers carry out these tasks themselves. However, this requires a staff and management structure which only very large companies can justify. For this reason most owners and charterers use one or more brokers. Since broking is all about information, brokers tend

CHAPTER 5

**Table 5.1** Voyage charter, time charter and bare boat cost distribution

| 1. Voyage Charter<br>*Master instructed by:-*<br>Owner | 2. Time charter<br>*Master instructed by:-*<br>Owner for ship and<br>charterer for cargo | 3. Bare boat<br>*Master appointed by:-*<br>Charterer |
|---|---|---|
| *Revenue depends on:*<br>Quantity of cargo & rate<br>per unit of cargo | *Revenue depends on:*<br>Hire rate, duration and<br>off-hire time | *Revenue depends on:*<br>Hire rate & duration |
| **Costs paid by owner:** | **Costs paid by owner:** | **Costs paid by owner:** |
| *1. Capital costs*<br>Capital<br>Brokerage | *1. Capital costs*<br>Capital<br>Brokerage | *1. Capital costs*<br>Capital<br>Brokerage |
| *2. Operating costs*<br>Wages<br>Provisions<br>Maintenance<br>Repairs<br>Stores & supplies<br>Lube oil<br>Water<br>Insurance<br>Overheads | *2. Operating costs*<br>Wages<br>Provisions<br>Maintenance<br>Repairs<br>Stores & supplies<br>Lube oil<br>Water<br>Insurance<br>Overheads | } Operating costs: note<br>that under bare boat<br>these are paid by the<br>charterer |
| *3. Port costs*<br>Port charges<br>Stevadoring charges<br>Cleaning holds<br>Cargo claims<br><br>*4. Bunkers, etc*<br>Canal transit dues<br>Bunker fuel | } Voyage costs: note that under time-<br>charter and bare boat contracts these<br>costs are paid by the charterer | |

4. **Contract of Affreightment** (COA): cost profile same as voyage charter

Source: Compiled by Martin Stopford

to gather in shipping centres. London remains the biggest, with other major centres in New York, Tokyo, Hong Kong, Singapore, Piraeus, Oslo and Hamburg.

Four types of contractual arrangement are commonly used, each of which distributes costs and responsibilities in a slightly different way, as shown in Table 5.1. Under a *voyage charter*, the shipowner contracts to carry a specific cargo in a specific ship for a negotiated price per ton which covers all the costs. A variant on the same theme is the *contract of affreightment*, in which the shipowner contracts to carry regular tonnages of cargo for an agreed price per ton, again covering all the costs. The *time charter* is an agreement between owner and charterer to hire the ship, complete with crew, for a fee per day, month or year. In this case the shipowner pays the capital costs and operating expenses, whilst the charterer pays the voyage costs. The owner continues to manage the ship, but the charterer instructs the master where to go and what cargo to load and discharge. Finally the *bare boat* charter hires out the ship without crew or any operational responsibilities, so in this case the owner just pays the capital costs – it is really a financing arrangement, requiring no ship management expertise on the part of the owner.

## The voyage charter

A voyage charter provides transport for a specific cargo from port A to port B for a fixed price per ton. For example, a grain trader may have 25,000 tons of grain to transport from Port Cartier in Canada to Tilbury in the UK. So what does he do? He calls his broker and tells him that he needs transport for the cargo. The broker will fix (i.e. charter) a ship for the voyage at a negotiated freight rate per ton of cargo, say $5.20. The terms will be set out in a charter-party and, if all goes well, the ship arrives on the due date, loads the cargo, transports it to Tilbury, discharges and the transaction is complete.

If the voyage is not completed within the terms of charter-party then there will be a claim. For example, if laytime (i.e. port time) at Tilbury is specified as 7 days and the time counted in port is 10 days, the owner submits a claim for 3 days' *demurrage* to the charterer. Conversely, if the ship spends only 5 days in port, the charterer will submit a claim for 2 days' *despatch* to the owner. The rates for demurrage and despatch are stated in dollars per day in the charter-party.

The calculation of demurrage and despatch does not normally present problems, but cases do arise where the charterer disputes the owner's right to demurrage. Demurrage becomes particularly important when there is port congestion. During the 1970s there were delays of up to 6 months in discharging cargo in the Middle East and Lagos, while during the coal boom of 1979–80 bulk carriers had to wait several months to load coal at Baltimore and Hampton Roads. These are extremes, but during very strong markets such as 2007 when Capesize bulk carriers were earning over $200,000 a day and iron ore ports were congested, even a few days demurrage can be significant. In cases where the demurrage cannot be accurately predicted it is important to the shipowner that he receives a demurrage payment equivalent to his daily hire charge.

## The contract of affreightment

The contract of affreightment is a little more complicated. The shipowner agrees to carry a series of cargo parcels for a fixed price per ton. For example, the shipper may have a contract to supply 10 consignments of 50,000 tons of coal from Colombia to Rotterdam at two-monthly intervals. He would like to arrange for the shipment in a single contract at an agreed price per ton and leave the details of each voyage to the shipowner. This allows the shipowner to plan the use of his ships in the most efficient manner. He can switch cargo between vessels to give the best possible operating pattern and consequently a lower charter rate. He may also be able to arrange backhaul cargoes which improve the utilization of the ship. Companies who specialize in COAs sometimes describe their business as 'industrial shipping' because their aim is to provide a service. Since a long-term contract is involved, COAs involve a greater commitment to servicing the shipper and providing an efficient service.

Most COA business is in the major dry bulk cargoes of iron ore and coal, and the major customers are the steel mills of Europe and the Far East. The problem in negotiating COAs is that the precise volume and timing of cargo shipments are not generally known in advance. Cargo volume may be specified as a range (e.g. 'minimum *x* and maximum *y* tons'), while timing may rely on generalizations such as 'The shipments under the contract shall be evenly spread over the contract period'.

### The time charter

A time charter gives the charterer operational control of the ships carrying his cargo, while leaving ownership and management of the vessel in the hands of the shipowner. The length of the charter may be the time taken to complete a single voyage (*trip* charter) or a period of months or years (*period* charter). When on charter, the shipowner continues to pay the operating costs of the vessel (i.e. the crew, maintenance and repair as detailed in Table 6.2), but the charterer directs the commercial operations of the vessel and pays all voyage expenses (i.e. bunkers, port charges and canal dues) and cargo-handling costs. With a time charter, the shipowner has a clear basis for preparing the ship's budget, since he knows the ship operating costs from experience and is in receipt of a fixed daily or monthly charter rate (e.g. $5,000 per day). Often the shipowner will use a long time charter from a major corporation, such as a steel mill or an oil company, as security for a loan to purchase the ship needed for the trade.

Although simple in principle, in practice time charters are complex and involve risks for both parties. Details of the contractual agreement are set out in the charter-party. The shipowner must state the vessel's speed, fuel consumption and cargo capacity. The terms of hire will be adjusted if the ship does not perform to these standards. The charter-party will also set out the conditions under which the vessel is regarded as 'off-hire', for example, during emergency repairs, when the charterer does not pay the charter hire. Long time charters also deal with such matters as the adjustment to the hire charge in the event of the vessel being laid up, and will set out certain conditions under which the charterer is entitled to terminate the arrangement – for example, if the owner fails to run the ship efficiently.

There are three reasons why subcontracting may be attractive. First, the shipper may not wish to become a shipowner, but his business requires the use of a ship under his control. Second, the time charter may work out cheaper than buying, especially if the owner has lower costs, due to lower overheads and larger fleet. This seems to have been one of the reasons why oil companies subcontracted so much of their transport in the 1960s. Third, the charterer may be a speculator taking a position in anticipation of a change in the market.

Time chartering to industrial clients is a prime source of revenue for the shipowner. The availability of time charters varies from cargo to cargo and with business circumstances. In the early 1970s about 80% of oil tankers owned by independent shipowners were on time charter to oil companies. Figure 5.2 shows that twenty years later the position had reversed and only about 20% were on time charter. In short, there had been a major change of policy by the oil companies, in response to changing circumstances in the tanker market and the oil industry.

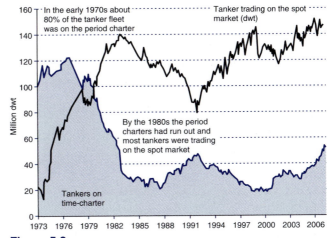

**Figure 5.2**
Independent tanker fleet trading on time charter and spot
Source: Drewry, CRSL 2007

## The bare boat charter

Finally, if a company wishes to have full operational control of the ship, but does not wish to own it, a bare boat charter is arranged. Under this arrangement the investor, not necessarily a professional shipowner, purchases the vessel and hands it over to the charterer for a specified period, usually 10–20 years. The charterer manages the vessel and pays all operating and voyage costs. The owner, who is often a financial institution such as a life insurance company, is not active in the operation of a vessel and does not require any specific maritime skills. It is just an investment. The advantages are that the shipping company does not tie up its capital and the nominal owner of the ship may obtain a tax benefit. This arrangement is often used in the leasing deals discussed in Chapter 7, page 307.

## The charter-party

Once a deal has been fixed, a charter-party is prepared setting out the terms on which the business is to be done. Hiring a ship or contracting for the carriage of cargo is complicated and the charter-party must anticipate the problems that are likely to arise. Even on a single voyage with grain from the US Gulf to Rotterdam any number of mishaps may occur. The ship may not arrive to load at the time indicated, there may be a port strike or the ship may break down in mid-Atlantic. A good charter-party will provide clear guidance on precisely who is legally responsible for the costs in each of these events, whereas a poor charter-party may force the shipowner, the charterer or the shipper to spend large sums on lawyers to argue a case for compensation.

For the above reasons the charter-party or cargo contract is an important document in the shipping industry and must be expertly drawn up in a way that protects the

| 1. Shipbroker | RECOMMENDED<br>THE BALTIC AND INTERNATIONAL MARITIME COUNCIL<br>UNIFORM GENERAL CHARTER (AS REVISED 1922, 1975 and 1994)<br>(To be used for trades for which no specially approved forms is in force)<br>CODE NAME: "GENCON" |
|---|---|
| | Part I |
| | 2. Place and date |
| 3. Owner's/Place of business (Cl. 1) | 4. Charters/Place of business (Cl. 1) |
| 5. Vessel's name (Cl. 1) | 6. GT/NT (Cl. 1) |
| 7. DWT all told summer load line in metric tons (abt.) (Cl. 1) | 8. Present position (Cl. 1) |
| 9. Expected ready to load (abt.) (Cl. 1) | |
| 10. Loading port or place (Cl. 1) | 11. *Discharging port or place (Cl. 1)* |
| 12. Cargo (also state quantity and margin in Owners' option, if full and complete cargo not agreed state "part cargo" (Cl. 1) | |
| 13. Freight rate (also state whether freight prepaid or payable on delivery) (Cl. 4) | 14. Freight payment (state currency and method of payment, also beneficiary and bank account) (Cl. 4) |
| 15. State if vessel's cargo handling gear shall not be used (Cl. 5) | 16. Laytime (if separate laytime for load. and disch. is agreed, fill in a) and b). If total laytime for load. and disch. fill in c) only (Cl. 6) |
| 17. Shippers/Place of business (Cl. 6) | (a) Laytime for loading |
| 18. Agents (loading) (Cl. 6) | (b) Laytime for discharging |
| 19. Agents (discharging) (Cl. 6) | (c) Total laytime for loading and discharging |
| 20. Demurrage rate and manner payable (loading and discharging)(Cl. 7) | 21. Cancelling date (Cl. 9) |
| | 22. General date (Cl. 12) |
| 23. Freight Tax (state if for the Owners' account (Cl. 13 (c)) | 24. Brokerage commission and to whom payable (Cl. 15) |
| 25. Law and Arbitration (state 19 (a), 19 (b) or 19 (c) of Cl. 19; if 19 (c) agreed also state Place of Arbitration) (if not filled in 19 (a) shall apply) (Cl. 19) | |
| (a) State maximum amount for small claims/shortened arbitration (Cl. 19) | 25. Additional clauses covering special provisions, if agreed |

It is mutually agreed that this Contract shall be performed subject to the conditions contained in this Charter Party which shall include PartI1 as well as Part II. In the event of a conflict of conditions, the provisions of part I shall prevail over those of Part II to the extent of such conflict.

| Signature (Owners) | Signature (Charterers) |
|---|---|

Printed and sold by FR. G. Knudtzons Bogtrykken A/S, 61 Vallensbaekvej, DK-2625 Vallensbaek,
Telex +45 43 66 07 08 by authority of The Baltic and International Maritime Council (BIMCO), Copenhagen

**Figure 5.3**
BIMCO Gencon charter-party form, Part I

position of the contracting parties. It would be too time-consuming to develop a new charter-party for every contract, particularly voyage charters, and the shipping industry uses standard charter-parties that apply to the main trades, routes and types of chartering arrangement. By using one of these standard contracts, proven in practice, both shipper and shipowner know that the contractual terms will cover most of the eventualities that are likely to arise in that particular trade.

An example of a basic general charter-party is the BIMCO 'Gencon'. This consists of two parts, Part I which sets out details of the charter, shown in Figure 5.3, and Part II which contains notes and is not reproduced. These templates used to be filled in by hand, but today are generally created using an electronic template, with any additional clauses typed up separately.

It is usual to specify the standard charter-party to be used at the time when the order is quoted – this avoids subsequent disputes over contractual terms, a very important point in a market where freight rates can change substantially over a short period and one of the contracting parties may look for a legitimate loophole. Because there are so many variants there is no definitive list of charter-party clauses.[4] Taking the Gencon charter-party as an example, the principal sections in the charter-party can be subdivided into six major components:

1.  Details of the ship and the contracting parties. The charter-party specifies:
    *   the name of the shipowner/charterer and broker;
    *   details of the ship – including its name, size and cargo capacity;
    *   the ship's position;
    *   the brokerage fee, stating who is to pay.
2.  A description of cargo to be carried, drawing attention to any special features. The name and address of the shipper is also given, so that the shipowner knows whom to contact when he arrives at the port to load cargo.
3.  The terms on which the cargo is to be carried. This important part of the voyage charter-party defines the commitments of the shipper and shipowner under the contract. This covers:
    *   the dates on which the vessel will be available for loading;
    *   the loading port or area (e.g., US Gulf);
    *   the discharging port, including details of multi-port discharge where appropriate;
    *   laytime, i.e. time allowed for loading and discharge of cargo;
    *   demurrage rate per day in US dollars;
    *   payment of loading and discharge expenses.
        If loading or discharge is not completed within the time specified the shipowner will be entitled to the payment of liquidated damages (demurrage) and the amount per day is specified in the charter-party (e.g. $5,000/day).
4.  The terms of payment. This is important because very large sums of money are involved. The charter-party will specify:
    *   the freight to be paid;
    *   the terms on which payment is to be made.

There is no set rule about this – payment may be made in advance, on discharge of cargo or as instalments during the tenure of the contract. Currency and payment details are also specified.

5. Penalties for non-performance – the notes in Part II contain clauses setting out the terms on which penalties will be payable, in the event of either party failing to discharge its responsibilities.

6. Administrative clauses, covering matters that may give rise to difficulties if not clarified in advance. These include the appointment of agents and stevedores, bills of lading, provisions for dealing with strikes, wars, ice, etc.

Time charter-parties follow the same general principles, but include boxes to specify the ship's performance (i.e. fuel consumption, speed, quantity and prices of bunkers on delivery and redelivery) and equipment, and may exclude the items dealing with the cargo.

Efficient business depends upon shippers and shipowners concluding the business quickly and fairly without resorting to legal disputes. In view of the very large sums of money involved in shipping cargo, this goal can be achieved only by detailed charter-parties that provide clear guidance on the allocation of liability in the event of many thousands of possible mishaps occurring during the transport of cargo across the world.

## Freight market reporting

The rates at which charters are fixed depend on market conditions, and the free flow of information on the latest developments plays a vital part in the market. Since the starting point for the charter negotiations is 'last done', shipowners and charterers take an active interest in reports of recent transactions. As an example of the way in which charter rates are reported we will take the daily freight market report published in *Lloyd's List*. Figure 5.4 shows a typical dry cargo market report, while Figure 5.5 shows a typical tanker chartering report.

### DRY CARGO MARKET REPORT

The report consists of a commentary on market conditions followed by a list of reported charters under the headings grain, coal and time charters. Not all charters will be reported. On this particular day the report comments: 'With a surfeit of cargoes and continued port congestion in Australia the capesize market has continued to surge this week and shows little sign of slowing'.

In the fixture report, the details of the charter are generally summarized in a specific order. For voyage charters we can illustrate this point by referring to the first example of an ore charter as follows:

> Seven Islands to Rotterdam – Rubena N, 180,000t, $19.50 per tonne, fio 7 days sc, 20-30 May. (TKS)

The vessel *Rubena N* has been chartered to load cargo at Seven Islands in Canada and transport it to Rotterdam. The cargo consists of 180,000 tonnes of iron ore, at a freight

# Capesize market milestone in sight

WITH a surfeit of cargoes and continued port congestion in Australia the capesize market has continued to surge this week and shows little sign of slowing, writes Keith Wallis in Hong Kong.

One Hong Kong broker said: "There are plenty of cargoes and the market is flying up. We expect it to break $60 per tonne soon."

Asked if the milestone could be broken next week, he would only say it would be "very soon", adding: "It is unbelievable".

Port congestion in eastern Australia has continued to play a key role in pushing rates higher. Officials at Newcastle in New South Wales said 70 ships were queuing last week to load while the average waiting time was nearly 26 days.

Brokers believed the present high rates could continue indefinitely.

Brazilian iron ore mining company CVRD postponed several cargoes from May to June, loading

suggesting there are plenty of cargoes still to come.

Fearnleys said a modern 172,000 dwt vessel was fixed at $110,000 a day for a round trip transatlantic voyage, while a 2001-built, 172,000 dwt vessel was chartered at $130,000 a day for a trip from Brazil to China.

The broker said there was also strong activity in the Pacific where a 2000-built, 170,000 dwt vessel achieved $106,000 a day for a round trip voyage to Australia .

But brokers also introduced a note of caution into the long-term sustainability of such high rates.

They pointed out that owners, especially European operators, were seeking long period charters of five to 10 years at rates of around $100,000 a day amid cautious sentiment that the market was reaching a peak.

One Hong Kong broker pointed out the Capesize sector could be

heading for overcapacity in the next two or three years and questioned whether demand could meet the supply of capesize bulk carriers.

He said the large number of newbuildings in 2009 and 2010, coupled with the arrival of several very large ore carriers and the possible conversion of very large crude carriers into bulkers, could bring overcapacity in the market.

This week's fixtures included time charter business such as the 1999-built, 171,000 dwt Anangel Dynasty which was fixed by K Line at about $140,000 dwt a day, higher than $130,000 quoted in some reports.

In period business, the 1996-built, 180,000 dwt Quorn was fixed and failed by Oldendorff for 11 to 13 months at $100,000 a day.

EDF fixed the 2004-built, 176,00 dwt KWK Providence for four to six months at a daily rate of $110,000.

**ORE**

Seven Islands to Rotterdam — Rubena N, 180,000t, $19.50 per tonne, fio 7 days sc, 20-30 May. (TKS)

Saldanha to Pohang - vesserl to be nominated, 160000t, $38,25 per tonne, fio scale/55000sc, 16-30 Jun. (Posco)

**TIME CHARTERS**

**Mineral Hong Kong** (175,000 dwt, 14/54.7L 14.5/47.3B, 2006

built) delivery worldwide 1 Nov-31 Dec 2008, redelivery worldwide, 3 years, $52,500 daily. (Glory Wealth)

**Fertilia** (171,565 dwt, 13/62L 13.75/59B, 1997-built) delivery HongKong 14-16 May, redelivery Taiwan, $100,000 daily. (China Steel)

**Anangel Dynasty** (171,101 dwt, 14.5158L 15/58B, 1999-built) delivery Cape Passero 15-17 May,

redelivery Japan, $130,900 daily. (K Line)

**Marijeannie** (74,540 dwt, 14/34.5L 14128.5B, 2001-built) delivery worldwide 1-30 Jun, redelivery worldwide, 2 years, $40,000 daily. (Hanjin)

**Theodoros P** (73,800 dwt, 14/34L 14.5/34B, 2002-built) delivery Qingdao 10-15 May, redelivery South East Asia, $44,500 daily. (Louis Dreyfus)

**Figure 5.4**
A dry cargo market report
Source: *Lloyd's List*, 11 May 2007

---

rate of $19.50 per tonne. According to the *Clarkson Bulk Carrier Register*, the *Rubena N* is 203,233 dwt, so this not quite a full cargo. The charter is free in and out (fio), which means the owner does not pay the cargo-handling costs which would have to be paid if it was a 'gross load'. Seven days are allowed for loading and discharge, Sundays and holidays included (sc). The vessel must present itself ready to load between 20 and 30 May and the charterers are Germany's ThyssenKrupp Steel (TKS).

The layout for time charters is slightly different, as we can see taking the first example:

**Mineral Hong Kong** (175,000 dwt, 14/54.7L 14.5/47.3B, 2006 built) delivery worldwide 1 Nov-31 Dec 2008, redelivery worldwide, 3 years, $52,500 daily. (Glory Wealth)

This is a period charter. The ship's details are given in brackets after its name, and in this case the vessel is a new 175,000 dwt bulk carrier delivered in 2006. The speed and fuel consumption are quoted, since these are significant in determining the charter rate. Operating at 14 knots loaded the ship burns 54.7 tons per day and in ballast at 14.5 knots it consumes 47.3 tons per day. The vessel is to be delivered to the charterer between 1 November and 31 December 2008 and to be redelivered 3 years later. Since this is a long charter the delivery and redelivery locations are just specified as 'worldwide'. For a shorter charter a specific port or geographical range would be specified in the charter-party. The charter rate is $52,000 per day, and the charterer is Glory Wealth.

Often the redelivery location is specified. For example, the next time charter for the *Fertilia* specifies 'delivery Hong Kong' 14–16 May, redelivery Taiwan. Note that the daily charter rate for the shorter *Fertilia* charter is twice the charter rate for the *Mineral Hong Kong*. Several of the time charters reported in Figure 5.4 are for a single round voyage, emphasizing the fact that the time charter is not exclusively a means of fixing vessels for long periods.

### TANKER MARKET REPORT

The tanker charter report in Figure 5.5 follows a similar pattern to that for the dry cargo market, though in this case the main division in the reported charter is between 'clean' and 'dirty'. The clean charters refer to products tankers carrying clean oil products such as gasoline, diesel fuel and jet fuel, while the dirty charters refer to crude oil and black products. Details of individual product volumes can be found in Table 11.7 (page 445). In this case the market commentary notes that Suezmax rates are under pressure, but are expected to improve.

Tanker fixtures for a single voyage are generally in Worldscale, an index based on the cost of operating a standard tanker on the route. However, the first item reported in the commentary is an exception to this rule. The 105,000 dwt *Galway Spirit* has fixed a 90,000 tonne parcel of clean products for a lump sum of $2.25 million for a voyage from the Middle East Gulf to the UK. This usually happens when the load and discharge ports are specified in the charter-party. The details reported for each charter follow a similar pattern to dry cargo. For example:

Middle East Gulf to Japan —**Falkonera**, 257,000t, W80, May 30 (Idemitsu)

This means that the motor ship *Falkonera* has been fixed for a voyage charter from Middle East Gulf to Japan. The cargo is 257,000 tonnes. Checking in the *Clarkson Tanker Register*, we see that *Falkonera* is a 1991-built single hull tanker of 264,892 dwt. The charter rate is Worldscale 80 and commences on 30 May. The charterer is Idemitsu. Note that the charter rate of WS 80 for this 257,000 tonne parcel is half the rate of WS 175 paid for the 52,000 tonne parcel of products shipped in the *BW Captain* on the same route, but the cargo is five times bigger, illustrating economies of scale.

# Suezmax rates live up to dire predictions

AS PREDICTED, Suez-max rates have continued their steady decline for a third week running, writes Mike Grinter in Hong Kong. However, indications are that the trade may be turning the corner. The threat of political unrest in the Bras River region of Nigeria led charterers to hold off, thereby precipitating another fall in Suezmax trade out of West Africa to The US Gulf and Europe.

The already dismal rates of the previous week that peaked at W117.5, plunged to W100, only recovering slightly to W107.5 as the week progressed.

A Norwegian broker insisted that the trade will probably move sideways until next week when there will be some potential for increases. Suezmax business cross-Mediterranean and on the Black Sea remains healthier with rates settling at around W125.

Here there is much more potential for improvement if only temporarily. Between May 20 and 25, a window has opened due to a number of Aframax cargoes faced with a lack of vessels in the region. Suezmax currently in the Mediterranean will get better rates for these cargoes when charterers stop seeking alternatives.

The worst performers this week were Suezmax running transatlantic. Owners struggled to achieve W100.

**CLEAN**
Middle East Gulf to UK Continent — **Galway Spirit,** 90,000t, $2,250,000 lumpsum May 24. (Fleet)
Middle East Gulf to Japan - **BW Captain,** 52,000t, W175, May 20. (St Shipping)
Middle East Gulf to Taiwan — **Promise,** 55,000t, W190, May 12. (CPC)
Black Sea to Mediterranean — **Indra,** 30,000t, W285, May 15. (Sibneft)
Black Sea to Mediterranean — Pride A, 26,000t, W275, May 12. (Palmyra)

**DIRTY**
Middle East Gulf to Ulsan - **Sunrise,** 260,000t, W80, Jun 7. (SE Corp)
Middle East Gulf to Japan — **Falkonera,** 257,000t, W80, May 30 (Idemitsu)
Middle East Gulf to Yosu - **Takayama,** 257,500t, W77.5, May 26. (GS Caltex)
Primorsk to UK Continent — **Lovina,** 100,000t, W150, May 20. (Sibneft)
Tuapse to Mediterranean - Thenamaris vessel to be nominated, 80,000t, W210, May 26. (Sibneft)
Sidi Kerir to Italy — **Iran Amol,** 80,000t, W220, May 18. (Eni)
Ceyhan to UK Continent - **Popi P,** 80,000t, W230, May 15. (Statoil)
Enfield to Philippines - **Lion City River,** 80,000t, W110, May 23. (Sietco)
TG Pelepas to Philippines - **South View,** 40,000t, $400,000 lumpsum May 10. (Vitol)

**Figure 5.5**
A tanker market report
Source: *Lloyds List* 11 May 2007

## Liner and specialist ship chartering

The biggest international charter market is in tanker and dry bulk tonnage, but there is also a significant and growing market for liner and specialist vessels. In the early days of containerization companies tended to own and operate their own fleets of container-ships, occasionally chartering additional ships to meet the requirements of an upswing in trade or to service the trade while their own vessels were undergoing major repairs. But as the business developed the major companies started to time-charter vessels from operators, often German KG companies, and by 2007 more than half the fleet of the top 20 service operators was provided in this way. For this reason there is an active charter market in 'tweendeckers, ro-ros and container-ships. The markets for the specialist vessels are reviewed in Chapter 12.

## Freight rate statistics

Shipowners, shippers and charterers take great interest in statistics showing trends in freight rates and charter rates. Three different units of measurement are commonly used. *Voyage rate statistics* for dry cargo commodities are generally reported in US dollars per tone for a standard voyage. By convention this is a negotiated rate covering the total transport costs. This measurement is commonly used in the dry cargo trades where, for example, brokers such as Clarksons report average rates on many routes each week, for example, $12 per tonne for grain from the US Gulf to Rotterdam or $5.50 per tonne for coal to Queensland to Japan etc. In contrast, *time-charter rates* are generally measured in thousand of dollars $000s per day. Time charterer rates are commonly reported for 'trip' (i.e. round voyage), 6 months, 12 months and 3 years.

## The Worldscale index

A third and more complex measure of freight rates is *Worldscale*. The tanker industry uses this freight rates index as a more convenient way of negotiating the freight rate per barrel of oil transported on many different routes. The concept was developed during the Second World War when the British government introduced a schedule of official freight rates as a basis for paying the owners of requisitioned tankers. The schedule showed the cost of transporting a cargo of oil on each of the main routes using a standard 12,000 dwt tanker. Owners were paid the rate shown in the schedule or some fraction of it. The system was adopted by the tanker industry after the war and has been progressively revised over the years, the last amendment being in January 1989 when 'New Worldscale' was introduced.

The Worldscale index is published in a book that is used as the basis for calculating tanker spot rates. The book shows, for each tanker route, the cost of transporting a tonne of cargo using the standard vessel on a round voyage. This cost is known as 'Worldscale 100'. Each year the Worldscale Panel meets in New York (which covers the Western Hemisphere) and London (which covers the rest of the world) and updates the book. The standard vessel has, from time to time, been updated. The one in use in 2007 is shown in Table 5.2. The Worldscale system makes it easier for shipowners and charterers to compare the earnings of their vessels on different routes. Suppose a tanker is available spot (i.e. waiting for a cargo) in the Gulf and the owner agrees

**Table 5.2** Worldscale basis tanker

| | |
|---|---|
| Total capacity | 75,000 tonnes |
| Average service speed | 14.5 knots |
| Bunker consumption | |
| steaming | 55 tonnes per day |
| other | 100 tonnes per round voyage |
| in port | 5 tonnes per port |
| Grade of fuel oil | 380 centistokes |
| Port time | 4 days for a voyage from one loading port to another discharging port |
| Fixed hire element | $12,000 per day |
| Bunker price | US$116.75 per tonne |
| Port costs | Most recent available |
| Canal transit time | 30 hours per Suez transit |

Source: Worldscale Association, London

a rate of WS 50 for a voyage from Jubail to Rotterdam. To calculate how much money he will earn he first looks up the rate per tonne for WS 100 from Jubail to Rotterdam. Consulting the appropriate entry he finds that it is $17.30 per tonne. Since he has settled at WS 50 he will receive half of this amount, i.e. $8.65 per tonne. If his ship carries 250,000 tonnes, the revenue from the voyage will be $2,162,500. It is an equally simple matter to make the same calculation for a voyage to Japan.

## 5.4 THE FREIGHT DERIVATIVES MARKET

Shipping markets have changed surprisingly little over the centuries. The issues raised in the 2000-year-old bill of lading discussed in Chapter 1 (Box 1.1) are not so very different from the charter–parties reviewed in Section 5.3. But occasionally a radical innovation appears, and the freight derivatives market is one of these. Derivatives can be pretty confusing, so we will start with the basics. A *derivatives contract* is a legally binding agreement in which two parties agree to compensate each other, with the compensation depending on the outcome of a future event. These contracts are used to hedge risk by compensating for the cost of a large adverse movements in the variable being hedged.

To illustrate the principle, suppose a shipowner has a racehorse which is favourite to win a race with a $1 million prize and a bookmaker has accepted $1 million bets that the horse will win. If the horse wins, the owner gets $1 million and the bookmaker loses $1 million, but if the horse comes second the owner gets nothing and the bookmaker makes $1 million. Neither is very happy with this 'all or nothing' situation, so they draw up a contract to share some of their risk. If the horse wins, the shipowner pays the bookmaker $0.5 million out of his winnings, and if it comes second the bookmaker pays the shipowner $0.5 million out of his profit. Thanks to the contract they both get $0.5 million regardless of whether the horse comes first or second. Basically that is what the FFAs discussed in this section do. They share the risk that freight rates (and hence the costs incurred by cargo shippers and the revenue received by shipowners) may go up or down unpredictably. Different derivatives markets specialize in different types of risk (e.g. currency, interest rates, commodities, oil prices etc). In this section we are concerned with the derivatives market for sea freight.

### The freight derivative contract

The freight derivatives market is used to arrange contracts settled against an agreed future value of a freight market index. This works because cargo owners and shipowners face opposite risks – when rates go up shippers lose and owners gain, when they go down the reverse happens. By contracting to compensate each other when rates move away from an agreed settlement rate shippers and owners can remove this volatility risk.

An example illustrates the process. Suppose a European trader buys 55,000 tonnes of maize in July 2002 for shipment from the US Gulf to Japan in March the following year.

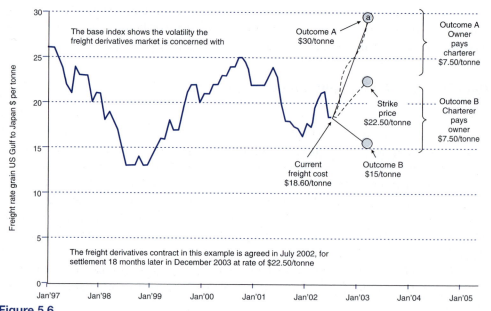

**Figure 5.6**
Example of freight derivative contract for charterer and shipowner
Source: Martin Stopford 2007

Although the grain price is fixed, by March the freight rate could easily double, wiping out his profit. So what are his options? One is to fix a ship for March loading, but owners may be unwilling to commit so far ahead. Anyway, if the trader sells the cargo before then he is left with a physical freight contract he does not want.

The alternative is to arrange a freight derivatives contract to hedge his spot market risk. In July 2002 the freight rate for grain from US Gulf to Japan was $18.60 per tonne, as shown in Figure 5.6. The trader calls his broker who finds a counterparty prepared to enter into a contract for settlement in March 2003 at $22.50 per tonne, with settlement against the US Gulf Japan freight index (the base index). The way the contract works is illustrated by the two possible outcomes illustrated in Figure 5.6. If on 31 March the base freight index is $30 per tonne (outcome A) the owner pays the trader $7.50 per tonne, but if the freight settlement index has fallen to only $15 per tonne (outcome B) the trader pays the owner $7.50 per tonne. This is a *freight derivative* contract because the amount of money which changes hands is 'derived' from the underlying market, as represented by the base freight index used for settlement. The idea is that both parties end up with $22.50 per tonne, since the financial payment covers the trader's extra freight if rates go up or the shipowner's loss if rates go down. In fact the actual freight rate in March 2003 was exactly $30 per tonne (you can just see it as the bendy dotted line in Figure 5.6), so the trader would have received $7.50 per tonne, which works out at $412,500 million for the 55,000 tonnes cargo. That sounds like a disaster for the owner, but provided the base index is accurate, the ship earns the extra $7.50 per tonne trading spot, so the owner still gets $22.50 per tonne, just as he planned. He may regret playing safe and missing out on the boom, but that's life.

Finally, we should note the difference between *hedging* and *speculating*. Hedging uses a derivatives contract to secure the cost of a physical position. If there is no physical position, the derivatives contract is a speculation on the shipping cycle.

## Requirements for a freight derivatives market

Because of the large sums involved and the risks, making derivatives work in practice is not easy. There are three practical problems which must be overcome. *Firstly* a reliable base index is required for settling the contract – suppose the charterer's broker claims the actual rate on the settlement day was $30 per tonne, but the owner's broker says it was only $29 per tonne. Which is correct? *Secondly* the market must be liquid enough to allow contracts to be placed reasonably quickly. In the physical market this is not a problem because the ships have to be fixed, but trading freight derivatives is optional. There is no guarantee that anyone will want to trade, so lack of counterparties can be a real problem. *Thirdly* there is a credit risk, which is much greater than in the physical market where time-charter contracts can be terminated if the charterer does not pay his hire. Some system is needed to ensure that on the settlement date the contracting parties can meet their obligations.

## Freight indices

Freight derivatives rely on indices which accurately reflect the risk being swapped. Any index can be used provided both parties agree, but there is a strong case for using indices developed by an independent party which are demonstrably representative of the freight being hedged and which cannot be manipulated. This service is provided by the Baltic Exchange in London. In 1985 the Baltic Exchange started to compile the Baltic Freight Index (BFI) shown in Figure 5.7. This index was designed as a settlement index based on a weighted average of 11 different trade routes (grain (four routes), coal (three routes), iron ore, and trip charter (three routes)) collected daily from a panel of brokers.

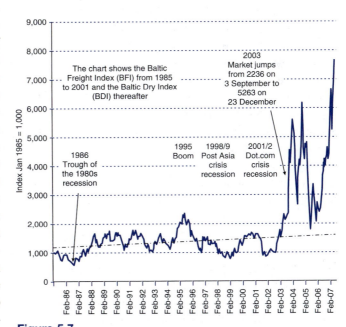

**Figure 5.7**
The Baltic Freight Index (BFI) and the Baltic Dry Index (BDI)
Source: Baltic Exchange

In October 2001 the single index was replaced by four dry cargo indices – the Baltic Exchange Capesize Index (BCI), the Baltic Exchange Panamax Index (BPI), the Baltic Exchange Handymax Index (BHMI) and the Baltic Exchange Dry Index (BDI) – all based on the weighted average of representative routes. For example the, BCI has ten routes which are weighted by their importance in the trade when calculating the average. The Baltic indices and the underlying route assessments from which they are compiled rely on estimated rates provided by independent competitive shipbrokers acting as panellists. They are given a standard ship specification and loading and cargo conditions are specified. The original BFI was discontinued in October 2001, but after this date the BDI can be used in its place, and this series is shown in Figure 5.7. Over the two decades 1987–2005 the average value of the index was 1787 and the standard deviation of the weekly index was 1210 points, showing a high degree of volatility. By 2007 the Baltic Exchange had expanded the range of indices published to 53 dry bulk and tanker routes with rates supplied by 47 panellists, all large companies, in 14 countries.[5]

## Development of the freight derives market

The freight derivatives market started when the BFI was first published in 1985. Initially it operated as a *freight futures* market, in which standard contracts could be bought and sold, and later as a market in FFAs, a more bespoke system which started to take over in the late 1990s.

## Freight futures trading

The first attempt at freight derivatives trading was through the Baltic International Freight Futures Exchange (BIFFEX) set up in 1985. In this market traders could buy and sell standard contracts for settlement against a 'base index', which in this case was the BFI. To deal with the credit risk issue, all traders were registered with a clearing house and their portfolio was 'marked to market' at the close of trading each day. If the account was in deficit, the trader had to deposit the difference in his account, reducing the credit risk to one day's trading. The BIFFEX market operated as a pool where contract units could be bought and sold, with units traded ahead for settlement at three-monthly intervals. The contract units were priced at $10 per BIFFEX index point and all trades were cleared. Shippers and owners could use contracts purchased through the exchange to hedge their freight risk. For example, an owner might sell contracts for settlement in July the following year at 1305. If by July the BIFFEX Index has fallen below 1305, he makes a profit on the transaction that compensates for the losses he will be making on chartering his ship at the lower freight rate, as described at the beginning of the section.

## Forward freight agreements

In the late 1990s FFAs took over from futures contracts as the main form of freight derivative, and by 2006 FFA market volume had reached an estimated $56 billion, with 287,745 lots traded over the counter and 32,200 cleared through clearing houses.[6] The key feature of FFAs (also known as freight *swaps*) is that they are principal-to-principal contracts, usually arranged by a broker, though they can also be traded on screens provided by a number of freight derivatives brokers. The process for arranging an FFA is similar to the way shipping has traditionally arranged time charters, but no physical commitment is involved. For example, the cargo owner wishing to hedge the freight on his cargo of ore calls his broker and outlines his requirements, which will include an indication of five parameters – the route (e.g. Richards Bay to Rotterdam); the price he would be willing to trade at (e.g. $33 per tonne); the contract month; the quantity required (e.g. 150,000 tonnes) and the period; and the settlement index (e.g. BCI C4). The broker will give him an idea of the depth of the market and the likely pricing, which may be quite specific if the broker has suitable counter-parties available, or vague if there have been no trades on those particular terms recently.

If the principal decides to proceed, the broker calls around to find a counter-party at the quoted terms. Market liquidity varies and the broker may take some time to come back with an offer, or may respond immediately – short periods on common routes are generally easier to place than longer contracts. However, this is also a matter of price, since somebody will generally step in if the price is right. FFAs can be tailor-made with customized cargo size and settlement dates, but trading standard contracts is now more common and offers more liquidity. In 2006 and 2007 the practice of passing FFA trades to clearing houses gathered momentum in response to growing concern about the credit risk inherent in the pure over-the-counter market for FFAs. In these circumstances, at the time of accepting the order, or during the trade process, the broker is advised that the trade is intended for clearing. Subsequent to execution the transaction is passed to a clearing house, usually via an intermediary 'clearing broker' with whom the principal has an account. During the term of the contract each party's portfolio is marked to market at the end of the day's trading, and margin calls are made as required. Often the clearing broker handles the day-to-day administration.

As a basis for marking contracts to market and for general guidance the Baltic Exchange publishes a daily 'forward rate assessment' for each of the settlement indices. An example of a report of trading on 31 August 2007 is shown in Table 5.3, covering the rate for the C4 Capesize bulk carrier route from Richards Bay to Rotterdam, and the

**Table 5.3** Baltic forward rate assessment examples

| | Capesize | | VLCC | |
|---|---|---|---|---|
| Parcel t | 150,000 | | 250,000 | |
| Route | C4 | | TD3 | |
| Unit | $/ton | | WS | |
| Period/Route | CS RBAY-RDM | | ME Gulf JAPAN | |
| Spot | 35.20 | | 57.94 | |
| Oct '07 | 35.28 | Oct '07 | 72.80 | |
| Nov (07) | 35.02 | Nov (07) | 87.20 | |
| Dec (07) | 34.55 | Dec (07) | 87.00 | |
| Jan (08) | 32.83 | Jan (08) | 80.00 | |
| Feb (08) | 31.85 | Feb (08) | 76.60 | |
| Mar (08) | 31.09 | Q1 (08) | 76.80 | |
| Apr (08) | 30.29 | Q2 (08) | 67.00 | |
| Jul (08) | 28.69 | Q3 (08) | 70.00 | |
| Cal 08 | 28.79 | Cal 08 | 74.00 | |
| Cal 09 | 23.87 | Cal 09 | 69.80 | |
| Cal 10 | 18.66 | Cal 10 | | |

Source Baltic Exchange

This BFA mark-to-market data is published daily

TD3 VLCC route from the Arabian Gulf to Japan. This shows that on the day in question the actual rate for the Richards Bay–Rotterdam index was $32.50 per tonne, with contract units for settlement at the end of November being traded at $35.02 per tonne, and for the full year 2008 the average was $28.79 per tonne. This implies a strong market continuing, but with some weakening, in 2008. For tankers the TD3 route was trading at WS 57.94 on 31 August, but contracts for January 2008 were trading at WS 80, suggesting that the market expects a seasonal improvement. These provide price guidelines at which buyers and sellers might start negotiating a trade and they are also used by the clearing houses to mark cleared contracts to market.

## 5.5  THE SALE AND PURCHASE MARKET

### What the sale and purchase market does

We now come to the sale and purchase market. In 2006 about 1,500 deep-sea merchant ships were sold, representing an investment of $36 billion. The remarkable feature of this market is that ships worth tens of millions of dollars are traded like sacks of potatoes at a country market. There are many bigger commodity markets, but few share the drama of ship sale and purchase.

The participants in the sale and purchase market are the same mix of shippers, shipping companies and speculators who trade in the freight market. The *shipowner* comes to the market with a ship for sale. Typically the ship will be sold with prompt delivery, for cash, free of any charters, mortgages or maritime liens. Occasionally it may be sold with the benefit (or liability) of an ongoing time charter. The shipowner's reasons for selling may vary. He may have a policy of replacing vessels at a certain age, which this ship may have reached; the ship may no longer suit his trade; or he may think prices are about to fall. Finally, there is the 'distress sale' in which the owner sells the ship to raise cash to meet his day-to-day commitments. The *purchaser* may have equally diverse objectives. He may need a ship of a specific type and capacity to meet some business commitment, for example a contract to carry coal from Australia to Japan. Or he may be an investor who feels that it is the right time to acquire a ship of a particular type. In the latter case his requirements may be more flexible, in the sense that he is more interested in the investment potential than the ship itself.

Most sale and purchase transactions are carried out through *shipbrokers*. The shipowner instructs his broker to find a buyer for the vessel. Sometimes the ship will be given exclusively to a single broker, but it is common to offer the vessel through several broking companies. On receipt of the instruction the broker will telephone or email any client he knows who is looking for a vessel of this type. If the instruction is exclusive, he will call up other brokers in order to market the ship through their client list. Full details of the ship are drawn up, including the specification of the hull, machinery, equipment, class, survey status and general equipment. Simultaneously the broking house will be receiving enquiries from potential purchasers. For example an owner may be seeking a 'modern' 76,000 dwt bulk carrier. The broker may have suitable vessels for sale on his own list, and would not pursue enquiries through other brokers. If no suitable candidates can be found, he may look for suitable candidates and approach their owners to see if there is any interest in selling.

## The sales procedure

Broadly speaking the procedure for buying/selling a ship can be subdivided into the following five stages:

1. *Putting the ship on the market.* The first step is for the buyer or seller to appoint a broker – or he may decide to handle the transaction himself. Particulars of the ship for sale are circulated to interested parties in the market.
2. *Negotiation of price and conditions.* Once a prospective buyer has been found the negotiation begins. There are no hard and fast rules. In a buoyant market the buyer may have to make a quick decision on very limited information. In a weak market he can take his time, inspecting large numbers of ships and seeking detailed information from the owners. When agreement has been reached in principle, the brokers may draw up a 'recap' summarizing the key details about the ship and the transaction, before proceeding to the formal stage of preparing a sale contract.
3. *Memorandum of Agreement.* Once an offer has been accepted a Memorandum of Agreement is drawn up setting out the terms on which the sale will take place. A commonly used pro forma for the Memorandum of Agreement is the Norwegian Sales Form (1993), though the shorter 1987 version is still in use. The memorandum sets out the administrative details for the sale (i.e. where, when and on what terms) and lays down certain contractual rights, such as the right of the buyer to inspect class society records. A summary of the key points covered in sales form documents is given in Box 5.2. At this stage the memorandum is not generally legally binding, since it will include a phrase to the effect that it is 'subject to …'
4. *Inspections.* The buyer, or his surveyor, makes any inspections which are permitted in the sales contract. This will generally include a physical inspection of the ship, possibly with a dry docking or an underwater inspection by divers to ensure that when delivered it complies with the requirements of its classification society. The buyer, with the seller's permission, will also inspect the classification society records for information about the mechanical and structural history of the ship. Sales often fail at this stage if the buyer is not happy with the results of the inspections, but much depends on the market. If the buyer has other offers, there may be no time for inspections and the bidder must take a chance, but in a depressed market any defects found during the inspection may be used to renegotiate the price.

## BOX 5.2 SALE AND PURCHASE MEMORANDUM OF AGREEMENT (MOA): EXAMPLE: NORWEGIAN SALES FORM 1993

This seven page pro-forma contract has 16 clauses covering the issues which can be problematic in selling a ship. The following summary refers to the Memorandum of Agreement as drafted. Individual clauses are generally modified during the negotiation, with terms added or removed.

**Preamble**: At the top of the form are spaces to enter the date, the seller, the buyer and details of the ship, including the name, classification society, year of build, shipyard, flag, registration number, etc.

1.  **Purchase Price**: The price to be paid for the vessel.
2.  **Deposit**: A 10% deposit to be paid by the purchaser; when it must be paid and where.
3.  **Payment**: The purchase money (amount and bank details stated) must be paid on delivery of the vessel, but not later than three banking days after the buyer has received the Notice of Readiness stating that the vessel is ready for delivery.
4.  **Inspections**: The buyer can inspect the vessel's class records and two options are provided, depending on whether this has already taken place. It also authorizes a physical inspection of the ship, stating where and when the vessel will be available for inspection and restricts the scope of the inspection (no 'opening up'). After inspection the buyer has 72 hours to accept in writing, after which, if not accepted, the contract is null and void. (*N.B.* In practice buyers generally inspect the ship before the Memorandum is drawn up, in which case this clause does not apply.)
5.  **Notices, place and time of delivery**: States where the vessel will be delivered (usually a range of ports over a period of time); the expected delivery date; and the date of cancelling (see clause 14). The seller must keep the buyer well informed of the vessel's itinerary before delivery and its availability for drydock inspections (see clause 6). The seller must provide a written Notice of Readiness confirming that the vessel is ready for delivery. If the ship is not delivered by the cancellation date, the buyer can cancel the purchase or agree a new cancelling date.
6.  **Drydocking/Divers Inspection**: This is a complex area and two alternative clauses are provided. Under clause a) the seller drydocks the vessel at the port of delivery, a bottom inspection is carried out by the Classification Society and the seller rectifies any defects which affect its Class. Clause b) applies if the ship is delivered without drydocking and permits the buyer to arrange an inspection by divers approved by the Classification Society. The buyer pays for the divers but any defects affecting Class must be put right by

## BOX 5.2—cont'd

the seller. A lengthy clause c) sets out the rules if the ship is drydocked. The buyer can ask for tailshaft inspection, even if the Classification does not require it, and has the right to observe the drydocking and to carry out hull cleaning and painting work as long as it does not interfere with the survey. Costs for the drydocking and any tailshaft inspection are distributed between the buyer and seller depending on whether defects which affect Class are discovered.

7. **Spares/Bunkers etc**: Names moveable items included in the sale and those which the seller can take ashore. Bunkers and lubricating oils are handed over at the market price in the delivery port.

8. **Documentation**: The seller must provide a bill of sale which is legal in the (named) country where the ship is to be registered. Other documents include a certificate of ownership; confirmation of Class within 72 hours of delivery; a certificate stating that the vessel is free from registered encumbrances; a certificate demonstrating that the vessel has been deleted from its current registry; and any other documents the new owners require to register the vessel.

9. **Encumbrances**: The seller warrants that the vessel is free from any third party claims which could damage its commercial value.

10. **Taxes**: Buyers and sellers are responsible for their own costs of registration etc.

11. **Condition on delivery**: The ship must be delivered in the condition in which it was inspected; it must be in class, and the Class Society must have been notified of anything which could affect its Class status.

12. **Name/Markings**: On delivery the buyer must change the name of the vessel and all funnel markings (i.e. so that it is clear that it is not still trading under the previous owner).

13. **Buyer's default**: If the buyer defaults and the deposit has not been paid, the seller can claim his costs from the buyer. If the deposit has been paid, but the purchase money is not paid, the seller can retain the deposit and claim compensation for losses, with interest, if the sum exceeds the deposit.

14. **Seller's default**: If the seller fails to provide a Notice of Readiness for Delivery for the vessel, or if the ship is not physically ready on the cancellation date stated in clause 5, the buyer has the option to cancel the contract and receive interest and compensation for expenses.

15. **Representatives**: Once the agreement has been signed the buyer can, at his expense, put two representatives on the vessel as observers. The place of boarding is stated.

16. **Arbitration**: Sets out the legal jurisdiction and the terms under which arbitration will be carried out.

5.  *Closing.* Finally, the ship is delivered to its new owners who simultaneously transfer the balance of funds to the seller's bank. At the closing meeting representatives of the buyer and seller on board ship are in telephone contact with a meeting ashore of representatives of sellers, buyers, current and prospective mortgagees and the ship's existing registry.

## How ship prices are determined

The sale and purchase market thrives on price volatility. 'Asset play' profits earned from well-timed buying and selling activity are an important source of income for shipping investors. Bankers are just as interested in ship values because a mortgage on the hull is the primary collateral for their loans.

There has always been plenty of volatility to attract investors and worry bankers. Early in the twentieth century Fairplay monitored the price of a 'new, ready 7,500 ton cargo steamer'. The price of this vessel increased from £48,000 in 1898 to £60,750 in December 1900, and then fell by one-third to £39,250 in December 1903.[7] The same vessel was worth £232,000 in 1919, £52,000 in 1925 and £48,750 in 1930. Over the last thirty years we find much the same sort of pattern. For example the price of a Panamax bulk carrier, shown in Figure 5.8, fell to $6 million in December 1977. Three years later in December 1980 the price had increased by 60% to $22 million, but by 1982 it was back down to $7 million, and did not reach $22 million again until late 1989, after which it was steady until the end

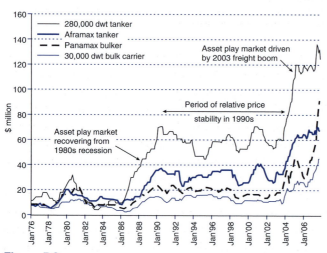

**Figure 5.8**
Price cycles for tankers and bulk carriers (five-year-old ships)
Source: Clarkson Research Services Ltd

of the 1990s, when it fell to $13.9 million in February 1999. From there prices surged, reaching $28 million at the end of 2003; $34.5 million in October 2004 and $92 million in December 2007. Interestingly the price of the cargo steamer at the 1919 peak was 5.9 times its 1903 trough price of £39,250, but the 2007 peak of $92 million for the bulk carrier was 15 times the 1977 trough. So these extreme fluctuations are very large.

If we express the price of a Panamax bulk carrier as a percentage deviation from a linear regression trend fitted over the period 1976–2007, the volatility becomes even clearer. In 1980 the price peaked at 90% above the trend, then in 1986 it fell to 60% below trend, eventually rising to 125% above trend in 2007 (Figure 5.9). There are no rules about how low or how high prices can go during these cycles. Like any commodity, the price is determined by a negotiation between a buyer and a seller. Where prices settle depends on who wants to sell and who is willing to buy. Obviously selling a ship at the bottom of a market cycle is disastrous for its owner and a great bargain for the buyer. No shipping company follows this suicidal course of action by choice. 'Distress' sales during market troughs are generally forced on companies by cashflow pressures

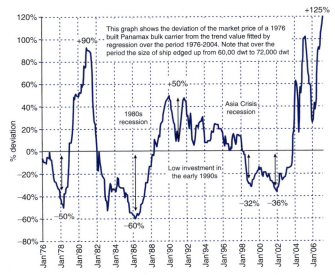

**Figure 5.9**

Bulk carrier price volatility, 1976–2007 (65,000 dwt bulk carrier)
Source: Clarkson Research Services Ltd

such as bunker bills or a banker who has foreclosed and taken possession of the fleet. For example, when the price fell 32% below trend in February 1999, only one ship was sold. Very high prices generally occur when there are plenty of buyers and firm market sentiment, so nobody wants to sell. It follows that the extreme price fluctuations shown in Figure 5.9 are very much a characteristic of the extreme cashflow fluctuations in the shipping industry. However the intervals between the more extreme fluctuations are sometimes long when measured in terms of the working life of managers and investors working in these markets, making it difficult for them to keep a balanced perspective.

Not surprisingly, movements in the price of different ship types tend to be closely synchronized. For example, the analysis in Box 5.3 shows that between 1976 and 2003, 79% of the price movements of a 65,000 dwt bulker and a 30,000 dwt bulker were correlated. In other words, the movement in the price of the 30,000 dwt ship explains 79% of the price movement of the Panamax bulk carrier. That is reasonable, since the two vessel types are close substitutes. The relationship is slightly weaker for the

---

**BOX 5.3 SECOND-HAND PRICE CORRELATION IN TANKERS AND BULK CARRIERS**

| Correlation of price movements 1976–2004 | Coefficient (R2) |
|---|---|
| 65,000 dwt and 30,000 dwt Bulk Carriers | 0.79 |
| 30,000 dwt and 280,000 dwt Tanker | 0.58 |
| 65,000 dwt Bulk Carrier and 280,000 dwt Tanker | 0.62 |
| 30,000 dwt Bulk Carrier and 30,000 dwt Products Tanker | 0.63 |

30,000 dwt and 280,000 dwt tankers, with 58% of the price movements correlated. Even tanker and bulk carrier prices show a correlation coefficient of 62% for the small vessels and 63% for large vessels[8]. Considering the long time period covered and the different character of the markets, the relationship is remarkably close. It raises an interesting question. If the prices of different types of ships are so highly correlated, does it really matter what ship type asset players buy? For really major swings in prices it probably does not matter because cashflow pressures work their way from one sector to another. However, there is plenty of room for independent price movement during the more moderate cycles. For example, between 1991 and 1995 bulk carrier prices held steady, while the price of large tankers fell. This is where the choice of market really does make a difference.

## Price dynamics of merchant ships

In the circumstances outlined above it is natural that second-hand prices play a major part in the commercial decisions of shipowners – very large sums of money are involved. What determines the value of a ship at a particular point in time? There are four factors which are influential: freight rates, age, inflation and shipowners' expectations for the future.

*Freight rates* are the primary influence on ship prices. Peaks and troughs in the freight market are transmitted through into the sale and purchase market, as can be seen in Figure 5.10 which traces price movements from 1976 to 2006 for a five-year-old bulk carrier, comparing the market price with the one-year time charter rate. The relationship is very close, especially as the market moves from trough to peak. When the freight rate fell from $8,500 per day in 1981 to $3600 per day in 1985 the price fell from $12 million to $3 million. Conversely, when the freight recovered to $8,500 per day the price increased to $15 million and when it went to $41,000 per day in 2007 the price jumped to $57 million. This correlation provides some guidance on valuing ships using the gross earnings method. Analysis of the past relationship between price and freight rates suggests that when freight rates are high the Sale and Purchase market values a five-year-old ship at about four to six times its current annual earnings, based on the one-year time-charter rate.

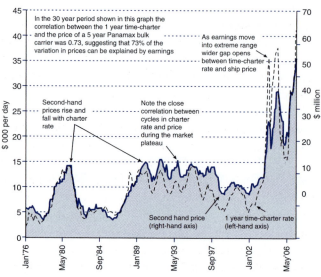

**Figure 5.10**
Correlation of second-hand price and freight rate (five-year-old 65,000 dwt bulk carrier)
Source: Clarkson Research Services Ltd

For example, if it is earning $4 million per annum it will value the ship at $24 million. But this depends on the stage in the cycle. Broadly speaking, when the market falls the earnings multiple tends to increase, and when it rises the multiple falls, but there can be no firm rules because it all depends on sentiment and liquidity.

The second influence on a ship's value is *age*. A ten-year-old ship is worth less than a five-year-old ship. The normal accountancy practice is to depreciate merchant ships down to scrap over 15 or 20 years. Brokers who value ships take much the same view, generally using the 'rule of thumb' that a ship loses 5–6% of its value each year. As an example of how this works in practice, Figure 5.11 shows the price of a 1974 built products tanker over the 20 years to 1994. The slope of the depreciation curve reflects the loss of performance due to age, higher maintenance costs, a degree of technical obsolescence and expectations about the economic life of the vessel. For a specific ship the economic life may be reduced by the carriage of corrosive cargoes, poor design, or inadequate maintenance.

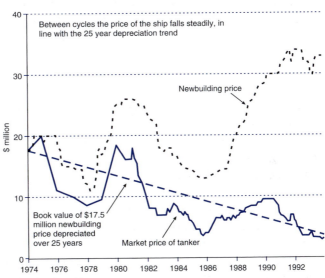

**Figure 5.11**
Price lifecycle and depreciated trend (30,000 dwt products tanker built 1974)

When the market value eventually falls below the scrap value the ship is likely to be sold for scrapping. The average age of tankers and bulk carriers scrapped in 2006 was 26 years, but in protected trades, such as the US domestic trades, the average scrapping age is up to 35 years. Ships operating in fresh water environments such as the Great Lakes last much longer.

In the longer term, *inflation* affects ship prices. To illustrate the point we can look at its effect on the market price of the second-hand Aframax tanker shown by the thick line in Figure 5.12. The price fluctuates wildly, starting at $20 million in 1979, falling to $8 million in 1985, shooting up to $34 million in 1990, wandering around $30–35 million until 2003, then suddenly doubling to $78 million in 2007. To identify the part inflation played in this volatility we first must decide what inflation index to use. One possibility is the US consumer price index, since the ship price is in dollars, but a more appropriate measure would be the shipbuilding price, since this determines the replacement cost of the ship. For example, if an investor sells a ship for twice what it cost, but has to pay twice as much for a new replacement, he has not really made a profit so by deflating the asset price by the newbuilding cost we get a clearer idea of whether the ship's economic value is going up or down. The deflated price of the five-year-old Aframax, using a newbuilding price index, is shown by the fine line in Figure 5.12. This inflation adjusted price has a much clearer trend,

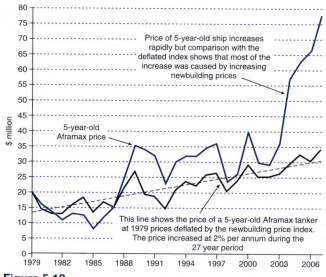

**Figure 5.12**

Price of five-year-old Aframax tanker adjusted for newbuilding price inflation

Source: Clarkson Research Services Ltd

increasing by 2% per annum over the 27-year period, which suggests for example that most of the big price movements such as those in 2003 and 2006 were driven by newbuilding price changes. In conclusion, although second–hand price statistics may suggest that asset values are increasing, when the effects of replacement cost inflation are taken into account that may not be the case. Inflation and freight cycles both have an effect which can, and should, be considered separately.

The fourth and in some ways most important influence on second-hand prices is *expectations*. This accelerates the speed of change at market turning points. For example, buyers or sellers may first hold back to see what will happen, then suddenly rush to trade once they believe the market is 'on the move'. The market can swing from deep depression to intensive activity in the space of only a few weeks, as the following newspaper report demonstrates:

> A very large crude carrier damaged in a Persian Gulf missile attack and destined to be broken up has become the subject of one of the year's most remarkable sales deals. Market sources believe that the buyer has paid $7 million for the tanker which, until the recent surge in demand for large tonnage, appeared to have no future. The rescue of the *Volere* is indicative of the continuing shortage of large tankers which has prompted many vessels to break lay-up. A month ago the 423,700 dwt *Empress* was brought from Taiwanese interests after being towed half around the world for intended demolition.[9]

The *Volere* was resold two months later for $9.5 million and second-hand tonnage was in very short supply as owners held back on sales to see how prices would develop. In short, although there is a clear correlation between second-hand prices and freight rates, the movement of prices is often not a leisurely process. Peaks and troughs tend to be emphasized by the behaviour of buyers and sellers.

## Valuing merchant ships

Valuing ships is one of the routine tasks undertaken by sale and purchase brokers. There are several reasons why valuations are required. Banks lending against a mortgage need to value the collateral and will probably continue to monitor the ship's value over the term of the loan. Prospectuses for public offerings of equity generally include a valuation of the company's fleet, as do the annual accounts of public companies. Finally, leases often require a view on the residual value of the ship at the end of the loan period, a much more complex and difficult task than simply appraising the current value. This is covered in Section 6.8 which deals with valuing ships and shipping companies, including the calculation of residual values and scrap values.

## 5.6 THE NEWBUILDING MARKET

### How the newbuilding market differs from sale and purchase

Although the shipbuilding market is closely related to the sale and purchase market, its character is quite different. Both markets deal in ships, but the newbuilding market trades in ships which do not exist. They must be built. This has several consequences. First, the specification of the ship must be determined. Whenever possible, the shipyards will press the buyer to take a yard standard design. This speeds up the negotiation, reduces the pressure on their design and estimating resources and is generally cheaper to build than a bespoke design. Totally new designs are tricky because the costs have to be estimated early in the negotiation and that involves a significant risk. Buyers can make modifications to the yard design, but will generally be charged extra for these. For the same reason, the shipyards prefer series orders. Second, the contractual process for such a major undertaking is more complex. Third, the ship will not be available for 2–3 years from the contract date, by which time conditions may have changed, so expectations are important.

### Buyers and sellers in the newbuilding market

The *purchaser* entering the newbuilding market may have several different motives. He may need a vessel of a certain size and specification, and nothing suitable is available on the second-hand market. This often happens when market conditions are firm and the supply of good-quality ships is restricted. Second-hand prices may even be higher than new prices, as discussed in the previous section. Another possibility is that the ships are needed for an industrial project. Steel mills, power stations, LNG schemes and other major industrial projects are generally developed with specific transportation requirements met by newbuildings. Some large shipping companies have a policy of regular replacement of vessels, but this is less common than it was when British shipping companies would replace their fleets at 10 or 15 years of age. Finally, speculators may be attracted by incentives offered by shipbuilders short of work – low prices and favourable credit are examples – or by the availability of profitable time charters, if they can only find a ship.

The shipyards form a large and diverse group. There are about 300 major shipyards and many smaller ones.[10] Their size and technical capability ranges from the small yards with a workforce of less than 200 employees building tugs and fishing boats, to major South Korean yards employing over 10,000 workers building container ships and gas tankers. Although some shipyards specialize in one particular type of ship, most are extremely flexible and will bid for a wide range of business. In adverse markets major shipyards have been known to bid for anything from floating production platforms to research vessels.

## The newbuilding negotiation

The negotiation is complex. Often owners appoint a broker to handle the newbuilding, but may deal direct, especially if they have an existing relationship with the shipyard and the expert resources to handle the negotiation, which can be time-consuming. The buyer may approach the shipbuilding market from several different directions depending on their circumstances and the state of the market. One common procedure is to invite tenders from a selection of suitable yards. The tender documentation is often very extensive, setting out a precise specification for the ship. Once tenders have been received the most competitive yards are selected and, following a detailed discussion of the design, specification and terms, a final selection is made. This whole process may take anything from six months to a year. In a sellers' market the tender procedure may not be possible. Buyers compete fiercely for the few available berths and shipyards set their own terms and conditions. Often shipyards take advantage of a firm market to insist upon the sale of a standard design.

The contract negotiation can be divided into four areas on which negotiations focus, the price, the specification of the vessel, the terms and conditions of the contract, and the newbuilding finance offered by the shipbuilder. In a weak market buyers will seek to extract the maximum benefit from their negotiating position in each area. Conversely in a strong market the shipbuilder will negotiate for the maximum price possible on a standard vessel, with favourable stage payments.

Price is the most important. Usually ships are contracted for a fixed price, payable in a series of 'stage payments' which spread payment over the construction of the vessel. The shipbuilder's aim is to be paid as he builds the ship, so that he does not need working capital, and will generally aim for stage payments along the lines shown in Box 5.4.

The pattern varies enormously with the market, but nowadays there are seldom more than five or six payments. In a seller's market the builder may demand 50% on contract signing, whilst low interest rates and a weak market in 2002 resulted in contracts with 10% payable at contract, keel lay and launch and the remaining 70 percent on delivery. The specification of the vessel is also important, because modifications to the design may add 10–15% to the

### BOX 5.4 TYPICAL PATTERN OF SHIPYARD STAGE PAYMENTS

| Stage in production | Payment due |
| --- | --- |
| Signing of contract | 10 per cent |
| Steel cutting | 22.5 per cent |
| Keel laying | 22.5 per cent |
| Launching | 22.5 per cent |
| Delivery | 22.5 per cent |

Source: H. Clarkson newbuilding department

cost. There are many negotiable elements in the contract, as discussed below. Finally, the provision of finance by the shipbuilders is a long-established way of securing business, especially by shipyards who are uncompetitive on price, or during recessions when customers find it difficult to raise finance. The financing of new ships is discussed in Section 8.4.

## The shipbuilding contract

Once the preliminary negotiations are complete, a 'letter of intent' is often drawn up as a basis for developing the details of the design and the construction contract. At this stage the letter of intent is not generally legally binding, though this can become a delicate issue, especially if the builder is devoting significant resources to working up a design to the buyer's specification. For example the cost of developing a detailed design for a ferry or a large containership can exceed $1 million.

Because the construction of a merchant ship can stretch over several years, things may not develop as expected, leading to design changes or disputes between the buyer and the builder. The shipbuilding contract must ensure that each of these disputes can be dealt with in a fair and orderly way which does not disrupt production or commercial relations. Inevitably the contract is more detailed than the brief sales form used for second-hand transactions, typically running to 70–80 pages, containing a preamble and various articles, each of which deals with a specific area where disputes have been found to arise. The general form of shipbuilding contracts is now well established, and Box 5.5 provides a broad summary of the issues dealt with, including procedures for resolving anticipated problems, whilst minimizing expensive legal disputes.

## Shipbuilding prices

Shipbuilding prices, like second-hand prices, are determined by supply and demand. However, in this case the sellers are not other shipowners, but shipyards. On the demand side, the key factors are freight rates, the price of modern second-hand ships, financial liquidity of buyers, the availability of credit and, most importantly, expectations. From the shipyard supply viewpoint the key issues are production costs, the number of berths available and the size of the orderbook. A yard with three years' work may be reluctant to offer a longer delivery because of the inflation risks, while another yard with only the ships under construction on order will be desperately keen to find new business. This balance is what drives shipyard prices. During booms when the yards have built up long orderbooks and many owners are competing for the few berths available, prices rise sharply. In a recession the opposite happens. Shipyards are short of work and there are fewer buyers, so the yards have to drop their prices to tempt in buyers.

As a result shipbuilding prices are just as volatile as second-hand prices and with good reason are closely correlated with them, as can be seen in Figure 5.13. This graph compares the new and secondhand price of an Aframax tanker over 18 years. This chart

**BOX 5.5 EXAMPLE OF A TYPICAL SHIPBUILDING CONTRACT. SEVERAL DIFFERENT STANDARD CONTRACTS ARE AVAILABLE, BUT MOST HAVE 'ARTICLES' DEALING WITH THE ISSUES LISTED BELOW**

Article 1: Description and Class. A detailed description of the ship, its yard number, registration and classification and the use of subcontractors (e.g. if part of the vessel is subcontracted).

Article 2: Contract price and terms of payment. Specifies the contract price, currency, the instalments and the method of payment for modifications, and premiums.

Article 3: Adjustment of the contract price. Sets out the liquidated damages and compensation which will be paid if the speed, deadweight, cargo capacity and fuel consumption measured on the sea trials do not exactly comply with the terms of the contract.

Article 4: Approval of plans, drawings and inspection during construction. This important section covers the procedures for approving plans and the rights of the buyer's supervisor to inspect the vessel during construction and attend tests and trials. The builder must send the buyer three copies of the plans and technical information for approval. One annotated copy must be returned to the builder within 21 days. During construction, defects noted by the supervisor must be notified in writing and a procedure is laid down for resolving disputes.

Article 5: Modifications. Lays down the rules for any modifications to the design requested by the buyer after the contract date, or to meet changing regulatory requirements. It gives the builder the right to charge for any changes and modify the building programme if necessary. The builder is also permitted to make minor specification and material changes if they do not affect performance.

Article 6: Trials and acceptance. Deals with sea trials, including the weather, the conditions under which tests will be carried out and the right of the builder to repeat trials or postpone them if necessary. The builder must notify the buyer that trials are complete within 5 days, following which the buyer must accept or reject the vessel, giving specific reasons. Dispute procedures are set out in Article 12.

Article 7: Delivery of the vessel. States where and when the vessel will be delivered and lists the documents to be given by the builder to the buyer.

Article 8: Delays and extension of time for late delivery. Defines *force majeure* (causes of delay) which may be acceptable reasons for late delivery and lays down procedures for notifying the buyer if the delivery date is postponed. The buyer has right to cancel if delivery, excluding permissible delays, slips by more than 210 days. Sets out the liquidated damages and premiums for late/early delivery. Permissible delays include strikes, extreme weather conditions and shortage of materials.

## BOX 5.5—cont'd

**Article 9: Guarantee.** Sets out the terms and period over which the vessel is guaranteed against defects due to bad workmanship or defective materials.

**Article 10: Cancellation by the buyer.** Within 3–4 months of signing the contract the builder must provide the buyer with a Letter of Refundment Guarantee from an acceptable bank. If the buyer cancels in writing for reasons acceptable under the contract and the builder accepts, all stage payments must be returned with 8% interest. Otherwise arbitration procedures are followed (Article 12).

**Article 11: Buyer's default and builder's default.** Defines the conditions under which the buyer or builder are deemed to be in default. Stipulates the interest rate at which late payments by the buyer will be charged and the terms under which the builder can rescind the contract and sell the vessel. Defines the rights of the buyer to be repaid with interest if the builder goes into liquidation or stops work on the vessel.

**Article 12: Arbitration.** Nominates the legal regime, and sets the conditions for appointing a classification society or technical expert to resolve any disputes over the construction of the vessel and the arbitration regime for any contract disputes.

**Article 13: Successor and Assignees.** Sets out the terms under which the buyer can sell the ship to a third party or assign the contract for financing purposes.

**Article 14: Property.** Defines who owns the plans, the working drawings and the vessel itself during construction. Alternative formats may be offered. The first specifies that the vessel belongs to the contractor until delivery; the second makes it the property of the purchaser, but gives the contractor a lien for any unpaid portion of the price; the third lays out a procedure for marking parts which become the purchaser's property held as security against instalments paid.

**Article 15: Insurance.** The builder is responsible for insuring the vessel and all associated components.

**Article 16: Contract expenses.** Allocates payment of taxes, duties, stamps and fees between the contractor and the purchaser.

**Article 17: Patents.** Makes the shipbuilder liable for any infringements of patent on his own work, but not on the work of suppliers.

**Articles 18–20.** Deal with various technicalities, including the terms on which the contract becomes binding, legal domicile of the purchaser and contractor, the purchaser's right to assign the contract to a third party, and addresses for correspondence.

**Figure 5.13**
Correlation of new and five-year-old Aframax tanker prices
Source: Clarkson Research

illustrates the distinction between the way the market treats the second-hand ship which is available immediately and the new ship which will not be available for 2–3 years, depending on the orderbook. Assuming a 25-year life, on average a five-year old ship should cost about 80% of the price of a new ship. But Figure 5.13 shows that in the early 1990s the price ratio fell to 60% because the market was depressed and investors did not want a prompt ship. They preferred a newbuilding that would not be delivered for a couple of years, by which time the market should have improved. However, by 2006 the second-hand price was higher than the newbuilding price because freight rates were very high and there was intense competition for prompt ships that could be chartered at a high rate.

## 5.7 THE DEMOLITION (RECYCLING) MARKET

The fourth market is demolition. This is a less glamorous but essential part of the business, now often referred to as the recycling industry. The mechanics are simple enough. The procedure is broadly similar to the second-hand market, but the customers are the scrap yards which dismantle ships (see Chapter 13) rather than shipowners. An owner has a ship which he cannot sell for continued trading, so he offers it on the demolition market. Usually the sale is handled by a broker, and large broking companies have a 'demolition desk' specializing in this market. These brokers keep records of recent sales and, because they are 'in the market', they know who is buying at any point in time. When he receives instructions from the owner the broker circulates details of the ship, including its lightweight, location and availability to interested parties.

The ultimate buyers are the demolition yards, most of which are located in the Far East (e.g. India, Pakistan, Bangladesh and China). However the buying is usually done by intermediaries, buying the ships for cash and selling them on to the demolition yards. Prices are determined by negotiation and depend on the availability of ships for scrap and the demand for scrap metal. In Asia much of the scrap is used in local markets where it provides a convenient supply of raw materials for mini-mills, or cold rolled for use in construction. Thus, demand depends on the state of the local steel market, though availability of scrapping facilities is sometimes a consideration.

Thus prices can be very volatile, fluctuating from a trough of $100/lwt in the 1980s to more than $400/lwt in 2007. The price also varies from ship to ship, depending on its suitability for scrapping.

As offers are received, the price firms up and eventually a deal is made. Although a standard contract such as the Norwegian Sales Form is sometimes used, so few of the clauses are relevant to a demolition sale that brokers tend to use their own simplified contract. On completion the purchaser takes delivery of the ship and, if he is an intermediary, makes the arrangements for delivering the ship to the demolition yard.

## 5.8 SUMMARY

In this chapter we have looked at the four shipping markets, the freight market (including the freight derivatives market), the sale and purchase market, the newbuilding market and the demolition market. Since markets are practical places, economists who want to understand how they work must study what actually happens. Starting from the definition of a market place, we examined how the four shipping markets go about the business of managing the supply of ships.

The *freight market* consists of shipowners, charterers and brokers. There are four types of contractual arrangement: the voyage charter, the contract of affreightment, the time charter, and the bare boat charter. The owners trading in the voyage market contract to carry cargo for an agreed price per tonne while the charter market involves hiring out the ships on a daily basis (time charter). The charter is legally agreed in a charter-party which sets out the terms of the deal. Freight rate statistics show the movement of prices over time, recorded in dollars per tonne, Worldscale, or time-charter earnings. Finally the freight derivatives market allows charterers and shipowners to hedge their freight risk or speculate by making forward freight agreements (FFAs) which are financial contracts settled against the value of a base index on the date specified in the agreement.

Second-hand ships are traded in the *sale and purchase market*. The buyers and sellers are shipowners. Broadly speaking the administrative procedures are similar to real estate, using a standard contract such as the Norwegian Sales Form. Ship prices are very volatile, and this makes trading ships an important source of revenue for shipowners, though these transactions do not affect the cashflow of the industry as a whole. The second-hand value of merchant ships depends on the freight rates, age, inflation and expectations.

The *newbuilding market* is quite different. The participants are shipowners and shipbuilders. Because the ship has to be built the contract negotiations are more complex than the sale and purchase market, extending beyond price to such factors as specification, delivery date, stage payments and finance. Prices are just as volatile as second-hand prices and sometimes follow the same pattern.

Finally we looked at the *demolition market*. Old or obsolete ships are sold for scrap, often with speculators acting as intermediaries between the shipowners and the demolition merchants.

C
H
A
P
T
E
R
5

   These four markets work together, linked by cashflow. The players are jostled in the direction the market wants them to go by a combination of cashflow and market sentiment, but the market does not have complete control. Ultimately what happens tomorrow depends on what people do today. In this respect shipping is just like the country market. By the time the farmer arrives at market with his pig and finds that all the other farmers have bred pigs, it is too late. Prices will fall, and the farmer, who has feed bills to pay, must accept the price on offer. But this situation was created a year earlier when prices were high and everyone started breeding pigs. The smart farmers saw what other farmers were doing and switched to chickens. This has nothing to do with the demand for pigs or chickens. It is a supply-side management and we will discuss how individual firms deal with it in Chapter 8. But for now we conclude that, like the farmer, the successful shipping company must know when to steer clear of pigs!

# Part 3

# SHIPPING COMPANY ECONOMICS

# 6 Costs, Revenue and Cashflow

*Annual income twenty pounds, annual expenditure nineteen nineteen six, result happiness.*
*Annual income twenty pounds, annual expenditure twenty pounds ought and six, result misery*

(Mr Micawber in *David Copperfield*)

## 6.1 CASHFLOW AND THE ART OF SURVIVAL

### The impact of financial pressures on shipowners' decisions

In this chapter we look at shipping economics from the perspective of the individual shipping company. Every company faces the challenge of navigating its way through the succession of booms, recessions and depressions which characterize the shipping market. During prosperous periods when funds flood in, it must meet the challenge of investing wisely for future growth and a commercial return on capital. The seeds of future problems are often sown under the heady influence of market sentiment at the peak of a cycle. In recessions the challenge is to keep control of the business when the market is trying to force surplus capacity out of the system by squeezing cashflow and take advantage of the opportunities. During these periods the shipping market is like a marathon race in which only a limited number of entrants are allowed to finish. The race has no fixed length, it goes on lap after lap until enough competitors drop out from exhaustion, leaving the surviving runners to pick up the prizes.

In the last resort what sorts out the winners from the losers is financial performance. The risks faced by shipping companies are illustrated by a ship sale decision reported in *Lloyd's List* during the 1980s recession (Figure 6.1). This was at a time when the freight market was very depressed, and the article reviews the considerations that entered into the decision by a shipping company to sell a VLCC from its fleet. Although this recession occurred many years ago, the circumstances are timeless and illustrate the issues facing shipping company management during depressions. The company was losing money – $14.5 million in the previous year – and the ship was laid up and generating a negative cashflow. For several years the company had accepted this drain

# Lofs is poised to sell 'London Pride'

By Tony Gray, Business Editor

1 FLEET pruning looks set to continue at London & Overseas Freighters, the UK tanker owner which suffered a loss of £14.5 million last year.

After yesterday's annual meeting Lofs managing director Mr. Miles Kulundis disclosed that the group was actively considering the sale of the VLCC *London Pride*.

2 This 12-year old 259,182-tonnes deadweight tanker is the group's largest and oldest vessel, and has been a drain on the group's financial performance.

For some years, Lofs harboured the belief that it would be able to cash in on the *London Pride's* earning potential once the market picked up. But, the depression in the tanker market has persisted, and the heavily over tonnaged VLCC size range has been the worst affected.

A hint that the *London Pride's* future in the Lofs fleet was in doubt came in the recent annual report.

The chairman's statement disclosed 3 the group's disenchantment with the vessel: "Our VLCC *London Pride*, is still laid-up and, with the benefit of hindsight, it is evident that our hopes for the future of the VLCC were ill-founded."

4 The *London Pride* has, in fact, been laid-up since December 1981. As she is turbine-powered, it seems likely that the vessel will be scrapped if Lofs proceeds with a sale. In current market conditions, a 5 demolition sale may bring in around £4m for Lofs.

A sale for further trading could involve 6 an additional $0.5m. Whatever the price achieved, it is likely to be below the sterling book value – of £3.56m at Mar 31 7 1983 – and a loss being carried into the current year's accounts.

However, the sale would have a 8 beneficial impact on the group's cash flow.

The departure of the *London Pride* would leave Lofs with a fleet comprising five tankers: the two 61,000-tonnes general purpose tankers *London Spirit* and *London Glory*; and the three 138,000-tonners – one of which is jointly owned – *London Glory*, *London Enterprise*, and *Overseas Argonaut*.

Lofs hopes that this will remain its core fleet for the anticipated recovery in freight rates later this year and next as oil re-9 stocking takes effect. The group placed all its eggs in one basket through the sale earlier this year of its dry bulk fleet to the Onassis group for $20.55m.

Lofs is not alone in discerning a more imminent recovery in the tanker market rather than for bulk carriers. Some fear the dry bulk market could be facing problems of a similar scale to those that have plagued tanker owners for so long.

It is vital for Lofs, after many years of losses and strain on the company's cash resources, that the tanker market does improve this winter.

Lofs has a versatile fleet that should be able to capitalise quickly on a rise in freight rates. A phase of oil re-stocking is expected to particularly benefit medium-sized tankers, and the group's 61,000 and 138,000-tonne vessels fit the bill.

**Figure 6.1**

Newspaper report illustrating the commercial influences on a scrapping decision

Source: *Lloyd's List*, July 1983

*Notes:* Influence on scrapping decision: 1 financial performance of the owner, 2 age and size of vessel, 3 market expectations, 4 operating costs (turbines use a lot of fuel), 5 scrap prices, 6 state of second-hand market, 7 book value of vessel in relation to its scrap or resale price, 8 cashflow of company, 9 management policies and attitudes

on its cashflow, in the hope that the market would improve, but the board had now decided that 'with the benefit of hindsight it is evident that our hopes for the future of the VLCC were ill-founded' and had decided to sell the vessel. Its sale would mean writing off as a loss the remainder of its book value not covered by the selling price, so the company would have to announce a large loss, but the proceeds from the sale would improve the cashflow.

Since the vessel was turbine powered and had been laid up for several years it was considered likely that at prevailing market prices the vessel would be sold for scrapping. In the final paragraph the article discusses a further significant decision by the group to sell its dry bulk fleet and concentrate entirely on the tanker market – a strategic decision to sacrifice one part of the business to provide cash to allow the remainder to continue, based on a belief that the prospects for the tanker market were better than those for the dry cargo market.

On the basis of this example, the challenge is to create sufficient financial strength when times are good to avoid unwelcome decisions such as selling ships for scrap when times are bad. It is the company with a weak cashflow and no reserves that gets pushed out during depressions and the company with a strong cashflow that buys the ships cheap and survives to make profits in the next shipping boom. It is not therefore the ship, the administration, or the method of financing that determines success or failure, but the way in which these are blended to combine profitability with a cashflow sufficiently robust to survive the depressions that lie in wait to trap unwary investors.

## 6.2 FINANCIAL PERFORMANCE AND INVESTMENT STRATEGY

If financial performance is the key to survival in the shipping market, then how is it achieved? The three key variables with which shipowners have to work are:

- the revenue received from chartering/operating the ship;
- the cost of running the ship;
- the method of financing the business.

The relationship between these cashflow items is shown diagrammatically in Figure 6.2. Revenue, represented by the box on the left, is received from trading the ship. Although shipowners do not generally control the price they receive per tonne of cargo, there are various ways of squeezing more revenue out of the ship. Increasing cargo capacity to achieve economies of scale is one solution. A few thousand tonnes of extra revenue-earning capacity can make all the difference. Increased productivity by operational planning, reducing backhauls, minimizing time off hire, improved deadweight tonnage utilization and cutting cargo-handling time are other possibilities. From the revenue earned by the ship must be deducted running costs and capital payments shown by the boxes in the centre of Figure 6.2. The costs include operating, voyage and cargo–handling costs, while capital repayments cover interest and periodic maintenance of the ship. What is left after these charges may be subject to taxes, though few shipowners are subject to this particular cost. The residual is paid out in dividends or retained within the business.

As we shall see, the way shipping companies manage these cost and revenue variables significantly influences the financial performance of the business. More specifically:

- The choice of ship influences the running cost. Day-to-day cash costs are higher for old ships with ageing machinery requiring constant maintenance; a rusty hull requiring regular steel replacement; and high fuel consumption. Modern vessels with fewer crew, more reliable fuel-efficient machinery and negligible maintenance cost less to run.
- Running a successful shipping operation is not just a matter of costs. It also involves squeezing as much revenue as possible out of the ship. Revenue may be steady on a long-time charter or irregular on the spot market. It may be increased

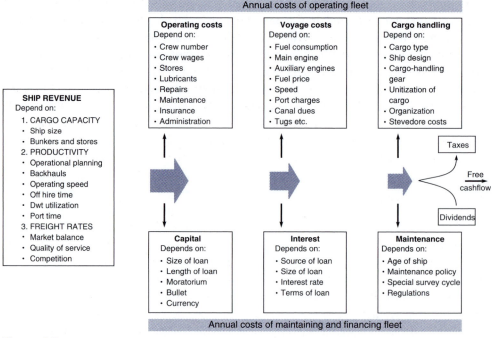

**Figure 6.2**
Shipping cashflow model, showing the revenue, operating and capital payments

by careful management, clever chartering and flexible ship design to minimize time in ballast and ensure that the vessel is earning revenue for a high proportion of its time at sea.

- Financing strategy is crucial. If the vessel is financed with debt, the company is committed to a schedule of capital repayments, regardless of market conditions. If the ship is financed from the owners' cash reserves or outside equity finance there are no fixed payments to capital. In practice if a shipping company has only limited equity capital, the choice is often between an old ship with high running costs but no debt and a new ship with low running costs and a mortgage.

The trade-off between new and old tonnage, single-purpose or sophisticated multi-purpose tonnage, and debt or equity financing offers an enormous range of possible ship investment strategies. Each shipping company makes its own choice, giving it a distinctive style of operation which soon becomes well known in the shipping market. However, once a fleet has been purchased and financed, many of these parameters are fixed and the options open to shipowners become more restricted.

The result can be a striking difference between the culture and approach of shipping companies. For example, some companies specialize in operating older tonnage with low debt and high equity. The low fixed capital cost makes it possible to lay the ships up during depressions with minimum cashflow and earn good profits during booms, often by the sale of the ship itself. However, the company must have the 'hands on' skills to manage old ships and deal with the problems of maintenance and reliability which an old fleet is likely to encounter. Other companies specialize in modern, highly sophisticated ships, which give the maximum revenue-earning potential through their high flexibility and ability to carry special cargoes. This strategy is capital-intensive and often involves a high degree of debt financing, with the result that the ships have to be operated continuously throughout depressions. Getting value for the investment involves strong management skills to build client relationships, careful quality management and often a corporate structure. This approach focuses on minimizing unit costs on a continuous basis, whereas the other is more concerned with cost minimization. Both carry cargo in ships, but they are worlds apart.

## The classification of costs

If we start with the basics, the cost of running a shipping company depends on a combination of three factors. First, the ship sets the broad framework of costs through its fuel consumption, the number of crew required to operate it, and its physical condition, which dictates the requirement for repairs and maintenance. Second, the costs of bought-in items, particularly bunkers, consumables, crew wages, ship repair costs and interest rates, are subject to economic trends outside the shipowner's control. Third, costs depend on how efficiently the owner manages the company, including the administrative overheads and operational efficiency.

Unfortunately the shipping industry has no internationally accepted standard cost classification, which often leads to confusion over terminology. The approach used in the present volume is to classify costs into five categories:

- Operating costs, which constitute the expenses involved in the day-to-day running of the ship – essentially those costs such as crew, stores and maintenance that will be incurred whatever trade the ship is engaged in.
- Periodic maintenance costs are incurred when the ship is dry-docked for major repairs, usually at the time of its special survey. In older ships this may involve con- siderable expenditure, and it is not generally treated as a part of operating expenses. Under international accounting standards an assessment must be made of the total periodic cost over the maintenance cycle and this is capitalized and amortized. The costs when actually incurred are treated as cash items separately from operating costs.
- Voyage costs are variable costs associated with a specific voyage and include such items as fuel, port charges and canal dues.
- Capital costs depend on the way the ship has been financed. They may take the form of dividends to equity, which are discretionary, or interest and capital payments on debt finance, which are not.
- Cargo-handling costs represent the expense of loading, stowing and discharging cargo. They are particularly important in the liner trades.

By analysing these different categories of costs we can develop a more thorough understanding of the market economics discussed in Chapter 5. In particular they provide an important insight into the shape of the short-run supply curve and decision process which drives the adjustment of supply and demand described in Figure 4.15. There are two central cost-related principles which we must explore, first the relationship between cost and age, and second the relationship between cost and size.

## Ship age and the supply price of freight

Within a fleet of similar sized ships, it is usual to find that the old ships have a different cost structure from the new ones. Indeed, this relationship between cost and age is one of the central issues in shipping market economics, since it defines the slope of the short-run supply curve shown in Figure 4.12 in Chapter 4. As the ship ages its capital cost reduces, but its operating and voyage costs increase relative to newer ships which are more efficient due to a combination of technical improvement since the ship was built (e.g. more efficient engines) and the effect of ageing.

An illustration of the way the cost profile changes with age is provided by the comparison of the annual costs of three Capesize bulk carriers, one 5-years-old, one 10 years and one 20 years, shown in Figure 6.3. All three ships are trading under the Liberian flag using the same crewing arrangements and charging capital at 8% per annum. The overall cost per day works out at about the same for the 5-year-old and 10-year-old ships but on these assumptions the 20-year-old ship is about 13% cheaper. However, the structure of costs of the new and old ships is quite different. If we consider only the direct cash costs and exclude capital costs and periodic maintenance, the modern ship is much cheaper to run, with operating expenses of only 18% compared with 31% for the old ship and bunkers 40% compared with 33% for the modern ship. This differential is due to the old ship's higher operating costs, larger crew, more routine maintenance and lower fuel efficiency (remember the owner trading spot gets paid per tonne of cargo, so fuel is an out-of-pocket expense). However, when we look at capital the position is very different, accounting for 47% of the cost of the modern ship but only 11% of the cost of the old ship. The obvious conclusion is that owners of new and old ships are in very different businesses.

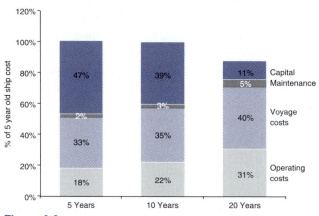

**Figure 6.3**
Capesize bulk carrier cost and age
Source: Clarkson Research Studies, Capesize Quality Survey (1993)

This cost differential plays an important part in the cashflow 'race'. If we ignore capital costs and periodic maintenance, the modern vessel can survive at freights which are way below the lay-up point for older ships. It is this differential which determines the slope of the supply curve. Because spot earnings have to cover operating and fuel costs, for any given spot rate the old ship generates less cash than the new ship. If gross earnings for a Capesize (i.e. before bunker costs) fall to the operating costs of the 20-year-old ship for any length of time, the owner of the 20-year-old ship, will probably lay it up, since revenue does not cover operating and voyage costs, but the modern ship with its lower operating expenses will be able to go on trading. Will the old ship come out of lay-up? This is where periodic maintenance costs come into play. Although these costs can be postponed, they cannot be deferred indefinitely. In this example, when the fourth special survey arrives at about 20 years, the ship faces a bill for, say, $2.2 million. This must be paid if the ship is to continue trading, so the owner must decide whether the repair is worthwhile. If he is pessimistic about the future and he expects more bills to follow, he may decide to sell for scrap. This is how the scrapping mechanism works. But if the market is strong he may decide to patch it up for a couple more voyages. For example, if he can convince himself that the rates will be $6,000 per day above operating costs for a year, that would pay the repair cost in full. So by adjusting rates the market can adjust the flow of ships leaving the market in response to the balance of supply and demand, and it relies on the astuteness of owners in estimating what will happen next to fine-tune this process. It is a very efficient system for squeezing the maximum economic value out of the ships, though in the end it is not a mechanical relationship, it depends on what owners and their financiers decide to do.

It is not just old ships that are on trial during recessions. Capital costs cannot just be written out of the picture. Ships financed with bank loans have a fixed cashflow which may exceed operating costs by a considerable margin. In these circumstances it is the owner of the modern ship who is on trial. If the freight is not enough to cover financing costs and the owner defaults, the bank may enforce its mortgage rights, seize the ship and sell it to cover the outstanding debt. In this way the market filters out the substandard owners as well as the substandard ships.

## Unit costs and economies of scale

Another economic relationship which dominates shipping economics and complicates life for shipping economists is the relationship between cost and ship size, usually referred to as economies of scale. Shipping is about moving cargo, so the economic focus of the business is unit cost, the cost per ton, per TEU or per cubic metre. That is where we will start. We define the annual cost per deadweight tonne of a ship as the sum of operating costs, voyage costs, cargo-handling costs and capital costs incurred in a year divided by the deadweight of the ship:

$$C_{tm} = \frac{OC_{tm} + PM_{tm} + VC_{tm} + CHC_{tm} + K_{tm}}{DWT_{tm}} \tag{6.1}$$

where $C$ is the cost per dwt (or other capacity measurement e.g. M3) per annum, $OC$ the operating cost per annum, $PM$ the periodic maintenance per annum, $VC$ the voyage costs per annum, $CHC$ the cargo-handling costs per annum, $K$ the capital cost per annum, *DWT* the ship deadweight, *t* is the year, and *m* stands for the *m*th ship.

This relationship is particularly important because operating, voyage and capital costs do not increase in proportion to the deadweight of the vessel, so using a bigger ship reduces the unit freight cost. For example, a VLCC of 280,000 dwt requires the same number of crew as a 29,000 dwt products tanker, and uses only a quarter as much fuel per deadweight tonne. Similarly, for dry bulk carriers in 2005 the annual cost for a 170,000 dwt Capesize bulker was about $74 per cargo tonne compared with $191 per cargo tonne for a 30,000 dwt vessel, as can be seen in Table 6.1. Capital, operating expenses and bunker costs all contributed to this. Provided the cargo volume and port facilities are available, the owner of a large ship has a substantial cost advantage, and can generate a positive cashflow at rates that are uneconomic for smaller ships. In this example, a hire of $44 per dwt per annum would cover a Capesize's operating and bunker expenses, but would only pay operating expenses for a 30,000 dwt bulk carrier, with nothing left for bunkers.

This explains why cargo ships tend to get bigger. In 1870 brokers talked about a 'handy' (i.e. flexible) vessel of 2,000 tons, but 130 years later a Handy vessel was approaching 50,000 tons. Since ships have grown steadily bigger over the years, in practice age/cost differentials and economies of scale have worked together. The penalty of size is the loss of flexibility, which impacts on the revenue side of the equation by limiting the ports that can be entered and making it more difficult to reduce ballast time by obtaining backhaul cargoes. Investors in the next generation of bigger ships always face the risk that they have overstepped the mark.

**Table 6.1** Economies of scale in bulk shipping (including bunkers)

| | Assumptions | | | Unit Costs ($/dwt p.a.) | | | | |
|---|---|---|---|---|---|---|---|---|
| Cargo capacity dwt | Investment $m[a] | Bunker cons tons/day | Operating $m p.a. | Operating cost | Bunker costs[b] | Capital cost[c] | Total cost $/dwt p.a. | Memo[d] daily cost $000/day |
| 30,000 | 26 | 21 | 1.2 | 40.6 | 56.7 | 93.5 | 191 | 11,494 |
| 47,000 | 31 | 24 | 1.4 | 30.3 | 41.4 | 71.4 | 143 | 13,657 |
| 68,000 | 36 | 30 | 1.8 | 26.0 | 35.7 | 58.2 | 120 | 16,360 |
| 170,000 | 59 | 50 | 2.0 | 12.0 | 23.8 | 38.2 | 74 | 24,374 |
| *Memo:* cost of 170,000 dwt ship as % 30,000 dwt ship | | | | | | | | |
| 567% | 231% | 238% | 168% | 30% | 42% | 41% | 39% | |

Source: various

[a]Cost of newbuilding in December 2005

[b]December 2005, assuming 270 days at sea per annum at 14 knots and bunkers at $300/tonne

[c]Capital costs at 5% depreciation plus interest at 6% p.a. over 365 days

[d]Time-charter rates are used for the economy of scale calculations

The history of freight cycles is an economic struggle between the big modern ships and earlier generations of smaller ships with outdated technology. Usually the combination of small size, which reduces revenue, and increasing maintenance cost makes the ship uneconomic when it reaches 20 or 25 years old, forcing it from the market. However, when the size of ships stops growing, as happened in the tanker market during the 1980s and 1990s, the economic advantage of the modern ships becomes less clearly defined, extending the economic life of ships.[1]

## 6.3 THE COST OF RUNNING SHIPS

The costs discussed in the previous section illustrate the general principles involved, but in practice all costs are variable, depending on external developments such as changes in oil prices and the way the ship's owner manages and finances the business. To understand ship investment economics we must look in much greater detail at the structure of costs. Figure 6.4 summarizes the key points we will consider. Each box in the diagram lists a major cost category, the variables which determine its value, and the percentage cost for a 10-year-old ship. In the remainder of this section we examine how the four main cost groups – operating costs (14%), periodic maintenance (4%), voyage costs (40%) and capital costs (42%) – are built up to determine an overall financial performance of the ship. Taken together these costs determine the cost of sea transport and they are extremely volatile, as is evident from the trends in fuel, capital and other costs shown in Figure 6.5. Between 1965 and 2007 the ship cost

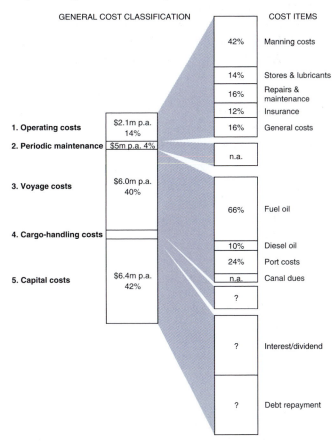

**Figure 6.4**

Analysis of the major costs of running a bulk carrier
Source: Compiled by Martin Stopford from various sources
*Note*: This analysis is for a 10-year-old Capesize bulk carrier under the Liberian flag at 2005 prices. Relative costs depend on many factors that change over time, so this is just a rough guide.

index increased by 5.5% per year, compared with 4.6% for the US consumer price index. However, the ship cost index was far more volatile, driven by the wild swings in fuel and capital costs which together account for close to two–thirds of the total.

## Operating costs

Operating costs, the first item in Figure 6.4, are the ongoing expenses connected with the day-to-day running of the vessel (excluding fuel, which is included in voyage costs), together with an allowance for day-to-day repairs and maintenance (but not major dry dockings, which are dealt with separately). They account for about 14% of total costs. The principal components of operating costs are:

$$OC_{tm} = M_{tm} + ST_{tm} + MN_{tm} + I_{tm} + AD_{tm}$$

(6.2)

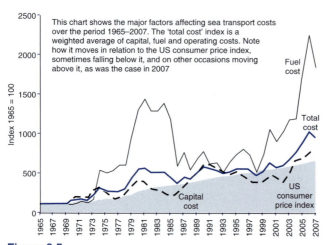

**Figure 6.5**

Inflation in shipping costs, 1965–2007

Source: Fuel costs based on marine bunker price 380 cSt, Rotterdam; capital costs based on Aframax tanker newbuilding price (in $); other costs based on US consumer price index

where $M$ is manning cost, $ST$ represents stores, $MN$ is routine repair and maintenance, $I$ is insurance and $AD$ administration.

An example of the operating cost structure of a Capesize bulk carrier is shown in Table 6.2, subdivided into these categories. In summary, the operating cost structure depends on the size and nationality of the crew, maintenance policy and the age and insured value of the ship, and the administrative efficiency of the owner. Table 6.2 shows the relative importance of each of these components in operating costs and compares them for ships of three different ages, 5, 10 and 20 years.

### CREW COSTS

Crew costs include all direct and indirect charges incurred by the crewing of the vessel, including basic salaries and wages, social insurance, pensions, victuals and repatriation expenses. The level of manning costs for a particular ship is determined by two factors, the size of the crew and the employment policies adopted by the owner and the ship's flag state. Manning costs may account for up to half of operating costs, depending on the size of the ship.

**Table 6.2** Operating costs of Capesize bulk carriers by age ($000 per annum)

| Age of ship | 5 Years | 10 Years | 20 Years | % Total Average |
|---|---|---|---|---|
| Crew cost | | | | |
| Crew wages | 544 | 639 | 688 | 30% |
| Travel, insurance etc | 73 | 82 | 85 | 4% |
| Victualling | 46 | 54 | 64 | 3% |
| Total | 743 | 871 | 956 | 41% |
| % | 32% | 31% | 26% | |
| | | | | |
| Stores & Consumables | | | | |
| General stores | 129 | 144 | 129 | 6% |
| Lubricants | 148 | 148 | 219 | 8% |
| Total | 277 | 292 | 348 | 15% |
| % | 12% | 11% | 9% | |
| | | | | |
| Maintenance & Repairs | | | | |
| Maintenance | 90 | 169 | 10 | 4% |
| Spares | 74 | 169 | 181 | 7% |
| Total | 164 | 338 | 393 | 14% |
| % | 9% | 15% | 13% | |
| | | | | |
| Insurance | | | | |
| Hull & machinery & war risks | 133 | 148 | 303 | 9% |
| P&I | 63 | 94 | 120 | 4% |
| Total | 196 | 243 | 423 | 14% |
| % | 32% | 32% | 44% | |
| | | | | |
| General Costs | | | | |
| Registration Costs | 17 | 17 | 17 | 1% |
| Management Fees | 255 | 223 | 255 | 12% |
| Sundries | 57 | 57 | 57 | 3% |
| Total | 330 | 298 | 330 | 15% |
| % | 14% | 11% | 9% | |
| Total per annum | 1,710 | 2,041 | 2,450 | 100% |
| Daily Costs (365 days) | 4,685 | 5,591 | 6,712 | 100% |

Source: Ten-year old ship, Moore Stephens, V Ships; 5- and 20-year-old ship costs estimated from various sources

The minimum number of crew on a merchant ship is usually set by the regulations of the flag state. However, it also depends on commercial factors such as the degree of automation of mechanical operations, particularly the engine room, catering and cargo handling; the skill of the crew; and the amount of on-board maintenance undertaken. Automation and reliable monitoring systems have played an important part in reducing crew numbers.[2] It is now common practice for the engine room to be unmanned at night, and various other systems have been introduced such as remote control ballast, single-man bunkering, rationalized catering and improved communications which remove the need for a radio officer. As a result crew numbers declined from about 40–50 in the early 1950s to an average of 28 in the early 1980s. Current levels of technology on modern ships allow a basic crew of 17 in a deep-sea vessel, while experimental vessels have been operated with a crew of 10. Under some flags manning scales govern the

**C H A P T E R 6**

numbers of personnel required on the various types and sizes of vessels, and any reductions must be agreed between the shipowners' organization and the seamen's unions.

An idea of the basic manning cost in 2005 is provided in Table 6.2. The figure for annual crew wages of $544,000 for a 5-year-old ship covers direct wages and employment-related costs. An additional $119,000 per annum is required to cover travel; manning and support; medical insurance and victualling; and the basic management costs that apply to crewing – crew selection, rotation, making travel arrangements, purchase of victuals and ship supplies. In total these add 16% to the crew cost for a 5-year-old ship.

**Table 6.3** Crew costs on 160,000 dwt bulk carrier, 2007 ($ per month)

| Rank | Note | Basic | Consolidated Allowances | Bonus (officers) | Provident Fund[b] | Totals[c] 2007 | 1993 | % ch |
|------|------|-------|-------------------------|------------------|-------------------|-----------------|------|------|
| Master | India | 1,967 | 3,933 | 300 | 35 | 6,235 | 3,644 | 171% |
| Chief officer[a] | | 1,294 | 3,206 | 200 | 35 | 4,735 | 3,025 | 157% |
| 2nd officer | | 1,077 | 1,773 | — | 35 | 2,885 | 2,338 | 123% |
| 3rd officer | | 1,030 | 1,320 | — | 35 | 2,385 | 1,650 | 145% |
| Radio officer | | radio officer no longer required in 2007 | | | | | 1,650 | 0% |
| Chief engineer | | 1,760 | 3,990 | 300 | 35 | 6,085 | 3,575 | 170% |
| 1st asst engr | 2nd eng. | 1,294 | 3,206 | 200 | 35 | 4,735 | 3,025 | 157% |
| 2nd asst engr | 3rd eng. | 1,077 | 1,773 | — | 35 | 2,885 | 2,338 | 123% |
| Bosun | Philippines | 670 | 649 | — | 182 | 1,501 | 1,521 | 99% |
| 5AB | | 558 | 542 | — | 171 | 6,353 | 6,479 | 98% |
| 3 oiler | | 558 | 542 | — | 171 | 3,812 | 3,888 | 98% |
| Cook/std | chief cook | 670 | 649 | — | 182 | 1,501 | 1,596 | 94% |
| Std | 2nd cook | 558 | 542 | — | 171 | 1,271 | 1,296 | 98% |
| Messman | | 426 | 378 | — | 158 | 962 | 1,071 | 90% |
| Total crew number modern ship: 20 | | | | | | 45,344 | 37,094 | 122% |
| *Additional crew for 10-year-old ship* | | | | | | | | |
| 3rd asst engr | India | 1,030 | 1,320 | — | 35 | 2,385 | 1,650 | 145% |
| Electrician | Elec. off. | 1,077 | 1,823 | — | 35 | 2,935 | 2,338 | 126% |
| AB | Philippines | 558 | 542 | — | 171 | 1,271 | 1,296 | 98% |
| 1 oiler | | 558 | 542 | — | 171 | 1,271 | 1,296 | 98% |
| Total crew number 10-year-old ship: 24 | | | | | | 53,205 | 43,673 | 122% |
| *Additional crew for 20-year-old ship* | | | | | | | | |
| 2 ordinary seamen | Philippines | 426 | 378 | — | 158 | 1,925 | 2,142 | 90% |
| 1 oiler | | 558 | 542 | — | 171 | 1,271 | 1,071 | 119% |
| 1 messman | | 426 | 378 | — | 158 | 962 | 1,071 | 90% |
| Total crew number 20-year-old ship: 28 | | | | | | 57,362 | 47,956 | 120% |
| Annual crew cost for 20-year-old ship | | | | | | 688,344 | 575,475 | 120% |

Notes

[a]Senior Officer based on 5 yr senority & Junior Officers 3 yrs seniority.

[b]Includes social costs

[c]1993 data from Stopford (1997, Table 5.3)

Source: V Ships

A more detailed breakdown of the crewing arrangements of three Capesize bulk carriers, one 5 years old, one 10 years old and one 20 years old, is provided in Table 6.3. The modern vessel has a crew of, comprising the master, four officers, three engineers, a bosun, eight seamen and three catering staff. The 10-year-old ship, where the maintenance workload is beginning to increase, might require a crew of 24, while a 20-year-old ship might have a crew of 28. The extra crew includes an additional engineer, an electrician, four seamen and one messman. They are needed to handle the repair and maintenance workload which is a continuous cycle on an old ship and can be carried out more cheaply at sea while the ship continues to trade. The total annual cost is $688,344 per year for the 20-year-old ship, a 20% increase on the costs in 1993.

The wages paid to the crews of merchant ships have always been controversial. The International Transport Workers' Federation (ITF) lays down minimum basic monthly rates of pay for all ranks, as well as paid leave, as part of its world-wide and Far East wage scale, but these are not universally accepted. There are, in fact, wide disparities in the rates of pay received by crews of different nationalities. The nationality of the crew is often governed by national statute of the country of registration and under some flags shipowners are prevented from employing non-nationals on their vessels. The cost per crew member may be 50% higher for a vessel registered under a European flag than for a comparable vessel 'flagged out' to one of the countries of open registration such as Liberia, Panama and Singapore, where employment regulations are less stringent. As the practice of flagging out became more widely accepted the cost differentials narrowed and quality became as much an issue as cost.

These costs are certainly not standards. Shipowners have far more opportunity than land-based businesses to determine manning costs by operating under a flag that allows the use of a low-wage crew and by shopping around the world for the cheapest crews available. Exchange rates will be an important factor here if wages are paid in a currency other than the one in which revenue is earned. Although shipping is a dollar-based business, shipping companies typically find themselves handling cashflows in many different currencies.

## STORES AND CONSUMABLES

Another significant cost of operating a vessel, accounting for about 15% of operating costs, is expenditure on consumable supplies. These fall into two categories, as listed in Table 6.2: General stores including cabin stores and the various domestic items used on board ship; and lubricating oil which is a major cost (most modern vessels have diesel engines and may consume several hundred litres of lube oil a day while at sea).

## REPAIRS AND MAINTENANCE

Routine maintenance, which accounts for 14% of operating costs, covers the routine repairs needed to maintain the vessel to the standard required by company policy, its classification society and the charterers of the vessel who choose to inspect it (it does not include periodic dry docking which is not generally considered an operating expense and is dealt with under 'periodic maintenance' below). Broadly speaking, maintenance covers the cost of routine maintenance, including breakdowns and spares:

- *Routine maintenance*. Includes maintaining the main engine and auxiliary equipment, painting the superstructure and carrying out steel renewal in those holds and cargo tanks which can be safely accessed while the ship is at sea. As with any capital equipment, the maintenance costs of merchant ships tend to increase with age.
- *Breakdowns*. Mechanical failure may result in additional costs outside those covered by routine maintenance. Work of this type is often taken by ship repair yards on 'open order' and is therefore likely to be expensive. Additional costs are incurred owing to loss of trading time.
- *Spares*. Replacement parts for the engine, auxiliaries and other on-board machinery.

The typical maintenance costs for a Capesize bulk carrier listed in Table 6.2 cover visits to repair yards, plus the cost of riding crews and work carried out on board. All items of maintenance costs increase substantially with age, and a 20-year-old vessel may incur twice the costs of a more modern one. Expenditure on spare parts and replacement equipment is also likely to increase with age.

### INSURANCE

Typically insurance accounts for 14% of operating costs, though this is a cost item which is likely to vary from ship to ship. Two-thirds of the cost is to insure the hull and machinery, which protects the owner of the vessel against physical loss or damage, and the other third is third party insurance, which provides cover against third party liabilities such as injury or death of crew members, passengers or third parties, pilferage or damage to cargo, collision damage, pollution and other matters that cannot be covered in the open insurance market. Additional voluntary insurance may be taken out to cover against war risks, strikes and loss of earnings.

Hull and machinery insurance is obtained from a marine insurance company or through a broker who will use a policy backed by underwriters in one of the insurance markets. Two important contributory factors in determining the level of hull and machinery insurance are the owner's claims record and the claimed value of the vessel. Ship values fluctuate with the freight market and the age and condition of the vessel.

The third party insurance required by shipowners falls under four headings: P&I cover, which is generally obtained through a club; collision liability cover; war P&I cover; and the provision of certificates of financial responsibility required to trade into the United States.

The P&I clubs, of which there are 13, are mutual insurance societies which settle third party claims for their members. They investigate claims on behalf of their shipowner members, provide advice during any negotiations or legal dispute over the claim and hold reserve funds to settle the claims on their members' behalf. This reserve is replenished through a subscription (known as the 'call') from members which varies, depending on the level of claims settled. The subscription for an individual member depends on the company's claims record and other factors such as the intended trading area, the cargo to be carried, the flag of registry and the nationality of the crew. Since settlement takes time, there may be a supplementary call on members and members changing clubs generally pay a 'release call' to settle their outstanding liabilities with the old club and an 'advance call' to the new club.

Because of the potential size of third party claims, the P&I clubs reinsure their exposure to very large claims. In 2005 individual clubs had a maximum liability exposure of $5 million. A pool of clubs covered larger claims of $5–$20 million, and claims of $20 million to a maximum of $4.25 billion were reinsured in the insurance market. The P&I clubs also obtain credit ratings from the rating agencies, which assist in marketing their services to members. Unlike other forms of insurance, P&I cover cannot be assigned to a mortgagee, though a comfort letter may be obtained. It is also subject to retrospective cancellation, for example if the club member goes bankrupt.

## GENERAL COSTS

A registration fee is paid to the flag state, the size of which depends on the flag. In Table 6.2 a fee of $17,000 per annum for a single ship is included under general costs.

Included within the annual operating budget for the ship is a charge to recover shore-based administrative and management charges, communications, owners' port charges, and miscellaneous costs. The overheads cover liaison with port agents and general supervision. The level of these charges depends on the type of operation. For a small tramping company operating two or three ships they may be minimal, whereas a large liner company will carry a substantial administrative overhead. With improved communications, many of these functions can now be undertaken by shipboard personnel in tramping companies. It is also an increasingly common practice for day-to-day management to be subcontracted to specialists for a predetermined fee.

## Periodic maintenance

Periodic maintenance, the second major cost item in Figure 6.4, involves a cash payment to cover the cost of interim dry docking and special surveys. It accounts for about 4% of costs, though this depends on the age and condition of the ship. To maintain a ship in class for insurance purposes, it must undergo regular surveys with a dry docking every 2 years and a special survey every 4 years to determine its seaworthiness. At the special survey the vessel is dry-docked, all machinery is inspected and the thickness of the steel in certain areas of the hull is measured and compared with acceptable standards. These measurements become more extensive with age and all defects must be remedied before a certificate of seaworthiness is issued. In older ships these surveys often necessitate considerable expense, for example in replacing steelwork that, owing to corrosion, no longer meets the required thickness standards. In addition, dry docking allows marine growth, which reduces the operating efficiency of the hull, to be removed.

**Table 6.4** Standard Capesize, lifetime periodic maintenance costs (1993 dollar prices)

| | Age of ship | | | | |
|---|---|---|---|---|---|
| | 0–5 | 6–10 | 11–15 | 16–20 | |
| Time out of service (days) | 20 | 23 | 40 | 40 | |
| Time in drydock (days) | 10 | 14 | 23 | 18 | Total |
| Cost Items (USD) | | | | | |
| Dry-dock charges | 62,000 | 68,000 | 81,500 | 74,000 | 285,500 |
| Port charges, tugs, agency | 70,000 | 73,300 | 92,000 | 92,000 | 327,300 |
| General services | 80,000 | 92,000 | 160,000 | 160,000 | 492,000 |
| Hull blast, clean & painting | 102,800 | 128,800 | 183,600 | 99,000 | 514,200 |
| All dry-dock paint | 164,100 | 175,500 | 207,000 | 194,100 | 740,700 |
| All steel replacement | 70,000 | 350,000 | 1,190,000 | 840,000 | 2,450,000 |
| Cargo spaces | 22,200 | 64,200 | 126,000 | 150,000 | 362,400 |
| Ballast spaces | 36,400 | 23,200 | 26,000 | 47,400 | 133,000 |
| Hatch covers & deck fittings | 28,000 | 56,320 | 60,560 | 60,560 | 205,440 |
| Main engine and propulsion | 46,000 | 42,000 | 48,000 | 48,000 | 184,000 |
| Auxiliaries | 27,000 | 34,000 | 134,000 | 44,000 | 239,000 |
| Piping & valves | 18,000 | 37,000 | 50,000 | 34,000 | 139,000 |
| Navigation & communications | 9,000 | 11,000 | 11,000 | 11,000 | 42,000 |
| Accommodation | 6,000 | 8,000 | 7,000 | 7,000 | 28,000 |
| Surveys & surveyors | 70,000 | 78,500 | 113,000 | 108,000 | 369,500 |
| Miscellaneous | 100,000 | 100,000 | 100,000 | 100,000 | 400,000 |
| Spare parts & subcontractors | 70,000 | 100,000 | 100,000 | 120,000 | 390,000 |
| Owner's attendance | 23,800 | 25,600 | 35,800 | 35,800 | 121,000 |
| Estimated total | 1,005,300 | 1,467,420 | 2,725,460 | 2,224,860 | 7,423,040 |
| Averaged annual cost | 201,060 | 293,484 | 545,092 | 444,972 | |
| Averaged daily cost | 551 | 804 | 1,493 | 1,219 | |

Source: Clarkson Research, Capesize Quality Survey (1993)

Table 6.4 shows how the periodic maintenance schedule for a Capesize bulk carrier evolves as the vessel ages. The sums shown cover the cost of both the interim dry dockings and the special surveys.[3] Eighteen cost areas are covered, some of which, such as the cost of using the dry dock ($62,000) vary only slightly with age, whilst others, such as steel replacement and work on the hatch covers, increase very sharply as the ship gets older. In this example the periodic cost increases from $1 million for the two surveys in the first five years to $2.7 million in the 11–15-year period. Naturally this depends on the ship. The average daily cost increases from $551 per day to $1493 per day. Owners who operate preventive maintenance policies may incur lower costs, while for ships in poor condition the costs may be much higher.

## Voyage costs

We now turn to voyage costs, the third cost item in Figure 6.4, which accounts for 40% of the total costs. These are the variable costs incurred in undertaking a particular voyage. The main items are fuel costs, port dues, tugs, pilotage and canal charges:

$$VC_{tm} = FC_{tm} + PD_{tm} + TP_{tm} + CD_{tm} \qquad (6.3)$$

where $VC$ represents voyage costs, $FC$ is the fuel costs for main engines and auxiliaries, $PD$ port and light dues, $TP$ tugs and pilotage, and $CD$ is canal dues.

## FUEL COSTS

Fuel oil is the single most important item in voyage costs, accounting for 47% of the total. In the early 1970s when oil prices were low, less attention was paid to fuel costs in ship design and many large vessels were fitted with turbines, since the benefits of higher power output and lower maintenance costs outweighed their high fuel consumption. However, when oil prices rose during the 1970s, the whole balance of costs changed. During the period 1970–85, fuel prices increased by 950% (Figure 6.5). Leaving aside changes in the fuel efficiency of vessels, this meant that, if fuel accounted for about 13% of total ship costs in 1970, by 1985 it had increased to 34%, more than any other individual item. As a result, resources were poured into designing more fuel-efficient ships and operating practices were adjusted, so that bunker consumption by the shipping industry fell sharply. In 1986 the price of bunkers fell and the level of interest in this aspect of ship design reduced, but in 2,000 bunker prices started to increase again (see Figure 6.5) and the importance of fuel costs increased.

The shipping industry's response to these extreme changes in bunker prices provides a good example of how the design of ships responds to changes in costs. Although shipping companies cannot control fuel prices, they have some influence on the level of fuel consumption. Like any other piece of complex machinery, the fuel a ship burns depends on its design and the care with which it is operated. To appreciate the opportunities for improving the fuel efficiency of ships it is necessary to understand how energy is used in the ship. Take, for example, a typical Panamax bulk carrier, illustrated in Figure 6.6. At a speed of 14 knots it consumes 30 tons of bunker oil and 2 tons of diesel oil in a day. Approximately 27% of this energy is lost in cooling the engine, 30% is lost as exhaust emission,

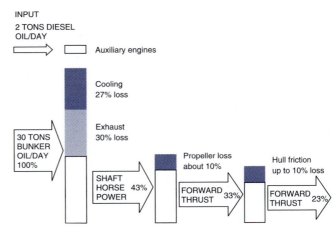

**Figure 6.6**
Energy losses in typical 1990s built Panamax bulk carrier, 14 knots design speed
Source: Compiled by Martin Stopford from various sources

10% is lost at the propeller, and hull friction accounts for an additional 10%. Only a residual 23% of the energy consumed is actually applied to propelling the vessel through the waves. Whilst this is a simplified view of a complex process, it identifies the areas where technical improvements can, and have, been made – the main engine, the hull and the propeller. The extent of the improvement can be judged from the fact that ships built in the 1970s typically consumed 10 tons per day more fuel than ships built in later years to achieve the same speed.

The design of the main engine is the single most important influence on fuel consumption. Following the 1973 oil price rises, and particularly since 1979, there were major improvements in the thermal efficiency of marine diesel engines. Between 1979 and 1983 the efficiency of energy conversion in slow-speed marine diesel engines improved from about 150 grams per brake horsepower per hour to around 127 grams per brake horsepower per hour. In addition to lower fuel consumption, engine operating speeds were reduced to below 100 rpm, making it possible to use more efficient large-diameter, slow-speed propellers without installing a gear box. The ability to burn low-quality fuel was also improved. In some cases the fuel savings achieved were quite spectacular. Diesel-powered 300,000 dwt VLCCs built in 2005 consumed 68 tons of bunkers a day at 15 knots, compared with fuel consumption of 130–150 tons per day by turbine-powered vessels built in the 1970s.

It is also possible to improve the fuel efficiency of a ship by fitting auxiliary equipment. One method is to install waste heat systems, which use some of the heat from the exhaust of the main engines to power a boiler that drives the auxiliary engines when the main engine is running, thus saving diesel oil. An alternative method is to use generators driven direct from the main engine while the vessel is at sea. This means that auxiliary power is obtained from the more efficient main engine rather than a small auxiliary engine burning expensive diesel fuel.

In operation, the ship's fuel consumption depends on its hull condition and the speed at which it is operated. When a ship is designed, naval architects optimize the hull and power plant to a prescribed design speed which may be, for example, 15 knots for a bulk carrier or 18 knots for a small container ship. Operation of the vessel at lower speeds results in fuel savings because of the reduced water resistance, which, according to the 'cube rule', will be approximately proportional to the cube of the proportional reduction in speed:

$$F = F^* \left( \frac{S}{S^*} \right)^a \qquad (6.4)$$

where $F$ is the actual fuel consumption (tons/day), $S$ the actual speed, $F^*$ the design fuel consumption, and $S^*$ the design speed. The exponent $a$ has a value of about 3 for diesel engines and about 2 for steam turbines. It follows from the cube rule that the level of fuel consumption is very sensitive to speed. For example, for a Panamax bulk carrier a reduction in the operating speed of 16 knots to 11 knots results in a two-thirds saving in the tonnage of fuel burnt per day, as shown in Table 6.5.

For any given speed, fuel consumption depends on hull design and hull smoothness. According to work carried out by British Maritime Technology, a reduction in hull roughness from 300 micrometres to 50 micrometers can save 13% on the fuel bill. Between dry docking, marine growth on the hull of the ship increases its water resistance, reducing the achievable speed by 2 or 3 knots in extreme cases. Even with regular dry docking, as the ship ages its hull becomes less smooth as the hull has been scraped and repainted many times. Self-polishing coatings and anti-fouling, which release a poison to kill marine growth and reduce hull fouling between dry dockings, are now widely used but are expensive to apply and have a limited life.

**Table 6.5** How speed affects fuel consumption for a panamax bulk carrier

| Speed knots | Main engine fuel consumption tons/day |
|---|---|
| 16 | 44 |
| 15 | 36 |
| 14 | 30 |
| 13 | 24 |
| 12 | 19 |
| 11 | 14 |

As a result of these factors there can be a wide disparity between the fuel consumption of vessels of a similar size and speed. For example, the fuel consumption of two Panamax bulk carriers operating at the same speed could differ by 20–30% depending on age, machinery and hull condition. Obviously the cost importance of this difference in efficiency depends on the price of fuel.

### PORT CHARGES

Port-related charges represent a major component in voyage costs and include various fees levied against the vessel and/or cargo for the use of the facilities and services provided by the port. Charging practices vary considerably from one area to another, but, broadly speaking, they fall into two components – port dues and service charges. Port dues are levied on the vessel for the general use of port facilities, including docking and wharfage charges, and the provision of the basic port infrastructure. The actual charges may be calculated in four different ways, based on: the volume of cargo; the weight of cargo; the gross registered tonnage of the vessel; or the net registered tonnage of the vessel. The service charge covers the various services that the vessel uses in port, including pilotage, towage and cargo handling.

The actual level of port costs depends on the pricing policy of the port authority, the size of the vessel, the time spent in port and the type of cargo loaded or discharged. For example, the typical port cost for a Panamax bulk carrier loading 70,000 tonnes of coal in Australia in 2007 and discharging in Europe would be about $147,000, roughly $2 per tonne. By convention, the allocation of port charges differs for different types of charter. Under a voyage charter, all port dues and charges related to the vessel are charged to the shipowner, while all charges on the cargo are generally paid for by the charterers, except for cargo-handling charges, which are generally agreed under the charter terms. Under a trip charter or time charter, all port charges are carried by the charterer.

The main canal dues payable are for transiting the Suez and Panama canals. The toll structure of the Suez Canal is complicated since it is based on two little-known units of measurement, the Suez Canal net ton and Special Drawing Rights (SDRs). Tariffs are calculated in terms of these. The Suez Canal net tonnage of a vessel is a measurement based on late nineteenth-century rules that were intended to represent the revenue-earning capacity of a vessel. It broadly corresponds to the cargo-carrying space below deck, though it is not directly comparable to the more normal measurement of cargo capacity (net tonnage).

The Suez Canal net tonnage of a vessel is calculated either by the classification society or by an official trade organization which issues a Suez Canal Special Tonnage Certificate. For vessels wishing to transit the canal that do not have a certificate, the calculation is provisionally done by adding together the gross and net tonnage, dividing by two and adding 10%. Tariffs are then calculated on the basis of SDRs per Suez net ton. SDRs were chosen as the currency unit in an attempt to avoid losses owing to fluctuations in exchange rates, as their value is linked to a number of major national currencies. Suez Canal toll charges per Suez net ton vary for different types and sizes of ships. For the Panama Canal a flat rate charge per Panama Canal net ton is used (see Chapter 8 for more details on the Suez and Panama canals).

## Cargo-handling costs

Finally, we come to cargo–handling costs, the fourth major cost item in Figure 6.4. The cost of loading and discharging cargo represents a significant component in the total cost equation, and one to which considerable attention has been paid by shipowners, particularly in the liner business. Cargo-handling costs are given by the sum of loading costs, discharging costs and an allowance for the cost of any claims that may arise:

$$CHC_{tm} = L_{tm} + DIS_{tm} + CL_{tm} \tag{6.5}$$

*where CHC* is cargo-handling costs, *L* is cargo loading charges, *DIS* is cargo discharge costs, and *CL* is cargo claims.

The level of these costs may be reduced by investment in improved ship design – to facilitate rapid cargo handling, along with advanced shipboard cargo-handling gear. For example, a forest products carrier with open holds and four cranes per hold can achieve faster and more economical cargo handling than a conventional bulk carrier relying on shore-based cranes.

## 6.4 THE CAPITAL COST OF THE SHIP

The fifth component in the cost equation for our 'typical' ship in Figure 6.4 is its capital cost. This accounts for 42% of total costs, but in economic terms it has a very different character from the other costs. Operating and fuel costs are necessities without which the ship cannot trade. Crew and bunker suppliers are generally the first creditors to be paid off in a financial crisis, because without them the ship is marooned. In contrast, once a ship is built, its capital costs are obligations which have no direct effect on its physical operation. That is why the costs are not specified in Figure 6.4. In practice these obligations take three forms as far as the shipping company's cashflow is concerned. First, there is the initial purchase and the obligation to pay the shipyard; second, there are the periodic cash payments to banks or equity investors who put up the capital to purchase the vessel; and third, cash received from the sale of the vessel. How these obligations appear in the cashflow is not determined by the ship's trading activities – as, for example, fuel costs are – they are the result of financing decisions made by the ship's owner, and there are many ways this can be handled as we will see in Chapter 7 which discusses financing ships and shipping companies.

## The distinction between profit and cash

Before discussing this process in detail we need to be clear about the distinction between cash and profit. Profit is a concept used by accountants and investment analysts to measure the financial return from a business. It is calculated by taking the total revenue earned by the business during an accounting period (e.g. a year) and deducting the costs which the accounting authorities consider were incurred in generating that revenue. The cashflow of a company, in contrast, represents the difference between cash payments and receipts in the accounting period. In surviving shipping recessions cash is what matters, while for companies with equity investors, providing a commercial return on assets is equally important. The main reason why cashflow differs from profit in a particular year is that some costs are not paid in cash at the time when the accountant considers them to have been incurred. In shipping the best example is the timing of payment for the ship. The cash transaction takes place when the ship is built and each year the ship grows older and loses a proportion of its value.

To give investors a fair account of whether the business is making money, accountants have developed procedures for reporting large capital items in the profit and loss account. When a capital item is purchased, its full cost does not appear in the profit and loss account. If it did, shipping companies would report a massive loss whenever they bought a new ship. Instead the cost of the ship is recorded in the company's balance sheet as a 'fixed asset' and each year a percentage of its value (e.g. 5%) is charged as a cost in the profit and loss account to reflect the loss of value during the accounting period. This charge is known as *depreciation* and is not a cash charge. The ship was paid for in cash long ago. It is just bookkeeping, so profit will be lower than cashflow by that amount.

If a merchant ship is depreciated (or written off) over 20 years on a linear basis (there are several methods, but this is the most common), it means one-twentieth of its original cost is included in the company's overhead costs each year for 20 years. For example, if the ship was purchased for $10 million cash and depreciated at the rate of $1 million per annum, the position might be as shown in Table 6.6. In each of the first two years

**Table 6.6** Example of profit (loss) account and cashflow for shipping company purchasing vessel for cash (equity) ($ million)

| | Profit (loss) account | | Cashflow | |
|---|---|---|---|---|
| | Year 1 | Year 2 | Year 1 | Year 2 |
| 1 Freight revenue | 10 | 10 | 10 | 10 |
| 2 Less: operating costs | 5 | 5 | 5 | 5 |
| 3    voyage costs | 3 | 3 | 3 | 3 |
| 4    depreciation[a] | 1 | 1 | 0 | 0 |
| 5 Total operating profit/cashflow | 1 | 1 | 2 | 2 |
| 6 Less capital expenditure on ship | None[a] | None | 10 | 0 |
| 7 Total profit/cashflow | 1 | 1 | (8) | 2 |

[a]Captal expenditure is covered by the depreciation item (see text)

the company has the same profit of $1 million, which is calculated by deducting costs, including depreciation, from the total revenue earned. However, the cashflow profile is quite different. The operating cashflow at line 3 is $2 million in each year because depreciation is not a cash item – it is simply a bookkeeping entry, so it does not appear in the cashflow calculation. From this is deducted the cash payment for the ship in year 1, giving a negative cashflow of $8 million in year 1 and a positive cashflow of $2 million in year 2.

However, this is not the whole story. Not many shipping companies buy their ships for cash. A particularly important aspect of cashflow is the method used to pay for the ship. In Table 6.6 the company pays cash on delivery and that shows up as a 'lump' in the cashflow, following which there is nothing more to pay for capital. If the ship is purchased with a loan, the cashflow profile changes because the cashflow now includes payment of interest and repayment of the loan. This situation is illustrated in Table 6.7

**Table 6.7** Example of profit (loss) account and cashflow for shipping company purchasing vessel on five-year loan ($ million)

| | Profit (loss) account | | Cashflow | |
|---|---|---|---|---|
| Line | Year 1 | Year 2 | Year 1 | Year 2 |
| 1 Freight revenue | 10 | 10 | 10 | 10 |
| 2 LESS:  operating costs | 5 | 5 | 5 | 5 |
| 3    voyage costs | 3 | 3 | 3 | 3 |
| 4    depreciation[a] | 1 | 1 | 0 | 0 |
| 5 Total operating profit/cashflow | 1 | 1 | 2 | 2 |
| 6 LESS interest at 10% | 1 | 0.8 | 1 | 0.8 |
| 7 Profit/cashflow after interest | 0 | 0.2 | 1 | 1.2 |
| 8 LESS capital repayment | None | None | 2 | 2 |
| 9 Total profit/cashflow | 0 | 0.2 | (1) | (0.8) |

[a]Captal expenditure is covered by the depreciation item (see text)

which shows what happens if, instead of paying cash, the ship is financed with a five-year loan. Although the company generates a positive operating cashflow of $2 million (line 5), after deducting interest (line 6) and capital repayments (line 8) it has a net cash outflow in both years. If the company has sufficient funds available, this negative cashflow required to meet finance payments may not present a serious problem. The problems arise if there is a negative cashflow but no cash reserves to meet it.

## Estimating a ship's depreciation

Equity investors in public shipping companies face a different problem. If they are investing for the long term they need to estimate how much profit the company is making, and that depends crucially on how much depreciation is deducted to arrive at a fair estimate of the profit earned. Eventually the ship wears out, so its cost must be deducted from profits at some point and the usual approach used by accountants is 'straight-line depreciation'. The ship is written off in equal proportions over its expected life. The longer it lasts, the less depreciation can be deducted each year. An example illustrates two important points about the depreciation of merchant ships. If we analyse the Panamax bulk carrier sales shown in Figure 6.7, we find that the relationship between year of build and sale price is approximately linear. The regression coefficient is 0.93, indicating a relatively good fit, suggesting that the depreciation curve is linear, and the expected life is about 25 years.

That is very typical because the fifth special survey involves heavy repairs, though market conditions are also influential. For example, between 1995 and 2000, a period of generally weak market conditions, bulk carriers were on average scrapped at 25.2 years of age and tankers at 24.7 years, but in 2006, a year of high earnings, the average scrapping age was 28 years for tankers and 30 years for bulk carriers. Specialized ships have longer lives, notably cruise ships which averaged 43.8 years, livestock carriers 33.9 years and passenger ferries 30 years. In these cases shipping companies may choose to refurbish their vessels rather than demolish them. This calls for a word of caution in determining the life expectancy of these specialized ships. Steel ships can be repaired at almost any stage in their life and there are examples of ships

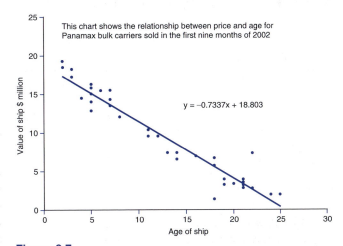

**Figure 6.7**
Market value and age of Panamax bulk carriers
Source: Clarkson Research Studies (1993)

operating in protected markets such as the United States coastal trades or the Great Lakes for more than 50 years. A shipowner may choose to refurbish an old vessel rather than build a new one, but it can be very costly and is all a matter of economics. So although specialist ships may appear to last more than 25 years we need to take the cost of life extension and refitting into account.

## Cashflow costs and gearing

Capital is the cashflow item over which the owner has the most control at the outset. Operating and voyage costs can be adjusted marginally, depending on the ship he buys, but the cash payments associated with capital can be very high or non-existent, depending on how the ship is financed. The initial purchase of the ship may be paid for with cash, either from reserves or, in the case of very large companies, from cashflow. In that case there is a one-off capital payment and no further cashflow relating to capital until the ship is sold. A shipowner who follows this route and purchases his ships for cash has no further cash costs and can survive on a freight rate equal to operating and voyage costs. For the 5-year-old Panamax bulk carrier in Table 6.1 the operating and bunker costs are $11,820 per day.[4] If instead of paying cash the shipowner borrows the full purchase price from a bank over 20 years the capital repayments would be $11,155, almost doubling the daily payments the company is committed to making to $22,975 a day. In a volatile market like shipping that would present a problem, since the company often would not be able to meet the payments out of trading income. That is why banks rarely advance the full capital cost of the vessel, requiring the borrower to meet a portion of the purchase price of the ship from equity. The ratio of debt to equity is referred to as *gearing*; the higher it is, the riskier it is.

## Security and bank lending policy

The terms on which bank loans are made available, and in particular the gearing they permit, are very important. We will discuss debt finance in Chapter 7, but it is worth previewing the way banks approach the repayment of interest and principal on a shipping loan. Since most commercial banks lend money at only 1 or 2 percentage points above the rate at which they borrow, there is little margin for risk – the bank must be sure before it lends that it will receive repayment of capital and interest in full. For this reason a major consideration in ship finance is the security against the loan. A shipowner borrowing money must be able to satisfy the lender that if he defaults the loan can be recovered. The following methods are used to provide security:

- Assignment of earnings, insurances, etc.
- The lender takes a first mortgage on the ship being purchased, giving him the first claim on the proceeds of the sale should the borrower default.

- A mortgage on other ships or assets may be offered. As with any security the bank must be convinced that in a forced sale the assets will realize sufficient cash to cover the outstanding debt.
- The income from a long charter with a 'blue chip' company is assigned to the lender and provides assurance that the cashflow will be available to service the loan.
- A guarantee of the loan may be given by the owner, shipping company, the ship-building company constructing the vessel or a government agency such as the UK's Export Credit Guarantee Department.

The choice of finance, and the obligations that arise as a result, have a tremendous impact on the shipowner's cashflow commitments. During recessions shipowners who fund investment with equity are safe so long as freight revenue is sufficient to cover operating and voyage costs. The ship may not be profitable, but at least the owner remains in control. The shipowner who has financed his investment from debt faces a very different situation. He must make regular payments to his banker to cover interest and capital repayments. If the freight rate only covers operating and voyage costs, as often happens during depressions, he must meet his financing costs from elsewhere or lose control of the business to his bankers. Thus two shipowners running identical vessels with similar operating and voyage costs face radically different cashflows during a depression if one has financed his fleet on an equity basis and the other using debt.

## Taxation

Taxation does not figure prominently in the accounts of most bulk shipping companies. The international nature of the business makes it possible to avoid tax by registering a company under one of the many open registry flags (see Section 16.5) which exempt shipping companies from tax. During the recession of the 1980s many shipping companies switched to flags of convenience which charged only a nominal tonnage tax; in 2005, 49% of world tonnage was registered in this way (see Table 16.4). In response some European countries started, with the approval of the European Union, to offer special taxation schemes for shipping companies registered under their domestic flag. These schemes had three components: a tonnage tax approximating to zero corporation tax; a reduction in social contributions for seafarers and shipping companies; and a reduction to zero of personal income tax for national seafarers.

For example, the Danish International Shipping Register (DIS), which was set up in 1988, exempted crew from national tax and in 2002 a tonnage tax scheme was introduced, basing taxation on the tonnage of ships the company was operating, at a specified rate per tonne, with no regard to the actual operating profits of the company. Germany, the Netherlands, Norway, the UK, Belgium and Greece have all introduced schemes. Other reasons for registering in a particular country are to take advantage of investment incentives available to local businesses, or where other business activities make this route economic.

## 6.5 THE REVENUE THE SHIP EARNS

### The classification of revenue

The first step is to define how revenue is received. As we saw in Chapter 5, there are several different ways a shipowner can earn revenue, each of which brings a different distribution of risk between the shipowner and the charterer and a different apportionment of costs. The risks are shipping market risk, which concerns the availability of cargo and the freight rate paid, and operational risk, arising from the ability of the ship to perform the transport. The costs are those discussed in the previous section. Each of the revenue arrangements deals with these items differently:

- *Voyage charter*. This system is used in the voyage-charter market, the specialist bulk market and in a rather different way in the liner trades. The freight rate is paid per unit of cargo transported, for example $20 per ton. Under this arrangement, the shipowner generally pays all the costs, except possibly cargo handling, and is responsible both for managing the running of the ship and for the planning and execution of the voyage. He takes both the operational and the shipping market risk. If no cargo is available, if the ship breaks down, or if it has to wait for cargo he loses out.
- *Time charter*. The charter hire is specified as a fixed daily or monthly payment for the hire of the vessel, for example $5,000 per day. Under this arrangement, the owner still takes the operational risk, since if the ship breaks down he does not get paid. The charterer pays fuel, port charges, stevedoring and other cargo-related costs. He takes the market risk, paying the agreed daily hire regardless of market conditions (unless the charter rate is linked to the market in some way).
- *Bare boat charter*. This is essentially a financial arrangement in which the charter hire only covers the financing cost of the ship. The owner finances the vessel and receives a charter payment to cover expenses. All operating costs, voyage costs and cargo-related costs are covered by the charterer, who takes both the operational and the shipping market risk.

A discussion of these revenue concepts can be found in Table 5.1. For simplicity the discussion in this chapter assumes that revenue is earned as a unit freight rate per ton mile of cargo carried.

### Freight revenue and ship productivity

The basic revenue calculation involves two steps: first, determining how much cargo the vessel can carry in the financial period, measured in whatever units are appropriate (tons, ton miles, cubic metres, etc.); and second, establishing what price or freight rate the owner will receive per unit transported. In more technical terms, the revenue per deadweight of shipping capacity can be viewed as the product of the ship's productivity, measured in ton miles of cargo transported per annum, and the freight rate per ton mile, divided by the ship's deadweight:

$$R_{tm} = \frac{P_{tm}.FR_{tm}}{DWT_{tm}} \qquad (6.6)$$

where $R$ is the revenue per dwt per annum, $P$ the productivity in ton miles of cargo per annum, $FR$ the freight rate per ton mile of cargo transported, $t$ the time period and $m$ the ship type.

The concept of a ship's 'productivity' is useful because it measures overall cargo-carrying performance, encompassing operating performance in terms of speed, cargo deadweight and flexibility in terms of obtaining backhaul cargoes. For example, a combined carrier potentially has a much higher productivity than a tanker because it can carry a backhaul of dry cargo if one is available. The analysis of productivity can be carried further by subdividing into its component parts as follows:

$$P_{tm} = 24 \cdot S_{tm} \cdot LD_{tm} \cdot DWU_{tm} \qquad (6.7)$$

where $S$ is the average operating speed per hour, $LD$ is the number of loaded days at sea per annum, and $DWU$ is deadweight utilization. This definition states that ship productivity, measured in terms of ton miles of cargo transported in year $t$, is determined by the distance the vessel actually travels in 24 hours, the number of days it spends loaded at sea in a year, and the extent to which it travels with a full deadweight of cargo. By further examination of each of these components a precise definition of productivity can be obtained.

### OPTIMIZING THE OPERATING SPEED

When a vessel is earning unit freight revenue, the mean operating speed of the ship is important because it determines the amount of cargo delivered during a fixed period and hence the revenue earned.

In a high freight rate market it pays to steam at full speed, whereas at low freight rates a reduced speed may be more economic because the fuel cost saving may be greater than the loss of revenue. This certainly happens in practice. For example, in early 1986 the VLCC fleet was operating at a speed of around 10 knots, but when freight rates rose in 1988–9 it speeded up to almost 12 knots. For the same reasons, a substantial increase in bunker prices will change the optimum operating speed for a particular level of freight rates because it increases the cost saving for a given reduction in fuel consumption.

The financial logic behind the optimum operating speed calculation can be illustrated with a simple example in Table 6.8 which shows the effect of speed on the cashflow of a ship for different fuel prices and freight rates. By slowing down from 14 knots to 11 knots, the amount of fuel used in a year is more than halved, from 33.9 tons per day

**Table 6.8** Effect of speed on cashflow for high and low freight and bunker costs

| Ship speed knots | Fuel consumption tons per day | FUEL COST SAVING by slowing down | | REVENUE LOSS by slowing down | |
|---|---|---|---|---|---|
| | | $/day | $/day | $/day | $/day |
| 14 | 33.9 | — | — | — | — |
| 13 | 27.2 | 2,697 | 674 | 1,440 | 4,320 |
| 12 | 21.4 | 5,016 | 1,254 | 2,880 | 8,640 |
| 11 | 16.5 | 6,979 | 1,745 | 4,320 | 12,960 |

*Assumptions:* 70,000 ton cargo; 300 days a year at sea; 10,000 mile round voyage

| bunker assumptions | | freight assumptions | |
|---|---|---|---|
| high | low | low | high |
| $400/ton | $100/ton | $10/ton | $30/ton |

to 16.5 tons per day, bringing a saving in bunker costs that depends on the level of fuel prices. There is, however, a corresponding loss of revenue, because at the lower speed less cargo is delivered. The size of this loss depends on the level of freight rates. As a result the shipowner is confronted by a trade-off between lower costs and lower income, and the balance will determine his decision.

To illustrate this point we can examine the circumstances set out in Table 6.8 under which it would pay the shipowner to slow down to 11 knots. Bunker costs are $400/ton (high) and $100/ton (low), whilst freight ranges from $30/ton (high) to $10 per ton (low).

- *Case 1*: fuel cost $100/ton and low freight rates – he would save $1.745 million on bunkers but would lose $4.3 million revenue, so it is not worth slowing down.
- *Case 2*: fuel cost $400/ton and low freight rates – he would save $6.9 million and lose $4.3 million revenue so it is worth slowing down.
- *Case 3*: fuel cost $400/ton and high freight rates – he would save $6.9 million costs but would lose $12.9 revenue, so it is not worth slowing down.

In fact, for any level of freight rates and fuel costs there is an optimum speed.

## MAXIMIZING LOADED DAYS AT SEA

A ship's time is divided between 'productive' loaded days at sea and unproductive days spent in ballast, in port, or off hire. A change in any of these variables will affect the number of loaded days at sea, *LD*, as follows:

$$LD_{tm} = 365 - OH_{tm} - DP_{tm} - BAL_{tm} \tag{6.8}$$

where *OH* is the number of days off hire per annum, *DP* the number of days in port per annum, and *BAL* the number of days in ballast per annum.

*Days off hire* reflect time spent for repairs, breakdowns, holidays, etc. A survey of bulk carriers showed an average of 24 days per annum off hire, though this figure can be expected to vary with conditions in the freight market. Owners will always attempt to minimize the time the vessel is not earning, but during periods of low freight market activity the ship may spend substantial time waiting for cargo, this being one of the major costs incurred during a market recession. For example, a ship that waits 12 days for a cargo with daily operating costs of $6,000 will have lost $72,000.

*Port days* depend upon the type of ship, the loading facilities available and the cargo being loaded. The more time the ship spends in port the less it spends carrying cargo. Homogeneous cargoes such as iron ore and grain can load very quickly where good facilities are available – iron ore loading rates of 6,000 tons per hour are common. Difficult cargoes such as forest products and general cargo may take weeks rather than days to load under some circumstances. Ships handling bagged sugar can spend a month loading or discharging.

*Days spent in ballast* is the third and most important determinant of loaded days at sea. For tankers and other single cargo ships it is a simple calculation, since backhauls are not generally available and the ship spends half its sea time in ballast. For combined carriers, most bulk carriers, reefers and liners the calculation is more difficult because these vessels can carry a wide range of different cargo types, and are often able to pick up backhaul cargo. Relatively little statistical information is available about the average time spent in ballast. A rule of thumb is 'the bigger the ship, the more time in ballast'. For example, a 30,000 dwt bulk carrier is always better placed to obtain a backhaul than a 160,000 dwt vessel since draught restrictions may limit the larger vessel's ability to pick up part cargoes.

The financial impact of obtaining a backhaul cargo can be illustrated by the example in Table 6.9 of a Panamax bulk carrier operating in the coal trade from Hampton Roads, USA, to Japan during the shipping depression in 1985. At a freight rate of $15 per ton this vessel would have a negative cashflow of $500,000 per annum when operating on a 50% ballast basis. However, by picking up a backhaul of coal from Newcastle, New South Wales, to Norway at a rate of $15 per ton, the vessel would generate a positive cashflow of $19,000 per annum.

## DEADWEIGHT UTILIZATION

This refers to the extent to which the vessel travels with a full payload of cargo. In other words, it is the ton mileage of cargo carried divided by the ton mileage of cargo that the

**Table 6.9** The effect of the backhaul on cashflow

|  | Cargo 000 tons per year | Freight per ton $ | Annual revenue $m | Annual cost $m | Cashflow $'000 |
|---|---|---|---|---|---|
| Backhaul | 308 | 15 | 4.62 | 4.43 | 19 |
| No backhaul | 252 | 15 | 3.78 | 4.28 | (500) |

vessel could have carried if it had always obtained a full payload. In practice, the dead-weight cargo capacity of a vessel represents a physical maximum, and it is a commercial decision whether this capacity is fully utilized. The shipowner always has the option to accept a part cargo and it is common practice in both the dry bulk and the tanker markets, especially during recessions. The change was particularly noticeable in the tanker market after the 1973 oil crisis, when the oil companies were no longer able to match cargo parcels to ships. Conversely during the 2003–7 boom there was enormous pressure to use ships as efficiently as possible by obtaining a full cargo.

An interesting example of deadweight utilization is the grain trade between the US Gulf and Japan. In the 1970s this trade was shipped in 25,000 dwt bulk carriers, but during the 1980s it was taken over by Panamax bulk carriers. Because the parcel size is restricted to 55,000 tons by the water depth in the Panama Canal, a 65,000 dwt Panamax cannot load a full deadweight, but in a relatively weak freight environment Panamax owners were prepared to settle for a part cargo. But by 2007 three things had happened. Handymaxes had edged up in size to 55,000 dwt; Panamaxes had increased to 75,000 dwt; and freight rates were much higher. As a result the part cargo trade was less attractive to the Panamaxes, but ideal for Handymaxes, which took it over. An unusual exception to the rule that ship sizes increase with time.

Products tankers also carry many part cargoes. Two popular parcel sizes in this trade are 33,000 and 40,000 tonnes, neither of which fills the popular 37,000 dwt and 47,000 dwt products tankers. The matter is further complicated by the high cubic of naphtha, a common oil products cargo (see Table 11.5). As a result products tankers often trade with a part cargo. With this in mind, some shipyards design products tankers with scantlings of 47,000 dwt and a hull optimized to 40,000 dwt, a reminder that the issue is not filling the ship, but making a profit.

In conclusion, investors face many decisions concerning the trade-off between revenue and cost variables. A combined carrier offers the shipowner the option to obtain very high deadweight utilization by carrying alternate cargoes of oil and dry cargo, while incurring higher capital and operating costs. Containerization involves heavy investment in cargo-handling efficiency, whereas the ro-ro combines some of the benefits of containerization with a higher degree of cargo flexibility. But many of the decisions are less dramatic but equally important – for example, paying extra for a faster bulk carrier that can make more trips during a boom, or a bigger products tanker that has the edge in long-haul trades even if it often carries part cargoes.

## 6.6 SHIPPING ACCOUNTS – THE FRAMEWORK FOR DECISIONS

So far we have focused on the cost and revenue relationships which determine how a shipping company or investment project performs financially. Now it is time to pull this together using the accounting framework which shipping companies and their investors use to take financial decisions.

## What company accounts are used for

First a brief note about the comparability of financial information. Shipping companies register in many countries around the world and different financial reporting standards mean that financial information is not always in a comparable form. However in recent years significant progress has been made in coordinating financial reporting standards through the International Accounting Standards Board (IASB). In 2003 the IASB published the first International Financial Reporting Standard (IFRS 1). This was adopted by the European Union for public companies in 2004 and by 2008 about 100 countries complied with this standard.

Company accounts are compiled for three quite different purposes, each calling for a different presentation of the information. One is to show the financial standing of the company. Potential creditors need to know if the company is financially sound and likely to meet its commitments. Most jurisdictions impose strict rules regarding the provision of this type of financial information, obliging limited liability companies to publish accounts and as noted above there are now international guidelines setting out what company accounts must contain. For example since January 2005 listed companies in the European Union must comply with the International Financial Reporting Standards (IFRS1). Naturally companies, know these accounts will be read by their competitors as well as their suppliers and generally prefer to reveal as little as possible.

The second purpose of accounts is for the assessment of tax. The tax authorities lay down rules for what is and is not permissible in a particular country regarding the calculation of the profit upon which tax is raised. This means that the published accounts of a company registered in that country reflect the accounting conventions of the local tax system, which may make them quite different from, and much less useful than, the accounts published by the company's internal management for the purposes of running the business.

Finally we have the 'management accounts', which are compiled to help the management of the company in their decision-making. This is the aspect of financial reporting we are most interested in. Three separate, but connected, financial statements are generally used by the accounting profession to supply information for management purposes; income statement, the balance sheet, and the cashflow statement. Each has its own 'slant' on the business.

In this section we will review these financial statements. Since shipping is a dollar denominated business we will use as an example the accounts of a company listed in the USA. Our aim is to understand the economics of the business but note that the accounts used, which were selected to illustrate the type of financial issues shipping companies deal with, predate IFRS 1.

## The income statement

The income statement, referred to in the UK as the profit and loss account, shows how much profit (net revenue) the company made during the accounting period. This tells us how much wealth the company created, a crucial piece of information since a company generating profits is increasing in value, whilst a company losing money is on the slippery slope. If we think of the company as a stream of net revenue, then the income

**Table 6.10** Shipping company income statement

| | Year end ($millions) | | |
|---|---|---|---|
| | **2003** | **2002** | **2001** |
| **Operating Revenue** | 1,576 | 783 | 1,039 |
| *less* Operating expenses: | | | |
| Voyage expenses | 395 | 239 | 250 |
| Vessel operating expenses | 211 | 168 | 155 |
| Time-charter hire expense | 305 | 50 | 66 |
| Depreciation and amortization | 191 | 149 | 136 |
| General and administrative | 85 | 57 | 49 |
| *Sub-total* **Income from operations** | **390** | **119** | **383** |
| Write-offs & gains on vessel sales | −90 | | |
| Restructuring charge | −6 | | |
| Equity income from joint ventures | 7 | 5 | 17 |
| *Sub-total* **operating revenue** | **300** | **124** | **401** |
| Interest expense | −81 | −58 | −66 |
| Interest income | 4 | 3 | 9 |
| Other loss | −45 | −16 | −7 |
| **Net income** | **177** | **53** | **337** |
| *Memo* | | | |
| Earnings per share – basic | 4.43 | 1.35 | 8.48 |

Source: based on the published accounts of a public shipping company

statement tells us the rate of flow of the stream. Table 6.10 shows the income statement for a large shipping company for three accounting periods, 2001–3. In 2003 the company earned $1.58 billion operating revenue from its ships, including both timecharter and spot income. From this they deducted five cost items: $395 million voyage expenses; $211 million operating costs; $305 million for ships chartered in; depreciation of $191 million; and general and administration costs $85 million. That leaves $390 million income from vessel operations. However, it is then necessary to make some other adjustments that had nothing to do with vessel operations, but affected the company's wealth. A major item was the write-off of $90 million on ships which were sold during the year for prices below their book value. There was also a $6 million restructuring cost for closing some overseas offices and $7 million joint venture income. After taking account of these the operating income was $300 million. Finally, the interest payments and 'other losses' (mainly tax) are deducted to give the net income for the company in 2003 of $177 million.

## The balance sheet

The balance sheet shows the company's wealth at a specific point in time, in this case 31 December 2001, 2002 and 2003 which was the company's year end. It starts by reporting the total assets of the business (i.e. everything the company owns), and then deducts the liabilities (i.e. money owed to third parties). Analysts are also interested in the balance sheet because it tells them how the company is holding its wealth. It is all very well having spectacular profits, but if a company has all its wealth tied up in ships and no cash to pay the bills, it could be a very risky situation.

Usually the balance sheet divides the calculation of wealth into three components. First, the current assets of the business are funds that can be realized quickly without changing the basic structure of the business or incurring penalties. Second, there are the 'fixed' assets which, for a shipping company, include the value of the vessels the company owns and other assets such as buildings and investments in other companies. Valuing the vessels raises issues about whether they should be valued at book value (i.e. acquisition cost less depreciation) or market value since the two methods can produce very different results (see Section 6.4 for a discussion of the calculation of depreciation). Finally, we deduct the liabilities (i.e. the money owed) which usually takes the form of any outstanding bills, debt, bonds and other financial commitments that must be met at some time in the future. The fact that the capital value of the ships is so high and subject to extreme volatility makes it difficult to disentangle the underlying value of the business, taking one cycle with another, from the cyclical elements that depress or increase returns.

Table 6.11 provides an example of a relatively complex shipping company balance sheet. The layout is conventional, with the assets listed at the top of the table in sections 1.1–1.3 and the liabilities in the second half of the table in sections 2.1 and 2.2. In this case the total assets in 2003 were $3.588 billion, and the sum of long- and short-term liabilities was $1.921 million. The difference between these two is shareholders' equity, which was $1.667 billion.

The current assets, shown in Section 1.1, include cash in the bank of $295 million, plus accounts receivable (i.e. invoices which have been presented, but not paid) of $147 million and some pre-paid expenses and other assets of $39 million, giving the company total current assets of $481 million. In section 1.2 the ships in the company's fleet are valued at $2.4 billion, based on cost less accumulated depreciation. This method of valuation, known as 'book value', is not always a reliable guide to the market value of the vessels. In fact the income statement included a write-off of $90 million from the sale of ships whose sale price was lower than the book value. In addition to the ships the balance sheet reports some capital leases, which nowadays have to be declared, and advance payments on some tankers currently under construction. Section 1.3 includes various other assets totalling $533 million in 2003, including $96 million worth of shares in other shipping companies and an investment in some financial leases. Unusually for a shipping company, there are also some intangible assets and 'goodwill'. Overall the company's assets consist of 13% cash and working capital, 70% ships, and the remaining 17% is various odds and ends.

On the liabilities side, by far the biggest liability in 2003 was $1.5 billion of long-term debt. In addition, there are various short-term obligations listed in section 2.1.

**Table 6.11** Shipping company balance sheet

| | Year end ($ millions) | |
|---|---|---|
| | **2003** | **2002** |
| **1. ASSETS** | | |
| *1.1 Current Assets* | | |
| Cash and cash equivalents (note 1) | 295 | 289 |
| Accounts receivable | 147 | 71 |
| Prepaid expenses and other assets | 39 | 28 |
| Total current assets | 481 | 388 |
| *1.2 Vessels* | | |
| Vessels at cost less depreciation | 2,387 | 1,928 |
| Vessels under capital leases, at cost, | 38 | |
| Advances on newbuilding contracts (note 3) | 151 | 138 |
| Total vessels | 2,575 | 2,067 |
| *1.3 Other assets* | | |
| Marketable securities (note 2) | 96 | 14 |
| Restricted cash | | 5 |
| Deposit for purchase of company (note 4) | | 76 |
| Net investment in direct financing leases (note 5) | 73 | |
| Investment in joint ventures (note 6) | 54 | 56 |
| Other assets | 60 | 30 |
| Intangible assets and goodwill (note 7) | 249 | 89 |
| Total other assets | 533 | 269 |
| **TOTAL ASSETS** | **3,588** | **2,724** |
| **2. LIABILITIES** | | |
| *2.1 Current liabilities* | | |
| Accounts payable | 52 | 22 |
| Accrued liabilities | 120 | 84 |
| Current portion of long-term debt | 102 | 84 |
| Current obligation under capital lease | 1 | |
| Total current liabilities | 275 | 190 |
| *2.2 Long term liabilities* | | |
| Long-term debt | 1,498 | 1,047 |
| Obligation under capital lease | 35 | |
| Other long-term liabilities | 113 | 45 |
| Total long-term liabilities | 1,646 | 1,092 |
| **TOTAL LONG- & SHORT-TERM LIABILITIES** | **1,921** | **1,281** |
| **Stockholders' equity** | **1,667** | **1,442** |
| **TOTAL LIABILITIES** | **3,588** | **2,724** |

1. The company has loans which specify a minimum cash balance
2. Shareholding in two other shipping companies
3. Payments already made to shipyard on new ships under construction
4. 10% deposit paid against the purchase of another shipping company
5. Capatilized value of investment in financing leases
6. The appraised value of a 50% holding in a joint venture company
7. Goodwill purchased with companies
Source: based on the published accounts of a public shipping company

1. less accumulated depreciation of $1,034,747 (2002; $940,082)
2. less accumulated depreciation of $438 (2002: nil)

## The cashflow statement

Finally there is the cashflow statement, which tells the analyst exactly how much cash the company paid in or paid out during the period, where the cash that was spent came from, and where it went. Often the trigger of bankruptcy for shipping companies is not the multi-million dollar debts owed to the bank, it is the bunker supplier who, faced with an unpaid bill, decides to arrest a ship. So it is always important to have enough cash in hand. The cashflow statement is in many respects similar to the income statement, but it deals strictly with cash payments, excluding certain items such as depreciation which are not actually paid in cash.

The cash flow statement in Table 6.12 is divided into three sections, each dealing with a different aspect of the company's activities. Section 1 deals with the cash provided by operating activities; section 2 deals with the cashflow arising from financing activities; and section 3 deals with the cashflow from investing activities. If we take each of these in turn, we can see how the company's business was developing.

The operating activities in section 1 generated $456 million in 2003. The key point here is that the cash flow from operating activities is quite different from the net income reported in Table 6.10. That showed net income of $177 million in 2003, but in section 1.2 the cash statement adds back non-cash items which appeared in the income statement, including depreciation of $191 million, losses on the write-down of vessels of $92 million (a pure balance-sheet item), and various other non-cash items. Changes in working capital and expenditure for dry docking are then deducted to give positive net cashflow from operating activities of $456 million – more than twice the net income.

In section 2 we see the cashflow arising from financing activities. In 2003 this was also strongly positive, with $447 million of cash generated. This cash was generated mainly by refinancing – they raised $1.98 billion of new long-term debt, $25 million by issuing common stock, made $63 million scheduled debt repayments, and prepaid $1.47 billion of debt, leaving $447 million free cash.

The way the company used the cash raised from operating and financing is shown in section 3. Investments made by the company in 2003 cost $895 million. They paid $730 million for new companies and $372 million for new ships. The sale of old ships generated $242 million. There were various other minor investments, including the purchase of shares and some leases.

Pulling all this together, the company generated $456 million cash from operating its ships; topped it up with $447 million of additional external finance; and invested $895 million in buying companies and ships. But despite all this activity the company's cash balance changed by only $8 million in the year. Somebody has done good job of balancing the books!

Not all companies publish accounts in this form, but the above examples illustrate the general principles of financial accounting in shipping. Whether the company has 40 ships or 400 the operating activities are about increasing revenues and squeezing costs to generate income; the financing activities are about managing funds, whether from a bond issue or an investment by a high net worth relative so that the company can do what it needs to when it needs to do it; and the investment activities are about implementing the

**Table 6.12** Shipping company cashflow statement

| | Year end ($ millions) | | |
| --- | --- | --- | --- |
| | 2003 | 2002 | 2001 |
| Cash provided by (or used for): | | | |
| **1. OPERATING ACTIVITIES** | | | |
| 1.1 Net income | 177 | 53 | 337 |
| 1.2 Non-cash items (to add back): | | | |
| Depreciation and amortization | 191 | 149 | 136 |
| (Gain) loss on sale of assets | −2 | 1 | −1 |
| Loss on write-down of vessels | 92 | | |
| Other non-cash items | 44 | 4 | 20 |
| total | 325 | 154 | 155 |
| 1.3 Change in working capital | −4 | 7 | 28 |
| 1.4 Expenditures for drydocking | −43 | −35 | −20 |
| Net cash flow from operating activities | 456 | 180 | 500 |
| **2. FINANCING ACTIVITIES** | | | |
| Net proceeds from long-term debt | 1,981 | 255 | 688 |
| Scheduled repayments of long-term debt | −63 | −52 | −72 |
| Prepayments of long-term debt | −1,467 | −8 | −752 |
| Decrease (increase) in restricted cash | 6 | −1 | −8 |
| Proceeds from issuance of Common Stock | 25 | 4 | 21 |
| Repurchase of Common Stock | | −2 | −14 |
| Cash dividends paid | −36 | −34 | −34 |
| Net cash flow from financing activities | 447 | 163 | −171 |
| **3. INVESTING ACTIVITIES** | | | |
| Expenditures for vessels and equipment | −372 | −136 | −185 |
| Proceeds from sale of vessels and equipment | 242 | | |
| Purchase of companies | −705 | −76 | −182 |
| Purchase of intangible assets | −7 | | |
| Purchase of available-for-sale securities | −37 | | −5 |
| Proceeds from sale of available-for-sale securities | 10 | 7 | 36 |
| Decrease (increase) in investment in joint ventures | 26 | −26 | |
| Net investment in direct financing leases (note 3) | −20 | | |
| Other | −5 | −2 | 0 |
| Net cash flow from investing activities | −895 | −233 | −336 |
| Cash and cash equivalents, beginning of the period | 285 | 175 | 181 |
| Cash and cash equivalents, end of the period | 292 | 285 | 175 |
| Increase (decrease) in cash and cash equivalents | 8 | 110 | −6 |

Source: based on the published accounts of public shipping company

company's strategy. Cashflow does not make a good business, but well-managed cashflow certainly smooths the way for good businessmen to get on with what they are good at.

## 6.7 FOUR METHODS OF COMPUTING THE CASHFLOW

Our aim in this chapter is to focus on how costs can be controlled and how revenue can be increased within the overall constraints imposed by the ship, the business organization and the legal jurisdiction under which a company's vessels operate. At the beginning of this chapter we discussed the importance of cash management in navigating through the shipping cycles that are such a feature of the business and examined the cost and revenue items that underlie a shipping business's cashflow. It now remains to discuss the practical techniques for preparing operational cashflow calculations that can be used as a basis for decision-making.

In shipping the usual measure of cashflow is *earnings before interest, tax, depreciation and amortization* (EBITDA). This measures the 'cash in hand' generated by the business during a period of time and is calculated by deducting out-of-pocket expenses from revenue. Four methods of cashflow analysis are widely used in the shipping industry, each of which approaches the cashflow from a different perspective:

- *The voyage cashflow (VCF) analysis* is the technique used to make day-to-day chartering decisions. It computes the cashflow on a particular ship voyage or combination of voyages. This provides the financial basis for operational decisions such as choosing between alternative charter opportunities where there are several options, or in a recession deciding whether to lay up the ship or fix it.
- *The annual cashflow (ACF) analysis* calculates the cashflow of a ship or a fleet of ships on a year-by-year basis. It is the format most often used for cashflow forecasting. By projecting the total cashflow for the business unit during a full financial year, it shows whether, on specific assumptions, the business as a whole will generate enough cash to fund its operations after taking account of complicating factors such as tax liabilities, capital repayments and periodic maintenance.
- *The required freight rate analysis* is a variant on the annual cashflow analysis. It focuses exclusively on the cost side of the equation, calculating the level of costs which must be covered from freight revenue. This is useful for shipowners calculating whether a ship investment will be profitable and bankers carrying out credit analysis to decide how much to lend. It can also be used to compare alternative ship designs.
- *The discounted cashflow (DCF) analysis* is concerned with the time value of money. It is used for comparing investment options where the cashflows differ significantly over time. For example, a new ship involves a large initial investment but is cheap to run, whereas an old ship is cheap to buy but has higher costs later in its life. DCF analysis provides a structured way of comparing the two investments.

These methods are complementary and each approaches the cashflow in a different way appropriate to the needs of different decisions.

## The voyage cashflow analysis

The VCF analysis provides information about the cash that will be generated by undertaking a particular voyage or sequence of voyages. Typically the owner with a ship which is open on a particular date will have brokers' lists showing cargoes available in the relevant loading area. Sometimes there will be one obvious cargo, so the decision is easy.

In most cases, however, there will be several alternatives, all possible but none ideal, so a decision is needed about which cargo to take. This means having to decide whether to accept the grain cargo from the US Gulf to Japan, or from the US Gulf to Rotterdam, whether to fix now or wait a few days to see if the rates improve, and whether to lay up the vessel or to continue to trade. By providing an estimate of the profitability of a particular voyage, the VCF analysis plays an essential part in making operating decisions.

An example of a voyage cashflow analysis is shown in Table 6.13. A Panamax bulk carrier is on a multi-leg voyage from the US Gulf to Japan with grain, then ballasting down to Australia, where it picks up another cargo of coal to deliver to Europe before returning in ballast to East Coast North America to reload grain. The aim is to estimate how much cash the voyage will actually generate.

This table is in a summarized form, and in practice a more detailed voyage estimating programme would be used, but it covers the main issues. The four sections of the table are reviewed below:

1  *Ship information*. Details of the ship size, speed, bunker consumption, etc. In this case the speed is 15 knots on the loaded and ballast voyages and a 5% sea margin is deducted to allow for weather conditions and other delays. The ship, which is relatively modern, burns 33 tons per day on the laden voyage and 31 tons on the ballast voyage. Operating costs are shown as a daily rate assuming 350 days a year on hire (note that the cashflow attributable to operating costs will not necessarily fall within the time-scale of the voyage). The bunker price is $338 per ton for bunker oil and $531 per ton for diesel oil for the auxiliaries. Bunker prices vary around the world and a bunkering plan will be considered, to ensure that the ship bunkers in the cheapest location.

2  *Voyage information*. This section shows details of the voyage – port days, distance, cargo carried, and the freight rate for each leg of the voyage. The port time of 3 days loading and 2 days discharging includes time waiting for a berth, documentation, loading and discharging cargo, bunkering and a day for transiting the Panama Canal. It is not always easy to estimate port times precisely. In this case the cargo is 54,000 tons of grain on leg 1 and 70,000 tons of coal on leg 3. A ship of this type would probably carry about 3,500 tons of bunkers and stores, leaving an available cargo capacity of 71,500 tons, so the vessel is not fully loaded on the first leg. On this voyage the ballast legs are much shorter than the cargo legs, which is good – the shorter, the better. The round voyage is calculated from the speed, less the sea margin for good weather, the voyage distance on loaded and ballast legs, and the port times. In addition, a congestion provision is shown in line 2.6 which could cover port time, delays at certain ports such as loading coal, or congestion at known chokepoints such as the Dardanelles for tankers leaving the Black Sea. In total the voyage is 31,089 miles, takes 116 days (90.9 days at sea and 25 days in port), transports 124,000 tons of cargo and the freight is $5.75 million.

3  *Voyage cashflow*. The freight earnings are repeated in line 3.1. From this are deducted the broker's commission, and voyage costs which include bunkers, diesel

**Table 6.13** Voyage cashflow analysis for 75,000 dwt bulk carrier (with backhaul), 4 May 2007

## 1. SHIP INFORMATION

| Ship Type | | Speed (knots) | | | Bunkers (tons/day) | |
|---|---|---|---|---|---|---|
| | Design speed | Sea margin | voyage speed | Main | Auxiliary |
| 1.1 Bulk carrier, 75,000 dwt | | | | | | |
| 1.2 Laden voyages | 15 | 5.0% | 14.25 | 33 | 1 |
| 1.3 Ballast voyages | 15 | 5.0% | 14.25 | 31 | 1 |
| 1.4 Operating cost $/day | | 5,620 | At 350 days on hire pa | | |
| 1.5 Bunker price $/ton | | | | 338 | 531 |

## 2. VOYAGE INFORMATION

| Route | col (1) Distance (miles) | col (2) Days at sea | col (3) Days in port | col (4) Cargo (tons) | col (5) Freight $/ton |
|---|---|---|---|---|---|
| 2.1 Port days/voyage - loading | | | 3 | | |
| 2.2 Port days/voyage - discharge | | | 2 | | |
| 2.3 Voyage details: | | | | | |
| Leg 1: US Gulf–Japan | 9,123 | 26.7 | 5 | 54,000 | 56.0 |
| Leg 2: Japan–Australia | 4,740 | 13.9 | 0 | Ballast | |
| Leg 3: Australia–Europe | 12,726 | 37.2 | 10 | 70,000 | 39.0 |
| Leg 4: Europe–East Coast North America | 4,500 | 13.2 | 0 | Ballast | |
| 2.4 Total loaded voyages | 21,849 | 63.9 | | | |
| 2.5 Total ballast voyages | 9,240 | 27.0 | | | |
| 2.6 Port congestion provision | | | 10 | | |
| 2.7 Total round voyage | 31,089 | 90.9 | 25 | 124,000 | 5,754,000 |

## 3. VOYAGE CASHFLOW

| | $ | Notes |
|---|---|---|
| 3.1 Freight earnings $ | 5,754,000 | From row 2.7 above |
| 3.2 *less* Broker's commission | 86,310 | At 1.5% |
| 3.3 *less* Voyage costs | | |
| Bunker oil for main engine | 995,674 | Days at sea *consumption*price |
| Diesel oil for auxiliaries | 48,270 | Days at sea *consumption*price |
| Port costs | 418,000 | Cost of four port calls |
| Canal dues | 80,000 | One Panama canal transit |
| Total | 1,541,944 | |
| 3.4 less operating costs | 651,378 | days on voyage * operating cost/day |
| 3.5 Voyage cashflow | 3,474,369 | Cash generated by voyage (less OPEX) |

## 4. VOYAGE EARNINGS

| | | |
|---|---|---|
| 4.1 memo: Days on the voyage | 116 | From line 2.7 including congestion |
| 4.1 Time-charter equivalent $/day | 35,596 | Equals (line 3.5/line 4.1) + row 1.4 |

Note: Freight rates shown are as on 4 May 2007

for auxiliaries, port and canal costs. Operating costs are then deducted in line 3.4 to calculate the net voyage cash flow.

4    *Voyage earnings.* Finally, in line 4.1 we calculate the time-charter equivalent for the round voyage, which is $35,596 per day.

In this example the freight rates are taken from a period of very strong earnings in May 2007. The ship would earn more than enough to cover its full capital costs. To put the voyage time-charter equivalent into perspective, on the same date, 4 May 2007, the 3-year time-charter rate for a modern Panamax bulk carrier was $34,000 per day, but the 1-year-rate was $41,750 per day.

So what does the owner do in this situation? Basically, money is flooding in and the ship is generating almost $10 million a year. The owner will earn a very decent return if he accepts the voyage at this level of freight rates, but he could match it with less trouble if he puts the ship out on a 3-year time-charter at $34,000/day and if he puts the ship out on a 1-year time-charter at $41,750/day he could get more. It all depends on what he thinks will happen in future, and that means anything from the end of this voyage to the next three years. He may remember that five years earlier in August 2002 the rate for US Gulf–Japan grain was $19.40 per tonne and the backhaul from Newcastle, NSW to Europe was $10.20 per tonne. Admittedly bunkers were cheaper at $153 for fuel oil and $213 for marine diesel oil, but at those rates the voyage would only pay $6357 per day. Could it happen again? Should he take a time-charter while the rates are so good? It's the million-dollar decision that shipowners ponder every day.

For older ships strong markets like this are very profitable. A few voyages generating over $3 million each soon generate more cash than the ship is worth in a normal market. It is easy to see why in strong markets old ships are rarely scrapped unless they have serious physical problems. But if we rerun the voyage estimate for the August 2002 scenario the ship does not earn enough to cover its operating costs. This puts the owner in a very difficult position. If he accepts the charter in these circumstances he will lose money on the voyage, even if things go as planned. With old ships he knows that things do not always go as planned. However, if he refuses the cargo he will be even worse off. His operating costs must be paid whether the ship has a cargo or not. One option is to send the ship to lay-up, saving a large part of operating costs, but unless the vessel is carefully maintained during lay-up its future value can be badly affected.

In these circumstances it is easy to see how during recessions the business becomes totally preoccupied with the problem of obtaining enough cash to pay each day's bills as they come in and with cutting costs wherever possible. The lesson relearned by each generation of over-leveraged shipowners and their bankers is that once the recession has started it is too late. There are no real options. With a real effort the owner might cut his annual operating costs, using a cheaper crew, defer all but the most essential repairs and tighten up on administration costs. However, if he is highly leveraged, whether the ship is new or old, the $1,500 per day he might save will not make much difference to his cashflow. Indeed, if he cuts costs too much it could lead to expensive operational problems.

If cash is not available elsewhere and the bankers press for payment, the only option may be to sell assets to raise cash. This usually means selling a ship, and brings us back to the sale and purchase decision that we discussed at the beginning of the chapter in Figure 6.1. The problem is that a ship that cannot generate a positive cashflow, even when well managed, will not command a high price on the market. As desperate owners are driven to sell their ships in order to raise cash, and as few potential purchasers can be found, the price falls. For newer vessels, a speculative investor will almost always be found, but for old ships whose economic life may not span the depression the demolition yard may be the only willing purchaser.

The moral is that financially shipping is a business of feast and famine. When times are good, as they are in the example in Table 6.13, the challenge is to invest the funds wisely. But surviving depressions depends upon being able to generate cash when other shipowners are losing money and, as we saw in Chapter 3, recessions are a regular feature of the shipping market. By the time the voyage decision arrives, it is too late. Banks rarely lend money to customers who are in financial difficulties and if they do, it is usually on very disadvantageous terms. Financial planning for such contingencies must be undertaken before the ship is purchased, when rates are high, and the shipowner still has some room for manoeuvre. Cashflow planning is the technique to use.

## The annual cashflow analysis

ACF analysis is concerned with calculating the cashflow generated by the business as a whole over a period of time. In this sense it is less concerned with the ship as an operating unit than with the total cashflow that the business must finance over a period of time, either months or years.

There are several different methods of calculating the annual cashflow, but the simplest is the receipts and payments method shown in Table 6.14 (a simpler version of the cashflow statement in Table 6.12). The top of the table shows cash revenue, the lower half of the table shows cash costs, and the bottom line indicates the cashbook balance carried forward from one year to the next in the company's bank account. This simple example illustrates the ACF technique for a one-ship company trading over a four-year period. The figures are loosely based on actual market conditions between 1990 and 1995, and the freight rates, prices, operating costs and the outstanding loan are shown as a memo item at the bottom of Table 6.14. For simplicity, inflation and bunker price changes have not been included in the analysis.

The shipping company has an opening balance of $8.5 million (line 1). On the last day of year 0 it purchases a 1992 built tanker of 280,000 dwt for $22 million. A bank loan is used to finance 70% of the purchase price, to be paid back in equal annual instalments of $3.08 million per annum over 5 years. The remainder of the purchase price is paid from the company's own cash reserve. Receipt of the loan from the bank is shown in line 2.2 as a capital receipt of $15.4 million, while the payment for the ship is shown in line 4.4 as $22 million. In year 1, freight rates are running at $31,824 per day and the ship generates total revenue of $10.8 million (line 2.1), more than enough to cover operating costs, voyage costs and capital charges, so the company ends year 1 with a positive bank balance of $4.45 million. However, freight rates fall to $12,727 per day in year 2, $17,768 per day in year 3 and $10,107 per day in year 4. Each year the company's bank balance is slowly eroded, so that by the end of year 3 the strong positive balance has disappeared and the company needs to raise an additional $798,000 in cash just to meet day-to-day commitments.

**Table 6.14** Annual cashflow analysis Case 1: 280,000 dwt tanker built 1976 scrapped at 4th survey

| $000s | Year 0 (1990) | Year 1 (1991) | Year 2 (1992) | Year 3 (1993) | Year 4 (1994) | Year 5 (1995) |
|---|---|---|---|---|---|---|
| 1 Opening balance | 8,500 | 1,900 | 4,450 | 815 | (798) | (1,487) |
| 2 Cash receipts | | | | | | |
| 2.1 Operating revenue (gross) | 0.0 | 10,820 | 4,327 | 6,041 | 3,436 | |
| 2.2 Capital receipts | 15,400 | | | | | |
| 2.3 Revenue from ship sale | | | | | 6,300 | |
| 3 TOTAL RECEIPTS | 15,400 | 10,820 | 4,327 | 6,041 | 9,736 | |
| 4 Cash payments | | | | | | |
| 4.1 Operating costs | | 3,650 | 3,650 | 3,650 | 3,650 | |
| 4.2 Dry docking | | | | | | |
| 4.3 Voyage costs | | | | | | |
| 4.4 Purchase of ship | 22,000 | | | | | |
| 4.5 Loan repayments | | 3,080 | 3,080 | 3,080 | 6,160 | |
| 4.6 Interest | | 1,540 | 1,232 | 924 | 616 | |
| 4.7 Tax payments | | | | | | |
| 5 TOTAL COSTS | 22,000 | 8,270 | 7,962 | 7,654 | 10,426 | |
| 6 CASHBOOK BALANCE AT YEAR END | 1,900 | 4,450 | 815 | (798) | (1,487) | (1,487) |
| *memo*    Charter rate / day | 22,883 | 31,824 | 12,727 | 17,768 | 10,107 | 15,789 |
| Days trading | | 340 | 340 | 340 | 340 | 340 |
| Second-hand price of ship | 22,000 | 20,000 | 9,500 | 11,000 | 8,000 | 10,000 |
| Operating costs $/day | 10,000 | 10,000 | 10,000 | 10,000 | 10,000 | 10,000 |
| Outstanding loan (year end) | 15,400 | 12,320 | 9,240 | 6,160 | 0 | 0 |
| Asset cover | 1.426 | 1.6234 | 1.02814 | 1.7857 | | |

At the end of year 4 the company is only generating enough cash to pay its operating costs and, to make matters worse, in year 4 it faces its fourth special survey, with an estimated cost of $5 million. Faced with a negative cashflow it cannot fund from its own cash reserves the company would be forced to make some major decisions of the type discussed at the beginning of the chapter. One option would be to sell. The second-hand price for a VLCC in average condition shown in the memo section of Table 6.14 is $8 million. However, a ship due for its fourth special survey is not in average condition and would not attract even that price – a scrap sale at $6.3 million would be more likely. With $3.08 million of the original loan still outstanding and debts of $798,000, a sale for $6.3 million would leave the shipping company with a loss of $1.487 million, compared with an opening balance of $8.5 million. Obviously this option would suit the bank, which would be repaid in full, but the shipping company would have lost heavily on the deal. By selling the ship any hope of recovering the losses would be gone.

**Table 6.15** Annual cashflow analysis Case 2: 280,000 dwt tanker built 1976 traded past 4th survey

| $000s | Year 0 (1990) | Year 1 (1991) | Year 2 (1992) | Year 3 (1993) | Year 4 (1994) | Year 5 (1995) |
|---|---|---|---|---|---|---|
| 1 Opening balance | 8,500 | 1,900 | 4,450 | 815 | (798) | (9,707) |
| 2 Cash receipts | | | | | | |
| 2.1 Operating revenue (gross) | 0.0 | 10,820 | 4,327 | 6,041 | 3,436 | 5,368 |
| 2.2 Capital receipts | 15,400 | | | | | |
| 2.3 Revenue from ship sale | | | | | | 11,000 |
| 3 TOTAL RECEIPTS | 15,400 | 10,820 | 4,327 | 6,041 | 3,436 | 16,368 |
| 4 Cash payments | | | | | | |
| 4.1 Operating costs | | 3,650 | 3,650 | 3,650 | 3,650 | 3,103 |
| 4.2 Dry docking | | | | | 5,000 | |
| 4.3 Voyage costs | | | | | | |
| 4.4 Purchase of ship | 22,000 | | | | | |
| 4.5 Loan repayments | | 3,080 | 3,080 | 3,080 | 3,080 | 3,080 |
| 4.6 Interest | | 1,540 | 1,232 | 924 | 616 | 308 |
| 4.7 Tax payments | | | | | | |
| 5 TOTAL COSTS | 22,000 | 8,270 | 7,962 | 7,654 | 12,346 | 6,491 |
| 6 CASHBOOK BALANCE AT YEAR END | 1,900 | 4,450 | 815 | (798) | (9,707) | 171 |
| memo Current account interest | 190 | 445 | 82 | (80) | (971) | 17 |
| memo Charter rate / day | 22,883 | 31,824 | 12,727 | 17,768 | 10,107 | 15,789 |
| Days trading | | 340 | 340 | 340 | 340 | 340 |
| Second-hand price of ship | 22,000 | 20,000 | 9,500 | 11,000 | 8,000 | 11,000 |
| Operating costs $/day | 10,000 | 10,000 | 10,000 | 10,000 | 10,000 | 8,500 |
| Outstanding loan (year end) | 15,400 | 12,320 | 9,240 | 6,160 | 3,080 | (0) |
| Asset cover | 1.4286 | 1.6234 | 1.0281 | 1.7857 | 2.5974 | |

The second option is to put the ship through survey and trade on. The cashflow in Table 6.15 shows what would happen in years 4 and 5 if the company followed this strategy. First, the owner would have to raise an overdraft of, say, $10.5 million cash to meet his negative cashflow in years 3 and 4. This will be difficult. Few bankers are willing to lend to a business with no assets and a negative cashflow. There is little that can be done to raise money within the business. Cost economies might be possible if the company is paying top rates to the crew and maintaining the vessel to a very high standard. Closing expensive offices is another source of economy. If rigorous cost-cutting saves $1,500 per day, that is worth $0.5 million in a full year. This might convince his bankers that he is determined to tackle the problem, but would not even pay the interest on his overdraft. The best the company can offer its bankers is a straight gamble on the market. Bankers do not generally gamble, but since the choice is between foreclosing and providing a $10.5 million overdraft, it is not so much a matter of gambling as choosing between unpalatable options. Such decisions test the concept of relationship banking which we discuss in Chapter 8.

On this occasion, if the bank decided to back the owner, it would pay off. The out-turn in year 5 (Table 6.15) shows how quickly a company's financial position can change in shipping. Freight rates increase to $15,789 per day in year 5, which brings in an extra $1.9 million income (line 2.1). In response to higher freights the market price of the ship goes up to $11 million. Since the ship has now passed survey, it would probably fetch this price if sold, so its real asset value has increased by 75% from $6.3 million to $11 million in a year, adding $4.7 million to the net worth of the company. Lower operating costs of $3.1 million contribute an extra $0.5 million, so the company's financial position has improved by $7.2 million. At the end of that year the last instalment on the loan is paid off, so there will be no more repayments. If the company sold the ship it would end the year with a balance of $17 million, from which it has to pay interest on its current account. However, the owner has no debt and the ship has passed its survey. He has survived and by taking a gamble he and his bankers have avoided taking a loss. If all goes well the owner will soon be a rich man and the banker will have a grateful client.

As always in recessions, the crucial issue is survival. By the time the unpaid bills start to pile up in year 4 it is too late to do very much – the right time to raise questions about costs, efficiency and working capital is before the ship is purchased. The example discussed in the preceding paragraphs shows how a realistic ACF analysis can provide the framework for thinking ahead and planning financial strategy in the shipping market. If the shipowner had borrowed less, or borrowed more and provided for emergency working capital at the outset, the problem would never have arisen. Or would it? We started this chapter by likening competition in a depressed shipping market to a marathon race with only a few prizes. Someone has to lose. It is through ACF analysis that shipping companies and their bankers can weigh up their fitness to finish the race, and identify those actions that can enhance their chances of future survival.

## The discounted cashflow analysis

So far we have concentrated on cashflow analysis which helps management to think through the implications of certain decisions in terms of the future cashflow of the business. But business is not just about surviving recessions. Staying in business also depends on making a commercial return on capital, and that calls for sound investment decisions. Often the decision facing management is a choice between investment projects where the future cashflows are well established, but different. For example, consider a shipowner who purchases a tanker for $45 million and is offered two different deals by oil companies, Big Petroleum and Superoil Trading:

- Big Petroleum offers to charter the ship for $18,000 per day for 7 years, trading 355 days a year. At the end of the charter the oil company guarantees to buy the ship for $35 million.

- Superoil Trading's proposal is a little more complex. To fit its trading patterns the company wants the owner to have the cargo tanks epoxy-coated. This will cost $3 million, bringing the total price up to $48 million. However, Superoil is willing to buy the ship at the end of the charter for $45 million. Also, they want to escalate the daily charter rate by $2,000 each year from $12,000 per day in year 1 to $24,000 per day in year 7.

The owner is particularly impressed by Superoil's contract. The charter revenue over the 7 years of $44.3 million is exactly the same as for the Big Petroleum deal. However, the buyback terms are far better. He loses only $3 million on the ship with Superoil, compared with $10 million in the Big Petroleum deal. It seems he will be $8 million better off with Superoil. Although this seems obvious, Superoil has a reputation for driving a hard bargain and the owner is worried. So he should be. He has ignored the time value of money.

If we take the time value of money into account, we find that there is less difference between the two offers than there appears at first sight, as we will demonstrate using DCF analysis. The principle behind this analysis is that because investors can earn interest on their money, cash paid on a future date is worth less than the same amount of cash paid today. For example, $1,000 invested today at 10% interest is worth $1100 in a year, but $1,000 paid in a year is worth $1,000. So $1,000 today is worth 10% more than $1,000 in a year's time. Putting it another way, the 'present value' of $1100 paid in a year is $1,000.

DCF analysis converts future payments into a 'present value' by discounting them. The method is as follows. The first step is to determine the 'discount rate', which represents the time value of money to the company. There are several ways of doing this. The simplest way, if the company has a cash surplus, is to use the interest rate which the company would receive if it invested the cash in a bank deposit. Or the discount rate might be set at a level which reflects the average return on capital obtained from investments in other parts of the business. Many businesses use 15% per year. Finally, if the company has to borrow to finance the project, the marginal cost of debt might be more appropriate.

Once the discount rate has been agreed, we can discount the future cashflows. In Table 6.16 we do this for the two contracts, and the two parts of the table have the same layout. In row 1 we show the purchase price of the ship, in row 2 the time-charter revenue, and in row 3 the total cashflow. In row 4 we use 12% per annum to calculate a 'discount factor' for each year. Row 5 shows the discounted cashflow, calculated by multiplying the cashflow in each year by the discount factor for that year. Finally this discounted cashflow is summed over all years to produce the net present value (NPV) of each project shown in row 6 in the year 0 column.

For the Big Petroleum contract the NPV is −$5,400. It seems he would be better off investing in stocks, though not by very much. However, the real surprise comes when we look at the Superoil Trading contract. The $8 million extra return from this project has completely disappeared. The NPV is $64,700, which on a $48 million project is insignificant. The reason why this project looked so good is that all the extra revenue

**Table 6.16** Example of discounted cashflow (DCF) analysis for tanker charter options ($000)

| Row | | Year 0 | Year 1 | Year 2 | Year 3 | Year 4 | Year 5 | Year 6 | Year 7 |
|---|---|---|---|---|---|---|---|---|---|
| *Big Petroleum* | | | | | | | | | |
| 1 | Ship purchase/sale | (45,000) | | | | | | | 35,000 |
| 2 | Timecharter revenue | | 6,390 | 6,390 | 6,390 | 6,390 | 6,390 | 6,390 | 6,390 |
| 3 | Cashflow | (45,000) | 6,390 | 6,390 | 6,390 | 6,390 | 6,390 | 6,390 | 41,390 |
| 4 | *Discount rate (at 12% pa)* | *1.00* | *0.89* | *0.80* | *0.71* | *0.64* | *0.57* | *0.51* | *0.45* |
| 5 | Discounted cash flow | (45,000) | 5,705 | 5,094 | 4,548 | 4,061 | 3,626 | 3,237 | 18,723 |
| 6 | Net Present Value (npv) | (5.4) | | | | | | | |
| | *memo: Time charter rate $/day* | | *18,000* | *18,000* | *18,000* | *18,000* | *18,000* | *18,000* | *18,000* |
| *Superoil Trading* | | | | | | | | | |
| 1 | Ship purchase/sale | (48,000) | | | | | | | 45,000 |
| 2 | Timecharter revenue | | 4,260 | 4,970 | 5,680 | 6,390 | 7,100 | 7,810 | 8,520 |
| 3 | Cashflow | (48,000) | 4,260 | 4,970 | 5,680 | 6,390 | 7,100 | 7,810 | 53,520 |
| 4 | *Discount rate (12% pa)* | *1.00* | *0.89* | *0.80* | *0.71* | *0.64* | *0.57* | *0.51* | *0.45* |
| 5 | Discounted cash flow | (48,000) | 3,804 | 3,962 | 4,043 | 4,061 | 4,029 | 3,957 | 24,210 |
| 6 | Net Present Value (npv) | 64.7 | | | | | | | |
| | *memo: Time charter rate $/day* | | *12,000* | *14,000* | *16,000* | *18,000* | *20,000* | *22,000* | *24,000* |

was received towards the end of the project and was heavily discounted. In financial terms Superoil's offer is not significantly better than the Big Petroleum deal.

### The internal rate of return

An alternative approach to calculating the return on investment projects is the internal rate of return (IRR). Whereas the NPV method starts from a net cashflow in current terms and calculates the value today, IRR technique works out the discount rate which gives an NPV of zero. The IRR in the two examples works out at 12% for both projects. This is exactly what we would expect since the NPV is close to zero in both cases using a 12% discount rate.

The calculation of the IRR is an iterative process, and rather more time-consuming than the NPV. Fortunately, most computer spreadsheet programs now have IRR functions which provide estimates quickly and easily.

## 6.8 VALUING MERCHANT SHIPS

### Estimating the market value of a ship

Valuing ships is one of the routine tasks undertaken by sale and purchase brokers. A merchant ship is a substantial physical asset and, as we have seen, values can change rapidly, so investors and bankers need to check how much the asset they are buying or financing is really worth. Valuation procedures are well established in the industry and merchant ships are bought and sold as 'commodities', so obtaining valuations does not usually present a particular problem. The banker, owner or investor can call up a broker and receive a valuation certificate within a few hours. However, like any valuation process there are hidden complexities which the prudent banker/investor takes into account.

The valuation establishes how much the ship is worth at a point in time and it has five common uses. The first is to establish the current market value of a vessel being purchased or offered as collateral against a loan. When drawing up a loan agreement, bankers seek an independent 'collateral value' of the ship. Second, loan documentation often includes a clause requiring the borrower to maintain collateral at a prescribed level. If a merchant ship is held as part of the collateral package, it is necessary to update the market value of the vessel to establish whether the collateral conditions are being met. A third use is to establish the market value of the fleet owned by a company making a public offering or issuing a bond, and the values will appear in the related documentation, for example the prospectus. Fourth, companies publishing their accounts may include a current market value of the fleet. Finally, an investor buying a second-hand ship may obtain a valuation as a check against the price, especially if there is not much else on the market.

Shipbrokers are the main source of valuations. For a fee, most shipbroking companies will issue a certificate indicating the market value of a named vessel. The first step in preparing a valuation certificate will be to consult the shipbroking company's reference databases to establish the ship's physical characteristics and recent sales of similar ships, including vessels currently in the market. During this process the valuer will note the following features of the ship:

- *Ship type.* For example, whether the ship is a tanker, bulk carrier, container-ship, chemical tanker, etc.
- *Ship size.* The size will normally be measured in the most appropriate unit – deadweight, TEU, cubic meter, cubic feet. Bigger ships are generally worth more than smaller ships.
- *Age.* The usual 'rule of thumb' is that ships lose about 4–5% of their value each year as they age, which is usually calculated from the year of build, not the anniversary of delivery. This suggests that the economic life of most merchant ships is about 20–25 years, by which time the vessel has depreciated to scrap value. Figure 6.7 shows the relationship between age and value for a sample of Panamax bulk carriers.
- *Yard of build.* The relationship between value and yard/country of build is difficult to establish. For ships built in Japan and Korea the yard of build does not make a great deal of difference. However, there are some countries whose ships sometimes sell at a discount. Brazil, Romania and China are three which come to mind. However, there are no hard and fast rules and this is more a caution rather than a prescription.
- *Specification.* The valuer will be looking for features of the ship which might affect its value because it does not match up to its peer group. Speed, fuel economy, cubic capacity, engine make, cargo-handling gear and tank coatings are areas where

differences may be found. For example, an unusual engine can be a problem, as can poor cubic capacity in a products tanker. This is all relative. Most small bulk carriers have cargo-handling gear so an ungeared Handy bulker may be more difficult to sell. Conversely there is no guarantee that a Panamax bulk carrier with cargo-handling gear will achieve a premium because most Panamaxes are not geared.

Valuers do not usually carry out a physical inspection of the vessel. Even if they have the time and resources to do so, shipbrokers are not usually qualified to carry out technical inspections and their valuation assumes the ship is 'in good and seaworthy condition'. The responsibility for establishing the physical condition of the ship lies with the purchaser, owner or lender. The exception is that if a special survey is imminent, this may be taken into account if the valuer believes the market would do so.

Valuations are made on a 'willing buyer, willing seller' basis. Shipping is a small market and if no 'willing buyer' is available, prices may be heavily discounted. Although the 'last done' is taken into account, the valuation reflects the broker's judgement of what the ship would sell for if put on the market at that date. This is important. In a rising market, the broker's valuation will generally lead the historic statistics. Conversely, in a falling market the broker's valuation may be lower. If there have been no sales of similar vessels for several months the valuation is entirely judgemental and two brokers may arrive at very different valuations, depending on how they believe the market would price the ship.

Although ship valuation is generally straightforward, problems arise from time to time due to the technical complexities of valuing a ship. One common issue is what to do if the ship has a current time charter. It is unrealistic to ignore the charter, but valuing it goes outside the normal shipbroking expertise. One method is to carry out an NPV calculation (see Section 6.7), based on the charter revenue and projected operating costs, but this raises two difficult questions – how to value the ship at the end of the charter and the creditworthiness of the charterer. Most brokers prefer to value vessels charter-free. Lack of liquidity is another problem. As mentioned above, some ship types are rarely sold, so differences of opinions as to the current market value are difficult to resolve. To deal with this problem bankers often ask for several shipbrokers to value the vessel and average their valuations. Complex ships are particularly difficult to value. For example, a chemical parcel tanker of 30,000 dwt may cost more than twice as much to build as a conventional products tanker of the same size. Because the market for specialized vessels is often thin, with only two or three buyers, brokers find it very difficult to provide valuations. A final issue is whether the valuation should reflect the 'quality' of the ship. Brokers are not in a position to judge the condition and quality of the ship. From a market viewpoint, quality ships generally sell more easily but do not necessarily obtain a better price, especially in a weak market. It is a difficult area and valuers usually fall back on the 'average condition' clause in the valuation certificate.

## Estimating the scrap value of a ship

Many banks and financial institutions valuing ships adopt a rule that after a certain age the ship is valued at its scrap value rather than its market value, also referred to as its demolition or recycling value. Sometimes the gap between market and scrap value may be very considerable. For example, a 20-year-old Panamax bulk carrier in August 2007 was worth $16 million, whilst its scrap value was only about $5 million. The rationale for valuing ships at scrap is that as the vessels become older the prices become more volatile. For example, a bank which lent an apparently prudent 50% against the $16 million Panamax bulk carrier could find that in less than 18 months the price has fallen to $5 million, which is insufficient to cover the outstanding loan.

Valuing at scrap involves two steps. Firstly the lightweight (lwt) tonnage of the ship must be established. This is the physical weight of the vessel (i.e. the amount of water it displaces). For example, a VLCC might have a lightweight of between 30,000 and 36,000 tons, depending on its method of construction. If the lightweight of the ship is not available it can be estimated by looking up the lightweight of similar ships, though this is not a precise process. Second the current scrap price for the ship must be established. Scrap prices are quoted in dollars per lightweight ton, and many brokers publish values and lists of ships sold for demolition. In practice, scrap prices are almost as volatile as second-hand ship prices. During the last 20 years the scrap price of tankers has swung between $100/lwt and $550/lwt. Finally, the scrap value is calculated by multiplying the lightweight of the ship by the scrap price. For example at a price of $430/lwt the scrap value of a Panamax bulk carrier of 12,300 lwt is $5.3 million.

## Estimating the residual value of a ship

So much for the current value of a ship, but what will it be worth in future, for example at the end of a 10-year lease? Since we cannot answer this question with certainty, we need an approach which gives an acceptable assessment of the likely value. The basic methodology is to use the three determinants of a ship's price: the depreciation rate, the rate of inflation and the market cycle. Take as an example a new bulk carrier costing $28 million in 1996 (see Table 6.17). If we assume that vessel depreciates at 5% per annum on a straight-line basis during the first 10 years of its life, by the end of 10 years its book value will have fallen to $14 million. However, during this time we assume that shipbuilding prices

**Table 6.17** Example of residual value calculation

|  | Value $ million |
| --- | --- |
| Age at which residual value calculated | 10 |
| Initial cost of the ship | 28 |
| Depreciation rate (% per annum) | 5% |
| Book value after 10 years | 14 |
| Inflation rate (% per annum) | 3% |
| Expected residual value | 18.3 |
| Cyclical trough margin, say | 70% |
| Resale price at trough | 5.5 |
| Value at cyclical peak | 70% |
| Resale price at peak | 31.1 |

have increased by 3% per annum, so the replacement cost after 10 years would be $18.3 million. This is the most likely value. However, we need to take account of the market cycle, which we have seen can affect the resale price by plus or minus 70%, if we take the most extreme price movements in Figure 5.9. A sale at the top of the market could bring a price of $31 million, which is higher than the initial purchase price of the ship. If, however, the sale occurs at the bottom of a trough and we allow for a price 70% below the trend value, the minimum resale value would fall to US$5.5 million, which is 20% of the initial cost.

This approach has many pitfalls. Depreciation rates and inflation are difficult enough to predict, but the market cycle is the real challenge. The cyclical value range of $5.6 million to $32 million is so wide that a view has to be taken on what cycles might lie ahead. This is pure shipping risk and it is up to the investor to decide what level of risk he is prepared to accept. For example, a cyclical trough margin of 70% has happened, but only in very extreme circumstances such as the mid-1980s depression. The view might be taken that this is unlikely to happen in the period under consideration, so a smaller residual value range would be appropriate. Study of the market cycles discussed in Chapter 3 and the market fundamentals in Chapter 4 can help to narrow the range, but will never entirely remove it. That is the judgement that no amount of statistical analysis will remove. Someone has to take a risk. That, after all, is what the shipping market is all about.

## 6.9 SUMMARY

In this chapter we have reviewed the shipowner's financial performance. We started by observing that shipping companies have a great deal of influence on their future cashflow when they frame their strategy. The choices between new ships and old, flexible ships and specialized, and debt and equity finance all make a difference. Once these major decisions are made an owner can use his management skills to optimize cashflow on a day-to-day basis through efficient ship management and resourceful chartering, but major cost and revenue items are beyond his control. They have already been determined by the initial investment decision. Once these particular decisions have been made, the owner is very much at the mercy of the market and his bankers.

Cash is the difference between costs and revenue. Costs are subdivided into operating costs (which represent the fixed costs of running a ship), voyage costs (which are variable, depending upon the way in which the ship is employed) and capital costs. Crew costs account for almost half of operating costs and the shipowner can reduce these by purchasing a highly automated ship, which reduces the number of crew required, or operating under a flag that allows the use of a low-cost crew. Voyage costs are dominated by bunker prices which can be controlled or reduced by investing in modern tonnage with the latest fuel-efficient machinery or by reducing the design speed. Both operating and voyage costs are likely to be substantially higher for an old ship than a new ship, while economies of scale lead to lower unit costs for bigger ships.

On the revenue side the owner can play the spot market, in which he accepts full market risk, or time charter, which shifts that risk to the charterer. Earnings also depend on the 'productivity' of the ship, that is, the number of tons of cargo it can carry in a year. Again we find that the initial investment decision has a part to play in determining productivity by investment for rapid cargo handling, greater cargo flexibility to enable the ship to pick up backhauls, and high speed (we will discuss this in Chapter 12, which deals with specialized shipping). Drawing these factors together with the influences on cost, we can deduce that in terms of the trading cashflow there are many options. Age, size, technical flexibility and cargo management all play a part in generating more revenue and cutting costs.

When we turn to the capital account, the picture changes substantially. The large modern ship financed by debt carries an annual cashflow for interest and debt repayment far in excess of its operating costs, whereas the small old vessel financed on equity would have no cashflow obligations on the capital account. As a result, during a depression the owner of a small, old vessel can afford to withdraw from the market and leave his vessel in lay-up until conditions improve, whereas the owner of the large, modern, debt-financed vessel faces a fixed capital charge that must be paid even if the ship is laid up.

We also discussed how the industry reports costs and revenues, covering the income statement (profit and loss account), the balance sheet and the cashflow statement. In addition, we reviewed cashflow forecasting techniques, including voyage cashflow analysis which addresses voyage decisions; annual cashflow analysis for longer-term planning; and discounted cashflow analysis for comparing projects when the timing of payments is an issue. Finally, we looked at methods for valuing ships and estimating their residual value.

The topics in this chapter may be dry, but they go to the heart of the business. In the last resort it is for the shipowner to blend the operating, commercial and financial aspects of the business into the business strategy that suits him best. The trade-off between cost minimization, revenue maximization and the approach to ship finance gives each shipping venture its own particular characteristics.

# 7 Financing Ships and Shipping Companies

*For the ordinary investor, the tramp company remains a form of investment to be avoided. It is a very special business and at its best financed and managed by those who are versed in its difficulties.*

(A.W. Kirkaldy, *British Shipping*, 1914)

## 7.1 SHIP FINANCE AND SHIPPING ECONOMICS

Ships tie up a lot of capital. Container-ships and tankers can cost up to $150 million each, about the same as a jumbo jet, while LNG tankers, the most expensive ships, cost $225 million each. In 2007 investment in new ships reached a new record of $187.5 billion,[1] and second-hand sales reached $53.5 billion (see Figure 7.1). As a result, capital can account for up to 80% of the costs of running a bulk shipping company with a fleet of modern ships, and decisions about financial strategy are among the most important that shipping companies make. But shipping has distinctive characteristics which make financing different from other asset-based industries such as real estate and aircraft. Broadly speaking, bankers like predictable earnings, well-defined corporate structures, high levels of disclosure and well-defined ownership, whilst investors look for consistent growth and high yields. However, many shipping companies do not meet these criteria. Because the ships are internationally mobile and their owners can choose their legal jurisdiction, shipping companies are able to adopt less formal corporate structures than are found in most other businesses employing such large amounts of capital. In addition the revenue flows are highly volatile, as are asset values. This history of volatility was described in Chapter 3. Thus, a ship is not just a transportation vehicle, it is a speculation. This makes life interesting for shipowners but difficult for potential lenders and investors who are used to dealing with more stable businesses. As a result, ship finance is generally regarded as a specialist business and, for example, the rating agency Moody's classifies it as 'exotic' finance.

This brings us face to face with a paradox. Given all these difficulties, raising finance should be difficult, but historically the industry has generally suffered from too much finance. In 1844 George Young complained to a British House of Commons Select

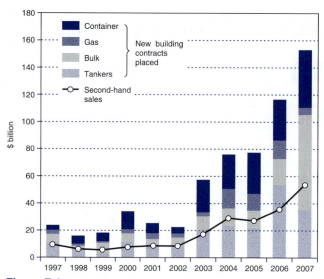

**Figure 7.1**
Investment in merchant ships, 1997–2007
Source: CRSL

Committee that during the period 1836–41 mortgages for the purchase of ships had led to an increase in the supply of shipping 'inducing persons without capital or with inadequate capital to press into shipowning, to the injury of shipowners in general'.[2] One hundred and sixty years later the same complaint could still be heard and even the bankers were complaining about the intense competition, with 150 banks targeting the ship finance market. There have been times when the industry has indulged in phases of wild speculation, often using borrowed money, but it would be wrong to say that ship finance drives the market – that responsibility lies firmly with the shipping investors. It does, however, help to grease the tracks of the shipping roller-coaster.

Our aim in this chapter is to explain the role of ship finance in the shipping market from the shipowner's and the ship financier's point of view. We will start by looking at how ships have been financed in the past, and then we will explain how ship finance fits into the world financial system alongside other forms of investment. Then, we will examine the options open to shipping companies wishing to raise finance. Finally we will draw some conclusions about the interplay between the activities of bankers on the shipping markets discussed in Chapter 4 and the way in which bankers should approach this form of lending.

## 7.2 HOW SHIPS HAVE BEEN FINANCED IN THE PAST

### Ship finance in the pre-steam era

Although the history of ship finance can be traced back to the joint stock companies of the sixteenth century, the logical starting point for a discussion of modern ship finance is the 1850s when steamships started to appear in significant numbers. A widely used technique was the 'sixty-fourth' company. In the United Kingdom a ship is registered as 64 shares, so an investor could buy part of a ship as a standalone investment. An investor who bought 32 sixty-fourths owned half the ship, while to hold 64 equal shares was to be a sole owner. Legally shareholders were tenants in common, each having a separate interest which could be sold or mortgaged without reference to other owners of the vessel.[3]

There were three ownership structures. Shares could be held by individuals on their own account, by individuals organized into partnerships, or by investors in a joint stock enterprise. However, most ships were owned by one person. According to records for ships registered in the City of London in 1848, out of 554 vessels, 89% were owned by individuals and 8% by trading partnerships. The remaining 3% were owned by joint stock companies. Only 18% of the vessels were mortgaged, mainly to cover the cost of repairs.[4] Where partnerships were used, they were generally limited to only two or three partners, possibly reflecting the difficulty of managing larger groups.

## The evolution of the shipping corporation

As ships grew in size during the second half of the century, the joint stock company rapidly became the preferred financial vehicle for raising the large sums of money required. A major factor in this development was the Companies Act 1862, which protected investors from liability claims by company creditors. This opened the way for small investors whose other assets were now protected, though share ownership in such a risky and individualistic business tended to be restricted to family and friends.

A good example is the Tyne Steam Shipping Company which was formed as a joint stock company with limited liability on 1 July 1864. The company was to carry the growing bulk export trade of bulk coal from Newcastle on Tyne. It owned the first bulk carrier, the *John Bowes* (see Chapter 10). The nominal capital of the company was set at £300,000 in 12,000 shares of £25 each. Initially 10,100 shares were issued on which £18 was paid up, raising £181,800. This was used to purchase 10 vessels for £150,000, leaving £30,000 working capital. Approximately one-quarter of the shares were taken by previous owners of the new company's steamers and the rest were sold, as far as possible, to the public locally because 'a shareholder at London, Liverpool or Manchester brings little business to the company'.[5] This company is typical of many others in the international shipping industry at this time. A few such as Cunard (now part of Carnival Cruise Lines) and Hapag-Lloyd are still in operation.

Although these companies were capitalized with equity raised from the public, share ownership was often closely controlled and many companies relied on self-financing or borrowing rather than share capital to finance expansion. For example, share ownership in the Charente Shipping Company Ltd, which was set up in 1884 with share capital of £512,000 and a fleet of 22 vessels, was 'limited to a small and closely-knit family group'.[6] In each subsequent year, with only two exceptions, the company ordered at least two new ships, and by 1914 the fleet had increased from 22 ships to 57. No further capital was raised and investment was paid for from cashflow, and despite the many cycles adequate investment funds were always available from internal funds (see Chapter 3 for a review of these cycles). Majority ownership remained with three families, the Harrisons, the Hughes and the Williamsons.

Other companies were less conservative. In the nineteenth century borrowing was common. According to Sturmey, during the long recession of 1904–11 many heavily indebted lines failed and 'the financially conservative men who controlled the major shipping lines observed the failure and took the lesson to heart'. For the next 50 years

British shipowners stuck firmly to the policy of financing investment from accumulated depreciation reserves. 'Borrowing became anathema'.[7] In 1969 the Rochdale Committee of Inquiry into Shipping found that only £160 million out of over £1,000 million capital employed by British owners was represented by loans, a 16% gearing rate.[8] The same financial conservatism was shared by many of the older established Greek names.

Although this policy provided protection against recessions, earnings were never strong enough to fund expansion or attract external equity. Between 1950 and 1970 the return on British shipping shares averaged only 6% per annum compared with 15% per annum for all companies. As a result, although most of the larger shipping companies were publicly listed, no cash was raised by issuing equity capital to the public[9] and the British fleet played little part in the post-war bulk shipping boom.

## Charter-backed finance in the 1950s and 1960s

In the 1950s the balance of financial conservatism, with its protection from market cycles and high leverage which boosts the return on equity, took a new turn. The rapidly growing industrial economies in Europe and Japan needed cheap raw materials. Industrial shippers, particularly oil companies and steel-makers, started to look abroad for new supply sources. As a result an important new player entered the ship financing game, the industrial shipper. As more raw materials were sourced abroad, shippers needed the cheapest possible transport, using very big ships operating between specialized terminals. Oil companies and steel mills offered shipowners time charters as an incentive to order these large ships, and the owners would raise a loan to buy the ship against the security of the time charter.

This was known as charter-backed finance and it typically involved ordering a new ship, obtaining a long-time charter for the ship from a creditworthy organization such as an oil company, and using the time charter and a mortgage on the hull as security to obtain a bank loan covering a high proportion of the purchase price of the ship. This allowed shipowners to expand their fleets with little equity and it played a major part in building up the independent bulk shipping fleet. It originated in the 1920s when the Norwegians started to build up a tanker fleet. In 1927, as part of their fleet replacement programme, Anglo Saxon Petroleum Ltd offered 37 ten-year-old tankers at between £60,000 and £70,000 each with 10-year time charters. The financing terms were 20% cash down and the balance over 5 years at 5% interest.[10] Twenty-six were bought by Norwegians, mostly newcomers to the business, who were able to borrow against the time charters. The process took another step forward after the Second World War when Norwegian owners could only obtain licences to order ships abroad if the vessels were 100% financed abroad. Soon adept Norwegian brokers perfected borrowing techniques based on pre-construction time charters. This initiated the great expansion of the Norwegian fleet which, during the 1950s, almost trebled in size, drawing heavily on finance raised from American banks.[11]

Greek shipowners were also quick to exploit this opportunity. A high proportion of tanker construction was financed with American loan capital and 'Greek owners appear to have operated largely on the basis of securing a time charter for 7 or even 15 years from an oil company, a 95 per cent mortgage from American financiers on the security of the time charter, then building to fit the charter and finally sitting back to enjoy the profits'.[12] US shipowners were equally active, though the charter-back system was refined to its most sophisticated form in the *shikumisen* arrangements developed between Japanese charterers and Hong Kong shipping entrepreneurs.

## The one-ship company

The aim of the time-charter system was to reduce transport costs and this led to a different form of legal and business organization. The most important innovation was the single-ship company. Using the flags of convenience developed for this purpose (see Chapter 16, Section 16.5), these one-ship companies became the building-blocks for complex shipowning empires. Each ship was registered as a separate company, with ownership vested in the group and management handled through an agency. This suited bankers because for financing purposes the ship could be treated as a separate company, secured by a mortgage on its hull and a time charter. Although organization structures were loose, with few published financial accounts and little financial transparency, very high leverage rates could be achieved because the bank had the security of both the hull and the time charter.

This phase of charter-backed finance dominated ship finance for about 20 years, but during the 1970s and 1980s gradually shrank in importance. There seem to have been three reasons. First, the charters had been made available during a period of structural change when charterers needed to encourage owners to order the large vessels they needed. By the early 1970s economies of scale had been pushed to their limit and it was no longer necessary for shippers to make this onerous commitment in order to secure the ships they needed. Second, after two decades of headlong growth in the bulk trades, there was a change of trend and the crude oil and iron ore trades stopped growing (see Chapter 4). Third, some shipowners who had expected to 'sit back and enjoy the profits' found themselves locked into contracts whose small profit margins were eaten away by inflation. Worse still was the failure of several charterers to honour their commitments, notably Sanko in the mid-1980s. As the market and the needs of charterers changed in the following decades, time charters became much more difficult to obtain and the financing structures used by the shipping industry changed.

## Asset-backed finance in the 1970s

In the early 1970s, after two decades of highly leveraged charter-backed finance, shipping bankers started to revise their lending policies. Instead of securing the loan against a long-term contract, for a brief but disastrous spell in the early 1970s many bankers were prepared to rely on the first mortgage on the hull, with little additional security. A prominent banker summarized the reasons for this change as follows:

> A long-term charter-party with no or few escalation clauses built into it can be disastrous to the shipowner … Inflation, engine breakdowns and other accidents as well as changes in currencies can very quickly alter or wipe out the best

planned cash flows … On the other hand, shipowners who run vessels on the spot market have recently been better off … Many bankers have objected to a gearing of 1 to 5, or lending of up to 80 per cent of the cost price or market value of the vessel… I believe that from a commercial bank's point of view this form of lending has caused no major disasters, and the main reason is perhaps that good, well maintained modern ships have retained their value or even appreciated.[13]

In short, bankers started to see shipping as a form of 'floating real estate'.

This was a fundamental change of policy because it removed the link between supply and demand. During the period of charter-backed finance, newbuilding was restricted by the availability of charters. If the hull was regarded as acceptable collateral, there was no limit to the number of ships which could be ordered from the slimmest equity base. When, in 1973, petrodollars flooded into the world capital markets, shipping seemed an obvious target. The tanker industry was swept away on a tidal wave of credit which allowed 105 million deadweight of tankers, representing 55% of the fleet, to be ordered in a single year. In the stampede for business, financing standards became so casual that loan syndications could be arranged by telephone with little documentation and few questions asked.[14] It took the tanker market 15 years to recover.

Unfortunately, that was not the end of the story. In the 1980s the shipping industry experienced its worst recession for fifty years just at a time when the capital markets were again awash with petrodollars, generated by oil at $40 per barrel, and desperate shipbuilders started to use credit as a thinly disguised way of building for stock. Mortgage-backed debt underpinned orders for 40 million deadweight of bulk carriers in 1983–4 when freight rates were at rock bottom. The rationale was counter-cyclical ordering, but the volume of orders was so great that the cycle did not turn. With so many deliveries, the recession dragged on through 1986 and the owners could not service their debt, causing many defaults and reducing second-hand ship prices to distress levels as owners were forced to sell ships to raise cash.

## Financing asset play in the 1980s

As the shipping market cycle bottomed out in the mid-1980s, the distress sales created opportunities for 'asset play' (i.e. buying ships cheaply and selling them at higher prices). The problem was that conventional sources of equity and debt had no interest in additional shipping exposure, so new sources of finance were required. One of the first devices to emerge was the self-liquidating ship fund. Bulk Transport, the first of these schemes, was set up in February 1984 and proved very successful, with assets appreciating to four times their purchase price during the following four years. As the success of the early schemes filtered into the market place, imitators appeared, using the same basic structure and offering equity to non-shipping investors. Ironically, as the market cycle matured and asset values increased it became progressively easier to place the equity. Eventually, a total of about $500–600 million was raised and invested in ships purchased at higher prices towards the top of the cycle. As a result few investors made a commercial return and some lost their money.

A parallel development was the re-emergence of the Norwegian K/S limited partnership as a vehicle for financing speculative investment in second-hand ships. K/S partnership structures were similar to ship funds, or indeed the trading partnerships of the 1840s, but had the added advantage that profits earned by investors were tax-free, provided they were reinvested within a specified period. At a time of high personal tax rates in Norway this was very attractive to private investors, many of whom invested in K/S companies set up to buy ships. Perhaps the most significant development was not so much the K/S structure, which had been available for many years, but the growth of the Norwegian banks during this period. At the beginning of the 1980s the Norwegian banks carried a shipping portfolio, variously estimated at around $1 billion. During the 1980s it grew to a peak of around $6–7 billion in 1989. The availability of this finance and the willingness of Norwegian banks to make advances to the K/S companies, despite their unconventional structure, must surely be one of the key factors in determining the phenomenal success of this market (see page 306 below for more details of the K/S structure).

## Developments of corporate finance in the 1990s

After the lengthy financial crisis of the 1980s, when financing had mainly been limited to small mortgage loans, in the 1990s the ship finance industry had to rediscover many of the more conventional ship finance techniques. Syndication of shipping debt is a good example of how things had changed. During the early 1970s large shipping loans were often syndicated, but this practice had lapsed during the recession, due mainly to the difficulty of placing assets trading in such a disturbed market. The widely publicized difficulties of mid-1970s syndications did not help. During the intervening period the value of shipping transactions was so low or so dubious that syndication virtually disappeared and had to be rediscovered by the new generation of shipping bankers who had taken over in the late 1980s. There was also a wave of KG companies set up in Germany to finance container-ships. These structures, based on German private partnerships, began to be used extensively in the early 1990s as a way of providing cost-effective and secure 'off balance sheet' finance for container-ship operators at a time when the fleet was expanding rapidly. Many of the costs of raising the finance are borne by private shareholders.[15]

After the disappointing performance of the ship funds, a few of which were public offerings, in the early 1990s there was little activity as the market weighed up the liability implications of the US Oil Pollution Act 1990 and the tightening regulatory environment. These developments probably encouraged a more corporate approach as a way of protecting the interests of high net worth shipping families operating tankers. In addition corporate structures began to look more acceptable to shipping companies operating at the quality/industrial end of the shipping market. This case was strongly argued by shipping experts such as Peter Stokes. From 1993 onwards there were a series of important IPOs including Teekay, Frontline and General Maritime, all of which grew into substantial public shipping companies. High-yield bonds also appeared in 1993, marking a major development in the ship finance business. Bankers who had learned their trade during the 1980s could hardly imagine that a bulk shipping company would be able to apply for a credit rating and issue bonds, but by the late 1990s they were doing so with regularity and even a few more exotic structures such as synthetic securitizations put in an appearance. So by the early years of the twenty-first century ship finance had become more sophisticated, though commercial bank debt continued to predominate.

## Shipbuilding credit

Finally, a source of ship finance available throughout the period was shipbuilding credit. During each of the recessions reviewed in Chapter 3 shipyards would compete by offering shipowners favourable credit. This practice was already common in the nineteenth century when some UK shipbuilders would, out of their own funds, allow a reliable client 25–30% credit for 3–5 years to tide them over a period of low freight rates. By the early twentieth century governments had decided that shipbuilding was an important strategic industry and became involved in the provision of subsidized credit. In the 1920s the German and French governments offered favourable credit terms to help their yards win business against the then dominant British shipbuilding industry. During the recession of the 1930s, the Danish, French and German governments all offered government credit schemes to owners. The practice of subsidizing credit reappeared in the first major post-Second World War recession of 1958–63 and was regulated by the OECD Understanding on Export Credit in 1969. The provision of credit is generally coordinated by a government-controlled credit agency (the Export Credit Guarantee Department in the UK, Hermes in Germany, COFACE in France, KEXIM in Korea, EXIM Bank in Japan, etc.). These agencies are responsible for coordinating the credit on behalf of the government and providing financial guarantees and interest rate support when appropriate.

## 7.3 THE WORLD FINANCIAL SYSTEM AND TYPES OF FINANCE

### Where does the money to finance ships come from?

This brief historical review has touched on many ways of financing shipping, showing how the financial techniques employed have changed from one decade to another. We now turn to a more rigorous discussion of the financial structures currently in use. Raising ship finance is essentially a matter of persuasion, so a good starting point is to return to two basic questions: 'where does the money to finance ships come from', and what do businessmen have to do to get it?

To answer these questions we need to look at the world financial system as a whole. The flow chart in Figure 7.2 shows how the different parts of the system fit together. Column 3 on the right shows the *source* investment funds; column 2 shows the markets where these funds are traded, while column 1 shows the arrangers who act as intermediaries and risk-takers in providing businesses needing capital, including the shipping companies, with access to the pool of funds in columns 2 and 3.

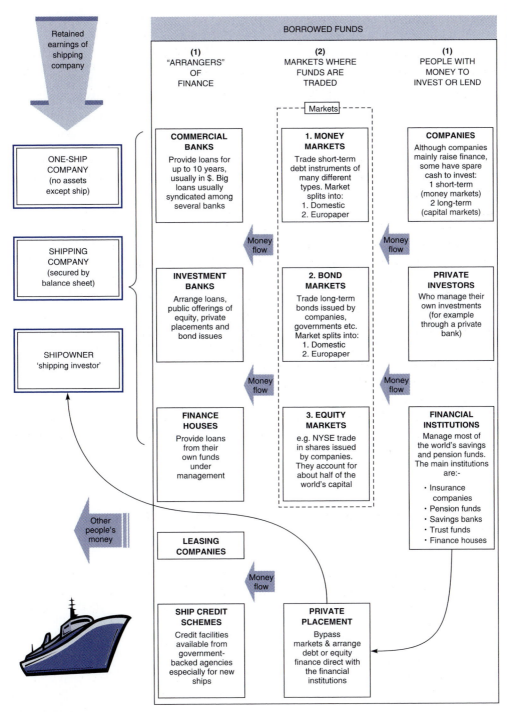

**FIGURE 7.2**
Where the money comes from to finance ships
Source: Martin Stopford 2007

## Investment funds come from savings

First the source: the money comes from corporate or personal savings which need to be invested. Some corporations and individuals handle the investment themselves. For example, an individual might buy a house as an investment and let it out. But nowadays about 80% of savings end up in the hands of professional investment managers such as insurance companies, pension funds, savings banks, finance houses, trust funds, mutual funds and commercial banks which take money on deposit, so-called 'institutional investors'.[16]

## Investors and lenders

These professional fund managers in column 3 of Figure 7.2 have two options. They can invest the money or they can lend it. The investor commits funds to a business venture in return for a share of the profits. Usually the only way to get this money back is to sell the 'equity' stake in the business to someone else (if the equity in the company is traded on an exchange it is called a public company and its shares can be bought or sold on the stock market where they were issued). In contrast, the lender advances money for a predetermined period in return for regular interest payments and a predetermined schedule for the repayment of the principal so that by the end of the agreed period the 'debt' has been repaid in full. This is an important distinction for anyone trying to raise finance because investors and lenders see the world from a very different perspective.

Investors take risk for profit, so they are interested in the upside. How profitable could the investment be? Is this a business which could make a 30% return? Is there a convincing reason why profits will be high? Lenders just get paid interest, so they want to be sure they will be repaid. This makes them more interested in the downside. Is the business sound? Could it survive in an adverse market? Are the borrowers taking risks that might damage their ability to repay? Since lenders do not share the profits they are less interested in this aspect of the business. Shipowners are often puzzled about why bankers are more interested in recessions than booms. This is the reason.

## Private placement of debt or equity

One method open to fund managers is to place the funds directly with companies which need finance. This is known as private placement and it is shown at the bottom of column 2 in Figure 7.2. The lender, which might be a pension fund or an insurance company, negotiates a financial agreement to suit both borrower and lender. The structure of this agreement could be either debt or equity. Whilst private placement is quite widely used, especially for long-term loans, as a general technique for managing investment, it presents practical difficulties. Fund managers face the administrative task of analysing detailed investment proposals. More importantly, the loan or investment is not liquid. Once the transaction is placed, there is little the investor can do to adjust his portfolio of such loans and investments. In practice this market is only accessible to shipping companies of investment-grade quality.

## The financial markets buy and sell packaged investment funds

An alternative is to use the financial markets. Ingeniously, the world financial system has succeeded in developing three markets which trade investments which have been processed as standard packages known as 'securities', a term used to refer to all standard investment instruments. The two main types of securities are 'stocks' which are packaged equities, and 'bonds' which are packaged loans. Packaging investment into securities is rather like containerizing cargo. It takes a unique investment package and processes it into a unit which conforms to rigid standards, making it easy to buy and sell without specialized knowledge. The capital markets where securities are traded are strictly regulated to ensure that the rules are followed. Each of the three markets shown in column 2 of Figure 7.2 trades in a different type of security.

- *Money markets* trade in short-term loans (less than a year). The 'market' consists of a loose network of banks and dealers linked by telephone, e-mail and computers (rather like the voyage charter market) who deal in any short-term debt securities such as bankers' acceptances, commercial paper, negotiable certificates of deposit, and Treasury bills with a maturity of 1 year or less and often 30 days or less.[17] It is where the banks trade with each other, but companies use it too. For example, a shipowner with spare cash who wants to keep his funds liquid can purchase 'commercial' paper which gives him a slightly better return than he would get on deposit. The markets trade funds held in local currency by local investors (the domestic market) and funds held outside the issuing country (in Europe the eurocurrency market). These markets have a different interest rates structure,[18] the eurodollar interest rate being the London Interbank Offered Rate (LIBOR).
- *Bond markets* trade in interest bearing securities with a redemption date of more than a year, often 10 or 15 years. Companies issue bonds or debentures (bonds not secured by collateral), via a dealer, and to make it tradeable a bond must have a credit rating (see Box 7.1). For example, bonds rated less than BBB– by Standard & Poor's (S&P) or Baa3 by Moody's are known as 'high-yield' bonds. Interest is obtained by redeeming coupons attached to the bonds and the rate of interest reflects the credit rating. For example, a bond rated AAA will pay lower interest than a bond rated BB. The bond is subject to a deed of trust between issuer and bondholder, known as the 'indenture'. This is designed to protect the bondholder with property pledges, protective covenants and working capital requirements, and it also sets out redemption rights. Dealings in off-shore funds are referred to as the 'eurobond' market.
- *Equity markets* trade in equities (also known as securities or stocks). This allows creditworthy companies to raise capital by means of a 'public offering' on the stock market. To raise capital in this way a company must follow regulations (e.g. laid down by the SEC in the United States) and convince the shareholder that the investment will be a good one.[19] Issues are made through an investment bank and the cost of underwriting, legal and auditing fees is usually about 7–9% of the sum raised.

## BOX 7.1 BOND RATINGS AND APPROXIMATE INTERPRETATION

| Moody's | S&P | Approximate interpretation | |
|---------|-----|---------------------------|---|
| Aaa | AAA | Capacity to service debt extremely | Investment Grade |
| Aa1 | AA+ | strong in all forseeable circumstances | |
| Aa2 | AA | | |
| Aa3 | AA– | | |
| A1 | A+ | *Getting more risky* | |
| A2 | A | | |
| A3 | A– | | |
| Baa1 | BBB+ | Debt service will be met, barring some serious and unpredictable catastrophe | |
| Baa2 | BBB | | |
| Baa3 | BBB– | *Medium grade* | |
| Ba1 | BB+ | Judged to have speculative elements | Speculative Grade |
| Ba2 | BB | | |
| Ba3 | BB– | Acceptable for now but easily foreseeable | |
| B1 | B+ | adverse conditions could impair capacity to | |
| B2 | B | service debt in future | |
| B3 | B– | | |
| Caa | CCC | | |
| Ca | CC | Highly vulnerable to non-payment | |
| C | C | | |
| | D | Payment is in default | |

Source: Compiled from rating agency material

Checked against

*Standard & Poor's* investment grade ratings in order from the highest to the lowest are: AAA, AA+, AA, AA–, A+, A, A–, BBB+, BBB and BBB–. Standard & Poor's non–investment grade ratings in order from the highest to the lowest are: BB+, BB, BB–, B+, B, B–, CCC+, CCC, CCC– CC, C, D and SD.

*Moody's Credit Ratings* - Moody's investment grade ratings in order from the highest to the lowest are: Aaa, Aa1, Aa2, Aa3, A1, A2, A3, Baa1, Baa2 and Baa3. Moody's non-investment grade ratings in order from the highest to the lowest are Ba1, Ba2, Ba3, B1, B2, B3, Caa1, Caa2, Caa3, Ca and C.

http://www.quantumonline.com/RatingsNotes.cfm

Over half the world's capital is held as investments traded in the securities markets, and in 2005 the world equities market totalled $55 trillion and corporate bonds about $35 trillion. That compares with $38 trillion of bank deposits, so the capital markets are the first choice of global investors.[20] Shipping only accounts for a small proportion of these funds. To put the annual financial requirements of the shipping industry into context, if the total world capital were $100, the transport industry, which includes airlines, shipping, ports, etc., would need to raise 18 cents. Obtaining even such a small sum is not easy. The job of the markets is to channel funds to where they can be used most productively. There are many other industries fishing in the same pool, so borrowers must offer a competitive rate of return. Raising money in the equity markets generally involves issuing a prospectus and selling the 'story' to investors. In the capital markets the main preoccupation of institutions buying the bonds is the risk that the company will be unable to repay the money it has borrowed, so to raise capital a shipping company must achieve recognized standards of credit-worthiness. It does this by obtaining a 'credit rating' from one of the credit rating agencies. This opens the door to the bond markets and determines the cost of finance to the borrower.

## The role of the credit rating agencies

For a bond to be placed by the issuer, the financial institutions which buy it must have a reliable indication of whether the yield (i.e. the coupon divided by the price) reflects the risk and whether the principal is likely to be repaid on time. To address this need a shipping company issuing bonds must obtain a credit rating for the transaction from one or more of the credit rating agencies. In return for a fee the credit rating agency evaluates the issuing company's credit history and its ability to repay, and issues a credit rating which provides a current opinion on the creditworthiness of the obligor with respect to the specific financial obligation, including an estimate of the risk of default. The credit rating generally takes the form of a letter to the bank handling the issue.

The four main credit rating agencies are Standard & Poor's, Moody's, Fitch, and Duff & Phelps, and there is generally a requirement to obtain a rating by at least two of these. The slightly different rating systems used by the two largest agencies are shown in Box 7.1 with a rough definition of what they mean. AAA ('triple A') is the best, and Baa3/BBB– and above are 'investment grade'. Investment-grade rating characteristics are such factors as reliability, strong debt cover, a strong market position for the company's products and the scale of the business. To get this rating the company must be strong enough to survive almost any imaginable crisis. In contrast, bonds with lower ratings have 'significant speculative characteristics'[21] and are referred to as 'high yield' because they require higher interest rates (they are also known as 'junk bonds'). In this way investments are 'packaged' before they are offered to the market. Because of the volatility of revenues and the competitiveness of the market, shipping companies are rarely awarded investment-grade ratings, though a few large and diversified shipping companies have achieved that distinction.

## Definition of 'shipowner' and 'shipping company'

Before proceeding with the discussion of financing techniques, we should clarify the distinction between a 'shipowner' and a 'shipping company'. These terms are used interchangeably in the business, but when we discuss finance it makes life much easier if we define them precisely.

A *shipowner* is an individual who owns a controlling interest in one or more ships. Part A of Figure 7.3 shows a typical structure. The ships are usually registered as one-ship companies in which the owner has the controlling interest, whilst the cash and other

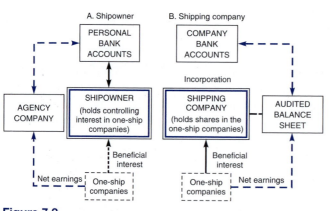

**Figure 7.3**
Definition of shipowner and shipping company
Source: Martin Stopford, 2007

assets associated with the shipping business are held separately, usually in bank accounts in tax-efficient locations. The two are quite separate, and an independent agency or management company is generally set up to deal with the day-to-day operations. Since this structure is not transparent to third parties, in order for the ships to trade, the owner and the agency must establish their creditworthiness. Hence the importance of the good name of a shipowner trading in this way. But the fact remains that the assets are dispersed and potential financiers have little control.

In contrast a *shipping company* of the type shown in part B of Figure 7.3 is a legal organization which owns ships. It may be a legal partnership, company or corporation in a jurisdiction with enforceable laws of corporate governance, with an audited balance sheet showing its controlling interest in the ships it operates and the status of its other assets, liabilities and bank accounts. Its executive officers are responsible for running the business and taking investment decisions. This distinction between the proprietor and the company exists in all businesses, but in shipping it is crucial and gives ship finance its unique flavour. As we saw in Chapter 2, *shipping businesses* (i.e. shipowners and shipping companies) vary enormously in size. In 2004, 32 had more than 100 ships, while 256 had 20–49 ships, 460 had 10–19 ships, and over 4,000 had fewer than five ships.

The main methods of raising ship finance are summarized in Figure 7.4 and include private funds, bank loans, the capital markets, and special purpose companies SPCs. *Private funds* include cash generated by the business, which is important during booms, and loans or equity from friends, relatives or venture capitalists. It is often the only source available to start-up businesses. *Bank loans* are a major source of finance for shipowners and shipping companies, with four types listed in Figure 7.4: mortgage loans secured against the ship; corporate loans secured against the company balance sheet; shipyard credit; and mezzanine finance. The market for commercial bank loans is very competitive and it is also flexible because the loans can easily be refinanced if circumstances change. Private placements with financial institutions are included under this heading. *Capital markets* can provide shipping companies with equity through an initial public offering (IPO) of shares or debt by issuing bonds. They work best for larger shipping companies, especially those with over $1 billion net worth. A final option is to use a special purpose vehicle (SPV) to own the ships and raise the finance. This technique is often used when shipping companies want the use of ships without having them on the balance sheet or when tax allowances are available. For example, UK tax leases and German KG partnerships fall into this category.

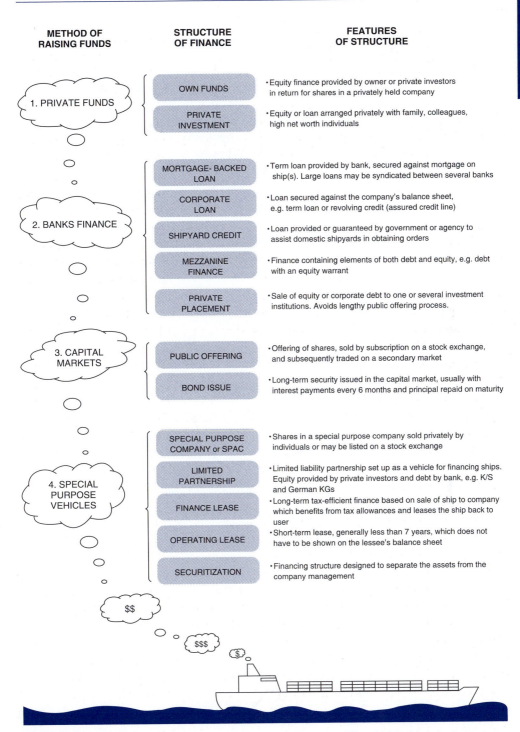

**METHOD OF RAISING FUNDS**

**STRUCTURE OF FINANCE**

**FEATURES OF STRUCTURE**

1. PRIVATE FUNDS

OWN FUNDS
- Equity finance provided by owner or private investors in return for shares in a privately held company

PRIVATE INVESTMENT
- Equity or loan arranged privately with family, colleagues, high net worth individuals

2. BANKS FINANCE

MORTGAGE- BACKED LOAN
- Term loan provided by bank, secured against mortgage on ship(s). Large loans may be syndicated between several banks

CORPORATE LOAN
- Loan secured against the company's balance sheet, e.g. term loan or revolving credit (assured credit line)

SHIPYARD CREDIT
- Loan provided or guaranteed by government or agency to assist domestic shipyards in obtaining orders

MEZZANINE FINANCE
- Finance containing elements of both debt and equity, e.g. debt with an equity warrant

PRIVATE PLACEMENT
- Sale of equity or corporate debt to one or several investment institutions. Avoids lengthy public offering process.

3. CAPITAL MARKETS

PUBLIC OFFERING
- Offering of shares, sold by subscription on a stock exchange, and subsequently traded on a secondary market

BOND ISSUE
- Long-term security issued in the capital market, usually with interest payments every 6 months and principal repaid on maturity

4. SPECIAL PURPOSE VEHICLES

SPECIAL PURPOSE COMPANY or SPAC
- Shares in a special purpose company sold privately by individuals or may be listed on a stock exchange

LIMITED PARTNERSHIP
- Limited liability partnership set up as a vehicle for financing ships. Equity provided by private investors and debt by bank, e.g. K/S and German KGs

FINANCE LEASE
- Long-term tax-efficient finance based on sale of ship to company which benefits from tax allowances and leases the ship back to user

OPERATING LEASE
- Short-term lease, generally less than 7 years, which does not have to be shown on the lessee's balance sheet

SECURITIZATION
- Financing structure designed to separate the assets from the company management

$$

$$$

$

**Figure 7.4**
Fourteen options for financing merchant ships
Source: Martin Stopford, 2007

## BOX 7.2 INSTITUTIONS PROVIDING OR ARRANGING SHIP FINANCE

**Commercial banks:** These are the most important source of debt finance for the shipping industry. Many have dedicated ship finance departments. They offer term loans of 2–8 years which they mainly finance by borrowing from the capital and money markets. This short-term funding limits the tenor of loans commercial banks are willing to take onto their balance sheet and most are uncomfortable with more than 5–6 years. A balloon payment is often used to lower the debt servicing burden on modern ships, but borrowers who want longer-term finance must look elsewhere such as the capital markets or leasing companies. Loans are generally quoted at a margin over LIBOR. Typical spreads range from 60 basis points to 200 basis points (a basis point is one hundredth of a percentage point). Sums of more than $100 million are generally syndicated between several banks. In addition to loans, banks now offer many other services, including risk management products, mergers and acquisitions, financial advisory services etc.

**Investment banks:** These arrange and underwrite finance but do not generally provide capital themselves. They will arrange loan syndications, public offerings of equity, bond issues in the capital market and the private placement of debt or equity with financial institutions or private investors. Some of the large Investment banks have specialist shipping expertise and a few smaller ones, such as Jefferies, specialize in this area.

**Ship credit banks:** In some countries credit is provided by specialist shipping banks which either obtain their funds in the market or issue bonds which have tax concessions for local investors.

**Finance houses and brokers:** Some financial institutions (GE Capital, Fidelity Capital, etc.) which have substantial funds under management have specialist shipping departments which lend direct to the industry. In addition there are a number of organizers and brokers of ship finance who specialize in putting together inventive financing packages.

**Leasing companies:** These specialize in leasing assets and some will arrange long-term leasing of ships. In addition, in Japan leasing companies are significant lenders. Since they are subject to different regulations they can offer long-term finance which commercial banks could not take onto their balance sheets.

**Shipbuilding credit schemes:** Some countries offer shipbuilding credit to domestic and foreign owners. The terms of export credit are agreed under the OECD Understanding on Export Credit and currently are set at 80% advance for 8.5 years (see page 296 which discusses newbuilding finance).

Larger companies have more options because they can access the capital markets, and investment banks help them to issue bonds, equity and private placements, whilst smaller shipping businesses mainly rely on loans from the commercial banks. There are at least 200 institutions world-wide with specialist expertise in some aspect of ship finance, usually through shipping departments. A brief description of the main ones and their activities is given in Box 7.2. In what follows we will go through the four ways shipowners and shipping company can raise finance, following the structure set out in Figure 7.4. We start with the two main sources of finance for established shipping companies, private equity (Section 7.4) and bank loans (Section 7.5), then we move on to capital markets (Section 7.6) and finish up with the various SPC financing structures (Section 7.7).

## 7.4 FINANCING SHIPS WITH PRIVATE FUNDS

The first and most obvious way of financing ships is with the owner's private resources, the earnings of other ships he owns, or an investment or loan from friends or family. This source of finance was widely used in the nineteenth century when investment by family members dominated many companies that were nominally public, and it is still the main source of start-up capital today. For example, Sir Stelios Haji-Ioannou, the well-known entrepreneur who founded Stelmar Tankers and Easyjet, got started in 1992 with $30 million capital from his father[22] which he paid back in 2004. Most shipping businesses finance at least part of their activities from internally generated equity, and family ownership remains a common form of finance in Greece, Norway, Hong Kong and other countries with a seagoing tradition. The advantage is that close friends and relations who understand shipping are more likely to tolerate the volatility of its returns. Occasionally companies may place equity privately on a broader basis, gathering together a group of investors who take a significant share in the business.

On a broader note, during the 2003–8 shipping boom private equity firms started to show more interest in the shipping business, primarily in more specialized sectors where cashflow volatility is seen to be lower than in mainstream bulk and container shipping. In the European ferry sector, for example, there was considerable amount of private equity activity: Grandi Navi Veloci was bought by Permira and then sold on to Investitori Associati; Scandlines was bought by 3i, Allianz Capital Partners and DSR; UN RoRo was bought by KKR; and Marfin purchased the Panagopulos stake in Attica Group. Elsewhere, 3i bought Dockwise and, in the services sector, Istithmar bought Inchcape Shipping Services from Electra and Exponent bought V Holdings from Close Brothers Private Equity.[23]

## 7.5 FINANCING SHIPS WITH BANK LOANS

Bank loans are the most important source of ship finance. They provide borrowers with quick and flexible access to capital, while leaving them with full ownership of the business. This is also an important business for banks, and in 2007 the various institutions lending to the shipping industry had loan portfolios ranging in size from $1 billion to $20 billion. Because ship finance is specialized (it has to cope with all those cycles we discussed in Chapter 3!), it is usually managed by a separate department. Typically the head of ship finance has a group of marketing officers who know the business; administrative staff to handle the portfolio; and credit officers who report to the credit side of the bank, but understand the shipping business. There are three main types of loans available to shipowners: *mortgage-backed* loans, *corporate* loans, and loans made under *shipyard credit* schemes. Occasionally a bank will arrange mezzanine finance.

Loans of this sort have three limitations. Firstly, banks will only advance limited amounts, so large loans must be syndicated amongst a group of banks. Managing large syndications can be difficult when the shipping market is poor. Secondly, loans are usually restricted to 5–7 years and an advance rate of 70–80%, both of which are limiting. Thirdly, the bank requires a mortgage against the ship, and restrictive covenants. This can become complex and inconvenient for large companies with many ships. In effect this is retail finance, with the commercial banks acting as the intermediaries between the capital markets and the small shipping companies.

## Mortgage-backed loan

A mortgage-backed loan relies on the ship for security, allowing banks to lend to one-ship companies which would not otherwise be creditworthy for the large loans required to finance merchant ships. As we noted in the previous section, there are many shipping businesses whose assets are held privately, with no audited accounts and no reliable way for the banker to access company funds in the event of a default. This sort of transaction will generally use a structure of the type set out in Figure 7.5. The borrower is a one-ship company registered in a legally acceptable jurisdiction such as Liberia. This structure isolates the asset from any claims arising elsewhere in the owner's business. Security may be sought both from the borrower and the owner.

To raise a loan the shipowner approaches the bank and explains his requirements. If the bank is prepared to consider a loan, the bank

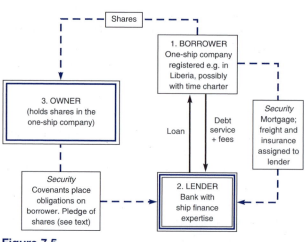

**Figure 7.5**
Mortgage-backed bank loan model
Source: Martin Stopford, 2007

officer draws up a proposal, discusses it with the borrower and negotiates any points which are not acceptable. Negotiating terms is an important part of the lending process. The lender obtains a valuation of the ship offered as collateral (see Section 6.8 for valuation methods) and decides what proportion of its current market value can safely be advanced. This will depend on the age of the ship and the state of the market. Some bankers consider that loans should not exceed 50% of the market value of the vessel unless additional security is available. Additional security in the form of a time charter, mortgages on other ships, a personal guarantee from the owner or a history of successful business with the owner, may persuade the bank to increase the loan to 60–80% of the ship's current value. In some exceptional circumstances bankers may lend 100%. However, there are no firm rules. Banking, like shipping, is a competitive market. If a competitor offers 80% against a first mortgage, that is the market rate.

A credit judgement must be made on whether the risk is acceptable to the bank. It is here that the real skill of ship finance lies. From the shipowner's point of view higher leverage is generally better, but only if the return on equity is higher than the cost of borrowing. If, for example, the business earns 10% per annum but borrows at 7% per annum, leveraging increases the return on equity. But if the average return is less than 7%, leverage actually reduces the return on equity. In shipping the return on assets is often dangerously close to the cost of funds, so borrowers walk a fine line.

Another consideration for the bank is the security of the transaction if things go wrong for the borrower. This involves a mortgage on the ship, assignment of insurance and earnings (freight) to the lender and various other covenants designed to ensure that the assets held as security are adequate if sold, to cover the outstanding loan. This includes covenants covering such issues as the loan to value ratio, conditions precedent to drawdown, and restrictions on dividends. They will also define the events which constitute a default.

The loan proposal, which is generally set out in a letter with a *term sheet* attached, generally covers the seven key issues listed below, with a disclaimer making it clear that the offer is subject to various conditions such as credit committee approval. The bank officer's challenge is to find a combination of terms which are acceptable to the customer and the bank's credit officer.

1.  The *amount*, or maximum size of the loan. This depends on security (i.e. the value of the ship, etc.) and the other factors listed below. Normally the advance will be 50–80% of the market value of the ship, depending on its age and the security available. The purpose of the loan and terms on which it can be drawn down are defined.

2.  The *tenor (term)*, the period over which the loan is to be repaid. Banks prefer to lend for no more than 5–7 years, since the bank funds its loans by borrowing short (see below), but longer terms may be approved for strong credits.

3.  The *repayment*, which determines how the loan is repaid. This is usually by equal instalments, probably every 6 months. For modern ships a 'balloon' repayment may

be used to reduce the annual principal repayments (e.g. repay half the principal at the end) and possibly a grace period at the start.

4.  The *interest rate*: loans are generally made at a 'spread' over the bank's funding cost, for example, LIBOR for a dollar loan. Spreads range from 0.2% (20 basis points) to 2% (200 basis points)

5.  The *fees* that are charged to cover the bank's costs in arranging and administering the loan. For example, a 1% arrangement fee, charged when the loan is drawn, and a commitment fee to cover the cost of tying up the bank's balance sheet, even if the loan is not drawn.

6.  The *security*: the loan agreement requires assets to be pledged as collateral to which the bank has legal access if the borrower defaults. This is usually a mortgage on the vessel, but other security may be sought.

7.  The *financial covenants*: the borrower pledges to do certain things and not to do others. Affirmative covenants pledge to comply with laws, maintain the condition and class of vessels held as collateral and maintain the value of collateral relative to the loan. Restrictive covenants limit third-party debt, cash dividends and the pledging of assets to third parties.

The term sheet only deals with the key issues, and once these are agreed a detailed loan agreement must be drawn up, which is likely to lead to more negotiations over the precise terms and the wording of covenants. Finally, before a firm offer can be made the bank officer must obtain *credit approval* from the bank's credit department. For a client well known to the bank, this will only take a few days, but for difficult or risky loans obtaining credit approval can be a lengthy process. The credit officers or credit committee review the borrower's ability to service the loan in all foreseeable circumstances and the security available in the event of a default. Cashflow projections will probably be used to review debt service obligations under different market scenarios. It simplifies the review if the ship has a time charter, provided the charterer is creditworthy. A shipbrokers' valuation is obtained to establish the ship's market value, and other security is reviewed, along with the covenants. The credit officer may ask for some terms to be revised, and this will need to be agreed with the borrower. When credit approval is obtained and the offer accepted, a closing is arranged at which evidence of security is provided, the papers are signed and the funds transferred. Repayment then proceeds in accordance with the loan agreement.

## The structure of commercial bank lending

In most businesses loans are made to a company, but shipping banks generally use the model shown in Figure 7.5. The ship to be financed is registered as a one-ship company under a flag (i.e. in a country) with well established and enforceable maritime law. The bank makes the loan to this company, taking a mortgage on the ship. Freight and insurances are assigned to the bank with a 'dividend stopper' to ensure that funds remain within the company and the bank takes a pledge of shares from the owner. In addition to giving the bank control in the event of a default, this insulates the ship from other claims on the owner's fleet. It suits the shipowner because the major flags of convenience are acceptable to most banks, so the ship can be registered in a low cost tax-free environment (see Chapter 16).

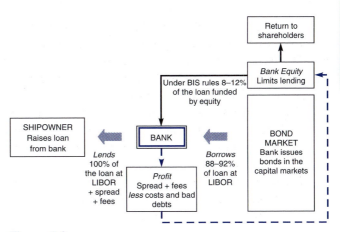

**Figure 7.6**
Bank funding model for ship loans
Source: Martin Stopford, 2007

Since bank loans play such a big part in financing the shipping industry, it is worth spending a little time understanding the economics which drive commercial bank lending. The basic model is shown in Figure 7.6. The capital the bank lends to the shipping industry comes from two sources: the bank's equity and bonds issued by the bank. By financing part of its loan portfolio with equity the bank ensures that it can absorb bad debts and still meet its obligations to bondholders. However, the bank's equity caps the amount of loans it can commit to at any time. During the last twenty years the international banking industry has been trying to establish minimum requirements for equity. In 1988 The Bank for International Settlements (BIS), which is located in Basel, established a guideline that 8% of the bank's portfolio must be funded with equity. This became known as BASEL I. Sixteen years later BASEL II introduced a more sophisticated guideline which took the riskiness of the bank's portfolio into account in arriving at its required equity. Under the new system some high-risk loans could require equity cover of up to 12%.

The bank makes a profit on loans in two ways. Firstly, it lends to shipowners at a 'spread' which is typically in the range 20–200 basis points over its financing cost, depending on the customer and the risk. Secondly, the bank charges fees for arranging and administering the transaction. On the cost side, the bank must pay its overheads and the cost of any loans which have to be written off. What is left after these charges is profit on equity. Clearly it is a very tightly balanced equation, with the bank juggling the potential revenues from interest and fees against the cost of overheads and the risk of bad debt. An example in Table 7.1 illustrates the economics for a $100 million loan.

The loan of $100 million is repaid in five $20 million instalments (row 2) and the bank receives a payment of 1% spread over LIBOR (row 3). LIBOR payments (row 3) are only shown on the equity portion of the loan because the remainder is paid out by the bank to service its bonds. An arrangement fee of 1% is charged in the first year (row 5). Administration expenses, shown in row 6, are $500,000 million in the first year, and thereafter $100,000 a year. The bank's net earnings are shown in row 7, which is the sum of interest and fees, less administration expenses.

**Table 7.1** Bank funding calculation on $100 million ship loan

| | $ million | | | | |
|---|---|---|---|---|---|
| | 1 | 2 | 3 | 4 | 5 |
| 1 Loan outstanding, 31 Dec | 100 | 80 | 60 | 40 | 20 |
| 2 Principal repayment, 31 Dec | 20 | 20 | 20 | 20 | 20 |
| *Bank receives revenue from:* | | | | | |
| 3 Interest spread over LIBOR (1%) | 1.0 | 0.8 | 0.6 | 0.4 | 0.2 |
| 4 LIBOR paid on the 8% of the loan covered by equity (1) | 0.5 | 0.4 | 0.3 | 0.2 | 0.1 |
| 5 Arrangement Fee (1%) | 1.0 | | | | |
| *Bank incurs costs on:* | | | | | |
| 6 Bank administration expenses | 0.5 | 0.1 | 0.1 | 0.1 | 0.1 |
| 7 Net earnings, after costs | 2.0 | 1.1 | 0.8 | 0.5 | 0.2 |
| *Return on capital calcualtion* | | | | | |
| 8 Bank equity committed | 8 | 6.4 | 4.8 | 3.2 | 1.6 |
| 9 Return on bank equity (before debt provision) | 24.8% | 16.9% | 16.4% | 15.4% | 12.3% |
| *Risk calculation* | | | | | |
| 10 Bad debt provision | 0.5% | 0.5% | 0.5% | 0.5% | 0.5% |
| 11 Return on bank equity (after provision) | 18.5% | 10.7% | 10.2% | 9.1% | 6.0% |

Note 1: LIBOR assumed at 6% pa

| Percentage of bank's equity reserved: | Return on bank's equity | | | | |
|---|---|---|---|---|---|
| 4% | 37.0% | 21.4% | 20.3% | 18.3% | 12.0% |
| 8% | 18.5% | 10.7% | 10.2% | 9.1% | 6.0% |
| 12% | 12.3% | 7.1% | 6.8% | 6.1% | 4.0% |

| Bad debt provision: | Return on bank's equity | | | | |
|---|---|---|---|---|---|
| 0.1% | 23.5% | 15.7% | 15.2% | 14.1% | 11.0% |
| 0.3% | 21.0% | 13.2% | 12.7% | 11.6% | 8.5% |
| 0.5% | 18.5% | 10.7% | 10.2% | 9.1% | 6.0% |
| 0.7% | 16.0% | 8.2% | 7.7% | 6.6% | 3.5% |

| Size of the loan | Return on bank's equity (before provision) | | | | |
|---|---|---|---|---|---|
| $100 million | 24.8% | 16.9% | 16.4% | 15.4% | 12.3% |
| $50 million | 18.5% | 15.4% | 14.3% | 12.3% | 6.0% |
| $25 million | 6.0% | 12.3% | 10.2% | 6.0% | −6.5% |

Source: Martin Stopford 2005

Next we come to the return on capital calculation. Under Basel I the bank must cover 8% of the loan from equity, which in this case is $8 million in the first year. As the loan is paid down, the allocation of equity also reduces. The return on equity (ROE) is calculated by dividing earnings (row 7) by equity (row 8), giving 24.8% in year 1, falling to 12.3% in year 5 (row 9). The return falls because the loan reduces in size, but the administration cost does not, which is probably a realistic assumption. In fact many shipping loans are paid down long before their full term. Although this is an impressive return we have not factored in the bank's risk. If any loans in the bank's shipping portfolio are not repaid, earnings are reduced. To deal with this we need to set aside a 'bad debt provision' reflecting the probability of the loan being written off. In this example a provision of 0.5% is shown in row 10. After deducting this provision the ROE in the first year falls to 18%. Still a pretty good return, but by year 5 it is down to just 6%.

Three ROE sensitivity analyses are shown at the bottom of Table 7.1. The first shows the effect of varying the bank's equity contribution between 4% and 12%. Clearly this has a massive effect on profitability, producing returns ranging from 37% to 12% in year 1. The second sensitivity table shows the effect of changing the bad debt provision. Reducing the provision to 0.1% (a one in one thousand chance of write-off) increases the return from 18.5% to 23.5%. Conversely increasing the bad debt provision from 0.5% to 0.7% reduces the return from 18.5% to 16%. Thirdly, we see the relationship between ROE and the size of the loan. The $100 million loan makes four times the ROE in the first year as the $25 million loan.

This analysis highlights three economic characteristics of commercial ship lending. Firstly it shows the importance of economies of scale in banking. The administrative work does not vary significantly with the size of the loan, so small loans are much less economic than big loans. Syndications are commercially attractive because the lead bank is paid for the administrative work, but only retains a small proportion of the loan on its balance sheet. This means that the fee revenue is high relative to the size of the loan actually booked. Secondly, the profitability of the loan diminishes with time because the sum outstanding reduces relative to the administrative cost. This suggests that the bank has an interest in recycling loans as quickly as possible. It also suggests that from the bank's point of view a balloon payment (e.g. a large lump-sum repayment at the end of the loan period) gives a better return because the sum outstanding remains higher. Thirdly it illustrates how sensitive the profitability of the loan is to risk management. A shipping bank which reduces its annual write-off to 0.1% of the portfolio can make a profit, whilst a bank with a higher write-off rates will consistently lose money (these are hypothetical examples). If nothing else, this emphasizes the importance of managing the portfolio in a way which ensures that even if there are defaults, there are few write-offs.

## Corporate bank loans

For large shipping companies, borrowing against individual ships is inconvenient because any change in the fleet involves a time-consuming loan transaction. For this reason large companies with well-established financial structures often prefer to borrow as a company, using their corporate balance sheet as collateral. Most liner companies and a few bulk shipping companies are able to access this type of finance. Mitsui OSK, OSG, General Maritime, A.P. Møller and Teekay are examples.

An example of a corporate loan is provided by a $300 million credit facility raised by General Maritime in June 2001. This credit facility consisted of two parts, a $200 million 5–year term loan and a $98.8 million 'revolving credit' allowing the borrower to draw up to the limit at any time. The term loan was to be repaid in equal quarterly instalments over the 5 years, whilst the principal drawn down against the revolving loan was repaid at maturity. Interest was payable at 1.5% over LIBOR, with a fee of 0.625% payable on the unused portion of the revolving loan, on a quarterly basis. In this case the loan was in fact secured by 19 tankers, with a pledge of the ownership interest in the subsidiaries owning the tankers and guarantees from the vessel-owning subsidiaries. In December 2002 the market value of the tankers was $464.3 million, 50% above the committed loans.[24]

The advantage of this type of arrangement is that it gives the company a flexible source of capital. The term loan has to be paid back relatively quickly, creating a substantial negative cashflow, but the revolving credit provided an overdraft facility which offers flexibility for the business, either to allow it to make unplanned purchases or to cover cashflow fluctuations. In fact in December 2002 they had $129.4 million outstanding on the term loan and $54.1 million on the revolving loan. Large loans are usually syndicated among several banks and have covenants which ensure that the company maintains a strong balance sheet. Typically these covenants cover the leverage rate, the earnings to interest ratio and the asset cover.

## Loan syndications and asset sales

Lenders like to diversify their risk and are generally unwilling to keep more than, say, $25–50 million of a particular transaction on their books. For larger loans the usual practice is to spread the risk by sharing the loan among a syndication of several banks. Asset 'distribution', as this is known, is thus used to split large loans into small packages which can be distributed around many banks. In addition to spreading the risk, it allows banks without the expertise to appraise shipping loans to participate in the business under the guidance of a lead bank that does.

Syndicating a large shipping loan of, say, $300 million is a complex task. In addition to the normal credit appraisal process, the lead bank must manage the relationship with the borrower, whilst organizing a syndicate of banks to provide the loan. The simplest way to explain the process is to work through an example of a typical syndication timetable, focusing on the key areas. The main items are as follows:

1. *Getting a mandate.* First the lead bank meets the client to discuss his financing needs. For example, a loan of $500 million might be required to finance a newbuilding programme. The bank's syndication department will be consulted about the terms on which the loan could be syndicated to other banks, and unofficial enquiries will be made to discover how difficult the loan will be to place and what

particular features in terms of pricing, etc. will be necessary. If the bankers are sure the loan can be placed they will offer to underwrite it. Otherwise the offer will be on a 'best efforts' basis. When the client is satisfied with the terms and conditions, he will issue a mandate letter.

2. *Preparation for syndication.* Next, documentation is prepared and the whole package is agreed with the client. Again this is a complex exercise involving the syndications department, the shipping department and the bank's credit control officers. It also requires skills in drafting documentation and preparing an information memorandum designed to answer the questions likely to be raised by participating banks.

3. *Syndicating the loan.* When the preparations are complete the terms will be circulated to those banks which the syndication department believes may be interested in participating. For a specialized business like shipping the list may extend to 20–30 banks which will be asked to respond by a given date, indicating their interest. In the meantime the lead bank will visit interested banks to discuss the proposal and the participating banks carry out their own enquiries, since they will have to process the loan through their own credit control system. Those banks prepared to participate will indicate the sum they are willing to take, and when sufficient commitments have been obtained a closing is arranged at which all banks and the owner sign the necessary documents.

4. *Administration, fees, etc.* The loan documentation sets out the procedures for administering the loan. As a rule the lead bank acts as agent and charges a fee for doing so. For large syndications a management group may be set up. Their task is to handle ongoing problems without the necessity for approaching every participant. The pricing of the loan and the split of fees, etc. between the lead bank and participants will form a key part of the offer documentation.

The time taken to arrange a syndication depends on its complexity. Some loans can be placed very quickly because they are readily acceptable in the market. Others may require many months to line up the full subscription. Obviously one problem to be faced is that the shipowner may not be in a position to wait many months.

Widely syndicated shipping loans can sometimes be difficult to manage. If the borrower runs into difficulties, the lead bank and management group may find it difficult to control a diverse group of participating banks, some of whom know nothing about the shipping market and its cycles. This makes borrowers uncomfortable, and it is often argued that it is better if syndication is restricted to club deals between banks that combine to offer joint financing. For example, five banks may join to finance a $150 million newbuilding programme, each taking $30 million.

## Asset sales (participation agreement)

Another form of distribution commonly used by banks is asset sales. The bank books the loan in the normal way, placing it on its balance sheet. For example, it may lend $50 million to a shipowner to purchase an $80 million tanker. If at some later date the bank decides to reduce its exposure to shipping risk, or to that particular client, it sells the loan to another bank which has room on its balance sheet for shipping risk. Large banks have an asset sales department which arranges the sale of loans. The bank officer in the asset sales department approaches banks that he knows are interested in taking shipping loans. When a buyer has been found the two banks sign a joint participation agreement, transferring a specified proportion of the loan, say $5 million, to the buyer, on agreed terms of interest and capital repayment. Naturally the bank which booked the loan will aim to sell it on favourable terms, retaining a margin for itself. The originating bank will continue to manage the loan in the normal way. In some cases the shipowner may not even be aware that his loan is now held by another bank.

## Financing new ships

Now we come to debt finance for newbuildings. Although the principles of financing a new ship are generally the same as for second-hand ships, there are two additional problems to overcome. First, the capital cost of a new ship is generally too high relative to its likely spot market earnings to be financed from cashflow, especially if the loan is amortized over the short periods of 5–7 years favoured by commercial banks. Unless a time charter is available, arranging security can be difficult, especially if a one-ship company structure is used. Second, the finance is needed before the ship is built, so there is a period before delivery when part of the loan is drawn but the hull is not available as collateral.

*Pre-delivery* finance is usually arranged separately. Shipyards generally require their customers to make 'stage payments' to the shipyard to pay for the material and labour required to build the ship. This involves a down payment to the builder for the purchase of materials on signing the contract, with the balance being paid in roughly equal instalments on keel laying, engine delivery, launching and delivery (see Chapter 14 for a discussion of this practice).

The pattern of stage payments is negotiable. If pre-delivery credit has been arranged, the purchaser makes the first payment from his own funds and the bank makes the remaining stage payments. The risk for the lender is that stage payments are made, but the ship is not completed, either because the shipyard goes bankrupt with a partly finished ship in the yard, technical problems, or because some form of civil or political disturbance prevents completion or delivery. With no ship to act as collateral, additional security is needed, and this is generally covered by a 'refund guarantee' issued by the shipyard's bank. However, problems may arise when dealing with shipyards where bankruptcy is a risk, or located in politically unstable areas. This is where a government guarantee is particularly valuable, or possibly the purchaser can arrange political risk insurance.

*Post-delivery* finance is generally drawn on delivery of the vessel. It may be obtained from three sources: a shipyard credit scheme, commercial bank credit or by leasing. Bank credit, and leasing are discussed elsewhere, so here we will focus on the shipbuilding credit schemes. There is a long history of governments offering credit to assist its shipyards in obtaining orders, though the availability of this facility is constantly changing. There are three ways in which a government can make its ship-building credit more attractive to the shipowner than commercial bank credit. They are:

1. *Government guarantee.* By obtaining a government guarantee of the loan, the shipowner can borrow from a commercial bank. The value of this guarantee to the borrower depends on the credit standards which the government agency applies in issuing the guarantee. Sometimes the standards are the same as those applied by commercial banks, so the guarantee has little value. If, however, the government wants to help the shipyard win the order, it may guarantee terms which the owner would not obtain from a commercial bank. In doing this the government takes a credit risk, which is in effect a subsidy.
2. *Interest rates subsidy.* Some government agencies offer subsidized interest. For example, a loan is raised from a commercial bank, which receives an interest rate make-up from the government to cover the difference between the agreed rate on the loan and the current market rate. In a low interest rate environment this is less useful.
3. *Moratorium.* In difficult circumstances the government may agree to a one-or two-year moratorium on interest or principal repayments.

Some governments have a bank – for example, the Export Credit Bank of Japan and the KEXIM bank in South Korea – which carries out credit analysis and makes the loan itself. Other governments use an agency which performs the credit analysis, but the loan is provided by local commercial banks. For example, the Export Credit Guarantee Department in the UK performs in this way, following the model illustrated in Figure 7.7.

Government credit schemes stretch back to the 1930s, but the modern shipbuilding credit regime developed in the 1960s when the Japanese shipyards took the first step by launching an export credit scheme offering customers 80% over 8 years at 5.5% interest. Fierce credit competition between Japanese and European shipyards followed, leading to the OECD Understanding on Export Credit for Ships in 1969 (see Chapter 13) which informally regulated

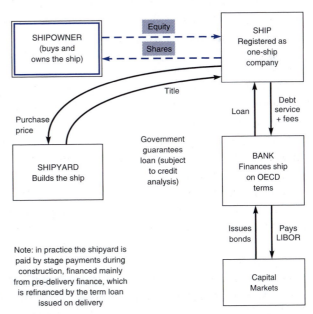

Note: in practice the shipyard is paid by stage payments during construction, financed mainly from pre-delivery finance, which is refinanced by the term loan issued on delivery

**Figure 7.7**
Newbuilding finance model
Source: Martin Stopford, 2007

inter-country competition in shipbuilding credit terms; this is still in force and was last updated in 2002.

The OECD Understanding defines a 'ship' as any seagoing vessel of 100 grt and above used for the transportation of goods or persons, or for the performance of a specialized service (e.g. fishing, icebreakers, dredgers). For many years the terms were capped at 80% over 8 years at 8.5% interest, but in 2002 shipbuilding export credit was brought in line with other capital goods and the new agreement approved 80% over 12 years, at the Commercial Interest Reference Rate (CIRR) plus a spread. The CIRR is based on the previous month's domestic bond rate for the appropriate term. Most European shipyards offer OECD terms, though with some local variations for domestic customers. Japan offers export finance in yen through the EXIM bank on OECD terms.

## Mezzanine finance structures

*Mezzanine finance* is a loosely defined term which usually refers to high-yielding debt, typically priced at several percentage points above LIBOR, often with some form of equity 'kicker' attached – for example, equity warrants. One such structure involved $40 million of senior debt, topped by $26 million of mezzanine finance in the form of cumulative participating *preference shares*. These preference shares, redeemable after 5 years, paid a basic 10% per annum dividend plus an additional 20% of cashflow after interest and principal repayment. They also included detachable 5-year warrants for 25% of the company at original cost. Despite the apparent generosity of this offer it was never placed and the company resorted to more conventional financing. Mezzanine finance has not been widely used in shipping and is not easy to place.

## Private placement of debt and equity

Finally, instead of borrowing from a bank it may be possible to arrange a private placement of debt or equity directly with financial institutions such as pension funds, insurance companies or leasing companies. An investment bank will normally be retained to handle the placement, which will involve the preparation of a prospectus and presentations to the potential investors. Private placements have the advantage that they do not need to be registered in the USA and avoid some of the lengthy processes required to place tradable securities. This allows established companies familiar to the financial institutions to raise funds quickly and inexpensively. Private placement of debt offers advantages such as fixed interest rate, long tenor and the corporate obligation which leaves individual assets unencumbered.

## 7.6 FINANCING SHIPS AND SHIPPING COMPANIES IN THE CAPITAL MARKETS

In most capital-intensive industries large companies use the capital markets to raise finance either by making a public offering of shares or by issuing bonds. The advantage of the capital markets is that once the company is known and accepted by the financial institutions, it offers wholesale finance and a quick and relatively inexpensive way of raising very large sums of money. However, most shipping companies are too small to require funding on this scale and can end up spending a great deal of time and money raising sums that could be obtained more easily from a commercial bank. In short, the capital markets are not a source of finance to be dabbled in. They are a way of life that must be embraced and that is not always easy, given the volatile characteristics of the shipping business.

## Public offering of equity

Shipping companies can raise equity by arranging a public offering of stock to be traded on one or more of the stock exchanges around the world. New York, Oslo, Hong Kong, Singapore and Stockholm are all used for public offerings of shipping stock. During the 1990s the shipping industry made real progress in developing this capital source, though it remains a minor player in ship finance. In 2007 there were 181 public shipping companies with a market capitalization (the number of issued shares multiplied by the market value per share) of $315 billion, as shown in Table 7.2. Two companies, Maersk and Carnival Corporation, accounted for $90 billion or 29% of the total market capitalization. Apart from these two, the biggest sector are 'multi-sector' companies. This sector includes large Asian conglomerates such as Mitsui OSK ($16.2 billion), NYK ($11.2 billion), COSCO ($10.5 billion) and China Shipping ($10 billion). Bulk shipping companies include Teekay ($4.2 billion) and Frontline ($3.4 billion). The liner companies include OOIL ($6.1 billion) and NOL ($6 billion). The top 20 companies account for two-thirds of the world market capitalization of shipping companies. This is a significant critical mass, and the public companies as a whole owned 472 million dwt of ships, accounting for 47% of the world fleet, so it is an important part of the shipping business.

If a private company wants to raise equity in the public markets, it must make an IPO. A prospectus is drawn up describing the company, its markets and its financial performance, and offering shares, to be listed on a specified stock exchange where they will be traded (this is important because it allows investors to get their money out whenever they wish to). For example, in 1993 Bona Shipholding Ltd issued a prospectus offering 11 million shares at a target price of $9 per share, to be listed on the Oslo Stock Exchange from 17 December 1993. Once the issue is made and trading starts, the shares are traded in the secondary market where the price is determined by supply and demand. By 1996 the stock in Bona Shipholdings Ltd was trading at $11.79, so investors had made a profit of $2.79 per share. The listing of equity allows investors to buy or sell shares at any time provided there is liquidity (i.e. buyers and sellers). For this to work the offering must be big enough to allow reasonable trading volume. Eventually the company was bought by Teekay.

A company wishing to issue a public offering of shares will first appoint an investment bank to act for it, preparing the prospectus, submitting it to the stock exchange authorities who regulate offerings on their exchange, and arranging for it to be 'placed' with financial

**Table 7.2** Top 20 public shipping companies 2007

| Short Name | Sector | Fleet | | Market % | |
| --- | --- | --- | --- | --- | --- |
| | | Ships | Dwt (m.) | Cap $ M. | Share |
| Maersk | Container | 841 | 38.0 | 50,125 | 16% |
| Carnival | Cruise | 102 | 0.7 | 40,821 | 13% |
| Mitsui OSK | Diversified | 620 | 44.8 | 16,254 | 5% |
| NYK | Diversified | 583 | 43.9 | 11,279 | 4% |
| China Cosco Holdings | Container | 152 | 6.5 | 10,502 | 3% |
| China Shipping Dev. | Tanker | 95 | 4.6 | 10,055 | 3% |
| Royal Caribbean | Cruise | 44 | 0.3 | 9,132 | 3% |
| K-Line | Diversified | 390 | 31.3 | 8,204 | 3% |
| MISC | Diversified | 167 | 13.1 | 7,572 | 2% |
| OOIL | Container | 95 | 5.0 | 6,115 | 2% |
| Hyundai MM | Container | 109 | 10.4 | 5,965 | 2% |
| NOL | Container | 117 | 5.5 | 5,802 | 2% |
| Cosco Singapore | Dry Bulk | 11 | 0.6 | 5,471 | 2% |
| Teekay | Tanker | 149 | 15.0 | 4,142 | 1% |
| Tidewater | Offshore | 493 | 0.6 | 4,074 | 1% |
| CSCL | Container | 120 | 4.9 | 4,006 | 1% |
| Bourbon | Offshore | 239 | 0.7 | 3,489 | 1% |
| Frontline | Tanker | 101 | 20.3 | 3,410 | 1% |
| Hanjin Shipping | Container | 149 | 11.1 | 3,180 | 1% |
| Star Cruises | Cruise | 26 | 0.1 | 2,746 | 1% |
| Others | | 4839 | 214.7 | 103,128 | 33% |
| Total | | 9442 | 472.1 | 315,474 | 100% |

Source: Clarkson Research Services

institutions which buy the stock at an agreed price. A major responsibility is pricing the shares. The starting point is to value the equity stake being sold, which is done by taking the market value of the ships, adding cash and other assets, and deducting bank debt and other liabilities to arrive at a value for the company. In the example in Figure 7.8 the company has $1 billion assets ($700 million in ships and $300 million in cash) and $500 million debt, so it ought to be worth $500 million. If 50 million shares are issued they should be worth $10 each, but will investors pay more or less than this value per share? The issuer may feel the company, with its dynamic track record, is worth more and ask for $11 per share,

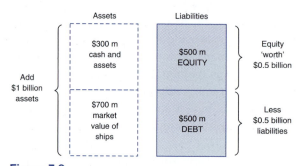

**Figure 7.8**
Valuing equity in shipping company
Source: Martin Stopford, 2007

but the investors may be concerned by the volatility of the shipping market and only prepared to offer $9.

Pricing an IPO is as much an art as a science, but three factors will generally be taken into account in pricing a shipping offering: the company's market-adjusted net asset value (NAV); the enterprise value based on the company's EBITDA compared to similar listed companies; and, in the case of offerings aimed at income funds and retail investors, the yields of comparable public companies. This establishes the full value of the stock but, except in a very hot new issue market, an IPO will generally have to be priced at a discount to full value in order to ensure that the offer is fully subscribed.

In the USA a preliminary prospectus, known as a 'red herring' (because preliminary portions are printed in red ink), is often issued containing all the details except the price of the shares. Feedback allows the pricing to be fine-tuned and a full prospectus can then be issued. After circulating the prospectus the shipping company generally goes on a 'roadshow' to present their company to institutional investors. These roadshows are often very demanding, involving a gruelling schedule of back-to-back investor meetings spread over one or two weeks. A successful listing depends on convincing institutions that the investment is sound, which depends in turn on the general case for investing in the shipping industry and whether the company looks well managed and has a good 'story'. Since the investors often know little about shipping, that has to be explained, as must the company strategy. A clear corporate structure, a well-defined strategy, a credible management track record, and plenty of information can all contribute to a successful outcome. Technical questions about the value of the fleet and the EBITDA levels must be answered along with more difficult questions like 'what if things go wrong – could you still carry out your plans?' The whole process including the roadshow takes about 10–15 weeks and in New York costs about 9% of the funds raised, though costs in London are closer to 7%. If enough investors are willing to purchase the stock at the offer price, the offering is a success. If not, it may be withdrawn. As the example in Box 7.3 illustrates, things do not always go smoothly. The purpose of the offering was to raise money to buy a fleet of double hull tankers. Since the shares were eventually placed at $11, well below the $13–15 per share target, the company had to borrow an additional $25 million from its bankers.

Raising shipping equity through the stock market has a mixed history, especially in bulk shipping and accessing the public equity markets is not easy. The large public shipping companies listed in Table 7.2 are mainly diversified corporates, with only three single-purpose companies. Two particular problems are the small size of many shipping companies, which excludes them from this type of finance, and the volatility of earnings and asset values. Volatility is an issue because although shipowners thrive on it, Stokes thinks that 'the essentially opportunistic nature of the tramp shipowning business somehow appears incongruous in the context of the stock market, where highly rated companies are those which are able to achieve consistent profit growth year after year'.[25] The corporate structures required by the equity markets can slow decision-making. There are also cultural issues to consider. If a shipowner has the skill to become very wealthy, why should he share his success with equity investors when cheap and flexible finance is available from commercial banks?

C H A P T E R 7

## BOX 7.3 IPO CASE STUDY

# Tough start for TOP float

**By Tony Gray**

THE flotation of TOP Tankers on the Nasdaq market has been successful – but at a cost. The Pistiolis family company sold the proposed 13.33m shares at $11 per share, substantially below its target range of between $13 and $15. After commencing trading on Friday afternoon [23 July], the shares closed 40 cents down at $10.60, a decline of 3.64%. The gross proceeds of the initial public offering (IPO) were $146.3m.

However, only $134.8m of this sum is to the company's account, as a shareholder sold 1.07m shares. The total could be raised by almost $22m through an underwriter's over-allotment option. The underwriters have a 30-day option to purchase up to an additional 1.54m and 454,545 shares. Based on the IPO price, TOP Tankers and its lender have agreed a $222m secured credit facility – this is $25m more than the $197m indicated in the prospectus.

TOP now intends to acquire 10 double-hull tankers for $251.2m. The 10 targeted tankers comprise eight handymaxes and two suezmaxes built between 1991 and 1992 by Hyundai Heavy Industries in South Korea and Halla Engineering & Heavy Industries respectively. This purchase will increase the size of TOP's fleet to 17 tankers of more than 1.1 m dwt, with 92% double-hulled compared with a global average of 61%.

Source: *Lloyd's List,* 26 July 2004

Despite these reservations, shipping is a key business in the world economy and financial institutions have a place in their investment portfolios for the equity of well-managed transport companies. From this perspective there is no doubt that the equity markets have a part to play in financing liner, bulk and specialist shipping.

### Raising finance by issuing bonds

Another way of accessing the capital markets is to issue bonds. A bond is a debt security (known as a 'note') redeemed on a specific date, say in 10 years' time, and on which the issuer pays interest. The basic structure is illustrated in Figure 7.9. The shipping company (the 'issuer') sells bonds to financial institutions (the bondholders) and pays them interest (known as the coupon). At the end of the term the capital is repaid to the bondholder. The bonds issued may be investment grade, sub-investment grade or convertible bonds (i.e. a bond that can be exchanged for common stock). Each has a different pricing and places different demands and obligations on the issuer.

In the USA a bond issue generally obtains a credit rating which determines the interest payable – investment-grade bonds can be placed at lower rates than 'high-yield' bonds. The bond will also include an 'indenture', which is a deed of trust designed to protect the bondholders. Typically it deals with property pledges, working capital requirements, and redemption rights. A trustee is appointed to represent the bondholders' interest and enforce the indenture.

Issuing a bond is in some ways similar to an IPO. An investment bank handles the placement, drawing up an offer document dealing with the following topics:

- overview of the company and its strategy;
- the terms of the note;
- risk sectors relating to the company and the industry;
- description of the company's business, operations and assets;
- overview of the company's market and regulatory environment;
- biographies of directors and executive officers;
- the indenture and financial tests;
- summary of financial data.

Once the offering memorandum is ready, the investment bankers and the company's top officers will go on the road to make presentations to institutional investors. Like an IPO roadshow, this often involves visiting several cities in one day and is both time-consuming and demanding. However, a well-established issuer who is well known to the investors may not need to do a roadshow. A conference call may be sufficient. Depending on the reception, the pricing and covenants are finalized and, if all goes well, finally the bond is placed.

Compared with bank debt, bonds have several advantages for established corporations. Firstly, they offer long-term finance: typically 10 years, and potentially 15 years. However, in shipping this is not necessarily an advantage since shipping companies like flexibility, and few bank loans run to their full term. More importantly, the principal is not repaid until the bond matures. This makes a difference to the cashflow of the company, especially during periods of low freight rates, as is illustrated in Figure 7.14 which compares debt service on a bond with the repayments

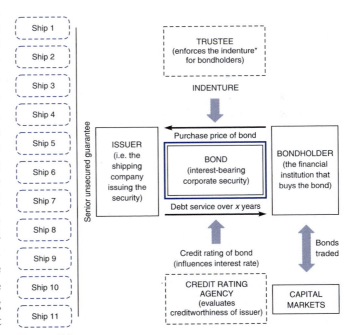

**Figure 7.9**

Basic structure of shipping bond issue

Source: Martin Stopford, 2007

*Indenture is the equivalent of the loan agreement, including, 'incurrence tests' and 'maintenance covenants'

**Table 7.3** Shipping high-yield bond issues

| | % Interest | Amount $ Million | Year | Maturity | Sector |
|---|---|---|---|---|---|
| Alpha Shipping | 9% | $175 | 1998 | 2008 | Multiple Sectors (5) |
| Amer Reefer Co. Ltd. (AMI RLF) | 10% | $100 | 1998 | 2008 | Reefers |
| American Commercial Lines (VECTUR) | 10% | $300 | 1998 | 2008 | Inland Barging |
| Cenargo Intl PLC (CENTNT) | 10% | $175 | 1998 | 2008 | Ferry |
| Enterprises Shipholding Inc | 9% | $175 | 1998 | 2008 | Reefers |
| Ermis Maritime (ERMIS) | 13% | $150 | 1998 | 2006 | Tanker |
| Gulfmark Offshore (GMRK) | 9% | $130 | 1998 | 2008 | Offshore Support |
| Hvide Marine (HMAR) | 8% | $300 | 1998 | 2008 | Chemical Tankers |
| International Shipholding (ISH) | 8% | $110 | 1998 | 2007 | Liner, Specialized |
| MC Shipping (MCX) | 11% | $85 | 1998 | 2008 | Gas Carriers |
| Millenium Seacarriers (MILSEA) | 12% | $100 | 1998 | 2005 | Drybulk |
| Pacific & Atlantic | 12% | $128 | 1998 | 2008 | Dry bulL, container, MPP |
| Premier Cruises (CRUISE) | 11% | $160 | 1998 | 2008 | Cruise |
| Sea Containers (SCR) | 8% | $150 | 1998 | 2008 | Diversified/Container Leasing |
| TBS Shipping (TBSSHP) | 10% | $110 | 1998 | 2005 | Break-bulk |
| Teekay Shipping Corp. (TK) | 8% | $225 | 1998 | 2008 | Tankers |
| Equimar Shipholdings Ltd. (EQUIMA) | 10% | $124 | 1997 | | Tanker |
| Global Ocean Carriers (GLO) | 10% | $126 | 1997 | 2007 | Dry Bulk, Containerships |
| Golden Ocean Group (GOLDOG) | 10% | $291 | 1997 | 2001 | Tankers/Drybulk |
| Navigator Gas Iransporr (NAVGAS) | 10.5% | $217 | 1997 | 2007 | Gas Carriers |
| Navigator Gas Transport (NAVGAS) | 12.0% | $87 | 1997 | 2007 | Gas Carriers |
| Pegasus Shipping (PEGSHP) | 12% | $150 | 1997 | 2004 | Tankers |
| Stena AB (STENA) | 9% | $175 | 1997 | 2007 | Tankers, Rigs, Other |
| Trico Marine | 9% | $280 | 1997 | | Offshore Support |
| Ultrapetrol (Bahamas) (ULTRAP) | 11% | $135 | 1997 | 2008 | Tankers |
| Sea Containers (SCR) | 11% | $65 | 1996 | 2003 | Diversified/Container Leasing |
| Transportación Maritima Mexicana (TMM) | 10% | $200 | 1996 | 2006 | Diversified, Container |
| International Shipholding (ISH) | 9% | $100 | 1995 | 2003 | Liner, Specialized |
| Pan Oceanic | 12% | $100 | 1995 | 2007 | Dry Bulk |
| Stena AB (STENA) | 11% | $175 | 1995 | 2005 | Tankers, Rigs, Other |
| Stena Line AB (STENA) | 11% | $300 | 1995 | 2008 | Tankers, Rigs Other |
| American President Lines (APL) | 8% | $150 | 1994 | 2024 | Container Shipping |
| Gearbulk Holding (GEAR) | 11% | $175 | 1994 | 2004 | Specialized Bulk |
| American President Lines (APS) | 7% | $150 | 1993 | 2003 | Container Shipping |
| Eletson Holdings (ELETSN) | 9% | $140 | 1993 | 2003 | Tankers |
| Overseas Shipholding Group (OSG) | 8% | $100 | 1993 | 2003 | Tankers |
| Sea Containers (SCR) | 10% | $100 | 1993 | 2003 | Diversified/Container Leasing |
| Transportación Maritima Mexicana (TMM) | 9% | $176 | 1993 | 2003 | Diversified, Container |
| Transportación Maritima Mexicana (TMM) | 9% | $142 | 1993 | 2000 | Diversified, Container |
| Sea Containers (SCR) | 13% | $100 | 1992 | 2004 | Diversified/Container Line |
| Total | | $6,331 | | | |

Source: A. Ginsberg, 'Debt Market Re-opens', *Marine Money*, June 2003

on a bank loan, and for comparison also shows a typical freight rate cycle (of course the bond will only get a credit rating if the company can demonstrate its ability to service the cashflow in these extreme circumstances). In the example of bond finance in Figure 6.14 case D the company is committed to repaying the full principal in year 15 and this would normally be done by refinancing, provided the company is in good financial shape. Ideally the bonds are rolled forward and each new issue should be cheaper if the company is doing a good job. Finally, once a company is established the bond markets offer very fast access to finance – shipping companies have raised sums in excess of $200 million in 24 hours.

For the shipping industry bonds can be used in two ways. The first is to provide creditworthy private companies which do not wish to go down the public equity route with access to capital market funding. During the 1990s about 50 companies followed this route, raising sums of $65–200 million, and a selection of the bonds issued are listed in Table 7.3). The results were mixed and in retrospect it seems that many were over-leveraged, perhaps because they regarded the bonds as quasi-equity. Interest rates were very high, averaging around 10% per annum, and in the difficult shipping markets of the late 1990s the debt could not always be serviced. The second use of bonds is by established public shipping companies with significant market capitalization which, as mentioned above, can use their credit status and relationship with investment institutions to raise relatively large amounts of capital quickly and easily. For them, bonds offer fast and flexible finance.

## 7.7 FINANCING SHIPS WITH SPECIAL PURPOSE COMPANIES

So far we have discussed how shipping companies raise finance. However, in this section we take a different approach, and discuss the use of special purpose companies (SPCs) as a means of raising finance to acquire ships. The type of structure we are dealing with is shown in Figure 7.10. The SPC buys the ships and either leases or time-charters them out. A manager is appointed to operate the ships and funds are obtained from equity investors, probably supplemented by a bank loan.

There are two reasons for using SPCs. The first is as a speculative shipping investment vehicle. Ship funds and Norwegian K/S partnerships are examples of structures which have been used in the past to allow private investors to invest in shipping. The structure is set up, the funds invested, and in due course the investment is liquidated. Second, SPCs are often used for off-balance-sheet financing. For example, during the 1990s liner

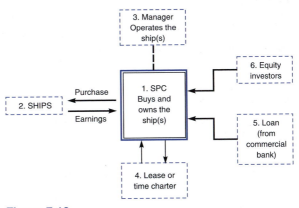

**Figure 7.10**
Special purpose company finance: basic model

companies preferred to charter ships rather than own them, and extensive use was made of leases and German KG partnerships as a way of securing the use of the ships without actually owning them. Finally, securitization structures take this a step further, but so far for shipping it has had limited success – there have been no securitizations of ships at time of publication, though there have been some of shipping debt.

## Ship Funds and SPACs

A *ship fund* is an investment vehicle designed to allow equity investors to invest in a specific investment opportunity. For example, Bulk Transport was set up during the tanker depression in 1984–5 to take advantage of very low second-hand prices by purchasing four ULCCs at prices just above scrap.[26] As an investment it proved extremely successful, with the assets appreciating to five times their purchase cost during the following 4 years. Between 1987 and 1989 a succession of funds were organized by US commercial and investment banks. In most cases the equity raised was $30 to $50 million, often topped up with 40–60% debt in order to improve the return to the investor. In total these funds raised about $500 million of equity capital. A more recent example is Sea Production Ltd, discussed below.

The structure is usually similar to Figure 7.10. An SPC is set up in a tax-efficient location (e.g. the Bahamas, Cayman Islands) and a general manager appointed to handle the buying, selling and operating of the company's ships. For this service he is paid a management fee - for example, one fund with four ships paid $100,000 plus 1.25% of revenue earned. Because ship funds are investment vehicles rather than shipping companies, the shareholders are given the option to wind up the company after 5–7 years, thus ensuring liquidity if the shares prove not to be tradable. To improve the return on equity most funds raised debt finance, increasing the risk–reward ratio for the equity investor.

A prospectus is drawn up setting out the terms on which shares in the business are offered for sale. This document may be anything from a few pages of typescript to a glossy brochure. It sets out the business in which the company is to operate, its strategy, the market prospects, the terms on which shares can be purchased, administrative arrangements, control mechanisms and winding-up arrangements. On the basis of this prospectus shares are sold by private placement to wealthy individuals or institutions, or in a few cases by public offering (see Section 5.4). Investment institutions have limited funds for high-risk ventures of this type, so ship funds depend heavily on wealthy individuals willing to back a good sales story. When sufficient funds have been raised, management purchases ships and operates the company according to the terms set out in the prospectus.

As a 'pure' investment vehicle ship funds face two problems. First, the equity must be raised before the ships are purchased, facing the organizers with the difficult task of finding good-quality ships at very short notice. To deal with this the transaction may be initiated by a company with assets it is willing to sell to the fund. Second, their commercial and management structure is ambiguous. They are not shipping companies because they have a limited life, but they are charged with running ships over a fairly long period. Both these problems arise from the perception of ships as commodities. Although ships are traded on the sale and purchase market as commodities, in terms of ongoing management they are complex engineering structures. Efforts to 'package' them as commodities bring a whole range of risks which need to be addressed.

But business moves on and in the more confident shipping markets of the early 2000s a new structure, the special purpose acquisition corporation (SPAC), has appeared to deal with the timing and corporate responsibility issues raised by ship funds. This is an enhanced version of the 'blind pool' in which the assets are not identified and acquired until after the funds have been raised. Corporate responsibility is provided by floating the SPAC as a fully reporting listed company, responsible for raising funds to acquire an operating business. The funds are escrowed; a proportion, say 80%, must be invested within a stipulated period, for example 18 months; and the investors must approve the acquisition. Once the ships have been acquired, the SPAC is listed on the NYSE or NASDAQ. This vehicle was used in 2005–6 by several Greek shipping companies to achieve a New York listing – for example, Navios International Shipping Enterprises (Angeliki Frangou), Trinity Partners Acquisition Company/Freeseas, Inc. (Gourdomichalis Bros and Ion Vourexakis) and Star Maritime Acquisition Corporation (Akis Tsiringakis and Petros Pappas). A transaction of this sort typically takes three to four months to complete and the fees are generally lower than for an IPO.

## Private placement vehicles

Special purpose companies are also used by public companies as a way of raising private equity by private placement, prior to a market offering. For example, in the USA a private investment in public equity (PIPE) involves the sale of stock in an SPC set up by a public shipping company to accredited investors[27] at a slight discount to the market price. Typically the securities are unregistered, but the company agrees to use its best efforts to register them for resale. In the case of a 'Registered Direct' (RD) placement the securities are registered with the SEC and can be resold to the public immediately. Because the offering is restricted there are fewer disclosure requirements than for a secondary offering; there is no need for a roadshow; and adjusting pricing in response to changing market conditions is easier than in the case of a secondary offering. The cost is generally 4–6% of the gross proceeds, which is cheaper than a secondary offering. All these factors can make a private placement attractive to established small- to medium-sized public companies, which find it difficult to access more traditional forms of equity financing.[28]

An example is the private placement of equity by Sea Production Ltd, a company set up by Frontline Ltd to acquire its floating production business consisting of two floating production, storage and offloading (FPSO) systems, two Aframax tankers for conversion, and a management organization. Sea Production financed the $336 million acquisition with a $130 million bond facility, a bank loan and a $180 million private placement of equity.[29] It was registered on the Oslo over-the-counter market in February 2007 with the aim of a listing on the Oslo Stock Exchange in the autumn. The placement was managed by three investment banks and was heavily oversubscribed, with Frontline taking 28% of the equity which it sold in June 2007. For a well-established company like Frontline the private placement was a quicker and less expensive way of raising the equity required by Sea Production Ltd than a public listing of shares. The number of shareholders is restricted by the regulatory authorities and the secondary market is generally limited.

## Norwegian K/S partnership structures

During the late 1980s substantial amounts of partnership capital were raised through the Norwegian K/S limited partnerships investing speculatively in the purchase of ships. It is estimated that during this period about half of the Norwegian shipping industry operated through K/S companies and during 1987–9 investors in K/S partnerships committed equity of $3 billion.

At the time the K/S partnership, a standard form of Norwegian company, offered investors tax advantages. The K/Ss were usually set up on a one-ship basis with management subcontracted. The organizer appointed a 'general partner' and invited equity partners to commit capital.[30] At least 20% of the committed capital had to be available in cash at the time of incorporation and another 20% within 2 years. The remainder was only called if needed.

As a rule 80% of the purchase price was raised as a bank loan and the remainder with cash drawn against the committed equity. For example the purchase of a $10 million ship requiring $0.5 million working capital might be financed as follows:

|  | $ million |
| --- | --- |
| Mortgage loan (80 per cent) | 8.00 |
| Called equity capital | 2.50 |
| Uncalled capital | 4.85 |

For tax purposes the committed capital could be depreciated at an annual rate of 25% on a declining balance basis. In addition, provisions could be made for classification costs, though allowable depreciation could not exceed the total capital committed.[31] The K/S shares could be sold, and there was a limited market within Norway through brokers or advertisements in Norwegian newspapers.

In the early 1990s these tax benefits were much reduced and the K/Ss, which had obtained a mixed reputation after a series of losses, fell out of favour, though interest has revived in recent years. They remain a fascinating example of opportunism in ship finance. The speed, flexibility, and relatively low cost of the K/S system were ideally suited to financing asset play during the period of escalating ship values in the late 1980s, allowing many small investors to become involved in shipping. Their weakness, from the investors' point of view, was the lack of the rigorous regulation which plays such an important part in protecting investors in the stock market.

## German KG funds

A form of the ship finance which emerged with great success in the mid-1990s was the German KG company, the German equivalent of the Norwegian K/S company. The structure is shown in Figure 7.11. A German registered limited liability partnership company purchases the vessel from a shipyard (or owner) and obtains a time charter. The purchase price is raised from a bank loan (usually about 50–70%), and equity raised from German high net worth investors and the general manager (usually around 30–50% between them).

By 2004 over 600 ships had been financed by KGs, typically $50–100 million in size. The scheme owes its success to a combination of circumstances. Firstly, during the 1990s the liner

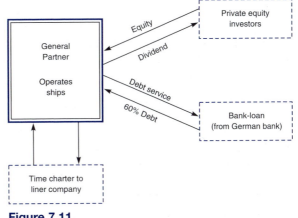

**Figure 7.11**
KG finance model

companies were earning poor returns and used KGs to move ships off their balance sheet – between 1991 and 2004 the proportion of the container fleet chartered in by liner service operators increased from 15% to over 50%. Secondly, the German shipyards had a very strong position in the container-ship building market, supported by the strong container-ship brokerage community in Hamburg. Thirdly, Germany had a pool of high net worth individuals facing high marginal tax rates and an equity distribution system run by small investment houses. Fourthly, the German banks were in an expansionist phase and willing to provide the loans required. In these circumstances the quick and tax-efficient KG company proved to be an ideal financing vehicle, providing the liner company with container-ships which were 'off the peg' and off the balance sheet. Private investors liked the return of 8% after tax so much that ships became the most popular investment, accounting for about 20% of private funds raised in Germany in 2003.

By 2007 the KG market continued to provide ship finance, especially for the container market, but its competitive position was under pressure as a result of reduced tax benefits, higher capital costs and increased competition from the listed container-ship operators discussed in the next section.

## Leasing ships

Leasing 'separates the use and ownership of the vessel'. This technique was originally developed in the property business where land and buildings are often leased. The lessor (i.e. the legal owner) hands the property over to the lessee who, in return for regular lease payments is entitled to use it as though it were his own (known legally as 'quiet enjoyment'). At the end of the lease the property reverts to the lessor. This technique is widely used for financing mechanical equipment, including ships. In arranging this sort of finance there are three main risks to consider: the revenue risk (will the lessor be paid in full for the asset he has purchased?); the operating risk (who will pay if it breaks down?); and the residual value risk (who gets the benefit if it is worth more than expected at the end of the lease?).

The two common types of leasing structures, the *operating lease* and the *finance lease*, deal with these risks in different ways. The operating lease, which is used for hiring equipment and consumer durables, leaves most of the risk with the lessor. The lease can usually be terminated at the lessee's discretion, maintenance is carried out by the lessor and at the end of the lease the equipment reverts to the lessor. This is ideal for big photocopiers where the lessor is an expert in all these practicalities and the lessee just wants to use it. Operating leases generally do not appear on the balance sheet and in shipping have been very widely used for container-ships. Finance leases are longer, covering a substantial part of the asset's life. The lessor, whose main role is as financier, has little involvement with the asset beyond owning it, and all operating responsibilities fall on the lessee who, in the event of early termination, must fully compensate the lessor. Finance leases are typically used for long-term finance of LNG tankers and cruise ships and will generally appear on the lessee's balance sheet.

The main attraction of finance leases to shipping companies is that they bring a tax benefit. Governments in some countries encourage investment by providing tax incentives such as accelerated depreciation, and companies with high profits but no suitable investment of their own can obtain tax relief by purchasing a ship, which they then lease to a shipowner who operates it as his own until the end of the lease. The lessor does not have to get his hands dirty, but, hopefully, he collects a tax benefit, some of which is passed on to the lessee in the form of reduced charter hire. Obviously this depends on the goodwill of the tax authorities. More recently leasing structures of 5–6 years have become more common.

A lease structure is shown in Figure 7.12. The ship, built to the lessee's specification, is purchased by the company providing the finance (the lessor) – a bank, large corporation or insurance company – and leased under a long-term agreement (e.g. a bare boat charter) to the shipping company (lessee). The lease gives the lessee complete control to operate and maintain the asset but leaves the ownership vested in the lessor who can obtain tax benefits by depreciating the ship against profits. Some of this benefit is passed on to the lessee in lower rental (charter) payments. A variant is the leverage lease which raises most of the cost of the ship in bank debt (e.g. 90%) and the lessor buys the equity at a price which reflects the tax benefits he gets from depreciating the whole ship.

This type of finance has several advantages. It provides funding for longer periods than is available from commercial banks, possibly as much as 15 years or even 25 years. Capital costs are reduced to the extent that any tax benefits are reflected in the charter-back arrangement.

It also has drawbacks. The lessor, who has no interest in the ship, must be

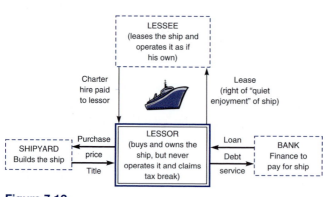

**Figure 7.12**
Typical lease finance model
Source: Martin Stopford, 2008

satisfied that the lessee will meet its obligations under the lease. Only financially sound shipping companies are likely to qualify. The lessee is tied into a long-term transaction, which makes life much more complicated than just buying the ship and owning it. For example, if he decides after a couple of years to sell the ship, he must go through the complex business of unwinding the lease. Another problem is that, since tax laws may change, the tax benefit is never quite certain, and this must be covered in the documentation. With so many eventualities to cover, the paperwork on leasing transactions can be prodigious. For this reason leasing works best for well-established shipping companies with a well-defined long-term need for the ships, for example to service an LNG project against a long-term cargo contract.

A new development in the early 2000s was the flotation of ship leasing companies based on the model used in the aircraft industry for financing aircraft. The container-ship operator Seaspan, which was floated in August 2005, was modelled on the International Lease Finance Corporation which provides aircraft to FedEx, DHL and UPS. When floated, Seaspan had 23 container-ships leased to major liner operators such as Maersk, Hapag-Lloyd, Cosco, and China Shipping at fixed rates for periods of 10, 12 and 15 years. Operating expenses and interest rates were also fixed, insulating the company from shipping cycles.[32] In 2007 Seaspan had 55 ships and was one of the world's largest container owning companies. Several other companies have followed this model, which provides an alternative to the KG system discussed above.

## Securitization of shipping assets

Asset-backed securitization is used to finance mortgage loans, auto loans, credit card receivables, and it has also been widely used in the aircraft industry, which has a similar asset base to shipping. The technique involves taking a portfolio of cash-generating assets (e.g. mortgage loans, aircraft, ships) and selling them to a bankruptcy remote trust which issues bonds serviced with the cashflow from the assets.

The process as it might apply to ships is illustrated in Figure 7.13. Step 1 is for the originator, an aircraft or shipping company, to appoint an investment bank to handle what might well be a lengthy and complex transaction. Step 2 is to set up an SPC and a trust. The trust is controlled by

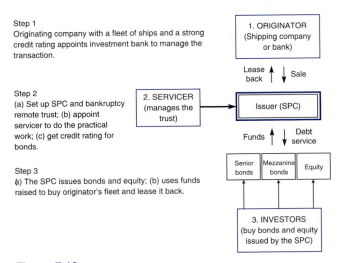

Step 1
Originating company with a fleet of ships and a strong credit rating appoints investment bank to manage the transaction.

Step 2
(a) Set up SPC and bankruptcy remote trust; (b) appoint servicer to do the practical work; (c) get credit rating for bonds.

Step 3
(a) The SPC issues bonds and equity; (b) uses funds raised to buy originator's fleet and lease it back.

**Figure 7.13**
Ship securitization financial structure
Source: Martin Stopford, 2007

a board and arrangements are made for a 'back-up servicer' to manage the assets in the event of a default by the lessee. The SPC raises finance by issuing bonds backed by the assets, known as asset-backed securities. These bonds may be issued in several tranches, each with different credit ratings. For example, a senior tranche structured to obtain an investment-grade rating; a second sub-investment-grade tranche which permits repayments to be suspended during difficult periods in the market; and a tranche of equity. The ability to obtain the required credit rating is crucial. In Step 3 the bonds and equity are issued and the SPC uses the funds to purchase the originator's fleet of ships which are then leased back to the originator.

This sort of structure offers long-term finance, plus a degree of flexibility to deal with the realities of a cyclical business. Although asset-backed securitization is often used in the airline industry, the first shipping transaction was only completed in 2006 by the container company CMA CGM to finance 12 new container-ships. An SPC, VegaContainerVessel 2006-1 plc, raised three layers of finance: $253.7 million in senior AAA rated notes; $283.3 million in mezzanine finance from a syndicated bank loan; and a tranche of subordinated equity notes purchased by CMA CGM with the proceeds from simultaneously issuing a $283 million corporate bond. Vega then made loans to 12 SPCs, each of which purchased a container-ship from CMA CGM and bareboat chartered it back. Although this is the first shipping market transaction of its type, similar structures have been used in the aircraft market by flag carriers Iberia (in 1999, 2000 and 2004) and Air France (in 2003).[33]

The reason why this technique is more widely used for aircraft than ships seems to be that the financing options open to shipping and aircraft companies are very different. In the aircraft industry small airlines pay very high spreads to borrow from banks, so asset-backed securitization structures offer cheaper finance. In shipping, debt finance from commercial banks is very competitively priced and the rating agencies are cautious about rating bonds whose cashflow ultimately depends on the spot market. Add the fact that shipowners prefer flexible finance and the limited role of securitization becomes more understandable.

## 7.8 ANALYSING RISK IN SHIP FINANCE

### The risk management options

Although we have discussed many techniques for financing ships, it is important not to lose sight of the fact that raising finance is ultimately a matter of persuasion. There are many opportunities out there and whether the investor is Aunt Sophie or a pension fund, they must be persuaded that the return justifies the risk. However, the justification required by investors and lenders is very different. Investors take a risk in the hope of making a profit. They want to be convinced about the upside potential. Lenders on the other hand, do not share the profits and just want to be repaid on time with interest, so their focus is on strategies to ensure repayment.

The starting point for any analysis, whether by an investor or a lender, is cashflow analysis. Because shipping is so capital-intensive, financial structure has a major impact

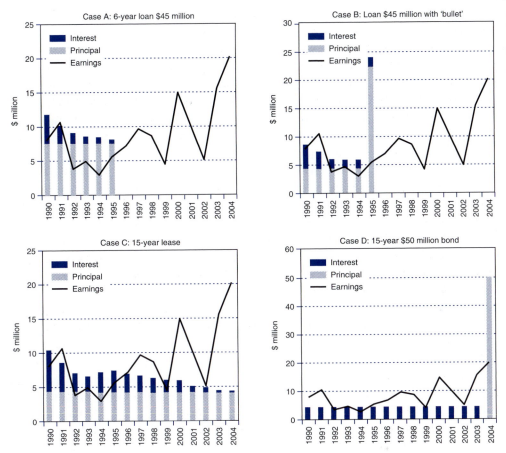

**Figure 7.14**
Four ship finance options for a new Aframax tanker

on the cashflow and it is only by carefully working through this that the true risks can be identified. To illustrate this point, Figure 7.14 compares four of the techniques for financing a new Aframax tanker valued at $65 million on delivery in 1990. The bars in each chart show the annual interest (at 1% over the prevailing LIBOR rate) and principal repayments, whilst the line shows the actual spot market earnings of the ship in each year, after deducting operating expenses of $6,000 a day in 1990, increasing to $7400 a day in 2004.

- Case A shows a 6-year term loan of $45 million, a 69% advance, amortized in equal payments of $7.5 million over the six years.
- Case B shows a $45 million 6-year term loan repaid at $4.5 million a year, with a $22.5 million 'bullet' payment in the last year.
- Case C shows a 15-year lease which repays the full $65 million in equal instalments of $4.3 million over 15 years and interest on a declining balance basis.
- Case D shows a 15-year bond for $50 million, a 75% advance, with the 9% coupon paid annually and the principal repaid in year 15 (i.e. 2004).

Comparing these techniques illustrates how the different structures cope with the same market cycle. The bank loan in case A is made at the top of a freight cycle, and even in the first year earnings do not quite cover debt repayments. Things get better in 1991, but from 1991 onwards they deteriorate and by 1995 earnings only cover half the debt service. The only comfort for the bank is that by 1994 over $30 million has been paid down, so the ship's market value of $20 million covers the outstanding $15 million. However, if the customer runs out of cash in 1993, that faces the bank with all the hassle and indignity of repossessing a ship, an act no banker wishes to contemplate. So a 6-year loan is not ideal for financing a new vessel.

Case B addresses the problem by introducing a bullet loan in which 50% of the principal is not repaid until the end of the term (a 'bullet loan' has a one-time re-payment of principal at its termination, in this case 50%). Debt service is much reduced and easily covered by earnings in the first two years, though there is still a small shortfall from 1992 to 1995. The problem comes when the bullet has to be repaid because the owner does not have the money – the cumulative deficit is $23 million. Of course the company could refinance, but after four years of recession the value of the ship has fallen to $18.5 million, less than is needed to cover the $23 million bullet. The new structure has 'reorganized the deckchairs', but the ship is still not generating enough cash to repay a 69% six-year term loan.

Case C takes a longer-term perspective, using a 15-year lease. This spreads the principal repayments over a much longer period. As with the bank debt, the transaction faces a problem between 1992 and 1996 when earnings are inadequate to cover lease payments. However, from 1996 to 2004 a substantial surplus is generated, and by the end of the transaction in December 2004 the obligation is fully paid down and the second-hand value of the 15-year old ship is now $20 million – a nice bonus for the lessor. Longer-term finance has evened out the long cycles, so although the market paid shipowners less revenue in the first half of the period, it came back in the second half. However, if the shipping company had no alternative source of funds, it would have defaulted on lease payments early in the period, so that is a problem. The fact that the lessor gets any residual profit is another.

Case D is a 15-year bond for $50 million. The principal is not repaid until the final year, so debt service is just the coupon which is fixed at 9%. In fact earnings are sufficient to pay interest every year except 1992 and 1995 when there is a very small deficit. Over the 15 years the ship generates $70 million after paying the coupon, enough to repay the $50 million bond and leave a $20 million surplus for the equity holders. Since the ship is now worth $20 million, this is a profitable transaction all round. So provided the company had $2 million working capital to cover the two bad years, the bond worked out pretty well, though this is just a hypothetical example. It is doubtful whether such a structure could be placed in the high-yield market without some partial amortization, due to the refinancing risk.[34]

The conclusion is simple enough. Shipping cycles cover long periods and are not always the extreme cycles of the 1980s. In this particular example earnings averaged $18,000 a day in the first half of the period and $32,000 a day in the second half, so any financial structure relying on earnings to repay interest and principal during the first half of the period was bound to run into problems (if this revenue sequence had been reversed it would have been a very different story). The bond works well because it defers repayment of principal until the end of the period, by which time in this example

## BOX 7.4 SHIPPING RISK CHECKLIST

*The following are some of the issues that should be considered when weighing up the risk in a shipping transaction:*

1. *Market risk*. Shipping markets face cyclical revenues and prices as discussed in Part 2 of this book. Cycles vary unpredictably in length and severity, which affects a company's ability to meet obligations and the value of collateral. What is the position in the cycle and its future development?

2. *Operating risk*. Technical problems can lead to off hire, reduced earnings, repairs and poor reputation with charterers. Failure to comply with regulations relating to safety and pollution can result in port state detention and problems with classification societies, insurance, pools and conferences.

3. *Counterparty risk*. Are charterers creditworthy and is the full charter status of the vessel known? For example, a vessel may have been sub-chartered several times.

4. *Competitive risk*. Shipping companies operate in a competitive environment which may affect their financial performance. Does the company have any protection from predatory competition or overinvestment?

5. *Diversification risk*. Market segments have different cycles, customers and ship types (see Chapter 12). Diversification reduces risk if the sector cycles are not highly correlated and specialization increases it (the 'portfolio effect').

6. *Operating and voyage cost risk*. How sensitive is the business model to cost changes (e.g. fast ships use a lot of fuel)? Fuel costs, crew costs, port costs, repair costs and insurance can all change.

7. *Ship size and age risk*. Is the fleet age profile balanced and how well equipped is the company to manage it? New ships carry a high capital cost, and are vulnerable to changes in capital costs. In contrast, old ships face lower capital costs and are vulnerable to operating, repair and regulatory costs.

8. *Financial structure*. How vulnerable is the company's financial structure (e.g. debt must be serviced regardless of market circumstances)? New fleet has a high breakeven point, old fleet vulnerable to repair costs.

9. *Workout risk*. How easy would the company be to deal with in the event of a default? This involves the relationship with management and the difficulty of repossessing and operating assets depending on the type and age of ships, flag, etc.

10. *Management risk*. How does performance compare with peer group and how vulnerable is the company in terms of succession and depth of the management team?

11. *Environmental risk*. Pollution liability is a major risk and for private companies the corporate veil can be pierced, but not public shipping companies. Cargo, geography and insurance all important.

the cash has accumulated; but in such a volatile business as shipping there is a risk that repayment coincides with an adverse market when the cash is not available and refinancing is difficult, so bondholders need to be happy with the company and its management.

In these circumstances lenders offering loans in a competitive banking market have little choice but to take a view on what lies ahead, and we discuss this in Chapter 17. There are many risks to consider. Shipping is vulnerable to *economic risk* caused by volatility of the world economy. *Operating risk* arises from problems with the ships and the companies which manages them. And of course there is *shipping market risk*. These are the main risks categories, but there are plenty of others to consider and Box 7.4 provides a checklist of the most important ones, covering everything from market cycles to the environment.

## 7.9 DEALING WITH DEFAULT

One of the cornerstones of ship finance is the fact that the loan or investment is secured by ships which are negotiable assets, and in the event of a default or business failure can be seized by the creditors and sold. However, the realizable value of this security depends to some extent on the practical ability of the mortgagee (or bondholders) to recover the assets, and it is worth briefly considering some of the issues which this raises.[35] The following comments refer mainly to situations where a borrower defaults on its debt obligations by failing to make the payments required under the loan agreement.

Because ships trade internationally and may be in a remote part of the world when the problem arises, the first practical issue in dealing with a default is to obtain accurate information about what is actually going on. The borrower is not impartial, so other information sources are needed if only to check the accuracy of information being provided. With large sums of money at stake, the situation can also change very rapidly, especially where other creditors are involved, so prompt action can play an important part in resolving the situation favourably. Broadly speaking, there are three ways a lender can minimize this sort of risk: by monitoring the performance of the borrower to give early warning that the risk of default is increasing; by putting controls in place to protect the lender's interests when things start to go wrong; and by having a well-thought-out strategy for managing any defaults which occur.

Monitoring the performance of a borrower is a delicate matter, but early warning of problems helps because by the time a default occurs some of the options for dealing with the situation are no longer available. Regular monitoring of vessel values against a minimum value clause in the loan documentation provides a warning of market weakening and can trigger a dialogue with the borrower in a falling market, though establishing the precise value of ships held as collateral can be contentious if the valuations obtained by the owner and banker are different. Obviously this does not identify problems caused by mismanagement. Some banks routinely check the financial strength of borrowers by a periodic review of the company's whole business, especially in a weak market. This is not easy but it may give early warning signals that things are not going well for the business as a whole. Another tactic is to inspect the ships regularly and look for signs of cash shortages – for example, a lack of spare parts or neglected maintenance. But this is expensive and requires a certain amount of tact.

Various steps can be taken to ensure that the lender has control in the event of a default. An enforceable mortgage on the ship and the assignment of all freights and insurances to the lender provide basic protection. Less common is a pledge of shares in the owning company, which the bank holds, with a letter of resignation from the directors. Or a personal guarantee from the shipowner may be requested. Guarantees of this sort are not easily obtained and can be difficult and unpleasant to enforce, but they may provide some leverage if things start to go wrong.

Once a default has occurred the lender as mortgagee must be prepared to deal with four practical issues, all of which are likely to require prompt action: the location of the ships; claims by other creditors; the condition of the ships and class; and the cargo aboard the ship.

The location of the ships is important because this determines the legal jurisdiction and, once the default has been declared, determines what the lender has a legal right to do. Some legal jurisdictions are better than others for arresting ships, so it may be advantageous to sail to a more favourable jurisdiction, if the ships can be moved. Other financial claims need to be addressed promptly because some, such as crew wages, rank ahead of the mortgagee's claim and must be settled first.

Trade creditors owed money for bunkers and stores must also be considered because if they are not paid there is the risk that these creditors will arrest the ship, creating a problem for the lender. Their services will be needed anyway if the ship is to continue trading. The third issue is the condition of the ships. Companies short of cash often defer maintenance and the supply of spares, so repairs may be needed, or worse the ship may not be in class. In that case it cannot be moved until repairs have been made. Finally, if there is cargo on board, that must be dealt with.

For all these reasons lenders often face a difficult and complex situation. Broadly speaking, there are three approaches, none of them attractive: (a) to provide the owner with the financial support to trade on; (b) to foreclose and trade on with a new company under new management; and (c) to foreclose and sell the assets either privately (which probably offers the best price) or through an Admiralty sale (which has the advantage of wiping out any claims against the ship). If the problem is market-driven and the relationship with the borrower is good, option (a) may make sense, provided there is upside in the assets, but if the problem is mismanagement, option (b) may be more appropriate. Either way, a decision to trade on means raising cash, and this can be done by selling off ships, negotiating with trade creditors to clear debts at a discount or supporting the owner until things get better. Otherwise a cash injection by the lender will be needed. The choice will depend on the circumstances. Selling ships under pressure can result in distress prices and is a poor option if the default takes place in a recession when the ships have upside potential. But if the default occurs in a normal market and assets can be sold for a fair price, this may be a more attractive option.

This is a superficial review of a difficult and complex subject but hopefully enough to demonstrate that managing default is one of the aspects of ship finance where practical skills are required, so ideally it is better for banks to choose clients who do not default!

## 7.10 SUMMARY

In this chapter we have discussed how the shipping industry finances its requirement for capital in a business which is volatile and historically has offered low returns. We started by reviewing the history of ship finance. This revealed that the type of finance available to the shipping industry has gone through distinct phases. As the world economy grew in the 1950s and 1960s there was a long phase of charter-backed investment, mainly initiated by the shippers. This was followed by new forms of asset-backed finance during the very volatile markets of the 1980s, notably ship funds and K/S companies. Finally, in the 1990s, shipping companies have shown more interest in corporate structures, with public offerings and corporate lending.

The money to finance ships comes from the pool of savings which are mainly held in three markets: the money markets (short-term debt), the capital markets (long-term debt) and the stock market (equity). Nowadays most of the investment is carried out by institutions such as pension funds and insurance companies, though there are a few private investors. Accessing these financial markets can be done directly by the shipping company, or indirectly through an intermediary such as a commercial bank. Direct access requires well-defined corporate structures which are less widely used in shipping than elsewhere. Shipping has traditionally relied heavily on bank debt, particularly bulk shipping. We divided the more detailed discussion of methods of ship finance into four broad groups.

Firstly, *private funds* represent an important source of financing. Initially the funds may come from a family member or a private investor, but subsequently the ships generate their own cashflow which can be used to develop the business.

Secondly, *commercial bank finance* is the most important source of funding for shipping companies. We drew the distinction between a 'shipowner' and a 'shipping company' and noted that commercial banks finance both, using the 'one-ship company' as a vehicle. Loans may be backed by a mortgage or the corporate balance sheet. For large loans a syndication can be arranged. Shipyard finance is sometimes used to finance new ships, since it addresses the difficult question of the pre-delivery guarantee, and credit terms are occasionally subsidized. Finally, we mentioned mezzanine finance, which is rarely used, and private placements, where financial institutions lend to or invest directly in shipping companies.

Thirdly, the capital markets allow established shipping companies to raise finance by issuing securities. Equity can be raised by an initial public offering of shares placed in the equity market, where the shares are subsequently traded in the secondary market. To raise debt finance a company with a credit rating from the rating agencies can issue bonds in the bond markets. These can be for 15 years or longer; the company pays interest (coupon) to the bondholder, and the sum advanced (the principal) is repaid in full when the bond matures.

Fourthly, we discussed *standalone structures*, set up for particular transactions. These include special purpose companies, limited partnerships such as Norwegian K/Ss or German KG, finance leases, operating leases, and securitization. Leasing offers the opportunity to reduce finance costs by transferring ownership of the vessel to a company which can use its depreciation to obtain a tax break.

The discussion was rounded up with a review of risk management issues, and the implications of financial structure for the volatile earnings flow in the shipping industry. We also reviewed a risk checklist and discussed the problems which confront a lender whose borrower has defaulted (workout). The conclusion is that ship finance, like everything else in shipping, moves with the times.

Finally, we reviewed the practical problems which arise when dealing with default. This is a difficult part of the business, made all the more challenging by the fact that it occurs infrequently.

# 8 Risk, Return and Shipping Company Economics

*A wise man will make more opportunities than he finds.*

(Sir Francis Bacon, English author, courtier, and philosopher, 1561–1626)

*The pessimist sees difficulty in every opportunity. The optimist sees the opportunity in every difficulty.*

(Sir Winston Churchill, British prime minister)

## 8.1 THE PERFORMANCE OF SHIPPING INVESTMENTS

### The shipping return paradox

In the early 1950s Aristotle Onassis, one of shipping's most colourful entrepreneurs, hatched a plan to take over the transport of Saudi Arabia's oil. On 20 January 1954 he signed the 'Jiddah Agreement' with the Saudi Finance Minister, establishing the Saudi Arabian Maritime Company (SAMCO) to ship Saudi oil. Initially Onassis was to supply 500,000 tons of tankers, and as the ARAMCO (the US-controlled Saudi oil concession) fleet became obsolete, SAMCO would replace their ships with its own. In May King Saud ratified the treaty and Onassis' biggest tanker, launched in Germany, was named the *Al Malik Saud Al-Awa* in his honour.

Needless to say, the oil companies did not welcome a private shipowner controlling this strategic oil resource, nor did the American government. ARAMCO turned away Onassis' tankers from its terminal and the US State Department pressed Saudi Arabia to drop the agreement. Onassis became the target of an FBI investigation and the coup became a disaster. As the shipping cycle turned down in the summer of 1956, Onassis's tanker fleet was laid up. Then he got lucky. On 25 July 1956 Egypt nationalized the Suez Canal, and in October Israel, Britain and France invaded Egypt to win back control. During this conflict Egypt blocked the Canal with 46 sunken ships and Middle East oil bound for the North Atlantic had to be shipped by the long route around the Cape of Good Hope. Tanker rates surged from $4 per ton to more than $60 per ton and Onassis was ideally placed to take advantage of the boom. In six months he made a profit of $75–80 million, equivalent to $1.5 billion at 2005 prices.[1]

This is the stuff of legends, and Onassis was not the only entrepreneur to make a fortune in shipowning. Livanos, Pao, Tung, Bergesen, Reconati, Niarchos, Onassis, Lemos, Haji-Ioannou, Ofer and Fredriksen are just a few of the families who have become fabulously wealthy in the shipping business during the last half century. But not everyone makes a fortune in shipping. As we saw in Chapter 3, shipping companies face endless recessions and average returns tend to be both low and risky in the sense that investors never know when the market will dive into recession. So why do they pour their money into the business? And how do fabulously wealthy shipowners like Aristotle Onassis and John Fredriksen fit into this business model? That is the shipping return paradox.

In explaining this paradox we turn to microeconomic theory to get a better understanding of what determines the behaviour of companies in the shipping market. First we will briefly review the industry's risk and return record to see what we are dealing with. Second, we will discuss how shipping companies make returns and work through an example; Third, we will discuss the microeconomic model to establish what determines 'normal' profits and the time-lags which contribute to the unpredictability of earnings; Finally, we will look in more detail at the part played by risk preference in pricing capital.

## Profile of shipping returns in the twentieth century

We start with a brief review of the shipping industry's financial performance over the last century – it has to be said at the outset that it makes gloomy reading. A.W. Kirkaldy's review of fifty years of British shipping, published in 1914, observed that in 1911, 'the best year for a decade', the returns were no better than could be obtained by investing in first-class securities and that "at times shipping had to be run at a loss".[2]Another study, by the Tramp Shipping Administrative Committee, found that, between 1930 and 1935, 214 tramp shipping companies had a return on capital of 1.45% per annum.[3] Admittedly the 1930s was a bad spell, but in the 1950s, a much better decade for shipping, things were not much better. Between 1950 and 1957 the *Economist* shipping share index grew at only 10.3% per annum compared with 17.2% for the 'all companies' index, and in the 1960s things got even worse. Between 1958 and 1969, the *Economist* shipping share index returned only 3.2% per annum, compared with 13.6% for all companies. A detailed analysis of private and public shipping companies by the Rochdale Committee reported a return of 3.5% per annum for the period 1958–1969 and concluded that 'the return on capital employed over the period covered by our study was very low'.[4]

In the 1990s, a period of expansion in the stock market generally, the Oslo Shipping Shares Index hardly increased and the return on capital employed by six public tanker owning companies published in 2001 showed an average return on equity of only 6.3%.[5] Another analysis of 12 shipping companies during the period 1988–97 concluded that the return on capital of six bulk shipping companies was 7% per annum, whilst six liner and specialized companies averaged 8% return on capital. It concluded that these returns were 'in most cases inadequate to recover capital at a prudent rate and retain sufficient earnings to support asset replacement and expansion'.[6] However, in 2003 the whole picture changed, revealing a very different side to the business. The boom of 2003–8 turned out to be an oasis in a desert of indifferent returns, and as earnings increased and asset values more than doubled it became, as we saw in Chapter 3, one of the most profitable markets in shipping history with investors trebling their capital in five years.

## Shipping risk and the capital asset pricing model

However there is more to the paradox than low returns. The capital asset pricing (CAP) model used by most investment analysts equates volatility with risk (we discuss the CAP model in Section 8.4), and shipping returns are very volatile. The sort of revenue volatility shipowners face is illustrated in Figure 8.1, which shows the earnings distribution for a shipping index covering the average earnings of tankers, bulk carriers, container-ships and LPG tankers. During the 820 weeks between 1990 and 2005 earnings averaged $14,600 per day but varied between $9,000 per day and $ 42,000 per day with a standard deviation of $5,900 per day. That is a very wide range. Extending the analysis to individual ship types, Table 8.1 compares the volatility of the monthly spot earnings of eight different types of bulk vessels using the standard deviation as a percentage of the mean earnings. This ratio ranges from 52% for a products tanker to 75% for a Capesize bulk carrier, and is extraordinarily high when compared with most businesses, where a month-to-month volatility of 10% would be considered extreme. To put it into perspective, if the average earnings are the revenue stream needed to run the business and make a normal profit (an issue we return to later in the chapter), shipping companies often earn 50% more or less than is required.

This volatility ripples through all the markets, producing a close correlation between the freight rate movements in different shipping market sectors. This point is illustrated by the correlation analysis in Table 8.2, which demonstrates the close correlation between the earnings of nine ship types. For example, the correlation between the earnings of a Panamax bulk carrier and a Capesize bulk carrier is 84%, so investing in Capesizes brings similar revenue risks

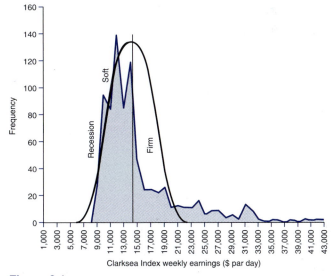

**Figure 8.1**
Distribution of shipping earnings, 1990–2005
Source: Martin Stopford, 2005 and Clarksons

**Table 8.1** Shipping earnings volatility by market sector, 1990–2005

| | Mean $/day | Standard deviation | |
|---|---|---|---|
| | | $/day | % mean |
| Capesize bulk carrier | 20,323 | 15,265 | 75% |
| Suezmax tanker | 25,257 | 17,479 | 69% |
| VLCC tanker (diesel) | 33,754 | 22,820 | 68% |
| Panamax bulk carrier | 11,552 | 7,485 | 65% |
| ULCC tanker (turbine) | 25,074 | 15,960 | 64% |
| Aframax tanker | 22,223 | 13,339 | 60% |
| Handymax bulk carrier | 11,435 | 6,853 | 60% |
| Clean products tanker | 15,403 | 8,048 | 52% |
| Average | 20,628 | 13,406 | 65% |

Source: Analysis based on CRSL data

to investing in Panamaxes. However, for some other ship types the revenue correlation is much lower. For example, VLCCs and Handymax bulk carriers have a correlation coefficient of −11% so their revenue fluctuations have tended to move in opposite directions. There is also a negative correlation between offshore and container-ships. In theory shipowners can reduce the volatility of their earnings by incorporating ships with low or negative correlations in their fleet. But investors may prefer not to reduce their volatility risk, since all that does is to lock in a low return, – a clue, perhaps, to how shipping investors view the business.

## Comparison of shipping with financial investments

This combination of volatile earnings and low returns distinguishes shipping from other investments. For example, the return on investment (ROI) summary over the period

**Table 8.2** Correlation matrix for monthly earnings of shipping market segments, 1990–2002

| | VLCC | Aframax | Products | Capesize | Panamax | Handymax | LPG | MPP 16kdwt | Container-ship |
|---|---|---|---|---|---|---|---|---|---|
| VLCC | 100% | | | | | | | | |
| Aframax | 84% | 100% | | | | | | | |
| Products | 59% | 80% | 100% | | | | | | |
| Capesize | 30% | 39% | 27% | 100% | | | | | |
| Panamax | 7% | 18% | 17% | 84% | 100% | | | | |
| Handymax | −11% | 4% | 8% | 70% | 86% | 100% | | | |
| LPG | 36% | 32% | 33% | 33% | 15% | −2% | 100% | | |
| MPP 16kdwt | −26% | −22% | −7% | 52% | 75% | 84% | −2% | 100% | |
| Containership | −9% | 9% | 14% | 59% | 68% | 71% | 14% | 68% | 100% |

**Table 8.3** Annual rate of return on various investments since 1975

|  | Period | ROI (%) | Standard deviation (%) |
|---|---|---|---|
| Inflation | 1975–2001 | 4.6 | 3.1 |
| Treasury bills | 1975–2001 | 6.6 | 2.7 |
| LIBOR (6 months) | 1975–2004 | 8.5 | 3.9 |
| Long-term gov bonds | 1975–2001 | 9.6 | 12.8 |
| Corporate bonds | 1975–2001 | 9.6 | 11.7 |
| S&P 500 | 1975–2001 | 14.1 | 15.1 |
| Bulk shipping | 1975–2004 | 7.2 | 40 |
| Tanker shipping | 1975–2002 | 4.9 | 70.4 |

Source: Ibbotson Associates

1975–2002 in Table 8.3 shows that Treasury bills, the safest investment, paid 6.6% per annum, whilst LIBOR (the London interbank offered rate), the eurodollar base rate used to finance most shipping loans, averaged 8.5% with a standard deviation of 3.9%. Corporate bonds paid 9.6%, but with a much higher standard deviation of 11.7%, and government bonds were much the same. By far the highest ROI was for the S&P 500 stock market index, which paid 14.1%. Shipping, as we have seen, is a very different story, with bulk carriers earning only 7.2%, with a standard deviation of 40%, making them twice as risky as the S&P 500. We will discuss how this return is calculated in the next section.

Because most investment is managed by financial institutions such as pension funds (see Chapter 7), the pricing of capital reflects the demand for the type of assets they invest in. The usual approach is to measure risk by volatility, using the standard deviation of the historic returns of the asset. They expect a higher return on volatile assets and a lower return on investments which are stable and predictable. To illustrate this point, Figure 8.2 plots the ROI against risk, measured by the standard deviation of the return over the period 1975–2002, on the horizontal axis and average return on the vertical axis.

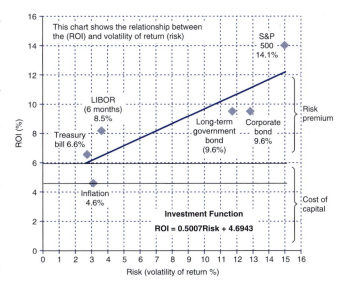

**Figure 8.2**
Risk pricing of various assets, 1975–2002
Source: Ibbotson, various

There is clearly a relationship. Treasury bills, with a volatility of only 3%, paid 6.6%, a premium 2% above the rate of inflation. That could be taken as the basic remuneration on a safe investment. As the volatility increases, so does the ROI, reaching 15% for the S&P 500, providing a risk premium of about 8% over inflation. A regression equation fitted to the points on the chart provides an estimate of the investment function over this period. On average the ROI increases by 0.5% for each 1% increase in volatility. If this model holds for shipping, a bulk carrier investment, with a volatility of 35%, should pay a return of about 22% (i.e. 6.6% cost of capital plus 17% risk premium). However, as we saw earlier in this section, it only paid 7.2%.

## 8.2 THE SHIPPING COMPANY INVESTMENT MODEL

### The shipping company's split persona

If investors can make 6.6% on safe Treasury bills and 15% on the S&P 500 (an index of US stocks), why should they invest in shipping, which offers a similar return but has 40% volatility? Generations of shipowners and their bankers must have seen something in the business, even in the hard times, and sure enough when we examine the microeconomic structure of the shipping market, we do indeed find an answer. In classical economics there is no 'right' level of profit. The 'normal profit' is whatever the participants in the market are prepared to settle for.

In many ways shipping companies are very similar to the 'firms' which classical economists had in mind when they developed their theory of perfect competition. In classical economic theory a firm is 'a technical unit in which commodities are produced. Its entrepreneur (owner and manager) decides how much of, and how, one or more commodities will be produced, and gains the profit or bears the loss which results from his decision'.[7] In other words, the firm transforms inputs into output and the owner pockets the profits or makes good the losses, and shipping remains this sort of business. Over 5,000 companies [8] compete fiercely in a market place where barriers to free competition such as tariffs, transport costs and product branding hardly exist.[9] Owning an average of only five ships, many of these companies bear an uncanny resemblance to Joseph Schumpeter's description of a typical firm operating in the market place of classical economics:

> The unit of the private property economy was the firm of medium size. Its typical legal form was the private partnership. Barring the 'sleeping' partner, it was typically managed by the owner or owners, a fact that it is important to keep in mind in any effort to understand 'classic' economics.[10]

This description fits many of the Greek, Norwegian and Asian shipping companies operating in the bulk shipping market in recent decades. Admittedly the specialized markets (see Chapter 12) and the liner business (see Chapter 13) do not fit this description so well, but bulk shipping certainly fits the classical economic model.

But the perfect competition model does not tell us how much that profit will be, just that it will tend towards the 'normal' level for the industry. This normal profit is the return needed to keep supply and demand in balance, and that means keeping investors in the business long term.[11] When supply and demand are out of line, the return moves temporarily above or below the normal profit for the business, and the market responds by correcting the imbalance. In the long run the normal profit earned by a specific company will average out of a level which reflects the company's performance in three aspects of the business: remuneration for the use of capital; the return for good management: and the risk taken (see Box 8.1).

> **BOX 8.1 THE THREE RS OF PROFIT**
>
> - **Remuneration** for the use of capital. Between 1975 and 2001 US Treasury bonds averaged 6.6% p.a. (Table 8.3) and inflation was 4.6% p.a. so the real return on capital was about 2% p.a.
> - **Return** for good management e.g. by reducing costs; using ships better and innovation to increase efficiency and improve cargo performance. These are important aspects of the business, but the returns are likely to be quite small, perhaps 1–2% p.a.
> - **Risk premium**. A venture capitalist whose whole investment could be lost might demand 20–30% return if the project succeeds. Because the shipping business is so volatile the rewards for playing the cycle correctly can be even larger if things go well.

Capital dominates the shipping business. In the classical model, entrepreneurs buy materials (factors of production) and add value to them. In shipping the factors of production are ships, and operating expenses and capital dominate the business, with operating expenses accounting for a small proportion of the cost of transport. So although the company's primary task is to provide transport, capital management dominates the business. The company might save a few hundred thousand dollars a year by careful ship management, but the value of a single ship can change by that amount in a few days. So a shipping company is really like Siamese twins - a sober transport provider twin joined at the hip to a high-rolling hedge fund twin who manages the capital portfolio. They are hard to separate and entrepreneurs who can do both jobs simultaneously are rare – many who succeed have a twin tucked away in the backroom running the business. This idiosyncratic combination probably accounts for the persistence of small business units in the shipping industry and its highly focused management style.

## The return on shipping investment model (ROSI)

The distinction between ship management and asset management is important because the shipping company Siamese twins are likely to produce very different financial returns. The transport provider twin who focuses only on transport, funded by equity, should expect low returns because the business is not very risky. But the hedge fund twin who focuses on asset management is in a very different business, offering very large returns to successful players prepared to take risks. It follows that the company's risk is determined by its business strategy, not the shipping cycle. Of course most companies face this sort of issue to some extent, but shipping is an extreme case because capital is so dominant and so liquid. The best way to illustrate the point is work through a practical example.

The return shipping investment (ROSI) can be split into four components and defined as follows:

$$ROSI_t = \frac{EVA_t}{NAV_t} = \frac{EBID_t - DEP_t + CAPP_t}{NAV_t} \times 100 \tag{8.1}$$

where *NAV* is the net asset value of the fleet at the end of accounting period and *EVA* is the economic value added. To obtain the economic value added we take earnings before interest and depreciation (*EBID*), which is the cash flow earned trading on the spot market or time-charter market after deducting operating expenses, subtract depreciation (*DEP*) to reflect the fact that during the year the company's ships age, reducing their value, and add capital appreciation (*CAPP*), the change in the company's asset value during the year. Capital appreciation in the hedge fund twin's territory; everything else is the realm of the transport provider twin. Multiplying by 100 expresses the return as a percentage.

To illustrate how this works in practice, Table 8.4 shows the calculation of ROSI for a hypothetical shipping company, Perfect Shipping, trading between 1975 and 2006. Since this includes the 1980s recession and the 2003–6 boom it illustrates how the company performed in extremely good and bad markets. In December 1975 the company bought a fleet of 20 bulk carriers for $162 million and traded them through to December 2006, by which time the fleet had a market value of $740 million. To keep things simple, the fleet purchases in 1975 included one ship of each age from 1 to 20 years, and each year Perfect Shipping sells its oldest ship for scrap and orders a new replacement. This deals with the tricky depreciation issue because it owns a fleet of 20 ships with an average age of 10 years throughout the period. Between 1976 and 2006 the ROSI, calculated by the internal rate of return method, is 7.3% per annum (see column 13 - the IRR calculation is shown at the bottom) and the volatility is 40%, so it was a high-risk, low-return investment. For comparison, between 1980 and 2006 the average value of the 6-month LIBOR interest rate was 6.9%, so the return was about the same as putting the funds on deposit.

However, when we examine the three components of this return, EBID (column 4), depreciation (column 7) and capital gain (column 10) we get some very interesting insights into the risk profile of the company. If by 'risky' we mean the chance of losing the investment, Perfect Shipping is not nearly as risky as the volatility suggests.

### Earnings before interest and depreciation (EBID)

The starting point is the EBID calculation shown in Table 8.4, column 4. This takes the earnings per day in column 2 and deducts operating expenses (OPEX) in column 3 to calculate EBID in millions of dollars per year. Over the period the company generated $1180 million but the cashflow was very volatile, swinging wildly from virtually nothing

# Table 8.4 Return on shipping investment for Perfect Shipping

| | 1 | 2 | 3 | 4 | 5 | 6 | 7 | 8 | 9 | 10 | 11 | 12 | 13 |
|---|---|---|---|---|---|---|---|---|---|---|---|---|---|
| | | | EBID | | | Depreciation (DEP) $ mill | | | Capital gain (CAPP) $ m. | | | Return (ROSI) | |
| | | Spot Earnings | less OPEX | EBID | Cost of replacing 1 ship | | | Price of 10-year-old ship | Value of fleet | Capital gain (loss) | Net EVA asset $ m. value | | ROSI% col 11 + col 12 |
| | Core fleet | $/day | $/day/ship | $ mlll | New ship | Scrap sale | Total | | | | | Net asset value | |
| t | $F_t$ | | $OPEX_t$ | $EBID_t$ | $NP_t$ | $S_t$ | $DEP_t$ | $P_t$ | $(P_t.N_t)$ | $CAP_t$ | 4+7+10 | NAV | $ROSI_t$ |
| 1975 | 20 | memo: purchase price of the fleet Dec 1975 ➤ 162.0 | | | | | | | | | (162) | 162 | |
| 1976 | 20 | 4,964 | 3,494 | 9.2 | 16.0 | 1.3 | (14.7) | 6.0 | 120.0 | −42 | (47) | 115 | −40% |
| 1977 | 20 | 3,814 | 3,984 | −2.4 | 16.0 | 1.3 | (14.7) | 4.1 | 82.7 | −37 | (54) | 60 | −66% |
| 1978 | 20 | 4,759 | 4,589 | −0.2 | 19.0 | 1.4 | (17.6) | 6.7 | 133.3 | 51 | 33 | 93 | 25% |
| 1979 | 20 | 9,888 | 5,079 | 32.1 | 26.0 | 2.3 | (23.7) | 10.8 | 216.0 | 83 | 91 | 184 | 42% |
| 1980 | 20 | 12,534 | 5,499 | 47.6 | 30.0 | 2.6 | (27.4) | 13.7 | 273.3 | 57 | 78 | 262 | 28% |
| 1981 | 20 | 11,540 | 5,152 | 43.2 | 29.0 | 1.8 | (27.2) | 8.7 | 173.3 | −100 | (84) | 178 | −48% |
| 1982 | 20 | 5,121 | 4,586 | 2.4 | 19.0 | 1.4 | (17.6) | 4.3 | 86.7 | −87 | (102) | 76 | −118% |
| 1983 | 20 | 5,129 | 4,406 | 3.7 | 18.0 | 1.5 | (16.5) | 5.2 | 104.0 | 17 | 5 | 80 | 4% |
| 1984 | 20 | 6,493 | 3,847 | 17.4 | 16.6 | 1.7 | (14.9) | 5.8 | 116.0 | 12 | 14 | 95 | 12% |
| 1985 | 20 | 5,803 | 3,409 | 15.7 | 15.0 | 1.6 | (13.4) | 4.1 | 81.3 | −35 | (32) | 62 | −40% |
| 1986 | 20 | 4,389 | 3,409 | 5.8 | 16.5 | 1.6 | (14.9) | 5.2 | 104.0 | 23 | 14 | 76 | 13% |
| 1987 | 20 | 6,727 | 3,519 | 21.4 | 21.0 | 2.2 | (18.8) | 8.7 | 173.3 | 69 | 72 | 148 | 42% |
| 1988 | 20 | 12,463 | 3,646 | 60.6 | 26.0 | 3.2 | (22.8) | 11.3 | 226.7 | 53 | 91 | 239 | 40% |
| 1989 | 20 | 13,175 | 3,865 | 64.0 | 29.0 | 3.3 | (25.7) | 14.0 | 280.0 | 53 | 92 | 331 | 33% |
| 1990 | 20 | 10,997 | 4,080 | 47.2 | 29.0 | 3.1 | (25.9) | 12.0 | 240.0 | −40 | (19) | 312 | −8% |
| 1991 | 20 | 12,161 | 4,950 | 49.0 | 34.0 | 2.3 | (31.7) | 16.0 | 320.0 | 80 | 97 | 409 | 30% |
| 1992 | 20 | 8,243 | 4,031 | 28.3 | 28.0 | 1.8 | (26.2) | 12.5 | 250.0 | −70 | (68) | 342 | −27% |
| 1993 | 20 | 9,702 | 4,413 | 35.7 | 28.5 | 2.0 | (26.5) | 13.0 | 260.0 | 10 | 19 | 361 | 7% |
| 1994 | 20 | 9,607 | 4,351 | 35.5 | 28.0 | 2.1 | (25.9) | 14.0 | 280.0 | 20 | 30 | 390 | 11% |
| 1995 | 20 | 13,934 | 4,654 | 63.6 | 28.5 | 2.3 | (26.2) | 14.3 | 286.7 | 7 | 44 | 434 | 15% |
| 1996 | 20 | 7,881 | 5,229 | 17.0 | 26.5 | 2.5 | (24.0) | 13.0 | 260.0 | −27 | (34) | 401 | −13% |
| 1997 | 20 | 8,307 | 5,377 | 18.9 | 27.0 | 2.0 | (25.0) | 15.8 | 316.0 | 56 | 50 | 451 | 16% |
| 1998 | 20 | 5,663 | 4,987 | 3.2 | 20.0 | 1.4 | (18.6) | 9.8 | 196.0 | −120 | (135) | 315 | −69% |
| 1999 | 20 | 6,370 | 5,000 | 8.1 | 22.0 | 1.9 | (20.1) | 12.0 | 240.0 | 44 | 32 | 347 | 13% |
| 2000 | 20 | 10,800 | 5,100 | 38.4 | 22.5 | 2.1 | (20.4) | 11.8 | 236.0 | −4 | 14 | 361 | 6% |
| 2001 | 20 | 8,826 | 5,202 | 23.8 | 20.5 | 1.7 | (18.8) | 9.5 | 190.0 | −46 | (41) | 320 | −22% |
| 2002 | 20 | 6,308 | 5,306 | 5.4 | 21.0 | 2.0 | (19.0) | 11.5 | 230.0 | 40 | 26 | 347 | 11% |
| 2003 | 20 | 17,451 | 5,412 | 82.6 | 27.0 | 3.4 | (23.6) | 20.0 | 400.0 | 170 | 229 | 576 | 57% |
| 2004 | 20 | 31,681 | 5,520 | 181.5 | 36.0 | 4.9 | (31.1) | 31.0 | 620.0 | 220 | 370 | 946 | 60% |
| 2005 | 20 | 22,931 | 6,000 | 116.7 | 36.0 | 4.3 | (31.7) | 24.0 | 480.0 | −140 | (55) | 891 | −11% |
| 2006 | 20 | 21,427 | 6,200 | 104.7 | 40.0 | 5.0 | (35.0) | 37.0 | 740.0 | 260 | 330 | 1221 | 45% |
| Number years | 31 | memo: closing value of the fleet | | | | | | | memo: closing NAV | | | | |
| Total $ mill | 2,234 | 1,053 | 180 | 772 | 72 | (700) | | | | | 578 | 1059 | |

## Notes on methodology

1. Number of ships in fleet
2. Average 1 year time-charter rate until 1989 and average weekly earnings for 10-year-old ship thereafter (all CRSL data)
3. Operating costs. 1976 to 1988 from Clarkson Research database. 1989 to 1998 from company records.
4. EBID is ((Col 2 × 350) − (Col 3 × 365) × Col 1) ÷ 1,000,000
5. Newbuilding price at year end. Should be lagged to take account of the delivery schedule, but for simplicity taken in year.
6. Shows the disposal value of one ship each year based on lightweight of 12,900 tons
7. 2nd hand price of 10-year-old vessel (year end). Until 1997 estimated from 5-year-old Panamax price.
10. Change in the value of total fleet during the year in $ million
11. Economic value added (EVA) Col 4 + Col 7 + Col 10
12. Net asset value is the current value of the fleet + EBID − DEP

in some years to over $50 million in others. But over the 31 years there were only two years when EBID was negative: $2.4 million in 1977 and $0.2 million in 1978. So with $3 million working capital, Perfect Shipping could have met its obligations every year, even in the appalling recession of the 1980s, which satisfies at least one of the criteria of an investment-grade credit rating – it could meet its obligations in all foreseeable circumstances, provided it was financed by equity and its only obligations are the operating costs.

## Depreciation

The reason why the company's trading cashflow cover is so strong is that a large proportion of its costs are capital. Normally depreciation is a non-cash item, but in this example replacement is dealt with out of cashflow. The fleet was bought for cash and each year a new ship is bought for cash at current market prices and the oldest ship is sold for scrap. Over the 31 years the replacement cost totalled $700 million, soaking up 59% of the company's $1180 million EBID. There are two points to make about this aspect of the model. First, the fleet retains exactly the same size and age profile over the period, so it is a true reflection of economic depreciation. Second, replacement is not necessarily a fixed cost and can be varied to fit with the company's cashflow. When cash is tight, replacement can be deferred and the oldest ships traded on for a few years. There were nine years when Perfect Shipping might have done this because trading cashflow did not cover replacement. During booms, when cash is plentiful, more ships can be ordered. This flexibility gives the company financial security.

## Capital gain

Finally, there is capital appreciation. By 2006 the fleet purchased for $162 million in 1975 had increased in value to $740 million. The fleet's asset value is calculated in Table 8.4 by multiplying the number of ships in the core fleet (column 1) by the market price of a 10-year-old ship (column 8) and the gain or loss each year is shown in column 10. It was a bumpy ride, with the fleet losing $100 million in 1981, gaining $220 million in 2004, losing $140 million in 2005 and gaining $260 million in 2006. But for Perfect Shipping this increase in asset values is not a true appreciation because the replacement cost of its fleet has also increased and the company has exactly the same physical assets it started with.

## Financial performance of Perfect Shipping

In summary, Perfect Shipping earned $1180 million before interest and depreciation (EBID). It spent $700 million cash replacing ships (i.e. the depreciation), leaving $480 million dollars free cashflow. The fleet increased in value to $740 million, an increase of $578 million, so the total economic value added was $1059 million and the net asset value increased from $162 million to $1221 million (column 12).

By capital markets standards it is a strange investment. The return of 7.3% IRR was very low compared with the other investments reviewed earlier in the chapter (see Table 8.3) and not much more than the dollars would have earned on deposit. The returns were unreliable. Earnings had a standard deviation of 40%, and 10 years into the investment in 1985 the NAV had halved to $76 million (column 12). It was not until 1987 that the original investment of $162 million was exceeded, so it needed very patient investors. These uneven returns over long periods would make shipping unsuitable as a pension investment, but it is surprisingly safe. The EBID was positive every year except 1977–8, and $3 million working capital would have covered that. There was no debt, and although there were years when replacement investment could not be funded from cashflow, that could be deferred allowing Perfect Shipping to navigate through recessions without running out of cash. In the past many shipping investors have adopted this sort of strategy of not borrowing. For example, after their experiences in the recessions which dominated the first half of the twentieth century, in the 1950s and 1960s many British shipping companies were very risk-averse, financing their investment mainly from cashflow,[12] and some Greek tramp owners followed the same sort of strategy.

But the redeeming feature of this idiosyncratic investment is the opportunity it presents to smart entrepreneurs. Perfect Shipping ended up with assets of over $1 billion, but it could be run by an owner, a couple of managers and 20–30 staff. Most businesses employing this amount of capital have thousands of staff and a large management structure to go with it. Slim returns by capital market standards are a small fortune for a single proprietor and the control of a business with all these assets presents endless opportunities. One obvious example is speculating in ships. If the company had bought five ships at the bottom of each cycle and sold them at the top it would have generated an extra $414 million over the period. Or if it had managed to make its ships last 25 years instead of 20, without spending more on maintenance, it would have made an additional $120 million. It could also have used the ships as collateral to borrow and enlarge the fleet. Then there is the cargo side – the opportunity to take cargo contracts and charter in ships to operate them at a profit. These activities do not require armies of managers; they call for an individual with a gift for spotting what to do next and the skill, luck and capital to do it.

So the reason for investing in a low-return, high-risk business is that owning a shipping company offers entrepreneurs a unique opportunity to put their talents to work. Proprietors and family investors in shipping companies who value security over ROI can play it safe, but ambitious shipowners can use their skills to trade the volatility of freight rates and ship prices. In doing so they add value by making shipping supply more responsive to economic trends – exactly what the market wants. If they get it right the market makes them rich – if not, there's always another cycle. So the ROSI model offers low return and low risk or high return and high risk. That, briefly, is the explanation of the *shipping return paradox*.

## 8.3 COMPETITION THEORY AND THE 'NORMAL' PROFIT

Our next task is to explore the economic trade-off between risk and return for shipping companies. In Chapter 5 we discussed the macroeconomic model and saw that the flow of cash is regulated by supply and demand which drives freight rates up and down. But that analysis did not tell us where freight rates and profits average out, nor did it discuss the risks of, for example, leveraging. So in this section we will apply the microeconomic theory to the firms in the shipping market to answer these questions.

## The Shipping company microeconomic model

Continuing with the Perfect Shipping case study, we will focus on the company's costs and revenues at a point in time. The business profile in Table 8.5 shows a fleet of 20 ships (column 1) with a book value of $246.8 million (the total of column 2). As before, the youngest ship is 1 year old and the oldest 20 years (column 3). Perfect Shipping's *variable costs* are shown in columns 4–6. Its office costs $3 million per annum to run, increasing to $4 million when all 20 ships are at sea (column 4). Operating costs (column 5) increase with ship age, almost doubling from $1.1 million per annum for the youngest ship to $2.05 million per annum for the oldest ship. The cumulative operating cost (column 6) reaches $31.4 million per annum when all 20 ships are in service. Since the older ships cost more to run, when freight rates are below variable costs the company can reduce its costs by laying up the least efficient ships. The *capital costs* of the business are summarized in section 3 at the bottom of Table 8.5. The annual cost of financing the $246.8 million fleet is $22.2 million, which assumes 5% interest and 4% depreciation, which must be paid regardless of how many ships are at sea.

On a day-to-day basis Perfect Shipping's main operating decision is whether to trade all its ships or move some of them into lay-up. It bases its decisions on two variables, the cost profile of its fleet and the level of freight rates. In Table 8.5, columns 7–9 show three cost functions which describe the company's cost profile, the marginal cost (MC) in column 8; the average variable cost (AVC) in column 9; and the average total cost (ATC) in column 10. These curves are illustrated graphically in Figure 8.3.

- The MC curve represents the cost of putting one more ship to sea. It is shown in column 7 of Table 8.5 and includes two items. The first is the cost per annum of each of the 20 ships, ranging from the cheapest, which costs $1.1 million per annum to run to the most expensive, which costs $2.05 million (Col 6). The second is the small increase in office costs as more ships are brought into service (calculated from the change in Col 4 as the fleet increases by one ship). In Figure 8.3 the MC curve is plotted using the MC data shown in Col 7 of Table 8.5. It appears as a straight line increasing from $1.1 million a year with only the cheapest ship at sea to $2.1 million a year when the least efficient ship is activated. When all 20 ships are at sea, the MC curve becomes vertical because the company has no more ships.
- The AVC is the average cost of the ships at sea, as shown in Col 8 of Table 8.5. It is the sum of office costs for the number of ships at sea (Col 4) and the total OPEX of those ships (Col 6) divided by the number of ships at sea. It falls from $4.15 million with one ship at sea to $1.77 million with 20 ships at sea, as plotted in Figure 8.3.
- The ATC is the sum of office costs, operating costs and capital costs, which are shown at the bottom of Table 8.5 divided by the number of ships at sea. Because capital costs

**Table 8.5** Perfect Shipping operating model

| 1 | 2 | 3 | 4 | 5 | 6 | 7 | 8 | 9 |
|---|---|---|---|---|---|---|---|---|
| **1. FLEET** | | | **2. VARIABLE COSTS** | | | **4. COST FUNCTIONS** | | |
| | | | Office | Operating costs | | | How costs develop as output expands | |
| Fleet profile | | | | | | | | |
| No. at sea | Book value $m/ ship | Age of ship years | Total costs in year | OPEX per ship of age in Col 1 | for fleet of ships at sea | MC equals Col 5 + extra office cost | AVC Col 4 + Col 6 ÷ Col 1 | ATC Cols 4 + 6 + 22.2 ÷ Col 1 |
| 1 | 20.0 | 1 | 3.1 | 1.10 | 1.1 | 1.10 | 4.15 | 26.36 |
| 2 | 19.2 | 2 | 3.1 | 1.15 | 2.2 | 1.20 | 2.67 | 13.78 |
| 3 | 18.4 | 3 | 3.2 | 1.20 | 3.4 | 1.25 | 2.20 | 9.60 |
| 4 | 17.6 | 4 | 3.2 | 1.25 | 4.7 | 1.30 | 1.97 | 7.52 |
| 5 | 16.8 | 5 | 3.3 | 1.30 | 6.0 | 1.35 | 1.85 | 6.29 |
| 6 | 16.0 | 6 | 3.3 | 1.35 | 7.3 | 1.40 | 1.77 | 5.47 |
| 7 | 15.2 | 7 | 3.4 | 1.40 | 8.7 | 1.45 | 1.72 | 4.90 |
| 8 | 14.4 | 8 | 3.4 | 1.45 | 10.2 | 1.50 | 1.70 | 4.47 |
| 9 | 13.6 | 9 | 3.5 | 1.50 | 11.7 | 1.55 | 1.68 | 4.15 |
| 10 | 12.8 | 10 | 3.5 | 1.55 | 13.2 | 1.60 | 1.67 | 3.89 |
| 11 | 12.0 | 11 | 3.6 | 1.60 | 14.8 | 1.65 | 1.67 | 3.69 |
| 12 | 11.2 | 12 | 3.6 | 1.65 | 16.4 | 1.70 | 1.67 | 3.52 |
| 13 | 10.4 | 13 | 3.7 | 1.70 | 18.1 | 1.75 | 1.68 | 3.38 |
| 14 | 9.6 | 14 | 3.7 | 1.75 | 19.9 | 1.80 | 1.68 | 3.27 |
| 15 | 8.8 | 15 | 3.8 | 1.80 | 21.7 | 1.85 | 1.70 | 3.18 |
| 16 | 8.0 | 16 | 3.8 | 1.85 | 23.5 | 1.90 | 1.71 | 3.10 |
| 17 | 7.2 | 14 | 3.9 | 1.90 | 25.4 | 1.95 | 1.72 | 3.03 |
| 18 | 6.4 | 16 | 3.9 | 1.95 | 27.4 | 2.00 | 1.74 | 2.97 |
| 19 | 5.6 | 18 | 4.0 | 2.00 | 29.4 | 2.05 | 1.75 | 2.92 |
| 20 | 3.6 | 20 | 4.0 | 2.05 | 31.4 | 2.10 | 1.77 | 2.88 |
| Total | 246.8 | | 3.0 | 31.40 | | | | |
| Percent of costs | | | | | | | | |

**3. CAPITAL COSTS**

The fleet's total annual capital cost is

| | £ mill |
|---|---|
| Interest at 5% p.a. | 12.3 |
| Depreciation at 4% pa | 9.9 |
| Total capital cost per annum | 22.2 |

**Definition of the 4 sections in this table**

**1. Fleet** shows a fleet of 20 ships with one ship of each age 1–20 years; **2. Variable Costs** show how ship specific costs vary for each age of ship; **3. Capital** is the fixed cost of $22.2 m which must be paid however many ships are at sea; **4. Cost functions** show how the company's cost per ship changes depending on the number of ships at sea, which is shown in Column 1

must be paid regardless of whether or not the ship is trading, it falls from a massive $26.36 million with one ship at sea to $2.88 million per annum with 20 ships at sea. The ATC curve in Figure 8.3 is plotted using the data from Col 9 of Table 8.5.

The graphical illustration of these three curves in Figure 8.3 summarizes the financial position on which Perfect Shipping bases its operating decisions. The AVC line shows the non-capital break-even point for the business during recessions (depending on the number

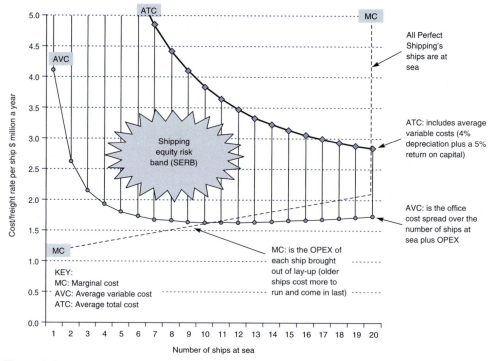

**Figure 8.3**
The perfect competition model MC, AVC and ATC curves

of ships at sea). But if we include the nominal allowance for capital, the relevant curve is the ATC line, that tells a very different story. At all output levels the break-even point is much higher. We will refer to the shaded area between these two curves as the shipping equity risk band (SERB), and the central issue for Perfect Shipping is how to finance this dominant element of its costs. The choice of debt or equity determines the business's break-even cashflow. If the SERB is financed mainly with debt the shipping company needs to invest less of its own capital, leveraging up its returns, but it is committed to a debt repayment schedule. For example, with nine ships at sea Perfect Shipping can survive on average earnings of $1.62 million a year, but if it is financed with 100% debt it must earn $4.09 million a year per ship to meet its obligations. So the company (and its bankers) must decide how much of the SERB can safely be financed by equity and how much by financial instruments involving fixed payment schedules.

## Freight revenue and the short-term cyclical adjustment process

If we introduce freight rates into the analysis (Figure 8.4), we see why the financial structure is so important. Four different levels of freight rates are represented by the horizontal lines labelled $P_1$–$P_4$. These freight rates are determined by supply and demand (see Chapter 5) but all Perfect Shipping sees is a horizontal price line which does not change, regardless of how many ships the company offers for hire.

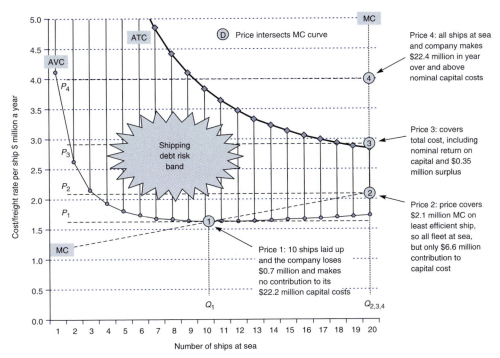

**Figure 8.4**
The perfect competition model with prices

The perfect competition model tells us that Perfect Shipping will maximize its profit (or minimize its loss) by producing at the level where its marginal cost equals the freight *rate*. At price $P_1$, which is $1.6 million per ship per annum, it should operate 10 ships because at that operating level its marginal cost of $1.6 million per annum equals the price. The economic logic is obvious. If it puts ten ships to sea, then the 11th ship costs $1.65 million to operate, so it loses $50,000 a year. Conversely if it puts only nine ships to sea, it loses the $50,000 revenue contribution obtained by trading ship 10. That is the basic decision process of companies operating in a perfect market – produce to a level at which marginal cost equals price.

With ten ships at sea, the AVC is $1.67 million per annum and the revenue is $1.6 million per ship, so the company loses a total of $ 0.7 million on the 10 ships at sea and makes no contribution to its $22.21 nominal capital cost. If the company is financed with equity there is no problem, but if any of the SERB capital is financed with debt, it cannot make its payments to the bank. If the payments are not made, a second decision-maker enters the market, Perfect Shipping's banker (a situation rather like the one faced by Perfect Shipping in 1977 in Table 8.4). This illustrates the position in recessions when the financial strength of shipping companies is tested and only the strongest survive. If the low rates persist the weak companies may end up selling their ships to the financially strong at distress prices, a game of pure Darwinian economics.

Moving on to $P_2$ in Figure 8.4, revenue increases to $2.1 million per ship, which equals the MC of the oldest ship, so the company puts all its ships to sea. Perfect Shipping can

**333**

now pay all its fixed and variable costs, but it only makes $6.6 million contribution to its $22.2 million nominal capital costs. It could probably pay some interest, but not repay principal, a situation the bank is unlikely to tolerate. At $P_3$ the earnings rise to $2.9 million per ship, so the company finally covers its nominal capital costs, whilst at $P_4$ the freight of $4 million per ship locks in a $22.4 million bonus profit for shareholders. Economists sometimes refer to this element of profit as 'rent'. At this point any leveraging pays off, since the owner or equity investor keeps this profit. As the money pours in the company is desperate to increase its earnings by expanding the fleet, and it has the funds to do it. Initially it bids for second-hand ships which can trade immediately, but eventually these become so expensive that newbuildings look more attractive. As the orderbook is delivered the market achieves its aim – capacity expands and earnings fall.

Since the financial structure determines a company's tolerance to freight cycles, this links their financial strategy to their view of the market. For example, companies which believe there will be no significant market disruption in the coming years may decide to cover a large proportion of their SERB with debt. If they are right, the owners will make big profits while companies taking a more conservative view will pay for their conservatism in low returns. If their shareholders become disillusioned, they might end up being bought out by their more aggressively financed competitors, or exiting the business. But if there is a market crisis, their conservative financial structure will let them survive and they may even be able to buy out their over-leveraged competitors. So shipping companies are differentiated and their financial strategy puts them in competition with each other as they make their way through the cycles. From this perspective shipping is more like poker, a game between the players.

## The long-term adjustment process

As the cashflow of the company swings from −$22.9 million at $P_1$ to $22.4 million at $P_4$, Perfect Shipping has to average out the good years with the bad. This is where the longer-term adjustment mechanism comes into play. Companies go on ordering ships as long as they can make a normal profit. If the freight rate moves above the ATC, companies will order more ships. Conversely if the rates stay below the ATC too long, investors become disillusioned and underinvest, cutting back on newbuilding and scrapping old ships. In this way the market squeezes out the inefficient ships and as the supply falls, earnings are driven up and a more cost-effective fleet moves into the upswing. Taking one cycle with another, the profits average out at the level which keeps investors coming back for more, and, given the structure of companies like Perfect Shipping, the idea that the normal profit settles at about the cost of borrowing plus a small margin is quite plausible.

## The link between the macroeconomic and microeconomic models

The link between the microeconomic and macroeconomic models is illustrated by the graphs in Figure 8.5. Figure 8.5(a) shows three prices being generated by the interaction of supply and demand at a macroeconomic level. Price 1 is determined by the intersection

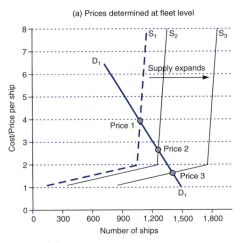
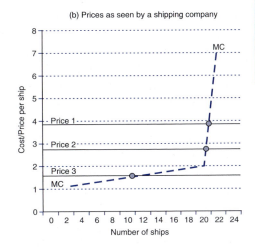

**Figure 8.5**
The long-term return ratchet

of $D_1$ and $S_1$, but as more supply is added in response to the high price, the supply curve moves to the right, generating price 2 at $S_2$ and price 3 at $S_3$. This process was discussed in Chapter 5. Figure 8.5(b) shows how this generates the market prices faced by the individual firm in Figure 8.4.

However, in practice the adjustment mechanism is not as clear-cut as the foregoing analysis suggests. At prices below $P_2$ the marginal benefit of laying a ship up is so small in relation to other costs the shipowner faces, the rational response is to keep all the fleet in service, just in case an unexpected surge in freight rates produces a spike. In these circumstances the process of selecting the ships to marginalize is left to charterers who take the best ships first and when there is surplus capacity, as there is at prices below $P_2$, leave the rest hanging around for a cargo. But that is not a great loss when rates are so close to operating costs. In these circumstances the shipping firm's position is like a poker player struggling with a bad run of cards and figuring out when to raise the bet and when to quit. On this analogy the 'normal' profit is the statistical margin that a professional gambler calculates he can win in the long run, and this is what determines whether he carries on gambling. But not all gamblers are strictly rational and the same probably applies to shipping investors, especially if there is a chance of getting $22.4 million on the next upswing.

## The cobweb theorem and the difficulty of defining returns

The market model in Figure 8.5 is static, so it does not show the time dimension that plays such an important part in the process of adjustment. The combination of unpredictable changes in demand and time-lags as supply responds, adds another dimension to the complexity facing firms in the shipping market. In Section 4.5 we defined three time-related equilibrium points: the *momentary* equilibrium which is only concerned with the ships in the loading zone; the *short run* in which ships can move in and out of lay-up; and the *long run* where new ships are built and delivered. The same lags operate at a microeconomic level, and the 'cobweb model' is often used by economists to describe the dynamic adjustment process when there is a time-lag in the response to supply and demand changes.[13]

The way the cobweb theorem works is illustrated in Figure 8.6. This figure is divided into two parts; Figure 8.6(a) shows the adjustment process for an individual company and Figure 8.6(b) shows what happens at industry level. The freight rate is in thousands of dollars per day on the vertical axis and the number of ships ordered or scrapped on the horizontal axis. We start with the market in equilibrium at $P_e$, a freight rate of $22,500 per day. At this freight rate demand equals supply and owners neither scrap nor order ships (i.e. it equates to $P_3$ in Figure 8.4, which just covers ATC). Then for some reason the price shoots up to $P_1$ ($30,000/day). At this profitable price level the supply curve shows that owners will rush to the shipyards and order four new ships (see point B on graph). But when the four ships are delivered the supply increases by four ships and the owners find they have to drop their price to $15,000 per day to get them all chartered (see intersection with demand curve at point C). With rates down at $15,000 a day the owners decide to scrap three ships (see supply curve at point D), reducing the fleet. But with three fewer ships available freight rates rise to $30,000 a day at point A! The owners order four ships ... and so it continues.

The graph in Figure 8.6(b) shows how these actions by individual shipping companies affect the general market balance (note that this chart is not really to scale). On the down stroke when the new ships are being delivered and supply is expanding, the extra ships move the supply curve to the right from $S_1$ to $S_2$, driving down rates. Then as the low rates force some old ships out of the market, the supply curve moves left from $S_2$ to $S_1$ pushing freight rates up from $P_2$ to $P_1$. This pumps money into shipowners' bank accounts, motivating the new orders. Because it takes a couple of years for the ships to arrive the boom is extended and many orders are likely to be placed. As all these new ships are delivered, the supply curve moves forward again to $S_2$, driving the price back

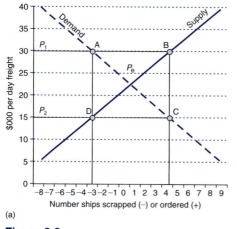

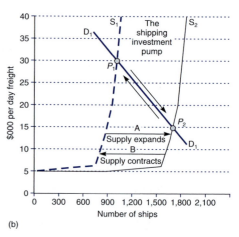

(a)        (b)

**Figure 8.6**
The cobweb model for the shipping market: (a) at company level; (b) at industry level

down to $P_2$. It may take owners a while to make the decision to scrap old ships, during which the recession drags on. In this way the investment pump manages fleet replacement, alternately sucking in the new ships and driving out the old ones.

But while this sub-plot of fleet replacement is going on, the market also has to deal with unpredictable changes in demand. In the example in Figure 8.6(b) the demand curve does not change – the adjustment is entirely driven by the supply mechanism. But in the real world the demand curve moves left and right in response to trade growth and business cycle recessions. This adds a second layer of complexity to the decision facing investors. Where will the demand curve be when the new ships are delivered? As we saw in Chapter 5, it is a mind-numbing calculation in which expectations play a major part. If all the old ships are scrapped as soon as rates fall, the cycle soon turns up. But if owners hang on in the hope of a demand-driven upturn, the recession drags on until a demand-driven recovery takes place. Pity the poor forecaster trying to reproduce this model, a cross between three-dimensional chess and stud poker.

Finally, we can note that the shipping supply curve is not just driven by freight rates, investor sentiment is also important. During a recession investors may decide the time is right for some counter-cyclical ordering, or they may panic and sell their older ships for scrap. Two very different freight scenarios would result, another reason why shipping cycles are so difficult to predict. However, one thing is clear. All the time the capacity pump is thumping away in the background, and since its pumping speed determines the ROSI we cannot expect the 'normal' profit to be consistent or well defined. All we know is that returns are sometimes very big, sometimes very small, and over the years there has never been a shortage of shipping investors willing to settle for these fuzzy terms.

### Returns earned in imperfect shipping markets

We noted at the beginning of this section that in the specialized and liner segments the requirements for perfect competition are not always met because product differentiation and barriers to entry exist to a greater or lesser extent in these sectors. So the foregoing analysis does not necessarily apply. Recent developments in microeconomics help bridge the gap between the perfectly competitive market, of which bulk shipping is an example, and the more complex oligopolistic world of specialized shipping companies. According to Porter, in any industry, whether it is domestic or international, the nature of competition and the return on capital are driven by five competitive forces: the threat of new entrants; the threat of substitute products or services; the bargaining power of suppliers; the bargaining power of buyers; and the rivalry among the existing competitors.[14] Porter argues that the strength of the five forces varies from industry to industry and determines long-term industry profitability. In industries in which the five forces are favourable, competitors are able to earn attractive returns on invested capital. Industries in which pressure from one or more of the forces is intense are those where few firms are very profitable for long periods.

The five competitive forces determine the industry profitability because they shape the prices firms can charge, the costs they have to bear and the investment required to compete in the industry. In industries such as soft drinks, pharmaceuticals, and cosmetics, Porter argues that the five forces are positive, allowing many competitors to earn attractive returns on invested capital. In others such as fabricated metal, aluminium and semiconductors the alignment of the five forces is unfavourable and profitability is weak. In effect, Porter's approach adapts the general principles of the perfect competition model to modern business. The threat of new entrants limits the overall profit potential because new entrants bring new capacity and seek market share, pushing down margins, whilst powerful buyers or suppliers bargain away the profits for themselves. The presence of close substitute products limits the price competitors can charge without inducing substitution. Industries which have some degree of protection from these five competitive elements are likely to have higher profits. This protection may take the form of barriers to entry, strong brand recognition, weak buyers and a degree of monopoly power. When none of these protective factors exist, the industry reverts to the classic perfect competition model.

Although specialized and liner shipping do not conform to the perfect competition model, they are vulnerable to similar competitive forces. Anyone who has studied the shipping market knows how vulnerable it is in these respects. Entry to even the most specialized services is relatively easy, requiring capital and expertise which can usually be acquired fairly easily. Customers are often large corporations importing cargo, who ruthlessly pursue any advantage. Admittedly there is no substitute for deep-sea service, but that is hardly a significant factor because the market place is very competitive. When we add the fact that many specialized shipping companies are privately owned, and thus the industry has a rather different yardstick for measuring profit from multinational corporations, the case is made.

## 8.4 PRICING SHIPPING RISK

### Differences in 'risk preference'

Shipping entrepreneurs are famous for taking risks, and during booms brokers' reports are full of comments about over-ordering which seem to suggest that the industry is run by irrational speculators who make the same overinvestment mistakes generation after generation. Can shipowners really be so irrational? Put so bluntly, it does not sound a very plausible theory, though there may be an element of truth in it. At the top of cycles investment sometimes gets out of hand, as it does in other markets, not least the stock markets. Taken to extremes that is bad because, as Keynes put it, 'When the capital development ... becomes a by-product of the activities of a casino, the job is likely to be ill done'.[15] But there is no clear line between gambling and taking economic risks, making it difficult to separate good luck from good judgement. However, economic progress relies on investors building ships which are not always needed,[16] and despite the occasional spectacular misjudgement such as the 1970s tanker bubble, there is little long-term evidence that in shipping the job has been 'ill done'. On the contrary, the history of shipping in Chapter 1 shows how effective the industry's risk taking has been in a world where nobody really knows what will happen next.

Shipping investors need to take risks and the world needs them to. In the sixteenth century when investors clubbed together to send ships to trade in distant lands it was an extremely risky investment which no prudent maritime economist would have dreamt of taking. Often the ship did not return and the investors lost everything. But sometimes it docked with a cargo worth many times the cost of the venture. These risk takers opened up the global economy and today's shipping investors are their direct descendants. Although it is easy to focus on Aristotle Onassis's good fortune in the 1956 Suez boom, remember how he earned the money. Without his ships the oil shortages in Europe would have been far more severe, and if Onassis had not had a taste for risk, his ships would not have been laid up in the first place. Freight rates shot up in 1956 because the ships were indispensable. Another example is illustrated in Figure 8.7 by the one-year time-charter rate distribution for a Panamax bulk carrier between 1990 and September 2002 shown. The charter rate averaged $9,571 per day and the standard deviation was $2,339 per day, so statistically we can be 99% certain that earnings would not exceed $16,588 per day.[17] Despite this unrewarding history, during the 1999 recession many new Panamax bulk carriers were ordered for delivery in 2002. But by the time they were delivered spot earnings were only $5,500 per day and it looked like a disaster. However, just two years later in 2004 the average one-year time-charter rate for a Panamax bulk carrier was $34,323 per day, and by 2007 it had reached $51,000 per day. So those seemingly irrational orders placed in 1999, some times at prices as low as $19 million, turned out to be inspired. In 2007 the ship could have earned $16.5 million in a single year, and where would the Asian economies have been without them?

In short, risk taking is the explosive that clears the path for economic progress, and like nitroglycerine it needs to be handled carefully! Not all investors are conservative pension funds – some are entrepreneurs who actually enjoy the thrill of handling high explosives and do not really mind losing the odd arm or leg! This provides a clue as to where we should look for the explanation in shipping's unusual risk–return profile. The explanation is that shipping entrepreneurs have different *risk preferences* from financial institutions, so they price investments differently.

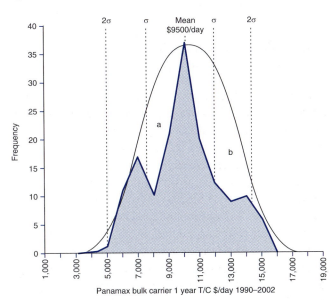

**Figure 8.7**
Risk profile of Panamax bulk carrier

## The capital asset pricing model

To clarify this point Figure 8.8(a) shows that most financial institutions approach risk by concentrating on the relationship between risk and return and require more volatile investments to pay higher returns. Risk, measured by the volatility of the investment, is shown on the horizontal axis, return on the vertical axis, and the graph is split into four risk/return 'options' –A (low risk, low return), B (high risk, high return), C (low risk, high return) and D (high risk, low return).

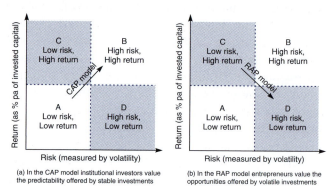

(a) In the CAP model institutional investors value the predictability offered by stable investments

(b) In the RAP model entrepreneurs value the opportunities offered by volatile investments

**Figure 8.8**
Risk, reward options, showing CAP and RAP models

Most conventional investments are priced along the diagonal shown by the arrow, between options A and B. This is known as the *capital asset pricing* (CAP) model, and it postulates that the more volatile the return on a stock, the higher its average return should be. Financial analysts use the relationship between volatility and return to price securities, calculating the value of a company share by comparing its return and volatility with a reference market index such as the S&P 500. Stocks with a bigger standard deviation are expected to pay a higher return and vice versa. For example an IT stock with a standard deviation of 35%, more than twice as high as the S&P 500, would be expected to pay a much higher average return.

## Risky asset pricing model

Shipping investors have different risk preferences, and we can introduce a new model to describe it. Working across the other diagonal from C to D, shown by the arrow in Figure 8.8 (b) the returns are negatively correlated with volatility, and we will call it the *risky asset pricing* (RAP) model. Shipping entrepreneurs are attracted to the high-risk and low-return option D by the opportunities offered by the volatility of the shipping cycles and its other characteristics, especially the liquid market for shipping assets which means that once in a while they can make fabulous profits. For example, a Panamax bulk carrier ordered in April 2003 for $23.5 million was resold on delivery in April 2005 for $55 million, a $52.5 million return on the $2.5 million deposit the owner paid when the ship was ordered. Investors choosing option D get a ticket to the big game and a few become billionaires.

But what about low risk, high return investments (option C)? The pricing in this box reflects the price of giving up the volatility. If a shipowner charters his ship for 10 years all he gets is the agreed charter hire. So naturally he might demand a higher return to compensate for the loss of flexibility and giving up his ticket to the big game. From this perspective the model makes perfect sense.

Shipping investors are not the only ones are willing to adopt the RAP model. Adam Smith pointed out that where the potential rewards are very great, 'the chance of loss by most men is under-valued'.[18] In other words, if there is a chance of getting really rich, a below average return may be acceptable. He gave the success of lotteries as evidence that 'the soberest people scarce look upon it as folly to pay a small sum for the chance of gaining ten or twenty thousand pounds; though they know that the small sum is perhaps twenty or thirty percent more than the chance is worth'.[19] And profit is not the only motivator. Risky trades in which there is an element of excitement often become so overcrowded that returns are lower than if there were no risks to be run. Alfred Marshall picked up this theme a century later, commenting that 'an adventurous occupation, such as gold mining, has special attractions for some people: the deterrent force of risks of loss in it is less than the attractive force of chances of great gain, even when the value of the latter estimated on the actuarial principle is much less a matter of the former'.[20] So there is nothing mysterious about shipping investors choosing the RAP model. After all volatility does not mean you lose your investment, it just means you are not sure when or how much you will be paid.

Shipping fits the RAP model pretty well, offering a few successful shipowners wealth beyond the dreams of lottery winners, whilst the less fortunate majority earn enough to survive and pay their bankers. In effect the market "sells" them the volatility which the institutional investors do not want because they cannot use it. But shipping entrepreneurs can and as the excitement of the poker table hooks investors, competition continually drives down the return on capital. This difference in risk pricing can be seen, for example, in the pricing of shares in publicly listed shipping companies which often trade at a discount to net asset value calculated on the basis of prevailing second-hand ship values. In other words given the same economic outlook, institutional investors are prepared to pay less for the assets than private shipowners buying the assets themselves.

And, of course, they like the business. Farmers are just the same, accepting a low return on the capital tied up in their farms because they value the way of life. It is a living and what would they do with the capital if they sold up? Many shipowners feel the same way. If you have $200 million in the business, what difference does it make if you make $10 million or $20 million in a year? And if you sell out, what do you do with the money? Where's the fun in owning stocks or a chain of supermarkets? Viewed in this way it is easy to see why the risk preferences of shipping investors are so different from those of fund managers. If they want to operate in box D, they are free to do so and history proves there is always a supply of investors ready to take their chances – if the supply dries up, the market just throws in a boom to kick-start the process.

But the last word goes to JP Morgan. Asked whether longshoremen were paid enough he replied: 'If that's all he can get, and he takes it, I should say it's enough'.[21] The same applies to shipping investors. A good outcome for consumers, which is exactly what market economics is about.

## 8.5 SUMMARY

In this chapter we have tackled the tricky issue of the return on capital. We started with the paradox that shipping is famous for its wealthy shipowners, but historically returns for such a volatile business have been low. Shipping investors often earned lower returns than, for example, the stock market. We called this the 'shipping return paradox' and set out to explain it.

The return on shipping investment (ROSI) model has four key components: EBID, CAPP, DEP and NAV. The core cashflow of any shipping company comes from earnings before interest and depreciation (EBID), but capital in the form of depreciation, capital appreciation and the net asset value of the fleet plays a dominant part in the financial performance of the business.

We used Perfect Shipping, a hypothetical shipping company which traded from 1975 to 2006 to illustrate the ROSI model. Over the 31-year period Perfect Shipping's annual ROSI was 7.3%, and its earnings were very volatile, even by equity standards, so this result is consistent with the history of low shipping returns. But we made a striking discovery. Despite the volatility of its earnings, Perfect Shipping was a very safe investment. There were only two years in 30 when its EBID was negative. Depreciation, which was dealt with by replacing one ship each year, could easily be deferred; the company's portfolio of real assets was a hedge against inflation; and sea transport is a core economic activity; so what more could an investor want? If we are concerned with the risk of loss, and can cope with a volatile revenue stream, Perfect Shipping is a pretty solid, if boring, investment.

We then discussed how the returns are determined. Although few modern industries conform to the famous perfect competition model developed by the classical economists in the nineteenth century, it fits shipping like a glove. With its many small companies, easy entry and exit, and flat medium-term supply curve, the shipping market operates like a pump, alternately sucking new ships in and pushing old ships out. The 'normal' profit is the lubricant needed to keep the pump operating efficiently. Basically companies keep investing until marginal cost equals price and in the long term marginal cost is the cost of capital. Interestingly, over the last fifty years, ROSI has fluctuated around the cost of interest.

Given the nature of the ROSI model, shipowners who want to make super-profits must be more adventurous than Perfect Shipping, and the ROSI model offers many opportunities for doing this. If they wish, shipowners can lead a Jekyll and Hyde existence. Dr Jekyll operates his fleet safely and efficiently, earning the normal profit, which is just sufficient to replace the fleet as it ages and pay a very modest return on capital. But the capital intensity of shipping provides Mr Hyde, the alter ego, with an ideal platform to operate as a speculator and entrepreneur, improving the EBID return by taking leveraged positions on time-charters or COA markets, and making capital gains through buying and selling ships on the side. Net asset value can be dramatically reduced by using old ships with low capital costs, but only if the shipowner can operate these old ships cost-effectively. Or the ships can be sold and chartered back, making the shipowner an operator.

This dual life is possible because the ROSI model offers the option to trade speculatively. Once shipowners go down this route their risk increases, but so do the potential profits. The problem is that as companies grow in size it becomes increasingly difficult to find attractive speculative opportunities of sufficient size to affect the company's bottom line, and the normal profits look unattractive. As a result, successful shipping companies often diversify into other industries, a tendency which keeps the size of shipping companies small!

In conclusion, shipping is as risky as the management make it and shipping investors enjoy one of the most exciting businesses in the world, whilst giving consumers a pretty good deal on their transport, so in the end everyone wins. But it is not a business for the faint-hearted!

# Part 4

# SEABORNE TRADE AND TRANSPORT SYSTEMS

# 9 The Geography of Maritime Trade

*Such therefore are the advantages of water carriage, it is natural that the first improvements of art and industry should be made where this convenience opens the whole world for a market to the produce of every sort of labor.*

(Adam Smith, *Inquiry Into the Wealth of Nations*, 1776)

## 9.1 THE VALUE ADDED BY SEABORNE TRANSPORT

When Vasco da Gama arrived in India in 1457 and found that he could buy pepper for 3 ducats in Calicut and sell it for 80 ducats in Europe (see Chapter 1), he was doing exactly what traders do today – using sea transport to exploit an interregional arbitrage. It was not just a commercial success. By bringing spices to the European population in far greater volumes than could be transported overland by camel, he made their lives better and, in modern economic jargon, 'added value'. Over the succeeding six centuries, as shipping became more efficient, the opportunities to add value by moving goods around the world increased and sea trade has grown, giving shipping a central role in the globalization of the world economy.

Today cargo moves between more than 3,000 major commercial ports, and to understand the economic mechanisms which drive this complex operation we need to know where goods move and why. Maritime economics is a practical discipline, and there is not much point in being an expert on the economics if we cannot find the ports on a map! So in this chapter we will study the oceans, continents, countries, manufacturing centres and ports which make up the maritime transport matrix. Starting with an overview of the trading world, we will then examine the 'spatial' geography of the Atlantic, Pacific and Indian oceans to get a sense of where the trading centres are located, the goods they trade and the time and cost of moving goods between them.

In this chapter we will review the physical framework within which the shipping industry operates, starting with the oceans, seas and transit times. We will then make a quick tour of the three major oceans, the Atlantic, the Pacific and the Indian, and discuss the economies of the main trading areas within them. In doing this we will refer to a series of maps and in particular four tables: Table 9.1 which contains an overview of regional trade; Table 9.4 which reviews the economies of the Atlantic countries; Table 9.5 which covers the Pacific economies; and Table 9.6 which contains details of the Indian Ocean economies.

## 9.2 OCEANS, DISTANCES AND TRANSIT TIMES

### Location of the major trading economies

Maritime trade is dominated by three economic centres, North America, Europe and Asia, strung out along the 'Westline' we studied in Chapter 1 (see Figure 9.1). The heavy black line in the map shows the shipping route between these three centres which is followed by container-ships and other specialized vessels such as car carriers and chemical tankers, carrying a wide range of merchandise. The lighter lines mark the main routes followed by bulk vessels carrying raw materials such as oil, iron ore, coal, grain and phosphate rock into the three economic centres. Europe, where it all started, lies in the centre of the figure, with North America on the left and Asia on the right. Together they have over 90% of the world's manufacturing industry and much of its technology. Their multinational corporations own most of the world's patents, develop most of the new technology, and one way or another they initiate and direct a large proportion of the investment and trade in raw materials and manufactures[1]. So naturally they also dominate sea trade.

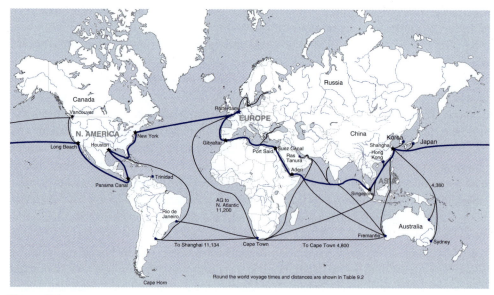

**Figure 9.1**
The world's major shipping routes, 2007
Source: Martin Stopford 2007

If we take imports as the yardstick, these three areas imported 88% of the 7 billion tons of cargo transported by sea in 2005. The detailed export and import statistics are summarized in Table 9.1, whilst the map in Figure 9.2 shows the share of each region in total imports and exports. This is the physical framework within which the shipping business operates, and analysing the efficient movement of cargo between the points on this map is the business of maritime economists, so we need to study it carefully. But before doing this, a word is needed about regional definitions, a source of endless difficulty for trade analysts. The issue is simple enough – which countries belong in which regions? The problem is that the statistics we use are often based on political groupings which change over time. A recent example is the break-up of the Soviet Union and the transfer of the central European countries into the European Union. In this chapter we will roughly

**Table 9.1** International seaborne imports and exports by region, 2005 (million tonnes)

| Region | Exports | | | | Imports | | | | Total Trade[a] | |
|---|---|---|---|---|---|---|---|---|---|---|
| | Oil | Dry | Total | % | Oil | Dry | total | % | mt | % |
| **1. Trade of the Atlantic** | | | | | | | | | | |
| North America[b] | 95 | 503 | 598 | 8% | 682 | 442 | 1,124 | 16% | 1,722 | 12% |
| Carib. & Cent. America | 169 | 65 | 234 | 3% | 73 | 86 | 159 | 2% | 393 | 3% |
| E. Coast S. America | 195 | 393 | 588 | 8% | 61 | 92 | 153 | 2% | 741 | 5% |
| West Africa | 198 | 20 | 218 | 3% | 8 | 42 | 50 | 1% | 268 | 2% |
| Northern Africa | 166 | 38 | 204 | 3% | 57 | 84 | 142 | 2% | 346 | 2% |
| Western Europe | 105 | 1,065 | 1,170 | 16% | 543 | 1,515 | 2,058 | 29% | 3,228 | 23% |
| Russia & E. Europe | 177 | 181 | 358 | 5% | 14 | 67 | 81 | 1% | 439 | 3% |
| Other Europe | 2 | 17 | 19 | 0% | 9 | 11 | 20 | 0% | 40 | 0% |
| Total Atlantic | 285 | 1,263 | 3,389 | 48% | 1,447 | 2,340 | 3,787 | 53% | 7,176 | 50% |
| **2. Trade of the Pacific & Indian Oceans** | | | | | | | | | | |
| West Coast | 32 | 120 | 152 | 2% | 22 | 35 | 56 | 1% | 209 | 1% |
| Japan | 4 | 186 | 190 | 3% | 248 | 585 | 832 | 12% | 1,022 | 7% |
| China[c] | 39 | 478 | 517 | 7% | 153 | 584 | 737 | 10% | 1,254 | 9% |
| S. & E. Asia | 172 | 762 | 934 | 13% | 469 | 915 | 1,384 | 19% | 2,318 | 16% |
| Total Asia[d] | 215 | 1,426 | 1,641 | 23% | 870 | 2,084 | 2,953 | 41% | 4,594 | 32% |
| Oceania (Dev.) | 4 | 2 | 6 | 0% | 6 | 6 | 12 | 0% | 18 | 0% |
| Australia & New Zealand | 14 | 604 | 618 | 9% | 40 | 48 | 88 | 1% | 706 | 5% |
| M. East (W. Asia) | 1,048 | 73 | 1,121 | 16% | 19 | 141 | 160 | 2% | 1,281 | 9% |
| East Africa | - | 9 | 9 | 0% | 6 | 21 | 26 | 0% | 36 | 0% |
| South Africa | - | 172 | 172 | 2% | 16 | 24 | 40 | 1% | 211 | 1% |
| Total | 1,314 | 2,406 | 3,720 | 52% | 979 | 2,356 | 3,335 | 47% | 7,055 | 50% |
| Total Sea Trade | 1,599 | 3,669 | 7,109 | 100% | 2,426 | 4,696 | 7,122 | 100% | | |
| Memo: Africa Total | 364 | 239 | 602 | 0 | 87 | 170 | 258 | | 860 | 6% |

Source: *Review of Maritime Transport 2006, United Nations Conference on Trade and Development*

[a]Total of imports and exports. Grand total not shown, since it double-counts imports and exports

[b]Includes Pacific coast

[c]Includes N. Korea & Vietnam

[d]maritime Asia is the sum of Japan, China and Southern & Eastern Asia

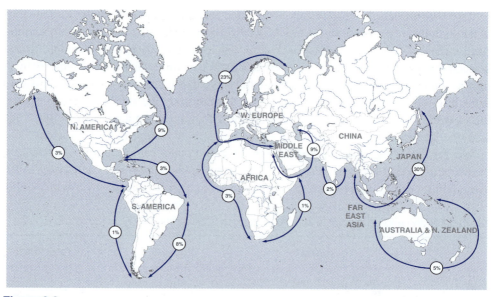

**Figure 9.2**
World seaborne trade by region, showing the share of maritime imports and exports 2005
Source: United Nations *Monthly Bulletin of Statistics*

divide the world into divisions based on the Atlantic, Pacific and Indian oceans, though the source data does not allow us to split the Pacific and Indian oceans. The 16 regions within these divisions are listed in Table 9.1, and although they do not support the divisional split precisely, they provide a rough idea of the distribution of trade around the world. The countries within the regions are defined further in Tables 9.4–9.6 which also show the area, population and GDP of each country and the region as a whole.

In 2005 trade was split roughly fifty-fifty between the Atlantic, with 7 billion tons of imports and exports, and the Pacific and Indian Oceans, with 7.1 billion tons. Atlantic trade was dominated by two big importers North America (1.1 billion tons) and Europe (2.1 billion tons), which together accounted for 45% of world imports, and the remaining Atlantic regions only 8% (note that North America, which has two coasts, is included in the Atlantic, overstating its importance). Exports were more widely dispersed, with Europe, North America and East Coast South America the most important. In the Pacific the dominant importers with a 41% trade share were Japan which imported 0.8 billion tons, China 0.7 billion tons and the cluster of Asian countries including South East Asia and India which imported 1.4 billion tons. Although the remaining regions, Africa, South America, Oceania, and the Middle East, include some very large land masses, their share of imports was quite small.

## Around the world in 80 days

Corporations and traders work on margins and are constantly scouring the regions of the world for cheaper suppliers and new markets where they can sell their products.

Distance, speed and the cost of sea transport all play a part in their calculations, and we will come across these variables time and again in our study of sea trade, ship design, and the market for sea transport. So it makes sense to start with two fundamental issues: how long does it take for cargo to move around the world, and how much does it cost? In fact sea transport is relatively slow, as we can see if we follow the round-the-world voyage shown by the broad line in Figure 9.1. It takes about 80.1 days to circumnavigate the world using a conventional bulk carrier travelling at 13.6 knots and 47 days using a container-ship operating at 23 knots.

The distances and travelling times are shown in Table 9.2. The individual legs of the bulk carrier journey give an idea of the times and distances involved in bulk transport. The voyage starts in Rotterdam and crossing the North Atlantic to New York is 3270 miles and takes 10 days, followed by a 1905 mile voyage to Houston in the US Gulf, taking 5.8 days. Houston to Long Beach is 4346 miles and takes 13 days. Crossing the Pacific to China is the longest single sea leg, with the journey from Long Beach to Shanghai covering 5810 miles and taking 17.8 days. From Shanghai to Singapore is 2210 miles, or 6.8 days steaming, and from there the trip through the busy Malacca Straits to Aden at the mouth of the Red Sea is 3627 miles, taking about 11 days. From Aden it is 8.9 days steaming to Marseilles on the Mediterranean coast of France, and 6.3 days to Rotterdam. The distance is 26,158 nautical miles and the total voyage time is 80.1 days at a cost of $25 per tonne of cargo carried round the world. This cost was calculated by dividing the bulk carrier's total costs on the voyage by the 70,000 tons of cargo it carried. It includes fuel and charter hire, but not canal and port costs (the assumptions for bunkers, ship costs, etc. are given in the footnotes to Table 9.2). If the shipper is in a hurry, a 23 knot container-ship could cut the voyage time to 47 days, but the cost per ton would more than double to $55 dollars due to the

**Table 9.2** Round-the-world voyage showing voyage times and total cost per tonne

| Trade route | | Distance, nautical miles[a] | Sailing Time (days) | | Total Cost $ mill | |
|---|---|---|---|---|---|---|
| From | To | | Bulker 13.6kts | Container 23 kts | Bulker[b] 13.6kts | Container[c] 23.0 kts |
| Rotterdam | New York | 3,270 | 10.0 | 5.9 | 0.22 | 0.32 |
| New York | Houston | 1,905 | 5.8 | 3.3 | 0.13 | 0.18 |
| Houston | Long Beach | 4,346 | 13.3 | 7.9 | 0.29 | 0.43 |
| Long Beach | Shanghai | 5,810 | 17.8 | 9.4 | 0.39 | 0.51 |
| Shanghai | Singapore | 2,210 | 6.8 | 4.8 | 0.15 | 0.26 |
| Singapore | Aden | 3,627 | 11.1 | 6.6 | 0.25 | 0.36 |
| Aden | Marseilles | 2,920 | 8.9 | 5.3 | 0.20 | 0.29 |
| Marseilles | Rotterdam | 2,070 | 6.3 | 3.8 | 0.14 | 0.20 |
| Total | | 26,158 | 80.1 | 47.0 | 1.78 | 2.55 |
| Cost: $/tonne for 70,000 tonnes bulk or 48,456 tonnes container cargo | | | | | 25.3 | 55.3 |

[a]A nautical mile is the length of a minute of the arc of a great circle of the globe, 6,080 feet
[b]Based on 74,000 dwt Panamax bulk carrier 2007 built averaging 13.6 knots and burning 33 tons/day heavy fuel oil at $250/tonne and chartered at $13,900/day, the TC rate of a Panamax bulk carrier over the 10 years April 1997 to April 2007
[c]Based on 4,048 TEU containership, 23 knots on 117 tonnes/day of heavy fuel oil at $250/tonne and 12 tonnes carried per TEU in a vessel chartered at $25,000/day

higher bunkers and the greater cost of chartering a container-ship capable of travelling at 23 knots.[2] Broadly speaking, 13.6 knots to 23 knots is the speed range within which merchant ships operate, though to trade efficiently at the opposite ends of this speed band requires significantly different hull and machinery designs. We reviewed these costs in detail in Chapter 6.

The average voyage on this journey is 3270 miles. However, there are some much longer trade routes in the bulk shipping business, a few of which are shown in Figure 9.1 by the light lines. They include oil from the Arabian Gulf to the North Atlantic via the Cape of Good Hope (12,000 miles or 37 days' steaming), grain from the US Gulf to Japan (9400 miles or 28 days' steaming) and iron ore from Brazil to Japan (11,500 miles or 34 days' steaming). But there are many shorter routes, and in 2005 the oil trade averaged 4989 miles and the major dry bulk trades 5100 miles.

## Transport demand and logistics

Although at first sight the link between distance and transport demand is quite straight-forward, appearances are deceptive. With over 3,000 major ports to consider, the trade matrix has, in principle, 4 million elements. Of course in practice some routes predominate, but even in a relatively simple trade such as oil the range of routes is enormous. For example, the oil tanker distance tables published by British Petroleum run to 150 densely packed pages!

At this point it is useful to introduce *logistics*, a science which deals explicitly with complex transport problems. The term, which is derived from the Greek word *logistikos* meaning 'calculatory' or 'rational', was adopted by the military to describe the science of planning the supply chain which supports combat troops. The term is now also used by commercial organizations to describe the process of rationalizing supply chains to support their commercial operations. Typically this involves integrating transport modes, storage facilities, cargo-handling facilities, information management, and performance measurement and monitoring. Of course this is easy enough to understand when dealing with an individual company and supply chain, but much more complex when operating across a global matrix with millions of elements. As an example, the distance matrix shown in Table 9.3(a) shows the distances between high-volume ports in Asia, Europe and the United States. On the horizontal axis, Asia is represented by Mumbai in India, Singapore (the crossroad port on the Malacca Straits) and Shanghai, which lies close to Japan and Korea, and thus represents a convenient reference point. Western Europe includes Rotterdam in the north-west and Fos, the port of Marseilles, in the Mediterranean. Finally, for the United States we include New York on the East Coast, New Orleans on the Gulf Coast, and Los Angeles on the West Coast. The vertical axis shows 12 ports in exporting areas. First is the Arabian Gulf, followed by Australia, Canada, USA, South America, Africa, the Black Sea and Europe. Although this matrix is a great oversimplification, it still has 90 elements and there is a lot of detail to absorb.

The shortest voyage in Table 9.3(a) is from Algiers to Fos (Marseilles) which is only 400 miles, and the voyage time matrix in Table 9.3(b) shows it takes only 1.3 days. Allowing for two days in port at either end of the voyage, a ship could complete

**Table 9.3(a)** Distance round voyage (nautical miles)

| | | ASIA | | | EUROPE | | UNITED STATES | | |
|---|---|---|---|---|---|---|---|---|---|
| | | India | S'pore | China | N. West | Med | E. Coast | US Gulf | W. Coast |
| Region | Port | Mumbai | | Shanghai | Rotterdam | Fos | N. York | New Orleans | L. Angeles |
| Arabian Gulf (1) | Ras Tanura | 1,352 | 2,435 | 5,852 | 11,170 | | 11,765 | 12,225 | |
| via Suez | Ras Tanura | | | | 6,412 | | | 9,543 | |
| Australia | Newcastle | 6,095 | 4,215 | 4,590 | 11,620 | 9,915 | 9,680 | 9,088 | 6,456 |
| Canada | Vancouver | 9,512 | 7,071 | 5,092 | 8,917 | 9,105 | 6,056 | 5,472 | 1,144 |
| US Gulf | N. Orleans | 9,541 | 11,514 | 10,080 | 4,880 | 5,300 | 1,707 | | 4,346 |
| East Coast South America | N. York | 9,541 | 10,169 | 10,669 | 3,270 | 3,825 | | 1,707 | 3,780 |
| West Coast South America | L. Angeles | 10,308 | 7,867 | 5,810 | 7,747 | 7,980 | 1,707 | 4,346 | |
| Brazil | Rio | 7,863 | 8,863 | 10,877 | 5,256 | 4,900 | 4,780 | 5,136 | 7,245 |
| W.Africa | Lagos | 7,188 | 8,188 | 10,202 | 4,310 | 3,810 | 4,883 | 5,749 | 8,006 |
| N. Africa | Algiers | 4,570 | 6,565 | 8,805 | 1,791 | 410 | 3,545 | 5,300 | 7,705 |
| B. Sea | Odessa | 4,230 | 6,214 | 8,465 | 3,508 | 1,720 | 5,265 | 6,740 | 9,450 |
| Europe | Rotterdam | 6,337 | 8,308 | 10,590 | | 2,070 | 3,270 | 4,880 | 7,747 |
| Asia | Osaka | 5,112 | 2,671 | 790 | 10,985 | 9,221 | 9,986 | 6,348 | 5,193 |
| | | | | | | | | | 6,671 |

**Table 9.3(b)** Days per single voyage (at 13 knots speed)

| | | ASIA | | | EUROPE | | UNITED STATES | | |
|---|---|---|---|---|---|---|---|---|---|
| | | India | S'pore | China | N. West | Med | E. Coast | US Gulf | W. Coast |
| Region | Port | Mumbai | | Shanghai | Rotterdam | Fos | N. York | New Orleans | L. Angeles |
| Arabian Gulf (1) | Ras Tanura | 4 | 8 | 19 | 36 | | 38 | 39 | |
| via Suez | Ras Tanura | | | | 21 | | | 31 | |
| Australia | Newcastle | 20 | 14 | 15 | 37 | 32 | 31 | 29 | 21 |
| Canada | Vancouver | 30 | 23 | 16 | 29 | 29 | 19 | 18 | 4 |
| US Gulf | N. Orleans | 31 | 37 | 32 | 16 | 17 | 5 | - | 14 |
| East Coast South America | N. York | 31 | 33 | 34 | 10 | 12 | 0 | 5 | 12 |
| West Coast South America | L. Angeles | 33 | 25 | 19 | 25 | 26 | 5 | 14 | 0 |
| Brazil | Rio | 25 | 28 | 35 | 17 | 16 | 15 | 16 | 23 |
| W.Africa | Lagos | 23 | 26 | 33 | 14 | 12 | 16 | 18 | 26 |
| N. Africa | Algiers | 15 | 21 | 28 | 6 | 1.3 | 11 | 17 | 25 |
| B. Sea | Odessa | 14 | 20 | 27 | 11 | 6 | 17 | 22 | 30 |
| Europe | Rotterdam | 20 | 27 | 34 | - | 7 | 10 | 16 | 25 |
| Asia | Osaka | 16 | 9 | 3 | 35 | 30 | 32 | 20 | 17 |
| | | | | | 30 | | | | |

Notes: (1) US Gulf (New Orleans),Distances via Suez Canal AG to Rotterdam 19.7 days; AG to New Orleans 30 days

**Table 9.3(c)** Number of round voyages a year (350 days trading, 2 days loading, 2 days discharge)

| | | ASIA | | | EUROPE | | UNITED STATES | | |
|---|---|---|---|---|---|---|---|---|---|
| | | India | S'pore | China | N. West | Med | E. Coast | US Gulf | W. Coast |
| Region | Port | Mumbai | | Shanghai | Rotterdam | Fos | N. York | New Orleans | L. Angeles |
| A. Gulf | Ras Tanura | 27.6 | 17.8 | 8.4 | 4.6 | | 4.4 | 4.2 | |
| *via Suez* | Ras Tanura | | | | 7.8 | | | 5.4 | |
| Australia | Newcastle | 8.1 | 11.3 | 10.5 | 4.5 | 5.2 | 5.3 | 5.6 | 7.7 |
| Canada | Vancouver | 5.4 | 7.1 | 9.6 | 5.7 | 5.6 | 8.2 | 9.0 | 30.9 |
| US Gulf | N. Orleans | 5.4 | 4.5 | 5.1 | 9.9 | 9.2 | 23.4 | — | 11.0 |
| East Coast South America | N. York | 5.4 | 5.1 | 4.8 | 14.0 | 12.3 | 87.5 | 23.4 | 12.4 |
| West Coast South America | L. Angeles | 5.0 | 6.4 | 8.5 | 6.5 | 6.3 | 23.4 | 11.0 | 87.5 |
| Brazil | Rio | 6.4 | 5.8 | 4.7 | 9.3 | 9.9 | 10.1 | 9.5 | 6.9 |
| W.Africa | Lagos | 7.0 | 6.2 | 5.0 | 11.1 | 12.3 | 9.9 | 8.6 | 6.3 |
| N. Africa | Algiers | 10.5 | 7.6 | 5.8 | 22.6 | 52.8 | 13.1 | 9.2 | 6.6 |
| B. Sea | Odessa | 11.2 | 8.0 | 6.0 | 13.2 | 23.3 | 9.3 | 7.4 | 5.4 |
| Europe | Rotterdam | 7.8 | 6.1 | 4.9 | — | 20.3 | 14.0 | 9.9 | 6.5 |
| Asia | Osaka | 9.5 | 16.6 | 38.6 | 4.7 | 5.5 | 5.1 | 7.8 | 9.4 |

52 voyages a year (Table 9.3(c)), spending only 137 days at sea and 211 days in port. This is quite a difference from the longest voyage from Ras Tanura (Saudi Arabia) to New Orleans (the LOOP oil terminal) which is 12,225 miles and takes 39 days for a single voyage. If the ship returns in ballast the round voyage takes 80 days so the ship will complete four voyages a year. No wonder analysts of the demand for oil tankers are very interested in whether the future trade growth will be from Africa to France or from the Middle East to the USA and whether refineries will be built close to the source of the crude! Finally, Table 9.3(c) shows the number of voyages completed per year at 13 knots.

How do you optimize transport logistics across this matrix? The four core variables in the maritime logistics model are distance, ship size, type and speed (see Figure 9.3). *Distance* is crucial because it affects cost and journey time. *Ship size* is important because bigger ships produce economies of scale and have lower unit costs per tonne on any route, but can enter fewer ports due to draft and length-overall constraints. In addition, on short-haul routes their economies are diluted because the ship completes more voyages and spends more time in port. They also deliver

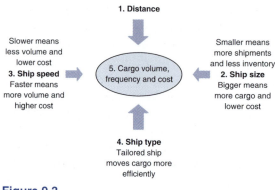

**Figure 9.3**
Four maritime logistics variables
Source: Martin Stopford, 2007

more cargo, which may be an issue. For example, a 300,000 dwt tanker (we discussed economies of scale in Chapter 2) delivers 1.25 million tons a year on the Arabian Gulf to USA route, but trading between the Arabian Gulf and Mumbai it transports 8.3 million tons a year. *Speed* determines the journey time, the bunker cost and the design of the ship. A 19-day transit from Los Angeles to Shanghai at 13 knots shrinks to 10 days at 24 knots, but fuel costs increase (see the discussion of the cube rule in Section 6.3); the 24 knot ship costs more; but it delivers more cargo by going faster, so there is a capital saving. Finally, ship *type* can affect logistical efficiency. A flexible ship can pick up a backhaul, for example carrying oil to New Orleans then loading a backhaul of grain to Japan. That would give an enormous increase in efficiency. Or a 39,000 dwt chemical parcel tanker with many 3,000 deadweight tanks could replace a fleet of 3,000 dwt vessels, increasing transport efficiency by grouping many small parcels in a big ship. But both these examples require all the links in the logistics chain to fit together, and the more links there are, the harder it is to achieve. Suppose you build the expensive flexible ship and the niche trade you had hoped to use disappears? Finally, it is a simple matter to develop a mathematical model relating the four variables to cargo volume, service frequency and unit cost. With such a model the service operator can develop the ideal logistics solution for the trade, for example using 22 knot, 3,000 TEU containerships on the shorter trades and 8,000 TEU, 24 knot vessels on the longer ones.

That is the theory, but reality is often less clear-cut. An example of the issues which shipping companies face in making these logistics decisions are those faced by liner companies in deciding how to route their Asia to East Coast North America container services. The first option is to ship their containers to West Coast North American ports and complete the journey to destinations on the US East Coast by rail or road. A second option is to sail direct to the US East Coast via the Panama Canal. Third, the carrier could sail direct to the US East Coast via the Suez Canal, with no call in Europe. In making this choice of routeing there are at least ten factors to be taken into account in arriving at the decision.[3] They are: (1) the level of freight rates on the trans-Pacific route and future rates which will depend on demand and capacity changes; (2) vessel size restrictions (the Suez Canal can accommodate post Panamax ships, whereas the Panama Canal cannot); (3) transit times and differences between the alternative routes; (4) Panama and Suez Canal tolls; (5) fuel costs (the Suez route is longer so bunker costs will be higher); (6) possible port disruption, a problem sometimes in certain areas, such as West Coast North America; (7) labour relations, which is related to the previous point; (8) the availability of container-ship capacity (if supply is short the focus will be on minimizing voyage time); (9) inland rail and road transport costs; (10) available capacity in key chokepoints. What this example demonstrates is that from the service operator's viewpoint shipping logistics is not a simple matter of optimizing the physical variables in Figure 9.3, possibly using a mathematical simulation model. That is the easy part. The much harder part is trading off the host of practical considerations which affect the variables in the model. How will canal charges develop? What about the risk of port disruption? Will it be possible to charter the right size of ship cheaply, or could charter rates escalate? These are the real questions which will determine service performance, and on many of them management will be guessing about what will happen. This is why they often fall back on the simple tried and tested practices in preference to optimization models which cannot really cope with these difficult-to-quantify variables. So logistics, like so many aspects of the maritime business, is as much an art as a science.

In summary, sea transport is a low-cost, high-volume business, preoccupied with small incremental savings that produce a competitive advantage – a little bit bigger, shallow draft, better cargo-handling gear, etc. – and it is through these small incremental changes that the market tackles this complex logistic task. This probably explains the technical conservatism which runs through the shipping business and the enthusiasm for; 'Handy' vessels which are cheap and versatile, a concept going back to the Dutch fly-boats of the sixteenth century, and tried and tested logistics solutions. Specialized vessels are all very well, and, as we see in Chapter 14, they have a role and shipping market, but operating specialized vessels usually goes much further than just owning ships. But there are no rules about this. It took a trucker, Malcolm McLean, to break the logistics mould of liner shipping and introduce containerization, a radically different logistics solution (see Chapter 13).

## 9.3 THE MARITIME TRADING NETWORK

At the heart of the maritime logistics model are the oceans and seas where the merchant ships operate. The Atlantic, the Pacific and the Indian Ocean cover 71% of the globe – 361 million square kilometres of the globe's surface area of 509 million square kilometres.[4] The Pacific is the largest, followed by the Atlantic, then the Indian Ocean. Each has a distinctive character and, as we saw in Figure 9.1, the trading centres are clustered in specific locations around the shores of the three oceans. In this section we will overview the three oceans to identify the main trading areas, the major ports and the distances. To keep the maps simple we focus on the big picture only, including just a few major ports as reference points for measuring distances – in Sections 9.4 – 9.9 we will include more detail about the economies, ports and trade. The distances shown on the maps are measured in days for a bulk carrier travelling at 13 knots.

### The Atlantic maritime area

The main countries of the Atlantic and its associated seas, the Baltic, the Mediterranean, and the Black Sea, are shown in Figure 9.4, whilst the economic statistics of the larger Atlantic economies are presented in Table 9.4. It is well suited to sea trade, being S-shaped and narrow in relation to its length, so the distance between the industrial economies on either side is little more than 3,000 miles or about 10 days' steaming for a 13 knot bulk carrier or 5 days for a fast container-ship. However, the north–south distances are much greater: from Rotterdam to Montevideo or Cape Town is 6,200 miles or about 19 days' steaming for a bulk carrier. Because the continents on either side of the North Atlantic slope gently towards its shores, it is well served by navigable rivers which provide cheap transport into the interior of the continents. In fact the 5.8 million hectares of land which drain into the Atlantic is only 20% less than the 7.1 million hectares draining into the

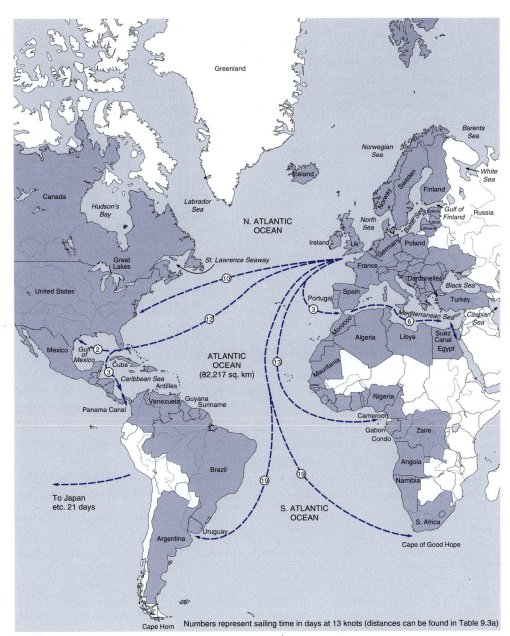

**Figure 9.4**
The major countries of the Atlantic
Source: Martin Stopford, 2007

**Table 9.4** The economies of the Atlantic trading countries 2005

| Country | Size | | Economic activity | | Country | Size | | Economic activity | |
|---|---|---|---|---|---|---|---|---|---|
| | Area m ha | Pop. million | GDP US$bill. | GNP/Cap US$ | | Area m ha | Pop. million | GDP US$bill. | GNP/Cap US$ |
| **1. North America** | | | | | Latvia | 7 | 2 | 16 | 6,870 |
| Canada | 998 | 32 | 1,115 | 34,844 | Estonia | 5 | 2 | 13 | 8,125 |
| USA | 937 | 297 | 12,455 | 42,007 | Lithuania | 7 | 3 | 26 | 7,500 |
| Total | 1935 | 329 | 13,570 | 41,309 | Poland | 31 | 38 | 299 | 7,832 |
| **2. Caribbean & Central America** | | | | | Total | 1786 | 157 | 1311 | 5,333 |
| Mexico | 196 | 103 | 768 | 7,456 | **6. Mediterranean Sea** | | | | |
| Guatemala | 11 | 13 | 32 | 2,462 | Turkey | 78 | 73 | 363 | 4,973 |
| Honduras | 11 | 8 | 8 | 1,000 | Greece | 13 | 11 | 214 | 19,455 |
| Nicaragua | 13 | 5 | 5 | 1,000 | Israel | 2 | 7 | 123 | 17,571 |
| Costa Rica | 5 | 4 | 19 | 4,750 | Syria | 19 | 19 | 26 | 1,368 |
| Panama | 8 | 3 | 15 | 5,000 | Cyprus | 1 | | | |
| Dominican Rep. | 5 | 28 | 28 | 1,000 | Jordan | 9 | 5 | 13 | 2,600 |
| El Salvador | 2 | 74 | 17 | 230 | | 122 | 115 | 739 | 6,426 |
| Trinidad & Tobago | 1 | 15 | 15 | 1,000 | **7. Black Sea** | | | | |
| Jamaica | 1 | 3 | 10 | 3,333 | Georgia | 7 | 5 | 6 | 1,422 |
| Puerto Rico | 1 | 4 | 8 | 2,000 | Bulgaria | 11 | 8 | 27 | 3,455 |
| Total | 267 | 269 | 929 | 3,454 | Romania | 24 | 22 | 99 | 4,565 |
| **3. E. Coast S. America** | | | | | Total | 102 | 81 | 213 | 2,637 |
| Brazil | 851 | 186 | 794 | 4,269 | **8. North Africa** | | | | |
| Venezuela | 91 | 27 | 139 | 5,148 | Egypt | 100 | 74 | 89 | 1,203 |
| Colombia | 114 | 46 | 122 | 2,652 | Algeria | 238 | 33 | 102 | 3,091 |
| Uruguay | 18 | 3 | 17 | 5,667 | Tunisia | 16 | 10 | 29 | 2,900 |
| Argentina | 277 | 39 | 5 | 128 | **9 West Africa** | | | | |
| Total | 1793 | 302 | 635 | 2,101 | Morocco | 45 | 30 | 52 | 1,733 |
| **4. Western Europe** | | | | | Mauritania | 103 | 3 | 5 | 1,800 |
| Germany | 36 | 82 | 2,782 | 33,927 | Senegal | 20 | 12 | 8 | 667 |
| United Kingdom | 24 | 60 | 2,193 | 36,550 | Guinea | 25 | 9 | 3 | 333 |
| France | 55 | 61 | 2,110 | 34,590 | Sierra Leone | 7 | 6 | 1 | 124 |
| Italy | 30 | 57 | 1,723 | 30,228 | Liberia | 10 | 3 | 1 | 333 |
| Spain | 50 | 43 | 1,124 | 26,140 | Cote d'Ivoire | 32 | 18 | 16 | 889 |
| Netherlands | 4 | 16 | 595 | 37,188 | Ghana | 24 | 22 | 11 | 500 |
| Belgium | 3 | 10 | 365 | 36,500 | Nigeria | 92 | 132 | 99 | 750 |
| Norway | 32 | 5 | 284 | 56,800 | Cameroon | 48 | 16 | 17 | 1,063 |
| Denmark | 4 | 5 | 254 | 50,800 | Gabon | 27 | 1 | 8 | 8,000 |
| Ireland | 7 | 4 | 196 | 49,000 | Congo | 34 | 58 | 7 | 121 |
| Portugal | 9 | 11 | 173 | 15,727 | Angola | 125 | 16 | 28 | 1,750 |
| Total | 256 | 354 | 11,799 | 33,331 | Namibia | 235 | 6 | 2 | 333 |
| **5. The Baltic Sea** | | | | | Total | 825 | 332 | 258 | 778 |
| Sweden | 45 | 9 | 354 | 39,333 | **10 South Africa** | 122 | 45 | 1,124 | 24,978 |
| Finland | 34 | 5 | 193 | 38,600 | **Total Atlantic** | 7,860 | 2,107 | 30,837 | 14,636 |
| Russia | 1708 | 143 | 764 | 5,333 | | | | | |

Source: Compiled from various sources, including the United Nations

Regional groupings based on data availability. Not all trading countries are shown

combined Pacific and the Indian oceans. The North Atlantic is particularly well served, with the rivers Rhine and Elbe providing water transport deep into Europe and the St Lawrence and Mississippi deep into North America. The five associated seas, the Baltic, the Mediterranean, the Black Sea, the Gulf of Mexico and the Caribbean, also play an important part in trade, extending the coastline accessible to merchant ships.

In 2005 the Atlantic region had a population of 2.1 billion and $31 trillion GDP (see Table 9.4).

There is heavy maritime traffic in both directions across the North-Atlantic, with smaller North–South liner trades. Containers are now one of the most important trades, but there are also substantial movements of oil and raw materials, with exports of grain, coal, iron ore and forest products from North America. In the east, the Suez Canal provides access to the Indian Ocean, via the Red Sea, and the Panama Canal provides a short cut to the Pacific in the East. The Mediterranean Sea is an important trading area in its own right, and the Black Sea, entered through the Dardanelles, is a busy waterway which carries heavy tanker traffic from Russia and the Caspian. To the north the Baltic Sea gives access to north-eastern Europe, Scandinavia and Russia via the Gulf of Finland, whilst northern Russia can also be reached via the Norwegian Sea. North-western Europe is well endowed with ports, and the Rhine and the Elbe are navigable deep into the continent. These routes will become increasingly important as the trade of Russia and the Baltic states develops. On the other side of the North Atlantic, Hudson's Bay and the Great Lakes provide seagoing vessels seasonal access two thousand miles into North America, and the East Coast is well endowed with ports. In the south the Gulf of Mexico provides excellent sea access, leading to the Panama Canal and on into the Pacific Ocean. The St Lawrence, Mississippi and River Plate are all major trading highways.

The South Atlantic is less busy than the North. We can see from Table 9.1 that East Coast South America accounts for only 5% of world trade, and the west coast of Africa only 2%. Little of this trade moves across the South Atlantic between the two, and most of the ship movements are container services, raw materials for export and through-traffic.

## The Pacific maritime area

The Pacific stretches from Balboa on the Panama Canal in the West to Singapore and the Straits of Malacca in the East, and it has a very different maritime character from the Atlantic. A map of the Pacific is shown in Figure 9.5 and some basic economic statistics of the larger countries can be found in Table 9.5. One obvious difference is size. The Pacific is twice as big as the Atlantic, occupying about one-third of the globe, so the distances are much greater. It is 10,300 miles from the Panama Canal in the East to Singapore in the West, and the Chinese coast where many of the busiest ports are located is 8600 miles or 27 days' steaming at 13 knots. But the map is visually misleading as the steaming times show. From Vancouver to Japan is half the steaming time of Balboa to Hong Kong.

The countries of the Pacific which trade by sea cover a smaller area than the countries of the Atlantic (2.7 billion hectares, compared with 7.9 billion hectares). In 2005 they had a similar population (1.9 billion compared with 2.1 billion) and roughly one-third of the GDP ($9.6 trillion compared with $31 trillion). China has half the region's population, with 1.3 billion people. Compared with the United States whose population is 297 million, China is a massive country, though the area of 9.6 million hectares is similar to the USA's 9.4 million hectares. Unlike the North Atlantic (and the Mediterranean in earlier times), the Pacific is not an ocean basin ringed by industrial economies. The 'rim' countries of West Coast America have little of the heavy industry

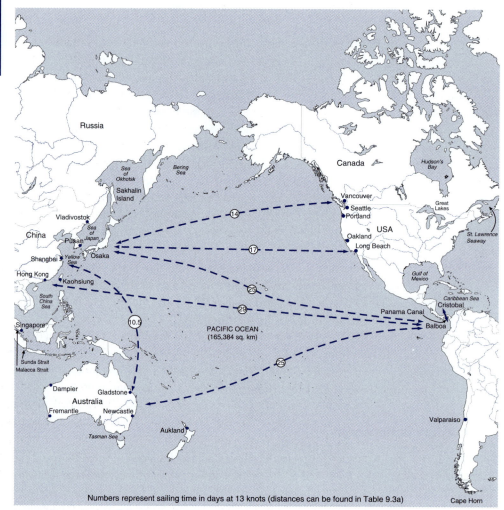

Numbers represent sailing time in days at 13 knots (distances can be found in Table 9.3a)

**Figure 9.5**
The major seas and ports of the Pacific Ocean
Source: Martin Stopford, 2007

which generates bulk trade, and most of the industry is found in a narrow 3,000 mile band stretching from the Sea of Japan in the north, through the South China Sea to the Straits of Malacca in the south (see Figure 9.5). This area, which has as coastal states Japan, South Korea, China, Hong Kong, Indonesia, Malaysia, Taiwan, the Philippines, Vietnam, Thailand and Singapore, generates seaborne inflows of energy, food and raw materials, matched by outflows of manufactured goods such as steel, vehicles, cement and general cargo. It also has the world's busiest concentration of container traffic. It has no geographical name, but for convenience we will refer to it as maritime Asia.

**Table 9.5** The economies of the Pacific trading countries 2005

| Country | Size | | | Economic activity | | |
|---|---|---|---|---|---|---|
| | Area mill HA | Pop. million | Arable m. ha | GNP US$ bill. | GNP/Cap US$ | Steel mt |
| **Asia** | | | | | | |
| Japan | 38 | 128 | 5 | 4,506 | 35,203 | 113 |
| China | 960 | 1,305 | 97 | 2,229 | 1,708 | 342 |
| Korea, Rep. | 10 | 48 | 2 | 788 | 16,417 | 48 |
| Indonesia | 190 | 221 | 22 | 287 | 1,299 | 3 |
| Hong Kong | 0 | 7 | 0 | 178 | 25,429 | 0 |
| Thailand | 51 | 64 | 20 | 177 | 2,766 | 1 |
| Malaysia | 33 | 25 | 5 | 130 | 5,200 | 1 |
| Singapore | 0 | 4 | 0 | 117 | 29,250 | 1 |
| Philippines | 30 | 83 | 8 | 98 | 1,181 | 1 |
| Vietnam | 33 | 83 | 6 | 52 | N/A | 0 |
| Korea, PDR | 12 | 22 | 2 | | N/A | 7 |
| Other | 198 | | 5 | | | 0 |
| Total Asia | 1556 | 1990 | 172 | 8562 | 4,303 | 517 |
| **Oceania** | | | | | | |
| Australia | 771 | 20 | 47 | 701 | 35,050 | 6 |
| New Zealand | 27 | 4 | 0 | 109 | 27,250 | 1 |
| Papua New Guinea | 46 | 6 | 0 | 5 | 833 | 0 |
| Other Oceania | 9 | | 1 | | | 0 |
| Total | 854 | 30 | 48 | 815 | 27,167 | 7 |
| **West Coast South America** | | | | | | |
| Ecuador | 28 | 13 | 3 | 36 | 2,769 | 0 |
| Bolivia | 110 | 9 | 2 | 9 | 1,000 | 0 |
| Peru | 129 | 28 | 4 | 78 | 2,786 | 0 |
| Chile | 76 | 16 | 4 | 115 | 7,188 | 1 |
| Total | 342 | 66 | 13 | 238 | 3,606 | 1 |
| Total Pacific | 2752 | 2086 | 234 | 9,615 | 4,609 | 525 |

Compiled from various sources

Regional groupings based on data availability. Not all trading countries are shown

Finally, nestling in the South-west corner of the Pacific (Figure 9.5), about 3,000 miles from the South China Sea, is the region known as Oceania. This grouping includes Australia, New Zealand, Papua New Guinea and various small islands. Because Oceania has only 30 million inhabitants (less than some Chinese provinces) and is rich in natural resources it is one of the principal suppliers of raw materials and energy to maritime Asia, with major exports of iron ore, coal, bauxite, grain forest products and gas. In 2005 Oceania exported 618 mt of cargo and imported 88 mt. Iron ore (241 mt), coal (233 mt) and grain (22 mt) are the major exports, though wool, meat and a range of other primary commodities are also traded.

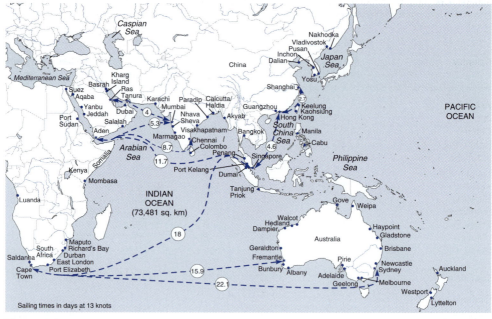

**Figure 9.6**
The major seas and ports of the Indian Ocean.
Note: Sailing times in days at 13 knots.
Source: Martin Stopford, 2007

## The Indian Ocean maritime area

The Indian Ocean is bounded by India, Pakistan and Iran to the north, eastern Africa to the west, Antarctica to the south, and Australia and Indonesia to the east (Figure 9.6). The eastern boundary with the Pacific is generally drawn through Malaya, Indonesia, Australia and the South East Cape of Tasmania to Antarctica. The six seas of the Indian Ocean, which have a long history in seaborne trade, are the Red Sea, the Arabian Gulf, the Arabian Sea (between Arabia and India), the Bay of Bengal (between India and the Thai peninsula), the Timor Sea, and the Arafura Sea (between Australia and Indonesia).

The countries of the Indian Ocean have a land area of 4.3 billion hectares, which is 56% bigger than the Pacific (excluding North America). However, the Indian Ocean itself is more compact than the Pacific and distances on the East–West routes fall midway between the Atlantic and the Pacific. From Singapore to Aden at the entrance to the Red Sea is 3600 miles via the Malacca Straits and takes 12 days at 13 knots, whilst the Cape of Good Hope is 5600 miles and takes 18 days.

Starting at the bottom left of Figure 9.6, the East African coast has few deep sea ports. This stretch of coastline runs from South Africa up to the Red Sea, and includes

**Table 9.6** The economies of the Indian Ocean trading countries, 2005

| Country | Size | | | Economic activity | | |
|---|---|---|---|---|---|---|
| | Area mill HA | Pop. million | Arable m. ha | GNP US$ bill. | GNP/Cap US$ | Steel mt |
| **S. Asia** | | | | | | |
| India | 329 | 1,095 | 170 | 785 | 717 | 38 |
| Pakistan | 80 | 156 | 21 | 111 | 712 | 1 |
| Sri Lanka | 7 | 20 | 2 | 23 | 1,150 | — |
| Bangladesh | 14 | 142 | 9 | 60 | 423 | 0 |
| Bhutan | 5 | 1 | 0 | 1 | 1,000 | — |
| Other | 2 | | 0 | | | — |
| Total | 515 | 1,414 | 213 | 980 | 693 | 14 |
| **Middle East** | | | | | | |
| Saudi Arabia | 215 | 25 | 2 | 310 | 12,400 | 4 |
| Iran | 165 | 68 | 15 | 196 | 2,882 | 9 |
| Kuwait | 2 | 3 | 0 | 75 | 25,000 | — |
| Yemen, Rep. | 53 | 21 | 2 | 14 | 667 | — |
| Qatar | 1 | 0 | 0 | 7 | 18,450 | 1 |
| Iraq | 44 | | 5 | | | — |
| Oman | 21 | 3 | 0 | | 0 | — |
| UAE | 8 | 5 | 0 | | 0 | — |
| Other M.East | 0 | | 0 | | | — |
| Total | 510 | 129 | 25 | 624 | 4,825 | 14 |
| **East Africa** | | | | | | |
| Sudan | 251 | 36 | 13 | 28 | n/a | — |
| Mauritius | 0 | 1 | 1 | 6 | 6,000 | — |
| Somalia | 64 | 1 | 1 | 8 | 8,000 | — |
| Kenya | 58 | 34 | 2 | 18 | 529 | — |
| Madagascar | 59 | 19 | 3 | 5 | 263 | — |
| Djibouti | 2 | 1 | N/A | 1 | 1000 | — |
| Mozambique | 80 | 20 | 3 | 7 | 350 | — |
| Total | 514 | 112 | 23 | 73 | 652 | — |
| Total Indian Ocean | 4359 | 1,751 | 322 | 2,730 | 1,559 | 258 |
| Pacific & Indian Ocean Total | 7,111 | 3,837 | 556 | 12,345 | | |

Source: Compiled from various sources

Regional groupings based on data availability. Not all trading countries are shown

Mozambique, Tanzania, Kenya and Somalia. These countries have an area the size of South Asia, a population of 112 million, and a GDP of $73 billion (Table 9.6). Despite their size, none of these countries have strong economies or rich reserves of primary commodities, so the volume of trade is very small – only 9 mt of exports and 23.9 mt of imports in 2005. The only ports of any size are Maputo, Beira, Dar es Salaam, Mombasa, and Mogadishu. The volume of cargo through these ports is small, the facilities are primitive, and they have little impact on the shipping market as a whole, other than as a continuing source of work for small general cargo ships.

Moving east, we come to the Red Sea, a busy highway for traffic through the Suez Canal linking the Mediterranean and the Arabian Gulf. This is a remote location,

12,000 miles from the USA and 6,000 miles from Asia, flanked by Egypt and Sudan to the west and Saudi Arabia to the east. Turning right past the entrance to the Gulf we come to Pakistan, India, Bangladesh, Myanmar (Burma) and various smaller countries. These densely populated countries have an area of 0.5 billion hectares and a population of 1.1 billion. They produce 254 mt of cereals, much the same as the USA as well as 229 mt of coal and 57 mt of iron ore. However, most of these commodities never enter trade, and India's GDP of $785 billion in 2005 was relatively low, about the same as South Korea's $788 billion. About half of the import volume is crude oil and oil products, since domestic reserves are very limited. There are sizable exports of iron ore from India.

India has 11 major sea ports: Kandla, Mumbai, Nhava Sheva, Marmagao, New Mangalore, and Kochi on the west coast, and Kolkata-Haldia, Paradip, Vishakhapatnam, Chennai, and Tuticorin on the east coast. The volume of trade is moderate and Mumbai, Vishakhapatnam, Chennai, and Marmagao are the most important ports in terms of cargo tonnage. Bulk cargo is dominated by iron ore exports from Marmagao, crude oil imports and oil products exports.

## The Suez and Panama canals

Finally, we must consider those two great works of engineering which provide short cuts between the oceans, the Suez Canal and the Panama Canal. The Suez Canal, which opened in 1869, links the Red Sea at Suez with the Mediterranean at Port Said, providing a much shorter route between the North Atlantic and the Indian Ocean than the alternative route round the Cape of Good Hope. For example, the Suez Canal reduces the transit distance from Rotterdam to Mumbai by 42%, and to Singapore by around 30%. Other examples of the saving in distance are shown in Table 9.7. It can accommodate vessels with beam up to 64 metres and draft up to 16.2 metres, which in practice means tankers up to 150,000 dwt fully loaded and 370,000 dwt in ballast. The canal is 100 miles long and transit takes 13–15 hours. Tolls are charged in US dollars based on the Suez Canal net tonnage of the ship, with separate rates for laden and ballast voyages (the Suez Canal net tonnage of a vessel roughly corresponds to the cargo carrying below deck space, though it is not directly comparable with the gross or deadweight tonnage. It is calculated by either the classification society

**Table 9.7** Distances saved by using Suez Canal (miles)

|  | By Cape | By Canal | Saving |
|---|---|---|---|
| *Rotterdam to:* |  |  | % |
| Mumbai | 10,800 | 6,300 | 42% |
| Kuwait | 11,300 | 6,500 | 42% |
| Melbourne | 12,200 | 11,000 | 10% |
| Calcutta | 11,700 | 7,900 | 32% |
| Singapore | 11,800 | 8,300 | 30% |
| *Marseilles to:* |  |  |  |
| Mumbai | 10,400 | 4,600 | 56% |
| Melbourne | 11,900 | 9,400 | 21% |
| *New York to:* |  |  |  |
| Mumbai | 11,800 | 8,200 | 31% |
| Singapore | 12,500 | 10,200 | 18% |
| Ras Tanura | 11,765 | 9,543 | 19% |

or an official trade organization which issues a Suez Canal Special Tonnage Certificate).

The Panama Canal, an even more challenging engineering feat, was opened in 1914, shortening the distance from the Atlantic to Pacific by 7,000–9,000 miles. It runs 83 kilometres from the Atlantic at Cristobal to the Pacific at Balboa, through a mountain range. Ships entering from the Atlantic sail down a channel to Gatun Locks where the ship is lifted to Gatun Lake. After crossing this lake the ship enters Gaillard Cut and runs about 8 miles to Pedro Miguel where another lock lowers it to a small lake. Across this lake at Mira Flores two more locks lower the vessel to the Pacific Ocean. A vessel of medium size can pass through the canal in about 9 hours and a transit booking system allows transit slots to be reserved. Although the nominal draft restriction is 11.28 metres (37 feet), the water level varies from 35 feet during droughts to 39 feet during wet spells. This means that a 65,000 dwt Panamax beam bulk carrier with a 43 foot draft cannot transit the canal fully loaded – the average bulk carrier with a draft of 37 feet is 40,000 dwt. Bigger ships often load part cargoes. The transit charges for the Panama Canal are based on a fixed tariff per (Panama Canal) net ton for vessels transiting laden and in ballast. In September 2007 work started on an eight-year project to develop the canal locks to accommodate vessels 427 metres long, 55 metres wide and 18.3 metres deep.

## 9.4 EUROPE'S SEABORNE TRADE

Europe, still one of the world's biggest trading regions, splits into three main areas which are defined in Table 9.4 as Western Europe, the Baltic Sea and the Mediterranean Sea. Western Europe accounts for 23% of world imports and exports, whilst Russia and Eastern Europe account for another 3% (see Table 9.1). This makes its trade twice the size of that of North America. Over the last 40 years exports have grown more consistently than imports which stagnated in the early 1970s, fell in the early 1980s and then resumed low growth (Figure 9.7).

In 2005 Europe imported 2.1 billion tonnes of cargo and exported 1.2 billion tonnes, explaining why European companies play a leading part in the shipping industry, owning 42% of the world fleet. Europe's importance in trade is explained

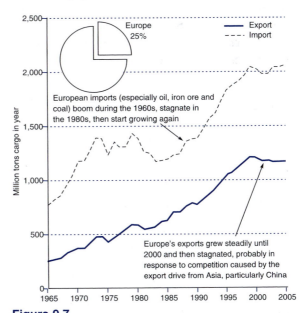

**Figure 9.7**
Europe's seaborne trade
Source: United Nations and UNCTAD

by its developed economy and large population which stretches its domestic resources, with the result that the region relies heavily on trade. The population of 353 million (excluding the Baltic, Mediterranean and Black Sea countries) produced a GDP of $11.8 trillion in 2005. The cereals crop is typically about 260 mt, slightly less than North America. Through intensive agriculture and protectionist policies the European Union region has achieved self-sufficiency, with a small exportable surplus. Although Europe was originally well endowed with all the major raw materials except bauxite, reserves are now depleted and expensive to produce.

Europe is very effective as a maritime area, with water on all sides except the border with Russia, as Figure 9.8 clearly shows. The west coast faces the Atlantic Ocean, with the Baltic Sea to the north, the Mediterranean Sea to the south and the Black Sea to the east. With so much water, maritime transport plays a major part in its economy; the economic data for these areas can be found in Table 9.4. Starting in the far north-east corner

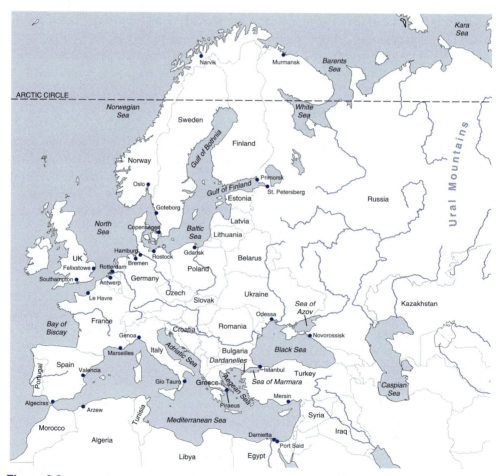

**Figure 9.8**
The major seas and ports of Europe
Source: Martin Stopford, 2007

of Figure 9.8, we find the north coast of Russia and Scandinavia. Narvik, the most northerly port, exports iron ore, and the opening of Russian oil trade in the 1990s gave Murmansk a new significance. Russia and eastern Europe, only account for about 3% of seaborne trade, but this is an important area of development and change. The opening up of the countries in this region to the global economy and free trade flows was a tremendously important development, given its geographical size and resource base.

Moving south, the Baltic ports handle the trade of Finland, Russia, the Baltic States (Latvia, Lithuania and Estonia), Poland, northern Germany and Sweden. The break-up of the Soviet Union changed the pattern of trade with these states, and the Gulf of Finland in the north Baltic gives sea access to the Russian ports. Forest products, oil, coal and general cargo are shipped through the ports of St Petersburg, Ventspils, Primorsk, Gdansk, Rostock, Świnoujście, Stockholm and Malmö. Moving south, Hamburg and Bremen, located on the rivers Elbe and Weser, serve Germany and its hinterland. These are important bulk ports, handling grain, fertilizers, steel and motor cars, but in recent years their real prominence has been in the container trade.

Europe's north-west coast is one of the busiest shipping areas in the world, with major ports at Hamburg, Bremen, Antwerp, Rotterdam and Le Havre. The Rhine, which is navigable by 2,000 ton barges for 800 km from Basel, enters the North Sea at Rotterdam. The Rhine handles over 500 mt of cargo a year, and Rotterdam is Europe's largest port. It is located on the New Rotterdam Waterway and the New Meuse, and the port itself is subdivided into three main areas, Maasvlakte at the entrance, Europoort and Botlek. Each contains a network of deep water specialist terminals, handling oil, grain, coal, forest products, motor vehicles, and petrochemicals. This is also the principal route for containers moving into Europe. In 2006 Hamburg handled 8.1 million TEU of containers, Bremerhaven 3.7 million TEU, Rotterdam handled 9.6 million TEU, while nearby Antwerp handled 6.5 million TEU. Le Havre is France's main northern port, handling 2.1 million TEU of containers, while the United Kingdom is served by Felixstowe, Southampton and Tilbury.

The ports of Mediterranean Europe serve the industrial areas in eastern Spain and the industrial belt running from Marseilles through to Trieste in Northern Italy. Marseilles, Genoa and Trieste are all important ports, handling grain, iron ore, oil, minor bulks and containers. The biggest container terminals are at Algeciras in southern Spain (3.2 million TEU in 2006) and Genoa in Italy (1.4 million TEU in 2006). Ten countries occupy the eastern and southern coasts of the Mediterranean (see Table 9.4), with GDP of about $1 trillion and a population of 238 million. This is a growing area for trade, with exports of oil, minerals and containers. Finally, the Black Sea provides sea access to southern Russia, Georgia, Ukraine, Bulgaria and Romania. It has a busy export trade for oil shipped from Russia and Kazakhstan.

In conclusion, western Europe is a major influence on the shipping market, still generating a large volume of seaborne trade. With the maturing of the economy the growth has moved from raw material imports to a more balanced trade in manufactures and semi-manufactures.

## 9.5 NORTH AMERICA'S SEABORNE TRADE

North America, which includes Canada and the USA, accounted for 12% of world seaborne trade in 2005, and its import trade grew from 294 mt in 1965 to 1124 mt in 2005, whilst exports are lower, increasing from 232 mt to 598 mt (Figure 9.9). It is the world's largest economic region, with a population of 329 million and a GDP in excess of $13.6 trillion, a quarter of the world's GDP. With a total area of 1.9 million hectares, it is eight times the size of western Europe. In 2006 the USA produced 100 mt of steel, 329 mt of cereals, 368 mt of oil, 951 mt of coal, 509 billion cubic metres of natural gas and 55 mt of iron ore. As one of the world's richest areas, the North American market for manufactures has grown rapidly and imports of motor vehicles and a wide array of containerized consumer goods have increasingly been supplied by Europe and the Far East.

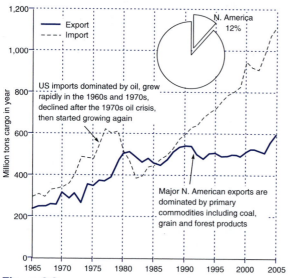

**Figure 9.9**
North America's seaborne trade
Source: United Nations and UNCTAD

Geographically North America falls into three areas – a hilly eastern strip where much of the heavy industry is located around the coal and iron ore fields near Chicago and Pittsburgh; a flat central area given over to farming, particularly grain; and a mountainous West, with the Rocky Mountains dividing the Pacific coast from the rest of North America (Figure 9.10). The central area and East Coast are served by two major waterways, the Great Lakes and the Mississippi-Missouri. In the north the St Lawrence Seaway, which stretches from Montreal to Lake Erie, gives access from the North Atlantic 2340 miles (3766 km) into the heartland of Canada and USA. In addition to providing an export route for grain, the lakes provide local transport for the heavy industrial belt of Pittsburgh, Chicago and Detroit. However, the locks can only handle vessels of about 32,000 dwt[5] and the navigation season is limited by ice to the period from April to early December; so much of the bulk cargo is transhipped at ports in the St Lawrence. The Mississippi and its tributaries give the central area, including most of the grain belt, water access to the US Gulf. The river system carried 615 mt of cargo in 2005, of which 150 mt was in foreign trade. Two intracoastal waterways link the US Gulf with the East Coast, extending from Boston, Massachusetts, to Key West, Florida, with many sections in tidal water or in open sea.[6]

Depletion of domestic oil reserves means that crude oil and products are the most important import, along with containers. Dry bulk exports include coal, grain, forest products, sulphur and various minor bulks such as steel scrap. North America is the world's largest grain exporter, with production from two grain belts running through the US Midwest and the Canadian Prairies, and the grain is exported through the Gulf, the Great Lakes or the Pacific Coast. Coal, mainly from Appalachian coalfields on the East Coast and Canadian coalfields in the west, is exported through ports such as Norfolk and Hampton Roads or US Gulf in the East and Vancouver in the West. Forest products are mainly shipped from the north-western ports, particularly Vancouver and Seattle, using container-ships or open hatch bulk carriers.

The locations of the main North American ports are shown in Figure 9.10. In the far north-east the port of Churchill in Hudson Bay lies close to Canada's western grain

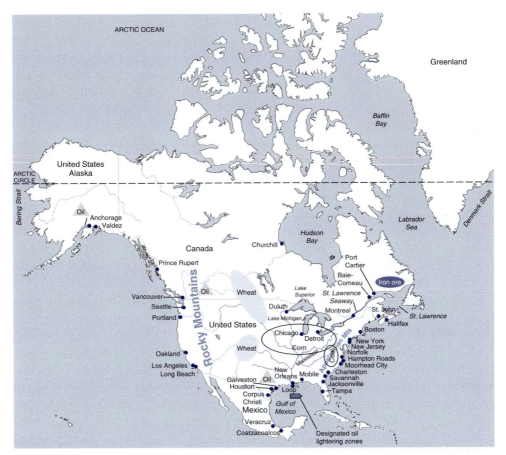

**Figure 9.10**
The major seas and ports of North America
Source: Martin Stopford, 2007

production, though the shipping season is limited by ice to July–October. Moving south, several important bulk ports are located in the Great Lakes and Thunder Bay and Duluth at the head of the Great Lakes handle grain exports and steel products. At the mouth of the St Lawrence Sept-Isles and Baie-Comeau are navigable all year and handle grain trans-shipment, iron ore and a wide range of other trades. To the south are Boston, New York, with its New Jersey container terminal, Philadelphia, Baltimore, Hampton Roads, Morehead City, Charleston and Savannah. Since this is a busy industrial area, all these ports have frequent container services. The largest in 2005 were New York (4.8 million TEU), Hampton Roads (2.0 million TEU) and Charleston (2.0 million TEU). The main bulk export volume is coal, shipped from Hampton Roads and Baltimore. All these ports have draft restrictions which mainly limit access to vessels of 60,000–80,000 dwt, thus excluding the largest bulk carriers and tankers.

Heading south from Jacksonville, we turn right into the US Gulf and come to Tampa, a cruise and container port, with some bulk trades such as steel. Beyond Tampa a string of oil and chemical terminals stretches along the Gulf, starting with the Louisiana Offshore Oil Port (LOOP) off New Orleans, Houston, Galveston and Corpus Christi. For historical reasons the US refinery and gas distribution systems centre on this area where imported oil is refined and distributed through a network of barge and pipeline services. The LOOP is located off the Louisiana coast near Port Fourchon and is the only deep water oil terminal in the USA capable of handling VLCCs, though lightering areas offshore allow VLCCs to be used in the trade and discharged into smaller tankers for delivery to the other more restricted terminals in the Gulf. Lightering is a way of delivering cargo in ships too big to access local terminals. The cargo is transferred from the large ships to smaller ships or barges which can access local terminals, usually in designated offshore zones. The LOOP handles about 1.2 million barrels a day, and connects by pipeline to 35% of the US refining capability. The Gulf is also an important export route for bulk cargoes. The Mississippi provides water transport deep into the continent carrying exports of coal and grain. Eleven grain export elevators capable of loading seagoing ships are strung along the river as far inland as Baton Rouge. Houston, the largest Gulf port, handles oil, grain, containers and chemicals.

Access to the West Coast of North America from the US Gulf requires a lengthy detour through the Panama Canal, and it has a very different maritime character. It is divided from the rest of the continent by the Rocky Mountains, with no major navigable rivers, so inland cargo mainly travels by rail or road. In the far north Valdez, the USA's most northerly ice-free port, is the export terminal for Alaskan crude oil, whilst Anchorage handles general cargo. Further south, Prince Rupert handles moderate quantities of Canadian grain exports, with the main traffic going through the port of Vancouver, located on the mainland opposite Vancouver island and handling about 80 million tons of cargo a year, mainly Canadian exports of coal, grain, forest products, potash and other minerals such as sulphur and 2.2 million containers in 2006. There are major coal-handling terminals at Roberts Bank and Neptune Terminals, and many smaller specialist terminals. Seattle, located 100 miles to the south, fulfils a similar function for the United States, with major exports of grain and forest products. It also has a large container terminal with shipments of 2 million boxes in 2006 as does Tacoma, a few miles to the south, which also lifted 2 million TEU in 2006. The fourth major port in this northern area is Portland, which handles grain and some container traffic. Further south, California's ports of Oakland, San Francisco and Los Angeles (Long Beach) all serve this thriving West Coast economy. There is some bulk cargo and oil into San Francisco and Los Angeles, but the main trade is container traffic. Oakland shipped over 2.4 million TEU in 2006. The main ports of California are San Francisco and Los Angeles, which service the rapidly growing economy of the south-western United States. These ports have facilities for handling imports of crude oil, vehicles and steel, and there are also major container terminals in Los Angeles and Long Beach. Both ports handled over 7 million containers a year, placing them in the top 20 container ports world-wide in 2006.

## 9.6 SOUTH AMERICA'S SEABORNE TRADE

South America has a very different trading pattern from North America. It is still mainly a primary producing region, generating about 974 mt of exports and 368 mt of imports each year, as shown by the graph in Figure 9.11. Over the last 40 years exports have followed a volatile path upwards, more than doubling between 1985 and 2005, whilst since the early 1970s imports have grown slowly. Broadly speaking, the region falls into three parts: the Caribbean and Central America; East Coast South America; and West Coast South America. Each has a very different character. The countries are shown in Figure 9.12 and their economic data in Table 9.4.

The Caribbean and Central America region starts with Mexico in the north, takes in the Caribbean islands and stretches down the coast-line to Belize, Honduras, Nicaragua, Costa Rica and Panama. The population of 269 million in 2005 and GDP of about $0.92 trillion, less than one-tenth the size of North America, is spread among many islands and the coastal states ringing the southern shores of the Gulf of Mexico.

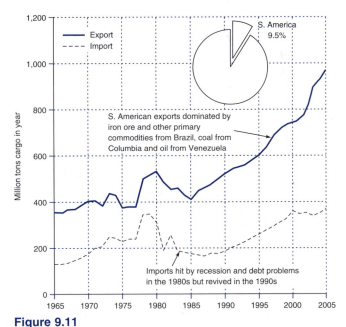

**Figure 9.11**
South America's seaborne trade
Source: United Nations and UNCTAD

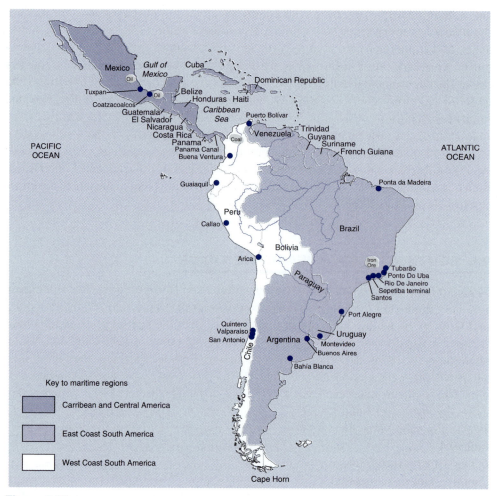

**Figure 9.12**
The main countries and ports of South America
Source: United Nations and UNCTAD

The main export trade is Mexico's oil mainly to the US Gulf and to a lesser extent Europe. Its oilfields were developed in the 1970s and 1980s and are now maturing. The oil is shipped principally from the port of Coatzacoalcos on the southern Gulf, which is the focal point for the seven major oilfields of Mexico. Other Caribbean exports are bauxite from Jamaica, crude oil imported by refineries in Trinidad and Tobago and Netherlands Antilles for refining and on shipment to the United States, sugar from Cuba and bananas.

Like North America, South America is split in two by a high mountain range, the Andes, which runs from north to south along the western coast, splitting it into two regions, East Coast South America and West Coast South America. Using the UNCTAD regional definitions, East Coast South America stretches along the Atlantic coast from Venezuela, Guyana and Surinam in the north through Brazil to Argentina in the south. With an area of 1.8 billion hectares and a population of

302 million, it is the same size as North America and drains into the Atlantic through three major river systems, the Orinoco, the Amazon and the River Plate. It is, however, a much smaller economy. South America's GDP of $0.6 trillion is only 5% of North America's. With so much space and so little economic activity, we would expect primary exports to predominate, and this is exactly what has happened. The trade of this very long coastline is dominated by exports of raw materials and semi-manufactures.

In 2005 East Coast South America exported 558 mt of cargo and imported 153 mt. Dry cargo exports of 393 mt were made up of iron ore from Brazil and Venezuela, and smaller quantities of coal, crude fertilizers, forest products, minor ores and crude minerals such as salt. A declining trend in oil exports was largely offset by a moderate increase in dry cargo. Brazil is the world's leading exporter of iron ore, and during the 1960s and 1970s developed iron ore deposits served by deep-water export terminals. Iron ore exports have grown from 7 mt in 1963 to 249 mt in 2006, accounting for over one-third of the global iron ore trade. The main iron ore export ports are Tubarão, Ponta do Uba, Sepetiba Bay and Ponta da Madeira. The area is well served by liner services linking it to North America, western Europe and Asia.

West Coast South America forms a thin coastal strip running from Columbia and Ecuador in the north, through Peru to Chile, which occupies over half its length. Its area is only 342 million hectares (see Table 9.5) with a population in 2005 of 66 million and GDP of $238 billion (about the same as Denmark), so it is much smaller than East Coast South America. The ports on this coast are relatively small, with few major primary commodity exports, so the volume of trade is restricted to servicing the local semi-industrial economy. In 2005 the region exported 152 mt of cargo and imported 56 mt. The main container ports are at Guayaquil, the principal port of Ecuador, Callao, the principal port of Peru, and Valparaiso and San Antonio, the principal ports of Chile. The biggest export is coal from Columbia, which has the largest coalmining operation in Latin America, El Cerrejón Norte. The mine is connected by a 150 km railway to Puerto Bolivar on Columbia's Caribbean coast, and unit trains are used to transport crushed coal from the mine to the port, which can handle 150,000 dwt ships.

## 9.7 ASIA'S SEABORNE TRADE

Geographically Asia stretches from Japan in the north down to Indonesia in the south and to India and Pakistan in the west (see Figure 9.13). Economically these countries cluster into four groups. The first consists of Japan and its near neighbour, South Korea. They are mature industrial economies, each supporting a major concentration of maritime activity, including two-thirds of the world's shipbuilding capacity. Second, China has a long coastline stretching from Dalian to Shenzen. Third, we have Thailand, Cambodia, Vietnam, Singapore and the Malacca Straits leading to the Indian Ocean (note that India and Myanmar are also included in the trade statistics in Figure 9.14). Finally, on the southern side of the China Sea are the heavily populated

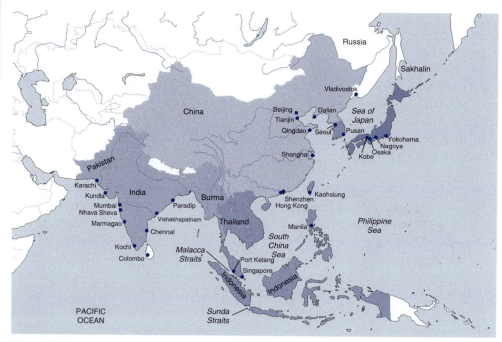

**Figure 9.13**
The main seas and ports of South and East Asia
Source: United Nations and UNCTAD

islands of Malaysia, Indonesia, and the Philippines. Taken together, Asia is the world's largest seaborne trading area, importing 2.9 billion tons of cargo in 2005 and exporting 1.6 billion tons, 50% more than western Europe. It is also growing rapidly (see Figure 9.14). The region covers 1.6 billion hectares, two-thirds of which is China, and in 2005 had a population of 2 billion and GDP of $8.6 trillion, of which half was Japan.

Between 1990 and 2005 Asia's exports trebled and imports doubled. The region is clearly moving through the material-intensive stages of the trade development cycle, a fact which becomes more apparent as we review the individual economies. The graphs of imports and exports in Figure 9.14 split the region into three parts – Japan, China and southern and eastern Asia. All three are net importers of energy, food and raw materials, with corresponding outflows of manufactured goods such as steel, vehicles, cement and general cargo.

## Japan

In 2005 Japan was the biggest economy in Asia with GDP of $4.5 billion, though China, still half this size, was catching up. Its seaborne imports of 832 million tons were also the largest, though again China was not far behind. Supporting this trade is an extensive

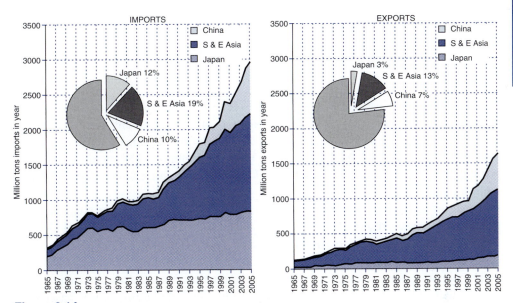

**Figure 9.14**
Asia's seaborne trade, 1965–2005
Source: United Nations and UNCTAD

industrial base. In 2006 Japan produced 115 mt of steel compared with 170 mt in western Europe and 100 mt in the United States. All the iron ore and coal for steel-making is imported, along with many other raw materials, including steam coal, oil, forest products, grain, non-ferrous metal ores and manufactures. Over the last 30 years Japan has been through a trade development cycle during which imports grew very rapidly during the 1950s and 1960s, reaching a peak of 588 mt in 1973. This was followed by a slump to 550 mt in 1983 after which growth resumed, though by 2005 imports had only edged up to 832 mt, an average growth rate of only 1% per annum. Of this total about two-thirds was iron ore, coal and crude oil. Export growth was more rapid, averaging 6% per annum between 1990 and 2005. Most of the export trade is manufactures and heavily concentrated in liner and specialist bulk cargoes, featuring motor cars, steel products, capital goods and the consumer goods for which the Japanese economy is famous.

All of the major Japanese ports are located in the industrial belt of Tokyo and Osaka-Kobe. In terms of cargo handled the biggest ports, shown in Figure 9.13, are Yokohama, Kobe, Nagoya, Osaka and Tokyo. These ports have many private terminals owned by the manufacturing companies. Yokahama is typical and its cargo gives a fair idea of the types of goods going through Japanese ports. In 2007 it handled about 90 mt of foreign cargo, with 43 mt of exports and 47 mt of imports. The imports include 6 mt of grain, 7 mt of crude oil, 6.5 mt of LNG and about 1.5 mt each of oil products, paper and pulp, processed foodstuffs, clothing, furniture, electrical machinery, non-ferrous metals, fruit and vegetables and animal feed. The exports included 14 mt of cars, 5 mt of auto parts, 5 mt of industrial machinery, 2 mt of chemicals, 1 mt of scrap and 1 mt of rubber products.

## China

In the 1990s, after five decades of virtual isolation, China emerged as the dominant maritime force in Asian trade. With a population of 1.3 billion and GNP in 2005 of $2.2 trillion growing at 9% per annum, it had an enormous impact on the maritime industry both locally and internationally. In 1990 China imported 80 mt of cargo by sea, but by 2006 imports had increased tenfold to 801 mt, and China's share of world seaborne trade increased from 1% to 10%.

Industrial activity is mainly in the coastal strip, particularly around Shanghai and Canton. Imports are resource-intensive, and 40% was associated with the steel industry and 21% with the oil industry. In 2001 China's steel production was 151 million tons, about the same as that of the European Union, but by 2006 it had reached 414 million tons, accounting for one-third of global steel production, having added capacity equivalent to that of the EU and Japan in just five years. Such rapid growth was based on a business model which was very different from the one used by Japan and South Korea in previous decades. In the 1990s the Chinese government adopted a development strategy based on a blend of state industry and private enterprise. This proved a powerful combination. Overseas investors provided technology, management skills and direct inward investment in joint venture companies which took advantage of China's low labour costs. The result was a rapidly growing export trade, mainly containerized, and a substantial trade surplus. Meanwhile the government sponsored a major infrastructure development programme spread across the provinces, designed to give the country the accommodation, roads, railways and port infrastructure needed to support economic growth. On the raw materials front China has substantial coal reserves amounting to 13% of the world total and relies mainly on coal for energy. Production was 2.2 billion tons in 2006. The country is less well endowed with oil, producing 3 million barrels per day from mature oilfields in the North West.

China has more than 40 ports, of which the biggest are Dalian, Tianjin, Shenzhen and Shanghai. Shanghai, located at the mouth of the Yangtze River, has the highest cargo volume, handling 537 million tons in 2006 and 21.7 million container lifts, making it one of the world's largest container ports. Dalian is now the largest petroleum port in China, and also the third largest port overall, handling 140 million tons of cargo in 2006. It is a natural harbour located on the southern tip of the Liadong Peninsula. Its oil terminal is at the terminus of an oil pipeline from the Daqing oilfields, and Dalian is a major centre for oil refineries, diesel engineering and chemical production.

Situated in the south of the Pearl River Delta in China's Guangdong province, Shenzhen Port is adjacent to Hong Kong. In 2004, the cargo throughput was 135 million tons, with 88.5 million tons of foreign trade. In 2006 the container throughput was 18.66 million TEU. The other major container port is Qindao. Major iron ore ports include Tianjin and the nearby Xingang, Qindao, Beilun, Dalian and Guangzho. Oil is mainly shipped in through Qindao, Huangpu, Xiamen and Tianjin.

## Southern and eastern Asia

In 2005 southern and eastern Asia[7] handled 934 mt of exports and 1384 mt of imports, making it a major maritime area. Between 1990 and 2005 exports grew by 5.3% per annum and imports by 6.1%, so the region is growing considerably faster than total sea trade. It is a region Adam Smith would have considered ideal for sea trade. The coast-line stretches through 18 countries (see Figure 9.13) mainly strung out along the bottom of the Asian continent, stretching from Indonesia in the east to Pakistan in the west. South Korea, something of an out-rider, lies to the north; India and Pakistan to the west; and the islands of Indonesia and Malaysia to the south. Singapore lies roughly at the centre. It is hard to imagine an arrangement better suited to seaborne trade. The trading countries spread around the shores of the South China and East China Seas have large, often well-educated, populations, but limited natural resources. Sea transport provides the coastal cities with easy access to materials and markets, without the need for major investment in transport infrastructure. The positions which Singapore, located at the southern tip of the Malaysian Peninsula, and Hong Kong, situated off southern China, have built up as trading and distribution centres echo the success of the city-states of Antwerp and Amsterdam in the growing North Atlantic trade and Venice and Genoa in the Mediterranean. In 2006 they were the world's two largest container ports, lifting over 23 million TEU in the year.

At the north-easterly end of the trading area lies South Korea. With a land area of 10 million hectares and GDP of $788 billion in 2005 it is about one-third the size of Japan. South Korea developed its economy in the 1970s using a model which closely matched the growth of Japan twenty years earlier. Like Japan, South Korea focused on steel, shipbuilding, motor vehicles, electronics and consumer durables, relying on aggressive export marketing of these manufactures to pay for imported raw materials and energy. Also like Japan, development was controlled by a few very large corporations, with close government involvement. The major ports of South Korea are Pusan, situated on the south-east corner of the Korean Peninsula, and Ulsan, situated 60 miles north. Pusan is the principal port of South Korea, handling about 100 million tons of cargo each year. Pohang is the cargo-handling terminal of the Pohang Steelworks (POSCO).

The remaining countries in the region are less developed. Vietnam is only just moving into the development cycle, but Thailand has a small but rapidly growing economy. Strung along the south-western boundary are Indonesia, Malaysia, the Philippines and Taiwan. However, to the west India with its population of 1.1 billion people and GDP of $785 billion in 2005, about one-third the size of China, is an area of potential growth and development in the coming decades. There is a major crude oil export trade from Indonesia and dry cargo exports include substantial quantities of forest products from Indonesia and the Philippines, and various manufactures and semi-manufactures.

## 9.8 AFRICA'S SEABORNE TRADE

Africa (see Figure 9.15) is a large continent covering 1.8 billion hectares, but its trade is smaller than might be expected from such a large continent. It is a poor region of the world, and in 2005 GDP was $758 per capita. Forty countries are engaged in seaborne trade, and in 2005 they imported 258 mt of cargo and exported 602 mt, accounting for 6% of world trade, split between North Africa (346 mt), West Africa (248 mt), East Africa (36 mt) and South Africa (211 mt) as shown in Table 9.1. Primary commodities dominate exports and three-quarters of the export cargo is oil from Algeria, Libya, Nigeria and Cameroon. Dry cargo exports are composed principally of iron ore, phosphate rock, bauxite and various agricultural products. Between 1990 and 2005 the trade volume of both imports and exports grew slowly at about 1% per annum, as shown in Figure 9.16.

West Africa stretches from Morocco in the north to Namibia in the south. The area covers 825 million hectares, three times the size of Europe, with a population of 258 million (see Table 9.4). To put this into perspective, their combined GDP was

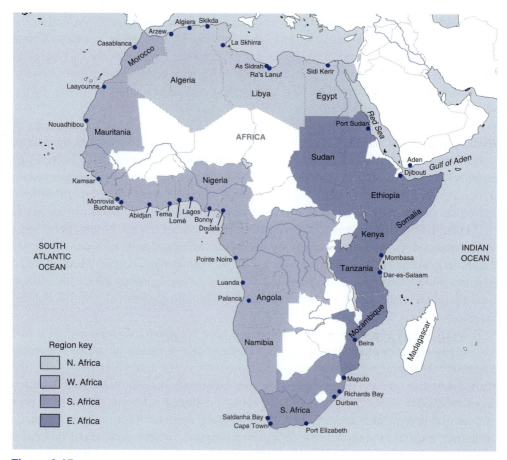

**Figure 9.15**
The main seas and ports of Africa
Source: United Nations and UNCTAD

$258 billion in 2005, the same as Denmark, and the average income was $778 per capita. As we would expect, the trade volume was also relatively low, accounting for 2% of the world total. In 2005 West Africa exported 218 mt of cargo and imported 50 mt. Two-thirds of the export cargo is oil from Nigeria. The remainder is dry cargo exports, mainly iron ore (Mauritania), phosphate rock (Morocco), bauxite (Guinea) and various agricultural products.

North Africa stretches from Egypt to Algeria, and the four countries have an area of 254 hectares and GDP of $220 billion. The average income in 2005 was over $2,000 per capita, much higher than West Africa, and Libya, a major oil exporter, had an income of $6500 per

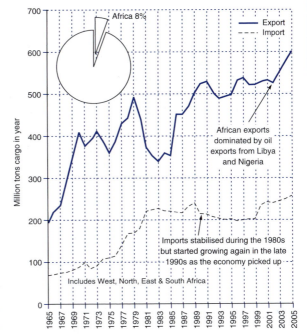

**Figure 9.16**
Africa's seaborne trade
Source: United Nations and UNCTAD

capita, making it one of the wealthiest countries in Africa. In terms of shipping North Africa exported 204 mt in 2005 and imported 142 million tons.

East Africa consists of six countries stretching from Sudan in the north to Mozambique in the south, plus two islands, Madagascar and Mauritius. It is a small economic region covering 514 million hectares, with GDP of only $73 billion in 2005 and a population of 112 million. Exports totalled 9 million tons and imports 26 million tons.

Finally, South Africa is by far the wealthiest country in Africa, with a population of 45 million and an average income of $25,000. This puts it in the same bracket as European countries in terms of size and wealth. It is an important dry bulk exporter of coal and iron ore, with deep-sea ports at Richards Bay and Saldanha Bay.

## 9.9 THE SEABORNE TRADE OF THE MIDDLE EAST, CENTRAL ASIA AND RUSSIA

The Middle East, central Asia and Russia form a convenient group because all three regional economies depend heavily on the export of oil. Between them they had 71.5% of the world's oil reserves in 2005, and in recent years they have been the marginal suppliers of this commodity to the world economy. The regional map shown in Figure 9.17 gives a rough idea of where the oil reserves are located. At the bottom of the map is the Middle East, with oilfields clustered around the Arabian Gulf in Saudi Arabia (35% of Middle East reserves), Iraq (15%), Kuwait (14%), and the United Arab Emirates (13%).

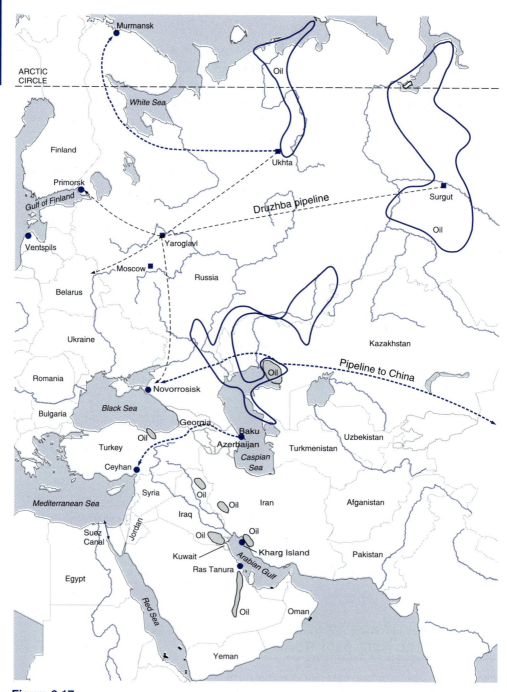

**Figure 9.17**
The countries and ports of the Middle East
Source: United Nations and UNCTAD

These oilfields are ideally located for sea transport, with relatively short pipelines moving the oil to deep-water terminals in the Arabian Gulf. Once on board ship, the journey times are relatively long, as we saw in Table 9.3(a), with voyage times of 19 days to Shanghai, 36 days to Rotterdam and 39 days to New Orleans.

Located north of the Arabian Gulf is the Caspian Sea, which has sizeable oilfields in Kazakhstan at its north-east corner. Although this was one of the original sources of crude oil in the nineteenth century, exports only started to become significant again in the 1990s, with shipments through three pipelines to Novorossiysk on the Black Sea, from Baku to Ceyhan in the East Mediterranean, and an eastward pipeline to north-west China.

At the top of the map Russia has major oilfields located to the north and north-west of the Caspian Sea, plus a third area of reserves located at Sakhalin Island on Russia's eastern coast and not shown on this map. These are located in or close to the Arctic Circle, and a long way inland from the ports of Primorsk, Ventspils, Murmansk and Novorossiysk on the Black Sea from which they are currently exported. The Druzhba pipeline provides a fifth outlet, carrying oil direct to north-west Europe. In all cases the oil must be transported long distances over land.

With the largest oil reserves and good sea access, in the last 20 years the Middle East has been an active area for the world shipping industry. The main trading countries are Bahrain, Oman, Qatar, Iran, Saudi Arabia, Iraq, UAE, Kuwait and Yemen. The Middle East has a population of 129 million, more than half of which is in Iran, and over 60% of the world's proven crude oil reserves. It is the largest oil exporting area, with total exports of 1121 mt in 2005 and imports totalling 160 mt, a 9% trade share (see Table 9.1), mainly due to oil exports. Figure 9.18 shows the development of imports and exports over the last 40 years. Exports of oil grew rapidly to reach 1 bt a year in 1973. Following the 'oil crisis' in that year imports halved to a trough of 440 mt in 1985 as coal was substituted for oil. However, the fall in oil prices in 1986 stimulated a recovery in export volume, and exports finally passed their previous peak in 2004. In contrast, the import trend has been upwards, stimulated by the sharp rise in oil revenues after the price increases in 1973 and 1979. During the three decades from 1975 to 2005 imports quadrupled from 58 mt to 160 mt. The commodity pattern of import

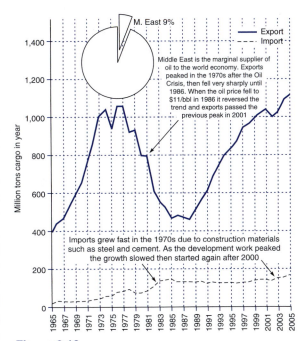

**Figure 9.18**
Middle East seaborne trade, 1965–2005
Source: United Nations and UNCTAD

trade of the Gulf states over the last decade closely reflects the pattern of economic development, with volume heavily concentrated in construction materials and food-stuffs. Construction materials account for a large proportion of imports, whilst the food and agricultural products comprise the second most important trade sector. These two commodity groups account for two-thirds of imports. The other two important categories are plant, machinery and vehicles, and chemicals and industrial materials.

Kazakhstan has an area of 270 million square hectares, similar in size to Saudi Arabia. In 2005 it had a population of 15 million and a GDP of $56 billion, about one-fifth the size of that of Saudi Arabia. Oil production increased from 100,000 barrels a day in the early 1990s to reach 1 million barrels a day in 2005, mainly shipped through pipelines to the Black Sea and the Mediterranean at Ceyhan.

Finally, Russia is an enormous country stretching from the Baltic Sea in the west to the Sea of Japan in the east. With a land area of 1.7 billion hectares, it is physically the world's largest country, almost twice the size of China. Its population was 143 million in 2005 and its GDP of $64 billion is approximately the same as that of Mexico. From a shipping point of view Russia's other distinctive feature is its northerly location and its widely dispersed access to the sea, with four separate routes to the sea: the first in the north through Murmansk and the White Sea; the second in the north-west through the Gulf of Finland; the third in the south through the Black Sea; and the fourth in the east through Vladivostok. The Gulf of Finland is ice-restricted for part of the year, but Murmansk is kept open by the Gulf Stream. Vladivostok in the East does not suffer from ice problems, but Sakhalin Island does.

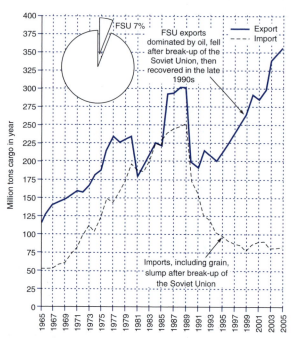

**Figure 9.19**
Russia and former Soviet Union sea trade, 1965–2005
Source: United Nations and UNCTAD

Russia's economic development strategy in the early twenty-first century focuses heavily on the export of primary commodities, particularly oil and gas, of which it has 13% of the world reserves. Figure 9.19 shows that following the break-up of the former Soviet Union, seaborne imports fell sharply from 250 mt a year to 75 mt a year in 2005, whilst exports initially fell from 300 mt to 200 mt, before recovering in the late 1990s and reaching a new peak of 360 mt in 2005. This mainly reflects the surge of oil exports through the Black Sea and the newly constructed export terminal at Primorsk in the Gulf of Finland.

## 9.10 THE TRADE OF AUSTRALIA AND OCEANIA

Australia has a population of 20 million and in 2005 its GDP was $701 billion, about the same as that of South Korea. However, it is physically almost the size of China, with a land area of 771 million hectares. It is well endowed with raw materials, and Australia is a leading exporter of primary commodities, principally iron ore, coal, bauxite and grain. It can be seen from Figure 9.20 that in the decade 1995–2005 exports doubled from 300 million tons to 600 million tons.

The location of the main primary resources which feed the exporting ports is shown in Figure 9.21. On the north-west coast of Western Australia there are major iron ore deposits, and in 2005 Australia had 38% of world iron ore export market, exporting 241 million tonnes of ore through Port Headland, Port Walcott and Dampier. Dampier handles about 80 million tonnes of iron ore a year and 11 million tonnes of LNG and LPG from the local gas

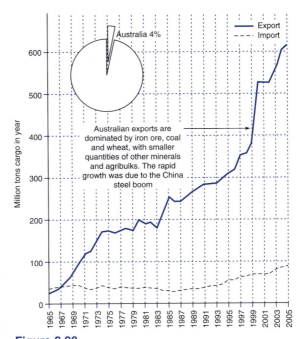

**Figure 9.20**
Oceania seaborne trade, 1965–2005
Source: United Nations and UNCTAD

fields. Coal deposits are mainly located in Queensland around the Gladstone area and in New South Wales inland from Sydney. The coal export ports are in this area – Gladstone, Abbott Point, Dalrymple Bay and Hay Point handle the Queensland exports, whilst Newcastle, Sydney and Port Kembla handle the New South Wales exports. This is a very big trade and in 2005 Australia exported 232 mt of coal, one-third of the world coal trade in that year. There are major bauxite deposits at Weipa in northern Queensland and at Bunbury near Perth – the Weipa bauxite is mainly shipped round to Gladstone for processing into alumina. Grain exports are smaller, totalling 22 million tons, shipped through various ports in the south-east and west.

## 9.11 SUMMARY

In this chapter we studied the geographical framework within which the maritime business operates. We started with the logistics model which is concerned with

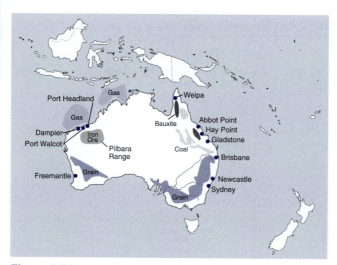

**Figure 9.21**
Oceania ports and resources
Source: United Nations and UNCTAD

the transport volume, frequency and cost per unit of transport. The four variables in the model are distance, speed, ship size and ship type, each of which has a part in determining the optimum transport solution for a particular trade. But we also saw that there are many other variables which determine the preferred solution, some of which involve judgements about the future, so shipping logistics, like market forecasting, is as much an art as a science and mathematical models are unlikely to provide decision-makers with a complete solution.

The focus of trade is created by the three economic 'superpowers' located in the temperate regions of North America, Europe and Asia. This means that the main trade routes are strung across the North Atlantic, the Pacific and the Indian Ocean, linked by the Panama and Suez canals.

The Atlantic, with imports of 3.7 bt and exports of 3.4 bt now has a 50% trade share. Much of the trade is generated by the mature economies ringing the North Atlantic which are exceptionally well served by rivers and ports. In 2005 the Pacific and the Indian oceans had the same total 50% share, but with imports of 3.3 bt and exports 3.7 bt. Distances in the Pacific are very large, but much of the trading activity is clustered in the area between Singapore and Japan. This region, which covers an area about the size of the Mediterranean, is now a major centre of maritime trade.

We reviewed the regions of the world, drawing attention to Europe which is still just the largest maritime trading area, but with a mature economy and relatively sluggish trade growth; North America which is also a mature economy with dynamic trade, due partly to the need to import raw materials such as oil and manufactured goods; South America which is a diverse low-income economy focusing on raw material exports; Asia which has become the powerhouse of growth in the twenty-first century; Africa which is a small economy largely focusing on the export of raw materials, especially oil; and finally, the Middle East, Central Asia and Russia which are the marginal suppliers of oil and gas.

This is the world within which the ships delivered today will earn their living over the next 25 years or so, and the political, geographical and economic environment that will determine the fortunes of shipowners.

# 10 The Principles of Maritime Trade

*A kingdom, that has a large import and export, must abound more with industry, and that employed upon delicacies and luxuries, than a kingdom that rests contented with its native commodities. It is, therefore, more powerful as well as richer and happier.*

(David Hume, *Essay of Commerce*, 1752)

## 10.1 THE BUILDING-BLOCKS OF SEA TRADE

Seaborne trade has a central place in our lives in the twenty-first century. Walk into any shop, and much of what you see will have come from overseas. Between 1950 and 2005 sea trade grew from 0.55 billion tons to 7.2 billion tons, an average of 4.8% per annum. This expansion was the result of the most fundamental redesign of the world's political and economic arrangements since the industrial revolution. The rapid economic growth and increasing consumer wealth which drove this change were, as we saw in Chapter 1, initiated at the Bretton Woods conference in 1944 which established the economic foundations for a period of economic stability which allowed companies and investors to operate freely across the globe. Three important developments helped:

- The world was progressively opened to free trade. The European empires were dismantled in the 1950s, removing a network of bilateral trade preferences, followed by the break-up of the Soviet Union in 1989 and the opening of the Chinese economy to free trade in the mid-1990s.
- Communications improved as telex, direct-dial telephony, fax, e-mail and the internet appeared in rapid succession. That process is taking another step forward with inter-regional broadband cabling.
- Cheaper transport. The falling cost of sea and air transport gave remote areas of the world access to world markets, making economic development possible. With the associated improvements in inland transport infrastructure, the catchment area for trade widened with each decade.

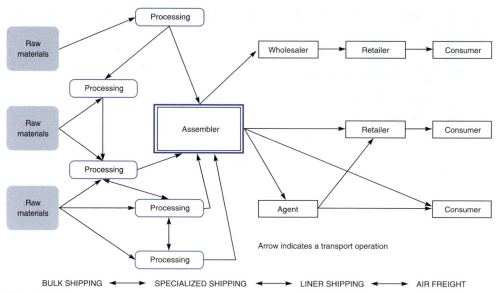

**Figure 10.1**
The shipping trade and transport system

In the quest to cut costs, corporations were able to shop around the world for components, raw materials and new markets. In doing so they brought new countries into the global system, generating new trade growth and giving rise to the trade system outlined in Figure 10.1. On the left are raw materials, which are shipped by sea to processing plants, often near the markets; in the centre are the assembly plants, and on the right the wholesalers and retailers. As sea transport costs fell, new opportunities for manufacturing were opened up, often involving multiple sea voyages. For example high-technology components are shipped to an assembler in a low-cost economy, processed, then exported as finished goods. This type of classic trade arbitraging is made possible by the transport network.

In this expanding global economy sea trade grew in pace with the world economy. For example, between 1986 and 2005 sea trade grew at an average of just over 3.6% per annum, very slightly faster than the growth of world GDP, which averaged just under 3.6% per annum. But when we dig deeper and look at the individual commodities shown in Table 10.1 we find that the rate of growth varied enormously. The phosphate rock trade declined, whilst coking coal grew at less than 2% per annum. Others grew very rapidly, for example the LNG trade grew at 6.8% per annum. A few new trades such as steam coal appeared and others such as asbestos disappeared. Containerized cargo grew at 9.8% per annum. Regional trade was also constantly on the move. Two of the biggest trading regions, western Europe and Japan, went through a cycle of growth until the early 1970s and stagnation for the next decade. New high growth economies emerged in other areas, notably in Asia and North America. Finally, although on average trade grew rapidly, its path was sometimes irregular, with deep recessions in the 1970s and 1980s.

## The theory of maritime trade

Changing trade flows set the framework for the sea transport business, and in this chapter our aim is to understand what drives change. This is not just a theoretical exercise. Liner companies planning new services, shipowners specializing in industrial shipping, shipbuilders planning capacity, and bankers financing fleet expansion all have an interest in understanding what drives trade. Because shipping is demand-derived, we must delve into the world economy for the explanation.

Over the last 200 years economists have developed an extensive body of international trade theory, and this is the starting point for our discussion. However, there are three significant differences between the approach of international economists and our focus as maritime economists. Firstly, maritime economists are primarily concerned with the physical quantity of cargo, whilst trade economists generally focus on the value of trade, which allows them to link their analysis to the economics of the trading economies. Since high-value commodities often have a low volume and vice versa, this inverts the importance of individual commodity trade flows. For example, iron ore exports from Brazil at $45 per ton represent a lot of cargo, but little value compared with manufactures at $20,000 per tonne. Secondly, maritime economists are interested in the way the detailed commodity composition of trade changes with economic circumstances while international economists are more interested in broad categories of trade, for example primary commodities, and manufactures. Thirdly, maritime trade analysis is more focused on geographical regions than political nation states – for example, whether trade is from the US East Coast or West Coast. None of this invalidates the body of trade theory, it simply changes the emphasis which we will place on these different economic tools in the course of this chapter.

Our basic aim is to answer the question 'What causes trade?', but before we do this we should consider the fact that, however powerful the economic arguments may be, if a country does not believe that trade is in its interest, it can close its borders. China, the former Soviet Union and Japan have all followed this policy, and at one time or another

**Table 10.1** World seaborne trade by commodity

| Million tonnes | 1986 | 2005 | % pa |
|---|---|---|---|
| Iron ore | 311 | 631 | 3.8% |
| Coking coal | 141 | 191 | 1.6% |
| Steam coal | 134 | 491 | 7.1% |
| Grain | 187 | 273 | 2.0% |
| Bauxite & alumina | 42 | 69 | 2.7% |
| Phosphate rock | 45 | 30 | –2.1% |
| Minor ores | 555 | 781 | 1.8% |
| Crude oil | 1030 | 1848 | 3.1% |
| Oil products | 401 | 672 | 2.7% |
| LPG trade | 22 | 37 | 2.7% |
| LNG trade | 38 | 132 | 6.8% |
| Containerized cargo* | 173 | 1015 | 9.8% |
| Other cargo | 555 | 995 | 3.1% |
| World sea trade | 3634 | 7163 | 3.6% |
| World GDP (1960=100) | 279 | 543 | 3.6% |

*estimate
Source: Clarkson Research Services Ltd

most Western countries have restricted trade in some way. A policy of not trading, or limiting trade by tariffs or quotas, is known as *protectionism*, or in its extreme form *isolationism*. It seeks to exclude the goods produced by foreigners from local markets in order to protect the livelihood of local producers or for political reasons. Over the last century isolationism in major regions such as the Soviet Union and China shaped the trading world and the opening up of these areas had a major impact on growth and development.

Protectionism is generally driven by the political influence of interest groups whose livelihood is threatened by trade. For example, protectionists may try to prevent the export of local resources which they argue are being exported by unprincipled traders, leaving nothing for the local inhabitants. When the reserves are all gone, the country will be left in poverty.[1] Or the aim may be to protect local jobs and skills which are threatened by cheap imports. If the local shipyard or car plant is about to close because it cannot compete with foreign facilities, offering subsidies or passing laws preventing imports is a natural response. After all, this could be just the beginning. Soon other industries will be under attack and then how will the country earn its living? Currency reserves will drain away and the country will be left in poverty, so trade must be prevented at all costs. Or must it?

## The arguments for free trade

Three hundred years ago this 'mercantilist' argument against free trade attracted much attention, and David Hume addressed it in his *Discourse on the Balance of Trade* (1752). Hume did not think much of the mercantilist approach, commenting:

> It is very usual in nations ignorant of the nature of commerce, to prohibit the exportation of commodities, and to preserve among themselves whatever they think valuable and useful ... There still prevails, even in nations well acquainted with commerce, a strong jealousy with regard to the balance of trade, and a fear, that gold and silver may be leaving them.[2]

In nineteenth-century Britain, as in many developing economies, free trade became a major political issue, centring on the question of whether the import of cheap grain should be permitted. Manufacturers in the towns were in favour because they wanted cheap food for their workers, but the domestic landowners, who stood to lose their protected market, were opposed. The issue split the country. Eventually free trade prevailed and in 1847 the Corn Laws, which prohibited imports, were repealed, helping Britain to develop as an industrial economy. Today the principles of free trade are broadly accepted through the World Trade Organization (WTO), but protectionism remains a live issue. In the West there are still concerns that developing economies in Asia will put the older industrial countries out of business, as demonstrated by the difficulties faced by the GATT negotiations over ten years. Apart from any personal considerations for the inhabitants of the developed countries, this would be very bad for shipping. Even where trade is relatively open, many countries protect inefficient industries whose output in a free market would be replaced by trade.

## 10.2 THE COUNTRIES THAT TRADE BY SEA

### The differences in maritime trade by country

There are currently about 100 countries which trade by sea. If every country is included, down to the smallest Pacific island, there are many more, possibly as many as 170. To explain their trade the starting point is to take a close look at the economic differences between the trading countries. Table 10.2 lists the imports and exports of 40 major trading countries, or in some cases groups of countries.[3] Together they account for 89% of world seaborne trade, so it provides a reasonable overview of the countries which trade by sea. Column 1 shows the country's rank; the second its name; columns 3 and 4 its seaborne imports and exports; and column 5 shows the total trade used in the ranking exercise. Columns 6–12 provide details of the geographical and economic size of each country in relation to its sea trade.

At the top of the list is north-western Europe with 1.91 billion tons of imports and exports, followed by the United States with 1.31 billion tons, the Middle East with 1.23 billion tons and China with 0.998 billion. Moving to the bottom of the list, we find some countries with very little trade, for example Cyprus with 6.7 mt and Brunei with 1.9 mt. To explain these trade volumes in a general way is difficult enough, but to do it well enough to forecast their future trade flows is a daunting task. Clearly a short cut is needed. We must look for a theory which will allow us to generalize about the factors which determine a country's trade. Armed with this theory, we can reduce the task to more manageable proportions. The starting point is to see how trade relates to the country's general economic structure, and for this purpose three economic indicators are shown in the table, land area (measured in thousands of hectares), population (measured in millions) and GDP (measured in billions of dollars). The final columns show three important ratios: population density, sea trade volume per capita and the trade per million dollars of GDP. In the following paragraphs we will examine each of these variables – the balance of trade, the size of the region, its level of economic activity, and of course its trade intensity – to draw some general conclusions about what determines the volume of sea trade.

### The balance of imports and exports

The first step is to examine the balance of trade. Figure 10.2 plots the imports and exports of the 40 trading countries accounting for 89% of world seaborne trade (see Table 10.2), with each dot representing a country or region. Imports are shown on the vertical axis and exports on the horizontal axis, so a country with balanced trade would fall on the dotted line which bisects the chart on the diagonal. In fact few do, especially amongst the bigger trading countries. The graph shows that trade volumes are very diverse, with one group of countries, including north-western Europe, USA, Japan, China and South Korea, strung out to the left of the dotted line and another group, including the Middle East, Australia and East Coast South America, strung out along the horizontal axis. This focuses on one of the main drivers of trade, the imbalance of supply and demand for resources between regions of the world. To the left of the dotted

**Table 10.2** Seaborne trade of 40 countries and regions ranked by trade volume

| (1) | (2) | (3) | (4) | (5) | (6) | (7) | (9) | (10) | (11) | (12) |
|---|---|---|---|---|---|---|---|---|---|---|
| 1 | 2 | Sea trade 2004 | | | Country size, 2004 | | | | Trade intensity | |
| | Country | Exports mt | Imports mt | Total | Area m HA | Pop. m | GDP US$ bill | Pop. Per HA | Trade intensity (tons) per capita | per $mn GDP |
| | Germany | 100 | 164 | 264 | 36 | 83 | 2,714 | 2.3 | 3.2 | 97 |
| | Belgium | 446 | 452 | 898 | 4 | 10 | 350 | 2.8 | 89.8 | 2,566 |
| | Netherlands | 102 | 329 | 431 | 3 | 16 | 577 | 5.2 | 26.9 | 747 |
| | France | 97 | 224 | 321 | 55 | 60 | 2,003 | 1.1 | 5.3 | 160 |
| 1 | Total NW Europe[a] | 745 | 1,168 | 1,913 | 97 | 169 | 5,644 | 1.7 | 11.3 | 339 |
| 2 | USA | 350 | 956 | 1,306 | 937 | 294 | 11,668 | 0.3 | 4.4 | 112 |
| 3 | Middle East | 1,084 | 148 | 1,231 | 730 | 294 | 600 | 0.4 | 4.2 | 4,188 |
| 4 | Japan | 178 | 829 | 1,008 | 38 | 128 | 4,623 | 3.4 | 7.9 | 218 |
| 5 | China | 352 | 646 | 998 | 960 | 1297 | 1,649 | 1.4 | 0.8 | 605 |
| 6 | S. Korea | 184 | 486 | 669 | 10 | 48 | 680 | 4.8 | 13.9 | 985 |
| 7 | Australia | 587 | 67 | 653 | 771 | 20 | 631 | 0.0 | 32.7 | 1,035 |
| 8 | E. Coast S. America[b] | 463 | 128 | 591 | 1,390 | 45 | 97 | 0.0 | 13.1 | 6,063 |
| 9 | Singapore | 197 | 197 | 393 | 0 | 4 | 107 | 58.8 | 98.3 | 3,680 |
| 10 | Spain | 108 | 258 | 366 | 50 | 41 | 991 | 0.8 | 8.9 | 369 |
| 11 | Indonesia | 246 | 82 | 328 | 190 | 218 | 258 | 1.1 | 1.5 | 1,275 |
| 12 | Central Asia[c] | 190 | 50 | 240 | 1,708 | 143 | 582 | 0.1 | 1.7 | 412 |
| 13 | W. Coast S. America[d] | 136 | 85 | 221 | 364 | 102 | 290 | 0.3 | 2.2 | 762 |
| 14 | Hong Kong | 86 | 135 | 221 | 0 | 7 | 163 | 62.5 | 32.1 | 1,355 |
| 15 | South Africa | 163 | 40 | 203 | 122 | 46 | 213 | 0.4 | 4.4 | 954 |
| 16 | Panama | 114 | 80 | 194 | 8 | 3 | 14 | 0.4 | 64.6 | 14,039 |
| 17 | Norway | 157 | 25 | 182 | 32 | 5 | 250 | 0.2 | 36.4 | 727 |
| 18 | Malaysia | 70 | 98 | 168 | 33 | 25 | 118 | 0.8 | 6.7 | 1,425 |
| 19 | Sri Lanka | 66 | 79 | 144 | 7 | 19 | 20 | 2.9 | 7.6 | 7,175 |
| 20 | Sweden | 65 | 71 | 137 | 45 | 9 | 346 | 0.2 | 15.2 | 395 |
| 21 | Finland | 43 | 53 | 96 | 34 | 5 | 187 | 0.1 | 19.2 | 514 |
| 22 | Iran | 33 | 58 | 91 | 165 | 67 | 163 | 0.4 | 1.4 | 561 |
| 23 | Turkey | 65 | 11 | 77 | 78 | 72 | 302 | 0.9 | 1.1 | 254 |
| 24 | Ukraine | 62 | 11 | 74 | 60 | 47 | 61 | 0.8 | 1.6 | 1,207 |
| 25 | Morocco | 28 | 37 | 65 | 45 | 31 | 50 | 0.7 | 2.1 | 1,305 |
| 26 | Latvia | 54 | 3 | 57 | 7 | 2 | 14 | 0.4 | 24.8 | 4,211 |
| 27 | Poland | 39 | 17 | 56 | 30 | 38 | 242 | 1.2 | 1.5 | 232 |
| 28 | Israel | 16 | 33 | 49 | 2 | 7 | 118 | 3.4 | 7.1 | 420 |
| 29 | Portugal | 10 | 39 | 49 | 9 | 10 | 168 | 1.1 | 4.9 | 290 |
| 30 | Estonia | 42 | 4 | 46 | 4 | 1 | 11 | 0.2 | 46.4 | 4,293 |
| 31 | Egypt | 13 | 29 | 41 | 100 | 69 | 75 | 0.7 | 0.6 | 549 |
| 32 | N. Zealand | 22 | 18 | 41 | 27 | 4 | 100 | 0.1 | 10.2 | 410 |
| 33 | Pakistan | 8 | 31 | 39 | 80 | 152 | 96 | 1.9 | 0.3 | 408 |
| 34 | Lithuania | 22 | 5 | 27 | 7 | 3 | 22 | 0.5 | 9.2 | 1,232 |
| 35 | Tunisia | 7 | 14 | 21 | 16 | 10 | 28 | 0.6 | 2.1 | 749 |
| 36 | Croatia | 7 | 13 | 20 | 6 | 4 | 31 | 0.8 | 4.5 | 646 |
| 37 | Bangladesh | 1 | 16 | 17 | 14 | 140 | 57 | 9.7 | 0.1 | 299 |
| 38 | Slovenia | 3 | 9 | 12 | 2 | 2 | 32 | 1.0 | 6.0 | 375 |
| 39 | Cyprus | 2 | 5 | 7 | 1 | 1 | 15 | 1.1 | 6.7 | 438 |
| 40 | Brunei | 0 | 2 | 2 | 1 | 0 | 5 | 0.4 | 5.4 | 386 |
| | Total 1–40 | 6,018 | 6,037 | 12,054 | 8,180 | 3,583 | 30,722 | | 3.4 | 392 |
| | Other countries | 741 | 750 | 1,491 | | | | | | |
| | World | 6,758 | 6,787 | 13,545 | | | | | | |

Source: World Bank (GDP), *UNCTAD Monthly Bulletin of Statistics,* UNCTAD (2005)
Notes:
[a]Total NW Europe includes only Germany, Belgium, the Netherlands and France
[b]East Coast S. America includes Guyana, Venezuela, Suriname, Argentina, Bolivia, Brazil, Uruguay
[c]Includes Russia, Kazakhstan, and various other central Asian countries
[d]West Coast S. America includes Chile, Columbia, Ecuador, Peru

line are the highly populated and wealthy regions of the world which are relatively resource-poor, whilst to the right are the resource-rich areas where demand is lower due to lower population (in the case of Australia) or income (in the case of East Coast South America).

## Wealth and seaborne trade

The obvious explanation of a country's seaborne trade is the size of its economy. Common sense tells us that bigger economies are likely to generate more trade. If we examine the

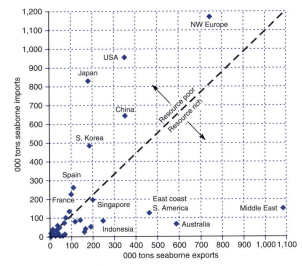

**Figure 10.2**
Seaborne imports and exports, 2004
Source: UN *Monthly Bulletin of Statistics*

relationship between seaborne imports and GDP, we find there is indeed a close relationship, as is demonstrated by Figure 10.3. This plots the seaborne imports of the 40 countries in 2004 against their GDP. As the level of GDP increases, so do imports. For example, the USA has a GDP of $11.66 trillion and imports of 956.2 mt, whereas the GDP of Cyprus was only $15 billion and its sea imports are 5.1 mt.

Taking the analysis a stage further and fitting a linear regression model of seaborne imports on GNP (see graph inset) we find that 71% of the variation in seaborne imports is explained by variations in GNP (this is $R^2$). The model implies that in 2004

seaborne imports start when GNP reaches $60 billion and increase by 110,500 tons for each $1 billion increase in GNP. The relationship is very approximate, but it is clearly significant and follows the sort of pattern we would expect. There are three reasons why rich countries with a high GNP might be expected to have a higher level of imports than a poor country with low GNP. First, a larger economy has greater needs in terms of the raw materials and manufactured goods which are shipped by sea. Some of these will not be available locally. Second, mature

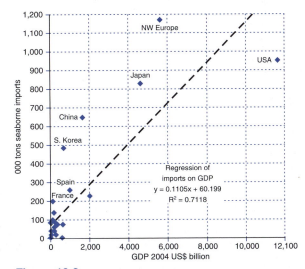

**Figure 10.3**
Seaborne imports and GDP, 2004
Source: UN *Monthly Bulletin*, World Bnak

economies which started out with plentiful local resources will eventually use them up, leading to the need for imports. For example, the USA started out with abundant oil reserves but now imports more than half its requirements. Third, a country with high GNP can afford to purchase imports and has more to export in return.

## Land area and sea trade

When considering the trade of a country, the next factor to consider is its physical size. We might expect the size of a country in terms of its land area to influence trade because it determines the amount of physical resources available locally. After all, reserves of energy, minerals and the production of agriculture and forestry are all likely to be greater in a large land mass than a smaller one. When we examine the correlation between sea trade and land area, (Table 10.2), we find that there are many countries that very obviously do not fit the model. For example, Singapore, a country with only 62,000 hectares, has roughly the same trade volume as Spain, which has an area of 50 million hectares.

But when we distinguish importers from exporters things start to make more sense. Figure 10.4 shows the relationship between seaborne imports and land area. Strung along the vertical axis of the graph are some quite small countries with big imports – north-western Europe, Japan, South Korea and Spain. Conversely, strung out along the horizontal axis are the countries with a big area and low imports, including the Middle East, Australia and Indonesia. In other words, imports are inversely related to country size, though the precise amount of trade arising from natural resources is also a matter of supply–demand economics. Where demand is high and no local reserves are available, as in the case of iron ore used by the Japanese steel industry or oil used by France and Germany, trade is directly related to demand. But often there is an economic choice between domestic and imported resources. For example, Europe has extensive coal deposits, but finds it more economic to import cheaper foreign coal. So we see the very high imports shown for north-western Europe, Japan and South Korea in Figure 10.4. Resource depletion is also an issue, and we have very large countries such as China and USA with abundant resources, but where imports are high because the resources are insufficient to meet domestic demand. In the case of China this is due to the high population and for USA the high GNP. In these large economies the domestic resources are diverted to the domestic market, whereas

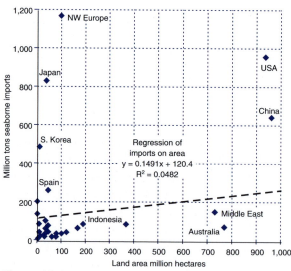

**Figure 10.4**
Seaborne imports and land area, 2004

for large landmasses with smaller population or GDP such as the Middle East, Australia and Indonesia, which appear at the bottom of the graph, local resources are the sufficient so there is little demand for imports. As we shall see when we study trade theory, factor endowments play a vital part in explaining trade, but this does not allow us to generalize about the relationship between resources and trade. The results of the regression analysis are a reminder of this fact.

So although common sense suggests that the area of a country should be important, it is not a simple relationship. Statistically there is almost no statistical correlation between a country's area and its volume of trade. But on reflection this is not really a surprising result. It reinforces the point that trade is about economic growth, not physical size. A country may be very large, but if it is mainly empty, there will not be very much import trade.

## Population and sea trade

Finally there is population. The idea that population and trade go hand in hand stretches back to the nineteenth-century trader's dream of 'oil for the lamps of China'. If there are enough people, it was argued, there is great trading potential. Much the same hopes were extended to South American countries such as Brazil. In both cases the expectations were disappointed and trade was slow to develop, despite the size of the population. For example, China has a population of 1.3 billion, ten times Japan's 128 million, but in 2004 it imported 25% less cargo (see Figure 10.5). A statistical analysis of the relationship between population and trade shows virtually no correlation. The correlation coefficient is 0.2. If nothing else, this demonstrates that sea trade is primarily an economic phenomenon.

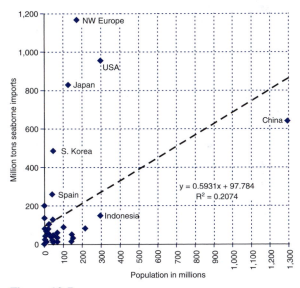

**Figure 10.5**
Seaborne trade and population, 2004
Source: *UN Monthly Bulletin*, World Bank

## 10.3 WHY COUNTRIES TRADE

### Trade theory and the drivers of trade

The conclusion from the brief overview of sea trade is that economic activity creates the demand for imports and the supply of exports, not numbers of people, or land area, though both have some influence. The countries that trade more than others generally have bigger economies (GDP), but trade volumes are also a matter of supply and demand. The USA, a major oil producer, imports oil because demand has outstripped supply. Similarly, China suddenly imported 60 mt of steel products in 2003 because local demand surged ahead of local steel production. That is fine for raw materials, and the bulk shipping industry, but what about manufactures? Why is the Japanese export trade in manufactures so high? Why does Europe import so many Japanese motor cars when it has a car industry of its own? These issues become more important when we study the container trade.

## The three fundamental reasons for trade

The starting point is that trade takes place because someone makes a profit from it. There are a few minor exceptions to this rule, such as food aid, but it applies to most trade and our quest to explain trade in theoretical terms starts here. That leads on to the question of what makes trade profitable, and the answer is generally a difference in costs. If it is possible to sell a foreign product for less than the price of locally produced goods, after deducting freight and duties, and make a profit, someone is going to do it. It does not need a model to figure that out, but it is useful to state the model anyway:

$$TR_{ij} = f(p_i, p_j, T_i, F_{ij})$$

(10.1)

This model stipulates that the trade ($TR$) between regions $i$ and $j$ depends on the price in country $i$ ($p_i$), the price in country $j$ ($p_j$), any tariffs between the two areas ($T_{ij}$) and the cost of freight ($F_{ij}$). So all we have to do is explain why products produced overseas cost less than their local counterparts. Of course, there are an infinite number of specific circumstances, but as far as explaining global sea trade of the type we reviewed in Tables 10.1 and 10.2 is concerned, three stand out: differences in manufacturing costs, differences in local natural resources, and temporary shortages or surpluses which disrupt the normal pricing process. We will consider each of these in the following sections, but a brief preview puts them into perspective:

1.  Differences in manufacturing costs. If one country can manufacture a product cheaper than another, for whatever reason, and the price difference is more than the transport costs and tariffs, trade is profitable. So we need to explain why certain goods cost more to manufacture in one area than another, an issue which has preoccupied trade economists more than any other.
2.  Differences in natural resources. Natural resources are not spread evenly around the world, so another set of trade flows developed moving them from where they are located to where they are needed. Unlike manufacturing plants which can be relocated, commodity trades are dictated by the distribution of resources. But the cost of recovering natural resources is important, too. If a country has no oil and there is a demand for motor cars, it has to import. But where there are local supplies, trade is determined by relative delivered costs of domestic and imported oil.

3.  Temporary imbalances. A third category of trade is a subset of item 2 which is important for shipping. Temporary local imbalances create a price differential between local and overseas products. This type of trade often happens during business cycles when, for example, shortages of chemicals, petroleum products or steel products result in imports of commodities, even if they can normally be manufactured competitively at home. However, cyclical patterns of trade also occur over much longer periods as economies develop, which we will refer to as the 'trade development cycle'.

These three types of trade are closely related, but each involves a slightly different theoretical model to explain how much trade, where and when. However, it is helpful to see them in the context of the transport system we reviewed at the beginning of the chapter (Figure 10.1). This highlighted the differences between the primary commodity trades which can generally be explained by a relatively simple model focusing on differences in primary commodities availability and the manufactures trades which involve a more complex trade model. The primary commodities are shipped from areas of low-price abundance to manufacturers who process them into semi-manufactures such as steel products, oil products, and chemicals. These are the backbone of the bulk trades discussed in Chapter 11. In contrast, the manufactured goods may be shuffled around the world between components manufacturers, assemblers and retailers, and we are interested in what determines who does what. From a shipping viewpoint the manufactures trade offers endless opportunities for sea transport, and before they reach the consumer, some components may have made several voyages and most are shipped in general cargo, which is discussed in Chapter 13. The specialized cargoes discussed in Chapter 12 fall somewhere between the two.

## 10.4 DIFFERENCES IN PRODUCTION COSTS

Interest in the 'who does what' aspect of trade was initially sparked during the industrial revolution in Britain because various parties stood to gain or lose a great deal of money from opening global free trade (there is nothing like hard cash to create economic controversy!). In the seventeenth and eighteenth centuries the dominant economic argument was that a country should encourage exports and discourage imports so that it could accumulate gold reserves and grow rich. Adam Smith coined the term 'mercantile system' to describe this trade theory.[4] The mercantilist theory suited the interests of the British landowners who were keen to prevent imports of cheap American corn, and they had the upper hand politically, so the country's policy was to restrict trade. But as the industrial revolution gathered force the merchants and producers became more powerful, and they wanted cheap grain to feed their workforce and a free world market to sell their goods. Naturally they became keen supporters of any trade theorists who argued that free trade was a beneficial strategy. Rarely have economic theorists been so close to frontline policy-making.

**C H A P T E R 10**

## The theory of absolute advantage

The best known of the early theories of the benefits of trade was developed by Adam Smith in *Wealth of Nations* and it is often referred to as the 'theory of absolute advantage'. At this time England was a rapidly growing industrial economy with a thriving export trade, and Smith treated the topic as a matter of common sense. He argued that countries are better off if they specialize, trading their surplus production for the other goods they need, because specialization makes them more productive. Although it might be possible to grow grapes in Scotland and make wine, the cost would be prohibitive and the quality poor. Importing wine and specializing in something the Scots are better able to produce means everyone benefits because the world's limited economic resources (factors of production) are used more efficiently. To illustrate the point he drew the analogy with tradesmen, who are better off if they specialize:

> It is the maxim of every prudent master of a family, never to attempt to make at home what it will cost him more to make than to buy. The tailor does not attempt to make his own shoes, but buys them from the shoemaker. The shoemaker does not attempt to make his own clothes, but employs a tailor. What is prudence in the conduct of every private family, can scarce be folly in that of a great kingdom. If a foreign country can supply us with a commodity cheaper than we ourselves can make it, better buy of them with some part of the produce of our own industry, employed in a way in which we have some advantage.[5]

Goods are cheaper because trade permits greater division of labour, allowing more to be produced with the same resources. So long as transport costs do not exceed the cost saving in production, trade is bound to be beneficial.

The point is easily demonstrated by the numerical example in Table 10.3. Two countries, Big and Bouncy, produce two goods, food and cloth. Both have 60 labourers. Bouncy, which is better at growing food, needs only 3 labourers per ton, whilst Big needs 4. But Big is better at cloth, using only 2 labourers per bale, whilst Bouncy needs 6. Assume that there are constant costs (i.e. they use the same labour per unit of output, regardless of volume). Big's production possibilities are 15 tons of food or 30 bales of cloth (or any combination). Write this as (15, 30). Bouncy's production possibilities are 20 tons of food or 10 bales of cloth (20, 10). They both need 12 tons of food to live on. Big uses 48 units of labour to produce its food and uses the remaining 12 units to produce 6 bales of cloth, so its output is (12, 6). But Bouncy only needs 36 units of labour to produce its food and uses the remaining 24 units to make 6 units of cloth (12, 6). So both states end up with exactly the same amount of food and cloth (12, 6).

Now we introduce trade and allow the two countries to specialize in their best products. Bouncy switches all its labour into food, producing 20 tons, consuming 12 and exporting 8 to Big. Thanks to the imports Big only produces 4 tons of food, using its remaining 44 units of labour to make 22 bales of cloth. It consumes 11 bales and exports 11 to Bouncy in return for the food. Thanks to trade Big and Bouncy now have 12 tons of food and 11 bales of cloth (12,11), almost twice as much cloth as previously. It's magic!

## The theory of comparative advantage

This theory leaves a crucial question unanswered. If Bouncy is better at producing food and Big at producing cloth there is no problem, but suppose one country is better at producing both goods? The mercantilists could still argue that under free trade the less efficient country would be driven out of both food and textile production, and would sink into poverty, so inefficient countries must avoid trade at all costs. In 1817, in his *Principles of Political Economy and Taxation*, David Ricardo came up with an elegant demonstration of why that was not the case. Trade is beneficial, he argued, even if one country is more efficient than its trading partners at producing all goods. If we rerun the example, but make the Bouncy better at producing both food and cloth, the countries are still richer with trade than without.

Bouncy now requires less labour than Big to produce both food and cloth. If there is no trade it can produce the 12 tons of food it needs and 24 bales of cloth (12, 24). Big would produce 12 tons of food, but only 6 bales of cloth (12, 6). However, if the countries specialize in the product in which they are *comparatively* more efficient, their production increases. Big is now relatively more efficient at food production, because it uses only twice as much labour as cloth, whereas Bouncy uses three times as much labour to produce food. So Big specializes in food, producing 15 tons, consuming 12 and exporting 3. With imports of 3 tons of food, Bouncy now cuts food production to 9 tons, requiring 27 units of labour. With the remaining 33 units of labour it produces 33 bales of cloth, nine more than previously. It exports 6 bales to Big in return for the 3 tons of food and is left with 3 more bales of cloth than it had

**Table 10.3** Absolute and comparative advantage

**1. Absolute advantage example**

| | Big | Bouncy |
|---|---|---|
| Available labourers | 60 | 60 |
| *Labour required per unit of output* | | |
| Food (tons) | 4 | 3 |
| Cloth (bales) | 2 | 6 |
| *Production possibilities* | | |
| Food production (tons) | 15 | 20 |
| Cloth production (bales) | 30 | 10 |
| *Production without trade (full output)* | | |
| Food production (tons) | 12 | 12 |
| Cloth production (bales) | 6 | 6 |
| Total (units) | 18 | 18 |
| *Production with trade* | | |
| Food production (tons) | 4 | 20 |
| Cloth production (bales) | 22 | 0 |
| Total (units) | 26 | 20 |
| Memo: exports | 11 | 8 |

**2. Comparative advantage example**

| | Big | Bouncy |
|---|---|---|
| *Labour required per unit of output* | | |
| Food | 4 | 3 |
| Cloth | 2 | 1 |
| *Production without trade (full output)* | | |
| Food production (tons) | 12 | 12 |
| Cloth production (bales) | 6 | 24 |
| Total (units) | 18 | 36 |
| *Production with trade* | | |
| Food production (tons) | 15 | 9 |
| Cloth production (bales) | 0 | 33 |
| Total (units) | 15 | 42 |
| Memo: extra output | | 3 bales of cloth |

without trade, so trade has increased output by 3 bales of cloth. The question is how much of this does Big get?

The heart of the theory is that free trade allows each country to specialize in its most competitive products. More wealth is created by trade because limited 'factors of production' are used more efficiently and all participants are better off than they would be without trade.[6] This has important implications for trade. The appearance of new competitors in the international market does not put existing traders out of business. Provided there are relative differences in efficiency it leads to more trade and greater wealth, though it does raise difficult questions about the redistribution of economic resources and how the gains from trade are distributed between the participating countries.

In reality free trade is often not all good news for individual interest groups. As the balance of comparative advantage adjusts, there are winners and losers. For example, the English landowners who resisted the repeal of the Corn Laws in the nineteenth century were right in thinking that they would suffer from free trade. After the Corn Laws were repealed in 1847, cheap foreign corn flooded into the country, depressing prices and impoverishing the countryside. Workers were forced to migrate to the towns, helping Britain to become even more successful as an exporter of manufactures. In the end Britain as a whole was better off for free trade, but the process of change left some individuals, particularly landowners, seriously worse off. There are parallels with the competition between European heavy industry and Far East in the 1970s and 1980s. European manufacturers were driven out of business by Far East competition. It is not much compensation to a redundant shipyard worker that he has lost his job because the country now has a comparative advantage in financial services, a business that has no call for welders. This is important because these side effects can lead to protectionism.

## Modern theories of manufacturing advantage

Comparative advantage is one of the most influential economic theories ever developed, providing the intellectual foundation for the free trade philosophy which has dominated political thinking over the last half century through the WTO. Much work has been done to extend the model to deal with multiple commodities and countries and to examine the effects of tariffs and imperfect competition. From a maritime perspective the important issue is the light it casts on why trade has grown so rapidly in the last fifty years. During this period of free trade improved transport and communications have stimulated growth by allowing global sourcing and marketing of products. The new technology also improved the services that support trade. Legally secure documentation, especially in such areas as establishing the ownership of goods, cheap direct-dialled phone calls, improved international banking, and more recently e-commerce have made global trading easier, especially for smaller companies.

Armed with these new services, industry can migrate to the remote corners of the globe where costs are low and many more towns and cities in these areas are continuously being drawn into the global trading system. Today trade growth in manufactures is driven by exploiting differences in labour costs between regions, but it does not rely exclusively on inter-country differences. Michael Porter's model of world trade attributes comparative advantage not only to local resources such as cheap labour, but also to expertise. He argues that clusters of companies specializing in a particular item, say ski boot clamps, develop a 'comparative advantage' in that product. With the right communications and transport, these clusters can exploit their advantage globally, leading to a broader trade matrix and improved global efficiency and trade growth even if wage cost differences are eliminated.[7] This process is dynamic. Once a particular company, country or cluster has become an established product area, it is difficult for others to build up sufficient volume of sales to break into that market. In the nineteenth century Britain developed mechanized textile manufacturing, and for some years gained a comparative advantage from this. Eventually other countries caught up. Today technical advance is continuous. The manufacture of medical equipment, the production of a particular type of rubber belt drive, and the manufacture of complex products such as cruise ships and aircraft are all examples where one country has developed a competitive advantage based on technical innovation and is protected by barriers such as the high cost of entry. In the case of particular inventions the manufacturing rights may even be covered by a patent.

A variant on this is driven not by production technology, but by *product differentiation* in the market. Motor cars are a good example, but petroleum products, electronic equipment and a whole range of consumer goods also qualify. In these cases the cause of trade is differences in tastes between countries. For example, motor car manufacturers face economies of scale, so low-volume production is expensive. If most Americans like to drive very big motor cars, while most Europeans prefer to drive small motor cars, then the minority in Europe who wish to purchase large motor cars can benefit from importing American cars and vice versa, especially if transport costs are low. This has had a tremendous impact on trade. In most countries consumers can now choose from twenty or thirty different brands of motor car, each sold at a highly competitive price. The production economics of car manufacture is such that if the market were fully supplied by UK manufacturers, there could only be a small number of different designs, and costs would almost certainly be higher. Similarly, if oil refineries are technically restricted to producing a mix of petroleum products which does not exactly match local demand, they will seek to export the products not needed locally.

## 10.5 TRADE DUE TO DIFFERENCES IN NATURAL RESOURCES

The classical economists were mainly interested in trade theory from a *normative* viewpoint and the theory of comparative advantage was a response to the political debate over free trade. Ricardo and other classical economists did not pay much attention to explaining what determines the comparative advantage a country may have. However, by the early twentieth century when the free trade battle had been won, economists became more interested in explaining trade patterns. The key issue turned out to be the assumption of constant costs, which is one of the basic building-blocks of Ricardo's model.

## Resource-based trade and the Heckscher-Ohlin theory

The theory of comparative advantage makes the important assumption that resources can be freely switched between the manufacture of different products without any loss of productivity. Even in the abstract world of economic theory this is clearly not realistic. In the 1920s two Swedish economists, Eli Heckscher and Bertil Ohlin, concluded that because countries have different endowments of factors of production, attempts to substitute one factor for another usually result in falling productivity or may not be possible at all. For example, America with its great prairies can expand grain production, but if the UK tries to switch more labour into agriculture, as we assumed in the example earlier in the chapter, yields would fall as the land was farmed more intensively. Conversely, although the UK with its abundant skilled labour can easily expand cloth production, the USA runs into diminishing returns due to the lack of suitable labour. Heckscher and Ohlin argued that these differences in the available factors of production (land, labour, etc.) can lead to differences in production costs between countries. All we need for trade to be beneficial is that economic resources are unevenly distributed between countries. Winters [8] summarizes these minimum conditions as follows:

1.  The production functions for the two products give constant returns to scale if both factors are applied proportionally, but diminishing returns to any individual factor (i.e. if a country runs out of land, but keeps applying more labour, fertilizers, machinery, etc., marginal returns fall).
2.  Goods differ in their requirements of different factor inputs (e.g. food production needs more land than textile manufacture).
3.  The countries have different relative factor endowments.

As an illustration, imagine the 'no trade' situation on two islands. Each island relies on its own domestic resources. Island A struggles to feed a large population by intensive agriculture on the limited land available. It mines coal from a few deep mines and manufactures a whole range of products, mainly on a small scale. In agriculture and labour the islanders face sharply increasing costs as they try to maintain growth by pouring more labour into fixed physical resources.

Island B has the same population but open-cast coalmines and better land. If trade is opened up the islands specialize. Because island A has few natural resources, its comparative advantage is in manufacturing. It imports coal and food from island B and switches the labour into manufacturing industry which for it (but not island B) is relatively more productive. In other words, it exports those goods whose production is relatively intensive in the factors with which it is well endowed. Island B opens more coalmines and switches labour into them, exporting coal. It all depends on their relative factor endowment. The precise definition of 'natural resources' raises all sorts of questions. In Chapter 1 we showed that the trading world is constantly on the move, so we should not rely too heavily on static models. However, the Heckscher-Ohlin theory suggests that in a free world market, countries must make the best of whatever resources they have, and this theory goes a long way towards explaining the diversity of trade in Figure 10.2. The countries on the left of the dotted line are like island A and the countries on the right of it are like island B.

## The commodity trade supply–demand model

This is a good point at which to discuss the commodity trade model. Raw materials account for a large part of seaborne cargo, and one of the main tasks of the bulk shipping industry is to anticipate future trade, so that efficient transport can be planned. For this reason alone shipping analysts often have to analyse trends in the commodity trades. The supply–demand model is the most commonly used technique for carrying out this analysis. For example, Japan has no local supplies of iron ore, so it must import what it needs from mines in Australia or Brazil. Iron ore is traded in an international market and supply and demand for the commodity are controlled by price movements. Thus the model consists of a demand function for the commodity, showing the relationship between demand and price, and a supply function, showing how supply responds to price changes.

The demand function describes the relationship between per capita income, commodity prices, and the consumption of the product and is generally referred to as the consumer demand function. It is expressed as

$$q_{it} = (p_{1it}, p_{2it}, y_{it}) \tag{10.2}$$

where $q$ is per capita consumption of the commodity, $p_1$ is its price in domestic currency, $p_2$ is the price of other commodities and $y$ is per capita income for the $i$th country in year $t$.[9] This function suggests that the demand for a commodity responds to changes in relative prices and income. To explain how demand responds to a change in price we need to introduce two economic concepts, the income elasticity and the price elasticity.

The income elasticity shows how consumers of the commodity adjust their consumption in response to a change in income. It is defined as the proportionate change in the purchase of the commodity such as energy for a change in income, with prices constant:

$$e_i = \frac{(\log q)}{d(\log y)} \tag{10.3}$$

In other words, the income elasticity is the percentage change in demand divided by the percentage change in income. The nature of this relationship varies from one commodity to another, with important consequences for trade. We can use the income elasticity to classify commodities into three different groups. *Inferior goods* have a negative income elasticity (i.e. less than 0), so when income rises, demand falls. For example, at higher incomes people typically consume less of basic foods such as bread and potatoes, switching their demand to other foodstuffs such as meat. *Necessities* are goods whose demand increases as income rises, but more slowly than income (i.e. the income elasticity is in the range 0–1). Finally, *luxuries* are goods for which demand grows faster as income rises (i.e. the income elasticity is greater than 1). These differences are important because they warn us to expect demand relationships to change when income changes. For example, the income elasticity of motor cars could be very high at low income levels because buying a motor car is a priority. When most people have a car the demand continues to rise with income as a few buy second cars, but the rate of increase slows and car demand eventually stagnates, or switches to higher value-added vehicles. The same is true of housing. For anyone modelling the demand for steel, much of which is used in construction and motor vehicle production, it is vital to model these relationships in a way which allows for these changing relationships.

The price elasticity shows how demand responds to a change in prices. It is derived from the demand function and represents the percentage change of consumption for a 1% change in prices. In mathematical terms the price elasticity can be expressed as follows:

$$e_p = \frac{d(\log p)}{d(\log q)} = \frac{p.dq}{q.dp} \tag{10.4}$$

where $e_p$ is the price elasticity, $p$ is the price of the commodity and $q$ the quantity consumed. It is possible to sub-divide the price elasticity into two components, the substitution effect and the income effect.

$$\frac{dq}{dp} = \frac{dp}{dq}\bigg|_u - \frac{dp}{dm}q \tag{10.5}$$

where $m$ is income. Equation (10.5) is known as the Slutsky equation. The first term on the right-hand side represents the *substitution effect* and the second the *income effect*. The substitution effect measures the extent to which a change in the price of a commodity results in the substitution (negative or positive) of other commodities in the total budget. The income effect measures the change in the level of consumption due to the change in real disposable income as a result of the price change.

This relationship is helpful to analysts in explaining and modelling sudden commodity price changes because it shows the different factors involved. For example, it was useful in explaining the crude oil trade during the two oil crises in 1973 and 1979 (see Figure 11.8, which shows the relationship between oil prices and seaborne crude oil shipments). When the price of oil increased sharply in 1973, the income effect was dominant because oil was a necessity and there was not very much substitution. Consumers spent more of their income on oil and had less to spend on other goods, triggering a recession in the world economy. But by the time the oil price went up again in 1979, the substitution effect was the dominant response because by that time it was technically possible to substitute coal and gas for oil. As a result consumers, particularly power stations, switched from high-priced oil to cheaper coal and gas and the crude oil trade fell sharply (see Figure 4.5 which shows how the oil trade declined), providing another different example of the two components of the Slutsky equation at work.

## Derived demand for a commodity

The next step in the commodity trade model is to reproduce the relationship between the demand for raw materials in an industry, and demand for the products of that industry which are sold to the final consumer. Industrial users often have a choice in sourcing their raw materials, raising the possibility that manufacturers will substitute one raw material for another. Heavy industries such as steel production and motor manufacturing are major users of raw materials, as is the transport industry (e.g. ships' bunkers). These industries will be concerned with minimizing their costs, and their demand for raw materials is derived from the underlying demand for the commodities the industry produces. The starting point is the cost function. For a given output level the cost function is

$$C = P_1 X_1 + P_2 X_2 + b \qquad (10.6)$$

where $C$ is the cost of production, $P$ is the price of each commodity, $X$ represents the quantities of factor inputs required at that price level and $b$ is capital cost, which is assumed to be fixed. Faced with a change in the price of raw material ($P_1$) and a fixed capital stock, the key issue for the industrialist will be whether it is cheaper to use less of one input ($X_1$) and more of some other input ($X_2$). The answer to this question is provided by the rate of technical substitution ($RTS$) which represents the extent to which commodity inputs can be substituted for each other with the available industry technology. It can be defined as

$$RTS = \frac{\mathrm{d}X_2}{\mathrm{d}X_1} \qquad (10.7)$$

We have already mentioned the example of power stations which can use oil, coal or gas. In 1973 when the oil price increased sharply, most power stations used oil and were not equipped to burn other fuels, so the substitution effect ($RTS$) was small. By 1979, when the price of oil rose to over $30 per barrel, most power stations had invested to allow other fuels such as coal or gas to be burned. As a result the substitution effect was very large and oil consumption fell sharply. But that substitution is a one-off change which could not be repeated when the oil price started to rise again twenty years later. Thus $RTS$ shows how the manufacturers respond to a change in the relative price of their raw materials. The relationship expressed in equation (10.7) is subject to the influence of technical development and change, which may significantly influence the amount of primary energy required to achieve a given effect – for example as a result of an improvement in the fuel conversion rate in marine diesel engines.

Picking up the example of forecasting Japanese iron ore imports, there is the impact of stock building during periods of economic change to consider. For example, as the Japanese economy matured in the 1980s, the growth rate of steel demand slowed. This caught out forecasters who, in the early 1970s, had assumed that steel demand in Europe and Japan would continue to grow at the same rate in the 1970s as it had in the 1960s. To meet this demand steel-makers planned to expand output from 110 mt to 180 mt.

But as the economy matured steel demand stopped growing and Japanese steel production never exceeded 120 mt. The same issue arose with the Chinese steel industry when it started to grow very rapidly in 2003–8. Analysts had to estimate how long the very rapid growth of steel production would continue. The problem was that the underlying demand was growing rapidly because the economy was building infrastructure, housing and durable goods stocks such as motor cars, and once the stocks were built up demand growth would slow. In both cases a carefully structured forecasting model would show how much of the demand growth was driven by stock building of steel-intensive products such as buildings and motor vehicles and how that trend might change as the economy matured. What it cannot usually do is predict how rationally people will approach the process of building the economy – whether it will be a sequence of boom and bust cycles or a carefully planned evolution. That is a matter of judgement.

Another potential trap for unwary forecasters is factor substitution. In addition to iron ore, there are other materials such as steel scrap which will do the same job. If the supply of steel scrap increases, this can be used instead of ore, making the iron ore demand forecast more complex. Or consider the thermal coal trade. There may be no local coal, but many power stations can use oil or gas in place of coal. Another complexity is the competition between domestic and foreign supplies. During the 2003–8 Chinese steel boom, international iron ore prices rose sharply and in 2005 there was a large increase in Chinese domestic iron ore production, which had previously been static, but which suddenly became very profitable. Sometimes technology changes alter the domestic or foreign production functions, with major consequences for trade. For example, the rise of 'mini-mills' using cheap scrap in Asia provides direct competition for blast furnace steel, changing the pattern of the iron ore trade. Similarly, new technology which reduced the cost of offshore production enabled Europe to increase its domestic oil production in the 1990s. Whilst these relationships are not easy to quantify, they illustrate the importance of gaining a thorough understanding of the demand relationships underlying the demand function for a commodity.

## 10.6 COMMODITY TRADE CYCLES

Another aspect we need to get to grips with in analysing trade is the trade cycle. When we discussed shipping cycles in Chapters 3 and 4, we saw that part of the cyclical effect filters through from the demand side of the shipping model. Trade is subject to cycles at three levels: seasonal cycles which occur regularly at particular times of the year; short-term cycles which accompany the international business cycle; and long-term waves arising from structural developments in the international economies.

### Seasonal and short-term cyclical trade

Seasonal cycles are well known in shipping and may arise from seasonal effects on the supply or demand side of the commodity market. An example of a supply-driven seasonal cycle is the summer lull in the bulk carrier market caused by the slow down of grain exports from the USA in July and August. This is when the US grain harvest takes place and by this time shipments from the previous season have usually run down but the new season shipments have not yet started. An example of seasonality in commodity demand is the cycle in world oil demand which results in lower trade in the second quarter of the year and higher trade as stocks are built up for the Northern Hemisphere winter in the fourth quarter. This is shown in Figure 10.6, which plots quarterly oil demand. These seasonal fluctuations are generally more noticeable when the oil market is just in balance and less apparent when it is very tight or in surplus.

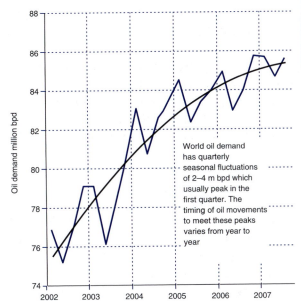

**Figure 10.6**
Quarterly cycles in world oil demand
Source: IEA Monthly Oil Market Report

Short-term volatility in commodity trades can also result from temporary local shortages of a product or commodity which could normally be obtained locally at a competitive price, but which temporarily is not available in sufficient quantities. Temporary shortages may arise from business cycles in demand, mechanical failure, disasters (e.g. the Kobe earthquake in 1994), poor planning or a sudden burst of commodity inflation which encourages manufacturers to build stocks of raw materials. In these circumstances the pattern of trade suddenly changes. For example, chemical manufacturers produce many different compounds and much of the seaborne chemicals trade is to supply temporary shortages for a particular compound or feedstock.

## Long-term influences on trade

There are also long-term cycles in trade. Our analysis of the 'causes' of sea trade at the start of this chapter identified economic activity (GDP) as by far the most important and that on average trade increases with GDP at an average rate of 104,300 tons for each extra $1 billion of GDP. One of the important lessons to be learned is that the relationship between trade and GDP is not static. As countries grow, their economies change and so does their trade. One of the most fundamental principles of trade forecasting is to recognize these changes and build it into the forecast. To do this we must understand the relationship between trade and GNP.

The key is to recognize the patterns in the way different parts of the economy develop over time. If we look more closely at the structure of world economic activity we can

C
H
A
P
T
E
R
10

## BOX 10.1  ISIC SECTORS

| ISIC | Sector | % Total GNP | Maritime intensity |
|------|--------|-------------|--------------------|
| 1 | Agriculture | 8 | High |
| 2–3 | Mining and utilities | 4 | High |
| 4 | Manufacturing | 28 | High |
| 5 | Construction | 6 | High |
| 6 | Wholesale and retail | 16 | None |
| 7 | Transport and comm | 7 | None |
| 8–9 | Other (services) | 31 | Very low |
| | TOTAL | 100 | |

immediately see why trade is likely to change as a country grows. Gross national product, a measure of the total economic output of a country, can be divided into the nine sectors shown in Box 10.1, which follow the International Standard Industrial Classification (ISIC). Each sector has a different propensity for maritime transport. Agriculture, mining and manufacturing are directly involved with trade because they produce and consume physical products which can be imported or exported. In contrast, businesses in the wholesale, retail, transport and service sectors produce services rather than physical goods. For example, the service sector consists of activities such as banking and insurance, public administration, social services, education, medicine, recreation facilities, and household services (repair, laundry) which have little if any impact on maritime transport. Of course, it is not quite that simple because a thriving service sector generates income which may be spent on physical goods, but often as income rises demand switches to services such as health care, education and eating out.

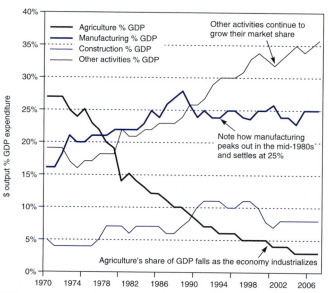

**Figure 10.7**
Structural GDP changes, South Korea, 1970–2006
Source: United Nations statistical database

When we examine the growth of modern economies we find that economic activity shifts away from the trade-intensive activities towards the service sector. It follows that we must expect the pattern of trade growth to change as the country grows and develops. To illustrate the nature of this change, Figure 10.7 shows how the GDP of South Korea changed between 1970 and 2006 when the country was going through its development cycle. In 1970 the South Korean economy was in the early stages of industrialization and the economy was dominated by agriculture, which accounted for 28% of GDP, while manufacturing was only 16% of GDP. But in the following decades agriculture declined to 3%, whilst manufacturing, construction and other service activities increased their share of GDP, changing South Korea from a rural society to a modern industrial economy. As a result, seaborne imports grew very rapidly at 11% per annum. But in the mid-1980s manufacturing's share stabilized at 25% and construction did much the same. But the other activities, which include many services such as education and healthcare, continued to grow, reaching 37% in 2006. Much the same development pattern was followed by Japan during its development cycle in the 1960s. Agriculture, mining, utilities, construction and manufacturing all peaked out, but services increased their share of GDP. In the USA, a very mature economy, services now have a dominant position, accounting for 56% of GDP in 2006, whilst agriculture, still a major US business, fell to 0.9% and manufacturing was only 13%. The development pattern is clear from these examples – agricultures give way to manufacturing and construction, which in turn give way to services.

However, this is not the whole story. As manufacturing industry loses market share, there is also a change in the type of goods manufactured. An analysis carried out by Maizels to establish a typical pattern of expansion of manufacturing industry, shown in Table 10.4, illustrates the point. At low income levels food manufacturing and textile industries are the most important when, in accordance with Engel's law, these products make up a large part of demand. Their share then declines rapidly, to be taken over by metals, metal products and chemical. At a certain income level the share of metals stabilizes, while the share of metal products continues to grow as more value is added to the basic materials. This implies that output becomes less resource-intensive at high income levels,

**Table 10.4** Pattern of manufacturing production per head, 1955 prices and percentages

|                     | $100 | $250 | $500 | $750 | $1,000 |
|---------------------|------|------|------|------|--------|
| Food and beverages  | 40   | 33   | 26   | 21   | 18     |
| Metals              | 4    | 5    | 7    | 7    | 8      |
| Metal products      | 4    | 10   | 18   | 24   | 29     |
| Chemicals           | 0    | 2    | 4    | 7    | 9      |
| Textiles            | 26   | 18   | 13   | 10   | 8      |
| Other manufactures  | 27   | 32   | 32   | 31   | 29     |
| Total               | 100  | 100  | 100  | 100  | 100    |

Source: Maizels (1971).

being directed towards value-added products. For example, motor car production progresses from economy models to executive limousines. Again we see evidence that we must expect the structure of economic activity to change with growth, bringing consequences for trade.

## The stages of economic development

Academics have spent much time discussing these changes to see if there is a consistent pattern of development. The 'stages of growth' theory developed by Rostow provides a useful starting point.[10] He argued that as economies grow they go through a series of different phases which he put into five categories according to the stage of economic development they had reached. The five stages are shown in Box 10.2.

There has been a good deal of discussion of Rostow's work. Like so many economic theories, Rostow's theory is based in a simple common-sense idea. As economies grow they start by producing necessities such as infrastructure which are resource-intensive, then progressively turn to the finer things of life (value-added products) as they become wealthier.

---

## BOX 10.2 ROSTOW'S FIVE STAGES OF ECONOMIC DEVELOPMENT

**Stage 1** *The traditional society*. This is a predominantly agricultural economy. Unchanging technology places a ceiling on the level of attainable output per head. This ceiling results from the fact that 'the potentialities which flow from modern science and technology are either not available or not regularly and systematically applied'. These societies devote a very high proportion of their resources to agriculture. They hardly trade by sea, except for food aid and the export of a few cash crops.

**Stage 2** *The pre-conditions of take-off established*. The second stage requires a surplus above subsistence, the development of education and a degree of capital accumulation to provide the foundation for economic growth. For example, in seventeenth-century England these conditions were established by a change in attitudes to investment, the emergence of banks and other institutions for mobilizing capital, etc. Sea trade is small but very active and growing fast.

**Stage 3** *The take-off*. In Rostow's analysis this stage is followed by a long interval of sustained but fluctuating progress as technology is extended over the whole front of economic activities. Increased investment permits output regularly to outstrip the increase in national population. New industries appear, older ones level off and decline. Changes take place in the external trade of the country, goods formerly imported are produced at home, new import requirements develop and new commodities are made for export.

**Stage 4** *Maturity*. After a period, which Rostow placed at 60 years after the beginning of take-off, maturity sets in. By this stage the economy has extended its range into more refined and complex processes, with a shift in focus from coal, steel and heavy engineering industries to machine tools, chemicals and electrical equipment. He thought Germany, Britain, France and the United States passed through this phase by the end of the nineteenth century or shortly afterwards. Depletion of raw materials may boost the import trade, while manufacture will dominate exports.

**Stage 5** *Mass consumption*. The fifth stage sees a movement of the leading sectors of industry towards durable consumer goods and services. A large proportion of the population can afford to consume much more than basic food, shelter and clothing, and this brings about changes in the structure of the working population, including a progressive movement into office and service work.

Maizels, who made a very long-term study of this hypothesis, explained it in the following terms:

> as a country becomes progressively more industrialised the proportion of the occupied population engaged in manufacturing does not rise indefinitely – there is an effective limit which may have been reached in a number of countries. This limit comes into operation for two reasons. Firstly as the economy grows and income rises the demand for workers in service operations such as doctors, typists, government officials increases as fast [as] or faster than the demand for manufactured goods. Secondly as productivity increases in manufacturing tend to outstrip the productivity increase in the distribution of goods from factory to the consumer, these workers tend to be absorbed in distribution to match the increased flow of industrial products.[11]

This reasoning suggests that the progress of economic growth will be associated with an increasing share for services and a corresponding decline in the growth rate of manufacturing industry and seaborne trade. Each development cycle is different, so it is not possible to set precise limits on the duration of a stage, or even to be sure when a new stage is about to begin, and the concept of a progression is helpful.

## The trade development cycle

If we apply the `stages of growth' concept to seaborne trade it is clear that, over a period of years, we must expect the trade of a country to change. How it changes depends on what stage the economy has reached in the economic growth cycle. The early stages of growth involve the import of all but the simplest items such as food and textiles, paid for by the export of whatever 'cash crops' are available – sugar, tropical fruit, oil, copper, jute and hardwood logs are typical examples. The availability of foreign exchange is the main constraint on trade and generally keeps trade at a low level. Countries such as Guinea, Togo and Cameroon in West Africa currently fall into this category.

As the economy develops through stages 2 and 3, the demand for raw materials such as iron ore, coal, non-ferrous metal ores and forest products increases as the industrial infrastructure is built up. If raw materials are not available locally they must be imported, as must the more sophisticated machinery, and paid for by exports of semi-manufactures and any primary exports which are available. The reconciliation of domestic and foreign markets thus forms a basic requirement of growth at this stage. Industries such as shipbuilding and automobiles are frequently developed as lead export earners, a pattern set by Japan in the 1950s and subsequently followed by South Korea, Poland and China.

When the economy matures, the character of seaborne trade changes again. In the course of time, whether 20 years or 50, the building-blocks of a capitalist economy are in place. Industrial infrastructure, housing, roads, railways and stocks of consumer durables such as motor vehicles and washing machines have reached a mature level.

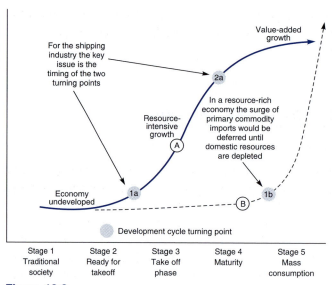

**Figure 10.8**
Seaborne trade development cycle
Source: Martin Stopford

Industries such as steel, construction and vehicle manufacture, which underpinned the growth during stage 2, stop growing and economic activity gravitates towards less material-intensive activities. Manufacturing gravitates towards the higher value-added end of the product range. How this affects trade depends on domestic resources. If the economy has always relied on imported raw materials, the growth rate of bulk imports slows, though the trade in manufacture shipped by liner and air freight will continue to grow. Typically this produces a trade development cycle of the type shown by curve A in Figure 10.8. However, the sea trade of countries which start out with extensive natural resources is likely to follow a different path. As industrialization consumes resources and domestic supplies become depleted, or better-quality materials become available abroad, bulk imports may start to increase. This happened in the USA when oil demand drew ahead of domestic production and imports started to grow rapidly after 1970. In such cases the trade development cycle may follow a path more like curve B in Figure 10.8.

Ultimately the seaborne trade development cycle is just a convenient way of summarizing certain common patterns which appear to occur in the world economy – it is not a law, nor does it apply in every case. Since economic development draws heavily on natural resources which are unevenly distributed between countries, we must expect each country to have a unique trade development cycle, determined by its factor endowments or other unique political and cultural characteristics. Thus the trade development cycle of a resource-rich economy which can draw on local raw materials in the early stages of growth, possibly with an exportable surplus, will be completely different from that of a country without raw materials. The shape of these 'trade development curves' can be seen in Figure 4.3 which shows the imports of western Europe, Japan, South East Asia and China between 1950 and 2005. The pattern is surprisingly similar considering the diversity of the countries and regions. Europe took a long pause in its development path between the mid-1970s and the mid-1980s and Japan's import path changed more dramatically than Europe's has done yet, probably because Europe is a much bigger economic unit with more domestic resources. Clearly there is much to consider in explaining the precise shape of these curves, but what we can be sure of is that economies are constantly changing and these changes have a major impact on the international transport industry.

## 10.7 THE ROLE OF SEA TRANSPORT IN TRADE

### Long-term price elasticity of sea transport demand

Finally, we should be aware of the part played by sea transport in facilitating trade. In the short term demand for sea transport is generally price inelastic, since once the cargo reaches the quayside shippers generally have few options other than shipping it. But in the longer term, trade volumes are price elastic and the price of freight plays a vital part in determining the growth and pattern of trade. The world trade model we discussed in Sections 10.4 and 10.5 suggests that the location of manufacturing processes will respond to the relative costs of factors of production between regions, and for many commodities the cost and availability of sea transport plays a part in that process. So the sea transport model should take account of this long-term relationship between transport costs and the volume of trade.

Because freight is part of the delivered cost of goods, a change in relative transport costs can affect the volume of cargo shipped. For example, in today's highly competitive world a television set assembled in Malaysia and exported to London could be competing in London shops with a similar set assembled in Wales. In one case the television set makes a 10,000 mile sea voyage, whilst the other only travels 200 miles from Wales to London. So we have two sets of relative costs to consider: the relative cost of manufacturing in Malaysia and Wales, and the relative cost of transport. If the c.i.f. price of the Malaysian product is lower than that of the Welsh product, the retailer will buy the Malaysian product in place of the Welsh one and sea trade will grow.

Viewed in this way, the liner trade is likely to be price elastic because lowering prices encourages the substitution of cheap foreign substitutes for local products. As manufacturers adjust their sourcing strategy to changes in relative c.i.f. costs and the transport element in this calculation falls, overseas suppliers will increase their market share, boosting trade. This resulted in the trade system we discussed at the beginning of the chapter (see Figure 10.1) with shipping providing the vital economic link between raw materials exporters, primary processing plants, assembly plants, wholesalers and retailers. As sea transport costs fell in real terms over the last fifty years, it opened up new opportunities for low-cost manufacturing, often involving multiple sea voyages. For example, in the present case, many high-tech components are shipped to China where they are processed and exported as finished goods. An extreme example is rough castings from Detroit, which are shipped to China for machining and then back to Detroit for finishing. This is just a simple arbitraging based on the reliability and cost of the transport network. So the liner operator who drives freight costs down by ordering bigger ships helps to generate new cargoes.[12]

## Unit costs and transport logistics

By far the most important way of reducing the price of sea transport is economies of scale, but when viewed in the context of the whole seaborne logistics operation, the relationship between ship size and unit cost is not simple. We touched on economies of scale in earlier chapters (Sections 2.6, 2.8, 6.2), but now it is time to analyse its impact on the operating economics of the bulk, specialized and liner trades we discuss in the next three chapters, using a modified version of the unit cost model discussed in Chapter 6.

The cost per tonne of cargo transported depends upon the annual cost of the ship itself plus the bunkers consumed in the year, divided by the tonnes of cargo transported:

$$\text{Cost per tonne} = \frac{\text{Ship cost p.a. } + \text{ Bunker cost p.a.}}{\text{Tonnes transported p.a.}} \qquad (10.8)$$

As we saw in Chapter 6, the cargo transported depends on the number of trips made in a year, multiplied by its cargo capacity, which in this case is measured in deadweight:

$$\text{Tonnes transported p.a.} = \frac{\text{Days on hire}}{\text{Days per trip}} \times \text{Ship size (dwt)} \qquad (10.9)$$

Finally, the days per trip depends on the distance, the speed and the port days:

$$\text{Days per trip} = \frac{\text{Distance per trip}}{\text{Speed} \times 24} \times \text{Port days per trip} \qquad (10.10)$$

The analysis in Table 10.5 illustrates the relationship between ship size, unit transport costs, and transport volumes which is an equally important part of the logistics problem facing the sea transport business. The analysis uses vessels ranging from 30,000 to 170,000 dwt and the general assumptions are shown in column 1 of Table 10.5(a). All ship sizes spend 6 days per trip in port, 350 days on hire per annum, and operate at 14 knots using bunkers costing $200 per tonne. Backhaul voyages are in ballast. The ship costs are shown in columns 2–5 of Table 10.5(a). Time-charter rates are taken from Table 6.1 and represent the break-even cost in 2005. Bunker costs shown in columns 5 and 6 are based on typical consumption rates for each size of ship. Finally, in column 7 we calculate the annual cost per deadweight for each ship size, which falls from $185 per deadweight per annum for a 30,000 dwt vessel to $66 per deadweight per annum for a 170,000 dwt bulk carrier. So transporting cargo in the Capesize bulk carrier saves about 65% compared with a 30,000 dwt bulk carrier because the unit costs of both the ship and bunkers are lower for the big ship.

Table 10.5(b) examines the impact of distance on transport costs and transport volumes. Voyages range from 4,000 miles per round trip to 11,000 miles. Part A shows that the number of trips per annum reduces from 30 for a 4,000 mile trip to 11 for an 11,000 mile trip. This covers the range of voyages normally undertaken by deep-sea bulk carriers.

**Table 10.5** Economies of scale model for different bulk carrier sizes and distances

| (a) Basic assumptions | 1 | 2 | 3 | 4 | 5 | 6 | 7 |
|---|---|---|---|---|---|---|---|
| | | | | Ship costs | | | |
| | *General assumptions* | *Ship size dwt* | *Timecharter hire (1)* $/day (1) $ mill pa | | *Bunker costs (2)* Tons/day $ mill pa | | *Total* $/dwt/pa |
| Port days per trip | 6 | | | | | | |
| Days on hire pa | 350 | 170,000 | 24,374 | 8.53 | 39 | 2.73 | 66 |
| Speed (knots) | 14 | 72,000 | 16,360 | 5.73 | 30.5 | 2.135 | 109 |
| Bunker price $/ton (1) | 200 | 46,000 | 13,657 | 4.78 | 24.3 | 1.701 | 141 |
| Backhaul % | 0 | 30,000 | 11,494 | 4.02 | 22 | 1.54 | 185 |

(b) Transport performance calculation

*Round trip distance*

| Ship size (dwt) | 4,000 | 5,000 | 6,000 | 7,000 | 8,000 | 9,000 | 10,000 | 11,000 |
|---|---|---|---|---|---|---|---|---|
| *A Trips per year (number)* | | | | | | | | |
| All sizes | 30 | 24 | 20 | 17 | 15 | 13 | 12 | 11 |
| *B Days at Sea per year (no Backhaul)* | | | | | | | | |
| All sizes | 170 | 206 | 230 | 247 | 260 | 270 | 278 | 285 |
| *C Tons of cargo transported per year (million tonnes)* | | | | | | | | |
| 170,000 | 5.09 | 4.07 | 3.39 | 2.91 | 2.54 | 2.26 | 2.03 | 1.85 |
| 72,000 | 2.15 | 1.72 | 1.44 | 1.23 | 1.08 | 0.96 | 0.86 | 0.78 |
| 46,000 | 1.38 | 1.10 | 0.92 | 0.79 | 0.69 | 0.61 | 0.55 | 0.50 |
| 30,000 | 0.90 | 0.72 | 0.60 | 0.51 | 0.45 | 0.40 | 0.36 | 0.33 |
| *D Total cost per tonne of cargo transported ($ per tonne)* | | | | | | | | |
| 170,000 | 2.21 | 2.77 | 3.32 | 3.87 | 4.43 | 4.98 | 5.53 | 6.09 |
| 72,000 | 3.65 | 4.56 | 5.47 | 6.38 | 7.30 | 8.21 | 9.12 | 10.03 |
| 46,000 | 4.71 | 5.89 | 7.06 | 8.24 | 9.42 | 10.59 | 11.77 | 12.95 |
| 30,000 | 6.20 | 7.75 | 9.29 | 10.84 | 12.39 | 13.94 | 15.49 | 17.04 |
| *E Cost per tonne ratios* | | | | | | | | |
| 170,000 | 35.7% | 35.7% | 35.7% | 35.7% | 35.7% | 35.7% | 35.7% | 35.7% |
| 72,000 | 58.9% | 58.9% | 58.9% | 58.9% | 58.9% | 58.9% | 58.9% | 58.9% |
| 46,000 | 76.0% | 76.0% | 76.0% | 76.0% | 76.0% | 76.0% | 76.0% | 76.0% |
| 30,000 | 100.0% | 100.0% | 100.0% | 100.0% | 100.0% | 100.0% | 100.0% | 100.0% |

Notes
1. Time-charter rates from the final column of Table 6.1 based on 2005 capital costs and OPEX
2. From 1990 to 2006 380cSt bunker oil in Rotterdam varied from $90/tonne to $340/tonne

Part (b) focuses on the time spent at sea, and this obviously depends on the time in port. On a 4,000 mile voyage the ship only spends 170 days at sea, compared with 285 days on an 11,000 mile voyage, so cargo handling is very significant on the shorter routes. This is one reason why ships used on long-distance trades generally do not have their own gear, whereas vessels likely to be used in short trades are generally geared. It also explains why vessels for short-haul routes are often designed with smaller engines and slower speeds and are less sensitive to fuel costs, and more sensitive to port turnaround times.

In Part C we look at the tonnes of cargo carried in a year, and the result is dramatic. The Capesize bulk carrier operating on a 4,000 mile trip transports 5 million tonnes of cargo, whilst the 30,000 deadweight vessel operating on a 11,000 mile trip transports only 300,000 tonnes. This reveals an important logistics characteristic of the economies of scale model. Big ships are cheaper in any trade, but the volumes of cargo they transport may be too large to provide a regular delivery service. In this example to permit a monthly delivery of cargo, the trade would need to be 60 million tonnes a year. This is an important constraint on ship size in both the liner and bulk markets. By the time you get down to the small and medium-size trades there just is not the cargo volume to support a bigger vessel. However, it does mean that small ship trades are always 'upsizing'.

Finally, the total cost per tonne of cargoes transported is shown in Part D. The cheapest transport is provided by the Capesize bulk carrier on the 4,000 mile round trip. It costs just $2.21 per tonne. At the other extreme, on the 11,000 mile round trip, the 30,000 dwt bulk carrier costs $17.04 per tonne. So economies of scale obviously do matter. A general point confirmed by the analysis is that economies of scale diminish as the size of ship increases. For example on the 11,000 mile voyage, by moving up from a 30,000 dwt bulk carrier to a 46,000 dwt bulk carrier the saving is $4.09/dwt, but increasing the ship's size by another 16,000 dwt to 72,000 deadweight only saves $2.90/dwt. Finally, the jump in size from Panamax to Capesize, an increase of 100,000 dwt, only saves another $3.94/dwt, roughly the same as increasing from Handy to Handymax. So the pressure to increase parcel size is at its most intense in the smaller sizes. There are many more of these vessels, which explains why size increases in the various bulk fleets occur in all size categories of vessels, not just the biggest.

From this analysis we can derive four conclusions on the role of economies of scale in sea transport:

1.  Big ships are always cheaper than small ships creating a financial incentive to use a bigger ship in a particular trade, other things being equal.
2.  In absolute terms, the economies of scale on short-haul routes are much smaller than on long-haul routes, so there is less financial incentive to invest in the necessary infrastructure to handle bigger ships.
3.  Short-haul trades spend less of their time at sea, therefore design should be focused on cargo handling.
4.  Delivery volumes increase rapidly as the voyage length reduces, so the ship size also depends on there being sufficient cargo to fully occupy bigger ships.

One way or another, these conclusions help to explain why the fleets of bulk ships which we will examine in the next two chapters include vessels of many different sizes. In every market we find size segments ranging from very small ships to very large ships, with new investment in every category. We also find that in most trades there is a steady upward drift as bigger ships slowly become substituted for smaller ships.

## 10.8 SUMMARY

In this chapter we have looked at sea trade from the viewpoint of the countries which trade. There are 100 countries and regions that trade by sea, but some are much bigger than others. In 2004 north-west Europe headed the list with 1.9 billion tonnes of imports and exports, while Brunei, the smallest, reported trade for only 2 million tonnes. When we looked for an explanation for the volume of trade it was clear that the level of economic activity, measured by GNP, was by far the most important. Two other explanatory variables, the size (area) of the country, and its natural resources, make a small contribution, explaining about a quarter of the variation in trade volume. This does not mean they are unimportant, but rather that their impact on trade cannot be reduced to a simple general rule. Population size, it seems, has no explanatory value whatsoever. In conclusion, we must expect sea trade to go hand in hand with economic growth, but modified by the availability of natural resources.

We then turned to trade theory for an explanation of why countries trade. The theory of absolute advantage shows that countries enjoy a higher living standard if they trade because it allows them to focus their scarce resources in the products they are most efficient at producing. Trade increases efficiency and everyone is better off. Taking this explanation a step further, the theory of comparative advantage shows that countries are better off with trade even if their competitors are more efficient at producing everything. All that is needed for trade to be beneficial is that they are relatively better at producing some goods than their competitors. Countries that fear that they will be reduced to poverty by foreign competition are wrong, though in a changing world, adjusting to new competitors can be painful and expensive for some parts of the economy.

What, then, determines the comparative advantage of a particular country? There are several different explanations. The Heckscher-Ohlin theorem argues that if goods require different factor inputs and there are diminishing returns when factors are substituted for each other, the comparative advantage is determined by the distribution of factors of production. Thus countries specialize in the goods which make the best use of their most abundant resources. Differences in technology, tastes, transport costs and cyclical surpluses and shortages are other reasons why countries trade.

We discussed the commodity supply and demand model which is often used for the analysis and forecasting of trade. The basic tool is supply–demand analysis, but we also examined the role of prices and substitution in this model, in particular the demand function which recognizes the impact of price changes on consumer demand and income (the Slutsky equation) and on the factor substitution by manufacturers.

We should expect the trade of a country to change over time. Starting from the proposition that GNP drives trade, we looked at the composition of GNP which we divided into nine categories. Some of these activities, especially manufacturing, make extensive use of sea transport, while others, such as services, do not. In practice, we find that as a country grows the structure of its economy changes. The early stages of growth tend to use large quantities of physical materials – infrastructure developments such as roads, railways, ports, and building a stock of cars, ships and industrial plant.

Consequently, there is a rapid expansion of import trade, matched by a corresponding export trade in primary produce or simple manufactures to pay for the imports. Whilst the early stages favour the bulk shipping business, when the economy reaches maturity, the liner business gains from the almost unlimited potential for shipping components and finished goods between developed markets.

The trade development cycle summarizes this dynamic relationship between the sea trade and economic growth. Each country has its own unique cycle which depends on its factors of production as well as cultural and commercial considerations. At the earliest stages of development, imports of manufactures are paid for by cash crop exports. As industry expands, raw materials generate demand for sea transport. The imports of countries with few natural resources slow down, but in countries which were initially resource-rich the depletion of domestic supplies may lead to growing imports of some commodities. Imports and exports of manufactures continue to grow as domestic import and export markets widen. Thus the trade development cycle has different implications for the bulk and liner businesses.

Finally, we explored some of the economics of shipping logistics that will enter into the discussion of the bulk, specialized and liner trades in the following chapters.

# 11 The Transport of Bulk Cargoes

*God must have been a shipowner. He placed the raw materials far from where they were needed
and covered two thirds of the earth with water.*

(Erling Naess)

## 11.1 THE COMMERCIAL ORIGINS OF BULK SHIPPING

There is nothing particularly new about bulk shipping. Cutting transport costs by
carrying cargo in shiploads is a strategy that has been around for millennia. The
grain fleet of ancient Rome,[1] the Dutch 'fly boats' of the sixteenth century, and the
nineteenth-century tea clippers are all examples. However the bulk shipping industry
which has such an important place in the shipping industry of the twenty-first century
has its roots in the eighteenth-century coal trade between the North of England and
London. At first the standard 'collier' was a wooden sailing collier brig, but between
1840 and 1887 the coal trade grew from 1.4 mt to 49.3 mt and better ships were needed.[2]
The new designs are recognizable as close relations of modern bulk carriers, incorporating screw propulsion, a double bottom for the carriage of water ballast and the
location of machinery fore and aft, leaving the entire hold amidships available for
the carriage of cargo.

Commercially the most successful of the pioneer designs was the *John Bowes*. Built
at Palmer's Shipyard in Jarrow in 1852, she was iron-hulled, screw-propelled and could
carry 600 tons of coal per voyage, compared with about 280 tons for a good sailing collier.
Independent of wind and with much greater carrying capacity, the steam colliers could
make many more round trips than a sailing vessel. These economic advantages more
than compensated for their higher capital cost,[3] making possible the rapidly growing
coastal trade between Newcastle and London. Since the nineteenth century the fleet of
general purpose bulk vessels has become one of the major components of the world
fleet, and bulk transport economics has been so successfully applied that coal can be
shipped across the world for much the same money price per ton as it would have cost
125 years ago.

Our aim in this chapter is to discuss the bulk fleet, the commodities traded, the general principles which drive bulk transport systems, and the transport of liquid and dry bulk commodities.

## 11.2 THE BULK FLEET

In July 2007 the bulk fleet consisted of 14,756 vessels divided into the segments shown in Figure 11.1. The two main fleets are tankers (8040 ships) and bulk carriers (6631 ships), with a smaller fleet of combined carriers (85 ships) which can carry both tanker and bulk carrier cargoes. There is also a sizeable MPP and tramp fleet which can carry dry bulk, general cargo and containers, providing a link between the dry bulk market and the container business. Finally, container-ships are a significant market force in some of the small bulk cargoes such as forest products.

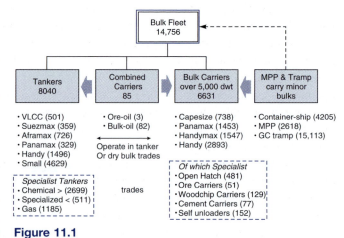

**Figure 11.1**
The bulk fleet showing main segments, 1 July 2007
Source: Table 2.5

The two defining characteristics of the 21 segments are ship size and hull design. Size is the dominant feature, and between 1976 and 2006 the average size of bulk carrier almost doubled from 31,000 dwt to 56,000 dwt, and the average tanker increased in size by 20% from 75,000 dwt to 90,000 dwt. As the ships got bigger the markets evolved into the ship size segments shown in Figure 11.1. The tanker fleet is divided into five main size segments: VLCCs which carry the long-haul cargoes; Suezmaxes which operate in the middle-distance trades such as from West Africa to the USA; Aframaxes which trade in shorter-haul trades such as across the Mediterranean; Panamaxes which trade in the Caribbean; and the Handy tankers which carry oil products. There is also a fleet of 4629 small tankers which operate in the short sea trades. In addition, there are a large number of specialized tankers. These are discussed in Chapter 12 and include a fleet of 2699 chemical tankers which transport chemicals, vegetable oils and other 'difficult' liquid cargoes, a small fleet of 511 specialized tankers built for a single commodity such as wine, and 1185 gas tankers which carry LNG, LPG, ammonia and other gases. Although these segmentations are generally accepted in the industry and, for example, shipbrokers often organize their broking desks around them, there is much overlap. Since the trend in size is generally upwards, typically the fleet segments with bigger ships grow faster as port improvements and increasing trade volumes widen their market, whilst the segments of smaller ships grow more slowly.

The dry bulk carrier fleet is divided into four main size segments 'Capesize, Panamax, Handymax and Handy', plus five groups of specialist bulk carriers, open hatch vessels, designed for unit loads; ore carriers, designed to carry high-density iron ore; woodchip carriers, designed for low-density wood chips; cement carriers, designed to handle cement efficiently; and self-unloaders capable of discharging cargo at very high rates using conveyor belts'. Finally, there is the swing tonnage. The small fleet of combined carriers can carry either oil or dry bulk, though the three remaining ore-oilers in 2007 were limited to iron ore. This fleet moves from dry to wet cargo depending on freight rates and the vessels can 'triangulate', carrying dry and wet cargo on alternate legs to reduce ballast time. In the depressed markets of the 1980s and 1990s this flexibility spread the surplus between markets and never produced the returns investors had hoped for, with the result that few replacement vessels were ordered and the fleet has been declining for 20 years. The link between the dry bulk trades and the general cargo trade is the fleet of MPP vessels and tramps which can carry dry bulk or containers, and operate in regular services carrying mixed general cargo or carrying dry bulk if freight rates are favourable, though container-ships increasingly carry minor bulk cargoes. Finally, there are the specialist bulk vessels distinguished by hulls designed for the carriage of specific cargoes such as gas, iron ore, forest products and cement. The self-unloaders carry their own high-speed cargo-handling gear. These vessels are discussed in Chapter 12, which examines the trades and markets, and Chapter 14, which discusses the economics of ship design.

Although Figure 11.1 presents the bulk fleet as having many segments, in practice ships can move between adjacent segments in response to changes in freight rates. For example, a VLCC might move into the West African oil trade, generally a Suezmax trade, if the freight makes it worth the effort, and the same is true of Panamax bulk carriers which compete closely with Handymax vessels and Capesize bulk carriers. In extreme circumstances chemical parcel tankers will even carry clean products and, during the boom of 2004, fuel oil, which would normally be transported in a 30,000 dwt vessel, was shipped in 440,000 dwt ULCCs. So the segments are a convenient way of recognizing demand differences within the trades, but not impenetrable barriers. If that was not the case, managing investment in bulk shipping would be far more difficult than it already is.

## 11.3 THE BULK TRADES

Our first task is to distinguish a 'bulk commodity' from a 'bulk cargo'. In the shipping industry a bulk commodity is a substance like grain, iron ore and coal which is traded in large quantities and has a physical character which makes it easy to handle and transport in bulk. Bulk commodities are generally carried in bulk carriers, in which case they are 'bulk cargo', but if they are shipped in a container they become 'general cargo'. So, strictly speaking, 'bulk cargo' describes the transport mode not the commodity type. In practice, commodities such as iron ore and coal are almost always shipped in bulk so the terms are often used synonymously – iron ore is referred to as a bulk cargo or a bulk commodity. But non-ferrous metal ores, for example, are often bagged and containerized, so the volume of cargo is different from the commodity trade. The distinction is even more blurred when we turn to commodities which can only be shipped in bulk if a special ship is constructed – for example, such diverse trades as meat, bananas, motor cars, chemicals and live animals. We refer to these as 'specialized cargoes' and discuss them in Chapter 12. This distinction between commodity and cargo is important even if we cannot always record it in statistical terms.

## The bulk cargoes shipped by sea

An idea of the sort of commodities shipped in bulk is provided by Table 11.1, which analyses 2549 bulk cargoes fixed in 2001 and 2002. The table lists 28 commodities along with details of the number of cargoes shipped and the average size. At the top of list is iron ore, with an average cargo size of 147,804 tonnes, followed by coal with an average cargo size of 109,046 tonnes. But the parcel sizes gradually diminish, with many parcels in the 20,000–45,000 tonne range, and the smallest is bagged rice with an average size of 7893 tonnes. This gives a sense of the variety and the range of parcel sizes carried by bulk carriers. Although the oil trade has fewer commodities, the range of parcel sizes is equally wide.

Some of the cargoes listed in Table 11.1 are also shipped by the liner services discussed in Chapter 13, or by the specialist carriers discussed in Chapter 12, the obvious cases being bagged sugar, steel pipes, fertilizers, scrap and agricultural products. From a transport viewpoint there are four main characteristics of bulk commodities which influence their suitability for transport in bulk:

- *Volume*. To be shipped in bulk there needs to be enough volume moving to fill a ship.
- *Handling and stowage*. Commodities with a consistent granular composition which can easily be handled with automated equipment such as grabs and conveyers are more suitable for bulk transport. Grain, ores and coal have these characteristics. Large units such as forest products (logs, rolls of paper, etc.) and vehicles can be shipped in conventional bulk carriers but cargo-handling efficiency and stowage can be improved by packing into standard units – timber may be packaged; ores and fertilizers put in large bags; or sacks loaded onto a pallet. In these cases ships can be designed to match the dimensions of the cargo. Cargoes susceptible to damage require special facilities. For example, alumina, sugar, manufactured fertilizers and grain need protected storage. Dangerous cargoes such as chemicals must be carried in ships which meet international regulations on the carriage of hazardous cargoes (see Chapter 16). Finally, some cargoes are very dense (e.g. iron ore), leaving much space in the hold if a standard ship is used. Others are very light (woodchips, naphtha), creating the need for a ship with a large volume that can carry a full cargo deadweight.
- *Cargo value*. High-value cargoes are more sensitive to inventory costs, which makes them advantageous to ship in smaller parcels, whereas low-value commodities like iron ore can be stockpiled.

**Table 11.1** Bulk cargoes fixed spot 2001–2

| Type of cargo | Number of cargoes | Tonnage of cargo (tonnes) | Average size (tonnes) |
|---|---|---|---|
| *Major Bulks* | | | |
| Iron ore | 889 | 131,397,500 | 147,804 |
| *Coal* | | | |
| Coking coal | 72 | 3,114,500 | 43,257 |
| Coal | 743 | 81,021,000 | 109,046 |
| *Grain* | | | |
| Oats | 2 | 197,000 | 98,500 |
| Grain | 326 | 16,540,135 | 50,737 |
| Heavy grain | 104 | 4,639,787 | 44,613 |
| Barley | 15 | 554,000 | 36,933 |
| Wheat | 64 | 2,175,960 | 33,999 |
| Corn | 14 | 444,000 | 31,714 |
| Maize | 13 | 322,000 | 24,769 |
| *Agribulks* | | | |
| Canola | 3 | 110,000 | 36,667 |
| Agriprods | 4 | 69,000 | 17,250 |
| Rice – bagged | 7 | 55,250 | 7,893 |
| *Sugar* | | | |
| Sugar – bulk | 116 | 1,981,400 | 17,230 |
| Sugar – bagged | 47 | 518,575 | 11,034 |
| *Fertilizers* | | | |
| Fertilizers | 18 | 468,000 | 26,000 |
| Phosphates | 7 | 168,000 | 24,000 |
| Phosphate rock | 8 | 171,000 | 21,375 |
| Urea | 16 | 287,000 | 17,938 |
| *Metals & minerals* | | | |
| Manganese ore | 9 | 185,000 | 20,556 |
| Concentrates | 2 | 160,000 | 80,000 |
| Pig iron | 2 | 75,000 | 37,500 |
| Cement | 4 | 261,000 | 65,250 |
| Bauxite | 20 | 1,097,000 | 54,850 |
| Petcoke | 13 | 600,000 | 46,154 |
| Coke | 7 | 198,000 | 28,286 |
| *Steel products* | | | |
| Scrap | 16 | 334,000 | 20,875 |
| Steel billets | 4 | 98,600 | 24,650 |
| Steel pipes | 4 | 91,000 | 22,750 |
| Grand Total | 2549 | 247,333,707 | 30,119 |

Source: Various

- *Regularity of trade flow.* Cargoes shipped regularly in large quantities provide a better basis for investment in bulk handling systems. For example, the sugar trade, which is very fragmented, has benefited less from bulk transport systems.

In most cases the overlap is relatively small, with the bulk shipping business focusing primarily on a few high-volume commodities, with the 'crossover' commodities occupying

**Table 11.2** Bulk commodities transported by sea

| Million tons | 1985 | 1990 | 1995 | 2004 | 2005 | Growth 1985–2005 (% pa) |
|---|---|---|---|---|---|---|
| **1. Liquid bulks** | | | | | | |
| Crude oil | 984 | 1,190 | 1,450 | 1,802 | 1,820 | 3.1% |
| Oil Products | 288 | 336 | 381 | 219 | 488 | 2.7% |
| Totals | 1,272 | 1,526 | 1,831 | 2,021 | 2,308 | 3.0% |
| **2. Three major bulks** | | | | | | |
| Iron ore | 321 | 347 | 402 | 589 | 650 | 3.6% |
| Coking coal | 144 | 342 | 160 | 186 | 184 | 1.2% |
| Thermal coal | 132 | | 242 | 475 | 498 | 6.9% |
| Grain | 181 | 192 | 216 | 273 | 242 | 1.5% |
| Total | 778 | 881 | 1,020 | 1,523 | 1,574 | 3.6% |
| **3. Minor bulks (see Table 11.12 for more details of the commodities)** | | | | | | |
| Agribulks | 79 | 87 | 106 | 136 | 158 | 3.5% |
| Sugar | 28 | 28 | 34 | 37 | 46 | 2.6% |
| Fertilizers | 96 | 90 | 93 | 100 | 109 | 0.6% |
| Metals and minerals | 170 | 188 | 217 | 235 | 310 | 3.1% |
| Steel and forrest products | 301 | 325 | 365 | 345 | 387 | 1.3% |
| Total | 673 | 719 | 815 | 852 | 1,010 | 2.0% |
| Total bulk trade | 2,723 | 3,126 | 3,666 | 4,396 | 4,892 | 3.0% |

Source: Major bulks, *Fearnleys Review* 2005, minor bulks Clarkson Research Studies, various

Note: The minor bulk data includes some land trade

a relatively small proportion of the businesses activity, and mainly in the smaller ship sizes. This point is apparent when we look at the statistics of the bulk commodities traded by sea in Table 11.2. In 2005 there were 4.9 billion tons of bulk commodities, about two-thirds of sea trade. This total included 2.3 billion tons of liquid, 1.6 billion tons of 'major' dry bulk commodities and 1 billion tons of 'minor' dry bulk commodities. The list of commodities is not comprehensive, but when viewed in the context of the cargo data in Table 11.1 it provides a more detailed account of the commodities most commonly traded in bulk carriers. The overlap is mainly in the minor bulks which only account for 17% of the bulk commodities. But the size of vessel required is also a central issue and in Chapter 2 we explored how the parcel size distribution function is determined by the commodity's economic and physical characteristics which influence the size and type of ship used to transport the cargo.

## 11.4 THE PRINCIPLES OF BULK TRANSPORT

At the heart of this analysis are the ships used by the transport system. A transport system is designed so that its parts work together as efficiently as possible, and sea transport is just one stage in the transport chain moving bulk commodities between producers and consumers. Cargo flows through the system as a series of discrete shipments, with the storage areas acting as buffers to allow for timing differences in the arrival and despatch of the commodity. For example in a grain system barges may be delivering grain every day, but the grain elevator may only load two ships a week.

The stages in a typical bulk transport system are shown in Figure 11.2. It consists of a sea voyage and two land journeys which could be by lorry, train, conveyor, or pipeline. There are four storage areas located at the origin (e.g. mine, oilfield, factory or steel mill), the loading port, the discharging port and the destination, and no less than 17 handling operations as the cargo moves through the system! These are listed in the diagram and include a ship loading and discharge; four handling operations on and off land vehicles, and eight movements to and from storage. No wonder transport system designers are so interested in finding ways to reduce this cost.

Building ships which fit into the bulk transport systems used by the cargo shippers presents shipowners with a challenge. For example, the transport system places constraints on ship size. The depth of water and berth length at the loading and receiving ends of the operation determine the maximum size of ship which can be used.

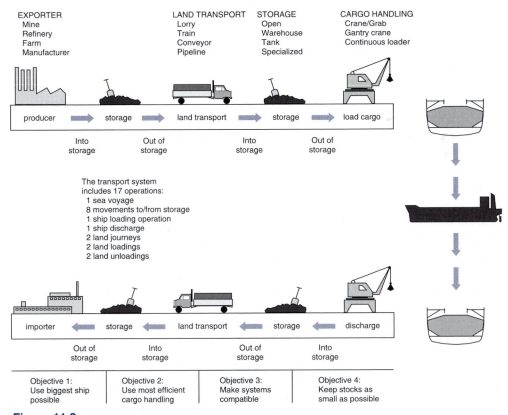

**Figure 11.2**
Elements in the bulk transport system

**Table 11.3** Examples of monthly plant throughput

| Commodity | Economic plant size ('000 tons) | | Typical ship size ('000 dwt) |
|---|---|---|---|
| | Year | Month | |
| Oil refining | 10,000 | 833 | 30–320 |
| Steel-making | 5,000 | 417 | 120–180 |
| Power station (coal) | 3,000 | 250 | 60–120 |
| Cement | 2,000 | 167 | 20–50 |
| Sulphuric acid | 1,000 | 83 | 20–50 |
| Automobiles (no. cars) | 1,000 | 83 | 1,000–6,000 cars |
| Sugar refining | 500 | 42 | 20–35 |
| Ammonium nitrate | 350 | 29 | 20–30 |
| Ethylene | 300 | 25 | 5–8 |
| Aluminium smelting | 200 | 17 | 20–30 |
| Synthetic fibres | 80 | 7 | Container |

Source: Compiled by Martin Stopford from various sources

Storage facilities are another potential constraint, since there must be enough storage capacity in the port to allow the ship to load and discharge its cargo. There is no point in shipping 70,000 tons of grain if the grain elevator in the terminal can only handle 60,000 tons. Another important issue is the amount of raw materials a manufacturing plant processes in a year, since this determines the size of cargo the plant will be able to absorb, placing a constraint on ship size even when the terminal facilities to handle big ships are available. The capacities of various manufacturing plants shown in Table 11.3 put this into perspective. A steel mill producing 5 million tons of steel a year needs roughly 700,000 tons of iron ore and 200,000 tons of coal each month. With these volumes it would make sense to use 180,000 dwt ships, even if they were not cheaper – managing 17 Handy bulk carrier shipments each month would be far too much trouble. However, a sugar refinery with an annual capacity of 500,000 tons and a monthly requirement for 42,000 tons of raw sugar is hardly likely to want 180,000 tons of raw sugar in a single cargo. It might well go for two 25,000 dwt bulk carrier shipments a month. With this sort of volume it is easy to see why the size of bagged sugar parcels in Table 11.1 is so small. So plant size is just as important as terminal facilities and economies of scale in determining the size of ship that can be used.

## Principles of bulk transport

Whether transport is between a coalmine and a power station or between a chemical plant and a fertilizer wholesaler, the aim is to move the cargo as cheaply and efficiently as possible. Inevitably this involves compromises. Each commodity and industry has specific transport requirements and no single system is ideal for every situation. But there are certain principles which make a useful 'checklist' when thinking about the transport systems in which bulk shipping plays a part. In this context there are four issues to consider: first, gaining maximum economies of scale by using a bigger ship; second, reducing the number of times the cargo is handled; third, making the cargo-handling operation more efficient; and fourth, reducing the size of stocks held. The problem for the system designer is that each of these objectives has a capital cost and some work in opposition. The challenge is to develop a system which gives the best overall outcome in terms of the transport user's priorities which are not only determined by cost.

## PRINCIPLE 1: EFFICIENT CARGO HANDLING

A fundamental principle of bulk transport is that unit costs can be reduced by increasing the size of the cargo on the shipping leg. Bigger ships have lower unit costs, and unit cargo handling and storage are also cheaper at high throughput volumes. As a result, the bulk trades are under constant economic pressure to increase the size of cargo consignments. But big is not always best. As we discussed in Chapter 10, the savings diminish as the ships get bigger, and big ships need more cargo to fill them. From the shipper's point of view delivery frequency is also important and bigger ships need fewer trips to deliver the same cargo volume. Cargo handling, which does not change with voyage distance, also becomes proportionally less important in the unit cost equation as the length of haul increases. So it is more important to have efficient terminals for products tankers operating in north-west Europe than for VLCCs plying between the Middle East and the US Gulf. Finally, very big ships are less flexible and have fewer trading options if their preferred trade disappears for some reason. All of which suggests that economies of scale must be viewed in the context of the transport system as a whole, and in practice the market provides its service with a portfolio of ships of different sizes.

A timeless example of the evolution of ship size is provided by the shipment of nickel matte (a concentrate of nickel ore) from Canada to a processing plant in Norway. The change from one transport system to another was described by an executive of the company in the following terms:

> As the size of the trade increased we decided to go from the barrel system to the bulk system of matte shipping and we proceeded to purchase a 9,000 ton vessel, which was to move matte from North America to our refinery at Kristiansand South, and return to North America with finished metal. As part of the overall operation, we had to provide a storage and loading facility at Quebec City; we had to increase our storage at Kristiansand, and we also had to consolidate our storage and handling facilities at a location just outside of Welland, Ontario. I would say not only the acquisition of the ship, but also the acquisition of the storage facilities at these various locations, has improved our metal and matte movements considerably.[4]

In this case we see bulk shipping as a natural stage in the development of the business and also the importance of making bulk shipping an integral part of the whole manufacturing operation. The same process is seen in the steel industry, where the size of ore carriers has increased from 24,000 dwt in the 1920s to 300,000 dwt in the 1990s.

Many of the bulk commodity trades discussed in this chapter travel partly in bulk and partly as general cargo, depending on the size of the individual trade flow. For example,

50,000 tons of wheat transported from New Orleans to Rotterdam would certainly travel in a bulk carrier, but 500 tons of malting barley shipped from Tilbury to West Africa would probably travel bagged on pallets or in containers. Because this depends on a commercial decision, there is no specific size at which a trade flow 'goes bulk'. In effect, the smallest practical bulk unit is a single bulk carrier hold; as the size of parcel falls below 3,000 tons it becomes increasingly difficult to arrange bulk transport. One expert puts the watershed at 1,000 tons.[5]

### PRINCIPLE 2: MINIMIZE CARGO HANDLING

Minimizing the cost of cargo handling is the second principle. Each time the product is handled during transport it costs money. The economic costs of cargo handling can be illustrated with an example from the grain trade. A 15,000 dwt 'tweendecker discharging in a small African port might take several weeks to discharge its cargo. Typically, the grain is unloaded on to the quayside with grabs, bagged by hand and transported to the warehouse by lorry. In contrast, a large modern grain elevator can discharge barges at the rate of 2,000 tons per hour and load ships at the rate of 5,000 tons per hour. With these facilities the same vessel could be handled in a day.

A radical solution is to reduce the number of transport legs by relocating the processing plant. Manufacturing plants such as steel mills can be relocated to coastal sites to avoid land transport of raw materials. Where cargo must be handled, the emphasis is on reducing cost by using specially constructed bulk handling terminals. Most large ports have specialist bulk terminals for handling crude oil, products, dry bulk and grain. The use of high-productivity cargo-handling equipment contributes to the overall cost efficiency of the operation by reducing the unit cost of loading and discharging, and minimizing the time the ship spends handling cargo.

Homogeneous dry bulks such as iron ore and coal can be handled very efficiently using continuous loaders and discharged with cranes and large grabs. Cargoes such as steel or forest products, which consist of large, irregular units, benefit from packaging into standard unit loads. In some cases, such as vehicles and refrigerated cargo, bulk shipping requires the construction of special vessels. Powdery cargoes like bulk cement shipped loose in a specially designed cement carrier can be discharged mechanically using pumps, stored in silos and loaded direct into suitable bulk railcars.

### PRINCIPLE 3: INTEGRATE TRANSPORT MODES EMPLOYED

Cargo handling can be made more efficient if care is taken to integrate the various stages in the transport system. One way to do this is to standardize cargo units. Cargo is packaged in a form that can easily be handled by all stages in the transport system, whether it be a ship, lorry or rail truck. Containerization of general cargo is an outstanding example of this principle. The standard container can be lifted off the ship and on to the lorry. In bulk shipping, intermediate units such as large bags, packaged lumber and pallets can be used to reduce handling costs.

Another is to design a system which covers all stages in the transport operation. This approach is used in many large industrial projects involving raw materials systems. Ships, terminal facilities, storage areas and land transport are integrated into a balanced system. The first integrated bulk transport system was probably in the iron ore trade. Through-transport from the iron ore mine to the steel plant was planned in detail at the time the plant was built. This approach works best where the cargo flows are regular, predictable and controlled by a single company, making it possible to justify special investment in ships and cargo-handling equipment. The key word here is *integration*. What matters is that the transport system is designed as a whole and sufficiently stable to operate as a whole.

### PRINCIPLE 4: OPTIMIZE STOCKS FOR THE PRODUCER AND CONSUMER

The transport system must incorporate stockpiles and parcel sizes which are acceptable to the importer and exporter. There are two issues to consider. One is the size of the trade flow. Although it would be cheaper to ship manganese ore in a 170,000 dwt bulk carrier, in practice steel-makers use much smaller ships – the parcel size in Table 11.1 is 20,000 tons. This is partly a matter of annual throughput which does not justify investment in high-volume cargo-handling facilities, but there are also inventory costs to consider. Even if the storage facilities are available to handle 170,000 tons of manganese ore, the cost of holding stock for a year could well exceed the freight saving. Under 'just in time' manufacturing systems the product should arrive at the processing or sales point as close as possible to the time when it is used, minimizing the need for stocks. This approach, which calls for a transport system with many small deliveries, conflicts with Principle 1 which favours a few very large deliveries.

The size of parcel in which a commodity is shipped is thus a trade-off between optimizing stockholding and economies of scale in transport. High-value cargoes, which are usually used in small quantities and incur a high inventory cost, tend to travel in small parcels. This is most noticeable in the minor bulk trades such as sugar, steel products and non-ferrous metal ores, where physical characteristics permit large bulk parcels but stockholding practices impose a parcel size ceiling on the trade. As far as the commercial structure of the transport of a commodity like iron ore is concerned, some is transported in ships owned by the steel mills; another proportion by ships on time charter to the steel mills; a third segment is moved on COA; and the remainder gets shipped through the spot market. Naturally the form which a particular commodity market takes makes a big difference to the shipowners offering transport.

## 11.5 PRACTICAL ASPECTS OF BULK TRANSPORT

### Participants in the transport system

The bulk transport system has four main participants. First there are the 'cargo owners', the businesses with bulk cargo to transport on a regular basis. Their approach to the business varies enormously. For basic industries such as oil refineries, steel mills or paper and pulp manufacturers, cost-effective transport of the raw materials and products is crucial. They need the cheapest possible transport, and generally have transport departments whose primary task is to minimize the cost of transport. Sometimes they approach this in a long-term manner by developing their own transport system. This involves the construction of specialist terminals, and obtaining a fleet of ships, either owned or on charter, under their own management. Many steel mills follow this approach. When there is a well-developed charter market, even very large businesses may choose to leave the task of owning ships and transport systems to other investors. They may prefer to charter ships on the spot market or, if they have a longer-term requirement for transport, arrange a COA, leaving responsibility for managing the ships with the shipowner.

A second important group of bulk transport users are commodity traders. They buy and sell commodities at different locations, and transport costs affect their margins. Traders are particularly active in the energy and agricultural commodity markets, where much of the cargo is bought and sold. In this case the charterers are rarely in a position to arrange long-term transport. Their focus is on the immediate cost of shipping today, so they generally use the spot market, though some build up fleets of chartered vessels.

The third participants are the shipowners who invest in ships to trade in the various markets described in Chapter 5. Their focus is on making the right investment and minimizing capital and operating costs.

Finally, sitting between the cargo owners and the shipowners are the bulk 'operators'. These are companies which do not own ships or cargo but take cargo contracts, often on a COA basis, and charter in ships to service them. They work at the margin, and this is risky business, but larger operators can use the size of their fleets and their knowledge of the trades to manage the risk and improve their margins, for example by developing favourable ballast patterns.

## Bulk shipping investment – the criteria and approach

Most bulk shipping investment does not follow the rigorous investment appraisal processes that would be used, for example, by charterers ordering ships for a specific trade such as an LNG plant. The investment proposal with operations analysis and discounted cashflows is not really appropriate for the sort of speculative investment that most bulk shipping investors are involved in.

Of course, this is not always the case. For regular cargo flows, such as iron ore shipments to a specific steel mill, analysing investment returns using an economic model is possible because the operating pattern of the ship is known in advance. However, for cargoes appearing on the market irregularly, the process is more complex. For most bulk shipping investors the market is a changeable mix of the cargoes listed in Table 11.1 and the variety is extreme.

Investors must look ahead and balance such issues as ship size, utilization of cargo space, backhaul, speed, cargo-handling gear and cargo access in a way that will work over whatever period the ship will be retained in the fleet. Developing a profitable fleet of bulk ships has at least three different dimensions. Size, as we saw earlier in the chapter, imposes many different constraints on the ship's operations, including the size of parcels of the commodities it is carrying, storage facilities, port draft, and trader preference. Utilization is another issue. Very big ships or specialized ships may be unable to get backhaul cargoes, so what they gain on economies of scale, they may lose on vessel utilization.

So how does the industry deal with this complex balance of issues? Shipping investors are inherently conservative and they often simplify the problem by operating a portfolio of ships of different sizes. In the bulk carrier market there are four sizes – Handy, Handymax, Panamax and Capesize – for bulk carriers, and five sizes – Handy, Panamax, Aframax, Suezmax and VLCC – in the tanker business. The way these size segments developed over the period from 1974–2005 is shown in Figure 11.3(a) for tankers and Figure 11.3(b) for bulk carriers. Investors must choose their segments and decide what type of fleet to develop. For example, in the second half of the 1990s Aframax tankers did particularly well thanks to the growing role of short-haul oil, especially Russian exports to Europe, much of which was best suited to the Aframaxes which took market share from the bigger VLCCs which focus on the long-haul Middle East export trades. Several companies built up very large fleets of Aframax tankers and did very well. But soon VLCCs started to move into the Atlantic shorter-haul trades, for example West Africa, demonstrating how the market is constantly adjusting to changing trade patterns.

Ultimately investors are paid for their ability to anticipate what ships will be needed in future. This is not an exact science and investment often follows cyclical patterns, with vessels being ordered through a combination of factors – market analysis, instinct and the availability of funds. The result can be a heavy ordering at the top of the market because the companies are liquid and finance is available, or at the bottom of the cycle because ships are cheap and recovery is thought to be in sight. But one way or another, the ships get ordered.

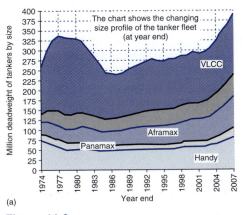

(a)

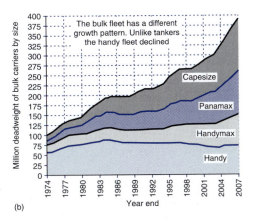

(b)

**Figure 11.3**
(a) The tanker fleet, 1974–2007; (b) The bulk carrier fleet, 1974–2007

**429**

Finally, we must not forget the specialized and MPP ships. In some trades the physical characteristics, volume and regularity of the cargo make it possible to customize or redesign the ship to suit that particular trade, giving rise to a substantial fleet of specialist bulk vessels. The more important of these specialist types are listed at the bottom of Figure 11.1 and their trades are discussed in more detail in Chapter 12. Bulk cargo is also sometimes transported in MPP vessels which can trade in both the liner and bulk segments and, at the other end of the scale, the combined carrier fleet which can move between the dry and oil markets. The hybrid tramp market in particular has recently been the focus of much new design work to develop vessels capable of operating effectively in bulk and general cargo trading under modern conditions, for example transporting heavy and awkward cargoes.

## Handling liquid bulk cargoes

Crude oil and oil products require different types of handling terminals. Since the carriage of crude oil uses very large tankers, loading and discharge terminals are generally found in deep-water locations with draft of up to 22 metres. Often these requirements can only be met by offshore terminals with strong fendering systems to absorb the berthing impact of large tankers. The berthing arrangements for a typical offshore oil terminal are shown in Figure 11.4. Storage tanks on land are linked by pipeline to the piers where tankers are berthed. These storage tanks must have enough capacity to service vessels using the port. There are two piers with four berths, one with a maximum size of 65,000 dwt, two 135,000 dwt berths and

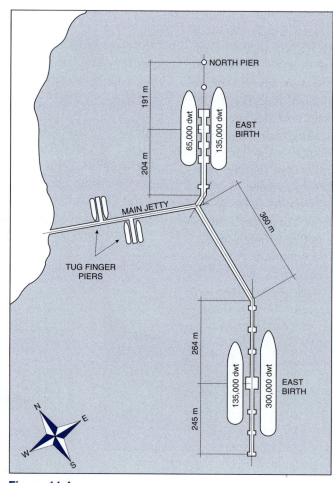

**Figure 11.4**
A crude oil export terminal
Source: UNCTAD (1985)

one VLCC berth. The exact combination would be adjusted to the trade. Note also the finger piers for tugs. Cargo is loaded by pumping oil from the storage tanks to the ship using the terminal's own pumping capacity. Discharge relies on the ship's pumps. Large tankers generally have four cargo pumps, located in a pump room between the engine room and the cargo tanks. Typical combined discharging rates are 6,500 cubic metres per hour for a 60,000 dwt tanker and 18,000 cubic metres per hour for a 250,000 dwt tanker.

Products terminals are generally smaller and as a result can often be accommodated within the port complex. Handling techniques are broadly similar to those of crude oil, but must be capable of dealing with smaller parcels of different products. These include black oils such as furnace oils and heavy diesel oils; and white oils, which include gasoline, aviation spirits, kerosene, gas oil and MTBE (an octane booster used in gasoline).

## Handling homogeneous dry bulk cargoes

Homogeneous dry bulks such as iron ore and coal are handled very efficiently using single-purpose terminals. The iron ore loading facility shown in Figure 11.5 illustrates the way the industry tackles the problems encountered in transferring cargo to and from the ship.

Cargo arrives at the terminal reception facility in railcars designed to tip or drop their cargo into a hopper below the track. From here the ore moves to the stockpile by wagon or, more usually, by conveyor. The stockpile acts as a buffer between the land and sea transport systems, ensuring the terminal has sufficient ore to load ships when they arrive. If stocks are inadequate, congestion builds up as ships wait to load cargo. In the iron ore terminal shown in Figure 11.5 the stockpile consists of long rows of ore, known as 'windrows'. Commodities such as grain require protection and are stored in silos.

Moving material into the stockpile is known as

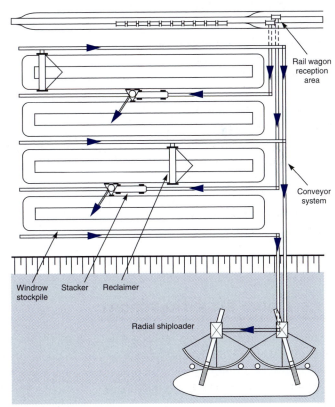

**Figure 11.5**
An iron ore export terminal
Source: UNCTAD (1985)

'spreading', while removing it is referred to as 'reclaiming'. Both processes are highly automated. The spreader moves slowly along the stockpile rows, receiving ore from the conveyor and dropping by gravity on to the stockpile at a rate of several thousand tons an hour. When the ore is needed the reclaimer, a revolving drum with buckets, moves along the wind-row, scoops ore from the stockpile and drops it on to a belt conveyor. From the conveyor the ore is taken to the quayside where it is loaded on to the ship. There are various other designs.

Material is weighed before loading or after unloading, to check shipping documentation, using an automatic weighing machine in the conveyor system. Sampling is also required to satisfy the purchaser that the material is in accordance with specifications.[6] The ship loader receives cargo from the conveyor and deposits it in the ship's holds in a planned sequence (the 'loading plan') which avoids putting structural stresses on the hull. Various loading systems are used. In the example illustrated in Figure 11.5 a radial arm loader is used. The ship is moored alongside the loader and the two loading 'booms' (i.e. arms which extend over the ship's hatches) move from hatch to hatch, loading ore by gravity. Other designs of loader use a loading arm on rails running alongside the berth. Loading rates of 16,000 tons an hour may be achieved, but at higher loading speeds a limit may be imposed by the rate at which the ship can be de-ballasted. During loading the boom moves from hatch to hatch. To allow for temporary interruptions to the loading operation, for example when moving from one hatch to another, there is generally a surge hopper in the system.

At the other end of the voyage the ore is unloaded with a grab unloader which picks material from the hold and discharges it into a hopper at the quay edge, from which it is fed onto a belt conveyor. The cargo-handling rate for a grab depends on the number of handling cycles per hour and the average grab payload. In practice, about 60 cycles per hour can be achieved. Grab designs range from light grabs for animal feedstuffs and grain, to massive 50-ton lift ore handlers. The grab unloader is used mainly for iron ore, coal, bauxite, alumina and phosphate rock. Other commodities handled by smaller mobile grabbing cranes include raw sugar, bulk fertilizers, petroleum coke and various varieties of bean and nut kernels. Pneumatic systems are suitable for handling bulk cargo of low specific gravity and viscosity such as grains, cement and powdered coal. Pneumatic equipment is classified into vacuum, or suction types and pressure, or blowing types.

## 11.6 LIQUID BULK TRANSPORT

Transporting liquids by sea raises a whole set of special challenges. There is a diverse fleet of tankers which transport crude oil, oil products, chemicals, liquid gases and specialist cargoes. Figure 11.6 shows how these ships serve the energy, chemical and agricultural businesses which are their main customers. The primary material production is shown in column 1, the primary sea transport in column 2, industrial processing in column 3, and secondary sea transport in column 4. The industrial processing plants are power stations, organic chemicals plants, inorganic chemicals plants, oil refineries,

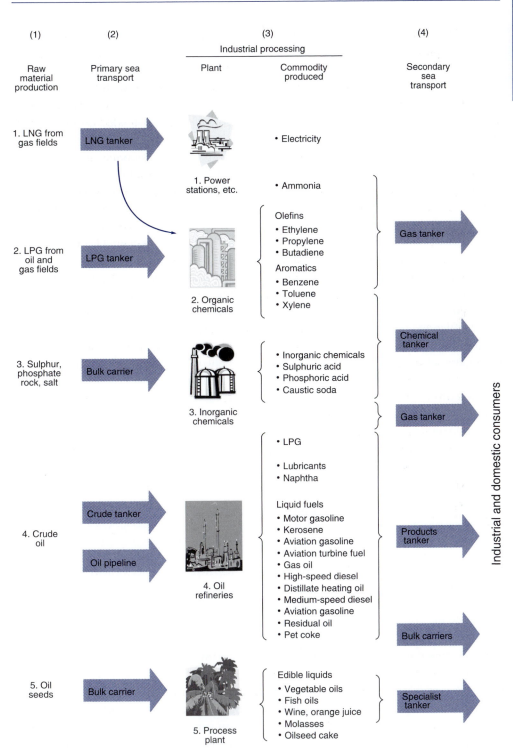

**Figure 11.6**
Principal sources of demand for tankers

and other processing plants. The purpose of Figure 11.6 is to summarize the part tankers play in these industries, making it clear why this is not an easy business to understand in detail.

Tankers are mainly employed carrying cargo between these three groups, ferrying in the raw materials and shipping out the product, as shown in columns 2 and 4. LNG tankers carry natural gas to power stations, though small amounts also go as a feedstock to chemical plants. Below that are LPG tankers carrying butane and propane from gas fields to petrochemical plants producing and exporting two main product groups, olefins (which are chemical gases) and aromatics (which are liquids). The gases travel in LPG tankers as semi-processed product, whilst the liquid aromatics travel in chemical tankers. Below that we come to the inorganic chemical trade, with bulk carriers and the various specialist tankers such as molten sulphur tankers, carrying raw materials to inorganic chemical plants which manufacture them into acids for onward shipment in chemical tankers. Then there is the crude oil trade, most of which is shipped to refineries, where it is refined into a whole range of products: LPG, liquid fuels, lubricants and heating oils. These are shipped on in gas tankers, chemical tankers or products tanker is as appropriate. Finally, at the bottom of the chart are the agricultural trades, notably vegetables, fish oils, wine, orange juice and molasses. Vegetable oils are the biggest trade, and recent regulations call for dedicated vessels which are not alternating with other chemical products.

All this adds up to a sophisticated transport network, operating the fleet of tankers discussed in Section 11.2 and ranging in size from the biggest crude oil tankers of 441,000 dwt at one extreme to a 2,000 dwt bitumen carrier at the other extreme. The task of shipping investors is to improve the efficiency of this transport business by improving the productivity of the transport system by means of better ships, greater flexibility and, where appropriate, specialized investment.

## 11.7 THE CRUDE OIL TRADE

### Origins of the seaborne oil trade

Crude oil was first produced commercially in 1859 when Colonel Edwin Drake struck oil at Titusville, Pennsylvania.[7] The first oil cargo was shipped two years later. Peter Wright & Sons of Philadelphia chartered the brig *Elizabeth Watts*, 224 tons, to load oil in barrels for London. Oil already had a reputation as a dangerous cargo and when that ship was ready for sea, her captain could not find seamen willing to sail with him. He enlisted the aid of a press gang and in November 1861 the first oil cargo sailed down the Delaware, and into history, with a drunken crew.[8]

For the next 25 years shipowners searched for better ways of transporting this disagreeable cargo.[9] Barrels, which were big and awkward to stow, were soon replaced by seven-gallon rectangular tins, packed in pairs in wooden cases. Known as 'case oil', these could be shipped as general cargo and for some years they became the standard cargo unit. As the trade grew, sailing ships were fitted with tanks, and some with cargo pumps, to carry petroleum 'without the aid of casks'. A few such as the *Ramsay* (1863) and the *Charles* (1869) were built for the trade but most were converted. The *Vaderland*, built in Jarrow in 1872 for Belgian owners, was the first effort to build an ocean-going tank steamer. It was designed to carry passengers to the USA and return with oil in tanks.[10]

The first purpose-built tanker to use the outer skin as the containment vessel was the *Glückauf*, 2307 tons, built for the German-American Petroleum Company and launched in 1886. As a safety measure, to avoid the build-up of dangerous gases, the double bottom was eliminated, except under the engine room. Several similar vessels, including the *Bakuin* built for Alfred Stuart and the *Loutsch*, were launched later in the year. [11]The savings by shipping bulk (4s. a barrel) were so great that within three years half of the oil imported into the UK came in bulk.[12] Thus started the era of bulk oil transport. From 12 bulk tankers in 1886, the fleet grew to 90 tankers operating in the Atlantic in 1891.

### The sea transport of oil, 1890–1970

Once the ships were available the newly emerging oil companies, which were deeply involved in distribution, were quick to see the advantages of bulk transport. In the late 1880s the US company Standard Oil, the world's biggest oil company, entered the tanker business.[13] They set up the Anglo-American Oil Co. Ltd and, in a typical grand gesture, purchased 16 tankers including the *Duffield* and the *Glückauf*.[14] At about the same time Marcus Samuel, who was distributing Russian case oil in the Far East, decided to build a fleet of tankers to transport Russian oil in bulk to the Far East, thus undercutting Standard Oil.[15] The first was the *Murex*, delivered in 1892, and by the end of 1893 ten ships had been launched for the Samuels.[16] In 1892 the Suez Canal permitted tankers to pass through, reducing the voyage to a competitive distance. Oil was loaded at the Black Sea port of Batum and delivered by tanker to the Far East. To improve profits, the tankers carried a backhaul of general cargo. After discharging oil at Bombay, Kobe, or Batavia, the tanks were steam-cleaned, white-washed and loaded with a backhaul cargo of tea, cereals or rice. In 1897 Shell Transport & Trading was formed and in 1907 Anglo-Saxon Petroleum Co. Ltd was formed by merging the Shell and Royal Dutch fleets, creating a total fleet of 34 ships.

Over the next 50 years the oil trade grew steadily, reaching 35 mt in 1920 and 182 mt in 1950 (Figure 11.7).

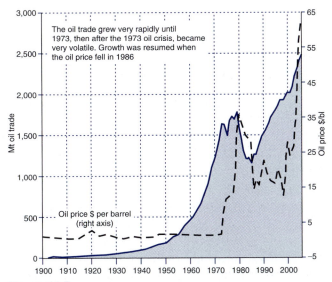

The oil trade grew very rapidly until 1973, then after the 1973 oil crisis, became very volatile. Growth was resumed when the oil price fell in 1986

Oil price $ per barrel (right axis)

**Figure 11.7**
World oil trade, 1900–2006
Source: Sun Oil, *Fearnleys Review*, CRSL

Trade was controlled by the 'oil majors' and transport dominated oil industry economics. In 1950 the cost of a barrel of oil in the Middle East was about $1. It cost another $1 to ship it to western Europe, so transport accounted for about half the c.i.f. price. Every cent shaved off transport costs contributed to profitability. Shipping was a 'core' business for the oil companies, who developed a policy of balancing owned ships with time charters to independent tanker owners. In the 1950s and 1960s the growth rate of trade increased to 8.4% per annum, compared with 5.9 per cent per annum previously, and since the Middle East was the marginal supply source, ton miles grew even faster. Planning the supply of transport became a major part of the oil industry's business, and they tackled it with characteristic thoroughness. In the 1950s the 'oil majors' set about creating a sophisticated machine for cutting the cost of oil transport. Their three guiding principles were as follows.

1. *Economies of scale*. Throughout the 1950s and the 1960s each generation of tankers was bigger than the last. The size increased from 17,000 dwt in 1950 to the first VLCC in 1966 and the first ULCC in 1976. The economics was simple and clear-cut. In 1968 an 80,000 dwt tanker such as the *Rinform* cost about 27s. 5d. per ton of oil to make the round trip from Rotterdam to Kuwait. On the same voyage a 200,000 dwt vessel returning via the Cape could do the voyage for 18s. 1d., a 34% saving.[17]

2. *Transport planning*. The majors developed a logistic network which used tankers to their maximum efficiency. They sailed with a full cargo; waiting time was negligible; regular maintenance minimized breakdown; and when problems occurred they were smoothly dealt with through inter-company cooperation. By the early 1970s the transport performance of the fleet was within a few per cent of the theoretical optimum.

3. *Subcontracting*. To avoid corporate overheads and to spread the risk, a large part of the fleet was subcontracted to independents, with Greeks and Norwegians serving the Atlantic market and Hong Kong serving Japan. To begin with in the 1950s the time charters were generally 5–7 years, but by the time VLCCs were being ordered in the 1960s charters of 15 or even 20 years were not uncommon. By the end of the 1960s the oil companies owned about 36% of the tanker fleet; they time-chartered another 52%; and they topped up their seasonal requirements from the spot market which accounted for about 12% of supply. The spot market was inhabited by the small, uneconomic elderly tankers and a few speculators trading modern tonnage through the boom and bust cycles.

This 'charter back' policy (*shikumisen* in Japan) enabled independent tanker owners to build up their tanker fleets by borrowing against the security of the oil company charter. By July 1971 there was a fleet of 178 m.dwt available for oil transport. The oil companies owned 48 m.dwt (27%), with an additional 79.8 m.dwt (45%) on time charter from independents. As fall-back, there was 19.5 m.dwt (11%) of the independent fleet trading spot, and 17 m.dwt of combined carriers.

Independent tankers thus outnumbered the oil company ships by a ratio of two to one. They made their profits by careful management and asset appreciation rather than speculation.[18] However, the oil companies were hard taskmasters. The charter rates they negotiated usually left little margin for error. As inflation and currency volatility developed in the late 1960s, some tanker owners became disenchanted with their role as subcontractors, especially as some owners seemed to be doing spectacularly well on the spot market.

## Growth of the tanker 'spot market',1975–2006

In the 1970s the factors that had worked so positively in favour of an integrated transport operation for oil were reversed. Everything went wrong. The oil trade fell sharply and at the same time supply got out of control, and the oil companies decided oil transport was no longer a core business and reduced their exposure to it. In the next 20 years the transport of oil changed from carefully planned industrial shipping to a market operation. As a result the independent tanker fleet, which in 1973 was mainly trading on time charter to the oil companies, gradually transferred to the spot market. By the early 1990s over 70% of this fleet was trading spot, compared with only about 20% in the early 1970s (see Figure 5.2).

This fundamental change in the organization of oil transport was precipitated by a period of volatility in the oil trade. Trade had reached 300 mt in 1960, and peaked at 1530 mt in 1978. From there it fell to 960 mt in 1983, then grew to 1480 mt in 1995 and 1820 mt in 2005 (Figure 11.8). The fall in the oil trade in the early 1980s had three causes. First, the European and Japanese energy markets were maturing. By the 1970s the transition from coal to oil was over, and lower growth was inevitable. Second, there were two deep economic depressions, one in the mid-1970s and the other in the early 1980s. Third, higher oil prices, which reached $30 per barrel in 1980, meant that other fuels were substituted for oil and fuel-saving technology became viable. In particular, the power station market was lost to coal, and technology reduced oil consumption in other areas.[19] In 1986 the oil price fell to $11 per barrel and remained in the $15–25 per barrel range until the end of the 1990s. This reversed the process of decline and the trade started growing again. But by the 1990s the oil trade had changed from the predictable trade for which transport was carefully planned by the oil companies to a volatile and risky business in which traders played a substantial part and transport was, to a large extent, left to the market place to manage.

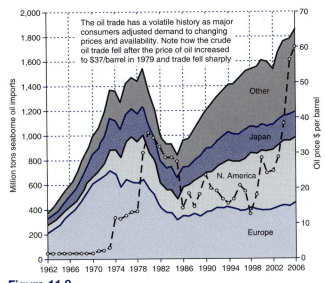

**Figure 11.8**
Crude oil imports, 1962–2005
Source: *Fearnleys Review* 2005 and earlier editions

### Geographical distribution of the crude oil trade

The geographical location of oil supplies plays an important part in determining the number of tankers needed to carry the trade. The location of the world's major oil exporting countries is shown in Figure 11.9, whilst the trade pattern in 2004 is shown in Table 11.4. The largest known source of crude oil outside the consuming areas is the Middle East. This region has 60% of world proven crude oil reserves and acts as marginal supplier of oil to the West, accounting for 47% of exports in 2004. No other supplier comes close to this. Most of the others are clustered around the North Atlantic, including Mexico, Venezuela, West Africa, North Africa, the North Sea and Russia (the main exporter in the 'others' category in Table 11.4). Finally, there are a few smaller producers in South East Asia, notably Indonesia, Australia and China. Since the Middle East lies further from the market than most of the other smaller export oil producers – it is 12,000 miles around the Cape to western Europe and over 6,000 miles to Japan – the ship demand depends upon the source from which oil is obtained and the route taken by the oil to market.

During the 1960s, the share of Middle East oil in the total trade grew very rapidly and the average haul for crude oil increased from 4500 miles to over 7,000 miles, giving a massive boost to ship demand. From a peak of 7,000 miles in the mid-1970s the average haul fell to a trough of 4450 miles in 1985. This fall was partly driven by increased

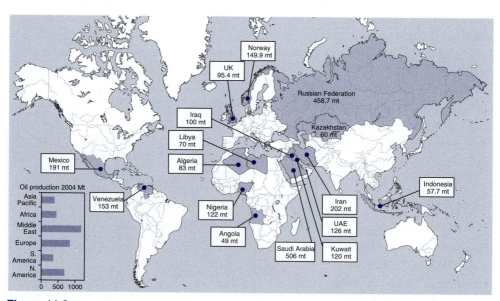

**Figure 11.9**
Major crude oil exporters, 2005
Source: BP Annual Review

**Table 11.4** Crude oil seaborne trade 2004 (million tonnes)

| To:<br>From: | Western<br>Europe | North<br>America | South<br>America | Japan | Other<br>Asia | Others | Total 2004<br>mt | Total 2004<br>% |
|---|---|---|---|---|---|---|---|---|
| Middle East | 129 | 130 | 11 | 180 | 353 | 30 | 832 | 47% |
| Near East | 11 | 1 | 0 | 0 | 0 | 0 | 12 | 1% |
| North Africa | 82 | 22 | 4 | 0 | 5 | 1 | 115 | 7% |
| West Africa | 26 | 92 | 9 | 8 | 67 | 4 | 206 | 12% |
| Caribbean | 14 | 189 | 13 | 0 | 6 | 0 | 222 | 13% |
| South East Asia | 0 | 5 | 0 | 10 | 25 | 15 | 56 | 3% |
| North Sea | 11 | 46 | 1 | 0 | 4 | 0 | 62 | 4% |
| Others | 155 | 40 | 14 | 2 | 32 | 6 | 250 | 14% |
| Total 2004 | 428 | 526 | 51 | 200 | 493 | 57 | 1,754 | 100% |
| % | 24% | 30% | 3% | 11% | 28% | 3% | 100% | |

Source: *Fearnleys Review* 2005

short-haul oil production. North Sea production started in 1975 and rose to 5.5 million barrels per day. At about the same time the Alaska North Slope came on stream, cutting US imports. Other factors contributing to the fall in ton miles were the reopening in 1975 of the Suez Canal which had been closed since 1967; the Sumed Pipeline which eventually carried 1.5 million barrels of oil per day to the Mediterranean; and in the 1980s the Dortyol pipeline built during the Iran–Iraq war diverted 1.5 million barrels of Arabian Gulf oil to the eastern Mediterranean. As a final complexity, in the early 1980s Saudi Arabia and Kuwait opened large refineries, with the capacity to export 100 mt of oil as products, not as crude. Taken together, over a period of 15 years these developments probably cut long-haul crude movements by about 10 million barrels per day. The cyclical role of the Middle East was repeated during the two decades from 1985 to 2005. After the oil price fell in 1986 there was a surge of Middle East exports which drove up ton miles and created demand for VLCCs. Then in the early 1990s there was a swing to short-haul oil, especially in the Atlantic, and ton miles fell as suppliers in the North Sea, West Africa and later Russia were able to meet the growing needs of the USA and Europe. Russia and Kazakhstan became the most important new exporters, with Russia shipping oil to Europe by pipeline, by sea through Primorsk on the Gulf of Finland and through the Black Sea. New supplies from Sakhalin on Russia's Pacific coast started to be shipped in 2006.

The position of the Middle East as marginal or 'swing' oil supplier and its geographical location relative to the other oil exporters creates a mechanism that we can refer to as the 'ship demand multiplier' – when oil exports are growing, the market share of the Middle East increases and the average haul rises; when the demand for imports is declining, the process goes into reverse. This means that upswings and downswings in the oil trade are intensified in terms of their impact upon the shipping market, and that predicting the demand for oil tankers must take account of the supply pattern for oil as well as the import requirement of each region.

Finally, we must say something about the control of the oil trade. Oil is a strategic business and market economics operate within a political framework. Until the 1970s the seven major oil companies were responsible for something like 80% of all oil processing in the world and they operated or controlled, through long-term charters, most of the seaborne oil transport.[20] However, in the last thirty years the control of oil transport has changed and their role in transport has been diluted. Oil producers, especially in the Middle East, now actively market their oil through distribution organizations in the consuming markets and several have built their own tanker fleets. New oil companies have emerged in the rapidly growing Asian markets, with their own transport policies. Finally, large volumes are now handled by oil traders, some working for the oil companies and others for independent traders such as Vitol or Glencore. They own much of the oil during shipment and since they are constantly buying and selling oil cargoes, it suits their business model to charter ships as required on a voyage by voyage basis, and this has encouraged the growth of the spot market. However, some take longer-term positions, especially products tankers, where their cargo volume allows them to obtain above-average utilization of the vessels.

## The crude oil transport system

Although seaborne oil transport is often thought of as a relatively straightforward business – and indeed, this is true of the crude oils – when we include all the various oil derivatives it really becomes a complex activity. The best way to understand the trade is to start by looking at its physical characteristics. From a transport viewpoint, oil cargoes can differ in two important respects: specific gravity;[21] and the standards of cleanliness needed to transport it. This point is illustrated in Table 11.5, which ranks oil cargoes by specific gravity. At the top end of the table are heavy fuel oils which have a specific

**Table 11.5** Oil product characteristics

| | Density at 15°C | | | | | | Stowage/tonne | |
| | Specific gravity | °API | Range + or – | Cargo type | Special characteristics | Typical cargo size- tons | Cu. ft | M³ |
|---|---|---|---|---|---|---|---|---|
| Heavy fuel oil | 0.98 | 13.53 | 3% | Dirty | Cargo heating | 50-80,000 | 32.8 | 0.93 |
| Heavy crude oil | 0.95 | 17.34 | 3% | Dirty | Cargo heating | 60-300,000 | 33.7 | 0.95 |
| Diesel oil | 0.86 | 32.92 | 3% | Dirty | | 40,000 | 37.2 | 1.05 |
| Light crude oil | 0.85 | 34.85 | 3% | Dirty | | 60-300,000 | 37.6 | 1.07 |
| Gas oil (light fuel oil) | 0.83 | 38.86 | 2% | Mainly clean | | 30,000 | 38.6 | 1.09 |
| Paraffin | 0.80 | 46.36 | 2% | Clean | Clean tanks | 30,000 | 40.3 | 1.14 |
| Motor spirit (petrol) | 0.74 | 59.58 | 5% | Clean | Clean tanks | 30,000 | 43.2 | 1.22 |
| Aviation spirit | 0.71 | 67.65 | 3% | Clean | Clean tanks | 30,000 | 45.1 | 1.28 |
| Naphtha | 0.69 | 73.43 | 4% | Clean | Clean tanks | 30,000 | 46.4 | 1.31 |

Source: Packard (1985, p. 129)

gravity close to 1, followed by heavy crude oil, diesel, and light crude oil. These are essentially the 'dirty' tanker products. Gas oil is a transitional product, in the sense that carrying several cargoes of gas oil helps to clean up the tanks after carrying a dirty cargo. Finally the lighter products fall into the 'clean' category, which simply means that the shippers are very sensitive that these products should not be polluted by any traces of the previous cargo. At the bottom of the table are petrol and naphtha, both of which have a substantially lower density than the dirty commodities. Finally, the table gives the typical parcel size in which these commodities are shipped. Crude oil is shipped in very large parcel sizes, typically over 100,000 tonnes, whilst most of the oil products are shipped in parcels of 30,000, 40,000 or 50,000 tonnes. However, diesel oil and heavy fuel oil are also shipped in relatively small parcels and need heating coils to keep the liquid at a pumpable viscosity.

These three characteristics – the density of the oil; the parcel size in which it is shipped; and the degree of care and cleanliness required in handling the cargo – set the framework for the oil transport system. Crude oil for export is usually transported from the oilfield to the coast by pipeline. A small-diameter pipe from each producing well connects to collecting stations from where it moves into large terminal areas with storage tanks capable of holding millions of barrels. The oil is then loaded into tankers and shipped to its destination, where it is offloaded into another bulk terminal. A typical 300,000 dwt VLCC would carry about 2 million barrels of oil, at a draught of about 22 metres, a speed of 15.8 knots and with a pumping capacity of between 15,000 and 20,000 tons per hour. The Suezmax tankers typically carry 1 million barrels with a loaded draught of 15.5 metres and a discharge pumping capacity of between 10,000 and 12,000 tons per hour.

Such large vessels require a dedicated port infrastructure and the terminals used in the oil trade, of the type illustrated in Figure 11.4, are often in remote locations, consisting of a tank farm for temporary oil storage and a jetty or single buoy mooring projecting into deep water where large tankers can load cargo. For example, Ras Tanura, the main export terminal of Saudi Arabia, has a series of jetties built offshore. From the discharge terminal the oil is delivered direct to a refinery, or to a crude oil terminal linked to refineries by a pipeline. In the early days of the oil industry much crude oil moved by rail tank car, but today pipelines, barges and ships dominate petroleum handling.

The deep draught of large tankers restricts their use of key shipping lanes such as the Straits of Dover, the Straits of Malacca and the Suez Canal. In the Straits of Dover, for instance, there is a maximum permissible draught of around 23–25 metres, which used to be on the margin for larger-size ULCCs, though in 2006 there were only four vessels of this draft in service. In the Straits of Malacca, on the route between the Middle East and Japan, the maximum draught of 21 metres precludes the larger ULCCs. However, from the shipping industry's point of view, the draught restrictions on the Suez Canal were the most important. Until the mid-1950s the Suez Canal was the main route for crude oil shipped from the Middle East to western Europe. At that time the draught was 11 metres, restricting the canal to loaded vessels of less than 50,000 dwt. The closure of the canal during the Six Day War in 1967 coincided with the trend to build VLCCs for the oil trade and as a result the imports of western Europe and the United States from the Middle East were diverted around the Cape of Good Hope.

After the Suez Canal was reopened in 1975, it was deepened to 16.2 metres, allowing vessels of up to 150,000 dwt to transit fully loaded, or larger vessels in ballast. As a result, shipments of oil through the canal edged up from 30 mt in 1976 to about 40 mt in 1995 and 85 mt in 2004, but remained well below the peak of 167 mt achieved before the canal was closed in 1967. This reflects the availability of bigger ships which cannot transit the canal fully loaded. One effect of the reopening of the Suez Canal was to generate a demand for intermediate-sized tankers of 100,000–150,000 dwt.

## 11.8 THE OIL PRODUCTS TRADE

The oil *products* trade is very different from the trade in crude oil. In 2005 about 500 mt of oil products were shipped by sea, about half of which were clean products and the other half dirty products. Clean products consist of the lighter distillates, principally kerosene and gasoline, which are usually shipped in vessels with coated, clean tanks. Dirty products include the lower distillates and residual oil, which can generally be shipped in conventional tankers, though the low viscosity sometimes necessitates steam-heating coils in the cargo tanks.

In the 1950s much of the oil trade was shipped as products, but as the market developed in the 1960s the oil company strategy was generally to ship crude oil to refineries located close to the market. Improved refining technology contributed to this trend, allowing the mix of refined products to be more closely matched to local demand and bigger crude oil tankers reduced transport costs, an important factor on the long sea journey from the Middle East to western Europe. Finally, politics played a part, since nationalization of the oil refineries of the Anglo-Iranian Oil Company in 1951 provided an incentive to locate refining capacity in the more politically secure consuming countries. As oil became more important to the economies of western Europe, so the degree of risk that they were prepared to accept became smaller. Thus 'there was an escalating interest in the development of market-based refineries, and by the end of the 1950s Western Europe had developed sufficient refinery capacity to meet its main oil products needs'. [22]

Despite these developments, in 2004 all the major oil-consuming areas imported products, notably the USA, Europe, China, Japan and the Asian tigers, whilst exports came from the Middle East, Venezuela, the Caribbean, Europe, Russia and India. This trade pattern, which is shown in Table 11.4, is shaped by a mix of economic and technical factors of which three are particularly important:

- *Refinery location.* There has been a gradual revival in the construction of export refineries located in producing areas, lead by the oil producers, for example in the Middle East, especially Saudi Arabia. Table 11.6 shows that in 2006 the Middle East was the biggest exporter, with a trade of 117 million tonnes, but India was also expanding its exports.
- *Balancing trades.* The mix of products refined from a barrel of oil does not always meet the precise market structure of the market adjacent to the refinery.

**Table 11.6** Oil products imports and exports, 2006 (million tonnes)

| | Imports | % | Exports | % |
|---|---|---|---|---|
| USA | 168.2 | 26% | 60.4 | 26% |
| Canada | 13.5 | 2% | 26.1 | 2% |
| Mexico | 20.1 | 2% | 6.9 | 2% |
| South & Central America | 24.0 | 3% | 63.8 | 3% |
| Europe | 131.4 | 22% | 75.9 | 22% |
| Former Soviet Union | 5.6 | 1% | 78.5 | 1% |
| Middle East | 7.3 | 1% | 116.7 | 1% |
| North Africa | 8.4 | 1% | 31.1 | 1% |
| West Africa | 7.5 | 2% | 7.5 | 2% |
| East & Southern Africa | 6.4 | 1% | 0.8 | 1% |
| Australasia | 13.9 | 2% | 4.1 | 2% |
| China | 45.9 | 9% | 13.5 | 9% |
| Japan | 48.4 | 9% | 5.5 | 9% |
| Singapore | 55.8 | 19% | 58.3 | 19% |
| Other Asia Pacific | 101.5 | 0% | 72.0 | 0% |
| Unidentified * | — | | 36.8 | |
| TOTAL WORLD | 657.8 | | 657.8 | |

Includes changes in the quantity of oil in transit, movements not otherwise shown, unidentified military use, etc.

Source: BP *Statistical Review of World Energy*, June 2007

For this reason there is a constant movement of specific oil products from areas of surplus to areas of shortage, driven by price differences.

- *Deficit trade*. Local shortages of refined products may occur either because demand grows faster than refining capacity can be expanded, or because the market is not large enough to support local refining operations. In these circumstances the import trade will take the form of oil products rather than crude oil.

The growth trends of the major importers are shown in Figure 11.10. Until the 1950s the principal products trades were from refineries in Venezuela and the Caribbean to the United States and from the Middle East to western Europe. The Caribbean to US trade built up to a peak of 150 mt a year in the early 1970s, then fell sharply to 75 mt as the US expanded its domestic refining capacity. However, in the 1990s the Clean Air Act legislation and the difficulty of building new refinery capacity started imports edging up again to 137 mt in 2004. European oil imports were mainly shipped as crude oil rather than products. Products imports fell to a trough of 35 mt in 1971, then revived to about 80 mt in the 1980s, compared with over 400 mt of crude imports. Towards the end of the 1990s European imports started to increase, following a similar pattern to the USA. The explanation of this trade pattern can be found in a combination of technical, economic and political factors. Figure 11.10 shows that a major change came in the 1980s when the 'other' countries' imports started to grow rapidly, quadrupling from 75mt in 1984 to 309mt in 2006. The split of the 2005 trade in Figure 11.10 shows that Asia accounts for two-thirds of this trade, in particular China, Korea and the many growing Asian economies which have a shortfall of particular product types.

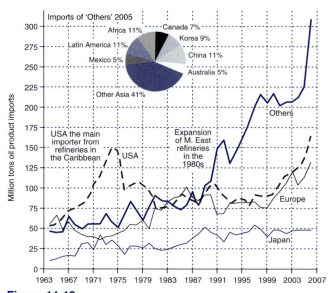

**Figure 11.10**
Oil product imports, 1963–2007
Source: BP, *Statistical Review*

Finally, we should note that to some extent this trade is supply-driven. Following the 1973 oil crisis several oil producers became interested in investing in refineries, which would enable them to export oil products rather than crude, increasing their value-added. The most prominent was Saudi Arabia, which has built a series of refineries aimed at the export market. In contrast, the US oil industry found itself with surplus refining capacity and started to withdraw from the refining operations in the Caribbean.

## The transport of oil products

The economics of the transport system for oil products is in many ways similar to that for crude oil, but there are some important differences. One is that most of the trade moves in small tankers of between 6,000 and 60,000 dwt, often with epoxy-coated tanks.[23] The size restriction arises from the smaller parcels of oil products traded by the oil industry and the many short-haul trades which limit economies of scale and terminal restrictions. However, there are no firm rules about size. Even VLCCs are occasionally chartered for long-haul parcels of fuel oil, and many Aframax tankers are coated to carry long-range products cargoes.[24]

An analysis in Table 11.7 of 11,577 vessels chartered in 2005–6 to carry oil products shows that gasoline is the biggest commodity, followed by fuel oil, gasoil and naphtha. The average parcel size was 44,600 tonnes, and the average ship size was 53,800 tonnes, so there was 18% 'dead freight' (un utilized space in the tankers). This is partly due to the low density of some oil products. For example, naphtha has a specific gravity of 0.69, and the dead freight for naphtha cargoes was 22%. The other reason for the high dead freight is that the available ships often do not exactly match the parcels for transport. For example, many 37,000 ton parcels of gasoline are shipped in products tankers of 48,000 dwt, and products tankers are sometimes designed with a hull optimized to a lower cargo parcel than the full deadweight (see Figure 14.7 for an example of a chemical tanker with a design deadweight 14% lower than its scantling deadweight). Products tankers trading switching from dirty to clean products need to go through a rigorous tank cleaning process.

**Table 11.7** Oil products cargo types Jan 2005 to July 2006

| | Ships fixed | | Cargo Mill. (t) | Cargo % dwt | Av. cargo '000 t | Av. ship '000 dwt |
|---|---|---|---|---|---|---|
| | Number | Mill. dwt | | | | |
| Gasoline | 5,390 | 254.5 | 198.5 | 78% | 36.8 | 47.2 |
| Fuel oil | 3,431 | 216.6 | 192.7 | 89% | 56.2 | 63.1 |
| Gasoil | 1,169 | 57.5 | 47.8 | 83% | 40.9 | 49.2 |
| Naphtha | 1,002 | 57.7 | 45.3 | 78% | 45.2 | 57.6 |
| Jet/kerosene | 393 | 22.2 | 19.1 | 86% | 48.5 | 56.6 |
| Condensate | 155 | 11.9 | 10.3 | 87% | 66.7 | 76.9 |
| Other | 37 | 1.8 | 2.9 | 166% | 79.5 | 47.8 |
| TOTAL | 11,577 | 622 | 517 | 83% | 44.6 | 53.8 |

Note: In some instances vessels have not been named for individual fixtures – as a result 'total vessel deadweight' may under-report actual tonnage used

Source: Sample of products tanker fixtures, 2005

The transport of oil products should be distinguished from the more specialized trade in small liquid parcels such as chemical and vegetable oils. These appear on the market in quantities which are large enough to make them prohibitively expensive to ship in drums or tank containers, but not in sufficiently large packages to justify the charter of a whole ship. This has led to the development of 'parcel' tankers which contain many segregated tanks, sometimes 30–40, with separate pumping arrangements, some of them with special coatings to resist toxic or corrosive liquids. This enables the shipowner to load many different cargoes of liquid into a single vessel. Some products tankers are designed with segregated cargo-handling systems which enable them to carry several different products or to trade in the easy chemicals market. A transport operation of this type is inevitably more complex, involving carefully planned investment decisions supported by a professional operating service to schedule the cargo and ensure that high utilization levels are achieved. The carriage of chemicals and other specialized liquid cargoes is discussed more fully in Chapter 12.

## 11.9 THE MAJOR DRY BULK TRADES

If oil is the energy of modern industrial society, the major bulks are the building-blocks from which it is constructed. *Iron ore* and *coking coal* are the raw materials of steelmaking, and steel is the principal material used in the construction of industrial and domestic buildings, motor cars, merchant ships, machinery and the great majority of industry products. *Steam coal* is a major energy source for power generation. The staple foods of the modern industrial society are bread and meat, both of which require large quantities of *grain* – for baking and as the raw material of the modern factory farming

**Table 11.8** The three 'major' bulk commodities shipped by sea (mt)

| Commodity | 1965 | 1975 | 1985 | 1995 | 2005 | % pa 1965–2005 |
|---|---|---|---|---|---|---|
| Iron ore | 152 | 292 | 321 | 399 | 650 | 3.7% |
| *growth % pa* | | 7% | 1% | 2% | 5% | |
| Coal | 59 | 127 | 272 | 403 | 690 | 6.3% |
| *growth % pa* | | 8% | 8% | 4% | 6% | |
| Grain | 70 | 137 | 181 | 184 | 242 | 3.1% |
| *growth % pa* | | 7% | 3% | 0% | 3% | |
| Total | 281 | 556 | 774 | 986 | 1,582 | 4.4% |
| *growth % pa* | | 7% | 3% | 2% | 5% | |

Source: Fearnleys *World Bulk Trades*, CRSL

of meat. It follows that in discussing these bulk trades we are concerned with the whole material development of the world economy that uses these materials.

Because of their volume, the three major bulk trades are the driving force behind the dry bulk carrier market. In 2005 the trade totalled 1.58 bt, accounting for almost one quarter of total seaborne cargo, and in terms of tonnage about the same as the crude oil trade. The tonnage of cargo in each commodity and its growth rate in each of the last four decades are shown in Table 11.8.

Over the four decades 1965–2005 the major bulk trades grew at an average of 4.4% per annum, but each followed a different growth pattern. Coal grew much the fastest (6.3% pa), followed by iron ore (3.7% pa) and grain (3.1% pa). In addition, the table shows that the rate of growth varied from decade to decade. For example, iron ore grew at 7% pa in the first decade, and 1–2% pa in next two, and 5% in the last. One of the principal reasons for studying commodity trade economics is to explain why such changes take place. As we shall see in the following brief review, there is no simple pattern. Each commodity has its own distinctive industrial characteristics, growth trends and impact upon the dry bulk shipping industry.

## The seaborne iron ore trade

Iron ore is the largest of the major bulk commodity trades and the principal raw material of the steel industry with a trade of 590 mt in 2004 (Table 11.9). Like crude oil, the iron ore trade is determined by the location of the processing plant in relation to raw material supplies. During the industrial revolution, steel plants were located on sites close to major sources of raw materials, notably iron ore, coal and limestone, and access to materials was a major concern in the economics of the industry. However, as transport technology developed, it became clear that the distance over which the materials were shipped was less important than the freight-rate structure, the transport service and the quality of the raw materials.[25]

Today developments in bulk shipping technology mean that steel plants located near to raw material supplies no longer have a significant cost advantage, particularly when land transport is required. For example, in the United Kingdom, Northamptonshire ores were trebled in cost by transport to Middlesbrough, making them unable to compete with high-grade ore shipped from Brazil to Middlesbrough by sea for around $7 per tonne. [26] As the demand for steel expanded in the twentieth century, the industry gravitated towards coastal steel plants, which could import raw materials at minimum cost by using a carefully planned integrated bulk shipping operation. This had the advantage that, with the resources of the world accessible by sea, it was possible to find higher-quality raw materials than were available locally, particularly in the traditional steel-making areas of western Europe where the better-quality ores were already depleted.

The prototype for the modern integrated dry bulk transport operation was the steel plant built by Bethlehem Steel at Sparrow's Point, Baltimore, in the early 1920s. This plant was designed specifically to import iron ore by sea from Cruz Grande in Chile, taking advantage of the newly opened Panama Canal. To service the trade, a contract was placed with the Brostrom group, which ordered two ore carriers of 22,000 dwt. At the time these were two of the world's largest ocean-going cargo ships. Details of the shipping operation are recorded as follows:

> The contract, signed in 1922, called for two ships to carry ore from Chile through the Panama Canal to Bethlehem Steel Company's plant at Sparrow's Point, Baltimore. The ships had no conventional cargo handling gear, and hinged corrugated steel hatch covers. These were the full width of the holds, weighed 8 tons apiece and were clamped down to thick rubber gaskets. The *Sveland* was delivered on 9th April 1925 and *Americaland* on 29th June and they promptly entered their designed service between Cruz Grande and Baltimore. It was an exacting schedule and the average time spent at sea each year was 320–330 days. At Cruz Grande the 22,000 tons cargo was normally loaded in two hours, though the record was 48 minutes. Discharging at the other end required about 24 hours. Routine engine maintenance was carried out at sea, one of the two engines being shut down for eight hours per trip. Painting was also carried out while underway. [27]

This strategy of using large, specially designed ships on a shuttle service between the mine and the steel plant has become standard practice in the steel industry and the size of ship increased from 120,000 dwt in the 1960s to 170,000 dwt in 2007, with some units of 300,000 dwt built for stable ore trades.

The East Coast development of the US steel industry proved something of a false start, and the major portion of US steel-making continued to be concentrated around the Great Lakes, using locally produced ores supplemented by imports from Canada via the St Lawrence Seaway when the Labrador iron ore fields were developed. As a result, the USA did not figure prominently in the post-war overseas iron ore trade.

In fact, the principal growth in imports of iron ore came from western Europe, Japan, Korea and most recently China, as can be seen in Figure 11.11. During the post-war period of industrial expansion, steel demand grew rapidly. In Europe and Japan this growth was met by building modern integrated coastal steel plants using imported raw materials. In Japan there was little choice since there were no domestic reserves of iron ore, but even in Europe where extensive iron ore reserves are available these were of

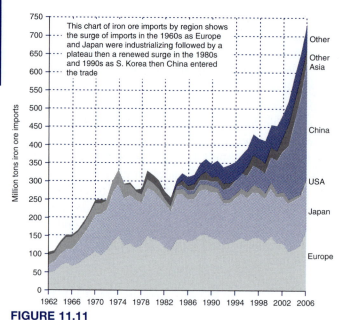

**FIGURE 11.11**

Iron ore imports, 1962–2005

Source: *Fearnleys Review* 2005 and earlier editions

lower quality than the imported variety. For new developments, the shorter land transit leg offered little cost advantage over seaborne transport using large bulk carriers. It was the rapid expansion of iron ore imports by the steel industry that underpinned the bulk carrier boom of the 1960s. The Japanese and European steel companies were prepared to offer long-time charters to meet the regular raw material requirements of the new coastal steel plants. These charters provided many growing bulk shipping companies with the stable foundation on which to base their fleet development strategy. In the early 1970s, however, the growth subsided. After a decade of expansion the steel companies found themselves facing excess capacity and for twenty years ore imports stagnated, as can be seen in Figure 11.11. The explanation is that steel production in Europe and Japan had reached a level which was sufficient to service their ongoing domestic needs: between 1975 and 2005, western European steel output fell from 170 mt to 162 mt; during the same period Japanese production fluctuated around 110 mt. [28] There are many reasons for this radical change of trend, but the most important was that the industries that use steel intensively (principally construction, vehicles and shipbuilding) had all reached a plateau in their output. [29] As a result, the growth had been removed from the largest iron ore importers.

The next turning point came in the 1980s when South Korean steel production started to grow, and a decade later that was dwarfed by the industrialization of China which, during a sudden burst of growth, added 300 mt of steel capacity in the four years 2002–6, driving the iron ore trade up to 720 mt.

Although we have concentrated on the demand for seaborne imports of iron ore, the trade also depends crucially upon the development of a global network of iron ore supplies, and the map in Figure 11.12 shows the pattern that developed. Generally at the initiative of the steel companies, iron ore resources were identified across the globe and the necessary capital raised to develop the mines and install the requisite transport infrastructure.

By far the largest iron ore exporters are Australia (206 mt in 2004) and Brazil (205 mt), together accounted for 70% of iron ore exports (Table 11.9). The Brazilian iron ore

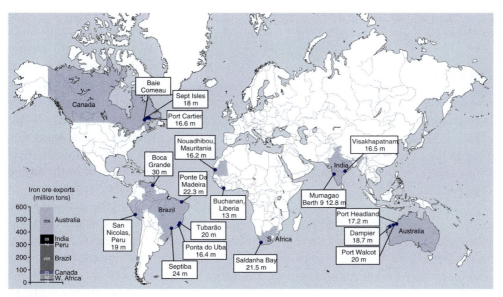

**FIGURE 11.12**
Major iron ore exporters and ports, 2005.
Note: The numbers against each port indicate the approximate maximum draft in metres.

reserves are located in the famous Iron Quadrangle of Minas Gerais which exports through the ports of Sepetiba and Tubarão Carajas, and a major iron ore development in the Pará region of Northern Brazil with port facilities at Itaqui geared to 300,000 dwt bulk carriers. Australia's mines are mainly located in north-west Australia, and its ore, exported mainly through the three ports of Port Hedland, Dampier and Port Walcott.

**Table 11.9** Seaborne iron ore trade 2004

| To: <br> From: | UK/ <br> Cont. | Mediter- <br> ranean | Other <br> Europe | USA | Japan | China | Other <br> Far East | Others | Total <br> mt | Total <br> % |
|---|---|---|---|---|---|---|---|---|---|---|
| Scandinavia | 7 | 1 | 1 | | | 1 | 0 | 7 | 16 | 3% |
| Other Europe | 0 | | | | | 0 | 1 | 3 | 5 | 1% |
| West Africa | 8 | | 1 | | | | | 3 | 11 | 2% |
| S. Africa | 7 | 0 | 3 | | 10 | 17 | 2 | 2 | 42 | 7% |
| North America | 12 | 1 | 0 | | 1 | 2 | 2 | 4 | 23 | 4% |
| Brazil | 46 | 2 | 8 | 7 | 27 | 54 | 21 | 38 | 205 | 35% |
| S.America Pac. | | | | 0 | 4 | 6 | 3 | 1 | 14 | 2% |
| India | 1 | 0 | | | 22 | 40 | 4 | 2 | 68 | 12% |
| Australia | 15 | 1 | 1 | 0 | 76 | 70 | 39 | 5 | 206 | 35% |
| Total 2004 | 95 | 6 | 14 | 8 | 140 | 190 | 71 | 66 | 590 | 100% |

Source: *Fearnleys Review*, 2005

The remaining third of the iron ore trade is supplied from a variety of smaller exporters, of whom the most important are India, South Africa, Liberia and Sweden.

## The transport system for iron ore

Iron ore is a low value commodity worth about $40 per tonne and very dense, with a stowage factor of 0.3 cubic metres per ton. It is almost always transported in bulk and in full shiploads. Over the past decade there has been great competition between suppliers in the Atlantic and Pacific for the markets in Asia and the North Atlantic, leading to increasing distance between source and markets and the employment of the largest ships possible.

At the mine earth-moving equipment removes the ore from open pits and transfers it to special trains or trucks that transfer it to port, where it is placed in storage areas. When needed it is reclaimed and transferred by conveyor to the quayside where it is loaded (see Figure 11.5) by gravity or cranes. The ship then steams to a port or coastal steel mill where the process is reversed. The entire system is geared to anticipate mill needs with a continuous flow of the ore from mine to mill. Discharge is at a special terminal similar to the loading terminal, but with grabs of up to 50 tons used to handle the cargo. The throughput of the system is determined by cargo-handling capacity, storage and the availability of ships.

Although the economies of scale which can be achieved through the use of large bulk vessels were well known in the 1950s, the transition from small vessels to the larger sizes was a slow process. In 1965, 80% of all iron ore was carried in vessels below 40,000 dwt; forty years on, by 2005, 80% was carried in ships over 80,000 dwt. The process of introducing large ships was gradual, with the bulk carriers built for the trade increasing steadily from around 30,000 dwt in the early 1960s to 60,000 dwt in 1965, 100,000 dwt in 1969, 1,50,000 dwt plus in the early 1970s, and 300,000 dwt in the 1990s. For example, the *Bergeland*, delivered in 1991, was a 300,000 dwt vessel designed exclusively for the carriage of iron ore, and in 2007 four 388,000 dwt bulkers were on order for the China trade. In fact the size of ship has grown with the volume of trade and the improvements in port facilities, though many small vessels built in previous periods continue to be used.

## The seaborne coal trade

Coal is the second largest dry bulk trade, with imports of 665 mt in 2004 (Table 11.10), principally into western Europe and Japan, as can be seen in Figure 11.13. It is a complex trade with two very different markets, 'coking coal' used in steel-making, and 'thermal coal' used to fuel power stations. As the inset chart in Figure 11.13 shows, in recent decades the two trades have followed very different growth paths, with the thermal coal trade growing rapidly at 9% per annum between 1980 and 2005, whilst the coking coal trade only managed 2% per annum.

Coking coal is a major raw material of the steel industry. The coal is first converted into coke in a coke oven, and then mixed with iron ore and limestone to form a charge that is fed into the top of the blast furnace. As the charge works its way down the blast furnace, the carbon in the coke combines with oxygen in the iron ore and at the bottom of the blast furnace the pig iron is drawn off, leaving a residue of slag. This process requires a special type of coal. To do its job satisfactorily the coke 'must be porous to allow air circulation, strong enough to carry the weight of the charge in the furnace without being crushed, and low in ash and sulphur'.[30] Many varieties of coal locally available do not meet these requirements, and some grades are naturally more satisfactory than others.

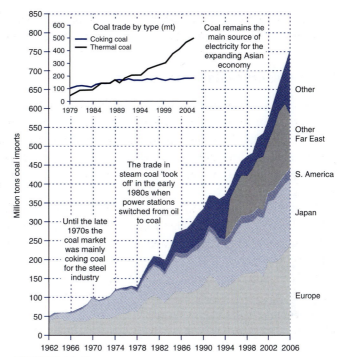

**FIGURE 11.13**
Coal imports, 1962–2005
Source: *Fearnleys Review* 2005 and earlier editions

By moving to coastal steel plants steel-makers can import the most suitable metallurgical grade coals from foreign mines and blend them to give the precise requirements for efficient steel-making. As a result, coking coal imports grew rapidly during the 1960s, but stagnated in the 1970s in the same way as the iron ore trade and for the same reason. However when China started to expand its steel industry in the late 1990s, coking coal imports did not expand because China has very large coal reserves (114 billion tons of recoverable coal in 2004) and was able to meet its coking coal requirements from domestic sources.

Coal is also widely burned in power stations and is in competition with oil and gas. During the 1950s the falling price of oil made coal uncompetitive, and by the early 1960s the thermal coal trade had disappeared. For the next decade almost the only coal moved by sea was for steel-making. With the increase in oil prices during the 1970s, however, coal became more competitive and its supply base more stable. It took several years to mobilize the necessary volume and handling infrastructure.[31] But from 1979 onwards there was a rapid increase in thermal coal imports, as is clearly visible in the inset graph in Figure 11.13.

The main coal importers and exporters are shown in Figure 11.14 and Table 11.10. Europe, Japan and other Far East countries are the main coal importers. Europe and Japan both use substantial amounts of coking coal, as does South Korea which is included in the 'other Far East' category, but power generation is also a substantial

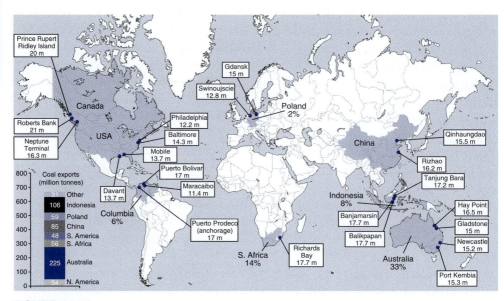

**FIGURE 11.14**
Major coal exporters and ports, 2005.
Note: The numbers against each port indicate the approximate maximum draft in metres.
Source: *Fearnleys Review* 2005

market and there are many power stations scattered across Asia which import coal by sea. Australia provides more than a third of the exports, followed by Indonesia and a number of smaller exporters such as Colombia (South American Caribbean) and Canada. One of the attractions of coal over oil is the wide range of different suppliers available. During the boom of 2006 China started to cut back on its exports and

**Table 11.10** Seaborne coal trade 2004

| To:<br>From: | Europe | South<br>America | Japan | Other<br>Far East | Others | Total<br>mt | % |
|---|---|---|---|---|---|---|---|
| N. America | 23 | 8 | 10 | 9 | 3 | 54 | 8% |
| Australia | 29 | 10 | 103 | 59 | 23 | 225 | 34% |
| S. Africa | 46 | 2 | | 1 | 6 | 56 | 8% |
| S. Am. Caribbean | 25 | 2 | 0 | 0 | 21 | 48 | 7% |
| China | 4 | 1 | 29 | 44 | 7 | 85 | 13% |
| FSU | 42 | 0 | 9 | 7 | 1 | 59 | 9% |
| Oth.E Europe | 13 | 0 | | | 1 | 14 | 2% |
| Indonesia | 14 | 1 | 25 | 55 | 10 | 106 | 16% |
| Others | 4 | 1 | 4 | 8 | 1 | 17 | 3% |
| Total | 200 | 26 | 180 | 184 | 75 | 665 | 100% |
| | 30% | 4% | 27% | 28% | 11% | 100% | |

Source: *Fearnleys Review* 2005

increase its coal imports. On the export side, Australia exported 225 mt of coal in 2004, accounting for one-third of the coal export trade, followed by Indonesia with exports of 106 mt and China with 85 mt, whilst South Africa, Colombia and Poland all supplied about 50 mt. In Australia, the major coal reserves are in Queensland and New South Wales which in 2004 produced 169 mt and 117 mt of coal respectively. South African coal is shipped by rail to Richards Bay for export. In Canada, the mines are mainly in British Columbia, where 20 bt of reserves are accessible to surface or shallow mining. Most of the coal exported from British Columbia comes from the Kootenay and Peace River coalfields which lie in the foothills of the Rockies. The coal is shipped 700 miles by rail for export through bulk handling terminals at Vancouver, mainly to Asian markets.

The bulk carriers used in the coal trade are generally smaller than in the iron ore trade – the analysis in Table 11.1 shows that ships transporting iron ore averaged 148,000 dwt compared with 109,000 dwt for coal. The main reason appears to be the smaller volume of coking coal used in the steel making process, relative to iron ore, its greater volume to stockpile, the higher value and the risk of spontaneous combustion in very large cargoes. An example of a coal transport system is provided by the Hunter Valley/Port of Newcastle complex in Australia. The Port of Newcastle services the export trade of over 30 coalmines located in the Hunter Valley behind Newcastle. The coal moves by rail through marshalling depots to two port stockpile areas. The port has three coal loaders loading up to four ships at once, ranging from vessels of only 10,000 dwt to coal carriers of 150,000 dwt. The water draught is maintained at 15.2 metres by a dredging programme which is paid for by the coal and steel companies. The cargo-handling equipment used for coal is very similar to the iron ore system described earlier.

## The seaborne grain trade

Although grain is grouped with iron ore and coal as one of the major bulks, in both economic and shipping terms it is a different business. Whereas iron ore and coal form part of a carefully structured industrial operation, grain is an agricultural commodity, seasonal in its trade and irregular in both volume and route. Consequently it is more difficult to optimize, or even plan, and the trade depends heavily on general-purpose tonnage drawn from the charter market.

In 2005, the grain trade was 236 mt (Table 11.1). Grain is used both as human food and as animal feed in the production of meat. Wheat accounted for about half of the grain trade, mostly destined for human consumption; the other half consisted of maize, barley and oilseeds, mainly for use as animal feed. The pattern of trade is shown in Figure 11.15. During the 1960s the grain trade was dominated by Europe and Japan, which accounted for more than two-thirds of grain imports. In tonnage terms this sector of the trade remained fairly static during the 1970s and early 1980s. Almost all of the growth in the volume of seaborne imports came from the entry of eastern Europe, including the USSR, and the developing countries into the market. After 1980 the trade grew more slowly and by 2005 the trade shares of Europe and Japan had fallen to 10%

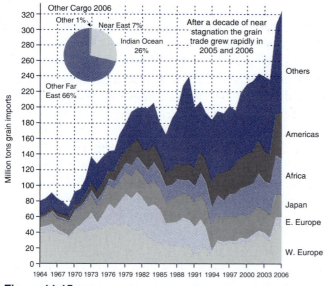

**Figure 11.15**
Grain imports, 1965–2005
Source: *Fearnleys Review* 2005 and earlier editions

and 12% respectively. Other Far East countries (29%), particularly China, the Americas (16%), and Africa (17%) had all become much more important (Table 11.11, right hand column).

The upward trend in seaborne grain imports shown in Figure 11.15 was to a large extent driven by the trend towards greater meat consumption at higher income levels. By commodity, in 2004 the seaborne grain trade was split between wheat (104 mt), and coarse grains (105 mt), most of which are fed to animals.[32]

The dietary pattern that underlies this situation, and its impact on grain demand in the post-1945 era, is described by Morgan as follows:

> Rising incomes put more money into people's pockets for buying food. Millions of families 'stepped-up' to diets that included more bread, meat and poultry. Livestock and poultry rather than people became the main market for American grain, and soya beans and corn ranked with jet aircraft and computers as the country's major exports. As more countries aspired to this grain based diet, the need for grain increased.[33]

Between 1950 and 2004, global meat production increased fivefold from 46 million tons to 248 million tons, and per capita production rates jumped from 18kg to 40.5 kg.[34] The 15 billion farm animals kept to supply this demand require on average about six units of feed for each unit of meat produced,[35] plus additional feed such as pasture in many cases. Broiler chickens are the most efficient, requiring 3.4 kg of feed (expressed in equivalent feeding value of corn) to produce 1 kg of ready-to-cook chicken. Pigs are the least efficient, with a feed to meat ratio of 8.4 : 1; eggs 3.8 : 1; beef about 7.5 : 1 and cheese, 7.9 : 1.

## The grain trade model

In view of the importance of the food–feed relationship in the grain trade, it is worth taking a look at the economics of the food trade. This is a typical supply–demand model of the type we discussed in Chapter 10. Food demand depends on income, population, prices, daily calorie intake and consumer tastes, while supply depends on land, yields, policies, prices and feed conversion efficiency.

The relationship between income and food demand is particularly important. The nineteenth-century statistician Ernst Engel discovered that as incomes rise the proportion spent on food declines.[36] He also found that within the food budget, the type of food purchased changes with income. At low income levels demand is for necessities such as rice, cereals and vegetables, but as income rises there is a tendency to substitute animal products such as meat and dairy for basic commodities such as cereals, root crops and rice. If we define 'income elasticity' as the percentage increase in demand for a 1% increase in income, we find that livestock-related food (i.e. meat and dairy products) tend to have a higher income elasticity than grains, vegetables and rice.[37] The feed conversion rates discussed in the previous paragraph mean that rapid growth in demand for these animal products as income rises has a multiplied effect on the demand for feedstuffs, and this filters through into the cereals trade.

The supply side of the food trade model is equally complex. Crop production depends upon crop yield and the area of agricultural land. Prices, political policies and stock changes are also important variables. Until the early years of the twentieth century most of the world's increase in crop production came from either an increase in land (e.g. the opening up of the North American grain lands) or from an increase in the amount of labour used. During the twentieth century, however, agricultural yields increased and the amount of arable land remained fairly constant. Higher yields were obtained from greater fertilizer application, improved seed varieties, mechanization, pesticides and better farming techniques. There are differences in productivity around the world. For example, the average level of France's cereal output per worker is ten times as great as in Japan and 40 times as great as in India.

Although in the short term the grain trade is influenced by local conditions such as harvests, in the longer term changing demand in response to income, prices, and, on the supply side, yields are more important. The rapid growth of imports by Asia, Africa and the Americas in the last twenty years (see Figure 11.15) was a response to rising incomes, the high income elasticity of animal products in these countries and the need to import animal feeds. As in the oil trade, the substitution effect of prices should not be overlooked.

## The transport of grain

Grain is traded on a wide range of routes, and the main trade volumes are shown in the matrix in Table 11.11. The United States is by far the biggest exporter, accounting for 46% of the trade, with other suppliers coming from Australia (10%) and South America, mainly Argentina. Imports are widely spread, with the Far East (29%) the biggest market, followed by Africa (17%), the Americas (16%), Japan (12%) and the Indian Ocean. The average trade flow is just 5 million tonnes, though the biggest route shown in this matrix is between the United States and the Far East.

Because this is an agricultural crop, subject to the vagaries of the weather and with many small ports, the transport system needs to be flexible. As an example of the grain transport system we can take the processing of Canadian wheat into consumer products. The wheat is harvested by large combines in the Canadian Prairies and moved by truck

**Table 11.11** Seaborne grain trade, 2004

| From: To: | USA | Canada | South America | Australia | Others | Total mt | % |
|---|---|---|---|---|---|---|---|
| Gulf/Continent | 2.8 | 0.7 | 6.0 | 0.0 | 0.3 | 9.8 | 4% |
| Total Europe | 5.0 | 1.8 | 8.9 | 0.7 | 7.4 | 23.9 | 10% |
| Africa | 14.6 | 2.2 | 7.4 | 3.8 | 12.0 | 40.1 | 17% |
| Americas | 26.5 | 3.2 | 7.8 | 0.2 | 0.2 | 37.9 | 16% |
| Near East | 3.6 | | 1.0 | 0.1 | 2.9 | 7.6 | 3% |
| Indian Ocean | 2.1 | 0.8 | 4.7 | 6.7 | 5.0 | 19.2 | 8% |
| Japan | 22.8 | 1.7 | 0.8 | 2.7 | 0.7 | 28.6 | 12% |
| Oth. FE | 30.1 | 5.2 | 16.4 | 9.9 | 6.7 | 68.4 | 29% |
| Oth. & Unspec. | | | | 0.5 | | 0.5 | 0% |
| Total | 107.6 | 15.7 | 53.0 | 24.6 | 35.1 | 236.0 | 100% |
| % total | 46% | 7% | 22% | 10% | 15% | 100% | |

Source: *Fearnleys Review* 2005

from the field to a storage elevator, into which it is transferred by conveyor or by an air pressure (pneumatic) system. During high harvests or when demand is low these storage facilities may become inadequate, and in the past farmers have been reduced to storing grain in sacks in any available covered storage. From the storage elevator the wheat is gravity fed to a railcar and shipped to port where it is offloaded from the railcar by opening a hopper in the bottom of the car to allow the grain to fall on to a conveyor under the rail track. From here the conveyor transfers the wheat into an elevator where it awaits transfer to a merchant ship. Naturally the elevator must hold enough grain to fill the ship.

At the other end of the voyage the process is reversed and the grain is offloaded from the ship into a storage elevator (i.e. silo) and shipped to a flour mill or feed compounder where it is again stored in silos. From the silos it moves to the grinding facility via a conveyor or an air slide. The finished flour coming from the end of the line is either packaged for the consumer market or shipped in bulk by rail and truck to bakeries, other large industrial users, or farmers.

At the bakery the flour is again placed in a silo or hopper, conveyed to a mixing unit for dough preparation, baked into bread or other products, sent to an automatic wrapping machine, and wheeled to trucks for delivery. In many cases the first time the product is handled as a single unit is when the consumer takes it from the shelf. Such an integrated transport system is made possible by meticulous attention to required materials handling systems within each process and to the transfers of material between processes.

Despite this organization, the sea transport of grain is not managed in the same carefully planned way as the industrial commodities. Because the trade is seasonal and fluctuates with the harvest in the exporting and importing regions, shippers rely heavily on the spot market, using the ships that are available. These fluctuations are not predictable, so planning transport is very difficult and complex. To load cargoes upwards of 70,000 tons involves careful scheduling of input barges or box cars from many different

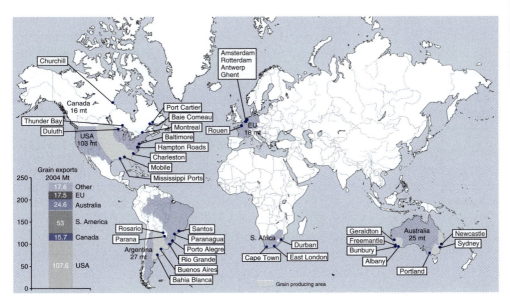

**FIGURE 11.16**
Major grain exporters and ports, 2005
Source: CRSL, *Dry Bulk Trade Outlook*, 2005

sources, often at the height of the season. Discharging can be equally hazardous since there are all the problems of ensuring the prompt arrival of a multitude of barges and coasters, and penalties for faulty consignment and demurrage charges grow more rapidly with large cargoes.[38] For this reason it is more difficult to introduce large ships into the grain trade than into the iron ore and coal trades and there is often congestion.

The major grain-exporting ports are shown in Figure 11.16 in relation to the grain-producing areas from which they draw their supplies. In 2004 over half of all grain exports were shipped out of Canada and the United States (see Table 11.11), so this is clearly the most important loading area. Essentially the US Gulf ports and the East Coast ports serve the southern end of the US grain belt, while the Great Lakes and the St Lawrence serve the north-east. Production from Saskatchewan and Alberta is shipped mainly through West Coast ports, especially Vancouver. Size limitations vary considerably, though ports on the lower St Lawrence and New Orleans can load vessels over 100,000 dwt. Argentina, Australia and the EU were the three other major exporters.

## 11.10 THE MINOR BULK TRADES

The third and most diverse sector of the bulk trades are the minor bulks, a mix of commodities which generated a billion tons of cargo in 2005, carried mainly by the smaller bulk carriers, but the container services also compete for many of these commodities. As Table 11.12 shows, this group comprises a mix of raw materials and semi-manufactures, divided into six groups: agribulks; sugar; fertilizers; metals and minerals; steel products; and forest products. This is not a complete list, and the statistics include some trade by land, but it covers the main items and gives a fair indication of

**Table 11.12** Selected minor bulk trades (mt)

|  | 1985 | 1990 | 1995 | 2000 | 2005 | % p.a. growth '85–'05 |
|---|---|---|---|---|---|---|
| **1. Agribulks** | | | | | | |
| Soya beans | 25.5 | 28.2 | 32.2 | 45.5 | 64.9 | 4.8% |
| Soya meal | 23.2 | 26.0 | 30.9 | 39.0 | 45.4 | 3.4% |
| Oilseed/meals | 19.0 | 21.0 | 21.9 | 28.3 | 19.8 | 0.2% |
| Rice | 11.3 | 12.1 | 20.9 | 22.8 | 27.8 | 4.6% |
| Total agribulks | 79.0 | 87.3 | 105.9 | 135.6 | 157.8 | 3.5% |
| Average % pa | | 2% | 4% | 6% | 3% | |
| **2. Sugar** | | | | | | |
| White sugar | 9.9 | 10.5 | 17.9 | 16.1 | 21.4 | 3.9% |
| Raw sugar | 17.0 | 18.0 | 16.1 | 20.4 | 24.9 | 1.9% |
| Total sugar | 27.8 | 28.5 | 34.1 | 36.5 | 46.3 | 2.6% |
| Average % pa | | 0% | 4% | 1% | 5% | |
| **3. Fertilizers** | | | | | | |
| Phosphate rock | 43.0 | 35.0 | 30.0 | 30.0 | 31.0 | −1.6% |
| Phosphates | 9.6 | 9.9 | 14.2 | 14.7 | 16.6 | 2.8% |
| Potash | 16.6 | 17.7 | 20.6 | 23.3 | 26.0 | 2.3% |
| Sulphur | 17.3 | 17.7 | 16.6 | 20.4 | 22.4 | 1.3% |
| Urea | 9.4 | 9.7 | 11.2 | 11.7 | 12.7 | 1.5% |
| Total fertilisers | 95.9 | 90.1 | 92.6 | 100.1 | 108.7 | 0.6% |
| Average % pa | | −1% | 1% | 2% | 2% | |
| **4. Metals & minerals** | | | | | | |
| Bauxite & alumina | 44.0 | 49.0 | 50.0 | 53.0 | 73.0 | 2.6% |
| Manganese ore | 8.2 | 7.1 | 5.4 | 6.7 | 11.0 | 1.5% |
| Coke | 12.5 | 11.8 | 17.2 | 24.4 | 24.7 | 3.5% |
| Cement | 50.0 | 49.0 | 53.0 | 45.5 | 60.0 | 0.9% |
| Scrap | 25.5 | 35.8 | 51.1 | 62.4 | 93.5 | 6.7% |
| Pig iron | 10.6 | 13.2 | 14.4 | 13.1 | 17.0 | 2.4% |
| DRI/HBI[a] | 0.8 | 1.8 | 3.8 | 6.7 | 7.2 | 11.6% |
| Salt & soda ash | 18.0 | 20.1 | 22.2 | 23.0 | 23.9 | 1.4% |
| Total metals & mins. | 169.6 | 187.8 | 217.1 | 234.8 | 310.3 | 3.1% |
| Average % pa | | 2% | 3% | 2% | 6% | |
| **5. Steel products** | | | | | | |
| Steel prods. | 170.0 | 168.0 | 198.0 | 183.7 | 217.0 | 1.2% |
| **6. Forest products** | | | | | | |
| Forest prods. | 131.0 | 157.0 | 167.0 | 161.0 | 169.9 | 1.3% |
| Total minor bulk | 673.3 | 718.6 | 814.6 | 851.7 | 1,010.1 | 2.0% |
| Average % pa | | 1.3% | 2.7% | 0.9% | 3.7% | |

Source: CRSL, USDA, IISI, IBJ and various

[a]Dry reduced/hot briquetted iron.

the growth trends. Not all of this cargo is shipped in bulk carriers. Shippers use whatever type of shipping operation is most economic for their particular cargo; usually they use bulk carriers, but containers or MPP services compete for smaller parcels. This variety of transport mode, combined with the fact that many of the minor bulk commodities are semi-processed, makes analysis more complex than for the major bulk trades.

## The agribulk trades

As a group the agribulk trades are nearly as big as the grain trade, with 158 million tonnes shipped in 2005 and an average growth rate of 3.5% per annum. The main commodities shipped are soya beans (65 mt), soya meal (45 mt), various other vegetable meals and rice. Soya beans are an important global crop, with world production in 2005 of 205 million tons. More than half is traded by sea, and the USA was the biggest producer with an output of 75 mt, followed by Brazil (50 mt), Argentina (38 mt) and China (17 mt). The beans are processed into vegetable oil and soya bean meal which is used as an animal feed. About 60% of the trade is shipped as soya beans which are processed at the market, and the other 40% is processed and shipped as oil (see chemical tankers in Chapter 12) and soya meal. China accounted for one-third of the imports, following a surge in domestic demand in the late 1990s and stagnant production. The imports came mainly from Argentina and Brazil. The EU is the other major importer, mainly for animal feeds.

The major importers of soya meal in 2005 were the EU (20–22 mt), central Europe (3.5 mt), Thailand (2 mt), South Korea (1.5 mt), Indonesia (1.5–2 mt), Japan (1–1.5 mt), the Philippines (1–1.5 mt) and Canada (1–1.5 mt). The major exporters are Argentina (19–20 million tons), Brazil (14–15 mt), USA (4–6 mt), India (3–4 mt) and the EU (2 mt).

## The sugar trades

Sugar consists of three trades: raw sugar (which is shipped loose in bulk in parcels averaging 12,200 tons), refined sugar (which is generally shipped in bags in parcels averaging 5600 tons) and molasses (which is a by-product of sugar refining and is shipped in tankers, so it is not covered here). The sugar trade demonstrates a pattern that we see again and again in the minor bulk trades. Over the 20-year period reviewed in Table 11.12, the volume of trade increased by 2.6% per annum. However, this was a trade-off between the raw sugar trade which, for part of the period was stagnant, and averaged only 1.9% per annum over the 20-year period, and the processed white sugar trade which grew at a brisk 3.9% per annum.

World sugar production in 2004 was 280 million tonnes, and the total trade in that year was 46 million tonnes, so only 16% of the total sugar crop is traded. The sugar itself is produced either from sugar beet in temperate areas or cane sugar in the tropics, so trade volumes depend heavily on the relative economic and political factors which determine the split between these two sources. For example, in 2004 the EU produced 22 million tonnes of sugar, imported 2.4 million tonnes, exported 4.3 million tonnes and consumed 17.7 million tonnes. This situation makes trade forecasting tricky.

**Table 11.13** Sugar Trade, 2004 (million tons)

| Exports | | Imports | |
|---|---|---|---|
| Brazil | 16.3 | Russian Fed. | 3.6 |
| Thailand | 4.9 | EU | 2.4 |
| Australia | 4.3 | Persian Gulf | 1.8 |
| EU | 4.3 | Indonesia | 1.7 |
| Cuba | 1.9 | Korea, Rep. of | 1.6 |
| Persian Gulf | 1.5 | U.S.A. | 1.4 |
| 91 others | 12.6 | 140 others | 33.2 |
| World | 45.8 | World | 45.9 |

Source: International Sugar Organization

Over 90 countries exported sugar in 2004, and the main ones are listed in Table 11.13. Brazil was much the biggest with 16 million tons of exports, followed by Thailand, Australia and the EU, all of which exported about 4 million tons. About a quarter of the trade is made up of 91 small exporters, mainly in the tropical areas. Many countries (such as Costa Rica, Pakistan and Indonesia) produce sugar as a cash crop and have exports of only a few hundred thousand tons at the most. Loading facilities in these countries are frequently very poor and, since the trade is seasonal and highly fragmented, there is little incentive to improve them. As a result, the trade mainly uses small ships. The import trade is very widely spread with over 140 countries importing sugar and the top six listed in Table 11.13 account for little more than a quarter. So this is a very diffuse trade which occupies the bottom end of the bulk shipping market, with a substantial overlap with the container sector.

## The fertilizer trades

The fertilizer trade was 77 mt in 2005 and, although relatively small, is a vital part of the world economy. Over the last fifty years the available arable land has not increased significantly and the growth of world food production depends on increasing yields, in which fertilizer application plays a major part and much of which travels by sea. The basic nutrients in fertilizer are nitrogen, which is obtained by fixation of atmospheric nitrogen; phosphate, which mainly comes from phosphate rock; potash; and sulphur. The manufacturing process is summarized in Figure 11.17. The intermediate products are ammonia, nitric acid, phosphoric acid and sulphuric acid which are used to manufacture the various fertilizers listed in column 3.

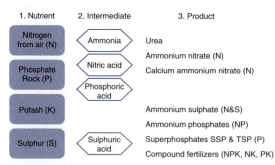

**Figure 11.17**
Manufactured fertilizer production processes
Source: European Fertilizer Manufacturers Association

These manufacturing processes can take place at source, near the market or at some intermediate location, and the location of these activities is subject to political as well as economic factors. Also the four intermediate products are toxic chemicals, usually carried in chemical or gas tankers (in the case of ammonia), as discussed in Chapter 12. Here we are mainly concerned with phosphate rock, phosphates, potash, sulphur and various manufactured fertilizers, of which ammonium sulphate and urea are the two most important. They are generally powdered or granular in form, and can travel loose or bagged in a bulk carrier or in containers.

### PHOSPHATE ROCK

Almost all phosphate fertilizers used today are derived from phosphate rock. The 'reserves' of phosphate rock (i.e. deposits which are viable with today's technology) are, according to a US Geological Survey, only 11 billion tons. Most of these reserves are located in Morocco (5.9 billion tons) and the USA (1.2 billion tons), though the USA produces slightly more rock than Morocco, despite its smaller reserves. Twenty years ago most phosphate rock was shipped raw to compound fertilizer plants located near the markets, but since then processing at source has become more common. In the case of the USA, for example, rock exports declined from 6.9 mt in 1990 to only 3,000 tonnes in 2004. As a result, between 1985 and 2005 the phosphate rock trade fell by −1.6% per annum (Table 11.12) from 43 mt to 31 mt, although it increased slightly during the last decade. Increased processing at source resulted in a growing trade in products such as phosphates and phosphoric acid, of which 5 mt was traded in 2005, mainly in Asia.

The main importers of phosphate rock are western Europe and Japan. Since the average size of fertilizer plant is comparatively small and they are often located in rural areas, the cargo parcel size remains small with little incentive to use very large bulk carriers except on major routes such as the North Atlantic. The main exporters of phosphate rock are Morocco, the USA and the USSR.

### PHOSPHATES

This trade grew from 9.6 mt in 1985 to 16.6 mt in 2005. It consists mainly of phosphate fertilizers such as diammonium phosphate exported from the USA, Africa and the former Soviet Union to a wide range of countries.

### POTASH

In the fertilizer trade the term 'Potash' refers to potassium fertilizers. Potassium is essential for plant growth, and potassium fertilizers improve growth. Approximately 95% of world potassium production is used for fertilizers, the remainder being used for various chemicals. Potassium chloride is the most common potassium fertilizer, followed by potassium sulphate. The world has 8.4 billion tonnes of commercially exploitable potassium-bearing rock reserves.

World output of potash (potassium oxide equivalent) is around 32 million tonnes a year, of which three-quarters is produced by Canada, Russia, Germany and Belarus. In 2005 the potash fertilizer trade was 26 million tonnes, of which 10 million tonnes was imported by Asia, 5 million tonnes by Latin America, 5 million tonnes by the United States and 3 million tonnes by western Europe. Much of the US trade is by land rather than sea.

## SULPHUR

Sulphur is a small bulk trade, with imports of 27 mt in 2005. The major importers are western Europe, various developing countries (particularly India and Brazil), Australia, New Zealand and South Africa. Sulphur is transported either in dry form (crushed, flaked, slated or pelleted), or as a molten liquid. Although dry sulphur can be shipped in conventional bulk carriers or two-deckers, it is not an easy cargo. It ignites easily, there is a danger of explosion from sulphur dust, it is extremely corrosive, and in conditions of excess moisture it may produce hydrogen sulphide gas which is poisonous. For this reason a number of special dry sulphur carriers have been built, incorporating various features such as a double skin (so that the interior skin can be easily cleaned and replaced when corroded), sealed hatches, special gas monitoring equipment, intensive hold-washing equipment and mechanical ventilation. Flaking and pelleting of sulphur have brought some improvements, though the commodity remains a difficult one to transport.

To ship sulphur in liquid form special tankers are required, with heating coils, stainless steel tanks, special valve gear, and inert gas systems to prevent explosions. Although these vessels can be used in other chemical trades, the reverse is not true – conventional chemical tankers are not generally suitable for sulphur transportation. In addition, special loading and discharging facilities are required, so that trade is generally conducted under long-term contract. This is, therefore, a trade for which ships must be especially built or converted.

There are few handling problems, though they usually require undercover storage, and ammonium sulphate in particular is likely to absorb water from the atmosphere if not protected. Since their final market is in agriculture, individual consignments tend to be relatively small, so this is not a commodity that is likely to be shipped in 40,000 ton lots. Many shipments are to small ports in rural areas and may be only a few thousand tons. Another factor limiting the size of vessel in the fertilizer trade is that 70% of the trade is into developing countries and half is to very small importers, even the larger ones taking only a few hundred thousand tons each. This results in the trade travelling predominantly in the 10,000–18,000 dwt size group of vessels, while part still travels by container.

## UREA

Urea is a widely traded nitrogen fertilizer with 46.4% nitrogen content. About 100 mt is produced annually from synthetic ammonia and carbon dioxide and it can be shipped as prills, granules, flakes, pellets, crystals or in solution. More than 90% of world production is used as a fertilizer, and in 2005 the sea trade was 12.7 million tons.

## The metals and minerals trade

This important and diverse group of minor bulks includes a mixture of metal industry related products and other industrial materials. In 2005 the trade was 310 million tonnes, having grown at 3.1% per annum during the previous 20 years. However the growth rate between 2000 and 2005 was almost twice as much, due in particular to a sharp increase in the trades in bauxite, cement, scrap and pig iron. This was certainly associated with the expansion of Chinese industry.

Bauxite ore is the raw material from which aluminium is made, while alumina is its semi-refined product. It takes about 5.4 tons of bauxite to produce 2 tons of alumina, from which 1 ton of aluminium can be smelted. Shipments of bauxite ore and alumina totalled 73 mt in 2004.

The trade in bauxite and alumina follows the familiar industrial pattern we have already discussed under the heading of oil, iron ore and coal, but with some special features. In the early 1950s the trade was dominated by North American imports from the Caribbean, but in the 1960s both Europe and Japan entered the trade on a major scale. Although aluminium is used in much smaller quantities than steel, it has been finding new markets; consequently demand grew very rapidly during the first six decades of the twentieth century. To meet this demand, during the 1960s aluminium companies in western Europe and Japan built domestic aluminium smelters, importing bauxite from the Caribbean, the traditional producer, and also from newly developed reserves in West Africa and Australia. As a result, there was a rapid growth in the seaborne bauxite trade. This pattern changed fairly dramatically in the 1970s as the bauxite producers moved downstream into alumina refining and the aluminium smelters in Europe and Japan proved uneconomic owing to the high cost of electricity for aluminium smelting, particularly after the 1973 oil crisis. As a result, although the demand for aluminium continued to grow, the sea trade in bauxite and alumina remained at the same level of around 42–44 mt for the decade 1974–1984. After this structural adjustment, growth resumed, with the trade reaching 49 mt in 1995 and 73 mt in 2004.

Aluminium production technology follows the classic pattern of industrial integration, and in principle it is generally possible to optimize the shipping operation by using vessels of Panamax size or above. The alumina trade, on the other hand, does not generally favour the use of vessels of Panamax size and over, since alumina has a high value, needs to be stored under cover and the quantities of raw material required by a smelter are too small to encourage large bulk deliveries. An aluminium smelter producing 100,000 tons of metal per annum would require 200,000 tons of alumina, hardly a sufficient volume to justify the use of Panamax bulk carriers.

Manganese has a high density, with trade of about 11 mt a year shipped mainly to Europe, Japan and the USA from South Africa, the former Soviet Union, Gabon and Brazil. It has a low average value and differs little from iron ore, except that it is used in much smaller quantities. Consequently manufacturers keep small stores and large shipments are inconvenient. Various other non-ferrous metal ores are shipped by sea, including nickel, zinc and copper concentrates. Not shown in Table 11.12, these trades generally travel in small parcels owing to their high value and the small stocks carried by refineries. Transport is by small bulk carrier, container or bags.

Cement is another sizeable minor bulk trade and reached 60 mt in 2005. The trade is composed mainly of shipments to construction projects in Africa, Asia and the Middle East. By its nature the trade is volatile and ships tend to be chartered for either the carriage of bulk or bagged cement. Although small bulk carriers and 'tweendeckers are still used, in recent years the parcel size has increased sharply with Panamax bulk carriers moving into this trade and vessels of 50,000 tons and more operating in the export trade from Asia to the USA.

Steel scrap is traded as a source of raw material for steel production. Scrap comes from two sources: primary scrap, which is produced during the manufacture of steel products, and is generally recycled; and secondary scrap, which is derived from the recycling of various consumer and business durables such as motor vehicles. The international scrap trade is mainly from the mature areas such as USA to the developing steel-making areas, such as Asia. The large increase in the scrap trade during the period to 2000–5 was largely shipments into China which was expanding its steel business very rapidly at the time.

The salt trade is mainly into Japan. The Mexican trade to Japan was the first to develop in the early 1960s from the Mexican solar salt plant Exportadora de Sal. The trade is something of an oddity among the minor bulks, since it is shipped in very large bulk carriers. Shortly after the Japanese started to import salt from Mexico in 1962, D.K. Ludwig, the American shipowner, realized that he could radically reduce the c.i.f. price of salt in Japan by adopting a plan that involved building a 170,000 dwt bulk/oil vessel, the *Cedros*, which was launched in 1965, renting a small Japanese island as a bulk terminal, and obtaining a backhaul of crude oil from Indonesia to Los Angeles. The trade grew steadily throughout the 1960s. Salt is also shipped from Australia to Japan.

## Steel products trade

A good example of a trade that straddles the bulk and liner sector is *steel products*. In tonnage terms, steel is the largest minor bulk trade, with total imports of approximately 217 mt in 2005, though some of this was by land. Although a trade of this size might be expected to travel in large bulk carriers, the shipment of steel products involves a wide range of shipping activities. Take the exports of a large European steel producer as an example:

> for large contracts shipped on deep sea routes – for example, structural steel sections or tin plate exported to the Far East or the US West Coast – bulk carriers of 25,000–30,000 dwt would be chartered; in minor trades over long distances where the market volume fluctuates from year to year, liner services would generally be used depending on availability, or small conventional vessels chartered if sufficient cargo is available; in the short sea trades – for example, involving

exports to continental Europe – small coasters of 500–3,000 dwt would be chartered; very small consignments on the short sea trades would be shipped on trailers using conventional ro-ro services; on deep sea routes, medium-size trades of, say, 50,000 tons per year may be sent by container or ro-ro service using half-size containers or other specially constructed stowage devices.[39]

## The forest products trade

Another high-volume minor bulk trade is forest products, of which approximately 169 mt a year were shipped in 2005. Forest products share many of the bulk handling problems raised by steel products. *Thomas's Stowage* lists 56 different types of timber, all with different weights per unit volume, and 26 forms in which they can be shipped, ranging from logs to batons and bundles.[40] Luan, the major export of Malaysia, has a density of about 1.25 cubic metres per ton, while Norwegian pine has a density of 1.8 cubic metres per ton. In practice, forest products stow at about 50% more than the above rates due to air space, which is high for logs and bundles and lower for loose sawn timber. Sawn timber packed to length, which is the practice of Canadian exporters, has a better stowage rate than timber that has been 'truck packed' – bundled together in different lengths. As a very rough guide, in purpose-built ships logs stow at 2.7 cubic metres per ton or more, bundled and sawn timber at 2.2 cubic metres per ton, and the best rate is rarely better than 1.7 cubic metres per ton.

In the 1950s the forest products trade consisted mainly of European imports, and formed a valuable backhaul cargo for liners that had discharged general cargo in Third World countries, for example West Africa. As the trade grew in the early 1960s it started to go bulk. Initially forest products shippers chartered in conventional tonnage, but this proved generally unsatisfactory. Since the mid-1960s there has been a trend towards building specialist ships, either small log carriers for use in South East Asia or specialized open hold bulk carriers with extensive cargo-handling gear for use in long-haul trades such as from West Coast North America to Western Europe.

As with other primary materials, the basis of the forest products trade is supply and demand. Much the largest component of the trade is within South East Asia, dominated by the Japanese who import logs from Malaysia, Indonesia and the Philippines. Japanese forests were depleted by over-cutting in the Second World War and the import trade developed through the established lumber mills. A trade also developed into Japan from West Coast North America, including a sizeable trade in woodchips, which were also imported from Australia and Siberia. A number of special woodchips carriers were built to service this trade, which requires a very high cubic capacity compared with normal bulk carriers. In total, Japanese imports account for about half of the forest products imports.

Europe is the other major importer of forest products, though on a much smaller scale. In Europe, much of the temperate forest is already intensively used, but northern Europe, particularly Scandinavia, is self-sufficient with an exportable surplus. Southern Europe has become a major importer, drawing imports from northern Europe, the former Soviet Union and North America, though some hardwoods come from West Africa and Asia. The West Coast North America to Europe trade is mainly lumber and pulp loaded at a number of ports in the Vancouver area and is almost entirely bulk. However, pulp, paper and logs continue to travel by liner in some cases.

In conclusion, the minor bulk trades form an important source of bulk carrier employment, particularly for smaller sizes of vessels. Because of the physical characteristics of some cargoes and the low volume, they offer many more opportunities for innovative shipping operations than the major bulk cargoes, but are subject to many constraints that limit them to small ships.

## 11.11 SUMMARY

The sophisticated transport system for bulk commodities is one of the great innovations in world trade over the last 50 years. As a result of investment in integrated systems, the size of parcel in many commodities has increased very substantially and, as we noted in Chapter 2, transport costs have grown much more slowly than other costs in the world economy. In this chapter we discussed in more detail the economics underlying these developments.

We started off by dividing the bulk fleets into tankers and bulk carriers, whilst noting that some commodities are also carried by specialist vessels discussed in Chapter 12 and the MPP and container ship fleets discussed in Chapter 13. We also discussed the distinction between a bulk cargo and a bulk commodity: a bulk commodity is a material which can be handled in bulk, and bulk cargo is a parcel actually transported in a single ship. If the trade flow is large enough almost anything can be shipped in bulk to reduce costs. The trades in motor vehicles and sheep, both shipped in specially built vessels, illustrate the point.

We discussed four characteristics which determine the suitability of a cargo for bulk transport: the volume of cargo; its physical handling and stowage characteristics (granularity, lumpiness, delicacy); the value of the cargo; and the regularity of the material flow. The balance of these four characteristics determines the stage at which it is worth making the step from liner transport to a bulk shipping operation. In addition, we reviewed four principles which guide the development of a bulk transport system: using the biggest ship possible; minimizing cargo handling; integrating transport modes; and keeping stocks as low as possible. Some of these principles conflict, so transport systems involve trade-offs.

There are three classes of bulk cargo: liquid bulk, major dry bulk and the minor bulks. Because each commodity needs a different bulk handling system to deal with its physical and economic characteristics it is very difficult to generalize about bulk transport. Our discussion of the cargoes started with liquid bulk transport. We reviewed the global model of the seaborne energy trade and the geographical pattern of trade in crude oil, as well as the transport system. Crude oil uses very large vessels and is a well-defined trade with relatively few loading and discharge zones. In contrast, the oil products trade is a semi-manufactured commodity and more complex, depending on refinery locations, balancing trades and deficit traits. Cargo parcels of oil products are much smaller than for crude oil, occupying the fleet below 60,000 dwt, though a few big ships are used.

The major dry bulk trades reviewed included iron ore, coal and grain. These are the building-blocks of the world economy, and each has a very different economic model and different transport systems. Finally, there are a large number of minor dry bulk trades, each with its own different economic model, and many straddle the liner and bulk systems. The minor dry bulk trades also offer opportunities for innovation and ingenuity on the part of the shipowner, and trades such as forest products, chemicals, vehicles and refrigerated cargo provide specialized shipping services. We discuss these trades in greater detail in the next chapter.

In conclusion, each shipper must select the system which gives the best commercial result for the particular industrial operation. These systems were broadly reviewed in this chapter, and the transport of the more specialized commodities is discussed more fully in Chapter 12.

# 12 The Transport of Specialized Cargoes

*It is difficult though not impossible to be both lower cost and differentiated with respect to competitors. Achieving both is difficult because providing unique performance, quality, or service is inherently more costly, in most instances, than seeking only to be comparable to competitors in such attributes.*

(Michael Porter, *The Competitive Advantage of Nations*, 1990, p.38)

## 12.1 INTRODUCTION TO SPECIALIZED SHIPPING

### What is specialized shipping?

Companies transporting the bulk cargoes discussed in Chapter 11 trade in perfectly competitive markets where hundreds of similar ships compete for homogeneous cargoes on an equal basis. There is little shipowners can do to differentiate their service, so they rely on the entrepreneurial skills needed to charter and trade the bulk cargoes. But some cargoes such as chemicals, gas, refrigerated cargo, forest products, vehicles, heavy lift and people are more demanding to transport, offering transport providers an opportunity to improve their service by investing in specialized ships and services.

This chapter discusses five groups of commodity trades which fall into this category: chemicals, liquefied gas, refrigerated cargo, unit load cargoes and passenger shipping. Table 12.1 summarizes the fleets of ships used to transport them: chemical tankers; gas tankers; refrigerated ships and containers; the unit load fleet which includes open hatch bulk carriers, ro-ros, pure car carriers (PCCs), MPP vessels and heavy lift; and the passenger fleet of ferries and cruise vessels. In total we are dealing with about 10,000 cargo and passenger vessels, accounting for about 25% of the deep sea fleet. These are some of the most expensive ships to build and they tie up a significant portion of the shipping industry's capital, so it is an important business. Our aim is to discuss the services they provide and to explain how their various markets work.

Each specialized trade has its own distinctive features arising from the character of the cargo and the way transport providers have adapted to improve their performance in carrying it. Chemical parcel tankers transport specialized liquid cargoes including chemicals,

**Table 12.1** Specialised Shipping Fleet 1 Jan 2006

| Design | Number | Capacity | Units |
|---|---|---|---|
| 1. Chemical tankers (see Table 12.3) | | | |
| Chemical Parcel >1k dwt | 1,015 | 15,274 | M dwt |
| Chemical Bulk | 179 | 2,395 | M dwt |
| Chemical products | 682 | 19,942 | M dwt |
| Unknown type | 699 | 5,703 | M dwt |
| Total | 2,575 | 43,314 | |
| 2. Gas Tankers | | | |
| LPG (see Table 12.5) | 993 | 14,612 | 000 m³ |
| LNG | 193 | 22,871 | 000 m³ |
| Total | 1,186 | 37,483 | |
| 3. Refrigerated ships | | | |
| Refrigerated >10k cuft | 1,242 | 333 | M Cu ft |
| Container | | 899 | M Cu ft |
| 4. Unit load vessels | | | |
| Open hatch bulk | 486 | 16,508 | M dwt |
| Ro-Ro | 1,040 | 9,183 | M dwt |
| PCC | 560 | 7,848 | M dwt |
| Multipurpose (>10k dwt) | 741 | 13,151 | M dwt |
| Heavy Lift | 193 | 3,113 | M dwt |
| Total | 3,020 | 49,803 | |
| 5. Passenger vessels | | | |
| Ferry | 2,300 | | Lane length |
| Cruise | 235 | | Berths |
| Total | 2,535 | | |
| Total | 10,558 | | |

Source: Clarkson Research Services Ltd
Note: ship numbers differ from Table 2.5 due to differences in the lower size limits and date

vegetable oils and oil products which must be transported separately, often to rigorous safety standards. Most have multiple tanks with segregated cargo handling and safety features to meet the regulatory codes for hazardous cargoes. The gas tankers transport liquefied gases at very low temperatures, particularly LNG, LPG, and chemical gases such as ammonia and ethylene which must be liquefied for transport. Refrigerated ships (reefers) transport perishable commodities including frozen meat, fruit, vegetables and dairy products, and are the subject of fierce competition between container services. Unit load vessels ship the large general cargo units which cannot travel by container, including forest products, cars and heavy lift items. Finally, the passenger vessels carry people either for transport or pleasure.

The economics of these specialized trades is quite subtle, so before delving into detail we will briefly examine the economic framework within which specialized shipping companies operate. Specialized ships come in all shapes and sizes and we will discuss their design features in Chapter 14, but there are three areas where investors can tailor the ship design for a specific cargo. The first is improved cargo handling. For example, chemical tankers allow small chemical parcels to be handled separately, without risk of contamination, or corrosive damage to the vessel. Or wheeled cargoes, which are an important specialist shipping sector, can be handled more efficiently with ro-ro access. Other examples are wide hatches with advanced crane systems and specialized handling systems. In each case the shipping company invests to improve cargo-handling economics and boost the productivity of the ship. Second, improved cargo stowage minimizes 'deadfreight' and reduces damage. Fitting refrigeration systems for perishable cargoes and or protective coating to prevent the cargo from corroding the hull are related possibilities. Third, the system can be adapted to integrate with the customer's inland transport operation. For example, a shipping company transporting cars is a vital link in the manufacturer's distribution chain and this has resulted in some specialist shipping companies entering the terminal and storage business. Providing these services requires an appropriate management structure and proven sector-specific expertise which acts as a barrier to entry, often leading to a higher concentration of ownership. As a result pools and cooperative arrangements are more common in the transport of specialized cargo, for example cars, chemicals and gas.

## The specialized shipping model

The starting point is not, however, the ships or the transport system, but the market. No matter how clever the hull design or cargo-handling systems are, if the company cannot make a profit the venture will fail. These specialized cargoes can usually be shipped in several different ways, so there are nearly always competitors. For example, chilled cargo can be shipped in refrigerated ships, container-ships, or air freight. All three compete and market economics determine who gets the cargo. Some chilled cargoes such as raspberries are delicate and favour air freight, whilst others such deciduous fruits, which are less demanding and more price sensitive, gravitate towards the reefer ships. Specialist shipping companies search out and exploit these differences. If the economics works and the venture thrives, a new specialist segment emerges, and most of the trades reviewed in this chapter developed like this. But sometimes the economics does not work. The ships are sold to the highest bidder and work out their physical lives in services for which they were not really designed. This complicates things for analysts because commodity flows cannot be neatly matched against the fleet of specialist ships, but it is a reality of the business which we must accept from the outset

The forest products trade provides a good example of how the economics of specialization works in practice. Like most of the specialized commodities in this chapter, forest products are semi-manufactures, and the trade mainly travels in units such as packaged lumber, pulp bales, rolls of paper, packaged plywood and particle board. This is high-value cargo, worth up to $1,000 a tonne, and vulnerable to damage. Conventional bulk carriers are not very efficient at handling and stowing unit load cargoes and forest products carriers (FPCs) target this weakness. To improve stowage they have box- shaped holds and hatches which extend to their full width, allowing the FPC to load about 20% more cargo than a conventional bulk carrier of the same deadweight. Cargo handling is also improved by the open holds, which allow packages to be dropped directly into place. As a result cargo-handling rates in excess of 450 tonnes per hour can be achieved, compared with 250 tonnes per hour for a conventional bulk carrier.[1] However these improvements increase the capital cost by 25–50% above a conventional bulk carrier of the same deadweight capacity. Is it worth the money?

Figure 12.1 compares the cost per tonne of transporting packaged forest products in a conventional 47,000 deadweight bulk carrier (the dashed line) and a 47,000 deadweight FPC (the solid line), assuming the performance levels listed at the bottom of

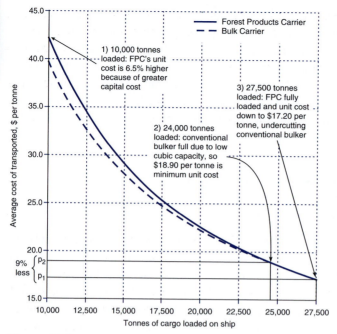

**Figure 12.1**
Specialized shipping competition model

the figure. The average cost per tonne is shown on the vertical axis, and the tonnes of cargo loaded into the ship on the horizontal axis. With a 10,000 tonne load the FPC has a higher cost per tonne ($42.30/tonne compared with $39.70/tonne), but as the cargo size increases the gap narrows due to the FPC's faster cargo handling. With both ships loading 24,000 tonnes of cargo the conventional bulk carrier is full, but thanks to its open holds the FPC keeps going and loads 27,500 tonnes of cargo, at which point its unit cost has fallen to $17.20 per tonne, under-cutting the bulk carrier costs of $18.90 per tonne by 9%. Although this calculation will vary with the precise assumptions, it makes the important point that investing in a tailored ship does not necessarily produce decisively cheaper transport. A better way to look at the investment is as a way of providing a better service for the same cost. In this example the FPC's open holds and sophisticated cargo-handling gear offer a faster service with less risk of damage for 9% less than the conventional bulk carrier. When dealing with high-value semi-processed products such as chipboard, plywood and newsprint this can be decisive.

In summary, specialized shipping companies operate on the two fronts: first, by undercutting the conventional operator on unit transport cost if they can; and second, by obtaining a premium over the freight rate offered by the conventional operator by offering a differentiated service, as illustrated in Figure 12.2. Neither is easy. In our example, to match

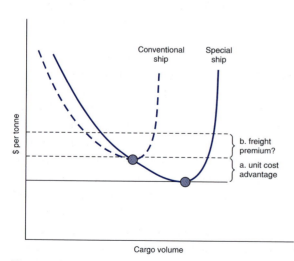

**Figure 12.2**
Specialized shipping model

the conventional bulk carrier's cost the FPC operator must run a tight voyage schedule, with only six days allowed for cargo handling. But success also depends on the customer's willingness to pay for the service offered, which is where the high value and delicacy of the cargo come into play. With cargo worth $1,000 per tonne, exporters may be willing to pay a freight premium for a fast service with good-quality ships and minimal damage risk. Arguably, specialized shipping sectors are the ones where shippers are prepared to pay this freight premium. This is the perspective from which we will approach the specialist segments in the following sections.

## 12.2 THE SEA TRANSPORT OF CHEMICALS

### The demand for chemical transport

The major chemical trades are between the USA, Europe and Asia, India, the Middle East and South America. Most specialist chemicals are used locally, but some are exported in response to local stock imbalances, or to areas where there is no local production of a particular chemical. Each year chemical tankers transport about 60 million tonnes of organic and inorganic chemicals and another 40–45 million tonnes of vegetable oils, alcohols, molasses and lubricating oils[2]. Clean petroleum products and lube oils also provide an important source of employment for the less sophisticated vessels in the chemical carrier fleet and a large proportion of the fleet can switch between these trades and chemicals or edible oils. Since there are so many products involved, a good starting point is an explanation of how they are produced and used (see also Figure 11.6 which describes the energy transport model).

*Organic chemicals* (also known as 'petrochemicals') contain carbon and are made from crude oil, natural gas or coal. The two main product groups are the olefins which include ethylene, propylene and butadiene; and the aromatics, named for their peculiar odour, which include benzene, toluene, xylene (known collectively as 'BTX') and styrene. These are used to manufacture virtually all products made with plastics and artificial fibres.

*Inorganic chemicals* do not contain carbon and are made by combining chemical elements. Phosphoric acid, sulphuric acid and caustic soda are three of the most common. Phosphoric acid and sulphuric acid are used in the fertilizer industry, whilst caustic soda is used in the aluminium industry. They present several transport problems. One is that they are very dense: phosphoric acid has a specific gravity of 1.8; caustic soda liquor 1.5; sulphuric acid 1.7–1.8 and nitric acid 1.5. Second, they are corrosive to metals such as iron, zinc and aluminium and must be carried in tanks coated with stainless steel, rubber or acid-proof paints. The others are less demanding in normal concentrations. The chemical tankers which carry these cargoes generally load and discharge through stainless steel pipes with typical handling rates of 600 tons per hour. In port the acids are stored in steel cisterns with a rubber lining standing in concrete tanks that can hold the contents in case of leakage.

*Vegetable oils* are derived from seeds of plants and used extensively both for edible and industrial purposes. Animal fats and oils are also transported. They include palm oil and soya bean oil.

*Molasses*, a by-product of the sugar refining operations, is a thick brown syrup which is fermented into alcohols such as rum but is traded mainly as an animal feed or in the production of organic chemicals.

These chemicals, especially the organics, often move in small parcels which must be handled separately and transported in segregated tanks which are meticulously cleaned between cargoes. An idea of what this means in practice is provided by Table 12.2 which shows a sample of 3,000 chemical 'parcels' (a parcel is an individual consignment). The average parcel was 1,475 tonnes but for different products the average ranges from 3,000 tonnes for caustic products to 279 tonnes for acetate. Over half the parcels are less than 500 tons and there are over a hundred different chemical and oil commodities in the sample (not all shown separately), some recognisable products like brake fluid, or liquid paraffin but many others that the average layman would not recognise. Chemical parcels of this sort are generally transported in small tankers under 10,000 dwt or in large 'parcel' tankers with many separate tanks. Tank containers are also sometimes used for parcels under 200 tonnes. The range of vessel sizes is illustrated in Table 12.2 which shows that, for example, the average 2925 tonne parcel of Caustic Products was carried in a 5736 dwt ship, occupying 51% of the cargo capacity. But some other commodities such as Paraffin wax, Toluene and Acetate travelled in parcel tankers of 35,000 dwt or more, occupying only 1–2% of the cargo space. This trade is also geographically complex with cargoes loading in the Middle East,

**Table 12.2** Sample of chemical parcels by size

Cargo parcel size analysis

| Cargo product group | Average parcel size, tonnes | Cargo % Ship |
|---|---|---|
| Caustic products | 2925 | 51% |
| Styrene products | 2195 | 35% |
| Formaldehyde | 1852 | 54% |
| MEG | 1836 | 12% |
| Ethylene products | 1485 | 40% |
| Paraffin wax | 1298 | 3% |
| Polypropylene | 1239 | 3% |
| Paraffin | 1217 | 12% |
| Resins | 955 | 26% |
| Polyol | 684 | 15% |
| Lube additive | 594 | 7% |
| Isopropyl alcohol | 579 | 6% |
| MEK | 578 | 3% |
| Toluene | 544 | 1% |
| Chlorinated organics | 514 | 15% |
| Xylene | 486 | 1% |
| Solvent naphtha | 429 | 1% |
| Additive | 367 | 2% |
| Brake fluid | 338 | 11% |
| Solvent | 336 | 1% |
| White spirit | 328 | 3% |
| Methyl isobutyl | 324 | 1% |
| Hexane | 314 | 4% |
| Alcohol | 313 | 2% |
| Acetone | 295 | 9% |
| Acetate | 279 | 1% |
| Grand Total | 1,475 | 24% |

Source: 1) Based on a sample of parcels transported on many routes over several years 2) The cargo type indicates the broad product category and in some cases covers a range of related products 3) The cargo % ship was calculated by dividing each cargo parcel by the dwt of the ship which carried it and averaging the resulting percentage over the cargo group.

Singapore, US Gulf, West coast North America, NW Europe and Asia and distributed to a large number of importers around the world. The cargo flow on individual routes is often small, which adds to the complexity of the transport operation. Finally, chemicals may explode, corrode, pollute, taint, and be toxic to the crew or marine life, so the transport of products with these characteristics is regulated under the IMO Code on the Carriage of Hazardous Cargoes. All these features of the trade make chemical transport by sea a complex business.

## Development of chemical transport

Chemical tankers were pioneered in the USA. During the 1920s and 1930s the US chemical industry grew rapidly, especially along the Gulf coast around the oil and gas fields of Texas and Louisiana. Since most plants had good water access, it was natural to transport the chemicals by sea, and by the early 1950s over 25 varieties of liquid chemicals were being shipped in purpose-built tankers.

These vessels differed from products tankers in several ways. Dense chemicals were carried only in the centre tanks, and to allow parcels of different chemicals to be carried in the same ship, longitudinal coffer dams (i.e. double skins) separated the centre tanks from the wings, and transverse coffer dams separated the centre line tanks. Double bottoms were also fitted. One of the earliest vessels, the 16,000 dwt *Marine Chemist*, was built in 1942.[3] These early chemical tankers often had special coatings, for example zinc silicate. In the 1950s an international trade in chemicals started to develop and the evolution of the first vessels for this trade are described by Jacob Stolt-Nielsen as follows:

> Before 1955 the international chemical trade was very small. The cargoes were tallow, grease, vegoils and 'solvents.' Chemicals or BTX were collectively known as 'solvents.' The trade was trans-Atlantic and was served by small 2/4000 dwt tankers. The ships had ring-lines from one or two pumprooms. The cast iron lines had expansion boxes and flanges, none of which could hold solvents. They leaked like sieves. As a consequence, the ships could only segregate one grade fore and one grade aft of the pumprooms. Since the cargo lots seldom were larger than 1,000 tons per parcel that determined the size of the ships.

> But the trade was growing fast. The owner who could find a way to use a 10/15,000 dwt ship, with a break-even rate half of that of a 4000 dwt ship, would make a fortune! ... I got the idea how to solve the problem from an article in Life magazine, about pumping water up from the depths under the desert: Deep-well-pumps. I persuaded Charles P. Steuber and Russel J. Chianelli (my partner) that with deep-well pumps we could carry as many grades as the ship had tanks. We time-chartered the 'M/T Freddy,' 13,000 dwt, from Erling Naess. The ship came to Todd's shipyard in Galveston, Texas, and I was waiting on the pier along with 18 brand new Byron Jackson deep-well pumps. I had no drawings, no marine architects, and no price from the yard. I had given them a verbal description of the

work to be done. Soon the big cranes were hovering overhead and ripping out the large cast iron pipelines. I cannot deny that I had butterflies in my stomach. This was in May 1955 and I was 24 years old.[4]

That was the beginning of the parcel tanker business. Stolt-Neilsen and Odfjell, two of the biggest companies today, both started operation in the 1950s and over the next two decades they developed and refined the chemical parcel tanker, a vessel with many tanks and segregations capable of carrying a mix of small parcels within the complex regulations laid down by the IMO.

## The chemical transport system

Today chemical transport has developed into a sophisticated and flexible transport operation capable of moving the wide range of different parcel sizes around the world. The diagram in Figure 12.3 shows how it works. On the right in column 5 are the chemical companies and a few of the hundreds of chemical commodities which they ship in a wide range of parcel sizes from a few hundred tons of MEK to 30,000 tons of MTBE. In column 2 is the fleet of ships used to transport them, consisting of a fleet of large 'parcel tankers' with many segregations; the bulk chemical tankers with a high proportion of segregated tanks, but bigger tanks of over 2700 cubic metres; and the chemical/product tankers which have big tanks, 50–75% of which are segregated.

The shipping companies involved in the chemicals trade are shown in column 3. This is a hybrid business, falling between the tanker market, with its aggressive focus on the spot market, and the liner business, with its tightly planned schedules. Transport is provided by three groups of shipping companies, each of which approaches the task in a different way. The first group, shown at the top of the figure, are the parcel tanker

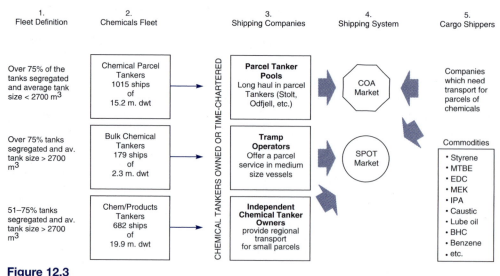

**Figure 12.3**
Chemical tanker sea transport system model, 2006

pools, operated by companies like Stolt and Odfjell. They offer liner services for small parcels, using fleets of parcel tankers. Transport is often arranged on a COA basis, with regular port itineraries worked out to meet the needs of the trade. However, they also take cargoes from the spot market where these are available at an acceptable rate and when the destination fits in with available capacity and the vessel operating pattern. The second group are tramp operators using medium-sized bulk chemical tankers, often of 10,000–20,000 dwt, which trade spot, grouping together several spot parcels on a voyage by voyage basis. Finally, there are the independent owners of small tankers which generally operate on the spot market, picking up whatever parcels are available, but may be engaged on a time charter or a consecutive voyage basis. These small vessels tend to operate within the regions, particularly Europe and Asia.

## Chemical fleet and supply

The fleet of about 2600 chemical tankers used to transport chemical cargoes, sometimes in shiploads using small tankers, but more often consolidating many small parcels of 100–5,000 tons in a single ship, is shown in Table 12.3. Although the transport of chemicals is different from the crude oil and product trades, there is some overlap, with 'swing tonnage' operating in either sector. This means we cannot define the chemical tanker fleet precisely, though many of the ships used in the chemical trade are built for the business and generally belong in a different investment category from crude oil and products tankers. Ships built specifically for the chemical business must satisfy the IMO regulations for the carriage of hazardous cargoes which are discussed in Chapter 14.

The fleet of 1015 chemical parcel tankers have average size of 15,000 dwt and are distinguished by having more than three-quarters of their tanks segregated with separate cargo-handling facilities; an average tank size of less than 2700 cubic metres; and some stainless steel tanks. The second is a group of 179 slightly smaller chemical bulk tankers averaging 13,380 dwt with segregated tanks, but all have tanks over 2700 cubic metres, enabling them to carry the bigger parcels. Finally, there are the

**Table 12.3** The chemical tanker fleet by vessel type, 2006

| Size | Chemical Parcel | | Chemical Bulk | | Chem. Products | | Unknown | | Total | |
|------|------|------|------|------|------|------|------|------|------|------|
| (000 dwt) | No. | '000 dwt | No. | '000 dwt | No. | '000 dwt | No. | '000 dwt | No. | '000 dwt |
| 1–4.9 | 192 | 639.9 | 62 | 200.7 | 56 | 187.1 | 393 | 880.0 | 703 | 1,907.7 |
| 5–9.9 | 304 | 2,278.1 | 39 | 289.3 | 89 | 616.9 | 176 | 1,258.3 | 608 | 4,442.6 |
| 10–19.9 | 279 | 4,232.2 | 36 | 489.5 | 102 | 1,489.3 | 53 | 758.5 | 470 | 6,969.5 |
| 20–29.9 | 70 | 1,761.2 | 23 | 589.0 | 32 | 841.7 | 16 | 425.0 | 141 | 3,616.9 |
| 30–39.9 | 130 | 4,619.1 | 4 | 141.5 | 163 | 5,910.1 | 35 | 1,266.5 | 332 | 11,937.2 |
| 40–49.9 | 40 | 1,743.6 | 14 | 633.5 | 224 | 10,037.1 | 26 | 1,114.7 | 304 | 13,528.9 |
| 50+ | – | – | 1 | 51.7 | 16 | 859.4 | – | – | 17 | 911.1 |
| Total | 1,015 | 15,274.1 | 179 | 2,395.3 | 682 | 19,941.6 | 699 | 5,703.1 | 2,575 | 43,314.0 |

Source: *Clarkson Research Services July 2006*

682 chemical/products tankers with fewer segregations (only 50–75% of their tanks are segregated) which can carry chemical parcels, or switch into the products tanker business. The distinction between these segments is fuzzy, but each group caters for a slightly different mix of cargoes. The design of these ships is discussed further in Chapter 14 (see Figure 14.7) which describes an 11,340 dwt chemical tanker of sophisticated design. The regulatory regime for carrying hazardous cargoes is discussed in Chapter 16.

## 12.3 THE LIQUEFIED PETROLEUM GAS TRADE

### The transport of LPG by sea

The LPG business has many similarities with the chemical trades discussed in the previous section. It supplies feed stock gases to the chemical industry and transports the intermediate gases produced by chemical plants and also gas for domestic and commercial use. On land these gases are generally transported by pipeline, but for sea transport they must be liquefied to reduce their volume by 99.8%. A bird's-eye view of the sea transport system is provided by Figure 12.4. The main cargoes – petroleum gases, ammonia and olefins – are listed in the right-hand column, which also notes that they may be transported by a COA, time charter or consecutive voyage charter. There is also

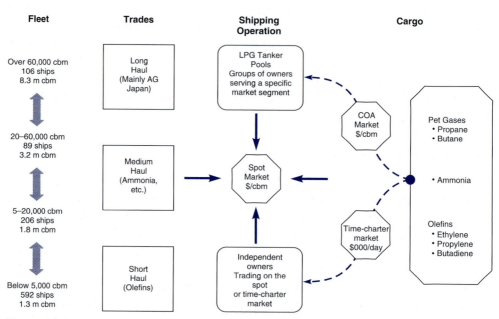

**Figure 12.4**
The LPG sea transport system model

**Table 12.4** Some major traded liquified gas commodities

| | Boiling point °C | Specific Gravity | Ship Type | Primary Markets |
|---|---|---|---|---|
| **1. Liquified petroleum gas** | | | | |
| Propane | −42.3 | 0.58 | LPG tanker | Feedstock & heating |
| Ethane | −88.6 | 0.55 | LPG tanker | Feedstock & heating |
| Butane | −0.5 | 0.60 | LPG tanker | Feedstock & heating |
| **2. Chemical gases** | | | | |
| Ammonia | −33.4 | 0.68 | LPG tanker | Fertilizer manufacture |
| **3. Olefines** | | | | |
| Ethylene | −103.9 | 0.57 | LPG tanker | Chemical feedstock |
| Propylene | −47 | 0.61 | LPG tanker | Feedstock |
| Butadiene | −5 | 0.65 | LPG tanker | Feedstock |
| Vinyl chloride monomer | −13.8 | 0.97 | LPG tanker | Feedstock |
| *Memo* | | | | |
| Methane | −161.5 | 0.48 | LNG tanker | Electricity generation |

some spot market business. The fleet of about 1,000 LPG tankers built to carry the liquid gases at the very low temperatures (listed in Table 12.4) is shown in the left-hand column. The ships fall into four segments: the big LPG tankers over 60,000 cubic metres which are used on long-haul trades, especially to Japan; the mid-size vessels of 20,000–60,000 cubic metres, used in medium-haul trades, particularly for ammonia; and the smaller sized vessels of 5,000–20,000 cubic metres which are used in the short-haul trades, especially for the transport of olefins. There is also a sizeable fleet of very small vessels which are used mainly in the coastal and short-sea trades. LPG tanker pools play a significant part in the supply of LPG transport, but there are also independent operators who play the spot market or time charters. Finally, in the centre of the Figure 12.4 are the shipping operations, focusing around the spot market, but also including COA and time-charter markets.

## The demand for LPG gas transport

Not only LPG but also many other gases are shipped in LPG tankers. The gases fall into the three groups shown in Table 12.4. Firstly, the three main *petroleum gases* are propane, ethane and butane whose main markets are in transportation, residential and commercial heating, and as a feedstock for the production of petrochemicals. Secondly, ammonia is a *chemical gas* which is produced in large quantities and used in the manufacture of fertilizers. Finally, the *olefins*, such as butadiene, ethylene oxide, vinyl chloride and acetaldehyde, are used to manufacture everything from plastics to rubber tyres. These tend to be shipped in the smaller LPG tankers. At the bottom of the table, for reference purposes, is methane which is not shipped in LPG tankers because it travels at lower temperatures. This trade is discussed in Section 12.4

*Propane and butane*, two major cargoes for LPG tankers, are mainly produced from crude oil, natural gas fields and oil refining. Because of the difficulty of transport they were often flared off, but nowadays most of the gas is either used in local chemical plants in oil-producing areas such as Saudi Arabia, or exported by pipeline or liquefied and shipped by LPG tanker. In 2006, 50% of the market was domestic, 12% in industry, 8% in transport and 27% as a feedstock. In the domestic and commercial energy markets the gas is used in restaurants, hotels and industry for cooking, heating and generally as an alternative to natural gas where that facility is not available. The demand for LPG as a chemical feedstock originated with the plastics revolution in the second half of the twentieth century, and this remains the main driving force behind demand. Petrochemical plants (ethylene crackers) produce the 'primary petrochemicals', especially ethylene, from which plastics, synthetic fibres and synthetic rubber are manufactured. The structure of the production process is briefly summarized in Table 12.5, which shows that the product mix of ethylene, propylene and butadiene varies depending on the proportions of ethane, propane, butane and naphtha used as feedstock. The early US plants used ethane which was plentifully available from natural gas fields, but modern plants are generally capable of adjusting their feedstock mix in response to price and availability. When LPG is used as a feedstock for chemical manufacture, price is important because supply and demand imbalances in the petrochemical industry lead to price differences between regions and, of course, LPG is in competition with other feedstocks such as naphtha. In the transport market LPG is used as a fuel for cars, trucks, taxis and industrial equipment such as fork-lift trucks. It has the advantage of cleanliness and low maintenance, and currently in some countries LPG users receive tax concessions.

North East Asia (Japan, China, and South Korea) is the world's largest importing region of LPG, followed by western Europe and the United States. The biggest market is Japan, which imported over 14 million tonnes in 2,000, accounting for over 72% of demand. Japan has a well developed market for LPG, which is imported in large LPG tankers to coastal cities and towns and distributed by a fleet of coastal tankers, mainly under 1,000 dwt, to the local wholesale and retail network. The commercial markets include fuel for motor vehicles, industrial fuel and chemical feedstock. It is also used in

**Table 12.5** Typical ethylene plant yield pattern weight % yield

| Product | Feedstock | | | | |
|---|---|---|---|---|---|
| | Ethane | Propane | *n*-Butane | Light Naptha | Typical end products produced from the primary chemical products shown on the left hand axis |
| Ethylene | 78 | 42 | 37 | 32 | Plastic bags, antifreeze, plastic packaging, etc. |
| Propylene | 2 | 16 | 17 | 16 | Polyurethane foam, plastic coatings, moulded plastics |
| Butadiene, etc.[a] | 3 | 11 | 19 | 30 | Tyres, nylon, detergents, fibreglass, pesticides |
| Fuel oil | 15 | 29 | 25 | 20 | heating, etc |
| Loss | 2 | 2 | 2 | 2 | |
| Total | 100 | 100 | 100 | 100 | |

[a] Includes Butylene, benzene, toluene, raffinate

power stations. In Europe the principal market is as a chemical feedstock, though there is a significant secondary market for butane and propane gas in domestic heating. In the absence of a pipeline distribution system, the LPG moves from import terminals in small coastal tankers of around 3,000 dwt, barges and railcars which use 100 cubic metre tank cars, or 50 cubic metre trucks which load 20 tonnes of LPG. In northern Europe LPG is frequently moved by barges along the Rhine. In the USA the main distribution system is by long-distance pipeline, although barges and rail trucks are used. LPG is produced primarily in the North Sea, as a result of natural gas production, and in the Middle East, as a refining by-product.

*Ammonia* is used to manufacture fertilizers, explosives, and in several chemical processes. It boils at −33°C and is usually shipped in medium-sized semi-refrigerated chemical tankers. Between 1987 and 2002 the world ammonia trade increased from 8.2 to 13.4 million tonnes. The biggest exporters of anhydrous ammonia were Russia, Canada, Trinidad and Tobago, and Indonesia, and the largest importer was the USA (5.5 mt in 2002), followed by India, South Korea, and Malaysia.

*Ethylene* is derived from the cracking of petroleum feedstocks (see Table 12.5). It has a very low boiling point of −103°C, the lowest in this group (see Table 12.4) and it is generally shipped by sea in small pressurized vessels which can handle the small parcels and very low temperatures. It is the key raw material for manufacturing many day-to-day items – two-thirds of global production is used to manufacture plastics and automobile parts and the remainder is used to produce antifreeze and various artificial fibres. The principal ethylene exporters are the Middle East, Europe and Latin America.

*Propylene* is a by-product of ethylene and gasoline manufacture and is used to manufacture polyurethane foam, fibres and moulded plastics for use in manufacturing such items as car parts, plastic pipes and household articles. Polypropylene is used as a feedstock for plastics and is imported by the Far East from the United States and Europe.

*Vinyl chloride monomer*, produced by the cracking of ethylene dichloride, is used to manufacture PVC which is widely used in the construction industry, for example for window frames. It is exported by the USA to South East Asia and Latin America.

*Butadiene* is mainly used to manufacture rubber for use in tyres, but it is also used in detergents and pesticides.

## The LPG fleet and ownership

The LPG fleet consists of a mix of large vessels for deep-sea shipments and medium and small tankers for short-sea and coastal shipments. The range of low temperatures required to transport liquid gases by sea also affects the composition of the fleet. As already noted in Table 12.4, the LPG gases boil at temperatures ranging from −103°C for ethylene to −0.5°C for butane. These low temperatures can be achieved by pressure, refrigeration or a combination of both. Until 1959 LPG ships were fitted with spherical pressure tanks which relied on compression to liquefy gases. These tanks protruded above the deck, making the tankers immediately recognizable.

**Table 12.6** LPG gas tankers – type and capacity analysis

| Capacity Range m³ | Pressurized | | Semi-refrigerated | | Fully-refrigerated | | Total | |
|---|---|---|---|---|---|---|---|---|
| | No. | m³ | No. | m³ | No. | m³ | No. | m³ |
| 0–5,000 | 466 | 917 | 114 | 344 | 12 | 20 | 592 | 1,281 |
| 5–20,000 | 50 | 336 | 150 | 1,356 | 6 | 92 | 206 | 1,783 |
| 20–60,000 | — | — | 16 | 353 | 73 | 2,914 | 89 | 3,266 |
| 60,000 plus | — | — | — | — | 106 | 8,283 | 106 | 8,283 |
| Total | 516 | 1,252 | 280 | 2,052 | 197 | 11,308 | 993 | 14,612 |

Source: Clarkson *Liquid Gas Carrier Register 2006*

Although cheap to run, the size and weight of fully pressurized vessels makes them uneconomic over 5,000 cubic metres. In 1959 the first semi-refrigerated LPG ship was built, and three years later the first fully refrigerated LPG ship came into service. The fully refrigerated ships carry the cargo at ambient pressure under refrigeration, whilst the semi-refrigerated ships can carry gases at different temperature and pressure combinations. For example, a 140 metre semi-refrigerated tanker can carry 6,000 tonnes of propane at −48°C or 7200 tonnes of ammonia at −33°C. Structural steel is brittle at these temperatures and the tanks are installed as separate insulated units.

In 2006 there were 993 LPG tankers, and Table 12.6 shows that the split between the three liquefaction systems – pressurized, semi-refrigerated and fully refrigerated – is correlated with size. Broadly speaking, the small tankers are pressurized, the medium-sized are semi-pressurised, and the largest are fully refrigerated. The way these vessels are used is summarized below.

- 0–5,000 cubic metres. The smallest class of vessels is the most numerous, but contributes less than 10% of the fleet in capacity terms. Of the 592 tankers in this segment two-thirds are fully pressurized and carry petrochemical gases such as vinyl chloride monomer and LPG. Another 20% are semi-refrigerated, including several 4,000 cubic metres ethylene-capable carriers. They trade mainly in the short-haul cross-trades in the Far East, the Mediterranean, north-western Europe and the Caribbean.

- 5,000–20,000 cubic metres. About 70% of the tankers in this segment are semi-refrigerated, but there are some fully refrigerated vessels which carry LPG and ammonia mostly on long-haul routes. The semi-refrigerated vessels carry petrochemical gases, including ethylene on short- and medium-haul routes. A few of these smaller semi-refrigerated vessels can carry ethylene at −104°C, and ethane at −82°C. To a lesser extent, these smaller vessels are also used to transport LPG and ammonia over short-haul routes.

- 20,000–60,000 cubic metres. Mid-size gas tankers form 22% of the fleet by capacity. Most of this fleet is fully refrigerated but there are a few semi-refrigerated vessels.

They transport LPG on long-haul trades between the Arabian Gulf and the Mediterranean and cross-trades in the North Sea and Europe, and ammonia in various typically shorter cross-trades.

- Very large petroleum gas carriers (VLGCs) over 60,000 cubic metres. The 106 biggest LPG tankers account for 56% of the LPG fleet by capacity. All are fully refrigerated and mainly carry LPG on the long-haul routes such as from the Middle East to Japan, and from Trinidad and Tobago to Europe.

The ownership structure of the VLGC fleet is highly concentrated, and there are several pools. For example, Bergesen, one of the largest owners of LPG tonnage, operated the VLGC pool which in 2003 included ships owned by Exmar, Mitsubishi, Yuyo Ship Management, Neste Sverige and Dynergy.

## 12.4 THE LIQUEFIED NATURAL GAS TRADE

Natural gas (methane) is the third major energy source transported by sea, after oil and coal which we discussed in Chapter 11. In 2005 the world consumed 2.5 billion tons of natural gas (oil equivalent), compared with 3.8 billion tons of oil and 3 billion tons of coal; since it burns cleanly, gas is the preferred energy source for power generation. Between 1990 and 2005 demand increased at 2.2% per annum which was faster than both coal (1.8% per annum) and oil (1.3% per annum) as shown in Figure 12.5. However, gas delivered to markets that cannot be reached by pipeline must be processed into LNG. Although this technology is well established and very reliable, it is expensive and inflexible. For example, over the last 20 years shipping oil from the Middle East to Europe cost on average $7–10 per tonne, whereas LNG cost $25–100 per tonne, depending on the distance.[5]

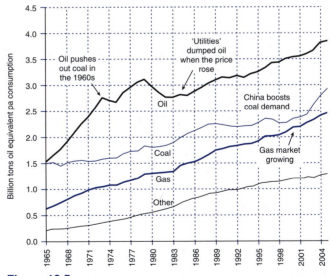

**Figure 12.5**
World energy consumption by commodity
Source: BP Annual Review of the World Oil industry

**Table 12.7** World natural gas reserves, demand and LNG trade 2006

| (1) | (2) | (3) | (4) | (5) | (6) | (7) | (8) |
|---|---|---|---|---|---|---|---|
| | Gas reserves | | Gas demand | | | LNG imports | |
| | Billion m³ | % | Billion m³ | Mtoe[a] | R/D years[b] | billion m³ | Mtoe[a] |
| USA | 5,925 | 3 | 630 | 566.9 | 9 | 16.6 | 14.9 |
| Russian Federation | 47,650 | 27 | 432 | 388.9 | 110 | 0.0 | 0.0 |
| Middle East | 73,471 | 41 | 289 | 260.3 | 254 | 0.0 | 0.0 |
| Japan | — | 0 | 85 | 76.1 | 0 | 81.9 | 73.7 |
| South Korea | — | 0 | 34 | 30.8 | 0 | 34.1 | 30.7 |
| European Union | 2,426 | 1.3 | 467 | 420.6 | 5 | 57.4 | 51.7 |
| China | 2,449 | 1 | 56 | 50.0 | 44 | 1.0 | 0.9 |
| Other Asia | 12,371 | 7 | 264 | 237.7 | 47 | 18.2 | 16.4 |
| Other | 37,300 | 21 | 604 | 543.6 | 62 | 1.9 | 1.7 |
| Total | 181,458 | 101 | 2861 | 2574.9 | 63.4 | 211.1 | 190.0 |

[a]Million tonnes of oil equivalent.

[b]R/D is the reserves to demand ratio in years.

Source BP *Annual Review* 2007

## Natural gas supply and demand

Natural gas has been used as an energy source since 1825 when small amounts were found in Fredonia, New York. Larger gas fields were discovered in Pennsylvania in the 1860s, and the first distribution system, a six-inch cast iron pipeline 17 miles long, was built in 1874 to ship gas from Butler County, Pennsylvania, to an iron mill at Etna near Pittsburgh.[6] It is now widely used in the USA, the EU Russia, the Middle East, Japan, South Korea and various other Asian countries (Table 12.7, col. 5). However, two-thirds of the gas reserves are in the Middle East (41%) and the Russian Federation (27%), with smaller quantities in Africa (8%); Asia (8%); North America (4.9%); South America (3.9%) and the EU (1.3%). Within the Middle East, Iran and Qatar each had 14% of world reserves in 2005. This pattern of demand and geographically dispersed supply creates the basic conditions for trade, especially since the USA and EU have limited reserves, whilst Japan, South Korea and China have almost none. However, despite this regional imbalance, in 2006 the LNG trade of 190 million tons was only 7.4% of world gas demand, well short of oil, whose trade was 63% of demand.[7]

## Development of LNG trade

To explain why the gas trade is so small, we need to look at the basic economics. Successful gas trade requires three conditions to be met. Firstly, a plentiful source of gas is needed at a price competitive with other energy sources such as coal. Secondly, there must be a market with a pipeline network capable of distributing the gas to domestic and commercial customers. Thirdly, it must be possible to raise funds for the required liquefaction and transport system. These conditions have been difficult to meet in the gas trade. Although there are plenty of reserves, they are in the wrong place and multi-billion dollar investment projects are needed to ship the gas to market. This locks investors into a very inflexible long-term commitment, so political stability and future pricing worries weigh heavily on their minds, often leading to delays. But price is the central issue and for many years Europe and the USA had access to cheap natural gas from domestic gas fields, so high-cost imported LNG struggled to be competitive in these important markets, especially from long-haul sources such as the Middle East.

The first LNG cargo was shipped in 1959 when the *Methane Pioneer*, a converted dry cargo ship, carried about 5,000 cubic metres of LNG from Louisiana to Canvey Island. The ship was a technical success, but was too small and too slow to be economically viable, and the operation was terminated after the first year and the ship switched to the LPG trade, though it later carried transatlantic LNG cargoes when freight rates were high. Five years later in 1964 the first large-scale liquefaction plant was built at Arzew in Algeria. It had a capacity of 1.1 million tonnes per annum divided over three trains (an independent unit for liquefying gas) and the gas was shipped between Algeria and Canvey Island in the UK using two purpose-built ships, the *Methane Princess* and the *Methane Progress*. This was followed by a scheme to export LNG from Brunei to Japan, which came on stream in 1969. Following these successes, plans were developed for exports from North Africa to the USA and Europe and from South East Asia for Japan, and forecasters were predicting that the LNG trade would reach 100 million tons by 1980. However, the 1973 oil crisis intervened and the uncertainty this created, especially over future gas export prices, resulted in projects being deferred or abandoned altogether, and by 2004 the trade was still only 50 billion cubic metres.

By 1983 a third of the LNG tanker fleet's 71 ships were laid up (Figure 12.6) and pricing disputes, breach of contract cases and the closure of two US reliquefaction terminals brought investment to a halt, especially in the Atlantic. Only two export projects were completed in the 1980s, one in Malaysia and the other in Australia, both for the Asian market. It was 20 years before any further development projects occurred in the Atlantic. However in the 1990s investor confidence revived and the LNG business got a new lease of life. Trade quadrupled

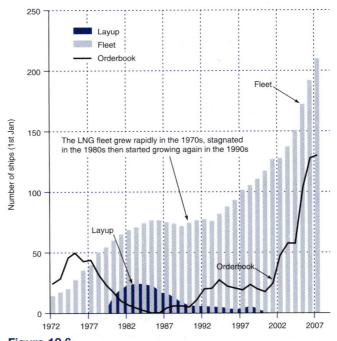

**Figure 12.6**
LNG fleet, 1972–2007
Source: Clarkson Research Gas Tanker Register

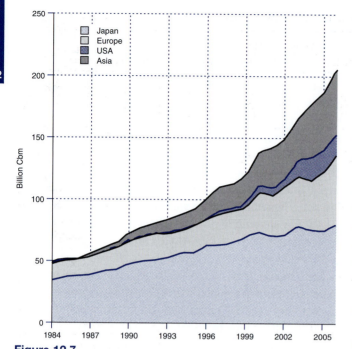

**Figure 12.7**
LNG trade, 1984–2006
Source: BP Annual Review of the World Oil Industry/Cedex

from 48 billion cubic metres in 1984 to 211 billion cubic metres in 2006 (Figure 12.7), finally reaching the forecast 100 million tons in 2000, twenty years behind schedule, with the long-awaited growth of the Atlantic market finally occurring in the mid-1990s. By 2006 the trade split roughly one-third in the Atlantic and two-thirds in the Pacific, as shown in the trade matrix in Table 12.8. Malaysia and Indonesia were the biggest exporters, with the Middle East accounting for less than a quarter of the trade. Japan remained by far the biggest importer, mainly from short-haul Asian sources, followed by Europe, and South Korea. The 13 countries shown in the matrix exported LNG to 48 import terminals, located in Japan (24 terminals), South Korea (4), Taiwan (1), India (1), Europe (13), and the United States (5). So this is a well-defined trade.

## The LNG transportation system

LNG transport involves four operations. Firstly, the natural gas is transported by pipeline from the gasfield to the plant. Secondly, the LPG and condensates are separated out and the methane gas is liquefied and stored ready for sea transport. Thirdly, the liquid gas is loaded onto ships for transport to its destination. Finally, the receiving terminal unloads the cargo, stores it and regasifies it. The costs are around 15% for production and transport to the export terminal, 40% for liquefaction, 25% for sea transport, and 20% for regasification.[8]

A liquefaction plant has one or more 'trains' which liquefy the gas. A train is a compressor, usually driven by a gas turbine, which compresses a coolant until it reaches −163°C, at which temperature the gas is reduced to 1/630 th of its original volume, and feeds it into cooling coils which liquefy the gas passing over them. A train might produce 4 million tons of LNG a year and a large facility will have several trains. The liquid gas is stored in refrigerated tanks until a ship arrives and carries it rapidly to its destination. LNG tankers rely on insulation to prevent the gas from reliquefying and the boil-off gas is burned in the engines of the vessel or reliquefied. Typical modern LNG tankers are

**Table 12.8** LNG trade movements, 2006 (billion cubic metres)

| to | Americas | | Middle East | | | North & West Africa | | | | SE Asia & Oceania | | | | Total |
|---|---|---|---|---|---|---|---|---|---|---|---|---|---|---|
| | USA | Trinidad | Oman | Qatar | UAE | Algeria | Egypt | Libya | Nigeria | Australia | Brunei | Indonesia | Malaysia | |
| *Atlantic* | | | | | | | | | | | | | | |
| USA | | 10.9 | | | | 0.5 | 3.6 | | 1.6 | | | | | 16.6 |
| Dom. Rep | | 0.3 | | | | | | | | | | | | 0.3 |
| Puerto Rico | | 0.7 | | | | | | | | | | | | 0.7 |
| Mexico | | 0.2 | | 0.1 | | | 0.2 | | 0.5 | | | | | 0.9 |
| Belgium | | 0.2 | | 0.4 | | 3.4 | 0.3 | | 0.2 | | | | | 4.3 |
| France | | | | | | 7.4 | 2.3 | | 4.2 | | | | | 13.9 |
| Greece | | | | | | 0.5 | 0.0 | | | | | | | 0.5 |
| Italy | | | | | | 3.0 | 0.1 | | | | | | | 3.1 |
| Portugal | | | | | | | | | 2.0 | | | | | 2.0 |
| Spain | | 3.0 | 1.0 | 5.0 | | 2.8 | 4.8 | 0.7 | 7.1 | | | | | 24.4 |
| Turkey | | | | | | 4.6 | | | 1.1 | | | | | 5.7 |
| UK | | 0.6 | | | | 2.0 | 1.0 | | | | | | | 3.6 |
| *Asia Pacific* | | | | | | | | | | | | | | |
| China | | | | | | | | | | 1.0 | | | | 1.0 |
| India | | | 0.2 | 6.8 | 0.1 | 0.1 | 0.6 | | 0.1 | 0.1 | | | 0.1 | 8.0 |
| Japan | 1.7 | 0.4 | 3.0 | 9.9 | 7.0 | 0.2 | 0.8 | | 0.2 | 15.7 | 8.7 | 18.6 | 15.6 | 81.9 |
| South Korea | | 0.1 | 7.1 | 9.0 | | 0.3 | 1.3 | | 0.2 | 0.9 | 1.2 | 6.7 | 7.5 | 34.1 |
| Taiwan | | | 0.2 | | | | 0.2 | | 0.4 | 0.4 | | 4.3 | 4.9 | 10.2 |
| TOTAL | 1.7 | 16.3 | 11.5 | 31.1 | 7.1 | 24.7 | 15.0 | 0.7 | 17.6 | 18.0 | 9.8 | 29.6 | 28.0 | 211.1 |

Source: BP and Cedigaz (provisional)

around 160,000 cubic metres, travelling at 19 knots and with a steam turbine engine or diesel and carrying about 115,000 tonnes of liquefied gas (1 million tonnes of LNG is equivalent to 1.38 billion cubic metres of natural gas) though in 2006 vessels twice this size were being built for the long-haul Middle East export trades. At the other end of the voyage the regasification plant turns the liquid back into gas, and feeds it to the power utility or the local pipeline system. All this equipment makes the LNG trade very capital-intensive relative to coal and inflexible at today's trade levels.

During the 1990s the cost of gasification plants fell by more than 30% for a 5 million tonnes per year plant, whilst the cost of LNG tankers varied from $250 million to $160 million. These developments, combined with the diminishing domestic reserves in Europe and the USA, resulted in a renaissance in the LNG trade during the early years of the twenty-first century. This was accompanied by changes in the LNG transportation market. Originally the LNG business was conducted with long-term contracts, usually 20 years, with fixed prices and rigid commitment to the contracted quantities. In these circumstances negotiating the price caused great difficulties, due mainly to the lack of any established 'norm'. Later as oil prices became market-driven, the price of the gas was indexed to oil in some way, for example a basket of oil prices, and the growth of forward markets in gas allowed pricing to be hedged. All of this, combined with the growing number of terminals, created a more flexible investment climate.

## LNG transport supply

In 2006 the LNG fleet consisted of 193 ships with another 140 on order. Because the LNG business is still built around major projects which can take as much as a decade to develop, it is relatively easy to see where the next tranches of business will come from. Since large sums of money are involved, the progress of these schemes is fraught with difficulty. The design of LNG tankers is discussed in Section 14.6.

## 12.5  THE TRANSPORT OF REFRIGERATED CARGO

### Demand for refrigerated transport

Refrigerated transport is another example of a trade created by transport technology. Perishable commodities could only be shipped between regions when it was possible to preserve them during transit, and when this technology became available new trades rapidly emerged. The trade developed for several different reasons. One is that some parts of the world could produce perishable foodstuffs much more cheaply than others. For example, New Zealand is a major international supplier of meat and dairy products to economies in the North Atlantic because it can produce these products much more cheaply. A second element in the trade is the movement of seasonal crops between the hemispheres, smoothing out the imbalances caused by the harvest cycles. This is particularly prominent in the citrus and deciduous fruit trades, where countries like South Africa produce their new crop during the Northern Hemisphere winter. Thirdly, there are climatic differences. For example, bananas, which can only be grown in tropical areas, are exported to the temperate zones. There is fierce competition for these cargoes between conventional reefer ships and refrigerated containers, and in many trades containers pushed the reefer ships into second place. Air freight has also become important for the high-value exotic fruits. As a result fast, cheap transport has opened up an enormous global market for seasonal vegetables at all times of the year, greatly widening the range of fresh foodstuffs available in most countries. In this section we will examine how the trade fits into this model in practice.

### Development of refrigerated transport

Refrigerated sea transport started in the meat trade in the nineteenth century. As Europe's urban population increased, local meat and dairy farmers could not feed the cities and the railways were opening up vast new food-producing areas of North America, South America, New Zealand, Australia and South Africa. With unsatisfied demand in Europe and meat supplies available overseas, all that was needed was a transport system. As in so many other specialist trades, it was the shippers who made the running. To begin with the meat was canned and shipped by liner. The first Australian canning company started in 1847, and in 1863 the Liebig beef extract process was established at Fray Bentos in Uruguay. Between 1868 and 1876 there were various experiments in shipping frozen meat, but the refrigeration equipment was unreliable and, even when it worked, the quality of the meat was poor.

By the end of the 1870s refrigeration technology was improving and the *Paraguay*, fitted with a Carre ammonia machine, carried a frozen cargo from France to Buenos Aires, returning to Le Havre with 80 tons of mutton which arrived in excellent condition. This marked the beginning of the seaborne reefer business. Two years later in 1880 Australia shipped its first cargoes in the *Strathleven* which loaded 40 tons of beef and mutton which was frozen on board and delivered to London in perfect condition. Later that year the *Protos* sailed for London with 4600 carcasses of mutton and lamb, stored in holds insulated with wool.[9] When the vessel arrived in London the cargo was discharged in excellent condition and the wool insulation was removed from the vessel and also sold – those old-time shipping entrepreneurs certainly knew how to squeeze an extra buck out of the business! The first New Zealand frozen cargo in 1882 sold in London for twice the market price in New Zealand, which gives an idea of the financial incentive driving the trade. This convinced the meat producers of South America, Australia and New Zealand that refrigerated transport was viable and within a few years a transport system had evolved. Freezing plants were established in the meat-exporting areas to supply wholesale markets with refrigerated storage and distribution facilities at the importing end. For example, Smithfield Market in London acted as the main centre for meat in the UK. In the 1970s palletization was introduced and ships, storage and cargo-handling facilities were all designed around the standard pallet sizes of 800 × 1200mm and 1000 × 1200mm agreed by the OECD.[10] This opened the way for greater mechanization of cargo handling, for example using fork-lift trucks and banana conveyors.

However, in the 1940s the land-based transport industry developed the portable refrigeration unit, initially in the form of an insulated trailer with an integral refrigeration unit, and this technology was to have a major impact on reefer trade. These refrigerated trailers, which kept produce fresh by saturating the air with moisture from the integral refrigeration unit, were introduced in 1942 for US troops stationed overseas and subsequently were adopted by the railways in the USA. In the 1950s the trucking business started to use them, and when diesel engines replaced gas-powered refrigeration in the late 1950s the technology became more reliable and cheaper to run, especially on long trips with high run hours.[11] This coincided with the start of containerization by sea, and from the outset the new seaborne container business carried refrigerated containers, competing with the conventional reefer ships.

## The reefer commodity trades

In 2005, 130 million tons of perishable cargoes were traded world-wide (Table 12.9), though these statistics are not precise because they include land trade and some cargoes that are not refrigerated. Broadly speaking, the refrigerated cargo trade falls into three groups: deciduous fruit, which accounts for about a third; meat and dairy produce, which account for another third; and fish, which accounts for the remainder. In addition, Table 12.9 shows 'other fruit and vegetables' as a memo item. This is a very large trade

**Table 12.9** World trade in perishable foodstuffs (mt)

| Year | Commodity | | | | | | | | Total growth Yr on Yr | Memo: Other Fruit & Veg. |
|------|---------|--------------|------------------|-------------|----------------|------|------|-------------|-----------------------|--------------------------|
| | Bananas | Citrus fruits | Deciduous fruits | Total fruit | Dairy products | Meat | Fish | Total trade | | |
| 1983 | 6 | 7 | 5 | 19 | 10 | 9 | 20 | 58 | | 59 |
| 1984 | 7 | 8 | 5 | 20 | 11 | 9 | 22 | 61 | 5.9% | 63 |
| 1985 | 7 | 7 | 5 | 19 | 12 | 9 | 25 | 64 | 5.1% | 66 |
| 1986 | 7 | 9 | 5 | 21 | 12 | 10 | 27 | 69 | 7.7% | 70 |
| 1987 | 8 | 8 | 6 | 21 | 12 | 10 | 28 | 71 | 2.8% | 73 |
| 1988 | 8 | 8 | 6 | 21 | 13 | 11 | 29 | 74 | 3.5% | 77 |
| 1989 | 8 | 8 | 6 | 22 | 13 | 11 | 31 | 77 | 4.5% | 81 |
| 1990 | 9 | 8 | 6 | 24 | 12 | 12 | 29 | 77 | −0.5% | 84 |
| 1991 | 10 | 8 | 7 | 25 | 13 | 13 | 29 | 81 | 5.1% | 88 |
| 1992 | 11 | 9 | 7 | 26 | 15 | 14 | 31 | 85 | 5.4% | 91 |
| 1993 | 12 | 9 | 8 | 29 | 15 | 14 | 34 | 92 | 7.8% | 96 |
| 1994 | 13 | 10 | 8 | 31 | 16 | 16 | 41 | 103 | 12.5% | 102 |
| 1995 | 13 | 10 | 8 | 32 | 16 | 17 | 38 | 103 | 0.0% | 101 |
| 1996 | 14 | 10 | 9 | 33 | 17 | 18 | 38 | 105 | 1.7% | 104 |
| 1997 | 15 | 10 | 9 | 34 | 18 | 19 | 39 | 110 | 4.5% | 107 |
| 1998 | 14 | 11 | 9 | 33 | 18 | 19 | 32 | 104 | −5.4% | 109 |
| 1999 | 14 | 10 | 9 | 34 | 19 | 21 | 36 | 110 | 6.1% | 115 |
| 2000 | 14 | 11 | 9 | 34 | 20 | 22 | 41 | 117 | 6.7% | 117 |
| 2001 | 15 | 11 | 10 | 35 | 20 | 22 | 41 | 118 | 0.9% | 123 |
| 2002 | 14 | 12 | 10 | 36 | 20 | 23 | 41 | 120 | 1.8% | 126 |
| 2003 | 15 | 12 | 11 | 38 | 21 | 24 | 41 | 124 | 3.0% | 129 |
| 2004 | 16 | 13 | 11 | 40 | 21 | 26 | 41 | 128 | 3.0% | 131 |
| 2005 | 16 | 14 | 11 | 41 | 21 | 27 | 41 | 130 | 1.4% | 133 |

Source: FAO Trade Yearbook and FAO Yearbook of Fishery Statistics.
Note: data includes land and seaborne trade.

which includes commodities such as manioc which are shipped in bulk. Between 1990 and 2005 the trade grew by an average of 3.6% per annum, making it one of the more rapidly growing segments of the business, driven by the high income elasticity of fruit and vegetables in the developed countries of the Northern Hemisphere.

Bananas provide a stable base load from exporters in the West Indies, South America and, to a lesser extent, Africa. Western Europe and the USA account for about two-thirds of the imports. Exports from the seasonal producing areas in the Southern Hemisphere such as South Africa are volatile. There is a major trade in oranges from the Mediterranean (especially Israel) and South Africa to Western Europe. Recently the trade in exotic fruits such as strawberries, raspberries and kiwi has grown rapidly as exporters have searched for value added. The 'other vegetable' trade includes a sizeable trade in manioc from South East Asia to western Europe where it is used as an animal feed – this is not refrigerated cargo. A wide range of other fruit and vegetables are also traded by sea, including potatoes. The fresh meat trade is principally from Australia, New Zealand and Argentina into the developed areas of western Europe, the USA and Japan. The trade accounts for only a very small proportion of meat consumption and growth has been more rapid into Japan and West Coast North America than elsewhere, benefiting particularly from the growth of the 'fast food' business. Fresh milk is hardly traded internationally (though there is a trade in powdered milk of over 2 mt per annum) and the main dairy trades are in butter and cheese. The traditional trade was from New Zealand or Australia into the UK, though this started to change when the UK joined the EEC.

Perhaps the most interesting aspect of the refrigerated cargo trade from the maritime economist's viewpoint is the competition between different transport modes for this type of cargo. Refrigerated cargo can be carried in reefer ships; refrigerated containers; refrigerated spaces in conventional liner and MPP vessels; and in refrigerated trucks on ro-ros. In recent years the container trade has become increasingly important, providing a fascinating example of the

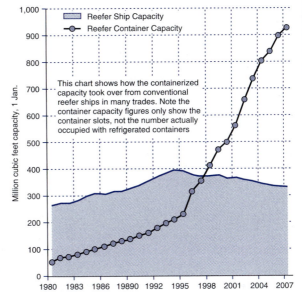

**Figure 12.8**
Reefer fleet and reefer container capacity, 1980–2007
Source: Clarkson Research Reefer and Container Registers

dynamics of competition in specialist shipping. For example, during the first half of the twentieth century there was intense competition between the liner services and the reefer fleet for the refrigerated cargo. The fleet of refrigerated vessels grew steadily and many cargo liners fitted refrigerated capacity if cargo was moving on their routes (see Chapter 13 and the discussion of the *Point Sans Souci* class of liners). In 1956 Sea-Land introduced the first refrigerated containers on its new container service, using 500 refrigerated trailer units with their own cooling system, adapted for sea transport. In the 1960s more reefer services were containerized, including the important Australia to Europe trade, and the reefer operators responded by palletizing the cargo and building ships designed to handle and stow pallets efficiently. Initially this defensive strategy was successful, but in 1999 container capacity finally overtook conventional reefer capacity, forcing a decline in the fleet of dedicated reefer ships (Figure 12.8).

## Reefer transport technology

The cargoes shown in Table 12.9 all need to be transported at carefully regulated temperatures, but they have very different requirements. Broadly speaking the refrigerated cargoes can be divided into three groups:

- *Frozen cargo.* Certain products such as meat and fish need to be fully frozen, and transported at temperatures of up to –26°C.
- *Chilled cargo.* Dairy products and other perishables are transported at low temperatures, though above freezing point, in order to prevent decomposition.

- *Controlled temperatures*. Fruit transported by sea is generally picked in a semi-ripe state, and allowed to finish ripening at sea at a carefully controlled temperature. For example, bananas require precisely 13°C.

Refrigerated ships remain the core source of transport for the high-volume trades. Temperatures must be maintained consistently throughout the ship to prevent deterioration of the cargoes, and even small temperature deviations can be disastrous, especially for tropical fruit. To achieve this, air passes over a bank of refrigerated pipes and is distributed through ducts to the cargo space, allowing both the temperature and the rate of air change to be controlled. The circulating air can also be adjusted for carbon dioxide content, which is important in the carriage of chilled meat and the controlled ripening of certain fruit. The cargo holds are generally lined with plywood and layers of polystyrene insulation (not wool!).

Two types of containers are used in the refrigerated container trade. 'Integral units' are fitted with their own refrigeration unit designed to meet ISO standards and to fit the container-ship cell guides. On board the ship, the refrigeration unit is plugged in to the ship's power supply, the size of which determines how many refrigerated containers the ship can carry. These units are expensive but flexible. 'Insulated containers' have no integral refrigeration unit, just insulation, and must be plugged into an air cooling system on the ship or terminal, or 'clip-on' refrigeration units can be used.

### Supply of refrigerated transport capacity

In 2006 the reefer fleet numbered 1,242 vessels with a capacity of 333 million cubic feet. However, as Figure 12.8 shows, the reefer fleet capacity had been declining since the mid-1990s and the container-ship fleet was expanding with capacity to carry 939 million cubic feet of containerized cargo, though how much of this is in use is not statistically recorded. It is, however, an excellent example of the continuous competition between different shipping services.

## 12.6 UNIT LOAD CARGO TRANSPORT

There are many large physical units such as package timber, bales of pulp, spools of paper, motor vehicles, heavy lift cargoes such as components for a petrol refinery, heavy units such as container cranes, earth-moving equipment, and the host of other large and awkward physical objects which need to move from one part of the world to another. Where volumes are sufficiently large it is often economic to build specialized vessels designed for the efficient transportation of the specific cargo, and over the years several specialized fleets totalling over 3,000 ships have developed to service these trades (see Table 12.1). The five we will cover are deep sea ro-ros used for a mix of cargoes including containers, forest products and wheeled cargo; open hatch bulk carriers, used principally in the forest products trades; PCCs and PCTCs; MPP vessels used for mixed cargoes and increasingly for heavy lift; and heavy lift vessels which focus on the transport of very large unit cargoes, sometimes weighing thousands of tons. All these vessel types are to some extent competing with each other, and the cargo flows are not clearly defined in statistical terms. So the following notes concentrate mainly on the development of the various fleets.

## Deep-sea ro-ros

Deep sea ro-ros were one of the first unit load cargo carriers to be developed. These vessels have multiple decks accessed by ramps in the stern, bow or side of the vessel and are very much in the cargo liner tradition, capable of transporting forest products, cars, containers, pallets and heavy lift cargoes. Forest products, containers and palletized cargo are loaded with fork-lift trucks, whilst cars, trucks and other wheeled cargo are driven on. Some also have hoistable decks to accommodate tall items of cargo.

All this versatility comes at a price and they are expensive to build. Although in the early days some enthusiasts saw the ro-ro as the natural successor to the cargo liner, it was pushed into the sidelines by the less versatile but ruthlessly efficient container-ship. Table 12.10 shows that by 2006 the fleet had edged up to 1040 vessels, but it had a sluggish growth record. Between 1996 and 2006 the ro-ro fleet grew at an average of only 1.7% per annum, compared with the 10% growth of the container-ship fleet. In addition, the average ship size remained small, edging up to 8800 dwt in 2006.

**Table 12.10** The cargo ro-ro fleet, 1996–2006

| 1 Jan. | No. | Dwt | Growth % p.a. | Av. dwt |
|--------|------|-------|------|---------|
| 1996 | 962 | 7,754 | | 8,061 |
| 1997 | 981 | 7,989 | 3% | 8,143 |
| 1998 | 996 | 7,984 | 0% | 8,016 |
| 1999 | 1,007 | 8,118 | 2% | 8,062 |
| 2000 | 1,036 | 8,401 | 3% | 8,109 |
| 2001 | 1,039 | 8,561 | 2% | 8,240 |
| 2002 | 1,034 | 8,716 | 2% | 8,429 |
| 2003 | 1,042 | 8,904 | 2% | 8,545 |
| 2004 | 1,039 | 9,016 | 1% | 8,678 |
| 2005 | 1,035 | 9,088 | 1% | 8,781 |
| 2006 | 1,040 | 9,183 | 1% | 8,830 |
| 2007 | 1,075 | 9,500 | 3% | 8,837 |

Source: CRSL Containership Register 2007, Table 5

The modern ro-ro type vessels were first built in volume by the US Army which in the 1940s used landing ship tanks (LSTs) to move tanks to beachheads and discharge them through wide bow doors.[12] An early commercial vessel to use this technology was the *Vacationland*, built in 1952 to trade on the Great Lakes. It had accommodation for 150 vehicles in eight lanes and 650 passengers. Cargo could be loaded and discharged via ramps at the bow and stern. By the end of the 1950s Scandinavian shipowners had started using small ro-ros to transport forest products, pulp and paper from Baltic ports to the Continent, with a backhaul of motor vehicles to Scandinavia. These vessels had large stern doors, 6–7 metres wide and 5 metres high, and could carry big trailers and heavy equipment of up to 70 or 80 tonnes on their ramps.

In the late 1960s the first large deep-sea ro-ro services were developed. Scandinavian owners Wallenius Line, along with Transatlantic AB and a group of European owners, set up Atlantic Container Line in 1967 using a fleet of ten large ro-ro vessels with stern ramps for stowing about two-thirds of the cargo below decks with containers on the deck.[13] The ships operated on the North Atlantic and their main aim was to speed up cargo handling and reduce stevedore costs, at a time when both of these factors were a major problem for the shipping industry. Shortly afterwards in 1969 Scanaustral set up a ro-ro service between Australia and Europe. The service was to handle cargoes of forest products, cars, and heavy lift southbound and return with wool, sheepskins, hides, canned and refrigerated foods and metal ingots or bars. After a careful study they concluded that although almost all of this cargo could in principle be containerized, the trade was imbalanced, and the ro-ro system offered better overall economics.[14] Although this logic seemed valid the critical mass built up by container services meant that this deep-sea ro-ro transport never developed as more than a niche.

However, this was not the end of the road for ro-ro transport. Whilst ro-ro vessels have a limited role on the deep-sea general cargo routes, the design has proved extremely effective in two other unit load areas: Firstly in the vehicle trades using PCCs and, more recently, PCTCs which are discussed below, and secondly, in the short-sea trades where ro-ro ferries carrying cargo and passengers now dominate sea transport over short distances.

## Pure car and truck carriers

With the opening of global markets in recent decades, the sea trade in cars and trucks has grown rapidly and has become one of the most important unit load cargoes. Vehicles are light, easily damaged and take a lot of space in a conventional cargo ship, typically stowing at 12 cubic metres to the ton. As a result the freight rates on conventional ships were very high and in the 1950s car exporters started to arrange their own transport, initially using bulk carriers with folding car decks which could be stowed when not in use and which could be prepared for cars in under an hour. In 1956 Wallenius built the first ocean-going vehicle carrier with a capacity for 260 vehicles, and in the following years their size and sophistication increased. By 1965 Japan's first car carrier, the *Opama Maru*, had a capacity of 1200 cars, with a stern ramps that allowed the cars to be driven on and off the ship and elevators to move them between decks where they were stowed. By 1970 car-carriers capable of carrying over 3,000 cars at 21 knots were being built and rapidly replaced the earlier lift-on, lift-off vessels. For example, *Lorita*, belonging to Uglands, carried 3200 motor cars on nine decks, each with deck headroom of 2.52 metres. Cars were loaded through side doors and internal ramps connected the decks, with final positioning by fork-lift truck. In January 2008 the fleet was 634 vessels of 9.1 million dwt (see Table 12.11), including both PCCs and PCTCs. During the previous decade it grew at over 6% per annum, and the largest ships could carry 7,000 vehicles. Most are owned by a small number of Japanese, European and Korean companies.

### DEMAND AND THE TRANSPORT SYSTEM

Car manufacturing is subject to scale economies, but consumers like variety and cars are traded in volume. The growth of international consumer markets in the 1970s and 1980s encouraged a rapidly growing interregional trade in vehicles. The trade is principally from Japan and South Korea to the USA and Europe, with a much smaller trade from Europe to North America. In 1996 the trade was 6.9 million vehicles, but in the next decade it grew rapidly, reaching 15 million units in 2005. The major import trades were 2.5 million units to Europe, 6.4 million units to USA and 2.9 million units to Far East countries. These deep-sea trades have all been growing rapidly. The main exporters in 2005 were Japan which exported 5.6 million units, South Korea which exported 2.6 million units and Western Europe which exported 1.9 million units. This trade pattern reflects the growing

**Table 12.11** The pure car carrier fleet, 1996–2006

| 1 Jan. | No. | Dwt | Growth<br>% p.a. | Av. dwt |
|---|---|---|---|---|
| 1996 | 379 | 4,552 | | 12,011 |
| 1997 | 381 | 4,636 | 2% | 12,168 |
| 1998 | 395 | 4,831 | 4% | 12,230 |
| 1999 | 436 | 5,298 | 10% | 12,151 |
| 2000 | 452 | 5,840 | 10% | 12,920 |
| 2001 | 476 | 6,291 | 8% | 13,217 |
| 2002 | 483 | 6,461 | 3% | 13,377 |
| 2003 | 494 | 6,627 | 3% | 13,416 |
| 2004 | 524 | 6,847 | 3% | 13,067 |
| 2006 | 526 | 7,266 | 6% | 13,814 |
| 2006 | 560 | 7,848 | 8% | 14,015 |
| 2007 | 599 | 8,700 | 11% | 14,524 |
| 2008 | 634 | 9,100 | 5% | 14,353 |

diversity of the market place, as discussed in Chapter 10, and the cost-effective transport system which makes manufacturing location less important than product differentiation.

This is a classic industrial shipping operation. As a cargo, cars are high-volume, low-density, and high-value. Vehicles move in large numbers out of western Europe and Japan, mainly shipped in purpose-built vehicle carriers. When operating at full capacity, a large-scale auto assembly plant can produce one car about every 40 seconds. This means that a full 24-hour production schedule results in a maximum daily production of 2160 cars. This level of production can be maintained for long periods despite differentiation in colour, style, accessories and trim. Materials handling to ensure that the right cars arrive at the right destination must be highly organized.

Finished cars cannot be economically stored at the plant and are moved to distribution points as quickly as possible. This extends to the carriage of export cars by sea, and the shipping operation must 'fit' the overall system with storage facilities at the port, fast cargo handling, timely arrival of ships and security for the valuable product in transit. Thus the vehicle carrier fleet operates to carefully scheduled timetables by professional management teams. The largest vessels carry up to 7,000 vehicles, often with hoistable decks which can be adjusted to transport trucks and earth-moving equipment, especially on the backhaul when the vessels are generally empty. Because of the high value of the cargo and age restrictions on vessels imposed by car exporters, car carriers are generally subject to quite rapid depreciation.

## SUPPLY AND OWNERSHIP

In January 2008, the car-carrying fleets stood at 634 ships of 9.1 m.dwt, with a capacity of about 3.0 million vehicles (see Table 12.11). As with other segments of the fleet, the size is dispersed, with vessels varying in size from 1,000 vehicles up to 7,000 vehicles.

In recent years there have been mergers and the carrier market is dominated by eight operators who control about 90% of capacity. Two, Nissan and Hyundai are manufacturers; three are Japanese shipowners, NYK, Mitsui OSK, K-Line; one South Korean shipping company, Cido Shipping; and two Scandinavian operators who specialize in car transport, Walenius and Leif Hoegh.

## Open hatch bulk carriers

### THE OPEN HATCH BULK SHIPPING

In 2006 there was a fleet of 486 open hatch bulk carriers of 16.5 million dwt, with an average ship size of 34,000 dwt, most of which work in the forest products trade. Vessels of this type first appeared in the early 1960s to speed up the transport of newsprint which is shipped in large rolls weighing 730 kilograms each. At the time cargo was handled by lifting each roll on rope slings, dropping it into the hold, then laboriously manoeuvring it into place. The hatch overhang made this very labour-intensive, which tied up the ship in port for long periods and the cargo was easily damaged. The first open hatch bulk carrier, the *Bessegen*, built in 1962, had hatch openings the full width of the ship and gantry cranes with grabs capable of lifting eight spools of paper and dropping them vertically into the hold. This transformed a danger-ous and labour-intensive process into a fast and highly automated one. There are several large operators which specialize in the transport of all types of forest products, but also carry other unit loads, including containers. Most of the fleet is owned or operated by specialist operators, including K.G. Jebsen Gearbulk (60 ships), Star Shipping (40 ships), Egon Oldendorff (18 ships) and NYK (21 ships).

This distinctive business focuses on the efficient handling and stowage of unit cargoes. Forest products form the base load of the business, but these vessels also carry steel products, containers and project cargoes. The vessels which range in size from 10,000 to 57,000 dwt are designed specifically for the efficient transport of these cargoes. They have open hatches and some can fit 'tweendecks into the holds, allowing several cargoes to be carried in a single hold, for example a bottom cargo of lumber, with wheeled cargo in the 'tween deck (the 'tween decks rest on fold-down supports and are dropped into place when needed). They also have a variety of different types of gear. About 40% are fitted with gantry cranes capable of lifting of up to 70 tons, and the remainder with con-ventional cranes. Special slings and 'spreaders' are used to speed the handling of specific cargoes such as rolls of paper and steel products. The impact this has on cargo-handling speeds is significant. A conventional bulk carrier with slewing cranes handles forest products at a rate of 250 tons per hour, taking 4 days to load a 25,000 ton cargo, whereas an open hatch bulk carrier with 40 ton gantry cranes can load at over 400 tons per hour, cutting the loading time to 2.4 days.[15] This reduction in ship time is mirrored by increased terminal throughput, which reduces the cost of the overall transport operation, and the economics of the operation has already been discussed in Section 12.1.

All of which makes it a specialized business, and the following brief review clarifies the different ways operators seek to differentiate their service:

> Star has more than 40 highly specialized Open Hatch vessels that are tailor made for the carriage of wood pulp, rolled paper and other forestry products.

In addition we carry a wide range of other unitized cargoes, project cargoes and containers. ... Our vessels have box shaped holds, gantry cranes with rain protection, dehumidification systems and state-of-the-art cargo handling equipment. This enables us to load and discharge the cargo with minimum handling, ensuring safe stowage and minimum delays. Additionally our latest generation will also be equipped with 'tween decks in some of the holds, enabling a mix of various fragile types of cargo in the same hold. Our Open Hatch business is based on long term contracts and strong relationships where high quality, efficiency, punctuality and flexibility are necessary to ensure our customers' satisfaction in the long run.[16]

### PACKAGE BULK CARGO TRANSPORT SYSTEM

This type of operation often involves investment in terminal facilities, since handling and storing packaged cargoes provides terminal operators with a different type of problem. The broad aims are the same, but the operational aspects are very different.

The Squamish Terminals Ltd in British Columbia illustrates the terminal requirements in the forest products trade. The terminal handles exports of pulp from British Columbia. Pulp is shipped from the pulp mill by rail. The railway line runs into the terminal alongside the warehouses. Bales of pulp are discharged from train to storage and then to the ship with a fleet of 34 fork-lift trucks and 14 double-wide tractor trailer units of 34 tons capacity, plus four extension trailers. Three warehouses provide covered storage for 85,000 tons of pulp, about two shiploads, since the vessels servicing the terminal are 40,000–45,000 dwt. However, the terminal operators found that, because the pulp mills have little storage, any stock-building on their part ends up at the terminal. A third warehouse was built as a buffer for this purpose.

Cargo is loaded from two berths, Berth 1 of 11.6 metres draft and Berth 2 of 12.2 metres draft. Because the terminal is serviced by a fleet of geared bulk carriers there is no need for cranes on the quayside. Ships come alongside the apron and cargo is loaded with the ship's gantry cranes. Berth 1 can handle ships up to 195 metres, with an apron 135 metres long, which is sufficient to give access to the cargo holds. Berth 2 handles ships up to 212 metres, with an apron of 153 metres.[17]

## Heavy lift

One of the most difficult segments for the shipping industry to deal with are the large structures which need to be moved around the world. We will define a heavy lift cargo as any unit too large to fit in a container because it exceeds $40 \times 8 \times 8.5$ feet in dimensions or 26 tons in weight. This includes three categories of cargo. Firstly, there are industrial cargoes, for example a 230 tonne reactor for a power plant, a refining column or a container crane. Secondly, there are offshore structures – jack-up rigs, semi-submersible rigs and other pieces of offshore equipment, for example single point moorings or a 56 metre steel jacket, that need to be moved around the world. Thirdly, there are small ships or dredgers, ferries, or yachts and small cargo ships where it is cheaper and safer to move the vessel on a heavy lift ship than take it under its own steam.

Heavy lift ships are concerned with the transport of all these cargoes. Broadly speaking, they fall into three categories: first, powerful tug barge systems which tow large structures around the world on barges; second, semi-submersible heavy lift ships which can be ballasted down, allowing the heavy cargo to be floated onto the deck on a pontoon, after which the vessel de-ballasts to its normal freeboard; and third, many of the large fleet of cargo ships are equipped with heavy lift cranes and they pick up the many small to medium-sized heavy lift cargoes.

*Ocean-going tugs* are very different from the tugs used for manoeuvring ships in port. Essentially they are floating power units with engines of over 4,000 hp. The wheelhouse must be positioned for maximum visibility and the afterdeck is kept clear of obstructions which might snag the tow wire. Reliability and the ability to sustain heavy workloads over long periods are vital, as is the ability to handle a very variable workload and large-capacity fuel tanks for undertaking long tows. Apart from the power unit, the tug will carry specialist equipment, depending upon the type of work it is intended to undertake. The flat-topped barges towed by tugs are fitted with ballast systems that allow them to submerge so that heavy equipment can be floated on. Simpler units submerge and rest on the bottom whilst the more sophisticated vessels can achieve float on without the aid of bottom support.

*Semi-submersible heavy lift ships* are also popular. These vessels do much the same job as a tug and barge system, but the power plant is integrated into the vessel, giving better sea-keeping capabilities. The ships are generally designed to be ballasted down, allowing the cargo to float on board. These vessels can be very powerful, with 8,000 to 23,000 bhp engines, and are capable of carrying very heavy loads.

*Heavy lift ships* are generally under 15,000 dwt and fitted with heavy cranes capable of working in tandem. The cargo holds have open hatches, allowing heavy units to be dropped into place, and the cranes will have a capacity of up to 1800 tonnes working together. Cranes are often mounted to the side of the vessel, allowing the cargo space to be unobstructed. To ensure stability during loading and discharging, the ships have anti-healing ballast tanks, and strengthened hatch covers to take heavy loads on deck. In addition to crane capacity, some heavy lift vessels have ro-ro access and strengthened ramps so that cargo can be rolled on. For example, vessels operated by BigLift group have ramps capable of carrying loads of up to 2500 tons weight, substantially more than can be achieved using cranes. The fleet numbers 193 vessels of 3.1 m. dwt. Because of the small size of the fleet and the global reach of the business, some owners increase efficiency and flexibility by operating in pools.

As always there is pressure to increase flexibility. Recently heavy lift ships have been built with container capacity, whilst some of the car carriers discussed earlier in this chapter have strengthened ramps and hoistable decks, allowing them to load heavy lift and project cargoes.

This is a convenient point to mention the *multi-purpose and tramp fleets* shown in Table 12.12 because these ships play an important part in servicing the smaller end of the heavy lift market. The vessels in this table are divided into three categories: the MPP fleet;

**Table 12.12** Multi-purpose and tramp fleet

| 1st Jan | MPP fleet | | Tramp fleet | | Liner fleet | | Total fleet | | |
|---|---|---|---|---|---|---|---|---|---|
| | No. | m dwt | No. | m dwt | No. | m dwt | No. | m dwt | % growth |
| 1996 | 1,955 | 19.8 | 678 | 7.5 | 1,111 | 15.9 | 3,744 | 43.2 | |
| 1997 | 2,025 | 25.3 | 632 | 6.8 | 1,044 | 15.0 | 3,701 | 42.0 | –3% |
| 1998 | 2,095 | 20.6 | 623 | 6.7 | 895 | 13.0 | 3,613 | 40.1 | –5% |
| 1999 | 2,170 | 21.1 | 618 | 6.3 | 786 | 11.4 | 3,574 | 38.8 | –3% |
| 2000 | 2,219 | 21.3 | 606 | 6.0 | 727 | 10.3 | 3,552 | 37.8 | –3% |
| 2001 | 2,296 | 21.6 | 598 | 5.7 | 624 | 9.1 | 3,518 | 36.5 | –4% |
| 2002 | 2,227 | 21.4 | 585 | 5.5 | 546 | 7.9 | 3,358 | 34.8 | –5% |
| 2003 | 2,346 | 21.5 | 571 | 5.3 | 492 | 9.0 | 3,409 | 33.7 | –3% |
| 2004 | 2,365 | 21.6 | 562 | 5.1 | 442 | 6.2 | 3,369 | 32.9 | –2% |
| 2005 | 2,424 | 22.1 | 575 | 5.2 | 425 | 5.9 | 3,424 | 33.3 | 1% |
| 2006 | 2,533 | 22.8 | 605 | 5.4 | 419 | 5.8 | 3,557 | 34.1 | 2% |

Source: CRSL Containership Register 2007, Table 5

the tramp fleet; and the multi-deck 'liner' fleet. These are flexible vessels generally with more than one deck and cargo-handling gear, often heavy cranes. It is a large fleet, with 3,521 vessels in 2006. The MPP fleet is now much the largest, with 2,533 vessels and a capacity of 22.8 m.dwt though many of these are below 10,000 dwt. Typically these ships carry a mix of unit load cargoes, including containers, heavy lift, motor vehicles, forest products and steel products. The size of cranes varies enormously: 30–60 ton cranes are common but some can lift 100 tons (see Figure 14.4). This MPP fleet is growing slowly, increasing from 19.8 m.dwt in 1996 to 22.8 m.dwt in 2006. In contrast, the tramp and liner fleets are declining, since during the last 20 years most new investment has focused on the MPP segment.

## 12.7 PASSENGER SHIPPING

### Development history

The passenger business has changed a good deal over the years. Until the 1950s passenger ships were the only way of crossing water, and in the early twentieth century passengers became the core business of many great shipping companies. The powerful liners built to transport passengers in luxury at 20 or even 30 knots made it one of the most evocative periods in shipping history. Many cargo vessels also had facilities to carry paying passengers. In 1950 ships still carried three times as many passengers as aircraft across the Atlantic. However, as intercontinental airlines developed in the 1950s, the economics moved decisively against passenger ships, which proved to be far too labour-intensive to survive in the post-war world (Section 1.6). By the 1960s ships carried few deep-sea passengers. Some companies left the business whilst others, such as P&O and Cunard, diversified into the cruise business. But although aircraft had a decisive economic long-haul advantage, for short-sea voyages sea transport remained competitive, especially for cars, lorries and wheeled cargo. As motor transport flourished in the 1950s

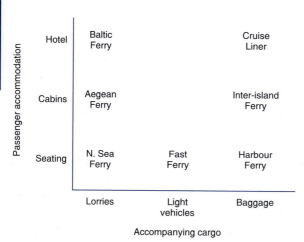

**Figure 12.9**
Passenger transport options

and 1960s, so did the ferry business. Today we have a whole spectrum of passenger vessels, ranging from commuter ferries to the luxurious 'resort' cruise liners dedicated to taking passengers on holiday.

To illustrate the diversity of passenger vessel types, Figure 12.9 concentrates on two key aspects of passenger ship design, the passenger accommodation, shown on the vertical axis of the diagram, and the accommodation for accompanying vehicles. There are three levels of accommodation. The most basic is seating with benches or overnight 'couchette' seats. At the second level cabins are provided, whilst the third level offers complete hotel accommodation with restaurants, shops and entertainment. It would be possible to extend the diagram one step further to the most modern development of 'resort' accommodation in which the ship is purpose-designed as a complete leisure resort, essentially a small town at sea. The other dimension identified is the accompanying cargo which ranges from hand baggage, through light vehicles such as motor cars, to lorries.

Using these broad criteria, the figure defines seven types of passenger vessel. On left-hand side of the diagram are the ferries designed primarily to carry cars and lorries. On the short routes such as the English Channel these will have seating accommodation, with associated restaurants, but no cabins, since the voyages are too short to include an overnight stay. At the second level of the 'Aegean Ferries' they have simple cabin accommodation, whilst at the third level the 'Baltic ferries' are designed to provide overnight accommodation with a full range of hotel-style services, entertainment, etc. These vessels are in effect cruise liners, but with roll-on roll-off accommodation for cars and lorries.

On the right hand side of the diagram are the vessels with no vehicle decks. At the lowest level is the harbour ferry, which has passenger seating accommodation and possibly some refreshment facilities. At the second level are Inter island ferries which have simple cabin accommodation, but no ro-ro facilities. Finally at the top are cruise liners with hotel accommodation and leisure activities.

The fundamental difference between these ship types is their role of transportation. Essentially, with the exception of the Cunard transatlantic service and the seasonal repositioning of vessels, the cruise liners are exclusively designed for leisure, with no transportation role, whilst all the others are primarily transport vessels which offer different degrees of leisure services to customers during their voyage. But they have many features in common.

## Passenger ferries

Ferries transport people, goods and vehicles over short distances by sea. They vary in size from small passenger ferries used to cross channels such as Hong Kong harbour, the Hudson River in New York, or the Bosphorus in Turkey, to very large ro-ro ferries which carry 3,000 passengers and 650 vehicles across the English Channel, the Baltic Sea or between the islands of Indonesia.

The vessels used in the ferry market share many common characteristics such as ro-ro access, vehicle decks, accommodation for passengers and entertainment facilities, but there are so many permutations of these basic characteristics that the ferry fleet is extremely diverse. As mentioned in the previous section, almost all ferries use ro-ro technology to allow motor vehicles and wheeled cargo to be loaded and discharged quickly and easily. Passengers arrive in motor transport which is stowed on vehicle decks designed with as few impediments as possible. Access is through a stern door which doubles as a loading ramp, possibly with a bow door arrangement which permits straight-through driving and parking. Accommodation is located above the car decks, and its design depends on the service for which the ferry is intended. This is where the ferry companies move into the entertainment business.

The opportunity to entertain passengers during their voyage and in so doing generate a profitable income stream is one of the prime considerations in the ferry business. Vessels used on short trips, for example across harbours or rivers, will have simple seating arrangements, but little entertainment. On short sea crossings taking a few hours, for example the English Channel, the accommodation typically focuses on restaurants, shopping facilities and seating areas for passengers. On longer voyages, for example across the Baltic, cabins are provided and the focus is on a offering customers a 'mini-cruise', with more exotic entertainment, discos, etc. Because of this distinction in commercial function, there are major differences between ferries used in these different markets, leading to a degree of market segmentation. In Europe the market splits into the Baltic market, which is relatively long distance and uses the most sophisticated overnight ferries; the North Sea which generally involves transit times of 3–8 hours, with less focus on passenger accommodation, and more on shopping and restaurants; and the Mediterranean, which has a mix of both.

The economics of the ferry business is complex. Because of the large amount of marketing required, and expense of the ships, ferry services are generally operated by large companies. There is generally intense competition with other ferry operators serving on the same routes or other routes to the same general destination. Speed, frequency of service and the levels of on-board accommodation are all key issues. Over the last 20 years the ferries built for these demanding markets have grown larger and more sophisticated. A typical example is the *Gotland*, a 196 metre vessel of 29,746 gross tonnes built in 2003 to operate between Visby on the Baltic island of Gotland and the Swedish mainland. It is capable of carrying 1500 passengers, 1600 metres of trailers or 500 cars at a speed of 28.5 knots and has 112 cabins with 300 berths. Ferries of this type have a variety of cabins, several restaurants and relaxation areas and luxurious public areas.

## The cruise business

Although it may seem surprising to include cruise liners in a book on maritime economics, that should not be the case. Cruise lies at the most sophisticated end of the specialized shipping market, and its principal assets are ships operated by seamen and moving from port to port. Like cargo vessels, cruise ships must load, discharge and operate to a tight schedule in all weathers. Viewed in this way cruise vessels and ferries are merchant ships. The difference is that passenger shipping is the only segment that deals directly with consumers and its competitors are not other shipping companies, but other holiday providers. But this is no different from the passenger liners of the previous century.

Sea cruising dates back to the nineteenth century when liner companies with spare passenger ships would offer occasional cruises. The first purpose-built cruise liner was the *Prinzessin Viktoria Luise*, built by Hamburg Amerika Line in 1901, with accommodation for 200 passengers. In the 1930s the *Arandora Star*, with 400 berths, was very successful, completing 124 cruises to the West Indies, the Canaries, the Mediterranean and the Norwegian fjords.[18] However, this was a very narrow market for the rich, and the real growth started with the tourism boom in the 1960s, with the highly successful development and marketing of Caribbean cruises. By 1980 the North American market was 1.4 million cruises a year, and Figure 12.10 shows that since then the number of passengers has grown at 8.2% per annum to 12 million cruises in 2006. In total 51 million people in North America (17% of the population) have taken a cruise, usually lasting an average of 7 days.

In 2006, over 15 million people worldwide took a cruise, with North America accounting for about 60% of the world cruise market, and another 15% overseas visitors flying to the USA to take a cruise (Figure 12.10, left-hand axis). From a company viewpoint the business is relatively consolidated. Carnival Cruise, the biggest brand and owner of several other brands, has 22 ships and 51,000 lower berths, giving it a 15% market share. Its market capitalization in 2007 was

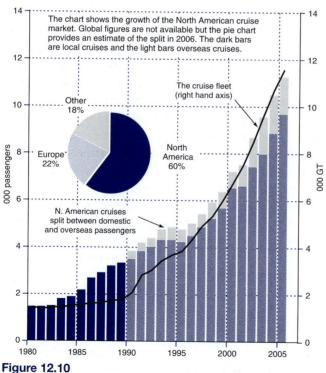

**Figure 12.10**
The North American cruise market
Source CLIA

$40 billion, making it the second biggest public shipping company after A.P. Møller-Maersk. The top five cruise companies owned 55% of the capacity and the top 10 have 74% of the capacity. This is a much higher concentration than is found elsewhere in the marine business and suggests that in the cruise business size brings a greater commercial advantage than in other segments of shipping. Concentration is even higher when considered on the basis of owning groups. The top three groups, Carnival, Royal Caribbean and Star, own 77% of the fleet capacity. Carnival alone owns 46%.

The cruise fleet capacity has also grown rapidly (see Figure 12.10, right-hand axis), averaging 8.7% per annum since 1980. In 2007 the 251 ships in the cruise fleet had 337,000 berths and a measurement of 12.8 million gross tonnes. The fleet is segmented by size, with 64 vessels over 2,000 berths, 76 with 1,000 to 2,000 berths, and 111 with under 1,000 berths. These are the most expensive merchant ships, costing around $280,000 per berth in 2007. On that basis a 3,000-berth vessel would cost close to $0.8 billion.

Traffic growth in the cruise business is driven by capacity. For all of the mass-marketed brands, where ticket prices are heavily discounted, it is imperative that the cruise lines fill their ships in order to take advantage of on-board spending in casinos, bars, spas, gift shops and for shore tours. High utilization rates in excess of 100% (possible because capacity is based on 2 per cabin, while third and fourth berths in a cabin are frequently used) ensure a steady stream of cash that can amount to as much as 25% of total revenue. High-end luxury brands tend to have lower utilization rates, which is viable because their higher *per diem* fares make them less dependent upon on-board spending.

Structurally, cruise liners must provide hotel accommodation and entertainment for the passengers whilst on board, and to achieve this the ships are arranged over multiple decks. A typical large cruise ship might have 10–12 decks available for passengers, though with the increasing size of ships and the popularity of balconies 12 or 13 decks are now the norm for new vessels and the largest have 15. The upper decks are devoted to sun decks, sports activities, observation decks and lounges, spa/fitness centres and a lido with swimming pools and casual buffet dining facilities. The next several decks would be devoted to passenger cabins, with balconies on most outside cabins. Two more decks are then typically devoted to public spaces, with casino, theatres, lounges and discos, cinema, library, shops and a range of restaurants. The remaining decks are devoted to passenger cabins, without balconies on the outside cabins. Passenger services (purser, shore excursions, forward bookings) are generally clustered on one of the lower decks around a central atrium that may extend up several decks and which often serves as the principal embarkation/debarkation area.

## 12.8 SUMMARY

Transport of specialized cargoes is one of the most challenging segments of the shipping market. Designing ships or whole transport systems to carry specific cargoes is not a recent development, but in the second half of the twentieth century the global economy developed in a way that has created many new opportunities for shipowners to offer specialized services which cut costs, improve quality and often make it economic to transport cargoes that otherwise could not be traded. The result is the fleet of over 10,000 specialized ships discussed in this chapter.

Specialist trades are often more difficult to analyse than bulk trades (see Chapter 11) because most are manufactures or semi-manufactures. In Chapter 10 we discussed why the economic model of the manufactures trade raises difficulties for the analyst. Competitive trades occur when cheaper supplies are available abroad, leading to trade flows which reflect these differences – for example, exports from chemical plants in the Middle East with low-cost raw materials such as gas available locally. Naturally these trades move when costs change. Deficit trade occurs when there is a temporary shortage of a product in one area and supplies are imported from another to fill the gap. This is very common in the oil products trades and forest products. Finally, differentiated trades develop because consumers like a choice. For example, many cars are shipped by sea because some consumers prefer the models that overseas manufacturers can offer. These are all issues which come up in discussing the trades carried in specialist vessels, so do not expect the trade analysis to be easy.

Most of these specialized trades segments face a degree of competition from other parts of the shipping market (LNG is the exception) and the main focus of the business model is to differentiate the service in a way which reduces costs per unit of transport and offers improved service in areas which are of importance to the customer. The chemical business invests in ships and terminals to handle small parcels of liquid cargo while complying with the various regulations for the transportation of hazardous substances by sea. It is very competitive, with parcel tankers competing with medium-sized tramp vessels and small tankers on short sea routes. Cargo handling and terminals play an important part in the business. Gas transport is also diversified. There is a large LPG trade from the Middle East mainly to Japan, whilst the mid-sized gas tankers focus on the ammonia trade and smaller vessels on ethylene and various industrial chemical gases. The gas tankers are pressurized; semi-pressurized or fully refrigerated. LNG is separate due to the low temperature of $-162\,°C$ at which methane liquefies.

The refrigerated cargo trade consists of frozen meat, chilled fruit and vegetables and fish. Purpose-built reefer ships are used for all three trades, but containerization has taken a growing market share. Car carriers move vehicles around the world as part of a tightly integrated transport operation. Many vessels now have hoistable decks to carry trucks, project cargoes and large units. Another segment which focuses on the 'large and awkward' cargo is the heavy lift business which moves very large structures around the world, employing several different types of ships. The basic heavy lift vessels are open hatch MPP ships with heavy lift gear and possibly a stern ramp. Other more sophisticated vessels allow cargo to be floated on. Open hatch bulk carriers are also used in the forest products trade where they offer very high productivity for the transport of package lumber, paper and, where appropriate, containers, steel products and other small unit cargoes. Finally, the ferry and cruise business has been developed as an important part of the shipping market, and the only one which deals directly with consumers.

The message of specialized shipping markets is that there are few clear boundaries. Shipowners invest to meet a market need, and many of them work off very tight margins. But there can be little doubt that the businesses discussed in this section differ substantially from the rough and tumble of the bulk markets discussed in Chapter 11.

# 13 The Transport of General Cargo

*The growing intricacy and variety of commerce is adding to the advantages which a large fleet of ships under one management derives from its power of delivering goods promptly, and without breech of responsibility, in many different ports; and as regards the vessels themselves time is on the side of large ships.*

(Alfred Marshall, *Principle of Economics*, 8th edition, 1890)

## 13.1 INTRODUCTION

General cargo accounts for about 60% of the value of goods shipped by sea, so it deserves special attention.[1] Most of this cargo is transported by containerized liner services which provide fast, frequent and reliable transport for almost any cargo to almost any foreign destination at a predictable charge. Thus, a Californian wine grower selling 2,000 cases of wine to a UK wholesaler knows that he can ship the wine by a liner service; that the journey will take 12–15 days, and he is quoted a through rate for the container. On this basis he can work out his profit and his cashflow and make the necessary delivery arrangements with confidence. If the destination was not Europe, but Iceland, Kenya or India, the procedure would be much the same – he could ship his wine on a regular service at a fixed tariff that may increase with inflation but will not go through the wild peaks and troughs encountered in the charter market. It is an important business for the world economy as well as the shipping industry.

This chapter examines how the liner business operates. We start with a brief review of the evolution from cargo liners to containerized transport. This is followed by a discussion of the economics of liner pricing and costs which are central to managing the business. We then look at the demand for liner services and supply in terms of ships and business organization. Finally, we examine the major liner routes, ports and terminals. Some of the technical terms used in the liner business are listed in the Glossary.

## 13.2 THE ORIGINS OF THE LINER SERVICE

Liners are a comparatively recent addition to the shipping business and we reviewed their development in Chapter 1. From the 1870s improving steamship technology made it possible for shipowners to offer scheduled services. Until that time a few shipowners such as the Black Ball Line had tried to run regular services with sailing ships, but most general cargo was carried by 'tramp' ships working from port to port. Developments in the commercial world also made a contribution. Steamship agents became better organized, with branches at key trading points in the Far East. The banking services for day-to-day business were greatly improved and the extension of the telegraph to the Far East enabled trading houses in China to sell by telegraphic transfer in London and India.[2]

Steamships created the supply, the new commercial systems stimulated demand and the shipping community was quick to seize the opportunity. The opening of the Suez Canal in 1869 demonstrated the advantages of steamships, and when this was followed by a freight market boom in 1872–3 there was a flood of orders for steamships to set up liner services on the prosperous Far East route. Once established, the network of liner services grew rapidly into the comprehensive transport system which exists today.

### The 'cargo liner' era

For a century until the 1960s liner companies ran fleets of multi-deck vessels known as *cargo liners*, versatile ships with their own cargo-handling gear (see Figure 1.9). Shipping had not subdivided into the many specialist operations we discussed in the previous two chapters and the liner services had to carry a mixture of manufactures, semi-manufactures, minor bulks and passengers. The trade routes were mainly between North America, the European countries and their colonies in Asia, Africa and South America, and on many of these routes trade was unbalanced with an outward trade of manufactures and a home trade of minor bulks. Filling the ship was the main aim and ship designers were preoccupied with building flexible vessels which could carry all sorts of cargo – even the first oil tankers built at this time were designed to carry a general cargo backhaul. The multi-deck 'cargo liner', with its capacity to carry both general cargo and bulks, was the preferred choice.

There was another aspect of the system which gave it great flexibility. Because the cargo liners were similar in size, design and speed to the 'tweendeckers used by tramp operators, the fleets were to a large extent interchangeable. A tramp could become a liner, and a liner could at times become a tramp.[3] This allowed liner companies to charter tramps to supplement their own fleets. For example, tramps returning from the UK to the River Plate to load grain would often carry a general cargo backhaul. Liner companies became charterers of tramp tonnage,[4] while tramp owners relied on the liner business as a cushion against the cycles in the bulk market and often built ships with 'tween decks and good speeds, which would fit conveniently into liner company schedules. Since the ships used in the bulk and liner markets were roughly the same size, this system of risk management worked well for both parties.

As trade grew in the twentieth century, the system was refined and developed. To improve productivity and widen their cargo base, liner companies built more sophisticated cargo liners, adding features such as tanks for vegetable oils, refrigerated holds, extensive cargo-handling gear, ro-ro decks and much automated equipment. They became increasingly complex and expensive. The *Pointe Sans Souci* class built in the early 1970s by Compagnie Générale Maritime (CGM) for their Europe-Caribbean service illustrates the extremes to which liner companies would go in their search for a more cost-effective cargo liner. These ships of 8,000 dwt were designed to carry cargo that had previously been carried by a mixed fleet of traditional liners and reefer ships. The forward holds were insulated to carry refrigerated cargoes, with collapsible container cell guides and electrical points for refrigerated containers. Doors for banana conveyors were let into the 'tween decks in each hold and side doors allowed the 'tween decks to be worked at the same time as the lower hold. Hatch covers were strengthened to take containers, and a 35-ton crane enabled the ship to be fully self-sufficient with container loads in the smaller ports of the West Indies. Holds aft of the bridge were devoted to palletized or vehicle cargo on two decks, with access by a wide stern ramp or a side door if the port did not have facilities for stern-to-quay loading. Below were tanks for carrying bulk rum.

Although the cargo liner was flexible, it was also labour- and capital-intensive. In the 1950s labour became more expensive and the trading world changed in a way which made flexibility less important than productivity. As the colonies gained independence the liner companies lost their privileged position in many of the core trades in which the cargo liners had been most effective. At the same time many of the minor bulk backhaul trades transferred to bulk carriers at rates the liners could not possibly match. As the bulk carrier fleet grew in size, the liner and bulk shipping industries grew apart. However, the most important change was in the pattern of trade. In the rapidly growing economy of the 1950s and 1960s, the real growth in trade was between the prosperous industrial centres of Europe, North America and Japan. Shippers in these trades needed fast, reliable, secure transport and the shortcomings of cargo liners became increasingly obvious. The cost, complexity and poor delivery performance of the cargo liner system became a major stumbling block. Shippers did not want to wait while their cargo made a leisurely progression round eight or ten ports, often arriving damaged, and shipowners found their expensive ships spending far too much time sitting in port.

For the liner companies, running cargo liners had become equally unrewarding. Expensive 'tailor made' ships spent up to 50% of their time in port, which tied up capital and limited the scope for economies of scale because doubling a cargo liner's capacity almost doubled its port time. There was not a great deal managers or naval architects could do to alleviate the fundamental problems of packing 10,000–15,000 tons of general cargo into a ship's hold.[5] By the 1960s the expense of the ships, the cargo-handling problems and the segregation of their cargo from the rest of the transport system had made the cargo liners technologically obsolete. This resulted in the complete restructuring of the shipping system which we discussed in Chapter 1 (see Figure 1.10) during which the liner and tramp system was replaced by the four business segments of bulk, specialized, containers and air freight.

## The container system, 1966–2005

For the liner business the solution was to unitize general cargo using containers. Standardizing the cargo unit allowed liner companies to invest in mechanized systems and equipment which would automate the transport process and raise productivity. The whole procedure was essentially an extension of the production line technology which had been applied so successfully in manufacturing industry and bulk trades such as iron ore. The new system had three components. First, the product transported, general cargo, was packed in *standard units* that could be handled across the whole transport operation. Several other systems such as palletization and barges were considered, but containers were chosen by all the major operators. Second, investment was applied at each stage to produce an *integrated transport system* with vehicles at each stage in the transport chain built to handle the standardized units. On the sea leg the investment was in purpose-built cellular container ships. On land it required road and rail vehicles capable of carrying containers efficiently. Finally, the third step was to invest in high-speed *cargo-handling facilities* to transfer the container between one part of the transport system and another. Container terminals, inland distribution depots and container 'stuffing' facilities where part loads could be packed into containers all played a part in this process.

The deep sea containerization system we have today drew on the experience that already existed in the USA where, by the mid-1960s, there was a box fleet of 54,000 units (see Table 13.1).[6] It was pioneered by a US businessman with no shipping experience in the face of general scepticism from the liner industry. Malcolm McLean had spent his life building up McLean Trucking, a road transport company with a fleet of 1,700 vehicles. In 1955 he sold it for $6 million and bought the Pan Atlantic Tanker Company, which owned several T2 tankers.[7] One of these tankers, the 10-year-old *Poltero Hills* (which McLean renamed the *Ideal-X*) had a deck built of spars over the piping and manifolds and McLean had it fitted to carry sixty 35-foot containers. On 26 April 1956

**Table 13.1** World container fleet, 1960–2005

| Year-end | Container box fleet (TEU) | Container ship fleet (TEU capacity) | Containers (TEU) Per slot |
|---|---|---|---|
| 1960* | 18,000 | | |
| 1965* | 54,000 | 16,000 | 3.4 |
| 1970 | 500,000 | 140,500 | 3.6 |
| 1975 | 1,300,000 | 366,000 | 3.6 |
| 1980 | 3,150,000 | 727,600 | 4.3 |
| 1985 | 4,850,000 | 1,189,384 | 4.1 |
| 1990 | 6,365,000 | 1,765,868 | 3.6 |
| 1995 | 9,715,000 | 2,492,649 | 3.9 |
| 2000 | 14,850,000 | 4,812,286 | 3.1 |
| 2005 | 28,486,000 | 8,116,900 | 3.5 |

Sources: US Steel Commercial Research Division and CI Market Analysis, MTR (1976), Vol 6 Table 51, CRSL
*estimate

the *Ideal-X* loaded 58 containers in New Jersey, and sailed for Houston, the first seaborne shipment of modern containers (although there are many earlier cases of cargo being shipped in standard boxes). The boxes weathered the 3,000-mile journey and handling costs were 16 cents per ton, compared with $5.83 per tonne for break-bulk cargo handling so it was a commercial success.[8] A second tanker was converted and on 4 October, 1957 the maiden voyage of the first fully cellular vessel the 226 TEU *Gateway City,* from Newark to Miami was watched by a crowd of 400 (including New Jersey governor Robert B. Meyner, who helicoptered to the pier to deliver an address)[9]. When it docked in Miami its cargo was delivered to the consignee within 90 minutes.

The established liner companies remained sceptical. Even in 1963 Ocean Transport and Trading, the leading liner company of its day, was still doubtful about the new system, probably because initially they approached it as a development of their existing cargo liner operations and from this perspective the economics looked less attractive.[10] But given dedicated container-ships, terminals, truck distribution networks and a fleet of boxes, the analysis looked very different, though it is easy to understand why such a radical change must have been unwelcome to companies with large fleets of cargo liners. Many other less radical systems were investigated, including palletization, in which cargo was shipped on standard pallets in pallet-friendly ships, and deep sea ro-ro services which allowed a wide variety of cargo to be loaded on fork-lift trucks. However, the economics did not work in practice and deep-sea ro-ros remained a niche business (see Section 12.6 for a brief review of the trade today).

However McLean pressed on, renaming his company Sea-Land and in April 1966 *SS Fairland*, the first transatlantic container service, sailed from its newly constructed Port Elizabeth terminal in New Jersey to McLean's new trailer terminal in Rotterdam. The cargo arrived at its destination 4 weeks in advance of a conventional cargo liner service. The major European liner shipping companies were by this time busy setting up their own container services. Because of the size of the investment in ships, terminals and of course the containers, consortia were formed. For example, Overseas Containers Limited (OCL), a joint venture between P&O, Ocean Transport and Trading, British and Commonwealth and Furness Withy, was formed in 1965 and its first container service started on 6 March 1969. Subsequent events illustrate the corporate changes which occurred as the container industry grew over the next thirty years. In the early 1980s P&O gradually increased its share and in 1986 bought the remaining 53% to form P&O Containers Ltd (P&OCL), which merged with Nedlloyd in 1996 to form P&O Nedlloyd N.V. Ten years later in 2005 this company and was bought by the A.P. Møller-Maersk Group and incorporated into Maersk Line.

### Developing the container service infrastructure

Developing a fleet of *container-ships* was a technical challenge because the structure, with its open hatches, was so different from the cargo liners shipyards were used to building. One of the earliest European orders by OCL, was for six 1600 TEU *Encounter Bay* class ships. They had open holds with cell guides so that the containers could be slotted in without clamping. Steel hatch covers fitted flush and provided a platform on which containers could be stacked four high and clamped in place. Although the ships were not big by the standards of tankers and bulk carriers, the open hold technology and cell guides were new and raised various technical problems. For the inland leg the investment in container-friendly trailers progressed rapidly and for their first service in April 1966 over 300 European truckers were signed up.[11]

The second vital component in the system was the *container terminal*. Previously liner ports had miles of wharves backing on to warehouses where ships would sit for weeks handling cargo. The container terminals were very different. Two or three berths, served by gantry cranes, backed on to open storage. To speed up the link with road transport Sea-Land stored the containers on trailers in a trailer park. Most other companies preferred to stack the containers three or four high, retrieving them from storage as required. Movement within the terminals was also mechanized, using fork-lift trucks, straddle carriers or, in a few cases, an automated gantry system. This system of cargo handling proved to be tremendously effective. Handling speeds vary from port to port, ranging from 15 to 30 lifts an hour, but averaging about 20 lifts per crane hour. The result was a dramatic improvement in productivity. Whereas general cargo berths typically handled 100,000–150,000 tons per year, the new container terminals were able to handle 1–2 million tons of cargo a year on each berth. Inter-modal compatibility was also greatly improved because the container itself is standardized. Forty years later in 2007 containers had taken over three-quarters of the general cargo trade and 4300 container-ships with a capacity of 10.6 million TEU were ferrying 35 million containers between 360 ports and carrying over 1 billion tons of cargo a year. Meanwhile Malcolm McLean had sold his share in Sea-Land for $160 million, so his pioneering efforts were well rewarded.[12]

Third, international agreement was needed on the sizes of *standard containers*. Because road regulations differed across the USA, various different sizes of container were in use, and McLean selected a 35 ft box for his first sea service because that was the best compromise. Eventually the ISO developed standards which applied to dimensions, corner casting strength, floor strength, racking tests and the gross weight of the container. Initially for general cargo the standard boxes were 8 ft high and 8 ft wide, with four optional lengths, 10 ft, 20 ft, 30 ft and 40 ft. In 1976, the height of standard containers was increased to 8 ft 6 ins, giving additional volume without altering the dimensions of the container. In recent years 20 ft and 40 ft containers have become the workhorses of the international container business. Out of a total container stock of 28.5 million TEU in 2004, 18 per cent were 20 ft units; 75 per cent were 40 ft units; 4 per cent were reefer containers and various specialized containers such as open top; and folding made up the balance (see Table 13.2). Containers generally have a life of 12–14 years. In Europe and the USA about half of the container fleet is leased.

Finally, the growth of the service depended on various technical developments which were taking place in the 1960s and 1970s. One was the communications and data processing revolution, discussed in Chapter 1. This made it possible to plan services, exchange detailed cargo manifests across the world and carry out the necessary paperwork in the much reduced time-scale required by containerization.

**Table 13.2** World container stock by principal type

| Container type 20-foot equivalent units ('000s) | | | | % in |
|---|---|---|---|---|
| | 1985 | 1995 | 2004 | 2004 |
| Standard | 4,090 | 8,050 | 26,699 | 94% |
| of which | | | | 0% |
| 20' 8'6" | | | 5,060 | 18% |
| 40' 8'6" (5.3 million units) | | | 10,620 | 37% |
| 40' 9'6" (5.2 million units) | | | 10,362 | 36% |
| 45' 8'6" | | | 639 | 2% |
| Open-top | 221 | 225 | 258 | 1% |
| Ventilated | 46 | 89 | 26 | 0% |
| Folding flatrack | 36 | 42 | 151 | 1% |
| Other | 115 | 112 | 217 | 1% |
| Integral reefer | 157 | 520 | 1,111 | 4% |
| Insulated reefer | 77 | 72 | 24 | 0% |
| Tank | 34 | 84 | — | — |
| Total | 4,776 | 9,194 | 28,486 | 100% |

Source: *Containerisation International* 2005
*World Container Census January 2005*

## The consequences of containerisation

Containerization was very successful in its main objective of reducing port time. A comparison of the operating performance of a *Priam* class cargo liner with the *Liverpool Bay* container-ship on comparable services published in 1985 illustrates the change. The 22,000 dwt cargo liner spent 149 days a year in port, 40% of its time. The 47,000 dwt containership reduced the port time to 64 days a year, just 17% of its time. As a result, a string of nine container-ships could do the work of 74 cargo liners.[13]

It also changed the way liner companies operated. First, and most importantly, unitization made 'door-to-door' service an essential part of the business. Previously most liner companies saw their responsibilities beginning and ending at the ship's rail, so the focus was on ships and shipping operations. The need to manage both the land and sea legs of the transport introduced logistics into the business, which in turn diluted the role of ships and changed the way companies approached pricing (see section 13.9). Second, the business consolidated into fewer companies. Hundreds of liner companies disappeared and liner shipping became the most concentrated sector of the shipping business. Third, the bustling ports of the cargo liner era disappeared, replaced by container terminals with few staff and fewer ships. Fourth, ships and shipowning slipped to the sidelines because the core business of liner companies was now through transport. Fifth, the tramp market for ships carrying containerizable cargoes disappeared. Container-ships could not switch between liner charters and bulk, so liner companies had to carry the marginal capacity they needed in their own fleets. Tramp operators turned to the bulk carrier or tanker markets. Sixth, minor bulk cargoes which had occupied the deep-well tanks, lower cargo holds and ro-ro decks of cargo liners moved into specialist vessels such as open hatch bulk carriers, parcel tankers, car carriers, MPP vessels and heavy lift ships (see Chapter 12).

Those were the effects on the shipping industry. But for the world economy the consequences were even more profound. Previously transport between regions had been slow, expensive and unreliable, with a high chance that delicate objects such as consumer electronics would be stolen or damaged during the lengthy process of loading and unloading a general cargo. Suddenly transport between regions became fast, secure and incredibly cheap. A few statistics put this into perspective. In 2004 packing 4,000 video-recorders into a 40 ft container reduced the freight cost from the Far East to Europe to around 83 cents per unit, whilst Scotch whisky could be shipped from Europe to Japan for 4.7 cents per bottle.[14] As a result, distance from the market and transport costs became a less important consideration in the location of manufacturing industry. As the container network grew in the 1980s and the 1990s, so did globalization.

## 13.3 ECONOMIC PRINCIPLES OF LINER OPERATION

Now it is time to take a closer look at the economics of the liner business. We start with a strict definition:

> A liner service is a fleet of ships, with a common ownership or management, which provide a fixed service, at regular intervals, between named ports, and offer transport to any goods in the catchment area served by those ports and ready for transit by their sailing dates. A fixed itinerary, inclusion in a regular service, and the obligation to accept cargo from all comers and to sail, whether filled or not, on the date fixed by a published schedule are what distinguish the liner from the tramp.[15]

This definition focuses on the ships rather than the logistics, because the sea transport leg remains the core activity of a liner company, distinguishing it from freight forwarders and logistics companies which focus purely on the through-transport management, relying on others to transport the cargo.

By the end of the twentieth century container services had largely replaced the conventional cargo liner services, so it is the container market model which we are concerned with in this chapter. Before going into detail, it is helpful to see how the pieces in the liner transport system fit together and the diagram of the container market model in Figure 13.1 identifies four: the cargo, the services, the liner companies, and the fleet.

We start with cargo at the top of Figure 13.1. General cargo still generates the basic demand for liner services, just as it did for cargo liners previously, but containerization had two important consequences for transport demand, the first concerning economies of scale and the second product differentiation. First, the use of much bigger ships with improved cargo handling meant that small end bulk and specialized cargoes have

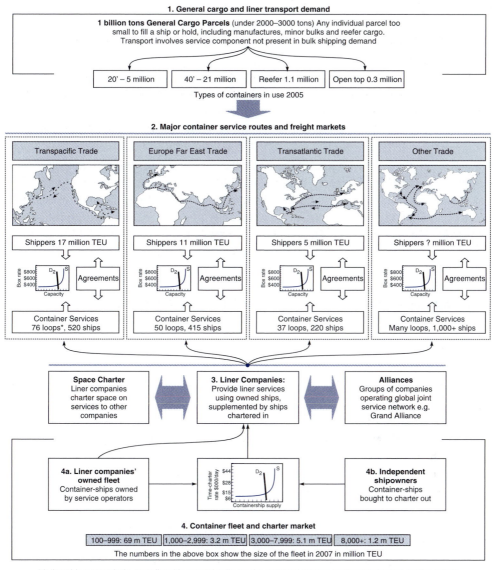

**1. General cargo and liner transport demand**

1 billion tons **General Cargo Parcels** (under 2000–3000 tons) Any individual parcel too small to fill a ship or hold, including manufactures, minor bulks and reefer cargo. Transport involves service component not present in bulk shipping demand

| 20' – 5 million | 40' – 21 million | Reefer 1.1 million | Open top 0.3 million |

Types of containers in use 2005

**2. Major container service routes and freight markets**

| Transpacific Trade | Europe Far East Trade | Transatlantic Trade | Other Trade |

| Shippers 17 million TEU | Shippers 11 million TEU | Shippers 5 million TEU | Shippers ? million TEU |

Agreements (×4)

| Container Services 76 loops*, 520 ships | Container Services 50 loops, 415 ships | Container Services 37 loops, 220 ships | Container Services Many loops, 1,000+ ships |

| **Space Charter** Liner companies charter space on services to other companies | **3. Liner Companies:** Provide liner services using owned ships, supplemented by ships chartered in | **Alliances** Groups of companies operating global joint service network e.g. Grand Alliance |

| **4a. Liner companies' owned fleet** Container-ships owned by service operators | | **4b. Independent shipowners** Container-ships bought to charter out |

**4. Container fleet and charter market**

| 100–999: 69 m TEU | 1,000–2,999: 3.2 m TEU | 3,000–7,999: 5.1 m TEU | 8,000+: 1.2 m TEU |

The numbers in the above box show the size of the fleet in 2007 in million TEU

*A 'loop' is a round trip, usually with several calls on the outward voyage and several more on the return

**Figure 13.1**
The liner transport system, 2007
Source: Martin Stopford, 2007, Fleet Figures 1st Sept 2007 CRSL, Service figures NYK

increasingly become potential targets for containerization. Second, the containers may all look the same, but their contents still retain their demand characteristics. Packing chicken and chips and a gourmet meal in similar cardboard boxes does not make them identical products – gourmet customers expect home delivery (perhaps in a monogrammed van?), whereas the chicken and chips clients probably prefer take-away. Exactly the same is true for containerized cargo. High-value and urgent cargoes are likely to have a different demand profile from low-value minor bulk cargoes.

At the heart of the liner system are the major routes, which Figure 13.1 divides into four categories: the transpacific trade; the Far East to Europe trade; the transatlantic trade; and other trades which include the North–South trades and a mass of short-and medium-distance trades within Asia and elsewhere. In each case we have shippers with volumes of cargo to transport – 17 million TEU in 2004 crossed the Pacific, and 5 million TEU the Atlantic. All this cargo travels on container services provided by liner companies, and shippers have many to choose from. For example, on the transpacific trade there were 76 loops served by 520 ships in 2004. These loops offer many different arrival and departure dates, ports called at and through services offered, so it can be a bit of a jungle for the shipper. Like any other market, rates are negotiated between shippers and carriers (illustrated diagrammatically by the small graphs in Figure 13.1), but as discussed at the beginning of the chapter, there is a long history of container services cooperating to fix prices, or more recently to exchange information (illustrated by the 'agreements' arrows). The regulation of these trades has been a hot issue for at least 150 years that we will discuss later in this chapter.

The liner companies are shown in the lower middle of Figure 13.1. They provide the liner services and face the enormously complex task of deciding which ships will call at which ports and on which dates. In 2006 the biggest liner company, Maersk, had a 16% market share, but many of the companies with only 4–5% market share operated thirty or forty different services.

Finally, the container fleet and its charter market are dealt with at the foot of Figure 13.1. In July 2007 the container fleet was 4,200 ships, about the same as the tanker fleet, with another 1,300 on the order and the fleet had many different ship sizes within it. Economies of scale are a major issue that we will discuss in some detail. One of the key strategic decisions for a liner company is whether to purchase their own ships or to charter them. Until the beginning of the 1990s most of the fleet was owned by the liner companies, but as the decade progressed ownership of the fleet was gradually taken over by operators, often using German KG finance, which owned the ships and chartered them to service providers. By 2007 these independent operators owned almost half the fleet, one effect of which was to create the charter market shown at the bottom of Figure 13.1. This is a separate market with independent shipowners on one side and liner companies on the other, and it deals in ships rather than cargo transport. In the following four sections we will discuss each of these four segments of the liner business in more detail.

## 13.4 GENERAL CARGO AND LINER TRANSPORT DEMAND

### General cargo and container movements

Between 1975 and 2007 the containerized cargo grew much faster than other parts of the shipping business. The number of containers lifted increased from 14.1 million TEU to 466 million TEU (Figure 13.2) and the average growth rate between 1990 and 2007 was 10.4% per annum. Analysing the trade presents many difficulties because anything that can physically go in a container is potential container cargo, and often other transport modes are competing for the same cargo. This means commodity analysis, even when it is possible for a few of the larger trades, does not tell the whole story and is not really practical. So we might as well accept at the outset that this is a highly complex business and analysts must expect problems getting to the bottom of it.

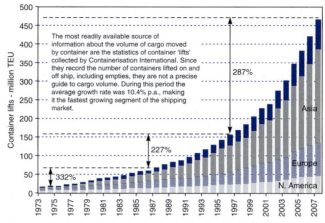

**Figure 13.2**
Liner trade, 1973–2007, and percentage growth per annum, 1981–2007
Source: Clarkson Research Services Ltd

A good starting point is the relationship between container cargo and world economic activity. Between 1983 and 2006 world GDP grew by 4.8% per annum and the value of manufactures exports grew by 6.6% per annum (Table 13.3), but container cargo grew much faster, averaging 10.1 per cent per annum for container lifts (column 4) and the volume of containerized cargo grew by 10.0 per cent (column 6). By 2005 the tonnage of containerized cargo had reached 1 billion tonnes[16] and the average tonnage per container lift in 2005 was only 2.7 tonnes per TEU, which reveals the underlying weakness of the container lift statistics as a measure of transport capacity. Container lifts include all container movements through ports, including double lifts when a container is trans-shipped from a deep-sea service to a feeder ship and containers returned empty on unbalanced trades. A 20 ft container can carry up to 24 tons, and 10 tons would be a more normal average.

Different shipping services compete for cargoes. Some cargoes, such as manufactured and semi-manufactured products, consumer goods, machinery, textiles, chemicals and vehicles have a very high value so they always travel by liner or possibly air freight which competes for the most urgent and high-value cargoes, especially on long routes. Clothing shipped from the Far East to Europe and electrical components are the sort of cargoes in this transport segment. Specialized shipping services are competitors for lower-value cargoes, including forest products, refrigerated cargo and wheeled cargo. The motor vehicle trade is a classic example, and the liner business lost most of the trade to specialized carriers using PCCs (see Chapter 12, page 494). At the other end of the scale, liner companies compete with bulk shipping for minor bulk cargoes such as steel products, building materials, foodstuffs such as coffee or empty gas canisters. Although these cargoes do not support high freight rates they provide what liner services used to call 'bottom cargo' which fills up the ship on routes where there is less cargo in one direction than the other. Whilst the core increase in container cargo volumes relies principally on the growth of the existing container cargo trades, especially the manufactured goods trade shown in Table 13.3, column 3, this is also topped up by the success

**Table 13.3** The container and break-bulk trades, 1983–2006

| | 1 | 2 | 3 | 4 | 5 | 6 | 7 | 8 | 9 | 10 | 11 |
|---|---|---|---|---|---|---|---|---|---|---|---|
| | World Economy % pa | | Containerized cargo movements (moves) | | | | | | | | |
| | GDP %pa | manufactures exports (value) | Container lifts TEU (m) | % pa | Container cargo mt | %pa | Tons per lift | Break bulk mt | Dry bulk mt | Total dry cargo mt | %pa |
| 1983 | 6.3% | 5.1% | 46 | | 127 | | 2.8 | 487 | 1,254 | 1,868 | |
| 1984 | 7.0% | 10.8% | 53 | 17% | 148 | 16% | 2.8 | 511 | 1,396 | 2,055 | 10% |
| 1985 | 4.0% | 4.8% | 57 | 7% | 160 | 8% | 2.8 | 549 | 1,461 | 2,170 | 6% |
| 1986 | 6.8% | 4.1% | 62 | 9% | 173 | 8% | 2.8 | 555 | 1,415 | 2,143 | −1% |
| 1987 | 7.6% | 6.3% | 68 | 10% | 192 | 11% | 2.8 | 549 | 1,472 | 2,213 | 3% |
| 1988 | 7.0% | 9.5% | 75 | 10% | 211 | 10% | 2.8 | 559 | 1,565 | 2,335 | 6% |
| 1989 | 5.2% | 7.8% | 82 | 9% | 231 | 10% | 2.8 | 578 | 1,610 | 2,419 | 4% |
| 1990 | 5.0% | 6.1% | 87 | 6% | 246 | 6% | 2.8 | 626 | 1,598 | 2,469 | 2% |
| 1991 | 4.6% | 3.6% | 96 | 10% | 268 | 9% | 2.8 | 653 | 1,625 | 2,546 | 3% |
| 1992 | 4.2% | 4.7% | 105 | 10% | 292 | 9% | 2.8 | 701 | 1,596 | 2,589 | 2% |
| 1993 | 3.8% | 4.1% | 115 | 10% | 322 | 10% | 2.8 | 715 | 1,616 | 2,653 | 2% |
| 1994 | 5.4% | 11.1% | 129 | 12% | 357 | 11% | 2.8 | 691 | 1,696 | 2,743 | 3% |
| 1995 | 5.0% | 9.0% | 141 | 10% | 389 | 9% | 2.8 | 861 | 1,805 | 3,055 | 11% |
| 1996 | 4.6% | 5.3% | 155 | 10% | 430 | 11% | 2.8 | 806 | 1,819 | 3,055 | 0% |
| 1997 | 4.5% | 11.0% | 169 | 9% | 470 | 9% | 2.8 | 872 | 1,916 | 3,258 | 7% |
| 1998 | 0.2% | 4.8% | 183 | 8% | 503 | 7% | 2.8 | 859 | 1,900 | 3,262 | 0% |
| 1999 | 5.5% | 5.1% | 205 | 12% | 560 | 11% | 2.7 | 877 | 1,896 | 3,334 | 2% |
| 2000 | 5.8% | 13.0% | 227 | 11% | 628 | 12% | 2.8 | 929 | 2,042 | 3,598 | 8% |
| 2001 | 1.1% | −1.4% | 239 | 5% | 647 | 3% | 2.7 | 910 | 2,095 | 3,652 | 1% |
| 2002 | 3.3% | 4.0% | 275 | 15% | 718 | 11% | 2.6 | 961 | 2,172 | 3,851 | 5% |
| 2003 | 2.6% | 4.9% | 303 | 10% | 806 | 12% | 2.7 | 955 | 2,291 | 4,052 | 5% |
| 2004 | 5.3% | 10.0% | 343 | 13% | 919 | 14% | 2.7 | 926 | 2,469 | 4,313 | 6% |
| 2005 | 4.9% | 6.0% | 381 | 11% | 1,017 | 11% | 2.7 | 920 | 2,564 | 4,502 | 4% |
| 2006 | 5.4% | 8.0% | 419 | 10% | 1,134 | 11% | 2.7 | 882 | 2,703 | 4,719 | 5% |
| Av. '83–'06 | 4.8% | 6.6% | | 10.1% | | 10.0% | | 2.6% | 3.4% | | 4.1% |

Notes

Col 2: manufactures exports show % change at constant prices; source World Bank

Col 3/4: shows container lifts, including empties

Col 5/6: shows container cargo moved in the year (estimate – the actual amount is not known)

Col 7: col 3 divided by col 5. 20' containers usually carry 10–12 tons, so there are many unexplained lifts

Col 8: break bulk cargo is the residual after deducting containerized cargo and bulk from col 10

Col 9: dry bulk commodities like ore, coal, grain etc.

Source: Cols 1 & 2 World Bank; cols 3–11 Clarksons SRO (spring 2006)

of liner operators in both generating new cargoes and winning cargo from the bulk and specialized segments.

## The characteristics of containerized cargo

As a practical example of the range of containerized cargoes, exports by commodity from the Port of Vancouver are shown in Table 13.4. The import trade includes all sorts of manufactured commodities, including consumer product, textiles, furniture, car parts, iron and steel, toys and a larger group of 'others' which are unidentified. This is typical of the import profile of a mature industrial economy. The exports have a very different character. Canada is a resource-rich country and exports many primary commodities – wood

**Table 13.4** Port of Vancouver trade

**13.4.1** Principal containerized commodities inbound

| Commodity ('000 metric tonnes) | 2003 | 2004 | 2005 | Increase 2004–5 |
|---|---|---|---|---|
| **A. Containerized commodities inbound** | | | | |
| Misc. consumer products | 586 | 605 | 687 | 14% |
| Home & bldg products | 419 | 506 | 620 | 23% |
| Furniture | 440 | 489 | 543 | 11% |
| Industrial machines/parts | 457 | 472 | 538 | 14% |
| Textile/clothing | 449 | 470 | 536 | 14% |
| Misc. industrial products | 239 | 312 | 338 | 8% |
| Autos/auto parts | 287 | 311 | 312 | 0% |
| Consumer electronics | 284 | 293 | 307 | 5% |
| Iron/steel | 196 | 247 | 231 | –6% |
| Toys/sports equipment | 198 | 200 | 205 | 2% |
| Others | 1,419 | 1,496 | 1,675 | 12% |
| Total | 4,974 | 5,401 | 5,992 | 11% |
| **B. Container movements ('000 TEU)** | | | | |
| Loaded with cargo | 713 | 783 | 857 | 9% |
| Empty containers | 35 | 42 | 27 | –36% |
| Total | 748 | 825 | 884 | 7% |
| Tons cargo per loaded TEU | 7.0 | 6.9 | 7.0 | 1% |

**13.4.2** Principal containerized commodities outbound

| Commodity ('000 metric tonnes) | 2003 | 2004 | 2005 | Increase 2004–5 |
|---|---|---|---|---|
| **A. Containerized commodities outbound** | | | | |
| Wood pulp | 1,646 | 1,966 | 1,840 | –6% |
| Lumber | 1,348 | 1,550 | 1,272 | –18% |
| Peas/beans/lentils | 448 | 427 | 524 | 23% |
| Waste paper | 408 | 376 | 510 | 36% |
| Hay/alfalfa | 241 | 356 | 401 | 13% |
| Fresh/frozen pork | 313 | 351 | 382 | 9% |
| Soya beans | 214 | 337 | 357 | 6% |
| Malt | 173 | 287 | 264 | –8% |
| Newsprint | 209 | 244 | 245 | 0% |
| Scrap metal | 193 | 231 | 229 | –1% |
| Others | 2,449 | 2,534 | 2,383 | –6% |
| Total | 7,642 | 8,659 | 8,407 | –3% |
| **B. Container movements (000 TEU)** | | | | |
| Loaded with cargo | 577 | 695 | 708 | 2% |
| Empty containers | 214 | 145 | 175 | 21% |
| Outbound containers (000 TEU) | 791 | 840 | 883 | 5% |
| Tons cargo per TEU | 13.3 | 12.5 | 11.9 | –5% |

Source: Port of Vancouver

pulp, lumber, soya beans, newsprint, scrap metal, and again a very large volume of unidentified commodities. Although these are low-value commodities, container-ships with plenty of spare capacity on the return leg to the Far East may well be prepared to heavily discount box rates. Finally, the growth rates of the different commodities vary considerably. For example home and building products grew by 23% per annum in 2005; auto parts imports were static; and toys grew by only 2%. Exports were equally variable – wastepaper declined in 2004, and then grew by 36% in 2005, whilst malt grew at over 50% in 2004 and declined by 8% in 2005. All of which leaves no doubt about the variability of this business and the wide range of cargoes transported.

The weight of the containers varies, depending on the contents. In 2005 Vancouver's average outbound container carried 11.9 tons of cargo, whilst the average inbound container carried 7 tons, reflecting the different characteristics of the inbound and outbound trades. The contents also vary in value. Electronic goods such as TV sets are worth over $30,000 per tonne, motorcycles $22,000 per tonne, basic clothing such as jeans $16,000 per tonne, and designer clothing perhaps $60,000 per tonne. At the other end of the scale, many of the export commodities are worth less than $1,000 per tonne, for example scrap metal $300 per tonne and steel products $600 per tonne. These differences are important because they affect transport pricing.

From an economic viewpoint, the general cargo trade, whether in boxes or break bulk, has two important differences from the bulk and specialized cargoes discussed in the previous chapters: first, transporting many small parcels requires a larger and more expensive administrative fixed cost; and second, the obligation to sail to a timetable makes capacity inflexible. This indivisibility arises because capacity expands in ship-sized increments, so when trade is growing, new ships must be ordered in multiples dictated by the service frequency, with sufficient capacity to cater for future growth. These are apparently small points which make a tremendous difference to the business model. Whereas the bulk market can respond to supply–demand imbalances by moving their least efficient ships into lay-up, liner companies must stick with their schedules. If it takes six ships to run a weekly service, they must operate six ships. From the outset this has created problems for liner operators, making capacity management a key feature of the business. The emergence of the two supporting markets shown in Figure 13.1, for container-ships and slot capacity, has helped to resolve this problem by introducing flexibility.

In addition to the usual trade cycles which affect all shipping business, there are two reasons why capacity management can be a problem. *Seasonality* occurs on many liner routes where cargo volume is higher at some times of the year than others. *Cargo imbalances* occur when there is more trade in one direction than the other, forcing ships to sail part loaded on the leg with the smaller trade flow. Both problems also occur in the bulk market, but they are quickly resolved by market forces as shipowners negotiate rates and move from trade to trade. Liner companies lack this flexibility. With so many customers it is not practical to negotiate a rate for every cargo. This combination of fixed prices and inflexible capacity leaves liner companies with a pricing problem which has dominated the industry since it started.

## Price, service and the demand for liner transport

Pricing is a central issue for liner service operators and we need to be aware of the total transport cost. Sea freight is only one part of the total cost invoiced to the shipper, which also includes inland transport costs at the origin and destination terminal service charges. The example in Table 13.5 shows that the terminal and inland transport costs can account for as much as the sea freight. In addition, surcharges such as currency adjustment factors) and (interim fuel participation also called bunker surcharges) may be a part of the freight costs, depending on whether a surcharge is in effect or not.

**Table 13.5** Example of container transport costs UK to Canada ($ per container)

|                                 | 20′  | 40′  |
|---------------------------------|------|------|
| Inland charges (origin)         | 225  | 225  |
| Terminal charges (origin)       | 248  | 340  |
| Ocean freight                   | 700  | 1100 |
| Terminal charges (destination)  | 121  | 121  |
| Inland charges (destination)    | 225  | 300  |
| Total                           | 1519 | 2086 |

Source: Canada-UK Freight Conference

The price that a shipper is prepared to pay depends to some extent on what is in the container. Although containers are physically homogeneous, their contents are not and have different characteristics in terms of price elasticity and service requirements. Shippers of high-value commodities are likely to be willing to pay more whilst for lower-value commodities, where the transport cost is a significant part of the delivered price, pricing is crucial. For example, a company distributing large tonnages of low-value cellophane rolls to processing plants in Europe might take the view that as long as they have a reasonable tonnage in the pipeline at any one time, considerations of service and claims experience are of far less importance than rate per ton.[17] For this type of commodity, prices are subject to intense competition and liner companies often discount heavily to win the business, especially where they have spare capacity on one leg of the voyage. Some examples of the price-sensitive cargoes that are containerized are as follows:

- *Wool.* A high proportion of the wool trade is containerized. Wool is 'dumped' (i.e. compressed) into bales which are packed into 20 ft containers, giving an average container weight of 18 tons.
- *Cotton.* US West Coast cotton exports are now containerized. A total of 82 standard dumped bales can be packed into a 40 ft container.
- *Wine.* This is shipped by container either in cases or in 5,000-gallon bulk container tanks. A 40 ft container can hold 972 cases of 1 litre bottles and 1,200 cases of 750 millilitre bottles.
- *Rubber.* This used to be shipped in bales. To facilitate containerization, some companies have now adopted standard bale sizes and pack the bales in shrinkfilm rather than timber crates. Latex is shipped in drums packed in containers.

However, for many cargoes, particularly those of high value, the shippers have more to lose if the service is poor than they could possibly gain from squeezing the price down a few per cent. For example a motor cycle manufacturer exporting components world-wide must be able to meet delivery schedules to its dealer network. Frequent services, sufficient volume of available shipping space, reliable advance information about vessel arrival and departure times, speed, and responsible management of cargo landed at the destination are all of crucial importance to a company distributing its products over a long distance. For example, a study comparing air and sea freight for the USA's merchandise trade concluded that each day saved is worth 0.8% of the ad-valorem for manufactured goods.[18] For a $30,000 per tonne container cargo that is a saving of $240 per tonne, a sizable sum of money. Whilst this sort of analysis must be applied with care, it does suggest that speed has a value to shippers of high-value commodities.

For this reason service requirements now dominate the liner business. Over the last 30 years international businesses have systematically tightened the management of product flows and inventory costs, often using 'just in time' control systems. Containerization played a major part in this process by allowing companies to access global markets through a fast, reliable transport network. Operating alongside the established freight forwarders, a new generation of logistics providers emerged. A good example of why customers are willing to pay extra for speed and reliability is illustrated by a freight forwarder dealing with the motor trade:

> We are heavily involved in spare parts traffic for the motor industry where in recent years inventory stocks have been reduced to the absolute minimum. This obviously has given quite substantial cost savings to importers and exporters. But they are prepared to spend some of this cost saving in additional freighting charges to ensure that their production lines are kept moving.[19]

Liners are part of a supply system and customers view the cost and benefits of transport in the context of the business as a whole.

## Product differentiation – the conflict of volume versus speed

It follows that there are two basic models of liner shipping. One is the low cost option and the other is where containers are treated as part of a package of services.[20] The challenge for liner companies operating under the second model is to find some way of differentiating their product that will support premium pricing. One method of doing this used by international businesses is to differentiate the products they offer to different market segments. For example, within a couple of years of Ford launching the Model T, Alfred Sloan of General Motors had used market segmentation to push Ford aside. He split his product range into five segments, with Cadillac at the top and Chevrolet at the bottom. It was an immediate success and car manufacturers still follow the same strategy. Similarly, passenger airlines segment their market by putting premium passengers at the front of the plane and calling it 'Business Class' and charging more for flexible tickets.

An example in the transport business is the parcel post market. In the 1970s FedEx segmented the parcel market by taking away the delivery of urgent and high-value merchandise from the US Postal Service which, preoccupied with the rapid growth of volume, had overlooked what seemed to be a minor niche.[21] At the time the big air freight operators like Pan Am were also convinced that shippers wanted cheaper transport using big cargo planes or traditional trucking lines such as UPS. The founder of FedEx, Fred Smith, studied each step in the collecting, transporting and delivering of packages and in billing for the work, and decided there was a market for a premium parcel service offering guaranteed fast delivery. He used small business jets that, although expensive, allowed FedEx to offer frequent services to smaller airports closer to the customer, without the big loads needed to fill the larger planes, thus demonstrating that market segmentation can be made to work in transport.[22]

The same issues of service differentiation are present in the liner shipping market and container transport can be viewed as a package of services which is likely to include the following seven characteristics:

- *Vessel on-time arrival.* On deep-sea routes the liner service is the customer's only direct link to his export market. Some customers are likely to value reliability of service. In terms of the transport service, adherence to fixed day schedules and on-time pick-up and delivery are important. The management of feeder services where these occur is also important.
- *Transit time door-to-door.* On long voyages, particularly for high-value products, speed of transit may be a major consideration owing to the cost of inventory. In this context, air freight may be a significant competitor, particularly where a shipping time of 4 weeks is involved in a Far East to Europe voyage.
- *Carrier cost per move.* The charge for transporting the container from origin to destination, including additionals.
- *Cargo tracking.* The ability of the shipper to check the progress of his cargo
- *Frequency of sailings.* Sea transport is one stage in the overall production process. Frequent sailings offer the manufacturer the opportunity to service one-off orders rapidly and enable him to reduce the level of stocks held at each end of the transport operation.
- *Reliability of administration.* Customers value prompt and accurate administration. The ability to provide timely quotations, accurate bills of lading, prompt arrival notices, accurate invoices and to resolve problems when they arise all play a part in the customer's evaluation of the liner company's performance.
- *Space availability.* The ability of the service to accept cargo, even at short notice, may be valued by businesses that are not able to plan their transport requirements far in advance.

A survey by the US Department of Transportation Marine Administration of companies serving the US liner trades in 2004 identified on-time arrival, cargo on-time delivery and cost reduction as the three areas which receive the greatest emphasis.[23] In practice, most shippers look for a combination of the above factors, though research suggests that there is no clear pattern of preferences which applies to all shippers and surveys of shippers' attitudes produce widely differing results. A survey of 50 shippers in the US domestic trades found that timeliness of service was the most important single factor,[24] but another study of the attitudes of shippers in North America and Europe found that cost of service and problem-solving capability were ranked most highly. Transit time, which had been placed third in an earlier survey carried out in 1982, had fallen to seventh place a decade later, suggesting that priorities change.[25] Common sense suggests that this must be the case. Price will only be a significant decision variable if different prices are quoted by different companies. More fundamentally, different shippers have different priorities, depending on the cargo and the nature of their business.

The practical difficulties of achieving these service levels are considerable. For example a survey of timekeeping of services in North America and the Far East found that in North America three-quarters of the vessels tracked arrived on or one day after their scheduled time. In the Far East ports 89% of the vessels arrived within a day of schedule.[26] At first sight it might seem surprising that timekeeping presents such a problem. However, liners work in such diverse conditions that it is difficult to plan for every contingency. Some delays are caused by breakdowns such as engine failure or dry dockings that overrun. Then there are accidents (e.g. collisions), natural disasters such as earthquakes, adverse weather, and congestion. Many of these are avoidable at a price. In the long-term powerful ships which can make up lost time and realistic schedules which incorporate a margin for delays are the solution. In the short term skipping ports is a common way of catching up on schedule, or for serious delays chartering a replacement ship, if one is available.

Two central issues for liner companies are whether customers will pay a premium for better service and how providing the higher service levels fits with the needs of the other market segments, in particular the low-value, high-volume cargoes. In theory high-value commodities should support premium freights but it is a complex issue. One ocean carrier summed up the problem in the following terms:

> We submit our rates (to the shipper) as required but often have no way of knowing if service profiles are also taken into account. Sometimes we don't even know the people we are addressing … Some global shippers claim that liner shipping is just a commodity as when a container is booked with any carrier, it is likely to be shipped on the same vessel as other carriers, from the same container terminal, in the same type of container from the same leasing company, and to the same container terminal at the port of discharge.[27]

## Containerizing minor bulk cargoes

Minor bulk commodities such as forest products, steel products, minor ores, soya beans, scrap metal and cotton are all potential cargoes for containerization, but each presents its own difficulties. This is a very different business. The low unit costs required to compete in these trades call for bigger ships which in turn need bigger arterial hubs. Inevitably this slows the transit times, especially for the unfortunate customers at the extremities of the feeder network. That is fine for the lower-value cargoes, but may not suit the shippers of premium cargoes who need speed and certainty. From the service operator's point of view it can be a slippery slope, putting container-ship operators on the same 'bottom cargo' treadmill that was such a problem for liner operators before containerization. The economic benefits of very big ships are surprisingly slim, and because ship-related costs can be less than a quarter of the total service cost, the financial benefits of size diminish as ships get bigger. We will develop this point in Section 13.8 below.

Despite these drawbacks, containerization of minor bulk cargoes plays an important part in helping service operators to obtain a balanced cargo payload, and new types of containers have been developed to allow the transportation of *low-value* or non-standard cargoes. The main types were summarized in Table 13.2. Open-top containers are used for heavy lift; reefer and ventilated containers are used for frozen and chilled cargo and various perishable agricultural crops; flat racks (a flatrack container has a load platform with a bulkhead at either end) are used for awkward cargoes; and tank containers are used for various bulk liquids such as wine and chemicals.

Containerizing cargoes not previously carried often involves research into packing, stowage and handling methods. For this reason the speed with which containerization has penetrated some trades, particularly the minor bulks, depends upon finding practical ways to allow difficult cargoes to be containerized. Sometimes the problem is the delicate nature of the cargo. For example, confectionery exports from the UK are containerized using insulated containers which need special handling to avoid condensation and tainting from previous cargoes.[28] Or it might be a matter of finding a way to reduce the cost by more effective stowage. Most of the motor cycle export trade from Japan is now containerized. By careful planning and some disassembly, a total of 28 large motor cycles or up to 200 small ones can be packed into a 40 ft container. This emphasis on efficient stowage led some manufacturers to take container dimensions into account in their design. However, the trend is not always towards packing more cargo into a container. In the integrated transport business, what matters is the total cost. High-density stowage which calls for some assembly at the destination can be expensive and difficult to control. As transport costs have fallen and labour costs have increased, many manufacturers have reverted to shipping motor cycles fully assembled and carefully packed.

An example of the practicalities of containerizing delicate cargoes is provided by the export of bulk coffee from Brazil to the USA.[29] Traditionally coffee beans were shipped in 60 kg bags, loaded into the hold of a general cargo ship. When containerization was introduced, the bags were packed into a container. Problems with condensation were overcome by using 'dry bags' which absorbed the moisture released by the coffee beans and a massive improvement in efficiency was achieved. Instead of having to individually handle about 250 sacks, the single container is dropped into place in the container-ship, an operation taking about 1½ minutes in a purpose-built container vessel. Then in the mid-1980s importers started looking for ways to reduce the labour required to 'stuff' and 'unstuff' containers with 60 kg bags. Eventually they developed a new cargo-handling system which loaded the container by gravity feed and discharged by a special chute, taking only a few minutes, compared with several hours and much more labour for manual handling. This example illustrates the important point that containerization does not just save transport costs. It has an impact on packaging costs and cargo-handling costs at either end of the cargo leg.

Finally, there is *project cargo*. Some specific items shipped by liners include, for example, equipment for two cement plants, electrification projects for Singapore and Korea, a water filtration plant for Hong Kong, a textile fibre plant for the Philippines, a telecommunications project for Malaysia and equipment for a mass transit railway system in Hong Kong. These cargoes can only be stowed on deck by container-ships and are generally transported by the MPP and heavy lift fleets discussed in Chapter 12.

## 13.5 THE LINER SHIPPING ROUTES

Providing liner services that cover the globe is a daunting task. In its annual *Maritime Transport Study* the United Nations identified 32 maritime coastal regions. There are 1024 potential liner routes between these areas, and some of the coastal regions cover thousands of miles of coastline with many ports. The task of the liner market is to sort out a route network which cost-effectively meets the changing needs of the shippers in these coastal regions.

The industry generally divides the trade routes into three groups, shown in Table 13.6. Firstly, there are the East–West trades. These include the prominent long-haul routes which use the biggest container-ships, account for almost half the containerized cargo and link the industrial centres of North America, western Europe and Asia. Secondly, there is a bewildering array of North–South services linking the economies of the Northern and Southern hemispheres and accounting for almost a quarter of the trade. They also fill the gaps where cargo volumes are lower, for example between South America and Australasia. Thirdly, there is the intraregional cargo, which is shorter-haul and uses smaller ships. It accounts for a third of the cargo volume in Table 13.6, but much less in terms of ship demand because the voyages are generally much shorter. This division of the liner trades is convenient, but in reality the global liner network is constantly adjusting to the changing needs of the world economy and if the network of routes fell into neat categories, the liner companies would not be doing their job properly. So we cannot define the routes precisely, but with this qualification the groupings in Table 13.6 provide a convenient framework for discussing the broad shape of the transport system.

### The East–West trades

By far the largest volume of trade is on the East–West routes. These trades dominate the liner business. Over the last 20 years they have grown enormously, underpinning the rapidly expanding trade links between these areas. These routes probably provide employment for over half of the container-ship capacity and provide the main employment for ships over 4,000 TEU.

**Table 13.6** Principal world container routes, 2004, showing approximate trade volumes

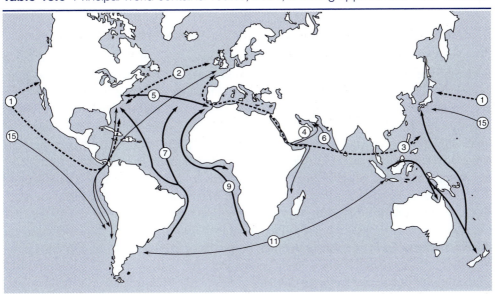

| | Route no | 1994 ‘000 TEU p.a. | 1994 % total | 2004 ‘000 TEU p.a. | 2004 ‘000 TEU p.a. | 2004 Total trade | 2004 % total |
|---|---|---|---|---|---|---|---|
| **1. East–West trades** | | | | *East* | *West* | | |
| Transpacific | 1 | 7,470 | 20% | 11,361 | 4,892 | 16,253 | 17% |
| Transatlantic | 2 | 3,030 | 8% | 2,473 | 3,228 | 5,701 | 6% |
| Europe–Far East | 3 | 4,895 | 13% | 3,538 | 7,510 | 11,048 | 12% |
| Europe–Mid East | 4 | 645 | 2% | 1,675 | 525 | 2,200 | 2% |
| NorthAmerica–Mid East | 5 | 205 | 1% | 160 | 287 | 447 | 0% |
| Far East–Mid East | 6 | 255 | 1% | 300 | 1,300 | 1,600 | 2% |
| Total | | 16,500 | 44% | 19,507 | 17,742 | 37,249 | 39% |
| **2. North–South trades** | | | | *North* | *South* | *Total* | |
| *Europe to* | | | | bound | bound | trade | |
| Latin America | 7 | 1,150 | 3% | 2,046 | 799 | 2,845 | 3% |
| South Asia | 8 | 475 | 1% | 910 | 600 | 1,510 | 2% |
| Africa | 9 | 950 | 3% | 770 | 1,487 | 2,257 | 2% |
| Australasia | 10 | 400 | 1% | 256 | 343 | 599 | 1% |
| Total | | 2,975 | 8% | 3,982 | 3,229 | 7,211 | 8% |
| *North America to* | | | | | | | |
| Latin America | 11 | 2,000 | 5% | 2,627 | 1,526 | 4,153 | 4% |
| South Asia | 12 | 250 | 1% | 533 | 216 | 749 | 1% |
| Africa | 13 | 100 | 0% | 149 | 189 | 338 | 0% |
| Australasia | 14 | 275 | 1% | 203 | 252 | 455 | 0% |
| Total | | 2,625 | 7% | 3,512 | 2,183 | 5,695 | 6% |
| *Far East to* | | | | | | | |
| Latin America | 15 | 725 | 2% | 1,100 | 850 | 1,950 | 2% |
| South Asia | 16 | 425 | 1% | 850 | 1,120 | 1,970 | 2% |
| Africa | 17 | 425 | 1% | 825 | 975 | 1,800 | 2% |
| Australasia | 18 | 875 | 2% | 785 | 800 | 1,585 | 2% |
| Total | | 2,450 | 7% | 3,560 | 3,745 | 7,305 | 8% |
| Total North–South Trades | | 8,050 | 22% | 11,054 | 9,157 | 20,211 | 21% |
| **3. Intra-regional** | | | | | | | |
| Asia | 19 | 6,750 | 18% | | | 28,154 | 29% |
| Europe | 20 | 4,250 | 11% | | | 7,675 | 8% |
| North America | 21 | 1,250 | 3% | | | 339 | 0% |
| Total intra regional | | 12,250 | 33% | | | 36,168 | 38% |
| Other | 22 | 300 | 1% | | | 1,957 | 2% |
| **Total container trade** | | 37,100 | 100% | | | 95,585 | 100% |

Source: Clarkson Research and various sources

## THE TRANSPACIFIC TRADE

Containerization started in the Far East trade in December 1968 when Sea-Land introduced the container service from Seattle to Yokohama and the Japanese shipping companies introduced six 700/800 TEU container ships into a service between California and Japan. Now the biggest deep-sea liner route is the transpacific trade between North America and the Far East, with 16 million TEU of trade, representing 17% of the world total. The services operate between North American ports on the East Coast, the Gulf and the West Coast, to the industrial centres of Japan and the Far East, with some services extending to the Middle East. Some services to the USA Atlantic coast operate direct by water through the Panama Canal, but other containers to US East Coast are shipped under one bill of lading to a US West Coast port and then by rail to the East Coast destination, thus avoiding the Panama transit. On the rail leg containers may be double-stacked. There is a substantial cargo imbalance on this trade, and in 2004 eastbound exports from the 10 major Asian economies[30] to the USA were 11.4 million TEU, whilst the westbound exports were only 4.9 million TEU. This creates significant opportunities for westbound minor bulk cargoes of the sort we saw in the Port of Vancouver trade data in Table 13.4.

In 2004, about 18 operators were servicing the trade, including Maersk, Evergreen, CMA, Mediterranean Shipping Company (MSC), the Grand Alliance and the New World Alliance. An example of a round voyage is provided in Figure 13.3. The service calls at five ports in South East Asia and two on the US West Coast, covering about 16,500 miles. At a speed of 21.5 knots the sea time is 27 days, with an additional 8 days in port, giving a

| Load | Discharge | Distance* | Sea days | Port days | Total |
|------|-----------|-----------|----------|-----------|-------|
| Sendai | Oakland | 4,800 | 9.3 | 1 | 10.3 |
| Oakland | Long Beach | 450 | 0.9 | 1 | 1.9 |
| Long Beach | Oakland | 450 | 0.9 | 1 | 1.9 |
| Oakland | Nagoya | 4,800 | 9.3 | 1 | 10.3 |
| Nagoya | Kobe | 450 | 0.9 | 0.5 | 1.4 |
| Kobe | Shanghai | 783 | 1.5 | 0.5 | 2.0 |
| Shanghai | Kobe | 783 | 1.5 | 1 | 2.5 |
| Kobe | Nagoya | 450 | 0.9 | 0.5 | 1.4 |
| Nagoya | Tokyo | 400 | 0.8 | 0.5 | 1.3 |
| Tokyo | Sendai | 600 | 1.2 | 1 | 2.2 |
| Total | | 13,966 | 27.1 | 8.0 | 35.1 |

Av. speed (knots) 21.5    *distance in nautical miles

**Figure 13.3**
Typical transpacific loop using five ships

round journey time of 35 days. Port-to-port delivery times range from 10 to 18 days, depending on where the ports lie in the schedule. To provide weekly 'express' sailings in this trade requires a fleet of five ships, though some services might increase the number of port calls so as to operate to a six-week round voyage which can be operated by six ships. The 'all water' services to the US East Coast continue on through the Panama Canal, adding another 5,000 miles and requiring nine vessels, and delivery times are very wide, ranging from 10 to 36 days at the extreme ends of the service. Because of the long voyage time the transpacific trade uses the biggest ships, with many 'post-Panamax' vessels over 4,000 TEU on this service, though the East Coast services are limited to Panamax vessels.

## THE NORTH ATLANTIC TRADE

The North Atlantic was the first route containerized in the mid-1960s, as one might expect, since at that time it linked the two major industrial centres of the world, East Coast North America and western Europe. In 2004 it had a trade of 5.7 million TEU, accounting for 6% of world container trade (Table 13.6). There is a trade imbalance westbound, reflecting the greater volume of cargo to North America. In 2004, for example, there was 3.2 million TEU of cargo travelling west between Europe and the USA and only 2.5 million TEU in the opposite direction.

Geographically, the North Atlantic trade covers the major European ports of Göteburg, Hamburg, Bremerhaven, Antwerp, Rotterdam, Felixstowe and Le Havre, though there are some other smaller ports included on the itineraries of certain liner companies. At the North American end of the operation it is organized into two sections covering northern Europe to US Atlantic and northern Europe to the St Lawrence. The principal Canadian ports serviced are Montreal and Halifax, while in the US Boston, New York, Philadelphia, Baltimore, Hampton Roads, Wilmington and Charleston are all regular port calls. Some services extend into the US Gulf, particularly to Houston and Mobile. A typical service is shown in Figure 13.4. It calls at three ports in Europe and

US Gulf to Europe Service:

Transport time between ports in days

| From/To | Antwerp | Southampton | Bremerhaven |
|---|---|---|---|
| Miami | 18 | 19 | 21 |
| Houston | 15 | 16 | 18 |
| Charleston | 11 | 12 | 14 |
| Norfolk | 9 | 10 | 12 |

Europe to US Gulf Service:

Transport time between ports in days

| From/To | Charleston | Miami | Houston | Norfolk |
|---|---|---|---|---|
| Bremerhaven | 10 | 12 | 15 | 21 |
| Southampton | 12 | 14 | 17 | 23 |
| Antwerp | 13 | 15 | 18 | 24 |

**Figure 13.4**
Typical transatlantic loop using five ships

four in the USA. The round voyage distance is about 8,000 miles, which can be completed in 18 days at a speed of 19 knots. Allowing 7 days for port time and a sea margin of 2 days, the round trip takes about 28 days, which could be serviced using a fleet of four ships.

There were 25 carriers operating 37 service loops in 2004 employing 220 ships, an average of six ships per loop. The current conference, the Trans Atlantic Conference Agreement (TACA) operates between US ports, including the Gulf and Pacific, and northern Europe, including the UK and Ireland, Scandinavia and Baltic ports. In 2004 the TACA members provided 11 service strings covering 16 ports in Europe and 13 in the United States. Anyone can join this conference and there are no trade shares.

## WESTERN EUROPE TO THE FAR EAST TRADE

This route covers the trade of northern Europe, stretching from Sweden down to St Nazaire in France, to the Far East, an enormous maritime area covering West Malaysia, Singapore, Thailand, Hong Kong, Philippines, Taiwan, South Korea, China and Japan. This was one of the first trades to be covered by a conference system, the Far East Freight Conference (FEFC), and in 2004 there were about 13 operators or consortia running about 400 ships on many different loops.

Three major operators in the Far East trade are the Grand Alliance, composed of NYK, Neptune Orient Lines and Hapag-Lloyd; the Global Alliance, consisting of MOL, OOCL, APL and MISC; and Maersk. The round-voyage time is over 60 days, requiring nine ships to provide a weekly sailing covering a full range of Asian ports, though a shorter service schedule using eight ships and fewer portcalls is often used. The major operators run separate weekly services direct to Japan and Korea, and to South East Asia. It is the large number of ships required to operate a regular service in this trade that necessitated the development of consortia. A typical round voyage (Figure 13.5) would involve calling at three European ports (e.g. Rotterdam, Southampton, and Hamburg), Singapore and eight or nine ports in South East Asia. The permutations are enormous, involving the option to stop off in the Middle East and the choice of which countries to visit in Asia.

## ROUND-THE-WORLD SERVICES

A seemingly logical development was to fuse these three main liner routes into a single global service. In the early 1980s several operators took this step, of which the most important were Evergreen and United States Lines. Evergreen set up a service with 12 vessels in each direction around the world with a round trip of 80 days, providing a 10-day service frequency in each direction. This service was initially introduced with eight ships in September 1984, but it rapidly became apparent that the 10-day service compared unfavourably with the seven-day service operated by competitors, particularly on the North Atlantic. As a result, in 1985 the number of ships was increased to 11 in each direction, and then to 12, giving a weekly service with a round trip time of 77 days. The ships used on the service were G-class vessels of 2700 TEU which were then lengthened to 3428 TEU. Going westbound, after calling at the UK and north continent ports, vessels proceeded down the East Coast of North America through the Panama Canal to the US West Coast, Japan, the Far East and through the Suez Canal to the Mediterranean.

For some years DSR-Senator and Cho Yang ran a round-the-world service, but with the notable exception of Evergreen this method of operation attracted few operators and in the 1990s it became clear that the round-the-world serv-

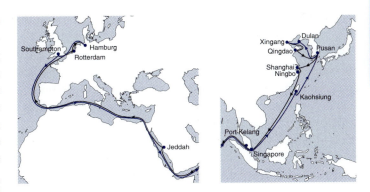

Transport time between ports in days

| From/To | Rotterdam | Hamburg | Southampton |
|---|---|---|---|
| Jeddah | 8 | 11 | 14 |
| Port Kelang | 15 | 18 | 21 |
| Singapore | 16 | 19 | 22 |
| Ningbo | 22 | 25 | 28 |
| Shanghai | 22 | 25 | 28 |
| Pusan | 24 | 27 | 30 |
| Qingdao | 27 | 30 | 33 |
| Xingang | 29 | 32 | 35 |
| Dalian | 30 | 33 | 36 |

**Figure 13.5**
Service loop to Europe from Far East trade

ice strategy faced two fundamental problems. First, the need to link services reduced flexibility over port calls, and balancing calls on the three routes added complexity. Second, the ships used on the arterial trades increased in size and the ships which could transit the Panama Canal became uncompetitive. The second problem will be removed when the development of the Panama Canal to handle bigger container-ships is completed.

## The North–South liner routes

The North–South liner services cover the trade between the industrial centres of Europe, North America and the Far East and the developing countries of Latin America, Africa, Far East and Australasia. There is also an extensive network of services between the smaller economies, especially those in the Southern Hemisphere. These trades, which are listed in Table 13.6, have a very different character. Cargo volumes are much lower, with the many routes together accounting for only 21% of the container cargo volume in 2004. However, this understates the importance of these trades to the shipping business. With many more ports to visit and often less efficient port itineraries, they generate more business than the container volume suggests. Although most trades are now containerized, a considerable amount of break-bulk cargo still cannot be handled in containers, so the liner services are more varied. These trades are too extensive to review in detail, so we will concentrate on one example, the Europe to West Africa service.

The Europe to West Africa trade operates between north-western Europe and the 18 countries of West Africa, stretching from Senegal down to Angola. Nigeria is comparatively rich, but many of the others are very poor with few ports and limited supporting transport infrastructure. European trade accounts for two-thirds of the seaborne traffic, with the remainder divided between the USA and a rapidly growing trade to Asia.[31] Southbound shipments include machinery, chemicals, transport equipment, iron and steel, machinery and various foodstuffs. The return cargo is principally composed of primary products and semi-manufactures such as cocoa, rubber, oilseeds, vegetable oil, cotton, petroleum products and non-ferrous metals. The volume of cargo southbound is higher than the volume northbound, which creates problems fully utilizing the vessels.[32]

In 2005 the main services were containerized, though ro-ros and MPP vessels continue to operate in the trade. These services tend to be more flexible than the deep-sea container services, varying the ships and services to meet the needs of the trade. For example, a typical service, shown in Figure 13.6, offers weekly container-ship sailings with less frequent break-bulk sailings. The ships load cargo in Europe at Felixstowe, Rotterdam, Antwerp, Hamberg and Le Havre. In West Africa the line offers shipment to virtually all major ports either direct or via a feeder system. The service in Figure 13.6 calls at Felixstowe, Antwerp and Le Havre in north-western Europe, whilst in West Africa the itinerary is Dakar, Abidjan, Lomé and Cotonou on the southbound leg, and Tema, Abidjan and Dakar on the northbound leg. To provide this service a fleet of five 1600 TEU containerships is used. Other services use break-bulk ships. For example, a service using six 660 TEU ro-ros offers sailings every 8 days, calling at 13 ports and carrying rolling stock and project cargo in addition to containers.

The imbalance of containerized cargo leaves the shipping line with empty containers to transport back to Europe, and strenuous efforts have been made to containerize return cargoes in order to utilize the container space on ships. On the West Africa to Europe leg the following commodities were containerized: coffee (bagged in containers), empty gas cylinders (returned for refilling), high-value veneers, ginger, cotton, and mail. Attempts to containerize cocoa were initially unsuccessful because the product sweats, while the large logs shipped from West Africa are not generally suitable for containerization. About two-thirds of the containers shipped out to West Africa thus travel back empty.

This is just one example of the North–South liner services. A sense of the way these services develop is given by the press release shown below:

Launch of Africa Service

Hapag-Lloyd is starting its new weekly service from Europe to South Africa in October 2006. The relevant organisation is already in place in South Africa.
[The new service will not use] charter ships as originally planned, but after further studying the market, as a space charterer from Mediterranean Shipping

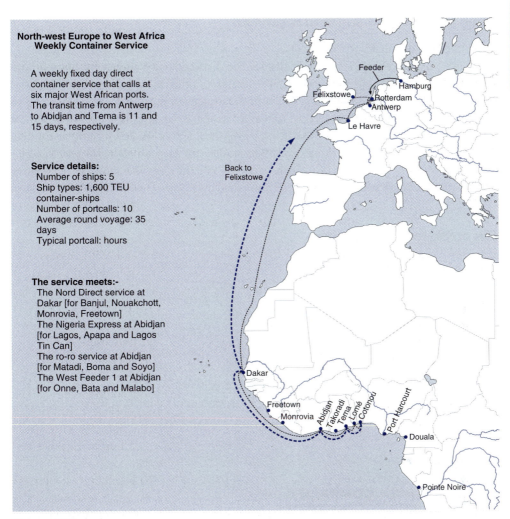

**North-west Europe to West Africa Weekly Container Service**

A weekly fixed day direct container service that calls at six major West African ports. The transit time from Antwerp to Abidjan and Tema is 11 and 15 days, respectively.

**Service details:**
Number of ships: 5
Ship types: 1,600 TEU container-ships
Number of portcalls: 10
Average round voyage: 35 days
Typical portcall: hours

**The service meets:-**
The Nord Direct service at Dakar [for Banjul, Nouakchott, Monrovia, Freetown]
The Nigeria Express at Abidjan [for Lagos, Apapa and Lagos Tin Can]
The ro-ro service at Abidjan [for Matadi, Boma and Soyo]
The West Feeder 1 at Abidjan [for Onne, Bata and Malabo]

**Figure 13.6**
Typical North–South Liner service, Europe–West Africa
Source: OTAL container services

Company (MSC), based in Geneva. As a result of the cooperation with MSC, we can offer our customers considerable service improvements with fixed day weekly sailings and refrigerated cargo capacity.

The South Africa Express service (SAX) will link the European ports [of] Felixstowe, Hamburg, Antwerp and Le Havre with Cape Town, Port Elizabeth and Durban. Transit time from Cape Town to Hamburg will be 18 days. The service will start with the first voyage from Felixstowe on Oct. 16th, the first north bound vessel will leave Durban on Oct. 29th.

Hapag-Lloyd has had its own organisation in South Africa with offices in Durban, Cape Town and Johannesburg since the beginning of July 2006.[33]

## Intraregional trades and feeder services

In addition to the deep-sea trades, the short-sea services are playing an increasingly important part in the business, especially for the distribution of containers brought into hubs such as Hong Kong, Singapore and Rotterdam. These have grown very rapidly as deep sea operators have moved to bigger ships and reduced their port calls, preferring to distribute cargo from base ports to out ports. Movement of cargoes between local ports is also growing rapidly in response to efforts by regional authorities, especially in Europe, to reduce congestion. Many of the short-sea trades use very small ships and voyages of only 3–4 days, but with the growth of cargo volumes a wide range of vessels of 1,500–2,000 TEU are being used in these trades and even some 3,000–4,000 TEU vessels.

## The break-bulk liner services

In discussing the liner trades it is easy to forget that cargo does not fall neatly into general cargo and bulk and there are many borderline trades which do not fit easily into either system. For example, Tasman Orient Line provides transport for New Zealand's forestry exports. It uses thirteen 22,000 dwt MPP liners with a capacity of 350 containers and 10,000 dwt of break-bulk cargo, a speed of 16 knots and 25–35 tonne cranes. The cargoes they carry include containers, reefer containers, car parts, machinery, vehicles, steel products, pulp, paper, lumber, cars, earth-moving equipment and heavy lift cargoes up to 120 tonnes. The vessels operate between New Zealand and South and East Asia. Services like this tend to be very fluid, constantly adjusting to the cargo flow. This is just one of many small and highly specialized liner services which serve the borders of the liner trades.

## 13.6 THE LINER COMPANIES

The liner companies which operate the services we discussed in the previous section are the third element in the container market model shown in box 3 of Figure 13.1. They have to decide which services to operate, which ships to use and whether to buy their own ships, charter them in, or just buy space on another service. They must also market their services, negotiate service contracts and undertake all the administration involved in the provision of services and the invoicing and accounting. Unlike bulk shipping companies which have a relatively simple management structure in relation to their assets (typically two ships at sea for each person on shore), liner companies are generally more complex and the shore–staff ratio is closer to 40 persons per ship. There are currently about 250 companies offering liner services of one sort or another and they should be distinguished from the independent shipowners in box 4b of Figure 13.1 who invest in container-ships and charter them to liner companies. These companies do not offer liner services themselves, and have more in common with the bulk shipping companies discussed in Chapter 11. A list of the 20 largest liner companies is shown in Table 13.7.

**Table 13.7** Twenty largest container fleet operators 1980, 2001, 2005 (year end)

| 1980 container fleet | | | | 2001 container fleet | | | | 2005 container fleet | | | |
|---|---|---|---|---|---|---|---|---|---|---|---|
| Company | No | '000 TEU | % | | No | TEU | % | | No | '000 TEU | % |
| 1 Sea-Land | 63 | 70 | 9.6% | Maersk-SL + Safmarine | 297 | 694 | 9.4% | Maersk | 586 | 1,665 | 16.4% |
| 2 Hapag Lloyd | 28 | 41 | 5.6% | P & O Nedlloyd | 138 | 344 | 4.6% | MSC | 276 | 784 | 7.7% |
| 3 OCL | 16 | 31 | 4.3% | Evergreen Group | 129 | 325 | 4.4% | CMA-CGM | 242 | 508 | 5.0% |
| 4 Maersk Line | 20 | 26 | 3.5% | Hanjin / Senator | 82 | 258 | 3.5% | Evergreen | 155 | 478 | 4.7% |
| 5 M Line | 17 | 24 | 3.3% | Mediterranean Shg Co | 138 | 247 | 3.3% | Hapag-Lloyd | 131 | 412 | 4.1% |
| 6 Evergreen Line | 22 | 24 | 3.2% | APL | 81 | 224 | 3.0% | China Shipping | 123 | 346 | 3.4% |
| 7 OOCL | 17 | 23 | 3.1% | COSCO Container Lines | 113 | 206 | 2.8% | NOL/APL | 104 | 331 | 3.3% |
| 8 Zim Container Line | | 21 | 2.9% | NYK | 86 | 171 | 2.3% | Hanjin | 84 | 329 | 3.2% |
| 9 US Line | 20 | 21 | 2.9% | CP Ships Group | 80 | 148 | 2.0% | COSCO | 126 | 322 | 3.2% |
| 10 American President | 15 | 20 | 2.8% | CMA-CGM Group | 81 | 142 | 1.9% | NYK | 118 | 302 | 3.0% |
| 11 Mitsui OSK | 16 | 20 | 2.7% | Mitsui-OSK Lines | 65 | 139 | 1.9% | Mitsui OSK | 80 | 241 | 2.4% |
| 12 Farrell Lines | 13 | 16 | 2.3% | K Line | 62 | 136 | 1.8% | OOCL | 65 | 234 | 2.3% |
| 13 Neptune Orient Lines | 11 | 15 | 2.0% | Zim | 75 | 132 | 1.8% | Sudamericana | 86 | 234 | 2.3% |
| 14 Trans Freight Line | 17 | 14 | 1.9% | OOCL | 48 | 129 | 1.7% | K Line | 75 | 228 | 2.2% |
| 15 CGM | 9 | 13 | 1.7% | Hapag-Lloyd Group | 32 | 116 | 1.6% | Zim | 85 | 201 | 2.0% |
| 16 Yang Ming | 9 | 13 | 1.7% | Yang Ming Line | 45 | 113 | 1.5% | Yangming | 69 | 188 | 1.9% |
| 17 Nedlloyd | 5 | 12 | 1.6% | China Shipping | 92 | 110 | 1.5% | Hamburg-Süd | 87 | 184 | 1.8% |
| 18 Columbas Line | 13 | 11 | 1.5% | Hyundai | 32 | 106 | 1.4% | HMM | 39 | 148 | 1.5% |
| 19 Safflarine | 5 | 11 | 1.5% | CSAV Group | 54 | 97 | 1.3% | PIL | 101 | 134 | 1.3% |
| 20 Ben Line | 5 | 10 | 1.4% | Hamburg-Süd Group | 45 | 80 | 1% | Wan Hai | 68 | 114 | 1.1% |
| Top 20 | 348 | 437 | 60% | Top 20 | 1,775 | 3,917 | 53% | Top 20 | 2,700 | 7,387 | 73% |
| All Other Operators | 497 | 290 | 40% | All Other | 1,135 | 3,475 | 47% | All Other | 938 | 2,777 | 27% |
| World Fleet | 845 | 726 | 100% | World Fleet | 2,910 | 7,392 | 100% | World Fleet | 3,638 | 10,164 | 100% |
| Average market share top 20 | | | 3.0% | | | | 2.6% | | | | 3.6% |
| Standard deviation top 20 | | | 1.9% | | | | 1.9% | | | | 3.4% |

Source: Pearson and Farsey (1983, Table 9.1, p. 196), CRSL, Martin Stopford

## Liner company size

When containerization started, the high capital investment required resulted in consolidation of trades and many hundreds of small liner companies disappeared. However, following this initial period of change, the size profile of the container companies settled down. Table 13.7, which compares the market shares of the 20 largest container companies in 1980, 2001 and 2005, shows that between 1980 and 2001 the size profile hardly changed. In 1980 the biggest operator was Sea-Land with a market share of 9.6% and the other 19 big players had shares ranging from 1.4% to 5.6%, with an average share for the top 20 of 3%. By 2001 Maersk had become the biggest liner company, with a share of 9.4%, having taken over Sea-Land in the late 1990s. P&O Nedlloyd was second with a fleet share of 4.6% and at the bottom of the top 20 was Hamburg-Süd with a fleet share of 1%. In fact during this period the share of the top 20 companies fell from 60% to 53% so the business was not consolidating and the average company had a market share of only 2.6%.

However, over the next five years the shares of the leading three companies increased rapidly. Maersk jumped from 9% in 2001 to 16% in 2005, mainly by acquiring P&O Nedlloyd. In second place in 2005 was MSC with a share of 8%, most of which was built up by acquisition of new and second-hand tonnage (MSC's share was only 3% in 2001). The other company which grew rapidly was CMA-CGM, which again built up capacity to around 5% by acquiring Delmas and buying ships. Despite these changes at the top, the companies in the middle of the table held onto their market share pretty well and many increased their share. It was the companies below the top 20 which lost market share, falling from 47% in 2001 to 26% in 2005. So the general conclusion from Table 13.7 is that the size distribution of liner companies does change, though not always in the same direction. In such a short period, dominated by unusual market circumstances, it is difficult to judge whether this sprint for growth has proved effective or not.

Finally, we can note that there was a trend for the larger liner companies to deal with the capital intensity problem by removing the ships from their balance sheet. This was achieved by leasing the ships or chartering them from independent operators. In the early 1990s few ships were chartered, but by 2005 about 50% of the container-ship capacity operated by the 20 largest container-ship companies was being time-chartered from independent owners, often financed through the German KG system (see Chapter 8).

## Strategic and global alliances

Under the commercial pressure to achieve greater economies of scale through bigger ships and at the same time provide more frequent global services, in the mid-1990s the medium-sized container companies started to form alliances. These agreements integrated the operational aspects of each participant's services, whilst leaving the commercial activities in the hands of the individual companies.[34] So the alliances typically cover operating joint services on the major liner routes, chartering in vessels, slot sharing, shared terminals, pooled containers, coordinated feeder and inland services where permitted, and information sharing. However, although there is often complete operational integration, each member retains its corporate identity and executive management, including sales and marketing, pricing, bills of lading and vessel ownership and maintenance.

The first of these, the Global Alliance, was formed by APL, OOCL, MOL, and Nedlloyd in May 1994, followed soon afterwards by the Grand Alliance consisting of Hapag-Lloyd, NOL, NYK, and P&OCL, and in 1995 a third alliance of Maersk and Sea-Land with a total of 206 ships. A decade later in 2006 there were three major alliances in operation, the Grand Alliance, the New World Alliance and CKYH. The Grand Alliance, with 152 ships, offered eight services between Europe and the Far East; 11 transpacific services, and four on the North Atlantic.[35] Its members controlled 17%

of the container tonnage. The New World Alliance had three members, APL, Hyundai Merchant Marine and Mitsui OSK Lines Ltd, and 90 ships, whilst the parent companies together controlled 6% of the container tonnage. The third, CKYH, included COSCO, K-Line, Yang Ming and Hanjin, and had 162 ships.

## The liner market model

Liner companies operate in a complex economic environment, and the business model helps to put the issues of company size and competition into perspective. Figure 13.7 sets out the basic elements of the model, with the market place for container transport in the centre of the diagram and the competitive process divided into two parts – part (a) is concerned with the market variables which set the tone of the market in which liner companies operate, whilst part (b) is concerned with the strategic variables over which liner companies have some influence. Part (a) identifies three factors which determine the market environment – (a1) the degree of rivalry between liner companies; (a2) barriers to entry; and (a3) the availability of substitutes such as air freight. Part (b) focuses on the company's bargaining power with suppliers (how powerful are they?) (b1); its bargaining power with customers (how strong is their bargaining position?) (b2); and the extent to which the company can differentiate its service and strengthen its competitive position (b3). Looked at in this way, we have the basic ingredients to explain such factors as market concentration, the company size profile and long-term profitability.

If profitability is any guide, competition in the liner market is severe and despite containerization, liner services are not much more profitable in the twenty-first century than they were in the 1960s before containerization appeared on the scene. In the 1960s British shipping companies earned a return of 6% on assets, about half the industrial average at that time. In the period 2000–5, a generally prosperous time for shipping, the profit earned by one of the largest container companies ranged from 4% to 10% of total assets.[36] Admittedly company rivalry (see (a1)) in Figure 13.7 is moderated by the various conferences

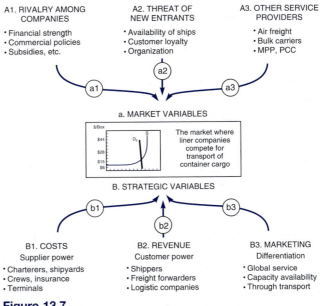

**Figure 13.7**
Liner industry business model
Source: developed from Porter (1990)

and alliances which were tolerated by regulators because they seemed to offer a degree of stability in a volatile business environment. However, new companies can enter the market with increasing ease (see (a2)). The container-ship charter market and a pool of skilled labour make setting up a new service relatively straightforward and the fragmented geographical route structure provides plenty of opportunities to compete against established companies on relatively equal terms. Finally, other service providers (see (a3)) such as air freight, bulk and multi-purpose operators compete for specialized cargoes. Of course this is a two-way street – their cargo is also a potential target for the container companies.

The strategic variables provide the liner companies with the raw material for competing in this market. As far as costs are concerned (see (b1)), the liner business is dealing with charterer-owners who provide ships; the shipbuilders who build new ones; crews, insurers, chandlers and bunker suppliers; terminals; and the sub-contractors such as road haulage. This is a difficult area because regional fragmentation probably dilutes the leverage big companies have over these suppliers. For example large supermarket chains can use their bulk purchasing power to exert pressure on suppliers, and companies with over 25% of the market are in a strong position. There is no parallel for this in the liner business and although size may be helpful, geographical fragmentation dilutes the benefits and consolidation does not necessarily add value in terms of enhancing the company's competitive position on individual routes.

On the revenue side (see (b2)), liner companies face powerful customers, including large cargo shippers, for example multinational corporations producing electronic goods, mechanical equipment, motorcycles and textiles. Customer strength is often a real issue because large cargo shippers run professional transportation operations and squeeze their transport budget very hard. One route to strength is service differentiation (see (b3)), though this is not easy. Ultimately the transport service provided is a commodity, so differentiation is difficult. Where shippers are smaller, freight forwarders and logistics companies provide the interface, and in a geographically fragmented market with many different routes, these intermediaries often have a strong negotiating position in their local area, though many are global in their spread. Company size only really matters when it generates strength in one of these areas.

In summary, there is plenty of flexibility over the way a liner company develops its business. On the cost side, it can use new or old ships, either purchased or on charters; it can select the size of ships it uses and tailor its approach to terminals. On the revenue side, the company can choose whether it specializes as a niche player on a small selection of local routes, or casts its role wider as a global carrier. Again there are many options which can be followed. Finally, there is the question of service differentiation, and the variety of cargoes offers range of potential markets. The way this works out in practice was illustrated in Table 13.7, which shows that the concentration of ownership is relatively low. In the retail business, for example, the top three or four retailers in national markets such as the USA often have a market share over 60%. Even with recent consolidation, the liner business has half that.

## 13.7 THE LINER FLEET

### Types of ship used in the liner trades

Now we turn to the fleet of ships used in these trades. Just as in other sectors of the shipping market, the fleet is not an optimum. It is the result of 20–30 years of investment decisions. Although some of the vessels in the fleet are now technically obsolete in some way or another, the fact that they are still trading is evidence that they retain economic value. Although predominantly container-ships, the fleet used in the liner trades actually includes six different types of ships, shown in Figure 13.8:

- *Container-ships.* Cellular 'lift on, lift off' container-ships are now the biggest and most modern part of the fleet, with 138 m.dwt in September 2007. All the ships in this fleet have open holds with cell guides and are designed exclusively for the carriage of containers.
- *Multi-purpose vessels.* There was a fleet of 2647 vessels of 24.1 m.dwt in September 2006. These are ships designed with a fast speed, good container capacity and the ability to carry break-bulk and other unitized cargo such as forest products. They were mainly built during

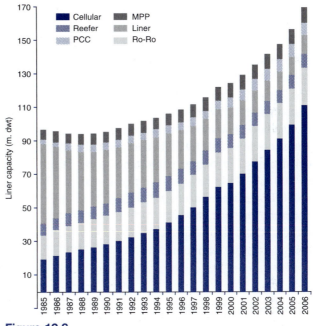

**Figure 13.8**
Liner fleet by vessel type, 1985–2006
Source: Clarkson Research Services Ltd

the early years of containerization when operators were handling a mix of containerized and break-bulk cargo, often with open holds without cell guides and often incorporating a 'tween deck. In the early twenty-first century the fleet found a new niche in the transport of heavy lift and project cargoes. MPPs are also used in services, for example, between Oceania and South East Asia where the ability to carry mixed break-bulk cargoes provides a competitive advantage. After some years of decline the fleet has started to grow again.

- *'Tweendeckers.* These flexible tramp vessels continued to be built until the 1980s, and in 2007 there was still a fleet of about 5.6 m.dwt in operation. Two standard designs, the SD14 and the Freedom, were very popular. 'Tweendeckers have two decks, narrow hatches, economical speed, limited container capacity and cargo gear.

- *General cargo liners*. These are purpose-built cargo liners still in service. They are fast with multiple decks, extensive cargo gear but poor container capacity and as the old ships were scrapped and not replaced the fleet shrunk to 5.5 m.dwt in 2007 (the *Pointe Sans Souci*, mentioned earlier in this chapter, was scrapped in 1996).
- *Ro-ros*. Multi-deck vessels in which the holds are accessed by ramps in the bow, stern or side. Although sometimes similar in design to car ferries, they have no accommodation or public areas and are designed primarily to carry cargo on deep-sea routes. The fleet, which includes ferries, edged up to 12.6 m.dwt in 2007.
- *Barge carriers*. A 1970s experiment which did not catch on, these carry 500-ton standard barges which are floated or lifted on and off the ship. There were about 50 of these vessels still operating in 2007 (including some heavy lift).

The number of container-ships increased from 750 in 1980 to 4208 in September 2007, and they now dominate the liner fleet, accounting for 60% of the total deadweight capacity. This compares with a tanker fleet of 4467 vessels and a bulk carrier fleet of 6557 vessels, making container-ships a very significant part of the merchant fleet. The container-ship fleet is usually measured in TEU. The ships have wide hatches designed to standard container dimensions and cell guides in the holds and sometimes on deck. An example of a 1769 TEU container ship is shown in Figure 14.3, along with technical details. The bigger ships tend to be faster. For example, Feeder container-ships of 100–299 TEU have an average speed of 13.8 knots, while many of the ships over 4,000 TEU have an average speed of 24 knots.[37] This reflects the fact that smaller ships generally operate on short routes where high speed brings fewer economic benefits.

### Container-ship size trends

One of the principal benefits of containerization is that it allows bigger ships to be used and the size of container-ships has increased steadily, following much the same process of evolving into size segments we have already seen in the tanker and bulk carrier markets, each serving a different part of the market. Figure 13.9 shows the segments developed between

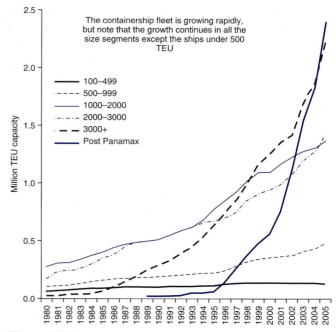

**Figure 13.9**
Container-ship fleet by ship size, 1980–2005
Source: Clarkson Research Services Ltd

1980 and 2005. The smaller sizes (Feeder, Feedermax and Handy) are mainly used in the short-sea trades and in draught-restricted ports on the North–South routes. The medium-sized vessels of 1,000–2,000 TEU are flexible enough for short-sea operations, large feeder services and North–South trading. The larger segments (sub-Panamax, Panamax, and post-Panamax) serve the long-haul deep-sea business. At the upper end, the Panamax fleet (over 3,000 TEU and able to transit Panama) has grown most rapidly in recent years, with a new generation of post-Panamax vessels appearing in the 1990s.

## 13.8 THE PRINCIPLES OF LINER SERVICE ECONOMICS

### The building-blocks of liner service economics

Liner service economics lies at the heart of the issues discussed in this chapter and a practical example helps put things into perspective. We will proceed in two stages, starting with the 'building blocks' from which the liner service is constructed and then build-ings a service cashflow model similar to the one used to analyse the bulk shipping industry in Chapter 5. As an example we will take a liner service operating on the transpacific trade and compare the cost structure for six sizes of ship – 1200 TEU, 2600 TEU, 4,000 TEU, 6,500 TEU, 8,500 TEU and 11,000 TEU. The eight main categories of building-block are shown in Table 13.8.

This is not a classification which appears in the accounts of any liner company, and in practice liner companies will not necessarily prepare their management accounts in this way. For example, ship capital costs would probably be allocated across a range of services, rather than attributing specific ships a specific service, as is done in Table 13.8. But in terms of understanding the economics of the business, this is a useful way to group the costs. Based on these operational and cost assumptions the voyage cash-flow for each vessel size is shown in Table 13.9 to give an idea of economies of scale. Of course liner companies operate many services and their published accounts are far more complex than this simple example. However, it serves the important function of identifying the economic variables involved in management decision-making and as the starting point for understanding the principles of liner service economics.

#### SHIP CHARACTERISTICS

The ship size, speed and cargo-handling efficiency set the economic framework for the service. Size ranges from 1,200 TEU to 11,000 TEU and the size, speed and fuel consumption of each size shown in Table 13.8 are based on averages for the fleet of vessels in 2006. The design speed increases by 38% from 18.3 knots for a 1200 TEU vessel to 25.2 knots for a 6,500 TEU vessel, after which it does not increase, whilst the design fuel consumption shown in the next row is 460% higher for the 6500 TEU ship. In the past a few container-ships were built with speeds over 30 knots, but the industry seems to have settled down at a 25 knot peak. The operating speed shown in the next row can be varied by service planners to leave a margin for weather and delays and also to fine-tune the voyage time to fit with the weekly sailing schedule adopted

**Table 13.8** The eight building-blocks of liner costs

| Vessel size (TEU) | | 1,200 | 2,600 | 4,300 | 6,500 | 8,500 | 11,000 |
|---|---|---|---|---|---|---|---|
| **1. Ship characteristics** | | | | | | | |
| Container-ship size | container-ship characteristics | 1,200 | 2,600 | 4,300 | 6,500 | 8,500 | 11,000 |
| Design speed (knots) | | 18.3 | 20.9 | 23.8 | 25.2 | 25.5 | 25.5 |
| Design fuel consumption (tons/day) | | 42 | 79 | 147 | 214 | 230 | 240 |
| Operating speed terminal to terminal | | 17.4 | 19.9 | 22.6 | 23.9 | 24.2 | 24.2 |
| Fuel Consumption (tons/day) | | 36.3 | 67.7 | 126.2 | 183.2 | 197.2 | 205.8 |
| Time per port call (days) | | 0.7 | 1.0 | 1.2 | 1.6 | 2.0 | 2.4 |
| **2. Service schedule** | | | | | | | |
| Distance of round trip | schedule | 14,000 | 14,000 | 14,000 | 14,000 | 14,000 | 14,000 |
| Service frequency | | weekly | weekly | weekly | weekly | weekly | weekly |
| Portcalls on round voyage | | 7 | 7 | 7 | 7 | 7 | 7 |
| Days at sea | performance variable | 33.6 | 29.4 | 25.8 | 24.4 | 24.1 | 24.1 |
| Days in port | | 5.0 | 6.7 | 8.7 | 11.4 | 13.8 | 16.9 |
| Total voyage time (days) | | 38.5 | 36.0 | 34.5 | 35.8 | 37.9 | 40.9 |
| Voyages per annum | | 9.5 | 10.1 | 10.6 | 10.2 | 9.6 | 8.9 |
| **Required number of ships in weekly string** | | **5.5** | **5.1** | **4.9** | **5.1** | **5.4** | **5.8** |
| **3. Capacity utilization (to calculate the number of loaded containers carried)** | | | | | | | |
| Eastbound Capacity Utilization (%) | how full ships are | 90% | 90% | 90% | 90% | 90% | 90% |
| Westbound Capacity Utilization (%) | | 40% | 40% | 40% | 40% | 40% | 40% |
| Containers shipped outward (TEU) | | 1,080 | 2,340 | 3,870 | 5,850 | 7,650 | 9,900 |
| Containers shipped back (TEU) | | 480 | 1,040 | 1,720 | 2,600 | 3,400 | 4,400 |
| Cargo transported per voyage (TEU) | | 1,560 | 3,380 | 5,590 | 8,450 | 11,050 | 14,300 |
| **Annual transport capacity per ship (TEU)** | | **14,785** | **34,232** | **59,097** | **86,235** | **106,391** | **127,467** |
| **4. Ship costs $ per day** | | | | | | | |
| 4.1 Operating costs (OPEX) $/day | | 4,643 | 5,707 | 6,000 | 6,500 | 7,000 | 7,500 |
| 4.2 Capital cost/$ day | capital cost | 8,904 | 17,096 | 23,863 | 31,699 | 39,178 | 46,301 |
| -Capital value $mill | | 25 | 48 | 67 | 89 | 110 | 130 |
| -Depreciation period (years) | | 20 | 20 | 20 | 20 | 20 | 20 |
| -Interest rate (% pa) | | 8% | 8% | 8% | 8% | 8% | 8% |
| 4.3 Bunker cost ($/day) | bunker cost | 12,690 | 23,700 | 44,160 | 64,110 | 69,000 | 72,000 |
| -Bunker price $/ton (average) | | 300 | 300 | 300 | 300 | 300 | 300 |
| 4.4 Total cost per vessel TEU capacity per day($/day) | | 648 | 496 | 457 | 433 | 395 | 360 |
| **4.5 Cost per container transported per annum ($)** | | **648** | **496** | **457** | **433** | **395** | **360** |

**Table 13.8** The eight building-blocks of liner costs—cont'd

| Vessel size (TEU) | | 1,200 | 2,600 | 4,300 | 6,500 | 8,500 | 11,000 |
|---|---|---|---|---|---|---|---|
| **5. Port & charges (excluding cargo handling)** | | | | | | | |
| Port cost $/TEU | | 22 | 15 | 12 | 11 | 11 | 10 |
| Port cost $/call | | 22,000 | 29,000 | 35,000 | 43,000 | 60,000 | 65,000 |
| **6. The deployment of containers** | | | | | | | |
| 20' containers (% ship capacity) | | 14% | 14% | 14% | 14% | 14% | 14% |
| '-Number of units loaded | | 168 | 364 | 602 | 910 | 1,190 | 1,540 |
| 40' containers (% ship capacity) | mix of boxes | 80% | 80% | 80% | 80% | 80% | 80% |
| -Number of units loaded | needed to | 480 | 1,040 | 1,720 | 2,600 | 3,400 | 4,400 |
| Reefer containers (% total) | operate | 6% | 6% | 6% | 6% | 6% | 6% |
| -Number of 40' units loaded | service | 36 | 78 | 129 | 195 | 255 | 330 |
| Total units on full vessel (all sizes) | | 684 | 1,482 | 2,451 | 3,705 | 4,845 | 6,270 |
| Container turnaround time (days/voyage) | efficiency variables | 75 | 75 | 75 | 75 | 75 | 75 |
| Inter-zonal repositioning (%) | | 10.0% | 10.0% | 10.0% | 10.0% | 10.0% | 10.0% |
| **7. The cost of containers and container handling** | | | | | | | |
| Container costs ($/TEU/day) | 20 foot | 0.7 | 0.7 | 0.7 | 0.7 | 0.7 | 0.7 |
| | 40 foot | 1.1 | 1.1 | 1.1 | 1.1 | 1.1 | 1.1 |
| | 40 foot reefer | 6.0 | 6.0 | 6.0 | 6.0 | 6.0 | 6.0 |
| Maintenance & repair ($/box/voyage) | | 50.0 | 50.0 | 50.0 | 50.0 | 50.0 | 50.0 |
| Terminal costs for container handling ($/lift) | | 220 | 220 | 220 | 220 | 220 | 220 |
| Refrigeration cost for reefer containers ($/TEU) | | 150.0 | 150.0 | 150.0 | 150.0 | 150.0 | 150.0 |
| Trans-shipment by sea ($/TEU) | | 225.0 | 225.0 | 225.0 | 225.0 | 225.0 | 225.0 |
| Inland intermodal transport cost ($/TEU) | | 220.0 | 220.0 | 220.0 | 220.0 | 220.0 | 220.0 |
| Interzone re-positioning ($/TEU) | | 240.0 | 240.0 | 240.0 | 240.0 | 240.0 | 240.0 |
| Cargo claims ($/box/voyage) | | 30 | 30 | 30 | 30 | 30 | 30 |
| **8. Administration costs** | | | | | | | |
| Administrative productivity (TEU/employee) | | 640 | 640 | 640 | 640 | 640 | 640 |
| Number of employees required | | 23 | 53 | 92 | 135 | 166 | 199 |
| Cost/employee $ per annum | | 60,000 | 60,000 | 60,000 | 60,000 | 60,000 | 60,000 |
| Administration cost ($000/voyage) | | 146 | 317 | 524 | 792 | 1,036 | 1,341 |

Source: CRSL, HSH Nordbanlk, Drewry Shipping Consultants

**Table 13.9** Liner voyage cashflow model ($000 per voyage)

| Vessel size (TEU) | 1,200 | 2,600 | 4,300 | 6,500 | 8,500 | 11,000 |
|---|---|---|---|---|---|---|
| | $000s | | | | | |
| **1. Cost of the ship on the voyage** | | | | | | |
| 1.1 Operating costs | 179 | 206 | 207 | 232 | 265 | 307 |
| 1.2 Capital costs | 343 | 616 | 824 | 1,134 | 1,485 | 1,896 |
| 1.3 Bunker costs | 426 | 696 | 1,139 | 1,562 | 1,662 | 1,734 |
| 1.4 Port costs | 154 | 203 | 245 | 301 | 420 | 455 |
| 1.5 Total ship costs | 1,102 | 1,721 | 2,415 | 3,229 | 3,832 | 4,392 |
| 1.6 Ship costs, % of total costs | 54% | 46% | 42% | 39% | 37% | 34% |
| **2. Costs of the containers on voyage** | | | | | | |
| 2.1 Cost of supplying containers | 32 | 65 | 104 | 162 | 225 | 314 |
| 2.2 Cost of container maintenance | 34 | 74 | 123 | 185 | 242 | 314 |
| 2.3 Total container cost | 66 | 139 | 226 | 347 | 467 | 628 |
| 2.4 Container cost, % of total cost | 3% | 4% | 4% | 4% | 4% | 5% |
| **3. Administration cost** | | | | | | |
| 3.1 Administrative cost per voyage | 146 | 317 | 524 | 792 | 1,036 | 1,341 |
| | 7% | 9% | 9% | 10% | 10% | 10% |
| **4. Cargo handling and onward transport** | | | | | | |
| 4.1 Terminal costs for container handling | 301 | 652 | 1,078 | 1,630 | 2,132 | 2,759 |
| 4.2 Refrigeration cost for reefer containers | 11 | 23 | 39 | 59 | 77 | 99 |
| 4.3 Inland intermodal transport cost | 343 | 744 | 1,230 | 1,859 | 2,431 | 3,146 |
| 4.4 Interzone repositioning | 58 | 125 | 206 | 312 | 408 | 528 |
| 4.5 Cargo claims | 47 | 101 | 168 | 254 | 332 | 429 |
| 4.6 Total handling & onward transport | 713 | 1,544 | 2,553 | 3,860 | 5,047 | 6,532 |
| 4.7 Handling and onward transport, % of total cost | 35% | 41% | 45% | 47% | 49% | 51% |
| **5. Voyage cost** | | | | | | |
| 5.1 Total voyage cost | 2,027 | 3,721 | 5,719 | 8,229 | 10,382 | 12,892 |
| 5.2 Cost Per TEU eastbound leg | 938 | 795 | 739 | 703 | 679 | 651 |
| 5.3 Cost Per TEU westbound leg | 2,111 | 1,789 | 1,662 | 1,582 | 1,527 | 1,465 |
| 5.4 Average cost/TEU | 1,299 | 1,101 | 1,023 | 974 | 940 | 902 |
| 5.5 % change in average cost/TEU | | −15.3% | −7.1% | −4.8% | −3.5% | −4.0% |
| **6. Voyage revenue ($000s)** | | | | | | |
| 6.1 Freight rate per TEU eastbound leg | 1,750 | 1,750 | 1,750 | 1,750 | 1,750 | 1,750 |
| 6.2 Freight rate per TEU westbound leg | 750 | 750 | 750 | 750 | 750 | 750 |
| 6.3 Total revenue eastbound leg | 1,890 | 4,095 | 6,773 | 10,238 | 13,388 | 17,325 |
| 6.4 Revenue westbound leg | 360 | 780 | 1,290 | 1,950 | 2,550 | 3,300 |
| 6.5 Total voyage revenue | 2,250 | 4,875 | 8,063 | 12,188 | 15,938 | 20,625 |
| **7. Voyage profit (loss) ($000s)** | | | | | | |
| Voyage profit (loss) | 223 | 1,154 | 2,344 | 3,959 | 5,555 | 7,733 |
| % total revenue | 10% | 24% | 29% | 32% | 35% | 37% |

in section 2 of the table. In this case as a neutral assumption the operating speed is set 5% below the design speed. Finally, the time per call shown in the last row of section 1 assumes half a day for entering and leaving port, plus one minute per lift, with 25% of the cargo being handled on each call. These assumptions will differ widely in practice.

## THE SERVICE SCHEDULE

The service schedule described in Table 13.8 is based on the 14,000-miles transpacific round voyage we reviewed in Figure 13.3. Service planners have to decide the frequency of sailings and the number of port calls, and this example is based on a weekly service with seven port calls on the round voyage (e.g. Shanghai, Kobe, Nagoya, Tokyo, Sendai, Oakland and Los Angeles), giving a round voyage time of 41.9 days for the slow 1,200 TEU ship and 42.3 days for the faster but much bigger 11,000 TEU ship. This raises the interesting point that the faster 11,000 TEU ship's shorter sea passage is offset by the longer port time needed to handle its cargo. From a practical viewpoint the 35.8 days for the 6,500 TEU ship fits pretty well with the actual schedule in Figure 13.3. The bottom line of section 2 in Table 13.8 shows that the number of ships required to run the service varies from 4.9 for the 4,300 TEU ship to 5.8 for the 11,000 TEU ship, reflecting the interplay between the speed and port time of the different ship sizes. In practice, the service planners would have to adjust the operating speed of the ships and the number of port calls to get the best balance. Or they could add a sixth ship to the string and operate at a lower speed, which would incur more capital costs, but save bunker costs. The possibilities are endless, but in this example for simplicity we will not do this.

## CAPACITY UTILIZATION

Getting the capacity right is crucial for service planners. There is no point in using big ships if you cannot fill them, but running out of space can be just as bad. For example, to fill the biggest ships, ten port calls might be needed rather than seven and since each port call takes an average of 1.25 days, this would extend the round voyage time to 40 days, requiring a six-ship string. One way round this is to set up regional hubs where cargo is collected for despatch on the deep-sea service, but that involves multiple handling and shippers often prefer direct services. Or a niche operator might decide to use a smaller ship and make only one port call at each end (a 'direct service'), cutting the round voyage time to around 25 days for the medium-size ships, allowing a string of four vessels to be used. There is also the issue of trade imbalances. For example in the transpacific trade there is always much more cargo moving east, and in Table 13.8 we assume 90% capacity utilization on the eastbound voyage and 40% on the westbound voyage. With these figures we can calculate the cargo transported on each voyage, and the annual transport capacity is shown in the final two rows of section 3. Each 1,200 TEU vessel transports 14,785 TEU in a year, whilst the 11,000 TEU vessel transports 127,467 TEU.

SHIP COSTS AND ECONOMIES OF SCALE

So far we have concentrated on the physical aspects of liner service, but the size of ship also has an economic dimension because some costs do not increase proportionally with the transport capacity of the ship. The economies of scale generated by the three main elements in the ship cost calculation – capital costs, operating expenses, and bunker costs – are examined in section 4 of Table 13.8:

- *Operating costs (OPEX)*. The operating expenses of the ship are crew, insurance, stores, maintenance and administration. Some of these items offer more scale economies than others. Administration, stores and crew generally do not increase very much as the ship gets bigger. For example the *Emma Maersk*, the industry's first 11,000 TEU container-ship, was designed for a crew of 13, significantly fewer than many 3,000 TEU ships. However, insurance and maintenance costs are likely to increase in line with the capital cost of the ship, though by less than the transport capacity of the ship. The OPEX numbers in Table 13.8, which are based on a survey of German containerships,[38] show that the daily cost increases from $4600 per day for a 1,200 TEU ship to around $7,000 per day for an 8,500 TEU ship, so there are significant scale economies here.

- *Capital costs*. Capital costs are subject to economies of scale because big ships cost less per container slot than small ones. For example, in 2006 a 1,200 TEU containership cost $25 million ($20,000 per slot) whilst a 6,500 TEU ship with five times the capacity cost about $89 million ($13,700 per slot). However, the saving diminishes as the ship gets bigger and beyond 5,000 TEU is not very great because the major fixed cost is the engine room and bigger ships are mainly adding more steel, which is not subject to the same degree of economies of scale.

- *Bunker costs*. Finally, there is fuel consumption and again we see the now familiar pattern of diminishing economies as the ship gets bigger. Figure 13.10 plots the average bunker consumption of ships in the container-ship fleet in 2006, adjusted to a standard 15 knot speed, against TEU

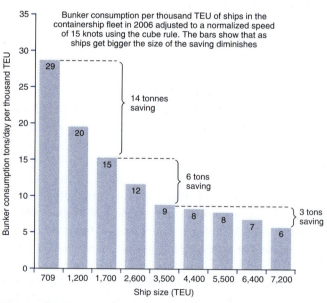

**Figure 13.10**
Bunker consumption of container-ships, 2006
Source: Clarkson Research Services Ltd

capacity for a sample of 2,500 container-ships.[39] Increasing the ship's capacity from 700 to 1700 TEU cuts bunker consumption by 11 tons per thousand TEU; from 1700 TEU to 3500 TEU by another 6 tonnes per thousand TEU; and from 3500 TEU to 7200 TEU by only 3 tons per thousand TEU. It follows that the biggest benefits come from upsizing the smaller segments of the container business.

The economies of scale for each size of ship are summarized in Figure 13.11 in terms of the cost per TEU transported in a year for each ship size (the numbers are in Table 13.8, row 4.5). The cost of $648 per TEU for a 1200 TEU vessel falls sharply to $498 TEU for a 2600 TEU vessel; $457 TEU for a 4,300 TEU vessel; and $360 TEU for an 11,000 TEU vessel. So the 11,000 TEU ship halves the cost of container transport. Beyond 2600 TEU economies of savings are roughly 5% for each additional 1,000 TEU capacity (but remember this is just an illustration and the savings depend on the assumptions). Finally, there

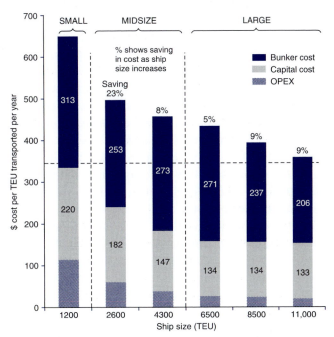

**Figure 13.11**
Container-ship cost per TEU transported
Source: Table 13.8

may be diseconomies of scale. Using very big ships means deep dredging of hub ports and necessitates feeder services to ports which cannot accommodate them. These feeder costs detract from the savings on using bigger ships on the deep-sea leg.

### PORT CHARGES

These are an item over which the shipowner has less control, since they vary from port to port, though big groups have a stronger negotiating position. Since port charges are generally levied on the basis of the ship's tonnage, this introduces an additional element of economies of scale, since the port costs per TEU reduce as the ship gets bigger. In Table 13.8, Section 5, we assume a reduction in the port costs per TEU from $22 for the 1,200 TEU ship to $10 for the 11,000 TEU ship. This creates an incentive to develop ship designs with a low tonnage relative to capacity, especially for distribution trades where the vessels make many port calls, encouraging designs with a low deadweight and gross tonnage per TEU.

## DEPLOYMENT OF CONTAINERS

This involves two main issues. First, there is the mix of container types for the trade. There are many different sizes of containers (see Table 13.1), including general purpose and specialized designs. In the transpacific trade the split is about 15% 20 ft containers, 80% 40 ft containers, and 6% refrigerated units, though the balance differs in other trades. For example, on the shorter transatlantic journey the proportion of 40 ft containers reduces to about 60%. There may also be a requirement for specialized containers, for example open-top containers or tanks. Most liner companies own a substantial proportion of their containers, since this is generally the cheapest option, and lease a proportion, say 20–30%.

Then there is the efficiency of container turn-around. Between voyages the containers must be delivered to the customer, collected and repositioned for the next cargo. This calls for a substantially greater container stock than the container capacity of the vessels employed in the trade. In this example, we assume a 75-day turn-around time for the cycle, of which 28 days are spent at sea and 47 days in transit to and from the customer. Naturally this will vary a great deal with the trade. Finally, trade imbalances on particular routes mean that some containers must be repositioned empty, which includes the significant cost of loading and unloading the empty container. In section 2 of Table 13.8 we assumed only 40% of the containers are filled on the westbound leg compared with 90% on the eastbound leg, so 50% of the westbound containers are empty. This is a classic opportunity for marginal cost pricing. If the container is travelling empty, any cargo which pays more than the handling charges is worth carrying. Hay, waste paper, building blocks, animal feeds and a host of other cargoes fall into this category. The danger arises when these marginal cargoes create hidden costs which are unseen by the salesman and end up being shipped at a loss.

## CONTAINER COSTS

These cover the capital cost of the containers; maintenance and repair; terminal costs for container handling (i.e. the cost of lifting it on and off the vessel); storage for reefer units; on-shipment costs by sea or inland; repositioning empty containers between zones; and cargo claims. The cost of the container itself depends on the purchase price, its economic life and the method of finance. In 2006 a 20 ft container cost about $2,000 and a 40 ft container about $3,200. Refrigerated containers are much more expensive, costing over $20,000 for a 40 ft unit. In practice containers have an average life of 12–16 years, at the end of which they have a scrap value of several hundred dollars. On these parameters the daily cost of a container can be calculated, working out at about 60 cents per day for a 20 ft unit and $1 per day for a 40 ft unit, whilst reefers are about $5.60. Like ships, containers and other equipment require continuous maintenance, for which an annual budget must be allowed.

Terminal and through transport costs vary enormously from port to port. Handling the container in the terminal includes the lift on or off the ship and the associated costs of moving, stacking and storing the container within the terminal. These costs depend on the facilities available and local stevedoring conditions. For simplicity the handling charges in Table 13.8 are limited to a single rate of $200 per lift. Refrigerated containers also require special terminal services which are costed here at $150 per unit. The on-shipment of the container is dealt with under three headings: trans-shipment by sea, inland inter-modal transport and inter-zone repositioning. These costs depend specifically on the trade and the method of pricing adopted by the company. Some operators charge separately for delivery, in which case the freight rate does not include the cost of on-transport. Other carriers offer 'door-to-door' rates. Since some cost will certainly be incurred, Table 13.8 assumes values of $225 per TEU for transhipment, $200 for inland transport, and $240 for inter-zone repositioning when regional imbalances appear and the containers have to be shipped to a different part of the world. Finally, there is an item for cargo claims. Concluding the discussion on container costs, perhaps the most significant feature is that because these costs are based on the standard container, they are not subject to economies of scale. The 11,000 TEU ship faces the same unit costs as the 1,200 TEU ship.

## ADMINISTRATION COSTS

Somehow the shipping company must recover the cost of running a global container service. If the profitability of each part of the business is to be calculated accurately, it is important to allocate costs fairly to those parts of the business which incur them so that the profitability of different parts of the business can be measured. One common way to do this is to charge an administration cost to each vessel on a proportional basis which recovers the full overheads of the company. This is the approach we use in Table 13.8, though the charging could also be done on a service basis.

A rough idea of the nature of these costs and the way they might be organized is given by the organization chart in Figure 13.12. The chart divides management responsibility between profit centres responsible for the trade routes on which the company is active and functional departments responsible for providing efficient and cost-effective services. Managers of the trade routes, shown in the first row of the organization chart, are responsible for running profitable services. They interface with the customers and carry out many functions locally. However, in the drive for efficiency, functional activities are managed and coordinated centrally on a matrix basis and their costs charged out to the profit centres. The example in the chart shows four functional departments, each responsible for a specific activity as follows:

- *Operations and logistics*. This covers the management of the ships, scheduling, cargo stowage and terminals. If the company has many terminals this could be a separate department. It is also responsible for the overall maintenance and control of the company's fleet of owned and leased containers, including maintenance, repair and scheduling.
- *Finance and admin*. A major activity including management accounts and budgeting; voyage accounts (e.g. booking, rating, tracking, billing.), compliance, human resources and general administration.
- *Global sales*. This covers the booking and documentation of cargo, plus dealing with insurance and conferences where appropriate, plus pricing, service agreements, public relations, and advertising and agents.

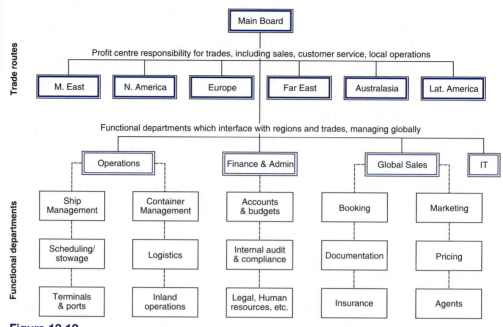

**Figure 13.12**
Liner company organization chart showing main regional and functional activities
Source: complied from various sources

- *IT.* This is a vital part of the modern global business, managing and developing the communications and computer systems used in the various offices.

The cost of these departments could be charged back to the trade route profit centres as a direct charge, or charged to the ships they use, as in Table 13.9.

Some companies carry out all of these activities themselves, while smaller companies may subcontract. As a result the numbers on the payroll vary a great deal. For example, in 1995 Atlantic Container Line shipped 224,000 containers on the North Atlantic and had a staff of about 380, a throughput of 588 TEU per employee. The salary cost was $91 per TEU. A decade later in 2005, Hapag-Lloyd shipped 2.67 million TEU with a workforce of 4,161, an average of 640 TEU per employee and we assume in Table 13.8, Section 8 that this applies to all ship sizes, requiring 23 employees for the 1,200 TEU ship and 199 for the 11,000 TEU ship.[40] With a cost per employee of $60,000 per annum the 1,200 TEU ship, which carries 1,560 TEU per voyage, will incur an administrative cost on the voyage of $146,000 (i.e. 38.5 days on the voyage at a daily cost of $3,797 per day).

## The liner voyage cash flow model

Now we can combine the costs with revenue to calculate the financial performance of the liner service just as we did for bulk shipping in Chapter 7 (see Table 7.11). The *voyage cashflow model* shown in Table 13.9 uses the cost information from Table 13.8

to calculate the cost of the ships (section 1), the cost of the containers (section 2), the administration cost (section 3) and the cargo-handling and onward transport cost (section 4). From these items we calculate the voyage cost per TEU in section 5 and add the voyage revenue based on the freight rate on each leg (section 6) to obtain the voyage profit or loss in section 7. Finally, to give a sense of how costs and profits can vary with ship size, Table 13.9 compares the results for the six vessel sizes. We will now discuss each of these items in more detail.

The ship costs shown in section 1 of Table 13.9 demonstrate why economies of scale are so important to liner operators. The 11,000 TEU ship costs four times as much as the 1,200 ship but carries nine times as much cargo. As a result the ship costs fall from 54% to 34% of the total. In contrast, the cost of containers shown in section 2 does not benefit from economies of scale and increases from 3% of total cost for the 1,200 TEU ship to 5% for the 11,000 TEU ship (Table 13.8, row 2.4). Administration costs, shown in section 3 of Table 13.9, charged on each TEU shipped, range between 7% and 10%. Finally, the various cargo-handling and distribution costs do not benefit from economies of scale and their share of costs increases from 35% for the 1,200 TEU ship to 51% for the 11,000 TEU ship. Drawing these costs together, the average cost per TEU shown in row 5.4 falls from $1,299 for the 1,200 TEU vessel to $902 for the 11,000 TEU vessel.

The freight rate shown in section 6 of Table 13.9, which is based on actual rates in the transpacific trade in late 2006, is $1,750 per TEU on the outward leg and $750 per TEU on the return leg. These are published averages and for many lines the rates would be fixed at different levels under service agreements with bigger shippers. To put these rates into context, about 4,400 DVD recorders can be packed into a 20ft container, so the sea freight would be around 40 cents per unit. On the return voyage around 15,000 bottles of wine can be packed into a container, so the freight per bottle would be 5 cents.[41] Such low levels of transport costs have certainly contributed to the growth of global trade.

At these cargo levels the 1,200 TEU vessel makes a profit of $223,000, a 10% return, while the 11,000 TEU vessel makes a profit of $7.7 million and a return of 37%, so the big ships pay off handsomely – that is, provided the company can fill the ship. In reality, what generally happens is that liner companies order bigger ships, bid competitively for cargo to fill them and slowly the price per TEU falls towards average cost. Once the 11,000 TEU vessels are in service the freight rates fall progressively more slowly towards $810 per TEU, the average cost. This is bad news for any owners who try to hang on with their 1,200 TEU ships. At that freight rate they would lose heavily on the voyage. But for the companies with ships over 4,000 TEU the economies of scale are more marginal. For example, the 6,500 TEU ship makes 32% profit compared with 37% for the much bigger 11,000 TEU ship and in a business of this complexity it is hard to be sure whether this relatively small increase in margin is worth the various limitations imposed by using the bigger ship.

## Conclusion

In this section we have focused on costs and revenues for a range of different ship sizes and in Tables 13.8 and 13.9 looked at a simplified example of the economics of running a liner service. We found that although there are strong economies of scale in some aspects of the liner shipping business, especially in the ships and their operating costs, economies of scale are not so strong in other areas, especially the deployment of containers and the costs of container handling and through transport. Since these account for up to two-thirds of the total cost budget, the benefit of using bigger ships is heavily diluted and the analysis demonstrates that economies of scale diminish with size and are more evident below 4,000 TEU than above. This suggests that for larger vessels, considerations such as the volume of cargo expected to be transported now and in future; the shipowner's assessment of the operational merits of running a single string of, say, 12,000 TEU ships compared with two strings of 6,000 TEU ships; and the extent with which diseconomies of scale such as feedering can be overcome are likely to be more decisive than the bottom-line 'theoretical' profitability of the different sizes. Liner investment decisions are a tough call and making these judgements is precisely what shipping companies get paid for.

## 13.9 PRICING LINER SERVICES

### Practical aspects of liner pricing

Now we come to the question of pricing for liner services. Ultimately liner prices, like bulk freight rates, are determined by competition in the market place. Shipping is a business which companies may enter or leave as they wish. However, because of the large fixed overhead and the need to operate regular services, the price-making process is more complex than for the bulk industry and the procedures are constantly changing in response to competitive and regulatory pressures.

During the cargo liner era a centralized system was developed for handling pricing. Liner conferences conducted the price negotiations, usually with a central body representing the shippers, for example a shippers' council. They would meet regularly to negotiate rates and agree 'general rate increases'. Outsiders, whether a small or a large part of the trade, followed an independent pricing policy. The introduction of containerization has diluted this process. Conferences still exist, but the price-making has become less structured, passing to a variety of discussion agreements, alliances and negotiated service agreements.

Liner companies generally try to base their pricing policy on the dual principles of *price stability* and *price discrimination*. The desire for price stability is obvious. Liner companies have fixed overheads, so why not fix prices? Anyway, with so many customers, negotiating every price is not practical. Ideally, once prices are set, they should change only when there is some valid reason, such as a change in the cost of providing the service or a major change in the underlying unit costs. The case for commodity price discrimination is equally obvious. Charge higher rates for commodities which can bear the cost, and discount low value commodities to attract a wider range of cargoes than would be economic if there was a single standard freight charge. By increasing the volume, this permits larger ships and more regular sailings. In this way the pricing policy supports the provision of a better service package for all customers, though the role of cross-subsidization remains one of active debate. The second type of price discrimination is between customers. Large customers, with whom it is worth negotiating, can be offered special discounts through service agreements.

For many years liner companies would set tariff classes and produce a rate book listing the tariff class to which each commodity belonged. The freight rate for a cargo was worked out by looking up the tariff for the commodity in the rate book, multiplying by the amount to be shipped, say 209.5 cubic metres, calculating the total freight and adding any additionals. However, containerization undermined this system by commoditizing the trade. If the tariff worked out at $10,000 to ship a 20 ft container when the shipper knows that boxes are being shipped on the same service for $1,500, it is bound to cause price resistance[42] and many liner companies now charge a standard box rate or apply a 'freight all kinds' tariff. But the fact remains that some shippers are more price sensitive than others (see Chapter 2, Section 2.4). An auto parts distributor might value reliability and service more than the shipper of a price-sensitive product such as cellophane rolls who just wants the cheapest freight. In a business offering a differentiated transport product there is certainly a case for a degree of price discrimination, but this can only work if the product and the pricing system can be adapted to the client's needs. One response has been to transact far more business through service agreements negotiated with each the customer and to offer a range of value added services. Ultimately it is a matter of what the market will bear, and whether the companies can find a form of service differentiation that shippers will pay for.

Even with a 'freight all kinds' rate, the freight invoice often includes charges for services and costs regarded as 'additional' to the basic transport service. Typically the invoice is either sent to the customer after delivery, or settled in advance with additionals invoiced afterwards, and will include some or all of the following items:

- *Freight charges.* The charge for transporting the box or cargo. Sometimes the customer is quoted a 'door-to-door' rate, but often there are separate charges for port-to-port transport, and collection or delivery.
- *Sea freight additionals.* Surcharges to cover unbudgeted costs incurred by the liner company. The *bunker adjustment factor* covers unexpected increases in the cost of bunker fuel, which accounts for a major proportion of operating costs on long routes. The *currency adjustment factor* covers currency fluctuations. The currency adjustment factor is based on an agreed basket of costs and is designed to keep tariff revenue the same, regardless of changes between the tariff currency rates of exchange. *Port congestion surcharges* may be charged if a particular port becomes difficult to access due to congestion.
- *Terminal handling charges.* These are charged per container in local currency to cover the cost of handling the container in the port. Within a region, ports may have different charges. Some operators absorb such changes into the through freight rate.
- *Service additionals.* If the shipper undertakes additional services for the customer – for example, storage of goods, customs clearance or trans-shipment – there would be an additional charge for this.

• *Cargo additionals*. Some cargoes such as open-top containers or heavy lift, attract additional charges because they are difficult or expensive to transport.

As mentioned above, to simplify the charging process companies frequently negotiate service contracts with major customers, offering discounts on volume or other concessions (see Case 4 below).

## The principles of liner pricing

The principles of liner pricing can be illustrated with the supply–demand charts shown in Figures 13.13 and 13.14. Consider the case of competing liner companies, each operating a single ship, say a 4000 TEU container-ship which makes five trips a year. Each ship costs $40,000 per day to run, including capital, operating costs and bunkers, and it costs $400 to handle each container. When the ship is full, no additional cargo can be shipped. The vertical axis of each graph shows the price (freight rate) or cost in dollars per TEU, while the horizontal axis shows the number of boxes shipped per trip.

The liner company must charge a price that covers its costs. If this objective is not achieved, in due course it will go out of business. Costs may be fixed or variable. In this simplified case the $40,000 per day cost of the ship is a *fixed cost*[43] because the company is committed to running the

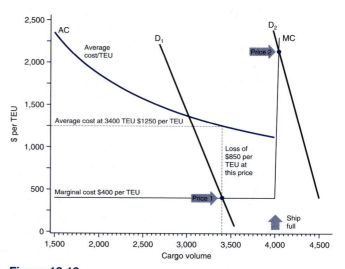

**Figure 13.13**
Liner pricing, Case 1: Marginal cost pricing
Source: Martin Stopford, 2006

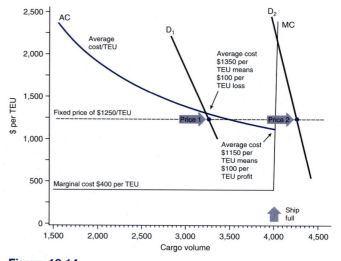

**Figure 13.14**
Liner pricing, Case 2: Fixed pricing
Source: Martin Stopford, 2006

service regardless of cargo volume, while the cargo-handling costs can be termed *variable costs* because these are not incurred if there is no cargo. This is a great simplification, but serves to illustrate the principle.

Because the company is already committed to the costs of the voyage, when the ship is part empty the only additional cost of accepting another container is the $400 per container cost of cargo handling. This is known as the *marginal cost* (MC). Once the ship is full the marginal cost rises sharply to, say, $2,500 per container, the cost of chartering another ship or hiring slots on another vessel. This is shown by the marginal cost curve (MC) in Figure 13.13. Note that the MC curve is horizontal at $400 from 1,500 TEU to 4,000 TEU when the ship is fully loaded; it then moves up vertically from $400 per TEU to $2,500 per TEU when the cargo load reaches 4,000 TEU. Also shown in Figure 13.13 is the average cost curve (AC), which shows, at each output level, the fixed and variable costs divided by the cargo volume. At low throughput levels the average cost is very high because a small number of containers must absorb the total cost of the ship. For example when the ship is only carrying 1,500 containers the average cost is $2,400 per TEU, but as the load factor increases the average cost falls steadily to $1,150 per TEU when the ship is full.

### CASE 1: MARGINAL COST PRICES

To make a profit, the liner company must generate enough revenue to cover the average cost. Figure 13.13 shows what happens in a free market (i.e. without conferences). When there is more shipping space than cargo, which is represented by the demand curve D1, the liner companies bid against each other for the available cargo. As they undercut each other the price falls to the marginal cost which in this example is $400 per TEU (i.e. the handling cost). At this price the cargo volume is 3,400 TEU, the point where the demand curve (D1) intersects the marginal cost curve. This is well below the average cost (AC) which at this throughput level is $1,250 per TEU, so the company makes a loss of $850 per container. With 3,400 containers to transport, that works out at a loss for the voyage of $2.9 million. When demand is high (D2) the price rises sharply to $2,250 per TEU as shippers bid for the limited 4,000 TEU capacity. At this volume the average cost is $1,150 per TEU, so the company makes a profit of $1,100 per container, which works out at $4.4 million on the voyage. To survive in a volatile market with prices determined by competition, the liner company must make enough profit during the good years to subsidize its operations during the bad years. In this case the profit of $4.4 million in the boom more than compensates for the $2.9 million loss in the recession, leaving a surplus of $1.5 million. Although cashflow will be very volatile, over time the entry and exit of liner companies should regulate the level of profit ensuring an adequate, but not excessive, return to efficient companies. That, at least, is the theory.

### CASE 2: FIXED PRICES

The alternative strategy is for liner companies to fix prices at a level which gives a reasonable margin over average cost. We see the consequences of this approach in

Figure 13.14 which has the same demand and supply curves. Suppose the company decides to impose a fixed price of $1,250 per TEU, shown by the dotted line. During the recession at a price of $1,250 per TEU demand falls to about 3,250 TEU (see the intercept between D1 and the fixed price curve). At this cargo volume the average cost is $1,350 per TEU, so the company makes a loss of $100 per TEU or $0.3 million on the voyage. During the boom (D2) at a price of $1,250 per TEU demand rises to 4,250 TEU (see the intercept between D2 and the price curve). Since the ship can only carry 4,000 TEU at an average cost of $1,150 per TEU, the voyage makes a profit of $100 per TEU or $0.4 million on the voyage. Thus at this price of $1,250 the company makes a net profit of $0.1 million on the two voyages, which is not as much as they would have made under the marginal cost pricing case. It seems they misjudged the price they should fix.

If the fixed prices are judged correctly and strictly maintained, this policy offers a practical way of stabilizing cashflow. The company makes a smaller loss during the recession and a smaller profit during the boom. Compared with the free market case, the cashflow cycles are reduced and customers have the benefit of stable prices. If there is free entry to the trade, the company does not end up making excess profits because new firms enter and existing firms expand capacity, wiping out the excess profits.

This is the positive side of price fixing. Making it work is an economist's nightmare. Fixed prices can only work if most shipowners comply with the policy, but during a recession with prices way above marginal cost, individual companies have a tremendous incentive to drop their prices and fill their own ships. Thus the 'price ring' is under continuous pressure. Even worse, during the boom there is a risk that outsiders will pile into the trade, soaking up the premium cargo at profitable prices, and the charter market for container-ships has made this much easier. If strict discipline cannot be enforced, the cartel is squeezed in both directions. Because each route is just a small island in a sea of liner capacity, efforts to enforce discipline from within or without are easily frustrated.

A simplified example illustrates the problem. Suppose there are three ships in a service, two in a conference (i.e. cartel) and the third an 'outsider'. Trade is depressed with only enough cargo to load 3,250 TEU per ship, and this demand level is fixed, that is, not price sensitive. If the conference holds, each ship charges a fixed price of $1,250 per TEU and loads 3,250 TEU, making a small loss of $100 per container on the voyage. If, however, the outsider offers a price of $1150 per TEU, the whole picture changes. At this price he will win enough cargo to fill his 4,000 TEU ship, so his average cost falls to $1,150 per container and he breaks even. But the conference members are left with only 2,875 TEU each (i.e. there is potentially 9,750 TEU cargo and the outsider takes 4,000 TEU, leaving 5,750 TEU for the two conference ships to share). With only 2,875 TEU per ship their average cost increases to $1,450 per TEU, but the rate is now $1,150 per TEU, so they lose $300 per TEU. They have been mugged by the outsider and there is nothing they can do about it. The examples we have considered so far relate to market cycles. Exactly the same principles apply to seasonal cycles or trade imbalances. This is a good example of a situation known in game theory as the Prisoner's Dilemma.[44]

## CASE 3: PRICE DISCRIMINATION

The third pricing option is *price discrimination*. One of the benefits of marginal cost pricing is that flexible prices help to coordinate cargo volume with the available capacity. Thus the low price during the recession in Figure 13.13 draws in marginal cargoes such as waste paper, hay or building-blocks, helping to fill up empty ships and generate extra revenue. As a result the cargo volume in the recession is 3,400 TEU compared with only 3,250 when the price is fixed at $1,250 per TEU. Conversely, during booms, high prices discourage cargo that will not bear the high freight rates, and the scarce capacity is taken by priority cargo, whereas the fixed price leaves the liner company with demand for 4,250 TEU, but only 4,000 slots. From this viewpoint flexible prices bring a positive benefit to the shipper and the liner company. One way to get the best of both worlds is to offer different prices for each commodity. Economists refer to this approach as price discrimination, and it is widely used in the transport system (e.g. business class versus economy class on the airlines). Low-value cargoes are offered cheap transport to fill empty capacity, while higher-value cargoes are charged a premium. Commodity price discrimination was widely used by cargo liner companies, though it has become more difficult since containerization has standardized the physical cargo. This aspect of pricing is particularly relevant to the containerization of minor bulk cargoes. Price discrimination can also be applied to customers. For example, special rates may be offered to customers who have large volumes of cargo. With all price discrimination the key is ensuring that the marginal revenue obtained from the cargo fully compensates the company for the cost of the service, including such hidden costs as repositioning containers. This is known as 'yield management'.

## CASE 4: SERVICE CONTRACTS

As containerization reduced the opportunities for price discrimination, a fourth pricing option emerged, the service contract. This approach builds on the fact that large shippers have as much interest in stability as the liner companies and uses a negotiated service contracts to fix price and volume guidelines. Initially this approach raised anti-trust issues, especially in the US trades, but the US Ocean Shipping Reform Act (1999) gave shippers the right to confidential service agreements and private shipper service contracts were widely adopted. However, a survey published three years later suggested that the level of definition of these contracts is generally very low. Only 44% of the respondents had a formal freight contract, the rest relying on informal arrangements and 'referring to conference [general rate increases] in various trades, instead of setting a rate for the movement of containers from A to B'.[45]

## 13.10 LINER CONFERENCES AND COOPERATIVE AGREEMENTS

The economic analysis in the previous section suggests that the managers of liner companies are 'between a rock and a hard place' in trying to meet the varying needs of a diverse customer base whilst operating regular schedules with relatively inflexible strings of ships and at the same time cover a sizeable administrative overhead. In free market trade cycles, seasonal cycles and trade imbalances produce volatile revenues. Living with a volatile cashflow is not particularly attractive and since they are in a position to form cartels this is an obvious strategy. As we have seen, efforts to take over from the market and 'manage' prices or capacity present great problems. But Figure 13.14 showed why economic forces do not favour stable liner price cartels. Companies which break the price ring reap such handsome profits at the expense of the cartel members that restraint never lasts long, especially in the age of containerization. With bank managers to pay, shareholder pressure for higher returns, or a government sponsor keen to see its domestic shipping company take a bigger share of the trade, there are too many temptations. In an industry where the barriers to entry are low, rate stability must be the exception rather than the rule.

Despite these difficulties, the quest continues. Over the years managers in the liner business have come up with a bewildering array of solutions. Some have concentrated on the revenue side, seeking to fix prices for the whole trade, often supported by a complex arrangement of loyalty rebates, commodity discounts, service agreements offering special rates to major clients, and other devices designed to blend fixed pricing with a degree of flexibility. Others have tackled capacity, attempting to strike at the root of the problem by fixing trade shares so that companies cannot compete for each other's cargo. From time to time there have been inter-company agreements to share shipping space and increase flexibility. Some major companies prefer independence and the free market, but one way or another most end up seeking ways to restrict market forces. In the next section we discuss these arrangements. Because they are constantly changing they are not easy to analyse or classify. We briefly review their history, more as an illustration of what can happen than as a definitive account of the system.

## Liner conferences

The *conference system*, which was developed in the mid-1870s, was the industry's first attempt to deal with the pricing problem. The major British shipping companies such as P&O, Alfred Holt and Glen Line, which set up the first liner services to the Far East in the early 1870s, found that, from the outset, competition was forcing tariffs to levels that would not cover their average costs. They faced all the problems mentioned in the previous section. There was overcapacity due to overbuilding; the trades were highly seasonal, particularly in agricultural products such as tea, so for part of the year the ships were only half full; and there was also an imbalance between the east-bound and the west-bound trade with the demand for shipping space to China falling short of the demand from China.[46] As a result, there was often more shipping capacity than cargo. Of course none of this was new. What had changed was the organization of the business. Because the newly emerging liner companies were operating in the same trades they were in a much better position to form a cartel to fix rates so that, in the words of John Swire, 'the companies may not ruin each other'.[47]

The first conference was formed in August 1875 by the lines trading between the United Kingdom and Calcutta. It was agreed to charge similar rates, to limit the number of sailings, to grant no preferences or concessions to any shippers and to sail on a given date regardless of whether they had a full load of cargo.[48] However, because of the over-tonnaging situation, this simply resulted in the major shippers, particularly the powerful Manchester merchants, threatening to use vessels outside the conference that would offer lower rates.[49] A custom already existed that the charge made for the use of ship's gear in loading and unloading was remitted to merchants who shipped regularly with the same company. In 1877 the conference used this as the basis for a rebate system. A reduction in rates of 10% was made to merchants who shipped exclusively with the conference for a period of six months, but the rebate was not paid until a further six months had elapsed, during which time the loyalty rebate was forfeit if the merchant used a ship owned by a firm not a member of the conference.[50] This meant that any shipper tempted by the cut-price rates of non-conference operators stood to lose a very substantial sum if they accepted.

This was only the beginning. Over the next century there was a constantly evolving network of agreements covering rates, the number of sailings, the ports served, the goods carried, and the sharing of freight revenues ('pool' agreements). *Closed* conferences control membership, share cargo and use price discrimination to encourage the major shippers to ship exclusively with the conference. For example, regular shippers might be charged a lower 'contract' rate, with a higher rate for shippers who sometimes used outsiders. The 'deferred rebate' developed in the Calcutta trade was also used. Loyal shippers receive a cash rebate, say 9.5%. *Open* conferences allow any company to join provided they comply with the rate agreements. Members are thus guaranteed the prices set by the conference but, since there is no control on the number of ships in service, open conferences are more vulnerable to over-tonnaging. By the early 1970s there were more than 360 conferences with membership varying from two to 40 shipping lines[51] and thirty years later in 2002, despite the inroads made by containerization, there were still 150 liner conferences operating world-wide, again with membership ranging from two to as many as 40 separate lines.[52]

However, the market changes which accompanied containerization, particularly the standardization of the market and global competition, weakened the industry's ability to enforce price cartels, and regulatory authorities have become less sympathetic to the arguments for exempting conferences from anti-trust legislation. As a result attention switched to strategies for reducing unit costs through consortia, alliances, and mergers which are acceptable to the regulatory authorities. A discussion of these issues can be found in Section 16.12.

## Global alliances

By the late 1980s the conference system had become seriously weakened,[53] and although efforts to resolve the pricing problem continued as actively as a century earlier, to the general disapproval of regulatory authorities, the industry changed its strategy. On the Pacific route a series of stabilization agreements were developed, no longer called conferences, the first being the Trans Pacific Discussion Agreement (TPDA). On the Atlantic the Trans Atlantic Agreement (TAA) subsequently became the

Trans Atlantic Conference Agreement (TACA). In the mid-1990s about 60% of the liner capacity on the major routes belonged to this sort of conference system, though the modern open conferences are very different from the tightly controlled closed conferences of the 1950s. Some act mainly as secretariats to the trades, administering rate agreements and dealing with the various regulatory bodies. In 2007 the two main conferences were the TSA (Transpacific Stabilisation Agreement) and the FEFC (Far East Freight Conference), but there were still many conferences covering smaller trades.

These arrangements, which we have already discussed in Section 13.6, are in many ways the industry's response to the changing requirements of containerized liner services. Unlike the old liner system which focused on individual routes, today competition is global and some of the larger companies develop alliances under which the members continue to run their own commercial operations, whilst sharing the management of services and container deployment. The Alliance agreements generally cover three main areas. Firstly, the service schedules including the type and size of vessel to be employed on each route; itineraries and sailing schedules; and ports and port rotations. Secondly, the various support services including chartering of ships; use of joint terminals; the management of containers; feeder services and the coordination of inland services. Thirdly, there may be restrictions on the activities of members such as the use of third-party carriers on specific routes subject to the consent of members and measures for capacity to deal with shortages and surpluses. This allows the members to use their combined size to improve the efficiency of global operations. The agreements do not generally cover sales, marketing or pricing, which are left to the individual members, as are invoicing and bills of lading. Ships continue to be owned and operated by the member companies which retain their own individual management functions.

## Principles for regulating liner competition

Since the beginning of liner services in the 1870s there has always been criticism of conferences by shippers' organizations, but a degree of cooperation between carriers was tolerated. There were several reasons for this, and a detailed study of liner shipping competition by the OECD in 2001 examined the economic evidence. It concluded that the underlying economics of the liner business were not fundamentally different from other transport sectors and that in fact the industry had become more competitive as conference power weakened and carriers turned to more flexible alliances aimed at gaining greater operational efficiency.[54] As a framework for designing the best solution they identified three issues:

- Freedom to negotiate. Rates, surcharges and other terms of carriage in liner shipping should be freely negotiated between shippers and carriers on an individual and confidential basis.
- Freedom to protect contracts. Carriers and shippers should be able to contractually protect key terms in negotiated service contracts including information regarding rates.

- Freedom to coordinate operations. Carriers should be able to pursue operational agreements with other carriers so long as these do not include price fixing or conferring market power on the parties involved.

If followed, these principles would, they argued, help to establish the right and equitable balance between the market power of shippers and shipowners. The regulation of liner shipping is discussed in Section 16.10.

In October 2008 the EU's repeal of regulation 4056/86 which removed the liner industry's block exemption from Articles 81 and 82 of the Treaty of Rome will take effect and conferences will be subject to these regulations. This change in the regulations governing liner services operating in and out of the EU will have a major impact on conferences such as the Far East Freight Conference. The regulatory issues are discussed in Section 16.10.

## 13.11 CONTAINER PORTS AND TERMINALS

### Port calls and liner pricing

Containerization changed the way the liner business managed its port itineraries. Previously cargo liners operated a port-to-port service, 'equalizing' prices by charging the same rate for all ports on their itinerary. Because shippers paid for the journey to and from the port they had an incentive to use a liner service which called at the local port. Each port had its own catchment area and to win a share of this cargo, liner services had to include that port on their itinerary. This pricing system encouraged lengthy itineraries and much duplication of port calls.

When containerization was introduced, the pricing system changed. Because the liner companies gained control of the land transport they could plan and adopt the itinerary which gave the cheapest overall unit transport cost. The result was to channel trade through fewer ports, each major port having a greatly enlarged catchment area. It also led to new competition between the ports to attract liner services. Choosing a port itinerary involves a trade-off between the cost of the call and the revenue obtained from providing a direct service to and from the port. Then there is the possibility of setting up intermediate distribution points to serve a third area. For example, the Arabian Gulf might be served by a feeder service from Jeddah in the Red Sea. In fact, we can define two levels of service:[55]

- *Load centres (base ports)*. These have a regular service with frequent loading and discharge of cargoes. The shipper is guaranteed a regular service at a fixed tariff, whether they are served directly or not. For example, Antwerp will attract the same rate as Rotterdam, even if the ship does not call there.
- *Feeder ports (outports)*. Some ports are not included in the normal service because they do not handle sufficient cargo to make this cost-effective. However, in order to

discharge their obligation to 'meet the requirements of the trade', the company accepts cargo at outports and provides a feeder service to a base port. These cargoes will be charged extra.

## The port infrastructure

Although there are currently about 400 ports which have a significant throughput of containers, the top 60 handle 98% of the throughput. Many countries now have only one or two major container ports serving the deep-sea trades, supported by a range of smaller ports handling short-sea and distribution trade. Table 13.10 lists the 36 most important container ports in 2005, organized by region. Between them these ports handled 194 million TEU in 2005, about 60% of the total container lifts, and between 1994 and 2005 their trade grew at 9.4% per annum. Interestingly the Middle East grew fastest with 13.4% growth per annum, followed by Asia at 9.6%, Europe slightly more slowly at 9.1% and North America fourth at 8.9%. The two largest container ports, Hong Kong and Singapore, each handled over 20 million TEU in 2005, acting as regional distribution centres for the predominantly maritime Asian distribution system. Shanghai was catching up fast and showed the fastest cargo growth of any port over the decade.

Container terminals generally have several berths, each served by one or more large cranes capable of lifting 40 tons. In an adjacent storage area the containers are stored to await collection. To carry the weight of the container crane it is generally necessary to strengthen the quay to support the container cranes. Several types of container terminal have been developed to meet differing requirements. One system is to lift the container off the ship on to a trailer chassis, which is then moved to a storage park to await collection. This has the advantage that the container is handled only once and it interfaces efficiently with the road haulage system. Its main drawback is that it uses a large amount of land and there is a significant investment in trailers. Where land is at a premium, containers could be stacked up to five high, using a system of gantry cranes which may also be used on the quayside, but the disadvantages of this system are the difficulty of obtaining random access to containers in the stack and the cost of multiple handling of individual units. The compromise is to stack containers two or three high, using 'straddle carriers', large fork-lift trucks or low loaders to move them from the quayside to the stack and retrieve them when required. In small ports an area of the quayside is often allocated for container storage.

In the advanced industrial areas of Europe, North America and the Far East, containerization has channelled trade through a small number of ports that have invested in high-productivity container terminals of the type outlined above. In the developing countries the problem is more complex, since the inland infrastructure is often not sufficiently developed to handle a sophisticated container network. As we saw in the example of the West Africa trade, cargo is not exclusively containerized. In such cases, even small ports need to be equipped to handle containers. This generally involves developing an existing berth for container handling, undertaking any necessary strengthening of the quay, the purchase of a suitable crane, often a mobile unit, and

**Table 13.10** Container traffic of 36 major ports, 1994 and 2005

| World rank 2005 | Country | | Traffic (lifts) M TEU | | | Region |
|---|---|---|---|---|---|---|
| | | | 1994 | 2005 | % pa | |
| | **Asia** | | | | | |
| 1 | Singapore | Singapore | 9.0 | 23.2 | 8.6% | Asia |
| 2 | Hong Kong | Hong Kong | 9.2 | 22.4 | 8.1% | Asia |
| 3 | Shanghai | PRC | 0.9 | 18.1 | 27.3% | Asia |
| 4 | Busan | S. Korea | 3.1 | 11.8 | 12.2% | Asia |
| 5 | Kaohsiung | Taiwan | 4.6 | 9.5 | 6.5% | Asia |
| 12 | Port Kelang | Malaysia | 0.8 | 5.5 | 17.9% | Asia |
| 15 | Tokyo | Japan | 1.5 | 3.6 | 7.7% | Asia |
| 16 | Tanjung Priok | Indonesia | 1.0 | 3.3 | 10.8% | Asia |
| 18 | Yokohama | Japan | 2.2 | 2.9 | 2.6% | Asia |
| 21 | Manila | Phillipines | 1.3 | 2.7 | 6.8% | Asia |
| 22 | Colombo | Sri Lanka | 0.9 | 2.5 | 9.6% | Asia |
| 23 | Nagoya | Japan | 1.2 | 2.3 | 6.3% | Asia |
| 25 | Kobe | Japan | 2.7 | 2.3 | -1.5% | Asia |
| 27 | Keelung | Taiwan | 1.9 | 2.1 | 1.1% | Asia |
| 33 | Bangkok | Thailand | 1.3 | 1.3 | 0.6% | Asia |
| | Total Asia | | 41.3 | 113.4 | 9.2% | |
| | **W. Europe** | | | | | |
| 6 | Rotterdam | Netherlands | 4.2 | 9.3 | 7.6% | Europe |
| 7 | Hamburg | Germany | 2.5 | 8.1 | 11.3% | Europe |
| 11 | Antwerp | Belgium | 1.9 | 6.5 | 11.9% | Europe |
| 14 | Bremerhaven | Germany | 1.4 | 3.7 | 9.7% | Europe |
| 17 | Algeciras | Spain | 0.8 | 3.2 | 13.2% | Europe |
| 20 | Felixstowe | UK | 1.6 | 2.7 | 4.6% | Europe |
| 26 | Le Havre | France | 0.9 | 2.1 | 8.1% | Europe |
| 36 | La Spezia | Italy | 0.8 | 1.0 | 2.5% | Europe |
| | Total Europe | | 14.0 | 36.6 | 9.1% | |
| | **Middle East** | | | | | |
| 8 | Dubai | UAE | 1.7 | 7.6 | 14.7% | Middle East |
| 19 | Jeddah | Saudi Arabia | 0.9 | 2.9 | 10.6% | Middle East |
| | Total Middle East | | 2.6 | 10.5 | 13.4% | |
| | **North America** | | | | | |
| 9 | Los Angeles | USA | 2.4 | 7.5 | 11.0% | N.America |
| 10 | Long Beach | USA | 2.1 | 6.7 | 11.3% | N.America |
| 13 | New York | USA | 2.0 | 4.8 | 8.4% | N.America |
| 24 | Oakland | USA | 1.3 | 2.3 | 5.2% | N.America |
| 28 | Seattle | USA | 1.2 | 2.1 | 5.6% | N.America |
| 29 | Tacoma | USA | 1.1 | 2.1 | 6.2% | N.America |
| 30 | Charleston | USA | 0.8 | 2.0 | 8.1% | N.America |
| 31 | Hampton Roads | USA | 0.8 | 2.0 | 8.8% | N.America |
| | Total N. America | | 11.6 | 29.4 | 8.9% | |
| | **Other** | | | | | |
| 32 | Melbourne | Australia | 0.7 | 1.9 | 9.3% | Oceania |
| 34 | San Juan | Puerto Rico | 1.6 | 1.3 | −1.8% | S. America |
| 35 | Honolulu | USA | 0.7 | 1.1 | 3.5% | N.America |
| | Total container lifts by 36 ports | | 72.5 | 194.0 | 9.4% | |

Source: CRSL, *Containerisation International*

straddle carriers or fork-lift trucks and the provision of a container-packing service for break-bulk cargo not delivered to the port in a container. The containers are then stacked in a suitable location.

## 13.12 SUMMARY

As we have seen in this chapter, liner companies carry 'general cargo' and operate in a market which has all the competitive edge of the bulk shipping market, but with two major differences which alter the market and the competitive process. First, the need to run a regular service makes liner capacity inflexible. Second, with so many customers, price negotiation is more restricted. With these restrictions the free market mechanism which regulates the bulk shipping market takes on a very different character in the liner business. When we examine the economic principles, we find that free market pricing would lead to a highly volatile cashflow, but that a system of fixed prices is difficult to enforce. That, in essence, has been the problem faced by the liner industry throughout its 125-year history.

Our review of the evolution of the liner business demonstrated the changes containerization has brought to the business, and we examined the global market model which now provides the framework for trade. This network of services is constantly changing to meet the needs of trade. The major liner routes, known as the East–West trades, operate between the three industrial centres of North America, western Europe and Asia. These are supplemented by a complex matrix of North–South trades serving the various developing countries. At the margin are the small services designed to meet particular local needs. A highly flexible supply system has evolved to service these trades involving alliances, space chartering arrangements and a charter market for the ships which grew from almost nothing in the early 1990s to over half the capacity in 2006.

Our review of the demand for liner services concluded that the 'commodity analysis' used to analyse the demand for bulk carriers is less appropriate as a methodology for the liner trades. There are so many commodities and so few statistics that detailed commodity analysis can hardly be expected to succeed. More importantly, the demand for liner transport is not determined by regional imbalances in supply and demand, but by the relative price and availability of goods. If a manufacturer in England can source more cheaply from Taiwan than from Scotland, he will choose Taiwan. In this sense the growth of demand depends on cost differences within the world economy, while inter-company competition revolves around a range of factors including price, speed, reliability and the quality of service.

The general cargo trade is carried by a fleet of ships comprising container ships, MPP vessels, 'tweendeckers, traditional cargo liners and ro-ros. Some of these vessels are designed to meet specific trading needs, while others are left over from another shipping era, serving out their useful lives. The whole liner business is supported by an extensive network of port facilities, ranging from the 'super-terminals' in Rotterdam, Hong Kong and Singapore to the many minor local ports which serve the feeder trades.

We examined the structure of liner costs and identified eight 'building-blocks' which contribute to the economics of a liner service: the ship characteristics, the service schedule, capacity utilization, ship cost per day, port charges, deployment of containers, container costs and administrative costs. The choices made by the liner company for each of these determines the cost profile of the operation. On the revenue side, the key principles are price stability and price discrimination. The pricing system, which involves differing degrees of discrimination by commodity and owner, has now been substantially modified by the widespread use of service contracts negotiated bilaterally between carriers and shippers.

The lessons from the liner business are simple enough. By using containers to mechanize the transport of general cargo, it has, in Adam Smith's words 'opened the whole world to a market for the produce of every sort of labour'. The financial return to liner companies may not be spectacular, but their contribution to the global trading economy is beyond question.

# Part 5

# THE MERCHANT FLEET AND TRANSPORT SUPPLY

# 14 The Ships that Provide the Transport

*Managers may believe that industry structures are ordained by the Good Lord, but they can – and often do – change overnight. Such changes create tremendous opportunities for innovation.*

(Peter Drucker, *The Profession of Management*, 1998, p. 58)

## 14.1 WHAT TYPE OF SHIP?

### The derived demand for ships

So far we have said much about shipping economics, but little about the ships themselves. A ship is a major investment, and with a wealth of different types and sizes on offer, investors are confronted with the difficult question of what type of ship to order. To help them in their decisions, they often ask shipping economists what will be the future demand, for example, for container-ships. The aim of this chapter is to discuss the different types of merchant ships and how their design features fit into the economic model discussed in Chapter 4.

First we must be clear about the meaning of *demand*. Although ships occupy centre stage, the product in demand is not a ship, but transport. It is not the container-ship that the customer wants; it is the transport of the container. Shipowners can use whatever ships provide the transport most profitably. Unfortunately this makes the shipping economist's job much more difficult. If containers could only be carried in container-ships, all the shipping economist would have to do is predict the trade in containers and work out the number of container-ships needed to carry the trade. But with several ship types available to carry the cargo which travels in containers, the demand calculation involves two additional questions. What options are open to the shipowner? And what economic criteria apply in choosing between them?

The answer depends on the type of shipping venture for which the vessel is intended. Although there are many different influences to consider, the most important can be summarized under the three following headings:

- *Cargo type.* The physical and commercial properties of the cargo to be transported set a limit on the ship types that can potentially be employed in the transport operation.

In a limited number of cases, such as liquid natural gas or nuclear waste, the cargo demands a specific type of ship, and the shipowner's choice is limited to general design and operating features such as speed and crew. For most cargoes, however, the shipowner can choose from several ship types. Crude oil can be carried in a specialist tanker or a combined carrier; dry bulk can be carried in a conventional bulk carrier, an open-hold bulk carrier or a combined carrier; containers in a container-ship, a 'tweendecker, an MPP vessel or a ro-ro.

- *Type of shipping operation.* In the previous paragraph we assumed that the shipowner knows the precise type of cargo to be carried, but in practice his knowledge of both the cargo and other physical operating constraints will depend upon the type of shipping operation for which the vessel is intended. There are several different types of shipping operation, for example: *long-term charters*, where the shipowner has some knowledge from the charterer of the cargoes to be carried and the ports to be used; *spot charter market operations*, where the owner has only a general idea of the type of cargo to be carried and no knowledge of the ports to be visited; and *liner operations*, where the owner has a specific knowledge of the ports to be visited and the likely cargo volume, but where both may change during the operational life of the vessel. The design criteria for a shipowner choosing a vessel for a long-term time charter are likely to be quite different from those for the owner intending to trade on the spot market. For example, the former will be preoccupied with optimizing the ship to a specific operation, whereas the latter will be more concerned with such factors as the vessel's acceptability to charterers, and its short-term resale value.

- *Commercial philosophy.* The way in which the shipowner or shipping company approaches the business may extend or limit the range of options. For example, one shipping company may prefer vessels that are highly flexible, servicing a number of different markets and thereby reducing the risk. This philosophy might lead the shipowner to prefer a more expensive open-hold bulk carrier, which can carry both dry bulk cargo and containers. Another owner may follow a policy of specialization, preferring a vessel that is in every respect designed for the efficient carriage of a single cargo, offering greater efficiency or lower costs but at the price of less flexibility.

It follows that shipping economists cannot forecast the demand for a particular type of ship just by studying cargo movements. In the real world the choice of a particular ship type depends on all three factors – cargo type, shipping operation and commercial philosophy. This makes it difficult to predict which factors will predominate in the final decision. Market research techniques of the type discussed in Chapter 17 will certainly form part of this process, as will fashion and market sentiment.

## The fleet by ship type

Since few ships are truly identical, one problem in discussing ship design is the sheer number of vessels involved.[1] So our first task is to classify the designs into types with common features, which we do in Figure 14.1. The world's 74,398 maritime vessels (Table 2.5) are first divided into the three groups of structures operating on the oceans: cargo shipping (group 1), offshore oil and gas structures (group 2) and non-cargo ships (group 3). Cargo ships, our main focus here, are split into four sectors based on economic activity: general cargo transport; dry bulk transport; oil and chemical transport; and liquid gas transport. At the third level the merchant ship sectors are divided into 19 ship types based on the physical design of the hull: for example, tankers have tanks, bulk carriers have holds and vehicle carriers have multiple decks designed to carry as many cars as possible. If this were a technical book we would probably stop there, but as economists we must recognize a fourth level of segmentation by ship size. Size restrictions on terminal facilities and waterways such as the Panama Canal divide ships of a particular type into segments.

This chapter is organized around the four sectors of the merchant fleet which transport general cargo, dry bulk, oil and chemicals, liquid gas, with a short section on non-cargo carrying vessels (see Figure 14.1). There are seven general cargo types, six dry bulk types, four oil and chemical types, two liquid gas types and four non-cargo types. Looking over this figure and Table 14.1, which shows how 19 segments of the fleet grew between 1990 and 2006 gives a sense of the way the ship type structure of the fleet is constantly changing. Between 1990 and 2006 the world fleet grew at an average of 2.7%

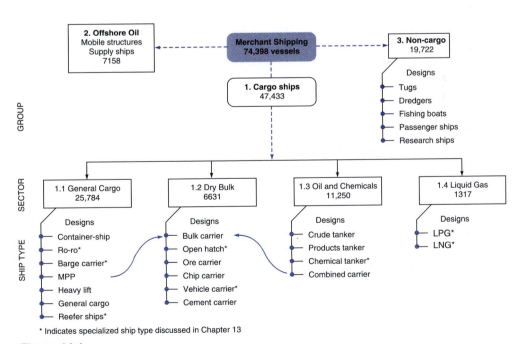

**Figure 14.1**
The commercial shipping fleet, 1 July 2007, classified by group, sector and ship type
Source: Ship numbers from Table 2.5

**Table 14.1** World cargo fleet showing growth rates 1990–2006 of 19 ship type segments

| | No. | Design Start | Fleet m.dwt 1990[a] | Fleet m.dwt 2006 | Number 2006 | Growth 1990–2006[b] | Key design issues |
|---|---|---|---|---|---|---|---|
| **1. General cargo** | 1 | 100–999 TEU | 5 | 9 | 1,167 | 4.2% | Slow, geared |
| Container | | 1,000–2,999 TEU | 17 | 41 | 1,659 | 5.8% | Faster, some geared |
| | | 3,000 + TEU | 4 | 61 | 1,113 | 18.0% | Fast (25 kts), no gear |
| | | Total container | 26 | 111 | 3,939 | 9.4% | |
| | 2 | Ro-ro | 7 | 9 | 1,109 | 2.1% | Ramp access to holds |
| | 3 | MPP | 17 | 23 | 2,533 | 2.0% | Open hatch, cargo gear |
| | 6 | Heavy lift | — | 1 | 53 | | 53 ships, excludes MMPs |
| | 4 | Barge carriers | | | 6 | | |
| | 5 | Gen. cargo | 27 | 11 | 1,024 | −5.3% | Includes liner types and tramps |
| | 7 | Reefer | 7 | 7 | 1,237 | −0.1% | Refrigerated, palletized |
| | | Total liner | 84 | 163 | 9,901 | 4.2% | |
| **2. Dry Bulk** | 8 | Capesize | 48 | 111 | 703 | 5.4% | Carry ore and coal |
| Bulk carrier | | Panamax | 43 | 94 | 1,386 | 5.1% | Coal, grain, few geared |
| | | Handymax | 31 | 67 | 1,488 | 5.0% | Workhorse, mainly geared |
| | | Handy | 82 | 74 | 2,762 | −0.7% | Smaller workhorse |
| *of which:* | 9 | Open hatch | — | 17 | 481 | | Designed for unit loads |
| | 10 | Ore carrier | 9 | 9 | 51 | −0.4% | Low cubic (0.6 m$^3$/tonne)) |
| | 11 | Chip carrier | — | 6 | 129 | | High cubic (2 m$^3$/tonne) |
| | 12 | Vehicle carrier | 4 | 8 | 594 | 4.2% | Multiple decks |
| | 13 | Cement carrier | | | 77 | | |
| | | Total dry bulk | 203 | 345 | 6,339 | 3.4% | |
| **3. Liquid Bulk** | 14 | VLCC | 114 | 143 | 483 | 1.4% | Long-haul crude oil |
| Crude | | Suezmax | 35 | 54 | 350 | 2.8% | Medium-haul crude |
| | | Aframax | 38 | 73 | 705 | 4.2% | Some carry products |
| | | Panamax | 14 | 23 | 305 | 3.0% | Very short haul |
| | | Handy | 50 | 76 | 2,414 | 2.6% | Mainly products |
| | | Total oil | 243 | 368 | 4,257 | 2.6% | |
| *of which:* | 15 | Products tanker | | 49 | 1,196 | | Some overlap with chemicals |
| | 16 | Specialized tanker | 10 | 41 | 2,517 | 9.1% | More tanks and pumps |
| | 17 | Oil/bulk/ore | 32 | 10 | 95 | −7.2% | dry and wet |
| | 18 | LPG | 7 | 11 | 1,030 | 3.2% | Several freezing systems |
| | 19 | LNG | 4 | 17.5 | 222 | 9.3% | −161°C |
| **World Fleet** | | | 573.1 | 914.7 | | 2.9% | |

[a]Container-ship dwt 1990 estimated from TEU statistics

[b]To show the growth rate since 1990 it was necessary to use slightly different statistical groupings from those shown in Figure 14.1 and Table 2.5.

Source: Clarkson Registers April 2006 and Shipping Review and Outlook Spring 2007, CRS, London

per annum, but the growth rate differed significantly between segments. The container-ship fleet averaged 9.4% per annum whilst the general cargo fleet declined at 5.3% per annum, so the liner fleet as a whole averaged 4.2% growth. In the bulk carrier segment the bigger sizes grew at about 5% per annum whilst the fleets of small bulk carriers and ore carriers both declined, so the dry bulk fleet averaged 3.4%. The tanker fleet grew even more slowly, averaging 2.6% per annum, with Aframax tankers showing the fastest growth and the VLCC fleet the slowest. The specialized fleets all grew at very different rates, with LNG tankers expanding fastest and the reefer fleet declining. All of which demonstrates the dynamic way the fleet structure evolves over time in response to the changing trade flows. This makes selecting the right type even more tricky.

## 14.2 SEVEN QUESTIONS THAT DEFINE A DESIGN

Broadly speaking, each ship is a bundle of features blended to achieve a specific objective, but, for the reasons discussed in the last section, the design parameters are not always clear-cut and designing a ship is not a precise science that can be reduced to purely economic criteria. Benford develops this point in the following way:

> Whether we use computers, hand held calculators, or backs of envelopes one rule applies: the decision will be made by some person, or group of persons, and will not hinge simply on the best numerical projection of some measure of merit. Like nearly all else in our business, there is art as well as science in this. Indeed – and roughly speaking – the more important the decision the greater is the reliance upon art. That is what makes ship design so fascinating.[2]

On this theme, before looking at individual ship types, it is helpful to review seven questions analysts should ask when defining the particular bundle of features the investor needs.

### How will the ship be traded?

The first question to ask is why the investor wants the ship. There may be lots of clever technology available which naval architects can use to produce the perfect ship, but investors have their own objectives. For example, they often value simplicity and robustness over technical perfection, in which case designing their ships is about optimizing commercial rather than technical performance. Clever and innovative technical designs make great conference papers but have a patchy history in the practical world of commercial shipping.

Anyway, investors often have only a rough idea about the type of cargo to be carried. If there is a *long-term charter* the shipowner probably knows the likely cargoes to be carried and possibly the ports to be used, but if the ship is to trade on the *spot market* there will be only a general idea of the type of cargo to be carried and no knowledge of the ports to be visited. In this case the investor is more interested in such factors as the vessel's acceptability to charterers and its short-term resale value. Ships built for *liner services* can often be designed for the particular route and tailored in such areas as reefer capacity, but these things change during the operational life of the vessel and container-ships are increasingly commoditized. The following examples illustrate some of the different angles from which investors may approach commissioning a new ship:

*Example 1*. A steel plant purchasing an iron ore carrier to service a long-term iron ore supply contract between Brazil and China. In this case, the cargo, the cargo volume and the trade route are all known in advance, and the ship will be dedicated to the trade over its life, so the design can be optimized to the shipping operation in terms of the cargo to be carried, the parcel size, the ports to be utilized and the opportunities for exploiting economies of scale. In addition, since the vessel is to be operated over a number of years, the shipowner is likely to take a close interest in any technology that will reduce operating costs – for example, automation and fuel-saving equipment.

*Example 2*. A dry bulk carrier operator purchasing a bulk carrier to trade on the voyage charter market. In this case, the shipowner has only a general idea of the cargoes and ports that the vessel will be required to service. Depending upon his style of operation, he may choose a small ship that can access many ports, or a larger ship that will be more competitive in some of the major bulk commodity trades. In particular, he wants the ship to be attractive to charterers, with a good resale value even after a short time. For this reason, a well-established standard design may be of interest and design features such as fuel saving equipment will only be of interest if they add to the ship's value in the second-hand market, which many do not.

*Example 3*. A company planning investment in a specialist bulk market such as motor vehicles or forest products may not have a precise future operating pattern, but will know what cargo features are needed to reduce operating costs and improve the service. This may lead to the design of a completely different type of ship such as a vehicle carrier, or a sophisticated version of a standard ship such as a forest products carrier. In such cases, the cargo figures prominently in the ship design, as do the range of ports, terminals and cargo-handling facilities servicing this particular trade.

Design sophistication comes at a price which makes it risky, and the preceding examples illustrate that investors have different requirements which determine how closely the ship is optimized to a particular cargo or trade route.

## What cargo will the ship carry?

Cargoes come in all shapes and sizes. Some, like grain, are homogeneous whilst others, such as logs or steel products, consist of large regular or irregular units that present the ship designer with a different challenge. This is not just about the commodity, because the same commodity can be transported in many different ways. For example, china clay can be loaded into bags transported loose, on a pallet, or in a container; shipped loose in the hold of a bulk carrier; or mixed with water and shipped in a tanker as slurry. These are all examples of 'cargo units', the term used to describe the physical form in which a commodity is presented for transport, and 12 of the most common ones are summarized in Box 14.1.

In a few cases, such as LNG or nuclear waste, the cargo demands a specific type of ship, and the shipowner's choice is limited to general design and operating features such as size, speed and crew. For most cargoes, however, the shipowner can choose from several ship sizes and types. Crude oil is carried in different sizes of tanker or even a combined carrier; dry bulk can be carried in a conventional bulk carrier, an open hold bulk carrier or a combined carrier; containers principally move in different sizes of container-ship, but MPP vessels and ro-ros carry them as well. The first six items on

## BOX 14.1 PHYSICAL UNITS IN WHICH COMMODITIES ARE SHIPPED BY SEA

| Cargo unit | Comment/commodity |
|---|---|
| *Natural cargoes:* | |
| General cargo | Small parcels of loose items – e.g. boxes, bags, packing cases, drums, a few cars, machines. |
| Dry bulk cargo | Cargo in ship- or hold-sized parcels that can be handled in bulk by gravity/pump loading and grab/suction/pump and stowed in its natural form – e.g. oil, iron ore, coal, grain and cargo. |
| Liquid bulk cargo | Liquid bulks raise four issues: parcel size which can vary from a few thousand tons to 300,000 tons; density of the liquids transported varies; some liquids are corrosive; some liquids are considered hazardous by regulators and require special transport. |
| Unit bulk cargo | Large quantities of units that must be handled individually – e.g. logs, sawn lumber, steel products, bales of wool or wood pulp. |
| Heavy and awkward cargo | Heavy loads up to 2,500 tons – e.g. project cargo, modular industrial plant, ship sections, oilfield equipment, locomotives, yachts, shiploader cranes. |
| Wheeled bulk cargo | Cars, tractors, lorries, etc. shipped in large quantities. |
| *Artificial units* | |
| Containers (ISO) | Standard boxes usually 8′ wide × 8′6″ high in lengths of 20′ and 40′, with a 20′ box typically handling 7–15 tons of cargo, typically stowing at 2.5–5 $m^3$ per ton. |
| Intermediate Bulk Container | Large bags typically 45″ in diameter with capacity of around 1 tonne of granular material and designed for efficient mechanical stacking, handling and discharging. |
| Pre-slung or banded | Usually used for sacks, bales and forest products, to speed up loading and discharge. The slings are left in place during transit. |
| Palletized cargo | Cargo is stacked on a pallet and usually held in place by steel or plastic bands or 'shrink fit' plastic – e.g. cartons of fruit. Can be handled by fork-lift truck. Dozens of sizes up to 6′ × 4′. Palletized cargo stows at about 4 $m^3$/ton. |
| Flats | Normally about 15′ × 8′, often with corner posts to allow stacking two high. Handled by fork-lift or crane. |
| Barges | LASH barges load about 400 tons cargo and Seabee about 600 tons. The barges are designed to be floated to the ship and loaded/discharged as a unit. Never caught on and now obsolete. |

the list are 'natural' cargo units, that is, the cargo is shipped in its natural form without pre-packing. General cargo consists of loose items such as bags or boxes, without any special packing. This type of cargo is the most difficult and expensive to transport by sea. Packing it into the hold of a ship is time-consuming, requires skill, and there are associated problems of loss and damage in transit, as was explained in Chapter 13.

A dry bulk cargo unit is a ship- or hold-size parcel of homogeneous cargo – for example, 150,000 tonnes of iron ore, 70,000 tonnes of coal, 30,000 tonnes of grain, 12,000 tonnes of sugar – whilst liquid bulk cargoes range in size from 500 tonnes of a chemical to 450,000 tonnes of crude oil. Homogeneous bulk cargoes can be loaded and unloaded using grabs or suction as appropriate, and the aim is generally to design a ship that can load its full cargo deadweight of a single commodity, though in some trades that does not always apply. For example, in oil products many ships carry cargo parcels that do not fully utilize the ship's deadweight, such as naphtha, and may be designed with this in mind. In practice, the hold is the smallest size unit for dry bulk cargo and the cargo tank the smallest unit for liquid bulk. Unit bulk cargoes consist of ship-sized parcels made up of units each of which must be handled individually – for example, steel products, forest products or bales of wool. In such cases it may be possible to design 'tailored' vessels offering improved stowage or faster cargo handling. Finally, the other natural cargo units are heavy and awkward cargoes and wheeled cargoes. Heavy and awkward cargoes are worth singling out because they present special shipping problems in terms of handling and stowing the cargo. For example, the tunnel kiln for a cement plant or a small warship being shipped from Europe to the Far East both present stowage problems.

The remainder of Box 14.1 is concerned with cargo that is pre-packed for transport, usually so that it can be handled mechanically rather than requiring skilled manual handling and stowage. Standardization also allows cargo units to be moved seamlessly between rail, road and sea vehicles, improving the efficiency of integrated 'door-to-door' transport services. In practice, there are six main forms of artificial cargo units: containers; intermediate bulk containers; pre-slung or banded; pallets; flats; and the now little-used barges.

By far the most important artificial unit is the *ISO container*. Standard 20 ft and 40 ft containers give the shipowner a homogeneous cargo that allows mechanized loading and discharging systems and produces a major improvement in efficiency. However, the uncompromising size, shape and weight of the container box presents designers with a specific set of problems.

*Intermediate bulk containers* are large bags made of flexible fabric, designed for mechanical filling, handling and unloading of solid materials in powder, flake, or granular form. They were first manufactured in the late 1950s and are mainly used for minor bulks such as chemicals and high-value ores.

The use of *pallets* and *flats* provides a degree of unitization without requiring the high capital costs incurred by containers and trailers, and there are fewer problems in returning the empty units. Pallets have not become established as a base unit for a sea transport system in the same way as containers except on individual routes where they meet a special need, for example in the refrigerated cargo trade. The cargo is loaded on to a pallet, of which there are a variety of sizes, and secured with bands or a plastic cover shrunk to protect the cargo. Loading and discharge are still labour-intensive operations and rely on the skill of stevedores to pack the pallets into the ship efficiently. It is, however, dramatically more efficient than the handling of individual boxes, drums, sacks or bales. Finally, *barges* were introduced in the 1960s in an attempt to cater for the small bulk packages of medium-value cargoes, especially where an inland waterway system allows through water transport to inland destinations, but were never widely adopted.

## How should the cargo be stowed?

The next issue is how best to tailor the cargo spaces to fit the cargo units the ship will carry. This presents more difficult choices because optimizing stowage often has adverse consequences for other aspects of the design. Buxton describes the problem in the following way:

> Merchant ships are mobile warehouses whose many different forms have evolved as a result of attempts to balance on the one hand the need for suitable storage capacity, against on the other hand the need for mobility. Thus a ship constructed as a simple rectangular box of appropriate dimensions could provide an ideal space for storing containers, but would be difficult to propel through the water, while an easily driven hull would offer relatively little useable cargo space. Ship design is largely a matter of solving such conflicts to produce vessels which are suited to the services in which they will be employed.[3]

A good starting point is the stowage factor, the volume of hold space in cubic metres occupied by a tonne of cargo. This varies enormously from one commodity to another, as the examples in Table 14.2 show. Iron ore, the densest cargo, stows at around $0.4 \, m^3$ per tonne, whilst wood chips stow at around $2.5 \, m^3$ per tonne and thus take up six times as much space. In between is heavy grain which stows at around $1.3 \, m^3$ per tonne. If a ship designed for grain is loaded with iron ore, much of the internal space will be empty. At the other end of the scale, light cargoes such as logs need a lot more space. So a bulk carrier designed with a cubic capacity of $1.3 \, m^3$ per tonne could take a full cargo of coal, but not a full deadweight of wood pulp which stows at $1.7 \, m^3$ per tonne.

If a ship is to be used exclusively to carry only iron ore, it can be designed as an ore carrier with cargo spaces stowing at, say, $0.5 \, m^3$ per tonne, but if it is to be used for other commodities such as coal or grain an internal cubic capacity of about $1.3 \, m^3$ per tonne might be preferred (see Table 14.9 for the average stowage of the bulk carrier fleet). The same problem arises with container-ships. Twenty-foot containers typically stow at around $1.6–3.0 \, m^3$ per tonne, one of the least dense commodities listed in Table 14.2. To utilize the ship's deadweight, containers are generally stacked on deck but the design deadweight per container slot is a matter of balance because the weight of cargo in the containers may change. We saw in Chapter 13 that the average container payload per TEU in the transpacific trade varies between 7 tonnes eastbound and 12 tonnes westbound. So a compromise is needed on the ship's loaded deadweight.

Hold dimensions are also important. Ships carrying containers, packaged timber or any standard unit must be designed with square 'open' holds that match the external dimensions of the units they are carrying and provide vertical access. For example, 'pallet-friendly' reefer vessels are designed with decks tailored to accommodate the maximum payload of standard pallets.

**Table 14.2** Stowage factors for various commodity trades

| Cargo type | Stowage factor | | Density index[a] |
|---|---|---|---|
| | Cu. ft/ton | Cu. m./tonne | |
| *Dry cargo* | | | |
| Iron ore | 14 | 0.40 | 31 |
| Bauxite | 28 | 0.80 | 62 |
| Phosphate (rock) | 30–34 | 1.00 | 77 |
| Soya beans | 44 | 1.20 | 92 |
| Grain (heavy) | 45 | 1.30 | 100 |
| Coal | 48 | 1.40 | 108 |
| Barley | 54 | 1.50 | 115 |
| Wood pulp (bales) | 60 | 1.70 | 131 |
| Copra | 73 | 2.10 | 162 |
| Pre-slung timber | 80 | 2.30 | 177 |
| China clay (bagged) | 80 | 2.30 | 177 |
| Paper (rolls) | 90 | 2.50 | 192 |
| Wood chips | 90 | 2.50 | 192 |
| Logs | 100 | 2.80 | 215 |
| Containers, 20 ft | 56–105 | 1.6–3.0 | 123–230 |
| Containers, 40 ft | 85–175 | 2.4–5.0 | 185–385 |
| Cars (vehicle carrier) | 150 | 4.2 | 323 |
| Toys, footwear | 300–400 | 8.5–11.3 | 230–869 |
| *Liquid cargo* | | | 0 |
| Molasses | 27.0 | 0.80 | 62 |
| Heavy fuel oil | 32.8 | 0.93 | 72 |
| Heavy crude oil | 33.7 | 0.95 | 73 |
| Diesel oil | 37.2 | 1.06 | 81 |
| Light crude oil | 37.6 | 1.07 | 82 |
| Gas oil (light fuel oil) | 38.6 | 1.10 | 84 |
| Paraffin | 40.3 | 1.14 | 88 |
| Motor spirit (petrol) | 43.2 | 1.23 | 95 |
| Aviation spirit | 45.1 | 1.28 | 98 |
| Naphtha | 46.4 | 1.32 | 101 |

[a]Density index based on grain (heavy) = 100. Big numbers take more hold space, whilst small numbers like iron ore take up little.

Source: Various

Where commodities with stowage factors that depart significantly from the average are shipped in large quantities, it may be economic to build specialist ships to carry them. Ore carriers, woodchip carriers and car carriers are three prominent examples, the first to deal with a high-density cargo and the latter two to deal efficiently with low density cargoes. Hoistable decks may be fitted to allow the head-room to be adjusted for different cargoes, for example to allow car carriers to transport larger units like trucks.

### How should the cargo be handled?

Getting the cargo on and off the ship is one of the most important aspects of ship design, involving both the cargo characteristics and the extent to which the transport operation is part of a wider integrated transport network. There are many ways ship designs can be developed to improve cargo-handling efficiency, provided the dimensions of the units are known in advance. Some of the most important are as follows:

- *Cargo-handling gear*. Jib cranes, heavy lift derricks, or other cargo-handling gear such as gantry cranes may be fitted to speed up the loading and discharge of dry cargo ships. For tankers the there are three main issues to consider – the capacity of the pumps; corrosion resistance of pipe work; and segregation of tank cargo-handling systems.
- *Hatch design*. Bulk carriers for transporting unit loads such as containers or packaged lumber may be designed with hatch coamings that match the standard package size, thus facilitating the efficient stacking of packages in the hold and on deck. Wide (sometimes called 'open') hatches provide vertical access to all parts of the hold.
- *Cell guides*. In the case of containers the process of integrating the hold design into the cargo-handling operation goes a step further, and to speed up handling on container-ships, cell guides are fitted in the holds and occasionally on deck so that containers do not need to be secured individually below deck.
- *Cargo access ramps*. Ramps may be fitted to allow cargo to be loaded by fork-lift truck, or to be driven aboard on its own wheels. They may be located at the bow, the stern or into the side of the vessel, accessed through watertight doors in the hull.
- *Tank segregations*. For liquid cargoes the provision of 'self-contained' tanks capable of handling many different liquid parcels within a single ship increases flexibility. This generally involves the installation of separate pumping systems for each tank using submerged pumps and special coatings such as zinc silicate or stainless steel to allow difficult chemicals to be carried.

This is not an exhaustive list, but it illustrates the way in which ships may be adapted to the carriage of cargoes.

## How big should the ship be?

With the issues over cargo handling and stowage out of the way, the next question facing the investor is the size of vessel to buy. There are numerous influences on the size of ship, but the principles of bulk shipping discussed in Chapter 11 suggest that the optimum size for a ship can be narrowed down to a trade-off between three factors: economies of scale; the parcel sizes in which cargo is available; and available port draught and cargo-handling facilities.

We discussed economies of scale in Chapter 7 and saw that substantial cost savings are achieved by using larger vessels, with the choice depending on the size of vessel used and the length of the voyage. The relative costs for large and small ships on short and long voyages are illustrated in Table 14.3. A 15,170 dwt vessel costs 2.7 times as much to run per ton of cargo as a 120,000 dwt ship on a 1000-mile round voyage, whilst on the 22,000 mile round voyage it costs 3.1 times as much.

**Table 14.3** Economies of scale in bulk shipping (% cost per ton mile)

| Round voyage (miles) | Ship size (dwt) | | | |
|---|---|---|---|---|
| | 15,170 | 40,540 | 65,500 | 120,380 |
| 1,000 | 100 | 53 | 47 | 37 |
| 6,000 | 56 | 34 | 27 | 20 |
| 22,000 | 52 | 30 | 24 | 17 |

Source: Goss and Jones (1971, Table 3).

This suggests that economies of scale are only slightly influenced by the length of haul, and the fact that smaller ships are generally used on short routes must have another explanation.

In practice, big ships face two important restrictions. The first is the maximum size of delivery that the shipper is able or willing to accept at any one time. If stockpiles are only 10,000 or 15,000 tonnes, a delivery of 50,000 tonnes would be too large. Second, there is the constraint on ship size imposed by port draught since deep-draught vessels, have access to fewer ports than shallow-draught vessels, as shown in Table 14.4. Limits may also be placed on overall length or beam or both (either by ports or by canals). The measure of accessible ports is very crude, since some ports are more important than others in the bulk trades and depth varies substantially from berth to berth within ports, but the broad relationship is valid. At the lower end of the scale, a small bulk carrier of 16,000 dwt is likely to have a draught of 7–9 metres and is able to access about three-quarters of the world's ports. A final point is that ship designers can vary the draught–deadweight ratio within certain limits by changing other aspects of the design such as the beam.

**Table 14.4** Relationship between ship draft and port access

| Ship draught | | Average size dwt | Standard deviation* dwt | % of world ports accessible |
|---|---|---|---|---|
| feet | metres | | | |
| 25–30 | 7.6–9.1 | 16,150 | 3,650 | 73 |
| 30–35 | 9.2–10.7 | 23,600 | 3,000 | 55 |
| 36–38 | 10.8–11.6 | 38,700 | 5,466 | 43 |
| 39–44 | 11.7–13.4 | 61,000 | 5,740 | 27 |
| 45–50 | 13.5–15.2 | 89,200 | 8,600 | 22 |
| 51–55 | 15.3–18.5 | 123,000 | 9,000 | 19 |

Source: Sample of bulk carriers from the Clarkson *Bulk Carrier Register* and *Ports of the World*
*Standard deviation is the spread of the average size

## How fast should the ship go?

In terms of cargo delivery economics, size and speed are to some extent interchangeable because a ship's transport capacity can be increased by increasing either its size or its speed. However, the two methods have very different economic and physical consequences. From a design viewpoint the fast ship will generally be more expensive to build and achieving the higher speed may call for a longer hull with less efficient cargo stowage. But the fast ship needs less cargo capacity to achieve a given cargo delivery volume and it can access shallower draft ports and make more frequent deliveries, reducing inventory requirements. Speed also reduces the transit time and the inventory cost of cargo in transit, which can be very significant for high-value cargoes such as television sets which can be worth around $44,000 per tonne (Table 14.5). If a company's cost of capital is 10% per annum, a 10-tonne cargo of television sets worth $44,000 per ton would, on a two-month voyage, incur interest charges of $7,000. Cutting the journey to one month saves $3,500, so the shipper should be willing to pay for faster transport. In fact air freight often competes with sea transport for this sort of cargo and, although the tonnages are small, the competition is significant because it is premium cargo. But these benefits of speed come at a cost. To be efficient, fast ships need a long hull and use far more fuel, as can be seen from Table 14.7 which shows the speed and fuel consumption of container-ships. For example, it shows that the average container-ship of between 6,000 and 12,000 TEU has a speed of 25.2 knots burns 211.3 tonnes a day, more than twice as much as a 15 knot VLCC.

At the other end of the range, some bulk commodities such as iron ore and coal have very low values, for example iron ore at $35 per tonne and coal at around $47 per tonne (Table 14.5). These commodities are generally shipped in very large consignments (up to 300,000 tonnes) and, since they have a low inventory cost, the emphasis is on minimizing the unit transportation cost by using the most economical speed. For these cargoes the relevant cost is the cost of the ship, not the cargo. Ship designers will generally work out the optimum operating speed for the vessel, taking account of the anticipated level of capital, operating and bunker costs on the assumption that the freight is not time sensitive. However, an important qualification is that if the ship is to

**Table 14.5** Value per ton of sea imports

| Commodity | $ per tonne f.o.b. | Quantity traded, (million tonnes) | Value trade $m |
|---|---|---|---|
| Stone, sand, gravel | 9 | 101 | 888 |
| Iron ore | 35 | 650 | 22,750 |
| Coal | 47 | 682 | 32,054 |
| Grain | 200 | 273 | 54,600 |
| TV sets | 43,076 | — | — |
| World imports | 1,341 | 6,893 | 9,244,700 |

Source: UNCTAD (2006) Table 41 and Annex 2 and various

be traded on the spot market the investor may specify a design speed above this minimum so that he can complete more voyages during periods of high freight rates when he is making premium profits.

## How flexible should the ship be?

Finally, there is the flexibility of the ship to consider – should the ship be designed to service several markets? Specialist tonnage is shut out from markets that could be serviced by more flexible vessels, or at least incurs a cost penalty, so naturally ship designers have devoted a great deal of attention to this question. This can raise issues over speed, cargo handling, cargo access, size, stowage and various less fundamental but expensive options such as tank coatings – for example, should a new Aframax tanker have tank coatings so that it can switch into the long-haul clean products trade?

A way of illustrating the degree of cargo unit flexibility of different ship designs is shown in Figure 14.2, which lists on the left-hand side the various cargo units we have discussed and on the right-hand side a range of recognized ship types. A line links each cargo unit to the various ships that are capable of transporting it, and for each ship type the lateral cargo mobility (LCM) coefficient records the number of different cargo units that the vessel can carry.

Four ships are sufficiently specialized to have an LCM rating of 1 – the container-ship, the vehicle carrier, the bulk carrier and the tanker. All these vessels are restricted to a single type of cargo unit. The combined carrier has an LCM rating of 2, reflecting its ability to switch between dry bulk and crude oil, while the open hatch bulk carrier can transport containers, pallets and pre-slung cargo in addition to dry bulk parcels. The ro-ro is even more flexible, with the ability to carry almost any cargo except bulk and barges, giving it an LCM rating of 6. However, the most flexible of all is the MPP cargo liner, which can carry everything except liquid bulk parcels and barges.

The trade-off between cost and operational performance in its main trade is central to the design of flexible ships. Often the flexible ship is more expensive

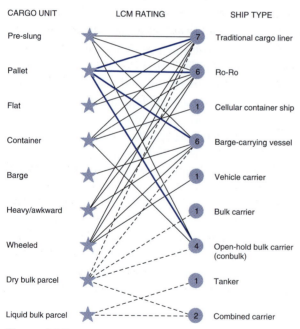

**Figure 14.2**
Analysis of flexibility
Source: Martin Stopford 2007
Note: Lateral cargo mobility (LCM) rating reflects the number of different types of cargo units that the vessel can carry, i.e. its flexibility. The higher the number, the greater the flexibility.

**Table 14.6** Principal dimensions of flat roof steel containers

| | Dimensions | |
|---|---|---|
| | 20′ × 8′ × 8′6″ | 40′ × 8′ × 8′6″ |
| Length (metres) | 6.1 | 12.2 |
| Width (metres) | 2.44 | 2.44 |
| Height (metres) | 2.6 | 2.6 |
| Cubic capacity (cubic metres) | 32.9 | 67 |
| Stacking capacity | 9 high | 9 high |
| Maximum weight (metric tonnes) | 24 | 30.5 |

Source: UNCTAD (1985, p.141).

to build and does not perform as well as a single purpose vessel in any of the trades for which it is built. So the key is whether it can gain benefits such as reducing ballast voyages or carrying more cargo (see the example of open-hatch bulk carriers at the beginning of Chapter 12). In this context, design technology can be important in addressing operational issues. Although the case for flexible ships which reduce risk and increase earnings sounds great, in practice relatively few shipping investors follow this strategy. Today the merchant fleet is dominated by single-purpose ships such as tankers, bulk carriers and container-ships, all of which have an LCM ratio of 1. In contrast, the flexible ship types such as cargo liners, ro-ros, barge carriers and combined carriers have recently been noticeably sluggish or in retreat. This suggests that in the modern shipping industry the economic benefits of specialization outweigh the economic benefits from flexibility – a useful reminder that simplicity is a guiding principle of successful ship design. Sophisticated ships make interesting conference papers, but in the harsh commercial world simple vessels which do one job well seem to do better.

## 14.3 SHIPS FOR THE GENERAL CARGO TRADES

This is the trade segment where ships have changed most in the last fifty years. Indeed, it is rare in shipping to find such a radical change as the substitution of container-ships for the flexible cargo liners which started in the 1960s. Like the switch from sail to steel, the transition took many years to accomplish and a large number of vessels left over from the cargo liner era continued to be used and in some cases were still being replaced fifty years after the first container was shipped in 1956. By 2006 the container-ships had taken over all but the fringe liner services, though there were still a few services using ro-ros, MPP vessels and even a handful of barge-carrying vessels (BCVs), and 'tweendeck tramps.

### Container-ships

All the major liner trades now use container-ships. A container-ship is, in principle, an open-top box in which containers can be stacked. It has hatches the width of the holds, fitted with cell guides so that containers can be dropped into place and held securely during the voyage without lashing. The hatches are sealed with strengthened hatch covers which provide the base for stacking more containers above deck. Since these have no supporting structure they must be lashed in place with twistlocks and wires. Some companies have experimented with hatchless designs which avoid the labour-intensive procedure of clamping containers.

Details of a large 8200 TEU container ship are shown in Figure 14.3. Since the sole purpose of this ship is to carry containers, its design centres on container dimensions. ISO standards identify a range of containers, the most widely used sizes being the 20 ft and 40 ft containers with dimensions as shown in Table 14.6. Container-ships are generally designed around the 8 ft 6 in. high module, though this also allows a mix of 8 ft and 9 ft 6 in. containers to be stowed as well. The containers are arranged in bays, with 30 forward of the accommodation and 10 at the stern. Below deck the containers are lowered into cell guides and the number of tiers which can be accommodated in the hold varies with the curvature of the hull, as illustrated by the longitudinal cross section in Figure 14.3. On-deck containers are stacked on the hatch covers and held in place by twistlocks and wires and stacked in tiers the height of which depends on visibility. In this example the number of tiers varies between five and seven. The ISO also specifies a weight standard, which is a maximum of 24 tonnes for 20 ft containers and 30 tonnes for 40 ft containers. These are well above the average values likely to be found in practice, which may range between 10 and 15 tonnes depending on the trade and the type of cargo. Although this ship has a nominal capacity of 8189 containers, its homogeneous capacity at 14 tons per TEU is 6,130.

At first, container-ship designs were categorized into 'generations', reflecting the evolving technology, but as the fleet grew to more than 4,000 ships in 2007 it polarized into size categories shown by the fleet statistics in Table 14.7. Each sector has a different place in the market. Smaller container ships of less than 1,000 TEU, often referred to as 'Feeder' (0–499 TEU) and 'Feedermax' (500–999 TEU) vessels, are generally used on short-haul operations. They distribute the containers brought to regional load centres or 'hub' ports such as Rotterdam by deep-sea services and carry coastal traffic. There is a sizeable fleet of Handy vessels of 1,000–3,000 TEU which are small enough to be used intraregionally, but large enough to be used in the North–South trades where port restrictions or cargo volume do not permit the use of a larger vessel. Bigger ships over 3,000 TEU are used on long-haul trades where they spend up to 80% of their time at sea. There are three groups of these vessels, referred to as Panamax (3,000–4,000 TEU) and post-Panamax (over 4,000 TEU), with an evolving group of very large box carriers (VLBCs) over 6,000 TEU. Since the different fleet segments have different functions they also have different design characteristics, especially speed and cargo-handling facilities.

Speed is a central feature of container-ship design; with the larger vessels having higher speeds, as can be seen in Table 14.7. In 2006 the average Feeder vessel had a speed of 14 knots, compared with an average speed of 24.5 knots for the average post-Panamax vessel. With each step up in size the speed increases, though the pace of increase slows sharply over 3,000 TEU. The economic explanation of this trend is that

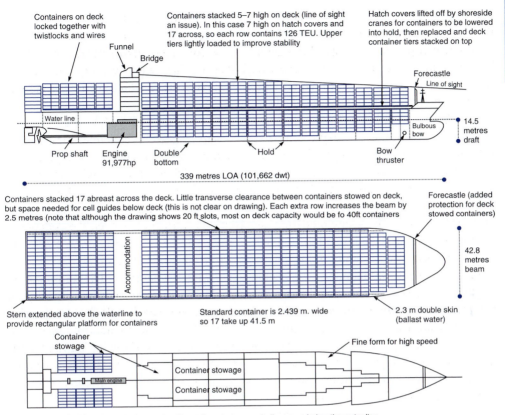

Containers on deck locked together with twistlocks and wires

Containers stacked 5–7 high on deck (line of sight an issue). In this case 7 high on hatch covers and 17 across, so each row contains 126 TEU. Upper tiers lightly loaded to improve stability

Hatch covers lifted off by shoreside cranes for containers to be lowered into hold, then replaced and deck container tiers stacked on top

Funnel

Bridge

Forecastle
Line of sight

Water line

Bulbous bow

14.5 metres draft

Prop shaft

Engine 91,977hp

Double bottom

Hold

Bow thruster

339 metres LOA (101,662 dwt)

Containers stacked 17 abreast across the deck. Little transverse clearance between containers stowed on deck, but space needed for cell guides below deck (this is not clear on drawing). Each extra row increases the beam by 2.5 metres (note that although the drawing shows 20 ft slots, most on deck capacity would be fo 40ft containers

Forecastle (added protection for deck stowed containers)

Accommodation

42.8 metres beam

Stern extended above the waterline to provide rectangular platform for containers

Standard container is 2.439 m. wide so 17 take up 41.5 m

2.3 m double skin (ballast water)

Container stowage

Fine form for high speed

Main engine

Container stowage

Container stowage

Plan view showing reduced container stowage as hull narrows below the water line

### 8,200 TEU Container-ship

17 containers abreast on deck but only 15 in holds

Hatch cover

2 m double bottom for water ballast

Transverse cross section

| HULL | CARGO | MACHINERY |
|---|---|---|
| Deadweight (design): 84,200 | Maximum TEU capacity: 8,189 | Engine: MAN-B&W |
| Deadweight (scantling): 101,662 | on deck 4,148 | Power output (hp): 91,977 |
| Gross tonnage: 88,600 | in holds | 4,041 at 97 rpm (67.6 MW) |
| *dimensions* | TEU capacity @14t per TEU: 6,130 | Six bladed propeller |
| Overall length (m): 339 | | Maximum speed (Kn): 25.4 |
| Overall beam (m): 42.8 | Container tiers/rows: | Speed, service 90% MCR* |
| | On deck: 7/17 | 15% sea margin 24.4 knots |
| Draft (m): scantling 14.5 | In holds: 8/15 | Consumption: 271 tons/day |
| Draft (m): design 13.0 | TEU bays on deck: 19 | Bunker capacity: |
| Width of double side: 2.23 m | TEU bays below deck: 18 | heavy oil 10,900 m³ |
| Height of double bottom: 2.00 m | Reefer containers: 700 electric | diesel oil 700 m³ |
| Percent high tensile steel 60% | sockets to supply 40' boxes | Diesel alternators 5 |
| | *complement* | Alternator output: |
| | Officers 16 | 3×2200 kW and 2×2800 kW |
| Tin free SPC paint, 5 year life | Ratings 18 | Exhaust gas scrubbing plant |
| | Suez crew 6 | Bow thruster 1×2500 kW |

*MCR is the maximum continuous rating i.e. maximum power

### Figure 14.3
Example of typical 8,200 TEU container-ship design
Source: Drawing by Martin Stopford, based on container-ships built by Hyundai Heavy Industries

**Table 14.7** The container-ship fleet, by size and hull characteristics

| Ship size TEU | | Container-ship fleet size | | | Hull characteristics | | | | | |
|---|---|---|---|---|---|---|---|---|---|---|
| | | No | Av. TEU | Tot TEU (000s) | Capacity dwt/TEU | Beam metres | Draft metres | Speed knots | Cons. t/day | % Geared |
| Feeder | 0–499 | 443 | 310 | 137 | 17.2 | 17.1 | 6.1 | 14.0 | 15.7 | 29% |
| Feedermax | 500–999 | 695 | 722 | 502 | 14.1 | 21.1 | 7.7 | 16.8 | 27.5 | 48% |
| Handy | 1000–1999 | 1012 | 1412 | 1429 | 14.9 | 26.3 | 9.7 | 19.0 | 49.2 | 53% |
| Sub-Panamax | 2000–2999 | 596 | 2504 | 1492 | 14.2 | 31.0 | 11.5 | 21.2 | 79.3 | 43% |
| Panamax | 3000–3999 | 297 | 3411 | 1013 | 13.8 | 32.3 | 12.0 | 22.5 | 104.5 | 9% |
| Post-Panamax | 4000–5999 | 533 | 4817 | 2567 | 12.9 | 35.4 | 13.3 | 24.5 | 159.5 | 0% |
| VLBC | 6000–12000 | 215 | 7419 | 1595 | 12.6 | 41.9 | 14.2 | 25.2 | 211.3 | 0% |
| Total | Grand total | 3791 | 2304 | 8736 | 13.6 | 27.6 | 10.0 | 19.7 | 64.5 | 34% |

Source: *Container-ship Register* 2006, Clarkson Research Services Ltd, London

the bigger ships are generally used on long-haul routes where speed is an important aspect of the service. High speed brings a cost penalty in terms of fuel consumption and restricted hull design, since high speeds require a fine hull form. For short-haul trades where there are many port calls, speed is less important than economy and cargo payload. Conversely, on long hauls speed is highly productive, reducing journey times and the number of ships required to run a service. Whatever the economic justification, and it is complex, the relationship between speed and size in container-ships is clear.

Cargo-handling gear also varies with size, following a similar pattern to the bulk carrier fleet. Many of the smaller vessels carry cargo gear and the larger container-ships rely exclusively on shore-based cargo-handling facilities. In 2006, 29% of the Feeder vessels, 48% of the Feedermaxes, 53% of the Handy container-ships, and 43% of sub-Panamax container-ships had cargo gear, but only 9% of post-Panamax container-ships.

One of the most important ways of increasing container-ship versatility is to carry *refrigerated containers*, enabling the container companies to compete with reefer operators for the trade in meat, dairy products and fruit. This can be achieved by insulating the containers which have their own refrigeration units that plug into a power plug on the ship. If a substantial regular volume of reefer cargo is available (e.g., on the Australia to UK route), a central refrigeration plant may be built into the ship. This blows cold air through ducts into the insulated containers. At the loading and discharging ports the insulated containers must be stored in special refrigerated reception facilities or portable refrigeration plants are used. Containers with their own refrigeration plant can be plugged into electrical socket adjacent to each container slot. In addition to fast cargo handling, refrigerated containers offer shippers precise temperature control through the journey and a better-quality product, which in the case of fruit and vegetables may result in a higher selling price.[4]

Finally, there has also been much research into containers for transporting small bulk cargoes. These include the use of ventilated containers for agricultural commodities such as coffee and cocoa beans, tank containers for bulk liquids, and containers with special loading and discharging facilities for the fast automated handling of minor bulk commodities. As we saw in Chapter 13, bulk cargoes such as wool, rubber, latex, cotton and some forest products can now be containerized.

## Other general cargo ships

Although container-ships dominate the transport of general cargo, in 2006 there was a fleet of 4717 other general cargo ship types operating in this market segment. The statistics are summarized in Table 14.8 which covers six ship types: ro-ro ships; MPP vessels; heavy lift; traditional liner types; tramps; and barge carriers. These fleet categories are not precise, since the dividing line between, for example, a liner type and a tramp is blurred. From the analyst's viewpoint this is a difficult segment because it has two different components. The first is a group of obsolete traditional liner vessels which, year by year, are being squeezed out by the more efficient container-ships. Liner types and tramps are obvious examples of vessels which fall into this category, and for them there is no question of replacement. But there is a second group of ships, possibly overlapping with the first group, which carry the cargo that container-ships cannot carry. Ro-ro vessels, MPPs and heavy lift ships all fall into this category. Unfortunately, in statistical terms we cannot precisely divide the fleet, but the consequences of this division are important for ship demand. Obsolete vessels will be replaced by container-ships, but the second group focusing on non-containerizable cargo is likely to continue to grow because there will always be a large number of cargos which do not conveniently fit in a standard container.

The key issue for vessels operating in these trades is the flexibility to carry containers, but the ability to also transport uncontainerizable general cargo which, for the reasons discussed in Section 12.6, cannot be transported in container-ships. Common examples are project cargos, forest products, palletized cargo, and wheeled vehicles. In the following paragraphs we will discuss seven different categories of ships which fall into this class.

### RO-RO SHIPS

Cargo ro-ros offer a more flexible alternative to containerization for transporting a mix of containerized and wheeled cargo with cargoes ranging from mini-bulks in intermediate

**Table 14.8** The general cargo fleet, by size and hull characteristics

| Type | TEU '000s | Number | Av. TEU | Av. dwt | Age (yrs) | Av. speed (units) |
|---|---|---|---|---|---|---|
| Ro-ro | 1,440 | 1,109 | 1,604 | 12,132 | 20 | 17.1 |
| MPP | 1,057 | 2,533 | 417 | 9,142 | 16 | 14.2 |
| Heavy lift | 15 | 40 | 364 | 18,031 | 21 | 13.9 |
| Liner type | 89 | 401 | 222 | 13,822 | 29 | 16.1 |
| Tramp | 93 | 624 | 149 | 8,970 | 16 | 12.9 |
| Barge carrier | 10 | 10 | 1,006 | 25,642 | 24 | 15.8 |
| Grand total | 2,703 | 4,717 | 627 | 14,623 | 21 | 15.0 |

Source: *Containership Register* 2006, Clarkson Research Services Ltd

bulk containers and pallets through to heavy lift units of 90 tonnes. These are interesting ships and several designs were developed, but in concept the ro-ro is a cargo liner with 'through decks' and roll-on access by means of ramps, rather than via hatches in the weather deck. Key design features are access ramps, open decks allowing fast manoeuvring of fork-lift trucks, tractor/trailers and wheeled vehicles, good access between decks, and deck and ramp loadings for heavy cargoes. They are particularly suitable for carrying any cargo that can easily be handled by a fork-lift truck (pallets, bales, containers, packaged timber, etc.) and also for wheeled cargo (cars, loaded trucks or trailers, tractors, etc.). A major advantage of the ro-ro vessel is its ability to provide fast port turnaround without special cargo-handling facilities.

Apart from some Scandinavian devotees, ro-ros never found a market in the deep-sea cargo trades (though they were more successful in the short-sea passenger-cargo ro-ro market) and in 2006 the fleet of 1109 vessels had an average age of 20 years, suggesting that the fleet is not being replaced (Table 14.8). There were only two small vessels on order. Although ro-ros have never been adopted on the scale of cellular container-ships, the existing fleet continues to be used in some trades where the cargo mix and port facilities favour this type of operation, for example the Atlantic Container Line ships discussed in Chapter 12. The explanation for this poor performance seems to be that although ro-ros have highly flexible cargo capacity, with an LCM coefficient of 6, and can handle cargo efficiently even in ports with very basic facilities, this flexibility has a price that makes it unacceptable to investors. The ships have much less efficient stowage than container-ships and, since the cargo is more difficult and labour-intensive to secure, the loading times are generally slower. In addition, ro-ros are very management-intensive, requiring careful stowage planning.[5] However, their greatest disadvantage is that they lack the simple integration with other transport systems which is the chief asset of the container-ship fleet. As a result the ro-ro fleet is very much smaller than the container fleet, and even on routes such as the West Africa trade where suitable conditions exist, ro-ros account for only about 10% of the tonnage employed.[6]

## MULTI-PURPOSE VESSELS

Where there is a continuing demand for flexible liner tonnage, MPP or lo-lo (lift on, lift off) vessels are used. Ships of this type are typically between 8,000 and 22,000 dwt with three to five holds, each containing a 'tween deck. The main difference from earlier traditional liners is that they are designed to carry a full load of containers as well as general cargo and heavy lift. This is achieved by designing the lower hold and the 'tween deck with dimensions compatible with containers and container cranes capable of 35–40 tonne lift. Table 14.8 shows that in 2006 there was a fleet of 2,533 MPP ships with an average size of 9,142 dwt and an average age of 16 years. The fleet grew at 2.6% per annum between 1996 and 2006 (Table 12.12), demonstrating that there is a positive demand which has become more apparent as the container business has matured.

In economic terms, MPP vessels are a compromise for use in trades that are partly containerized, especially for heavy and awkward cargoes which cannot be containerized, and their ability to pick up bulk cargoes helps to increase deadweight utilization.

The downside is reduced efficiency handling containers, since they do not have cell guides and they are expensive to build. However, even basic MPPs often have a lateral cargo mobility rating of 5, with the ability to carry pre-slung cargo, palletized cargo, flats, containers, heavy and awkward cargo, and wheeled vehicles, but designs vary a great deal. Since there are many permutations it is useful to review some examples which illustrate the principal features of this ship type and how they can be varied.

An example at the top end of the size range is a 23,700 dwt MPP vessel aimed mainly at the container and packaged bulk cargo markets. It has a container capacity of 1050 TEU, five holds with mechanically operated 'tween decks and a relatively fast speed of 18.5 knots on 50 tons a day. The cranes are of 35 tonne and 26 tonne capacity, so this is quite a high specification. In addition to containers, the vessel can carry wood products, steel products, construction materials, general cargo and project cargo including yachts and heavy machinery. Fragile or non-unitized cargoes such as packaged consumer items, perishable produce and chemicals can also be accommodated and the ship has capacity for 150 refrigerated containers. Containers can be stacked up to four high in the holds and three high on the hatch covers, and the holds and open hatches are designed to accommodate containers of 20 ft or 40 ft in length.

Figure 14.4 shows outline drawings for a smaller MPP aimed more at the heavy lift and project cargo markets. It is 12,000 dwt and can carry 684 TEU. Two cranes capable of lifting up to 80 tonnes, a big open deck and removable 'tween decks allow it to service a whole range of project and heavy lift cargoes. This particular vessel has been designed to a gross tonnage of 8,999, to comply with the Dutch manning requirements, and it has a crew of 13.

Basically this is a single-deck open-hatch design, with two very long holds, hydraulic folding hatch covers, and a removable 'tween deck. The 'tween deck is made up of 15 panels which can be lifted out and stowed at the aft end of no. 2 hold when not in use. The design is heavily focused towards the transport of containers, carrying 372 TEU on deck and 312 TEU in the holds. Four tiers of containers can be stacked in the hold, two below the 'tween deck and two above, allowing mixed container and unit cargoes to be carried in the holds when the 'tween deck is in place. Another two to four tiers of containers can be stacked on the deck, with the height of the forward tiers reduced for better visibility from the bridge. There are also 80 reefer plugs. Six rows of containers can be accommodated in the hold and seven rows on deck.

For project and heavy lift cargoes, the ship has two electric hydraulic deck cranes, each capable of lifting 30–80 tonnes (at 80 tonnes the lift is restricted to a 14 metre radius, whilst at 30 tonnes the radius extends to 32 metres). In order to leave the stowage space on deck open for project cargos, the cranes are built into the side shell (i.e. the double side – see Figure 14.4). This means that the ship has an open deck/hatch area over 100 metres long on which to carry project cargoes. An anti-heeling pump for use during cargo operations is located in the space between holds nos 1 and 2 along with air drying equipment.

The advantage of this arrangement is that the vessel can carry a mix of containers and general cargo in the hold, whilst having the option to carry heavy project cargos on deck, or a full load of containers if no such cargoes are available. Taken together, this

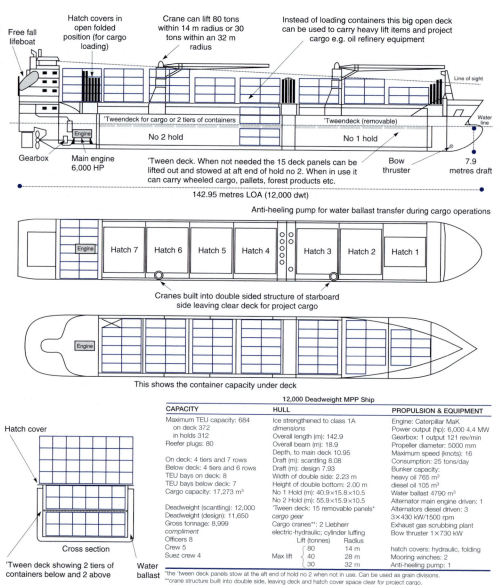

This shows the container capacity under deck

| | 12,000 Deadweight MPP Ship | | |
|---|---|---|---|
| **CAPACITY** | **HULL** | | **PROPULSION & EQUIPMENT** |
| Maximum TEU capacity: 684 | Ice strengthened to class 1A | | Engine: Caterpillar MaK |
| on deck 372 | *dimensions* | | Power output (hp): 6,000 4.4 MW |
| in holds 312 | Overall length (m): 142.9 | | Gearbox: 1 output 121 rev/min |
| Reefer plugs: 80 | Overall beam (m): 18.9 | | Propeller diameter: 5000 mm |
| | Depth, to main deck 10.95 | | Maximum speed (knots): 16 |
| On deck: 4 tiers and 7 rows | Draft (m): scantling 8.08 | | Consumption: 25 tons/day |
| Below deck: 4 tiers and 6 rows | Draft (m): design 7.93 | | Bunker capacity: |
| TEU bays on deck: 8 | Width of double side: 2.23 m | | heavy oil 765 m³ |
| TEU bays below deck: 7 | Height of double bottom: 2.00 m | | diesel oil 105 m³ |
| Cargo capacity: 17,273 m³ | No 1 Hold (m): 40.9×15.8×10.5 | | Water ballast 4790 m³ |
| | No 2 Hold (m): 55.9×15.9×10.5 | | Alternator main engine driven: 1 |
| Deadweight (scantling): 12,000 | 'Tween deck: 15 removable panels* | | Alternators diesel driven: 3 |
| Deadweight (design): 11,650 | *cargo gear* | | 3×430 kW/1500 rpm |
| Gross tonnage: 8,999 | Cargo cranes**: 2 Liebherr | | Exhaust gas scrubbing plant |
| *compliment* | electric-hydraulic; cylinder luffing | | Bow thruster 1×730 kW |
| Officers 8 | | Lift (tonnes) Radius | |
| Crew 5 | | 80 14 m | hatch covers: hydraulic, folding |
| Suez crew 4 | Max lift { | 40 28 m | Mooring winches: 2 |
| | | 30 32 m | Anti-heeling pump: 1 |

*the 'tween deck panels stow at the aft end of hold no 2 when not in use. Can be used as grain divisions.
**crane structure built into double side, leaving deck and hatch cover space clear for project cargo.

**Figure 14.4**

Multi-purpose heavy lift ship, 12,000 dwt

Source: Drawing by Martin Stopford, based on Damen Shipyard Combi-Freighter design

offers a high degree of flexibility and good operating efficiency, but it is a very different design philosophy from the dedicated container-ship reviewed in Figure 14.3. Ships of this sort fill an important role in the shipping market and because they are generally expensive to build and require careful marketing to achieve the best mix of cargo, the business philosophy is very different from the deep-sea container and commodity trades.

## HEAVY LIFT VESSELS

Heavy lift ships focus exclusively on large awkward cargo items. They range from items of industrial plant to offshore equipment, project cargo, and container cranes. As far as the ship design is concerned, there are basically three ways of dealing with heavy unit loads. The first is to lift it on and off the ship, generally using cranes with a high lifting capacity. MPP vessels with heavy lift capacity and ro-ros can carry unit loads of up to 100 tonnes, but there is a demand for small vessels capable of carrying much larger loads (e.g. up to 500 tonnes) or on routes where liner companies do not offer heavy lift capabilities. The second is to roll the cargo on or off the ship using a strengthened ramp, of the type fitted to some ro-ros. Modern vehicle carriers often have strengthened ramps and hoistable decks so that they can load heavy wheeled vehicles and industrial plant. The third is the float-on, float-off method in which the ship itself is submerged, allowing the heavy unit such as dredging plant to be floated on to the vessel for loading, and then removed in the same way. The market for these vessels is discussed in Section 12.6.

## CARGO LINER TYPES

Finally, we come to the general cargo fleet, which in 2006 was 401 ships with an average size of 13,800 dwt and an average age of 29 years (Table 14.8). These are history, the last remnants of the multi-deck ships used in the liner services, for example Ocean's *Priam* class cargo liner built in the 1960s. They had 'tween decks for mixed general cargo, tanks for carrying liquid parcels, refrigerated capacity and could also carry small bulk parcels (e.g. minor amounts of ore, copra, steel) in the lower hold. Often they had cargo-handling gear with heavy lift ability, but little attention was paid to container capacity. Some are still in service but, needless to say, they are not being replaced.

## 'TWEENDECKER TRAMPS

The 'tweendecker tramps are simpler versions of the cargo liner types. In 2006 there were over 624 ships of 5.5 m.dwt in service. Typically these vessels range in size from 10,000 to 22,000 dwt and are essentially small bulk carriers with a 'tween deck so that they can carry a mix of general cargo and bulk cargoes such as grain. Since the mid-1950s, the rapid growth of parcel size in the bulk trades and containerization of general cargo has resulted in the 'tweendecker being replaced by MPP vessels, but the type is still used in some trades. In 2006 the average fleet age was 16 years and the average ship was 8970 dwt with a speed of 12.8 knots trading largely in the Third World.

## BARGE-CARRYING VESSELS

The 1960s was a decade of great experimentation in the liner trades. The barge carrier was an extreme design developed to extend the benefits of unitization to the mini-bulk cargoes previously carried as bottom cargo. The concept involved grouping 'floating holds' (i.e. barges), generally of 400–1,000 tonnes, within a single ship. These barges could be filled with general cargo or small bulk parcels, making barge systems at least as flexible as the traditional cargo liner in terms of range of cargoes carried. The main design feature is the method employed for getting the heavy barges into the barge carrier – the LASH system used a shipboard crane, and the BACAT system floated the barges on to the ship. The barge carrier system has not been widely adopted. In 2006 there were only ten barge carriers, but not all were operating.

### REFRIGERATED VESSELS

Refrigerated vessels (reefers) were developed in the late nineteenth century to carry meat from New Zealand and Australia to the UK (see Chapter 12 for a discussion of the trade). Reefer cargo is frozen or chilled, in which case the temperature is maintained just above freezing. To achieve this reefer vessels have insulated cargo holds with cargo handled horizontally through side ports and vertically through hatches.

Modern vessels have their cargo spaces designed for palletized cargo and there may also be reefer container capacity on deck or in the holds plus conventional container capacity. For example a 14,800 dwt vessel delivered in 2006 had 460,000 cubic feet of refrigerated capacity, 880 TEU, and 144 reefer plugs. The speed was 20.5 knots on 67 tons per day. For fruit and vegetables the cargo continues to ripen during transit, so the refrigeration system must maintain a precisely controlled temperature in all parts of the cargo spaces. Since fruit cargoes such as bananas are frequently loaded in developing countries with poor port facilities, there is often a need to make the ships self-sufficient in terms of cargo handling. Cars are often carried as a backhaul.

Although reefers dominated the refrigerated cargo trade, the fleet of 1,800 vessels is now very old, with an average age of 23.9 years (see Table 2.5). Refrigerated foods are increasingly transported in reefer containers.

## 14.4 SHIPS FOR THE DRY BULK TRADES

In the bulk cargo market, the focus is on low-cost transport. The bulk carrier fleet (Table 14.9) consists of over 6,000 vessels of 369 m.dwt. The fleet falls into four main parts generally referred to as Handy bulk carriers (10,000–39,999 dwt), Handymax bulk carriers (40,000–59,999 dwt), Panamax (60,000–99,999 dwt)[7] and Capesize (over 100,000 dwt). These ships carry a wide spectrum of bulk cargoes ranging from grain, phosphate rock, iron ore and coal, to parcels of chemicals, with a premium on economy and flexibility.

### The bulk carrier

Nowadays the major bulk cargoes and the great majority of minor bulk cargoes are transported in bulk carriers. These are all single-deck ships with a double bottom, vertical cargo access through hatches in the weather deck and speeds generally in the range of 13–16 knots, though the average for most sizes is about 14.5 knots. Since the mid-1960s

**Table 14.9** Bulk carrier fleet, February 2007, by size and hull characteristics

| Size | Bulk carrier fleet size | | | Hull characteristics | | | | | | |
| | No | Av.dwt 000s | Total dwt | Length m. | Beam m. | Draft m. | Speed knots | Cons. t/day | Cubic m³/tonne | % geared |
|---|---|---|---|---|---|---|---|---|---|---|
| *Handy* | | | | | | | | | | |
| 10–19,999 | 611 | 15,679 | 9.6 | 136 | 22 | 8.7 | 14.1 | 22.5 | 1.22 | 73% |
| 20–24,999 | 487 | 23,025 | 11.2 | 154 | 24 | 9.7 | 14.3 | 26.1 | 1.27 | 89% |
| 25–29,999 | 820 | 27,627 | 22.7 | 166 | 25 | 9.9 | 14.3 | 28.6 | 1.28 | 93% |
| 30–39,999 | 917 | 35,270 | 32.3 | 178 | 27 | 10.7 | 14.4 | 31.3 | 1.25 | 87% |
| *Handymax* | | | | | | | | | | |
| 40–49,999 | 969 | 44,761 | 43.4 | 182 | 31 | 11.4 | 14.4 | 30.4 | 1.31 | 94% |
| 50–59,999 | 498 | 53,026 | 26.4 | 186 | 32 | 12.1 | 14.5 | 34.4 | 1.28 | 80% |
| *Panamax* | | | | | | | | | | |
| 60–79,999 | 1,292 | 71,350 | 92.2 | 218 | 32 | 13.4 | 14.4 | 36.7 | 1.18 | 7% |
| 80–99,999 | 121 | 87,542 | 10.6 | 230 | 37 | 13.7 | 14.3 | 42.0 | 1.14 | 2% |
| *Capesize* | | | | | | | | | | |
| 100–149,999 | 173 | 137,714 | 23.8 | 257 | 43 | 16.6 | 14.2 | 49.8 | 1.10 | 2% |
| 150–199,999 | 468 | 170,227 | 79.7 | 276 | 45 | 17.6 | 14.5 | 53.9 | 1.09 | 0% |
| 199,999+ | 74 | 229,096 | 17.0 | 303 | 52 | 18.9 | 14.0 | 60.3 | 0.87 | 1% |
| Grand total | 6,430 | 57,355 | 368.8 | 191 | 30 | 11.9 | 14.4 | 33.4 | 1.18 | 60% |

Source: *Bulk Carrier Register* 2006, Clarkson Research Studies, London

there has been a steady upward trend in the size of ship used in most bulk trades. For example, in 1969 only about 5% of the iron ore was shipped in vessels over 80,000 dwt, but by the early 1990s over 80% of the trade was shipped in vessels of this size, mainly 150,000–180,000 dwt.

In fact the bulk carrier market has evolved into several different size bands, each focusing on a different sector of the trade, and as a result the ships in the bulk carrier fleet are spread fairly evenly across the size range, with the greatest concentration by numbers in the smaller sizes as shown in Table 14.9. At the smaller end of the range, Handy bulk carriers of 10,000–40,000 dwt fill the role of flexible workhorses in trades where parcel size and draft restrictions demand small ships. Typically they carry minor bulks and smaller parcels of major bulks such as grain, coal and bauxite and in busy maritime areas such as Asia can often complete two loaded voyages for every ballast voyage. This is a great improvement over the larger bulk carriers which often alternate loaded and ballast voyages.

As ports have improved over the last 20 years, a new generation of larger 40,000–60,000 dwt Handy bulkers has emerged, generally referred to as Handymax bulk carriers. Like the Handy bulkers, these vessels are generally geared. In the centre of the market are the Panamax bulk carriers of 60,000–100,000 dwt, which service the trades in coal, grain, bauxite and the larger minor bulk parcels. These medium-sized ships are named Panamaxes because they can transit the Panama Canal, but vessels at the larger end of the range are too big to do so, at least until the Canal is extended. The upper end is served by bulk carriers of 100,000–300,000 dwt, which are heavily dependent on the iron ore and coal trades. There is a good deal of interchange between these size groups and in the last resort the choice is a trade-off between unit cost and cargo flexibility: the small vessel is flexible but expensive to run, while the large vessels become progressively cheaper and more inflexible.

Bulk carriers are generally designed for cheapness and simplicity. Key design features are cubic capacity, access to the holds, and cargo-handling gear. Hold design is important because cargoes such as grain can easily shift and, if unchecked, can capsize the ship. To prevent this, bulk carriers generally have self-trimming holds in which the topside wing tanks are sloped in such a way that granular cargoes can be loaded by gravity without having to trim the cargo out into the wings of the hold.

On conventional bulk carriers, hatch openings are generally 45–60% of the beam (width) and around 65–75% of the hold's length. This arrangement has the disadvantage that hatch openings are too narrow to allow vertical access to all parts of the cargo hold, with the result that it is difficult to handle large cargo units such as rolls of paper, steel products, pre-slung timber, cars loaded in pallets or containers in a single operation. However, because the deck makes an important contribution to the structural strength of the ship, wider hatches can only be accommodated by adding structural steel to reinforce the vessel, considerably increasing costs. The hatch widths described above represent a trade-off between cargo-handling speed and building cost that has been found to work well in practice.

Most bulk carriers are fitted with steel hatch covers, of which there are several designs available. The self-supporting type is the most popular. Each hatch cover has four to six sections extending across the hatchway, with rollers operating on a runway. The covers are opened by rolling them to the end of the hatch where they tip automatically into a vertical position so that they are not in the way during cargo handling. Another consideration is whether or not to fit cargo-handling gear. Cargo-handling gear is normally fitted to smaller bulk carriers, since they are more likely to operate into ports with inadequate shore-based facilities. Table 14.9 shows that few bulk carriers over 50,000 dwt have cargo-handling gear, compared with 80–90% of smaller vessels. This is because the transport operations for bigger ships generally involve specialist terminals with purpose-built cargo-handling facilities so that they can turn around quickly.

The cargo gear is generally cranes, since derricks are now largely obsolete. A common arrangement for Handymax bulk carriers is to fit four 30- or 35-tonne cranes serving holds 1–4 and 5. Occasionally gantry cranes on rails are fitted, especially for the forest products trade, whilst continuous self-discharging bulk carriers take an even more radical approach to cargo handling. They use a shipboard conveyor system fed by gravity from the bottom of the holds. This allows them to unload cargo at rates of up to 6,000 tonnes per hour, though the high cost and the weight of the cargo-handling equipment mean that they are most economic in short-haul trades involving many cargo-handling operations.

The bulk carrier illustrated in Figure 14.5 is a 77,000 dwt Panamax vessel, one of the new generation with a double hull. It has seven holds, each with a grain capacity of around 13,000 cubic metres, or around 11,000 tonnes of cargo, depending on density.

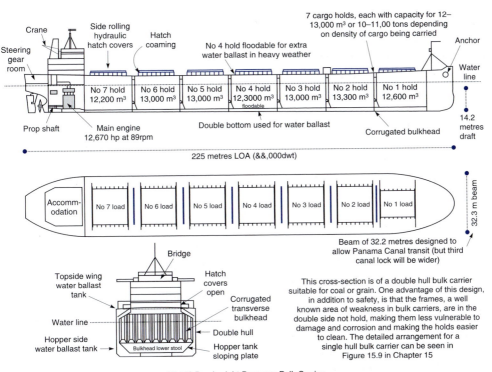

**77,000 Deadweight Panamax Bulk Carrier**

| HULL | CARGO | MACHINERY & EQUIPMENT |
|---|---|---|
| Deadweight (summer draft): 77,053 | Strengthened for heavy cargoes | Engine: MAN B&W 5S60MC-C two-stroke |
| Deadweight (winter draft): 75,073 | Bale capacity: 89,121 m³ | Power max (hp): 12,670@89 rpm (9.32 MW) |
| Gross tonnage: 40,424 | *hatches* | Power continuous: 10,135@83 rpm (7.45 MW) |
| Net tonnage (international): 25,482 | Hatch dimensions: 1 18.8×14.1 | Maximum speed (knots): 14.5 (15% SM) |
|  | 6 17.9×19.3 | Fuel consumption: 35 tons/day |
| *dimensions (all in metres)* | hatch covers: side rolling, hydraulic |  |
| Length, overall (m): 225.0 | *Cargo capacity of holds* | *auxiliary engines* |
| Length between perpendiculars: 220.0 | Grain 000 m³ 000 tonnes | Generators: 2 AC generators 475 KVA |
| Overall beam (m): 32.3 | No 1 Hold: 12.6 10.5 at 1.2m³/t | Generator engines: 2×570 hp diesels |
| Summer draft (m): scantling 14.19 | No 2 Hold: 13.3 11.1 typical of | Aux boiler: 1 cylindrical composite boiler |
| Winter draft (m): scantling 13.90 | No 3 Hold: 13.0 10.9 coal | Emergency generator: 120 KVA |
|  | No 4 Hold: 12.3 10.3 | Ballast pumps: 2 centrifugal type 800 m³/h |
| *tank capacities* | No 5 Hold: 13.0 10.9 | Fire pumps: 2 centrifugal type |
| heavy oil 2,193 m³ | No 6 Hold: 13.0 10.9 | *Crew* |
| diesel oil 145 m³ | No 7 Hold: 12.2 10.2 | Officers: 9 |
| lubricating oil 114 m³ | Total 89.5 74.6 | Petty officer: 3 |
| water ballast 37,164 m³ | Holds, Nos 2, 4 and 6 may be empty | Ratings, pilot, 2 spare 14 |
|  | with dense iron ore in holds 1, 3, 5, and 7 | Total 24 + 2 spare |

## Figure 14.5
Panamax bulk carrier (77,000 dwt), built 2006
Source: Drawing by Martin Stopford based on vessel built by Oshima Shipbuilding Co., Japan

The holds are separated by corrugated bulk heads and the hatch covers are very wide, about 60% of the beam of the vessel, giving improved vertical access to the holds. Since this is a Panamax vessel the beam is 32.3 metres, the maximum which can transit the Panama Canal (before it is widened). The vessel has a slow-speed two-stroke engine generating 12,670 hp at 89 rpm and the speed is a comparatively modest 14.5 knots on a consumption of 35 tonnes per day, which is normal for a bulk carrier. There are two AC generators driven by diesel engines, an auxiliary boiler and an emergency generator. In addition, the ship has two ballast pumps handling 800 cubic metres an hour and ballast water is carried in the topside tanks, the double bottom and hopper side tanks and a floodable hold for use in heavy weather.

## The open hatch bulk carrier (conbulker)

There was a fleet of 480 open hatch bulk carriers in 2006 ranging in size from 10,000 to 69,000 dwt. They are designed to offer direct access to the hold through hatches which extend the full width of the vessel, allowing large cargo units to be lowered into place. Where possible the holds/hatches are designed around standard cargo unit sizes, including containers, with special attention paid to shipboard cargo-handling gear, and sometimes a gantry crane is fitted. All this is expensive because when the hatches are widened extra steel is needed to provide strength and the cargo-handling gear adds to the cost. As a result, a high-specification open-hatch bulk carrier can cost up to 50% more than a conventional vessel of the same size. Typically the 'open' hatches extend the full width of the vessel. This is particularly useful for forest products, which stow at anything from 2.3 cubic metres per tonne for pre-slung timber to 2.8 cubic metres per tonne for logs, and the heavy units are difficult to handle through the narrow hatches of a conventional bulk carrier or 'tweendecker. Open-hatch bulk carriers can also be used to carry containers on the outward leg, and dry bulk on the return leg which is particularly useful for repositioning empty containers between regions.

## Woodchip carriers

Woodchip carriers have a high internal cubic capacity to accommodate the low-density woodchips. There were 129 ships in the bulk fleet in 2006 ranging in size from 12,000 to 74,000 dwt and typically cargo stows at around $2.5 \, m^3$ per deadweight compared with $1.3 \, m^3$ per deadweight for a general-purpose bulk carrier. Some are fitted with gantry cranes, though shore-based pneumatic handling equipment is often used.

## Ore carriers

Ore carriers originally found a market because of the high density of iron ore, which stows at approximately $0.5 \, m^3$ per tonne, compared with a normal bulk carrier's capacity of $1.3–1.4 \, m^3$ per ton. They are built with holds designed for this high-density cargo, though general-purpose bulk carriers with strengthened holds or combined carriers are preferred owing to their more flexible trading opportunities. A few very large ore carriers have been built and some converted from single-hull tankers. In 2006 there were about 51 ore carriers in the fleet.

## Pure car carriers

Another trade for which specialized bulk ships have been built is wheeled cargo. This is a rapidly growing segment, with 594 vessels in 2006. Initially cars were shipped in cargo liners but, as the volume of seaborne trade increased in the 1960s, bulk shipment became economically viable. The first development was to fit bulk carriers with car decks that could fold up to allow other bulk cargoes to be carried – a classic combined voyage was cars from Emden to San Francisco, returning with grain to Rotterdam. However, the low carrying capacity of car bulkers (one car per 13 dwt), combined with the additional weight of the decks, the slow loading and a high risk of damage in transit, made them a poor compromise.

As the car trade grew in size in the 1970s, vehicle carriers were purpose-built to carry new cars and small commercial vehicles such as vans and pick-ups. They have multiple decks (anything from 4 to 13 depending on size) with a high cubic capacity to dead-weight ratio (e.g. one car per 3 dwt), high speed (around 20 knots for the bigger ones), ro-ro loading/discharging facilities, and internal decks and ramps carefully designed to speed cargo handling and minimize damage.

The fleet varies in size and operation from ships of 499 grt with four decks each, carrying 500 cars in the European short-sea trades, up to Wallenius' *Madame Butterfly* of 27,779 dwt carrying 6,200 cars world-wide, though in 2008 the largest vessels on the orderbook were 29,000 dwt with a capacity of 8,000 vehicles. Specialization brought a cost in terms of restricting the cargo to motor cars and light trucks. With the more volatile market of the late 1970s there was a move towards developing vehicle carriers capable of handling a wider range of cargo. The *Undine* (2003) can carry 7200 cars on 13 decks. To carry large, heavy cargoes the stern ramp can carry loads up to 125 tonnes. Decks 4, 6 and 8 are strengthened and their height is adjustable by hoistable sections in decks 5, 7 and 9. This allows bulk parcels of cars to be supplemented by consignments of large vehicles such as trucks, buses, agricultural machinery and heavy plant, which cannot be accommodated between the low-headroom decks of a conventional car carrier.

## Cement carriers

Cement is a difficult and dusty cargo to handle, and some specialist cement carriers have been built. Typically they use pneumatic cargo-handling gear with totally enclosed holds and moisture control systems. For example, a 20,000 dwt bulk cement carrier might have four pairs of cargo holds and be designed to handle two grades of Portland cement, with a weight of up to 1.2 tonnes per cubic metre. Shore-based chutes deliver the cement to a single-point receiving system on each side of the ship at a rate of 1,000 tonnes per hour. A dust collection system may also be fitted. The cement is discharged at a rate of 1,200 tonnes per hour using the ship's own cargo-handling gear. Aeration panels in the tank top of each hold fluidize the cargo, allowing it to be pumped out of the hold by blow pumps located in a pump room amidships and discharged to shore-based reception facilities using the ship's boom conveyor. In principle, ships like this can be used to carry any cargo with a fine particle size.

## 14.5 SHIPS FOR LIQUID BULK CARGOES

The transportation of bulk liquids by sea generally requires the use of tankers. The main types of tanker are for the transport of crude oil, oil products, chemicals, LPG and LNG.

### Crude oil tankers

Oil tankers (Table 14.10) form by far the largest fleet of specialist bulk vessels, with over 6,000 vessels, accounting for 37% of the merchant fleet measured in tonnes deadweight. The size of individual tankers ranges from below 1,000 dwt to over 400,000 dwt; up to 1,245 feet (380 metres) in length; up to 222 feet (68 metres) in breadth; and drawing up to 80 feet (24.5 metres) of water.[8] This fleet can usefully be subdivided into six segments: small tankers (under 10,000 dwt), Handy (10,000–59,999 dwt), Panamax (60,000–79,999 dwt), Aframax (80,000–119,999 dwt), Suezmax (120,000–199,999 dwt), and VLCC (over 200,000 dwt). Each of these segments operates as a separate market and, from a ship design viewpoint, each has its own specific requirements.

**Table 14.10** The tanker fleet, January 2006

| Size 000 dwt | Tanker fleet size | | | Hull characteristics | | | Performance | | |
| | No. | Total dwt (mill.) | Av dwt | Age 2006 | Beam m | Draught m | Capacity 000 bbl | Tanks (number) | Speed (knots) | Fuel cons (t/day) |
|---|---|---|---|---|---|---|---|---|---|---|
| *Small* | | | | | | | | | | |
| 1–5 | 921 | 2.6 | 2,783 | 19 | 12.7 | 5.1 | 19 | 11 | 12.2 | 7.9 |
| 5–9 | 1115 | 7.7 | 6,867 | 16 | 17 | 6.8 | 48 | 13.6 | 13 | 13 |
| *Handy* | | | | | | | | | | |
| 10–19 | 728 | 11 | 15,051 | 14 | 21.7 | 8.6 | 106 | 16.5 | 14 | 22.5 |
| 20–29 | 313 | 8.3 | 26,611 | 19 | 25.5 | 10.3 | 201 | 19 | 14.7 | 29.9 |
| 30–39 | 589 | 21 | 35,626 | 13 | 28.8 | 11 | 254 | 18.1 | 15.1 | 37 |
| 40–60 | 740 | 34 | 45,895 | 9 | 31.8 | 12.1 | 320 | 13.4 | 14.7 | 34.1 |
| *Panamax* | | | | | | | | | | |
| 60–79 | 325 | 22.6 | 69,466 | 11 | 32.8 | 13.4 | 482 | 10.9 | 14.8 | 39.1 |
| *Aframax* | | | | | | | | | | |
| 80–120 | 721 | 72.9 | 101,100 | 10 | 41.7 | 14.3 | 702 | 10.9 | 15 | 46 |
| *Suezmax* | | | | | | | | | | |
| 120–200 | 361 | 54.4 | 150,673 | 10 | 46.7 | 16.6 | 1,011 | 11.9 | 14.9 | 62.9 |
| *VLCC* | | | | | | | | | | |
| 200+ | 488 | 142.7 | 292,412 | 9 | 58.4 | 21.2 | 2,040 | 14.2 | 15.3 | 85.7 |
| Total/Av. | 6,301 | 377 | 59,834 | 12.9 | 31.7 | 11.9 | 518 | 13.9 | 14.4 | 37.8 |

Source: Clarkson Research Studies, *Tanker Register* 2006, London

The Handy tankers under 50,000 dwt are mainly used for the transport of oil products (see the next section for details) and the larger vessels for the transport of crude oil.

There are two different designs for oil tankers, single hull and double hull. Until the 1990s most crude tankers had a single skin, using the hull as the main containment vessel. The single hull design had longitudinal bulkheads running the length of the ship from the bow to the engine room, dividing the hull into three sets of tanks, the port wing tanks, the centre tanks, and the starboard wing tanks. Transverse bulkheads running across the ship divide these three sets of tanks into separate cargo compartments. In single-hull vessels two or more sets of wing tanks act as 'segregated ballast tanks', which means they are only used for ballast water.

Single-hull tankers are now obsolete. IMO Regulation 13F required tankers ordered after 6 July 1993 to have double hulls as a protective measure against oil loss. A typical arrangement is shown in Figure 14.6. The regulations lay down precise rules regarding the width of the double sides and the double bottom, but the principle is simple enough. There must be a second skin to limit the outflow of oil in the event of collision or grounding damage to the outer hull. In December 2003 IMO passed Resolution MEPC.111(50) to phase out all remaining single-hull tankers by 2010, though it allowed local administrations to permit continued trading on a bilateral basis.

Cargo handling is an important aspect of tanker design. Rapid loading and discharge requires powerful pumps. Crude tankers rely on shore-based facilities for loading, but carry their own cargo pumps for discharge. The pumps are generally located in a pump room between the cargo tanks and the engine room, though tankers carrying different cargo parcels in different holds often have submerged deep well pumps. Pipes running along the deck link the cargo tanks to two banks of manifolds, one on each side of the ship. To load or discharge cargo the manifolds are connected to the shore-based storage tanks by flexible hoses, or fixed Chicksan arms, which are handled by the ship's cranes. The flow of oil is controlled by valves operated from a panel in the cargo control room and must conform to a plan which minimizes stress on the hull – an incorrect load or discharge sequence can literally break a ship in two.[9]

Figure 14.6 shows an example of a 157,800 dwt Suezmax tanker delivered in 2006. This is a medium-sized crude tanker, but the broad design features do not differ significantly for the smaller Aframax and the larger VLCC designs. The tanker has a double skin and scantling deadweight of 157,800 tonnes, with a cargo capacity of $175,000\,m^3$. However the design of the hull is optimized to a smaller 145,900 dwt, which would allow the ship to carry a 1 million barrel parcel of light (API 30) crude oil. This is a commonly traded parcel size and the arrangement gives the ship the flexibility to carry a full parcel of heavier crude oils than the design standard or extra cargo deadweight if necessary. This arrangement is very common in ships designed for the products trade where some cargoes such as naphtha have a very low specific gravity (see Table 11.5). It is all a matter of deciding what cargoes are likely to be carried and finding the best trade-off between tank volume and design cargo deadweight.

The hull was constructed using 53% high tensile steel, which is relatively high, but the structure was designed for a fatigue life of 40 years, with particular attention paid

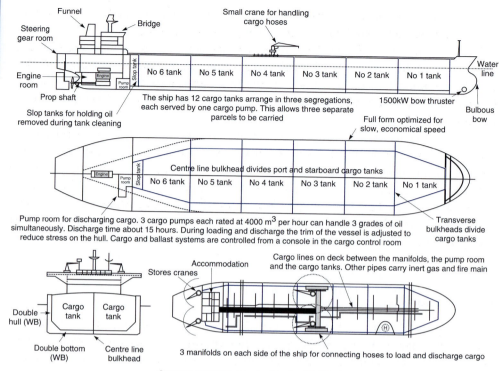

**Figure 14.6**
'Suezmax' crude oil tanker (157,800 dwt) design
Source: Drawing by Martin Stopford, based on design by DSME Shipbuilding Group, S. Korea

Suezmax 157,800 dwt crude oil tanker (87,167 gt)

| HULL | | MACHINERY | | OTHER | |
|---|---|---|---|---|---|
| Main Dimensions (m) | | Speed & Main Engine | | Navigation Equipment | |
| Deadweight (design) | 145,900 dwt | Speed, | 15.2 kts 15% sea margin | Radar plant | 2 |
| Scantling (scantling) | 157,800 dwt | Engine Type | Man B&W 6S70MC-C | Auto pilot/Gyro compass | 1 |
| Length over all (m) | 274 | Power output | 22,920 bhp×91 rpm (16.8 MW) | DGPS navigator | 2 |
| Length between perp. | 264 | NCR (90% DMCR) | 20,630 bhp×87.9 rpm (15.2 MW) | Painting System | |
| Breadth, moulded (m) | 48 | D.F.O.C at NCR | 60.5 MT/day | Under water hull: epoxy anti-corrosive | |
| Depth, moulded (m) | 23.2 | Cruising range | 22,900 NM | Antifouling | + Tin free SPC |
| Draught (design) (m) | 16 | | | Cargo tanks | Tar free epoxy |
| Draught (scantling) (m) | 17 | Main generators | Diesel: 3 Sets × 950 kW | Water ballast tanks: Tar free epoxy | |
| Tank Capacity (m³) | | Emergency generator | 1 Set × 300 kW | (Bottom & up to 0.5 m deck head | |
| Cargo tanks inc. slop | 175,000 | Steam Generating Plant | | and down to 1.7 m only) | |
| Heavy fuel oil tanks | 4,300 | Aux. boiler | : 2 Sets × 35 ton/h | | |
| Diesel oil tanks | 200 | Economizer: | 1 Set × 1.8 ton/h | Crew 28 | |
| Fresh water tanks | 400 | Water Ballast System | | % high tensile steel 53% | |
| Ballast water tanks | 54,500 | System | Two main line | | |
| Cargo System | | Pump | 2 pumps × 2,500 m³/h × 30m head | | |
| Segregation | Three groups | | Vertical centrifugal type | | |
| Pump | 3 Sets × 4,000 m³/h × 135mc | | 1-Electric motor driven | | |
| Vertical centrifugal, steam turbine driven | | | 1-Steam turbine driven | | |

to known areas of weakness such as the end connections of the longitudinal stiffeners to the transverse webs and bulkheads. It has 12 cargo tanks plus two slop tanks, arranged in three segregations. Three steam turbine pumps are located in the pump room between the engine room and the cargo tanks. Each pump serves a separate segregation, allowing the ship to handle three grades of cargo simultaneously, which is useful for carrying a combination of smaller parcels and for multi-port discharge. The cargo tanks are coated with tar-free epoxy, another useful extra.

The speed of 15.2 knots on 60.5 tonnes per day is typical for a ship of the size, as can be seen from Table 14.10. Electrical supplies are obtained from three 950 kW diesel generator sets, with one smaller emergency back-up generator and two auxiliary boilers. In addition, a waste heat economizer is fitted, another useful extra to improve fuel efficiency.

A final and less usual feature of a tanker this size is its ice class 1A classification. This means the hull is strengthened and an ice knife is built into the stern. In addition, all deck equipment can operate at –30°C. For example, deck hydraulics are heated to prevent freezing and electric motors are used in preference to air motors. The ice class certification makes the tanker acceptable to charterers for trades where ice is a problem, and is more common on the smaller products tankers, especially those trading in the Baltic. However, new trades are developing, especially out of Russia, where the bigger ships can be used.

## Products tankers

Products tankers form a separate category of vessel within the oil tanker fleet, but one which is not clearly defined in statistical terms because the distinction between crude, products tankers and chemical tankers is blurred. Products tankers are similar to crude oil tankers but generally smaller and are divided into clean products tankers, which carry light products such as gasoline and naphtha, and dirty products tankers, which carry the black oils such as fuel oil (see Table 11.5 for details) and a submerged cargo pump in each hold (deep well pumps), allowing separate grades of cargo to be carried on each voyage. Products tankers generally have tank coatings to prevent cargo contamination and reduce corrosion.

## Chemical tankers

In Chapter 12 we reviewed transport of chemicals by sea and in Table 12.3 split the fleet into three categories of vessels – chemical parcel tankers, chemical bulk tankers, and chemical/products tankers. These categories, which are mainly based on the number of segregations in the ship, make a good starting point, but when we dig a little deeper we find at least six characteristics of this trade which influence ship design:

- Many different types of chemicals are shipped, including products such as vegetable oils, lube oils, molasses, caustic soda, BTX, styrene and a whole range of specialist chemicals (see Chapter 12).
- Values are high, often over $1,000 per tonne, and the products transported are sensitive to cargo contamination.
- Parcel sizes are small, ranging from 300 tonnes to 6,000 tonnes, with a few larger industrial chemical trades such as caustic soda and MTBE which travel in parcels of up to 40,000 tonnes.

- Small parcels are frequently traded interregionally, and if a small chemical tanker of the appropriate size is used, the freight cost is very high, on a long journey from Europe to the Far East reaching as much as $150 per tonne.
- Some chemicals are corrosive and require special cargo handling and tank characteristics.
- Some chemicals are subject to the IMO regulations on the transport of hazardous cargoes, as discussed below.

Starting with the commodities, the chemicals to be transported vary enormously. The products carried by the chemical tanker fleet were discussed in Chapter 12 and include some bulk chemicals such as naphtha, BTX, alcohols and a large number of specialized chemicals, many of which travel in small parcels and require special handling because of physical characteristics which can damage the ship, the environment or both. In addition, liquid cargoes such as lubricating oils, vegetable oils and molasses fall into this trade group, along with cargoes such as molten sulphur which need much higher temperatures (80°C and above) than other cargoes. As a result, the design of chemical tankers involves many compromises to provide a design which will offer the right balance of cargo flexibility and capital costs.

In addition the ship design must comply with IMO regulations for the carriage of dangerous substances. Carriage of chemicals in bulk is covered by IMO regulations in SOLAS Chapter VII (Carriage of Dangerous Goods and MARPOL Annex II (Regulations for the Control of Pollution by Noxious Liquid Substances in Bulk); see Chapter 16. Both conventions require chemical tankers built after 1 July 1986 to comply with the International Bulk Chemical Code, which gives international standards for the safe transport by sea in bulk of liquid dangerous chemicals, by prescribing the design and construction standards of ships involved in such transport and the equipment they should carry so as to minimize the risks to the ship, its crew and to the environment, having regard to the nature of the products carried. The ship must be capable of dealing efficiently with four hazardous properties of commodities transported: flammability, toxicity, corrosivity, and reactivity. Chemical tankers are classed as being suitable for the carriage of IMO Type 1, Type 2, or Type 3 chemical and oil products, depending on their design characteristics.

All of this leaves the designers juggling characteristics such as cargo tank size and segregations; heating coils; tank coatings; special valve operating gear; and safety systems. In addition to carrying many cargo parcels, chemical tankers tend to load and discharge at several ports, and often different berths within the port. To achieve this flexibility, each cargo tank has a separate cargo-handling system, allowing the ship to carry many small chemical parcels on a single voyage. Vessels operating in liner services on long-haul routes may have 30 or 40 segregated tanks, allowing them to carry a wide range of regulated cargoes. Tank coatings are used to deal with corrosivity and reactivity and three different tank protection methods are used – stainless steel for corrosive cargo and zinc silicate or epoxy coatings which suit most others. Tanks for the most toxic and pervasive substances classified as Type 1 by IMO must be located not less than one-fifth of the ship's breadth from the ship's sides, measured at the water line. All in all it is a complex business for both the investor, who must decide what level of sophistication makes commercial sense, and the designer, who must create a ship which will operate successfully for 20–30 years.

The main features of the sophisticated chemical tanker illustrated in Figure 14.7 will be familiar from the discussion of the crude oil tanker earlier in this section. The ship has a double hull with cargo tanks laid out either side of a corrugated longitudinal bulkhead, separated by corrugated transverse bulkheads. However, this chemical tanker has a number of very significant features which differentiate it from the crude tanker.

The ship is designed to carry IMO Type 2 cargos in 18 tanks and two slop tanks, all constructed from stainless steel with stiffeners on the outside (for example, they can be seen on the deck), giving smooth internal surfaces for easy tank cleaning and stainless steel heating coils to maintain the cargo at 82°C. Heavy cargoes with a specific gravity of up to 1.55, for example caustic soda, can be loaded in all tanks. Each of the 18 tanks has a separate cargo-handling system with its own submerged cargo pump and separate pipelines to the manifold located amidships, where the cargo lines can be connected to hoses leading to storage tanks onshore. There are two cranes to handle the hoses and the manifold has ten hose connections, five on each side of the ship. All the pipes and valves are constructed of stainless steel, and five pumps can work simultaneously to discharge cargo through the five manifold outlets giving a total discharge rate of 1500 $m^3$ per hour.

Propulsion is provided by a medium-speed diesel engine operating at 500 rpm, with a gearbox which reduces the propeller speed to 140 per rpm. The operating speed is 14.2 knots on 20.5 tonnes of fuel per day, and electricity for ship equipment is provided by three diesel-powered alternators. There is also a shaft generator which provides electricity when the main engine is running. The gearbox also has a power 'take in' which in an emergency can use electricity from the three alternators to drive the vessel at 7 knots, or to top up the power of the main engine.

Since the vessel was designed to operate in the Baltic Sea, encountering ice regularly, it is ice class 1A. In addition to the features mentioned for the crude oil tanker in Figure 14.6, its deck cargo lines and valves are encased in a tunnel running from the poop deck to the enclosed forecastle, an unusual feature, but an interesting example of an owner paying for an extra feature that will make the ship easier and safer to operate in difficult weather conditions. In summary, this is a very sophisticated tanker, designed with specific operating conditions in mind, and the owner made a considerable investment to achieve this performance.

## Combined carriers

Combined carriers deserve a section to themselves, if only as an example of the problems facing investors in ships for niche markets (see Section 14.2). To give the ships greater flexibility, oil/bulk/ore carriers (often referred to as OBOs or combined carriers) are designed to carry a full cargo of dry bulk or crude oil. This means the ships can

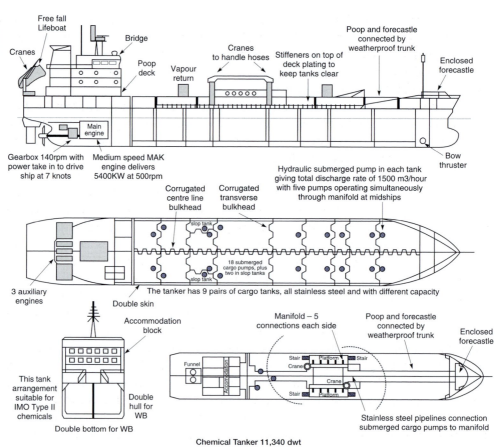

The tanker has 9 pairs of cargo tanks, all stainless steel and with different capacity

Chemical Tanker 11,340 dwt

| HULL | | MACHINERY | | OTHER | |
|------|------|-----------|------|-------|------|
| **Main Dimensions (m)** | | **Propulsion Machinery** | | **Cargo System** | |
| Gtoss tons | 7,903 gt | Speed, | 14.17 kts 90% MCR | Tank segregations | 18 plus 2 slop tanks |
| Deadweight (design) | 9,751 dwt | Engine Type | Caterpillar MAK 6M43 | Tanks on deck | $2 \times 120\,m^3$ |
| Scantling (scantling) | 11,339 dwt | Power output | 5400 kW at 500 rpm | Cargo grades | IMO II and oil products |
| Length over all (m) | 126.2 | Fuel Consumption – main | 20.5 MT/day | Pumps (submerged) | 18 plus 2 slop tanks |
| Length between perp. (m) | 119.2 | – auxiliaries | 2.9 MT/day | Pump capacity | $14 \times 300\,m^3/hr$ and |
| | | | | | $6 \times 100\,m^3/hr$ |
| Breadth, moulded (m) | 19 | Cruising range | 9,124 NM | Total discharge rate | 1500 $m^3$ per hour |
| Depth, moulded (m) | 10.7 | Prop shaft | 140 rpm | Vapour collector for shore return | |
| Draught (design) (m) | 7.6 | -shaft generator | 1000 kW | 2 tank washing appliances per tank | |
| Draught (scantling) (m) | 8.34 | -emergency prop motor | 1000 kW | Stainless steel heating coils to | |
| | | | | maintain tanks at 82°C | |
| Lightweight (tonnes) | 4,300 | -main engine boost | 5,400 kW + 1000 kW | Vertical centrifugal, steam turbine driven | |
| **Tank Capacity (m³)** | | Propellor diameter | 4,600 mm | Fire extinguishing system | |
| Cargo tanks | 12,120 | **Power Supply** | | Fire detection system | |
| Tank construction | Stainless, inc. pipes | Shaft generator | 1000 kW at 1800rpm | **Complement** | |
| Heavy fuel oil tanks | 550 | Diesel alternators | $3 \times 660$ kW at 900 rpm | Officers | 6 |
| Diesel oil tanks | 162 | | $3 \times 600$ kW at 900 rpm | Ratings | 8 |
| Ballast water tanks | 4300 | Power take-in on gearbox can drive ship at 7 kts | | Spare | 3 |
| **Paint System** | | Boilers | $2 \times 6$ ton/h | Total | 17 |
| Under water hull: epoxy anti-corrosion | | | | Class: Ice Class 1A | |
| Antifouling | + Tin free SPC | Bow thruster | $1 \times 600$ kW | High tensile steel | 8% |
| Cargo tanks | Tar free epoxy | | | | |
| Water ballast tanks: | Tar free epoxy bottom & up to 0.5 m, deck head and down to 1.7 m only | | | | |

## Figure 14.7

Chemical parcel tanker, 11,340 dwt

Source: Drawing by Martin Stopford, based on vessel built by INP Heavy Industries Co. Ltd, S. Korea

triangulate, for example shipping oil from the Middle East to Europe and returning to Asia with a cargo of Polish coal. They could also switch between the tanker and dry bulk markets to take advantage of a rate differential, or to reduce ballast time by carrying dry and liquid cargoes on alternate legs ('triangulation voyages'). In practice, the rewards for flexibility have been slim.

The concept of flexible ships carrying oil on the main leg and returning with a different cargo date back to the early days of the oil trade and in general has not been very successful. The first ocean-going tank steamer, the *Vaderland* (1872), was designed to carry passengers from Belgium to the USA and return with a cargo of petroleum. Unfortunately the owners could not obtain a licence to carry passengers and oil in the same ship so the *Vaderland* ended up carrying general cargo in the petroleum tanks.[10] In the 1920s two ore/oilers, the *Svealand* and the *Amerikaland*, were designed to carry iron ore from Peru to Baltimore, returning with a cargo of oil. This time the plan was frustrated by the high transit charges for the Panama Canal and they never carried oil. However, in the 1950s and 1960s combined carriers achieved greater success, capitalizing on the newly emerging oil and dry cargo trades.

Two different designs were used. The first to enter service in the 1950s were the ore/oilers. These vessels had holds in the centre of the ship to carry high-density iron ore, with side and bottom tanks designed to carry a full cargo of oil. The use of separate compartments avoided the need for cleaning between cargoes, but was wasteful of space and the dry leg was limited to high-density iron ore. The second design, which appeared in the mid-1960s, was the OBO which carried oil or dry bulk in the same cargo spaces. Typically these vessels have double bottoms and holds to carry oil, of which up to six can be used for ore or dry bulk. Hatch covers are oil-tight and gas-tight. Because they could switch between wet and dry markets, they made handsome profits during the three tanker booms in 1967, 1970 and 1973 (see Chapter 2).

So great was the enthusiasm for combined carriers that by the mid-1970s a fleet of 49 m.dwt had been built. Unfortunately this fleet far exceeded the available return cargoes, so the competitive advantage was lost. In addition, the time and difficulty of cleaning the cargo holds when switching between oil and dry cargo made the vessels difficult to charter, especially to oil companies. The resulting indifferent commercial performance of combined carriers was compounded by the fact that the ships were complex to build, maintain and operate, costing about 15% more to run than a comparable tanker or bulk carrier and oil charterers preferred a conventional tanker. In the early 1990s operators of combined carrier fleets were reporting a 10–15% revenue premium (say $2,000–3,000 per day), which paid the extra cost of operating the ship, but left little surplus to cover the higher capital cost. To make matters worse, the large combined carrier fleet ensured that surplus capacity was transmitted between the tanker and dry bulk markets, helping to moderate market peaks. As a result, from the mid-1970s onwards few new ships were ordered and by 2007 the combined carrier fleet had fallen to 8 m.dwt. In retrospect the commercial failure of the combined carrier fleet had less to do with the concept, which was perfectly sound, than with the economic obstacles it faced in a competitive market such as shipping.

C
H
A
P
T
E
R
14

## 14.6 GAS TANKERS

### Basic gas tanker technology

Transporting liquid gas by sea presents many complexities, one of which is the number of different cargo systems which are currently in use. So at the outset it is useful to define the various options available. The starting point is the containment system, and there are three options. The first is to use a 'self-supporting' tank system, which sits on a cradle which separates it from the hull. The second is the 'membrane' system which moulds the tank to the hull, which provides its strength, with insulation sandwiched between the tank membrane and the hull. The membrane must be able to cope with extreme temperature changes. The third option is the 'prismatic' system, which is a hybrid, using self-supporting tanks with an inner and outer skin, but tied into the main hull structure. Although the design details vary enormously, all gas tankers fall into one of these categories.

The gas is liquefied onshore prior to loading and there are three ways to keep it liquid during transport: by pressure;[11] by insulating the tanks; or by reliquefying any gas which boils off and returning it to the cargo tanks (petroleum gas remains liquid at around −48°C). In practice it is all a matter of economics, and various different permutations of refrigeration and pressure are used. Some small LPG tankers rely entirely on pressure, but this is uneconomic for large cargo parcels which use an on-board refrigeration plant to reliquefy boil-off gas and return it to the cargo tanks. Prior to 2006 LNG tankers did not carry refrigeration equipment, relying entirely on speed and heavy insulation to minimize the boil-off. Any burned-off gas was burnt in the ship's boilers.

### Liquid petroleum gas tankers

The term 'LPG tanker' is confusing because gas tankers carry a mix of petroleum gases such as propane, butane and isobutene and chemical gases such as ammonia, ethylene, propylene, butadiene and vinyl chloride. Most of these gases liquefy at temperatures ranges from −0.5°C to −50°C (see Table 12.4), but some liquefy at much lower temperatures (e.g. ethylene at −103.9°C). Gas tankers must be able to maintain gas at the required temperature during transport. In addition to temperature, the volume of cargo and the distance over which it is transported are also important. For example, LPG is shipped in large volumes on long-haul routes, especially from the Arabian Gulf to Japan, and the biggest LPG tankers are built for these trades. From a design viewpoint the LPG tankers in common use can be divided into four groups, depending largely on the size of the cargo being shipped.

*Fully pressurized vessels* carry liquefied gas in pressure tanks strong enough to prevent the gas cargo regasifying, even at ambient temperatures – typically 20 bar is required. The tanks are very heavy and this method is mainly used for small LPG tankers. In 2006 there were 540 pressurized vessels in the gas fleet, ranging in size from 100 to 11,000 m³. LPG and anhydrous ammonia are the most common cargoes, and the design pressure is optimized for propane at about 18 bar. Pressurized tankers have two to six cylindrical carbon steel pressure vessels resting on saddles built into the hull, or on deck. Cargo is carried at ambient temperature, and a compressor is usually provided to pressurize the cargo tanks during discharge or to transfer the cargo vapour when loading or discharging. Cargo handling is important because these short-haul ships make many port calls in a year. Because the cylindrical pressure tanks use the under-deck space inefficiently and are heavy, with a cargo to tank weight ratio of about 2 : 1, this system is mainly used for smaller ships.

*Semi-refrigerated vessels* have pressurized tanks constructed of carbon steel (typically 5–7 bar) with insulation to slow the boil-off and refrigeration plant to reliquefy the gas that escapes and return it to the tanks. These lighter-pressure vessels are located inside the hull (the cargo to tank weight ratio is typically about 4 : 1), and this is the preferred system for medium-sized LPG tankers. There were 280 semi-refrigerated ships in 2006, ranging in size from 1,000 to 30,000 m³. Depending on ship size and specification, the cargo is carried at minimum temperatures of about −50°C. Cargo handling is an issue, and when cargoes are loaded from fully pressurized storage tanks on shore it may also be necessary to refrigerate the cargo during loading by drawing off the vapours from the top of the tank. This process usually determines the size of the refrigerating plant if a reasonable loading rate is to be maintained.

*Fully refrigerated vessels* are generally built for the long-haul trades. In 2006 there were 197 fully refrigerated LPG vessels, ranging in size from 1,000 m³ to 100,000 m³. For example, a typical 82,276 m³ LPG tanker delivered in 2003 was 224 metres in length with a service speed of 16.75 knots. LPG weighs 0.6 tonnes per m³, so it was only 59,423 dwt with a draft of 12.6 metres (a similar sized crude oil tanker would be 87,000 dwt with a draft of 15.6 metres).[12] Cargo is carried at −46°C in unpressurized free-standing prismatic cargo tanks built of heat-treated carbon steel or alloy with centre line and transverse bulkheads to prevent 'sloshing'. The space between the hull and the tanks is insulated. Refrigeration plant reliquefies the boil-off gas and a cargo heater may also be fitted for discharging to storage tanks not constructed of low-temperature materials. The liquid gas is discharged through thermally insulated land-based pipes using the ship's pumps.

Ethylene an important intermediate product of the petrochemicals industry, which liquefies at −104°C and usually travels in small *ethylene carriers* ranging in size from about 2,000 m³ to 30,000 m³ (see Section 12.3). These are sophisticated vessels and some can carry ethane, LPG, ammonia, propylene butadiene, vinyl chloride monomer and even LNG. The tanks are insulated and may be self-supporting, prismatic or membrane type. Impurities such as oil, oxygen and carbon dioxide must be kept within acceptable limits when pumping, refrigerating, purging and inerting the gas cargo.

The choice between these four systems is a trade-off between the initial cost, cargo flexibility and operating cost, but the pressurized system is generally more economic for small ships and refrigeration for big ones. Broadly speaking, petrochemical gases are transported in semi-refrigerated or fully pressurized vessels under 20,000 m³, and LPG and ammonia gases are transported in fully refrigerated vessels, ranging in size from 20,000 to 80,000 m³, for long-haul, large-volume transportation. Some semi-refrigerated vessels can carry ethylene (−104°C) and ethane (−82°C); and in a few cases LNG. To a lesser extent, these smaller vessels are sometimes used to transport LPG and ammonia over short-haul routes, where the fully pressurized vessels mainly operate.

## Liquefied natural gas tankers

Natural gas is primarily an energy source. It is a high-volume commodity and very price-sensitive, so the cost of transport plays a major part in the trade's economics and ship design. LNG tankers generally form part of a carefully planned gas supply operation involving a substantial investment in shore-based liquefaction and regasification facilities. In 2007 there was a fleet of 240 vessels, with another 140 on order. These are the biggest gas tankers and in 2007 they ranged in size up to 153,000 m$^3$, with a new generation of 270,000 m$^3$ vessels on order for the long-haul Middle East to USA trades.

Natural gas liquefies at $-161.5°C$, at which temperature it is reduced to 1/630 times its original volume. However, this low temperature raises various issues for the ship designer. Before loading, the methane gas is liquefied by refrigeration in the terminal (the plant which does this is called a 'train') and pumped into the ship's insulated tanks at atmospheric pressure. Apart from keeping the gas at the required temperature, the tank system must be able to deal with the large temperature changes which occur when cargo is loaded and unloaded. LNG tankers rely on insulation and up to 0.3% of the cargo boils off per day. In the past LNG tankers did not reliquefy this gas as LPG tankers do, because of the high power required to do this.[13] Instead they burned it in the ship's boilers, which explains why steam turbines survived so long in this trade. Although less efficient than diesel engines, the boil-off provided 75% of the daily fuel consumption of a 75,000 m$^3$ vessel, making this an economic solution. However, the first LNG tankers with medium-speed diesel engines were delivered in 2006, and ships with reliquefaction plant and conventional slow-speed diesel engines in 2007.

Self-supporting, membrane and prismatic tank systems are all used for LNG tankers. The Moss system uses distinctive self-supporting spherical tanks with a single insulation layer. The membrane tank system offered by Gaz Transport has a primary and secondary thin membrane made of Invar (36% nickel iron) with insulation constructed of plywood boxes filled with Perlite, whilst the Technigaz system uses a stainless steel membrane. The two companies merged in 1994. IHI offers a prismatic system. In 2003 the Moss system had a 51% market share, whilst Gaz Transport had 37% and Technigaz 11%.

An example of an LNG tanker using the membrane system is shown in Figure 14.8. The vessel has a double skin with top and bottom wing tanks to carry water ballast. There are four cargo tanks separated by coffer dams and constructed in accordance with the GTT Mark 3 containment system for the carriage of LNG cargos. The tanks extend above the deck and are enclosed in a trunk which provides both protection and access passages.

The cargo tanks are moulded to the inner hull of the ship and insulated by the four-layer system described in previous paragraphs. A primary membrane protects the primary insulation, behind which is a secondary membrane and the secondary insulation which is attached to the ship's inner hull. With this level of insulation the boil-off gas is restricted to 0.15% of the cargo volume, and this is burnt in the ship's engine. However, some recent designs have reliquefaction equipment and return the gas to the cargo holds. It is all a matter of economics. The liquid gas is discharged using the ship's

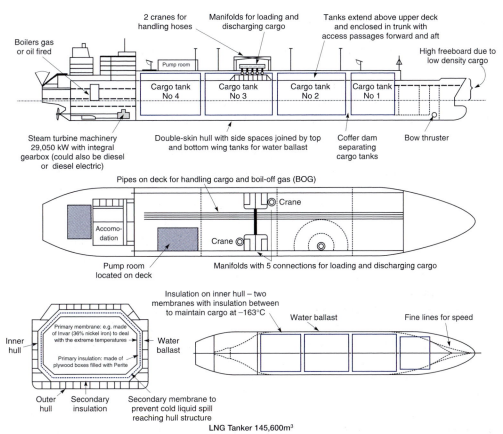

**Figure 14.8**
LNG tanker design with membrane tank system, 145,600 m³ capacity, with steam turbine
Source: Drawing by Martin Stopford, based on vessel built by Samsung Heavy Industries Co. S. Korea

| HULL | | MACHINERY | | OTHER | |
|---|---|---|---|---|---|
| Main Dimensions (m) | | Propulsion Machinery | | Cargo System | |
| Deadweight (design) | 71,450 dwt | Speed, | 20.6 kts 85% MCR | Cargo tanks | 4 IMO Type 2 Membrane |
| Scantling (scantling) | 81,450 dwt | Engine Type | Steam turbine | Pump type | submerged electric |
| Gross tons | 95,508 gt | Power output | 39,500 hp, 29,050kW | Pump capacity | 8×1800 m³/hr |
| Length over all (m) | 283 | Main boilers | 2×66 tonnes sleem/hour | Discharge rate | 12,100 m³/hour |
| Length between perp. | 270 | Consumption – main | 171.1 MT/day | Boil off rate per day | 0.15% |
| Breadth, moulded (m) | 43.4 | Cruising range | 9,124 miles | | |
| Depth, moulded (m) | 26 | Prop shaft | 90 rpm | Bow thruster | 1×2500KW |
| Draught (design) (m) | 11.4 | Propellor diameter | 8,600 mm fixed pitch | Complement | |
| Draught (scantling) (m) | 12.4 | Power Supply | | Crew | 41 |
| Lightweight (tonnes) | 30,740 | Turbo alternators | 2×3450 kW at 1800 rpm | Suez crew | 6 |
| Tank Capacity (m³) | | Diesel alternator:- | | | |
| Cargo tanks | 145,600 | - engine | 1×3664 kW at 720 rpm | | |
| Tank construction | GTT Membrane | - alternator | 1×3450 kW at 720 rpm | | |
| Heavy fuel oil tanks | 7,490 | | | | |
| Diesel oil tanks | 440 | | | | |
| Ballast water tanks | 57,000 | | | | |

eight submerged electric cargo pumps, each with a capacity of 1700 m³ per hour, and the cargo can be discharged in 12 hours.

Propulsion is provided by a traditional steam turbine system. Two water tube boilers, which burn fuel oil or boil-off gas, provide steam to a reversible steam turbine engine. The gearbox is integrated with the turbine, outputting 91 rpm to the propeller. The service speed of the ship is 20 knots and the consumption is 171 tons of fuel oil per day. Although turbines are the traditional power source for LNG tankers, diesel engines and diesel electric systems are also used.

This LNG tanker is a very sophisticated and expensive vessel, but the broad features are similar to the other tankers discussed in this chapter. The big difference is the engineering skills, materials and technology required to load, transport and discharge a liquid cargo at a temperature of −161.5°C.

## 14.7 NON-CARGO SHIPS

Non-cargo and service vessels cover a wide variety of ships from a 200 grt tug to a 100,000 gt cruise liner. This makes it difficult to analyse the demand for each type with any authority. Although these vessels represent only 7% of the fleet in gross tonnage terms, they are much more important to the industry in value and number. Over 70% of non-cargo carrying vessels may be under 500 gt, but by number they make up nearly half of the world's shipping fleet.

### The fishing fleet

Fishing vessels account for nearly half the non-cargo carrying fleet by tonnage. The fleet includes both fishing vessels and fish factories. The world fishing fleet grew rapidly at 15% per annum in the 1960s and then started to stabilize in the face of overfished oceans, escalating costs and the uncertainty of offshore limits.

### Supply ships and service craft

Supply ships and service vessels such as anchor handling tugs are used in the offshore oil and gas industry, and in July 2007 there was a fleet of 4394 of these vessels. With the increasing depth and distance from shore at which the work is taking place, proportionally more and larger vessels are needed. There has also been a trend towards building more highly powered, sophisticated, MPP vessels, especially for use in the bad weather areas of the North Sea and Gulf of Alaska.

### Tugs and dredgers

Tugs, dredgers and research craft form part of the fleet related to the coastal seabed activity, and there has also been a growing demand from harbour and canal authorities. One of the reasons for the faster growth was the change in trading patterns towards the developing countries and the use of larger ships. The growing interest in the resources of the seabed also generated a growing market for research, survey vessels and icebreakers.

## 14.8 ECONOMIC CRITERIA FOR EVALUATING SHIP DESIGNS

So far we have discussed the options that may confront a shipowner contemplating an investment decision. For the many practical reasons discussed, it is not easy to evaluate these options in financial or economic terms, and there is a temptation to suggest that ship design is a matter for commercial flair or 'gut feeling' rather than rigorous economic analysis. But despite this the commercial world expects such major investment decisions to be supported by some form of economic analysis.

There is substantial literature on the evaluation of alternative ship designs.[14] For practical purposes, the analysis needs to be carried out at two levels, which we will refer to here as market research and financial analysis.

### Market research

Market research is concerned with analysing the economic performance of the ship within the company's overall shipping activities. For a charter market operator this analysis might involve an examination of the type of vessel that will be easy to charter and its potential resale value. A liner operator might study the size of ship required to handle changes in the pattern of trade or competition on major routes and features such as speed and reefer capacity. This is closely aligned to the market research analysis described in Chapter 17. Through market research the owner can develop a specification for the type of shipping operation in which the vessel is to be used and the performance parameters that the vessel must satisfy.

### Financial analysis

The next step is to identify the ship design that meets the performance requirements most effectively, using some form of financial measure of merit. For example, the designer may be told that the owner requires a product tanker with the following features: a draught of not more than 10 metres; a length of not more than 170 metres; ability to carry simple chemicals such as caustic soda; cargo tanks that are cheap to clean; an operating speed of 14 knots; and design optimized to a 40,000 ton cargo of naphtha, but capable of carrying a 45,000 dwt of denser cargo. Although this list of requirements appears to be highly specific, in practice there may not be a unique solution. On examination, it may transpire that some of the requirements are inconsistent or very difficult to achieve. For example, it may be difficult to achieve the design draught within the other specified parameters, or doing so may result in a vessel with poor fuel economy. Did the shipowner appreciate this when he laid down the specification and is he prepared to pay the cost? These are all issues that have to be tackled at the operational analysis stage.

The task of the ship designer is to evaluate the various options in economic terms to see which gives the best overall result, recognizing both cost and operational performance. Buxton suggests two different ways of doing this, depending on the circumstances, net present value and required freight rate.[15]

*The net present value* technique, which is discussed in Section 6.7, involves setting up a projected cashflow for each of the options under consideration. Revenues and costs are projected on an annual basis over the life of the ship and the net cashflow in each year is calculated, taking account of capital payments, trading income, expenditure, taxation (if any) and probably the final resale value of the vessel. These annual cashflows are then discounted back to the present (using a minimum acceptable rate of return, for example 10% per annum) and summed, giving the NPV of each of the options. The option giving the highest NPV is generally preferred.

The advantage of this method is that it takes account of both the cost and revenue flows and produces a single figure, which makes the comparison of options a simple matter. On the negative side, if the revenue flow is difficult to predict, especially for vessels trading on the spot market, with the results that some near-arbitrary assumption about the potential earning power of the vessel is made, this can distort results. For this reason, the NPV approach is most appropriate when evaluating ships being constructed for a long-term time charter.

*The required freight rate* method avoids the problem of predicting revenue by comparing the relative unit transport cost of different ship types. The RFR is calculated by computing the annual average cost of running the ship (operating plus voyage costs), adding the capital costs and dividing by the annual tonnage of cargo transported to calculate the cost per tonne of cargo. These costs can then be discounted in exactly the same way as the NPV calculation and a discounted RFR calculated. There are several different ways of carrying out this calculation, but all aim to show which ship design will give the lowest unit transportation cost within the parameters specified by the owner. It is left to the investor to weigh up whether the project has a reasonable chance of earning enough revenue to cover the RFR. This may be an absolute evaluation, or used for comparing alternative designs or investment projects. For example is it better to order a new floating production, storage and offloading system or to buy a second-hand tanker and convert it? Although there are many very subjective variables in such an analysis, the process of working through the financial comparison can help to clarify the decision.

There are several variations on these two methods, notably the yield or internal rate of return, which is closely related to the NPV method (being the interest rate that produces an NPV of zero), and the permissible price (i.e. the maximum price payable for a ship to yield the required rate of return), which can be derived from either method.

## 14.9 SUMMARY

This chapter has reviewed the ships used in the shipping business. We started with two important observations. First, because the demand for merchant ships is derived from the demand for transport, we cannot determine the demand for merchant ships simply by examining the cargo flows. Shipowners are free to use whatever ships they think will provide the service most profitably. We must consider a wider range of economic factors which include the type of cargo, the type of shipping operation and the owner's commercial philosophy. Second, ship types should not be viewed in terms of physical design characteristics. From the shipowner's point of view, ships of the same type are substitutes in the market place. In particular, size plays an important part in determining ship type.

An examination of the relationship between cargo units and ship types shows that some ships, such as the MPP cargo liners or ro-ros, are highly flexible and capable of carrying six or seven different types of cargo units, while others, such as the container-ship, the gas carrier or the crude oil tanker, are highly specialized and are capable of carrying only one cargo. In terms of the revenue maximization calculations described in Chapter 3, the flexible ship has a better chance of achieving a high level of loaded days at sea and deadweight utilization because it is capable of carrying many different cargo types. The cost of this flexibility occurs in terms of higher capital cost per unit of capacity and, in some cases, lower operating efficiency than the more specialized vessel. Recently the trend has been decisively towards specialized ships with low LCM ratings.

In the liner business, the three main types of purpose-built vessels are container-ships, MPP cargo ships and ro-ros. Most of the ships employed in the liner trades are purpose-built within these general categories. There used to be an enormous number of different and unique ship specifications designed to fit particular trades, but container-ization has brought a high degree of standardization to ships used in the liner trades. There are still a few ships in the fleet designed for cargo flexibility, notably the MPP ships which can carry general cargo, project cargo, containers and even dry bulk. The popularity of these ships with investors declined during the 1980s, but the fleet has started to grow again.

In the dry bulk market, the trend towards single-purpose vessels continues. The general-purpose bulk carrier dominates the business, despite being restricted to the carriage of dry bulk cargoes and specialized bulks such as forest products and steel products. More flexible dry bulk vessels are the 'tweendecker which can trade either in bulk or general cargo; the open-hold bulk carrier which can trade in homogeneous dry bulk; containers and specialized bulks such as forest products; and the combined carrier which can alter-nate between dry bulk and crude oil and other liquids. All have been losing market share, especially the combined carrier.

Finally, there is a range of specialist ships designed for the bulk transport of specific cargoes. The most prominent of these are liquefied gas carriers, refrigerated cargo ships, car carriers, heavy lift ships, and cement carriers. In some cases, such as gas carriers, these ships are totally specialized and are in competition only with other ships of the same type, whereas others, such as the refrigerated cargo ship, the car carrier and the heavy lift vessel, face competition from MPP vessels.

The key point in all of this is that most cargoes can be transported in several different types of ship. In the last resort, the ship in which the cargo travels is determined by commercial performance rather than its specific technical design characteristics.

# 15 The Economics of Shipbuilding and Scrapping

*Build me straight, O worthy Master!*
*Staunch and strong, a goodly vessel,*
*That shall laugh at all disaster,*
*And with wave and whirlwind wrestle!*

*Day by day the vessel grew,*
*With timbers fashioned strong and true,*
*Stemson and keelson and sternson-knee,*
*Till, framed with perfect symmetry,*
*A skeleton ship arose to view!*

*And around the bows and along the side*
*The heavy hammers and mallets plied,*
*Till after many a week, at length,*
*Wonderful for form and strength,*
*Sublime in its enormous bulk,*
*Loomed aloft the shadowy hulk!*

('The Building of the Ship', Henry Wadsworth Longfellow,
*The Poetical Works of Longfellow*, Frederick Warne & Co.,
London 1899, p. 143)

## 15.1  THE ROLE OF THE MERCHANT SHIPBUILDING AND SCRAPPING INDUSTRIES

The shipbuilding industry supplies new ships, while shipbreakers ('recyclers') are the last-resort buyers of old ships which cannot be operated profitably in the shipping market. In terms of their economic structure, the two industries are very different. Shipbuilding is a heavy engineering business, selling a large and sophisticated product built mainly in facilities located in the industrialized countries of Japan, Europe, South Korea and now China. It requires substantial capital investment and a high level of technical and management expertise to design and produce a merchant ship. The ship scrapping industry, in contrast, is located mainly in the low-cost countries, particularly the Indian subcontinent, and is one of the world's most labour-intensive industries – in some countries ship scrapping takes place on the beach, with labour equipped with only the most primitive of hand tools and cutting equipment.

In the first part of this chapter we will examine the regional distribution of shipbuilding capacity and the relationship between the level of shipping and shipbuilding activity. We then consider shipbuilding market economics, looking in particular at the shipbuilding market cycle, the price mechanism and the influences on the supply of and demand for shipbuilding output. The section on shipbuilding ends with a discussion of competitiveness and the related issues of capacity measurement, the production process and international comparisons of productivity. The final section discusses how ships are scrapped, the market for scrap products and the international structure of the ship scrapping industry. Finally, in this chapter we introduce a new unit of measurement, the compensated gross ton (cgt). The compensated gross tonnage of a ship is derived from its gross tonnage (gt), but weighted to take account of the work content of that particular ship type – detailed definitions can be found in Appendix B.

## 15.2 THE REGIONAL STRUCTURE OF WORLD SHIPBUILDING

### Who builds the world's merchant ships?

About 30 countries have a significant merchant shipbuilding industry (see Table 15.1), and it has a changeable history. Ship production trebled from 8.4 million gt in 1960 to 27.5 million gt in 1977, then halved to 13 million gt in 1980, edged up to 16 million gt by 1990 and more than doubled to 44.44 million gt in 2005. This volatility was accompanied by a realignment of regional shipbuilding capacity. Europe's market share fell from 66% to 10% while Asia's grew from 22% to 84%. Japan and South Korea now dominate the industry, between them producing over two-thirds of the world's ships, with China coming up very fast and trebling its production between 2000 and 2005, aiming to be the biggest shipbuilder. The remaining production is spread over many countries, mainly in eastern and western Europe. The shipbuilding output of most European countries declined during the 1980s, and several, including Sweden, stopped building merchant ships. Meanwhile Asia's dominant role increased as South Korea and China grew rapidly despite the general market problems in the shipbuilding industry. Finally, the market upturn in the early 2000s, during which newbuilding berths were in short supply, brought a surge of new Asian shipyards in emerging countries such as Vietnam, the Philippines and India.

Shipbuilding is a long-cycle business. Ships take several years to deliver, and once built they remain in service for 25–30 years. Since ships trickle in and out of the merchant fleet at only a few per cent a year, the pace of change in shipbuilding demand is slow. Trends develop over decades rather than years, and we need to step well back

## Table 15.1 Merchant ships completed during years, 1960–2005 ('000 GT)

| | 1960 | 1977 | 1980 | 1985 | 1990 | 1995 | 2000 | 2005 |
|---|---|---|---|---|---|---|---|---|
| *Asia* | | | | | | | | |
| Japan | 1,839 | 11,708 | 6,094 | 9,503 | 6,663 | 9,263 | 12,020 | 16,100 |
| South Korea | — | 562 | 522 | 2,620 | 3,441 | 6,264 | 12,228 | 15,400 |
| Chinese PR | — | 110 | — | 166 | 404 | 784 | 1,647 | 5,700 |
| Taiwan | — | 196 | 240 | 278 | 685 | 488 | 603 | 500 |
| Singapore | — | | | | 49 | 99 | 17 | |
| Total Far East | 1,839 | 12,576 | 6,856 | 12,567 | 11,242 | 16,898 | 26,515 | 37,700 |
| % world | 22% | 46% | 52% | 69% | 70% | 75% | 84% | 85% |
| | | | | | | | | |
| *Europe* | | | | | | | | |
| Belgium | 123 | 132 | 138 | 133 | 60 | 11 | 0 | 0 |
| Denmark | 214 | 709 | 208 | 458 | 408 | 1,003 | 373 | 500 |
| France | 429 | 1,107 | 283 | 200 | 64 | 254 | 202 | 0 |
| Germany FR | 1,124 | 1,595 | 376 | 562 | 874 | 1,120 | 974 | 1200 |
| German DR | — | 378 | 346 | 358 in German FR | | | | |
| Greece | — | 81 | 25 | 37 | 19 | 0 | 0 | 0 |
| Irish Republic | — | 40 | 1 | 0 | 0 | 0 | 0 | 0 |
| Italy | 447 | 778 | 248 | 88 | 392 | 395 | 569 | 300 |
| Netherlands | 682 | 240 | 122 | 180 | 190 | 205 | 300 | 200 |
| Portugal | — | 98 | 11 | 41 | 74 | 18 | 47 | |
| Spain | 173 | 1,813 | 395 | 551 | 366 | 250 | 462 | 100 |
| UK | 1,298 | 1,020 | 427 | 172 | 126 | 126 | 105 | 0 |
| Finland | 111 | 361 | 200 | 213 | 256 | 317 | 223 | 0 |
| Norway | 254 | 567 | 208 | 122 | 91 | 147 | 114 | 100 |
| Sweden | 710 | 2,311 | 348 | 201 | 27 | 29 | 33 | 0 |
| Total Europe | 5,565 | 11,230 | 3,336 | 3,316 | 2,945 | 3,875 | 3,402 | 4,400 |
| % world | 66% | 41% | 25% | 18% | 18% | 17% | 11% | 10% |
| | | | | | | | | |
| *Eastern Europe* | | | | | | | | |
| Bulgaria | — | 144 | 206 | 173 | 92 | 92 | 21 | 0 |
| Poland | 220 | 478 | 362 | 361 | 141 | 524 | 630 | 700 |
| Romania | | 296 | 170 | 204 | 175 | 229 | 139 | 0 |
| USSR/Russia | | 421 | 460 | 229 | 430 | | | |
| Yugoslavia | 173 | 421 | 149 | 259 | 462 | | | |
| Russia | | | | | | 83 | 17 | — |
| Ukraine | | | | | | 185 | 5 | 0 |
| Croatia | | | | | | 179 | 342 | 600 |
| Total | 393 | 1,760 | 1,347 | 1,226 | 1,300 | 1,291 | 1,154 | 1,300 |
| % world | 5% | 6% | 10% | 7% | 8% | 6% | 4% | 3% |
| | | | | | | | | |
| *Others* | | | | | | | | |
| Brazil | | 380 | 729 | 581 | 255 | 172 | 10 | 0 |
| USA | 379 | 1,012 | 555 | 180 | 23 | 7 | 92 | 300 |
| Other countries | 586 | 573 | 278 | 286 | 288 | 225 | 523 | 744 |
| Total | 965 | 1,965 | 1,562 | 1,047 | 566 | 404 | 626 | 1,044 |
| % world | 12% | 7% | 12% | 6% | 4% | 2% | 2% | 2% |
| World total | 8,382 | 27,531 | 13,101 | 18,156 | 16,053 | 22,468 | 31,696 | 44,444 |

Source: Lloyd's Register of Shipping, Clarkson *World Shipyard Monitor*

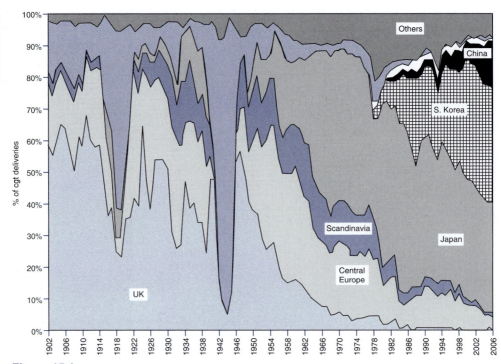

**Figure 15.1**
Shipbuilding market shares, 1902–2006
Source: Lloyd's Register of Shipping, Clarkson Research

to see them. Nowhere is this more apparent than in the changing regional location of shipbuilding activity, shown vividly in Figure 15.1. A century ago, shipbuilding was dominated by Great Britain. Gradually Continental Europe and Scandinavia squeezed Britain's share down to 40%. Then in the 1950s Japan overtook Europe, achieving a market share of 50% in 1969.

In the 1980s South Korean shipbuilding output grew rapidly, challenging Japan's dominant position and finally establishing the Far East as the centre of world shipbuilding. Then in the 1990s China started to increase in importance, achieving a 14% market share in 2006. Following this sequence of events we might ask what it is about shipbuilding that allows a single country to obtain the commanding position achieved by Britain, Japan, South Korea and China; and why has the balance changed so much over the years? To answer these questions it is instructive to take a brief look at the recent history of the shipbuilding industry, and in particular the relationship between the shipping and shipbuilding industries.[1]

## The decline of British shipbuilding

In the early 1890s Britain dominated the maritime industry, producing over 80% of the world's ships and owning half the world fleet. In 1918 the Board of Trade Departmental

Committee on Shipping and Shipbuilding commented: 'there are few important industries where the predominance of British manufacture has been more marked than shipbuilding and marine engineering'.[2] Britain held this dominant position until 1950 when it started to lose market share. The downward trend is apparent in Figure 15.2, as is the close correlation with the decline of the UK merchant fleet. At the beginning of the twentieth century, the UK merchant fleet had a 45% market share and shipbuilding about 55%, but by the end of the century the share had dwindled to virtually nothing.

It is not difficult to explain how British shipping achieved this dominant position. In the 1890s the Empire was at its height and Britain controlled massive trade flows, giving its shipping companies effective control of many liner routes in the Atlantic and Pacific, particularly between the colonies. In the tramp shipping market, Britain – an island nation – was the major importer of raw materials and foodstuffs such as grain, while the export trade in manufactures and coal was equally prominent. As the control of trade slipped away, so did shipping. With each world war the British Empire diminished in size, the merchant marine was weakened by wartime losses and its trading partners became better able to carry their own trade.[3] By 1960 the UK fleet had slipped to only 20% of world tonnage and British shipbuilding accounted for about the same proportion of world shipbuilding output, and by 2005 its market share of shipping had fallen below 2% and merchant shipbuilding was limited to very small ships.

One reason put forward for the decline of British shipbuilding was the industry's failure to graduate from a production process based on manual skills to the more closely integrated production technology that was developed in Sweden and Japan during the twentieth century.[4] But there was also a link between the fortunes of shipping and shipbuilding. Discussing the rise of the British shipbuilding industry during the nineteenth century, Hobsbawm argues strongly for the existence of this link in the following terms:

> During the age of the traditional wooden sailing ship Britain had been a great, but by no means unchallenged producer. Indeed her weight as a shipbuilder had been due not to her technological superiority, for the French designed better ships and the USA built better ones ... British shipbuilders benefited rather because of the vast weight of Britain as a shipping and trading power and the preference of British shippers (even after the abrogation of the Navigation Acts, which protected the industry heavily) for native ships.[5]

This link between trade, shipping and shipbuilding is too common to be a coincidence. In Britain relationships existed between shipowners and shipbuilders that went beyond normal competitive ties. Many British shipping lines had a long association with particular shipyards, which reinforced the tradition of building at home. Even in the 1970s there were shipyards in Britain that relied heavily on one or two domestic owners. As we shall see when we look at other regions, this was not a uniquely British state of affairs and shipbuilders are very dependent upon the fortunes of their home fleet.

But the commercial performance of the shipyards is also important and Britain was slow in adapting to the new highly competitive shipbuilding market after the

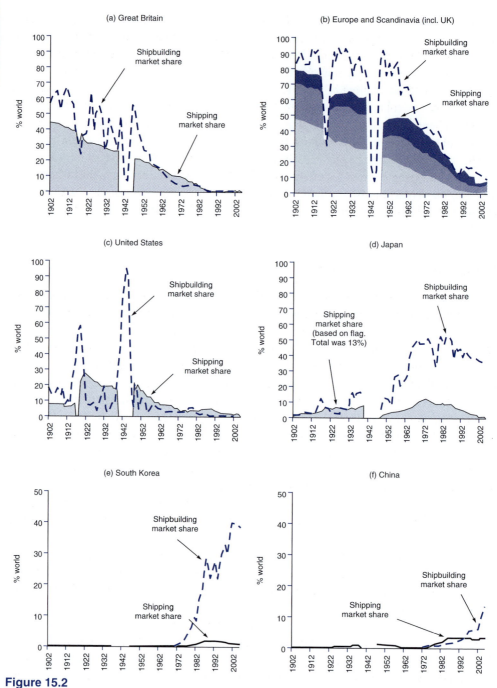

## CHAPTER 15

**Figure 15.2**

The link between shipping and shipbuilding market shares by region

Source: Lloyd's Register of Shipping

Note: This figure shows, for each region, the merchant fleet as a percentage of the world fleet and shipyard output as a percentage of world output.

Second World War. The battle was probably lost in the 1960s when British manufacturing industry as a whole was struggling with entrenched management practices and confrontational labour relations. Despite considerable capital investment, the British yards never achieved the high productivity levels of the German or Scandinavian yards. Typically it took twice as many man-hours to build a ship in the United Kingdom as in Scandinavia or Japan. A major strategic loss was the first container-ship which was started in the UK, but had to be towed to Germany to be completed. German shipyards continued to dominate the container business in Europe for the next 30 years.

The final blow was the UK's strong exchange rate when North Sea oil came on stream during the 1980s, at the trough of the 1980s recession. In 1988 the sterling price of a 30,000 dwt bulk carrier, £8 million, was only sufficient to buy the materials and left no margin for labour and overheads, an impossible position.[6] Slowly the industry slipped away.

## European shipbuilding, 1902–2006

In Europe as a whole shipbuilding went through much the same cycle of growth and decline as in the UK. No individual country achieved prominence in the shipbuilding market on a scale comparable with Japan or the UK, but in the early 1900s European shipyards, including the UK, accounted for over 80% of world production, similar to the market share the Asian shipyards achieved a century later. This is shown in Figure 15.1 along with the market share of their shipping fleets. Until 1945 the shipbuilding market share was 20–30% higher than the shipping market share, and Europe was a net exporter of ships. But by the late 1950s this export dominance had been lost and the decline of the European shipping fleet in the 1960s and 1970s was accompanied by a decline in the market share of shipbuilding. By 2005 the market share of the fleet had fallen to 14% of the gross tonnage delivered, whilst the shipbuilding share was reduced to 6%. Of course these statistics have limitations, since during this period much of the fleet 'flagged out' (see Chapter 16) and gross tonnage does not fully reflect the high value-added of European shipbuilding, but there is no doubt that over the period Europe switched from being a net exporter to an importer of ships.

The experience of the Scandinavian shipbuilding industry was similar. Although none of the Scandinavian countries has sufficient population or heavy industry to make it a major participant in seaborne trade, they all have a strong maritime tradition. In this sense, the Scandinavian fleets may be regarded as part of the international shipping industry, in much the same way as Greece. In 1902 the Scandinavian shipyards had only a 3% market share, well below the 10% share of the Scandinavian merchant fleet. Shipbuilding capacity lagged behind the merchant fleet during this period because the Scandinavian shipyards had difficulty switching from wooden ships to the more capital-intensive process of building steel ships. Petersen comments:

> In the 1870s Norway had a large number of small shipyards employing expert master carpenters and experienced workers. These men were able to build all the sailing ships Norway needed, using only simple tools and home grown timber.

The building of steam ships, on the other hand, demanded the import of raw materials and the erection of large shipyards with expensive, heavy machinery, and cranes. Steamship building did not gain momentum until the 1890s.[7]

Shipbuilding output in Scandinavia remained nominal until the First World War, when the industry started a rapid growth that eventually reached a peak market share of 21% in 1933. This position was maintained until the early 1970s when Scandinavian shipyards led the world in terms of productivity and production technology. For example Kockums shipyard in Sweden, which specialized in VLCCs, was generally regarded as the most productive yard in the world. But this success could not offset the high labour costs, and a decline in the market share of the Scandinavian fleet coincided with a fall in the market share of Scandinavian shipbuilding.

The fall in the European fleet, due partly to the transfer of registration to flags of convenience, was accompanied by a decline in Europe's market share, especially in the high-volume bulk markets. This undoubtedly reflects the growing competitive strength of the Japanese industry, and demonstrates that high productivity alone is not enough to maintain market share. But although many yards closed, some were successful in diversifying into high value-added ships for niche markets in which the Far East yards did not compete. These markets included container-ships, cruise ships, gas tankers, chemical tankers and many small vessels such as dredgers. All of these vessels are equipment-intensive, and this allowed the European equipment industry to maintain a leading role in design and development, for example in engines, cranes and engine room equipment.

## Merchant shipbuilding in the United States

Historically the USA has had an unusual role in world shipbuilding. Apart from a spell in the early nineteenth century as the leading shipbuilder, which was brought to an end by the Civil War (1861–5), in peacetime the USA was not internationally prominent as a merchant shipbuilder or shipowner. With the exception of the two wars and the inter-war period, Figure 15.2(c) shows that its market share was only a few per cent. Of course, the USA had major shipping interests but, as we will see in Chapter 16, US shipowners were at the forefront of developing international registries. Despite this, much of the world's shipping and shipbuilding technology originated in the USA and during the two world wars the USA demonstrated its ability to mount a massive, if rather expensive, shipbuilding programme.

During the First World War, US shipbuilding output increased from 200,000 grt in 1914 to 4 million grt in 1919 – the USA alone produced 30% more ships in that year than the whole of world shipbuilding output before the beginning of the First World War. Production on this scale was achieved by using standard ships and standard production methods at the Hog Island complex which consisted of 50 building berths in five groups of ten along the Delaware River. The complex built a standard merchant ship in three sizes constructed as far as possible from flat plate. The building time was approximately 275 days. This was the first step towards standardized shipbuilding practices, though the yards did not achieve the degree of prefabrication introduced later.

The Second World War saw an even more extensive shipbuilding programme for the American Liberty ship, which was a standard dry cargo vessel of 10,902 dwt, and the T2 tanker of 16,543 dwt. These ships were mass-produced, with major sub-assemblies constructed off the berths – a development made possible by introducing welding in place of riveting. Production commenced in 1941 and reached a peak in 1944 when a total of 19.3 million grt of new ships were launched in the US – almost ten times the total world shipbuilding output in 1939. A total of 2,600 Liberty ships and 563 T2 tankers were built. After the war some of the Liberty ships were sold to private operators, others were traded, and the remainder, about 1,400, were laid up as part of the US strategic reserve fleet. By the 1960s their slow speed of 11 knots and full-bodied design made them unattractive in commercial operation and a series of Liberty replacement designs such as the SD14 and the Freedom took their place.

The activities of the US merchant shipbuilding industry during the twentieth century demonstrate two important points. The first is the speed with which, given the right circumstances, a major shipbuilding programme can be set up and dismantled. On these two occasions the USA developed a massive shipbuilding capacity and dismantled it again within an equally short period. The second is that, despite the obvious efficiency of the US shipbuilding industry, it could not compete commercially in the world shipbuilding market. In the 1930s, and again during the post-war era, the US government provided construction subsidies to US merchant shipbuilders to offset the difference between the construction in American and foreign yards. At different times the levels of subsidy varied from 30% to 50% of the cost of construction.[8] Like Scandinavian shipyards, high productivity was not enough, though the isolation of the industry from international market forces and the focus on the very different craft of warship building make it very difficult to judge what the underlying competitiveness of the industry really was.

## The Japanese shipbuilding industry

The rise of Japan as the dominant force in the world shipbuilding market provides yet another example of the shipbuilding growth model. Like Britain, Japan is an island nation and the growth of the economy after the Second World War made intense demands on seaborne transport. Initially the development of the Japanese shipbuilding industry drew strength from a coordinated shipping and shipbuilding programme. For example, Trezise and Suzuki comment:

> In the early post war period … the industries selected for intensive governmental attention included the merchant shipping industry. A planned shipbuilding programme for the merchant fleet was instituted during the occupation, in 1947, and is still being pursued essentially along the lines laid down at this time. Each year the government – that is to say the Ministry of Transport – in consultation with its industry advisors in [the] Shipping and Shipbuilding Rationalisation

Council – decides on the tonnage of ships to be built, by type (tankers, ore carriers, liners, and so on) and allocates production contracts and the ships among the applicant domestic shipbuilders and shipowners. The selected shipping lines receive preferential financing and in turn are subject to close government supervision.[9]

During the period 1951–72, 31.5% of the total loans made by the Japan Development Bank were for marine transportation. This domestic shipbuilding programme undoubtedly contributed to the success of the Japanese shipbuilding industry, but the Japanese merchant marine never achieved the degree of market domination that the British merchant fleet had established in the nineteenth and early twentieth centuries. One reason was that by the 1960s the growth of flags of convenience and high Japanese costs meant that much of the fleet was chartered in from independent shipowners, especially in Hong Kong, under *shikumisen* contracts. Figure 15.2(d) shows that, although the market share of the Japanese fleet increased from 1% in 1948 to 10% in 1984, this fell well short of the 50% market share achieved by Japanese shipbuilders in the 1980s.

There are two explanations for this. One is that the Japanese flag was uncompetitive and many of the ships commissioned for the carriage of Japanese trade were purchased by international owners in Hong Kong or Greece and registered under flags of convenience. In 2005, 89% of the Japanese-owned fleet was operating under foreign flags, so the low shipping market share in Figure 15.2(d) is misleading. The second is that the Japanese shipbuilding industry became highly competitive and built for the emerging export market, particularly the market for large tankers and bulk carriers bought by independent European, US and Hong Kong shipowners. Their strategy was similar to their approach in other major industries. They built large modern shipyards and used the domestic market as the volume baseload for selling highly competitive ships into the export market. The new facilities had building docks capable of mass producing VLCCs and large bulk carriers at a rate of 5–6 vessels per annum. Production engineering, strict quality control, sophisticated material control systems and pre-outfitting were all used effectively to reduce costs and maintain delivery schedules. Some shipyards were built in the main industrial centres (e.g. the Mitsui Shipyard at Chiba, the IHI Shipyard at Yokohama and the Kawasaki Shipyard at Sakaide), while others were in remote areas (e.g. the Mitsubishi Shipyard at Koyagi).

During the 1990s Japan was challenged by South Korea, and its shipyards faced high labour costs and a strengthening currency. However, the Japanese shipyards were remarkably successful in maintaining their competitive position despite these disadvantages. Unlike the European yards which focused on high value-added ships, such as cruise liners, the medium-sized Japanese yards developed a very successful business building bulk carriers, generally regarded as the simplest of vessels. By employing production planning, production engineering and subcontracting they increased productivity and in 2005 Japan was still the market leader, producing 16.1 million gross tons of ships, compared with South Korea's 15.4 million gross tons (see Table 15.1).

## The rise of South Korean shipbuilding

The entry of South Korea into the world shipbuilding market was, like that of its near-neighbour Japan, the result of a carefully planned industrial programme. In the early 1970s a major investment programme was planned, starting with the construction of the world's largest shipbuilding facility by Hyundai at Ulsan, designed in the UK, with a 380 metre dry dock capable of taking vessels up to 400,000 dwt. Later in the decade a second major facility was built by Daewoo, with a 530 metre dry dock capable of taking vessels up to 1 m.dwt. This started production in the early 1980s. Two other South Korean industrial groups, Samsung and Halla Engineering, built new shipbuilding facil-ities and by the mid-1990s South Korea had a 25% market share and four out of the world's five largest shipyards.[10] By 2005 South Korea had matched Japanese output in gross tons and overtaken Japan in cgt terms.

Perhaps the most interesting aspect of the South Korean shipbuilding development model is that from the outset it focused on the export market. This is clearly visible in Figure 15.2(e). Unlike Britain or Japan, which had, to different degrees, built up their shipbuilding capacity to service domestic customers, from the beginning Korea targeted the export market. Whilst South Korea has a rapidly growing economy, this remains very much smaller than the Japanese or European in terms of trade volume. The suc-cess of Korean shipbuilding almost certainly reflects the growing internationalization of the bulk shipping industry where, with the development of international registries and multinational companies, the link between ship, shipowner and national interest is increasingly tenuous. The industry was also much more focused, with a small number of very large yards focusing on large vessels for the international market. In 2005 Hyundai, Samsung and Daewoo were the world's three largest shipbuilders and accounted for two-thirds of South Korea's production.

## The Chinese shipbuilding industry

In the shipbuilding market there is always a new entrant preparing to challenge the market leaders and in the 1990s China emerged as the next challenger. However China's approach was very different from that of South Korea. It has a long history of shipbuild-ing, stretching back to the fifteenth century and the construction of Admiral Zheng He's famous treasure ships, some of which were reportedly up to 540 feet long, with a capac-ity of 1,500 tons, though the size of these ships is controversial.[11] During the 1980s and early 1990s China had an active shipbuilding industry, with many domestic yards and a full infrastructure, including research institutes. Some ships were built for export, at very competitive prices, but the volume of business was limited and Chinese-built ships generally sold at a discount in the second-hand market.

The major expansion of China's shipbuilding capacity gathered speed in the late 1990s, as part of the Chinese industrial expansion. Initially the expansion came from existing shipbuilding facilities, with just one major new shipyard built, the Dalian New yard. However expansion of the existing Chinese shipyards allowed shipbuilding pro-duction to increase from 784,000 gt in 1995 to 5.7 million gt in 2005 and 11 million gt in 2007. At that stage over 90 established shipyards in China were building a wide range of vessel sizes and types and about 30 major new shipyards were under construction, or at an advanced stage of planning. Shipbuilding is in three areas spread around the Bohai Rim in the North, Shanghai, and with a few shipyards in the Pearl River in the South. It is widely anticipated in the shipbuilding market that the Chinese industry will take a leading share of the world market within the coming decade.

## Other countries

Eastern Europe is a long established participant in the world shipbuilding market, with a development pattern closer to western Europe than Asia. In fact Table 15.1 shows that between 1980 and 2005 eastern Europe's production was steady at about 1.3 million gt per annum. Poland increased its output, but others such as Ukraine declined under pressure from rising wage rates and exchange rates. However, in 2008 a number of new shipbuilding countries were emerging in Asia, including Vietnam, the Philippines and India, whilst Russia and Pakistan are developing plans to enter the shipbuilding market.

## Conclusions from a century of shipbuilding development

This short overview of the evolution of shipbuilding suggests that the business lends itself to a few dominant producers, with a succession of new challengers creating a highly competitive market environment which drives technical change. It also suggests that the market focus on domestic customers in the first half of the twentieth century gave way in the second half to the broader role of the export market which exists today. However, the individual regions dealt with this complex commercial environment in very different ways.

Britain built its supremacy early in the century on its large home market which allowed it to develop craft-based skills, but then failed to evolve technically, leaving the industry vulnerable to recessions and adverse currency movements. The European and Scandinavian yards were more effective in improving their production technology, but ultimately this could not overcome their high labour costs and aggressive competition from efficient Asian yards using the same techniques. Many European yards closed, but others developed successful niche markets and survived, leaving Europe with a substantial market share in the high value-added ships. Japanese yards were very successful in developing sophisticated production systems, but also drew commercial strength from their strong home market which acted as a base for winning export orders. As South Korean competition and Japanese labour costs increased, the Japanese yards adopted a very different defensive strategy from the Europeans, concentrating on mass-producing highly engineered bulk vessels, especially dry bulk carriers. Starting with low labour costs and large, efficient facilities, South Korea was the first to build its business primarily around the export market, with a product range focused on large vessels. China followed on with many more yards but much the same formula.

So there are many permutations, but the common theme is that newcomers combine low labour costs and decent capital investment with the capacity to work hard and move with the market. Whatever the technology, shipbuilding remains a business where someone has to get their hands dirty.

## 15.3 SHIPBUILDING MARKET CYCLES

From a commercial viewpoint, these changes in the regional structure were accompanied by long periods of intense competition as each new entrant, Continental Europe, Scandinavia, Japan and then South Korea, fought for market share. This harsh commercial climate was intensified by the cyclical nature of shipbuilding demand. Over the last century there have been 12 separate cycles which are charted in Figure 15.3 and summarized in Table 15.2. The left-hand half of Table 15.2 shows the peak of each cycle, the number of years to the next trough, and the percentage fall in world shipbuilding output at the trough, whilst the right-hand half shows the same information for each trough and upswing. The length of each cycle from peak to peak is shown in the last column.

The average cycle lasted 9.6 years from peak to peak, but the spread was very wide, ranging from 5 years to over 25 years. The average reduction in output from peak to trough was 52%, and the maximum peacetime reduction was 83% during the recession of the early 1930s. As with the shipping cycles we discussed in Chapter 4, these cycles were not just random fluctuations designed to make life difficult for the shipyards, but are part of the mechanism for adjusting shipbuilding capacity to the changing needs of world trade. During the period since 1886 there were four periods of change which drove this process.

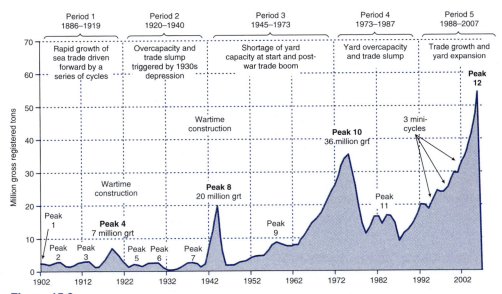

**Figure 15.3**
World shipbuilding launches, 1902–2007
Source: Lloyd's Register of Shipping

# ECONOMICS OF SHIPBUILDING AND SCRAPPING

**Table 15.2** Shipbuilding cycles, 1902–2007

| Cycle no | Cyclical peak and downswing | | | | Cyclical trough and upswing | | | | Full cycle years |
|---|---|---|---|---|---|---|---|---|---|
| | Year | Peak '000 grt | Peak to next trough years | % | Year | Trough '000 grt | Trough to next peak years | % | |
| 1 | 1901 | 2,617 | 3 | −24% | 1904 | 1,987 | 2 | 47% | 5 |
| 2 | 1906 | 2,919 | 3 | −45% | 1909 | 1,602 | 4 | 108% | 7 |
| 3 | 1913 | 3,332 | 2 | −59% | 1915 | 1,358 | 4 | 426% | 6 |
| 4 | 1919 | 7,144 | 4 | −77% | 1923 | 1,643 | 1 | 37% | 5 |
| 5 | 1924 | 2,247 | 2 | −26% | 1926 | 1,674 | 4 | 73% | 6 |
| 6 | 1930 | 2,889 | 3 | −83% | 1933 | 489 | 5 | 520% | 8 |
| 7 | 1938 | 3,033 | 2 | −42% | 1940 | 1,754 | 4 | 1057% | 6 |
| 8 | 1944 | 20,300 | 3 | −90% | 1947 | 2,092 | 11 | 343% | 14 |
| 9 | 1958 | 9,269 | 3 | −14% | 1961 | 7,940 | 14 | 352% | 17 |
| 10 | 1975 | 35,897 | 4 | −67% | 1979 | 11,787 | 3 | 47% | 7 |
| 11 | 1982 | 17,289 | 5 | −43% | 1987 | 9,770 | 20 | 534% | 25 |
| 12 | 2007 | 61,900 | Based on the orderbook output likely to double by 2010 | | | | | | |
| *Analysis of cycles* | | | | | | | | | |
| Average length | | | 3.1 | −52% | | | 6.5 | 322% | 9.6 |
| Standard deviation | | | 0.9 | 25% | | | 5.9 | 313% | 6.4 |

Source: Compiled by Martin Stopford from Lloyd's Register and other sources

The first period, which is only partly shown in Figure 15.3, lasted from 1886 to 1919 and was a period of 'cyclical growth', with output increasing with each peak, interspersed by periods of recession. As we saw in Chapter 1, this was a period of very rapid technical change as steel-hulled steamships of rapidly increasing size and efficiency replaced sail. The shipbuilding cycles seem to have followed the world trade cycles and the level of output responded sharply to each change in the market. During this period the cycles drove investment by drawing in a flood of new ships with the latest technology during the market peaks and then driving out the old and technically obsolete vessels during the lengthy troughs – a crude but effective way of adopting new technology, while deriving the maximum economic value from the existing stock of ships.

During the second period, from 1920 to 1940 the industry faced persistent market problems dominated by the 1931 depression. The period started with overcapacity because Europe had expanded its shipyards to replace wartime shipping losses and in 1919 the industry was capable of producing 7 million grt of ships a year, three times the underlying level of peacetime demand. In addition, the war had convinced some European governments that it was important to have a domestic maritime capability, and they devoted public funds to building up their industries. When combined with volatile trade, this capacity pressure contributed to two decades of almost continuous problems in the shipping market, with slumps interspersed by periods of moderate market improvement. Contemporary press statements illustrate the mood of the period. For example:

In the early part of 1924 it was generally believed that depression in the shipbuilding industry had touched its lowest point. It could not be imagined that the signs of revival would be so short lived ... the immediate outlook is now exceedingly grave.[12]

The year 1926 was one of great depression in shipbuilding.[13]

As far as shipbuilding is concerned 1930 has been a most trying time ... only one berth in four occupied.[14]

The year 1935 in the shipbuilding industry may be regarded as a year of marking time with only one-third of the greatly reduced capacity being utilised.[15]

In Britain, which dominated the shipbuilding market at that time, shipbuilding employment fell steadily from 300,000 in 1920 to 60,000 in 1931.[16] Unlike the pre-war period, this was not simply cyclical unemployment that was soon absorbed by the next boom; it was a steady downward trend. Broadly speaking, the 1920s were dominated by removing the surplus shipyard capacity. There was intense international competition, indicated by 'incidents' such as a Furness Withy order placed in Germany in 1926 at a price 24% below the lowest British price with marginal overhead recovery. Then in the 1930s the Great Depression undermined demand and resulted in an 83% fall in shipbuilding output between 1930 and 1933, the biggest of any of the 12 cycles shown in Table 15.2.

The third period, covering the period from 1945 to 1973, was one of exceptional growth. Although the industry started with output of 7 million grt (more than six times the pre-war level of demand – Figure 15.3), three-quarters was built under the US wartime construction programme, and at the end of the war the US effectively withdrew from the world shipbuilding market. Since war damage had reduced the output of the German and Japanese industries, there was an acute shortage of shipbuilding capacity. This persisted into the late 1950s and, for a few years it was a seller's market. It was not until 1958 that a major economic recession in the US, and over-ordering of tankers following the Suez closure in 1956, precipitated the first post-war shipbuilding depression, which lasted into the early 1960s. World shipbuilding output fell from a peak of 9 million grt in 1958 to a trough of 8 million grt in 1961 (Figure 15.3). By 1963, however, trade grew rapidly as Europe and Japan modernized their economies, bringing a steady upward trend in orders that resulted in an unprecedented expansion of shipbuilding capacity to 36 million grt in 1975 – in a single year the industry produced more shipping tonnage than was built in the whole period between the two wars.

The fourth period, which started after the 1973 oil crisis and continued until 1987, was grim for the shipyards. Trade growth was sluggish, volatile and unpredictable. The pace of technical obsolescence slowed, with few major advances in ship technology and a more stable size structure, especially in the tanker fleet. Shipyard overcapacity was increased by the entry of South Korea as a major shipbuilder. In these circumstances the shipbuilding industry swung sharply from rapid growth to deep recession.

At the start of this period in 1975, world shipbuilding output peaked at 36 m.grt, representing 50–100% overcapacity. After two decades of continuous growth, seaborne trade first stagnated and then abruptly declined, particularly in the oil sector, and the demand for new ships fell sharply from the pre-1975 level. This already difficult situation in the shipbuilding market was further aggravated by the entry of South Korea with a bid for a major share of the world market. As a result there was a three-way battle between Japan, Korea and western Europe for a share of the diminishing volume of orders.

During the late 1970s the restructuring of shipbuilding capacity started. Many shipyards were closed and output fell by 60% to 14 million grt in 1979. The time taken for this decline to occur reflects the large orderbook held by the world shipbuilding industry in 1974. A recovery in the world economy during the late 1970s brought renewed trade growth which, combined with the sizeable reduction in world shipbuilding capacity, was sufficient to produce a brief recovery in the world shipbuilding market. Laid-up tonnage fell to a minimal level, and during 1980–1 the world shipbuilding industry enjoyed a brief revival. However, following the brief market peak in 1980–1, demand again declined, fuelled by the collapse of world seaborne trade which fell from 3.8 bt in 1979 to 3.3 bt in 1983, a reduction of 13%. Severe downward pressure on shipbuilding prices and new ordering drove shipyard output in 1987 to a trough of 9.8 million gross tons, the lowest since 1962 and a decline of 73% from the 1975 peak. Employment in the world shipbuilding industry halved[17] and many of the marginal shipyards were closed. In 1986 new ships could be bought for prices not far above the cost of materials, and even the highly competitive South Korean shipyards announced major losses.

Following this appalling episode, the fifth period, from 1987 to 2007, saw an equally dramatic revival of world shipbuilding capacity as the expansion of Asia and China generated a recovery in trade, and this coincided with more capacity being needed to replace the ageing fleet built during the 1970s construction boom. By 1993 the volume of output had doubled to 20 million gt and by 2007 it had reached 62 million gt, five times the 1987 trough. In the process South Korea had consolidated its position as the leading shipbuilder, with China positioning itself in a bid for market leadership, opening the way for the next phase of competition.

Which leaves the question of how this fifth period will develop. Readers may know the answer to this, but in 2007 investors were still not sure. Some saw the cycle ending with a lengthy period of overcapacity, but others believed it was a new situation and still had a long way to go. Such uncertainty is the main reason why shipbuilding, like shipping, is a risky business. In a century of shipbuilding it is difficult to find many 'normal' years. The 12 cycles may have averaged 9.5 years in length, but they came in all shapes and sizes, driven by long-term swings in trade growth, combined with capacity imbalances caused by shipping market cycles. Add a constantly changing competitive structure and we can only conclude that shipbuilding is not a business for the faint hearted.

## 15.4 THE ECONOMIC PRINCIPLES

### Causes of the shipbuilding cycle

It is easy to understand why the shipbuilding market is so volatile. The market mechanism uses the volatility to balance the supply and demand for ships, whilst at the same time drawing in new low-cost shipbuilders and driving out high-cost capacity. This mechanism is basically unstable, as can be illustrated with a simple example. If the merchant fleet is 1,000 m.dwt and sea trade grows by 5%, an extra 50 m.dwt of ships are needed. If, in addition, 20 m.dwt of ships are scrapped, the total shipbuilding demand is 70 m.dwt. But if sea trade does not grow, no extra ships are needed and shipbuilding demand falls to 20 m.dwt. So a 5% change in trade produces a 70% change in shipbuilding demand. Five per cent changes in seaborne trade are common, and sometimes much larger swings occur (see Figure 4.2).

This basic instability is reinforced by two other characteristics of the shipbuilding market. Because new ships are not delivered until several years after they are ordered, investors really have no way of knowing whether they will be needed or not, and, in the absence of believable forecasts, market sentiment often takes over. As a result, ordering often peaks at the top of a cycle, but by the time the ships are delivered the business cycle is already driving demand down and the flood of new ships increases the surplus and prolongs the downturn. This process is reinforced by the inflexibility of modern shipyard capacity. Because it is difficult for the shipyards to adjust output, they often drop their prices to encourage speculative 'counter-cyclical' orders and liquid investors often take advantage of the bargains. This combination of demand-side opportunism and supply-side inflexibility tends to slow the market adjustment process, leading to some very long shipbuilding cycles.

Shipbuilding cycles are, of course, close relatives of the shipping cycles discussed at length in Chapter 3, but with special features due to the industry's different economic structure. Volk, in a lengthy study of shipbuilding cycles, takes much the same view, concluding that: 'Shipbuilding is characterised by heavy fluctuations of demand over the short-term and by high inertia of supply. This fact leads to brief phases of prosperity and long phases of depression.'[18] In one sense, this is all there is to be said. Until the demand for ships becomes regular or shipyards find a way of adjusting their capacity when it is not needed, the shipbuilding industry must live with long cycles. From an economic perspective, however, this is just the beginning of our study. In the previous section we saw that over the course of the last century this simple mechanism has produced radically different commercial environments. Applied economists in shipping or shipbuilding who understand the underlying relationships can recognize the way a particular market is likely to develop. This is what we will focus on in the remainder of this chapter, starting with the general economic relationships and then going on to a discussion of the microeconomic aspects of shipyard production.

## Shipbuilding prices

Shipbuilding cycles are controlled by the price mechanism, and this is where we must start. Shipbuilding is one of the world's most open and competitive markets. Shipowners invariably take several quotations before ordering a ship, and there are not the usual trade barriers in the form of distance, transport costs and tariffs to provide shipbuilders with a protected home market. Prices swing violently upwards or downwards depending upon the number of shipyards competing for a given volume of orders.

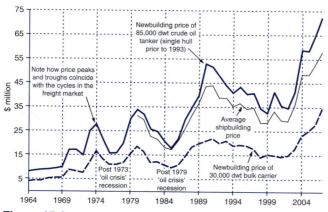

**Figure 15.4**
World shipbuilding prices, 1964–2007
Source: compiled from several sources including Fearnleys, CRSL

This point can be illustrated by following the development of the contract price for a 30,000 dwt bulk carrier and an 85,000 dwt tanker during the period 1964–2007 (Figure 15.4). Between 1969, when a 85,000 dwt tanker cost $10 million, and 2007, when it cost $72 million, we see price fluctuations on a scale which few capital goods industries can match. The price of the ship almost trebled to $28 million in 1974, fell to $16 million in 1976, increased to $40 million in 1981, fell to $20 million in 1985, increased to $43 million in 1990 and then edged down to $33 million in 1999, before more than doubling to $72 million in 2007. Faced with such volatile prices, it is hardly surprising that shipbuilders and their customers have difficulty in planning for the future. Because price movements for different types of ships are closely correlated – when the price of tankers goes up, so does the price of bulk carriers and ro-ros – there is no real refuge in finding market 'niches'. Most shipbuilders can compete for a wide range of ship types and, if their orderbook is short, will bid for ships they would not normally consider building.

These price fluctuations, and the large sums involved, make the shipbuilding market a tricky place to do business, and shipyards have to be very clever in their price strategy. In rising markets shipyards run the risk of filling their orderbook with ships contracted at low prices, only to find that by the time they deliver the ships, prices have doubled and costs have also increased. This happened to some shipyards in 2003 when they sold VLCCs for $70 million, only to find when they delivered them in 2006 that their value had escalated to $125 million and rising steel prices meant they had made a loss. Investors face the opposite problem – investors who ordered new tankers at the top of the cycle often found that by the time their tankers were delivered their value has slumped. But, of course, they can never be sure.

## Shipbuilding demand, supply and the price model

In this highly competitive market, the price at which a new ship is sold depends on the trade-off between the demand for new ships (i.e. the orders placed in a year) and the available supply of newbuilding berths for that particular ship type. If there are more potential orders than berths, the price rises until some investors drop out, and if there are more berths than orders, prices fall until new buyers are tempted into the market.

So explaining price movements depends on understanding what determines the demand for building slots and the supply of berths.

Because shipbuilding is a capital goods industry selling to an international market, its price model is more complex than the freight rate model we discussed in Chapter 4. However, the experience of the last two decades tells us that, for a given price, shipbuilding demand is influenced by shipping freight rates, second-hand prices, market expectations and sentiment, and liquidity and credit availability, while shipbuilding supply is influenced by available shipbuilding berths, shipyard unit costs, exchange rates, and production subsidies.

The way *freight rates* influence the demand for new ships is easy to understand – as earnings increase, ships become more profitable and shipowners want to increase the size of their fleets. The longer high freight rates persist, the more cash they have to do this. Historically there has been a close relationship between peaks in the freight market and peaks in ordering new ships. However, the time-lag between ordering and delivery and the long service life of ships mean that current freight rates are only a partial influence on new prices. The second major influence is *second-hand prices*. Potential investors want ships immediately, so initially when freight rates rise they try to buy second-hand ships, bidding up prices. Only when second-hand prices increase do newbuildings start to look a better deal and the rise in second-hand prices works through into newbuilding prices (note also that at high freight rates old ships which would otherwise have been scrapped continue trading, maintaining the supply). Because the new ships do not arrive immediately, they are not a precise substitute, which means that how keen investors are to order new ships depends on *market expectations*, the third major influence on newbuilding demand. A convincing 'story' about why the future will be prosperous can be very important and explains bouts of heavy ordering when freight rates are low, as happened in the early 1980s, or for bulk carriers in 1999. Finally, the *availability of credit* allows owners to leverage up their internally generated revenue, and broadens the market to include many entrepreneurial shipowners without large sums of capital.

Turning to shipbuilding supply, there are also four influences to consider. Firstly there is available *shipyard capacity*. In the short term, supply depends on how many shipyards are operational, their forward orderbook and how many berths they are willing to sell at prevailing prices. In physical terms, production facilities place an upper limit on output, whilst productivity determines the number of ships built. But the available capacity at a point in time also has an economic dimension. Shipyard *unit costs* depend on labour costs, labour productivity, material costs, exchange rates, and subsidies (which determine whether the shipyard is able to sell at prices which result in an acceptable return on capital). It does not matter how many facilities a shipyard has, or how high its productivity is – if the price on offer does not cover its costs, it will not bid. So capacity is not an absolute, it is a function of price. *Exchange rates* are enormously important because they determine the cash the shipyard receives in local currency. A 5% weakening of the domestic currency is equivalent to a 5% increase in the dollar price. The exception is if the shipyard is prepared to make a loss, for example to avoid cutting the workforce. This is an expensive strategy, but may be the cheapest option if the yard wants to keep its skilled workforce intact until the market recovers. Finally, local or state governments may decide to offer *production subsidies* to support their shipyards through a difficult patch, artificially flattening the supply curve.

The whole process is dynamic. Across the market shipowners ponder possible future earnings and whether it is better to buy a prompt second-hand ship, order a new ship which will not arrive for several years, or sell a second-hand ship, or do nothing. Depending on all these factors, they make their bid and if market sentiment is strong many others will be thinking along the same lines. Since owners are competing for limited second-hand ships or newbuilding berths, prices start to rise and vice versa. The speed with which this can happen is illustrated by price movements during the dry bulk boom in 2007. In January a five-year-old Panamax bulk carrier cost $37 million and a newbuilding for delivery in 2010 was $40 million. But freight rates surged during the year and by December the price of the second-hand ship had almost doubled to $72 million, whilst the new price had increased by 37% to $55 million. Clearly the market had made a judgement that the value of a prompt second-hand ship had increased considerably more than the value of a ship which would not arrive for three years.

On the other side of the negotiation, the shipyards are anxiously weighing up how many berths to offer for sale. Again price is the focus. If their orderbook is very short they may be under pressure to sell berths immediately, which puts them in a weak negotiating position and they may have to drop their price to attract a buyer. But if they have a long orderbook they must decide whether to sell the berths now or wait in the hope that prices will rise. For example, if they are confident about the future they may decide not to offer any berths, in the hope that the price will rise. That means investors are competing for fewer berths, pushing up the price. For this reason expectations are just as important in determining the supply of berths for sale.

Finally, we can define the time-scale for adjusting supply. In the *short term*, either the shipyard berths are full and supply is inelastic or some shipyards have empty berths and are desperate to fill them, leading to price cutting. In the *medium term* (two or three years' time) the yards have berth spaces and the price depends on the level of demand relative to the available berths. If there is a shortage, raising prices brings in the high-cost yards, expanding supply. In the *long term*, shipbuilders which are profitable at current prices can expand their capacity and unprofitable builders can close uneconomic yards. These are the general factors involved in the shipbuilding price model and in the rest of this section we will look more rigorously at how it works.

## The shipbuilding supply function

The first question is how many ships will be supplied or, in other words, how much capacity is available. The answer is provided by the *shipbuilding supply function.*[19] A typical short-term supply function (S1) is shown in Figure 15.5, which illustrates the relationship between the capacity available at a point in time, shown on the horizontal axis in million cgt of ships supplied, and the price. The bars show the capacity available in each of the shipbuilding areas, China, South Korea, Japan and Europe. They all have different cost levels. In China the average ship costs $34 million, compared with

$36 million in South Korea, $38 million in the small Japanese yards, and $43 million in the big Japanese yards. The European yards have costs of $52 million, but they mainly build specialized ships so that is what bulk ships would cost if they switched capacity into the bulk market. Assuming yards only bid when they can at least break even, the available capacity increases from 5 million cgt at a price of $33 million for a standard

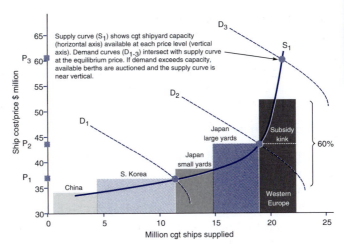

**Figure 15.5**
Short-run bulk shipbuilding demand and supply functions
Source: Martin Stopford 2007

ship to 22.5 million cgt at $52 million. The supply curve (S1) links these points. Note that when demand hits 25 million cgt and all the yards are bidding, there is an auction for any remaining berths that the yards have held back in the hope of such a situation arising. At this point the supply function is nearly vertical.

## The short-term shipbuilding demand function

The *shipbuilding demand function* shows how many ships investors will want to buy. Three examples of demand functions are shown in Figure 15.5, labelled D1, D2 and D3. For example, the demand curve D2 shows that if the ship price is $50 million investors will only order 14 million cgt, but if the price drops to $35 million orders will increase to 24 million cgt. This demand curve implies that price does have an effect on ordering activity, and economists analyse this degree of responsiveness by calculating the demand curve's *price elasticity* which is defined as the percentage change in demand divided by the percentage change in price:

$$e_{sbp} = \frac{\% \text{ change orders}}{\% \text{ change price}} \tag{15.1}$$

If the price elasticity is greater than 1 demand is price elastic, and if it is less than 1 it is price inelastic. In this example demand is relatively price elastic, but it is very difficult to be sure because so much depends on expectations. If shipping investors have plenty of funds and positive expectations they may order the same amount of ships regardless of price, in which case the demand curve would be vertical. But the usual assumption is that as prices rise the financial case for investment weakens and only those investors with a very profitable market opportunitiy or an urgent need for new ships are willing to pay. Others prefer to take their chances and wait until prices fall, by perhaps extending the life of their existing ships, especially since rising prices are generally associated with a long delivery date. Conversely, as the price falls the financial case for new orders improves and the demand for new ships increases until, at some point, constraints on finance or market expectations limit the number of new orders placed and no further ships are ordered however low the price falls.

## Shipbuilding market short-term equilibrium

Putting the supply and demand curves together, we have a sort of battlefield in which yards with different cost levels compete for business at the best price they can negotiate with their customers, the shipowners. There always seems to be a spectrum of yards with different cost levels and market cycles forming the backdrop to a running battle between low-cost new entrants and the established builders. Five hundred years ago it was the Dutch newcomers versus the Venetians. Later it was the Japanese newcomers versus the Europeans, then the South Koreans versus the Japanese. Over long periods shipbuilding cycles work like a pump, sucking the low-cost capacity in and pumping the high-cost capacity out. When demand is strong enough at D3 in Figure 15.5 even the high-cost yards can fill their berths and survive, limping from one peak to another. But they are vulnerable to recessions, and if demand falls to D2 the highest-cost yards will lose money and eventually give up, making way for the low-cost newcomers which enter the market because at D2 demand levels they can make a very decent profit.

As the low-cost yards make more profits they start to expand, moving the supply curve to the right and undermining the position of the high-cost yards even more. Meanwhile, the newcomers which entered the market during the boom when prices were at D2 have their own obstacles to overcome. Some will be small established yards moving into the international market place, and they will have to establish a reputation for quality and delivery that will carry them through recessions when orders are hard to get. Others will be 'greenfield' yards established to develop a country's industrial base. In the latter case the new shipyards carry high capital costs and may need to import specialized materials and marine equipment during the startup-up phase. Governmental financial aid is sometimes available to assist the development of upcoming yards. But all must find a way to compete. No wonder the shipbuilding market feels like a battlefield.

In the short run, equilibrium is achieved at the price where the demand for new ships equals the supply offered by shipbuilders. This is illustrated in Figure 15.6. At a price of $1,000 per cgt the 32 million cgt offered by the shipyards exactly matches the 32 million cgt the owners are willing to buy. If the shipyards try to increase prices to $1,500 per cgt, demand falls to only 20 million cgt, leaving shipyards with 10 million cgt of unutilized capacity. Conversely, at $750 per cgt the owners would want to order 37 million cgt, but the shipyards would offer only 30 million cgt of ships. There would be a shortage of berths and the price would be bid up. In this way the price mechanism matches existing capacity to demand on a day-to-day basis.

In the longer term, the shipyards respond to the market cycles by adjusting capacity. The low-cost shipyards which are profitable even in weak markets build new facilities, or expand existing ones, moving the supply curve to the right. For example, in Figure 15.7(a) we see an initial supply function (S1) with the equilibrium price of P1. At this price the low-cost shipyards make excess profits, but as they add new capacity, the supply curve moves to the right and at this increased level of output the equilibrium price falls from P1 to P2. As supply expands and prices fall, the high-cost yards start to make losses and eventually some of them will close or diversify – the market has replaced high-cost yards with low-cost yards, which is exactly what the market process is all about. Through this ratchet process capacity expands and the competitive yards gradually drive out the inefficient ones, making better use of economic resources.

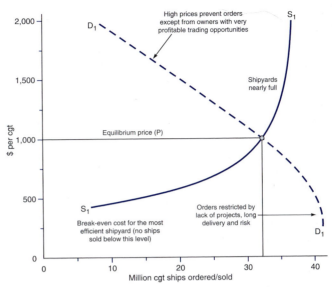

**Figure 15.6**
Shipbuilding supply and demand functions
Source: Martin Stopford 2007

But demand also plays a part in this market adjustment process. For example, the demand curve D1 in Figure 15.7(b) represents a situation where ship demand is growing at 3% per annum, requiring Q1 cgt of new ships (about 33 million CGT) at an equilibrium price of P1. But if total ship demand growth slips to a new trend of 2.8% per annum, only 30 million cgt of deliveries are needed each year and the demand curve

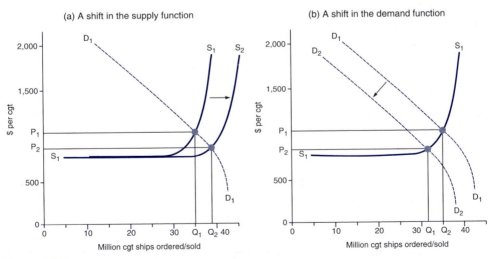

**Figure 15.7**
The effect on price of movements in shipbuilding supply and demand
Source: Martin Stopford 2007

moves left to D2. As a result the equilibrium price falls to P2. At this lower price the high-cost shipyards cannot cover their costs and eventually they close.

Putting the supply and demand dynamics shown in Figure 15.7 together, we have the basic model which drives the shipbuilding cycles we reviewed in Figure 15.3. During periods of expansion such as the long upswing from 1963 to 1977, or from 1988 to 2007, the demand curve is constantly moving to the right, with the shipyard capacity unable to keep up. As demand surges ahead so do prices, but when supply surges ahead, prices slump. The shape of the curves makes volatility normal.

## The long-term shipbuilding demand

The volatility of shipbuilding demand means that planning ahead is a priority for the shipbuilding and the marine engineering industries, and that calls for long-term forecasts of demand for new ships. The long-term demand forecasting model splits shipbuilding demand into two parts: *expansion demand* ($X$) which is the tonnage of new ships needed to carry trade growth in a given period, and *replacement demand* ($R$), which is the tonnage of new ships required to replace ships scrapped or removed from the fleet in the same period. Both are important. For example, between 1963 and 2005 expansion demand accounted for 57% of demand for new merchant ships and replacement demand for 43%. Using this model, which is discussed further in Appendix A, shipbuilding demand forecasts are made by estimating future values of $X$ and $R$.

This long-term shipbuilding demand forecasting model is given by

$$SBD_t = X_t + R_t \qquad (15.2)$$

where

$$X_t = \frac{\partial DD_t}{P_t} = \frac{DD_t - DD_{t-1}}{P_t} \qquad (15.3)$$

$$R_t \approx F_{t-\sigma} \qquad (15.4)$$

Here, for forecast year $t$, $SBD$ is the requirement for new ships (in deadweight or compensated gross tonnage terms, for example) $X$ the expansion demand, $R$ the replacement demand, $DD$ is the tonnage of cargo transported, $P$ is ship productivity (measured by dividing weight of cargo delivered by ship deadweight), $F$ is the fleet of ships by year of delivery, and $\sigma$ is the economic life of ship in years (e.g. 25 years).

Shipbuilders often use this basic model to forecast shipbuilding requirements for their own strategic planning and as a basis for international discussion of capacity levels. Expansion demand is estimated from trade growth and the incremental shipping capacity needed to carry it is calculated by applying the productivity factor $P_t$. So if trade is projected to grow by 70 million tonnes and the productivity is 7 tonnes per deadweight per annum, the expansion demand forecast for year $t$ would be 10 million deadweight. Forecasting replacement demand involves two steps. First, the economic life of the fleet is determined and its age profile is used to estimate the tonnage of ships likely to be replaced in the forecast period. For example, if tankers have an expected economic life of 25 years and the fleet has 10 m.dwt of tankers 25 years old, the expected replacement demand would be 10 m.dwt. Put the two together as shown in equation (15.2) and the forecast shipbuilding demand in year $t$ is 20 m.dwt.

Like so many aspects of shipping economics, the long-term shipbuilding model is simple in principle, but complex in practice. The model is illustrated in Table 15.3 which calculates shipbuilding demand from expansion demand and the replacement demand. We start in column 1 with a memo item, the actual growth of the world fleet between 1990 and 2006. The total at the bottom of this table shows that the fleet increased by 308 m.dwt during this period. This gives us a base in reality with which to compare our shipbuilding demand calculations. Next, in columns 2–4, we calculate the expansion demand. Column 2 shows total world trade, whilst column 3 estimates ship demand, by assuming the average ship carries 7 tonnes of cargo per deadweight per year. Analysts often employ complex commodity-based models to make this calculation, but we will keep it simple. Shipbuilding expansion demand is shown in column 4. It is quite volatile from year to year, but the trend

**Table 15.3** Shipbuilding demand model, 1990–2006, showing expansion and replacement demand in million deadweight (except where otherwise stated)

| | 1 | 2 | 3 | 4 | 5 | 6 | 7 | 8 | 9 |
|---|---|---|---|---|---|---|---|---|---|
| | *memo:* | Expansion demand | | | Replacement demand | | | Total ship-building demand $SDM_t$ | *memo:* ship-building deliveries |
| | Fleet (1st jan) | World trade (Mt) | Total ship demand | Expansion demand $X_t$ | Ships scrapped | Other removals | Total replacement $R_t$ | | |
| 1990 | 587.2 | 4,126 | 589 | 10.6 | 4.6 | 1.4 | 6.1 | 16.6 | 20.7 |
| 1991 | 603.2 | 4,313 | 616 | 26.7 | 3.8 | 4.5 | 8.2 | 34.9 | 20.6 |
| 1992 | 617.7 | 4,479 | 640 | 23.8 | 15.8 | 0.9 | 16.7 | 40.5 | 24.2 |
| 1993 | 626.2 | 4,623 | 660 | 20.6 | 16.8 | 1.2 | 18.0 | 38.5 | 27.5 |
| 1994 | 636.6 | 4,690 | 670 | 9.6 | 18.9 | 2.3 | 21.2 | 30.8 | 27.6 |
| 1995 | 639.4 | 5,083 | 726 | 56.1 | 15.5 | 1.2 | 16.7 | 72.9 | 33.0 |
| 1996 | 663.6 | 5,218 | 745 | 19.2 | 17.9 | 3.5 | 21.4 | 40.6 | 37.4 |
| 1997 | 679.7 | 5,506 | 787 | 41.2 | 15.7 | 4.0 | 19.7 | 60.9 | 36.5 |
| 1998 | 696.4 | 5,666 | 809 | 22.8 | 24.9 | 1.5 | 26.4 | 49.2 | 34.8 |
| 1999 | 704.5 | 5,860 | 837 | 27.7 | 30.4 | 1.1 | 31.5 | 59.2 | 39.8 |
| 2000 | 712.7 | 6,273 | 896 | 59.0 | 22.2 | 1.4 | 23.6 | 82.6 | 44.4 |
| 2001 | 733.8 | 6,167 | 881 | -15.2 | 28.1 | 4.2 | 32.3 | 17.1 | 44.6 |
| 2002 | 746.4 | 6,276 | 897 | 15.6 | 28.2 | 2.6 | 30.8 | 46.4 | 48.4 |
| 2003 | 764.1 | 6,598 | 943 | 45.9 | 26.9 | 2.4 | 29.4 | 75.3 | 55.6 |
| 2004 | 787.6 | 6,893 | 985 | 42.3 | 9.8 | 3.8 | 13.6 | 55.9 | 61.8 |
| 2005 | 834.0 | 7,122 | 1,017 | 32.7 | 5.7 | 3.2 | 8.9 | 41.6 | 70.2 |
| 2006 | 895.4 | 7,407 | 1,058 | 40.7 | 6.5 | 2.7 | 9.2 | 49.9 | 75.3 |
| Total increase | 308.2 | | | 479.3 | 291.6 | 42.1 | 333.8 | 813.1 | 702.4 |

Notes

| | | | | |
|---|---|---|---|---|
| Col. 1 | Clarkson fleet at year end from SRO | | Col. 6 | Other removals in year |
| Col. 2 | World Trade UNCTAD | | Col. 7 | Sum col. 5 and col. 6 |
| Col. 3 | Ship demand based on 7 tons per dwt pa | | Col. 8 | col. 4 + col. 7 |
| Col. 4 | Increase in col. 3 since previous year | | Col. 9 | Memo: deliveries in year |
| Col. 5 | Demolition in year | | | |

moves from around 20 m.dwt in the early 1990s to around 40 m.dwt per annum in 2006. Then, in columns 5–7 we calculate the replacement demand. Since we are dealing with history, scrapping and removals are used as the indicator of replacement demand. However, forecasters would use a model based on the life expectancy of ships.

Total shipbuilding demand is shown in column 8, and this model can be used to project scenarios of future shipbuilding requirements by forecasting the components in columns 2–7 at whatever level of detail is appropriate (many of the considerations about the shipping supply and demand model discussed in Chapter 4 are relevant to such an analysis).

This analysis raises two problems with this sort of long-term forecasting. Firstly, we must be very careful to define where supply and demand were at the start of the forecasting period. Estimated expansion demand between 1990 and 2006 shown at the bottom of column 4 is 479.3 m.dwt, but during this period the fleet only grew by 308.2 m.dwt. The explanation is that in 1990 there was surplus shipping capacity, which during the decade was gradually removed. Such factors need to be taken into account, which is not easy. Secondly, scrapping is not a precise indicator of replacement demand, since it includes a market component. As the markets tightened towards the end of the period, scrapping fell, possibly creating a backlog of 'over-age' tonnage. For both reasons what happens in practice can differ from the theoretical shipbuilding demand calculation, and these dynamic issues need to be taken into account. Finally, actual shipbuilding deliveries in column 9 provide a 'reality check' to see how the estimated demand compares with actual deliveries. It looks as though deliveries were below demand for the first half of the period, but drawing ahead towards the end.

## 15.5 THE SHIPBUILDING PRODUCTION PROCESS

For a better understanding of the shipbuilding supply model, we must now turn to the production process. In 2006 there were over 250 major merchant shipyards world-wide. The number of docks/berths and the layout and equipment of the shipyard place an upper limit on the number of vessels which can be built over any given period. There is great diversity. Some yards are fully operational, while others are uncompetitive and underutilizing their facilities.

### Categories of shipyard

Although modern shipyards are highly flexible in the type of ship they build, physical and commercial factors tend to subdivide the shipbuilding market into a number of sectors. The world's shipyards today fall broadly into three categories – small, medium and large.

Small shipyards specialize in vessels below about 10,000 dwt. These facilities generally have a workforce of below 1,000 employees, sometimes as few as 100–200. Some specialize in particular ship types, such as dredgers or offshore supply craft, but the product range is very wide, comprising small cargo ships, mini-bulkers, chemical tankers and a whole range of service craft such as tugs and dredgers. Consequently, most small shipyards tend to be very versatile in their product range. This sector is comparatively self-contained and it is unusual to find large shipyards competing for orders in the small ship market.

Medium-sized shipyards build vessels in the size range 10,000–40,000 dwt, although some may take vessels up to Panamax size. The constraint is usually the size of berth/dock and the facilities to process large quantities of steel. Typically, medium-sized shipyards have a workforce of about 500–1,500, though this varies greatly. In product terms the mainstay of these yards are container-ships, bulk carriers and small tankers. More sophisticated yards handle vessels such as short-sea ro-ros, ferries and gas tankers.

Finally, some very large shipyards have docks capable of accommodating tankers of up to 1 m.dwt and in a few cases a workforce of 10,000 or more, though some have fewer than 1,000. These facilities generally have highly automated equipment for steel preparation and assembly.

## The ship and the shipyard

The merchant ship is the world's largest factory-produced product. A 30,000 dwt bulk carrier might typically contain 5,000 tons of steel and 2500 tons of other components, ranging from the main engine to many thousands of minor items of cabling, pipes, furniture and fittings – and, by modern standards, this is a small vessel. Over half of the cost of the ship is materials. Figure 15.8 shows a rough breakdown of the main items. Steel represents about 13% of the cost, the main engine 16% and other materials 25–35%. The remainder of the cost is direct labour and overheads. The material content is higher for high-outfit ships such as cruise liners and lower for simple cargo ships such as large bulk carriers. Because of their size and value, virtually all merchant ships are built to order and the construction period is a long one, falling anywhere in the range 12 months to 3 years, depending on the ship size and the length of orderbook held by the shipbuilder.

The hull of a merchant ship is basically a box built from thin steel plate, reinforced by internal bulkheads and sections to give strength. Within the hull are various items of equipment required to propel and control the ship, handle cargo, accommodate the crew and monitor performance. The complexity in shipbuilding lies in minimizing the materials

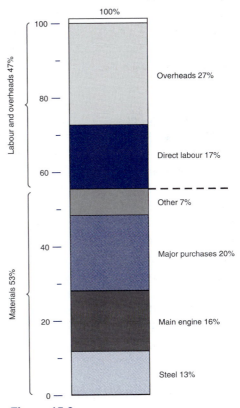

**Figure 15.8**
Cost structure of merchant ship
Source: Complied by Martin Stopford from various sources

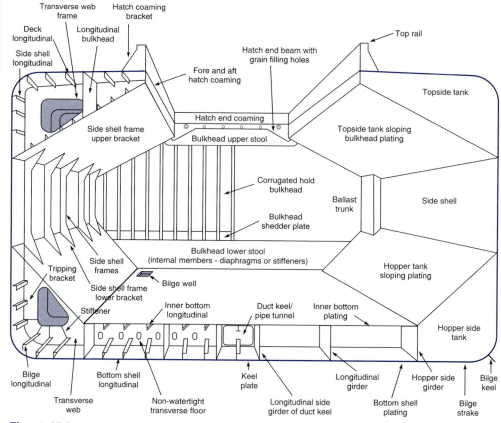

**Figure 15.9**
Cross-section of bulk carrier hull
Source: Lloyd's Register of Shipping

and labour required to construct a ship to the structural standards ('scantlings') laid down by the classification societies. The way naval architects resolve this problem depends on the ship. The bulk carrier hull shown in Figure 15.9 uses steel plate to construct the sides, double bottom, sloping plates, bulkheads and shaped components such as the transverse web. Sections are welded to the flat plate, for example as side or bottom shell longitudinals, to give rigidity. Although this structure looks simple, its structure is complex. The main deck is broken up by hatch openings and the hull derives its strength from the double bottom, the hopper tanks, the hatch coamings and the frames which run along the hull. Into the hull are fitted the many components, main engine, auxiliaries, pipe work, control systems, wiring and pumps. The entire structure must be coated with an efficient paint system, offering a long working life with minimum maintenance.

## The shipbuilding production process

To build ships the shipyard must accomplish three main tasks – the design and planning of the ship, the construction of the steel hull, and the outfitting of the hull with machinery, equipment, services and furnishings. These operations are not necessarily sequential and there is much overlap. An example of a shipyard layout is shown in Figure 15.10, with arrows indicating how work flows from the delivery of materials to the steel stockyard through to the assembly of the ship in the dock. This shipyard layout illustrates the different stages unusually well, though not all shipyards are designed in such a logical way. It is common to find these facilities spread around the yard, with units moved from one location to another on low loaders. The ten manufacturing stages are itemized in Box 15.1 and the numbers in brackets following the stage titles refer to the location in the shipyard diagram in Figure 15.10 where that stage takes place.

The production process is essentially one of assembly, and few of the individual tasks require sophisticated technical skills, though some automation of cutting, welding and repetitive assembly is possible. The skill comes in planning and implementing the tens of thousands of operations that contribute to the production of a merchant ship – materials must be ordered and arrive on time; steel parts, fabrication and pipe work must fit accurately without the need for rework and must be delivered to the work

## BOX 15.1 TEN STAGES IN THE SHIPBUILDING PRODUCTION PROCESS

The notes below are designed to be read in conjunction with the shipyard layout plan in Figure 15.10.

Stage 1: *Design and estimating (1)*

The design, cost estimates and vessel building strategy and production plans are produced by shipyard staff, initially in outline and then, if the ship is sold, gradually developed in greater detail to produce detailed working drawings and parts lists. Computer graphic equipment allows digital information developed during the design and estimating process to be used to plan and control the production of the vessel. Materials are ordered. Developing comprehensive and accurate information at an early stage in the design programme is one of the most crucial areas for improving productivity and product quality in modern shipbuilding.

Stage 2: *Materials reception (2, 15)*

Materials account for about 50–60% of the cost and labour and overheads for the remainder (see Figure 15.8), and a large merchant ship may involve several thousand separate purchase orders. A cost estimate must be prepared, often before the full design has been finalized, and materials, particularly long lead items such as the main engine, must be ordered. Items of equipment are delivered to the shipyard's material reception facility (2) where they are stored until needed. Pipes and other subcontracted components are delivered to the outfit storage area (15). The prompt delivery of materials is essential, as is quality control. Material supply problems can disrupt production programmes.

Stage 3: *The steel stockyard (3, 4)*

The steel is one of the first items to be ordered, and when it arrives it is stored in the steel stockyard. The two principal steel components used in ship manufacture are

**BOX 15.1—cont'd**

plates and rolled sections, which are used primarily to stiffen the plates. They are delivered to the yard by sea or road. The stockyard is laid out in an orderly manner and materials are retrieved using an overhead gantry crane.

Stage 4: *Surface preparation (5)*
Steel plates and sections are retrieved from the steel stockyard and processed through a surface preparation plant to ensure they meet the precise standards required for construction. This involves rolling plates and straightening sections to ensure that they are true, followed by shot blasting to remove rust and priming to protect the plate from further rusting and provide a foundation for paint. The edges of plate to be welded are chamfered ready for the welding machines.

Stage 5: *Plate and stiffener preparation (6)*
The primed steel plates are cut to the precise required size using numerically controlled profile burning machines. Any plates that do not need cutting are transferred to the flame planer to have their rough edges removed, and create the proper edge profile for welding. If required, they are bent to shape using a press or rolls. Framing members (e.g. as shown on the left-hand side of Figure 15.9) are prepared from steel sections, cut to size and then bent to shape using a frame-bending machine. By this process the many thousands of steel components for constructing the ship's hull are prepared, cut to size and numbered in accordance with the drawings. In practice, this is a flow process with a steady stream of components moving through the steel preparation bays.

Stage 6: *Assembly into blocks (7, 8, 9)*
The next stage is to build the steel components into the 'sub-assemblies' and 'blocks' weighing up to 800 tons from which the ship is constructed in the dry dock. The larger flat plates that make up most of the hull are transferred to the panel assembly line (7) where they are welded together, and framing members are welded in place to form 'straight hull blocks'. Shaped steel used to build curved hull blocks (e.g. bow and stern sections, double bottoms) requires different processes such as line heating which are carried out in the curved hull assembly shop (9). Smaller sub-assemblies are constructed in the sub-assembly shop (8). As each block is finished it is taken to the storage area (10) where it waits until the next stage of processing.

Stage 7: *Coating (11, 12)*
Once the blocks have been assembled all surfaces must be treated with anti-corrosion coatings under carefully controlled conditions, ideally in a properly designed paint cell. From a production viewpoint, this is particularly challenging because coatings are easily damaged and can become a production bottleneck. The blocks and sub-assemblies are taken to the block surface preparation unit (11) where surfaces are prepared and coatings applied under controlled conditions. Depending on the coatings used they will then be taken to the accelerated

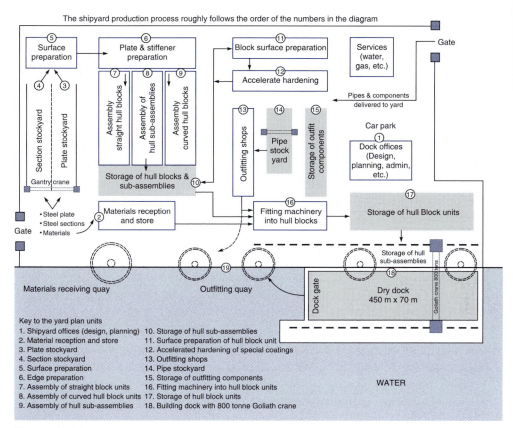

The shipyard production process roughly follows the order of the numbers in the diagram

Key to the yard plan units
1. Shipyard offices (design, planning)
2. Material reception and store
3. Plate stockyard
4. Section stockyard
5. Surface preparation
6. Edge preparation
7. Assembly of straight block units
8. Assembly of curved hull block units
9. Assembly of hull sub-assemblies
10. Storage of hull sub-assemblies
11. Surface preparation of hull block unit
12. Accelerated hardening of special coatings
13. Outfitting shops
14. Pipe stockyard
15. Storage of outfitting components
16. Fitting machinery into hull blocks
17. Storage of hull block units
18. Building dock with 800 tonne Goliath crane

**Figure 15.10**
Shipyard layout plan
Source: loosely based on Odense Lindo shipyard, part of A.P. Møller

---

### BOX 15.1—cont'd

hardening unit (12) to finish the process. When complete the blocks are taken back to the storage area (10) to await the next stage.

Stage 8: *Pre-outfitting (13, 16)*

The next step is to fit into the blocks and sub-assemblies as many as possible of the thousands of outfit items such as pipes, electrical cables, switchboards, furnishings and machinery. Most of this is done in the block outfitting hall (16). Blocks are brought there from the storage area and pipes and components from the pipe stockyard (14) and storage area (15) are fitted into them. This method allows better access and material scheduling control than is possible when working on the hull in the dock and is an important way of increasing shipyard productivity. Advance outfit requires sophisticated information management, accuracy control and tight organization. Plans must be made, and materials ordered and delivered to the work zone at precisely the right moment so that assembly can proceed smoothly. When materials

> **BOX 15.1—cont'd**
>
> arrive in the yard they must be precisely as specified and fit into the assembly with-out adjustment or rework. However, in the real world things inevitably go wrong and the greatest skill is the ability to adjust schedules when things do not go as planned. This sounds easy, but calls for great care in planning and accuracy control. After pre-outfitting the blocks are taken to the storage area (17).
>
> Stage 9: *Assembly in the dock (18)*
> Finally, prefabricated sections of the ship, together with those items of outfitting already installed, are lifted into the assembly dock and lowered in place, using the 800-tonne Goliath crane. They are carefully aligned, then welded into position. Outfit installations such as pipe runs are linked up.
>
> Stage 10: *Outfit at outfit quay (19)*
> When the hull is complete, the dock is flooded and the vessel is floated to the outfit quay where the outfitting of the ship is completed, systems are commissioned to ensure that on-board systems are operating correctly, and basin (or dock) trials of the main engines and auxiliary machinery are carried out.

station exactly when they are needed. Achieving this day after day is not as easy as it sounds, requiring considerable effort at the design and planning stage along with a production capability to manage material handling and production planning.

The major advances in shipbuilding techniques have been in planning and managing this process – for example, the introduction of pallets for material handling; the pre-outfitting and painting of assemblies before installation in the ship; and information systems to support these processes. The application of these techniques can yield dramatic results in terms of the man-hours required to build the ship.

## 15.6 SHIPBUILDING COSTS AND COMPETITIVENESS

In practice the level of efficiency and costs varies considerably from one yard to another. Although attention often focuses on the facilities as the main determinant of competitiveness, in reality there are many factors to consider. Broadly speaking, the price competitiveness of a shipyard depends on the key variables summarized in Figure 15.11 – material supply, facilities, availability of skilled labour, wage rates, labour productivity, cross exchange rates and, in some cases, subsidy all play a part in determining the cost and the revenue received by the shipbuilder.

### Material costs

Materials account for 60% or more of costs. Countries with large numbers of shipyards such as Japan, South Korea and China can support a full range of material suppliers, including engine builders, equipment manufacturers, subcontractors and manu-facturers of specialist items such as stern frames. Long production runs give these suppliers a competitive advantage, as does the ability to deliver a wide range of components from stock. Equipment which requires high levels of research and development is often supplied by local manu-facturers operating under licence. For example, marine diesel engines are developed and marketed by B&W MAN and Wärtsilä which have a major market share, and production is undertaken locally to their specifications. Shipyards in areas with little ship-building activity have a more difficult time. Even if they can obtain supplies abroad, timing and delivery issues can make this a difficult strategy to implement.

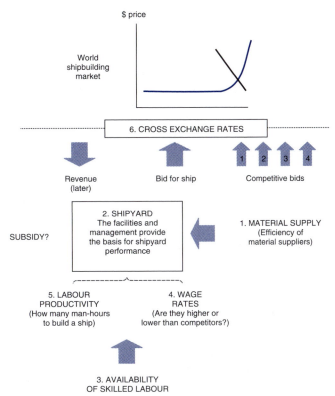

**Figure 15.11**
Influences of shipbuilding competitiveness
Source: Martin Stopford 2007

## Shipbuilding productivity

There are enormous differences in the productivity of shipyards around the world. Facilities explain some of these differences, setting an upper limit on the size and volume of ships that can be built. However, the productivity of the shipyard is more important. Unlike a process industry where achieving maximum production merely involves switching on the machinery and feeding in the required volume of raw materials, building a merchant ship requires the managerial skills to organize and control the fabrication and assembly process. Ultimately the maximum throughput will depend not just upon the size of the facilities, but upon the efficiency with which they are used. Some shipyards take ten times as many man-hours as others to build the same ship.

This naturally raises the question of how productivity can be measured As a rule, labour productivity is measured in man-hours per unit of output. Unfortunately there are practical difficulties in applying this formula to measuring and comparing shipyard productivity on an international basis. There are four main problems:

- *Output measurements.* There is no standard unit of shipyard production, and this is even more problematic at an industry level where production consists of a variable mix of large ship types. Although there have been a few successful standard ship designs such as the SDI4, even where ships have an apparently similar specification, for example Panamax bulk carriers, there is considerable scope for varying the design, machinery and general quality of finish. The best measure currently available is compensated gross tons (cgt), but this has limited value when dealing with sophisticated or complex ships.
- *Differences in subcontracting.* Shipyards differ in the amount of work that is subcontracted and there are few consistent detailed statistics about the labour used. For example, a shipyard which subcontracts electrical and joinery work will spend fewer man-hours building the ship, but its material costs will increase. The accounting practice of most shipyards is to treat subcontract labour as 'outside goods and services' and to include it in material costs. As a result, a comparison of man-hour productivity between two ships will be distorted if such differences in subcontracting are not taken into account, and this is extremely difficult to do at an international level.
- *Delivery peaks and troughs.* Ship deliveries from a yard may not represent the underlying level of production owing to the size and mix of ships. It is possible for a shipyard to be productively employed all year but not actually deliver any ships because of the irregular distribution of delivery dates. For this reason, throughput needs to be calculated from several years' deliveries if an accurate figure is to be obtained.
- *Joint product manufacture.* There are practical difficulties in measuring employment engaged on merchant shipbuilding because many shipyards undertake other activities such as warship construction, offshore and ship repair.

For these reasons any calculation of shipbuilding productivity and cost competitiveness is unlikely to be very accurate. However, to illustrate the general method involved, Table 15.4 shows the calculation of average shipbuilding productivity for some of the major shipbuilding countries in 2005. The first column estimates employment on merchant shipbuilding, while the second shows the tonnage completed in each country. Finally, productivity measured in cgt/per man-year is calculated in column 3 by dividing completions by employment. The range of productivity is very wide. Japan is at the top of the list with productivity of 183 cgt per employee, followed by S. Korea at 145 cgt per employee and Denmark at 91 cgt per employee. At the bottom of the range is Poland with 42 cgt per employee. For the reasons mentioned above, the productivity figures should only be regarded as a rough guide to the differences between shipyards, but they do at least illustrate the diversity that exists within the industry.

## Labour costs and competitiveness

Labour accounts for 40–50% of the cost of the ship, so wages have a major impact on competitiveness. The labour cost determines the total wage bill for producing the ship and depends upon the basic wage, to which must be added overtime payments and any bonuses paid to the workforce. In order to compare hourly wage costs it is necessary to convert them to a common currency; for present purposes, the US dollar has been used. There are significant differences in the wage rate in different countries, as can be seen in the right-hand half of Table 15.4. Applying the labour cost per man-year to the cgt productivity per man year gives an estimate of the labour cost per cgt, which is shown in column 5 of Table 15.4.

Shipyards facing competitive pressures due to rising wage rates, materials costs, or increasing price competition from other yards will, if they are to survive, have to reduce the man-hours required to build the ship. This can be done by improving facilities, systems and labour productivity. Automation is important, but improved organization, systems and product development may all play a part. For example, some Japanese shipyards tackled the challenge of rising labour costs by developing bulk carrier designs which were heavily engineered to assist the production process and thus reduce man-hours. In contrast, the Italian shipyards focused on the cruise market and mastering the skills needed to bring together the production of the hull with the very different task of outfitting the ship as a seagoing hotel and leisure centre. One way or

**Table 15.4** Merchant shipbuilding productivity by country

| | 1 | 2 PRODUCTIVITY | 3 | 4 LABOUR COST | 5 |
|---|---|---|---|---|---|
| | Numbers employed on merchant new work, 2005 | Tonnage completed 2005 | Productivity cgt per man-year | Hourly pay 2005 | Labour cost $ per CGT |
| Country | | ('000 cgt) | | US$[a] | |
| South Korea[b] | 38,600 | 5,600 | 145.1 | 13.56 | 159 |
| Poland | 11,818 | 500 | 42.3 | 4.54 | 182 |
| Japan[c] | 14,605 | 2,668 | 182.7 | 21.76 | 202 |
| Spain | 2,222 | 200 | 90.0 | 17.78 | 336 |
| Italy | 8,689 | 500 | 57.5 | 21.05 | 622 |
| Denmark | 3,300 | 300 | 90.9 | 33.47 | 626 |
| France | 3,500 | 200 | 57.1 | 24.63 | 733 |
| Germany | 14,600 | 1,100 | 75.3 | 33.00 | 745 |
| Netherlands | 4,300 | 300 | 69.8 | 31.81 | 775 |
| Finland | 4,290 | 200 | 46.6 | 31.93 | 1,164 |
| Total | 65,153 | 11,568 | 177.6 | | |

Source: CESA, KSA (all figures are approximate)

[a]Hourly pay is very sensitive to exchange rate of local currency against the US$

[b]Data for 2001 employment excludes 25,300 subcontractors source KSA

[c]Japanese data for 1998, Source KSA 'Proposal for the criteria of the derivation of productivity'

another these very different solutions increase the value added by the yard, but there is no simple formula for increasing productivity to offset high wage rates. Each shipyard must find its own solution.

## Currency movements and competitiveness

Although currency movements seem far removed from the shipyard, they are the single most important factor in determining shipbuilding cost competitiveness. Since the world economy moved to floating exchange rates after the breakdown of the Bretton Woods system in 1971, shipbuilders have faced a major problem with exchange rates. Unit costs vary proportionately with the exchange rate, and given the volatility of exchange rates during the 1980s and 1990s this is clearly a very major factor in determining shipbuilding cost competitiveness.

An example illustrates the point. A shipyard was negotiating the sale of a small bulk carrier. The yard's cost was £10 million and the $/£ exchange rate was 1.40, so the best price they could offer was $14 million. Unfortunately the owner would not pay more than $10 million, so to win the order the shipyard needed to cut its price by 30%. Since bought-in materials accounted for 60% of the shipyard cost, that was not possible, but while the negotiation dragged on over a period of six months the exchange rate fell to 1.06. At this exchange rate the shipyard could offer a price of $10 million and the contract was signed. Although such large currency movements are uncommon, it demonstrates just how vulnerable shipyards are to exchange rate fluctuations.

As we pull all of these factors together we build up a picture of how the competitive structure of the world shipbuilding industry really operates. At one extreme there are shipyards with low productivity but wages so low that man-hours hardly matter. They can undercut all comers. At the other end there are the high-productivity yards with even higher wage costs, which are slowly going out of business. This happened to the Swedish shipyards in the early 1980s, despite the fact that they had the highest productivity in the world. Between lie a whole range of shipyards with different combinations of wage costs and productivity. Washing over the whole industry are the waves of exchange rate movements that can sweep shipyards up and down the competitiveness league table in a matter of months. All of this combines to make shipbuilding a tough business that requires great management skill. Despite all these problems, or perhaps because of them, shipbuilders are some of the most tenacious businessmen in the maritime industry.

## 15.7 THE SHIP RECYCLING INDUSTRY

Compared with shipbuilding, shipbreaking (sometimes referred to as 'demolition' or 'recycling') is a rough business. The ships are sold at a negotiated price per light-weight ton (see Section 5.7 for a discussion of the commercial process). Shipbreakers mainly rely on manual labour to dismantle ships in whatever facilities are available, often a suitable beach. Although it is possible to increase productivity by using mechanized shipbreaking methods, these are capital-intensive and the investment has not generally been thought economic, given the volatility and small margins in the shipbreaking business.

The process of non-mechanized shipbreaking falls into three stages. At the preparatory stage, the owner of the vessel should undertake various operations including stopping up all intake apertures; pumping out all bilge water; blocking off intakes and valves; and removing all non-metal objects together with potentially explosive materials. If the vessel is a tanker it must be cleared of potentially dangerous gases. This work is often subcontracted.

The next stage is to beach the ship and remove large metal structures such as masts, pipes, superstructure, deck equipment, main engine, ancillary equipment of machinery room, decks, platforms, transverse bulkheads, propeller shafts, propeller shaft bearings, upper hull sections, bow and stern end sections. The remainder of the ship is then hauled by winches or lifted on to dry land by means of slipways, ramps or dry docks and cut into large sections. In some of the less sophisticated shipbreaking operations the vessel is simply winched on to the beach. Although this process can be undertaken satisfactorily on a beach or alongside a quay, the availability of a dry dock is a considerable advantage in terms of efficiency, safety and control of spillages.

Pumps, auxiliary engines and other equipment are removed and sold. Finally, the panels and sections obtained from the ship are cut into smaller pieces as required, using manually operated propane cutters. The scrap is then assembled for transport to its ultimate destination.

## The market for scrap products

Ships provide very high-quality steel scrap, especially tankers which have large flat panels. Sometimes the scrap is simply heated and rerolled into reinforcing rods for sale to the construction industry. Rerolled steel is also ideal for sewage projects, metal roads and agricultural needs. Smaller pieces are melted down. Much of the shipbreaking industry is located in the Far East and Indian subcontinent where there is a sizeable market for reprocessed steel products of this type. In the advanced countries of Europe, scrap is generally completely melted down to make fresh steel.

Although the scrap steel provides most of the value of the ship, the most lucrative return comes from the equipment and the 2% of non-ferrous items. Diesel engines, generators, deck cranes, compasses, clocks and furniture can also be resold. Again, the market for such equipment is stronger in Asian countries than in the developed countries, where technical standards are more demanding, the costs of refurbishing are higher and there is less demand for the second-hand equipment reclaimed from the ship.

## Who scraps ships?

For these reasons most shipbreaking occurs in low-wage countries in Asia where shipbreakers have a local market for their product and cheap labour to dismantle the ships.

**Table 15.5** Shipbreaking, by country, (1985–2005)

| | 1986 | | 1991 | | 1995 | | 2005 | |
|---|---|---|---|---|---|---|---|---|
| | GT | % | GT | % | GT | % | GT | % |
| Taiwan | 7,773 | 38 | 48 | 2 | – | 0 | 0 | |
| China | 4,567 | 23 | 172 | 7 | 754 | 9 | 200 | 3% |
| South Korea | 2,658 | 13 | 8 | 0 | 3 | 0 | 0 | |
| Pakistan | 861 | 4 | 445 | 19 | 1,670 | 20 | 0 | |
| Japan | 770 | 4 | 81 | 3 | 146 | 2 | 0 | |
| India | 636 | 3 | 695 | 29 | 2,809 | 33 | 1000 | 16% |
| Spain | 581 | 3 | 13 | 1 | 40 | 0 | 0 | |
| Turkey | 418 | 2 | 77 | 3 | 207 | 2 | 0 | |
| Italy | 311 | 2 | 8 | 0 | 1 | 0 | 0 | |
| Bangladesh | 268 | 1 | 512 | 22 | 2,539 | 30 | 4600 | 75% |
| Others | 1,444 | 7 | 306 | 13 | 354 | 4 | 300 | 5% |
| Total | 20,287 | 100 | 2,365 | 100 | 8,523 | 100 | 6,100 | 100% |

Source: Lloyd's Register of Shipping

This is a relatively mobile industry. Table 15.5 shows that during the recession in the mid-1980s when scrapping was very high, almost three-quarters of the shipbreaking industry was located in Taiwan, China and South Korea. Ten years later Taiwan and South Korea had left the industry. China's market share had fallen to 9% and India, Bangladesh and Pakistan had taken over as market leaders. By 2005, when the shipping industry was booming and demolition had fallen to 6.1 million gt, Bangladesh dominated the industry.

The explanation is that this very basic industry gravitates towards countries with low labour costs. Taiwan's development as a shipbreaker illustrates the point. The shipbreaking business got started with the dismantling of ships damaged during the Second World War and expanded rapidly after import controls were lifted in 1965. Encouraged by the government to meet rising domestic scrap demand and benefiting from a purpose-built site and from plentiful cheap labour, the industry established itself as the world's leading shipbreaker, with highly efficient facilities. Demolition took place in two state-owned sites at the deep-water port of Kaohsiung, using specially built berths and dockside cranes. The ships to be demolished were moored two abreast along the quay-side and systematically dismantled, with a breaking cycle of 30–40 days. With each decade the working conditions improved.[20] As the economy grew and labour costs increased, shipbreaking became less attractive and in the early 1990s Taiwan closed the demolition yards and replaced them with a container terminal. South Korea was a more recent entrant to the Far East scrapping business, but the story is much the same. In the 1980s South Korea was the third biggest shipbreaker with a 13% market share, mainly carried out in two demolition yards owned by Hyundai. As wages rose in the late 1980s and the shipbuilding industry expanded, the demolition yards were closed.

The People's Republic of China entered the ship demolition market in the early 1980s and rapidly became the world's second largest buyer of ships for scrap. There was a considerable domestic demand for steel products and, in fact, the China Steel Corporation was already importing a considerable amount of scrap steel from Taiwan. Although China continued to operate demolition yards in the 1990s, the scale of the business was restricted by government regulations controlling currency for the purchase of ships and strict environmental regulations, and China's market share fell from 23% in 1986 to 9% in 1995 and 3% in 2005.

In 2005 the main ship demolition sites were located in Pakistan, India and Bangladesh (Table 15.5), though the level of activity varies with the volume of ships available to scrap. Pakistan's main site is at Gadani Beach, with up to 100 scrapping plots, each plot covering 2500 square yards. Gadani Beach has no electricity supply or water mains and only a few plots have electric generators. Ship demolition takes place at the most basic level. Ships are driven on to the beach where an army of workers dismantle them. During busy periods, up to 15,000 labourers are employed breaking up the ships with the aid of very little mechanization. Much of the scrap material is moved manually, with the assistance of king-post trucks, blocks and pulleys, but the more profitable plots have now moved into mechanization and are using fork-lift trucks and mobile hydraulic cranes. Alang in India's Gujerat State was opened in 1983 and has 170 ship breakers along the 10 km of coastline on the west coast of the Gulf of Cambay. Strong tides and gently sloping beaches allow ships to be beached under their own motors or by tugs. The workers have access to them at low tide. There were 50,000 workers on this site in the 1990s but by 2006 that had shrunk to between 5,000 and 10,000. The Bangladeshi ship recycling yards are located near the port of Chittagong, and are the nation's main source of steel. Rerolling mills in Chittagong and Dhaka produce over 1 million tons of reinforcing rods for the construction industry.

Little shipbreaking is carried out in western Europe, owing to high labour costs and the lack of a ready market for recycled material. There are also various difficulties associated with health and safety legislation and environmental protection, both of which are more prominent than in the countries scrapping ships in Asia. The only European country of any significance in breaking activity in the recent past is Turkey. There are, however, a number of small shipbreaking companies scattered around the UK and continental Europe, mainly with 10–100 employees, specializing in breaking warships, fishing vessels and other high-value vessels.

Several features of the shipbreaking industry have recently raised concerns over the release of polluting materials such as heavy fuel oil and the effect of hazardous substances such as asbestos on workers. The IMO is currently developing a convention providing global ship recycling regulations for international shipping.

## The regulation of shipbreaking

Much of the ship dismantling nowadays takes place on tidal beaches and under primitive conditions and this presents society and policy-makers with a dilemma. On the positive side, the industry provides thousands of jobs for migrant workers and recycles valuable materials, including steel, other scrap metal and equipment which can be refurbished. However, the conditions in which this is done mean that workers employed in the industry face high accident rates and health risks from the dismantling of ships containing many hazardous materials, including asbestos, polychlorinated biphenyls, tributyl, tin and large quantities of oils and oil sludge. Protection for the environment is also a problem, with the pollution of coastal areas.

Work is ongoing, involving inter-agency cooperation between the ILO, IMO and the Secretariat of the Basel Convention, to establish mandatory requirements at a global level to ensure an efficient and effective solution to the problem of ship recycling. The IMO has adopted Guidelines on Ship Recycling and a new IMO Convention on ship recycling will include regulations for the design, construction, operation and preparation of ships so as to facilitate safe and environmentally sound recycling, without compromising the safety and operational efficiency of ships; the operation of ship recycling facilities in a safe and environmentally sound manner; and the establishment of an appropriate enforcement mechanism for ship recycling.

## 15.8 SUMMARY

In this chapter we have discussed the international shipbuilding and scrapping industries. Although shipbuilders face the same market volatility as their customers, the shipowners, it is a very different business with large fixed overheads and many employees.

Our review of the regional structure of world shipbuilding showed a clear regional pattern. During the first half of the twentieth century the industry was dominated by Europe, then in the second half the focus moved to Asia, with Japan leading the way, followed by South Korea which took over the dominant position at the beginning of the twenty-first century, by which time China was making a bid for market leadership, with a number of smaller Asian countries also entering the market.

This process of regional change was driven by a succession of shipbuilding market cycles, first generating growth which allowed new entrants to win market share, and then recessions during which the less efficient shipyards were forced out of the business. There were 12 of these cycles during the period 1901–2007, with an average length of 9.5 years. The cycles are driven by the interaction of supply and demand and coordinated by price movements. The shipbuilding supply function reflects differences in international cost competitiveness and typically has a J shape, whilst the demand curve is more difficult to define but is generally thought to be relatively inelastic. Movements in the demand curve result in changes in ship prices, which in turn move the supply curve to the left (reducing supply when prices are low) or the right (increasing supply when prices are high).

Shipbuilding production is an assembly process involving 10 steps. However, the competitiveness of the shipyard does not just depend on how efficiently it assembles the ship. Wage rates, the cost and availability of good-quality materials, and, most importantly, the exchange rate all play a part. Labour costs and productivity vary enormously from one country to another.

Finally, we discussed the shipbreaking industry, a very different industry from shipbuilding. Although ideally demolition takes place in a dry dock, gently sloping sandy beaches are often used. The industry at the beginning of the twenty-first century was mainly located in areas with plentiful cheap labour and a market for the steel and equipment recovered from the ship. India, Pakistan and currently Bangladesh undertake most of the ship demolition. Regulation governing health and safety in the recycling yards and the construction of ships from recyclable materials is increasing.

In conclusion, shipbuilding and demolition are fascinating industries, in some ways very close to shipping, and in others very different. Their global location is constantly shifting and this, combined with fixed capacity and a volatile market, makes it a tough business. But the shipbuilders, who are tough people themselves, do not seem to mind that, and as long as there is seaborne trade and salt water, they will remain a distinctive and essential part of the maritime business.

# 16 The Regulation of the Maritime Industry

*Whosoever commands the sea commands the trade; whosoever commands the trade of the world commands the riches of the world and consequently the world itself.*

*(Judicious and Select Essays and Observations by the Renowned and Learned Knight Sir Walter Raleigh, upon the First Invention of Shipping, H. Moseley, 1650)*

## 16.1 HOW REGULATIONS AFFECT MARITIME ECONOMICS

Shipowners, like most businessmen, find that regulation often conflicts with their efforts to earn a reasonable return on their investment. When Samuel Plimsoll first started his campaign against the notorious 'coffin ships' in the 1870s, British shipowners argued that the imposition of load lines would put them at an unfair competitive advantage. Fayle, writing in the 1930s, observed that:

> In their efforts to raise both the standard of safety and the standard of working conditions afloat, the Board of Trade frequently found themselves, during the last quarter of the nineteenth century, at loggerheads with the shipowners. They were accused of cramping the development of the industry by laying down hard-and-fast rules which in effect punished the whole of the industry for the sins of a small minority, and hampering British shipping in international competition, by imposing restrictions from which foreign ships were free, even in British ports.[1]

The same, sometimes legitimate, resistance to regulation is found in most industries, but the world's oceans provide the shipping industry with an unrivalled opportunity to bypass the clutches of regulators and gain an economic advantage. The goal of maritime regulators is to close the net and ensure that shipping companies operate within the same standards of safety and environmental responsibility which apply on land. As a result, in the last 50 years the regulatory regime has played a significant part in the economics of the shipping market.

It would, however, be wrong to think that the regulatory process is only concerned with pursuing villains. A few regulations are made in response to particular incidents.

The *Titanic*, the *Torrey Canyon*, the *Herald of Free Enterprise*, the *Exxon Valdez*, the *Erica* and the *Prestige* all provoked a public outcry which led to new regulations. But these are the exceptions. Over the last century the shipping industry and the maritime states have gradually evolved a regulatory system covering all aspects of the shipping business. Ship design, maintenance standards, crewing costs, employment conditions, operating systems, company overheads, taxation, oil pollution liability, environmental emissions and cartels are all subject to regulation in one way or another. However, the emphasis changes and during the last decade the environment, emissions by ships, ballast water, and ship recycling have all received more attention. Needless to say, all of this has economic consequences and a knowledge of maritime regulation is an essential part of the maritime economist's toolkit.

## 16.2 OVERVIEW OF THE REGULATORY SYSTEM

The aim of this chapter is to discuss the international regulatory system and the legal and political issues that have influenced, and in some cases dominated, the maritime scene since the mid-1960s. The chapter seeks to answer three questions: *Who* regulates shipping and commerce? *What* do they regulate? *How* do regulations affect shipping economics?

The first step is to identify the regulators more precisely. In an ideal world there would be a supreme legislative body which makes a single set of international laws, with an international court that tries cases and an enforcement agency. Reality does not live up to this ideal, and some experts doubt whether what passes for international law is really 'law' at all.[2] There is an International Court of Justice, but its rulings on shipping matters are purely advisory. We should not be surprised at this state of affairs. Each of the 166 countries with an interest in shipping has its own priorities. Gaining agreement on a body of international law, far less approving an international executive to enforce the laws, is hardly likely to succeed.

Maritime regulation is currently organized through the more pragmatic system set out in Figure 16.1. The difficult task of coordinating the many interests and gaining agreement to a consistent body of maritime law falls to the United Nations. The United Nations Convention on the Law of the Sea (UNCLOS 1982) sets the broad framework, whilst the task of developing and maintaining workable regulations within this framework is delegated to two UN agencies, the IMO and ILO. The IMO is responsible for regulations on ship safely, pollution and security and the ILO is responsible for the laws governing the people on board ships. These two organizations produce 'conventions' which become law when they are enacted by each maritime state.[3] The enactment of the maritime conventions is in some cases patchy because not all the 166 states sign up to some conventions, but the major ones such as SOLAS and MARPOL (see Table 16.5 below) have been made law by every significant flag state.

Each maritime state has two different roles, first as a 'flag state' and second as a 'coastal state' (see centre of Figure 16.1). As a 'flag state' it makes and enforces laws governing ships registered under its flag. For example, as a flag state Greece is legally

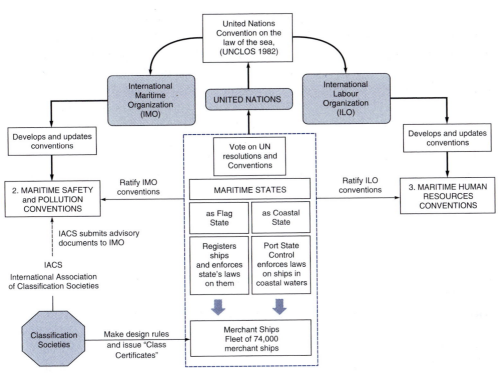

**Figure 16.1**
The maritime regulatory system showing the role of the 166 maritime states
Source: Martin Stopford 2007

responsible for ships flying the Greek flag, wherever they are in the world, whilst as a coastal state it enforces maritime laws on ships in Greek territorial waters. This is known as 'port state control'. Generally the laws maritime states enforce comply with maritime conventions, but not always. For example when the USA passed the Oil Pollution Act (1990), a law designed to phase out single-hull tankers in US waters, there was no maritime convention on this issue.

The other major 'players' in the regulatory process are the classification societies. Most major maritime nations have their own classification society and they are, in effect, the technical advisers to the maritime regulators. Over the last decade their role as recognized organizations (ROs) has increased and they assist the regulators in making and implementing maritime laws with a technical, human or environmental focus. In addition, they develop technical standards in their own right and award the classification certificate which is required by insurance underwriters. They are paid for these services, but have no legal powers of enforcement beyond withdrawing their services.

In summary, the regulatory system discussed in this chapter involves six principal participants in the regulatory process:

- The *classification societies*: the shipping industry's own system for regulating the technical and operational standard of ships. The classification societies make rules for ship construction and maintenance and issue a classification certificate to reflect compliance.

- The *United Nations*, which sets the broad framework of maritime law.
- The *flag states*. The primary legal authority governing the activities of merchant ships is the state in which the ship is registered, the flag state. By custom this state is responsible for regulating all aspects of the commercial and operational performance of the ship. International laws are developed by the participation of flag states in treaties or conventions.
- The *coastal states*. A ship is also subject to the laws of the coastal state in whose waters it is trading. The extent of each state's territorial waters and the scope of regulation vary from one country to another.
- The *IMO*, the UN agency responsible for safety, the environment and security.
- The *ILO*, responsible for regulations governing people on board ship.

In the following sections we will consider each of these regulatory regimes.

## 16.3  THE CLASSIFICATION SOCIETIES

The shipping industry's own regulatory system arose from the efforts of insurers to establish that the vessels for which they were writing insurance were sound. In the mid-eighteenth century they formed the first classification society and during the intervening period their activities have become so closely involved with the regulatory activities of governments that it is often difficult for laymen to understand the difference between the two. In this section we will focus on the role of classification societies and explain why they were set up, how they have evolved, the functions they undertake today and their impact on maritime regulation.

### Origin of the classification societies

Like many other shipping institutions, the classification societies are the product of their past, so knowing something of their history helps to explain the current structure. Lloyd's Register of Shipping, the first classification society, can trace its origins back to Lloyd's Coffee House in the early 1700s. The proprietor, Edward Lloyd, presumably in an effort to attract clients, started to circulate lists giving details of vessels which might appear for insurance.[4] The next step came in 1764 when a committee of London insurers and insurance brokers compiled a book containing details of ships that might require insurance. When published the book was known as *Lloyd's Register*. This register classified ships according to their quality, listing a grade 'conferred on the ship by the Committee's appointed surveyors'.[5] The condition of the hull was classified A, E, I, O or U, according to the excellence of its construction and its adjudged continuing soundness (or otherwise). Equipment was graded G, M or B – good, middling or bad. Any ship classified AG was thus as sound as it could be, whilst one rated UB was obviously a bad risk from the underwriter's point of view. In time, G, M and B were replaced by 1, 2 or 3.[6]

The 'green book', as it was known, was compiled by insurers for the sole use of members of the society and contained details of 15,000 ships. All went well until the 1797–8 register introduced a new grading system which based the ship's class on its river of build, favouring ships built on the Thames. This was disputed by many shipowners, and in 1799 a rival register was published, the *New Register Book of Shipping*, known as the 'red book'. A period of punitive competition followed, bringing both registers close to bankruptcy. In 1834 the differences were settled and a new society was set up to produce a shipping register which was acceptable to all sections of the industry. The new publication was Lloyd's *Register of British & Foreign Shipping* and its governing body had 24 members, eight each from the merchants, the shipowners, and the underwriters. This made it representative of the shipping industry as a whole.[7]

The new society had 63 surveyors and a system of regular inspection for ships was instituted. The main function continued to be the production of a register grading ships, but a new classification system was introduced. Under this system, ships that had not passed a prescribed age and had been kept in the highest state of repair were classed A; ships which, though not fit for carrying dry cargo, were considered perfectly safe for carrying cargoes not damaged by the sea were classed E; and ships unsuitable for dry cargo, but fit for short voyages (not out of Europe) were classed I. The condition of the anchor cables and stores when satisfactory was indicated by 1 and when unsatisfactory by 2. This system gave rise to the familiar expression 'A1 condition'. In the first five years 15,000 vessels were surveyed and 'classed'.

As the class movement developed in the nineteenth century, the role of classification societies changed. At first the main job was to grade ships. As time passed they started to set the standards to which ships should be built and maintained. Blake comments:

> As its authority grew, the Committee took upon itself something like disciplinary powers. Any new vessel for which an A1 classification was sought must undergo *a survey under construction*, which meant in effect that its progress was closely inspected at least three times while the hull was still on the stocks.

A1 became a requirement rather than a grade in a scale.

Technical committees were set up to write rule books setting the precise standards to which merchant ships should be built and maintained. These rules set the standards and the society policed them through their network of ship surveyors.

Other classification societies were set up in the nineteenth century. The American Bureau of Shipping (ABS) has its origins in the American Ship Masters Association which was organized in 1860 and incorporated in 1862 through an Act of Legislature of the State of New York. Like Lloyd's Register of Shipping it is a non-profit making organization with general management vested in the membership comprising individuals prominent in the marine and offshore industries and related fields. Most class societies today are managed by a Board drawn from all parts of the maritime industry – shipbuilders, shipowners, insurers, etc. Although underwriters still participate in general management through membership of these boards, the classification societies can no longer be seen as acting exclusively for the insurers.

## The classification societies today

There are currently more than 50 classification societies operating world-wide, some large and prominent, others small and obscure. The list of the ten larger societies and the number of cargo ships they class, shown in Table 16.1, gives a rough idea of the relative prominence of the various institutions. These are all well-known names in shipping circles and together they cover over 90% of the cargo and passenger fleet (note that these numbers do not include the many small non-cargo-carrying vessels which the societies also class).

Today the main job of the classification societies is to 'enhance the safety of life and property at sea by securing high technical standards of design, manufacture, construction and maintenance of mercantile and non-mercantile shipping'. The classification certificate remains the mainstay of their authority. A shipowner must class his vessel to obtain insurance, and in some instances a government may require a ship to be classed. However, the significance of the classification certificate extends beyond insurance. It is the industry standard for establishing that a vessel is properly constructed and in good condition.

In addition to their role as regulators, the major classification societies also represent the largest single concentration of technical expertise available to the shipping industry. For example, Lloyd's Register, the largest classification society, has over 5,400 people, of whom half are qualified engineers, operating from 240 offices in 80 countries world-wide. They class ships against their own rules (around 6600 ships annually),

**Table 16.1** The major classification societies, November 2006

| | | Fleet classed | | Average ship | |
|---|---|---|---|---|---|
| | | Number | Million gt | Thousand gt | Age |
| *IACS members* | | | | | |
| Nippon Kaiji Kyokei | NK | 6,494 | 142.9 | 22.0 | 12.8 |
| Lloyd's Register (LR) | LR | 6,190 | 125.8 | 20.3 | 18.4 |
| American Bureau of Shipping | ABS | 6,292 | 103.2 | 16.4 | 19.6 |
| Det Norske Veritas | DNV | 4,010 | 102.0 | 25.4 | 16.5 |
| Germanischer Lloyd | GL | 4,712 | 54.9 | 11.7 | 16.5 |
| Bureau Veritas | BV | 4,877 | 46.6 | 9.5 | 18.9 |
| Korean Register | KR | 1,648 | 21.9 | 13.3 | 17.4 |
| China Classification Society | CCS | 1,897 | 21.6 | 11.4 | 19.4 |
| Russian Register | RS | 3,174 | 12.5 | 3.9 | 25.2 |
| Registro Italiano | RINA | 1,345 | 12.0 | 9.0 | 23.8 |
| *Others* | | | | | |
| Indian Register | | 352 | 1.5 | 4.2 | 17.6 |
| 11 Others (under 1,000 ships) | | 1,819 | 5.3 | 54.6 | 24.8 |
| Total | | 42,810 | 650.2 | 15.2 | 0 |

Note: The statistics cover only vessels included in Clarkson Registers

carry out statutory certification against international conventions, codes and protocols, and offer a range of quality assurance, engineering and consultancy services. In 2007, ABS and its affiliated companies had a global staff of more than 3,000 people, primarily surveyors, engineers and professionals in the areas of risk assessment and mitigation. ABS maintains offices or is represented in more than 80 countries. To put this into perspective, the IMO has a permanent staff of about 300 and many important bulk shipping companies have fewer than 100 shore-based staff. In these circumstances it is easy to see why, in addition to the classification role, the class societies have a major role as technical advisers to shipowners and undertake technical inspection work on behalf of governments. Since government regulations cover much of the same ground as classification rules, this sometimes leads to confusion over the role of the classification societies and government regulators.

Although the major societies do not distribute profits, they depend on selling their services to cover their costs and are subject to commercial pressures. As self-funding organizations, their survival depends on maintaining a sufficiently large fee-paying membership to recover their costs. There is, therefore, intense competition between classification societies to attract members, leaving them in the tricky position of competing for the business of shipowners on whom they will often have to impose financial penalties as a result of their regulatory inspections.

## The regulatory activities of the classification societies

The role of the class societies today has two fundamental aspects, developing rules and implementing them.

*Developing rules* includes both new initiatives and the continuous updating of existing rules to reflect changes in marine technology and conventions. Procedures vary, but most societies develop their rules through a committee structure, involving experts from various scientific disciplines and technical activities including naval architects, marine engineers, underwriters, owners, builders, operators, materials manufacturers, machinery fabricators and individuals in other related fields. This process takes into account the activities of IMO and IACS unified requirements.

The second stage involves applying the rules to practical shipbuilding and shipping activities. This is a four-step procedure:

1. *Technical plan review.* The plans of new ships are submitted to the classification society for inspection to ensure that the structural details in the design conform to the society's rules. If the plans are found satisfactory they are passed and construction can proceed. Sometimes modifications are required, or explanations required on certain points. Alternatively, the society may be asked by the shipyard to help out in developing the design.
2. *Surveys during construction* to verify that the approved plans are implemented, good workmanship practices are employed and rules are followed. This includes the testing of materials and major components such as engines, forgings and boilers.

3. *Classification certificate.* On satisfactory completion of the vessel the class is assigned and a certificate of classification is issued.

4. *Periodic surveys* for the maintenance of class. Merchant ships are required to undergo a scheme of surveys while in service to verify their acceptability for classification. The ship's classification society carries out these inspections and keeps records which, for example, a prospective buyer of the ship may ask to inspect.

The classification procedures for existing ships are, in general terms, agreed by IACS for its members and associates. The regulations typically require a hull and machinery annual survey, a hull and machinery special survey every 5 years, a dry-docking survey every 2½ years, a tail shaft inspection every five years, and a boiler survey every 2½ years. The hull and machinery survey is very demanding, involving detailed inspection and measurement of the hull.

As the ship grows older, the scope of this inspection widens to cover those areas of the ship which are known to be most vulnerable to ageing. For example, as oil tankers grow older the area of the deck plates subject to tests for corrosion increases. To avoid the lengthy time out of service, the classification societies allow owners to opt for a *continuous survey* consisting of a programme of rolling inspections covering one-fifth of the ship each year.

As more governments have become involved in flag state regulation over the last 30 years, the activities of classification societies as government representatives has increased. The most common authorizations are in connection with tonnage measurement and load lines, SOLAS, MARPOL and IMO set standards on the transportation of dangerous goods. In carrying out statutory work, the classification society applies the standards relevant to the country of registry.

Finally, it is worth mentioning the vetting inspections carried out by charterers of ships, particularly corporations in the oil and steel industries.

## The International Association of Classification Societies

Over the last thirty years classification societies have been under pressure from shipowners and regulators to standardize their rules. Non-standard rules mean design work classed by one society may not be acceptable to another, causing unnecessary cost and inconvenience. For regulators legislating on the technical standards of ship construction, particularly through the IMO, the lack of a common standard complicates their job. To address this problem, in 1968 the International Association of Classification Societies was set up. Its ten members are listed in Table 16.1 and account for about 90% of world classification activity. The IACS has two main aims: to introduce uniformity into the rules developed by class societies and to act as the interface between class societies. A related function is to collaborate with outside organizations and in particular IMO. In 1969 IMO granted IACS 'consultative status'. The fact that it is the only non-governmental organization with observer status at the IMO neatly illustrates the position of the classification societies as intermediaries between the commercial shipping industry and governments.

Over the last 30 years IACS has developed more than 160 sets of unified requirements. These relate to many factors, of which a few are minimum longitudinal strength, loading guidance information, and the use of steel grades for various hull members. However, a significant step forward came in December 2005 when the IACS Council adopted Common Structural Rules for tankers and bulk carriers. For the first time this integrated the rule-making activities of the societies into a single design standard. The Common Structural Rules were implemented on 1 April 2006.

## 16.4  THE LAW OF THE SEA

### Why the law of the sea matters

Since maritime law is made and enforced by nation states, the next task is to examine the legal framework which determines the rights and responsibilities of nations for their ocean-going merchant ships. There are two obvious questions. First, which nation's law applies to a ship? Second, what legal rights do other nations have over that ship as it moves about the world? The answers were not developed overnight, they were evolved over the centuries as a set of customary rules known as the *law of the sea*.

### The law of the sea: flag state versus coastal state

The debate over the legal responsibility for ships stretches back to the days when naval power was the deciding factor. A country's navy protected the ships flying its flag and this established the principle, which survives today, of flag state responsibility. However, coastal states also had a claim over ships visiting their ports or sailing in their coastal waters, if only because they could sink them with their cannons if they did not behave. Indeed, early writers suggested that the distance controlled by shore-based cannons should be the criterion for determining the extent of the coastal seas. In a world of rapidly growing commerce, agreeing the rights of the flag and coastal states has become a major issue. Can a country ban alcohol on board foreign ships in its territorial waters? If it considers a foreign ship unsafe, has it the right to detain it? The answers to these questions, in so far as there are answers, are to be found in the UN Convention on the Law of the Sea (UNCLOS 1982), the culmination of three Conferences on the Law of the Sea, referred to as UNCLOS I (1958), UNCLOS II (1960) and UNCLOS III (1973).

The process of developing these conventions started in 1958 when the United Nations called the UNCLOS I. Eighty-six states attended. The aim was to define the fundamental issues of the ownership of the sea, the right of passage through it and the ownership of the sea bed. The latter issue was becoming increasingly important as offshore oilfields started to be developed. Four conventions were eventually finalized, dealing with the Territorial Sea and Contiguous Zone, the High Seas, the Continental Shelf, and Conservation of Fisheries.

A second conference, UNCLOS II, was called in 1960 to follow up on some items not agreed in UNCLOS I. In the 1960s the growing awareness of the mineral wealth on the sea bed placed new significance on the law of the sea, and in 1970 the United Nations convened a third conference to produce a comprehensive Convention on the Law of the Sea. Work started in 1973 (UNCLOS III), attended by 150 states. With so many participants, discussion was extended. It was not until 1982 that the UNCLOS 1982 was finally adopted, to enter into force 12 months after it had been ratified by 60 states. It finally came into force on 16 November 1994, at last providing a 'comprehensive framework for the regulation of all ocean space … the limits of national jurisdiction over ocean space, access to the seas, navigation, protection and preservation of the marine environment'.[8]

As far as the flag of registration is concerned, UNCLOS 1982 endorses the right of any state to register ships, provided there is a 'genuine link' between the ship and the state. Since the flag state can define the nature of this link, in practice it can register any ship it chooses. Once registered, the ship becomes part of the state for legal purposes. The flag state has primary legal responsibility for the ship in terms of regulating safety, labour laws and on commercial matters. However the coastal state also has limited legal rights over any ship sailing in its waters.

The rights of the coastal states are defined by dividing the sea into the 'zones' shown in Figure 16.2, each of which is treated differently from a legal point of view: the

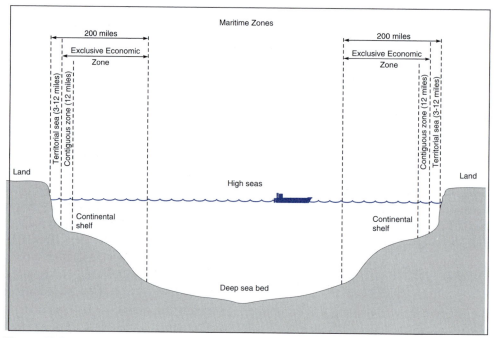

**Figure 16.2**
Maritime zones
Source: Martin Stopford 2007

# BOX 16.1  MARITIME ZONES RECOGNIZED BY THE UN CONVENTION ON THE LAW OF THE SEA 1982

*The territorial sea*

This is the strip of water closest to the shore. UNCLOS recognizes a maximum width of 12 nautical miles, but in practice countries use many different limits, as can be seen in Table 16.2. Three miles is the smallest limit, 12 miles the most common, while 200 miles is the furthest. Ships have the right of innocent passage through territorial waters. Coastal states only have the right to enforce their own laws relating to specific topics listed in Article 21 such as safe navigation and pollution. They are entitled to enforce international laws.

*The contiguous zone*

This is a strip of water to the seaward of the territorial sea. It has its origins in the eighteenth-century 'Hovering Acts' enacted by Great Britain against foreign smuggling ships hovering within distances of up to 8 leagues (i.e. 24 miles) from the shore. Coastal states have limited powers to enforce customs, fiscal, sanitary and immigration laws.

*The exclusive economic zone*

The exclusive economic zone (EEZ) is a belt of sea extending up to 200 miles from the baseline (i.e. the legally defined shoreline). It is mainly concerned with the ownership of economic resources such as fisheries and minerals. Within this zone third parties enjoy freedom of navigation and the laying of cables and pipelines. From a shipping viewpoint the EEZ is more like the high seas. However, the exception concerns pollution. Article 56 confers on the coastal state 'jurisdiction as provided for in the relevant provisions of this convention with regard to the protection and preservation of the marine environment'. The 'relevant provisions' relate to the dumping of waste and other forms of pollution from vessels. This gives the coastal state the right to enforce oil pollution regulations in the EEZ, a matter of major economic importance for shipowners.

*The high seas*

The high seas are 'all parts of the sea that are not included in the exclusive economic zone, in the territorial sea or the internal waters of a state'. In this area vessels flying a particular flag may proceed without interference from other vessels. This convention establishes the basis on which nationality can be granted to a merchant ship and the legal status of that ship. Article 91 of the 1982 Convention on the High Seas states that:

> Each state shall fix the conditions for the grant of its nationality to ships, for the registration of ships in its territory, and for the right to fly its flag. Ships have the nationality of the state whose flag they are entitled to fly. There must exist a genuine link between the state and the ship.

This paragraph was unchanged from the 1958 Convention and was the end-product of a heated debate about whether countries such as Liberia and Panama had the right to establish open registries. Since the Convention does not define what constitutes a 'genuine link' between state and ship, it was left to each state to define this link for itself.

territorial sea (the strip closest to land); the contiguous zone; and the exclusive economic zone. The fourth zone is the high seas, which nobody owns. None of the zones are precisely defined. Although the 1982 Convention fixes the limit to the territorial sea at 12 miles, Table 16.2 shows that many different limits are in use. The most common is 12 miles, but a few countries have adopted much more extensive limits. The contiguous zone and the exclusive economic zone are mainly of interest to shipowners because pollution control and prevention rights are granted to the coastal states in these areas. These zones are briefly defined in Box 16.1.

**Table 16.2** Limits of the territorial sea

| Distance miles | Number countries |
| --- | --- |
| 3 | 20 |
| 4 | 2 |
| 6 | 4 |
| 12 | 81 |
| 15 | 1 |
| 20 | 1 |
| 30 | 2 |
| 35 | 1 |
| 50 | 4 |
| 70 | 1 |
| 100 | 1 |
| 150 | 1 |
| 200 | 13 |
| None | 5 |
| Total | 137 |

Source: Churchill and Lowe, (1983, Appendix)

## 16.5 THE REGULATORY ROLE OF THE FLAG STATE

### Economic implications of flag state regulation

In recent years the flag state issue has been crucial for maritime economics because it provided shipowners with a way of reducing their costs. When a ship is registered in a particular country (the flag state), the ship and its owner must comply with its laws. The unique feature of shipping is that because the ship moves around the world anyway, it is easy to change legal jurisdiction. For a shipowner there are four principal consequences of choosing to register a ship in one state rather than another:

1. *Tax, company law and financial law.* A company that registers a ship in a particular country is subject to that country's commercial laws. These laws will determine the company's liability to pay tax and may impose regulations in such areas as company organization, auditing of accounts, employment of staff and limitation of liability. All of these affect the economics of the business.

2. *Compliance with maritime safety conventions.* The ship is subject to any safety regulations the state has laid down for the construction and operation of ships. Registration under a flag that has ratified and rigidly enforces the 1974 Safety of Life at Sea (SOLAS) Convention means complying with these standards. Conversely, registration under a flag state that has not ratified SOLAS, or does not have the means to enforce it, allows shipowners to set their own standards on equipment and maintenance (but they are still subject to port state regulation).

3. *Crewing and terms of employment*. The company is subject to flag state regulations concerning the selection of crew, their terms of employment and working conditions. Some flag states, for example, insist on the employment of nationals.

4. *Naval protection and political acceptability*. Another reason for adopting a flag is to benefit from the protection and acceptability of the flag state. Although less important today, there were examples during the war between Iran and Iraq in the 1980s when shipowners changed to the US flag to gain the protection of US naval forces in the Gulf.

Any of these factors may be sufficient to motivate shipowners to seek a commercial advantage by changing their flag of registry. Table 16.3 shows that this has a long history, and one that gathered momentum during the twentieth century as taxation and regulation came to play an increasing part in the shipowner's commercial operations. This naturally raises the question whether a shipowner is free to change his flag. To answer this question we must look at how ships are registered. In some countries the shipowner is subject to the same legal regime as any other business, while in others special legislation is introduced covering merchant shipping companies.

## Registration procedures

A ship needs a nationality to identify it for legal and commercial purposes, and it is obtained by registering the ship with the administration of a national flag. The way registration works varies from one country to another, but the British regime provides an illustration.

Under the Merchant Shipping Act 1894, British ships must be registered within Her Majesty's dominions (in practice, because of the constraints presented by the legislation of UK Dependent Territories, that registration may have to be in the UK). A peculiarity of British registration is that the ship is registered as 64 shares, at least 33 of which must be owned by a British subject or a company established under the law of some part of Her Majesty's dominions and having its principal place of business in those dominions.[9] Under the UK Companies Acts, any person of any nationality may register and own a company in the United Kingdom, so a national of any country may own a British ship.

Interestingly, there are no legal penalties for failing to register a ship, possibly because it was felt that the practical penalties are such that no legal enforcement is required to provide an additional inducement. A ship registered in the UK can fly the British flag, i.e. the Red Ensign, but is not obliged to do so. Nor is there any legal constraint on a British subject or British companies registering ships outside Britain if they wish to do so. All that is necessary is for the requirements of the recipient register to be met.

There is much variation in the requirements for registration. Some flag states require the ship to be owned by a national. This is the case in Liberia, but nationality is easily established by setting up a Liberian company, which qualifies as a national for the purposes of registration. Panama has no nationality requirements, while the Greek flag falls

**Table 16.3** History of ship registration and port state control

| Period | Flag of registry | Motivation |
|---|---|---|
| 16th century | Spanish | English merchants circumvented restrictions limiting non-Spanish vessels from West Indies trade. |
| 17th century | French | English fishermen in Newfoundland used French registry as a means to continue operation in conjunction with British registry fishing boats. |
| 19th century | Norwegian | British trawler owners changed registry to fish off Moray Firth. |
| Napoleonic War | German | English shipowners changed registry to avoid the French blockade. |
|  | Portuguese | US shipowners in Massachusetts changed registry to avoid capture by the British. |
| 1922 | Panamanian | Two ships of United American Lines changed from US registry to avoid laws on serving alcoholic beverages aboard US ships. |
| 1920–1930 | Panamanian | US shipowners switched registry to reduce operating costs by employing cheaper shipboard labour. |
| 1930s | Panamanian | Shipowners with German-registered ships switched to Panamanian registry to avoid possible seizure. |
| 1939–1941 | Panamanian | With encouragement from the US government, shipowners switched to Panamanian registry to assist the Allies without violating the neutrality laws. European shipowners also switched to Panamanian registry to avoid wartime requisitioning of their vessels. |
| 1946–1949 | Panamanian | More than 150 ships sold under the US Merchant Sales Act of 1946 were registered in Panama - as it offered liberal registration and taxation advantages. |
| 1949 | Liberian | Low registration fees, absence of Liberian taxes, absence of operating and crewing restrictions made registry economically attractive. |
| 1950–late 1970s | Flags of convenience develop as preferred registration for the independent shipping industry | As registry in USA and other countries became increasingly uneconomical, many countries competed to become 'flags of convenience' for ship registrations; only a few succeeded in attracting significant tonnage. |
| 1982–2007 | National flags start to enforce regulations on ships in their coastal waters | 1982 Paris Memorandum of Understanding in which 14 European states agreed to work together to ensure that ships visiting their ports complied with international conventions on safety and pollution. Others followed. |

Source: Cooper (1986)

somewhere between the two, requiring 50% ownership by Greek citizens or legal entities.[10] Dual registration is also possible to deal with situations where, for example, the ship is financed under a different jurisdiction from its legal ownership (dual registration is discussed below).

In 2004 the IMO adopted a scheme for issuing a unique number to each company and registered owner. Its purpose is to assign a permanent number for identification purposes to each company and/or registered owner 'managing ships of 100 gross tonnage and inwards ... involved in international voyages'.[11]

## Types of registry

Ship registers can be broadly divided into three groups: national registers, international registers and open registers.

- *National registers* treat the shipping company in the same way as any other business registered in the country. Certain special incentives or subsidies may be available but, broadly speaking, the shipping company is subject to the full range of national legislation covering financial, company and employment regulations.
- *International registers* were set up by some national flag administrations to offer their national shipowning companies an alternative to registering under open registries. They treat the shipping company in broadly the same way as an open register, generally charging a fixed tax on the tonnage of the ship (tonnage tax) rather than taxing corporate profits. The aim is to provide a national flag environment which offers shipowners the commercial advantages available under an open register. In 2005 there were eight international registers, of which Singapore, Norwegian International Registry, Hong Kong, Marshall Islands and the Isle of Man were the biggest.
- *Open registers (flags of convenience)* offer shipowners a commercial alternative to registering under their national flag, and they charge a fee for this service. The terms and conditions depend on the policy of the country concerned. The success of an open register depends on attracting international shipowners and gaining the acceptance of the regulatory authorities. In 2005 there were 12 open registries, which are listed in Table 16.4. Panama, Liberia, Bahamas, Malta and Cyprus were the biggest.

The distinction has more to do with how registered ships are treated than access to the flag. Most national registers are open to any shipowner, whatever his nationality, who wishes to apply for registration and satisfies the necessary conditions. For example, the United Kingdom is open to any Greek, Norwegian or Danish shipowner who wishes to register his vessels under the UK flag, provided he satisfies certain requirements.[12] Confronted with a choice of flags under which to register, the shipowner must weigh up the relative advantages and disadvantages of each of the alternatives.

# REGULATION OF THE MARITIME INDUSTRY

**Table 16.4** World merchant fleet by ownership and registration, January 2005

| (1) | (2) | (3) | (4) | (5) |
|---|---|---|---|---|
| Flag state | | '000 dwt | | |

## 1. NATIONAL REGISTERS

| | Registered | | | % on home |
|---|---|---|---|---|
| | Home | Overseas | Total | register |
| Greece | 50,997 | 104,147 | 155,144 | 33% |
| Japan | 12,611 | 105,051 | 117,662 | 11% |
| Germany | 9,033 | 48,878 | 57,911 | 16% |
| China | 27,110 | 29,702 | 56,812 | 48% |
| United States | 10,301 | 36,037 | 46,338 | 22% |
| Norway | 14,344 | 29,645 | 43,989 | 33% |
| Hong Kong | 17,246 | 23,747 | 40,993 | 42% |
| Republic of Korea | 10,371 | 16,887 | 27,258 | 38% |
| United Kingdom | 10,865 | 14,978 | 25,843 | 42% |
| Singapore | 12,424 | 9,909 | 22,333 | 56% |
| Russian Federation | 6,845 | 10,022 | 16,867 | 41% |
| Denmark | 8,376 | 8,491 | 16,867 | 50% |
| India | 11,729 | 980 | 12,709 | 92% |
| Sweden | 1,530 | 3,889 | 5,419 | 28% |
| Others | 70,915 | 80,963 | 151,877 | 47% |
| Total national registers | 274,697 | 523,326 | 798,022 | |

## 2. INTERNATIONAL REGISTERS

| | | Fleet Owned by | | % owned by |
|---|---|---|---|---|
| | Total | Nationals | Foreigners | nationals |
| Singapore | 40,934 | 12,424 | 28,510 | 30% |
| Norwegian Int. Registry | 21,262 | 12,424 | 8,838 | 58% |
| Hong Kong (China) | 43,957 | 17,246 | 26,711 | 39% |
| Marshall Islands | 38,088 | 10,828 | 27,260 | 28% |
| Isle of Man | 12,073 | 4,700 | 7,373 | 39% |
| Danish Int. Ship Registry | 8,859 | 8,330 | 529 | 94% |
| French Antarctic Territory | 5,427 | 1,769 | 3,658 | 33% |
| Netherlands Antilles | 2,132 | 616 | 1,516 | 29% |
| Total international registers | 131,798 | 55,913 | 75,885 | 42% |

## 3. OPEN REGISTERS ('FLAGS OF CONVENIENCE')

| | | Fleet Owned by | | % owned by |
|---|---|---|---|---|
| | Total | Nationals | Foreigners | nationals |
| Panama | 177,866 | 0 | 177,866 | — |
| Liberia | 76,372 | 0 | 76,372 | — |
| Bahamas | 41,835 | 0 | 41,835 | — |
| Malta | 30,971 | 0 | 30,971 | — |
| Cyprus | 31,538 | 459 | 31,079 | 1% |
| Bermuda | 6,206 | — | 6,206 | — |
| St Vincent & Grenadines | 6,857 | 0 | 6,857 | 0 |
| Antigua & Barbuda | 8,383 | 0 | 8,383 | 0 |
| Cayman Islands | 4,040 | 0 | 4,040 | 0 |
| Luxemburg | 794 | 0 | 794 | 0 |
| Vanuatu | 2,077 | 0 | 2,077 | 0 |
| Gibraltar | 1,281 | 0 | 1,281 | 0 |
| Total open registers | 388,220 | — | 387,761 | 0% |
| World total* (sum of col 2) | 794,715 | | | |

Source: United Nations Review of Maritime Transport, 2005. Section 1 "National Registers" is from Table 16, p. 33; Sections 2 "International Registers" and 3 "Open Registers" are from Table 18 p. 37

* Of which: National registers 35%; International registers 17%; Open registers 48%

## The economic role of open registers

The movement towards open registers started in the 1920s, when US shipowners saw registration under the Panamanian flag as a means of avoiding the high tax rates in the United States, while at the same time registering in a country within the stable political orbit of the United States. There was a spate of registrations during this period, but the real growth came after the Second World War when the US government sold off Liberty ships to US owners. Anxious to avoid operating under the American flag, US tax lawyers approached Liberia to set up a ship register designed to attract shipowners to register under that flag on the payment of an annual fee.[13] Shortly afterwards, Panama adapted its laws to attract shipowners from anywhere in the world, and thus the two major international open registers were established.

The use of an open register generally involves payment of an initial registration fee and an annual tonnage tax, which enables the register to cover its costs and make a profit. In return, the register offers a legal and commercial environment tailored to the requirements of a shipowner trading internationally. There are major differences in the way registers approach this task, but in general the areas addressed are:

- *Tax.* There are generally no taxes on profits or fiscal controls. The only tax is the subscription tax per net registered ton.
- *Crewing.* The shipping company is free to recruit internationally. There is no requirement to employ nationals either as officers or crew. However, international conventions dealing with crew standards and training may be enforced, depending on the policy of the register.
- *Company law.* As a rule, the shipping company is given considerable freedom over its corporate activities. For example, ownership of the stock in the company need not be disclosed; shares are often in 'bearer' form, which means that they belong to the person who holds them; liability can be limited to a one-ship company; and the company is not required to produce audited accounts. There are generally few regulations regarding the appointment of directors and the adminis-tration of business.

In effect, open registers are businesses and the service offered is determined by the register's maritime laws and the way they are enforced. Supervising safety standards is expensive and during the 1980s recession some open registers paid little attention to this aspect of the business, but this has proved a difficult stance to maintain. To be successful an open register's ships must be acceptable in the ports of the world and to bankers lending against a mortgage on the ship. As the scrutiny of ships by shippers and port authorities has increased it has become more important for open register flags to comply with international conventions, and most open registries, whilst offering shipowners freedom in the areas of taxation and company law, enforce legislation regarding the operational and environmental safety of ships registered under their flag.

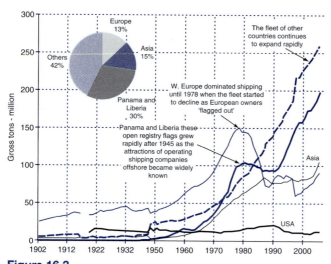

**Figure 16.3**
World merchant fleet by flag, 1902–2006
Source: Lloyd's Register of Shipping and CRSL

Figure 16.3 shows that by the late 1950s the Panamanian and Liberian fleets had reached 16 million grt and open registers were becoming a major issue for the established shipping states. Inevitably the question was raised whether a country such as Liberia has the right to offer registry to a shipowner who is not a national of that country. This issue was discussed at UNCLOS I in 1958 and put to the test in 1959 when the newly formed Inter-governmental Maritime Consultative Organization (IMCO) met in London and elected its Maritime Safety Committee. The terms of the election of the Committee stated that eight members of the committee should be the largest shipowning nations. Initially the eight nations elected were the USA, UK, Norway, Japan, Italy, the Netherlands, France and West Germany. However, objections were raised that Liberia, which ranked third in world tonnage, and Panama, which ranked eighth, should have been elected instead of France and Germany.

The dispute was submitted to the International Court of Justice for an opinion on whether the election was legal in terms of the 1948 Convention that established the IMCO.[14] It was argued by the European shipowners that for a ship to register in a country there had to be a 'genuine link' between registration and ownership, and that in the case of international open registry flags this link did not exist. Predictably Liberia, Panama, India and the USA took the opposite view. The European argument was not accepted by the Court which by a 9–5 vote held that, by not electing Liberia and Panama to the Maritime Safety Committee, the IMCO assembly had failed to comply with Article 28(a) of the 1948 Convention. As a result, international open registry flags were legitimized in international law.

In a world of high taxation, offshore registration was enormously attractive, and once this facility became available it was widely adopted. Today about half the world merchant fleet is registered under open registers. The principal open registry flags, Panama, Liberia, Bahamas, Malta, Cyprus, and Bermuda, plus half a dozen smaller flags including St Vincent and Antigua, are listed in Table 16.4. The fact that so few ships under these flags are owned by nationals confirms their status as open registries (see Table 16.4.3, column 3). Because in addition to tax concessions open registers allowed freedom in crew selection, in the 1980s and 1990s many large shipping corporations bowed, often reluctantly, to commercial pressures and abandoned their national flag in favour of open registers.

Although open registers acquired a mixed reputation in the 1980s, their success could not be overlooked and several established maritime nations set up their own 'international registry', designed to offer similar conditions and bring shipowners back under the national flag. The eight listed in Table 16.4 show that by 2005 these international registers had been successful in attracting 17% of the world fleet, though the fleet under open registers is considerably bigger and many shipowners in Greece, Japan, and the USA continue to register under their domestic flags. In the meantime the open registers have, in the main, fallen in line with regulatory practice and this form of ownership has become less controversial than it was a decade ago.

## Dual registration

In some circumstances it is necessary for a shipowner to register a ship under two flags. For example, the owner may be required to register the ship under his domestic flag, but this flag may not be acceptable to the financing bank, so for mortgage purposes it is registered under a second jurisdiction. The way this works is that the ship is first registered in country A and its owning company then issues a bare boat charter which is registered in country B where it enjoys the same rights, privileges and obligations as any other ship registered under the flag. Obviously this only works if the registration authorities in country B are prepared to accept a bare boat charter, but several flags such as Malta and Cyprus are willing to do so for registration purposes, provided the registers are compatible.[15] Separating ownership from operation in this way can be used, for example, to allow the company to register in country A to maintain the nationality of the ship, whilst using the second register to circumvent restrictive national regulations such as crewing or to gain access to certain ports.

## Company structures associated with ship registration

The use of open registers in shipping has given rise to a distinctive structure of company organization designed to protect the 'beneficial owner'. A typical company structure is shown in Figure 16.4. There are four active components:

1. *The beneficial owner*. The ultimate controlling owner who benefits from any profits the ship makes. He may be located in his home country or an international centre such as Geneva or Monaco.

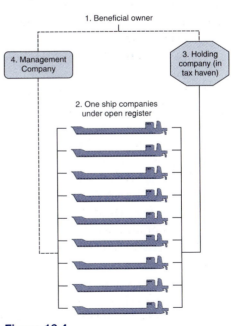

**Figure 16.4**
Shipping company ownership structure
Source: Martin Stopford, 2007

2. *One-ship company*. A company, usually incorporated in an open registry country, set up for the sole purpose of owning a single ship. It has no other traceable assets. This protects the other assets of the beneficial owner from claims involving the one-ship company.[16]

3. *Holding company*. A holding company is incorporated in a favourable tax jurisdiction for the purpose of owning and operating the ships. The only assets of this company are the shares in each one-ship company. The shares in this company are held by the beneficial owner, which could be a company or an individual.

4. *Management company*. Day-to-day management of the ships is carried out by another company established for this purpose. Usually this company is located in a convenient shipping centre such as London or Hong Kong.

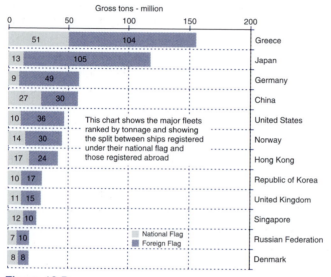

**Figure 16.5**
National merchant fleets using open registry flags, 2005
Source: Table 16.4

Beneficial ownership of the shipowning, management and holding companies takes the form of bearer shares. This device is used to insulate the beneficial owners of the ships from authorities seeking to establish tax and other liabilities. Its use is not universal and depends on the relative merits of the domestic flag. If we take the largest shipowning nations in 2005, we find that most had some vessels registered under foreign flags (Figure 16.5). For example, Greece, the nation with the biggest merchant fleet, had 67% of the tonnage registered abroad, leaving 33% under the domestic flag, whilst Japanese and US owners, both exceptionally high-cost flags, had had 89% and 78% registered abroad respectively. Germany had over 80% of its fleet flagged out. Norway had 67% flagged out, but many Norwegian owners use the Norwegian International Ship Register (NIS). In 1987 the Norwegian government, concerned about the trend towards flagging out, set up the NIS to give Norwegian owners most of the benefits they would receive under an international flag. Several other countries followed suit and their 'international flags' are listed in Table 16.4, including the Danish International Registry, Singapore, Hong Kong, Marshall Islands (the United States), Isle of Man (UK), French Antarctic Territory, Netherlands Antilles, and Belgium. All of these were established with the specific intention of providing a national alternative for domestic shipowners on commercial terms comparable with those available from open registries. There is a stark contrast between the open registries, which have few nationals using their flag, and the national registers shown at the top of Table 16.4 where most of the registered tonnage belongs to domestic shipowners (though more is flagged out).

## 16.6 HOW MARITIME LAWS ARE MADE

### The role of maritime laws

There are good practical reasons for developing an internationally accepted body of maritime law. It is common sense that if ships are to trade efficiently, the maritime states they trade between should have the same regulations on such matters as safety and the environment. Different rules about, for example, how hazardous cargoes should be stowed or the hull design mean that a ship complying with one country's rules could not trade with another, wasting economic resources. It would also make designing specialized ships more difficult because the designer needs to know precisely where it will trade. But an enforceable body of maritime law must also be seen as just by the various maritime interests involved in carrying world trade, and the institutions which enforce those laws must be accepted as satisfying the same principles of justice.[17] History proves that the shipping industry is too diverse to police autocratically, so the regulatory process must carry the shipping industry as well as the regulators with it.

Persuading maritime states to agree the conventions which are the framework of maritime law will never be easy. The issues dealt with are often controversial, emotional and involve commercial interests, especially those triggered by a particular maritime incident, so developing a workable solution calls for patience and pragmatism. In the nineteenth century, British law was widely used as the framework for national maritime law, providing a common base. More recently, governments of maritime nations have taken more formal steps to standardize maritime law. This is achieved by means of international 'conventions', which are jointly drawn up between maritime states, setting out agreed objectives for legislation on particular issues. Each country can, if it wishes, introduce the measures set out in these conventions into its own national law. All nations that do this (known as signatories to the convention) have the same law on the subject covered by the convention.

### The topics covered by maritime law

Today's body of maritime law has evolved gradually. Taking Britain as an example, in the mid-nineteenth century there were few rules and regulations and virtually no construction or safety standards for merchant ships. Many were sent to sea badly built, ill found, grossly overloaded and often over-insured. These 'coffin' ships 'frequently took their unfortunate crews to the bottom of the oceans of the world'.[18] As a result of the agitation for reform from a Member of Parliament called Samuel Plimsoll, the

'Plimsoll Act' became law in 1876 and the Board of Trade was empowered, as the responsible government department, to survey ships, pass them fit for sea, and have them marked with a load line indicating the legal limit to which they could be submerged.

In due course other laws were introduced as they became necessary, and the UK built up a body of maritime law which was specifically geared to tackling the problems that arise when operating an extensive merchant shipping fleet. As other countries developed their own laws they often drew on British practical experience as a basis for drafting their legislation. The first step towards a system of internationally accepted regulations (conventions) came in 1889 when the US government invited 37 states to attend an international marine conference. On the agenda at this conference was a list of problem areas in the maritime industry where it was felt that the standardization of the international regulations would be an advantage, including:

- rules for the prevention of collisions;
- regulations to determine the seaworthiness of vessels;
- draught to which vessels should be restricted when loaded;
- uniform regulations regarding the designation and marking of vessels;
- saving life and properties from shipwrecks;
- necessary qualifications for officers and seamen;
- lanes for steamers and frequented routes;
- night signals for communicating information at sea;
- warnings of approaching storms;
- reporting, marking and removing dangerous wrecks and obstructions to navigation;
- notice of dangers to navigation;
- the uniform system of buoys and beacons;
- the establishment of a permanent international maritime commission.[19]

In fact the conference succeeded in dealing with only the first item on the agenda, but the full agenda neatly illustrates the areas that were thought to be important and that were addressed by subsequent international conferences and conventions. But the most important outcome was to set the pattern for the present system under which maritime laws are developed by consensus between maritime states.

## Procedures for making maritime conventions

The conventions which form the building blocks of maritime law are not laws; they are internationally agreed 'templates' which maritime states use as a base for enacting their national maritime legislation. This does not guarantee that every country will have exactly the same maritime law since some modify it and others do not even sign up. But it helps to avoid badly thought-out and inconsistent maritime legislation and on important issues such as safety, most maritime countries now have the same maritime law. The procedure for making or changing a maritime convention involves four steps, which are broadly summarized in Box 16.2.

## BOX 16.2 FOUR STEPS IN MAKING A MARITIME CONVENTION

Step 1: *Consultation and drafting convention*. The issue requiring legislation is identified by interested governments and a conference is called to discuss it, at which written submissions from various interested states and parties are discussed. If there is enough support the agency (e.g. IMO or ILO) drafts and circulates to member states a convention setting out in detail the proposed regulation or an amendment or annex to an existing regulation.

Step 2: *Adoption of draft convention*. The conference is reconvened to consider the draft regulation, and when agreement has been reached on the text, it is adopted by the conference. The discussion serves the dual purpose of showing whether or not there is a consensus that the regulation is required and, if so, refining the form it should take.

Step 3: *Signature*. The convention is 'opened for signature' by the governments; by signing, each state indicates its intention to ratify the convention by making it legally binding in its own country.

Step 4: *Ratification*. Each signatory country ratifies the convention by introducing it into its own domestic legislation so that it becomes part of the law of the country or dominions, and the convention comes into force when the required number of states (usually two-thirds) have completed this process – the precise conditions of entry into force form part of the original adoption of the convention. Once the necessary conditions have been met, the convention has the force of law in those countries that have ratified it. It does not apply in countries where it has not been ratified and any legal cases must be tried under the prevailing national law.

An example of this process is provided by UNCLOS 1982 discussed in section 16.4. This was instigated by UN General Assembly Resolution 2749, which noted the 'political and economic realities' of the preceding decade and 'the fact that many of the present State Members of the United Nations did not take part in the previous United Nations Conferences on the law of the sea'. It called for a new conference on the law of the sea. The conference was convened in 1973, and discussions continued until 30 April 1982 when the draft convention was adopted by vote (130 in favour, 4 against, with 17 abstentions). The convention was opened for signature in Montego Bay, Jamaica, on 10 December 1982. On the first day signatures from 117 states were appended. In addition, one ratification was deposited.

Considerable time and effort is required to organize conferences, draft conventions and resolve differences and misunderstandings. This work is carried out by the IMO and the ILO. Each deals with a particular range of maritime affairs, as detailed in the following sections.

C
H
A
P
T
E
R
16

## 16.7 THE INTERNATIONAL MARITIME ORGANIZATION

### History and organization of IMO

The IMCO came into operation in 1958, with responsibility for adopting legislation on matters relating to maritime safety and pollution prevention on a world-wide basis and acting as the custodian of a number of related international conventions. Subsequently, in 1982, the IMCO changed its name to the International Maritime Organization (IMO). It has been responsible for developing a large number of conventions, ranging from the Convention for the Safety of Life at Sea (SOLAS) to conventions on tonnage measurement and oil pollution.

The IMO has 166 member states and two associate members. Its governing body is the Assembly, which meets every two years. In between Assembly sessions a Council, consisting of 32 member states elected by the Assembly, acts as the governing body. The technical and legal work is carried out by five committees:

- The *Maritime Safety Committee* deals with a whole range of issues concerning safety at sea. Sub-committees deal with a wide range of issues which cover safety of navigation; radio communications and life-saving; search and rescue; standards of training and watch keeping; ship design and equipment; life-saving appliances; fire protection; stability and load lines; fishing vessel safety; carriage of dangerous goods, solid cargoes and containers; carriage of bulk liquids and gases; and flag state implementation.
- The *Marine Environment Protection Committee* deals with all issues relating to pollution, particularly oil.
- The *Technical Co-operation Committee* handles the technical cooperation programme which is designed to help governments implement the technical measures adopted by the organization.
- The *Legal Committee* is responsible for considering any legal matters within the scope of the organization.
- The *Facilitation Committee* is concerned with easing the flow of international maritime traffic by reducing the formalities and simplifying the documentation required of ships when entering or leaving ports or terminals.

To support these committees the IMO has a secretariat of about 300 staff located in London.

In its early years the IMO developed a comprehensive body of maritime conventions, codes and recommendations which could be implemented by member governments. The 16 most important conventions are listed in Table 16.5 along with a brief summary of their scope and the percentage of world tonnage which has ratified each one. Its most important convention, SOLAS, is now accepted by countries whose combined merchant fleets represent 98.8% of the world total. Although the initial emphasis was on drafting conventions, since the 1980s the focus has changed. By then the IMO had developed a comprehensive series of measures covering safety, pollution

**Table 16.5** Major IMO conventions relating to maritime safety and pollution prevention for merchant shipping

| No. | Instrument | | Entry into force | |
| --- | --- | --- | --- | --- |
| | | | Date | % fleet |
| 1 | SOLAS | International Convention for the Safety of Life at Sea, 1974* as amended, and its Protocols (1978, 1988) | 25/05/80 | 99 |
| 2 | SAR | International Convention on Maritime Search and Rescue, 1979 | 22/06/85 | 52 |
| 3 | INTERVENTION | International Convention relating to Intervention on the High Seas in Cases of Oil Pollution Casualties, 1969, and its Protocol (1973) | 06/05/75 | 73 |
| 4 | MARPOL | International Convention for the Prevention of Pollution from Ships, 1973, and its Protocol (1978) Annex I (2 Oct. 1983); Annex II (6 April 1987) Annex III (1 July 1992); IV; Annex V (31 Dec. 1988) | 02/10/83 | 98 |
| 5 | CSC | International Convention for Safe Containers (1972) | 06/07/77 | 62 |
| 6 | OPRC | International Convention on Oil Pollution Preparedness, Response and Co-operation, 1990 | 13/05/95 | 65 |
| 7 | LC | Convention on the Prevention of Marine Pollution by Dumping of Wastes and Other Matter, 1972 as amended, and its Protocol (1996) | 30/08/75 | 69 |
| 8 | COLREG | Convention on the International Regulations for Preventing Collisions at Sea, 1972, as amended | 15/07/77 | 98 |
| 9 | FAL | Convention on Facilitation of International Maritime Traffic, 1965, as amended | 05/03/67 | 69 |
| 10 | STCW | International Convention on Standards of Training, Certification and Watchkeeping for Seafarers, 1978, as amended | 28/04/84 | 99 |
| 11 | SUA | Convention for the Suppression of Unlawful Acts against the Safety of Maritime Navigation, 1988, and its Protocol (1988) | 01/03/92 | 92 |
| 12 | LL | International Convention on Load Lines, 1966, as amended, and its Protocol (1988) | 21/07/68 | 99 |
| 13 | TONNAGE | International Convention on Tonnage Measurement of Ships, 1969 | 18/07/82 | 99 |
| 14 | CSC | International Convention for Safe Containers, 1972 as amended | 06/09/77 | 62 |
| 15 | SALVAGE | International Convention on Salvage, 1989 | 14/07/96 | 38 |
| 16 | ISM Code | Management Code for the Safe Operation of Ships and Pollution Prevention | 01/12/09 | |

Status as at October 2006

Source: International Maritime Organization (London)

prevention, liability and compensation. It was recognized that legislation is of little value unless it is enforced so, in 1981, the Assembly adopted Resolution A500(XII) which redirected activity towards the effective implementation of the conventions. This resolution was reaffirmed for the 1990s and 'implementation' has become the major objective of IMO.[20] To promote the task the Maritime Safety Committee established a flag state implementation subcommittee.

The coverage of the conventions is briefly described in the following paragraphs.

## The Safety of Life at Sea Convention (SOLAS)

The first conference organized by the IMO in 1960 adopted the International Convention for the Safety of Life at Sea 1960, which came into force in 1965 and covered a wide range of measures designed to improve the safety of shipping. This important convention has 12 chapters dealing with:

Chapter I – General Provisions
Chapter II:1 Construction: subdivision and stability, machinery and electrical installations
Chapter II:2 – Fire protection, fire detection and fire extinction
Chapter III – Life-saving appliances and arrangements
Chapter IV – Radio communications
Chapter V – Safety of navigation
Chapter VI – Carriage of cargoes
Chapter VII – Carriage of dangerous goods
Chapter VIII – Nuclear ships
Chapter IX – Management for the safe operation of ships
Chapter X – Safety measures for high-speed craft
Chapter XI:1 – Special measures to enhance maritime safety
Chapter XI:2 – Special measures to enhance maritime security
Chapter XII – Additional safety measures for bulk carriers.

SOLAS was updated in 1974 and now incorporates an amendment procedure whereby the convention can be updated to take account of changes in the shipping environment without the major procedure of calling a conference. The 1974 SOLAS Convention entered into force on 25 May 1980, and by October 2006 had been ratified by states representing 99% of the registered merchant fleet. A protocol relating to the Convention in 1978 entered into force on 1 May 1981.

With the growing recognition that loss of life at sea and environmental pollution are influenced by the way companies manage their fleets, in the 1990s the IMO took steps to regulate the standards of management in the shipping industry. At the SOLAS Conference held in May 1994, the International Safety Management (ISM) Code was formally incorporated into Chapter IX of the SOLAS regulations. The Code requires shipping companies to develop, implement and maintain a safety management system which includes:

- a company safety and environmental protection policy;
- written procedures to ensure safe operation of ships and protection of the environment;
- defined levels of authority and lines of communication shore and shipboard personnel;

- procedures for reporting accidents and non-conformities (i.e. errors which occur);
- procedures to prepare for and respond to emergency situations.

The ISM Code became mandatory for tankers, bulk carriers and passenger ships over 500 gross tons on 1 July 1998 and for most other ships trading internationally on 1 July 2002. Approximately 12,000 ships had to comply by the first deadline and the second phase of implementation brought in another 13,000 ships.[21] Previously safety regulations had tended to focus on the physical rather than the managerial aspects of the shipping business, so the ISM Code represented a new direction in maritime regulation. Inevitably it raised many new problems over the implementation and policing of such a complex system.

## Collision avoidance at sea

Collisions are a common cause of accidents at sea. Measures to prevent these occurring were included in an Annex to the 1960 Safety of Life at Sea Convention, but in 1972 IMO adopted the Convention on the International Regulations for Preventing Collisions at Sea (COLREG). Included in this convention were regulations to introduce traffic separation schemes in congested parts of the world. These 'rules of the road' have substantially reduced the number of collisions between ships.[22]

## Ships' load lines

The problem of dangerously overloading ships encountered in the nineteenth century was referred to earlier in the chapter. In 1930 an International Convention on Load Lines was adopted, setting out standard load lines for different types of vessels under different conditions. A new updated convention was adopted in 1966 and came into force in 1968.

## Convention on Tonnage Measurement of Ships, 1969

Although this might seem an obscure subject for an international convention, it is one of great interest to shipowners because ports, canals and other organizations fix their charges on the basis of the ship's tonnage. This created an incentive to manipulate the design of ships in such a way as to reduce the ship's tonnage while still allowing it to carry the same amount of cargo. Occasionally this was at the expense of the vessel's stability and safety.

In 1969 the first International Convention on Tonnage Measurement was adopted. It proved to be so complex and so controversial that it required 25 states with not less than 65% of the world's gross merchant tonnage to ratify it before it became law. The required number of acceptances was not achieved until 1980 and the Convention came into force in 1982. The Convention established new procedures for computing the gross and net tonnages of a vessel and for the allocation of an IMO number to each ship, so that vessels could be uniquely identified.

## Convention on Standards of Training, Certification and Watchkeeping for Seafarers (STCW), 1978

The aim of this Convention was to introduce internationally acceptable minimum standards for the training and certification of officers and crew members. It came into force in 1984. Amendments in 1995 complemented the ISM Code initiative by establishing verifiable standards, structured training and shipboard familiarization.

## International Convention for the Prevention of Pollution from Ships

This convention, knowns as MARPOL, is the main international convention covering the prevention and minimization of pollution of the marine environment by ships from operational or accidental causes. It is a combination of two treaties adopted in 1973 and 1978 and updated by amendments through the years. It currently has six technical annexes which set out the detail of the regulations:

Annex I: Regulations for the Prevention of Pollution by Oil
Annex II: Regulations for the Control of Pollution by Noxious Liquid Substances in Bulk, including a list of 250 regulated substances
Annex III: Prevention of Pollution by Harmful Substances Carried by Sea in Packaged Form (shipped in drums, etc.)
Annex IV: Prevention of Pollution by Sewage from Ships
Annex V: Prevention of Pollution by Garbage from Ships
Annex VI: Prevention of Air Pollution from Ships.

As the volume of oil shipped by sea increased in the 1950s and 1960s, regulations on marine pollution were needed. A conference to discuss the matter was held in London in 1952 and this resulted in the 1954 Convention for the Prevention of Pollution of the Sea by Oil (OILPOL). The main problem addressed by this convention was the uncontrolled discharge of oily ballast water. At the time tankers generally carried ballast water in their cargo tanks and discharged it outside the loading port. Because the ballast water contained small amounts of crude oil, it polluted the sea and beaches in these areas. To prevent this pollution OILPOL established 'prohibited zones' extending at least 50 miles from the nearest land. These regulations were progressively updated during the next 20 years.

During the 1960s, it became evident that there was a need for a wider-ranging convention on marine pollution, and in 1973 MAPROL was adopted. This convention applies to all forms of marine pollution except land-generated waste and deals with such matters as: the definition of violations; certificates and special rules on the inspection of ships; enforcement; and reports on incidents involving harmful substances. It required all tankers to have slop tanks and be fitted with oil discharge and monitoring equipment, whilst new oil tankers over 70,000 dwt must be fitted with segregated ballast tanks large enough to hold all ballast water for normal voyages – oil tanks could only be used for water ballast in extreme weather. At the next international conference on tanker safety and pollution prevention in 1978 additional measures were added in the form of a

Protocol to the 1973 Convention. The lower limit for tankers to be fitted with segregated ballast tanks was reduced from 70,000 dwt to 20,000 dwt and existing tankers were required to fit crude oil washing equipment.

Following a number of major oil pollution incidents, in particular the *Exxon Valdes*, in the early 1990s attention turned to tanker regulations to reduce the risk of oil spills resulting from tanker collisions and groundings. A new Annex I to MARPOL (73/78) was drafted, introducing two new regulations designed to reduce oil spills of this type. Regulation 13F required new tankers ordered after 6 July 1993 to have double hulls built to specified design parameters including a requirement that vessels over 30,000 dwt have a two-metre space between the cargo tanks and the hull. Regulation 13G created two age 'hurdles' for existing single hull tankers. As a defensive measure, at 25 years 30% of the side or the bottom area must be allocated to cargo-free tanks; and at 30 years all tankers must comply with Regulation 13F by fitting a double hull. The Annex was adopted on 1 July 1992.

Two major oil pollution incidents in European waters, the *Erika* in 1999 and the *Prestige* in 2002, resulted in the IMO Marine Environmental Protection Committee making further amendments to Annex 1 of MARPOL 73/78.

Firstly, the phasing-out of single hull tankers was accelerated. Under a revised Regulation 13G of Annex I of MARPOL, which entered into force in April 2005, the final phasing-out date for Category 1 tankers (pre-MARPOL tankers) was brought forward from 2005 to 2007. The final phasing-out date for Category 2 and 3 tankers (MARPOL tankers and smaller tankers) was brought forward from 2015 to 2010, though they were permitted to trade beyond the anniversary date of their delivery in 2010 at the discretion of port state administrations (double-bottomed and double-sided vessels were allowed to trade to 25 years or 2015). This was controversial because some single hull tankers would only be 15–20 years old in 2010. Secondly, it adopted the Conditional Assessment Scheme requiring a more detailed inspection of Category 2 (non-MARPOL compliant) and Category 3 (MARPOL compliant) single-hull tankers. Thirdly, a new Regulation 13H prohibited single hull tankers over 5,000 dwt from carrying heavy grades of oil from 5 April 2006 and smaller tankers of 600–5,000 dwt from 2008. These amendments entered into force on 5 April 2005. Note that in January 2007 the names of the regulations changed – Regulation 13F became Regulation 19, Regulation 13G became Regulation 20, and Regulation 13H became Regulation 21, all in MARPOL Annex 1.

In addition to oil pollution, in the late 1990s the IMO started to focus on the environmental impact of emissions from ships, including air emissions and ballast water. MARPOL Annex VI sets limits on sulphur oxide and nitrogen oxide emissions from ship exhausts and prohibits deliberate emissions of ozone-depleting substances. The annex includes a global cap of 4.5% on the sulphur content of fuel oil by weight and requires IMO to monitor the worldwide average sulphur content of fuel. In 2007 air emissions by ships were at the top of the IMO's agenda and were being studied by a working group on air pollution. Their agenda included nitrogen (NOx) emission limits for new and existing engines; sulphur and fuel oil quality; emission trading; and emissions of volatile organic compounds from tankers. The aim was to propose amendments to existing regulations for implementation in 2008.

## 16.8 THE INTERNATIONAL LABOUR ORGANIZATION

Since the 1920s the terms and conditions of employment for seafarers have been dealt with by the International Labour Organization (ILO), making it one of the oldest inter-governmental agencies now operating under the United Nations. Its principal concern is with the welfare of the 1.2 million people who work at sea. It was originally set up in 1919. During the twentieth century it developed 32 maritime labour conventions and 25 maritime labour recommendations dealing with working and living conditions at sea, manning, hours of work, pensions, vacation, sick pay and minimum wages.

By the end of the twentieth century the maritime industry and governments were finding this complex body of maritime conventions difficult to ratify and enforce, and it became apparent that the industry needed a more effective system if it was to elimi-nate substandard ships. In 2001 the international seafarers' and shipowners' organiza-tions presented a joint resolution at ILO calling for 'global standards applicable to the entire industry'. As a result, the ILO was charged with developing 'an instrument to bring together into a consolidated text as much of the existing body of ILO instruments as it proves possible to achieve'. The comprehensive new Maritime Labour Convention for the maritime industry was adopted in 2006 and comes into force after being ratified by 30 ILO member states with a total share of at least 33% of world gross tonnage. By mid-2008 it had been ratified by Liberia, Bermuda and the Marshall Islands and was expected to be in force by August 2011 (this section focusses on the new regulations, but a list of the existing regulations can be found in *Maritime Economics*, second edition, Table 12.6 or on the ILO website).

The 2006 Consolidated Convention aimed to maintain existing maritime labour standards, while giving countries more discretion to establish national laws adapted to local circumstances. It applies to all publicly or privately owned commercial ships, but excludes traditional vessels (e.g. dhows and junks), warships, naval auxiliaries and ships under 200 gross tons in domestic trades. Fishing boats are covered in a separate convention.[23] A 'seafarer' is defined as 'any person who is employed, engaged or works in any capacity on board a ship that is covered by the Convention'. Much of the new convention is devoted to a more structured version of the existing 68 ILO maritime conventions and recommendations, and gives countries flexibility to harmonize the new maritime legislation with national labour laws.

The convention has five 'titles', summarized in Table 16.6, setting minimum stan-dards for seafarers, including conditions of employment, hours of work and rest, accom-modation, recreational facilities, food and catering, health protection, medical care, welfare and social security protection. It sets legally binding standards but also incor-porates guidelines, a significant departure from traditional ILO conventions. It also introduces procedures to simplify amending the regulations, allowing amendments to come into effect within three to four years from the proposal date.

A major innovation is Title 5, which deals with compliance and enforcement of the regulations. Any ships over 500 gross tons trading internationally must carry a maritime labour certificate and a declaration of maritime labour compliance, setting out the shipowner's plans for ensuring that national regulations are complied with. The ship's

**Table 16.6** ILO Consolidated Maritime Labour Regulations, 2006*

*Title 1. Minimum requirements for seafarers to work on a ship*
- Minimum age
- Medical certificate
- Training and qualifications
- Recruitment and placement

*Title 2. Conditions of employment: seafarers' employment*
- Wages
- Hours of work and hours of rest; entitlement of leave
- Repatriation
- Seafarer compensation for the ship's loss; manning levels
- Career and skill development and opportunities for seafarers' employment

*Title 3. Accommodation, recreational facilities, food and catering*
- Accommodation and recreational facilities
- Food and catering

*Title 4: Health protection*
- Medical care, welfare and social security protection
- Medical care on board ship and ashore
- Shipowner's liability
- Health and safety protection and accident prevention
- Access to shore-based welfare facilities
- Social security

*Title 5. Compliance and enforcement*
Flag state responsibilities
- General principles
- Authorization of recognized organizations
- Maritime labour certificate and declaration of maritime labour compliance
- Inspection and enforcement; on-board complaint procedures; marine casualties

Port state responsibilities
- Inspections in port
- Onshore seafarer complaint-handling procedures
- Labour-supplying responsibilities

Note: This regulation was adopted in 2006, but is not expected to come into force until 2011 when the necessary ratifications have been achieved

master is responsible for carrying out these plans and keeping records as evidence of compliance. The flag state is responsible for reviewing the plans and their implementation. To encourage compliance by operators and owners, the Convention sets out mechanisms dealing with on-board and onshore complaint procedures; port state inspection; and the flag state's jurisdiction and control over vessels on its register.

## 16.9 THE REGULATORY ROLE OF THE COASTAL AND PORT STATES

### The rights of coastal states over foreign ships

Now we come to the 'coastal states' and the part they play in regulating merchant shipping. UNCLOS 1982 allows coastal states to legislate for the 'good conduct' of ships in their territorial seas, but otherwise not to interfere with them. The Convention lists eight specific areas in which legislation is permitted – the main ones are safety of navigation; protection of navigational aids; preservation of the environment and prevention, reduction and control of pollution; and the prevention of infringement of customs and sanitary laws, etc. However Article 21 of UNCLOS 1982 specifically states that the legislation of coastal states 'shall not apply to the design, construction, manning or equipment of foreign ships, unless they are giving effect to generally accepted international rules or standards'. This is intended to prevent a 'nightmare scenario' in which ships are subject to different construction and crewing standards in different territorial waters. However, it also endorses the coastal state's right to enforce international regulations in its territorial waters, and this gave rise to the port state control movement.

The port state control movement was a response to the growing number of ships registered under flags of convenience, and the recognition that some of these flags were not, for whatever reason, enforcing international maritime regulations. This made the traditional supervisory role of the flag states less reliable than previously and in response the port states started to play an increasingly important part in the regulatory system.

## The port state control movement

The port state control movement started in 1978 when eight European states located around the North Sea informally agreed to inspect foreign ships visiting their ports and share information about deficiencies. In 1982 the arrangement was formalized with the signing of the Paris Memorandum of Understanding (MOU) in which 14 European states agreed to work together to ensure that ships visiting their ports comply with international conventions on safety and pollution.

Signatories to the Paris MOU undertake to maintain an effective system of port state control by ensuring that foreign merchant ships calling at their ports comply with the standards laid down in the 'relevant' maritime conventions and their protocols which they define as the Load Lines Convention 1966; SOLAS 1974; MARPOL 1973/78; STCW 1978; COLREG 1972; the International Convention on the Tonnage Measurement of Ships 1969; and the ILO Convention No. 147 Merchant Shipping (Minimum Standards), 1976. Details of the first five conventions can be found in Table 16.5, whilst ILO Convention 147 is concerned with the crew safety, employment and welfare issues dealt with under Titles 1–4 of the new consolidated regulation in Table 16.6. Each participating state undertakes to inspect 25% of the foreign merchant ships entering its ports, basing the number on the average number of port calls during the previous three years. They also agree to work together, to exchange information with other authorities and to notify pilot services and port authorities immediately if they find deficiencies which may prejudice the safety of the ship or pose a threat of harm to the marine environment.

By 2007 the number of signatories to the Paris MOU had increased to 27, stretching from Russia to Canada, and the MOU has been updated regularly. In the meantime additional port state control MOUs have been established in the following areas:

- the Mediterranean MOU (10 participating countries);
- the Tokyo MOU (18 participants);

- the Caribbean MOU (11 participants);
- the Latin American agreement (12 participants);
- the Indian Ocean MOU (11 participants).

The United States controls its own programme.

## Port state control inspections

In 1995 the IMO adopted a resolution providing basic guidance on port state control inspections to identify deficiencies in ship, its equipment or its crew should be conducted. The aim was to ensure that the inspections are consistently applied across the world from port to port. These procedures are not mandatory, but many countries have followed them.[24] The range of inspections is now very broad with over 50,000 ships a year being inspected, a significant proportion of the international fleet. For example, the Paris MOU undertakes about 20,000 inspections a year, identifying an average of 3.5 deficiencies per inspection. Ships with serious shortcomings are detained and a small number are banned. Lists of detained ships are published on a website. The Tokyo MOU undertakes a similar number of inspections.

The ships to be inspected are selected from lists of vessels arriving in the port, often using statistical techniques to identify higher-risk vessels. For example, the Paris MOU uses a target factor calculator which takes into account such factors as flag, age and ship type, weighting each characteristic on the basis of previous association with defects.

The inspection has three parts: a general external inspection of the ship on boarding; a check of certificates; and a more thorough 'walk around' to inspect the condition of exposed decks, cargo-handling gear, navigation and radio equipment, life-saving appliances; fire-fighting arrangements; machinery spaces; pollution prevention equipment; and living and working conditions. Under each heading the inspector works through a detailed checklist and notes any deficiencies. A 'deficiency' exists when some aspect of the ship does not comply with the requirements of a convention. If the inspector finds significant deficiencies, a more detailed inspection may be required, and if the ship is considered too unsafe to be allowed to proceed to sea, a detention order will be made. For example, a detention could be ordered under the Load Lines Convention if some structural shortcoming is apparent such as serious pitting in the deck plating; or under MARPOL if the remaining capacity in the slop tank is insufficient for the intended voyage; or under SOLAS if the engine room is not clean, with oily water in the bilges and pipe work installation contaminated by oil.

## The US Oil Pollution Act 1990

Pollution is an area in which coastal states are very active. One of the most forthright initiatives in recent years has been the US Oil Pollution Act 1990. This legislation was formulated in response to the public concern following the grounding of the *Exxon Valdez* in the Prince William Sound, Alaska, in March 1989.

The Act applies to oil spills in US inland waters; up to 3 miles offshore; and the 'exclusive economic zone' up to 200 miles to sea from the shoreline. The LOOP

Terminal is not included. It lays down wide-ranging regulations for the handling of oil spills. The 'responsible party', defined as the owner or operator of the tanker, is required to pay for the clean-up, up to a liability limit of $10 million or $1200 per gross ton, whichever is the greater. However, if there has been gross negligence these limits do not apply.

In addition to making shipowners responsible for the cost of pollution incidents, the Act laid down specific requirements for ships operating in US waters. Each ship must carry a certificate of financial responsibility, demonstrating that it has sufficient financial means to pay a claim. There was also a requirement that vessels ordered after 30 June 1990 or delivered after 1 January 1994 should have double hulls and a schedule for phasing out single-hull tankers by 2010. The coastguard is required to evaluate the manning standards of foreign vessels and to ensure that these are at least equivalent to US law. All tankers are required to carry a contingency plan for responding to an oil spill.

This legislation, particularly the requirement for double-hulled tankers, caused great controversy. However, the effect was to focus the attention of the shipping community far more rigorously on the risks associated with oil pollution. In particular, for the first time, shipowners were faced with the possibility of unlimited liability for the cost of any oil spill they are involved in. The high cost of cleaning up after the *Exxon Valdez* spill put a financial dimension on the possible scale of this problem.

## 16.10 THE REGULATION OF COMPETITION IN SHIPPING

The final regulatory issue we will mention in this chapter is competition. Although the shipping industry is very competitive, parts of the business have a history of collusion, notably the liner business (Chapter 13) and some of the specialist shipping segments (Chapter 12). Even bulk shipping has various pools and cartels. Most countries have some legislation dealing with these issues, but the competition policy of the European Union and the anti-trust legislation in the United States are the two areas we will concentrate on in this section.

### Regulatory control of liner cartels, 1869–1983

When liner conferences were set up in the 1870s (see Section 13.10) they immediately came under attack. In 1879 the *China Mail*, a Hong Kong newspaper, set the tone for a debate which lasted a century by describing the China Conference as 'one of the most ill-advised and arbitrary attempts at monopoly which has been seen for many a year'.[25] The first legal challenge came in 1887 when the Mogul Line sought an injunction to stop the Far East Freight Conference, which had seven members, from refusing rebates to shippers using Mogul vessels. The background was that when in 1885 Mogul Line had applied for admission to the conference, it was refused because it did not bear a full share of running regular services during off-peak periods. This led to a rate war and the Conference's Shanghai agents issued a circular warning that shippers who used Mogul ships would forfeit their rebates. Mogul applied for an injunction to stop the Conference refusing the rebates, but it was refused, confirming the legality of the Conference. Some years later, however, a British Royal Commission on Shipping Rings was set up to investigate the rebate system. Its report in 1909 again confirmed that the commercial relationship between shippers and conferences was justified and that the possible abuses of the deferred rebate system should be tolerated in the interests of achieving a strong liner system.[26]

The conference system reached its peak during the 1950s. The prominence which the liner conferences had achieved by this time is demonstrated by the UNCTAD Code of Conduct for Liner Conferences which was initiated at the first UNCTAD Conference in Geneva in 1964 (see Section 12.9). Many of the developing countries which had gained independence during the previous decade had balance of payments problems and were searching for solutions. Sea freight played an important part in the price of the primary exports on which most of them relied. In addition, the freight itself was a drain on their scarce foreign currency reserves. Setting up a national shipping line seemed the obvious solution to both problems. However, the liner conferences were not generally sympathetic and the emerging nations lacked the experience in the liner business to press their case. This led to political action by the 'Group of 77', a pressure group of developing countries within UNCTAD, the result of which was the UNCTAD Code which aimed to give each country the right to participate in liner conferences servicing their trade.

The UNCTAD Code was developed in the 1960s and 1970s and covered four major areas of liner shipping. It provided the right to automatic conference membership for the national shipping lines of the countries served by the conference. A cargo-sharing formula gave national shipping lines equal rights to participate in the volume of traffic generated by their mutual trade, with third parties carrying the residual. For example, under a 40:40:20 cargo-sharing agreement the bilateral traders reserved 40% of the cargo for their national vessels and 'cross traders' carried the remaining 20% of the cargo. Finally, shipping conferences were required to consult shippers over rates, and national lines had the right of consent on all major conference decisions affecting the countries serviced.

The Code took almost 20 years to develop and by the time it came into force in 1983 the liner business had changed out of all recognition. It has never been ratified by the USA and implementing a convention of this complexity, which involved agreeing and measuring trade shares, was too difficult. Despite this, the Code achieved two things. First, it gave rights to the emerging Third World shipping industry at a time when this recognition was needed. Second, it was the first international effort to regulate the extensive, and overly weighty, system of closed conferences. By opening the conferences to new participants, it weakened the tight control which had developed and set the scene for a new regulatory attitude towards the conference system.

## US regulation of liner shipping, 1983–2006

From the 1970s onwards the USA became determined to open the newly containerized liner services to market forces and to curb, but not entirely prohibit, the activities of conferences. Under US anti-trust laws, agreements which restrict competition are illegal, but the US Merchant Shipping Act 1984 excluded liner conferences from US anti-trust legislation and allowed inter-modal rate making. However, the legislation placed severe limitations on conference activities, making closed conferences and loyalty rebates illegal. In addition, tariffs fixed by conferences operating into the USA were required to be filed with the Federal Maritime Commission FMC along with all service contracts, and made public. This changed the nature of the conferences operating on the Atlantic and the Pacific, producing the various alliances discussed in Section 13.10. The Ocean Shipping Reform Act which took effect on 1 May, 1999 was another step towards making the liner shipping industry more market-driven. The new law retained the antitrust exemption for the ocean liner industry and still required service contracts to be filed, but allowed their terms to remain confidential. A subsequent study found that as a result most shippers negotiated one-on-one confidential service contracts with individual carriers, instead of negotiating with rate-setting conferences or groups of carriers. In the two years following the regulation the number of these service contracts and amendments increased by 200%.[27]

## European Union regulation of shipping competition

European regulations governing competition are set out in Articles 81 and 82 of the Treaty of Rome (1958). Article 81 makes it illegal for companies to cooperate to 'prevent, restrict or distort' competition by fixing prices, manipulating supply or discriminating between parties. Article 82 makes it illegal for a company to use its dominant position to undermine free competition by price fixing, manipulating supply or other abuses. In 1962, Regulation 17 gave the EU powers to enforce these articles but specifically excluded the transport industries, and it was not until 1986 that the EU Regulation 4056/86 set out 'detailed rules for the application of Articles 81 and 82 of the Treaty to maritime transport'. This regulation excluded tramp shipping because prices were 'freely negotiated on a case by case basis in accordance with supply and demand conditions'. Liner shipping was included, but, like most regulators before them, the EU accepted that conferences were in the interest of consumers, providing stability. As a result, the liner companies were given a 'block exemption' from Article 81, permitting them to fix rates, regulate capacity and collude in ways which would otherwise be illegal under the Treaty of Rome (although some shipping companies were fined for fixing prices outside liner conferences).

In 2004 the EU launched an initiative to review this special treatment received by the tramp shipping and liner industries. After consultation with the liner and tramp shipping industries, the EU concluded that:

> no credible consideration has been put forward in response to the consultation to justify why these services would need to benefit from different enforcement rules than those which the council has decided should apply to all sectors. On that basis the intention would be to bring maritime cabotage and tramp vessels services within the scope of the general enforcement rules.[28]

In September 2006, Regulation 4056/86 was repealed. The tramp shipping exemption lapsed on 18 October 2006, facing companies with the possibility that Articles 81 and 82 of the Treaty of Rome might be enforced against shipping pools, of which a number were operating in the tanker, dry bulk and specialist markets.

For the rapidly growing container industry the Commission's discussion paper published in 2005 argued that

> even if conferences were to provide for pro competitive effects in terms of e.g. price stability, reduced uncertainty about trade conditions, possible more accurate forecasts of supply and demand, reliable and adequate services, this would appear in itself not to be sufficient to conclude that the second condition of Article 81(3) on the treaty is fulfilled, since it has not been established that the net effect on consumers (transport users and end consumers) is at least neutral.[29]

After a lengthy investigation they ruled that price agreement was no longer necessary and that the industry and consumers would benefit from free competition. The repeal of Regulation 4056/86 removed the block exemption with effect from 18 October 2008. From this date all shipping companies operating on routes into and out of Europe cannot operate in conferences that fix price and capacity. This will apply equally to EU and non-EU based carriers. Liner shipping conferences outside of Europe are not affected but are subject to their own anti-trust laws.

## EU regulation of tramp shipping pools

For tramp shipping the loss of the exemption from Articles 81 and 82 raised questions about the legality of the pools operated in the tanker and bulk carrier markets. Tramp shipping pools bring together similar vessels under different ownership. They are placed under a single pool manager, though the ships generally continue to be operated and crewed by the owners. The nature of pool agreements in tramp shipping varies widely, but the main principles were discussed in Section 2.9.

Article 81(1) of the Rome Treaty explicitly prohibits price fixing and sharing markets between competitors, unless the pool produces genuine benefits as defined in Article 81(3). In effect, pool members must be able to demonstrate: that their pool produces efficiency gains; that these benefits are passed on to transport users, for example as lower transport costs or new logistic solutions; that there is no less restrictive way of obtaining these efficiencies; and that the pool does not have an unreasonably large market share which inhibits free market competition.

Generally the EU took the view that tramp pool agreements that have very low market shares are unlikely to raise competition problems, provided the agreement does not contain provisions regarding joint price fixing and/or joint marketing or if the participants cannot be considered actual or potential competitors.[30] In September 2007 the EU published draft guidelines setting out the principles that the EU will follow when defining markets and assessing cooperation agreements in the maritime transport services sectors affected by the repeal of Regulation 4056/86.[31]

## 16.11 SUMMARY

In this chapter we have moved outside the conventional framework of market economics to examine the regulatory system that plays such a vital part in the economics of the shipping industry. We started by identifying three regulatory regimes which operate in the shipping industry: the classification societies, the flag states and the coastal states.

The classification societies are the shipping industry's internal regulatory system. The mainstay of their authority is the classification certificate which is issued when the ship is built and updated by means of regular surveys throughout the life of the ship. Without a class certificate a ship cannot obtain insurance and has little commercial value. But they are also the industry's largest technical resource, and in their role as recognized organizations they play an increasingly important part in the regulation of safety and security.

Flag states make the laws which govern the commercial and civil activities of the merchant ship. Because different countries have different laws, the flag of registration makes a difference. Registers can be subdivided into national registers, which treat shipping companies in the same way as other national industries; open registers (flags of convenience) such as Liberia and Panama, which are set up with the specific objective of earning revenue by offering commercially favourable terms of registration as a service to shipowners; and international registers set up by maritime states to offer their domestic shipowners comparable commercial terms to the open registers. With the increasing globalization of the maritime industry, open registers have become more prominent and half the world merchant fleet is now registered under a foreign flag, which in practice usually means a flag of convenience.

Although each nation makes its own maritime laws, on matters such as safe ship design, collision avoidance, load lines, pollution of the sea and air, tonnage measurement and certificates of competency it would be hopelessly impractical if each country had different laws. Developing a framework of international law which avoids this problem is achieved by means of international conventions. Maritime nations meet to discuss the draft convention, which is finally agreed. Each country then ratifies it and in doing so undertakes to incorporate the terms of the convention into its own national legislation. International conventions drawn up since the mid-1960s cover a wide range of different subjects including the safety of life at sea, load lines, crew training, tonnage measurement, terms and conditions of employment of crew, oil pollution and the conduct of liner conferences. The organizations active in developing these conventions are the International Maritime Organization and International Labour Organization.

Although major conventions such as SOLAS (1974) are ratified by 99% of the eligible countries, others are controversial and some countries choose not to ratify them, or allocate sufficient administrative resources to enforcing them, leaving 'loopholes' in the system.

Shipowners registered in these countries are, in principle, able to operate outside the convention, but they are still subject to a third form of regulation, by the coastal state in whose waters their ship is trading. The Law of the Sea permits coastal states to pass legislation concerning the 'good conduct' of ships in its territorial waters. One important area of legislation is pollution control, notably the US Oil Pollution Act 1990. In addition, since the 1970s there has been a trend towards 'port state control'. The movement started with the Paris MOU under which a group of European states agreed to work together to ensure that ships visiting their ports complied with international conventions on safety and pollution. There are now similar MOUs covering most parts of the world and over 50,000 ships a year are inspected.

Finally, the competitive practices of the shipping industry are also subject to regulation, and the United States and Europe are particularly active in this area. The principal area of concern is the liner conferences which fix prices and capacity levels. During the cargo liner era this was accepted as necessary to provide stable services and pricing, but with the advance of containerization the regulatory authorities are less willing to exempt the liner and tramp shipping industry from anti-trust regulations, and in 2006, for example, the EU made liner conferences and tramp shipping pools subject to its competition laws.

# Part 6

# FORECASTING AND PLANNING

# 17 Maritime Forecasting and Market Research

*The wretched boatmen do not know,*
*Their rudder gone at Yura Strait,*
*Where will their drifting vessel go.*
*And where my love, and to what fate?*

(Sone no Yoshitada, *One Hundred Poems from One Hundred Poets*)

## 17.1 THE APPROACH TO MARITIME FORECASTING

For most shipping investors forecasting is not optional. It is how they earn their living. Whether it is an investment decision like ordering a ship, or deciding which charter to take, the better they anticipate the future, the more profit they make. In fact if they cannot do that, what is the point? But it is not just shipowners who are in the forecasting business. Bankers lending money, shipyards developing designs, engineering companies selling equipment, rating agencies calculating the risk of default on a bond and ports developing their facilities will all be more successful if they can predict the future better than their competitors.

### The poor track record of shipping forecasts

Considering the importance of these decisions it is not surprising that shipping executives are preoccupied with the future. But to be realistic, maritime forecasting has a poor reputation, and the sense that forecasts are usually wrong is too widely held in the industry to be taken lightly. However, it is not just the maritime industry that has this problem. Peter Beck, Planning Director at Shell UK, came to the same conclusion when trying to find forecasts for the oil industry, commenting:

> When looking at forecasts made in the 1960s and early 1970s, one can find many failures but few successes. Indeed one may be shocked at the extent to which the most important forecasts and their surrounding assumptions had turned out to be wrong.[1]

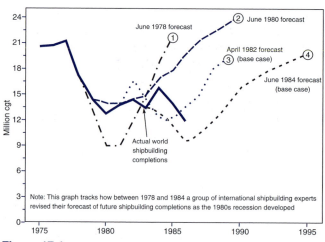

**Figure 17.1**
Comparison of forecasts of world shipbuilding completions

In the shipping and ship-building industries some forecasts have turned out to be wildly wrong, whilst others are right, but only by a fortunate combination of inaccurate assumptions. As an example, we can take four forecasts of the demand for new ships produced between 1978 and 1984, summarized in Figure 17.1. Each successive forecast predicted a different pattern of demand over the next seven years.

The 1980 forecast predicted 50% more demand in 1986 than the 1982 forecast, and even this proved to be too optimistic. The line showing actual world shipbuilding completions barely touches any of the forecast lines. In defence of the experts who produced these forecasts, there were developments in the world economy and the oil trade that they could not reasonably have anticipated. However, the fact remains that the forecasts were a poor guide to what was about to happen in the shipbuilding industry.

Long-term forecasts do no better. Later in the chapter we will see how inaccurate some predictions for the 1980s made in the mid-1960s proved to be. They predicted widespread supersonic air travel but gave the computer only a passing mention and completely misjudged the two major economic developments of the 1970s, inflation and unemployment. Similarly, in 2002 the oil industry based its long-term oil demand forecasts on an oil price of $25 per barrel, only to see the price rise to $70 per barrel over the next three years. With such a poor track record it is difficult not to agree with Peter Drucker that, the further ahead we try to predict, the more tenuous the forecasts become:

> If anyone suffers from the delusion that a human being is able to forecast beyond a very short time span, look at the headlines in yesterday's paper, and ask which of them anyone could have possibly predicted a decade or so ago … we must start out with the premise that forecasting is not a respectable human activity and not worthwhile beyond the shortest of periods.[2]

## The challenge of dealing with the unknown

The problem for maritime forecasters is that unfortunately Peter Drucker is right – there are important aspects of the future of the maritime industry that are not predictable. Future freight rates depend on how many ships are ordered, a behavioural variable which at the extremes of shipping cycles is totally unpredictable,[3] and developments in the world economy which, with its business cycles and crises, are far too complex for mere mortals to predict with any degree of certainty. In these circumstances even the most sophisticated scientific forecasting methods will have limited success.

This is not a new problem, and leaders of the ancient world developed all sorts of prophetic techniques to help them with imponderable decisions about how to conduct their lives and their military campaigns. Two thousand years ago there were oracles scattered all over Greece and Italy and some, such as Delphi and Trophonios, grew into large and wealthy organizations. Their sages would answer questions about what would happen in future, often as part of an elaborate ritual. For example a contemporary account of the Oracle of Trophonios, which was located underground at Lebadea in Greece in AD 150, describes the ritual an 'enquirer' went through to get a forecast. First, he spent several days in a special building purifying himself and making sacrifices. Then he was sent underground, feet first through a hole in the ground, to consult the oracle in a cavern full of smoke and mirrors. After the consultation he returned, again feet first, 'so possessed with terror he hardly knows himself or anything around him. Later he comes to his senses, no worse than before and can laugh again'.[4] Ancient decision-makers took their forecasts seriously!

The Babylonian, Greek, Roman and Etruscan civilizations used divination by entrails. The cuneiform literature of Mesopotamia in the twentieth century BC contains many accounts of divination in which a sheep's liver or other object (e.g. the behaviour of a drop of oil in a beaker of water) was used to make predictions: 'The king will kill his dignitaries and distribute their houses and property among the temples'; 'A powerful man will ascend the throne in a foreign city'.[5] Divination was a sophisticated skill. A Babylonian clay model of a sheep's liver in the British Museum, London, believed to have been used for training purposes, has 50 zones marked on it, each presumably with a different significance.

In the East equally sophisticated techniques were developed for predicting the future. Oracle bones were widely used in China three thousand years ago. The shoulder bone of an ox was trimmed to flatten it and several small cavities were gouged into its surface. Predictions were made by plunging a red hot iron into these cavities and interpreting the cracks which appeared on the underside of the bone. Nobody knows exactly how the cracks were interpreted, but over 1,15,000 oracle bones have been discovered, indicating the scale of this 'industry'.[6]

One of the most interesting ancient predictive systems is the Chinese 'Book of Change' or *I Ching*, which reduced the process of consulting fate to a system and the equally old 'Book of History' or *Shu Ching*. These classic books, written in China over 3000 years ago, focus on the process of change and include much that is relevant to the modern forecaster. Change is seen as continuous – 'Let him be wary and fearful, remembering that in one or two days there may occur 10,000 springs of things'[7] – and we are all responsible for our own actions: 'Calamities sent by Heaven may be avoided, but from calamities brought on by one's self there is no escape'.[8] The key issue is the right moment to act – 'The case is like that of sailing a boat; if you do not cross the stream at the proper time, you will destroy all the cargo'.[9] Once change has commenced we can sometimes tiptoe round it and get out of the way, or even manipulate it in our direction if it appears favourable.

In conclusion, the problems of making decisions about an uncertain future are as old as the shipping industry, and even Alexander the Great, a man of action whom any shipping magnate can admire, took divination very seriously.[10] Today's analysts with their computer models are the latest in a long line of intelligent individuals who minister to the needs of the decision-makers and perhaps we should not be too dismissive of these ancient rituals (or at least be more clear-sighted about our own). Strange though divination by bones or entrails may seem to us, are these rituals really any stranger then punching numbers into a plastic box and gazing at the digits which appear on a screen?

## The forecasting paradox

Although this may seem a discouraging way to introduce a discussion of forecasting techniques, at least we are getting off on the right foot by accepting that our forecasts will often be wrong. It is a certainty because, paradoxically, forecasters are only called in when the future is unpredictable. When the future is predictable, which it often is, nobody bothers with forecasts. For example, investors in a liquid natural gas project secured by long-term cargo contracts do not hire a forecaster to predict future cargo volume; they hire engineers to work out how many ships will be required. But when there is no cargo contract and it is not clear how much LNG the project will be able to sell, the engineers are pushed aside and the forecasters are called in. They have a trickier task than the engineers because they are not dealing with the immutable laws of physics. If the LNG trade grows rapidly, new tankers will be needed and the investors will be able to charter the ships at high rates. But if there is some change in the world energy economy the ships will not be needed. How can they hope to predict that accurately every time?

Obviously they cannot, so their forecasts are bound to be wrong sometimes. Indeed a forecaster who was always right would be in a very strange position. So if by 'forecasting' we mean predicting *exactly* what will happen, Peter Drucker is right. Mortals cannot see into the future. But that is a bit like saying that if man were meant to fly he would have been given wings. Humans cannot fly themselves, but with a little lateral thinking they came up with airplanes which are almost as good (and much better on a transpacific trip!). In coming to terms with forecasting we need to do the same sort of lateral thinking.

## Rational forecasting to reduce uncertainty

The first step in this process is to recognize that the goal of making precise predictions of the sort illustrated in Figure 17.1 is a red herring.[11] An interesting technical diversion but, like flapping your arms in an attempt to fly, it is unlikely to succeed. Shipping investors know very well that they are not dealing with certainty. In fact they are in much the same position as a poker player making an educated guess about his opponent's cards. The poker player knows he cannot identify the hand exactly, and the game would be pointless if he could. But a professional uses every scrap of information to make an educated guess about the range of possible hands. Although he will often be wrong, over a period of time this information helps him to come out ahead.[12] Shipping investors play the odds in much the same way – they know they will not win every hand but they also know that the right information plays an essential part in narrowing the odds.

That is where 'forecasters' come in, and one final example illustrates how information about the past can help decision-makers deal with the future. Suppose a driver wants to park in a restricted area. Nobody can predict for certain whether his car will be towed away, but accurate information about how often traffic wardens visit each street clarifies the risk – 'if you park there, you are almost certain to get a ticket because a traffic warden visits the street every ten minutes'. Quantifying the frequency with which traffic wardens visit the street clarifies the possible future outcomes and is precisely the type of relevant information analysts can provide. We are not talking about a precise forecast of the type 'your car will be towed away at 10.15 a.m.' Such a prediction would, as Peter Drucker points out, almost certainly be wrong and the driver would probably not believe it anyway. But knowing that the street is patrolled every ten minutes is believable and gives the decision-maker information to weigh up the risk of leaving his car for five minutes while he pops into a shop. So the purpose of *rational forecasting* is not to predict precisely, but to reduce uncertainty.

Over the last fifty years great progress has been made in developing rational forecasting systems. As data gathering improved in the decades after the Second World War and computers became available, forecasters developed economic models which could summarize the complex economic and behavioural relationships which determine what happens in the economy. This approach relies on recognizing patterns or trends in the past and capturing them in a model for making future projections. Sometimes forecasts focus on the short term, for example the spot tanker market, but they also need to deal with longer-term changes. Strategic decisions are among the most difficult to make, especially for companies well established in their business, but the brief history of shipping in Chapter 1 demonstrated that *I Ching* was right – things change, and when this happens inaction can be just as risky as action.

For decision-makers understanding and accepting analysis which indicates change requires vision and courage. For example, in the 1950s and 1960s liner companies were swept along by a tide of change caused by low-cost air travel, the independence of the colonies and containerization. In less than 20 years the economic framework of their business changed and companies which did not adapt disappeared. But it takes great resolve to abandon an apparently solid business and start building a new one. With or without forecasters, management can never be sure what is really happening. In such cases monitoring change is the key and acting hastily with the wrong information and analysis is as bad as doing nothing.

## The importance of information

All of the foregoing suggests that forecasting is not about the future, it is about obtaining and analysing the right information about the present. The right information is not always easy to come by, but it is important. Few investors would be rash enough to buy a ship without the information provided by a physical inspection, and exactly the same is true of decisions which depend on economic developments.

An example illustrates the point. In Chapter 8 we left Aristotle Onassis at the height of a winning streak in 1956, with a profit of $80 million in the bank, thanks to the closure of the Suez Canal. But that was not the end of the story. Believing that the Egyptian government was not capable of reopening the Canal, Onassis expected it to be closed for several years, leading to a strong tanker market. When his aide Costa Gratsos urged him to take some time-charter cover, he told him: 'I'm hot, Costa, I'm in front of the parade. I've got the touch; I don't even have to breathe hard. Why the hell should we crap out now?' Costa Gratsos did not agree and secretly chartered 12 tankers to Esso for 39 months. When he found out, Onassis hit the roof, but he had misjudged the capability of the Egyptian government. The Canal was reopened only a few months later in April 1957, just as the US economy was slipping into its deepest recession since the 1930s and tanker rates slumped. Onassis had allowed himself to be caught up in a wave of market sentiment. Reluctantly he admitted, 'you read it right. I read it wrong'.[13] He had misjudged Egypt's ability to reopen the canal, a matter which the right information and analysis could have addressed (though to be fair this is more obvious with hindsight than it was at the time). The trouble is that information of this type is difficult to obtain and analyse, especially against the background of a booming market, so forecasters have to be versatile.

This example raises another issue, the interplay between sentiment and rational analysis in shipping decisions. Some economists now argue that economic theory should recognize the influence of emotions on decisions. They speculate that the section of the brain known as the amygdala – a source of emotional conviction – fights for supremacy with the more deliberative prefrontal cortex which controls analytical thought.[14] However the decision is arrived at, we should be realistic about these human aspects of the process.[15]

But the market does not really care how the decision was made. As economists we know that in the long term it rewards players who get it right, and although a few get lucky the long-term winners are the ones who do their homework. The market's goal is to make sure that the minimum resources are used to carry the world's trade. Companies which use information and analysis to achieve that goal are rewarded because they save valuable economic resources. And if they act irrationally and waste resources by, for example, ordering more ships than are needed they are punished. That is all there is to it – the law of the economic jungle rules! Information can help decision-makers find their way through the jungle, so they need forecasts and analysts, despite the fact that they are often wrong.

## 17.2 KEY ELEMENTS OF THE FORECAST

### Three principles of forecasting

So how do we set about producing the right information for decision-makers? The first point to recognize is that if the results of the study are to be used in making a decision, and because there are so many different decisions to be made, no single methodology will produce a useful result in every case. There are, however, three principles that can be used to judge whether a forecast is likely to be useful.

1.  *Relevance*. The first step in any forecast is to find out exactly what aspect of the future the decision-maker is interested in. For example, a forecast that predicts the level of shipbuilding output five years ahead may not be what a shipbuilder really wants to know. He may be much more interested in the prices at which ships will be sold so that he can calculate whether he can make a profit, and what share of the market he might win. In this case a relevant forecast would concentrate on price and competitor activity as well as the demand for new ships.
2.  *Rationale*. There must be a convincing reason why the predicted developments may happen. Decision-makers have to decide how much weight to place on the analysis and they can only do this if there is some sort of rationale. Without it the forecaster is in the business of prophecy rather than economic analysis.[16] There are many ways of doing this. A quantitative forecast made with a model is appropriate in some cases and a set of scenarios in others. Or a credit-rating agency may insist on the probability of a particular event, say a default, being quantified in statistical terms.
3.  *Research*. Information reduces uncertainty, so careful research is important. Although this sounds obvious, it is surprising how often decisions are taken without researching key variables. Like any other job in business, forecasting requires an adequate input of skilled man-hours. Referring back to the traffic warden example earlier in the chapter, it is not much help to tell a motorist parking his car in Kensington, London, that the number of traffic wardens in the UK went up by 2.8% last year. He needs specific data about Kensington.

These principles are not about accuracy; they are about establishing the ground rules for producing information and analysis which will be useful to a maritime decision-maker. Forecasting is part of the decision process and is about applying economic resources to reduce uncertainty.

## Identifying the economic model

Identifying the underlying economic model is a vital part of the process because it tells us what information to collect and analyse. In fact we use this process all the time in our everyday life, using models founded on the principle of 'constant conjunction' first observed by the eighteenth-century philosopher, David Hume, in his *Treatise on Human Nature*. Hume concluded that we conduct our lives on the assumption that future events will generally follow the patterns we have observed in the past. As we gain experience we are constantly updating our range of constant conjunction models. For example, we expect rain because it is cloudy and we associate clouds with rain. In shipping, we may predict that trade will increase when the world economy recovers because this has always happened in the past. This form of verbal reasoning is the basis of most economic analysis and we often extend the model by taking account of additional information – are some cloud types more likely to produce rain than others?

Once we start asking questions like this, the problem becomes more complex. The first step is to specify the precise nature of the model by identifying the variables which we believe are related to the subject of the forecast and, from what we know, guessing the nature of the relationship between them. In the case of the weather model, one variable might be the percentage of blue sky visible in the morning and the other the hours of rain during the day. If we can quantify these two variables, for example by keeping records of their values every day for a year, we can analyse the data to measure the relationship (the number relating the variables is known as a parameter) and test it. The point of the test is to see whether the relationship between them is significant (are the variables really related?) and stable (will the parameter keep changing?). If the model does not pass these tests we might try a different specification. Other variables affecting the weather might be the temperature and the barometric pressure. If a more consistent relationship emerges, we have the basis for making a more authoritative forecast: 'If the pressure is falling and there is 100% cloud cover, we can expect rain'. Although they are not always correct, such forecasts can be helpful to us in taking day-to-day decisions like whether to wear a raincoat. Precisely the same principles apply in making business forecasts, but the time-scale is longer and there are many more variables to analyse.

## Types of relationships and variables

Successful modelling depends on recognizing the nature of the variables and applying the appropriate analytical techniques. There are four different types, which we can refer to as 'tangible', 'technological', 'behavioural' and 'wild card'. Each of these has a different character. *Tangible* variables are physically verifiable and thus, in theory, have a high degree of predetermination. For example, the distance from the Middle East to China or India and the maximum operating speed of an oil tanker can all be precisely defined. For this reason, tangible variables tend to be reasonably predictable provided sufficient research is carried out – we are talking here about predicting such factors as the tonnage of tankers needed to carry China and India's imports. Unfortunately, the information about this type of variable can sometimes be inaccurate or misleading. The register book may say a tanker's speed is 15.5 knots, but in service it may only average 13 knots.

A typical *technological* variable is the amount of energy used per unit of industrial output. These relationships are often treated as parameters in forecasting models, but they can change substantially over time. Thus forecasters confronted with the problem of predicting how the world economy would respond to higher oil prices face questions such as whether the automobile industry will be able to make vehicles more fuel efficient. The rate at which innovation could be introduced in response to a major price change is difficult to predict; nevertheless, with careful research, it is possible to form a reasoned view.

*Behavioural* relationships depend on the way people behave. Suppose a forecasting agency predicts a boom in tanker freight rates. Shipowners see the forecast and order more tankers, and the resulting oversupply drives down freight rates. The forecast is wrong simply because shipowners are free to change their behaviour after the forecast has been made, so attempts to predict them can be are self-defeating. Consequently, behaviourals of this type are not reliably predictable.

Finally, there are *wild cards*. There can be sudden departures from the established 'norm', for example hurricanes or revolutions. By definition they are unpredictable and there is really very little that can be done about them – life is, by its nature, a risky business.

## 17.3 PREPARING FOR THE FORECAST

Three practical steps must precede the forecast. The first is to define the decision to be made; the second is to determine who is qualified to make the forecast; and the third is to establish that the things we are trying to forecast really are predictable.

### Defining the decision

What exactly do shipping decision-makers want from their forecasters? That depends on who they are and what decisions they are making. There are many different decision-makers in shipping, each with a different forecasting requirement. Some of the more prominent ones are listed below.

- *Shipping companies* make decisions about the sale and purchase of ships; ordering newbuildings and whether to enter into long-term charters or COAs. These decisions depend on future freight rates, newbuilding prices and second-hand prices.
- *Cargo owners* are interested in the future cost and availability of suitable transport. Companies which ship cargo in sufficient volume will be concerned about future transport costs. For example, shippers may choose to cover a proportion of their shipping requirements by running their own ships, and using the charter market to meet fluctuations in demand. Once this approach has been adopted, the companies are faced with decisions about the size and type of fleet to maintain.
- *Shipbuilders* have to decide whether to expand or reduce capacity and whether to invest in new product development in certain areas. This involves the future demand for new ships, prices, currencies, subsidies, the demand for specific ship types and competition from other shipbuilders.
- *Bankers* make decisions about whether to approve a loan application and the level of security required. This involves decisions about future cashflow and whether the shipowner has the financial and managerial skills to survive recessions; often the question being asked is how bad things could get. If, in due course, the shipowner fails to service his loan owing to a protracted depression, then the banker faces another decision: whether to foreclose now and take a loss on the ships or wait in the hope that the market will improve.

- *Governments* are often confronted by difficult decisions about the shipbuilding industry. These decisions involve issues such as whether or not to provide subsidy and whether or not to cut capacity. Governments may also be involved in shipping decisions such as whether or not to set up an international shipping register and how to manage it. All these decisions involve weighing short-term benefits against long-term risks. If a minister decides to subsidize a shipyard rather than allow it to close, he avoids a short-term political problem, but ties himself into a longer-term problem if, in fact, the shipyard remains unprofitable.

- *Port authorities* are concerned with port development. There is intense competition between ports to attract cargo by offering advanced cargo-handling facilities for containers, large bulk carriers and specialist product terminals. The provision of these facilities involves major capital investment in terms of civil engineering, cargo-handling equipment and dredging. As a result, decisions about port development depend crucially on traffic forecasting to find out the volume of cargo, the way it will be packed and the ship types used. For example, the decision on whether or not to invest in a specialist container terminal involves such questions as: How much container cargo will be moving through our part of the coast? What volume of this cargo can we attract through our port? What facilities will we need to offer in future to attract this share of the cargo?

- *Machinery manufacturers* are faced with decisions about what type of products to develop and how to manage their capacity. Merchant ships are massive engineering structures and, with a total fleet of 72,000 vessels, there is an enormous industry world-wide manufacturing components for fitting into new ships – engines, generators, winches, cranes, navigation equipment, etc. – and spare parts and equipment to upgrade the existing fleet. Manufacturers must look at trends in ship construction, future developments in operational management of ships, ship operating economics and the activity of competitors.

- *International organizations* such as the OECD, EU and the IMO do not actually make commercial decisions, but they are invariable drawn into the discussion of maritime policy. For example, the European Union produces Directives on Aid to Shipbuilding and has commissioned forecasts for this purpose.[17]

For all the diversity of this group there is one aspect of the decision process which is of particular importance, and that is whether the real decision authority lies with an individual or a group of decision-makers. We consider this important distinction in the following paragraphs.

## Who makes the forecast?

Many shipping companies have a sole proprietor, the 'shipowner', who makes the decisions himself. These shipowners have so much riding on their decisions that they often do their own forecasting. Some have MBAs or degrees in economics and may even use the formal techniques discussed in this chapter, but most base their decisions on experience, common sense and 'gut feelings'. They are constantly on the lookout for information which gives an insight into what is really going on. There are several reasons why this approach works. Firstly, some key aspects of shipping markets are too subtle to capture in statistical models, for example the effect of congestion and supply shortages which disrupt the demand side of the model and cause unexpected changes in the market. Secondly, statistical data is limited and often arrives too late to be useful to a company trying to keep ahead of the pack. Thirdly, some variables such as market sentiment are too mercurial to capture in a formal forecasting model, so an experienced businessman close to the market has a far better chance of grasping what is really happening than a team of analysts struggling to fit a model to inadequate data.

But although this is a powerful argument, it has drawbacks. Sentiment can influence judgement, and decision-makers sitting too close to the market risk losing perspective. They need objective information and advice. Supporting balanced market decisions during periods of intense market sentiment is one of the most practical, and thankless, functions of shipping economics.

Although independent shipowners are an important group of maritime decision-makers, there are many others working in large shipping corporations, banks or bureaucracies whose approach to forward-looking decisions is very different. Entrepreneurs like Onassis have only themselves to convince, but decision-makers who share responsibility must carry their colleagues with them. Bankers, government officials, shipbuilding executives and board members of oil companies, steel mills and shipping conglomerates all participate in these forward-looking decisions but do not have the time or expertise to research them personally.

These decision-makers delegate the analysis and expect to be presented with predictions based on recognized analytical techniques, in a form which can be circulated to colleagues and independently checked. Even shipping entrepreneurs raising finance may be drawn into this process of structured market analysis. If they are borrowing from a bank, the bank's lending officer and its credit control department will expect to see a structured analysis of the prospects for their business. Or if the funds are to be raised by an IPO or from the bond market, financial institutions must be convinced and that means explaining how the markets work and what the risks are. In such cases forecasts, however inadequate, become part of the decision process.

## What decision-makers use forecasts for

The range of maritime business activities which require forecasts or 'forward-looking views' is extraordinarily wide, particularly if we take into account the activities of banks, governments, port authorities, shippers and other organizations with an interest in the shipping market. Some of the more important commercial decisions are listed below and it is apparent that each involves a very different approach to forecasting:

- *Spot-chartering ships.* This is one of the fundamental shipping decisions, and judging what will happen next is crucial. Waiting a couple of days can sometimes result in a better rate and there is the question of which discharge port will leave the ship best positioned. This requires a short-term view of the market and conventional forecasting techniques are not much help. Little reliable data is available in the time-frame and decision-makers generally rely on their own intuitive models and gut feeling of brokers working the markets, though modelling is not entirely out of the question for big companies or pools with a strong information base.

- *Time-chartering ships.* This covers a longer period and provides an ideal opportunity to take a reasoned view of market prospects. It is a central use of forecasting, focusing on the probable future level of spot earnings over the time-charter period compared with the available time-charter rate and the residual value of the ship at the end of the charter.

- *Sale and purchase.* Deciding when to buy or sell ships is another prime application for shipping forecasts. In this case the focus is on how second-hand prices will develop and identifying market turning points. Market players need to decide where they are in the cycle and whether prices represent good value in relation to long-term trends.

- *Budgets.* Most companies produce some sort of budget for the following year. Shipping companies with ships on the spot market need to estimate earnings and costs in the budget year, and shipbrokers whose commission is a percentage of freight rates have the same interest. Both may be interested in how second-hand prices will develop. Shipyards need to predict sales volumes and prices, whilst marine equipment manufacturers are interested in sales of the ship types which use their equipment.

- *Strategic and corporate planning.* This is moving into more specialist territory. Usually planning systems are used by larger corporates which need to involve the whole organization in thinking through how the business should develop. A few large shipping companies in the bulk, liner and specialist markets do strategic planning, but the technique is more commonly used by major charterers such as oil companies and steel mills; shipyards and marine equipment manufacturers; and ports. They use longer-term market forecasts or scenarios as the starting point for their planning activities.

- *Product development.* Shipyards, shipping companies and equipment manufacturers developing new products need market analysis of ship types that will sell well in future.

- *International negotiations.* Forecasts have a role in many international negotiations and formulating regulations. For example, shipbuilders use market forecasts as the basis for international discussions about capacity and regulators developing phase-out schedules for single-hull tankers needed to understand the impact the proposed regulations would have on the availability of transport capacity.

- *Government policy-making.* Market forecasts are sometimes required as an input to government policy decisions on shipping and shipbuilding.

- *Industrial relations.* Negotiations with shipping and shipbuilding unions often involve a view of market prospects.

- *Bank credit analysis.* Banks lending money to shipowners (or deciding whether to foreclose) must take a view on the risk. This involves appraising the future strength of the market, freight rates and ship prices; a market forecast provides a good starting point for discussing loans that involve a degree of commercial risk.

## 17.4 MARKET FORECASTING METHODOLOGIES

### The forecasting time-scale

Time has a special place in forecasting and has major significance for the forecasting methodology adopted. Although decisions are made in the present,[18] the distance their consequences stretch into the future affects the forecaster's task because important short-term variables often do not matter in the long term and vice versa. The three shipping market time-scales we defined in Section 4.5, p. 163 – momentary, short term and long term – provide a logical way of defining the forecasting time horizon, though it is useful to add a fourth, the medium term.

*Momentary* forecasts are concerned with days or even hours. This is the time-scale of charterers, shipbrokers and traders who have to decide whether to fix a ship or cargo. Chartering brokers, who work on very short-term decisions, deal with this sort of forecast every day. Should their client accept the offer or wait? Maybe he should ballast to another loading zone. Confronted with chartering options in the spot market, he must choose which part of the world is best for the ship to end up in. Or should he just put the ship on time charter? This is forecasting at the sharp end, at the frontiers of information availability, with no time for thick reports. A risky profession, but very rewarding for those who are good at it!

*Short-term* forecasts in shipping generally cover a period of months – for example, the remainder of the current year and next year. It is a popular time-frame because it covers the budget year, a forecasting activity most companies get involved in. From the forecaster's point of view there is more to work with and a better chance of being right because the market fundamentals such as the business cycle and the shipyard orderbook are sometimes well defined. The 'future' is close enough to make forecasts based on fundamentals plausible, increasing the chance of harnessing information to make accurate forecasts. Since there is plenty of data available it is an ideal time-frame for modelling.

*Medium-term* forecasts generally cover a time-scale of 5–10 years. They span an average shipping market cycle, which we know from Chapter 3 could be 4–12 years. Bankers lending to the shipping industry are fascinated by the shape and timing of the next cycle, and shipyards have a similar interest. If the shipowner buys bulk carriers, what is the chance of a protracted recession? Will he have the cashflow to survive a depression? How will operating costs compare with those of competitors? Forecasts over this time-scale often make use of either supply–demand models or some sort of econometric model.

*Long-term* forecasts have a logical span of 25 years, the life of a merchant ship. By the end of a 25-year forecast there will be little left of the current fleet, so anything is possible! This is 'think tank' territory, and major changes do happen from time to time. Over the last twenty years shipping has seen steam coal grow rapidly; the container charter market develop; reefers lose market share to container-ships; and cruise developed as a new segment. These longer-term developments are relevant for large bulk shipping companies, the shipbuilders, and service providers such as the container business and ports. Governments developing or reviewing maritime policy often want a long-term perspective. Although models are often used for long-term forecasts, they are

**Table 17.1** The forecasting applications matrix

| | Time-scale | | | |
|---|---|---|---|---|
| | Momentary 1 week | Short 18 Months | Medium 5–10 Years | Long 20 Years |
| Bulk shipping companies | Chartering | Budget | Investment | Strategy |
| Liner shipping companies | | Budget | Investment | Strategy |
| Cargo owner | Chartering | Budget | Investment | Strategy |
| Trader | Charteing | Advisory | Business Plan | Strategy |
| Shipbroker | Chartering | Advisory | Business Plan | Strategy |
| Shipyard | | Budget | Business Plan | Strategy |
| Equipment manufacturer | | Budget | Business Plan | Strategy |
| Port/terminal | | Budget | Business Plan | Strategy |
| Government | | Budget | Policy | Policy |
| Total | 4 | 8 | 7 | 1 |

little more than a convenient way of presenting conclusions drawn from less formal analysis.

A summary of how these different timescales apply to different decision makers is shown in Table 17.1. Easily the most popular is the short term. Almost everyone uses that at some time or other. Most of the support industries are also interested in the medium term, whilst only governments and large corporations venture into the long-term scenarios.

## Three different ways of approaching the forecast

Since decision-makers have such varied needs, covering such different time-scales, we must think carefully about how each forecast is prepared and presented. Even if it turns out to be wrong, the forecast is adding value if it gives decision-makers a better understanding of the decision they are making. In this sense forecasting has an educational element and analysts must think carefully about the methodology that is likely to give the maximum benefit. There are three different ways of approaching this task, each of which has specific advantages and disadvantages. We will call them the market report; the forecasting model; and scenario analysis.

*A market report* is a written study designed to provide the client with enough information to form his own views about what might happen in future. It will answer such questions as: How does the business work? How fast is it growing and why? What is the competitive structure and who are the market leaders? How are things likely to develop? What are the risks? A report dealing with these issues is necessarily descriptive, but will generally include some statistical analysis and forecast tables, though not necessarily produced with an integrated model.

A more structured approach is to model a segment of the maritime business mathematically. Several companies offer *forecasting models* of the whole shipping market, and shipping companies sometimes develop their own sector models, for example of the oil trade, the dry bulk trade or the shipbuilding market. Because models are easily updated, sensitivity analysis can be used to show the responsiveness of the results to changes in key assumptions. However, they also have three disadvantages. First, however sophisticated the model, the forecast is no better than the assumptions – typing numbers into a computer does not, in itself, add much value. Second, when forecasting freight rates and prices, supply–demand models can be so sensitive to very small assumption changes that the link between the assumptions and the forecast can become tenuous! Third, models cannot address the issues for which no data is available, however important they may be. Demand information is a particular problem.

*Scenario* analysis takes a different approach. Instead of starting from a preconceived model, it starts by identifying the critical issues that the decision-maker may have to respond to in future, then works backwards to analyse the forces which lie behind each issue, evolving a scenario. For example, if pollution risk was identified as a key issue for a tanker company, the scenario would examine how regulatory pressures and commercial trends might impact on the business. What is the probability of a serious pollution incident? How would regulators and shipowners respond? The analyst constructs a scenario illustrating how these factors might interact. The advantage of scenario analysis is that it allows 'lateral thinking' and can move into areas which are less well defined quantitatively. The disadvantage is that scenarios are complex to produce, and not all decision-makers are prepared to enter into the spirit of this wide-ranging technique.

From a methodological viewpoint there is a fundamental distinction between market forecasting and market research and Figure 17.2 summarizes some of the practical differences. In terms of objectives, market forecasts often have rather general terms of reference, whereas market research is generally linked to a defined business decision. The methodology of the market forecast tends to be dominated by statistical analysis, since statistics are the best way of representing large groups where the law of large numbers can be assumed to apply. Consequently, analysis is numerical and often involves computer modelling. In contrast, market research tends to be more closely concerned with technical and behavioural variables, which are less easily represented in statistical terms – models can be used to establish the framework, but the central issues are questions like 'How will competitors or charterers react?' which are best dealt with by research into the current views and behaviour patterns of the relevant decision-makers. Numerical analysis is still important but is generally of a financial nature.

In preparing a market research study it is generally necessary to narrow down the area of analysis to make the task manageable in terms of the volume of information to be handled. This leads to one of the most important functions of the market forecast, which is to set the scene for the more detailed market research study. However thorough the market research may be, it cannot afford to ignore trends in the market as a whole. If we take an analogy from road transport, the market forecast is equivalent to the road map that establishes where the main roads go, whilst the market research is equivalent to the route plan a driver prepares before setting out on a long journey. He will certainly refer to the roadmap, but his route plan will be unique. It will deal with a specific journey and, to be successful, must take account of such details as expected traffic density, speed limits, short cuts and road repair work which might cause delays, none of which are

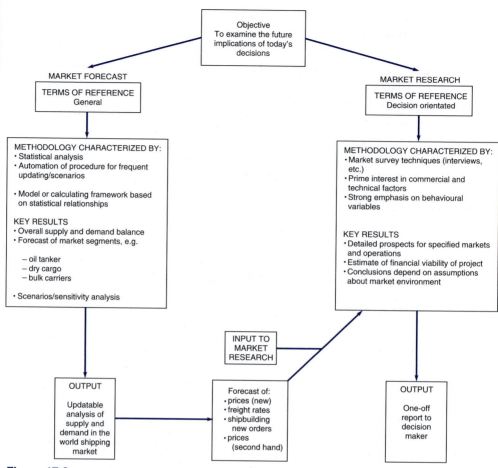

**Figure 17.2**
Differences between maritime market forecasting and market research
Source: complied by Martin Stopford from various sources

shown on the map. Of course, motorists going on long journeys do not have to consult maps or prepare route plans Many just set off and follow the road signs, hoping not to get lost. Much the same is true of decision-makers in the shipping market.

In the following sections we discuss each of the approaches in more detail.

## 17.5 MARKET RESEARCH METHODOLOGY

A market research report is as much about education as prediction. The aim is to summarize all the relevant facts about the market, examine trends, and draw conclusions about what might happen in the future.

Preparing this type of study requires a combination of commercial and economic knowledge. The statistical techniques we discuss in later sections are useful, but the emphasis is on identifying the factors that will significantly influence the success or failure of the commercial decision, gathering information and assessing how these may develop. A systematic procedure for carrying out a market research study is shown in Box 17.1, which lists the six main tasks involved.

*Step 1* is to establish the terms of reference of the study. What decision is to be made, and how will the study contribute? A great deal depends upon the stage of thinking that has been reached. For example, a liner company considering setting up a new service would need to decide what type of operation to set up and how much to invest in it. In this case some of the questions it must answer are the following:

- How big is the accessible market and what share might the company win?
- How will freight rates and volume develop on that route?
- What aspects of the service will be most important in achieving future sales?
- What ship type will be most cost-effective in providing this service?
- How will competitors react to a new entrant to the trade?

---

**BOX 17.1 STAGES IN PREPARING A SHIPPING MARKET REPORT**

1 Establish terms of reference
  1.1 Discuss the study with the decision-maker.
  1.2 Identify type of information required.
  1.3 Specify means by which results are to be presented.
  1.4 Estimate time and resources required for study.
  1.5 Ensure resources are available.
2 Analyse past trends
  2.1 Define market structure/segmentation.
  2.2 Identify competition.
  2.3 Compile database and tabulate.
  2.4 Calculate trends and analyse their causes.
  2.5 Extract cyclical effects.
3 Survey competitors' plans and opinions of experts
  3.1 Identify main competitors.
  3.2 Survey opinions of experts on future developments.
  3.3 Survey plans of companies operating in market.
  3.4 Prepare summary of the industry's view of the business.
4 Identify influences on future market development
  4.1 Determine future market environment.
  4.2 List key factors that will influence future outcome.
  4.3 Prioritize variables in terms of potential future impact.
5 Combine information into forecast
  5.1 Think through forecast theme (what will happen?).
  5.2 Develop detailed forecast tables.
  5.3 Write up forecast as clearly as possible.
6 Present results
  6.1 Executive summary.
  6.2 Detailed report.
  6.3 Verbal presentation.

---

Setting out the terms of reference in this way makes it clear that the decision-maker is seeking more than a simple forecast of trade. He needs advice on how the competitive position is likely to develop and how the commercial environment in which he will be operating will change.

*Step 2* is to assemble whatever information is available and analyse past trends. Defining the market segment can often be quite difficult. For example, an investor thinking of buying a small products tanker to trade on the spot market may not be sure what type of vessel is best. Should it be able to trade in chemicals? Is it for clean or dirty products? How much attention should be given to tank size, number of segregations and pump capacity?

Once the market segment has been defined, the third step is to identify the competition. The shipowner may find himself squeezed out of the market by cut-throat competition or over-ordering by competitors. In the case of a shipbuilding company, this may involve identifying other shipyards with a known capability in the market segment and assembling information about their commercial performance. In a bulk shipping project, it may involve identifying the fleet of ships able to trade in this market and analysing the future orderbook and the strategy of other operators.

The compilation of the database for all this work is often difficult because information is incomplete or unavailable, but it should aim to provide an overview of what is happening in the market, which the analyst can then investigate and explain. A final step is to consider any cyclical effects which may be at work – for example, recent strong growth may be due to the economic business cycle rather than a long-term trend.

*Step 3* takes the study into the activities of competitors. Statistics are not usually helpful for analysing this type of information, and a more productive approach is to survey the opinions of people involved in business about the plans of companies operating in the relevant market segment. This involves:

- identifying the relevant experts to question;
- deciding on a list of the questions that need to be answered;
- selecting the most appropriate method of surveying opinions.

There are many established techniques for surveying opinion, ranging from the personal interview to the general questionnaire.[19] For example, an opinion survey of the ferry market revealed that the commercial trend was strongly towards treating the cruise ship as a 'floating hotel' in order to maximize on-board expenditure by passengers. This provided the basis for a new line of investigation about how this trend would develop over the next decade.

The first three stages in Box 17.1 lay the foundation for the study by defining its aims, analysing statistical trends, obtaining the views of experts, and identifying the plans of competitors operating in the market. It remains to prepare the report, and this is subdivided into three steps. *Step 4* involves the future market environment and questions such as: How sensitive is this market to commercial conditions in other sectors of the shipping market? For example, during the 1990s the market for small products tankers proved to be comparatively robust against the surplus of VLCCs that developed early in the decade. *Step 5* singles out the factors that are likely to be most important in determining the future outcome for the project and draws conclusions about how these will develop.

Finally, *Step 6* is the crucial task of presenting the results. Usually a report is prepared with an executive summary for busy decision-makers who do not want to read the whole thing. That does not mean they do not want the detail. The ability to have an independent expert check the methodology is important and a report setting out the detailed research gives credibility to the conclusions. The summary may include a risk analysis. For example, suppose some of the key influences on the market develop unfavourably, what would happen and how would the company be able to react? Suppose, the company buys products tankers but one or more of the growth markets for products imports fails to develop. Would it matter? Is there any action that can be taken now to guard against such an event? This is not easy to carry out but it is a valuable addition to the 'spot prediction' technique.[20] In addition to the written report, a verbal presentation with slides is often provided.

## 17.6 FREIGHT RATE FORECASTING

Probably the most common requirement is for a forecast of freight rates. Freight rate forecasts are extensively used by banks, shipping companies, civil servants and consultants commissioned to produce commercial studies. There are several market forecasting models commercially available which allow users to enter their own assumptions. Although these models vary enormously in detail, most use a methodology based on forecasting the supply and demand for merchant ships and using the supply–demand balance to draw conclusions about developments in freight rates. This provides a consistent framework for preparing a market forecast of the shipping market and can be developed in appropriate detail to produce projections that are significant for particular purposes. Although forecasts of this type are produced in precise detail they are often wildly inaccurate. Their detail is the result of the way they are produced and not an indication of their accuracy.

### The classic maritime supply–demand model

For some purposes a computer model is more useful than a report. All economic forecasts are based on some sort of model, which provides a simplified image of the world we are seeking to forecast, but in this case we are aiming to develop a working model that will successfully reproduce the relationship between the key variables in the segment of the shipping market under investigation, often including prices and freight rates.

The shipping supply–demand model was discussed at length in Chapter 4. We reviewed the key variables and the relationships between them and this model is summarized in Figure 17.3. The main variables 'V' are shown by rectangular boxes and the relationships 'R' which form the links in the model by arrows. The principal demand variables are the world economy, the commodity trades and ship demand, whilst the main supply variables are scrapping, orders, and the merchant fleet. In addition to 'normal' values of these variables there may be wild cards, which are sudden and unexpected changes in

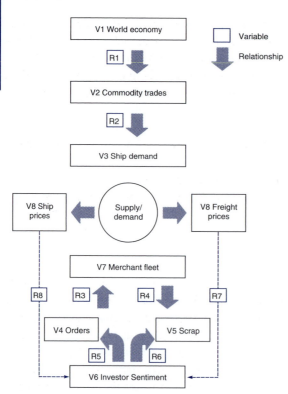

**Figure 17.3**
Macroeconomic shipping model

any of these key variables (see Section 17.2). The important point about wild cards is that although their timing is unpredictable, their occurrence is not. For example, it is impossible to predict exactly when political disruption will occur in the Middle East, but it has happened seven times over the last 50 years (1952, 1956, 1967, 1973, 1979, 1980 and 2001), so it is likely to happen again at some point. A parallel example is designing a ship to deal with 'super-waves'. The designer does not know when a ship will be hit by one, but if it is likely to happen eventually, the design must be able to cope with it. So timing is not the only issue.

Relationships link the variables together. The key relationships in the macroeconomic model in Figure 17.3, shown by the arrows, are the links between the world economy and commodity trade; commodity trade and ship demand; shipowner investment, orders and scrapping. Finally there is the crucial relationship between the supply–demand balance, freight rates, prices and investor sentiment. This feeds back into the supply side of the model through the relationship between freight rates, prices and investment sentiment shown by the dotted lines. This is one of the most difficult parts of the model. Obviously there are many ways the model can be developed in greater detail. For example, the world economy can be divided into regions or countries, commodity trades can be split into many commodities, each dealing with the industrial sector concerned in detail, and ship demand can be split by cargo type, for example containers, bulk and specialized cargoes. On the supply side, the fleet can be split by ship type and size, and such issues as fleet productivity can be developed in detail. Taken to extremes, the result could be a model with many thousands of equations, though as we will see in what follows, detail does not necessarily make models more accurate.

## Five stages in developing a forecasting model

In principle, supply–demand modelling can be applied to any segment of the shipping industry, but success depends on quantifying the variables at a significant level of desegregation, and in practice this is easier for some segments than others. Shipping segments such as crude oil tankers and bulk carriers which operate in well-documented markets are the easiest to model, whilst specialist vessels such as container-ships, vehicle carriers and chemical tankers are more difficult to model as a whole due to the lack of published information and the more complex relationships involved. Having said this, it is often possible to model parts of these complex sectors. The five stages in preparing a model are summarized below:

1. *Design model.* Draw a flow chart of how the model works. This helps to think about the structure and ensures that all possible influences on the dependent variables are considered. What variables are important? Does the model make economic sense?
2. *Define relationships and collect data.* At this stage the structural form of the model is established as a set of related equations. This stage is shown in parallel with data collection in Figure 17.3 because the form of the model will be influenced by data availability – there is no point in specifying equations which cannot be fitted because no statistical information is available. Once the structural equations have been established it is usual to recast the model into reduced form, by algebraic manipulation, to derive a model in which each endogenous variable has a separate equation in terms of exogenous variables. This can help to avoid statistical problems.[21]
3. *Estimate equations and test parameters.* This stage is usually carried out using a computer package which estimates the parameters and automatically provides a range of test statistics. In addition to the correlation coefficient and the 't'-test, various statistics are used to test for particular econometric problems – for example, the Durbin-Watson statistic to identify autocorrelation. The results of these tests will determine whether the equations are useful.
4. *Validate model.* In addition to statistical tests, it is good practice to test the model by carrying out a simulation analysis, ideally using data which was not used to estimate the equations. Following this stage, the model structure is finalized.
5. *Prepare forecast.* To make a forecast of the dependent variables it is necessary to forecast values for the exogenous variables. For example, this might include predictions of industrial production, commodity trade, and ship investment. The study of the appropriate values for the exogenous variables is therefore a vital stage.

## Example of a forecasting model

The practical procedure for producing a forecast using the shipping market model SMM described in Appendix A involves working through nine separate stages.

### STAGE 1: ECONOMIC ASSUMPTIONS

The first step is to decide what period the forecast is to cover and to discuss what assumptions should be made about the way in which the world economy will develop during this period. Specific requirements of the forecasting model are an assumption about the rate of growth of gross domestic product (GDP) and industrial production in the main economic regions. Deciding which regions to include and in how much detail is a key task. Oil prices may also play an important part, as will views on such issues as political instability, passage through the Suez Canal, etc.

### STAGE 2: THE SEABORNE TRADE FORECAST

The next step is to forecast seaborne trade during the period under review. The simplest method is to use a regression model of the following type:

$$ST_t = f(GDP_t) \tag{17.1}$$

where $ST$ is seaborne trade and $GDP$ is gross domestic product, both in year $t$.

Suppose, for example, we assume that there is a linear relationship between seaborne trade and gross domestic product. The linear equation which represents this model is:

$$ST_t = a + bGDP_t \tag{17.2}$$

This model suggests that the two variables, seaborne trade and gross domestic product move together in a linear way. For example, if industrial production increases by $1 billion, seaborne trade increases by 100,000 tons; whilst if industrial production increases by $2 billion, seaborne trade increases by 200,000 tons. The precise nature of the relationship is measured by the two parameters $a$ and $b$. Using past data and the linear regression technique we can estimate the value of these parameters. As an example, Figure 17.4(a) shows this model fitted to data for the period 1982–1995 using a linear regression:

$$ST_t = -26.289 + 30.9. GDP_t \tag{17.3}$$

What does this model tell us? The estimate for $b$ shows us that during the period 1982–1995, for each 1 point increase in the GDP index, seaborne trade increased by 30.9 million tonnes. The 'fit' of the equation is excellent, with a correlation coefficient of 0.99, which means that changes in industrial production 'explain' 99% of the changes in sea trade. If we accept the model, a forecast of seaborne trade can then be made by substituting an assumed value of GDP and calculating the associated level of seaborne trade.

How reliable is this model? One way to test it is by carrying out a simulation analysis. We feed the actual GDP index for the years 1995–2005 into the equation and compare the predicted level of sea trade with the actual trade volume. The comparison of projected with actual trade growth in Figure 17.4(a) shows that the model worked very well. Anyone who used it in 1995 to forecast trade volume would have been correct to within 0.1%. There were a few small divergences along the way, as the dotted line showing the predicted trade shows – the prediction was low in 1997 and high in 2002. But overall the model works very well, and provided the correct assumptions were made about GDP the result would have been very accurate.

**718**

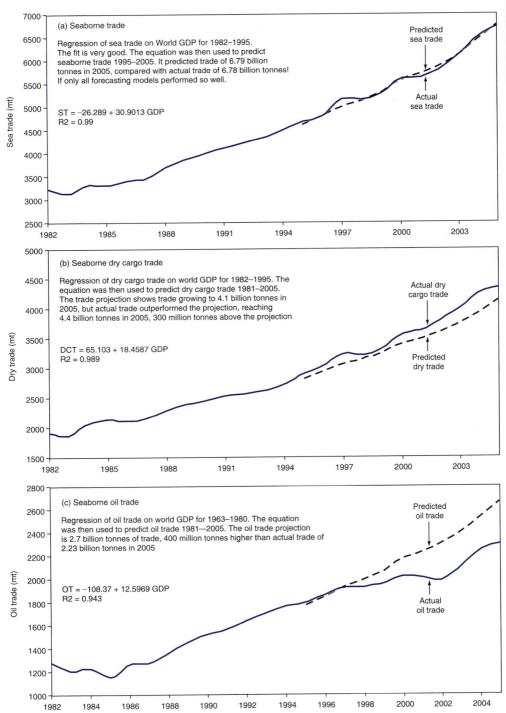

**(a) Seaborne trade**

Regression of sea trade on World GDP for 1982–1995. The fit is very good. The equation was then used to predict seaborne trade 1995–2005. It predicted trade of 6.79 billion tonnes in 2005, compared with actual trade of 6.78 billion tonnes! If only all forecasting models performed so well.

ST = −26.289 + 30.9013 GDP
R2 = 0.99

Predicted sea trade

Actual sea trade

**(b) Seaborne dry cargo trade**

Regression of dry cargo trade on world GDP for 1982–1995. The equation was then used to predict dry cargo trade 1981–2005. The trade projection shows trade growing to 4.1 billion tonnes in 2005, but actual trade outperformed the projection, reaching 4.4 billion tonnes in 2005, 300 million tonnes above the projection

DCT = 65.103 + 18.4587 GDP
R2 = 0.989

Actual dry cargo trade

Predicted dry trade

**(c) Seaborne oil trade**

Regression of oil trade on world GDP for 1963–1980. The equation was then used to predict oil trade 1981–-2005. The oil trade projection is 2.7 billion tonnes of trade, 400 million tonnes higher than actual trade of 2.23 billion tonnes in 2005

OT = −108.37 + 12.5969 GDP
R2 = 0.943

Predicted oil trade

Actual oil trade

**Figure 17.4**
Seaborne trade models comparing projections with actual trade growth
Source: World Bank and Fearnleys Annual Review, various editions

The problem with simple models of this type is that we have no way of checking in advance whether the relationship will be valid in future. A more thorough approach, which helps to check out the model, would be to subdivide the trade into separate commodities (crude oil, oil products, iron ore, coal, grain, etc.), and to develop a more detailed model of the type discussed in Section 10.5, for each commodity trade. For example, we might start by splitting seaborne trade into dry cargo and oil and estimating the regression model separately for each commodity, again using data for the period 1982–1995.

The result of this analysis for dry cargo is shown in Figure 17.4(b). For the years 1982–95 we estimate the relationship between the tonnage of dry cargo trade each year and world GDP. Once again the fit is excellent, with a regression coefficient of 0.989. However, when we use the equation to project seaborne trade through to 2005 using actual GDP the projection proves to be less accurate. The model predicts seaborne dry cargo trade of 4.1 billion tonnes in 2005, compared with actual trade of 4.4 billion tonnes. Admittedly a 7% error over 10 years is a better result than most economists would dare to hope for, but in real life it is unlikely that the GDP assumptions would be precisely correct and any errors here would be reflected in the projection.

When we extend the exercise to the oil trade the result is even less satisfactory, as can be seen in Figure 17.4(c). Although the model fits quite well during the base period 1982–95, with an $R^2$ of 0.94, the projection for 2005 is 400 million tonnes too high, an error of 20%. Between 1995 and 2000 the trade hardly grew, then it picked up between 2001 and 2005. There is really no choice but to dig deeper, perhaps by developing a regional oil trade model. During the first half of the projection period Japan and Europe hardly increased imports and a properly specified model of the type discussed in Section 10.5 would incorporate regional analysis to pick up these trends, thus providing a more informed basis for making forecasts

Some of the more sophisticated market forecasting models subdivide trade into many commodities and forecast each commodity trade using a set of equations. In theory more information should lead to a more reliable result. The danger is that it is very time-consuming and can easily generate so much detail that the underlying rationale of the forecast is lost. The key issue is to identify a significant level of detail to work at. Finally, we can note that we got a bit lucky with the total sea trade projection in Figure 17.4(a). The amazingly accurate projection in Figure 17.4(a) was the result of a dry cargo forecast which was 300 million tonnes too low and an oil trade forecast which was 400 million tonnes too high.

## STAGE 3: AVERAGE HAUL FORECAST

There are two alternative ways of forecasting average haul. The simple way is to project historic trends in the average haul for each commodity, attempting to identify the factors that might cause the average haul to increase or decrease. In the case of the crude oil trade, for example, an increase in the market share of Middle East oil producers would increase the average haul and vice versa.

Another approach is to analyse the trade matrix for each commodity, and from this to calculate the average haul. This is technically possible and probably worthwhile for some of the larger commodities such as oil, iron ore, coal and grain. For others it is extremely difficult because the information about the trade matrix is difficult to obtain, and the time taken to produce a matrix forecast is disproportionate to the small amount of trade involved. A compromise is to study the average haul of the major commodities in some detail, whilst extrapolating past trends for the remainder of the trade.

### STAGE 4: THE SHIP DEMAND FORECAST

As we saw in Chapter 4, ship demand should be measured in ton miles of cargo to be transported. The total requirement for transport is calculated by multiplying seaborne trade by the average haul. Some forecasters take an additional step and calculate the ship requirement in deadweight tons. This presents conceptual problems because the productivity of the fleet is a supply variable – it is the shipowner who decides how fast his ship should travel – but it is easier for users to understand because it can be compared directly with the fleet. Typically the merchant fleet transports about 7.3 tons per deadweight each year and that is a useful rule of thumb for converting tons of cargo into deadweight demand (see stage 6).

### STAGE 5: THE MERCHANT FLEET FORECAST

The supply side of the forecast starts by taking the available merchant fleet in the base year, adding the predicted volume of deliveries and subtracting the forecast volume of scrapping, conversions, losses and other removals. Forecasting scrapping and deliveries is complicated because these are behavioural variables. The minute freight rates go up, shipowners stop scrapping and start ordering new ships. For this reason the forecast needs to be made on a dynamic basis, preferably year by year using a computer model that adjusts scrapping and new ordering in line with the overall supply–demand balance.

### STAGE 6: SHIP PRODUCTIVITY FORECAST

As we saw in Chapter 4, the productivity of a ship is measured by the number of ton miles of cargo carried per deadweight of merchant shipping capacity per annum. There are two forecasting methods. The simplest is to take a statistical series of the past productivity of the merchant fleet either in tons per deadweight or ton miles per deadweight (see Figure 4.8) and project this forward, taking account of any changes of trend that may be thought appropriate. Since productivity depends on market conditions, the forecast ought to be developed on a dynamic basis that recognizes that when market conditions improve the fleet will speed up and vice versa. A more thorough methodology for building up a forecast of productivity in this way would use an equation like (6.7) in Chapter 6.

## STAGE 7: THE SHIPPING SUPPLY FORECAST

The shipping supply is calculated in ton miles by multiplying the available dead-weight tonnage of ships by their productivity. By definition, supply must equal demand. If supply is greater than demand, the residual is assumed to be laid up or absorbed by slow steaming; if supply is less than demand, the fleet productivity must be increased.

## STAGE 8: THE BALANCE OF SUPPLY AND DEMAND

As we have already stressed, a supply–demand model of this type contains behavioural variables, particularly the scrapping and investment variables. This is the most difficult part of the model. We know that supply must equal demand, and if the forecast level of supply does not match the forecast level of demand, then we must go back through the whole process again and make the adjustments that we believe the market would make in response to financial stimuli such as asset prices, freight rates and market sentiment.

## STAGE 9: FREIGHT RATES

Now we come to the heart of the forecast, the level of freight rates which will accompany each level of supply and demand. We discussed the relationship between supply, demand and freight rates in Chapter 4, relating demand to the shipping supply function and showing how prices are established in different time-frames. This is the method which should be used. From a technical viewpoint the most difficult element to model accurately is the J shape of the supply curve. Regression equations relating freight rates to laid-up tonnage do not generally work very well due to the difficulty of finding a functional form which picks up the 'spiky' shape of freight graph. Simulation models offer a more satisfactory solution.

A typical market forecast generally includes predictions of the rate of growth of ship demand, the requirement for newbuilding tonnage and the overall balance of supply and demand. There may also be scenarios of freight rates and prices.

Finally, a word of caution. Analysts who successfully design and use a model of this type will learn an important lesson about the freight market which only becomes obvious when the relationships are quantified. As the market modelled approaches balance, the freight rates become so sensitive to small changes in assumptions that the only way to produce a sensible forecast is to adjust the assumptions until the model predicts a level of freight rates which is determined by the forecaster. That is the nature of the market. When there are two ships and two cargoes freight rates are determined by market sentiment at auction, and economics cannot tell us how the auction will develop. At their best shipping market models are educational in the sense that they help decision-makers to understand in simple graphic terms what could happen, but when it comes to predicting what will actually happen to freight rates they are very blunt instruments.

## Sensitivity analysis

Forecasting models can be used to develop sensitivity analyses which explore how much the forecast changes as a result of a small change in one of the assumptions. A 'base case' forecast is first established using a reasonable set of assumptions, then small changes are made to the input assumptions and the resulting changes in the target variable are recorded. For example, the model might be used to explore the impact of lower industrial growth or higher scrapping on projected freight rates and a table compiled showing the change in each exogenous variable and the corresponding change in the target variable.

In theory this technique allows the user of the forecast to understand the sensitivity of the forecast to small changes in assumptions, but in the maritime economy there are many interrelationships which cannot be quantified with sufficient clarity to make this sort of sensitivity analysis totally 'automatic'. A change in the assumption for world industrial growth might reduce trade and trigger a fall in freight rates. However, in the real world lower freight rates may result in higher scrapping, so the market mechanism compensates for the lower growth in subsequent periods. Models are rarely capable of reflecting these behavioural interrelationships automatically and just changing one assumption whilst leaving everything else the same does not necessarily accurately reproduce the way the market mechanism works.

## 17.7 DEVELOPING A SCENARIO ANALYSIS

A third approach to forecasting is scenario analysis. The problem it deals with is communication between the analyst and the decision-maker. By the end of his market study the forecaster may be an expert, but how does he convey this knowledge to the decision-maker? And how does he take advantage of the decision-maker's own knowledge? Scenario analysis tackles this problem head on by involving the decision makers in the forecasting process. Scenarios are developed in a seminar forum with executives working alongside analysts. This avoids the rigidity of formal models which can over-simplify complex issues and be biased towards quantifiable variables. It also provides a better opportunity to focus on weighing up which issues are likely to be important.

The scenario approach was developed by Herman Kahn in his work for the Rand Corporation in the 1950s. He borrowed the term 'scenario' from the film industry, where the 'scenario' of a film outlines its plot and the mood of each successive scene. Khan's scenarios aimed to deal with the future in the same sort of way. Over the years this approach has been adapted and developed, often by big corporations (though nobody has yet tried producing feature length movies!). One approach is to start with a base-case scenario which takes the current 'plot' and develops it forward into a 'surprise-free' scenario which continues much as the past. From this base, alternative scenarios are developed by systematically discussing the developments which could produce different scenarios. Generally the scenarios are developed in clusters of two or three, normally covering long periods.

A systematic methodology for scenario analysis might consist of phases as follows:

1. A group of analysts manage the analysis and ask the assembled group of experts and managers to name the issues which they feel will be most important in determining how events will develop over the time-scale of the forecast. This can be done by splitting the group into working parties and asking each to report back with a list of issues.

2. Compile a list of 'key' issues based on the responses of the various groups and discuss the significance of each. The aim of this part of the analysis is to establish the facts that will be important in future, for example demographics, geography, political alignments, industrial developments, and resources.

3. Feed the edited list back to the working party and ask them to rank the issues in order of importance, using weights on the scale 1 to 10. Analyse the results and identify the variables on which there is greatest consensus, and those on which there is least agreement.

4. From this base develop a social, technical, economic and political 'no change' scenario, and alternatives in which the most important variables are changed, and prepare a report summarizing the results.

Scenario analysis is a way of encouraging management and staff in large organizations to become more aware of the issues which will be facing the company in future. Because it is based on 'systematic conjecture' it is much easier to range widely, but it requires skill and judgement to narrow down the range of possible trends to the few which are significant.

In conclusion, scenario analysis can be a useful way of defining the long-term business risks and opportunities. However, it is demanding in terms of time, calls for intellectual energy, and the results are difficult to encapsulate and distribute. The risk of a single quantified model forecast is that it ignores key issues. The risk of a scenario analysis is that it becomes so blurred that it is of little value.

## 17.8 ANALYTICAL TECHNIQUES

We will now briefly review the analytical techniques which are available. Four of the most popular forecasting techniques are summarized in Table 17.2. A brief review of their different capabilities will help to give newcomers to forecasting an idea of what to expect.

- *Opinion surveys* ask people 'in the know' what they expect to happen. Lots of shipping people do this informally, but there are structured methodologies such as the Delphi technique or opinion surveys. This technique is particularly useful for picking up emerging trends that are obvious to specialists but are not apparent from past data. The approach can be formal, using a panel, or informal.

**Table 17.2** Overview of five analytical techniques used in shipping

| Analytical technique | Main characteristic |
|---|---|
| **1  Opinion survey** | |
| Delphi technique | Discussion session in which group of experts make a consensus forecast |
| Opinion surveys | Send questionnaire to selection of experts and analyse results |
| **2  Trend analysis** | |
| Naive | Simple rule e.g. 'no change', or 'if earnings are more than twice OPEX they will fall' |
| Trend extrapolation | Fit a trend using one of several methodologies and extrapolate forward |
| Smoothing | Smooth out fluctuations to obtain average change, and project this |
| Decomposition | Split out trend, seasonality, cyclicality and random fluctuations, and project each separately |
| Filters | Forecasts are expressed as a linear combination of past actual values and/or errors |
| Autoregressive (ARMA) | Forecasts expressed as a linear combination of past actual values |
| Box–Jenkins model | Variant of the ARMA model, with rules to deal with the problem of stability |
| **3  Mathematical model** | |
| Single regression | Estimated equation with one explanatory variable to predict target variable |
| Multiple regression | Estimated equation with more than one independent variable to predict target variable |
| Econometric models | System of regression equations to predict target variable |
| Supply–demand models | Estimate supply and demand from their component parts and predict change in balance |
| Sensitivity analysis | Examine the sensitivity of the forecast to different assumptions |
| **4  Probability analysis** | |
| Monte Carlo | Probability analysis used to calculate the likelihood of a particular outcome occurring. |

- *Trend analysis* identifies trends and cycles in past data series (time series). The naive forecast extrapolates recent trends into the future, a quick approach because there are no tricky exogenous variables to forecast, but it gives no indication of when or why the trend may change. More sophisticated trend analysis analyses the underlying trends, cycles and the unexplained residuals. With one grand gesture the trends and cycles tell us what will happen, but the forecaster still has to decide whether past trends will change.
- *Mathematical models* go a step further and explain trends by quantifying the relationships with other explanatory variables. For example, how much does the oil trade grow if world industrial production increases? By estimating equations which quantify relationships like this we can build a model to predict the oil trade.
- *Probability analysis* uses a completely different approach. Instead of predicting what will happen, probability analysis estimates the chance of a particular outcome occurring. For example, probability analysis might tell the decision-maker that

there is a 20% chance that freight rates will be $20,000 per day next year. This approach only works if you can find a way of calculating probability in numeric terms.

Analysts can approach each of these techniques at several different levels. In all cases there is a quick approach which requires little special skill and yields nearly instant results, and a sophisticated version which is a specialist subject in itself. In this section we will concentrate on the quick forecasting methods and limit the discussion of the sophisticated methods to a review of the general issues involved.

## Opinion surveys

Opinion surveys involve canvassing the opinion of other experts. This is a good way of investigating issues that are constantly changing, and this approach is a firm favourite with shipping decision-makers who are constantly on the lookout for insights from experts. For analysts it can be a useful way of finding market intelligence, and opinion surveys approach the task in a structured way designed to provide a balanced appraisal of what experts in the industry think is important. Of course there is no guarantee that the issues identified will be correct, but in an industry driven by sentiment, knowing what others think has its uses (but see the dangers of consensus forecasting in Section 17.9).

## Time series analysis

Statistical techniques for analysing time series range from the straightforward to the highly sophisticated. In its simplest form trend extrapolation requires little technical knowledge, while the more sophisticated forms of exponential smoothing are complex, involving advanced mathematical skills.

### TREND EXTRAPOLATION

The simplest time series technique is trend extrapolation. A forecast is made by calculating the average growth rate between two points in a time series and extrapolating into the future. That is all there is to it, and it is very handy. When there is no data to build a more complex model, or there are hundreds of target variables to predict, it may be the only option. For example, a forecaster predicting the throughput of container terminals in the Mediterranean may have little choice but to extrapolate trends in the trade on each route, because all he has is a time series of past container lifts and no idea what is in them. Trend extrapolation may be simplistic, but it is better than nothing.

However, it is important to be aware of the pitfalls. A time series may look simple, but often there are several different components at work below the surface. Figure 17.5 illustrates the point. The line $A_1A_2$ shows the linear trend ($T$) in the data series; the curve shows the cycle (C) superimposed on the trend; and a small section of a seasonal cycle (S) is also shown. So at any point in time $t$, the value of variable $Y$ will be a mixture of the trend, the two cycles, plus an error term $E$ to reflect the random disturbances that affect all time series, thus:

$$Y_t = T_t + C_t + S_t + E_t \qquad (17.4)$$

In shipping the cycles $C_t$ are the shipping cycles we discussed at length in Chapter 4; the seasonal cycles $S_t$ are found in many trades in agricultural commodities, and especially in oil demand in the Northern Hemisphere; and the trend $T_t$ reflects long-run factors such as the trade development cycle we discussed in Chapter 10.

Because time series mix trends and cycles, extrapolation must be carried out with care. A forecast based on one phase of a cycle, for example between points $B_1$ and $B_2$ in Figure 17.5, is highly misleading because it suggests faster growth than the true trend $A_1A_2$. In fact the cyclical component $C_t$ changes from negative at $B_1$ to positive at $B_2$. Just after point $B_2$ the cycle peaks and turns down, so it would not be correct to extrapolate this trend. This is not just a fanciful example; it is one of the 'bear traps' with which maritime forecasting is littered. The economic

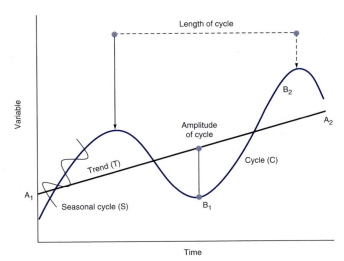

**Figure 17.5**
Cyclical components in a time series model

world dangles the 'bait' of rapid exponential growth in front of forecasters, who are delighted to predict a positive outlook. After all, that is what their clients usually want to hear. But no sooner have they made their positive forecast than the ground opens under them and they are in the trap. Our discussion of 'stages of growth' in Chapter 9 showed that growth rates often change as economies and industries mature, so the fact that a trade has grown at 6% per annum for 10 years does not really prove anything. Trends change.

In conclusion, trend extrapolation is handy for quick forecasts, but the 'bear trap' awaits forecasters who rely on it for long-term structural forecasts. Remember the second principle of forecasting – there must be a rational explanation for the forecast. Data series must be examined to establish what is driving the growth, including cyclical influences, and, as far as possible, these must be taken into account. Fortunately there are well-established techniques for doing this.

## EXAMPLE OF TIME SERIES ANALYSIS

Now we will analyse a time series in a different way, known as 'decomposition analysis'. Figure 17.6 shows a 16-year series for the freight rate for grain from the US Gulf to Japan.

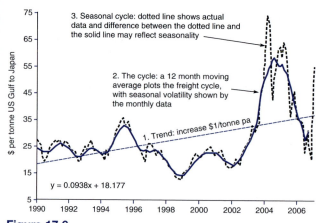

**Figure 17.6**

Grain freight rates – trend and seasonal volatility

Source: CRSL, monthly grain rates US Gulf to Japan

Brokers watch this series carefully for signs that rates are moving in or out of a cycle. We have three components to think about: the trend; some big cycles which seem to peak in 1995, 2000 and 2004; and what looks like short-term volatility which may turn out to be seasonal.

The starting point is the *trend* shown by the flat dashed line on the chart. It increases from $17 per tonne in 1990 to $36 per tonne in 2007. This trend was fitted by linear regression, which we will discuss below. However, it could easily have been drawn in by hand. It increases at a rate of $1 per tonne each year, so if we extrapolate it we find that in 10 years' time, cycles aside, the grain rates will have increased to around $46 per tonne. That is a very significant forecast for anyone running Panamax bulk carriers used in this trade, since it suggests they will be very profitable over the next decade. Naturally that invites the question 'why'. If we had fitted the trend to a slightly shorter data set of data ending in 2002 the positive slope would have disappeared and the rate would be stuck at around $24 per tonne. So have we found a significant trend caused by, for example, the emergence of China as a major importer and exporter? Or it could just be a cyclical effect caused by bulk carriers having an exceptional cycle between 2003 and 2007. Time series analysis gives trends, but not explanations, and a serious forecaster would not let the matter rest there. Research is needed.

Next we can look for signs of *cycles* which are shown by the 12-month moving average. As already noted, Figure 17.6 shows a cycle which peaks in 1995, falls to a trough in 1999, peaks again in 2000, declines in 2002, then finishes with a spectacular peak in 2004. Unfortunately, there is not very much consistency in these cycles, a conclusion that will not surprise readers of Chapter 3 where we argued that shipping cycles are periodic rather than symmetrical.

Finally, there is the *seasonal cycle*. The usual technique for revealing the seasonal cycle is moving averages. The method is simple. Using a monthly time series, we take a 12-month moving average of the US Gulf–Japan freight rate, centring the average in June (a 'centred' moving average calculates the average freight rate for an equal number of months either side of the target date, so if you start in June, the average would be taken from January to December). The resulting 12-month moving average, shown by the solid line in Figure 17.6, has smoothed out the seasonal fluctuations in the data, and we can see how the actual rate shown by the dotted line fluctuates around the 12-month trend. Computation of a moving average helps to squeeze a little extra information out of the data by a separating the seasonal and the trend components.

The next step is to calculate the seasonal cycle by averaging the deviation from the trend for each calendar month, to produce the pattern shown in Figure 17.7. By the magic of statistical analysis the random fluctuations of the dotted line in Figure 17.6 are transformed into the well-defined seasonal cycle in Figure 17.7. It shows that the US Gulf–Japan

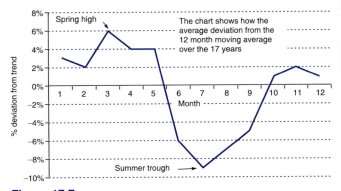

**Figure 17.7**

Grain trade seasonal cycle, 1990–2007

Source: CRSL, monthly grain rates US Gulf to Japan

rate is above trend for the first five months of the year and then dips below trend during months 6–9, before recovering in months 10, 11 and 12. That is exactly what we would expect. The US grain harvest is ready for Gulf loading in October and shipments build up during the following months, reaching a peak in January. They then slump in the last months of the agricultural year when there is less grain to ship. So the statistical analysis supports a common-sense view of what is likely to happen, and we may choose to accept this for forecasting. The cycle in Figure 17.7 can be used to 'correct' trend forecasts and make allowance for seasonal factors. The dip over the summer is quite significant.

## EXPONENTIAL SMOOTHING

This technique is similar to moving averages, but instead of treating each (for example). monthly observation in the same way, a set of weights is used so that the more recent values receive more emphasis than the older ones. This notion of giving more weight to recent information is one that has strong intuitive appeal for managers, and adds credibility to the approach. It is useful for short-term forecasting jobs when there are many target variables.

## AUTOREGRESSIVE MOVING AVERAGE

This takes the whole process of time series analysis a step further. Although the underlying approach is the same as for exponential smoothing, a different procedure is used to determine how many of the past observations should be included in the forecast and in determining the weights to be applied to those observations. The most commonly used technique is the procedure developed by Box and Jenkins.[22] They devised a set of rules for identifying the most appropriate model and specifying the weights to be used. This technique assumes that there are patterns buried in the data. It is particularly good for forecasting large numbers of variables when these are elements of cyclical activity. For example, the sales of many retail products are seasonal and large stores handling

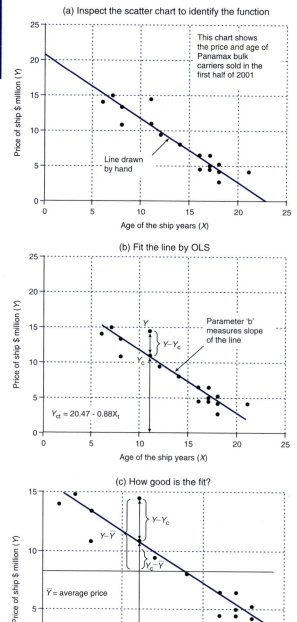

(a) Inspect the scatter chart to identify the function

This chart shows the price and age of Panamax bulk carriers sold in the first half of 2001

Line drawn by hand

(b) Fit the line by OLS

Parameter 'b' measures slope of the line

$Y_{ct} = 20.47 - 0.88X_t$

(c) How good is the fit?

$\bar{Y}$ = average price

**Figure 17.8**
Three steps in fitting a regression equation

thousands of product lines often use this technique to predict sales levels for inventory management.

## Regression analysis

Regression analysis is a useful statistical technique for modelling the relationship between variables in the shipping market. Spreadsheets make estimating regression equations straightforward and, with so much data available in digital form, regression analysis has suddenly gained a new lease of life. Developing big models has become much easier, but regression can also be used for simple jobs. So it is worth looking carefully at the application of this technique. There are excellent textbooks which discuss the methodology in detail, so here we will only deal with the broad principles.

Regression analysis estimates the average relationship between two or more variables. An example explains how this is done. Suppose you are asked to value a Panamax bulk carrier and have available the data on 21 recent ship sales shown by the dots in Figure 17.8(a) – the price is on the vertical axis and age is on the horizontal axis. The ships range in age from 6 to 21 years, and the prices paid range from $2.8 million to $15 million. How do you do it? By fitting a regression equation to the data to estimate the *average* relationship between the dependent variable $Y$ (the sale price) and the independent variable $X$ (the age of the ship when it was sold). Thus we aim to reduce the relationship between $Y$ and $X$ to an equation of the form

$$Y_t = a + bX_t + e_t \qquad (17.5)$$

In this equation, which represents a straight line, '$a$' and '$b$' are parameters (i.e. constants) and $e$ is the error term. The parameter '$a$' shows the value of $Y$ when $X$ is zero (i.e. where the line cuts the vertical axis), the parameter $b$ measures the slope of the line (i.e. the change in $Y$ for each unit change in $X$), and $e$ is the difference between the actual value and the value indicated by the estimated line. This is 'simple regression'. If we have several independent variables it is a 'multiple regression'. The aim is to find the line which fits the data best.

### FITTING A REGRESSION EQUATION

The three main steps are set out below and illustrated graphically in Figure 17.8.

Step 1: *What type of function?* The first step is to plot the data on a scatter diagram and examine it to see whether there appears to be a relationship. In this case the data is plotted in a scatter graph shown in Figure 17.8(a), with the price of the ship ($Y$) on the vertical axis, and the age ($X$) on the horizontal axis. We seem to have a negative linear relationship, since as the variable $X$ increases, the variable $Y$ declines. The points are scattered about, but there is clearly a relationship. If we draw a line by hand we can see if the relationship makes sense. The line crosses the $Y$ axis at about $21 million, which is the value of the parameter $a$, or in economic terms the value of the ship when $X$ (its age) equals zero, that is, the ship is new. It then falls steadily to cross the $X$ axis at about 22.5 years, which is the age of the ship when it has no value. That certainly makes sense. A new Panamax bulk carrier cost about $22 million in the second half of 2001, and on average Panamax bulk carriers get scrapped at about 25 years old. By fitting a regression equation we can estimate the line that fits the data best.[23]

Step 2: *What Equation?* To fit the equation we use the 'ordinary least squares' (OLS) technique. This method calculates the line that produces the smallest difference between the actual values $Y$ and the calculated value which we refer to as $Y_c$ (see Figure 17.8(b)). The values of these parameters which minimize the squared differences $(Y-Y_c)^2$ can be found by solving the 'normal equations' for '$a$' and '$b$'. This can be done using the Regression 'Add-in' provided by most spreadsheet packages. The results are as follows:

$$Y = 20.47 - 0.88X \qquad (17.6)$$

In this case the estimated value of $a$ is $20.47 million and the value of $b$ is $-0.88$, (see Table 17.3) which means that the value of the ship falls by $0.88 million a year. That is very close to the line we fitted by eye.

Step 3: *How good is the fit?* Having found the line which fits the data most closely, the third stage is to examine just how close the fit really is. The OLS technique splits

**Table 17.3** Example of regression statistics for 2 variable equation
SUMMARY OUTPUT (regression of Panamax price on ship age)

**(a) Regression statistics**

| Number of observations | | 21 | |
|---|---|---|---|
| Multiple R | 0.95 | Adjusted R² | 0.90 |
| R² | 0.90 | Standard error | 1.43 |

**(b) Analysis of variances (ANOVA)**

| Row label | df | SS | MS | F | Significance F |
|---|---|---|---|---|---|
| Regression | 1 | 355.6 | 355.6 | 173.3 | 5E-11 |
| Residual | 19 | 39.0 | 2.1 | | |
| Total | 20 | 394.5 | | | |

**(c) Parameter estimates and test statistics**

| Row label | Coeff-icients | Standard error | t stat | P value | Lower 95% | Upper 95% |
|---|---|---|---|---|---|---|
| Intercept | 20.47 | 0.90 | 22.63 | 3.3336E-15 | 18.57 | 22.36 |
| X variable 1 | −0.88 | 0.07 | −13.17 | 5.3277E-11 | −1.02 | −0.74 |

Source: Based on output of regression function produced by popular spreadsheet 'add in'

the variation in $Y$ from its mean into two parts: the part explained by the regression equation, and the 'error' term $e$ which is not explained. This is shown diagrammatically in Figure 17.8(c). From this basic information we can derive three central test statistics, the standard error, the $t$-test, and the correlation coefficient ($R_2$) (see Box 17.2 for definitions). These statistics are a quick way of summarizing how good the fit is. The test statistics in Table 17.3 were obtained for the regression of Panamax price on age illustrated in Figure 17.7. The standard error is 1.43, which tells us that on average $1.43 million variance in the price of a Panamax is not explained by the equation. The $t$ statistic is the value of $b$ divided by its standard error. It should be at least 2 in absolute value. In this case it is −13.2, which is highly significant. Finally, the $R_2$ is 0.9, which tells us that 90% of the variation in $y$ is explained by the equation. So overall the equation works pretty well.

**CALCULATING THE REGRESSION EQUATION**

Although it is quite straightforward to calculate the parameters and test statistics using a spreadsheet, it is easier to use a statistical package which automatically calculates the estimated parameters and a table of test results.[24] The example of a standard table shown in Table 17.3 has three parts. Part (a) shows the number of data observations, which in this case is 21, and the regression statistics – the correlation coefficient and the standard error of regression. Part (b) is an analysis of variance (ANOVA) table describing the relationship between $Y$, $Y_c$ and its mean, as discussed in Figure 17.8. Finally, part (c) shows the coefficients $a$ (the intercept) and $b$, along with their test statistics.

## BOX 17.2 SUMMARY OF TEST STATISTICS

**Test 1: Standard error.** The standard error of the regression measures how well the curve fits the data by calculating the average dispersion of the Y values around the regression line. It is given by:

$$SER = s_Y = \sqrt{\frac{\Sigma(Y - Y_c)^2}{N - K}}$$

where N is the number of observations and K is the number of parameters estimated.

**Test 2: Standard error of the regression coefficient.** Although the standard error is an interesting descriptive statistic, it does not in itself test the equation for significance. To do this we need to establish the confidence limits which can be placed on the estimated value of the regression parameters a and b. If we can make the assumption that b is normally distributed, it is possible to estimate its standard error:

$$s_b = \frac{s_y}{\sqrt{\Sigma x^2}}$$

**Test 3: The t-test.** If the independent variable does not contribute significantly to an explanation of the dependent variable we would expect the estimated value of b to equal zero (i.e. X will vary randomly in relation to Y). To test whether b could have come from a population in which the true value was zero we use the t-test. Divide the coefficient by its standard error ($s_b$)

$$t = \frac{b}{s_b}$$

and look up the resulting ratio in the t-table for N–K degrees of freedom. As a rule of thumb the value of t needs to be at least 2 to pass the test at the 5% significance level. If it is less than 2 the estimated parameter is probably not worth using.

**Test 4: The F statistic.** An alternative test statistic to the t test is the F statistic which is defined as follows:

$$F = \frac{\text{Variance explained}}{\text{Variance unexplained}}$$

Typically F will be a number in the range 1–5, with higher numbers indicating better fit. The statistic is tested by looking up the value of F In a table of critical values for the appropriate degrees of freedom of the numerator and the denominator.

*Continued*

---

**BOX 17.2—cont'd**

Test 5: The coefficient of correlation ($R^2$). A more general measure of the relationship between two variables is the coefficient of correlation. This statistic shows the average variation in $Y$ from its mean as a proportion of the total variation in $Y$:

$$R^2 = \frac{\Sigma(Y_c - \overline{Y})}{\Sigma(Y - \overline{Y})}$$

A little reflection will make it clear that the value of $R$ will fall between 0 and 1 (or −1). This makes the statistic particularly easy to interpret, and probably accounts for its popularity. It can, however, be misleading in time series analysis, since the variances are calculated in relation to the mean and two time series which are changing rapidly will invariably give a higher value of $R$ than two time series which are not growing. For this reason the correlation coefficient should be treated with some caution. In multiple regression the correlation coefficient shows the overall fit of the equation, and is a quick test to see how successful additional variables are in explaining variation in $Y$.

Test 6: The Durbin–Watson statistic. This a test for autocorrelation of the residuals. This statistic should show a value of about 2 and is defined as follows:

$$D = \frac{\Sigma(e_t - e_{t-1})^2}{\Sigma(e_t^2)}$$

$D$ takes values between 0 and 4. Values of $D$ below 2 indicate that the residual values ($e$) are close together and that there is positive autocorrelation which causes bias in the parameter estimates. Values of $D$ above 2 indicate negative autocorrelation.

---

We have already discussed Regression statistics. The correlation coefficient $R^2$ in Table 17.3(a) explains the variation of the dependent variable $Y_c$ from its mean, as a percentage of the total variation. In this case an $R^2$ of 0.9 tells us that 90% of the variation in $Y$ was explained by variations in $X$, which is a good result.

The first column of the ANOVA table in Table 17.3(b) shows the row labels; the second shows the degrees of freedom (df) accruing to the sum of squares appearing in the corresponding row; the third states the sum of squares (SS) of the regression and the residual. The bigger SS is for the regression and the smaller the summed square of the residuals the better; the 4th column shows the mean square (MS). The final column shows the value of $F$, which is the mean square of the regression divided by the mean square of the residual (355.6/2.1), which is a test of goodness of fit and should be looked up in a table of the $F$ distribution for the number of degrees of freedom for the numerator and denominator.

Table 17.3(c) shows the coefficients in the second column and the standard error, the $t$ statistic, $p$ value and the 95% confidence limits. The latter show that we can be 95% certain that the intercept lies in the range 18.57 to 22.36 and the $b$ coefficient lies in the range −1.02 to −0.74. These are useful results.

## MULTIPLE REGRESSION ANALYSIS

Regression analysis can be extended by adding more explanatory variables. Continuing with second-hand prices, we can construct a time series model to forecast the price of a five-year-old Aframax tanker using the data shown in Figure 17.9. This time series starts in 1976, showing many fluctuations in the price over the years which the model needs to explain. In Chapter 4 it was argued that two key

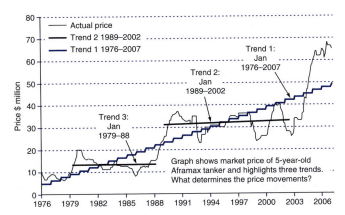

**Figure 17.9**
Example of time series trend analysis
Source: CRSL 5 year old Aframax price

variables drive second-hand prices, newbuilding prices and earnings. To model this we run a multiple regression analysis using the five-year-old price of an Aframax tanker as the dependent variable ($Y$) and the newbuilding price ($X_1$) and one-year time-charter rates ($X_2$) as the independent (exogenous) variables:

$$Y_t = a + b_1X_{1t} + b_2X_{2t} \tag{17.7}$$

where $Y$ is the second-hand price, $X_1$ is measured in millions of dollars and $X_2$ in thousands of dollars per day. Running this regression produces a high $R^2$ of 0.92 and significant $t$ test results for all the parameters. The equation we estimate is

$$Y_t = -10.6 + 0.589X_{1t} + 1.1478X_{2t} \tag{17.8}$$

This equation tells us that on average the second-hand price of the ship increases by $0.589 million for each $1 million increase in the newbuilding price, and $1.148 million for each $1,000 increase in the one-year time charter rates. When we compare the estimated past values shown by the dotted line in Figure 17.10, it is clear that the fit is reasonably close. Throughout the 22-year period the equation explains the main cycles in second-hand prices very well. Its weakness is that it sometimes overestimates the second-hand price at the peak of cycles, and underestimates it at the trough. These are quite significant differences.

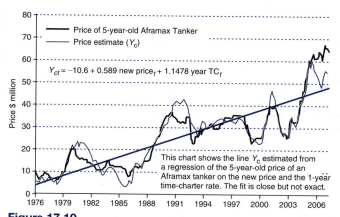

$$Y_{ct} = -10.6 + 0.589 \text{ new price}_t + 1.1478 \text{ year TC}_t$$

This chart shows the line $Y_c$ estimated from a regression of the 5-year-old price of an Aframax tanker on the new price and the 1-year time-charter rate. The fit is close but not exact.

**Figure 17.10**
Example of time series trend analysis
Source: CRSL and estimate

However, there are two important matters to consider before we risk using this model for forecasting. The first is the specification of the model. We have assumed that new prices influence second-hand prices, and got an equation with a good fit. However, in Chapter 15 we argued that shipbuilding prices are influenced by second-hand prices. So which is it? Unfortunately statistical analysis will not answer this question. It is an economic question which we have to resolve by examining how the economics of the shipbuilding price model really works. In fact in, Section 15.4 we suggested that shipyard prices are determined by the interaction of shipbuilding demand and supply functions and one of the demand variables is the second-hand price – when second-hand ships become too expensive shipowners start to buy new ships. So there is much more that could be done to develop this simplistic model before relying on it too much.

This leads on to another common problem, autocorrelation. Since both time-charter rates and newbuilding prices are influenced by the shipping market cycle, they are likely to be correlated (i.e. they move in the same direction at the same time). When this happens it is possible that the parameters are not estimated accurately in the equation. The Durbin-Watson statistic is used to test for autocorrelation. In this case it shows a very low value of 0.12 (ideally it should be about 2), which indicates significant autocorrelation. The value is small because the value of $e_t$ is often very close to the value of $e_{t-1}$. This is a matter which should be addressed.

Unfortunately, in this text space prevents us from exploring this type of modelling further, and indeed many practical forecasters would find the degree of analysis carried out here sufficient for their purposes. The model fits the data well enough, and although it may not work perfectly in some circumstances, as long as we are aware of the underlying risks, we might decide to use the equation anyway to predict second-hand prices in future. After all, there is no point in pouring an enormous amount of effort into a statistical analysis when the estimates for the newbuilding prices and time-charter rates which we feed into the model are likely to be wide of the mark!

Hopefully, this brief review has given readers who are not familiar with statistical analysis a sense of the way it can be used for modelling purposes and the precautions which must sensibly be taken. Sometimes regression equations are used as part of a comprehensive model, but often they can be used in a piecemeal way in different parts of a market report. Or maybe just as a 'rule of thumb' for making a quick forecast 'on assumptions' – for example, to project iron ore imports into Japan, or US oil demand. If nothing else, this type of simple analysis illustrates relationships that have existed in the past, and that is bound to be helpful to the decision-maker who is trying to weigh up what might happen in future.

Regression analysis is simple to apply, but a more thoughtful investigation reveals the fundamental problem that the analyst does not know with any certainty the true relationship between variables, and has available only a limited amount of statistical data from which to estimate these relationships. It is all too easy for these estimated relationships to be biased, producing results which are inaccurate and possibly misleading. Econometrics is the branch of economics which deals with these problems and offers a collection of skills and techniques which allow the practising economist to avoid the pitfalls outlined in the previous example. There are also some excellent texts available on econometric modelling,[25] and many excellent articles on this subject in shipping journals.[26]

## Probability analysis

We began this chapter by observing that forecasts are bound to be wrong sometimes, and this raises the question of probability. Some future events are reasonably predictable. For example, deliveries of ships next year are quite easy to predict because the orders have already been placed. But other shipping variables such as freight rates and prices are much less predictable, changing dramatically from month to month. Faced with this uncertainty, decision-makers might reasonably ask for an analysis of how predictable or unpredictable events are. That, essentially, is the role of probability analysis.

The basic technique involves taking a sample of data, either a time series or a cross-section, and calculating the number of times a particular event occurs. For example, if the basic data is a time series of tanker freight rates, you calculate how often during the sample period freight rates were above or below a particular level. If VLCC freight rates exceeded $60,000 per day 10 times in a data series with 100 entries, then on the basis of this sample, you can say there is a 10% chance that freight rates will exceed $60,000 a day.

As an example, suppose we take a time series of monthly earnings for tankers and bulk carriers, and analyse them into the histograms shown in Figure 17.11. On the horizontal axis this shows monthly earnings divided into $2,000 per day bands. The vertical axis shows the number of months when earnings fell into each band. For example, there were seven months when tanker earnings fell into the $10,000–$12,000 per day band. This frequency distribution gives us a snapshot of the earnings profile of these two market segments, and at a glance it conveys some significant information. Firstly, tankers obviously earned more than bulk carriers. In fact, the average tanker earnings were $21,800 per day, whilst the average bulk carrier earnings were $10,900 per day. Secondly, the earnings profile for tankers is much more widely distributed, ranging from $10,000 per day at the lower end to $68,000 per day at the upper end. In contrast,

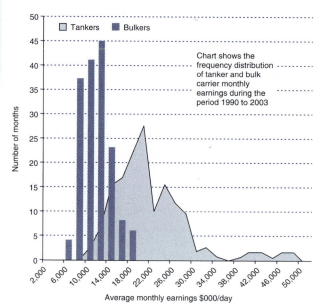

Chart shows the
frequency distribution
of tanker and bulk
carrier monthly
earnings during the
period 1990 to 2003

**Figure 17.11**
Earnings frequency distribution, 1990–2003
Source: CRSL and estimate

the bulk carrier distribution ranges from $4000 per day at the bottom to $18,000 per day at the top. Third, the bulk carrier at distribution is much more compact, with over 40 months in the $10,000–$12,000 per day band, whilst the most heavily populated tanker band has only 28 observations in it.

In fact this data is just a sample, but by using statistical analysis we can calculate the probability of earnings falling within a particular range. For example, if the frequency distribution is normally distributed, the mean and standard deviation can be used to calculate the probability of a particular event occurring. If the break-even earnings of a bulk carrier company are $7,500 per day, we can calculate the probability of earnings falling below that level. The mean bulk carrier earnings are $10,109 per day and the standard deviation is $2,708 per day, so $7,500 per day falls one standard deviation below the mean, which has a 66% chance of occurring. This is fine in theory, but the events of 2003–8 (see Figure 5.7, p. 195) showed that historic probabilities are not always a guide to the future.

This is a simplistic example, but statisticians have developed an extensive body of statistical analysis so that the analysis of probability can be applied to business problems. For example, a shipping banker trying to weigh up the credit risk on a particular loan may know that if the shipowner defaults on his repayments, his main source of collateral is the mortgage on the ship. As the mortgagee, he is entitled to seize the ship and sell it. So he is interested in three questions. First, what is the probability that during the five-year period following the shipowner will default? Second, in the event of a default, what is the probability that the resale value of the ship will equal or exceed the outstanding loan? Third, are there any actions he can take now which will improve the chances of a successful outcome? In such cases probability analysis and more sophisticated uses of it, such as Monte Carlo analysis, can be helpful.

## 17.9 FORECASTING PROBLEMS

There are many obstacles to producing worthwhile forecasts and it is useful to round off our discussion of forecasting methods with a review of some of the errors that can easily trap the unwary, including behavioural issues, problems with model specification and the difficulties of monitoring results:[27]

## Problems with behavioural variables

We will start with a few home truths about our own capabilities. It seems that most of us are programmed to feel overconfident in our ability to make accurate estimates and find it hard to accept that we know so little about the future, preferring to give forecasts that are unrealistically specific.[28] Behavioural economists illustrate this point by asking a group to estimate the value of something they know nothing about (say the length of cable on a VLCC's anchor). Rather than playing safe with a wide range, most participants give a narrow one and miss the right answer. Because we are unwilling to reveal our ignorance by specifying the very wide range, we choose to be precisely wrong rather than vaguely right.[29] The same sort of thing happens with forecasts, and we need to be careful not to be misled. The solution to this problem is to test strategies under a much wider range of forecast scenarios for example by adding 20–25% more downside (or upside) to the extreme cases.

The next problem is *status quo bias*. It is always tempting to forecast that the future will be like the past, even when common sense says that it will not be. When freight rates are high at the top of a cycle we assume that they will always be high, and when low that they will always be low. To make things worse, we often evaluate new developments in the context of the present system and conclude that the new way will not work. This happened to some shipping companies when containerization started to appear in the 1960s. They concluded it would not work because they evaluated it within the framework of the cargo liner system.

The *herding instinct* reinforces status quo bias and is well known in markets, including shipping. When markets are high, there is peer pressure to produce more positive forecasts. Conversely, during recessions forecasts tend to be downgraded. The desire to conform to the behaviour and opinions of others is a fundamental human trait, and when sentiment is pessimistic it is natural to want to fit in. Warren Buffet made the point neatly when he wrote: 'failing conventionally is the route to go; as a group, lemmings may have a rotten image, but no individual lemming ever has received bad press'.[30] This is particularly relevant to shipping cycles. It suggests that forecasters should look to the periphery for innovative ideas and look particularly carefully at counter-cyclical cases.

Finally, we have the issue of *false consensus*. The similarity of forecasts published by several different agencies may give the impression that a particular outcome is likely, but in reality it is often caused by the uncertainty of the agencies as a result of which each keeps an eye on what the other is saying. P.W. Beck, Planning Director for Shell UK Ltd, found that there were few 'uncorrelated estimates' in the work done by so-called independent forecasters.[31] He argued that, uncertain about what to predict, agencies check what other forecasters are saying and follow the consensus. In such cases the fact that all the forecasts are the same is not evidence of a strong case for that particular outcome; it just means nobody is sure what to think.

## Problems with model specifications and assumptions

Another obvious danger area lies in developing the framework (or model) and deciding what assumptions to use. The following problems often occur:[32]

- *Incorrect or superficial model specification.* The forecast may analyse and measure only surface factors and ignore important underlying forces. For example, when considering the future of the seaborne coal trade, it is important to take account of new technology which may, for example, change the type or volume of coal used in steel-making.
- *Too much detail.* There is a research rule of thumb that the researcher will identify 80% of the facts in 20% of the time required to obtain 100% of the facts. Put another way, it is easy to spend a long time investigating interesting but unimportant matters and lose sight of the overall objective.
- *Unchallenged preconceptions.* It is all too easy to assume that certain assumptions or relationships are correct and to accept them without question. Careful examination may show that under some circumstances they may be wrong (look how often forecasters have been caught out by oil price changes). Recall Aristotle Onassis's the assumption in 1956, mentioned earlier in this chapter, that Egypt could not reopen the Suez Canal for several years when in fact they reopened it in a few months.
- *Attempting to predict the unpredictable.* Some variables, such as the actions of small groups of people, are intrinsically unpredictable, and to attempt to predict them can create a false sense of security for decision-makers who assume that the forecast has a 'scientific' basis.

The forecaster needs constantly to ask the question: Am I falling into one of these traps?

## The problem of monitoring results

When we look at past forecasts, we see just how difficult forecasting really is. Even deciding whether a forecast was right is not as easy as it seems. The problem was neatly summarized in an article reviewing the forecasting record of the UK National Institute of Economics and Social Research over a period of 23 years.[33] The article comments:

> It might be imagined that it must be possible, after a certain time has elapsed, to conclude in an unambiguous way whether a forecast has turned out to be correct or not. Unfortunately, the comparison of forecasts with actual results is not nearly as straightforward as it sounds. The first difficulty is that official statistics often leave a considerable margin of doubt as to how big the increase or decrease in output has been. The three measures of GDP (from expenditure, income and output) often give conflicting readings. Moreover the estimates are frequently revised, so that a forecast which originally appeared wrong may later appear right and vice versa. Another difficulty is that forecasts, which were pre-budget, were

conditional on unchanged policies. Since policies often did change it would be inappropriate to compare the forecasts directly with what actually happened.

Assessing the accuracy of shipping forecasts presents just as many problems. In some cases we find that the forecasts are of ship demand, but there are no published statistics of ship demand with which we can compare the forecasts to judge their accuracy. In others, the statistical database has been so manipulated that it requires a considerable effort to reduce currently available statistics to a form comparable with the forecast.

The difficulty of making accurate comparisons of the predictions with actual events led M. Baranto to comment: 'The analysis of forecasting errors is not a simple process – ironically it is as difficult as making forecasts'.[34] Care is needed to produce forecasts that are capable of being monitored quickly and easily by users.

## Objectivity: the problem of escaping from the present

Another challenge facing any forecaster is to escape from the present. An illuminating example of this is provided by a forecast of the British economy in 1984 which was published in the early 1960s. Although this is a long time ago, the study is of particular interest because it was so wide-ranging and explicit in both its assumptions and its predictions. Reviewing the book 20 years later, Prowse draws the following conclusions:[35]

- Some of the basic assumptions that appeared unquestionable at the time have proved to be very wide of the mark. For example, the study contains the passage: 'It has been assumed throughout that no Government in power will permit unemployment to rise above 500,000 (2 per cent of the labour force) for any length of time'. In a similar vein, it assumed that there would be an 'average rise in retail prices of 1–2 per cent per annum'. Neither of these assumptions looked unreasonable in terms of the statistical trends evident in 1964. In fact, by 1984 Britain had unemployment of 10–15% in many areas of the country, while a reduction of the annual inflation rate to 5% per annum was regarded as a major achievement.

- In the area of technological change, the forecasts proved to be equally wide of the mark. Written at a time when the Concorde supersonic liner project was at the development stage, the study anticipated the use of vertical take-off passenger airliners crossing the Atlantic in 1½ hours. As it turned out the airlines, like shipping, preferred economies of scale to cutting-edge technology. In 1984 no new Concordes had been built, and transit times had hardly changed, but 'jumbo jets' had made cheap air travel available on an unprecedented scale. In the motor industry it was the same story. The study anticipated the replacement of the petrol engine by the fuel cell. By 1984 the cars were still basically the same as in the 1960s, but their design had evolved, making them more fuel efficient, better built and relatively cheaper. In all these cases revolution was predicted, but the commercial world chose evolution. Yet some revolutions were overlooked. The potential of computers was recognized in the statement that 'By 1984 the electronic computer will have come into its own', but the study did not anticipate the revolutionary impact which the microchip revolution has had on almost every area of business.

- Another area where problems arose was in the long-term projections of economic growth. The study predicted that UK productivity would increase by 2½% per annum, and taken together with a 17% rise in the labour force, it was expected that real GDP would double by 1984. As it turned out, the stagnation of demand during the 1970s and the failure of productivity increases to materialize meant that the increase in output was only about one-third during the period.

At the time these forecasts were prepared, inflation was running at 1% and within living memory prices had actually fallen; Concorde was the big technical phenomenon; and the first generation of nuclear power stations had been highly successful. In short, the forecasts seemed reasonable and it is easy to see the problems of following any alternative line of thought. A forecast in the mid-1960s that anticipated inflation rates of 20%, or the virtual stagnation of the nuclear power programme, would have been extremely difficult to justify. The one certainty is that things will change and we must not be surprised by surprises.

## 17.10 SUMMARY

Francis Bacon, the sixteenth century man of letters, said that 'if a man will begin with certainties, he shall end in doubts; but if he will be content to begin with doubts, he shall end in certainties'. How right he was. We began with doubts about whether it is sensible to make shipping forecasts, and ended with the certainty that many of the issues confronting forecasters are impossible to predict reliably. But that does not mean forecasting is pointless. Since forecasters are only called on to predict things which are unpredictable, they must expect to be wrong (the forecasting paradox). Their task is not to predict precisely, it is to help decision-makers to reduce uncertainty by obtaining and analysing the *right information* about the present and show how that information can help to understand the future.

All forecast analyses should satisfy three simple criteria: they should be *relevant* to the decision for which they are required; they should be *rational* in the sense that the conclusion should be based upon a consistent line of argument; and they should be based upon *research* at a significant level of detail.

We discussed the preparations for the forecast. The first step is to carefully define the decision being made. Decision-makers have very different requirements and forecasts are used for many different purposes, ranging from speculative investments to budgets and product development by shipbuilders. The forecasting time-scale is also important and we identified four different time horizons: momentary, which is concerned with days or even hours; short term, which is concerned with a period of 3–18 months; medium term, which covers a typical shipping cycle of, say 5–10 years; and long term, which spans the life of a merchant ship. Each time-scale requires a different forecasting technique.

There are three different types of analysis: the market report, a written study designed to provide the client with enough information to form his own views about what might happen in the future; the forecasting model, which uses economic analysis and a computer program to model some aspect of the business in numerical terms; and scenario analysis, which is designed to involve the decision-maker in the process of developing different scenarios about the future. We discussed each of these methodologies in some detail.

We also discussed analytical techniques. Opinion surveys are a good way to identify issues. Time series analysis is an easy way to make a quick forecast, and may be the only viable technique if there are many variables to predict, but can be misleading if several cycles are combined in a single series. Regression analysis is used to model relationships, and requires technical skills to fit regression equations and use the test statistics needed to determine if the equation is valid. Probability analysis takes a different approach. It is used to calculate the chance that a particular outcome will occur. Finally, scenario analysis builds 'future histories'.

These techniques are all useful in developing market models and market reports. Market models typically use a supply–demand framework to model the major market sectors such as crude oil tankers, and bulk carriers. They generally predict freight rates and ship prices. An eight-step programme for developing a market forecasting model was discussed, using the supply–demand analysis developed in Chapter 4 and described in mathematical form in Appendix A.

Market reports generally concentrate on a specific topic and use a less formal structure. They provide information and analysis in a logical framework, leading to conclusions. We discussed a six-stage procedure for planning and developing a study of this type.

In the last section of the chapter we discussed forecasting problems. Many problems are behavioural and arise because we are not as rational as we like to think. For example, we are over-confident about our ability to predict the unpredictable. Other problems arise because the model is incorrectly specified and misses out a key variable; uses consensus assumptions; has too much detail; or accepts assumptions that should be challenged. Monitoring forecasts against actual developments can be difficult. Care must be taken to ensure that predictions are made in a form that is directly comparable with regularly published information.

So forecasting really does matter. The market has just one objective, to reduce the resources used in transportation and get a better deal for the consumer. Gamblers take a chance and speculate, but shipping investors do their homework, calculate the odds, reduce uncertainty and take less risk. So, on average, their decisions should be better. Shipping forecasts have a part to play during those periods when market sentiment is running at the extremes of optimism or pessimism. Clear-sighted analysis and the willingness to take a well-thought-out risk are what mark out the professional investor. He may not get his picture on the front of *Forbes* magazine, but he can still leave a sizeable fortune to his children!

# A An Introduction to Shipping Market Modelling

The early chapters of this book, and particularly Chapter 4, were devoted to a discussion of the economic principles that underlie the shipping market. With the increasing power of microcomputers it has become possible to develop shipping market models that can assist in judging future trends in the shipping market. This appendix provides a brief description of the basic supply–demand framework, using numerical examples. This is not intended to be a complete model, but rather a skeleton that can then be developed in a number of different ways.

Since for most cargoes there is no viable alternative to ships on deep-sea routes, the supply and demand for sea transport can be defined in the following way:

$$DD_t = f(CT_t, AH_t) \tag{A.1}$$

$$SS_t = f(MF_t, P_t) \tag{A.2}$$

where, for year $t$, $DD$ is demand for seaborne transport, $CT$ the tonnages of cargo transported, $AH$ the average haul of cargo, $SS$ the supply of seaborne transport, $P$ is ship productivity and $MF$ the size of the merchant fleet.

Demand, measured in ton miles of transport required, is determined by the tonnage of cargo to be moved and the average distance in miles over which each ton of cargo is transported. The supply of shipping capacity, measured in cargo ton miles, is determined by the merchant fleet capacity measured in deadweight tonnage and fleet performance, which is the average ton miles of cargo delivered per deadweight per annum. Market balance occurs when demand ($DD$) equals supply ($SS$). The cycles which dominate shipping markets are driven by the endless adjustment of these two variables in pursuit of equilibrium. This dynamic process is one of most difficult parts of the shipping market to reproduce in a model.

These definitions are highly simplified, but they make the important point that, in economic terms, although the physical supply of ships is fixed at a given point in time, the available transportation capacity is flexible. As we saw in Chapter 4, transport supply depends on fleet performance, which is in turn determined partly by market variables and partly by physical characteristics of the ships in the fleet.

Building on the definition of supply and demand in equations (A.1) and (A.2), we can specify the basic structural equations of the macro model as follows. The demand equations are:

$$CT_{tk} = f(E_t, ...) \tag{A.3}$$

$$CT_t = \sum_k (CT_{tk}) \tag{A.4}$$

$$DD_{tk} = CT_{tk} - AH_{tk} \tag{A.5}$$

$$DD_{tm} = \sum_k (A_{tkm} DD_{tk}) \tag{A.6}$$

$$A_{tkm} = \frac{DD_{tkm}}{DD_{tk}} \tag{A.7}$$

The supply equations are:

$$MF_{tm} = MF_{(t-,1)m} + D_{tm} - S_{tm} \tag{A.8}$$

$$AMF_{tm} = MF_{tm} - L_{tm} \tag{A.9}$$

$$SS_{tm} = AMF_{tm} - P_{tm} \tag{A.10}$$

Finally, an equilibrium condition is required:

$$SS_{tm}(FR_{tm}) = DD_{tm}(FR_{tm}) \tag{A.11}$$

In the above equations, again for year $t$, $E$ is an indicator of economic activity, $A$ is the market share of ship type $m$ *(tankers, ...)*, $D$ represents deliveries of merchant ships (m.dwt), $S$ the amount of scrapping of merchant ships, $P$ is ship productivity as in equation (A.2), $AMF$ represents the active merchant fleet (m.dwt), $L$ the laid-up tonnage, $FR$ the freight rate, and $k$ is an index representing the commodities (oil, ...).

Dealing first with the demand side of the model, in equations (A.3) and (A.4) we define seaborne trade as the aggregate of $k$ individual commodity trades. The simplest forecasting model would treat seaborne trade in aggregate, as we did in the example in Chapter 14. This simulation analysis emphasized the importance of treating major commodity trades separately. Clearly the oil trade should be modelled separately in a way which takes account of developments in the energy market such as changing energy prices.

**746**

A more detailed discussion of the approach to specifying the form of the functions in equation (A.3) is presented in Chapter 7. If this approach is followed the trade model can become complex and very time-consuming to update. Alternatively, the volume of seaborne trade by commodity may be treated as an exogenous variable, and obtained from some other source, for example by using forecasts of trade published by consultancy organizations.

Moving on to equation (A.5), the volume of ship demand generated by each commodity, $k$, and measured in ton miles is the product of the tonnage of cargo of each commodity and its average haul. At this stage, demand is expressed in terms of the total ton miles of demand generated by each commodity, $k$, and it is still necessary to transform this into demand by ship type, $m$. This is done in equation (A.6), which shows that the demand for ship type $m$ is defined as the market share of that ship type in each commodity trade, summed over all commodities. This is a simple relationship to write in algebraic terms, but is much more difficult to define in practice. In reality trade will be carried in whatever ships are available, which depends on what shipowners order, so analysing investment trends may be the answer.

We pick this up on the supply side of the model in equation (A.8), which defines the fleet of ship type $m$ as equalling the fleet in the previous year, plus deliveries minus scrapping during the year. This fleet includes all vessels of type $m$ potentially available, but at any given time part of the fleet will not be trading. Equation (A.9) derives the active merchant fleet by deducting laid-up tonnage from the total merchant fleet. This equation could be extended to include other categories of inactive tonnage, for example oil tankers in storage. Finally, equation (A.10) shows that the supply of shipping capacity for ship type $m$ is determined by the product of the active fleet and the productivity of that fleet, measured in ton miles of cargo delivered per annum.

The balancing condition in the model is shown in equation (A.11), which specifies that the available ton mile supply of transport capacity of type $m$ equals the ton mile demand at the equilibrium freight rate. If too much supply is available, the freight rate will fall until equilibrium is achieved, by additional vessels being laid up or reduced steaming speeds. Conversely, if there is too much demand, the freight rate will rise until the demand is satisfied, though in the extreme case this may not be possible owing to the time-lag in delivering new ships.

The simple model set out in equations (A.3)–(A.11) is deterministic, in the sense that the key equations take the form of simple algebraic identities. The model is also closed, in the sense that any change in demand must be matched by an identical change in supply, and vice versa.

As a practical illustration of the basic shipping market model, we can take the three market segments for oil tankers, combined carriers and dry cargo vessels. The model calculations are illustrated for tankers in Table A.1 and can be briefly summarized as follows:

1. Starting from the oil trade in column 1 and average haul in column 2, the oil trade is calculated in billions of ton miles in column 3. A forecast would require predicting both of these variables exogenously.

**Table A.1**  Supply–demand model, tanker fleet

| Year | Trade volume mt | Av. haul miles | Transport required btm | combined carriers btm | Total demand btm | Fleet productivity tm dwt per annum | Active tanker fleet | less: laid up | less: storage & grain | Total tanker fleet |
|---|---|---|---|---|---|---|---|---|---|---|
| | (1) | (2) | (3) | (4) | (5) | (6) | (7) | (8) | (9) | (10) |
| 1963 | 582 | 4,210 | 2,450 | – | 2,450 | 35,871 | 68.3 | 0.7 | 1.0 | 70 |
| 1964 | 652 | 4,248 | 2,770 | – | 2,770 | 37,534 | 73.8 | 0.5 | 1.7 | 76 |
| 1965 | 727 | 4,292 | 3,120 | 24 | 3,096 | 38,128 | 81.2 | 0.4 | 3.4 | 85 |
| 1966 | 802 | 4,152 | 3,330 | 53 | 3,277 | 36,330 | 90.2 | 0.4 | 3.4 | 94 |
| 1967 | 865 | 4,775 | 4,130 | 162 | 3,968 | 39,171 | 101.3 | 0.3 | 1.4 | 103 |
| 1968 | 975 | 5,077 | 4,950 | 358 | 4,592 | 40,565 | 113.2 | 0.2 | 0.6 | 114 |
| 1969 | 1,080 | 5,194 | 5,610 | 400 | 5,210 | 40,671 | 128.1 | 0.2 | 0.7 | 129 |
| 1970 | 1,193 | 5,440 | 6,490 | 465 | 6,025 | 40,709 | 148.0 | 0.2 | 0.8 | 149 |
| 1971 | 1,317 | 5,664 | 7,460 | 714 | 6,746 | 40,541 | 166.4 | 1.2 | 0.4 | 168 |
| 1972 | 1,446 | 5,982 | 8,650 | 920 | 7,730 | 42,034 | 183.9 | 1.4 | 0.7 | 186 |
| 1973 | 1,640 | 6,232 | 10,220 | 1,255 | 8,965 | 41,834 | 214.3 | 0.3 | 1.4 | 216 |
| 1974 | 1,625 | 6,535 | 10,620 | 1,084 | 9,536 | 37,707 | 252.9 | 0.7 | 0.7 | 254 |
| 1975 | 1,496 | 6,504 | 9,730 | 826 | 8,904 | 33,856 | 263.0 | 26.8 | 1.1 | 291 |
| 1976 | 1,670 | 6,695 | 11,180 | 841 | 10,339 | 36,951 | 279.8 | 38.5 | 2.2 | 321 |
| 1977 | 1,724 | 6,647 | 11,460 | 912 | 10,548 | 35,160 | 300.0 | 30.3 | 1.6 | 332 |
| 1978 | 1,702 | 6,251 | 10,640 | 676 | 9,964 | 34,205 | 291.3 | 32.8 | 4.5 | 329 |
| 1979 | 1,776 | 5,912 | 10,500 | 635 | 9,865 | 33,947 | 290.6 | 14.8 | 21.4 | 327 |
| 1980 | 1,596 | 5,783 | 9,230 | 404 | 8,826 | 28,582 | 308.8 | 7.9 | 8.0 | 325 |
| 1981 | 1,437 | 5,699 | 8,190 | 368 | 7,822 | 26,408 | 296.2 | 13.0 | 11.0 | 320 |
| 1982 | 1,278 | 4,914 | 6,280 | 389 | 5,891 | 23,744 | 248.1 | 40.8 | 12.0 | 301 |
| 1983 | 1,212 | 4,587 | 5,560 | 328 | 5,232 | 23,922 | 218.7 | 52.4 | 15.0 | 286 |
| 1984 | 1,227 | 4,603 | 5,648 | 285 | 5,363 | 26,051 | 205.9 | 46.0 | 17.0 | 269 |
| 1985 | 1,159 | 4,450 | 5,157 | 304 | 4,853 | 24,779 | 195.9 | 34.9 | 15.0 | 246 |
| 1986 | 1,263 | 4,675 | 5,905 | 479 | 5,426 | 26,208 | 207.0 | 20.8 | 14.0 | 242 |
| 1987 | 1,283 | 4,689 | 6,016 | 480 | 5,536 | 25,669 | 215.7 | 11.0 | 14 | 241 |
| 1988 | 1,367 | 4,770 | 6,510 | 355 | 6,155 | 26,717 | 230.4 | 4.0 | 11 | 245 |
| 1989 | 1,460 | 4,984 | 7,276 | 316 | 6,960 | 28,523 | 244.0 | 2.3 | 7.2 | 254 |
| 1990 | 1,526 | 5,125 | 7,821 | 445 | 7,376 | 29,995 | 245.9 | 2.3 | 11.7 | 260 |
| 1991 | 1,573 | 5,268 | 8,287 | 403 | 7,884 | 30,360 | 259.7 | 2.2 | 5.4 | 267 |
| 1992 | 1,648 | 5,217 | 8,597 | 398 | 8,199 | 31,221 | 262.6 | 5.8 | 4.5 | 273 |
| 1993 | 1,714 | 5,266 | 9,026 | 411 | 8,615 | 32,057 | 268.8 | 4.5 | 5.2 | 278 |
| 1994 | 1,771 | 5,189 | 9,190 | 314 | 8,876 | 33,145 | 267.8 | 3.5 | 3.6 | 275 |
| 1995 | 1,796 | 5,105 | 9,169 | 212 | 8,957 | 33,674 | 266.0 | 2.5 | 6.5 | 275 |
| 1996 | 1,870 | 5,099 | 9,535 | 319 | 9,216 | 33,782 | 272.8 | 2 | 3.9 | 279 |
| 1997 | 1,929 | 5,122 | 9,880 | 378 | 9,502 | 34,756 | 273.4 | 3 | 4.4 | 281 |
| 1998 | 1,937 | 5,090 | 9,859 | 403 | 9,456 | 33,629 | 281.2 | 1.6 | 3.1 | 286 |
| 1999 | 1,965 | 5,107 | 10,035 | 387 | 9,648 | 33,961 | 284.1 | 1.5 | 3.2 | 289 |
| 2000 | 2,027 | 5,064 | 10,265 | 382 | 9,883 | 33,776 | 292.6 | 1.4 | 1.8 | 296 |
| 2001 | 2,017 | 5,047 | 10,179 | 408 | 9,771 | 34,023 | 287.2 | 2 | 1.7 | 291 |
| 2002 | 2,002 | 4,944 | 9,898 | 374 | 9,524 | 32,769 | 290.6 | 3 | 1.5 | 295 |
| 2003 | 2,113 | 5,007 | 10,580 | 293 | 10,287 | 33,976 | 302.8 | 0.4 | 0.6 | 304 |
| 2004 | 2,254 | 4,925 | 11,100 | 106 | 10,994 | 34,415 | 319.5 | 0.1 | 0.5 | 320 |
| 2005 | 2,308 | 4,965 | 11,460 | 109 | 11,351 | 33,120 | 342.7 | 0.1 | 0.5 | 343 |

| | | | |
|---|---|---|---|
| (1) | Fearnleys Annual Review - oil and products | (6) | (5)/(7)×1,000 |
| (2) | (3)/(1) | (7) | (11)–(8)–(9) |
| (3) | Fearnleys Annual Review - oil and products | (8) | Fearnleys Review |
| (4) | Fearnleys Review 2006, assumes 4,551 average haul | (9) | Fearnleys Review incl. tankers in Grain |
| (5) | (3)–(4) | (10) | CRSL Shipping Review and Outlook |

2. Oil tanker demand in column 5 is calculated by deducting combined carrier cargo (column 4) from oil trade (column 3). This calls for a judgement about how the combined carrier fleet will change in size and how it will be distributed between the oil and dry cargo trades. This is usually a matter of relative freight rates, which means that so long as there is a combined carrier fleet the tanker market cannot be treated in isolation from the rest of the market (though as the combined carrier fleet shrinks the link is becoming more tenuous).

3. The supply of tanker capacity starts from the total fleet in column 10, deducts tankers in grain (a rarity nowadays) and tankers in oil storage (column 9) and tankers laid up (column 8), deriving the active tanker fleet in column 7.

4. Fleet productivity is shown in column 6 in ton miles per deadweight per annum and tanker supply in column 6 in billion ton miles.

The statistics in this table provide historical trends showing the relationships between the variables and the way they have changed in the past. To make a forecast requires input assumptions for the tanker fleet, trade and the combined carrier fleet in oil. From these variables surplus tonnage can be calculated as the balancing item, on the assumption that supply must equal demand. Substituting these into the model, the volume of surplus tonnage can be calculated. This supply–demand model can be progressively enlarged so that it generates its own forecasts of the key assumptions, for example by introducing equations to predict the future level of oil trade, average haul, fleet growth, etc. (see Chapter 14). Since the variables on the supply side include behavioural variables, automating them is very difficult.

Once the level of surplus tonnage has been established, an estimate can be made of the level of freight rates. In extreme cases where there is a very large surplus this is easy. We know that freight rates will fall to operating costs. The difficulty lies in modelling market behaviour when the demand curve is hovering in the 'kink' of the supply curve. Sometimes this is done with regression equations, but a simulation model is likely to work better. Whatever method is used, the first lesson modellers learn is that when the market is close to balance, tiny changes in supply or demand send rates shooting up or down, which makes forecasting very difficult. Unfortunately, that is how the shipping market works. If it was easy to predict, there would be no need for a market!

# B Tonnage Measurement and Conversion Factors

A problem that recurs frequently in the shipping industry is the need to measure the size of a ship or the size of a fleet of ships. One reason for doing this is to measure the cargo-carrying capacity, but there are many other commercial reasons. For example, port authorities will wish to charge large ships higher wharfage fees than small ships, and the same applies to the Panama and Suez canal authorities. To meet these needs a whole range of different measurement units have been developed in the shipping industry, each adapted to some particular need. Here we briefly review the principal units currently in use.

## GROSS REGISTERED TONNAGE

One major issue of concern to shipowners, particularly liner companies handling low-density cargo, is the internal volume of the ship, and before 1969 this was recorded by the gross registered tonnage (grt). This was a measure of the total permanently enclosed capacity of the ship and consists of:

- underdeck tonnage;
- 'tweendeck tonnage;
- superstructures;
- deckhouses and other erections.

Certain spaces such as navigational spaces (wheel-house, chart rooms, etc.), galleys, stairways, light and air spaces are exempted from measurement, in order to encourage their adequate provision. The official gross tonnage of a vessel is calculated by the government surveyor when it is first registered. One ton equals 100 cubic feet of internal space.

## GROSS TONNAGE

The 1969 IMO Tonnage Convention introduced a new simplified standard procedure for calculating gross tonnage (gt), and this is now used in all countries that are signatories to the convention. Instead of going through the laborious process of measuring every open space in the ship, the gross tonnage is calculated from the total volume of all enclosed spaces, measured in cubic metres, using a standard formula. For some ship types, especially those with complex hull forms, the gt and the grt may be significantly different.

## NET REGISTERED TONNAGE

Under the existing rules, net registered tonnage is supposed to represent the cargo volume capacity of the ship and is obtained by deducting certain non-revenue-earning spaces from the grt. The net registered tonnage is expressed in units of 100 cubic feet.

## NET TONNAGE (1969)

A formula introduced by the 1969 Tonnage Convention gives net tonnage (1969) as a function of the moulded volume of all the ship's cargo spaces, with corrections for draughts less than 75% of the ship's depth and for the number of berthed and unberthed passengers. The net tonnage so calculated cannot be less than 30% of gt. The net tonnage is also dimensionless.

## DEADWEIGHT

In many trades the principal concern is with measuring the cargo-carrying capacity of a fleet of ships, and for this purpose deadweight tonnage (dwt) is used. The deadweight of a ship measures the total weight of cargo that the vessel can carry when loaded down to its marks, including the weight of fuel, stores, water ballast, fresh water, crew, passengers and baggage.

As a rule, the non-cargo items account for about 5% of the total deadweight in medium-sized ships, although the proportion is lower in large vessels. As an example, a 35,000 dwt bulk carrier would probably be able to carry about 33,000 dwt of cargo.

Deadweight can also be measured as the difference between the loaded ship displacement and its lightweight (see below for definition).

## COMPENSATED GROSS TONNAGE

This is a measure of shipbuilding output which takes account of the work content of the ship. In the early 1970s, shipbuilders in Europe and Japan had reached the conclusion that inter-country comparisons of shipbuilding output, measured in deadweight or gross registered tonnage, were unreliable because some ships had a higher work content per gross ton than others. For example, a passenger ferry of 5,000 gross tons may involve the shipbuilder in as much work as a bulk carrier of 15,000 gross tons. To overcome this problem, a new standard unit called compensated gross tonnage (cgt) was developed. This is calculated by multiplying the gross tonnage of a ship by an appropriate conversion ship factor for that ship type.

A set of standard cgt conversion factors were agreed in 1984, but in 2005 they were replaced by a formula which is used to calculate the compensated gross tonnage of the ship from the gross tonnage:

$$\text{cgt} = A \times \text{gt}^B \tag{B.1}$$

where $A$ represents the influence of ship type, and $B$ the influence of ship size and gt is the gross tonnage of the vessel. ($B$ is itself defined as $B=b+1$ where $b$ represents the diminishing influence of ship size on the work input required to build a single gross ton, this factor having been derived from a substantial sampling of shipyard outputs.) The internationally agreed $A$ and $B$ parameters developed on the basis of sampling shipyard output are shown in Table B.1. For example, using this formula and the parameters in Table B.1, a crude oil tanker of 157,800 dwt (see Figure 14.6), of 87,167 gross tons would have a cgt coefficient of 0.36 and a cgt of 31,423.

**TABLE B.1** cgt parameters 2005

| Ship type | A | B |
|---|---|---|
| Oil tankers (double hull) | 48 | 0.57 |
| Chemical tankers | 84 | 0.55 |
| Bulk carriers | 29 | 0.61 |
| Combined carriers | 33 | 0.62 |
| General cargo ships | 27 | 0.64 |
| Reefers | 27 | 0.68 |
| Full container | 19 | 0.68 |
| Ro-ro vessels | 32 | 0.63 |
| Car carriers | 15 | 0.7 |
| LPG carriers | 62 | 0.57 |
| LNG carriers | 32 | 0.68 |
| Ferries | 20 | 0.71 |
| Passenger ships | 49 | 0.67 |
| Fishing vessels | 24 | 0.71 |
| Non-cargo vessels | 46 | 0.62 |

Some examples of cgt coefficients calculated using the formula are summarized in Table B.2. The cgt coefficients in this table were obtained by calculating the cgt and dividing it by the gt to get the cgt coefficient shown in the table. For each ship type the cgt coefficient changes. For example a 50,000 gt container-ship has a cgt coefficient of 0.7, whilst a 50,000 gt tanker has a lower cgt coefficient of 0.46, indicating the lower work content per gross ton. The highest coefficients are for the LNG tankers and the passenger ships. So this table also gives a useful insight into the relative work content of different ship types.

## LIGHTWEIGHT

A ship's lightweight is the weight of the vessel as built, including boiler water, lubricating oil and the cooling system water.

**Table B.2** Approximate cgt coefficients calculated using the 2005 formula

| Ship type | Parameters | | Ship size (gt) | | | | | | |
|---|---|---|---|---|---|---|---|---|---|
| | $A$ | $B$ | 4,000 | 10,000 | 30,000 | 50,000 | 80,000 | 100,000 | 150,000 |
| Crude oil tankers (double) | 48 | 0.57 | 1.36 | 0.91 | 0.57 | 0.46 | 0.37 | 0.34 | 0.29 |
| Chemical tankers | 84 | 0.55 | 1.48 | 1.46 | 1.42 | 1.41 | 1.40 | 1.39 | 1.38 |
| Bulk carriers | 29 | 0.61 | 0.57 | 0.60 | 0.64 | 0.66 | 0.68 | 0.69 | 0.71 |
| Combined carriers | 33 | 0.62 | 1.24 | 1.25 | 1.26 | 1.27 | 1.27 | 1.28 | 1.28 |
| General cargo | 27 | 0.64 | 0.97 | 0.98 | 1.01 | 1.02 | 1.03 | 1.03 | 1.04 |
| Reefers | 27 | 0.68 | 1.39 | 1.45 | 1.51 | 1.54 | 1.57 | 1.58 | 1.61 |
| Container-ships | 19 | 0.68 | 0.70 | 0.70 | 0.70 | 0.70 | 0.70 | 0.70 | 0.70 |
| Ro-o | 32 | 0.63 | 1.11 | 1.06 | 1.01 | 0.98 | 0.96 | 0.95 | 0.93 |
| Car carriers | 15 | 0.7 | 0.84 | 0.89 | 0.96 | 1.00 | 1.03 | 1.05 | 1.08 |
| LPG carriers | 62 | 0.57 | 1.41 | 1.25 | 1.08 | 1.01 | 0.95 | 0.93 | 0.88 |
| LNG carriers | 32 | 0.68 | 1.29 | 1.42 | 1.60 | 1.70 | 1.79 | 1.83 | 1.91 |
| Ferries | 20 | 0.71 | 0.80 | 0.82 | 0.85 | 0.86 | | | |
| Passenger ships | 49 | 0.67 | 1.76 | 1.69 | 1.62 | 1.59 | | | |
| Fishing vessels | 24 | 0.71 | 0.68 | 0.71 | 0.74 | 0.76 | | | |
| Other non-cargo | 46 | 0.62 | 0.91 | 0.84 | 0.76 | 0.72 | | | |

Note: The cgt of a ship is calculated by multiplying the gross tonnage by the appropriate factor in the table. For ship sizes not shown, the cgt coefficients can calculated by interpolation.

## STANDARD DISPLACEMENT

This is the theoretical but accurate weight of the vessel fully manned and equipped, with stores and ammunition but without fuel or reserve feed water.

## SUEZ AND PANAMA TONNAGES

For ships transiting the Suez and Panama canals, different systems of measurement are used to assess the dues payable. All ships have to be specially measured for the assessment of their dues when passing through these areas.

# C Maritime Economics Freight Index, 1741–2007

| Index (market prices) | | | Index (2000 prices) | | Index (market prices) | | | Index (2000 prices) | |
|---|---|---|---|---|---|---|---|---|---|
| Year | Index | % | Deflator | Index | Year | Index | % | Deflator | Index |
| 1741 | 100 | | | | 1776 | 155 | 6% | 1,658 | 2,565 |
| 1742 | 83 | −17% | | | 1777 | 172 | 11% | 1,628 | 2,798 |
| 1743 | 148 | 79% | | | 1778 | 158 | −8% | 1,598 | 2,522 |
| 1744 | 113 | −24% | | | 1779 | 158 | 0% | 1,516 | 2,393 |
| 1745 | 91 | −19% | | | 1780 | 202 | 28% | 1,478 | 2,980 |
| 1746 | 80 | −12% | | | 1781 | 213 | 5% | 1,516 | 3,222 |
| 1747 | 70 | −12% | | | 1782 | 136 | −36% | 1,386 | 1,884 |
| 1748 | 88 | 24% | | | 1783 | 144 | 6% | 1,431 | 2,057 |
| 1749 | 94 | 7% | | | 1784 | 131 | −9% | 1,543 | 2,025 |
| 1750 | 80 | −15% | 1,887 | 1,504 | 1785 | 116 | −12% | 1,556 | 1,799 |
| 1751 | 78 | −2% | 1,971 | 1,540 | 1786 | 113 | −3% | 1,478 | 1,663 |
| 1752 | 69 | −12% | 2,218 | 1,525 | 1787 | 113 | 0% | 1,504 | 1,691 |
| 1753 | 67 | −2% | 2,218 | 1,490 | 1788 | 119 | 6% | 1,478 | 1,756 |
| 1754 | 111 | 65% | 1,868 | 2,072 | 1789 | 141 | 18% | 1,556 | 2,189 |
| 1755 | 152 | 37% | 1,829 | 2,772 | 1790 | 141 | 0% | 1,556 | 2,189 |
| 1756 | 159 | 5% | 1,792 | 2,856 | 1791 | 133 | −6% | 1,539 | 2,044 |
| 1757 | 163 | 2% | 1,774 | 2,883 | 1792 | 192 | 45% | 1,574 | 3,025 |
| 1758 | 150 | −8% | 1,658 | 2,487 | 1793 | 200 | 4% | 1,428 | 2,856 |
| 1759 | 113 | −25% | 1,658 | 1,865 | 1794 | 213 | 6% | 1,399 | 2,973 |
| 1760 | 147 | 31% | 1,628 | 2,391 | 1795 | 192 | −10% | 1,204 | 2,315 |
| 1761 | 175 | 19% | 1,658 | 2,902 | 1796 | 166 | −14% | 1,194 | 1,978 |
| 1762 | 108 | −38% | 1,628 | 1,755 | 1797 | 166 | 0% | 1,307 | 2,164 |
| 1763 | 130 | 20% | 1,628 | 2,111 | 1798 | 273 | 65% | 1,283 | 3,507 |
| 1764 | 119 | −8% | 1,658 | 1,969 | 1799 | 294 | 7% | 1,108 | 3,255 |
| 1765 | 106 | −11% | 1,690 | 1,795 | 1800 | 186 | −37% | 917 | 1,706 |
| 1766 | 91 | −15% | 1,690 | 1,531 | 1801 | 172 | −8% | 888 | 1,526 |
| 1767 | 98 | 9% | 1,690 | 1,663 | 1802 | 239 | 39% | 1,135 | 2,714 |
| 1768 | 89 | −10% | 1,706 | 1,519 | 1803 | 222 | −7% | 1,117 | 2,478 |
| 1769 | 108 | 21% | 1,810 | 1,952 | 1804 | 225 | 1% | 1,117 | 2,513 |
| 1770 | 130 | 20% | 1,774 | 2,301 | 1805 | 222 | −1% | 1,018 | 2,260 |
| 1771 | 120 | −7% | 1,774 | 2,135 | 1806 | 236 | 6% | 1,026 | 2,421 |
| 1772 | 97 | −19% | 1,706 | 1,653 | 1807 | 256 | 9% | 1,057 | 2,709 |
| 1773 | 102 | 5% | 1,690 | 1,716 | 1808 | 303 | 18% | 955 | 2,896 |
| 1774 | 106 | 5% | 1,706 | 1,813 | 1809 | 294 | −3% | 894 | 2,625 |
| 1775 | 145 | 37% | 1,706 | 2,479 | 1810 | 280 | −5% | 905 | 2,532 |

*Continued*

# MARITIME ECONOMICS FREIGHT INDEX, 1741–2007

| Index (market prices) | | | Index (2000 prices) | | Index (market prices) | | | Index (2000 prices) | |
|---|---|---|---|---|---|---|---|---|---|
| Year | Index | % | Deflator | Index | Year | Index | % | Deflator | Index |
| 1811 | 228 | −18% | 955 | 2,179 | 1858 | 88 | −13% | 1,588 | 1,390 |
| 1812 | 242 | 6% | 845 | 2,045 | 1859 | 97 | 11% | 1,531 | 1,483 |
| 1813 | 303 | 25% | 820 | 2,484 | 1860 | 103 | 6% | 1,465 | 1,511 |
| 1814 | 263 | −13% | 899 | 2,361 | 1861 | 106 | 3% | 1,478 | 1,570 |
| 1815 | 178 | −32% | 1,065 | 1,898 | 1862 | 97 | −9% | 1,428 | 1,384 |
| 1816 | 150 | −16% | 1,164 | 1,746 | 1863 | 97 | 0% | 1,405 | 1,361 |
| 1817 | 180 | 20% | 1,049 | 1,886 | 1864 | 108 | 11% | 1,371 | 1,478 |
| 1818 | 166 | −7% | 996 | 1,657 | 1865 | 105 | −2% | 1,428 | 1,506 |
| 1819 | 154 | −7% | 1,082 | 1,667 | 1866 | 97 | −8% | 1,416 | 1,372 |
| 1820 | 161 | 4% | 1,204 | 1,938 | 1867 | 95 | −2% | 1,440 | 1,373 |
| 1821 | 157 | −3% | 1,385 | 2,169 | 1868 | 91 | −5% | 1,465 | 1,328 |
| 1822 | 160 | 2% | 1,574 | 2,513 | 1869 | 94 | 3% | 1,478 | 1,385 |
| 1823 | 174 | 9% | 1,413 | 2,454 | 1870 | 97 | 3% | 1,504 | 1,457 |
| 1824 | 172 | −1% | 1,358 | 2,332 | 1871 | 88 | −10% | 1,504 | 1,316 |
| 1825 | 160 | −7% | 1,226 | 1,955 | 1872 | 109 | 25% | 1,395 | 1,521 |
| 1826 | 147 | −8% | 1,385 | 2,041 | 1873 | 124 | 14% | 1,342 | 1,661 |
| 1827 | 141 | −4% | 1,399 | 1,970 | 1874 | 114 | −8% | 1,384 | 1,582 |
| 1828 | 133 | −6% | 1,443 | 1,916 | 1875 | 105 | −8% | 1,441 | 1,510 |
| 1829 | 132 | −1% | 1,443 | 1,898 | 1876 | 104 | −1% | 1,478 | 1,533 |
| 1830 | 130 | −1% | 1,458 | 1,898 | 1877 | 105 | 1% | 1,441 | 1,510 |
| 1831 | 139 | 7% | 1,458 | 2,032 | 1878 | 96 | −8% | 1,543 | 1,486 |
| 1832 | 125 | −10% | 1,506 | 1,882 | 1879 | 90 | −7% | 1,630 | 1,466 |
| 1833 | 113 | −9% | 1,556 | 1,763 | 1880 | 92 | 2% | 1,571 | 1,447 |
| 1834 | 117 | 3% | 1,592 | 1,866 | 1881 | 92 | 0% | 1,600 | 1,473 |
| 1835 | 125 | 7% | 1,630 | 2,037 | 1882 | 86 | −7% | 1,586 | 1,359 |
| 1836 | 135 | 8% | 1,458 | 1,975 | 1883 | 79 | −7% | 1,615 | 1,282 |
| 1837 | 145 | 7% | 1,474 | 2,130 | 1884 | 68 | −15% | 1,780 | 1,205 |
| 1838 | 153 | 6% | 1,413 | 2,164 | 1885 | 67 | −2% | 1,896 | 1,264 |
| 1839 | 144 | −6% | 1,332 | 1,915 | 1886 | 62 | −6% | 2,005 | 1,252 |
| 1840 | 136 | −5% | 1,345 | 1,828 | 1887 | 69 | 10% | 2,052 | 1,411 |
| 1841 | 109 | −20% | 1,413 | 1,546 | 1888 | 80 | 17% | 2,005 | 1,612 |
| 1842 | 105 | −4% | 1,556 | 1,629 | 1889 | 79 | −1% | 1,960 | 1,555 |
| 1843 | 97 | −7% | 1,731 | 1,677 | 1890 | 68 | −15% | 1,960 | 1,327 |
| 1844 | 108 | 11% | 1,710 | 1,844 | 1891 | 67 | −2% | 1,896 | 1,264 |
| 1845 | 116 | 7% | 1,669 | 1,930 | 1892 | 58 | −13% | 2,005 | 1,167 |
| 1846 | 106 | −8% | 1,611 | 1,711 | 1893 | 63 | 9% | 2,052 | 1,303 |
| 1847 | 127 | 19% | 1,428 | 1,807 | 1894 | 61 | −3% | 2,180 | 1,336 |
| 1848 | 103 | −19% | 1,689 | 1,742 | 1895 | 59 | −3% | 2,236 | 1,325 |
| 1849 | 98 | −5% | 1,872 | 1,843 | 1896 | 59 | 0% | 2,295 | 1,360 |
| 1850 | 98 | 0% | 1,872 | 1,843 | 1897 | 59 | 0% | 2,265 | 1,342 |
| 1851 | 92 | −6% | 1,868 | 1,722 | 1898 | 72 | 21% | 2,180 | 1,569 |
| 1852 | 95 | 3% | 1,847 | 1,761 | 1899 | 69 | −4% | 2,208 | 1,519 |
| 1853 | 128 | 34% | 1,517 | 1,944 | 1900 | 80 | 17% | 2,028 | 1,631 |
| 1854 | 138 | 7% | 1,416 | 1,947 | 1901 | 60 | −25% | 2,101 | 1,268 |
| 1855 | 130 | −6% | 1,428 | 1,852 | 1902 | 52 | −14% | 2,101 | 1,090 |
| 1856 | 119 | −8% | 1,428 | 1,696 | 1903 | 52 | 0% | 2,101 | 1,090 |
| 1857 | 100 | −16% | 1,371 | 1,371 | 1904 | 52 | 0% | 2,076 | 1,077 |

| | Index (market prices) | | Index (2000 prices) | | | Index (market prices) | | Index (2000 prices) | |
|---|---|---|---|---|---|---|---|---|---|
| Year | Index | % | Deflator | Index | Year | Index | % | Deflator | Index |
| 1905 | 54 | 4% | 2,076 | 1,121 | 1952 | 99 | −36% | 650 | 641 |
| 1906 | 55 | 2% | 2,005 | 1,103 | 1953 | 77 | −22% | 645 | 495 |
| 1907 | 57 | 4% | 1,917 | 1,095 | 1954 | 82 | 6% | 640 | 523 |
| 1908 | 48 | −17% | 1,982 | 944 | 1955 | 113 | 39% | 643 | 729 |
| 1909 | 49 | 2% | 1,960 | 954 | 1956 | 133 | 18% | 633 | 845 |
| 1910 | 53 | 9% | 1,875 | 992 | 1957 | 109 | −18% | 613 | 668 |
| 1911 | 61 | 16% | 1,855 | 1,139 | 1958 | 68 | −38% | 596 | 406 |
| 1912 | 83 | 34% | 1,762 | 1,454 | 1959 | 69 | 2% | 592 | 410 |
| 1913 | 72 | −13% | 1,744 | 1,255 | 1960 | 72 | 4% | 582 | 418 |
| 1914 | 71 | −1% | 1,722 | 1,221 | 1961 | 74 | 2% | 576 | 423 |
| 1915 | 211 | 49% | 1,705 | 3,590 | 1962 | 68 | −8% | 570 | 386 |
| 1916 | 386 | 0% | 1,580 | 6,102 | 1963 | 68 | 0% | 563 | 382 |
| 1917 | 735 | 0% | 1,345 | 9,895 | 1964 | 73 | 7% | 555 | 405 |
| 1918 | 795 | 0% | 1,140 | 9,063 | 1965 | 87 | 19% | 547 | 474 |
| 1919 | 519 | 0% | 995 | 5,161 | 1966 | 74 | −15% | 531 | 393 |
| 1920 | 396 | 0% | 861 | 3,408 | 1967 | 84 | 13% | 516 | 433 |
| 1921 | 176 | 66% | 962 | 1,690 | 1968 | 60 | −29% | 495 | 297 |
| 1922 | 138 | −22% | 1,025 | 1,410 | 1969 | 58 | −3% | 469 | 273 |
| 1923 | 130 | −5% | 1,007 | 1,311 | 1970 | 95 | 63% | 444 | 422 |
| 1924 | 128 | −2% | 1,007 | 1,289 | 1971 | 44 | −54% | 425 | 186 |
| 1925 | 116 | −9% | 984 | 1,145 | 1972 | 42 | −5% | 412 | 171 |
| 1926 | 141 | 21% | 973 | 1,369 | 1973 | 135 | 225% | 388 | 524 |
| 1927 | 129 | −8% | 990 | 1,278 | 1974 | 168 | 24% | 349 | 586 |
| 1928 | 119 | −8% | 1,007 | 1,194 | 1975 | 73 | −57% | 320 | 232 |
| 1929 | 122 | 3% | 1,007 | 1,226 | 1976 | 72 | −1% | 303 | 218 |
| 1930 | 98 | −19% | 1,031 | 1,015 | 1977 | 71 | −2% | 284 | 201 |
| 1931 | 95 | −3% | 1,133 | 1,079 | 1978 | 98 | 39% | 264 | 259 |
| 1932 | 93 | −2% | 1,257 | 1,171 | 1979 | 152 | 55% | 237 | 361 |
| 1933 | 90 | −3% | 1,325 | 1,192 | 1980 | 207 | 36% | 209 | 432 |
| 1934 | 90 | 0% | 1,285 | 1,156 | 1981 | 178 | −14% | 189 | 337 |
| 1935 | 93 | 4% | 1,239 | 1,154 | 1982 | 117 | −34% | 178 | 208 |
| 1936 | 109 | 17% | 1,239 | 1,350 | 1983 | 118 | 2% | 173 | 205 |
| 1937 | | | 1,196 | | 1984 | 108 | −9% | 166 | 180 |
| 1938 | | | 1,221 | | 1985 | 98 | −10% | 160 | 157 |
| 1939 | | | 1,239 | | 1986 | 74 | −25% | 157 | 116 |
| 1940 | | | 1,230 | | 1987 | 116 | 58% | 152 | 176 |
| 1941 | | | 1,171 | | 1988 | 164 | 41% | 146 | 239 |
| 1942 | | | 1,056 | | 1989 | 183 | 11% | 139 | 254 |
| 1943 | | | 995 | | 1990 | 167 | −9% | 132 | 220 |
| 1944 | | | 978 | | 1991 | 189 | 13% | 126 | 239 |
| 1945 | | | 957 | | 1992 | 154 | −19% | 123 | 188 |
| 1946 | | | 883 | | 1993 | 175 | 14% | 119 | 209 |
| 1947 | 100 | | 772 | 772 | 1994 | 174 | 0% | 116 | 203 |
| 1948 | 79 | −21% | 715 | 564 | 1995 | 236 | 35% | 113 | 267 |
| 1949 | 71 | −10% | 724 | 517 | 1996 | 172 | −27% | 110 | 189 |
| 1950 | 74 | 4% | 715 | 530 | 1997 | 166 | −4% | 107 | 178 |
| 1951 | 154 | 108% | 662 | 1,023 | 1998 | 110 | −34% | 106 | 116 |

*Continued*

# MARITIME ECONOMICS FREIGHT INDEX, 1741–2007

| Index (market prices) | | | Index (2000 prices) | | Index (market prices) | | | Index (2000 prices) | |
|---|---|---|---|---|---|---|---|---|---|
| Year | Index | % | Deflator | Index | Year | Index | % | Deflator | Index |
| 1999 | 135 | 23% | 103 | 140 | | | | | |
| 2000 | 164 | 21% | 100 | 164 | | | | | |
| 2001 | 145 | −12% | 97 | 141 | | | | | |
| 2002 | 155 | 7% | 96 | 148 | | | | | |
| 2003 | 253 | 63% | 92 | 233 | | | | | |
| 2004 | 425 | 68% | 89 | 379 | | | | | |
| 2005 | 355 | −16% | 86 | 307 | | | | | |
| 2006 | 283 | −20% | 83 | 236 | | | | | |
| 2007 | 587 | 107% | 81 | 477 | | | | | |

Sources

A. 1741–1817 Tyne coal trade freight statistics in shillings per chaldron converted to shillings per ton at 0.85 tons per chaldron; Beveridge *et al*. (1965, pp. 264–95).

B. 1818–1835: Tyne coal trade freight rates from the testimony of James Bentley before the Select Committee on the Coal Trade, *Parliamentary Papers*, 1836, XI, p. 98.

C. 1836–1837: Tyne coal trade freight rates from the testimony of James Bentley before the Select Committee on the Coal Trade (Port of London) Bill, *Parliamentary Papers*. 1837-8, XV, p. 79.

D. 1838–1868: Tyne coal trade freight rates extracted by C.K. Harley from freight quotations in the *Newcastle Courant*, average of six quotes (first week of Jan., May, July, Sept., Nov. or nearest available date).

E. 1869–1936: A composite global freight index compiled by Isserlis (1938).

F. 1947–1959: A dry bulk freight index published monthly as the Norwegian Shipping New's Worldwide Dry Cargo Tripcharter Index July/December 1947=100, average of monthly rates, reproduced from summary tables published in *Norwegian Shipping News* no. 10C, 1970.

G. 1960–1985: Grain freight statistics for a voyage from the US Gulf to Japan via the Panama Canal published in *Fearnleys Review* 1966, Table 9, based on fixtures of vessels 15,000–25,000 dwt and free discharge. Data for later years was reported in subsequent editions of this publication.
By the early 1980s the vessel referred to was a Panamax bulk carrier.

H. 1986–2007: Grain freight statistics for a voyage from the US Gulf to Japan via the Panama Canal published in *Clarkson's Shipping Review and Outlook*, spring 2008, Table 30.

Price deflator: The freight index at 2006 constant prices shown in Figure 3.5 calculated using a composite price deflator based on US and UK prices by Randy Young, Civil Maritime Analysis Department, US Office of Naval Intelligence.

Note: sources A–D were published in summary as a series by Harley (1988).

# Notes

## 1 SEA TRANSPORT AND THE GLOBAL ECONOMY

1 Radcliffe (1985).
2 Drury and Stokes (1983, p. 28) discuss the case of Tidal Marine, which collapsed in 1972, raising many questions about the basis on which loans had been obtained.
3 Figure 2.4 in Chapter 2 shows that the cost of transporting coal and oil between 1947 and 2007 did not increase significantly over this period until the boom of 2004–8.
4 Launching a large ship into a narrow river is a tricky process involving 'sliding ways that usually extend from the bilge to bilge of the ship. By shaping and greasing surfaces of both ways, any movement of the vessel at right angles to the direction of motion is prevented' (Hind 1959, p. 45).
5 Needless to say, the author does not really believe that the following account of maritime history is complete, accurate or balanced. There are better historians who can do that. This overview simply aims to demonstrate the common theme of economics running through 5000 years of history, and this at least provides perspective.
6 Smith (1998, Book 1, Chapter III, p. 27).
7 Smith (1998, Book 1, Chapter III, p. 27).
8 Unsourced quotation attributed to Winston Churchill in the 1999 Christmas broadcast of Queen Elizabeth II.
9 Braudel (1979, p. 21).
10 McEvedy (1967, p. 26).
11 McEvedy (1967, p. 26).
12 Nawwab et al. (1980, p. 8).
13 Haws and Hurst (1985, Vol. 1, p. 18).
14 Lindsay (1874, Vol. 1, p. 4). According to R.I. Bradshaw it was located on two islands 600–700 m from the mainland and 40 km south of Sidon, with an estimated population of 30,000 in its heyday. It had two ports, but lacked agricultural land and an adequate supply of fresh water and fuel.

15 McEvedy (1967, p. 44).

16 Haws and Hurst (1985, p. 36). Herodotus described the Greek trading methods in a detailed account written c.620 BC.

17 McEvedy (1967, p. 54).

18 McEvedy (1967, p. 70, footnote).

19 Some historians attribute this to a period of extreme bad weather between 536 and 545, possibly caused by the Earth passing through an asteroid belt which affected harvests in northern areas (Bryant 1999).

20 Byzantium was the old Greek name for Constantinople.

21 McEvedy (1961, p. 58).

22 Venice's power as a shipowner was demonstrated in 1202 when the Fourth Crusade contracted for a Venetian fleet to transport its army of 4,000 knights, 9,000 squires and 20,000 foot soldiers to recapture Jerusalem at a cost of 5 marks per horse and 2 marks per man. When the army arrived in Venice for transport the crusaders could not pay the freight and the Venetians persuaded them to help them recapture the city of Zara from the Hungarians and then to take Constantinople, which they did in 1204.

23 Braudel (1979, p. 99).

24 McEvedy (1972, p. 12).

25 Needham (1954, p. 481). These dimensions were apparently confirmed by the discovery in 1962 of a rudder post of one of Zheng He's treasure ships at the site of one of the Ming shipyards near Nanking. It was 36.2 feet long, suggesting a ship length of 480–536 ft, depending upon its draught. But there is no other evidence that a vessel of this size was actually built and operated successfully, and Professor Ian Buxton of Newcastle University points out the difficulty of building long structures in timber capable of withstanding waves. The biggest wooden ships built in the nineteenth century, the 336 foot HMS *Orlando* and HMS *Mersey*, suffered from structural problems. Since the Ming shipyards had no special construction techniques such as iron strapping for supporting the wooden hulls of these treasure ships, the Ming texts may have been reporting a project which was never successfully carried out (see Gould 2000, pp. 198–9).

26 The Ming maritime voyages are very well documented in the form of maps, charts and travel records.

27 Although the voyages were remarkable, there is plenty of evidence that these seas had been navigated before. The Chinese and the Arabs had probably sailed into the Atlantic at earlier dates, but reaching Asia from Europe was not easy.

28 Marco Polo travelled 24,000 miles between 1275 and 1295 and published an account in 'Description of the World'. See Humble (1979, p. 27).

29 The Benguela current runs north along the West African coast and the SE Trades oppose a sailing ship heading south.

30 According to Lindsay (1847, Vol. 1, p. 559), citing R.H. Major, the astrolabe was invented by Beham about the year 1480, with the aid of two physicians, Roderigo and Josef Lindsey.

31 Lindsay (1874, Vol. 1, p. 549).

32  Madeira was discovered in 1418 by Jo„o Zarco and Tristao Vaz, who were blown onto it in a storm; the Cape Verde Islands were discovered in 1441 and the Azores in 1449 (Lindsay 1874, Vol. 1, p. 551).

33  Columbus studied the writings of Ptolemy, Pliny and Strabo.

34  Lindsay (1874, Vol. 1, pp. 561–3).

35  Written in 1410 by Pierre d'Ailly.

36  Humble (1979, p. 56).

37  Irving (1828, p. 24).

38  Humble (1979, p. 60).

39  Humble (1979, p. 102).

40  Minchinton (1969, p. 2).

41  Braudel (1982, p. 362).

42  Braudel (1984, p. 143)

43  Barbour (1950, pp. 95–122).

44  Van Cauwenbergh (1983, p. 16).

45  *Le Guide d'Amsterdam*, 1701, pp. 1–2.

46  Braudel (1984, p. 190).

47  J.N. Parival, *Les Délices de la Hollande*, 1662, p. 36

48  McEvedy (1972, p. 38) says that the newbuilding price and operating costs of Dutch ships were a good third below anyone else's.

49  Braudel (1984, p. 191).

50  Braudel (1984, p. 207).

51  McEvedy (1972, p. 38).

52  Haws and Hurst (1985, p. 270).

53  Deane (1969, p. 89).

54  Minchinton (1969, p. 62, Table 6).

55  Minchinton (1969, p. 18).

56  Fayle (1933, p. 218).

57  Fayle (1933, pp. 202–5).

58  Soudon (2003, p. 22).

59  Fayle (1933, p 207).

60  Blake (1960, p. 4).

61  Fayle (1933, p. 217).

62  MacGregor (1961, p. 157).

63  A Gould, Angier & Co. (1920) freight report for 1871 comments: 'the great progress made in the transition from the use of sailing to steam vessels stands out as the salient feature of the trade'.

64  This account is based on a speech given in 1863 by the builder of the *John Bowes*, C.M. Palmer, published in 1864: 'On the construction of iron ships and the progress of iron shipbuilding' (see Craig 1980, pp. 6–7).

65  Kirkaldy (1914, p. 159).

66  Jennings (1980, p. 20). This service meant that a ship could be despatched from London for the East and orders sent out by this service would reach the ship's destination before her arrival.

67 MacGregor (1961, p. 44). Grant's Trans Mongolian Telegrams advertised a 10-day delivery for cables to the Far East.

68 Dugan (1953, p. 167). The cable company raised $3 million. The *Great Eastern*, Brunel's massive iron ship, was chartered for the job. Daniel Gooch offered the ship free if she failed to lay the cable. If she succeeded he asked for $250,000 cable stock.

69 Comparing prices over such a long period is difficult. A composite US dollar price index shows a multiple of 45 for the price increase between 1865 and 2003, but Buxton (2001) indicates a multiple of 60, as used here.

70 The 1865 cable lasted until 1877 and the 1866 cable lasted until 1872.

71 The 1911 edition of *Encyclopaedia Britannica* quotes Sir Charles Bright as stating that by 1887, 107,000 miles of submarine cable had been laid, and 10 years later 162,000 miles of cable were in existence, representing a capital of £40 million, 75% of which had been provided by the UK. Most of the cable was manufactured on the Thames.

72 Fayle (1933, p. 228).

73 Lindsay (1874, Vol. 4, p. 273).

74 Immigration into the USA amounted to 5.2 million in 1881–1990, 3.7 million in 1891–1900, and 8.8 million in 1901–1910.

75 Wall (1977, p. 34).

76 Deakin and Seward (1973, p. 13)

77 Dugan (1953, p. 187). The submarine cable to China opened in 1871 and charged £7 per message. In 1872 the charge was reduced to £4 6*s.* for 20 words.

78 Based on the Captain's accounts for the voyage of the *Nakoya* to South America between October 1870 and 20 July 1871, which showed seamen earning £2 2*s.* a month and the mate £6.

79 Barty-King (1994, p. 3).

80 Barty-King (1994, p. 10).

81 Horace Clarkson, aged 28, joined the Baltic in 1858.

82 Clarkson (1952, p. 20).

83 In that year the expenditure on telegrams was £5,300 and on wages £5,000

84 One of the techniques was the Boe code, a system which reduced lengthy messages to a few words.

85 Gripaios (1959, p. 25).

86 Harlaftis (1993, p. 1).

87 This example is based on a tramp itinerary described by Fayle (1933, p. 264).

88 McKinsey (1967, pp. 3–4) makes these points in its analysis of the possible effects of containerization.

89 Sklar (1980).

90 US Council on Foreign Relations council memorandum, July 1941, quoted in Sklar (1980).

91 Maber (1980, p. 50).

92 Corlett (1981, p. 7).

93 Rochdale (1970, p. 87).

94  UN *Statistical Yearbook* 1967, Table 156; and 1982, Table 179.

95  Fearnleys *World Bulk Trades* 1969, p. 13, shows that in 1969 61% of the grain trade was in vessels below 25,000 dwt and only 1% in vessels over 60,000 dwt. The 1985 edition of the same report shows 40% of all shipments in vessels over 60,000 dwt.

96  Graham and Hughes (1985).

97  Falkus (1990, p. 360).

98  Graham and Hughes (1985, pp. 19, 95).

99  Graham and Hughes (1985, pp. 95).

100  American President Lines, 'Intermodal Information Technology: A Transportation Assessment', May 1997, p. 7.

101  Proulx (1993, p. 202).

102  Smith (1998, Book 1, Chapter III, page 28).

## 2  THE ORGANIZATION OF THE SHIPPING MARKET

1  Zhou and Amante (2005).

2  For example, according to the US Navy website (http://www.navy.mil), its mission is to 'maintain, train and equip combat-ready Naval forces capable of winning wars, deterring aggression and maintaining freedom of the seas'.

3  Clarkson Research Services, *World Shipyard Monitor*, December 2007, p. 9.

4  *UNCTAD Review of Maritime Transport*, 2002, Table 41 page 66 and estimates by the author.

5  Maritime ton miles from *Fearnleys Review* 2005, p. 49 and air freight from Boeing.

6  Tinsley (1984).

7  An integrated transport system consists of a series of components (e.g. road, sea, rail) designed for the efficient transfer of cargo from one system to another. 'Intermodalism' refers to the specific elements in this system concerned with the transfer of cargo from one mode to another.

8  Rochdale (1970).

9  Neresian (1981, p. 75) discusses the importance of flexibility in ship types. See also the discussion in Chapter 7 of the present text.

10  To link this diagram with world economic statistics published by the United Nations (UN) and OECD, the economic groupings are based on the Standard Industrial Classification (SIC) and the trade groupings are based on the Standard International Trade Classification (SITC).

11  Porter (1990, p. 72).

12  'Underlying … the phenomenon of clustering is the exchange and flow of information about needs, techniques, and technology among buyers, suppliers and related industries' (Porter 1990, p. 153).

13  For a more extensive discussion of the PSD function, see Stopford (1979a) particularly Appendix C, 'A model of dry cargo ship demand' (pp. 366ff.), which analyses the PSD function for 55 commodity groups.

14  Rochdale (1970).

15 Graham and Hughes (1985, p. 17) discuss the problems faced by conventional liner owners in the 1960s.

16 'Steel trades: the choice of ship type', *Lloyd's Shipping Economist*, July 1984, p. 16, provides a well-documented illustration of how this works in the steel products trade, describing the shipment of steel products in containers, bulk carriers, ferries and ro-ros.

17 UNCTAD, *Review of Maritime Transport*, 2006, Table 41. Note that their estimate of the value of freight is lower than the estimate in Table 2.1.

18 In 1960 the cost of freight Arabian Gulf (AG) west was $0.57 per barrel and the oil price was $1.90 per barrel, so freight was 23% of the c.i.f. price.

19 These figures were provided by the Far East Freight Conference. They are undiscounted, so a big shipper would expect to pay much less.

20 See Buxton (2004).

21 Neresian (1981, Ch. 14) gives a particularly vivid account of the debate over whether an oil company should buy its own ships.

22 'Mitsui OSK', *Lloyd's Shipping Economist*, March 1981, p. 37.

23 Packard (1989, p. 5).

## 3 SHIPPING MARKET CYCLES

1 This comment was made in conversation with the owner of a North American shipowning company in spring 1995.

2 J.C. Gould, Angier & Co., market report, 31 December 1894.

3 J.C. Gould, Angier & Co., *Angier Brothers' Steam Shipping Report*, 31 December 1900.

4 This figure was taken from the market reports of J.C. Gould. It reported a freight rate of 50 shillings per ton at an exchange rate of $4.75 per pound sterling.

5 These comments apply principally to charter market operations where the decisions are few but the consequences of errors are large. In liner companies, a multitude of decisions have to be made daily, but for the most part the consequences of error are less onerous.

6 Petty (1662).

7 Nerlove *et al.* (1995, p. 1).

8 Cournot (1927, p. 25).

9 Braudel (1979, p. 80).

10 Schumpeter (1939).

11 Braudel (1979, Chapter 1).

12 According to Schumpeter (1954), an early use of the word 'cycle' in this context was by Petty (1662).

13 Braudel (1979, p. 80).

14 Schumpeter (1954, p. 744).

15 Gould, Angier & Co. (1920).

16 Kirkaldy (1914).

17 Fayle (1933, p. 279).

18 Cufley (1972, p. 408).

19  Cufley (1972, p. 408).

20  Hampton (1991, p. 1).

21  Hampton (1991, p. 2).

22  This quotation was adapted from Downes and Goodman (1991, p. 380) where risk is defined as 'the measurable possibility of losing or not gaining value. Risk is differentiated from uncertainty which is not measurable.' In later editions the requirement that risk is measurable is dropped from the definition, but in shipping it is appropriate to retain the distinction because the value of the assets at risk can be measured, even if the probability of loss cannot always be accurately quantified

23  Chida and Davis (1990, p. 177).

24  Zannetos (1973, p. 41).

25  Rochdale (1970, para. 565).

26  Isserlis (1938).

27  Davis (1962, p. 295).

28  Schumpeter (1960).

29  Schumpeter (1960, Table 1, p. 15).

30  The rate for a coal cargo from South Wales to Singapore confirms the trend. In 1869 the freight was 27 shillings per ton, but by 1908 it had fallen to a low of 10 shillings.

31  Gould, Angier & Co (1920), annual reports for years stated.

32  Rogers (1898, p. 109).

33  The early steam engines had worked at below 5 lbs/in pressure and consumed 10 lbs of coal per horsepower hour. They could carry little but bunker coal. By 1914, pressures had increased to 180 lb/in and coal consumption had fallen to 11/2 lb per horsepower hour, giving the steamer a decisive economic advantage, despite its high capital costs.

34  Smith and Holden (1946).

35  These fleet figures understate the true growth of shipping supplies. According to contemporary estimates, the productivity of a steamer was four times as high as a sailing ship, so in real terms the available sea transport capacity increased by 460%. No doubt much of this was absorbed by increasing ton miles as more distant trades were opened up, though unfortunately no ton-mile statistics were collected at this time.

36  The brokers' reports for the 45-year period paint a consistently gloomy picture. There are only a handful of years that do not warrant a complaint about the state of the market. As time progresses the complaints about over-building intensify. A comment on 1884 from Gould, Angier & Co. (1920) is typical: 'This state of things was brought about by the large over-production of tonnage during the three previous years, fostered by reckless credit given by the banks and builders and over-speculation by the irresponsible and inexperienced owners.'

37  Gould, Angier & Co. (1920).

38  MacGregor (1961, p. 149).

39  Gould, Angier & Co. (1920).

40  Gould, Angier & Co. (1920).

41  Gould, Angier & Co. (1920).

42  Gould, Angier & Co. (1920).

43 Gould, Angier & Co. (1920).

44 Gould, Angier & Co. (1920).

45 Gould, Angier & Co. (1920).

46 Gould, Angier & Co. (1920).

47 Gould, Angier & Co. (1920).

48 Jones (1957).

49 'Fluctuations in shipping values', *Fairplay*, 1931.

50 Given that the freight index fell to 80 in the 1930s recession, and assuming that this represented the operating cost of the marginal ship, the operating margin for capital in the 1920s must have been about 30 points.

51 Jones (1957).

52 Angiers Report for 1936, published in *Fairplay* (see Jones 1957, p. 56).

53 Jones (1957, p. 57).

54 This conclusion was based on an unpublished analysis of the force of the cycles between 1741 and 2005 carried out by the author.

55 Platou (1970, p. 158).

56 Platou (1970).

57 Platou (1970, p. 162).

58 Platou (1970, p. 200).

59 Platou (1970).

60 Platou (1970).

61 Tugendhat (1967, pp. 186–7).

62 Platou (1970).

63 Tugendhat (1967, p. 186).

64 Hill and Vielvoye (1974, pp. 119–120): sterling prices of £11 million, £25 million and £30 million converted to US dollars at exchange rate of $2.45 to the pound.

65 *Fearnleys Review* 1977, p. 9

66 *Fearnleys Review* 1980.

67 *Fearnleys Review* 1974, p. 8

68 *Fearnleys Review* 1981, p. 9.

69 *Fearnleys Review* 1982, p. 9.

70 *Fearnleys Review* 1986.

71 The yen strengthened from ¥232 to the dollar in 1983 to ¥156 to the dollar in 1986, increasing the price of a ¥2 billion ship from $8.5 million to $12.9 million.

72 The 64,000 dwt *Pacific Prosperity* built in 1982 sold in August 1986 for $6.2 million.

73 By 1987 the *Pacific Prosperity* was worth $12 million, by 1988 $17.2 million, and by 1989 $23 million.

74 *Fearnleys Review* 1981, p. 12.

75 *Fearnleys Review* 1986.

76 Clarkson Research Studies, *Shipping Review and Outlook*, Autumn 1999, p. 1.

77 Alderton (1973, p. 92).

78 'We have a saying in Greek: "we get the light from above"… when we buy we buy because a vessel is cheap, that is the main consideration: when we consider it a bargain' (statement by Greek shipowner).

79 *Webster's Dictionary* offers two definitions, one of which implies regularity and the other does not. The first focuses on regular time intervals and defines a cycle as 'an interval of time during which one sequence of a regularly recurring sequence of events or phenomena is completed'. For example, we talk of the 'special survey cycle' of a ship, meaning a sequence of ship inspections and dry dockings in accordance with a regular timetable. However, there is another meaning of the word which has nothing to say about timing or regularity. It defines a cycle as 'a recurrent sequence of events which occur in such an order that the last event of one sequence precedes the recurrence of the first event in the new series'. For example, when we discuss the building cycle of a ship (keel lay, launch, sea trials, delivery, etc.) we make no comment on how long each of these stages will take. It depends on the shipbuilder. Knowing that the keel has been laid is little help in predicting the launch date.

80 Cufley (1972, pp. 408–9).

81 Kepner and Tregoe (1982, p. vii).

## 4 SUPPLY, DEMAND AND FREIGHT RATES

1 Hampton (1991).

2 Isserlis (1938).

3 Samuelson (1964, p. 263).

4 Pigou (1927).

5 Samuelson (1964, p. 251).

6 Isserlis (1938, p. 76).

7 Maizels (1962).

8 European Commission (1985, p. 18).

9 Kindleberger (1967, p. 24).

10 MARPOL Paragraph 13G.

11 Platou (1970, p. 180).

12 Platou (1970, p. 183).

13 In the present context the 'productivity' of a fleet can be defined as the total ton miles of cargo shipments in the year divided by the deadweight fleet actively employed in carrying the cargo.

14 Information provided in a personal communication from a medium-sized private shipping company.

15 Clarkson Research Studies Ltd, 'VLCC Investment: a scenario for the 1990's' London, 1993.

16 *Webster's Dictionary* defines a retailer as someone who sells small quantities direct to the ultimate consumer at a price customarily charged by the retailer.

17 In this section the discussion is restricted to a graphical discussion of the supply–demand model. A mathematical treatment can be found in Evans and Marlow (1990, Chapter 6).

18 Evans and Marlow (1990, Chapter 7).

19 A notable exception to this is the oil trades.

20  One possible solution to forcing up freight rates at this stage in the market is the formation of a cartel. However, efforts by owners to control the market by forming 'stabilization pools' of vessels that remain permanently out of the market have never been successful.

21  For the reasons discussed in the previous section, freight rates and supply should be expressed per ton mile.

22  Hampton (1991).

23  J. Tinbergen, 'Ein Schiffbauzyklus?' *Weltwirtschaftliches Archiv*, July 1931, quoted in Schumpeter (1954).

24  Smith (1998).

25  Marshall (1994, p. 28).

## 5  THE FOUR SHIPPING MARKETS

1  Jevons (1871, Ch. IV).

2  At least that is the case if there is no bank lending. If the buyer borrows 60% of the purchase price of the ship, repayable over 5 years, this increases the short-term liquidity of the shipping industry. For example, if an owner purchases a $10 million tanker and finances the transaction with a $6 million loan plus $4 million of his own equity, the effect is to increase the industry's short-term cash balance by $6 million. If we look at the industry balance sheet as a whole, the effect of this sale and purchase transaction is to increase the current assets by $6 million, which is precisely offset by a $6 million increase in net liabilities.

3  The sale and purchase market has an important economic role as the mechanism used by the market to filter out unsuccessful shipowners. During recessions the financially weak owners are obliged to sell to the financially strong at bargain prices.

4  Ihre and Gordon (1980) provide a more detailed discussion of the charter-party practices.

5  The Baltic freight market information is controlled by the Freight Indices and Futures Committee (FIFC), which is made up of five Baltic Exchange directors and in turn reports to the Baltic Board.

6  FFA Brokers Association reported in Baltic Exchange press release, January 2007.

7  Fluctuations in shipping values, *Fairplay*, 15 July 1920, p. 221.

8  See Chapter 17 for a brief review of regression and correlation techniques for analysing maritime data.

9  *Lloyd's List*, 4 July 1986.

10  *World Shipyard Monitor* reports the orderbook of 300 shipyards each month.

## 6  COSTS, REVENUES AND CASHFLOW

1  This is evident in the USA where the domestic market was for many years closed off from the world shipping market by the Jones Act. Faced with high replacement costs and little change in size, ships often trade to 30 or 40 years of age.

2 The first steps in ship automation were made in the early 1960s, and in 1964 the East Asiatic vessel *Andorra* was the first ship to go into service without an engine-room watch below. To facilitate this, the ship had an elaborate system of malfunction alarms with indicator relayed to strategic points in the accommodation. At this time the main emphasis was on improving crew conditions and freeing them from the unproductive routine task of engine-room watchkeeping in order to carry out maintenance work elsewhere on the vessel.

3 Unfortunately it was not possible to update this table for the present edition, but although the dollar costs will have changed the relative costs probably have not.

4 These figures are calculated by converting the annual cost in dollars per deadweight in Table 6.1 into dollars per day on the basis of 355 operating days a year.

## 7 FINANCING SHIPS AND SHIPPING COMPANIES

1 According to *World Shipyard Monitor*, in 2003 the shipping industry invested $59 billion in new ships and $16.7 billion in second-hand vessels.

2 Select Committee on Employment of British Shipping, 1844, D111Q55.

3 G. Atkinson, *The Shipping Laws of the British Empire* (1854), p. 122, quoted in Palmer (1972, p. 49).

4 Palmer (1972).

5 Northway (1972, p. 71).

6 Hyde (1967, p. 99).

7 Sturmey (1962, p. 398).

8 Rochdale (1970, para. 1270).

9 Rochdale (1970, para. 1270).

10 Haraldsen (1965, p. 35).

11 See Petersen (1955, p. 197). Owners applying for a licence to build abroad were required to obtain foreign currency loans.

12 Sturmey (1962, p. 223).

13 Arnesen (1973).

14 Examples of this practice were provided verbally by the head of a major shipping bank active at the time in ship finance.

15 CRSL (2006) *KG Finance & Shipping*, p. 3.

16 These investors are spread around the financial centres of Europe, North America and the Far East. Their investment behaviour is restricted and to some extent determined both by the regulatory framework within which they operate (which is different in Tokyo, London and New York) and the policies implicit in their own particular business. For example, liquidity is less important to institutions such as life insurance companies which invest huge amounts of money for the 'long haul'. On the contrary, liquidity will be of prime importance to the corporate treasurer investing spare cash which he may need to draw on at any time. Other complications are the currency in which assets are held and commitments must be paid.

17 Because it is an efficient market, at any given time there is a standard price for a given combination of liquidity, risk and yield.

18 If we lived in a world without regulation and taxes the two markets would be the same – the interest rate on a eurodollar loan would have to be the same as an equivalent domestic dollar loan, etc. This is not the case because governments use domestic interest rates to regulate domestic bank lending, resulting in pools of currency held off-shore where rates are determined by supply and demand.

19 Usually this demands evidence that the company has a profitable trading record in an industry which is considered to have a profitable future.

20 *McKinsey Quarterly*, January 2007 Mapping the Global Capital Markets Farrell, Lund, Maasry Exhibit 7.

21 Standard and Poor's April 1998 'Launching into the Bond Market' p. 28

22 'If I had to go back and ask for funds every time, he would have been in charge,' [Stelios] says. 'The only condition he imposed, which I accepted, was, "If you are financially successful, I want your brother and sister to benefit. This is family wealth, not your own." My father was hedging his bets. He had two sons. He wanted to see who would do better' (Morais 2001).

23 The author is grateful to Peter Stokes of Lazards for his assistance with this section.

24 These terms are quoted in the General Maritime Preliminary Offering Memorandum for $250 million bonds dated 3 March 2003.

25 Stokes (1992).

26 The fund was marketed in Europe and South East Asia but, according to the organizers, interest from South East Asia was virtually nil, and it was not much better in Norway. Eventually a total of $21.25 million was raised mainly from UK institutions, but with the help of two substantial subscriptions from Germany and Saudi Arabia.

27 An 'accredited investor' is a wealthy investor who meets certain SEC requirements for net worth and income. This includes institutional investors and high net worth individuals.

28 Dresner and Kim (2006).

29 Frontline Ltd press release, 5 February 2007. The placement was made in February 2007.

30 The liability of the general partner is unlimited, but for equity partners it is limited to the sum committed.

31 In November 1989 the Aarbakke Committee recommended that the depreciation rate in the K/S should be reduced to 10% and the classification fund provision should not be allowed. In June 1991 it was announced that the cutback would be to 20%.

32 Based on interview of Gerry Wang, President of Seaspan, by Peter Lorange, President of IMD, in *European Business Forum*, 2007

33 Freshfields (2006) CMA CGM hails a CABS structure deal and diversifies its ship funding sources.

34 I am grateful to Peter Stokes for this observation.

35 I am grateful to Jean Richards for her practical thoughts and advice on this topic.

## 8 RISK, RETURN AND SHIPPING COMPANY ECONOMICS

1  Evans (1986, p. 111).
2  Kirkaldy (1914, p. 176).
3  The Tramp Shipping Administrative Committee was set up in 1935 with the task of securing closer cooperation between all sections of the British tramp shipping industry. In 1936 it published a report on the financial performance of over 200 British tramp shipping companies 1930–5, reported in Jones (1957, Table VI, p. 36).
4  Rochdale (1970, p. 332, para. 1251). This was one of the most comprehensive studies of the shipping industry carried out in the last 50 years. By sector they reported that the return was 4.1% for cargo liners, 3.3% for bulk carriers, 18.7% for ore carriers and 4.2% for tankers. The exceptionally high return for ore carriers was explained by the fact that most of the vessels were on long-term charters designed to produce a reasonable return on capital. However, the tankers were also mainly on long-term charter to international oil companies, so time charters were no guarantee of high returns. One reason for the poor performance of British shipowners was thought to be their unwillingness to borrow: in 1969 the companies surveyed had only £160 million debt, compared with £1000 million of assets.
5  In a paper to the Marine Money Conference on 18 October 2001, Jeffries & Co. reported the average return on capital employed of six public tanker companies as 6.3% and the return on equity as 6.7%.
6  Stokes (1997).
7  Henderson and Quandt (1971, p. 52).
8  See Table 3.9 for a discussion of the size of companies in the shipping industry.
9  The formal conditions for perfect competition are a competitive market, identical products, free entry and exit, and perfect information – and shipping companies meet them pretty well. The companies are small – arguably each ship is a separate company – and the liquidity of the assets makes it easy to move in and out of the shipping market. Anyone with capital can set themselves up as a shipowner in a few weeks. The product is fairly homogeneous and the information flow is good. So we have something approaching a perfect market, in bulk shipping at least.
10 Schumpeter (1954, p. 545).
11 Rather confusingly, economists also refer to the normal profit as a zero economic profit. By this they mean that on average investors will earn the normal profit for the business and nothing more.
12 Rochdale (1970, p. 338, para. 1270) commented that the gearing of British shipping in the 1960s was only 16%.
13 McConville (1999, p. 298).
14 Porter (1990).
15 Keynes (1991, p. 158).
16 Drucker (1977, p. 433).
17 This is based on the mean earnings plus three standard deviations.
18 Smith (1998, p. 104).

19  Smith (1998, p. 104).
20  Marshall (1994, p. 332).
21  Peter (1979, p. 85).

## 9  THE GEOGRAPHY OF MARITIME TRADE

1  Independent Commission on International Development Issues (1980, p. 32).
2  Based on *Oriental Bay*, 4038 TEU, consuming 117 tons per day at 23 knots and $25,000 per day charter rate.
3  This analysis was suggested by Berrill (2007).
4  Couper (1983, p. 26).
5  The dimensions of the locks are: length 233.48 m; width 24.38 m; depth over sill 9.14 m.
6  The Gulf Intracoastal Waterway comprises large sheltered channels running along the coast and intersected by many rivers giving access to ports a short distance inland. New Orleans is reached by the Tidewater Ship Canal, a more direct and safer waterway than the Mississippi Delta. The Pacific coast canals are not linked with the national network.
7  This regional grouping is based on the UNCTAD classification of countries and territories published in Annex 1 of the *UNCTAD Yearbook*.

## 10  THE PRINCIPLES OF MARITIME TRADE

1  David Hume, *Political Discourses* (1752), reprinted in Meek (1973, p. 61).
2  Meek (1973, p. 61).
3  Some entries in the table refer to country groups (e.g. Middle East) because country data was not available. Since the trade of Belgium and the Netherlands includes substantial amounts of cargo passing through Germany and France, their trade is totalled.
4  Smith (1998, Book IV, Chapter VIII, pp. 374–375).
5  Smith (1998, Book IV, Chapter II, p. 292).
6  The factors of production required to produce a product are the costs which the manufacturer must pay, organized into convenient groups. In a very general way, labour and capital are the main factors.
7  Porter (1990, p. 162).
8  Winters (1991, p. 31). Three other assumptions are: perfect competition in factor markets; no impediments to trade such as tariffs or transport costs; and that there are two factors and two countries.
9  This function is discussed in Henderson and Quandt (1971, ch. 2).
10  Rostow (1960).
11  Maizels (1971, p. 30).
12  Thornton (1959, p. 239).

## 11  THE TRANSPORT OF BULK CARGOES

1  McEvedy (1967, p. 70).
2  Craig (1980).
3  McCord (1979, p. 113).
4  P.J. Raleigh of Falconbridge Nickel Mining, quoted in Kirschenbaum and Argall (1975, p. 127).
5  H.E. Tanzig, 'Imaginative bulk parcel ocean transportation' in Kirschenbaum and Argall (1975, p. 290).
6  A typical sample consists of a scoop which is quickly swung through the material on the belt and deposits its contents into a sample box for analysis.
7  McCord (1979, p. 130).
8  Dunn (1956, p. 18).
9  Dunn (1956, p. 19).
10  Blake (1960, page 83). Unfortunately, this clever idea did not work. The Belgian authorities refused permission for storage tanks and the American authorities refused a licence for passenger carriage. When the *Vaderland* arrived in Philadelphia, the pumping apparatus was not ready, so they loaded general cargo. The owners then got a mail contract from the Belgian government and the ship never traded in oil.
11  The *Loutsch* was still trading in Russian hands in the early 1950s.
12  Kirkaldy (1914, p. 126).
13  Strictly speaking, the first 'oil company' to get involved with tankers was the Swedish Nobel brothers, of explosives fame. They exported oil from the Russian oilfields, which involved a difficult journey to the Caspian Sea, down the Volga and through the Black Sea to Europe. Starting with barges and sailing ships on the Volga, in 1878 they built the *Zoroaster*, a tank steamer that burned fuel oil and carried 250 tons of kerosene in 21 vertical cylindrical tanks. By 1882 they had 12 tank steamers trading in the Caspian.
14  Hunting (1968) and Dunn (1956).
15  Howarth (1992, p. 23).
16  Howarth (1992, p. 28).
17  Tugendhat (1968, p. 187).
18  At the time tanker owning was not particularly risky because most of the tanker owning industry's revenue covered by long-term contracts. Zannetos (1973) confirmed this view by stating 'I know of few industries which are less risky than the oil tank transportation industry'.
19  For example, the thermal coal trade for power stations increased from almost nothing in 1971 to 236 mt at the time of writing.
20  Odell (1981, p. 13).
21  The specific gravity of a liquid represents its density as compared with water, which has a specific gravity of 1. Liquids which are less dense than water have a specific gravity less than 1, whilst 'heavy' liquids have a specific gravity greater than 1.
22  Odell (1981, p. 120).

23 Tankers under 60,000 dwt are often referred to as MRs, which stands for medium range.

24 Tankers over 60,000 dwt used in the products trade are referred to as LRs, which stands for long range.

25 Estall and Buchanan (1966, p. 156).

26 Bernham and Hoskins (1943, p. 104).

27 Dunn (1973, p. 195).

28 International Iron and Steel Institute, *Steel Statistical Yearbook* (1985), Table 9.

29 Maritime Transport Research (1976, Vol. 3, Appendix E).

30 Steven (1969, p. 108).

31 Stopford (1979b).

32 OECD (1968, Annex 5, Table 1).

33 Morgan (1979, p. 137).

34 Between 1950 and 2004 world population increased less than threefold, from 2.55 billion to 7.1 billion. Per capita consumption rates were provided by the FAO.

35 For example, to produce 31.2 million tons of carcass meat in 1993, US farm animals were fed 192.7 million tons of feed concentrates, mostly corn.

36 Income–consumption curves showing income on one axis and consumption on the other are often referred to as 'Engel curves'. Typically calorie intake rises from a subsistence level of 2,000 calories to reach a plateau at around 3,500 calories per day.

37 Inferior goods are the cheapest commodities, with an income elasticity below 0 – consumption declines as income rises. Necessities are commodities with an income elasticity between 0 and 1 – consumption increases with income, but at a slower rate of growth. Luxuries are commodities with an income elasticity in excess of 1 – consumption grows faster than income.

38 Maritime Transport Research (1972, p. 36).

39 'Steel trades: the choice of ship type', *Lloyd's Shipping Economist*, July 1984, p. 16.

40 Thomas (1968).

## 12 THE TRANSPORT OF SPECIALIZED CARGOES

1 These figures were provided by Star Shipping as rough examples. Industry practice varies.

2 Drewry Shipping Consultants (1996, Table 1.1).

3 La Dage (1955, p. 49).

4 Jacob Stolt-Nielsen, 'History – Timeline Stolt Parcel Tankers', December 2005.

5 This cost is based on a cost of $0.52–$1.8 per million BTU provided by LNG Solutions, London, converted at 52 million BTU per tonne of LNG.

6 Nuttall, B.C. (2003) *Oil and gas history of Kentucky: 1860 to 1900*. http://www.uky.edu/KGS/emsweb/history/1860to1900.htm (accessed 24 April 2008).

7 In 2005, according to the BP *Annual Review of the World Oil Industry*, total oil demand was 3.86 billion tons and the inter-regional oil trade was 2.461 billion tons.

8 Information provided by LNG Solutions, London.

9 Thomas, O.O., 'The carriage of refrigerated meat cargoes' in Kummerman and Jacquinet (1979, pp. 123–9).

10 Recommendation of the Council on the Standardization of Packaging for the International Transport of Fresh or Refrigerated Fruit and Vegetables, OECD, Paris, 30 July 2006.

11 See http://www.thermoking.com.

12 La Dage (1955, p. 44).

13 Kummerman, H. (1979, Ed) The Evolution of the Deep Sea ro/ro Vessels B.W. Tornquist p. 144 MacGregor Publications, London.

14 Scanaustral, 'Why Scanaustral chose roro' in Maritime Transport Research (1976, Vol. 6, Appendix G, p. 133).

15 Star Shipping, 'A Long Term Industrial Concept', company presentation, 2007.

16 Star Shipping website, June 2006.

17 Source: Squamish Terminals Ltd website.

18 Gardiner (1992, p. 93).


## 13 THE TRANSPORT OF GENERAL CARGO

1 In 2005, 1 billion tons of containerized cargo was shipped. Assuming an average box cost of $1200 and 10 tons per box, that gives a value of $120 billion, compared with bulk freight of about $80 billion, giving containers a 60% share of total revenues.

2 Jennings (1980, p. 16).

3 Kirkaldy (1914, p. 179).

4 Gripaios (1959, pp. 38–39).

5 McKinsey (1967).

6 'A commemoration of 40 years of containerisation', *Containerisation International*, April 1996, p. 65.

7 A T2 tanker was a standard tanker of 9,900 GRT and 16,000 dwt which was mass produced in the USA in World War II.

8 *The Economist*, 31 May 2001

9 Information from the Sea-Land alumni website.

10 For example, the head of Ocean's cargo-handling department published a paper in 1963 arguing that 3,000 miles was the effective limit of commercially viable containerization (Falkus 1990, p. 360).

11 'A commemoration of 40 years of containerisation', *Containerisation International*, April 1996, p. 9.

12 The sale took place in 1968. Asked in the mid-1990s when the idea for containerization first occurred to him, McLean said there was no particular time. It was all the inlets his trucking fleet had to negotiate on the US East Coast that got him thinking about it.

13 Meek (1985).

14 These figures are for the third quarter of 2004. 15,500 bottles of Scotch whisky shipped Europe to Far East at $735/TEU works out at 4.7 cents per bottle.

4403 video recorders shipped in a 40 ft container from the Far East to Europe at $1826/TEU works out at 83 cents per unit.

15  This definition is an updated version of the definition given in Fayle (1933, p. 253).

16  These container cargo statistics in column 5 of Table 13.3 were estimated by Clarkson Research and may not be very precise.

17  Bird (1988, p. 111).

18  Hummels (2001).

19  Bird (1988, p. 111).

20  David Lim, President of NOL, quoted in *Containerisation International*, August 2006, p. 32.

21  Drucker (1986, p. 336).

22  Drucker (1992, p. 277).

23  US Department of Transportation Maritime Administration (2004, p. 9).

24  Collinson (1984).

25  Brooks (1995).

26  Bird (1988, p. 111).

27  *Containerisation International*, August 2006, p. 32.

28  'Lifting the lid on the chocolate box', *Containerisation International*, May 1983, p. 67.

29  *Containerisation International* (1985), p. 51.

30  The ten were Singapore, Philippines, Malaysia, Indonesia, Thailand, South Korea, Taiwan, Japan, Hong Kong and China.

31  Drewry Shipping Consultants (1979, p. 51).

32  Drewry Shipping Consultants (1979, Table 4.1).

33  'Launch of Africa service', Hapag-Lloyd press release, 30 August 2006. http://www.hapag-lloyd.com/daily/i_news_060830_africaservice.pdf (accessed 28 April 2008).

34  OECD (2001, p. 23) discusses the role of alliances.

35  'Grand Alliance member lines expand service network in 2006', Hapag-Lloyd press release, 25 January 2006.

36  Based on A.P. Møller-Maersk profits 2001–5 which were 3.7–7.1% of assets and 4.4–9.7% of operating revenues.

37  Clarkson Research (1996).

38  'Operating costs study 2006: a study on the operating costs of German container-ships', compiled by HSH Nordbank, Ernst & Young, and Econum.

39  The vessel speed was normalized to 15 knots using the cube rule to remove differences in the speed of containerships in the sample

40  Hapag-Lloyd Corporate Review 2005, p. 1. The numbers are based on the first half year.

41  These container capacity figures were provided by the Far East Freight Conference in 2006.

42  Bird (1988, p. 121).

43  Strictly speaking, we should also include the various administrative costs of running a liner business in this item, although doing so would not alter the principles we are discussing.

44 Fisher and Waschik (2002, p. 70).

45 CI (Nov 2002) (Petersen, logistics manager Arla foods overseas division, Denmark)

46 Marriner and Hyde (1967, p. 141).

47 Jennings (1980, p. 23).

48 Deakin and Seward (1973, p. 24).

49 Sturmey (1962, p. 324).

50 Briggs and Jordan (1954, p. 295).

51 Deakin and Seward (1973, p. 1).

52 OECD (2001).

53 One freight forwarder interviewed in this survey commented: 'There are not many shippers left who would say that they are 100 per cent loyal to the conferences they have signed for. The problem is that it is such a difficult thing for the conference to police' (Bird 1988, p. 119).

54 OECD (2001).

55 Deakin and Seward (1973, p. 54).

## 14 THE SHIPS THAT PROVIDE THE TRANSPORT

1 Gardiner (1994, p. 7).

2 Benford (1983, p. 2).

3 Buxton *et al.* (1978, p. 25). This book provides a detailed technical discussion of many of the design features discussed in Chapter 7.

4 'UNCTAD reviews the banana trade and favours boxes', *Containerisation International*, August 1982, p. 41.

5 Graham and Hughes (1985, p. 20).

6 'West Africa – a difficult market for ro-ros', *Lloyd's List*, 13 May 1986, p. 8, contains a discussion of the use of containers in the West African trade.

7 The size range on the Panamax fleet, extending up to 100,000 dwt, includes ships of 80,000 dwt too large to transit the Panama Canal. However, Panama transits are much less common than previously and the large Panamax vessels are competing with the 80,000–100,000 dwt vessels in many trades and are included in the fleet for this reason.

8 Dimensions based on the *TI Europe*, 441,561 dwt, built in 2002.

9 For example the *Betelgeuse*, a 1968 built tanker of 121,432 dwt, broke up while discharging cargo in Ireland in 1979. One of the causes of the incident identified by the Irish government inquiry was incorrect unloading sequences and ballasting, resulting in the buoyancy of the hull becoming uneven and the hull therefore strained.

10 Dunn (1956).

11 For example, petroleum gas liquefies at around 18 bar, 1.01325 bar being equivalent to atmospheric pressure.

12 Based on the *Hellas Nautilus*; details from the Clarkson *Gas Carrier Register* 2007.

13 Approximately 5,000 kW power would be required to maintain the cargo temperature of a 100,000 m$^3$ vessel.

14 See, for example, Buxton (1987) and Benford (1983).

15 Buxton (1987).

## 15 THE ECONOMICS OF SHIPBUILDING AND SCRAPPING

1 A more detailed discussion can be found in Stopford and Barton (1986).

2 Board of Trade, Departmental Committee on Shipping and Shipbuilding, Report (1918), pp. 35–6.

3 Sturmey (1962), particularly Chapter 2, provides a vivid description of the link between British shipping and trade.

4 This explanation of the decline in British shipbuilding was put forward by Svensson (1986).

5 Hobsbawm (1968, pp. 178–9).

6 In March 1988 the price of a 30,000 dwt bulk carrier was $14.5 million and the $/£ exchange rate was 1.88, so the sterling price was £8 million, which was the cost of the materials at that time.

7 Petersen (1955, p. 47).

8 Jones (1957, p. 72).

9 Trezise and Suzuki (1976).

10 *World Shipyard Monitor*, February 1996, p. 12.

11 These dimensions were confirmed by the discovery in 1962 of a rudder post of one of Zheng He's treasure ships at the site of one of the Ming shipyards near Nanking. It was 36.2 feet long, suggesting a ship length of 480–536 feet, depending upon its draught (Needham 1954, p. 481).

12 *Glasgow Herald Trade Review*, 31 December 1924.

13 *Glasgow Herald Trade Review*, 31 December 1924.

14 'Shipbuilding notes', Shipbuilding Employers' Federation press release, December 1930 (unpublished).

15 'Shipbuilding notes', Shipbuilding Employers' Federation press release, December 1936 (unpublished).

16 Shipbuilders' and Repairers' National Association employment statistics (unpublished).

17 Stopford (1988, p. 22).

18 Volk (1994).

19 For a discussion of the principles of supply–demand analysis, see Evans and Marlow (1990, Chapter 5).

20 Geff Walthow, a demolition broker dealing with Taiwan from the early 1950s until 1994, describes how the living standards of workers at the Kaohsiung yard improved as the shanty town in which they lived gradually gave way to purpose-built apartments.

## 16 THE REGULATION OF THE MARITIME INDUSTRY

1 Fayle (1933, p. 285).
2 "International Law of the Sea" John Hopkins, Senior Tutor, Downing College, Cambridge March 1994, Cambridge Academy of Transport.
3 A convention is a template outlining the content of a particular maritime law, whilst a law is a statute enacted by a sovereign state.
4 The earliest list in existence dates from 5 October 1702 (Blake 1960, p. 3).
5 Blake (1960, p. 5).
6 International Association of Classification Societies (2007, p.4).
7 Blake (1960, p. 22).
8 United Nations (1983).
9 Stephenson Harwood (1991, p. 212).
10 Stephenson Harwood (1991, Chapter 9).
11 IMO Resolution MSC.160(78): Adoption of IMO Unique Company and Registered Owner Identification Number Scheme.
12 A few national flags restrict registration to nationals of the country. For example, a Greek shipowner could not register under the Soviet flag, even if he wished to. Note that the term 'flag of convenience' is commonly used to refer to registers that, under the terminology used in this chapter, would be defined as 'open registers'.
13 Cooper (1986).
14 Gold (1981, p. 258).
15 Usually legal issues regarding title over the ship, mortgages and encumbrances are governed by the underlying registry, while the vessel itself falls under the jurisdiction of the bare boat charter registry.
16 The International Convention relating to the Arrest of Seagoing Ships provides that 'a claimant may arrest either the particular ship in respect of which the maritime claim arose, or any other ship which is owned by the person who was, at the time when the maritime claim arose, the owner of the particular ship' (Stephenson Harwood 1991, p. 10).
17 Rawls (1971, p. 5).
18 Gold (1981, p. 119).
19 *Protocol and Proceedings, International Marine Conference 1889*, 3 vols (Washington, DC: US Government Printing Office, 1890), Vol. 1, pp. ix–xiii.
20 Mitropoulos (1994).
21 'Shipping enters the ISM Code era with second phase of implementation', IMO press briefing 2002.
22 Mitropoulos (1985, p. 11).
23 This proposed convention was discussed at the International Labour Conference in 2007.
24 Kidman (2003, p. 6).
25 *China Mail*, 22 November 1879.
26 Sturmey (1962, p. 327).

27 Federal Maritime Commission (2001, p. 2).

28 *The EU's New Competition Regime for Maritime Transport: Options and Opportunities for the Shipping Industry* (2nd edition), December 2005, p. 37, para. 154.

29 *The EU's New Competition Regime for Maritime Transport.*

30 Guidelines on the application of Article 81 of the EC Treaty to maritime transport services 2007/C 215/03 EU MEMO/07/355, Brussels, 13 September 2007 'Antitrust: Draft Guidelines for maritime transport - frequently asked questions'.

31 On 14 September 2007 the European Commission issued draft guidelines on the application of Article 81 of the EC Treaty to maritime transport services.

## 17 MARITIME FORECASTING AND MARKET RESEARCH

1 Beck (1983).

2 Drucker (1977).

3 Decisions made during extreme periods are often irrational. Many investment decisions made during the dot-com bubble in the late 1990s were based on unfounded beliefs which the decision-makers never really challenged, for example that internet business could be developed in a shorter time-scale than normal businesses, an assumption which turned out to be incorrect.

4 Paget (1967, p. 76).

5 'History of Mesopotamia and Iraq', *Encyclopaedia Britannica* (1975), Volume 11, p. 976.

6 Temple (1984, p. 154).

7 Waltham (1972, p. 134) quoted in Temple (1984, p. 28).

8 Waltham (1972, p. 79) quoted in Temple (1984, p. 135).

9 Waltham (1972, p. 90) quoted in Temple (1984, p. 136).

10 Plutarch, 'Life of Alexander', Chapters 73–4, in *Lives*, trans. Aubrey Stewart and George Lang, Bohn's Library, London, 1889, Vol. II, pp. 61–2.

11 Something that distracts attention from the real issue (from the practice of drawing a red herring across a trail to confuse hunting dogs).

12 Sklansky (1987).

13 Evans (1986, p. 158).

14 These issues were discussed at the Neurobehavioural Economics Conference, Pittsburgh, 30 May 1997, reported in *Business Week*, 16 June 1997, p. 45.

15 Bechara and Damasio (2005).

16 Temple (1984) provides a discussion of the use of these techniques in decision-making.

17 Stopford and Barton (1986).

18 Although forecasts refer to the future, the decisions they relate to are firmly rooted in the present. The ship may be delivered in two years and trade for 20 years, but the decision to order it is made today.

19 For a detailed discussion of these techniques, see Tull and Hawkins (1980), particularly Chapter 10.

20 For a discussion of scenario techniques, see Beck (1983) and Linnerman (1983, p. 94).

21 See Seddighi *et al.* (2000, pp. 145–52) for a discussion of the use of reduced form to deal with autocorrelation.

22 See Box *et al.* (1994).

23 This is a linear relationship. Other possible relationships are inverse linear, exponential, and log inverse.

24 This example was run using the Regression program in Microsoft Excel, but most spreadsheets have similar functions.

25 A useful text to pursue this subject further is Seddighi *et al.* (2000). See especially Chapter 1 which introduces the subject and Chapter 5 which gives some practical examples of estimating a supply–demand model for a commodity.

26 Beenstock (1985).

27 Moyer (1984, p. 17) contains a more detailed discussion of these problems.

28 Roxburgh (2003, p. 29).

29 In a 1981 survey, for example, 90% of Swedes described themselves as above-average drivers.

30 Warren Buffet, 'Letter from the Chairman', *Berkshire Hathaway Annual Report* 1984.

31 Beck (1983).

32 See also Moyer (1984, p. 17).

33 Savage (1983).

34 Baranto (1977).

35 Prowse (1984).

# References and Suggested Reading

Note: suggested reading is denoted by an asterisk

*Alderton, P.M. (2004) *Sea Transport Operation and Economics*, Fifth edition, (London: Witherby).

Arnesen, F.W. (1973) Bankers' view of ship finance. Paper presented to Seatrade Money and Ships Conference, 26 March.

Baranto, M. (1977) How well does the OECD forecast real GNP? *Business Economist*, 9.

Barbour, V. (1950) *Capitalism in Amsterdam in the Seventeenth Century* (Baltimore, MD: Johns Hopkins Press).

Barty-King, H. (1994) *The Baltic Story – Baltic Coffee-House to Baltic Exchange, 1744–1994* (London: Quiller Press).

Beughen, S. (2004) Shipping Law (Cavendish Publishing Ltd).

Bechara, A. and Damasio, A.R. (2005) The somatic marker hypothesis: A neural theory of economic decision. *Games and Economic Behavior*, 52, 336–372.

Beck, P.W. (1983) Forecasts: opiates for decision makers. Lecture to the Third International Symposium on Forecasting, Philadelphia, 5 June.

Beenstock, M. (1985) A theory of ship prices. *Maritime Policy and Management*, 12(3), 215–25.

Benford, H. (1983) A Naval Architect's Introduction to Engineering Economics (Ann Arbor: University of Michigan, College of Engineering), No. 282.

Bernham, T.H. and Hoskins, G.O. (1943) *Iron and Steel in Britain 1870–1930* (London: Allen & Unwin).

Berrill, P. (2007) Suez Canal transits 'more viable option'. *TradeWinds*, 20 April. Beveridge, W.H. *et al*. (1965) *Prices and Wages in England, from the Twelfth to the Nineteenth Century*, Vol. 1, 2nd impression (London: Frank Cass).

Bird, J. (1988) Freight forwarders speak: the perception of route competition via seaports in the European Communities Research project – Part II. *Maritime Policy and Management*, 15(2), 107–125.

Blake, G. (1960) *Lloyd's Register of Shipping 1760–1960* (London: Lloyd's Register of Shipping).

Box, G., Jenkins, G.M. and Reinsel, G. (1994) *Time Series Analysis: Forecasting and Control*, 3rd edition (Englewood Cliffs, NJ: Prentice Hall).

*Branch, A.E. (2006) *Elements of Shipping* (London: Routledge)

*Braudel, F. (1982) *Civilisation and Capitalism 15th–18th Century, Vol. 2: The Wheels of Commerce* (London: Collins).

# REFERENCES AND SUGGESTED READING

*Braudel, F. (1982) *Civilisation and Capitalism 15th–18th Century, Vol. 3: The Perspective of the World* (London: Collins).

Briggs, M. and Jordan, P. (1954) *The Economic History of England* (London: University Tutorial Press).

Britannic Steamship Insurance Association (2005) *A Concise History of Modern Commercial Shipping* (London).

Brooks, M.R. (1995) Understanding the ocean container market – a seven country study. *Maritime Policy and Management*, 22(1), 39–49.

*Brooks M. (2000) *Sea Change in Liner Shipping: Regulation and Managerial Decision-making in a Global Industry* (Oxford: Pergamon)

Bryant, G. (1999) The Dark Ages: Were they darker than we imagined? *Universe*, September.

Buxton, I.L. (1987) *Engineering Economics and Ship Design*, 3rd edn (Wallsend: British Maritime Technology).

Buxton, I.L. (2001) Ships and efficiency – 150 years of technical and economic developments. *Transactions of the Royal Institute of Naval Architects B*, 143, 317–338.

Buxton, I. (2004) Will ships always grow larger? *Naval Architect*, April.

Buxton, I.L., Daggitt, R.P. and King, J. (1978) *Cargo Access Equipment for Merchant Ships* (London: E&FN Spon).

Chancellor, E. (1999) *Devil Take the Hindmost: A History of Financial Speculation* (New York: Farrar, Straus Giroux).

Chida, T. and Davies, P.N. (1990) *The Japanese Shipping and Shipbuilding Industries* (London: Athlone Press).

Churchill, R.R and Lowe, A.V. (1983) *The Law of the Sea* (Manchester: Manchester University Press).

Clarkson, H. & Co. Ltd (1952) *The Clarkson Chronicle 1852–1952* (London: Harley Publishing).

Collinson, F.M. (1984) Market segments for marine liner service. *Transportation Journal*, 24, 40–54.

*Collins, N. (2000) *The Essential Guide to Chartering and the Dry Freight Market*, London: Clarkson Research Services Ltd.

Cooper, G.B.F. (1986) *Open Registry and Flags of Convenience* (Cambridge: Seatrade Academy).

Corlett, E. (1981) *The Ship, 10: The Revolution in Merchant Shipping 1950–80* (London: HMSO).

Couper, A. (1983) *The Times Atlas of the Oceans* (London: Times Books).

Cournot, A. (1927) *Researches into the Mathematical Principle of the Theory of Wealth* (New York: Macmillan).

Craig, R. (1980) *The Ship, 5: Steam Tramps and Cargo Liners 1850–1950* (London: HMSO).

Cufley, C.F.H. (1972) *Ocean Freights and Chartering* (London: Staples Press).

*Cullinane, Kevin (2005) *Shipping Economics (Research in Transportation Economics)* (Greenwich, CT: JAI Press).

Davis, R. (1962) English foreign trade, 1700–1774. *Economic History Review*, New Series, 15(2), 285–303.

Deakin, B. M. and Seward, T. (1973) *Shipping Conferences: A Study of Their Development and Economic Practices* (Cambridge: Cambridge University Press).

Deane, P. (1969) *The First Industrial Revolution* (Cambridge: Cambridge University Press).

*De Wit R. (1995) *Multimodal Transport*, (London: LLP).

Dougan, D. (1975) *The Shipwrights: The History of the Shipconstructors' and Shipwrights' Association, 1882–1963* (Newcastle upon Tyne: Graham).

*Downes, J. and Goodman, J.E. (2007) *Dictionary of Finance and Investment Terms*, 3rd edition (New York: Barron's).

Dresner, S. and Kim, K.E. (2006) *PIPEs: A Guide to Private Investments in Public Equity* (Princeton, NJ: Bloomberg Press).

Drucker, P. (1977) *Management: Tasks, Responsibilities, Practices* (New York: Harpers College Press).

Drucker, P. (1986) *The Executive in Action* (New York: HarperCollins).

Drucker, P. (1992) *Managing for the Future* (Harmondsworth: Penguin).

Drucker, P. (1998) *Peter Drucker on the Profession of Management* (Boston: Harvard Business School Press).

Drury, C. and Stokes, P. (1983) *Ship Finance: The Credit Crisis* (London: Lloyd's of London Press).

Dugan, J. (1953) *The Great Iron Ship* (New York: Harper & Brothers).

Dunn, L. (1956) *The World's Tankers* (London: Adlard Coles).

Dunn, L. (1973) *Merchant Ships of the World in Colour 1910–1929* (London: Blandford Press).

Estall, R.C. and Buchanan, R.O. (1966) *Industrial Activity and Economic Geography* (London: Hutchinson).

European Commission (1985) Progress towards a Common Transport Policy: Maritime Transport, Commission to Council, Com(85)90 Final (Brussels, March).

Evans, J.J. and Marlow, P.B. (1990) *Quantitative Methods in Maritime Economics*, 2nd edn (London: Fairplay Publications).

Evans, P. (1986) *Ari: The Life and Times of Aristotle Onassis* (London: Charter Books).

Falkus, M. (1990) *The Blue Funnel Legend* (Basingstoke: Macmillan).

Fayle, E.C. (1933) *A Short History of the World's Shipping Industry* (London: George Allen & Unwin).

Federal Maritime Commission (2001) *Impact of the Ocean Shipping Reform Act of 1998.* http://www.fmc.gov/images/pages/OSRA_Study.pdf (accessed 1 May 2008).

Fisher, T.C.G. and Waschik, R.G. (2002) *Managerial Economics: A Game Theoretic Approach* (London: Routledge).

Fujiwara, S. (1957) *One Hundred Poems from One Hundred Poets* (Tokyo: Hokuseido Press).

*Gardiner, R. (ed.) (1992) *The Shipping Revolution: The Modern Merchant Ship* (London: Conway Maritime Press).

Gardiner, R. (ed.) (1994) *The Golden Age of Shipping* (London: Conway Maritime Press).

Gold, E. (1981) *Maritime Transport: The Evolution of International Maritime Policy and Shipping Law* (Lexington, MA: D.C. Heath).

Goss, R.O. and Jones, C.D. (1971) *The Economics of Size in Bulk Carriers*, Government Economic Services, Occasional Paper No. 2 (London: HMSO).

J.C. Gould, Angier & Co., Ltd (1920) Fifty years of freights reproduced in *Fairplay*, 8 January–10 June 1920.

Gould, R.A. (2000) *Archaeology and the Social History of Ships* (Cambridge: Cambridge University Press).

Graham, M.G. and Hughes, D.O. (1985) *Containerisation in the Eighties* (London: Lloyd's of London Press).

*Grammenos, C.Th. (ed.) (2002) *The Handbook of Maritime Economics and Business* (London: LLP).

*Greve M., Hansen M.W., Schaumburg-Muller H. (2007) *Container Shipping and Economic Development: A Case Study of A.P.Moller-Maersk* (Copenhagen: Copenhagen Business School Press).

Gripaios, H. (1959) *Tramp Shipping* (London: Thomas Nelson).

Hampton, M.J. (1991) *Long and Short Shipping Cycles*, 3rd edition (Cambridge: Cambridge Academy of Transport).

Haraldsen, R.B. (1965) *Olsen & Ugelstad 1915–1965* (Oslo: Grondahl & Sons).

Harlaftis, G. (1993) *Greek Shipowners and Greece* (London: Athlone Press).

Harley, C.K. (1988) Ocean freight rates and productivity, 1740–1913: The primacy of mechanical invention reaffirmed. *Journal of Economic History*, 48(4), 851–76.

Haws, D. and Hurst, A.A. (1985) *The Maritime History of the World*, 2 vols (Brighton: Teredo).

Henderson, J.M. and Quandt, R.E. (1971) *Microeconomic Theory: A Mathematical Approach*, 2nd edition (New York: McGraw-Hill).

*Hill C. (2004) *Maritime Law*, Sixth edition (London: LLP).

Hill, P. and Vielvoye, R. (1974) *Energy in Crisis* (London: Robert Yateman).

Hind, J.A. (1959) *Ships and Shipbuilding* (London: Temple Press).

Hobsbawm, E. J. (1968) *Economic History of Britain, Vol. 3: Industry and Empire* (London: Penguin).

Hosking, R.O. (1973) *A Source Book of Tankers and Supertankers* (London: Ward Lock).

Howarth, S. (1992) *Sea Shell: The Story of Shell's British Tanker Fleets, 1892–1992* (London: Thomas Reed Publications).

Humble, R. (1979) *The Explorers* (Amsterdam: Time-Life Books).

Hummels, D. (2001) Time as a trade barrier, Unpublished paper, Purdue University. http://www.mgmt.purdue.edu/faculty/hummelsd/research/time3b.pdf (accessed 25 April 2008).

Hunting, P. (1968) *The Group and I* (London: John Wallis).

Hyde, F.E. (1967) *Shipping Enterprise and Management* (Liverpool: Liverpool University Press).

Ihre, R. and Gordon, L. (1980) *Shipbroking and Chartering Practice* (London: Lloyd's of London Press).

Independent Commission on International Development Issues (1980). *North–South: A Programme for Survival* (Oxford: Oxford University Press).

International Association of Classification Societies (2007) *Classification Societies – What, Why and How?* Updated edition (London: IACS).

Irving, W. (1828) *Life of Columbus* (London).

Isserlis, L. (1938) Tramp shipping, cargoes and freights. *Journal of the Royal Statistical Society*, 101, 53–146.

Jennings, E. (1980) *Cargoes: A Centenary Story of the Far East Freight Conference* (Singapore: Meridian).

Jevons, W.S. (1871) *The Theory of Political Economy* (London and New York: Macmillan).

Jones, L. (1957) *Shipbuilding in Britain: Mainly between the Wars* (Cardiff: University of Wales Press)

Kahre G. (1977) *The Last Tall Ships* (London: Conway Press).

*Kavussanos, M. and Ilias, D.V., (2006) *Derivatives and Risk Management in Shipping* (Witherby, London)

Kepner, C.H. and Tregoe, B.B. (1982) *The New Rational Manager* (London: John Martin).

Keynes, J.M. (1991) *The General Theory of Employment, Interest, and Money* (San Diego: Harcourt Brace).

*Kendall L.C. and Buckley J., (2001) *The Business of Shipping* (Centreville, MD: Cornell Maritime Press)

Kidman, P. (2003) *Port State Control: A Guide for Cargo Ships*, Second edition (London: Intercargo).

Kindleberger, C.P. (1967) *Foreign Trade and the National Economy* (New Haven, CT: Yale University Press).

Kirkaldy, A.W. (1914) *British Shipping* (London: Kegan Paul Trench Trubner & Co.). Reprinted by Augustus M. Kelly, New York, 1970.

Kirschenbaun, N.W. and Argall, G.O. (eds) (1975) *Minerals Transportation*, Vol. 2 (San Francisco: Miller Freeman).

Kummerman, H. and Jacquinet, R. (1979) *Ship's Cargo, Cargo Ships* (London: E & FN Spon).

La Dage, J.H. (1955) *Merchant Ships: A Pictorial Study* (Cambridge, MD: Cornell Maritime Press).

*Leggate H, McConville J, Morvillo A, (2005) *International Maritime Transport Perspectives* (London: Routledge).

*Levinson M., (2008) *The Box: How the Shipping Container Made the World Smaller and the World Economy Bigger* (Princeton, NJ: Princeton University Press).

Lindsay W.S. (1874) *History of Merchant Shipping and Ancient Commerce*, 4 vols (London: Simpson Low, Marston, Low and Searle).

Linnerman, R.E. (1983) The use of multiple scenarios by US industrial companies: a comparison study 1971–1981. *Long Range Planning*, 6.

*Lorange P., (2005) Global Management Under Turbulent Conditions (Oxford: Elsevier).

Maizels, A. (1962) *Growth and Trade* (Cambridge: Cambridge University Press).

Maizels, A. (1971) *Industrial Growth and World Trade* (Cambridge: Cambridge University Press).

*Mandaraka-Sheppard A., (2007) *Modern Maritime Law* (London: Routledge-Cavendish).

Maber, J.M. (1980) *The Ship – Channel Packets and Ocean Liners, 1850–1970* (London: HMSO).

MacGregor, D.R. (1961) *The China Bird: The History of Captain Killick and the Firm He Founded* (London: Chatto and Windus).

Major, R.H. (ed.) (1847) Select Letters of Christopher Columbus (London: Hakluyt Society).

Maritime Transport Research (1972) *The Sea Trades in Grain* (London: MTR).

Maritime Transport Research (1976) *Dry Cargo Ship Demand to 1985*, Vol. 3: *Raw Materials* (London: Graham & Trotman).

Maritime Transport Research (1977) *Dry Cargo Ship Demand to 1985*, Vol. 6: *Ship Demand* (London: Graham & Trotman).

Marriner, S. and Hyde, F.E. (1967) *The Senior John Samuel Swire, 1825–98. Management in Far Eastern Shipping Trades* (Liverpool: Liverpool University Press).

Marshall, A. (1994) *Principles of Economics*, Eighth edition (London: Macmillan Press). Reprint of Eighth edition originally published in 1920.

*McConville J. (1999) *Economics of Maritime Transport* (London: Witherby).

*McConville J, and Rickaby G. (1995) *Shipping Business and Maritime Economics* Annotated International Bibliography (London: Mansell).

McCord, N. (1979) *North East England: The Region's Development 1760 to 1960* (London: Batsford).

McEvedy, C. (1961) *The Penguin Atlas of Medieval History* (Harmondsworth: Penguin).

McEvedy, C. (1967) *The Penguin Atlas of Ancient History* (Harmondsworth: Penguin).

McEvedy, C. (1972) *The Penguin Atlas of Modern History* (Harmondsworth: Penguin).

McKinsey and Co. (1967) *Containerisation: The Key to Low Cost Transport* (London: British Transport Docks Board).

Meek, M. (1985) Operational experience of large container ships. Paper presented to Institute of Engineers and Shipbuilders in Scotland.

Meek, R.L. (1973) *Precursors of Adam Smith 1750–1775* (London: Dent).

Minchinton, W.E. (ed.) (1969) *The Growth of English Overseas Trade in the Seventeenth and Eighteenth Centuries* (Oxford: Oxford University Press).

Mitropoulos, E.E. (1985) Shipping and the work of IMO related to maritime safety and pollution prevention. Paper presented to the Maritime Economists' Conference on the State and the Shipping Industry, London, 1–2 April.

Mitropoulos, E.E. (1994) World trends in regulation of safety at sea and protection of the environment. Paper presented to Sea Japan Conference, 9 March.

*Molland A.F. (2008) *The Maritime Engineering Reference Book: A Guide to Ship Design, Construction and Operation* (Oxford: Butterworth-Heinemann).

Morais, R.C. (2001) Proving Papa wrong. *Forbes*, 19 June.

Morgan, D. (1979) *Merchants of Grain* (London: Weidenfeld & Nicolson).

Moyer, R. (1984) The futility of forecasting. *Long Range Planning*, 17,(1), 65–77.

# REFERENCES AND SUGGESTED READING

Nawwab, I.I., Speers, P.C. and Hoyle, P. F. (1980) *ARAMCO and its World* (Dhahran, Saudi Arabia: ARAMCO).

Needham, J. (1954) *Science and Civilisation in China*, Vol. 4 (Cambridge: Cambridge University Press).

Neresian, R. (1981) *Ships and Shipping: A Comprehensive Guide* (New York: Penwell Press).

Nerlove, M., Grether, D.M. and Carvalho, J.L. (1995) *Analysis of Economic Time Series: A Synthesis* (San Diego: Academic Press).

Northway, A.M. (1972) The Tyne Steam Shipping Co: a late nineteenth-century shipping line. *Maritime History*, 2(1).

Odell, P. R. (1981) *Oil and World Power* (London: Pelican)

OECD (1968) *Agricultural Commodity Projections 1975 and 1985: Production and Consumption of Major Foodstuffs* (Paris: OECD).

OECD (2001) *Liner Shipping Competition Policy Report* (Paris: OECD, Directorate for Science, Technology and Industry/Division of Transport).

*Packard, W. V. (2006) *Sale and Purchase*, Third edition (Colchester: Shipping Books).

*Packard, W.V. (2004) *Sea Trading, Volume 2: Cargoes*, Second edition (London: Shipping Books).

Packard, W.V. (1989) *Shipping Pools* (London: Lloyd's of London Press).

Paget, R.F. (1967) *In the Footsteps of Orpheus* (London: Robert Hale).

Palmer, S.A. (1972) Investors in London shipping, 1820–50. *Maritime History*, 2(1).

Pearson, R. and Fossey, J. (1983) *World Deep-Sea Container Shipping* (Aldershot: Gower).

Peter, L.J. (1979) *Quotations for Our Time* (London: Macdonald & Co.).

Petersen, K. (1955) *The Saga of Norwegian Shipping* (Oslo: Dreyers Forlag).

Petty, Sir W. (1662) *Treatise of Taxes and Contributions* (London: N. Brooke).

Pigou, A.C. (1927) *Industrial Fluctuations* (London: Macmillan).

Platou, R.S. (1970) A survey of the tanker and dry cargo markets 1945–70.
Supplement published by *Norwegian Shipping News*, No. 10c in 1970

Porter, M. (1990) *The Competitive Advantage of Nations* (New York: Free Press).

Proulx E.A. (1993) *The Shipping News* (London: Fourth Estate).

Prowse, M. (1984) The future that Britain never had. *Financial Times*, 17 August.

Radcliffe, M. A. (1985) *Liquid Gold* (London: Lloyd's of London Press).

Raleigh, Sir W. (1650) *Judicious and Select Essayes and Observations by that renowned and learned knight, Sir Walter Raleigh, upon the first invention of shipping, the misery of invasive warre, the Navy Royall and sea-service* (London: H. Moseley).

Rawls, J. (1971) *A Theory of Justice* (Cambridge, MA: Belknap Press).

Rochdale, Viscount (1970) *Committee of Inquiry into Shipping. Report*, Cmnd 4337 (London: HMSO).

Rogers, J.E. (1898) *The Industrial and Commercial History of England*, Volume I (London: T. Fisher Unwin).

Rostow, W.W. (1960) *Stages of Economic Growth* (Cambridge: Cambridge University Press).

Roxburgh, C. (2003) Hidden flaws in strategy. *McKinsey Quarterly*, no. 2, 27–39.

Samuelson, P. A. (1964) *Economics: An Introductory Analysis* (London: McGraw-Hill).

Savage, D. (1983) The assessment of the National Institute's forecasts of GDP, 1959–1982. *National Institute Economic Review*, no. 105.

Schumpeter E.B. (1960) *English Overseas Trade Statistics 1697–1808* (Oxford: Oxford University Press).

Schumpeter, J.A. (1939) *Business Cycles: A Theoretical, Historical and Statistical Analysis of the Capitalist Process* (New York: McGraw-Hill).

Schumpeter, J.A. (1954) *History of Economic Analysis* (London: Allen & Unwin).

Seddighi, H.R., Lawler, K.A. and Katos, A.V. (2000) *Econometrics: A Practical Approach* (London: Routledge).

Sklansky, D. (1987) *The Theory of Poker* (Henderson, NV: Two Plus Two Publishing).

Sklar, H. (ed.) (1980) *Trilateralism: The Trilateral Commission and Elite Planning For World Management* (Boston: South End Press).

Smith, A. (1998) *An Inquiry into the Nature and Causes of the Wealth of Nations* (Oxford: Oxford University Press).

Smith, J.W. and Holden, T.S. (1946) *Where Ships are Born* (Sunderland: Weir Shipbuilding Asociation).

Soudon, D. (2003) *The Bank and the Sea: Royal Bank of Scotland* (London: Shipping Business Centre, Royal Bank of Scotland).

Stephenson Harwood (1991) *Shipping Finance* (London: Euromoney Books).

Steven, R. (1969) *Iron and Steel for Operatives* (London: Collins)

Stokes, P. (1992) *Ship Finance: Credit Expansion and the Boon–Bust Cycle* (London: Lloyd's of London Press).

Stokes, P. (1997) A high risk low return industry – Can the risk/reward balance be improved? Paper presented at the LSE Shipping Finance Conference, 20 November.

Stopford, R.M. (1979a) Inter regional seaborne trade – a disaggregated commodity study. PhD thesis, London University.

Stopford, R.M. (1979b) New designs and newbuildings. In *Commodities and Bulk Shipping in the'80s* (London: Lloyd's of London Press).

Stopford, M. (1988) Yard capacity – is it enough to meet future needs? *Fairplay*, 15 December.

Stopford, M. (1997) *Maritime Economics*, 2nd edition (London: Routledge).

Stopford, R.M. and Barton, J.R. (1986) Economic problems of shipbuilding and the state. *Journal of Maritime Policy and Management* (Swansea), 13(1), 27–44.

Sturmey, S.G. (1962) *British Shipping and World Competition* (London: Athlone Press).

Svensson, T. (1986) Management strategies in shipbuilding in historical and comparative perspective. Lecture to the fourth International Shipbuilding and Ocean Engineering Conference, Helsinki, 8 September.

Temple, R.K.G. (1984) *Conversations with Eternity* (London: Rider Press).

Thomas, R.E. (1968) *Stowage: The Properties and Stowage of Cargoes*, Sixth edition revised by O.O. Thomas (Glasgow: Brown, Son and Ferguson).

Thornton, R.H. (1959) *British Shipping* (Cambridge: Cambridge University Press).

Tinsley, D. (1984) *Short-Sea Bulk Trades* (London: Fairplay Publications).

Trezise, P. H. and Suzuki, Y. (1976) Politics, government and economic growth in Japan. In H. Patrick and H. Rosovsky (eds), *Asia's New Giant* (Washington, DC: The Brookings Institution).

Tugendhat, C. (1968) *Oil: The Biggest Business*, Second edition (London: Eyre & Spottiswoode).

Tull, D.S. and Hawkins, D.L. (1980) *Marketing Research* (London: Collier Macmillan).

*Tusiani, Michael D., (1996) *The Petroleum Shipping Industry: Operations and Practices (Petroleum Shipping Industry)* (Tulsa, OK: Penwell Books).

UNCTAD (1985) *Port Development: A Handbook for Planners in Developing Countries*, 2nd edition (Geneva: UNCTAD).

United Nations (1983) *The Law of the Sea: Official Text of the United Nations Convention on the Law of the Sea with Annexes and Index* (London: Croom Helm).

US Department of Transportation Maritime Administration (2004) Mainstream Container Services 2003. http://www.marad.dot.gov/marad_statistics/Mainstream_Container.pdf (accessed 25 April 2008).

Van Cauwenbergh, G. (1983) *Antwerp, Portrait of a Port* (Antwerp: Lloyd Anversois S.A.).

*Van Dokkum, K. (2006) *Ship Knowledge – A Modern Encyclopedia. Covering ship design, construction and operation*, Third edition (Netherlands: Dokmar).

Volk, B. (1994) *The Shipbuilding Cycle – A Phenomenon Explained* (Bremen: Institute of Shipping Economics and Logistics).

Wall, R. (1977) *Ocean Liners* (London: Quarto).

Waltham, C. (1972) *Shu Ching. Book of History* (London: George Allen & Unwin).
*Wilson, J. (2004) *Carriage of Goods by Sea*, Fifth edition (Harlow: Longman)
*Willingale, M. (2005) *Ship Management*, Fourth edition (London: LLP).
Winters, L.A. (1991) *International Economics*, Fourth edition (London: Harper Collins).
*Wood P. (2000) *Tanker Chartering* (London: Witherby).
Zannetos, Z.S. (1973) Market and cost structure in shipping. In P. Lorange and V.D. Norman (eds), *Shipping Management* (Bergen: Institute for Shipping).
Zhou, M. and Amante, M. (2005) Chinese and Filipino seafarers: A race to the top or the bottom? *Modern Asian Studies*, 39, 535–57.

## Magazines and Periodicals

*Cargo Systems & International* Freighting (weekly) – valuable source of information on the container industry, port development and intermodalism.
*Containerisation International* (monthly) – the leading international publication devoted to the container business and excellent source of practical information about container transport (also publishes a very useful Yearbook).
*Fairplay* (weekly) – lively, long established practical shipping journal.
*International Bulk Journal* (monthly) – in-depth articles on the bulk trades, bulk handling and logistics; particularly good on minor bulks, providing a feel for the practicalities of the business.
*Lloyd's List* (daily) – newspaper covering shipping and the transport industry. Essential reading for keeping up to date, it also includes many supplements, features, articles and conference reviews.
*Lloyd's Shipping Economist* (monthly) – a good source of statistics and feature articles for the practical shipping economist.
*Maritime Policy and Management* (quarterly) – wide-ranging academic quarterly
*Motor Ship* (monthly) – mainly technical, provides detailed design drawings of ships and also feature articles.
*Petroleum Economist* (monthly) – definitive journal dealing with the oil industry and oil trade by sea; includes statistics of oil production and prices.
*Seatrade* (monthly) – established shipping magazine.
*UNCTAD Review of Maritime Transport* (annual) United Nations E.86.1I.D3 – annual review of shipping industry.

## Maritime Geography and Ports

*Guide to Port Entry* (Shipping Guides Ltd, Reigate, UK) – book and CD provide extensive details of ports, plans and port conditions.
*Lloyds Maritime Atlas* (LLP, 2007) – details of port, terminal and trade of ports, by country.
*Times Atlas of the Oceans* (Times Press, London).

## Maritime Statistics

British Petroleum Ltd, *Statistical Review of the World Energy Industry*, annual (London: BP).
Calvert, J. and McConville, J. (1983) Shipping Industry Statistical Sources (Sir John Cass Faculty of Transport, City of London Polytechnic).
*Clarkson Registers* – Clarkson Research Services Ltd (CRSL) publishes annual registers on Tankers, Bulk Carriers, Gas Tankers, Containerships, Reefers Offshore Vessels in hard copy and digital format (St Magnus House, 3 Lower Thames St, London).

*Containerisation International Yearbook* (National Magazine Company, London) – contains detailed statistics of world container industry.

*Fearnleys Annual Review*, annual (P.O. Box 1158, Sentrum 0107 Oslo, Norway) – provides a range of up-to-date shipping statistics with some series stretching back to the 1960s.

Fearnleys, *Monthly Report* – covers tankers, dry bulk, gas and containers (PO Box 1158 Sentrum, 0107 Oslo 1, Norway).

International Iron and Steel Institute, *World Steel Statistics and Steel Statistical Yearbook*, annual (IISI, Brussels).

Lloyd's Fairplay, *Statistical Tables* (London) – annual summary of world merchant fleet.

Lloyd's Register, *Casualty Return* (London) – details of ships totally lost, broken up, etc.

OECD, *Main Economic Indicators* (OECD, Paris).

Platou, R.S., *The Platou Report*, annual (R.S. Platou, Oslo) – source of market information.

*Shipping Intelligence Weekly* (CRSL St Magnus House, 3 Lower Thames St, London) – provides a wide ranging source of market, economic and fleet statistics.

United Nations, *Monthly Bulletin of Statistics* (New York: UN).

*World Shipyard Monitor* (CRSL St Magnus House, 3 Lower Thames St, London) – provides comprehensive monthly shipbuilding statistics and orderbook lists.

# Index

ABS *see* American Bureau of Shipping
added value 347
administration costs of liner services 547–8
advance calls 231
affect of regulations on maritime economics 655–6
Aframax tankers 70, 75, 168, 205–6, 209–12, 305, 311, 418, 429, 444, 570, 580, 596–7, 735
Africa's seaborne trade 378–9
*Agamemnon* 27, 31
ageing of ships 71–3
agribulk trades 459
agricultural 58
air freight 50–51
air transport, 1950–2006 35–44; *see also* container transport, 1950–2006
*Al Malik Saud Al-Awa* 319
Alexander the Great 9, 700
American Bureau of Shipping 35, 659
American Ship Masters Association 659
American War of Independence 109
*Amerikaland* 447, 603
ammonia 481
Amsterdam 6, 18–20, 45, 48, 377; and Dutch trade 18–20
analysing risk in ship finance 310–314; risk management options 310–314
analysts' views of short shipping cycles 99–101
analytical techniques 724–38; opinion surveys 726; probability analysis 737–8; regression analysis 730–37; time series analysis 726–30

Anglo-American Oil Co. Ltd 435
Anglo-Saxon Petroleum Co. Ltd 435
annual cashflow analysis 257–60
anti-trust laws 690
Antwerp 6, 18–19, 45, 82, 367, 377, 527, 530–31, 560
approach to maritime forecasting 697–702; challenge of dealing with the unknown 698–700; forecasting paradox 700; importance of information 701–2; poor track record of shipping forecasts 697–8; rational forecasting to reduce uncertainty 700–701
approaches to the forecast 710–712
*Aquitania* 26, 111
Arabian Gulf 7–9, 11–13, 127, 162–4, 362–4, 483, 559, 604; oil transportation 77, 124, 146, 352–5, 380–81, 439
arguments for free trade 388
aromatics 434
around the world in 80 days 350–52
arranging employment for a ship 181–3
asbestos 386, 651–2
Asia's seaborne trade 373–7; China 376–7; Japan 374–6; southern and eastern Asia 377
asset play 274–5
asset sales 292–4; participation agreement 293–4
asset-backed finance in the 1970s 273–4
assumptions 740
Athens 6, 9
Atlantic Container Line 548
Atlantic maritime area 356–9
Aurelius Heracles 5

Australia 383
autocorrelation 717, 734, 736
autoregressive moving average 729–30
availability of credit 631
average haul and ton miles 146–7
average haul forecast 720–21
avoiding collisions at sea 681
awkward cargo 523

Babylon 6–8, 699
balance of imports and exports 389–91
balance of supply and demand 722
balance sheet 248–50
balancing trades 442–3
Baltic Coffee House 32, 180
Baltic Exchange 32–4, 41, 46, 180, 195–7
Baltic Exchange Capesize Index (BCI) 196
Baltic Exchange Dry Index (BDI) 196
Baltic Exchange Handymax Index (BHMI) 196
Baltic Exchange Panamax Index (BPI) 196
Baltic Freight Index (BFI) 195
Baltic International Freight Futures Exchange
    (BIFFEX) 196
Baltic Sea 6, 11–12, 19–22, 24, 358–9, 365–6,
    382, 501, 601
Bangladesh 212, 364, 650–53
bank credit analysis 708
bank lending policy 240–41
bank loans 285–96
bare boat charter 185, 242
barge-carrying vessels 538, 589–90
barges 574
base ports 559
Basel Convention 652
basic gas tanker technology 604
bear trap 727
beginnings of sea trade 7–8
behavioural variables 704, 739
beneficial owner 673
Bergesen, Sigval 123, 320, 483
Bessegen 496
Bethlehem Steel 447
'between a rock and a hard place' 555–6
bill of lading AD236 5, 44
BIMCO 'Gencon' 187
Black Ball Line 506
Black Sea 10–12, 24, 33, 254, 352, 356–9,
    366–7, 381–2, 435, 439
Blue Funnel Line 32
Board of Trade Departmental Committee on
    Shipping and Shipbuilding 616–17
Boer War 132

Bombay 27, 435; see also Mumbai
bond ratings 280
'Book of Change' 699
'Book of History' 699
Bosphorus 501
bourses 18–19
Braudel, Ferdinand 6–7, 96
break-bulk cargo 65, 82, 509, 530, 532,
    537–8, 562
break-bulk liner services 532
breakdowns 33, 230
Bremen 82, 367
Bretton Woods 36–7, 44–6, 385, 648
Britannia 30
British Empire 617
Brostrom group 447
budgets 708
building ships 156–60
building-blocks of liner service economics
    539–48; administration costs 547–8; capacity
    utilization 543; container costs 546–7;
    deployment of containers 546; port charges
    545; service schedule 543; ship
    characteristics 539–40; ship costs and
    economies of scale 544–5
building-blocks of sea trade 385–8; arguments
    for free trade 388; theory of maritime trade
    387–8
bulk cargo transport 417–68
bulk carriers 590–94
bulk fleet 418–19
'bulk shipping': definition 64
bulk shipping economics 78–90
bulk shipping investment 428–30
bulk shipping market cycles, 1945–2007
    118–30; cycle 15: 1945–51 121; cycle 16:
    1952–5 121–2; cycle 17: 1957–69 122–3;
    cycle 18: 1970–2 123–4; cycle 19: 1973–8
    124–6; cycle 20 (bulk carriers): 1979–87
    126–7; cycle 20 (tankers): 1979–87 127–8;
    cycle 21: 1988–2002 128–30; cycle 22:
    2003–2007 130; short-term cycles,
    1945–2007 121; technological trend,
    1945–2007 119–21
bulk trades 419–22; bulk cargoes shipped by
    sea 420–22
bulk transport, 1950–2006 35–44; see also
    container transport, 1950–2006
bunker adjustment factors 551
bunker costs 156, 223, 240, 244, 355, 412,
    543–5, 549
butadiene 481

butane 480
buyers and sellers in the newbuilding market 207–8
Byzantine Empire 10–12, 71

Cadiz 8, 18, 22
Caesar Gaius Julius Verus Maximus the Pious 5, 44
calculating the regression equation 732–5
Calcutta 34, 80, 556–7
canal dues 236
capacity utilization 543
Cape of Good Hope 13–19, 122, 146, 148, 162, 319, 352, 362, 364, 436–8, 442
Cape Town 356, 532
Capesize tankers 41, 60, 70, 76–8, 88, 120, 129, 183, 188, 197, 222–32, 321–2, 412–14, 429, 590
capital asset pricing model 321–2, 340
capital cost of ships 236–41, 544; cashflow costs and gearing 240; distinction between profit and cash 237–9; estimating a ship's depreciation 239–40; security and bank lending policy 240–1; taxation 241
capital gain 328
capital markets and financing ships 296–303; public offering of equity 297–300; raising finance by issuing bonds 300–303
cargo access ramps 577
cargo additionals 552
cargo imbalances 518
cargo liner era 506–7
cargo liner services 31–2
cargo liner types 589
cargo stowage 575–6
cargo tracking 521
cargo value 420
cargo-handling costs 236
cargo-handling gear 577
Carnival Corporation 271, 297, 502–3
Carriage of Dangerous Goods 600
carrier cost per move 521
case oil 434–5
cash crops 409
cashflow 217–68; and art of survival 217–19
cashflow costs and gearing 240
cashflow statement 251–2
Caspian Sea 359, 381
categories of shipyard 638–9
causes of the shipbuilding cycle 628–9
caustic soda 473, 599
cell guides 577

cellular 'lift on, lift off' ships 537
cement carriers 595–6
central Asia 379–82
century of shipbuilding development 624–5
CGM see Compagnie Générale Maritime
challenge of dealing with the unknown 698–700
challenge of successful risk management 133
changing shipping company organization 43–4
characteristics of containerized cargo 516–18
characteristics of liner ships 539–40
characteristics of sea transport demand 53–61; commodities shipped by sea 56–8; global sea transport demand model 53–6; parcel size distribution 58–60; product differentiation in shipping 60–1; sea transport product 53
characteristics of shipping business 3–4
characteristics of shipping market cycles 94–101; analysts' views of short cycles in shipping 99–101; components of economic cycles 94–5; long shipping cycles 95–6; seasonal shipping cycles 97–8; short shipping cycles 96–7
charter-backed finance in the 1950s and 1960s 272–3
charter-party 185–8
chartering terms 176
checklist for shipping risk 313
chemical fleet and supply 477–8
chemical tankers 599–601
chemical transport system 476–7
chemicals transport 473–8
chilled cargo 491
China 376–7
China Ocean Shipping Company see COSCO
China Shipping 84, 297, 309
Chinese New Year 144
Chinese shipbuilding industry 623–4
Churchill, Winston 5, 319
CIRR see commercial interest reference rate
Civil War 620
Clarkson Bulk Carrier Register 189
Clarkson Tanker Register 190
classic maritime supply–demand model 715–16
classification certificates 662
classification of costs 221–2
classification of revenue 242
classification societies 657–63; classification societies today 660–61; International Association of Classification Societies 662–3; origin of classification societies 658–9; regulatory activities of classification societies 661–2

closed conferences 557
closing 202
coastal state 658, 663–6, 685–8; regulatory role of 685–8; rights over foreign ships 685–6; versus flag state 663–6
cobweb theorem 335–7
Code on the Carriage of Hazardous Cargoes 475
Code of Conduct for Liner Conferences 689
Code of Hammurabi 8
coefficient of correlation 734
coffee 523–4
'coffin ships' 655, 675
coking coal 445–8
collapse 98
collision avoidance at sea 681
COLREG see Convention on the International Regulations for Preventing Collisions at Sea
Columbus, Christopher 3, 15–16
combined tankers 601–3
commercial bank lending 288–91
commercial interest reference rate 296
commercial origins of bulk shipping 417–18
commercial philosophy 568
commodities shipped by sea 56–8
commodity trade cycles 404–411; long-term influences on trade 405–7; seasonal and short-term cyclical trade 404–5; stages of economic development 407–9; trade development cycle 409–411
commodity trade supply–demand model 401–2
Common Structural Rules, 2006 663
Compagnie Générale Maritime 507
company law 666, 671
company structures associated with ship registration 673–5
comparison of shipping with financial investments 322–4
compensated gross tonnage 752–3
competition regulation 688–92
competition theory 329–38; cobweb theorem and the difficulty of defining returns 335–7; freight revenue and the short-term cyclical adjustment process 332–4; link between the macroeconomic and microeconomic models 334–5; long-term adjustment process 334; returns earned in imperfect shipping markets 337–8; shipping company microeconomic model 330–32
competitiveness 130, 644–8; see also currency movements; labour costs; material costs
compliance with maritime safety conventions 667

components of economic cycles 94–5
computing cashflow 252–62; annual cashflow analysis 257–60; discounted cashflow analysis 260–2; internal rate of return 262; voyage cashflow analysis 253–7
conbulkers 594
Concorde 741–2
conference systems 556–7
conflict of volume versus speed 520–22
consequences of containerization 511–12
Constantinople 10–12
consumables 229
container costs 546–7
container ports and terminals 559–62; port calls and liner pricing 559–60; port infrastructure 560–62
container system, 1966–2005 508–9
container transport, 1950–2006 35–44; changing shipping company organization 43–4; containerization of general cargo 41–2; development of bulk transport systems 39–41; growth of air transport between regions 37–8; growth of seaborne trade, 1950–2005 38–9; new trade environment created at Bretton Woods 36–7; rationale for sea transport integration 35–7; shipping's 'industrial revolution' 39; transport of specialized cargoes 42–3
container-ship size trends 538–9
container-ships 537, 581–5
containerization of general cargo 41–2
containerized cargo's characteristics 516–18
containerizing minor bulk cargoes 522–4
contiguous zone 665
contract of affreightment 183–4
control inspections by port states 687
control movements by port states 686–7
controlled temperature cargo 492
Convention on the International Regulations for Preventing Collisions at Sea 681
Convention on the Law of the Sea 656, 663–6
Convention on Load Lines 681, 687
Convention for the Safety of Life at Sea 678
Convention on Standards of Training, Certification and Watchkeeping for Seafarers, 1978 682
Convention on Tonnage Measurement of Ships, 1969 681
conversion factors 751–4
cooperative agreements 556–60
corn bin of Europe 19
Corn Laws 388, 398

corporate bank loans 291–2
corporate finance 275–6
correlation of price in tankers and bulk
    carriers 203
COSCO 84, 297, 309, 535
cost of freight 73–5
cost of running ships 225–36; cargo-handling
    costs 236; operating costs 226–31; periodic
    maintenance 231–2; voyage costs 232–6
cost of sea transport 73–80; bulk shipping
    economics 78–80; liner shipping economics
    80; sea transport unit cost function 76–8;
    ship size and economies of scale 75–6; world
    trade and cost of freight 73–5
costs 172, 217–68; capital cost of the ship
    236–41; cashflow and the art of survival
    217–19; cost of running ships 225–36;
    financial performance and investment strategy
    219–25; methods for computing cashflow
    252–62; revenue and cashflow 217–68;
    revenue the ship earns 242; shipping accounts
    246–52; valuing merchant ships 262–6
cotton 519
countries producing world's merchant ships
    614–16
countries that scrap ships 649–51
countries that trade by sea 389–93; balance of
    imports and exports 389–91; differences in
    maritime trade by country 389; land area and
    sea trade 392–3; population and sea trade
    393; wealth and seaborne trade 391–2
coverage of maritime laws 675–6
creation of maritime convention 677
crew costs 226–9
crewing 667, 671; and terms of employment 667
criteria and approach of bulk shipping
    investment 428–30
crude oil tankers 596–9
crude oil trade 434–42; crude oil transport
    system 440–42; geographical distribution of
    the crude oil trade 438–40; growth of the
    tanker 'spot market', 1975–2006 437; origins
    of the seaborne oil trade 434–5; sea transport
    of oil, 1890–1970 435–7
crude oil transport system 440–42
cruise liners 502–3
Cruz Grande 447
Cunard 30–31, 37, 271, 499–500
currency adjustment factors 551
currency movements 648
current classification societies 660–61
cycle 8: 1873–9 112–13

cycle 10: 1889–97 113–14
cycle 11: 1898–1910 114–15
cycle 12: 1911–14 115
cycle 13: 1921–5 116–17
cycle 14: 1926–37 117–18
cycle 15: 1945–51 121
cycle 16: 1952–5 121–2
cycle 17: 1957–69 122–3
cycle 18: 1970–2 123–4
cycle 19: 1973–8 124–6
cycle 20 (bulk carriers): 1979–87 126–7
cycle 20 (tankers): 1979–87 127–8
cycle 21: 1988–2002 128–30
cycle 22: 2003–2007 130

da Gama, Vasco 16, 347
Daewoo 623
Danish International Shipping Register 241
Dardanelles 254, 359
Darwinian economics 333
Darwinian purpose 99
days off hire 245
days spent in ballast 245
'dead cat bounce' 97
dead freight 444, 470
deadweight 752
deadweight utilization 156, 245–6
dealing with default 314–16
dealing with the unknown 698–700
debt 296
decision makers 85, 150–1; supply controllers
    150–1
decisions facing shipowners 175–7
decline of British shipbuilding 616–19
decomposition analysis 727–9
deep-sea cables revolutionize shipping
    communications 27–8
deep-sea ro-ros 493–4
deep-sea shipping 50–51
default 314–16
deferred rebate 558
deficit trade 443
defining forecasting decision 705–6
delivery peaks and troughs 646
Delphi technique 724
demand and the car and truck carrier transport
    system 494–5
demand for chemical transport 473–5
demand for general cargo and liner transport
    514–24; characteristics of containerized
    cargo 516–18; containerizing minor bulk
    cargoes 522–4; general cargo and container

movements 514–16; price, service and the demand for liner transport 519–20; product differentiation – conflict of volume versus speed 520–22

demand for LPG gas transport 479–81

demand for refrigerated transport 488

demand for sea transport 139–50; average haul and ton miles 146–7; impact of random shocks on ship demand 147–9; seaborne commodity trades 143–6; transport costs and long-un demand function 149–50; world economy 140–3

demolition 648–52; see also recycling industry

demolition market 212–13

demurrage 176–7

deployment of containers 546

depreciation 328

depreciation of ships 239–40

depression 131

derived demand for a commodity 403–4

derived demand for ships 567–8

Det Norske Veritas 35

determining ship prices 202–4

developing a forecasting model 716–17

developing container service infrastructure 509–510

developing rules 661–2

developing scenario analysis 723–4

development of bulk transport systems 39–41

development of chemical transport 475–6

development of freight derivatives market 196

development of LNG trade 484–6

development of passenger shipping 499–500

development of refrigerated transport 488–9

developments of corporate finance in the 1990s 275–6

DHL 309

Diaz, Bartholomew 3, 15

differences in maritime trade by country 389

differences in natural resources 399–404; commodity trade supply–demand model 401–2; derived demand for a commodity 403–4; resource-based trade and the Heckscher-Ohlin theory 400–401

differences in production costs 395–9; modern theories of manufacturing advantage 398–9; theory of absolute advantage 396–7; theory of comparative advantage 397–8

differences in 'risk preference' 338–9

differences in subcontracting 646

different character of the four shipping markets 180

different ways of approaching forecast 710–712

difficulty of defining returns 335–7

DIS see Danish International Shipping Register

discharging facilities 584

discounted cashflow analysis 260–62

Discourse on the Balance of Trade 388

diseconomies of scale 545, 550

distances and transit times 348–56

distinction between profit and cash 237–9

'distress' sales 203

distribution key 85, 87–8

diversified shipping group 86

division of labour 4

Dr Jekyll and Mr Hyde 342

Drake, Colonel Edwin 434

Drucker, Peter 698–701

dry bags 523

dry cargo market report 188–90

dry docking 33, 162, 200, 221, 226, 230–32, 251, 522, 623, 649–52, 662

dual registration 673

Duff & Phelps 281

Duffield 435

'dumped' wool 519

Durbin–Watson statistic 717, 734, 736

Dutch East India Company 19–20

Dutch trade 18–20

dynamic adjustment process 171–2

dynamic links in the shipping model 138–9

earnings before interest and depreciation 326–8

East India Company 20, 23

eastern Asia 377

East–West trades 524–9; North Atlantic trade 527–8; round-the-world services 528–9; transpacific trade 526–7; Western Europe to the Far East trade 528

easyJet 285

EBID see earnings before interest and depreciation

economic assumptions 717–18

economic criteria for evaluating ship designs 609–610; financial analysis 609–610; market research 609

economic cycle components 94–5

economic framework of shipping market 47

economic implications of flag state regulation 666–7

economic Jurassic Park 3

economic model for sea transport 61–4

economic principles 628–38; causes of the shipbuilding cycle 628–9; long-term

shipbuilding demand 636–8; shipbuilding demand, supply and the price model 630–32; shipbuilding market short-term equilibrium 634–6; shipbuilding prices 629–30; shipbuilding supply function 632–3; short-term shipbuilding demand function 633–4
economic principles of liner operation 512–14
economic role of open registers 671–3
economics of discovery 15
economics of shipbuilding and scrapping 613–53; economic principles 628–38; regional structure of world shipbuilding 614–25; role of merchant shipbuilding and scrapping industries 613–14; ship recycling industry 648–52; shipbuilding costs and competitiveness 644–8; shipbuilding market cycles 625–8; shipbuilding production process 638–44
economies of scale 436, 545; and liner ship costs 544–5; and ship size 75–6; and unit costs 223–5
EEZ see exclusive economic zones
effect of sentiment on supply curve 168–9
efficient cargo handling 425–6
Elbe (river) 357, 359, 367
elements involved in ship production 640–44
Elizabeth Watts 434
Emma Maersk 544
Encounter Bay class ships 509
encumbrance 201
energy trades 58
English Channel 500–501
equilibrium 163–8, 634–6; long-run equilibrium 166–8; momentary equilibrium 163–5; shipbuilding market short term 634–6; short-run equilibrium 165–6
equity 278, 296–300
equity 'kickers' 296
Erika 656, 683
escaping from the present 741–2
estimating a ship's depreciation 239–40
estimating market value of a ship 262–4
estimating residual value of a ship 265–6
estimating scrap value of a ship 265
ethylene 481, 606
EU see European Union
Euphrates (river) 7–8
eurobond market 279
Europe discovers sea route to Asia 13–14
European shipbuilding, 1902–2006 619–20
European Union 88–9, 690–91; regulation of shipping competition 690–91; regulation of tramp shipping pools 691

Europe's seaborne trade 365–7
Evergreen 526, 528–9
evolution of the shipping corporation 271–2
example of time series analysis 727–9
Exchange Handymax Index (BHMI) and the Baltic
exchange rates 631
exclusive economic zones 665–6, 687
expansion demand (X) 636–7
expectation curve 164
exponential smoothing 729
Export Credit Bank of Japan 295
Export Credit Guarantee Department 241, 295
Exxon Valdez 656, 683, 687–8

F statistic 733
Facilitation Committee (of the IMO) 678
Falklands War 149
false consensus 739
Far East Freight Conference 558–9
fast food 490
Fearnleys Review 125
Federal Maritime Commission 690
FedEx 309, 521
feeder ports 559–60
feeder services 532
Feeders 538–9, 582, 584
Feedmaxes 539, 582, 584
FEFC see Far East Freight Conference
Felixstowe 5, 367, 527, 532
fertilizer trades 460–63; phosphate rock 461; phosphates 461; potash 461–2; sulphur 462; urea 462–3
fifteenth-century global economy 12–13
financial analysis 609–610
financial investments and shipping investments compared 322–4
financial law 666
financial markets and packaged investment funds 279–81
financial performance 219–25; classification of costs 221–2; ship age and supply price of freight 222–3; unit costs and economies of scale 223–5
financial performance of 'Perfect Shipping' 328–9
financial pressures and shipowners' decisions 217–19
financing asset play in the 1980s 274–5
financing new ships 294–6
financing ships and shipping companies 269–318; analysing risk in ship finance

310–14; dealing with default 314–16; financing ships with bank loans 285–96; financing ships with private funds 285–6; financing ships with special purpose companies 303–10; how ships have been financed in the past 270–6; ship finance and shipping economics 269–70; world financial system and types of finance 276–85

financing ships with bank loans 285–96; asset sales (participation agreement) 293–4; corporate bank loans 291–2; financing new ships 294–6; loan syndications and asset sales 292–3; mezzanine finance structures 296; mortgage-backed loan 286–8; private placement of debt and equity 296; structure of commercial bank lending 288–91

financing ships with private funds 285

financing ships with special purpose companies 303–310; German KG funds 306–7; leasing ships 307–9; Norwegian K/S partnership structures 306; private placement vehicles 305–6; securitization of shipping assets 309–310; ship funds and SPACs 304–5

First World War 27, 105, 114–17, 148, 620

fishing fleet 608

Fitch 281

fitting a regression equation 731–2

fixed prices 553–4

flag state 658, 663–75; economic implications of regulation 666–7; regulatory role of 666–75; versus coastal state 663–6

flagging out 619, 674–5

flags of convenience 36, 43–6, 71, 92, 241, 273, 289, 620–22, 669, 686

flats 574

fleet by ship type 568–71

fleet productivity 154–6

fleet replacement 71–3

flexibility of ship 580–81

flotation 300

FMC see Federal Maritime Commission

forecast preparation 705–8; defining the decision 705–6; what decision makers use forecasts for 707–8; who makes the forecast? 706–7

forecasting and planning 695–744; maritime forecasting and market research 697–744

forecasting model 717–22; average haul forecast 720–21; balance of supply and demand 722; economic assumptions 717–18; freight rates 722; merchant fleet forecast 721; seaborne trade forecast 718–20; ship

demand forecast 721; ship productivity forecast 721–2; shipping supply forecast 722

forecasting paradox 700

forecasting problems 738–42; objectivity: the problem of escaping from the present 741–2; problem of monitoring results 740–41; problems with behavioural variables 739; problems with model specifications and assumptions 740

forecasting time-scale 709–710

forest products trade 67, 465–6

forestry trades 58

forward futures agreements 196–8

four shipping markets 175–214; decisions facing shipowners 175–7; demolition (recycling) market 212–13; four shipping markets 177–80; freight derivatives market 193–8; freight market 180–93; newbuilding market 207–12; sales and purchase market 198–207

framework for decisions 246–52

Fredriksen, John 320

free passage 162

freight charges 551

freight derivative contract 193–5

freight derivatives market 178, 193–8; development of freight derivatives market 196; forward futures agreements 196–8; freight derivative contract 193–5; freight futures trading 196; freight indices 195–6; requirements for a freight derivatives market 195

freight futures trading 196

freight indices 195–6

'freight market': definition 180–1

freight market 180–93; arranging employment for a ship 181–3; bare boat charter 185; charter-party 185–8; contract of affreightment 183–4; freight market reporting 188–91; freight rate statistics 192; liner and specialist ship chartering 191; time charter 184–5; voyage charter 183; what is the freight market? 180–1; Worldscale index 192–3

freight market reporting 188–91; dry cargo market report 188–90; tanker market report 190–1

'freight of all kinds' tariff 551

freight rate forecasting 715–23; classic maritime supply–demand model 715–16; example of a forecasting model 717–22; five stages in developing a forecasting model 716–17; sensitivity analysis 723 freight rate mechanism 160–72; dynamic adjustment process 171–2; effect of sentiment on supply curve 168–9; equilibrium and importance of time 163–8; long run prices and costs 172; shipping cycle model 169–71; supply and demand functions 161–3

freight rate statistics 192

freight rates 111–12, 135–74, 631, 722; 1869–1913 111–12

freight revenue 160, 178, 242–6; deadweight utilization 245–6; maximizing loaded days at sea 244–5; optimizing operating speed 243–4; and ship productivity 242–6; and the short-term cyclical adjustment process 332–4

freight swaps 196

Frontline 275, 297, 305–6

frozen cargo 491

fuel costs 233–5

fully pressurized vessels 604

fully refrigerated vessels 605

functions of supply and demand 161–3

fundamentals 130–1

Gadani Beach 651

game theory 555

gas tankers 604–8; basic gas tanker technology 604; liquefied natural gas tankers 606–8; liquid petroleum gas tankers 604–5

GATT see General Agreement on Tariffs and Trade

Gaz Transport 606

gearing 240

General Agreement on Tariffs and Trade 37, 388

general cargo and container movements 514–16

general cargo trades ship types 581–90

general cargo transport 505–564

general costs of running a ship 231

General Council of British Shipping 115

General Maritime 275, 292

General Motors 520

General Shipowner's Society 22

geographical distribution of the crude oil trade 438–40

geography of maritime trade 347–84; Africa's seaborne trade 378–9; Asia's seaborne trade 373–7; Europe's seaborne trade 365–7; maritime trading network 356–65; North America's seaborne trade 368–71; oceans, distances and transit times 348–56; seaborne trade of Middle East, Central Asia and Russia 379–82; South America's seaborne trade 371–3; trade of Australia and

Oceania 383; value added by seaborne transport 347–8

German KG funds 306–7

German-American Petroleum Company 435

getting a mandate 292–3

Global Alliance 529, 535

global alliances 534–5, 557–8

global economy 3–46; in the fifteenth century 12–13

global market place 32–5

global sales 547

global sea transport demand model 53–6

Glückauf 27, 435

good and bad decades 130–31

good conduct 685, 692

goodwill 249

government guarantee 295

government policy-making 708

governments' role in shipping 89

grain trade model 454–5

Grand Alliance 526, 529, 535

Great Depression 115, 117–18, 627

Great Eastern 27–8

Great Lakes 205, 240, 359, 368–70, 447, 457, 493

Greek shipping 9–10

gross registered tonnage 751

gross tonnage 751–2

growth of air transport between regions 37–8

growth of sea trade in the nineteenth century 23–5

growth of seaborne trade, 1950–2005 38–9

growth of the tanker 'spot market', 1975–2006 437

Guidelines on Ship Recycling 652

Gulf of Finland 359, 367, 382, 439

Gulf War 120, 149

Haji-Ioannou, Stelios 285, 320

Hamburg 12, 31, 48, 82, 182, 307, 367, 527, 529, 532

Hamburg Süd 32, 533

handling homogeneous dry bulk cargoes 431–2

handling liquid bulk cargoes 430–31

Handy bulk carriers 41, 76, 78, 264, 424, 590–91

Handymax bulk carriers 70, 78, 88, 246, 300, 322, 414, 419, 429, 590–92

Hanjin 535

Hanseatic League 6, 11–12; AD 1000–1400 11–12

Hapag-Lloyd 271, 309, 529, 532–5, 548

hatch design 577
heavy lift 497–9
heavy lift vessels 588
Heckscher-Ohlin theory 400–401, 415
Her Majesty's dominions 667
*Herald of Free Enterprise* 656
herding instinct 739
high seas 666
historical financing of ships 270–76; asset-backed finance in the 1970s 273–4; charter-backed finance in the 1950s and 1960s 272–3; developments of corporate finance in the 1990s 275–6; evolution of the shipping corporation 271–2; financing asset play in the 1980s 274–5; one-ship company 273; ship finance in the pre-steam era 270–1; shipbuilding credit 276
history and organization of IMO 678–80
history of classification societies 658–9
history of maritime development 5–7
history of shipping 1–90; organization of the shipping market 47–90; sea transport and the global economy 3–46
holding company 674
homogeneous dry bulk cargoes 431–2
Hong Kong 6, 44, 48, 51, 82–3, 182, 273, 285, 297, 359, 376–7, 436, 501, 524, 528, 532, 560–63, 622, 674
'Hovering Acts' 665
how cargo should be handled 576–7
how cargo should be stowed 575–6
how company accounts are used 247
how maritime laws are made 675–7; procedures for making maritime conventions 676–7; role of maritime laws 675; topics covered by maritime law 675–6
how newbuilding differs from sale and purchase 207
how ship prices are determined 202–4
how ships are traded 571–2
Hume, David 385, 388, 703; *see also* mercantilism
Hunter Valley 453

*I Ching* 699–701
IASB *see* International Accounting Standards Board
*Ideal-X* 508–509
identifying economic model 703–4
IFRSs *see* International Financial Reporting Standards
ILO *see* International Labour Organization

*Imago Mundi* 15
IMCO *see* Intergovernmental Maritime Consultative Organization
IMO *see* International Maritime Organization
impact of financial pressures on shipowners' decisions 217–19
impact of random shocks on ship demand 147–9
implementing rules 661–2; classification certificate 662; periodic surveys 662; surveys during construction 661; technical plan review 661
importance of information 701–2
importance of law of the sea 663
importance of market intelligence 132–3
importance of time 163–8
income effect 402–4
income statement 247–8
Indian Ocean maritime area 362–4
indivisibility 518
industrial relations 708
'industrial revolution' of shipping 39
inferior goods 401
inflation 205
information 701–2
inland waterway systems 575
inorganic chemicals 473
inspections 199–200
institutions providing ship finance 284
insurance 230–31
integration of shipping markets 178–80
integration of transport modes 51–2
integration of transport modes of cargo handling 426–7
interest rates subsidy 295
Intergovernmental Maritime Consultative Organization 672
intermediate bulk containers 574
internal rate of return 262
International Accounting Standards Board 247
International Association of Classification Societies 662–3
International Bulk Chemical Code 600
International Convention for the Prevention of Pollution from Ships 682–4
International Court of Justice 672
International Financial Reporting Standards 247
International Labour Organization 658, 684–5
International Lease Finance Corporation 309
International Maritime Organization 150–51, 658, 678–84; collision avoidance at sea 681; Convention on Standards of Training,

Certification and Watchkeeping for Seafarers (STCW), 1978 682; Convention on Tonnage Measurement of Ships, 1969 681; history and organization of IMO 678–80; International Convention for the Prevention of Pollution from Ships 682–4; Regulation 13G 150–51; Safety of Life at Sea Convention (SOLAS) 680–81; ships' load lines 681
International Monetary Fund 37
international negotiations 708
international registers 669
International Safety Management 680
International Standard Industrial Classification 406; sectors 406
international transport industry 50–52; deep-sea shipping and air freight 50–51; land transport and integration of transport modes 51–2; short-sea shipping 51
intraregional trades and feeder services 532
introduction to general cargo 505
introduction to specialized shipping 469–73; specialized shipping model 471–3; what is specialized shipping? 469–71
invasion of Iraq 120
investment funds from savings 278
investment strategy 219–25; see also financial performance
investors and lenders 278
Iran Revolution 149
iron ore 445–8
ISIC see International Standard Industrial Classification
ISM see International Safety Management
ISO container 574
isolationalism 388
issuing bonds 300–303

Japan 374–6
Japan Development Bank 622
Japanese shipbuilding industry 621–2
John Bowes 26, 66, 271, 417
joint product manufacture 646
joint ventures 85–9
junk bonds 281

K-Line 84, 496, 535
Kawasaki Shipyard 622
key elements of maritime forecast 702–5; identifying the economic model 703–4; three principles of forecasting 702–3; types of relationships and variables 704–5

key influences on supply and demand 136–9; dynamic links in the model 138–9
Keynes, John Maynard 338
Kobe earthquake 405
Kockums Shipyard 620
Kommandit-gesellschaft 138
Kondratieff, Nikolai 95–6

labour costs 647–8
land area and sea trade 392–3
land transport 51–2
large local port 83
large regional port 83
last-resort buyers 158–60, 613–54
law of the sea 663–6; flag state versus coastal state 663–6; why the law of the sea matters 663
Le Havre 367, 527, 530, 532
leasing ships 307–9
Legal Committee (of the IMO) 678
lessons from 5000 years of commercial shipping 44–5
lessons from two centuries of cycles 130–1; fundamentals set the tone for good and bad decades 130–1
Liberty ships 110, 121–3, 154, 621, 671
LIBOR see London interbank offered rate
lightweight 753–4
limitations of transport statistics 67–8
liner and shipping system emerges 28–9
liner cartel regulation, 1869–1983 688–9
liner chartering 191
liner companies 532–6; liner company size 533–4; liner market model 535–6; strategic and global alliances 534–5
liner company size 533–4
liner conferences 555–9; conference systems 556–7; global alliances 557–8; principles for regulating liner competition 558–9
liner fleet 537–9; container-ship size trends 538–9; types of ship used in the liner trades 537–8
liner market model 535–6
liner pricing 560
liner ship characteristics 539–40
'liner shipping': definition 64–5
liner shipping, 1833–1950 23–35; cargo liner services 31–2; deep-sea cables revolutionize shipping communications 27–8; four innovations transform merchant shipping 23; growth of sea trade in the nineteenth century 24–5; liner and shipping system emerges

28–9; passenger liner services 29–30; regulation of shipping 35; steam replaces sail in the merchant fleet 25–7; tramp shipping and global market place 32–5
liner shipping economics 80
liner shipping routes 524–32; break-bulk liner services 532; East–West trades 524–29; intraregional trades and feeder services 532; North–South liner routes 529–31
liner voyage cashflow model 548–9
link between the macroeconomic and microeconomic models 334–5
liquefied natural gas tankers 606–8
liquefied natural gas trade 483–8; development of LNG trade 484–6; LNG transport supply 488; LNG transportation system 486–7; natural gas supply and demand 484
liquefied petroleum gas trade 478–83; demand for LPG gas transport 479–81; LPG fleet and ownership 481–3; transport of LPG by sea 478–80
liquid bulk cargoes 430–31
liquid bulk transport 64, 432–4
liquid paraffin 474
liquid petroleum gas tankers 604–5
Liverpool 20, 22, 29, 82, 271
Liverpool Bay 511
Lloyd's Coffee House 658
Lloyd's Demolition Register 159
Lloyd's List 22, 188, 217
Lloyd's Register of British & Foreign Shipping 659–62
Lloyd's Register of Shipping 22, 25, 658
LNG transport supply 488
LNG transportation system 486–7
load centres 559
load lines 681
loaded days at sea 156, 244–5
loading facilities 584
loading plan 432
loan syndications 292–3
location of the major trading economies 348–50
logistics 547; and operations 547; and transport demand 352–6; unit costs and transport logistics 412–14
logistikos 352
London interbank offered rate 279, 288–9, 323
long run prices and costs 172
long shipping cycles 95–6
long-run demand function 149–50
long-run equilibrium 166–8

long-term adjustment process 334
long-term charter 571
long-term influences on trade 405–7
long-term price elasticity of sea transport demand 411
long-term shipbuilding demand 636–8
LOOP terminal 354, 370, 687
losses 158–60
Louisiana Offshore Oil Port terminal see LOOP terminal
LPG fleet and ownership 481–3
luxuries 401–2

McLean, Malcolm 356, 508–510
Madame Butterfly 595
Maersk 84, 297, 309, 503, 509, 514, 526, 529, 533–4
Magellan, Ferdinand 3
maintenance 229–30
major dry bulk trades 445–57; grain trade model 454–5; seaborne coal trade 450–53; seaborne grain trade 453–4; seaborne iron ore trade 446–50; transport of grain 455–7; transport system for iron ore 450
major trading economies' location 348–50
making maritime forecasts 706–7
malting barley 426
management company 674
Marco Polo 13, 15
marginal cost prices 553
Marine Dow Chem 42, 67, 475
Marine Environment Protection Committee 678
maritime conventions 676–7
maritime economics freight index, 1741–2007 755–8
maritime forecasting and market research 697–744; analytical techniques 724–38; approach to maritime forecasting 697–702; developing a scenario analysis 723–4; forecasting problems 738–42; freight rate forecasting 715–23; key elements of the forecast 702–5; market forecast methodologies 709–712; market research methodology 712–15; preparing for the forecast 705–8
Maritime Labour Convention 684
Maritime Safety Committee 678
maritime supply–demand model 715–16
maritime trading network 356–65; Atlantic maritime area 356–9; Indian Ocean maritime area 362–4; Pacific maritime area 359–61; Suez and Panama canals 364–5

*Maritime Transport Study* 524
maritime zones recognized by the UN
 Convention on the Law of the Sea, 1982 665
'market': definition 177
market expectations 631
market forecasting methodologies 709–712;
 forecasting time-scale 709–710; three
 different ways of approaching the forecast
 710–712
market for scrap products 649
market intelligence 132–3
market price 172
market reports 710, 713; stages in preparation
 713
market research 609, 695–744; methodology
 712–15; *see also* maritime forecasting and
 market research
market research methodology 712–15
market structure 102–4
market value of a ship 262–4
mass consumption 408
mass psychology 141–2
material costs 644–5
materials reception 642
maturity 408
*Mauritania* 30–31
maximizing loaded days at sea 244–5
Mediterranean Shipping Company 526, 532
Mediterranean trade 8–10; during the Roman
 Empire 10; opening of 8–9
membrane system 604
memorandum of agreement 199–201
mercantilism 388, 395, 397; *see also* Hume,
 David
merchant fleet 23, 25–7, 68–73, 151–4,
 565–694; by ship type 568–71; price
 dynamics of merchant ships 204–6; and
 transport supply 565–694; valuing merchant
 ships 206–7, 262–6
merchant fleet forecast 721
merchant scrapping industry 613–14
merchant shipbuilding in the United States
 620–21
Merchant Shipping Act, 1894 667
Mesopotamia 5, 7, 44, 699; Maritime Code 44
metal industry trades 58
metals and minerals trade 463–4
mezzanine finance structures 296
Middle East 379–82
minimal cargo handling 426
minor dry bulk trades 457–66; agribulk trades
 459; fertilizer trades 460–63; forest products

trade 465–6; metals and minerals trade
 463–4; steel products trade 464–5; sugar
 trades 459–60
Mitsubishi Shipyard 622
Mitsui 79, 84, 292, 297, 496, 535
Mitsui Shipyard 622
MOA *see* memorandum of agreement
model specifications and assumptions 740
modern theories of manufacturing advantage
 398–9
Mogul Line 688–9
molasses 474
momentary equilibrium 163–5
monitoring results 740–41
Monte Carlo analysis 738
Montreal 368, 528
Moody's 279, 281
moratorium 295
Morgan, J. P. 341
mortgage-backed loans 286–7
Moss system 606
motor vehicles 66–7
MSC *see* Mediterranean Shipping Company
multi-purpose vessels 537, 586–8
multiple regression analysis 735–7
Mumbai 352, 355, 364
*Murex* 435

naphtha 246, 420, 441, 444, 480, 574, 597,
 599–600, 609
Napoleonic Wars 105, 108–9
NASDAQ 305
National Institute of Economics and Social
 Research 740
national registers 669
natural gas supply and demand 484
natural price 172
naval protection 667
necessities 401
Nedlloyd 509, 533, 535
negotiation in the newbuilding market 208–9
negotiation of price and conditions 199
net registered tonnage 752
net tonnage (1969) 752
new directions in European trade 17–18
*New Register Book of Shipping* 659
new trade environment created at Bretton
 Woods 36–7
New World Alliance 526, 535
New Worldscale 192
New York 6, 21–3, 29, 37, 48, 86, 182, 192,
 297–9, 305, 351–2, 370, 484, 501, 528, 659

New York Stock Exchange *see* NYSE
newbuilding market 207–212; buyers and
    sellers in the newbuilding market 207–8;
    how newbuilding differs from sale and
    purchase 207; newbuilding negotiation
    208–9; shipbuilding contract 210–11;
    shipbuilding prices 209–12
newbuilding negotiation 208–9
Newcastle, NSW 34, 181, 245, 256, 383, 453
Newcastle on Tyne 18, 21, 108, 271, 417
Niarchos, Stavros 3, 44, 320
non-cargo ships 608–9; fishing fleet 608;
    supply ships and service craft 608; tugs and
    dredgers 608–9
normal profit 329–38; *see also* competition
    theory
North America's seaborne trade 368–71
North Atlantic trade 527–8
North–South liner routes 530–31
Norwegian International Ship Register 674
Norwegian K/S partnership structures 306
Norwegian sales form 1993 200–201
nuclear power 742
NYSE 86, 305

objectivity 741–2
obsolescence of ships 71–3
Ocean Shipping Reform Act, 690, 1999
Ocean Transport and Trading 509
ocean-going tugs 498
Oceania 350, 383, 537
oceans, distances and transit times 348–56;
    around the world in 80 days 350–52; location
    of the major trading economies 348–50;
    transport demand and logistics 352–6
Ofer Group 84, 320
'oil for the lamps of China' 393
oil products trade 442–5; transport of oil
    products 444–5
Old Black Ball Line 29
olefins 479
Onassis, Aristotle 3, 44, 319–20, 339, 702, 707,
    740
one-ship company 273, 674
OPEC 125, 148
open conferences 557
open hatch bulk carriers 496–7, 594; open
    hatch bulk shipping 496–7; package bulk
    cargo transport system 497–8
open hatch bulk shipping fleet 496–7
open registers 669, 671–3; *see also* flags of
    convenience

opening up global trade, 1450–1833 13–23;
    Amsterdam and Dutch trade 18–20;
    economics of discovery 15–16; Europe
    discovers sea route to Asia 13–14; new
    directions in European trade 17–18;
    Portuguese expeditions 14–15; Portuguese
    trade network 16; rise of Antwerp 18; rise of
    independent shipowner 21–3; sea trade in the
    eighteenth century 20–1
operating costs 226–31, 544; crew costs 226–9;
    general costs 231; insurance 230–1; repairs
    and maintenance 229–30; stores and
    consumables 229
operating speed 243–4
*operations and logistics 547*
OPEX *see* operating costs
opinion surveys 724, 726
optimal stocks for producer and consumer 427
optimizing operating speed 243–4
options for risk management 310–314
Oracle of Trophonios 699
ore carriers 594
organic chemicals 473
Organization of Petroleum Exporting Countries
    *see* OPEC
organization of the shipping market 47–90;
    characteristics of sea transport demand
    53–61; cost of sea transport 73–80;
    economic framework of 47; international
    transport industry 50–2; overview of
    maritime industry 48–50; role of
    governments in shipping 89; role of ports in
    the transport system 81–3; sea transport
    system 61–8; shipping companies that run
    the business 83–9; world merchant fleet
    68–73
origin of classification societies 658–9
origins of the liner service 506–512; cargo liner
    era 506–7; consequences of containerization
    511–12; container system, 1966–2005
    508–9; developing the container service
    infrastructure 509–510
origins of sea trade, 3000 BC to AD 1450
    7–12; Arabian Gulf 7–8; the beginning 7–8;
    Byzantine Empire 10–11; Mediterranean
    trade during the Roman Empire 10; opening
    Mediterranean trade 8–9; rise of Greek
    shipping 9–10; Venice and the Hanseatic
    League 11–12
origins of the seaborne oil trade 434–5
Oslo 48, 182, 297, 305, 320
Oslo Stock Exchange 297, 305

other countries' shipbuilding activity 624

other general cargo ships 585–90; barge-carrying vessels 589–90; cargo liner types 589; heavy lift vessels 588; multi-purpose vessels 586–8; refrigerated vessels 590; ro-ro ships 585–6; 'tweendecker tramps 589

Ottoman Empire 12–13

outports 559–60

output measurements 646

over-trading 98

overview of maritime industry 48–50

overview of regulatory system 656–8

overview of shipping cycles, 1741–2007 104–7; shipping cycles in practice 107

ownership of the world fleet 71

Oxyrhynchus 5

P&I clubs *see* protection and indemnity clubs

P&O 27, 32, 499, 509, 533–4, 556

Pacific maritime area 359–61

package bulk cargo transport system 497–8

packaged investment funds 279–81

pallets 574

Palmer's Shipyard 417, 435

Pan Atlantic Tanker Company 508

Panama Canal 34, 246, 254, 355–9, 364–5, 527–9; canal dues 236; size restrictions on 539, 591–3; tonnages 754

Panamax bulk carriers 41, 70, 75–8, 88, 93, 126–7, 154, 181, 202–3, 233–5, 239–40, 245–6, 254–6, 263–5, 321–2, 339–40, 365, 418–19, 429, 463–4, 539, 582–4, 590–96

Pao, Y. K. 44, 320

parcel size distribution 58–60

Paris Memorandum of Understanding 686–7

participants in the transport system 427–8

participation agreement 293–4

passenger ferries 501

passenger liner services 29–30

passenger shipping 499–503; cruise business 502–3; development history 499–500; passenger ferries 501

*Pax Romana* 10

peaks 98

performance of shipping investments 319–24; comparison of shipping with financial investments 322–4; profile of shipping returns in the twentieth century 320–21; shipping return paradox 319–20; shipping risk and the capital asset pricing model 321–2

periodic maintenance 231–2

periodic surveys 662

Persian Gulf 8, 16, 206

Peter Wright & Sons of Philadelphia 434

petrochemicals 473

Phoenician trade 8–9

physical units in which commodities are shipped by sea 573

Pigou, Arthur Cecil, 141–2

Piraeus 48, 182

plateaux 98

Plimsoll Act, 89, 1870

Plimsoll mark 35, 89, 655, 675–6

*Pointe Sans Souci* class of liners 491, 507, 538

political acceptability 667

pollution 89, 657, 682, 687–8

'pool' agreements 557

pools 85–9

poor track record of shipping forecasts 697–8

population and sea trade 393

port calls 559–60

port charges 235, 545

port congestion surcharges 551

port days 245

port infrastructure 560–62

port states 685–8; control inspections 687; control movement 686–7

port time 156

Porter, Michael 337–8, 399, 469, 536

ports' role in the transport system 81–3

Portuguese expeditions 14–15

Portuguese trade network 16

'post-Panamax' vessels 355, 527, 539, 582, 584

practical aspects of bulk transport 427–32; bulk shipping investment – criteria and approach 428–30; handling homogeneous dry bulk cargoes 431–2; handling liquid bulk cargoes 430–31; participants in the transport system 427–8

practical aspects of liner pricing 550–52

pre-conditions of take-off 408

pre-outfitting 643–4

pre-packing 573

pre-steam era ship finance 270–71

prediction of shipping cycles 131–3; challenge of successful risk management 133; importance of market intelligence 132–3

preparation for syndication 293

preparing for forecast 705–8

preparing shipping market report 713

press gangs 434

*Prestige* 656, 683

price and demand for liner transport 519–20

price discrimination 550, 555

price dynamics of merchant ships 204–6
price elasticity 633; of sea transport demand 411
price model 630–32
price of shipbuilding 209–12, 629–30
price stability 550
pricing liner services 550–55; practical aspects of liner pricing 550–52; principles of liner pricing 552–5
pricing shipping risk 338–41; capital asset pricing model 340; differences in 'risk preference' 338–9; risky asset pricing model 340–41
Primorsk 367, 381–2, 439
principles of bulk transport 422–7
principles of liner pricing 552–5; fixed prices 553–4; marginal cost prices 553; price discrimination 555; service contracts 555
principles of liner service economics 539–50; building-blocks of liner service economics 539–48; conclusions 549–50; liner voyage cashflow model 548–9
principles of maritime trade 385–416; building-blocks of sea trade 385–7; commodity trade cycles 404–411; countries that trade by sea 389–93; differences in production costs 395–9; role of sea transport in trade 411–14; trade due to differences in natural resources 399–404; why countries trade 393–5
*Principles of Political Economy and Taxation* 397
principles for regulating liner competition 558–9
prismatic system 604
Prisoner's Dilemma 554
private bulk company 86
private funding 282, 285
private placement of debt 278, 296
private placement vehicles 305–6
probability analysis 737–8
procedures for making maritime conventions 676–7
product development 708
product differentiation 60–61, 520–22; conflict of volume versus speed 520–22
production of ships 638–44
production subsidies 632
productivity 242–6, 645–6; *see also* freight revenue and ship productivity
products tankers 599
profile of shipping returns in the twentieth century 320–21

prohibited zones 682
project cargo 524
propane 480
propylene 481
prosperity 13
protection and indemnity clubs 33, 230–31
protectionism 388
provision of ships' finance 284
PSD *see* parcel size distribution
Ptolemy 16
public offering of equity 297–300
pure car and truck carriers 494–6; demand and the transport system 494–5; supply and ownership 495–6
pure car carriers 595
Pusan 377
putting the ship on the market 199

*Queen Elizabeth 2* 37
questions that define a design 571–81; how big should the ship be? 577–8; how fast should the ship go? 579–80; how flexible should the ship be? 580–81; how should the cargo be handled? 576–7; how should the cargo be stowed? 575–6; how will the ship be traded? 571–2; what cargo will the ship carry? 572–5

raising finance by issuing bonds 300–303
Rand Corporation 723
random shocks 136, 142, 147–9
RAP model *see* risky asset pricing model
rational forecasting to reduce uncertainty 700–701
rationale 703
rationale for sea transport integration 35–7
reasons for trading by sea 393–5; three fundamental reasons for trade 394–5; trade theory and drivers of trade 393–4
recession 44, 80, 93–4, 96–7, 100–101, 109–114, 626
reclaiming 432
recovery 98
recycling industry 648–52; market for scrap products 649; regulation of shipbreaking 651–2; who scraps ships? 649–51
recycling market 212–13; *see also* demolition market
Red Ensign 668
red herrings 299
reducing uncertainty 700–701
reefer commodity trades 489–91
reefer transport technology 491–2

refinery location 442

refrigerated cargo transport 67, 488–92

refrigerated vessels 584, 590

regional distribution centre 83

regional structure of world shipbuilding 614–25; Chinese shipbuilding industry 623–4; conclusions from a century of shipbuilding development 624–5; decline of British shipbuilding 616–19; European shipbuilding, 1902–2006 619–20; Japanese shipbuilding industry 621–2; merchant shipbuilding in the United States 620–21; other countries 624; rise of South Korean shipbuilding 623; who builds the world's merchant ships? 614–16

registration procedures 667–9

regression analysis 730–37; calculating the regression equation 732–5; fitting a regression equation 731–2; multiple regression analysis 735–7

regularity of trade flow 421

regulation of competition 688–91; EU regulation of tramp shipping pools 691; European Union regulation of shipping competition 690–91; regulatory control of liner cartels, 1869–1983 688–9; US regulation of liner shipping, 1983–2006 689–90

regulation of shipbreaking 651–2

regulation of shipping 34–5

regulation of the maritime industry 655–94; classification societies 658–63; how maritime laws are made 675–7; how regulations affect maritime economics 655–6; International Labour Organization 684–5; International Maritime Organization 678–84; law of the sea 663–6; overview of regulatory system 656–8; regulation of competition in shipping 688–91; regulatory role of coastal and port states 685–8; regulatory role of the state flag 666–75

Regulations for the Control of Pollution by Noxious Liquid Substances in Bulk 600

regulatory activities of classification societies 661–2

regulatory control of liner cartels, 1869–1983 688–9

regulatory role of coastal and port states 685–8; port state control inspections 687; port state control movement 686–7; rights of coastal states over foreign ships 685–6; US Oil Pollution Act, 1990 687–8

regulatory role of flag state 666–75; company structures associated with ship registration 673–5; dual registration 673; economic implications of flag state regulation 666–7; economic role of open registers 671–3; registration procedures 667–9; types of registry 669–71

release calls 231

relevance 703

reliability 61, 521

relocation 145

repairs 229–30

replacement demand (R) 636–7

required freight rate analysis 253

requirements for a freight derivatives market 195

research 703

residual value of a ship 265–6

resonant frequency 148

resource-based trade and the Heckscher-Ohlin theory 400–401

return 319–44

return on shipping investment model 325–6

returns earned in imperfect shipping markets 337–8

revenue 217–68

Rhine (river) 11–12, 357, 359, 367, 481

Ricardo, David 397, 399

rights of coastal states over foreign ships 685–6

*Rigoletto* 42, 66

*Rinform* 436

rise of Antwerp 18–19

rise of Greek shipping 9–10

rise of independent shipowner 21–3

rise of South Korean shipbuilding 623

risk 101–4, 310–314, 319–43; analysis in ship finance 310–314; competition theory and 'normal' profit 329–38; performance of shipping investments 319–24; pricing shipping risk 338–41; risk distribution and shipping strategy 104; shipping company investment model 324–9; shipping risk and market structure 102–4

risk distribution and shipping strategy 104

risk management 133; options 310–314

risky asset pricing model 340–41

roadshows 299

Rochdale Committee of Inquiry into Shipping 272

role of credit rating agencies 281

role of governments in shipping 89

role of maritime laws 675

role of merchant shipbuilding industry 613–14

role of ports in the transport system 81–3
role of sea trade in economic development 4–5
role of sea transport in trade 411–14; long-term price elasticity of sea transport demand 411; unit costs and transport logistics 412–14
Rome 5–6, 10–11, 45, 417, 699
ro-ros 493–4, 538, 585–6
ROSI *see* return on shipping investment model
Rostow's five stages of economic development 408
Rotterdam 34, 51–2, 82–3, 93, 181, 185, 188, 192–3, 197, 254, 351–2, 356, 364, 367, 381, 426, 509, 527–32, 560, 582, 595
round-the-world services 528–9
routine maintenance 230
Royal Caribbean 503
Royal Commission on Shipping Rings 689
Royal Dutch 435
rubber 519
*Rubena N* 188–9
Rules for Iron Ships, 1855 35
Russia 379–82

S&P *see* Standard & Poor's
Safety of Life at Sea Convention 678, 680–81
sailing ship cycles, 1741–1869 108–110
St Lawrence Seaway 357, 359, 368, 370, 447, 457, 528
Sakhalin 381–2, 439
sale and purchase market 198–207, 708; how ship prices are determined 202–4; price dynamics of merchant ships 204–6; sales procedure 199–202; valuing merchant ships 206–7; what it does 198–9
sale and purchase memorandum of agreement 200–201
sales procedure 199–202
Saudi Arabian Maritime Company 319
SAX *see* South Africa Express service
Schumpeter, J.-A. 95
scrap products market 649
scrap value of a ship 265
scrapping 158–60, 613–54; and losses 158–60; role of merchant scrapping industries 613–14
SDRs *see* special drawing rights
sea freight additionals 551
sea route to Asia 13–14
sea trade in the eighteenth century 20–1
sea trade's role in economic development 4–5
sea trading countries 389–93
sea transport 3–46, 150–60; container, bulk and air transport 35–44; and global economy

3–46; global economy in the fifteenth century 12–13; lessons from 5000 years commercial shipping 44–5; liner and tramp shipping 23–35; opening up global trade and commerce 13–23; origins of sea trade 7–12; supply of 150–60
sea transport demand price elasticity 411
sea transport integration 35–7
sea transport of chemicals 473–8; chemical fleet and supply 477–8; chemical transport system 476–7; demand for chemical transport 473–5; development of chemical transport 475–6
sea transport of oil, 1890–1970 435–7
sea transport product 53
sea transport system 61–8; definition of 'bulk shipping' 64; definition of 'liner' shipping 64–5; definition of 'specialized' shipping 65–7; economic model for sea transport 61–4; limitations of transport statistics 67–8
sea transport unit cost function 76–8
Sea-Land 41, 491, 509–510, 526, 533–4
seaborne coal trade 450–53
seaborne commodity trades 143–6
seaborne grain trade 453–4
seaborne iron ore trade 446–50
seaborne trade and transport systems 345–564; geography of maritime trade 347–84; principles of maritime trade 385–416; transport of bulk cargoes 417–68; transport of general cargo 505–64; transport of specialized cargoes 469–504
seaborne trade forecast 718–20
seaborne trade of the Middle East, central Asia and Russia 379–82
search for signposts to shipping market 135–6
seasonal shipping cycles 97–8
seasonal trade 404–5
seasonality 143, 518
Seaspan 309
Second World War 37, 40, 45, 64, 105–7, 118–19, 192, 276, 619–21
second-hand prices 631; correlation in tankers and bulk carriers 203
'secular trend' 94, 95
securitization of shipping assets 309–310
security 61
security and bank lending policy 240–41
self-supporting tank system 604
semi-public shipping group 87
semi-refrigerated vessels 605
semi-submersible heavy lift ships 498

sensitivity analysis 723
sentiment 168–9
service additionals 551
service and demand for liner transport 519–20
service contracts 555
service schedule 543
setting the tone 130–31
Shanghai 6, 48, 82, 351–2, 355, 376, 381, 543, 562, 624, 688
Shell 123, 435, 697, 724, 739
*shikumisen* 103, 273, 436, 622
ship age and the supply price of freight 222–3
ship and shipyard 639–40
ship costs and economies of scale 544–5
ship demand forecast 721
ship finance 269–70; in the pre-steam era 270–1
ship flexibility 580–81
ship funds 304–5
ship information 254
ship market modelling 745–50
ship prices 202–4
ship productivity forecast 721–2
ship size and economies of scale 75–6, 577–8
ship speed 579–80
ship types in the world fleet 68–71
ship types used in the liner trades 537–8
shipbreaking 648–52; *see also* recycling industry
shipbuilding contract 209–211
shipbuilding costs and competitiveness 644–8; currency movements and competitiveness 648; labour costs and competitiveness 647–8; material costs 644–5; shipbuilding productivity 645–6
shipbuilding credit 276
shipbuilding cycle: causes 628–9
shipbuilding demand 636–8; long term 636–8
shipbuilding demand and supply 630–32
shipbuilding market cycles 625–8
shipbuilding market short-term equilibrium 634–6
shipbuilding prices 209–12, 629–30
shipbuilding production 156–60
shipbuilding production process 638–44; actual production process 640–44; categories of shipyard 638–9; ship and the shipyard 639–40
shipbuilding productivity 645–6
shipbuilding supply function 632–3
'shipowner': definition 281–5
shipping accounts 246–52; balance sheet 248–50; cashflow statement 251–2; income statement 247–8; what company accounts are used for 247

shipping as business 3–7; characteristics of the business 3–4; history of maritime development 5–7; role of sea trade in economic development 4–5; the Westline 5–7
shipping communications 27–8
shipping companies 83–9, 269–318; financing 269–318; joint ventures and pools 85–9; types of shipping company 83–4; who makes the decisions? 85
'shipping company': definition 281–5
shipping company economics 215–344; costs, revenue and cashflow 217–68; financing ships and shipping companies 269–318; risk, return and shipping company economics 319–44
shipping company investment model 324–9; capital gain 328; depreciation 328; earnings before interest and depreciation (EBID) 326–8; financial performance of 'Perfect Shipping' 328–9; return on shipping investment model (ROSI) 325–6; shipping company's split persona 324–5
shipping company microeconomic model 330–32
shipping company's split persona 324–5
shipping corporate 86
shipping corporations 271–2
shipping cycle model 169–71
shipping cycles between wars (1920–40) 115–16
shipping cycles in practice 107
shipping division 86
shipping economics 269–70
shipping investment performance 319–24
shipping market cycles 93–134; bulk shipping market cycles, 1945–2007 118–30; characteristics of shipping market cycles 94–101; lessons from two centuries of cycles 130–1; overview of shipping cycles, 1741–2007 104–7; pervasion of market cycles 93–4; prediction of shipping cycles 131–3; sailing ship cycles, 1741–1869 108–10; and shipping risk 101–4; tramp market cycles, 1869–1936 110–118
shipping market economics 91–214; four shipping markets 175–214; shipping market cycles 93–134; supply, demand and freight rates 135–74
shipping market model 135–6; search for signposts 135–6
shipping market, organization of 47–90
shipping market report 713

shipping return paradox 319–20
shipping returns in the twentieth century 320–21
shipping risk and market structure 102–4
shipping risk and the capital asset pricing model 321–2
shipping risk checklist 313
shipping strategy 104
shipping supply forecast 722
shipping's four market places 177–8
shipping's 'industrial revolution' 39
ship's articles 210–11
ships for dry bulk trades 590–96; bulk carrier 590–94; cement carriers 595–6; open hatch bulk carrier 594; ore carriers 594; pure car carriers 595; woodchip carriers 594
ships for general cargo trades 581–90; container-ships 581–5; other general cargo ships 585–90
ships for liquid bulk cargoes 596–603; chemical tankers 599–601; combined tankers 601–3; crude oil tankers 596–9; products tankers 599
ships' load lines 681
ship's revenue 242–6; classification of revenue 242; freight revenue and ship productivity 242–6
ships that provide transport 567–612; economic criteria for evaluating ship designs 609–610; gas tankers 608–9; seven questions that define a design 571–81; ships for general cargo trades 581–90; ships for liquid bulk cargoes 596–603; what type of ship? 567–71
shipyard capacity 631
shipyards and ships 639–40
short shipping cycles 96–7; analysts' views of 99–101
short-run equilibrium 165–6
short-sea shipping 51
short-term cycles, 1945–2007 121
short-term cyclical adjustment process 332–4
short-term cyclical trade 404–5
short-term shipbuilding demand function 633–4
*Shu Ching* 699
Siamese twins 325–6
significant speculative characteristics 281
Silk route 7, 11–13
Six Day War 123, 148, 441
size of ship 75–6, 577–8
Sloan, Alfred 520
Slutsky equation 402, 415
small local port 82–3

Smith, Adam 4–5, 21, 45–6, 172, 341, 377, 395–6, 563
smuggling 665
SOLAS *see* Safety of Life at Sea Convention
Sophocles 3
sources of finance for ships 276–7
South Africa Express service 532
South African War 99, 114, 124, 132
South America's seaborne trade 371–3
Southampton 37, 367, 529
southern Asia 377
space availability 521
SPACs 304–5
spares 230
special drawing rights 236
special purpose acquisition corporations *see* SPACs
special purpose companies 282, 303–310
specialist ship chartering 191
specialized cargoes shipping 469–504
'specialized shipping': definition 65–6, 469–71
specialized shipping model 471–3
speed of ship 61, 155–6, 579–80
Spice Islands 13, 15, 17
Spice route 7, 11–13
'spot' cargoes 23
spot-chartering ships 707–8
spreading 432
*SS Fairland* 509
stages in a typical shipping cycle 98
stages in developing a forecasting model 716–17
stages in preparing shipping market report 713
stages in shipbuilding production process 641–4
stages of economic development 407–9
standalone structures 282
Standard & Poor's 279, 281, 323–4
standard displacement 754
standard error 733
Standard Oil 435
Standards of Training, Certification and Watchkeeping for Seafarers, 1978 682
Star Shipping 67, 79, 496, 503
status quo bias 739
STCW *see* Standards of Training, Certification and Watchkeeping for Seafarers, 1978
steam coal 445–8
steam replaces sail in the merchant fleet 25–7
steel products trade 464–5
stockbuilding 141
stores 229
stowage 420, 575–6
straddle carriers 510, 560, 562

straight-line depreciation 239
Straits of Dover 441
Straits of Magellan 19
Straits of Malacca 351–2, 359, 362, 373, 441
strategic and corporate planning 708
strategic and global alliances 534–5
*Strathleven* 67, 489
structure of commercial bank lending 288–91
subcontracting 436, 646
substitution effect 402–4
Suez Canal 8, 46, 112, 120–23, 162, 339,
    363–5; canal dues 236; closures of 120–23,
    134, 145, 152–4, 439; crisis 122–3, 148;
    draught restrictions on 441–2; nationalization
    of 120, 148, 319; opening of 25–7, 112, 364;
    strategic importance of 148; tonnages 754
Suezmax tankers 70, 75, 175, 190, 300,
    418–19, 429, 441, 596–8
sugar trades 459–60
summary of test statistics 733–4
super-waves 716
supply and demand 135–74; balance of 722;
    classic maritime supply–demand model
    715–16; demand for sea transport 150–60;
    freight rate mechanism 160–72; functions
    161–3; key influences 136–9; shipbuilding
    and the price model 630–32; shipping market
    model 135–6
supply and demand functions 161–3
supply and demand of natural gas 484
supply and ownership of car and truck carriers
    495–6
supply controllers 150–51
supply curve 168–9
supply of refrigerated transport capacity 492
supply of sea transport 150–60; decision-
    makers who control supply 150–1; fleet
    productivity 154–6; freight revenue 160;
    merchant fleet 151–4; scrapping and losses
    158–60; shipbuilding production 156–8
supply price of freight 222–3
supply ships and service craft 608
surveys during construction 661
survival 217–19; impact of financial pressures
    on shipowners' decisions 217–19
*Sveland* 447, 603
Swire, John 556
Sydney 27, 34, 383
syndicating the loan 293

t-test 732–3
TAA *see* Trans Atlantic Agreement

TACA *see* Trans Atlantic Conference Agreement
take-off 408
tangible variables 704
tank segregations 577
tanker market report 190–91
Tap Line 124, 148
Tasman Orient Line 532
tax 666, 671; company law and financial law 666
taxation 241
Technical Co-operation Committee 678
technical plan review 661
Technigaz 606
technological trend, 1945–2007 119–21
technological trend in freight rates, 1869–1913
    111–12
technological variables 704
Teekay 84, 275, 292, 297
tenor of the loan 287
terminal handling charges 551
terms of employment 667
territorial sea 665
test statistics 733–4
Thames (river) 659
theories of manufacturing advantage 398–9
theory of absolute advantage 396–7
theory of comparative advantage 397–8
theory of maritime trade 387–8
theory of non-compensated errors, 141–2
*Thomas's Stowage* 465
three principles of forecasting 702–3; rationale
    703; relevance 703; research 703
three Rs of profit 325
ThyssenKrupp Steel 189
Tidal Marine 3
Tigris (river) 7
Tilbury 183, 367, 426
time 163–8
time charter 184–5, 242
time series analysis 726–30; autoregressive
    moving average 729–30; example of time
    series analysis 727–9; exponential smoothing
    729; trend extrapolation 726–7
time-charter market 178
time-chartering ships 708
*Titanic* 656
Tokyo 6, 48, 182, 375, 543, 686–7
ton miles and average haul 146–7
tonnage measurement 751–4; compensated
    gross tonnage 752–3; deadweight 752; gross
    registered tonnage 751; gross tonnage 751–2;
    lightweight 753–4; net registered tonnage
    752; net tonnage (1969) 752; standard

displacement 754; Suez and Panama tonnages 754

topics covered by maritime law 675–6

*Torrey Canyon* 656

TPDA *see* Trans Pacific Discussion Agreement

trade of Australia and Oceania 383

trade development cycle 409–411

trade due to differences in natural resources 399–404

traditional society 408

tramp ship cycles, 1869–1936 110–118; cycle 8: 1873–9 112–13; cycle 10: 1889–97 113–14; cycle 11: 1898–1910 114–15; cycle 12: 1911–14 115; cycle 13: 1921–5 116–17; cycle 14: 1926–37 117–18; shipping cycles between wars (1920–40) 115–16; technological trend in freight rates, 1869–1913 111–12

tramp shipping, 1833–1950 23–35; and global market place 32–5; *see also* liner shipping

Tramp Shipping Administrative Committee 320

tramp shipping pool regulation 691

Trans Atlantic Agreement 557

Trans Atlantic Conference Agreement 528, 558

Trans Pacific Discussion Agreement 557

transformation of merchant shipping 23

transit times 348–56; door-to-door 521

Transpacific Stabilisation Agreement 558

transpacific trade 526–7

transport costs and long-un demand function 149–50

transport demand and logistics 352–6

transport logistics 412–14

transport of bulk cargoes 417–68; the bulk fleet 418–19; bulk trades 419–22; commercial origins of bulk shipping 417–18; crude oil trade 434–42; liquid bulk transport 432–4; major dry bulk trades 445–57; minor dry bulk trades 457–66; oil products trade 442–5; practical aspects of bulk transport 427–32; principles of bulk transport 427–32

transport of general cargo 505–564; container ports and terminals 559–62; economic principles of liner operation 512–14; general cargo and liner transport demand 514–24; introduction to general cargo 505; liner companies 532–6; liner conferences and cooperative agreements 555–9; liner fleet 537–9; liner shipping routes 524–32; origins of the liner service 506–512; pricing liner services 550–55; principles of liner service economies 539–50

transport of grain 455–7

transport of LPG by sea 478–80

transport of oil products 444–5

transport of refrigerated cargo 488–92; demand for refrigerated transport 488; development of refrigerated transport 488–9; reefer commodity trades 489–91; reefer transport technology 491–2; supply of refrigerated transport capacity 492

transport of specialized cargoes 42–3, 469–504; introduction to specialized shipping 469–73; liquefied natural gas trade 483–8; liquefied petroleum gas trade 478–83; passenger shipping 499–503; sea transport of chemicals 473–8; transport of refrigerated cargo 488–92; unit load cargo transport 492–9

transport planning 436

transport supply and the merchant fleet 565–694; economics of shipbuilding and scrapping 613–54; regulation of the maritime industry 655–94; ships that provide transport 567–612

transport system for crude oil 440–42

transport system for iron ore 450

transport system participants 427–8

Treaty of Rome, 1958 559, 690–91

trend extrapolation 726–7

troughs 98

truck packed timber 465

TSA *see* Transpacific Stabilisation Agreement

tugs and dredgers 608–9

Tung, Chee-hwa 44, 320

'tweendecker tramps 506, 537, 589

Tyne Steam Shipping Company 271

types of finance 276–85

types of registry 669–71

types of relationship and variable in forecasting 704–5

types of ship used in the liner trades 537–8

types of ship used in the merchant fleet 567–71; derived demand for ships 567–8; fleet by ship type 568–71

types of shipping company 83–4

types of shipping market 177–80; definition of market 177; different character of the four markets 180; how the four shipping markets integrate 178–80; shipping's four market places 177–8

typical pattern of shipyard stage payments 208

typical shipbuilding contract 210–11

typical shipping company structures 86–7

Tyre 5–6, 8–9

UN Convention on the Law of the Sea, 1982 665
uncertainty reduction 700–701
UNCTAD 89, 372, 689
Understanding on Export Credit for Ships, 276, 295, 1969
*Undine* 595
unit costs and economies of scale 223–5
unit costs and transport logistics 412–14
unit load cargo transport 492–9; deep-sea ro-ros 493–4; heavy lift 497–9; open hatch bulk carriers 496–7; pure car and truck carriers 494–6
United Nations 524, 656, 658, 663, 677
UPS 309, 521
Uring, Captain Nathaniel 22–3, 32
US Department of Transportation Marine Administration 521
US Geological Survey 461
US Gulf 93, 144, 181, 185–7, 192–4, 246, 254–6, 351–2, 368, 372, 435, 457, 475, 528, 727–9
US Merchant Shipping Act, 1984 690
US Ocean Shipping Reform Act, 1999 555
US Oil Pollution Act, 1990 89, 657, 682, 687–8, 693
US Postal Service 521
US regulation of liner shipping, 1983–2006 689–90
use of company accounts 247
uses of maritime forecasts 707–8

*Vacationland* 493
*Vaderland* 435, 603
value added by seaborne transport 347–8
valuing merchant ships 206–7, 262–6; estimating market value of a ship 262–4; estimating residual value of a ship 265–6; estimating scrap value of a ship 265
Vancouver 359, 369–70, 453, 457, 466, 516–18, 526
vegetable oils 473, 599
Venice 5–6, 11–12, 15–19, 22–3, 45, 71, 377, 634; trade between AD 1000–1400 11–12
vessel arrival on time 521
vinyl chloride monomer 481
volume versus speed 520–22
voyage cashflow analysis 253–7, 548–9
voyage charter 183, 242
voyage costs 232–6; canal dues 236; fuel costs 233–5; port charges 235

voyage information 254
voyage rate statistics 192

Wall Street Crash 117, 147
Wallenius lines 42, 79, 493–4, 595
ways of approaching the forecast 710–712
weakness 131
wealth and seaborne trade 391–2
*Wealth of Nations* 4, 21, 396; *see also* Smith, Adam
Wear (river) 111–14
Western Europe to the Far East trade 528
Westline 5–7, 10, 44, 348
what cargo ships will carry 572–5
what decision makers use forecasts for 707–8
what sale and purchase market does 198–9
what specialized shipping is 65–6, 469–71
White Star 30, 37
why countries trade 393–5
wild cards 704–5, 715–16
wine 519
woodchip carriers 594
wool 519
World Bank 37
world economy 140–43
world financial system 276–85; definition of 'shipowner' and 'shipping company' 281–5; financial markets and packaged investment funds 279–81; investment funds come from savings 278; investors and lenders 278; private placement of debt or equity 278; role of credit rating agencies 281; where money comes from to finance ships 276–7
*World Janker Fleet Review* 156
world merchant fleet 68–73; ageing, obsolescence and fleet replacement 71–3; ownership of the world fleet 71; ship types in the world fleet 68–71
world trade and cost of freight 73–5
World Trade Organization 388
Worldscale 100 192
Worldscale 125–6, 190, 192–3
WS *see* Worldscale
WTO *see* World Trade Organization

yield management 555
Yokohama 375, 526, 622
Yom Kippur War 120, 124–5, 148